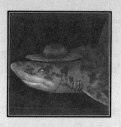

You can't see your own face in profile with one mirror.
Is that really true? What if I whip around really quickly like
this...wip!! And wip!! If I look toward the mirror like that...!
Wouldn't I be able to see an afterimage or something?!
Wip!! Wip!! Krak!! ...!!

— *Eiichiro Oda, 1998*

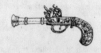

· AUTHOR BIOGRAPHY ·

Eiichiro Oda began his manga career in 1992 at the age of 17,
when his one-shot cowboy manga *Wanted!* won second place in
the coveted Tezuka manga awards. Oda went on to work as an
assistant to some of the biggest manga artists in the industry,
including Nobuhiro Watsuki, before winning the Hop Step
Award for new manga artists. His pirate adventure *One Piece*,
which debuted in *Weekly Shonen Jump* magazine in 1997,
quickly became one of the most popular manga in Japan.

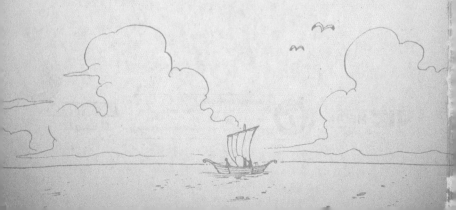

EAST BLUE ONE PIECE

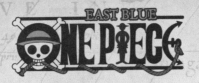

## ONE PIECE: EAST BLUE 7-8-9

SHONEN JUMP Manga Omnibus Edition
A compilation of the graphic novel volumes 7–9

STORY & ART BY EIICHIRO ODA

English Adaptation: Lance Caselman
Translation: Naoko Amemiya
Touch-up Art & Lettering: Mark McMurray
Additional Touch-up: Josh Simpson and Walden Wong
Design: Frances O. Liddell (Omnibus edition), Sean Lee (graphic novel volumes 7–9)
Editor: Megan Bates (volume 7), Megan Bates and Yuki Takagaki (volumes 8–9)



Printed in the U.S.A.

Published by VIZ Media, LLC
P.O. Box 77010
San Francisco, CA 94107

13
Omnibus edition first printing, March 2010
Thirteenth printing, August 2021

VIZ MEDIA
viz.com



SHONEN JUMP

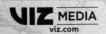

# Vol. 7
# THE CRAP-GEEZER

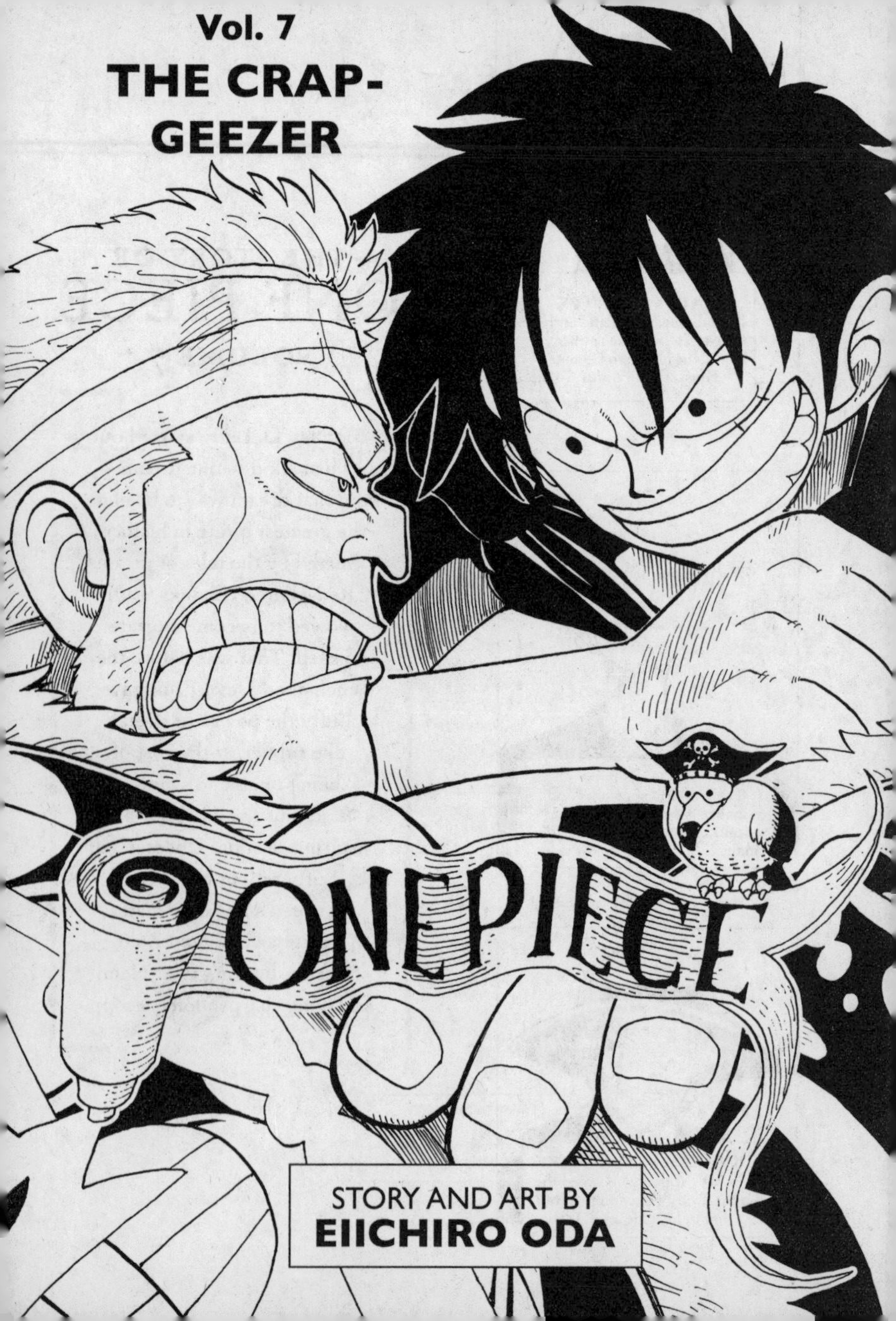

# ONE PIECE

STORY AND ART BY
**EIICHIRO ODA**

# THE STORY OF ONE PIECE

## · VOLUME 7 ·

Monkey D. Luffy started out as just a kid with a dream—and that dream was to become the greatest pirate in history! Stirred by the tales of pirate "Red-Haired" Shanks, Luffy vowed to become a pirate himself. That was before the enchanted Devil Fruit gave Luffy the power to stretch like rubber, at the cost of being unable to swim—a serious handicap for an aspiring sea dog. Undeterred, Luffy set out to sea and recruited some crewmates: master swordsman Zolo, treasure-hunting thief Nami and lying sharpshooter Usopp.

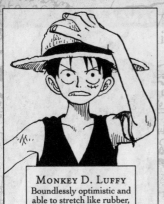

MONKEY D. LUFFY
Boundlessly optimistic and able to stretch like rubber, he is determined to become King of the Pirates.

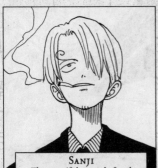

SANJI
The merciful sous-chef and maitre d' on the oceangoing restaurant Baratie. He's a ladies' man with a keen sense of taste.

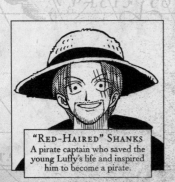

"RED-HAIRED" SHANKS
A pirate captain who saved the young Luffy's life and inspired him to become a pirate.

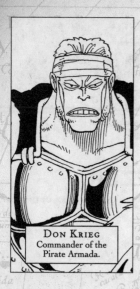

**DON KRIEG**
Commander of the
Pirate Armada.

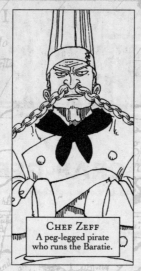

**CHEF ZEFF**
A peg-legged pirate
who runs the Baratie.

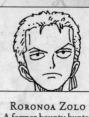

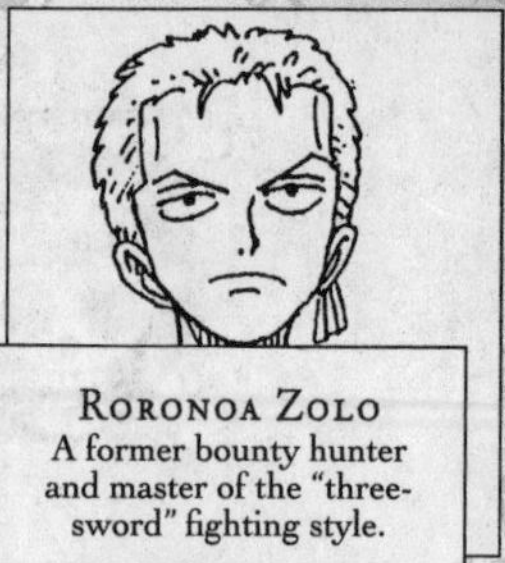

**RORONOA ZOLO**
A former bounty hunter
and master of the "three-
sword" fighting style.

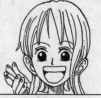

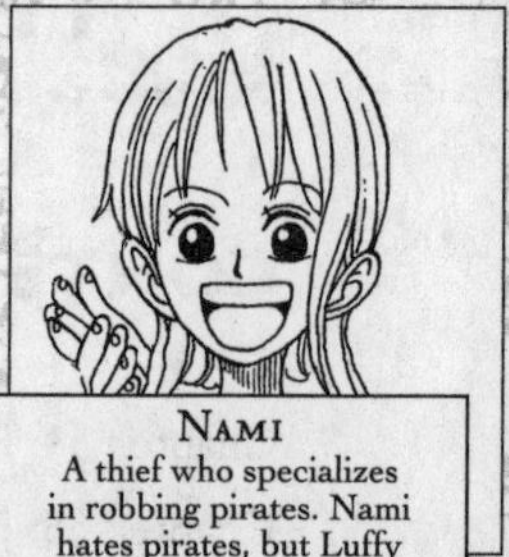

**NAMI**
A thief who specializes
in robbing pirates. Nami
hates pirates, but Luffy
convinced her to join his
crew as navigator.

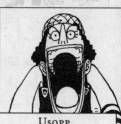

**USOPP**
The newest addition to
Luffy's crew, Usopp's known
for his tall tales, but he
has a way with a slingshot
and a heart of gold.

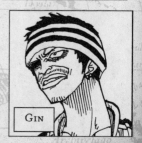

**GIN**

Luffy and his crew sail to Baratie,
the oceangoing restaurant, to find
themselves a ship's cook. There Luffy
takes a liking to the arrogant-but-
merciful Sanji and asks him to join the
crew. Unfortunately, before he can be
recruited, Don Krieg and his 5,000
pirates arrive on the scene. After Sanji
takes pity on the starving Krieg and
gives him food, Krieg is completely
revitalized. But the pirate repays good
with evil by trying to take over the ship!
So the battle for the Baratie begins.
Then suddenly the sea rumbles and
"Hawk-Eye" Mihawk, reputed to be the
world's greatest swordsman, appears.
Zolo, who aspires to win that title for
himself, challenges Mihawk. Zolo is
defeated, but vows never to lose again.
Mihawk departs and the deadly battle
with Krieg's pirates resumes…

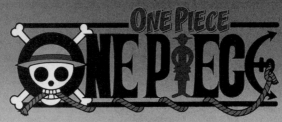

## Vol. 7
# THE CRAP-GEEZER

## CONTENTS

| | |
|---|---|
| Chapter 54: Pearl | 7 |
| Chapter 55: Jungle Blood | 27 |
| Chapter 56: I Refuse | 47 |
| Chapter 57: If You Have a Dream | 69 |
| Chapter 58: The Crap-Geezer | 89 |
| Chapter 59: Sanji's Debt | 109 |
| Chapter 60: Resolution | 129 |
| Chapter 61: The Demon | 149 |
| Chapter 62: MH5 | 171 |

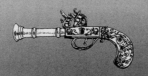

# Chapter 54: PEARL

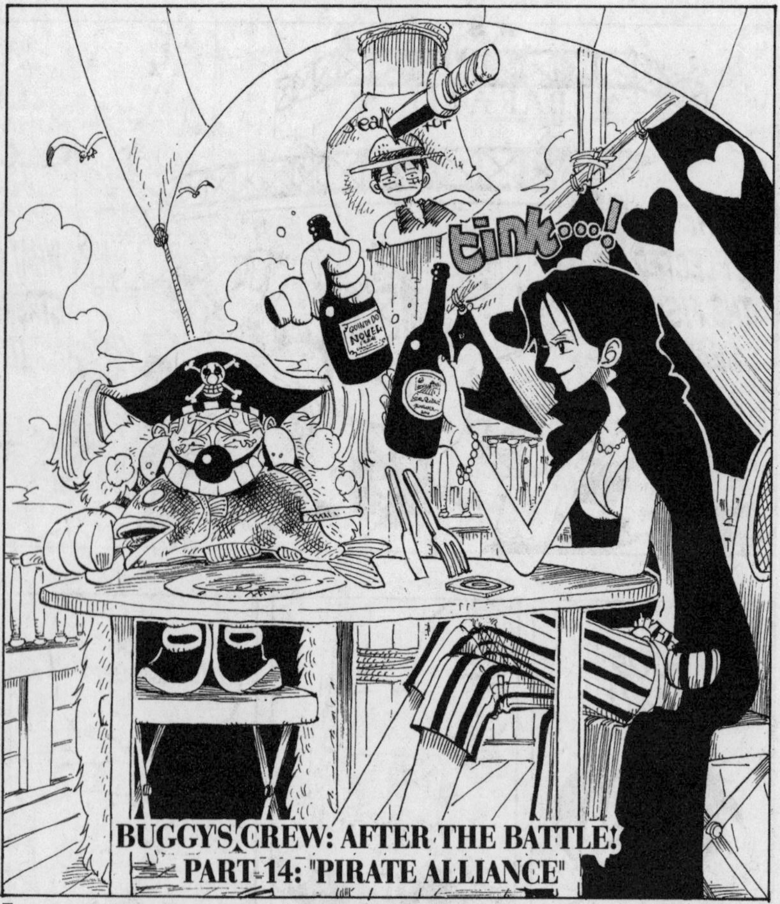
tink...!
BUGGY'S CREW: AFTER THE BATTLE!
PART 14: "PIRATE ALLIANCE"

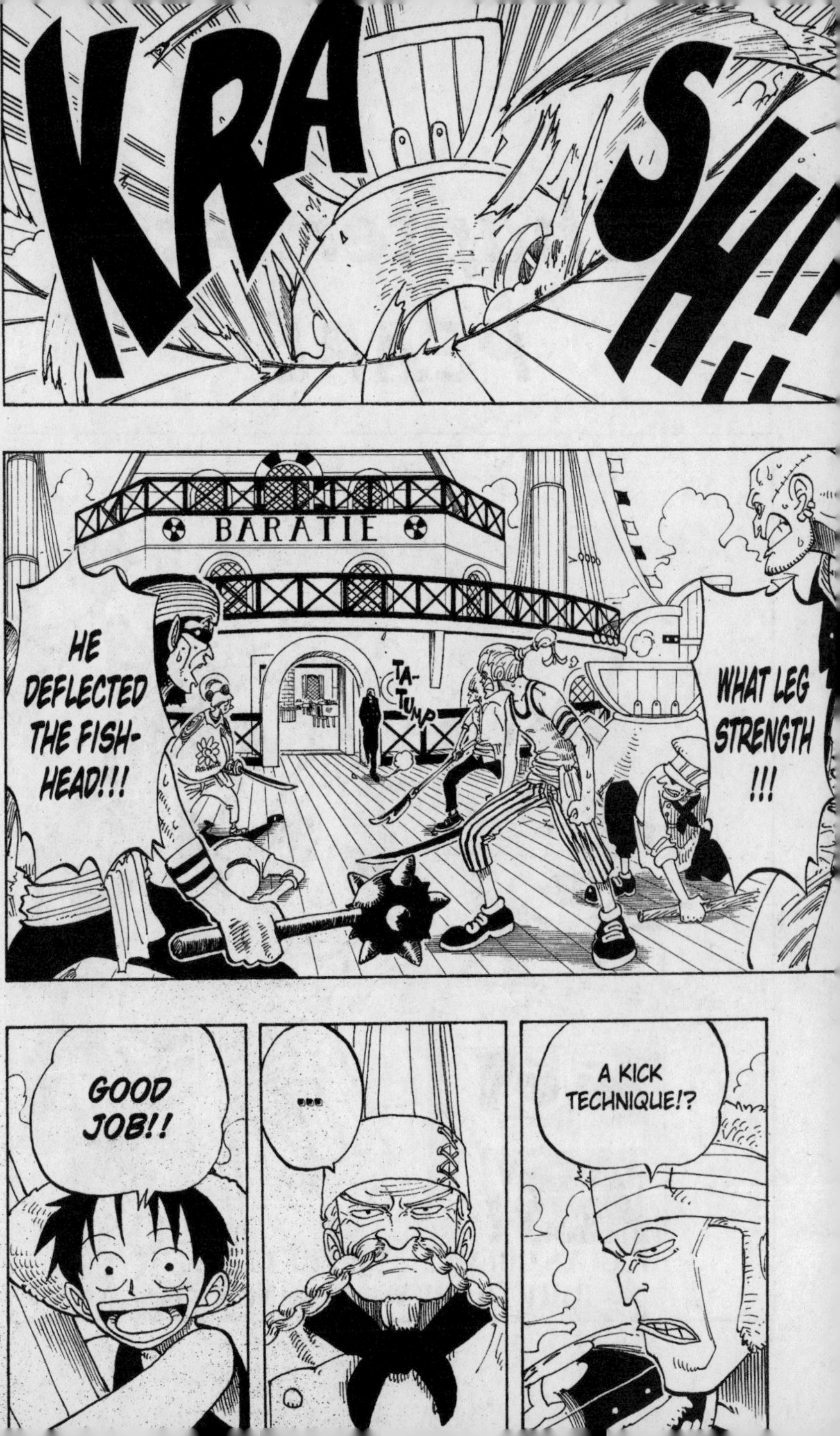
KRASH!!
WHAT LEG STRENGTH!!!
TA-TUMP
HE DEFLECTED THE FISH-HEAD!!!
BARATIE
A KICK TECHNIQUE!?
...
GOOD JOB!!

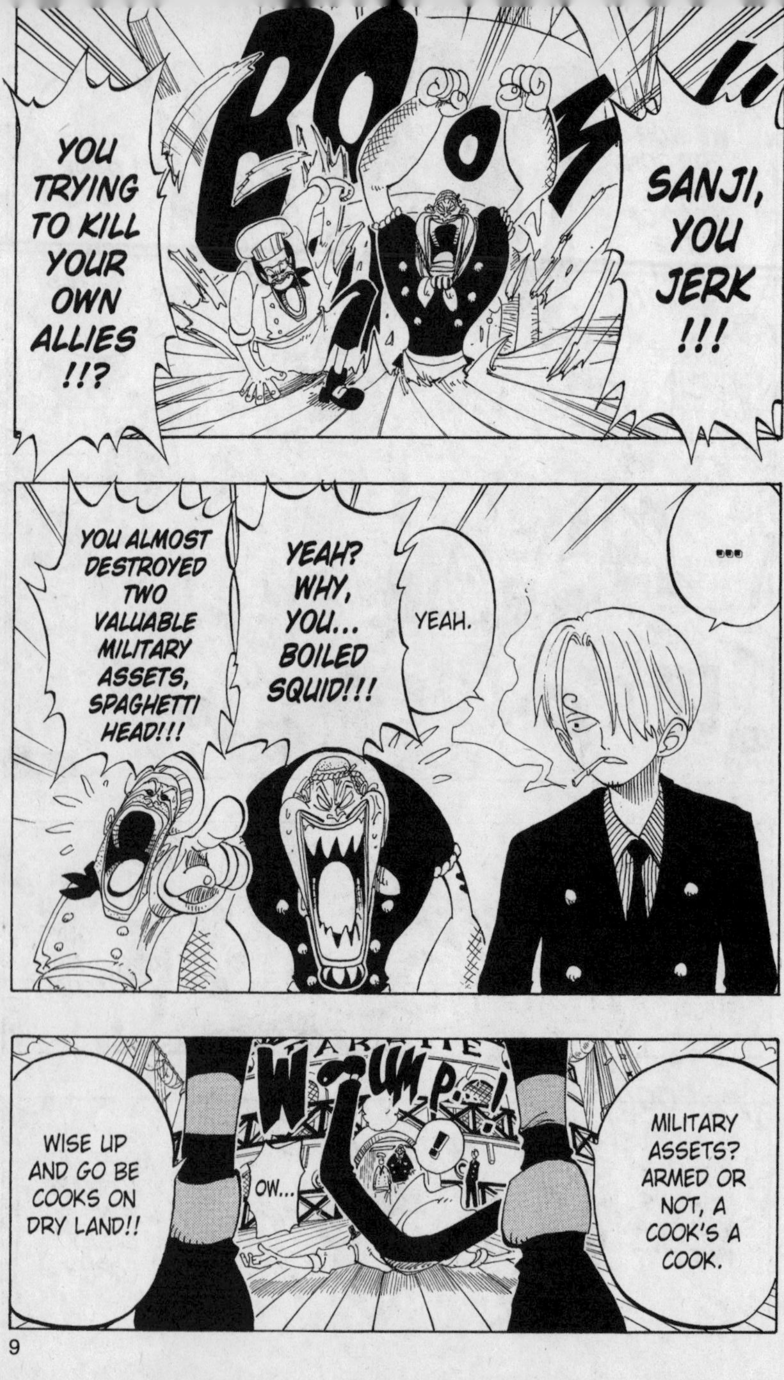
BOOM!!
SANJI, YOU JERK!!!
YOU TRYING TO KILL YOUR OWN ALLIES!!?
...
YEAH.
YEAH? WHY, YOU... BOILED SQUID!!!
YOU ALMOST DESTROYED TWO VALUABLE MILITARY ASSETS, SPAGHETTI HEAD!!!
MILITARY ASSETS? ARMED OR NOT, A COOK'S A COOK.
WUMP!
!
OW...
WISE UP AND GO BE COOKS ON DRY LAND!!

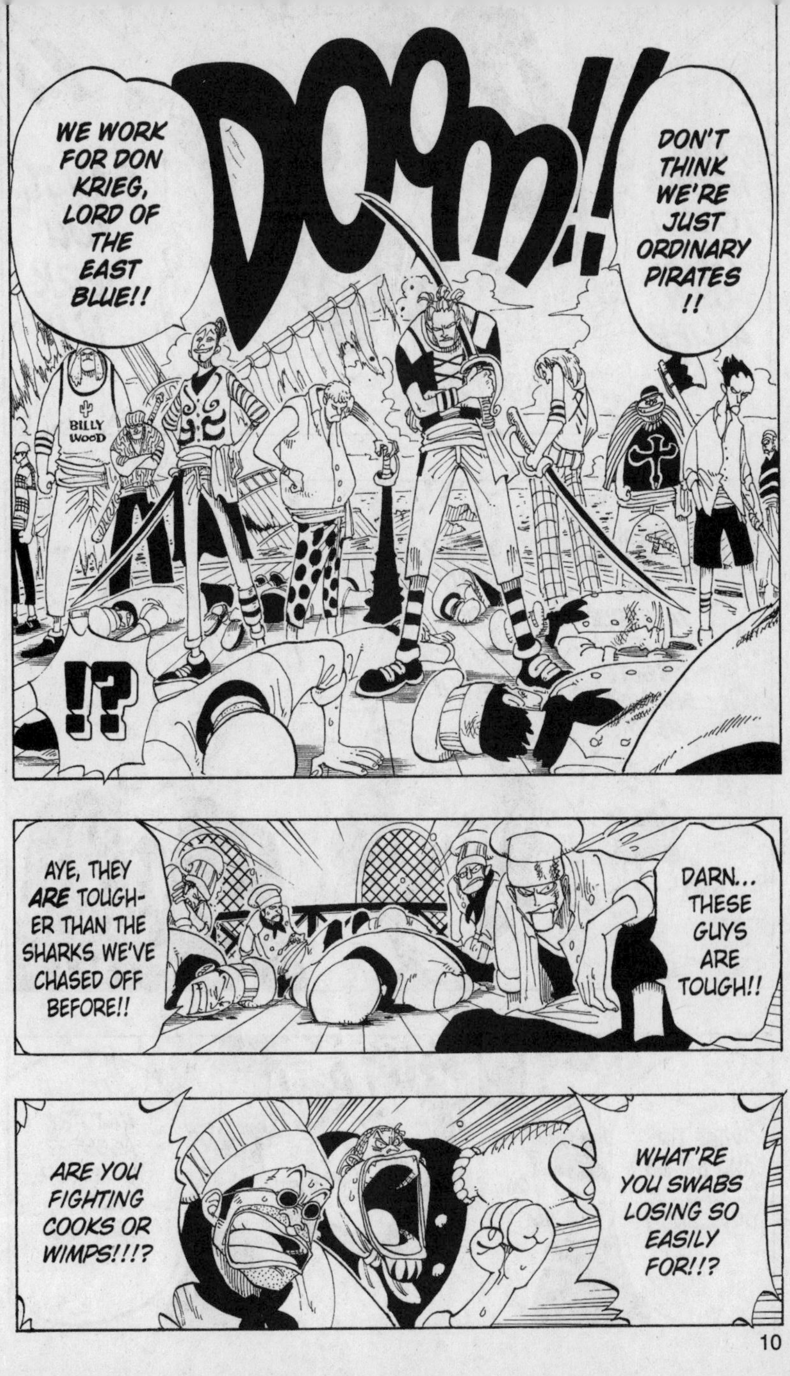
DOOM!!
DON'T THINK WE'RE JUST ORDINARY PIRATES!!
WE WORK FOR DON KRIEG, LORD OF THE EAST BLUE!!
!?
DARN... THESE GUYS ARE TOUGH!!
AYE, THEY ARE TOUGHER THAN THE SHARKS WE'VE CHASED OFF BEFORE!!
WHAT'RE YOU SWABS LOSING SO EASILY FOR!!?
ARE YOU FIGHTING COOKS OR WIMPS!!!?

READ THIS WAY

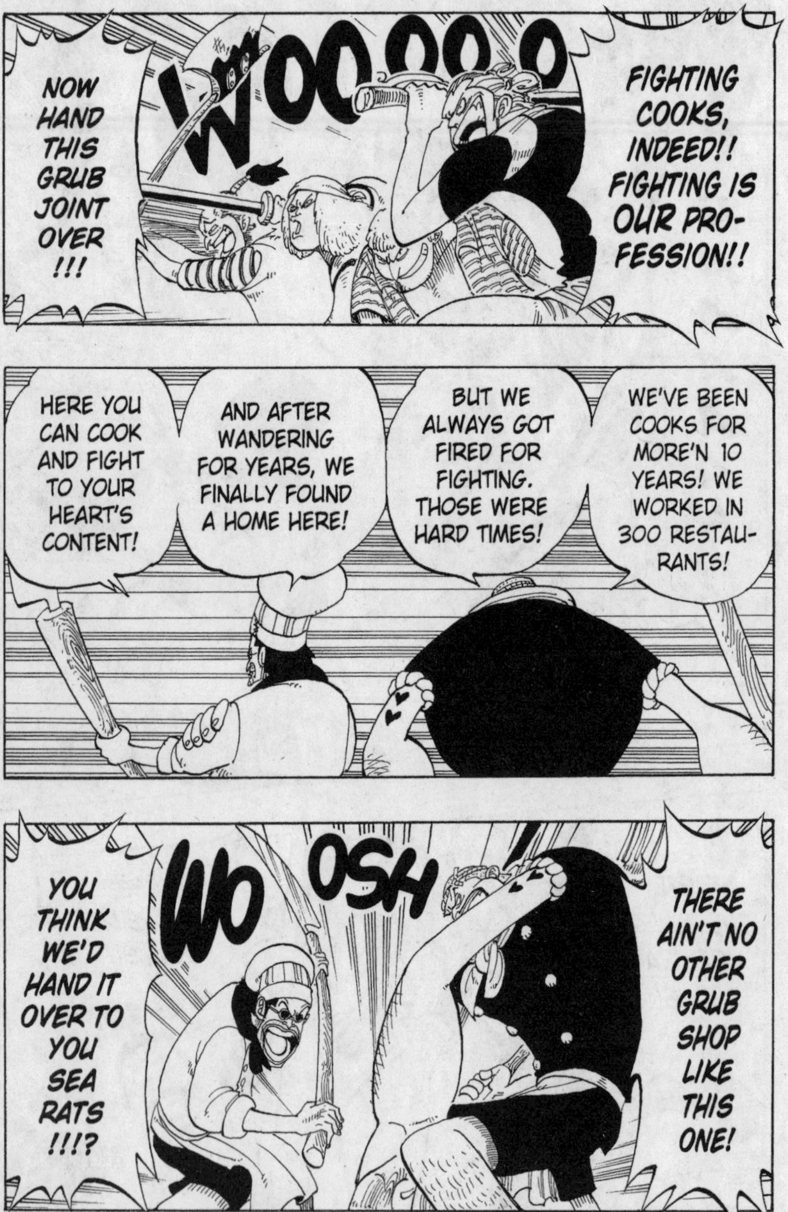
WOOOOOO
FIGHTING COOKS, INDEED!! FIGHTING IS OUR PRO-FESSION!!
NOW HAND THIS GRUB JOINT OVER!!!
WE'VE BEEN COOKS FOR MORE'N 10 YEARS! WE WORKED IN 300 RESTAU-RANTS!
BUT WE ALWAYS GOT FIRED FOR FIGHTING. THOSE WERE HARD TIMES!
AND AFTER WANDERING FOR YEARS, WE FINALLY FOUND A HOME HERE!
HERE YOU CAN COOK AND FIGHT TO YOUR HEART'S CONTENT!
THERE AIN'T NO OTHER GRUB SHOP LIKE THIS ONE!
WOOSH
YOU THINK WE'D HAND IT OVER TO YOU SEA RATS!!!?

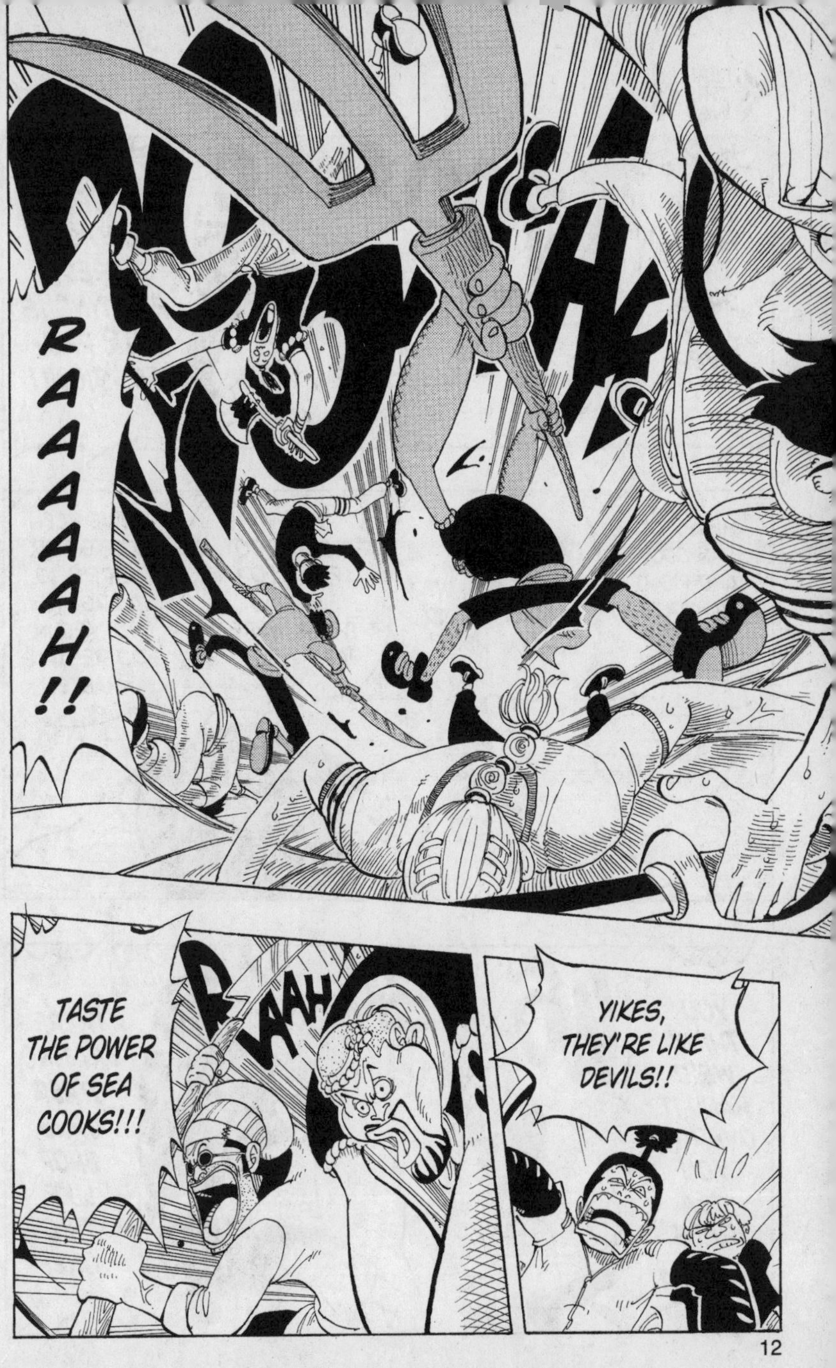
RAAAAAH!!
YIKES, THEY'RE LIKE DEVILS!!
TASTE THE POWER OF SEA COOKS!!!

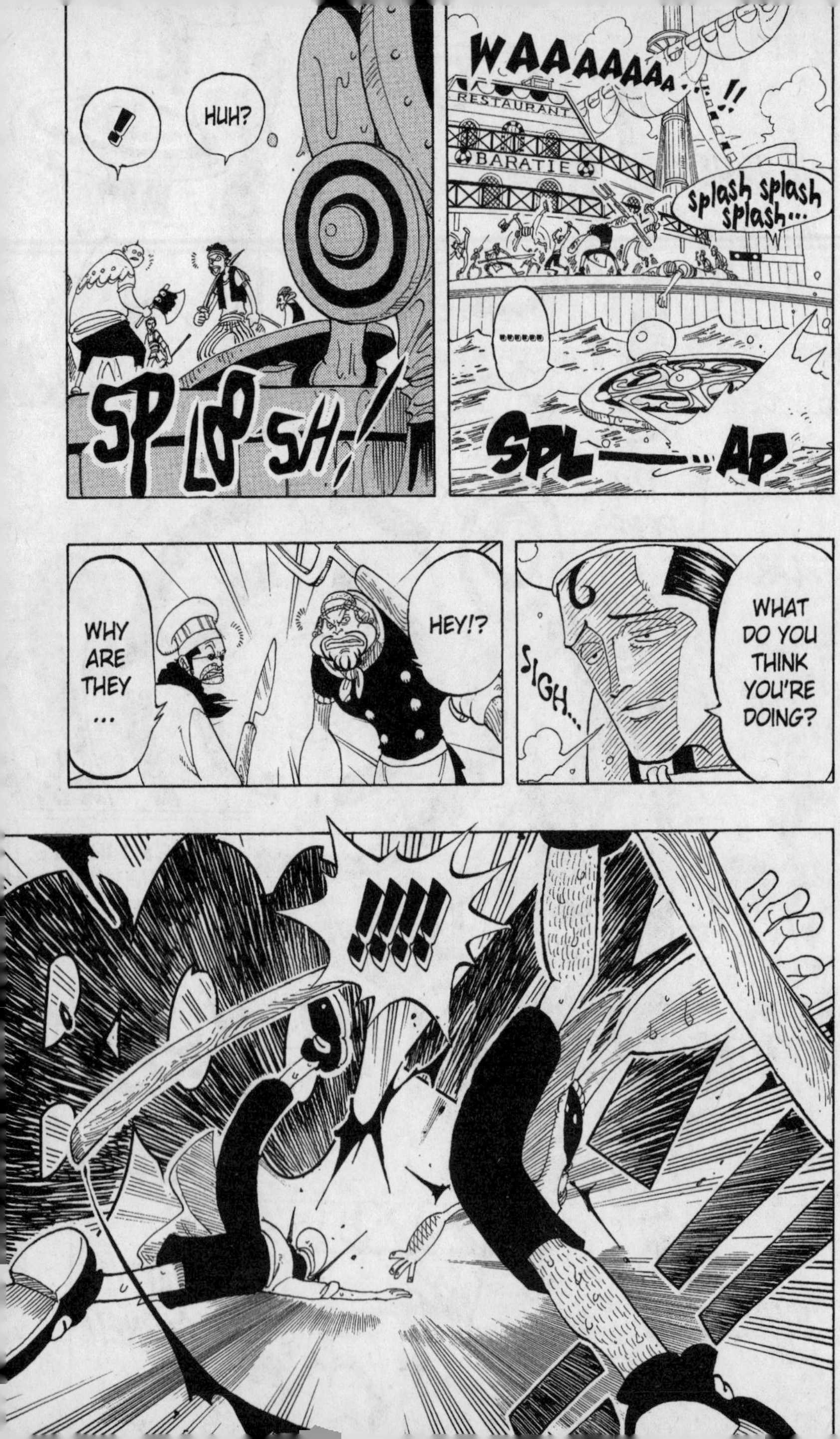
WAAAAAAA...!!
RESTAURANT
BARATIE
splash splash splash...
......
SPL——...AP
HUH?
!
SPLOPSH!
WHAT DO YOU THINK YOU'RE DOING?
SIGH...
HEY!?
WHY ARE THEY ...
!!!!

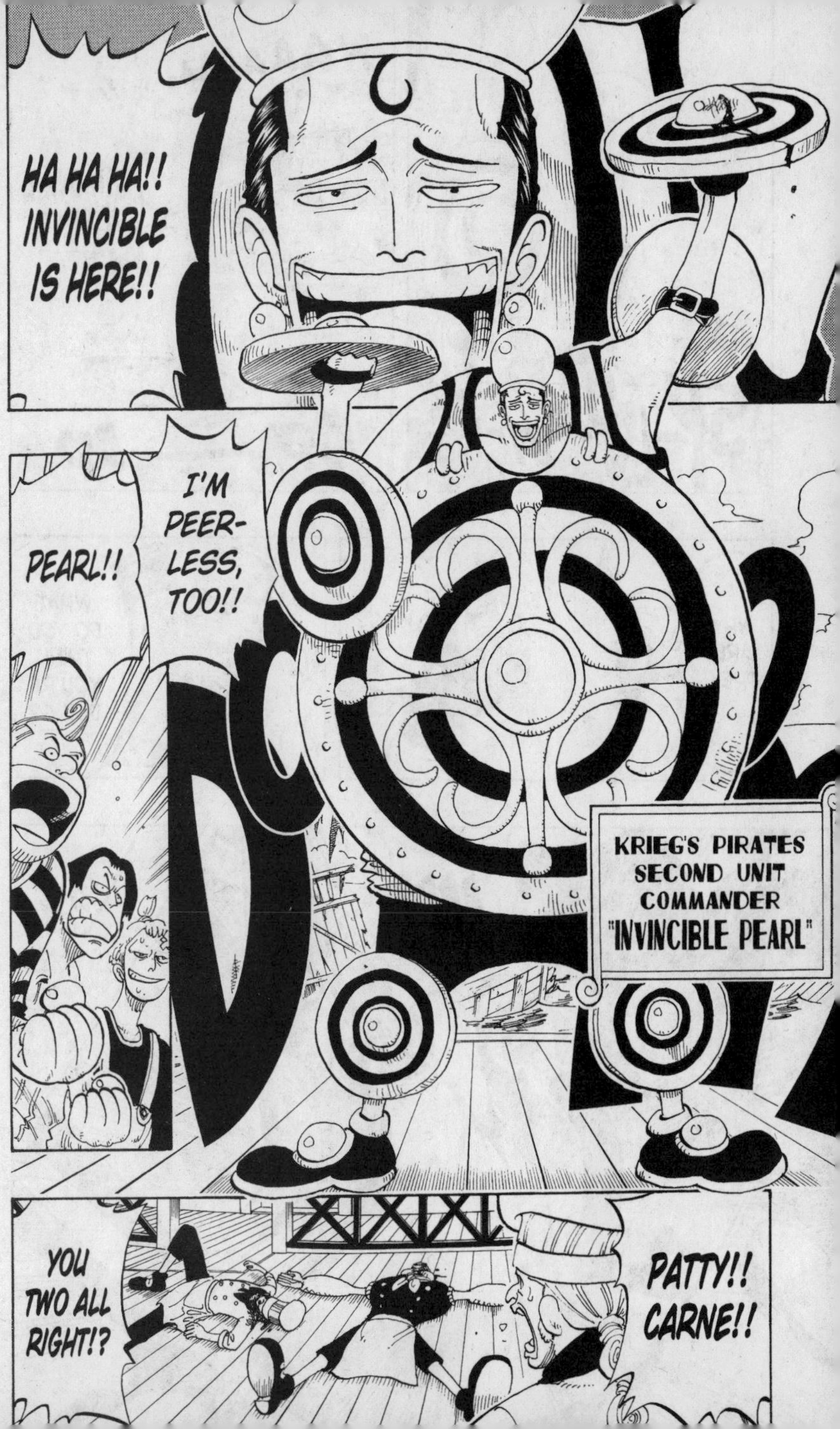
HA HA HA!! INVINCIBLE IS HERE!!
I'M PEERLESS, TOO!!
KRIEG'S PIRATES SECOND UNIT COMMANDER "INVINCIBLE PEARL"
PEARL!!
PATTY!! CARNE!!
YOU TWO ALL RIGHT!?

READ THIS WAY

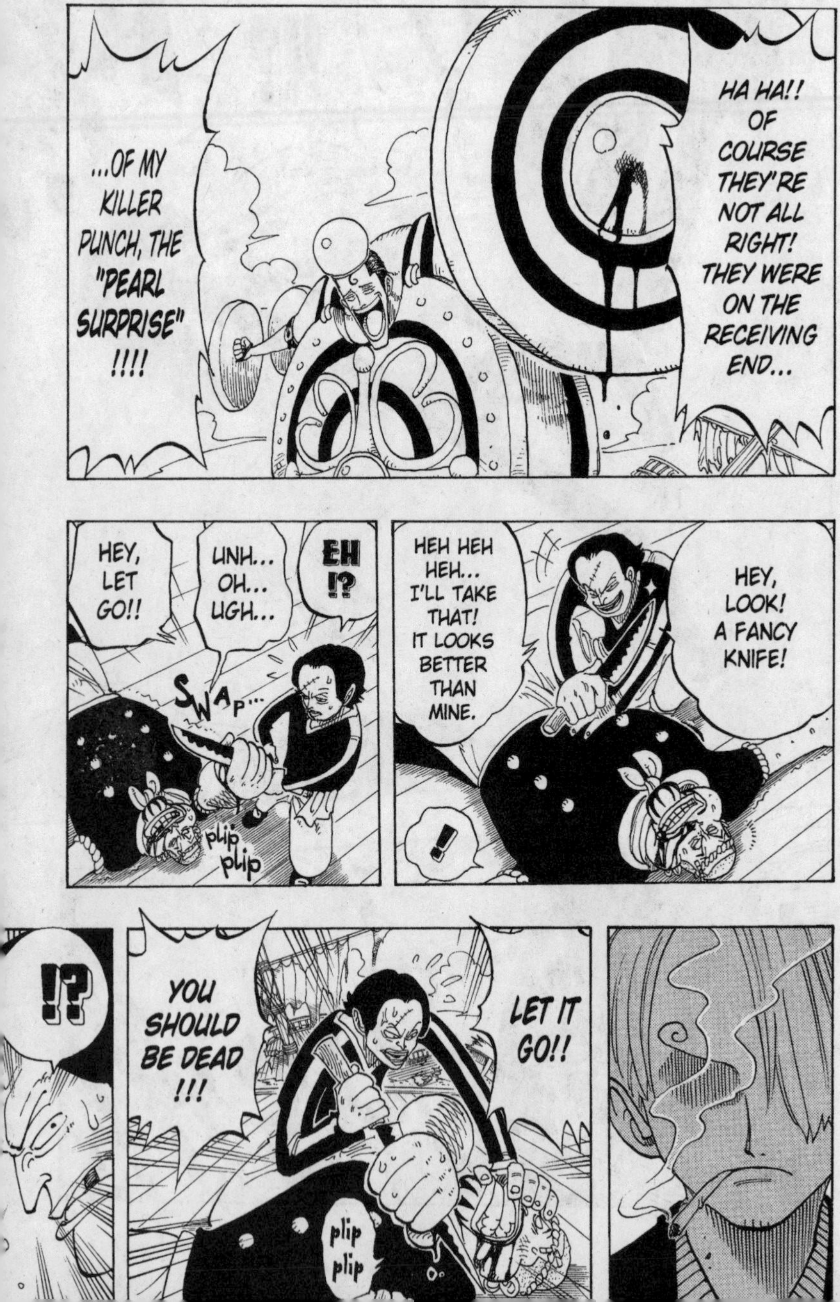
HA HA!! OF COURSE THEY'RE NOT ALL RIGHT! THEY WERE ON THE RECEIVING END...
...OF MY KILLER PUNCH, THE "PEARL SURPRISE" !!!!
HEY, LOOK! A FANCY KNIFE!
HEH HEH HEH... I'LL TAKE THAT! IT LOOKS BETTER THAN MINE.
!
EH !?
UNH... OH... UGH...
HEY, LET GO!!
SWAP...
plip plip
LET IT GO!!
YOU SHOULD BE DEAD !!!
plip plip
!?

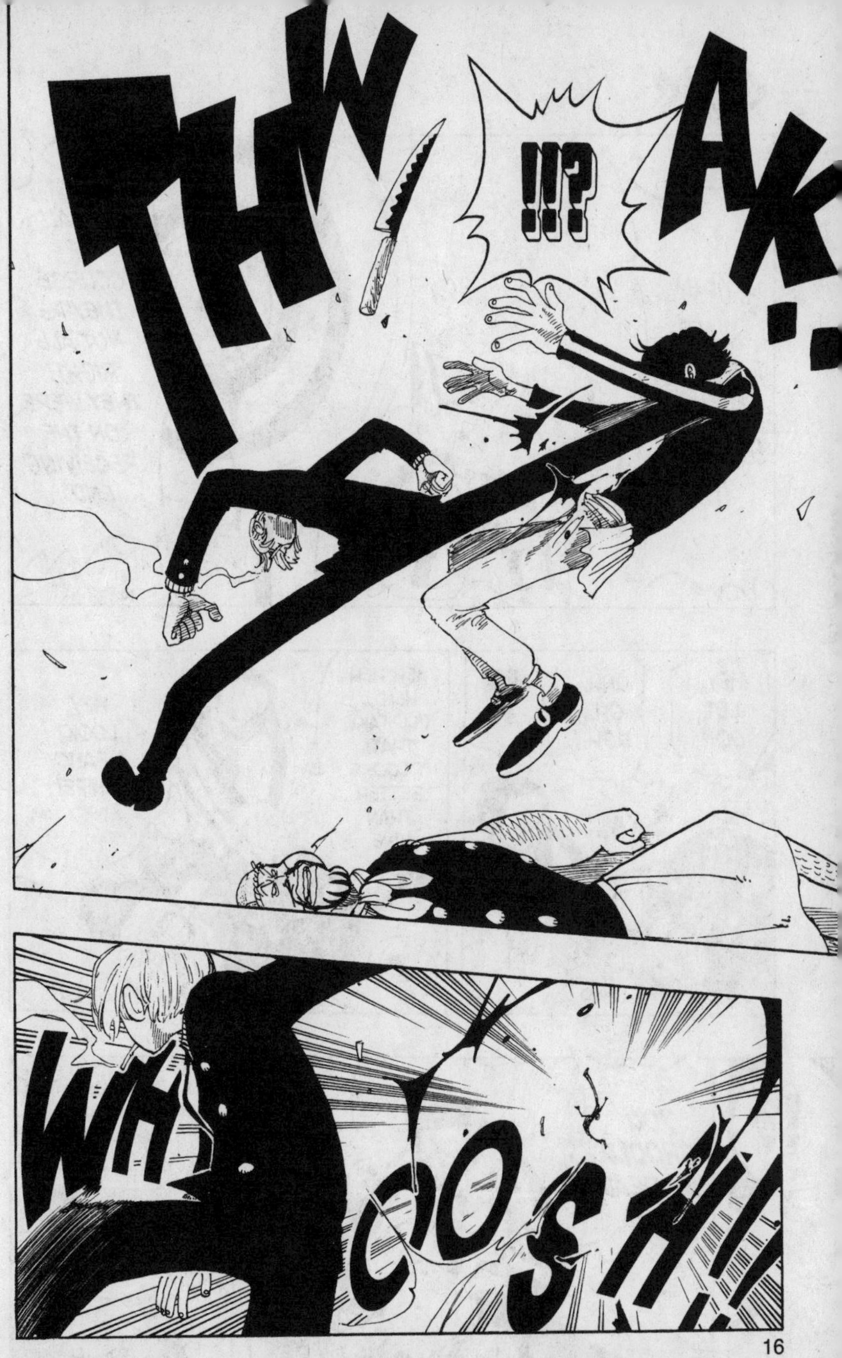
THWAK..
!!?
WHOOSH!!

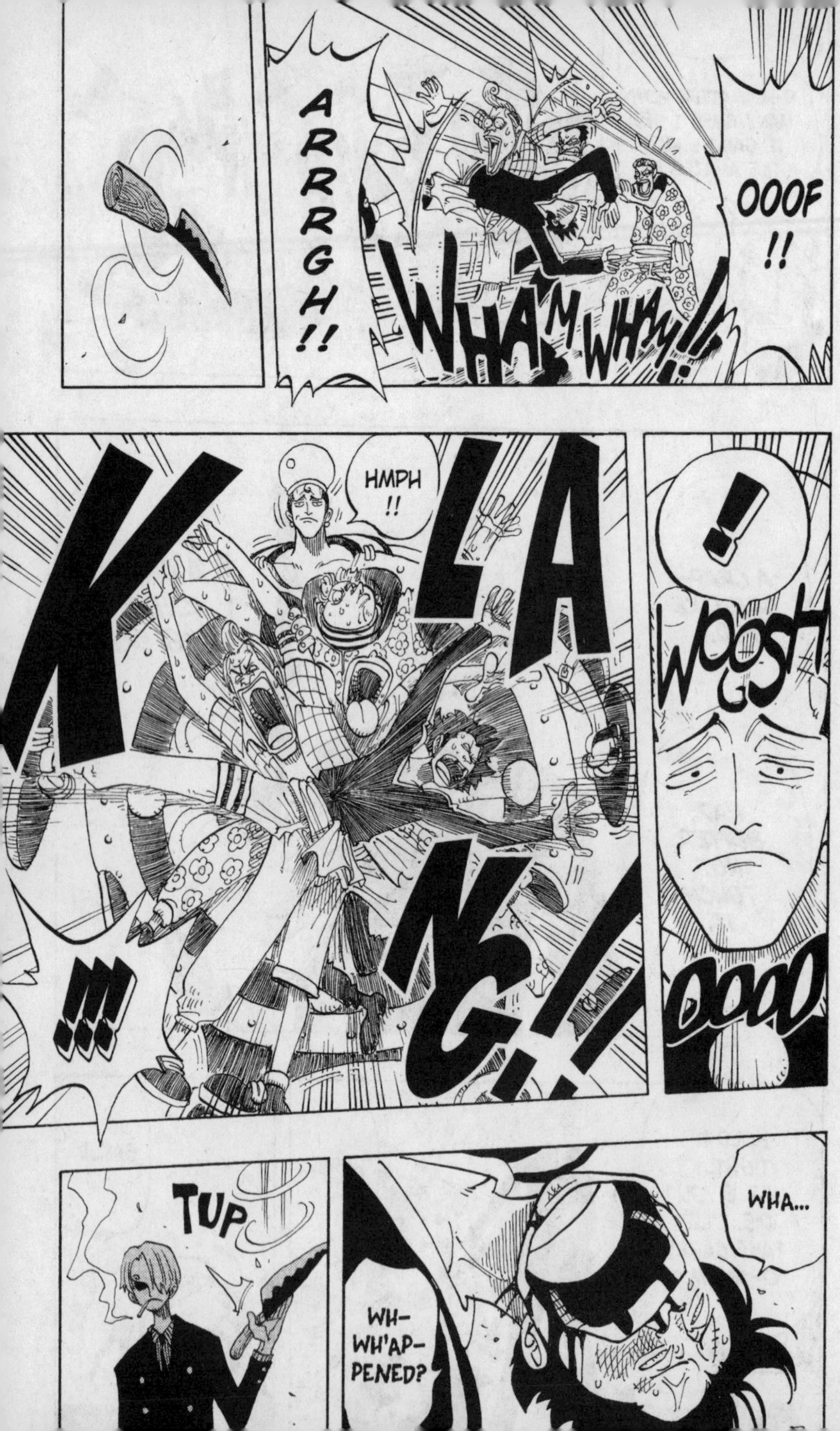
OOOF!!
ARRRGH!!
WHAM WHAM!!
!
WOOSH!
DOOO
HMPH!!
KLANG!!
!!!!
WHA...
WH-WH'AP-PENED?
TUP

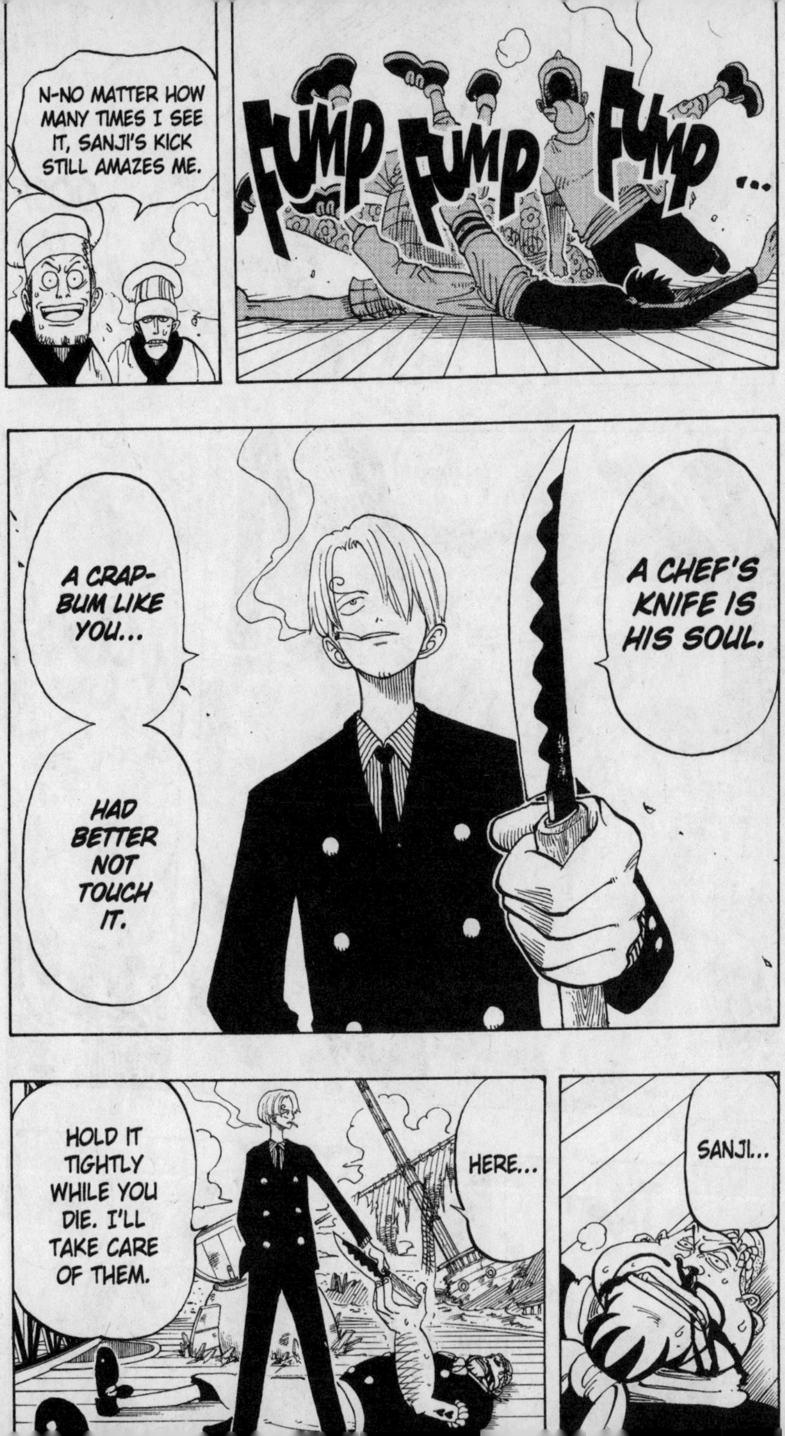
FUMP FUMP FUMP...
N-NO MATTER HOW MANY TIMES I SEE IT, SANJI'S KICK STILL AMAZES ME.
A CHEF'S KNIFE IS HIS SOUL.
A CRAP-BUM LIKE YOU...
HAD BETTER NOT TOUCH IT.
SANJI...
HERE...
HOLD IT TIGHTLY WHILE YOU DIE. I'LL TAKE CARE OF THEM.

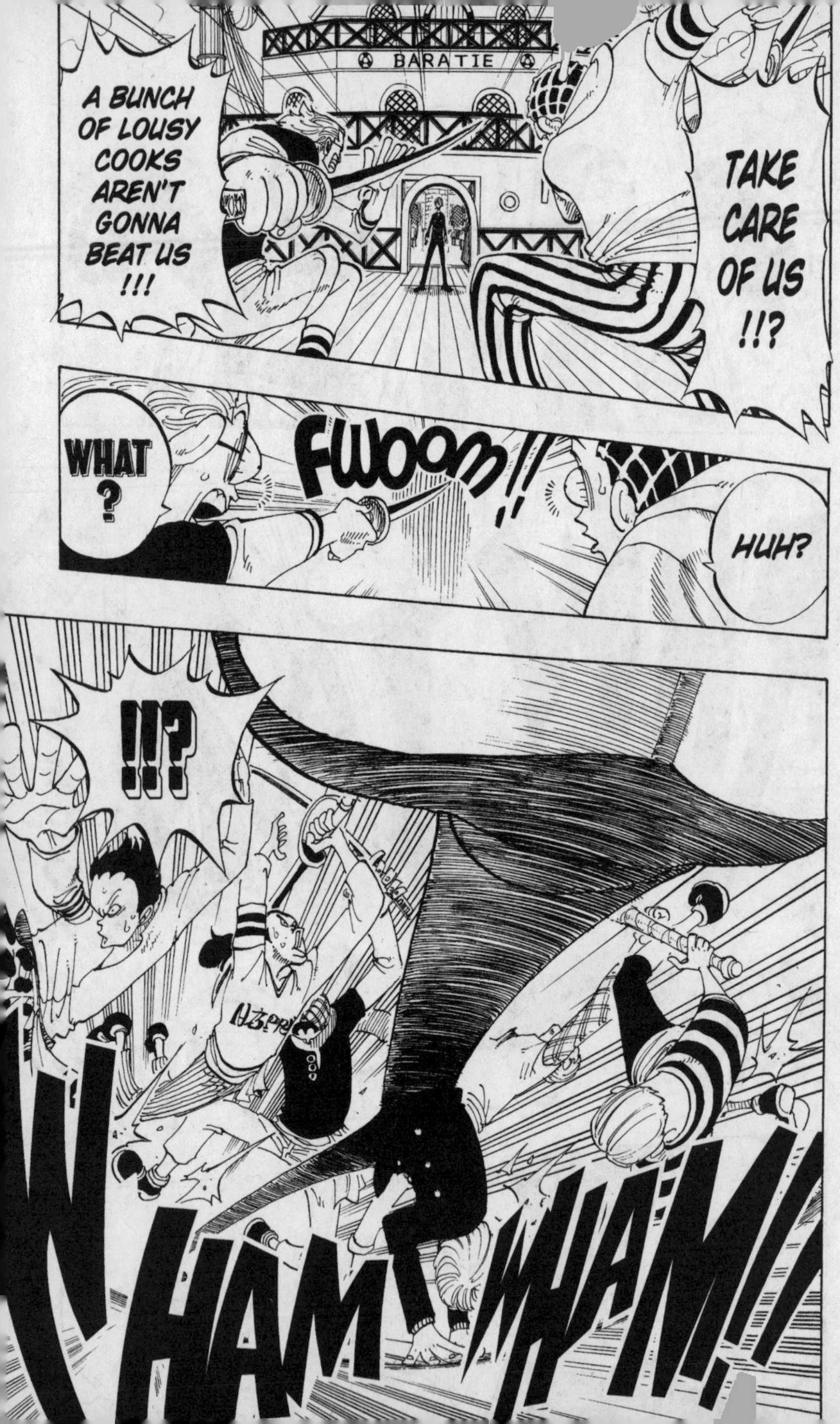
BARATIE
TAKE CARE OF US !!?
A BUNCH OF LOUSY COOKS AREN'T GONNA BEAT US !!!
HUH?
FWOOM!!
WHAT?
!!?
WHAM WHAM!!

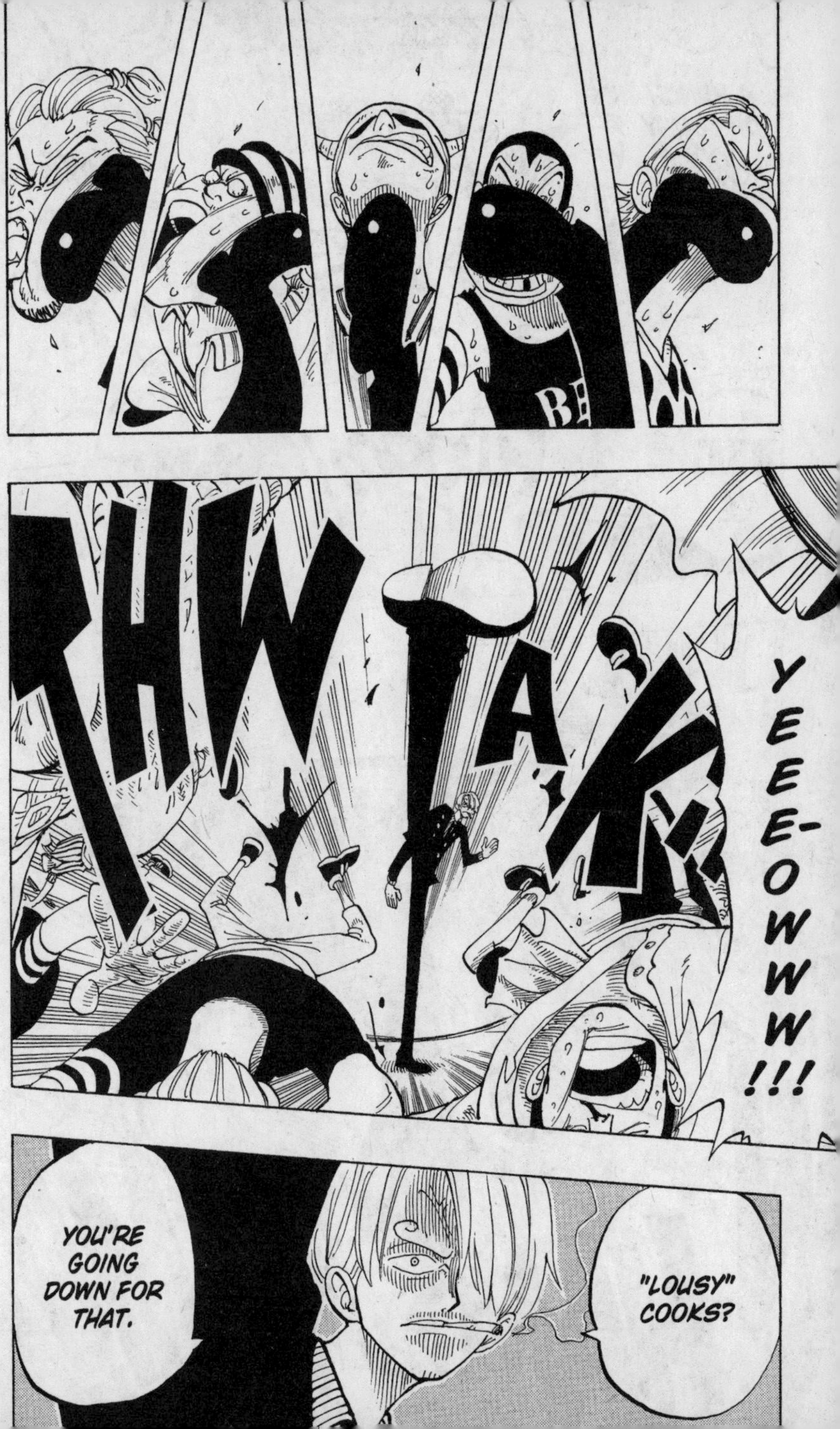
YEEEOWWW!!!
THWAK
"LOUSY" COOKS?
YOU'RE GOING DOWN FOR THAT.

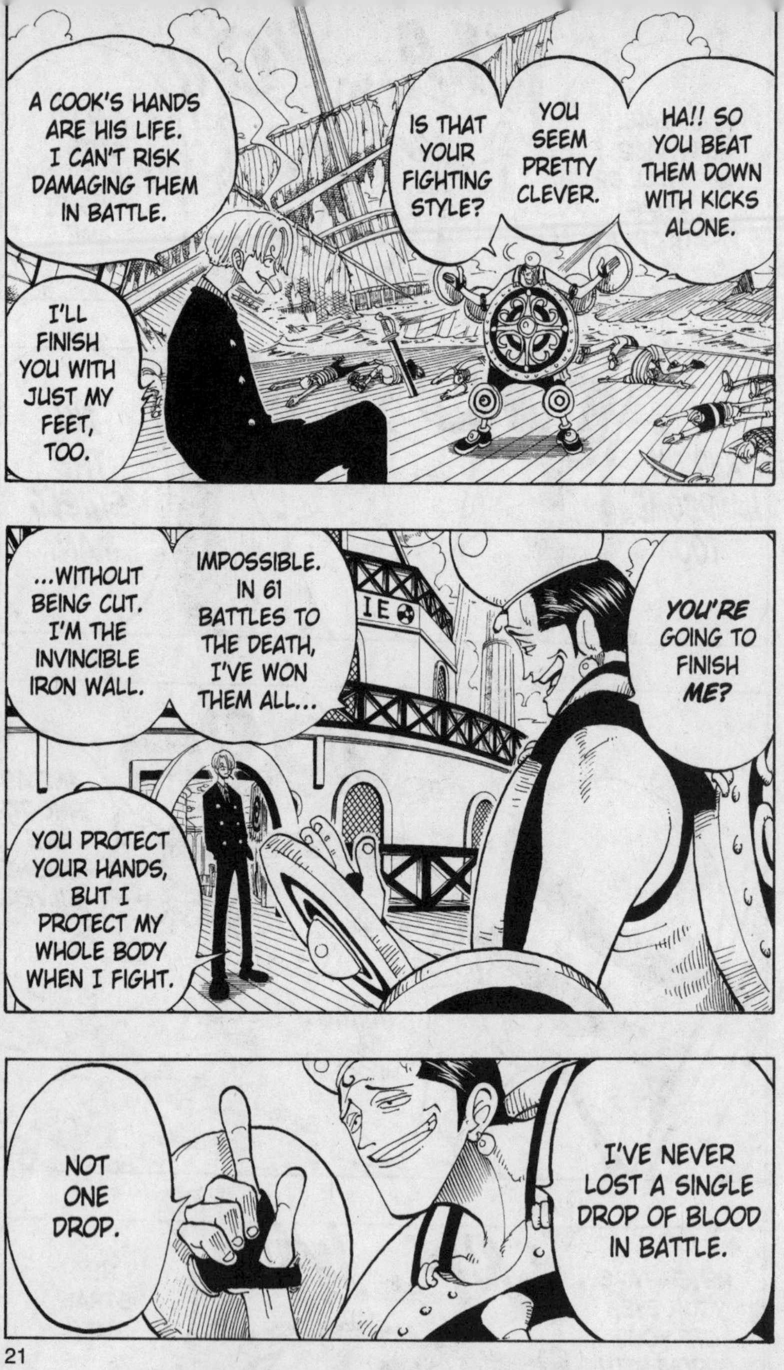
HA!! SO YOU BEAT THEM DOWN WITH KICKS ALONE.
YOU SEEM PRETTY CLEVER.
IS THAT YOUR FIGHTING STYLE?
A COOK'S HANDS ARE HIS LIFE. I CAN'T RISK DAMAGING THEM IN BATTLE.
I'LL FINISH YOU WITH JUST MY FEET, TOO.
*YOU'RE* GOING TO FINISH *ME?*
IMPOSSIBLE. IN 61 BATTLES TO THE DEATH, I'VE WON THEM ALL...
...WITHOUT BEING CUT. I'M THE INVINCIBLE IRON WALL.
YOU PROTECT YOUR HANDS, BUT I PROTECT MY WHOLE BODY WHEN I FIGHT.
I'VE NEVER LOST A SINGLE DROP OF BLOOD IN BATTLE.
NOT ONE DROP.

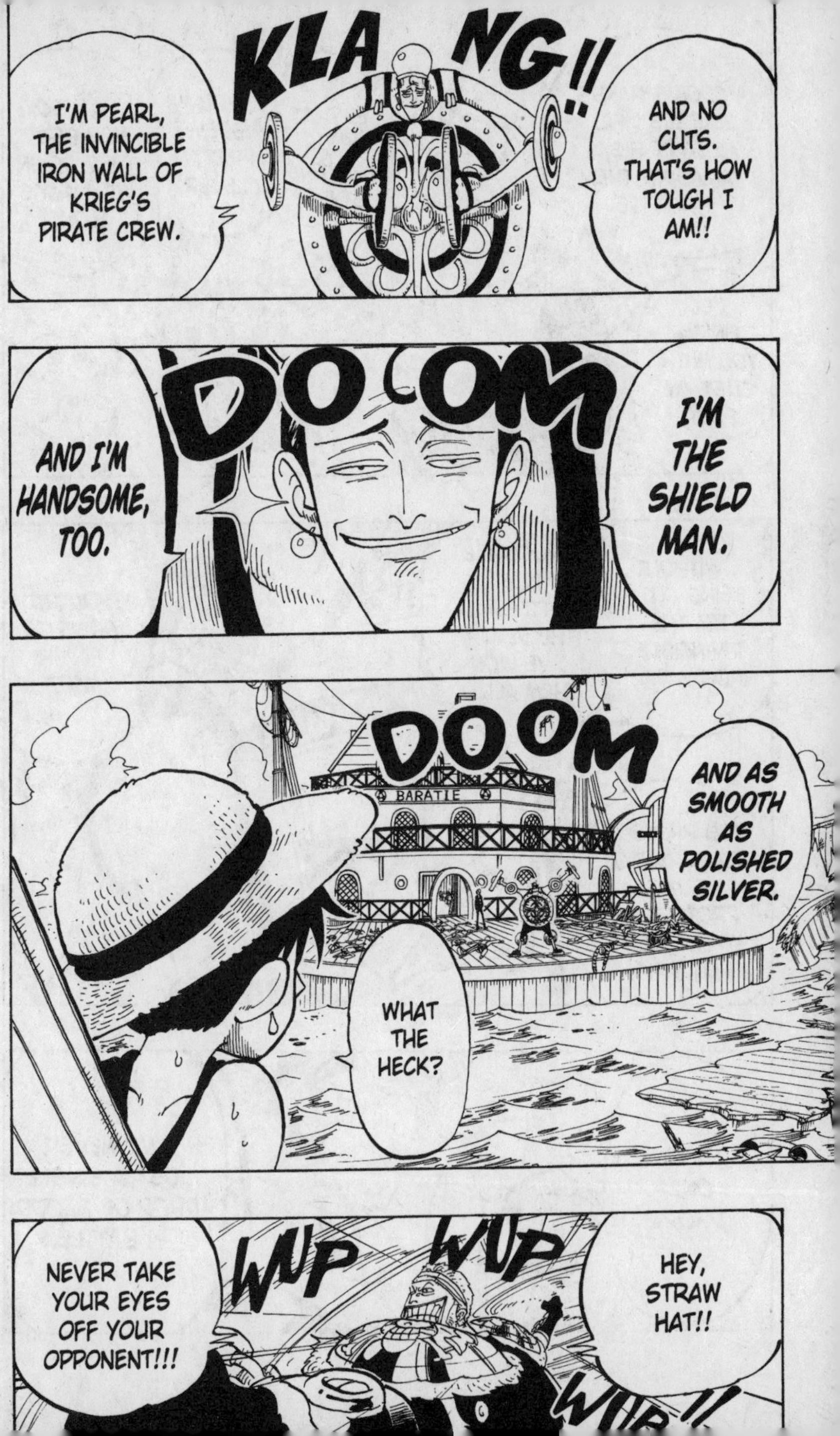
KLANG!!
AND NO CUTS. THAT'S HOW TOUGH I AM!!
I'M PEARL, THE INVINCIBLE IRON WALL OF KRIEG'S PIRATE CREW.
DOOM
I'M THE SHIELD MAN.
AND I'M HANDSOME, TOO.
DOOM
BARATIE
AND AS SMOOTH AS POLISHED SILVER.
WHAT THE HECK?
WUP WUP
HEY, STRAW HAT!!
NEVER TAKE YOUR EYES OFF YOUR OPPONENT!!!
WUP!!

READ THIS WAY

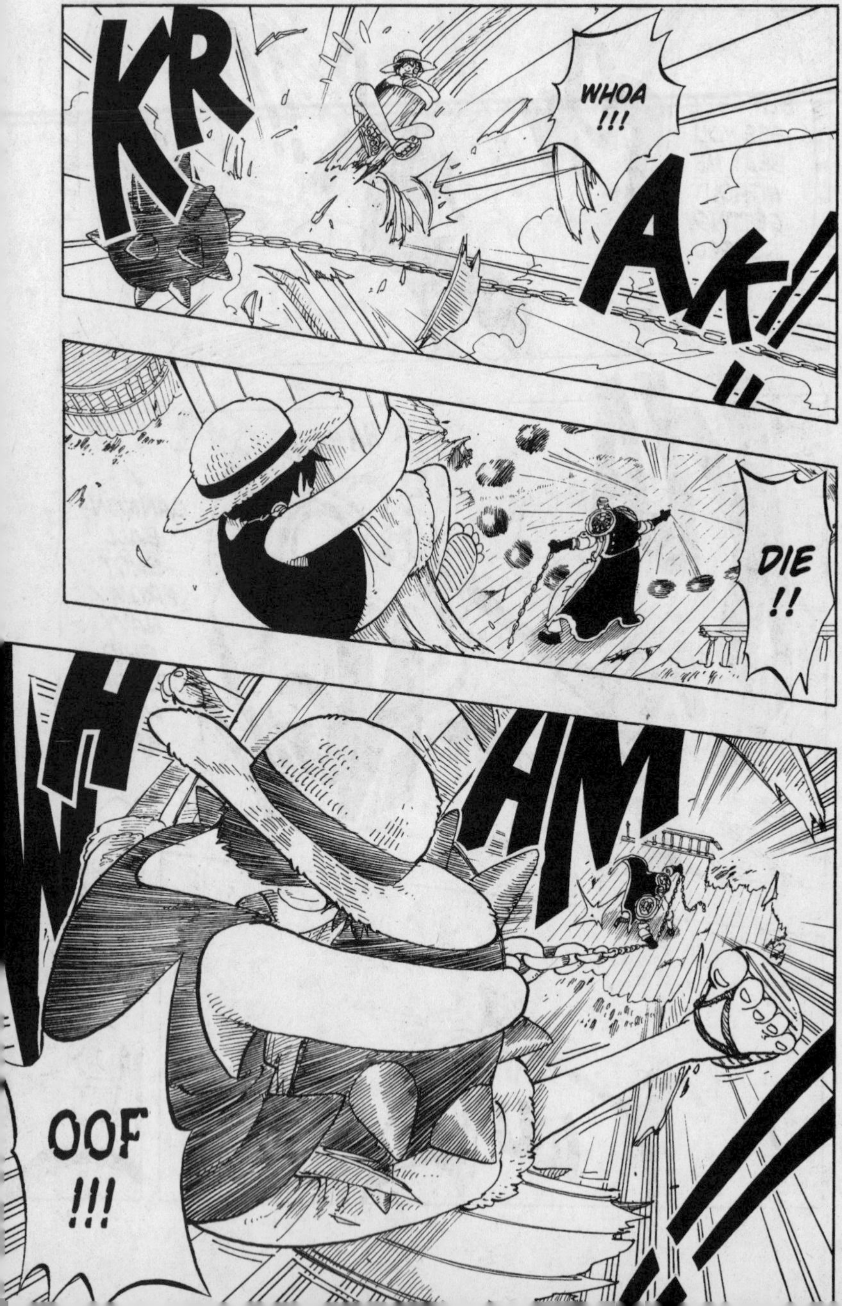
WHOA !!!
KRAK!!
DIE !!
WHAM!!
OOF !!!

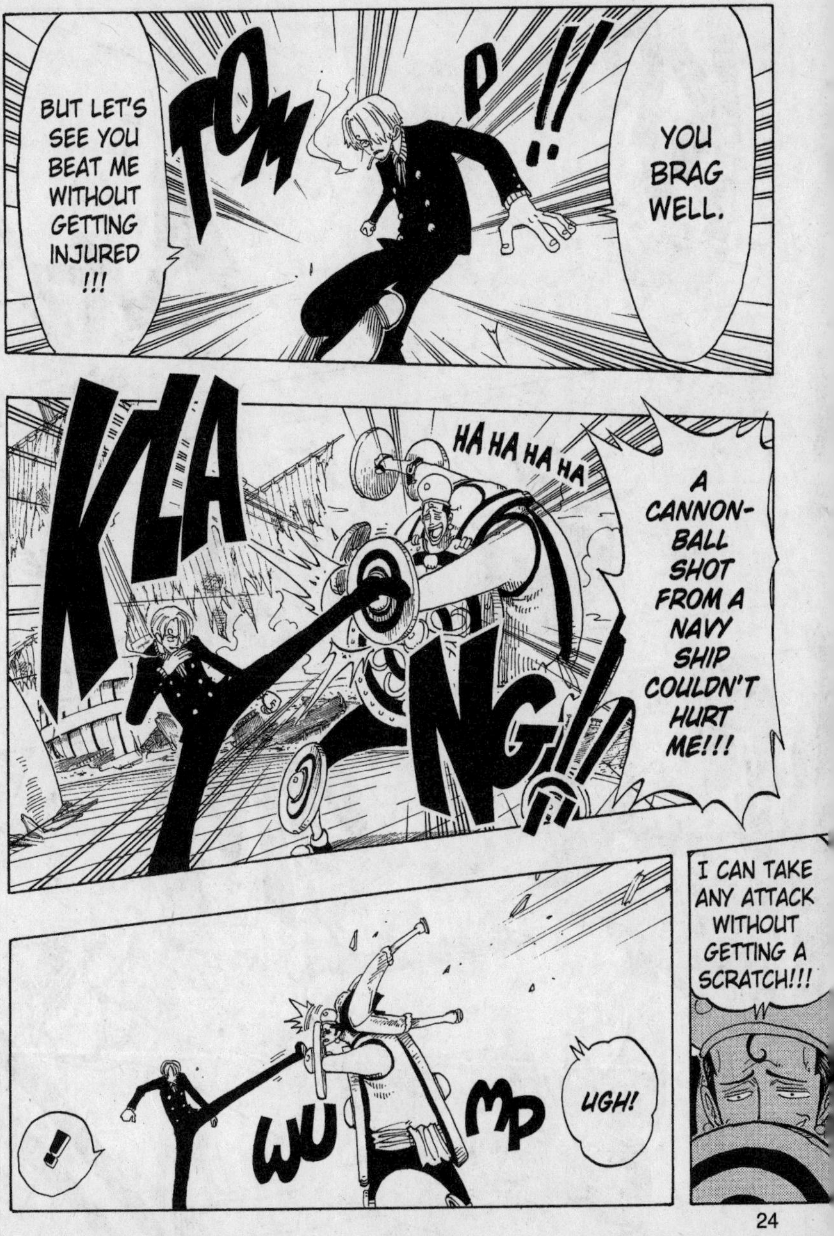
YOU BRAG WELL.
TOMP!!
BUT LET'S SEE YOU BEAT ME WITHOUT GETTING INJURED!!!
A CANNON-BALL SHOT FROM A NAVY SHIP COULDN'T HURT ME!!!
HA HA HA HA
KLANG!!
I CAN TAKE ANY ATTACK WITHOUT GETTING A SCRATCH!!!
UGH!
WUMP
!

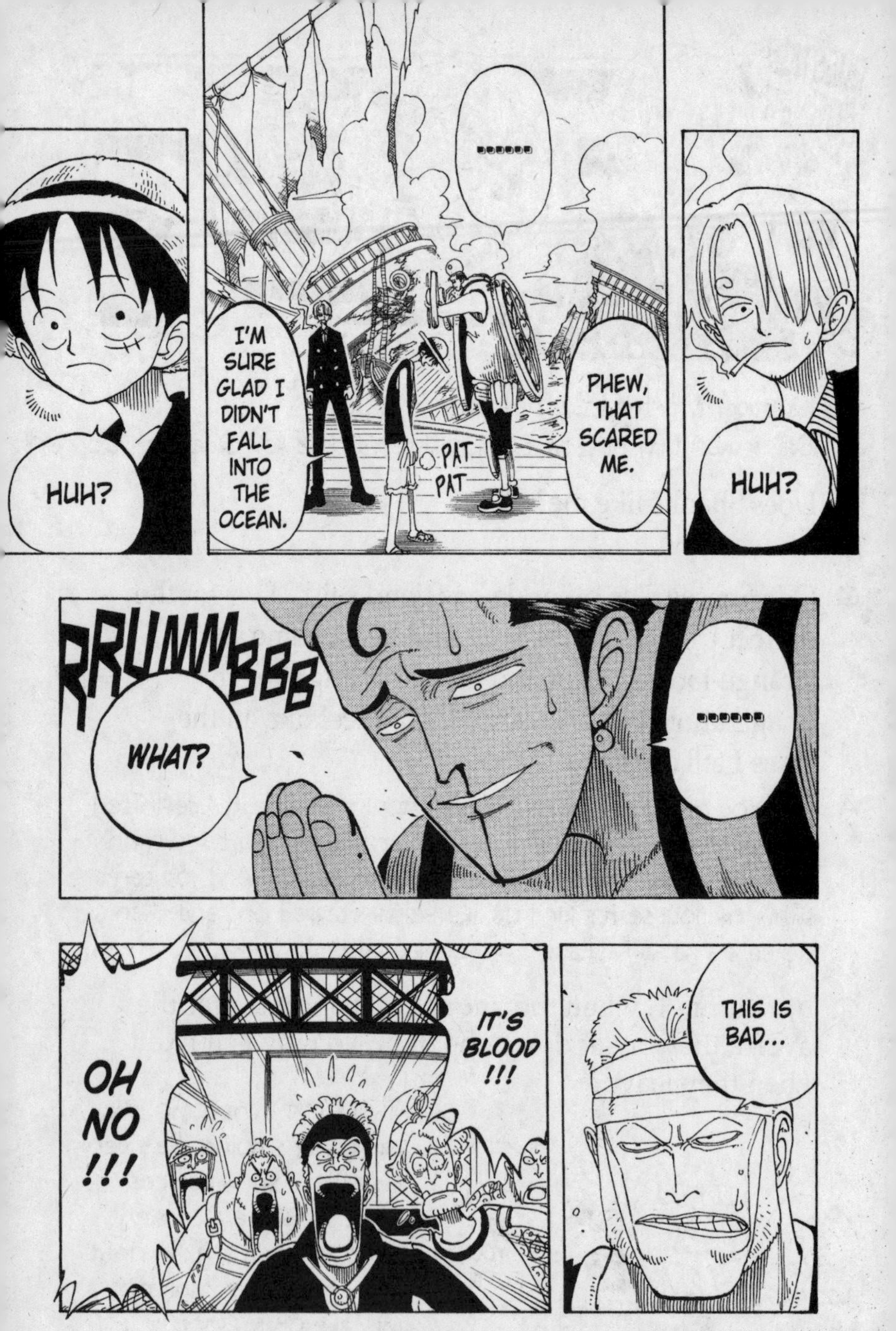
HUH?
......
PHEW, THAT SCARED ME.
PAT PAT
I'M SURE GLAD I DIDN'T FALL INTO THE OCEAN.
HUH?
......
RRUMMBBB
WHAT?
THIS IS BAD...
IT'S BLOOD!!!
OH NO!!!

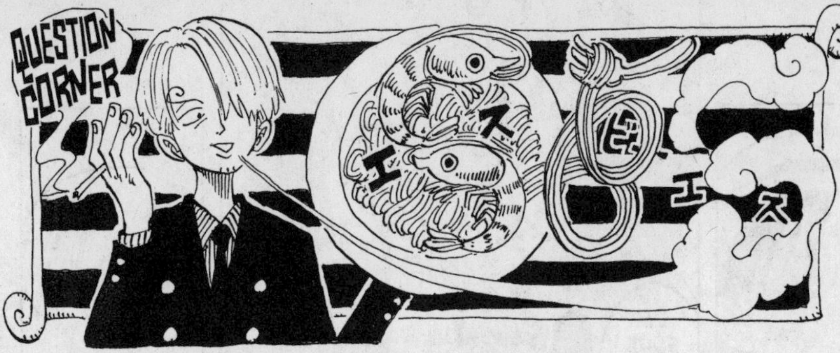
QUESTION CORNER

Q: (Question) Master Ei, what time is it now?

A: (Oda's answer) Um, nine past...midnight! It's time for Question Corner!!

Q: Does Shanks like me?

A: I don't know.

Q: Oda Sensei! The other day a friend said, "I've got the perfect Devil Fruit for you" and he gave me some strange-looking fruit and I ate it. It might be my imagination, but ever since then, I feel like all the jokes I tell are flops.

A: Oh...You ate that one, eh? Yes, I know that one. It's definitely a Samu-Samu (chilly-chilly) Fruit. When you eat that fruit, only really bad (chilly) jokes come out of your mouth. And you can't swim, of course. It's kind of like being stepped on...and then kicked. Ha ha ha ha! Laugh. Go on, laugh! Ha ha ha ha.

Q: In volume 1, when the mountain bandits enter the tavern, they break down the door, so why is it fixed when they leave?

A: That's Mr. Minatomo, the carpenter's doing. He's very impatient, so if he sees something like a broken door, he has to fix it right away. It was certainly not a mistake on my part.

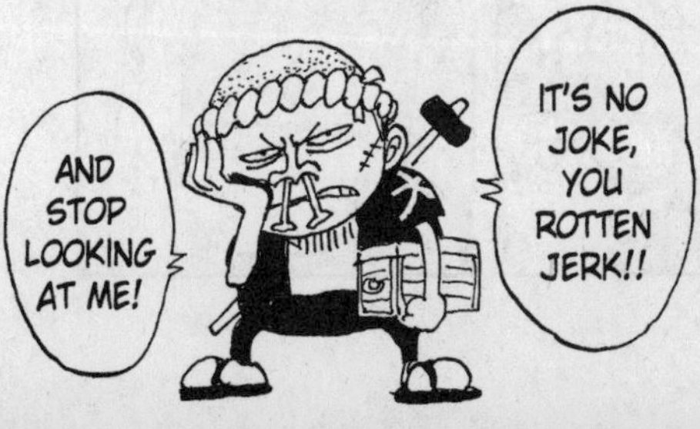
IT'S NO JOKE, YOU ROTTEN JERK!!
AND STOP LOOKING AT ME!

# Chapter 55:
# JUNGLE BLOOD

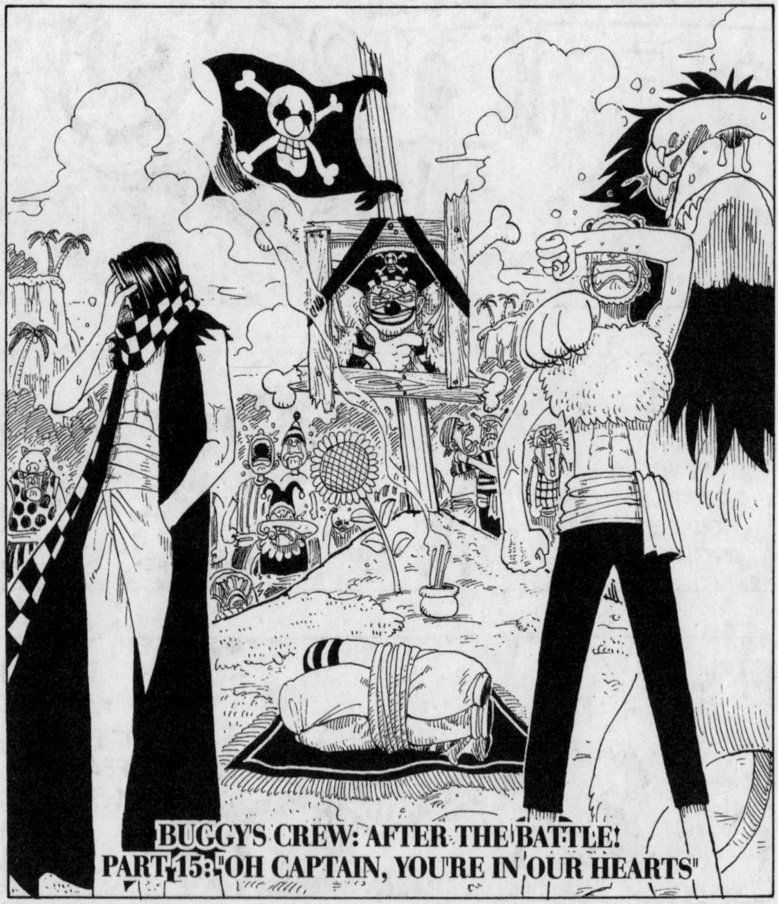
BUGGY'S CREW: AFTER THE BATTLE!
PART 15: "OH CAPTAIN, YOU'RE IN OUR HEARTS"

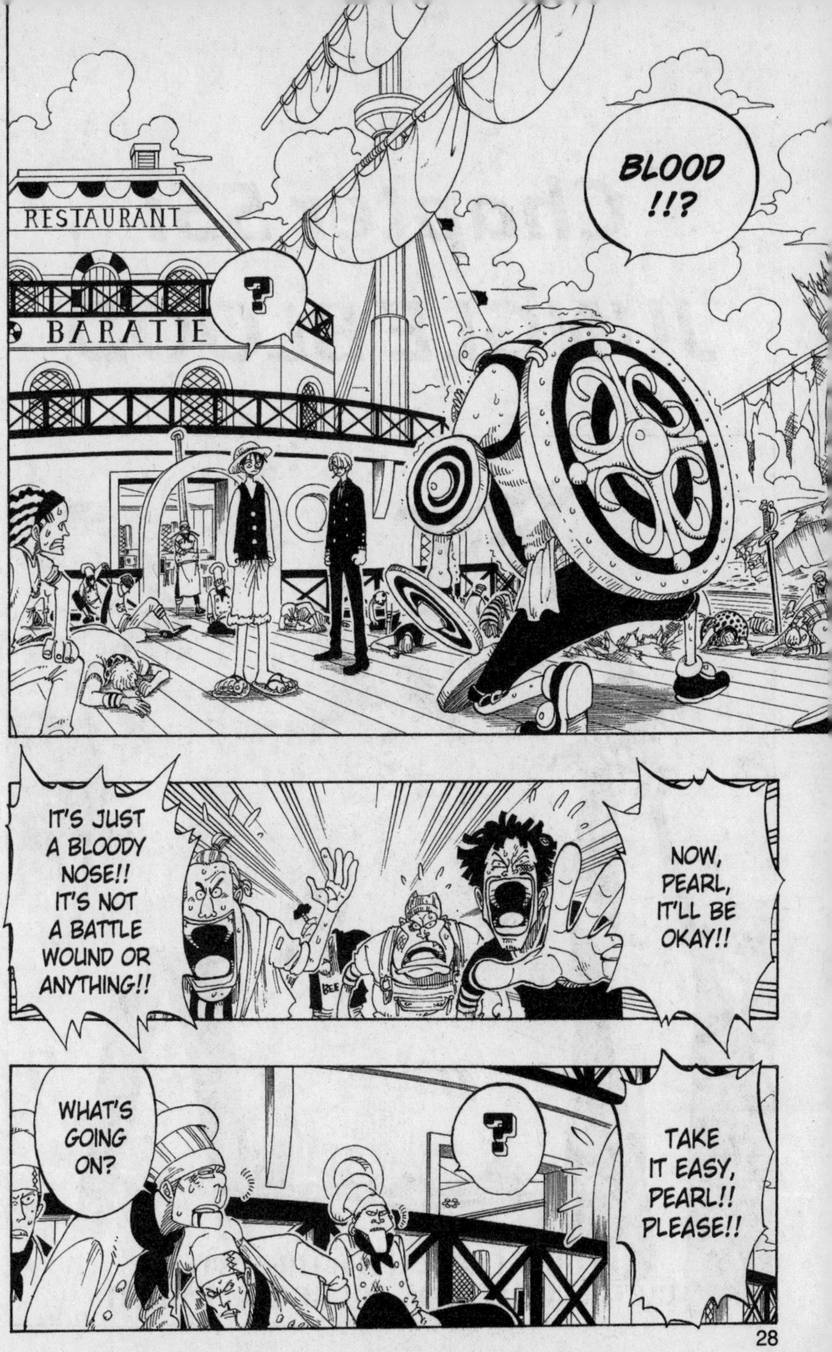
BLOOD !!?
RESTAURANT
?
BARATIE
NOW, PEARL, IT'LL BE OKAY!!
IT'S JUST A BLOODY NOSE!! IT'S NOT A BATTLE WOUND OR ANYTHING!!
TAKE IT EASY, PEARL!! PLEASE!!
?
WHAT'S GOING ON?

READ THIS WAY

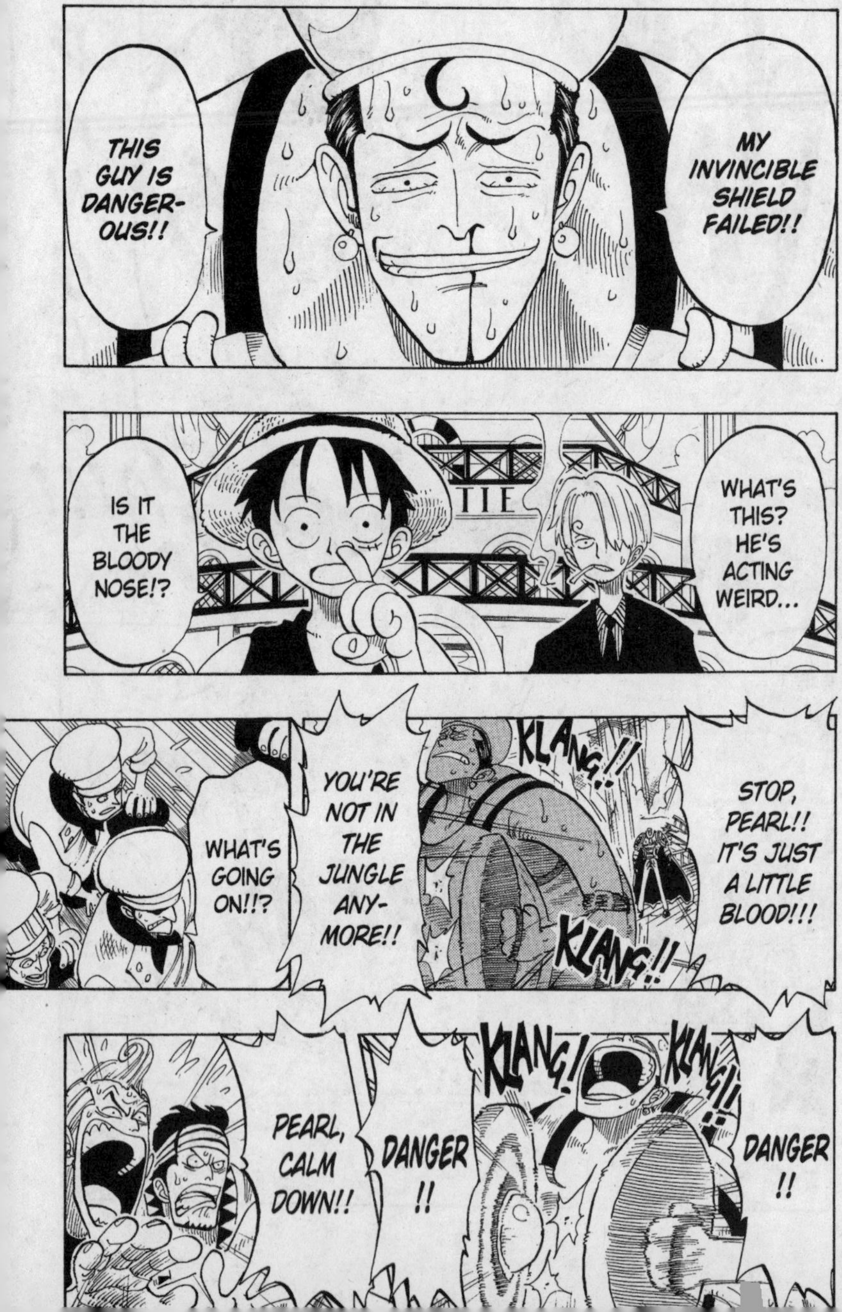
MY INVINCIBLE SHIELD FAILED!!
THIS GUY IS DANGER-OUS!!
WHAT'S THIS? HE'S ACTING WEIRD...
IS IT THE BLOODY NOSE!?
STOP, PEARL!! IT'S JUST A LITTLE BLOOD!!!
KLANG!!
KLANG!!
YOU'RE NOT IN THE JUNGLE ANY-MORE!!
WHAT'S GOING ON!!?
DANGER!!
KLANG!!
KLANG!
DANGER!!
PEARL, CALM DOWN!!

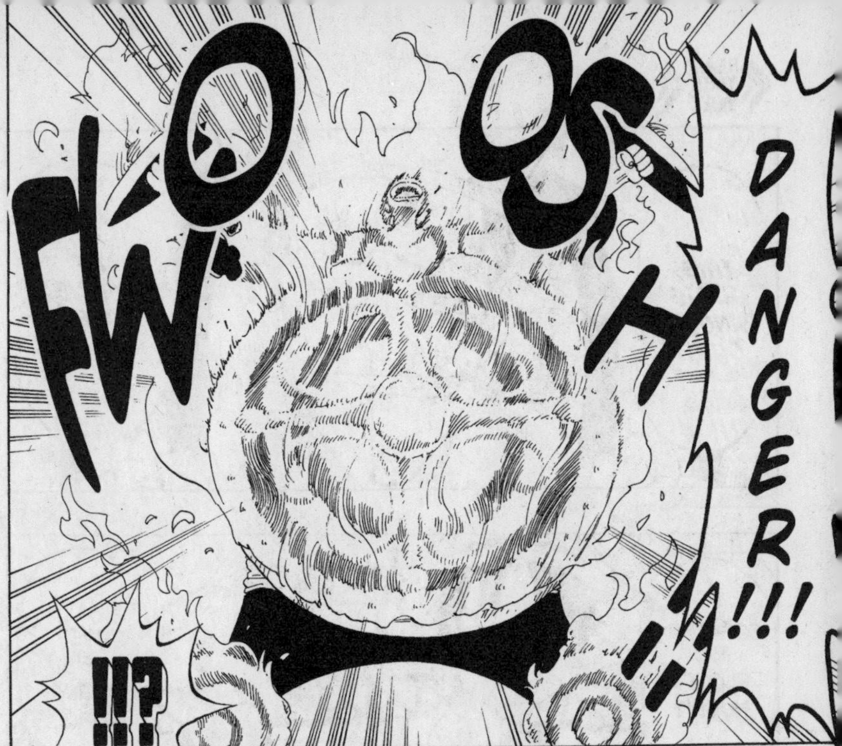
DANGER!!!
FWOOSH!!
!!?

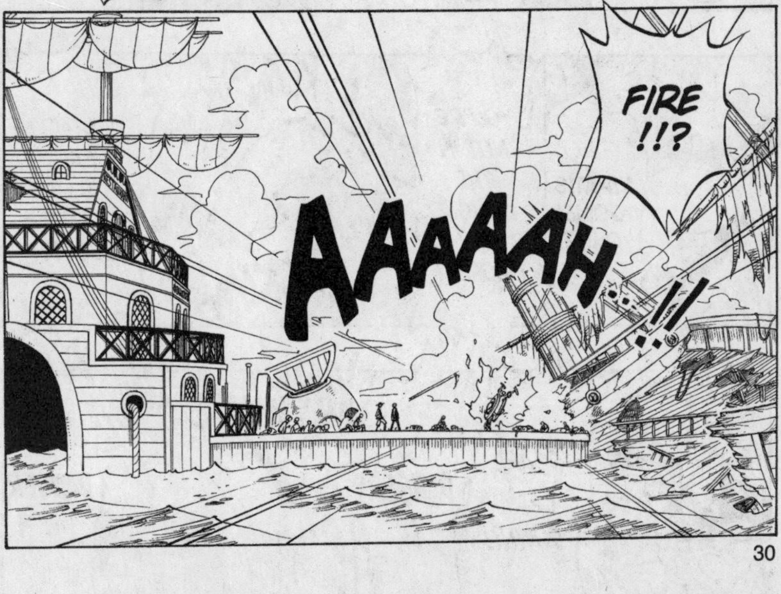
FIRE!!?
AAAAAH...!!

READ THIS WAY

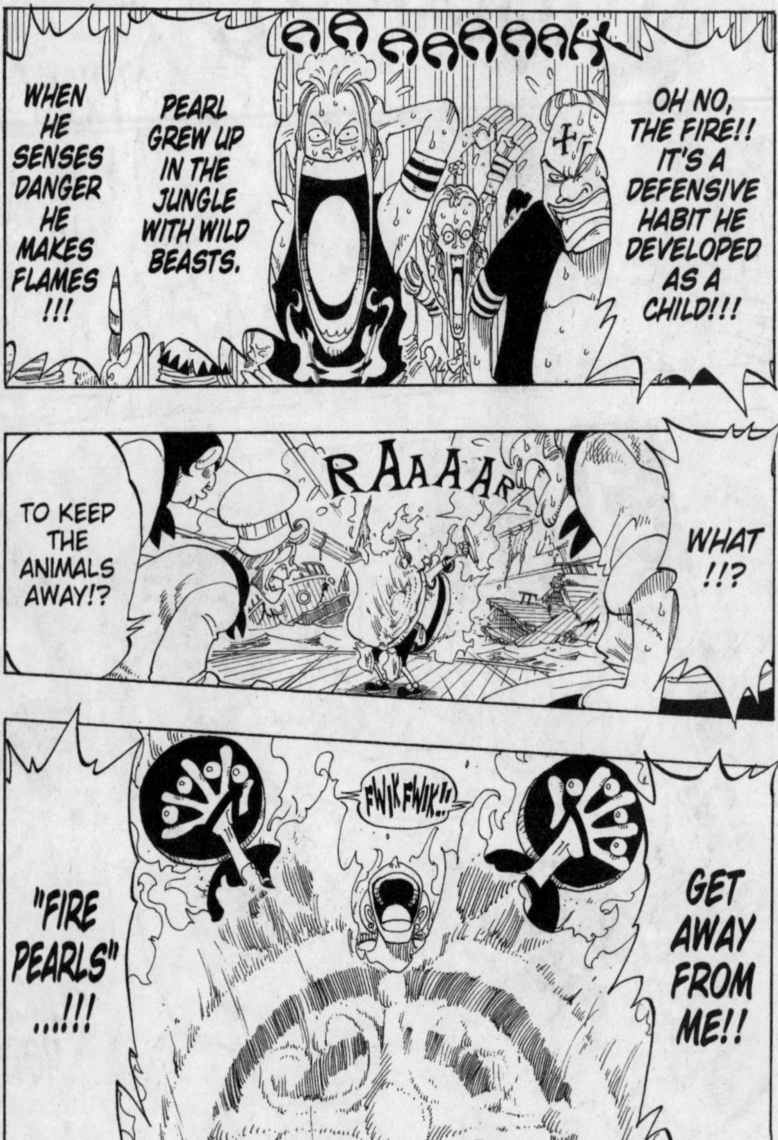

AAAAAAAAH
OH NO, THE FIRE!! IT'S A DEFENSIVE HABIT HE DEVELOPED AS A CHILD!!!
PEARL GREW UP IN THE JUNGLE WITH WILD BEASTS.
WHEN HE SENSES DANGER HE MAKES FLAMES!!!
WHAT!!?
RAAAAR
TO KEEP THE ANIMALS AWAY!?
GET AWAY FROM ME!!
FWIK FWIK!!
"FIRE PEARLS"...!!!

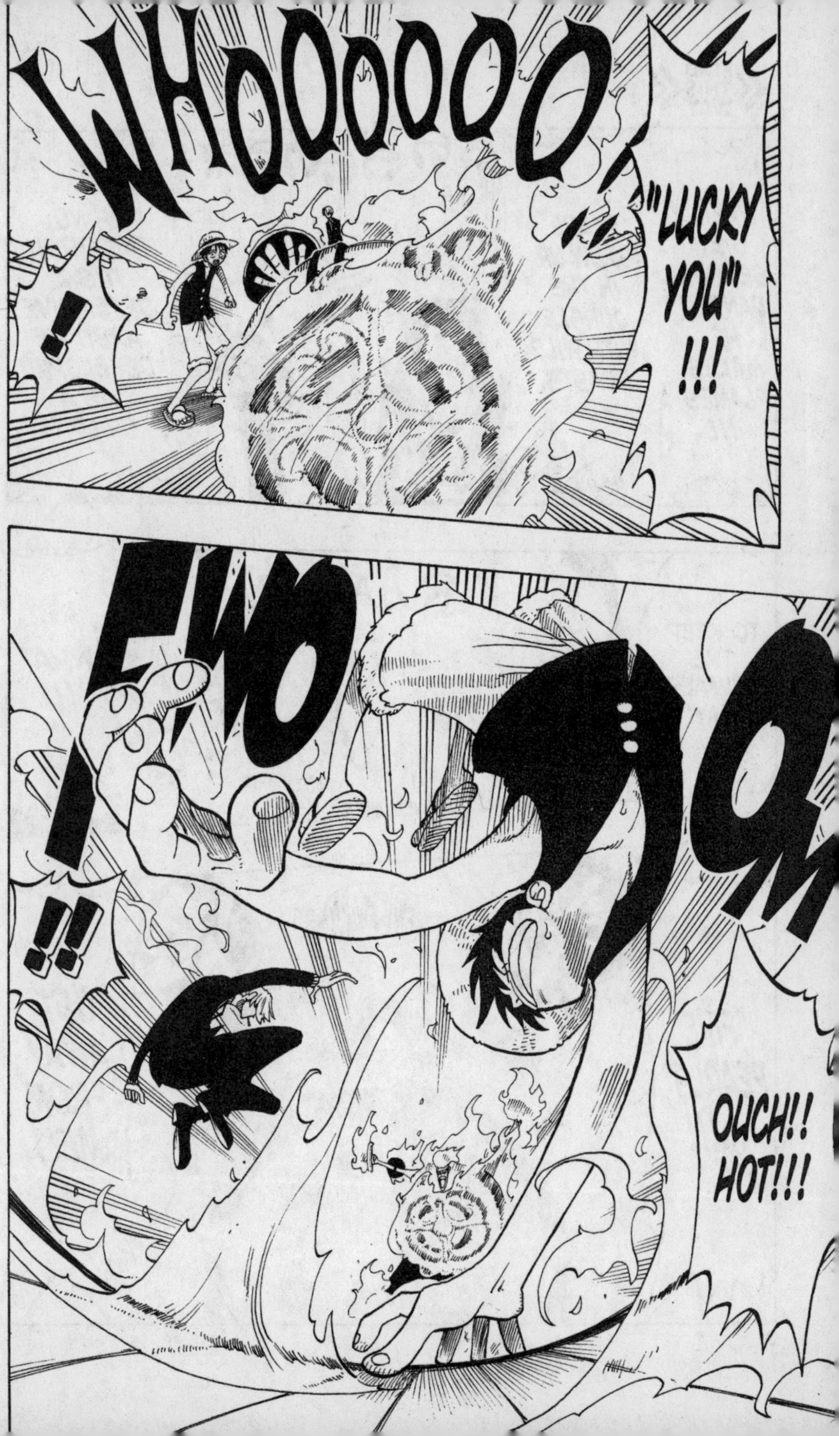
WHOOOOOO!!
"LUCKY YOU"!!!
!
FWOOM!!
OUCH!! HOT!!!

READ THIS WAY

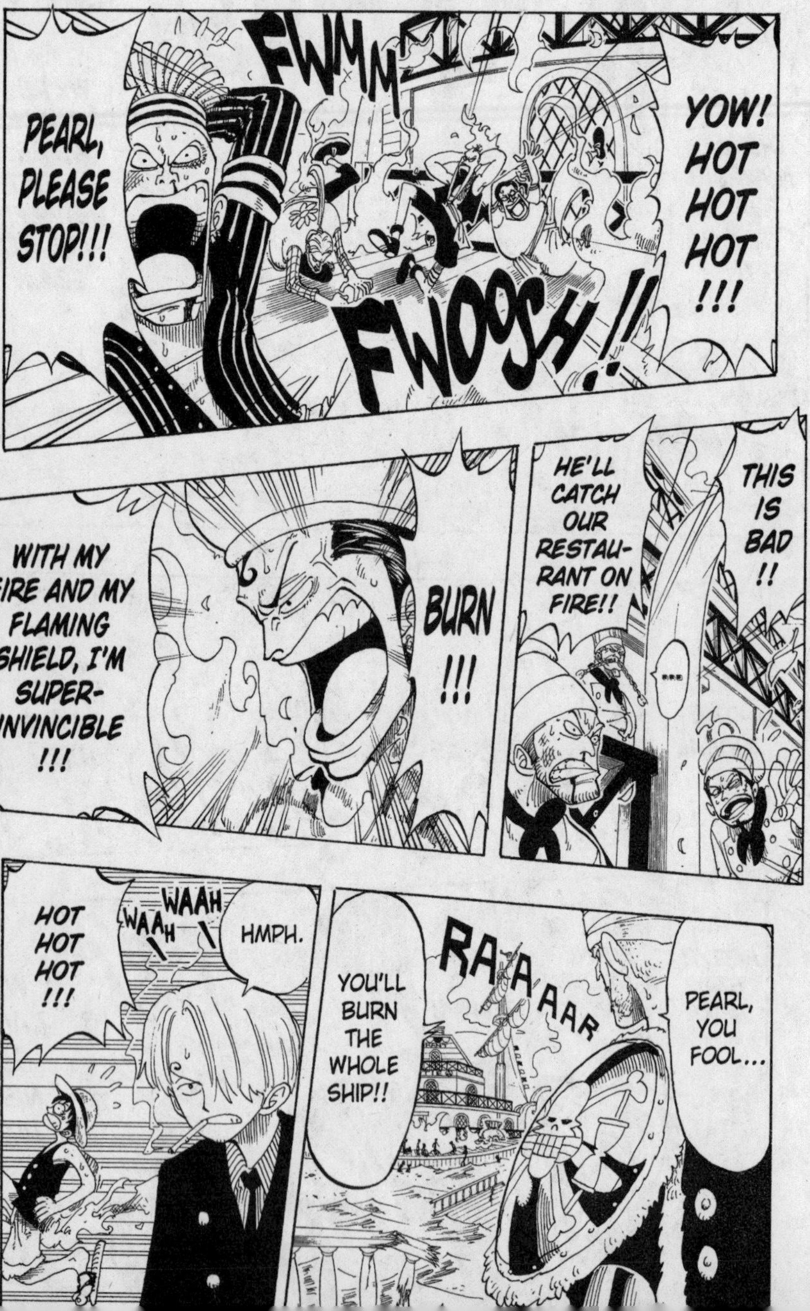
YOW! HOT HOT HOT!!!
FWMM
PEARL, PLEASE STOP!!!
FWOOSH!!
THIS IS BAD!!
HE'LL CATCH OUR RESTAU-RANT ON FIRE!!
...
BURN!!!
WITH MY FIRE AND MY FLAMING SHIELD, I'M SUPER-INVINCIBLE!!!
PEARL, YOU FOOL...
RAAAAAR
YOU'LL BURN THE WHOLE SHIP!!
HMPH.
WAAH WAAH
HOT HOT HOT!!!

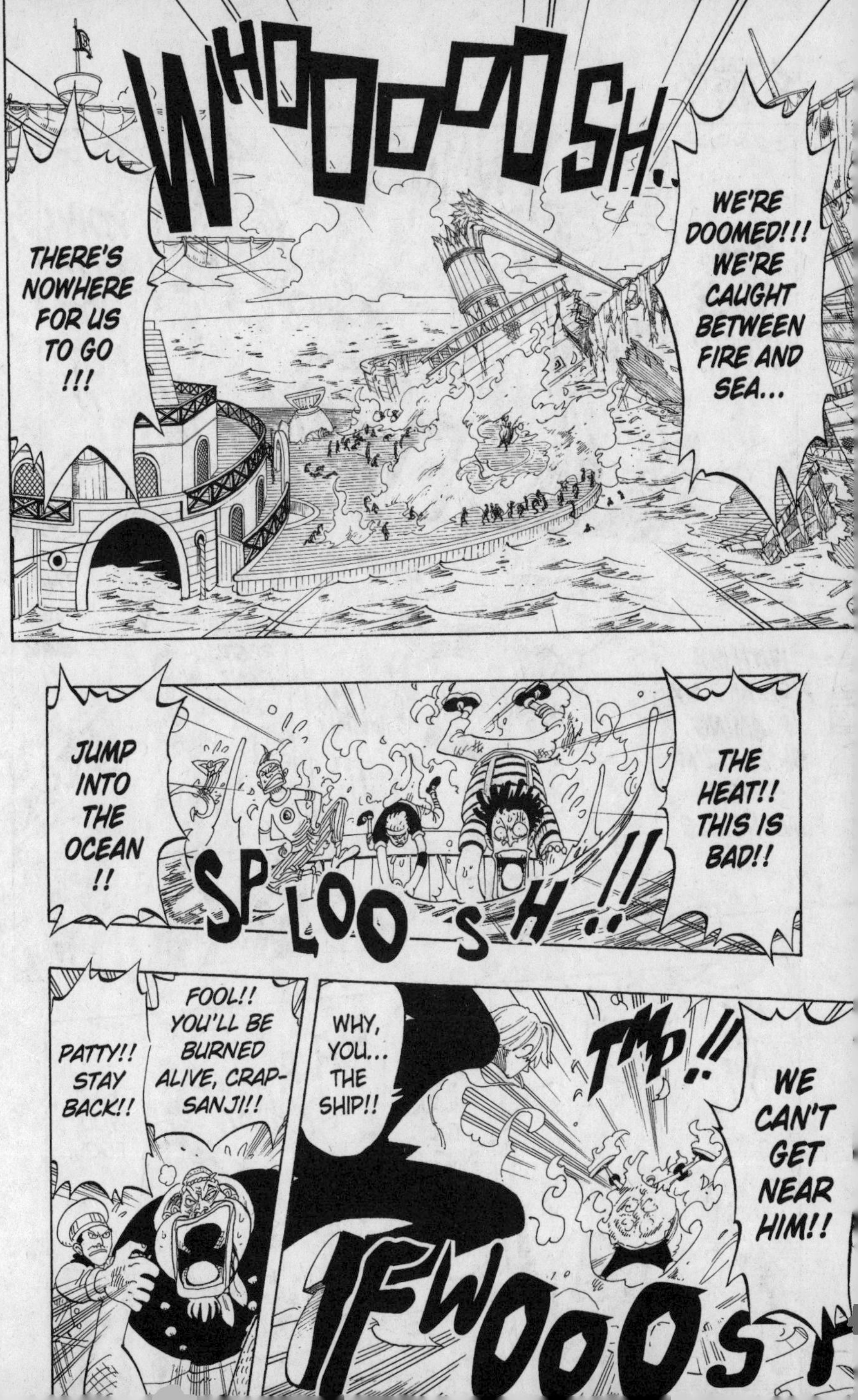
WHOOOOOSH
WE'RE DOOMED!!! WE'RE CAUGHT BETWEEN FIRE AND SEA...
THERE'S NOWHERE FOR US TO GO !!!
THE HEAT!! THIS IS BAD!!
JUMP INTO THE OCEAN !!
SPLOOSH!!
WE CAN'T GET NEAR HIM!!
TMP!!
WHY, YOU... THE SHIP!!
FWOOOS
FOOL!! YOU'LL BE BURNED ALIVE, CRAP-SANJI!!
PATTY!! STAY BACK!!

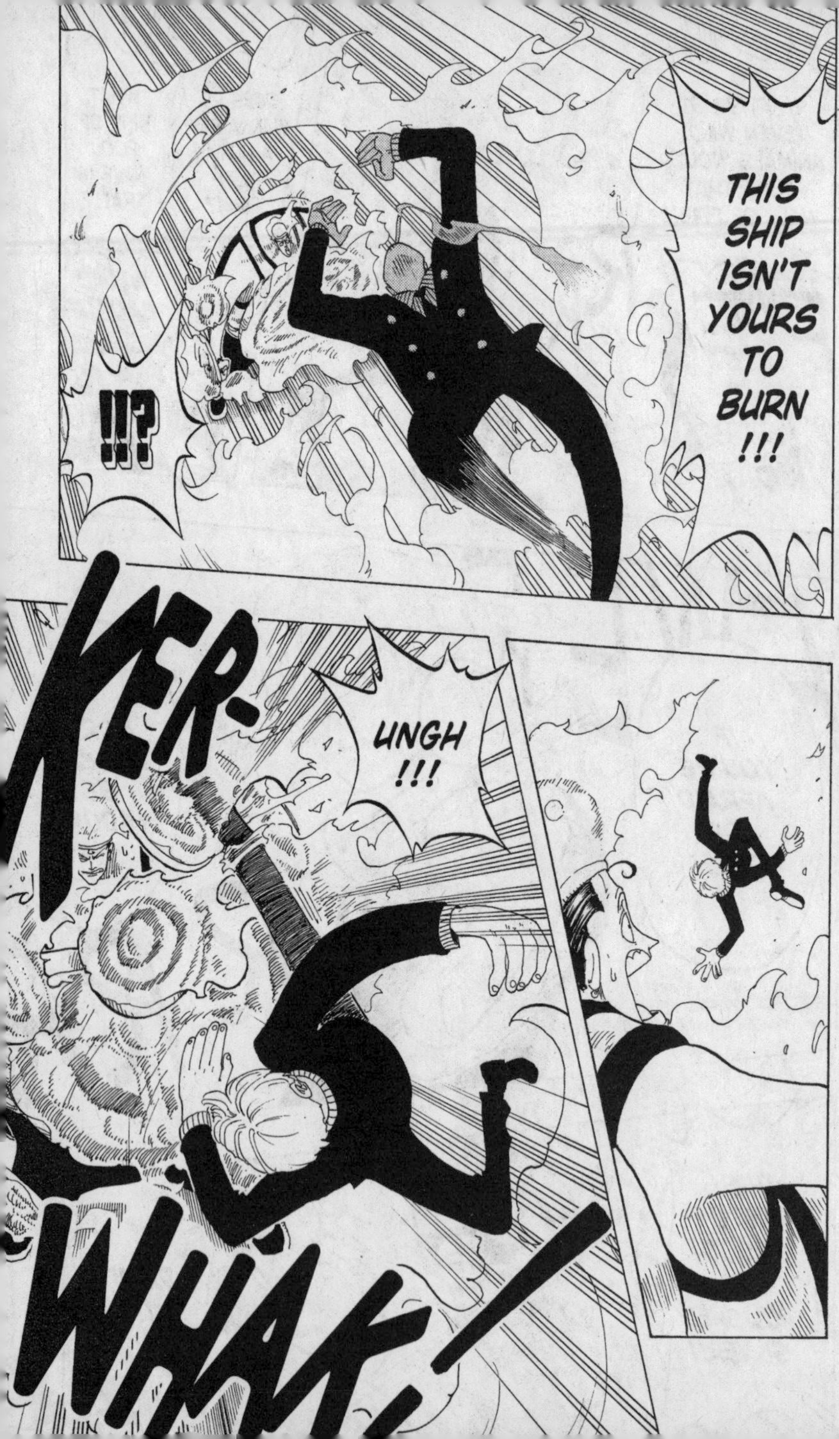
THIS SHIP ISN'T YOURS TO BURN !!!
!!?
UNGH !!!
KER-
WHAK!

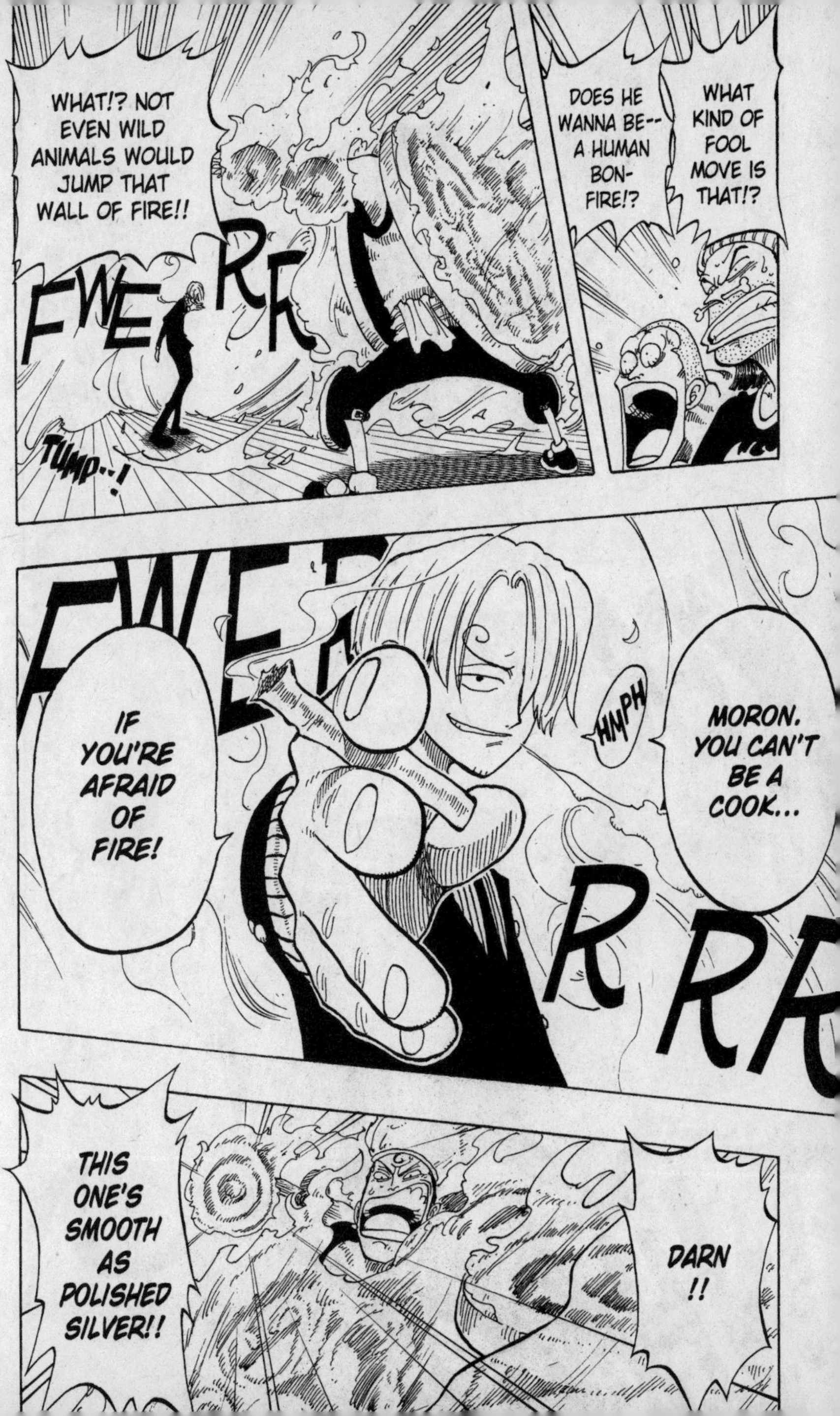
WHAT KIND OF FOOL MOVE IS THAT!?
DOES HE WANNA BE-- A HUMAN BON-FIRE!?
WHAT!? NOT EVEN WILD ANIMALS WOULD JUMP THAT WALL OF FIRE!!
FWERR
TUMP..!
MORON. YOU CAN'T BE A COOK...
HMPH
IF YOU'RE AFRAID OF FIRE!
FWERRRR
DARN!!
THIS ONE'S SMOOTH AS POLISHED SILVER!!

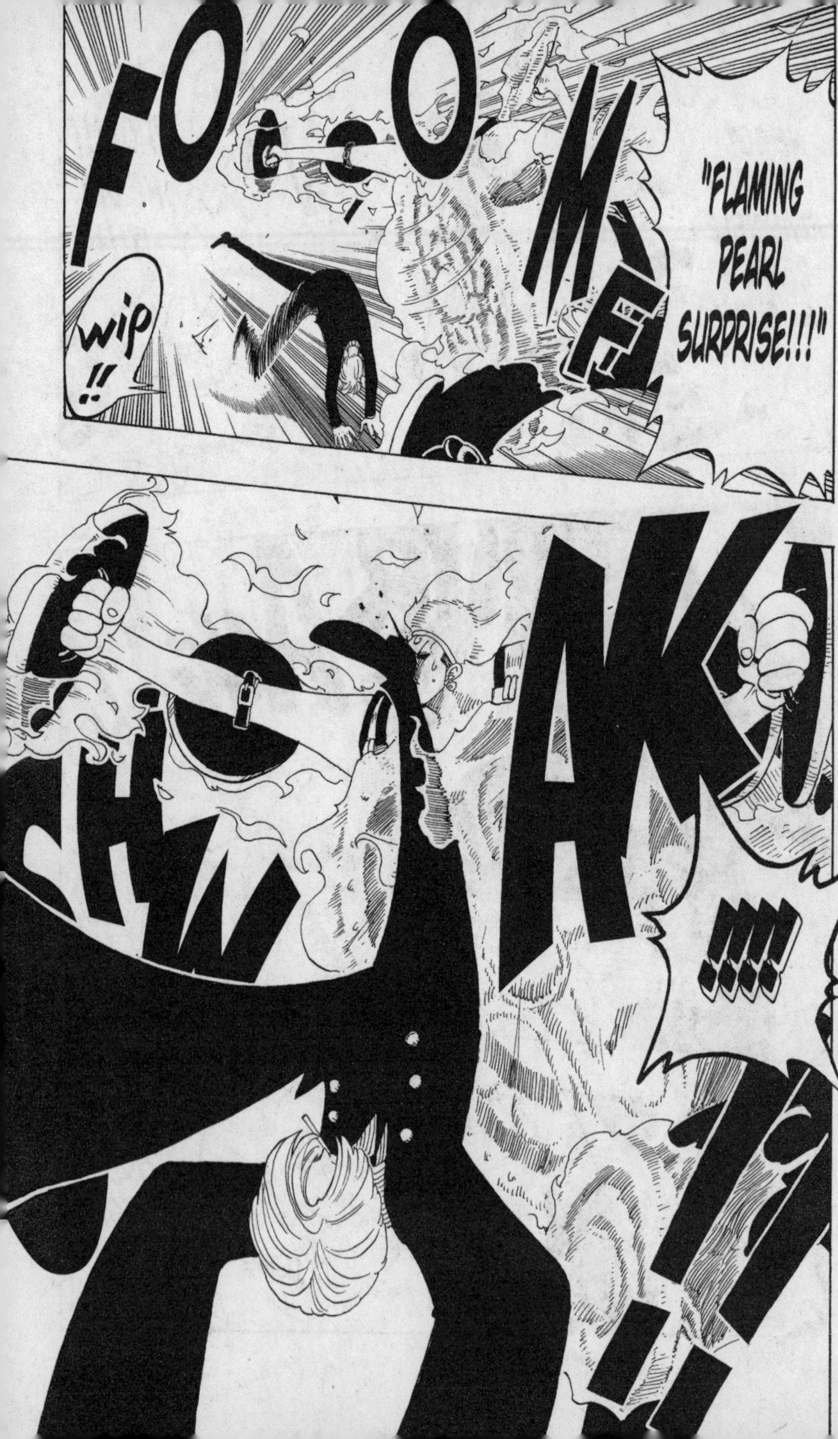
"FLAMING PEARL SURPRISE!!!"
FOOOM
wip!!

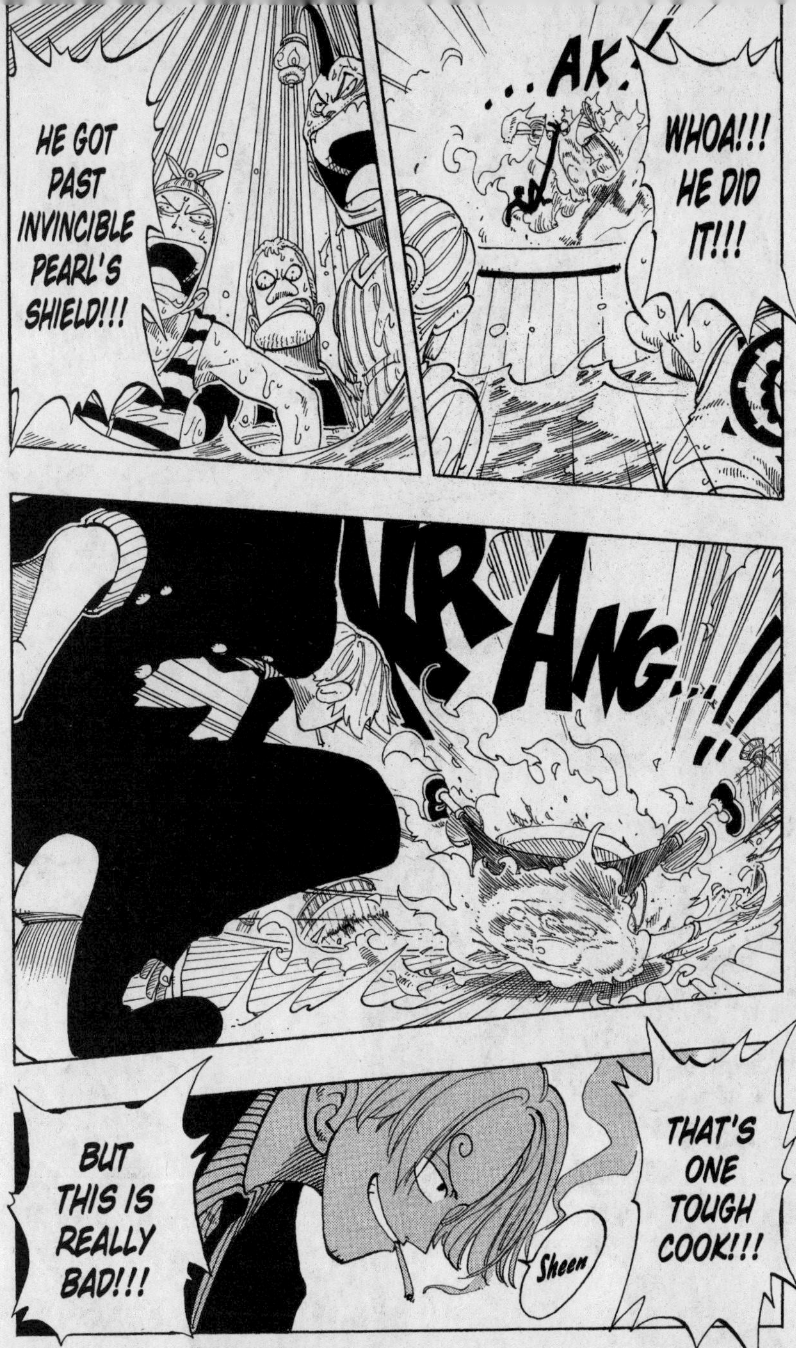

...AK.
WHOA!!! HE DID IT!!!
HE GOT PAST INVINCIBLE PEARL'S SHIELD!!!
RANG...!!
THAT'S ONE TOUGH COOK!!!
Sheen
BUT THIS IS REALLY BAD!!!

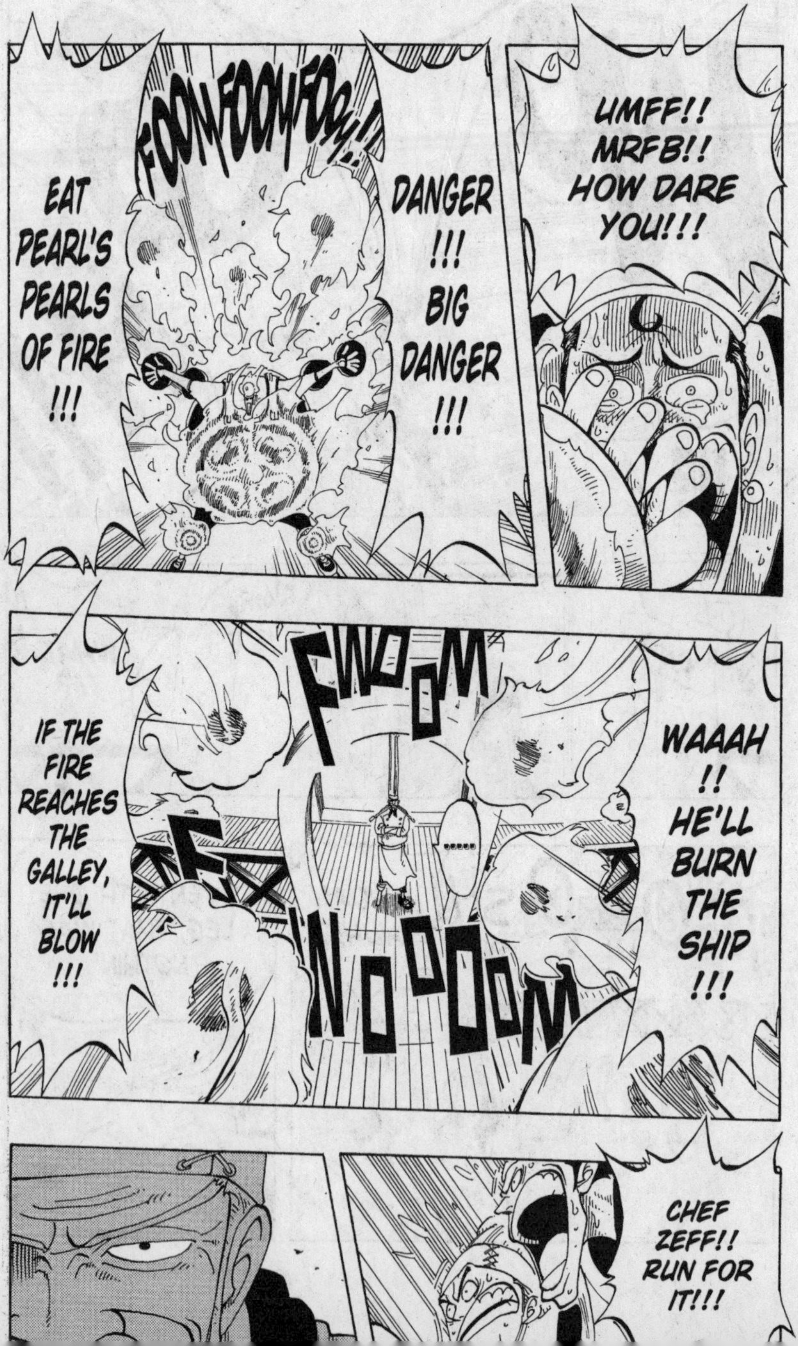
UMFF!! MRFB!! HOW DARE YOU!!!
FOOMFOOMFOOM!!!
DANGER!!! BIG DANGER!!!
EAT PEARL'S PEARLS OF FIRE!!!
WAAAH!! HE'LL BURN THE SHIP!!!
FWOOM
.....
IF THE FIRE REACHES THE GALLEY, IT'LL BLOW!!!
CHEF ZEFF!! RUN FOR IT!!!

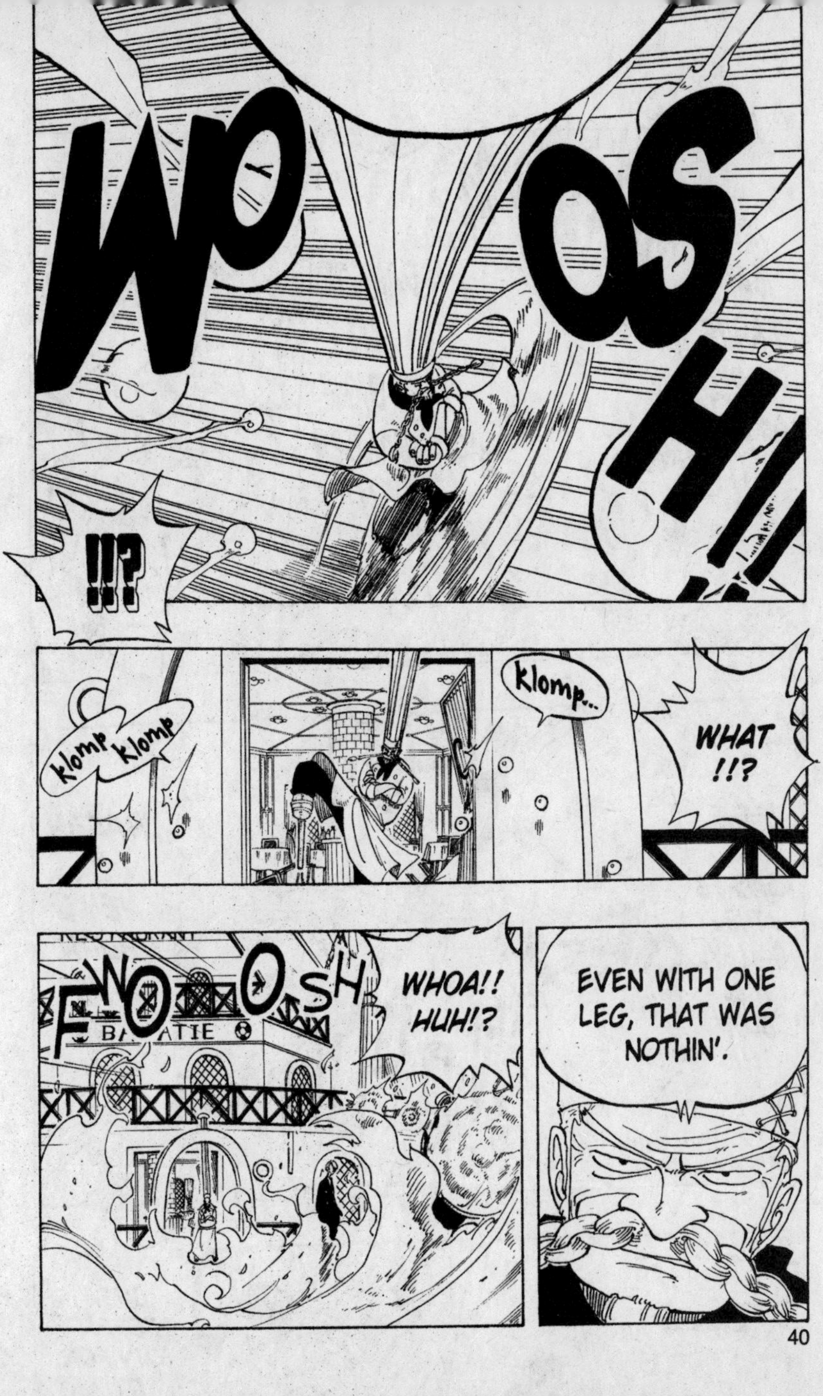
WOOSH!!
!!?
WHAT !!?
klomp...
klomp klomp
EVEN WITH ONE LEG, THAT WAS NOTHIN'.
WHOA!! HUH!?
FWOOSH

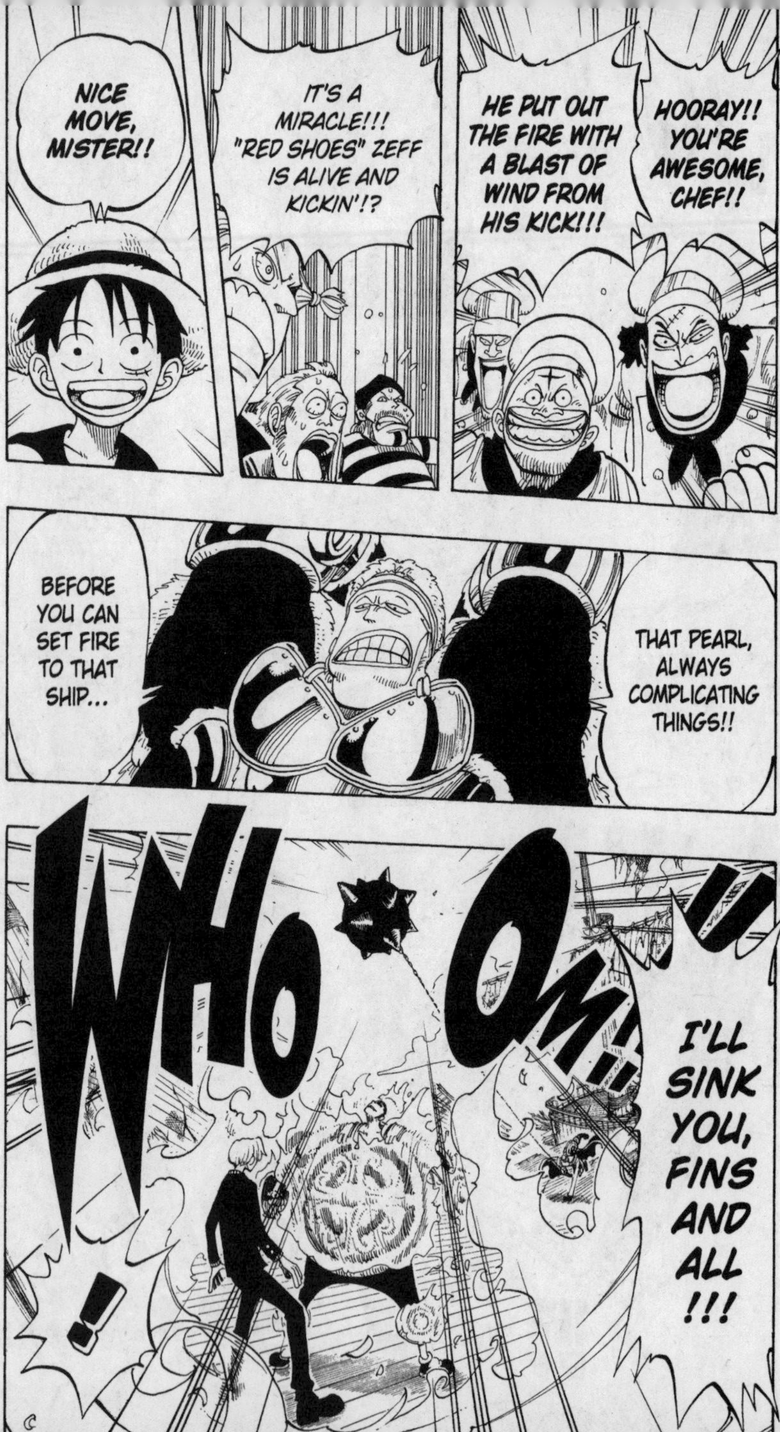
HOORAY!! YOU'RE AWESOME, CHEF!!
HE PUT OUT THE FIRE WITH A BLAST OF WIND FROM HIS KICK!!!
IT'S A MIRACLE!!! "RED SHOES" ZEFF IS ALIVE AND KICKIN'!?
NICE MOVE, MISTER!!
THAT PEARL, ALWAYS COMPLICATING THINGS!!
BEFORE YOU CAN SET FIRE TO THAT SHIP...
WHOOM!!
I'LL SINK YOU, FINS AND ALL!!!
!

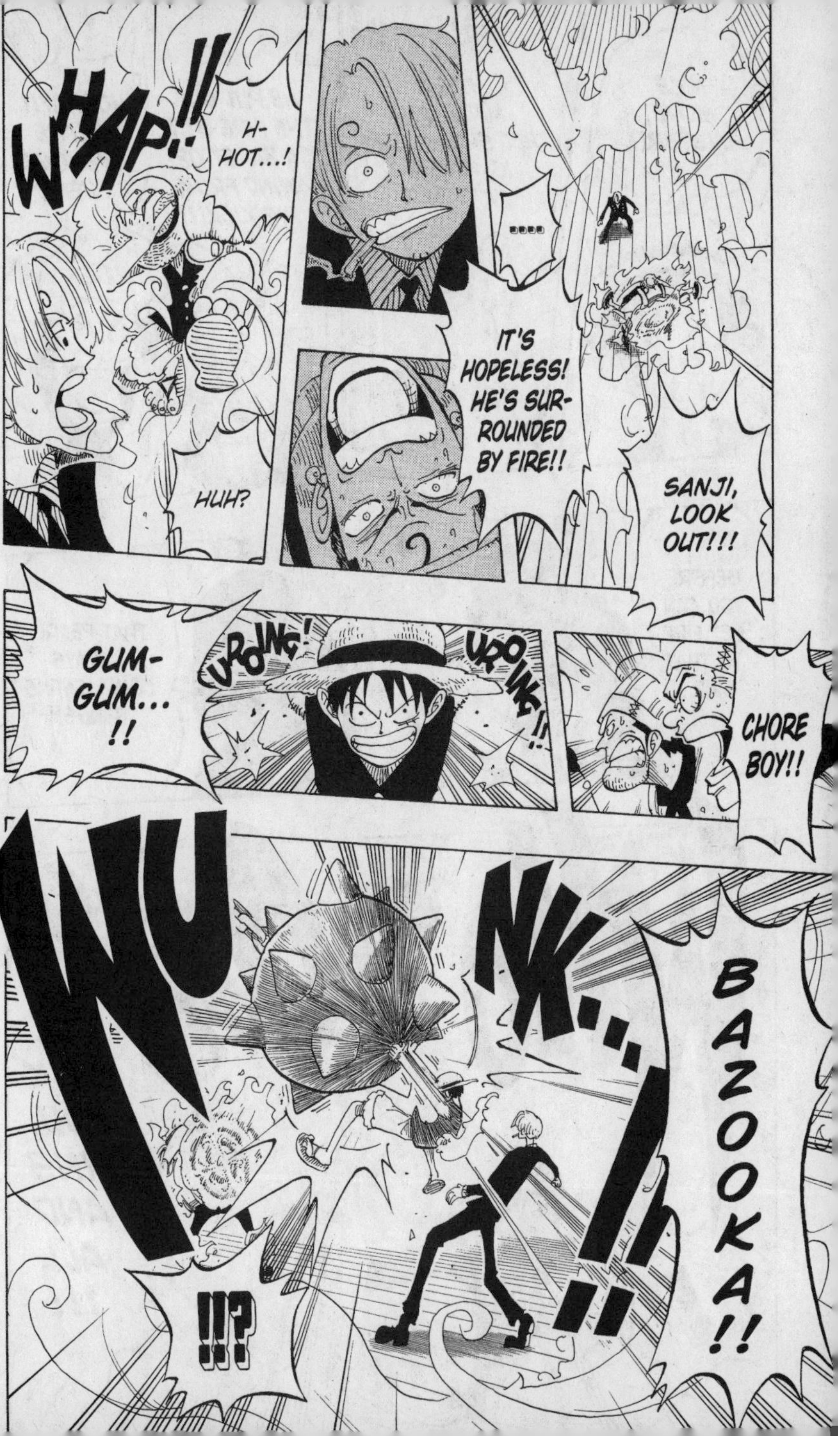
.....
SANJI, LOOK OUT!!!
IT'S HOPELESS! HE'S SUR-ROUNDED BY FIRE!!
WHAP!!
H-HOT...!
HUH?
CHORE BOY!!
VROWNG!!
VROING!
GUM-GUM... !!
WUNK...!!
BAZOOKA!!
!!?

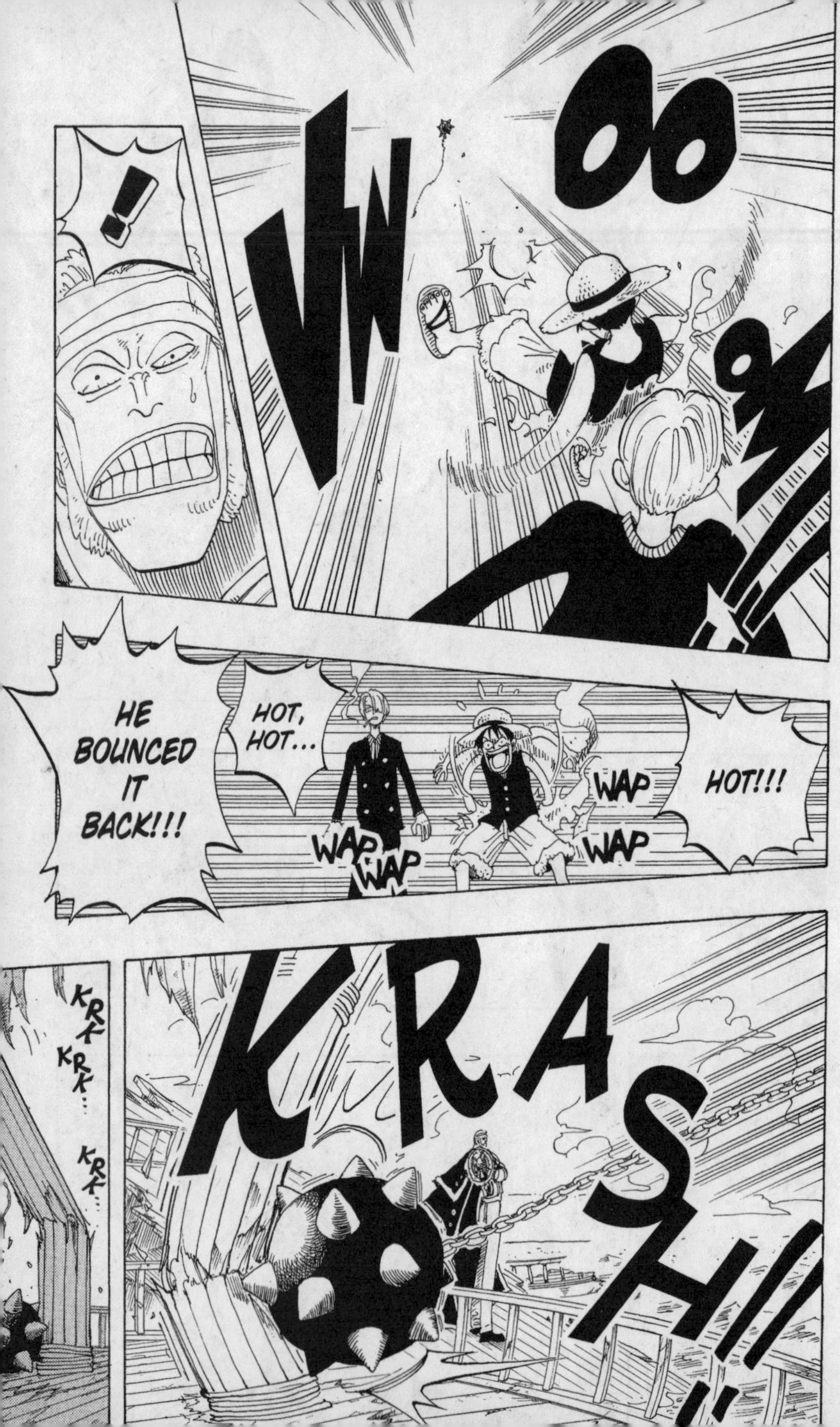

VWOOOM!!
!
HOT!!!
WAP
WAP
WAP
WAP
HOT, HOT...
HE BOUNCED IT BACK!!!
KRASH!!
KRK
KRK
KRK...

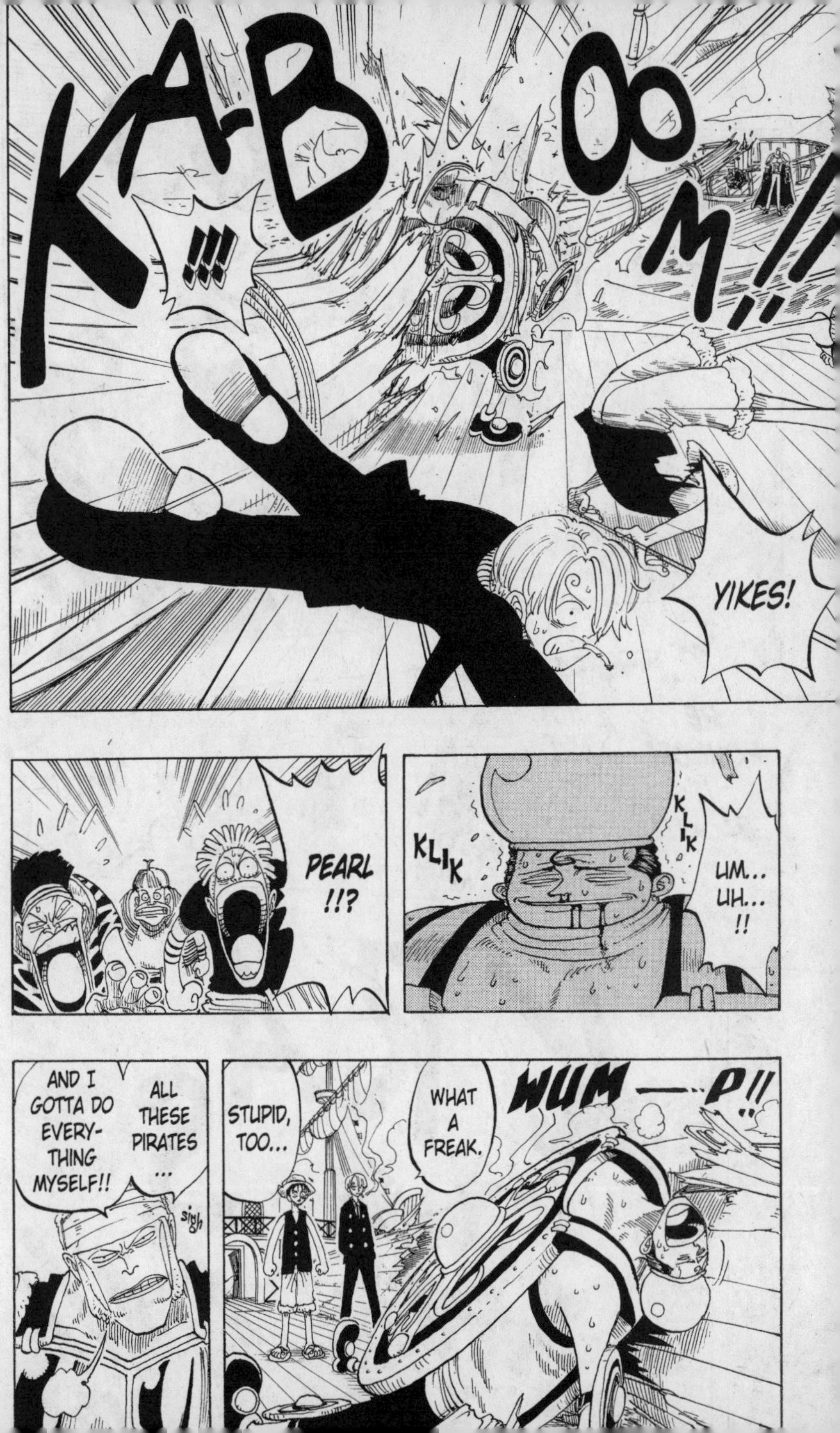
KA-BOOOM!!
!!!
YIKES!
KLIK
KLIK
UM... UH... !!
PEARL !!?
WUM—P!!
WHAT A FREAK.
STUPID, TOO...
ALL THESE PIRATES...
AND I GOTTA DO EVERY-THING MYSELF!!
sigh

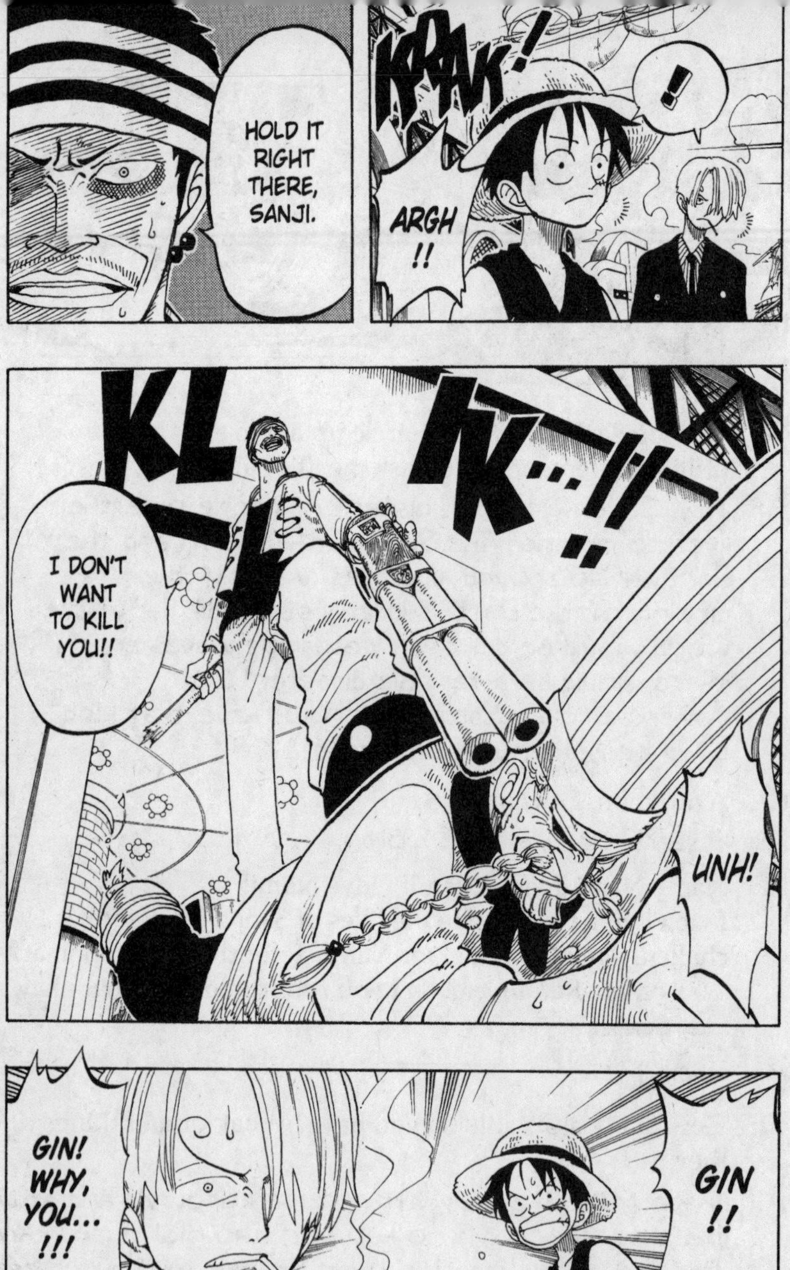
KRAK!
!
ARGH!!
HOLD IT RIGHT THERE, SANJI.
KLNK...!!
UNH!
I DON'T WANT TO KILL YOU!!
GIN!!
GIN! WHY, YOU...!!!

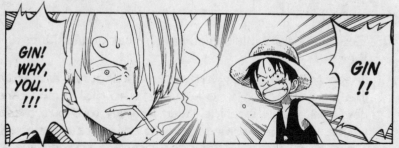

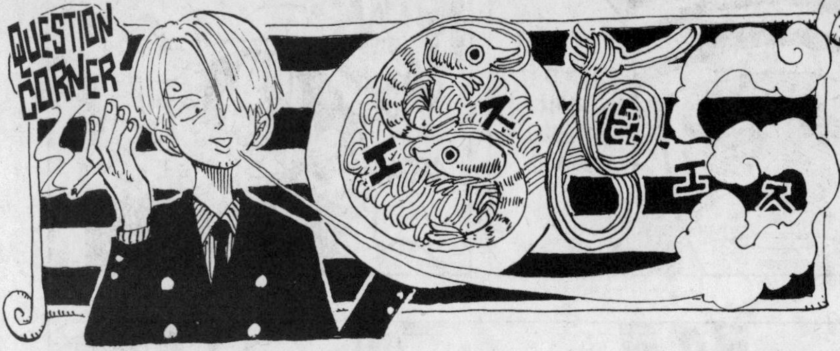
QUESTION CORNER

Q: Why do Sanji's eyebrows circle up at the ends? Is it a fashion statement? If you ask me, it's lame!!

A: Hey!! Sit down, now!! Listen!! All people owe their lives to circling!! The Sun and the Moon and the Earth all go around in circles. What if the circling of the Earth suddenly stopped!! The whole world would be deluged by gigantic waves and there would be a terrible disaster!! So remember that Sanji's eyebrows have that kind of energy!! Repent!! Dismissed!!

Q: A question. How old is Sanji?

A: 19 years old--just like Zolo.

Q: Nami, Nami, Nami, Nami! I love Nami!
I won't give Nami up to the likes of Sanji!! Therefore, I challenge him to a duel for Nami. Tomorrow afternoon at 3:00, on the Red Line. Don't you run from me! Is that okay, Oda Sensei?

A: Okay!! Fight!!

Q: How many assistants do you have? What kind of things do they do?

A: I have four. They help with the backgrounds and stuff like that. They come to help for two nights and three days each week, sleeping over. Frankly, without these people it would be impossible to complete a script in a week. But it's a really goofy workplace, so we have a lot of fun working on the manga.

# Chapter 56:
# I REFUSE

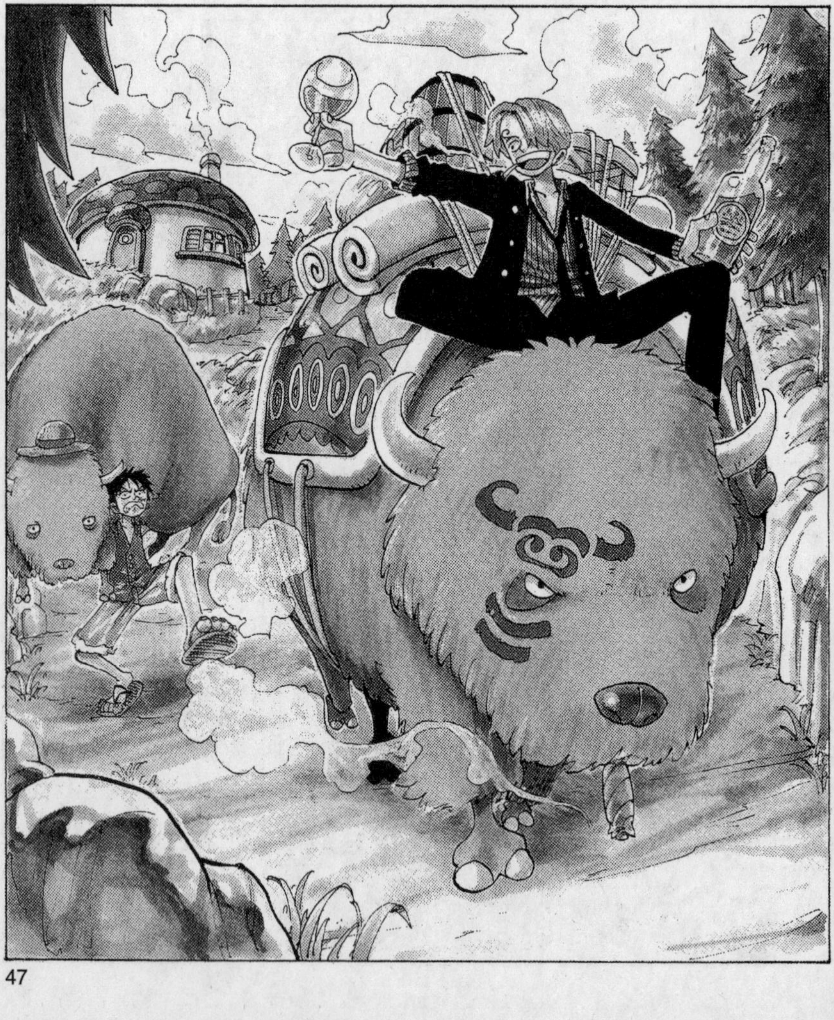

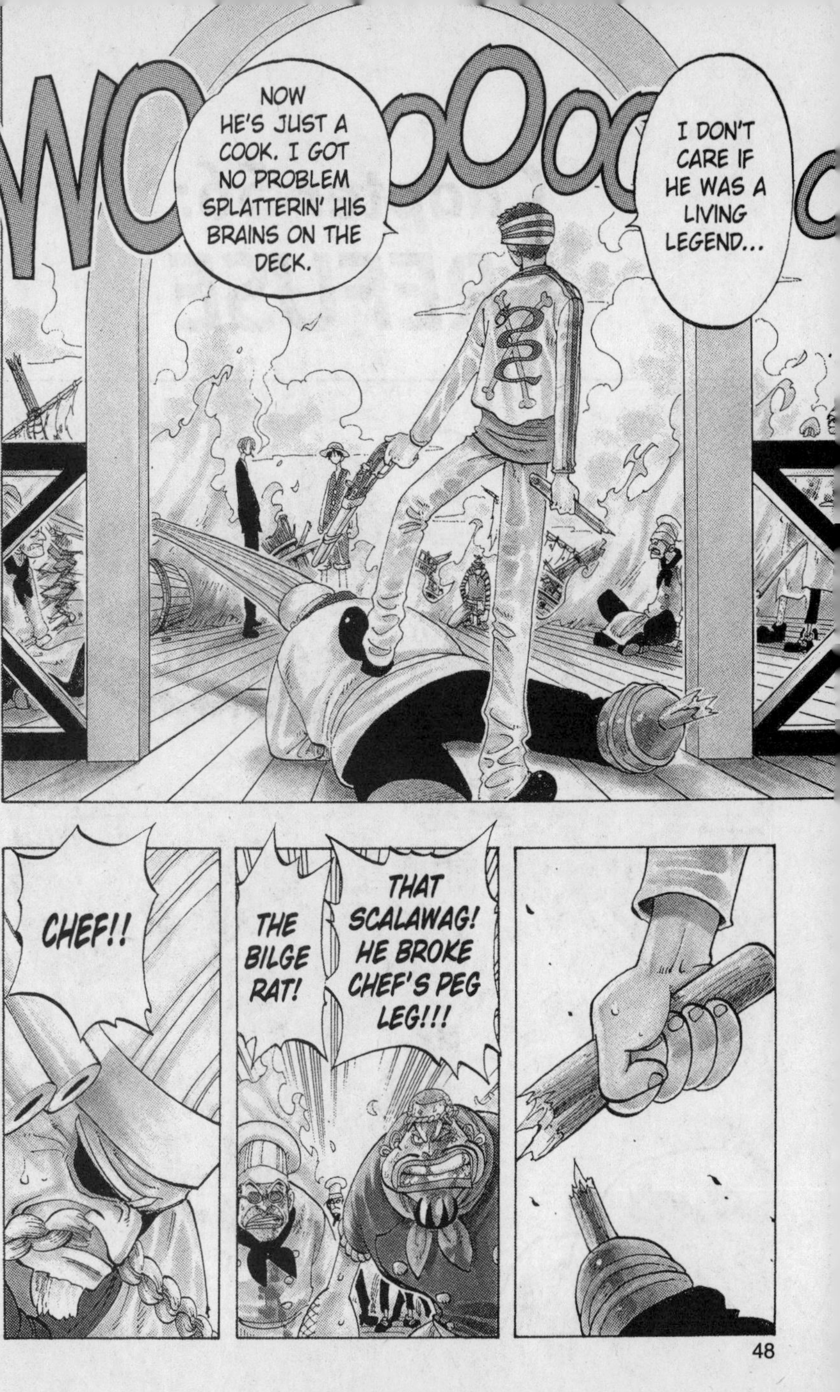
I DON'T CARE IF HE WAS A LIVING LEGEND...
NOW HE'S JUST A COOK. I GOT NO PROBLEM SPLATTERIN' HIS BRAINS ON THE DECK.
THAT SCALAWAG! HE BROKE CHEF'S PEG LEG!!!
THE BILGE RAT!
CHEF!!

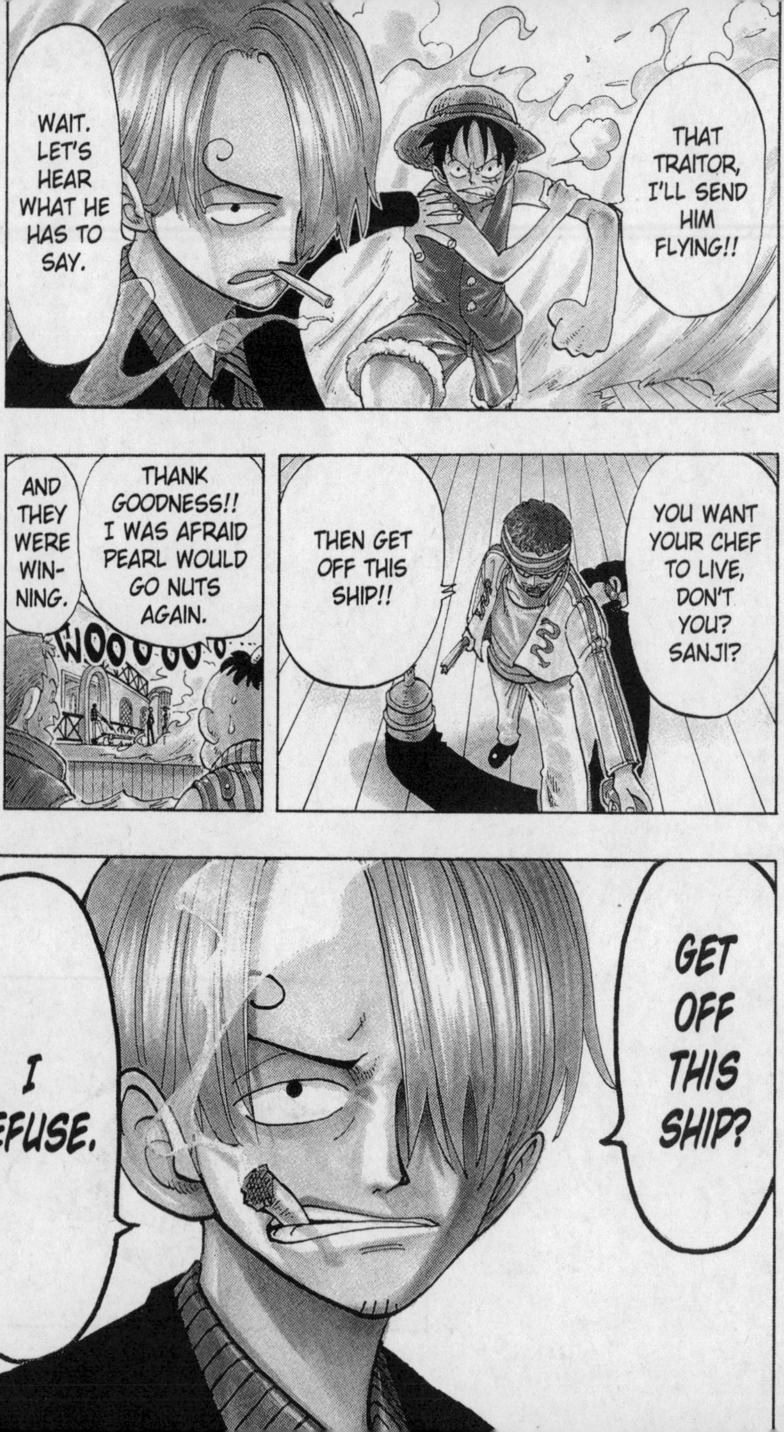
THAT TRAITOR, I'LL SEND HIM FLYING!!
WAIT. LET'S HEAR WHAT HE HAS TO SAY.
YOU WANT YOUR CHEF TO LIVE, DON'T YOU? SANJI?
THEN GET OFF THIS SHIP!!
THANK GOODNESS!! I WAS AFRAID PEARL WOULD GO NUTS AGAIN.
AND THEY WERE WIN-NING.
GET OFF THIS SHIP?
I REFUSE.

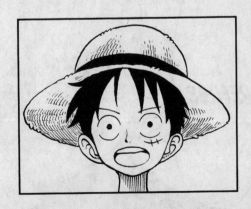

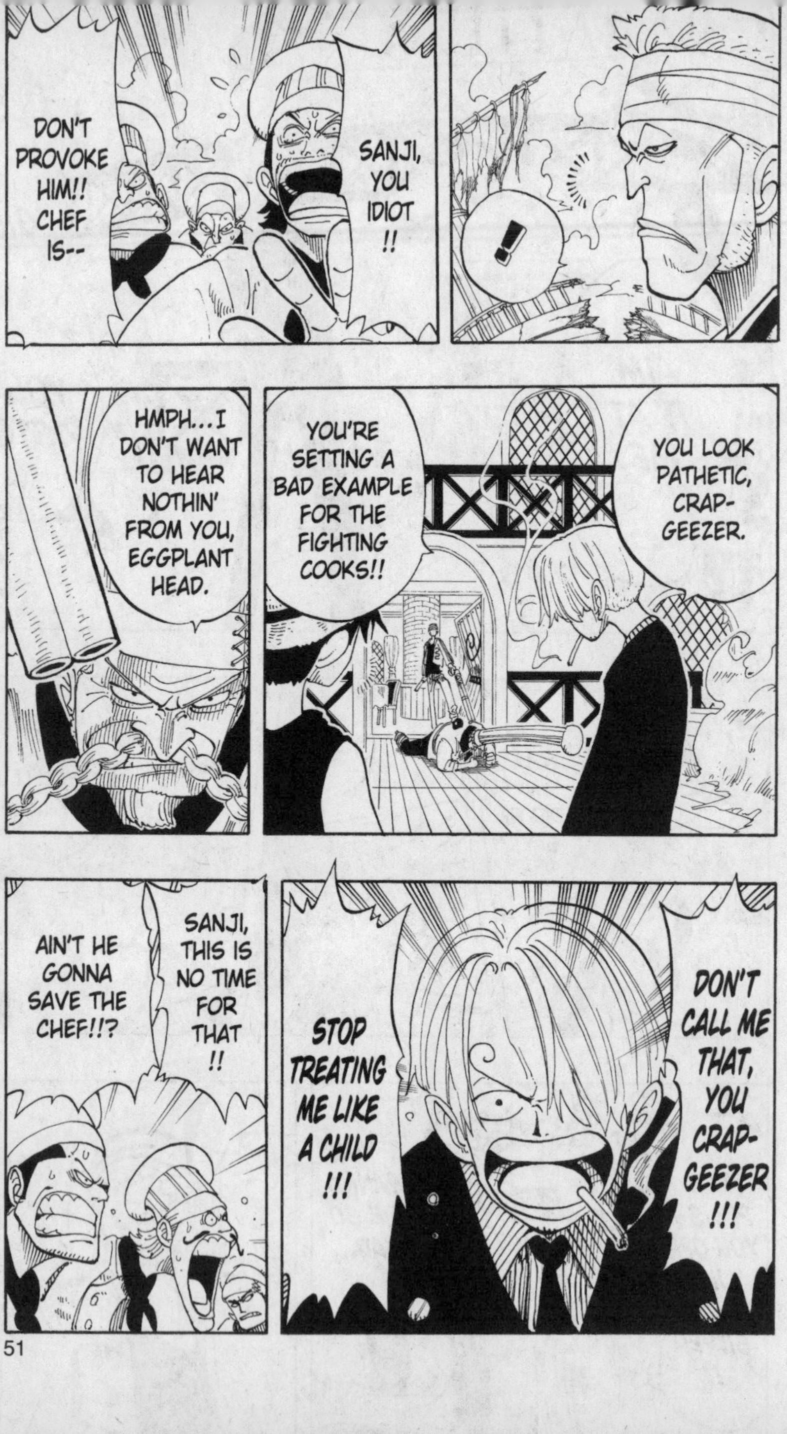
!
SANJI, YOU IDIOT!!
DON'T PROVOKE HIM!! CHEF IS--
YOU LOOK PATHETIC, CRAP-GEEZER.
YOU'RE SETTING A BAD EXAMPLE FOR THE FIGHTING COOKS!!
HMPH...I DON'T WANT TO HEAR NOTHIN' FROM YOU, EGGPLANT HEAD.
DON'T CALL ME THAT, YOU CRAP-GEEZER!!!
STOP TREATING ME LIKE A CHILD!!!
SANJI, THIS IS NO TIME FOR THAT!!
AIN'T HE GONNA SAVE THE CHEF!!?

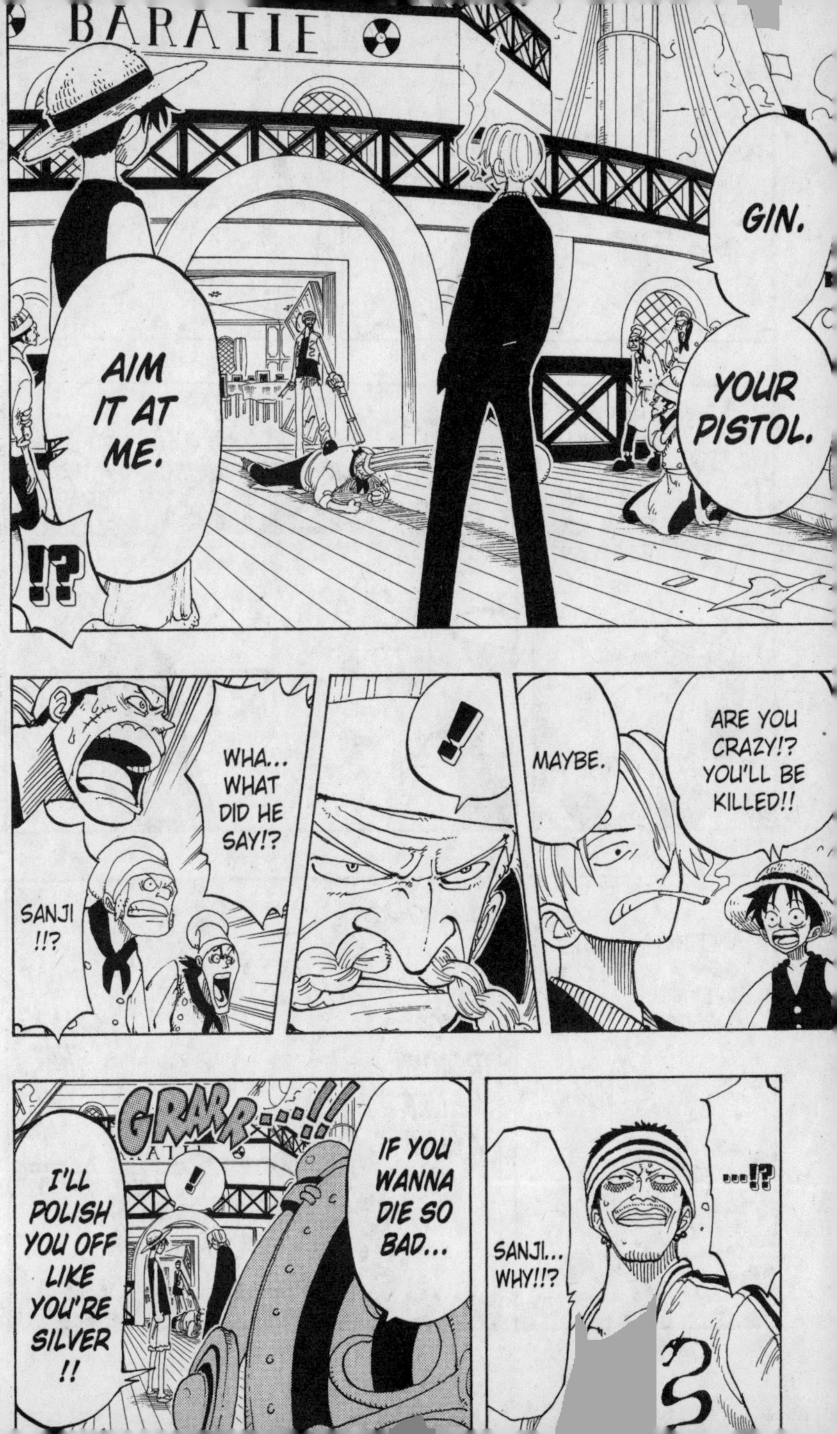
BARATIE
GIN.
YOUR PISTOL.
AIM IT AT ME.
!?
ARE YOU CRAZY!? YOU'LL BE KILLED!!
MAYBE.
!
WHA... WHAT DID HE SAY!?
SANJI !!?
...!?
SANJI... WHY!!?
IF YOU WANNA DIE SO BAD...
GRARR...!!
!
I'LL POLISH YOU OFF LIKE YOU'RE SILVER !!

READ THIS WAY

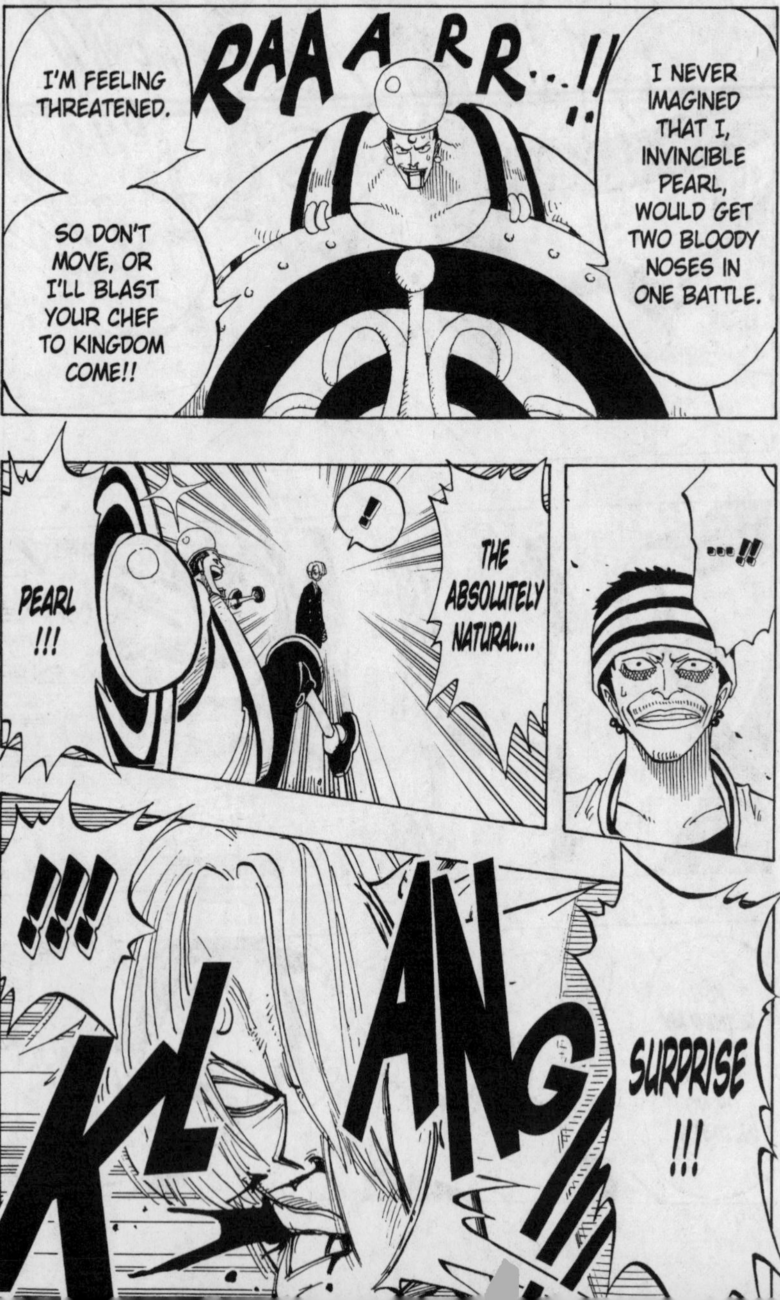
I NEVER IMAGINED THAT I, INVINCIBLE PEARL, WOULD GET TWO BLOODY NOSES IN ONE BATTLE.
RAAARR...!!
I'M FEELING THREATENED.
SO DON'T MOVE, OR I'LL BLAST YOUR CHEF TO KINGDOM COME!!
...!!
!
THE ABSOLUTELY NATURAL...
PEARL !!!
SURPRISE !!!
KLANG
!!!

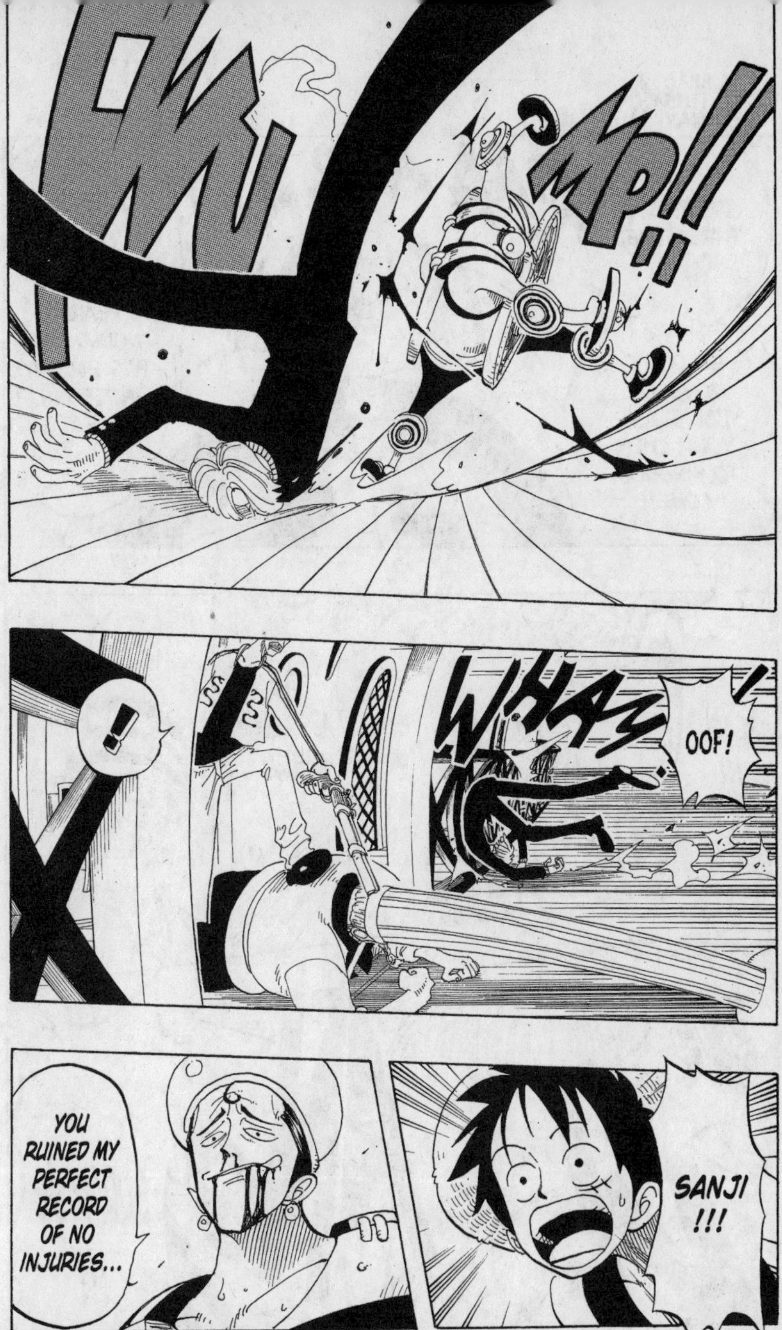
THWUMP!!
!
OOF!
WHAM
SANJI!!!
YOU RUINED MY PERFECT RECORD OF NO INJURIES...

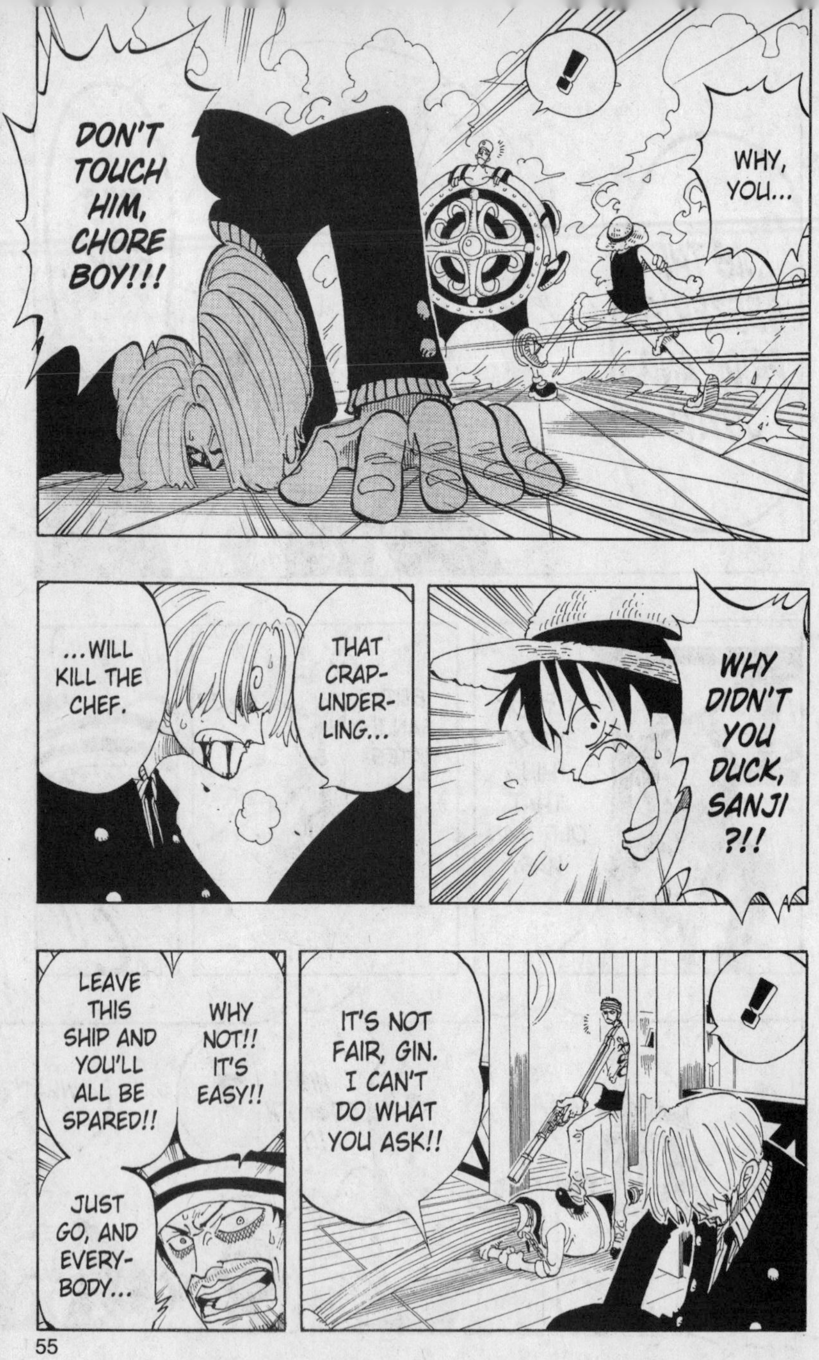
!
WHY, YOU...
DON'T TOUCH HIM, CHORE BOY!!!
WHY DIDN'T YOU DUCK, SANJI?!!
THAT CRAP-UNDERLING...
...WILL KILL THE CHEF.
!
IT'S NOT FAIR, GIN. I CAN'T DO WHAT YOU ASK!!
WHY NOT!! IT'S EASY!!
LEAVE THIS SHIP AND YOU'LL ALL BE SPARED!!
JUST GO, AND EVERYBODY...

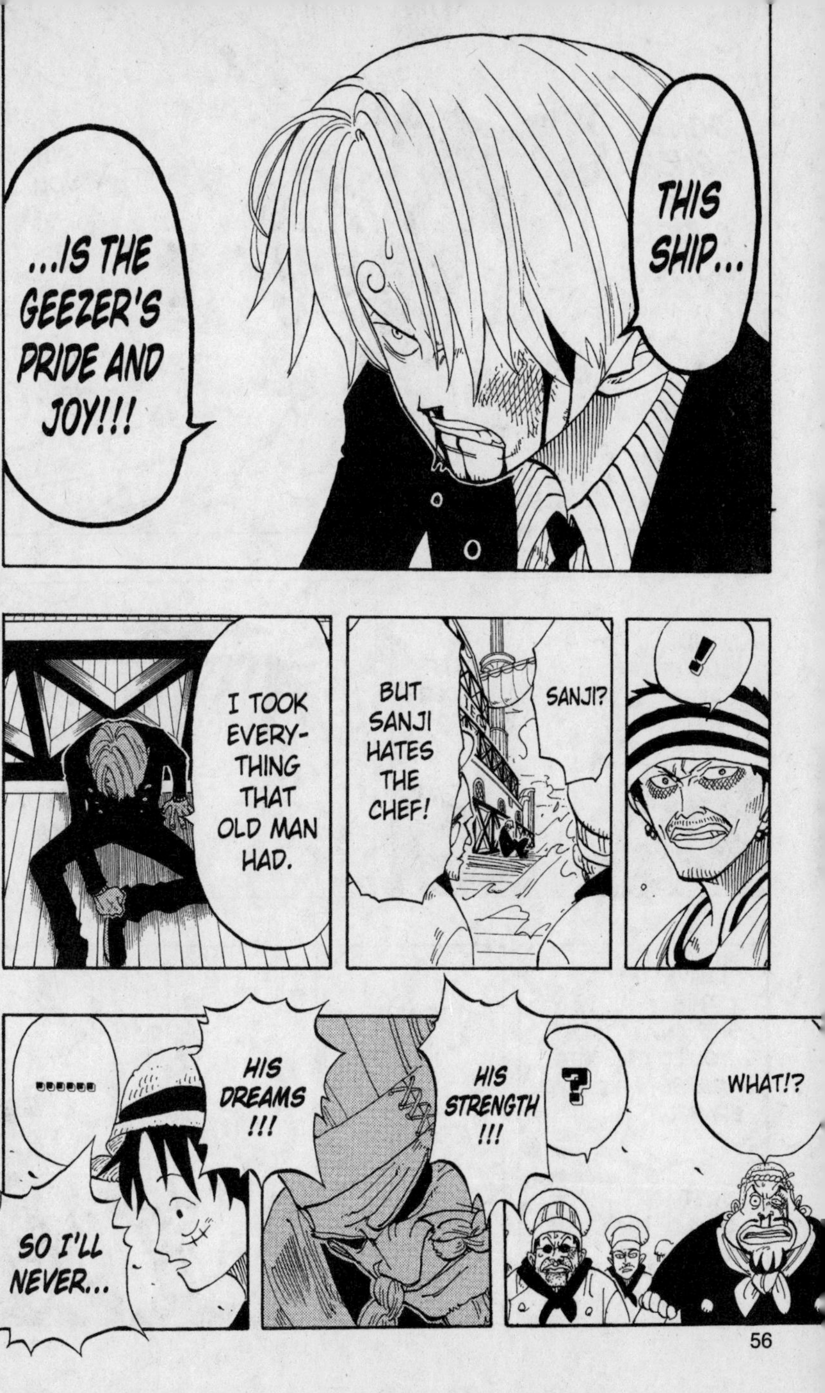

THIS SHIP...
...IS THE GEEZER'S PRIDE AND JOY!!!
!
SANJI?
BUT SANJI HATES THE CHEF!
I TOOK EVERY-THING THAT OLD MAN HAD.
WHAT!?
?
HIS STRENGTH!!!
HIS DREAMS!!!
......
SO I'LL NEVER...

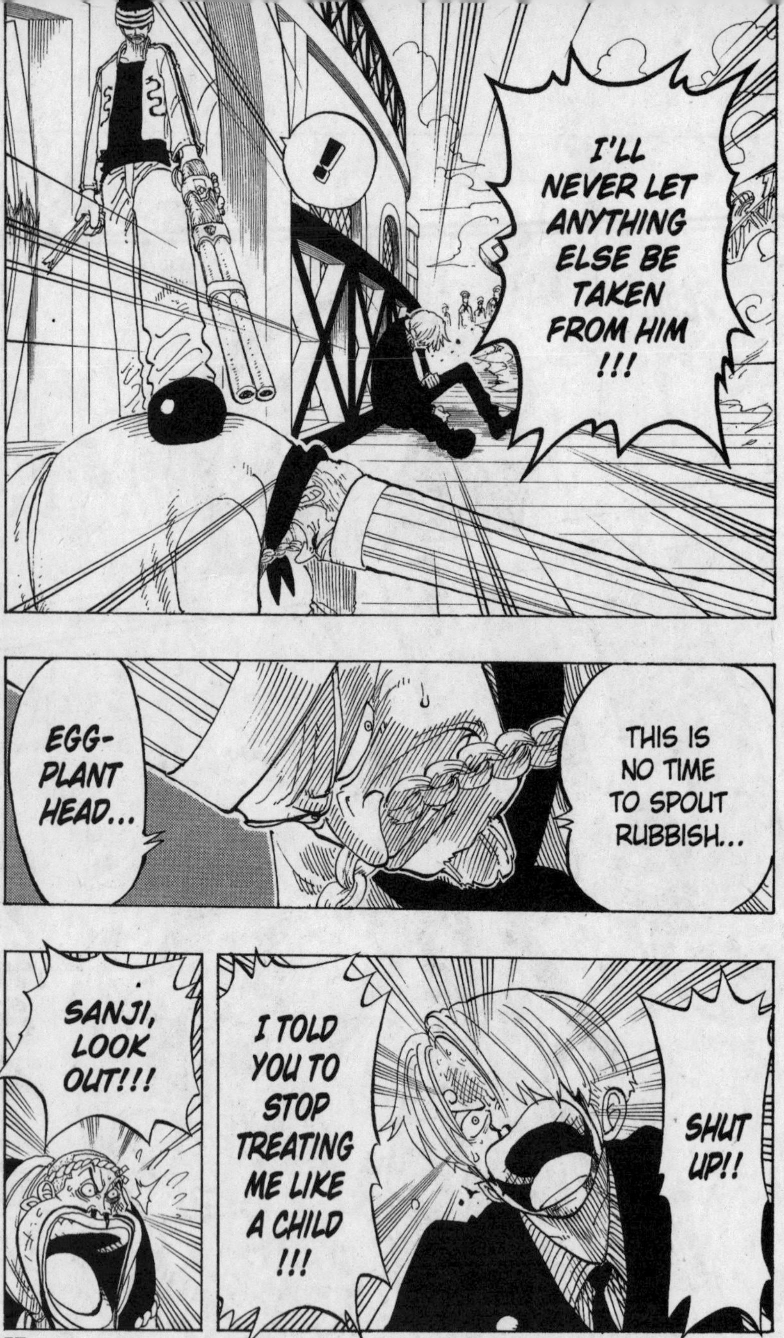
I'LL NEVER LET ANYTHING ELSE BE TAKEN FROM HIM !!!
!
THIS IS NO TIME TO SPOUT RUBBISH...
EGG-PLANT HEAD...
SHUT UP!!
I TOLD YOU TO STOP TREATING ME LIKE A CHILD !!!
SANJI, LOOK OUT!!!

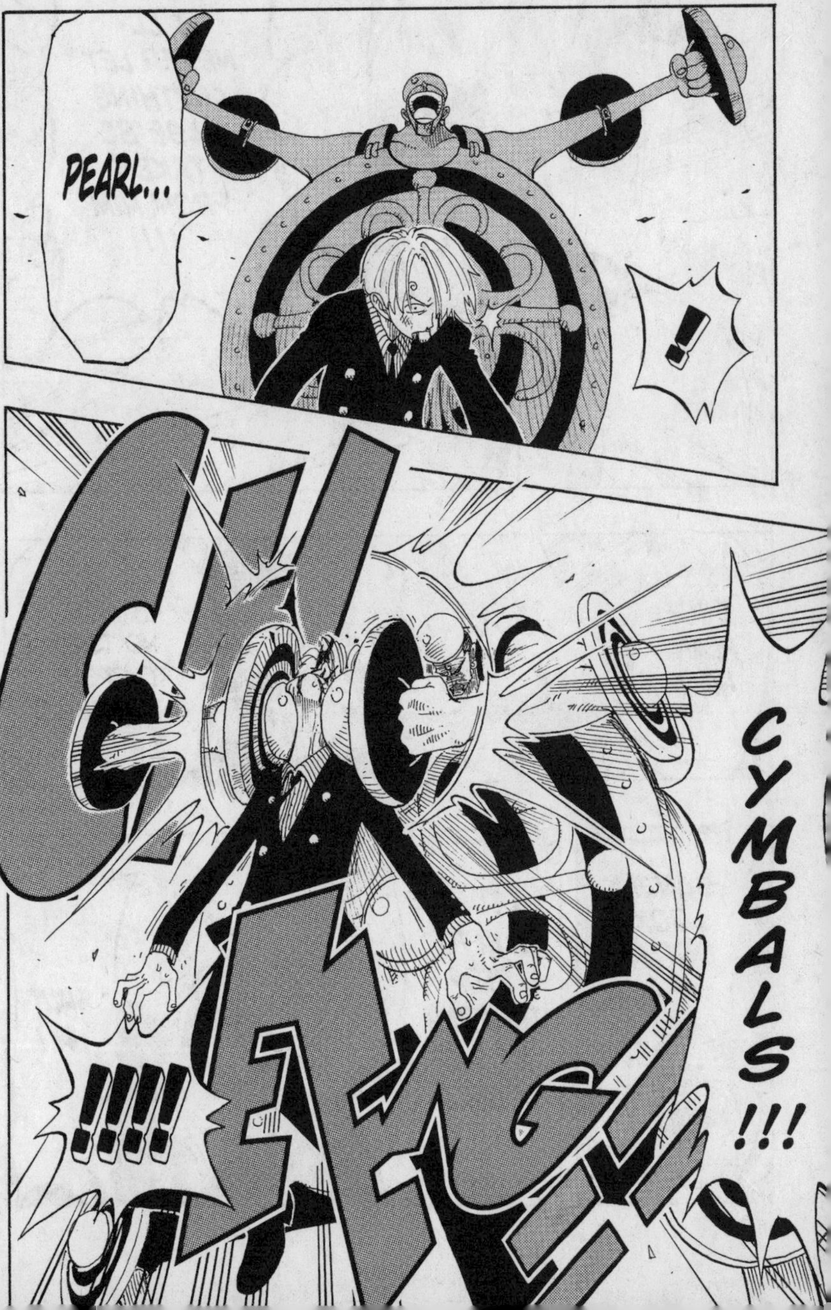
!
PEARL...
CYMBALS!!!
!!!!

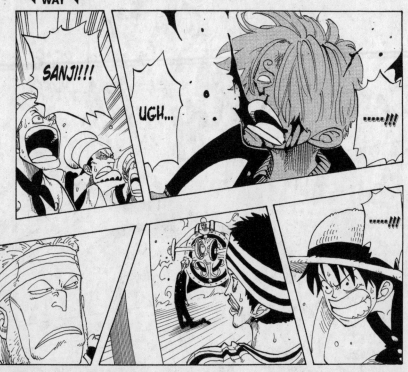

SANJI!!!

UGH...

......!!!!

......!!!!

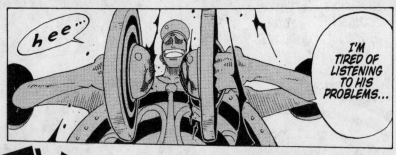

*hee'''*

I'M TIRED OF LISTENING TO HIS PROBLEMS...

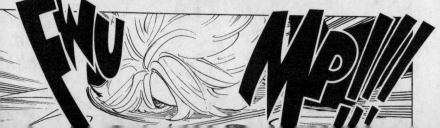

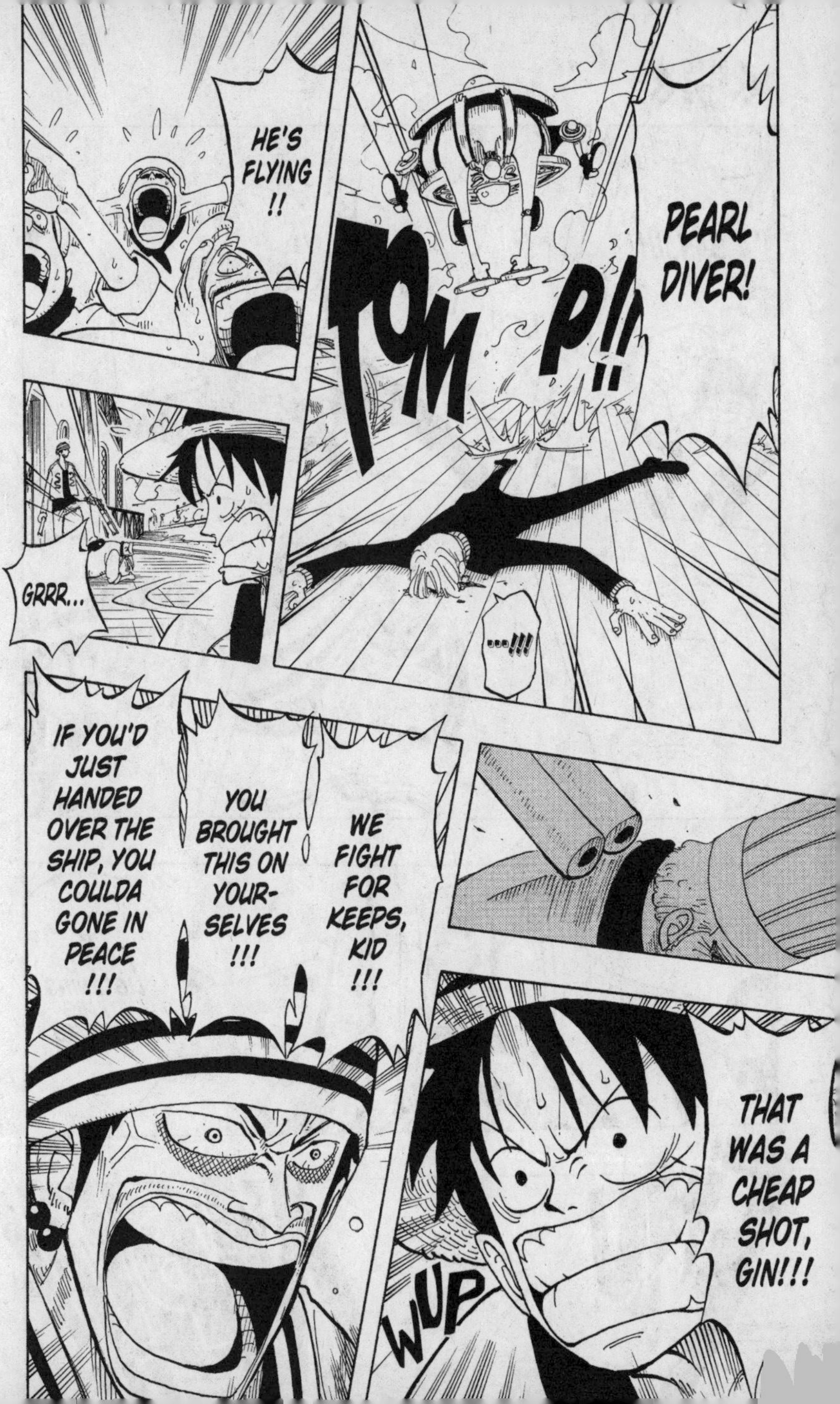
PEARL DIVER!
TOMP!!
...!!!
HE'S FLYING!!
GRRR...
THAT WAS A CHEAP SHOT, GIN!!!
WUP
WE FIGHT FOR KEEPS, KID!!!
YOU BROUGHT THIS ON YOURSELVES!!!
IF YOU'D JUST HANDED OVER THE SHIP, YOU COULDA GONE IN PEACE!!!

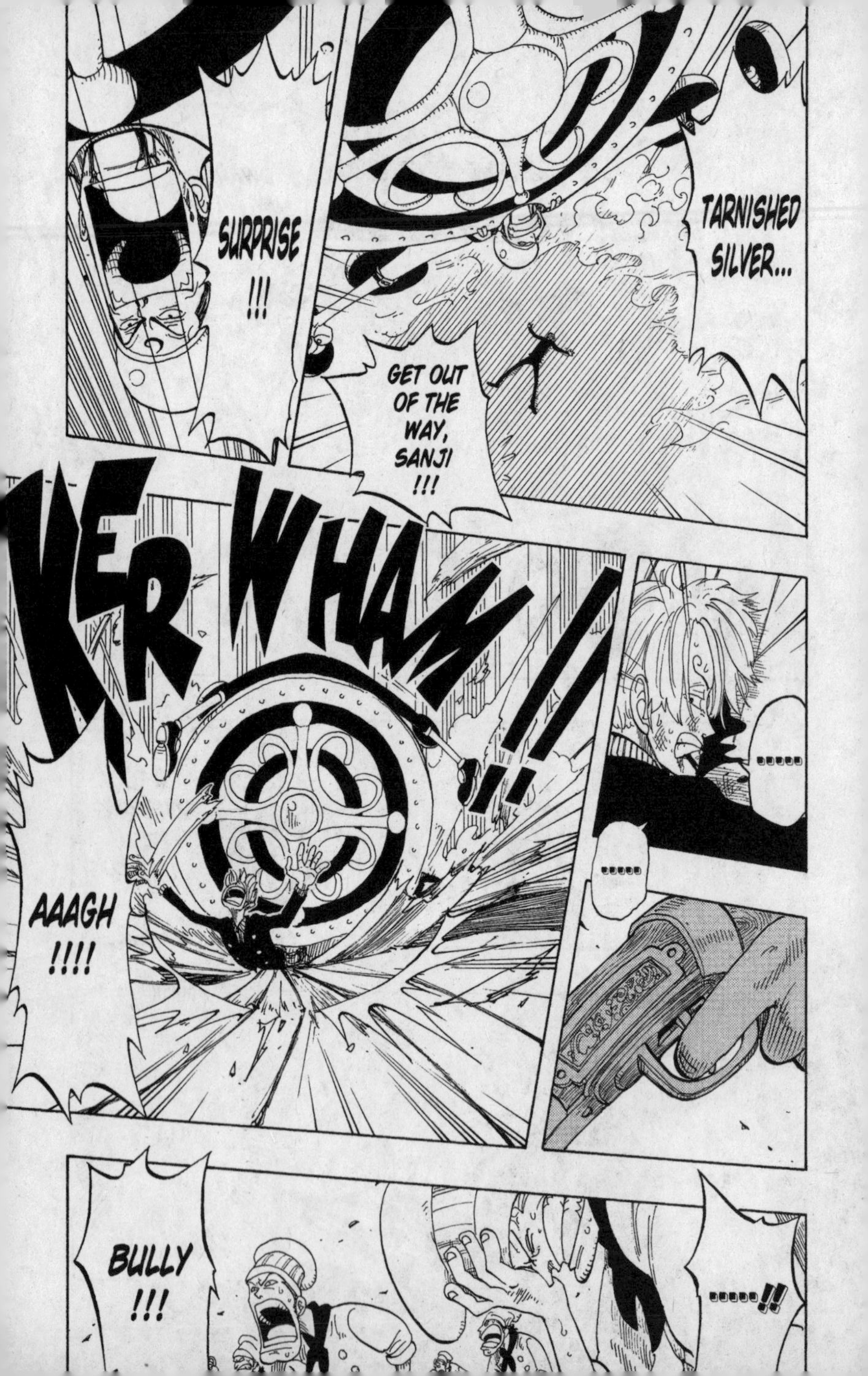
TARNISHED SILVER...
GET OUT OF THE WAY, SANJI !!!
SURPRISE !!!
.....
.....
KER WHAM!!
AAAGH !!!!
.....!!
BULLY !!!

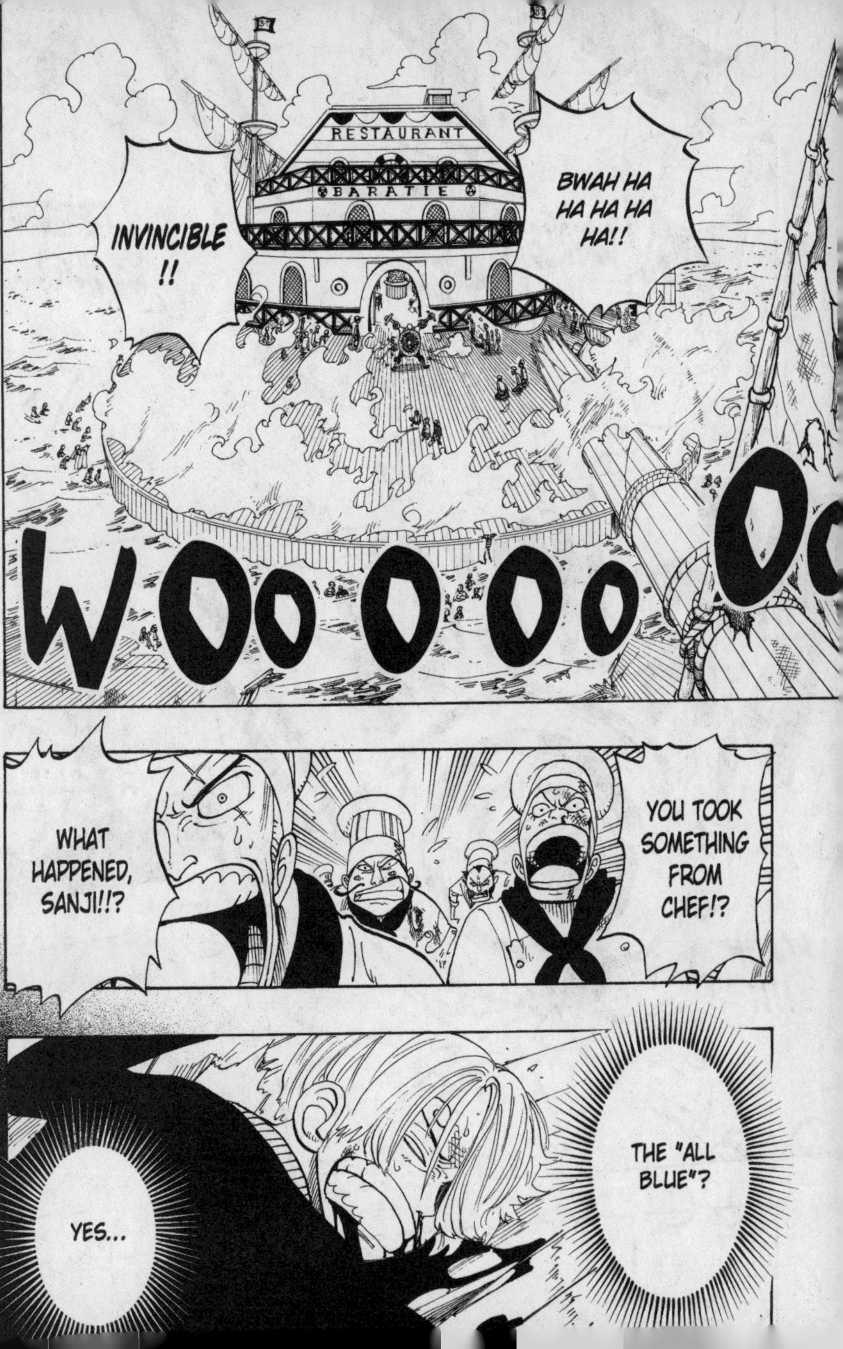
RESTAURANT
BARATIE
BWAH HA HA HA HA HA!!
INVINCIBLE !!
WOOOOOOO
YOU TOOK SOMETHING FROM CHEF!?
WHAT HAPPENED, SANJI!!?
THE "ALL BLUE"?
YES...

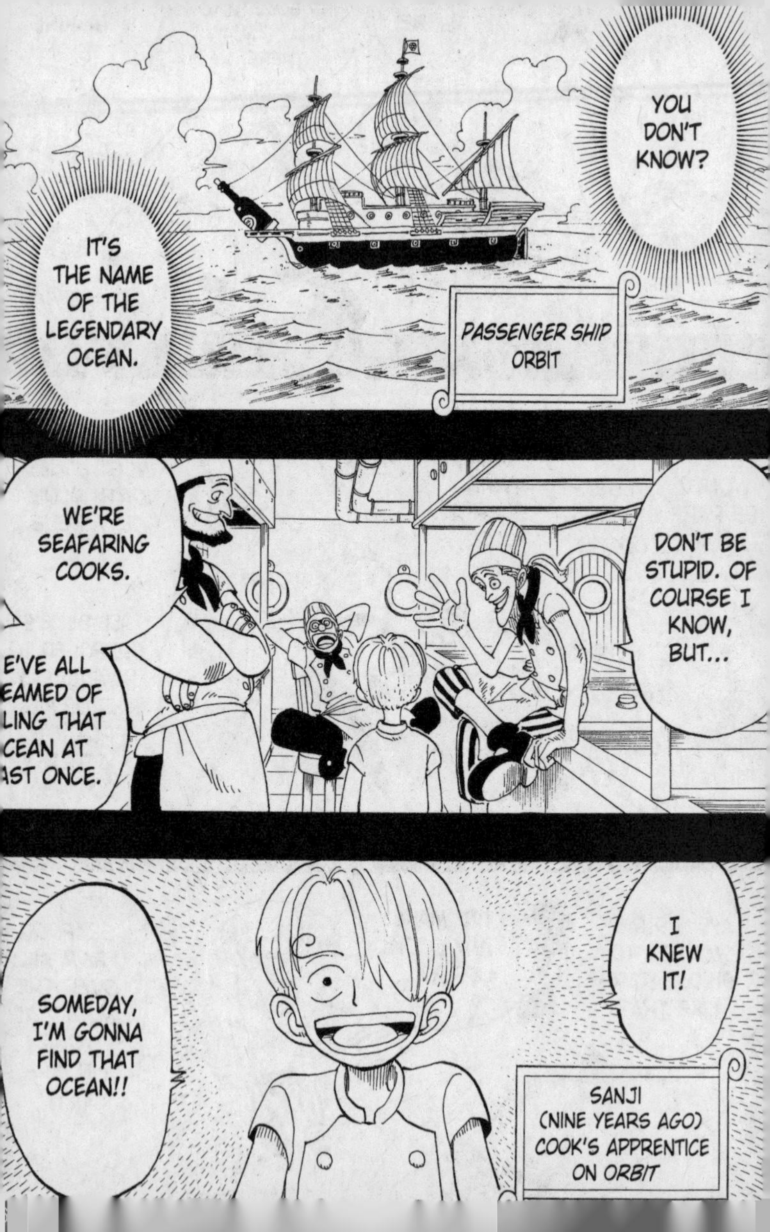
YOU DON'T KNOW?
PASSENGER SHIP ORBIT
IT'S THE NAME OF THE LEGENDARY OCEAN.
DON'T BE STUPID. OF COURSE I KNOW, BUT...
WE'RE SEAFARING COOKS.
E'VE ALL EAMED OF LING THAT CEAN AT AST ONCE.
I KNEW IT!
SOMEDAY, I'M GONNA FIND THAT OCEAN!!
SANJI (NINE YEARS AGO) COOK'S APPRENTICE ON ORBIT

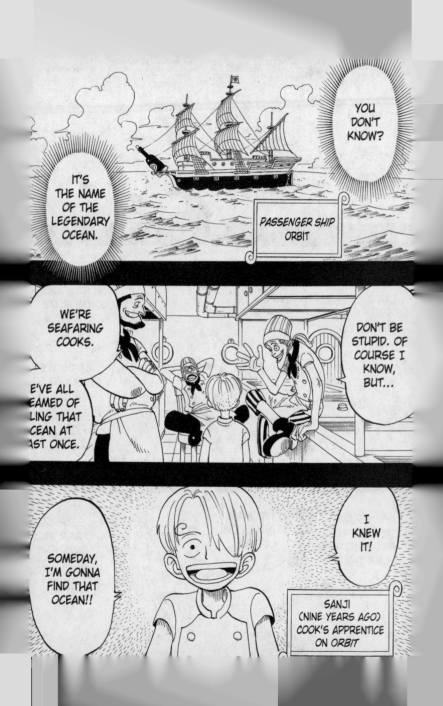

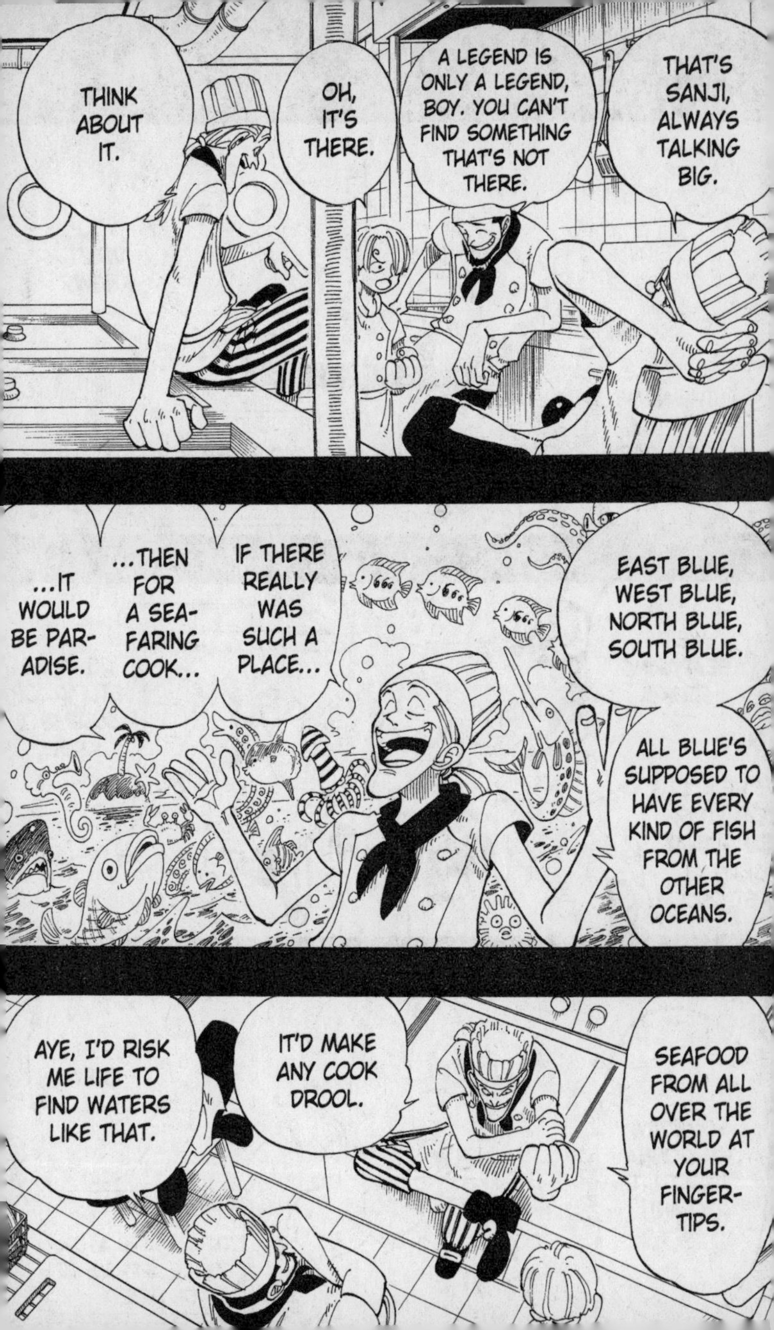
THAT'S SANJI, ALWAYS TALKING BIG.
A LEGEND IS ONLY A LEGEND, BOY. YOU CAN'T FIND SOMETHING THAT'S NOT THERE.
OH, IT'S THERE.
THINK ABOUT IT.
EAST BLUE, WEST BLUE, NORTH BLUE, SOUTH BLUE.
ALL BLUE'S SUPPOSED TO HAVE EVERY KIND OF FISH FROM THE OTHER OCEANS.
IF THERE REALLY WAS SUCH A PLACE...
...THEN FOR A SEAFARING COOK...
...IT WOULD BE PARADISE.
SEAFOOD FROM ALL OVER THE WORLD AT YOUR FINGERTIPS.
IT'D MAKE ANY COOK DROOL.
AYE, I'D RISK ME LIFE TO FIND WATERS LIKE THAT.

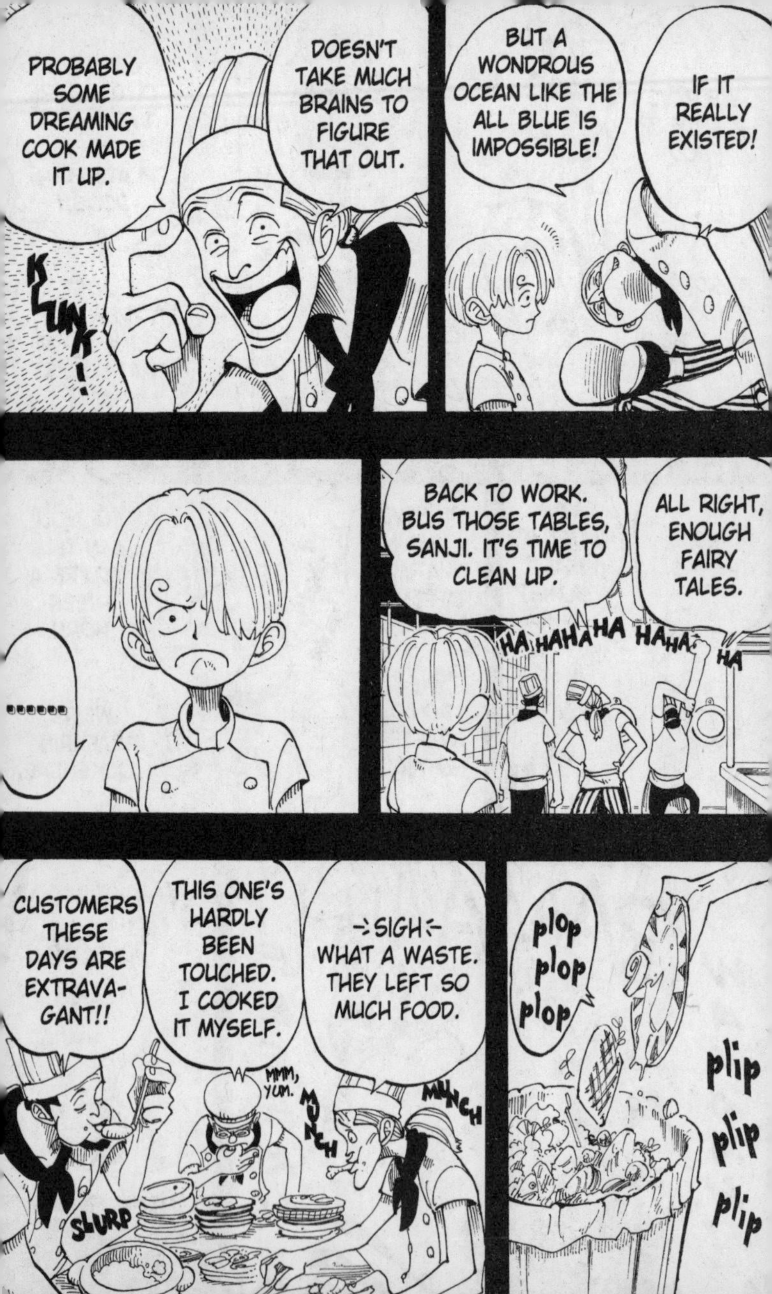
IF IT REALLY EXISTED!
BUT A WONDROUS OCEAN LIKE THE ALL BLUE IS IMPOSSIBLE!
DOESN'T TAKE MUCH BRAINS TO FIGURE THAT OUT.
PROBABLY SOME DREAMING COOK MADE IT UP.
KLUNK!!
ALL RIGHT, ENOUGH FAIRY TALES.
BACK TO WORK. BUS THOSE TABLES, SANJI. IT'S TIME TO CLEAN UP.
HA HAHAHA HA HAHAHA HA
......
plop plop plop
plip plip plip
SIGH WHAT A WASTE. THEY LEFT SO MUCH FOOD.
MUNCH
MMM, YUM.
MUNCH
THIS ONE'S HARDLY BEEN TOUCHED. I COOKED IT MYSELF.
CUSTOMERS THESE DAYS ARE EXTRAVA-GANT!!
SLURP

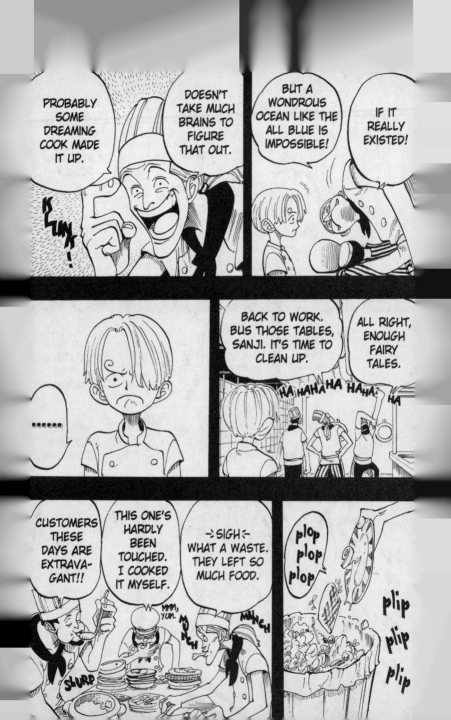

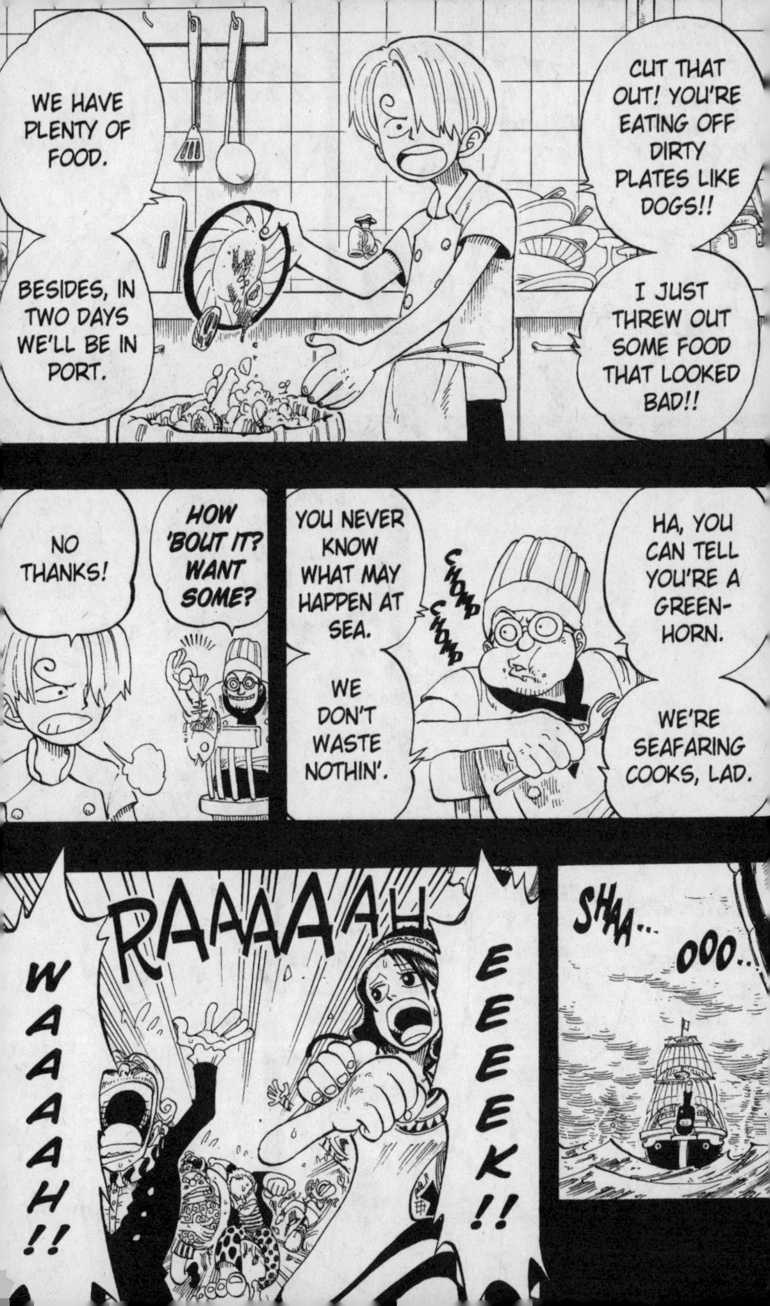
CUT THAT OUT! YOU'RE EATING OFF DIRTY PLATES LIKE DOGS!!
I JUST THREW OUT SOME FOOD THAT LOOKED BAD!!
WE HAVE PLENTY OF FOOD.
BESIDES, IN TWO DAYS WE'LL BE IN PORT.
HA, YOU CAN TELL YOU'RE A GREEN-HORN.
WE'RE SEAFARING COOKS, LAD.
CHOMP CHOMP
YOU NEVER KNOW WHAT MAY HAPPEN AT SEA.
WE DON'T WASTE NOTHIN'.
HOW 'BOUT IT? WANT SOME?
NO THANKS!
SHAA... OOO...
EEEEK!!
RAAAAAH
WAAAAAH!!

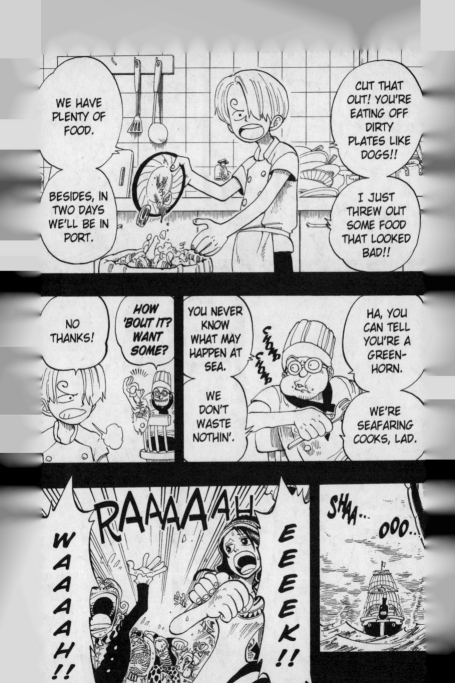

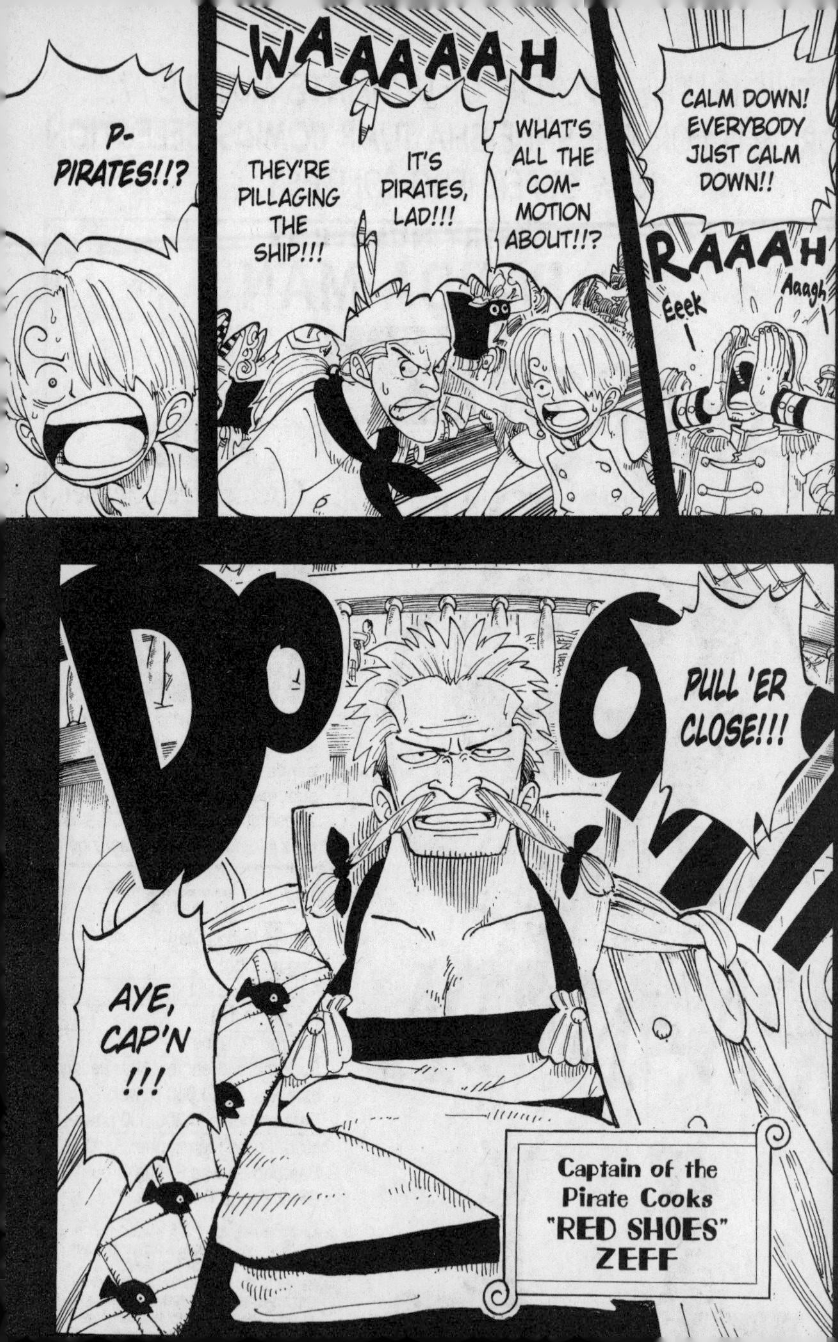
CALM DOWN! EVERYBODY JUST CALM DOWN!!
RAAAH
Aaagh
Eeek
WAAAAAH
WHAT'S ALL THE COM-MOTION ABOUT!!?
IT'S PIRATES, LAD!!!
THEY'RE PILLAGING THE SHIP!!!
P-PIRATES!!?
PULL 'ER CLOSE!!!
AYE, CAP'N!!!
Captain of the Pirate Cooks "RED SHOES" ZEFF

☆ THIS IS "THE MYSTERY OF ULTIMATE MUSCLE 77."
I DREW IT FOR THE SHUEISHA JUMP COMICS SELECTION
NEW SUPERHERO CONTEST.

## ENTRY NUMBER 12
# PANDA MAN

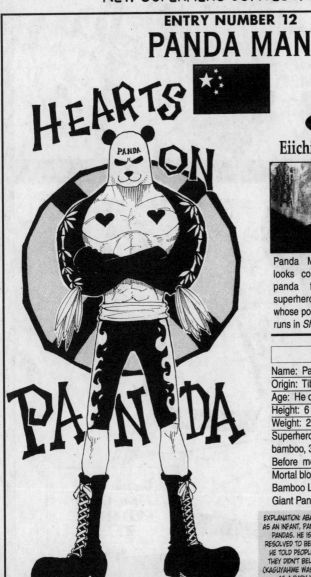

*Conceived by*

### Eiichiro Oda Sensei

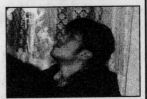

Panda Man, who somehow looks cool despite having a panda face, is the new superhero from Oda Sensei, whose popular ONE PIECE also runs in *Shonen Jump* magazine.

| DATA |
|---|
| Name: Panda Man |
| Origin: Tibet |
| Age: He doesn't know |
| Height: 6 ft. 6 in. |
| Weight: 270 lbs. |
| Superhero strength: After eating bamboo, 3,300,000 power. Before meals, 3,300,000 power. |
| Mortal blow techniques: S.P.D.-- Bamboo Leaves Panda Drop, Giant Panda Deathlock. |

EXPLANATION: ABANDONED IN A BAMBOO THICKET AS AN INFANT, PANDA MAN WAS RAISED BY GIANT PANDAS. HE IS A DEMON SUPERHERO WHO RESOLVED TO BECOME STRONG BECAUSE WHEN HE TOLD PEOPLE HE HAD SEEN KAGUYAHIME, THEY DIDN'T BELIEVE HIM AND PICKED ON HIM. (KAGUYAHIME WAS A PRINCESS WHO WAS FOUND AS A BABY INSIDE A BAMBOO STUMP.)

# Chapter 57:
# IF YOU HAVE A DREAM

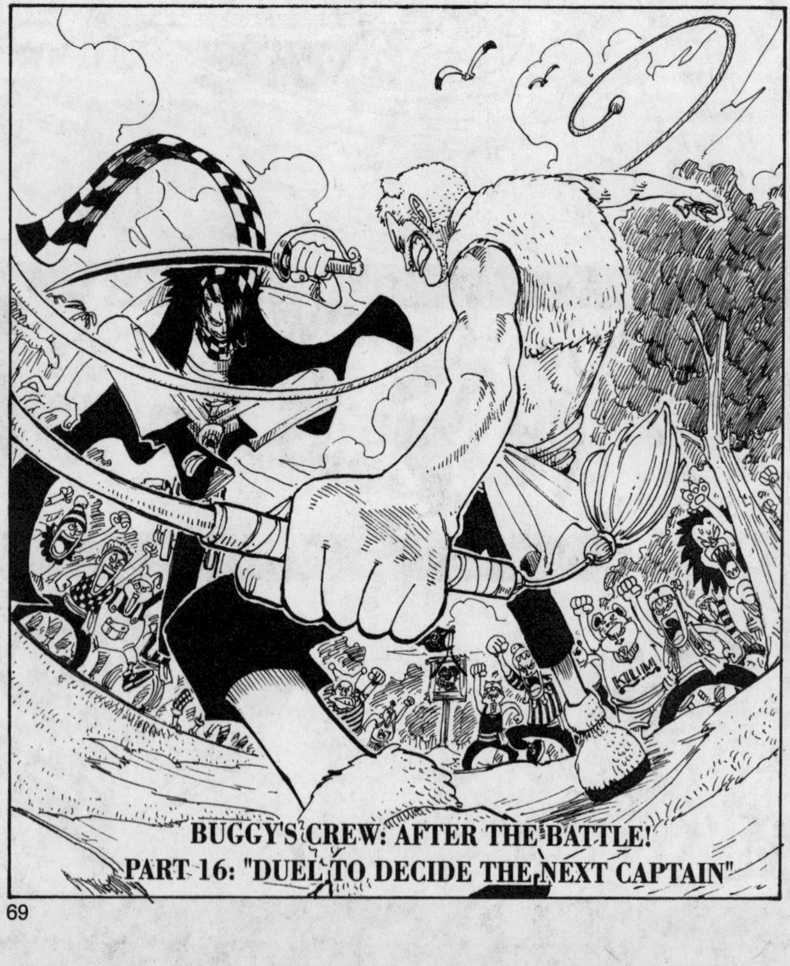
BUGGY'S CREW: AFTER THE BATTLE!
PART 16: "DUEL TO DECIDE THE NEXT CAPTAIN"

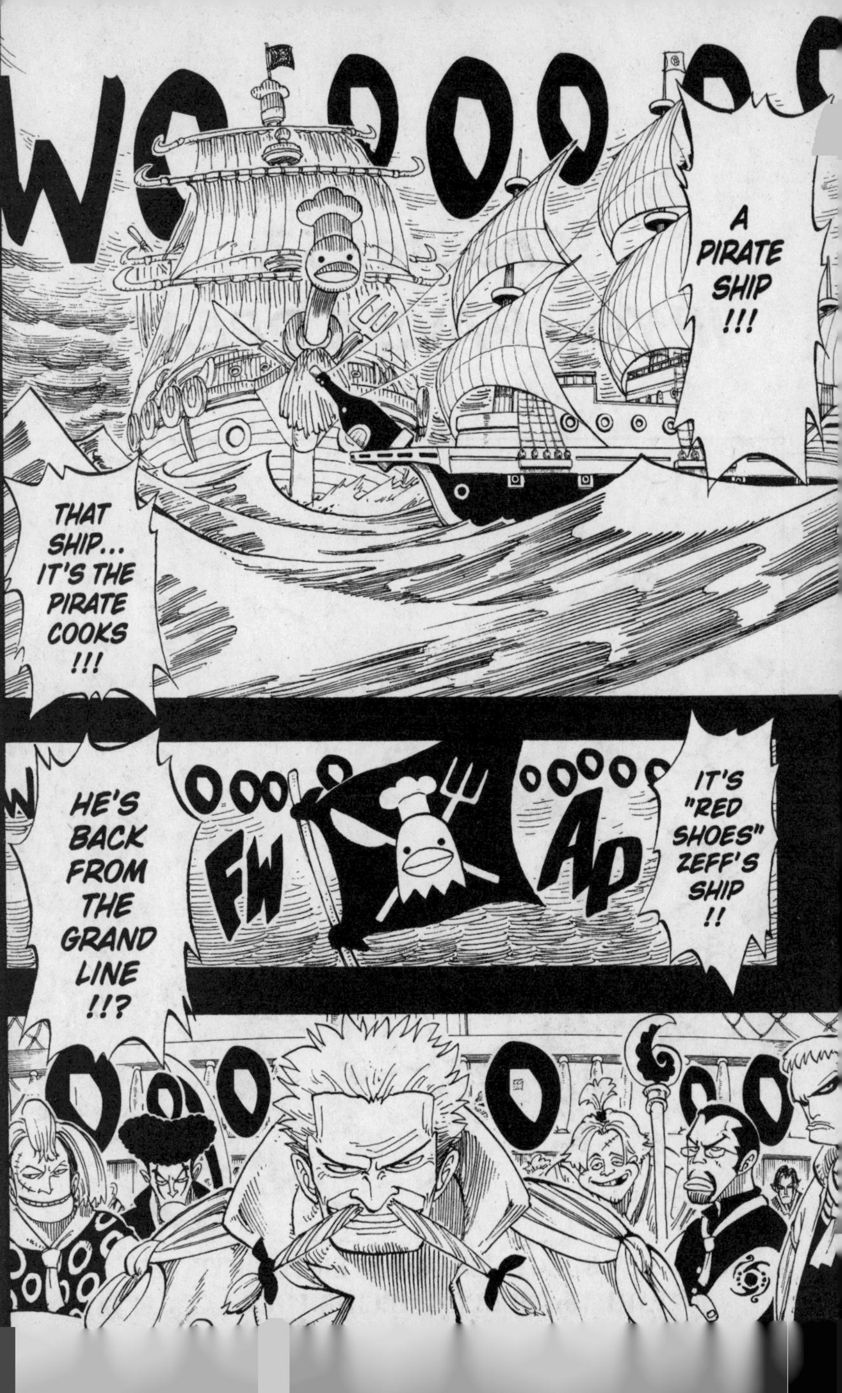

A PIRATE SHIP!!!
THAT SHIP... IT'S THE PIRATE COOKS!!!
IT'S "RED SHOES" ZEFF'S SHIP!!
FWAP
HE'S BACK FROM THE GRAND LINE!!?

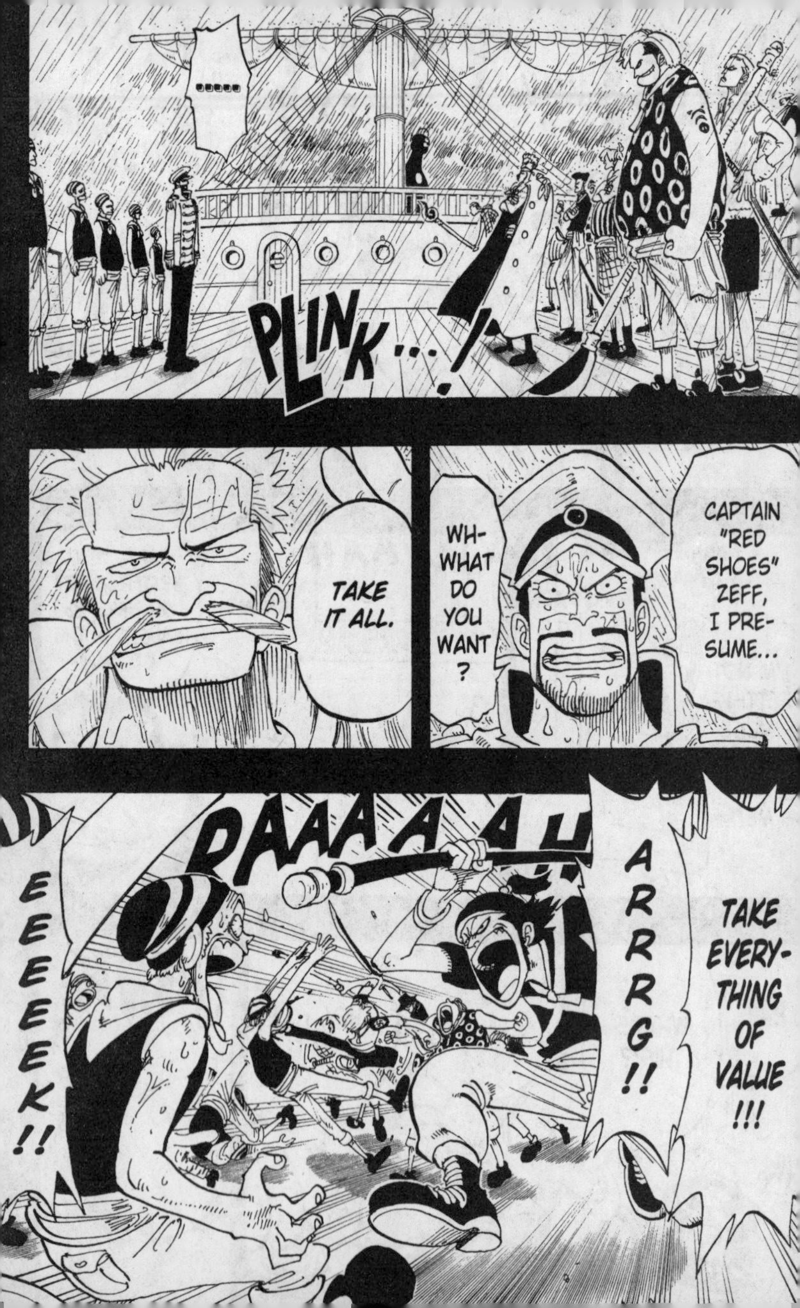
.....
PLINK...!
CAPTAIN "RED SHOES" ZEFF, I PRESUME...
WH-WHAT DO YOU WANT?
TAKE IT ALL.
TAKE EVERYTHING OF VALUE!!!
ARRRG!!
DAAAAAH
EEEEEEK!!

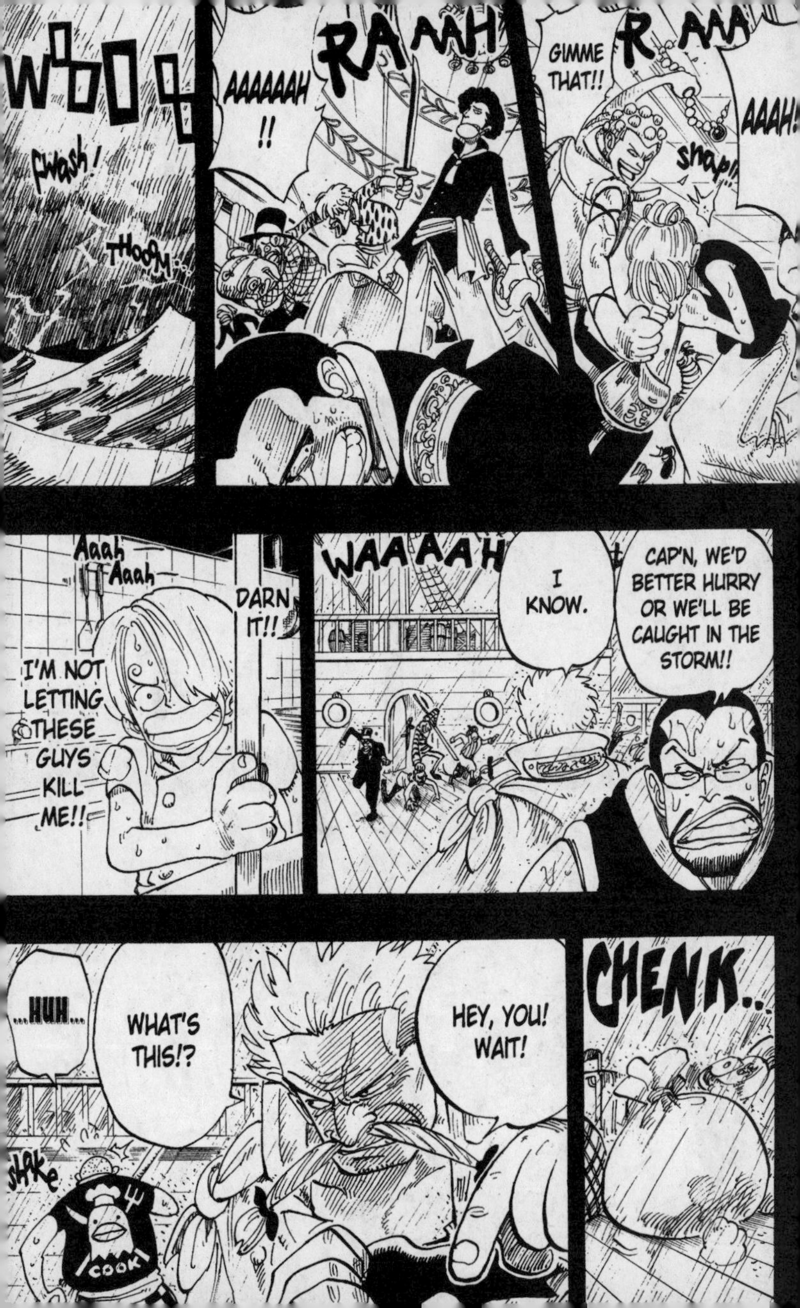

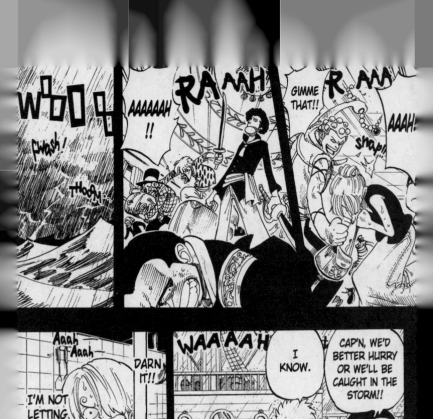

GIMME THAT!!
RAAA
AAAH!
snap!!
RAAAH
AAAAAAH !!
fwash!
THOOM...
WAAAAH
CAP'N, WE'D BETTER HURRY OR WE'LL BE CAUGHT IN THE STORM!!
I KNOW.
Aaah Aaah
DARN IT!!
I'M NOT LETTING THESE GUYS KILL ME!!
CHENK..
HEY, YOU! WAIT!
WHAT'S THIS!?
...HUH...
shake
COOK

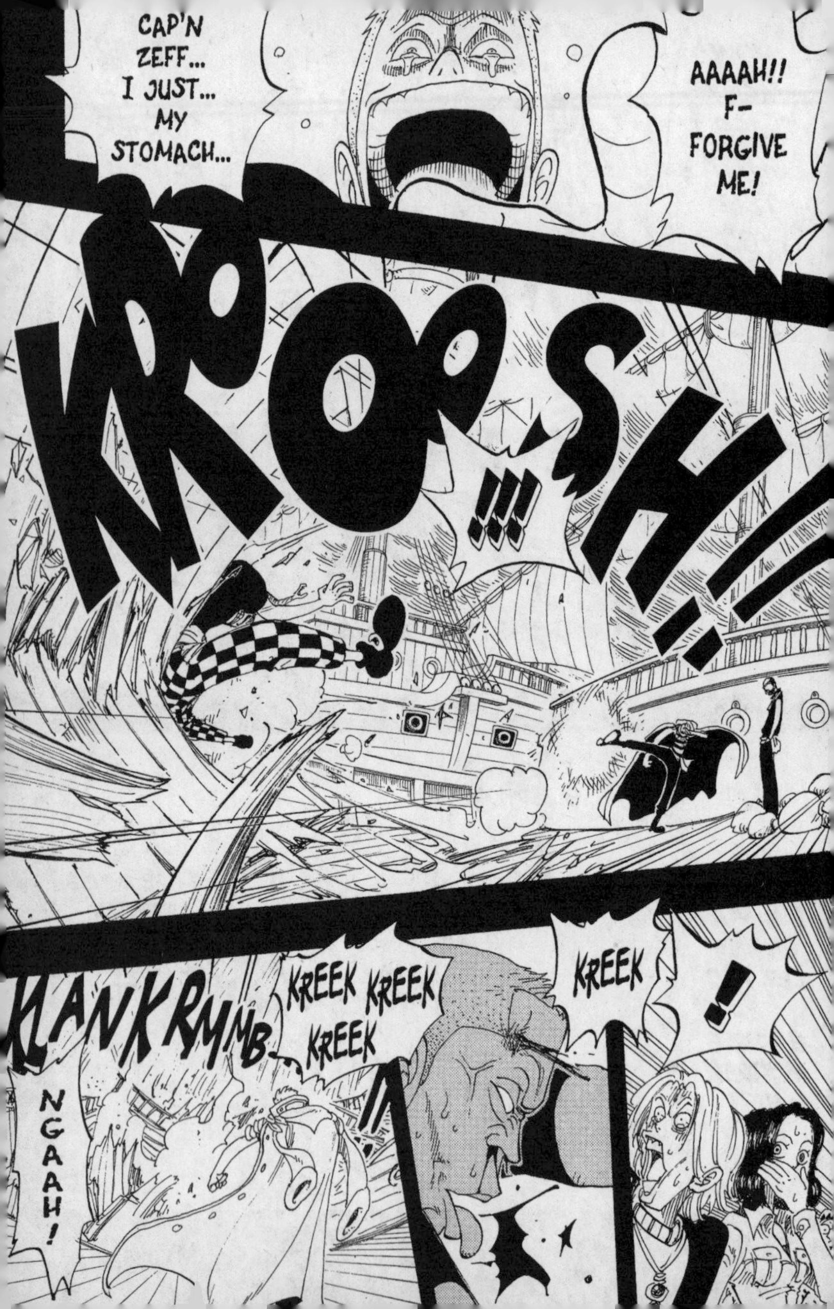
AAAAH!! F- FORGIVE ME!
CAP'N ZEFF... I JUST... MY STOMACH...
KROOOSH!!!!
!
KREEK
KREEK KREEK
KREEK
KLANK KRYMB...
NGAAH!

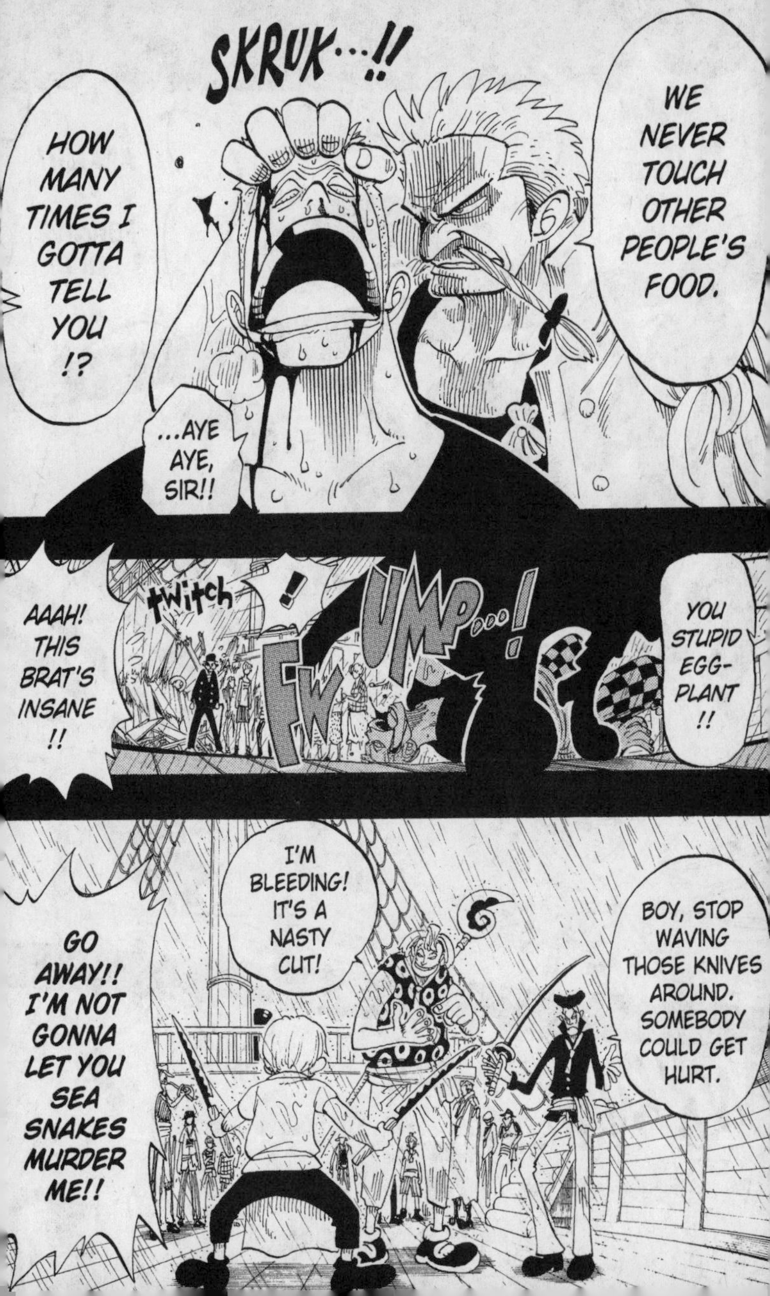
SKRUK...!!
WE NEVER TOUCH OTHER PEOPLE'S FOOD.
HOW MANY TIMES I GOTTA TELL YOU!?
...AYE AYE, SIR!!
YOU STUPID EGG-PLANT!!
FWUMP...!
!
twitch
AAAH! THIS BRAT'S INSANE!!
BOY, STOP WAVING THOSE KNIVES AROUND. SOMEBODY COULD GET HURT.
I'M BLEEDING! IT'S A NASTY CUT!
GO AWAY!! I'M NOT GONNA LET YOU SEA SNAKES MURDER ME!!

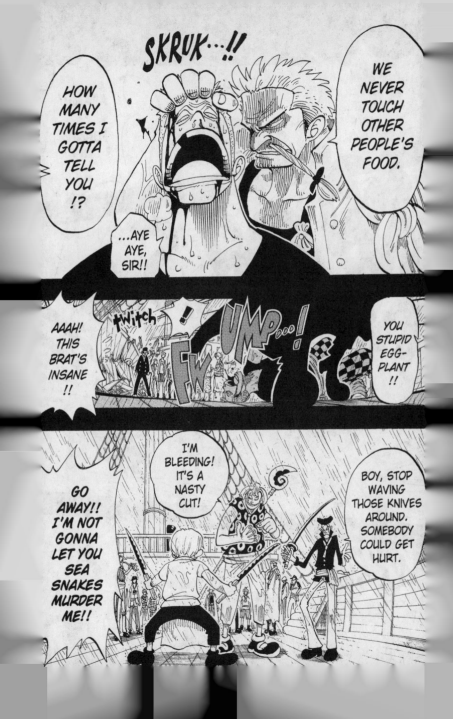

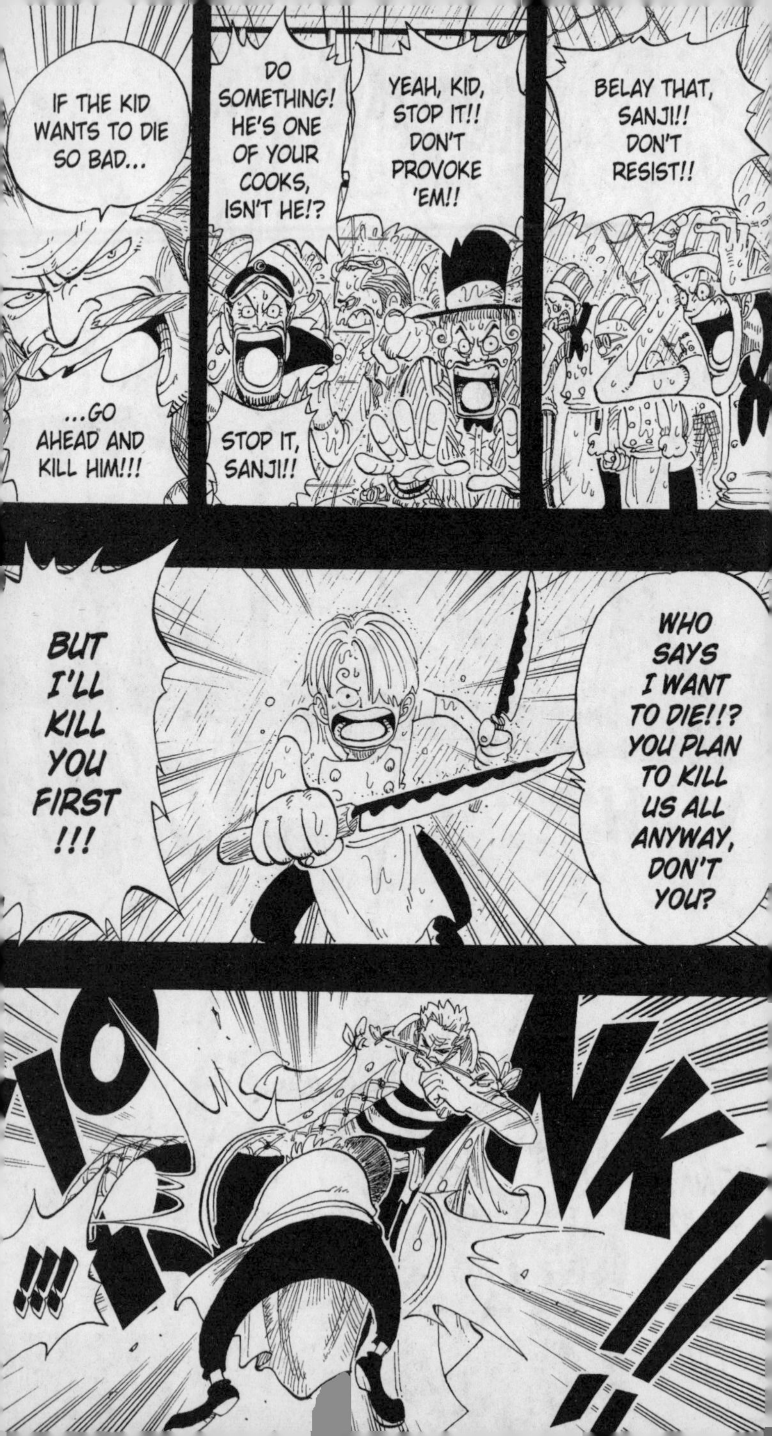
BELAY THAT, SANJI!! DON'T RESIST!!
YEAH, KID, STOP IT!! DON'T PROVOKE 'EM!!
DO SOMETHING! HE'S ONE OF YOUR COOKS, ISN'T HE!?
STOP IT, SANJI!!
IF THE KID WANTS TO DIE SO BAD...
...GO AHEAD AND KILL HIM!!!
WHO SAYS I WANT TO DIE!!? YOU PLAN TO KILL US ALL ANYWAY, DON'T YOU?
BUT I'LL KILL YOU FIRST!!!

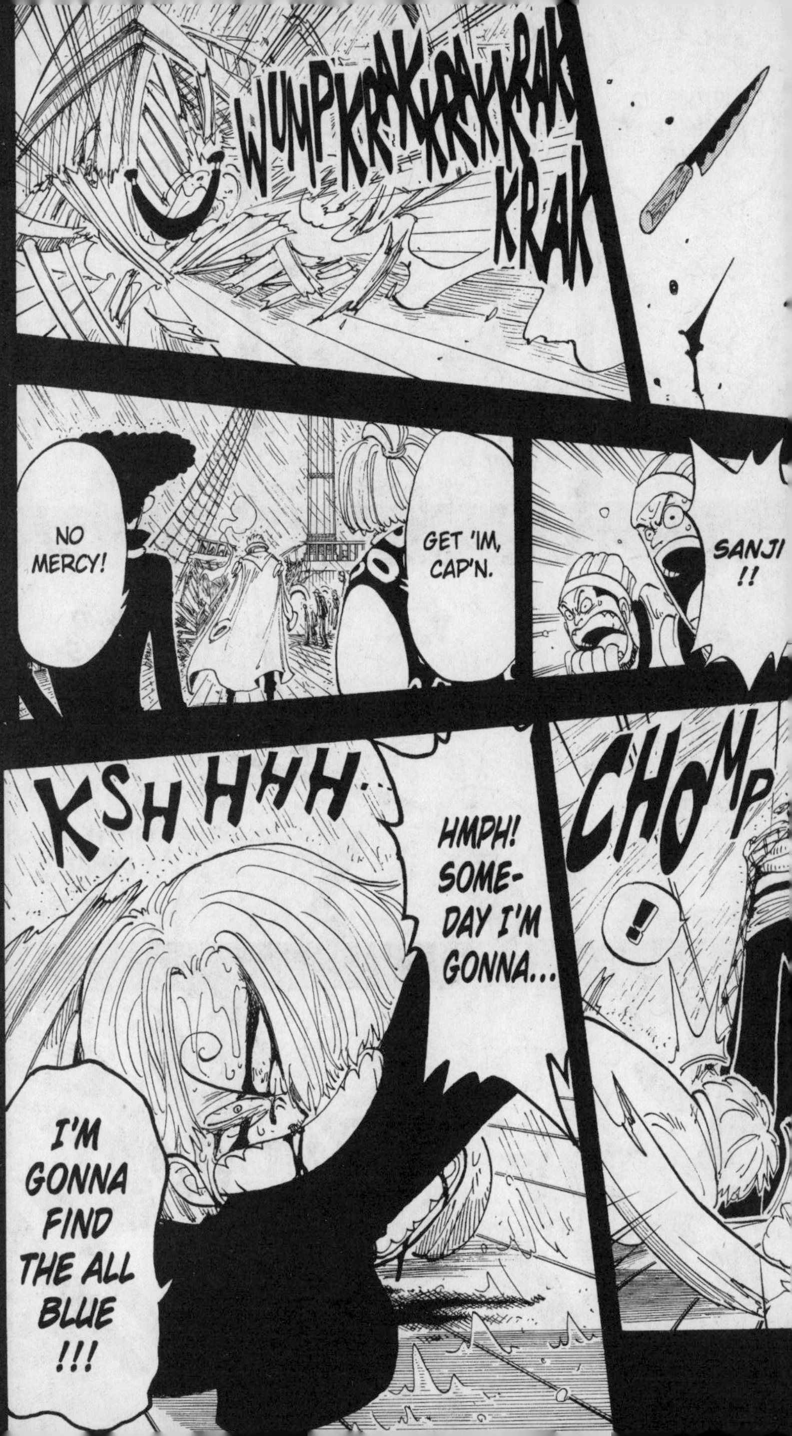
WUMP KRAK KRAK KRAK KRAK
SANJI !!
GET 'IM, CAP'N.
NO MERCY!
CHOMP
!
KSHHHH...
HMPH! SOMEDAY I'M GONNA...
I'M GONNA FIND THE ALL BLUE !!!

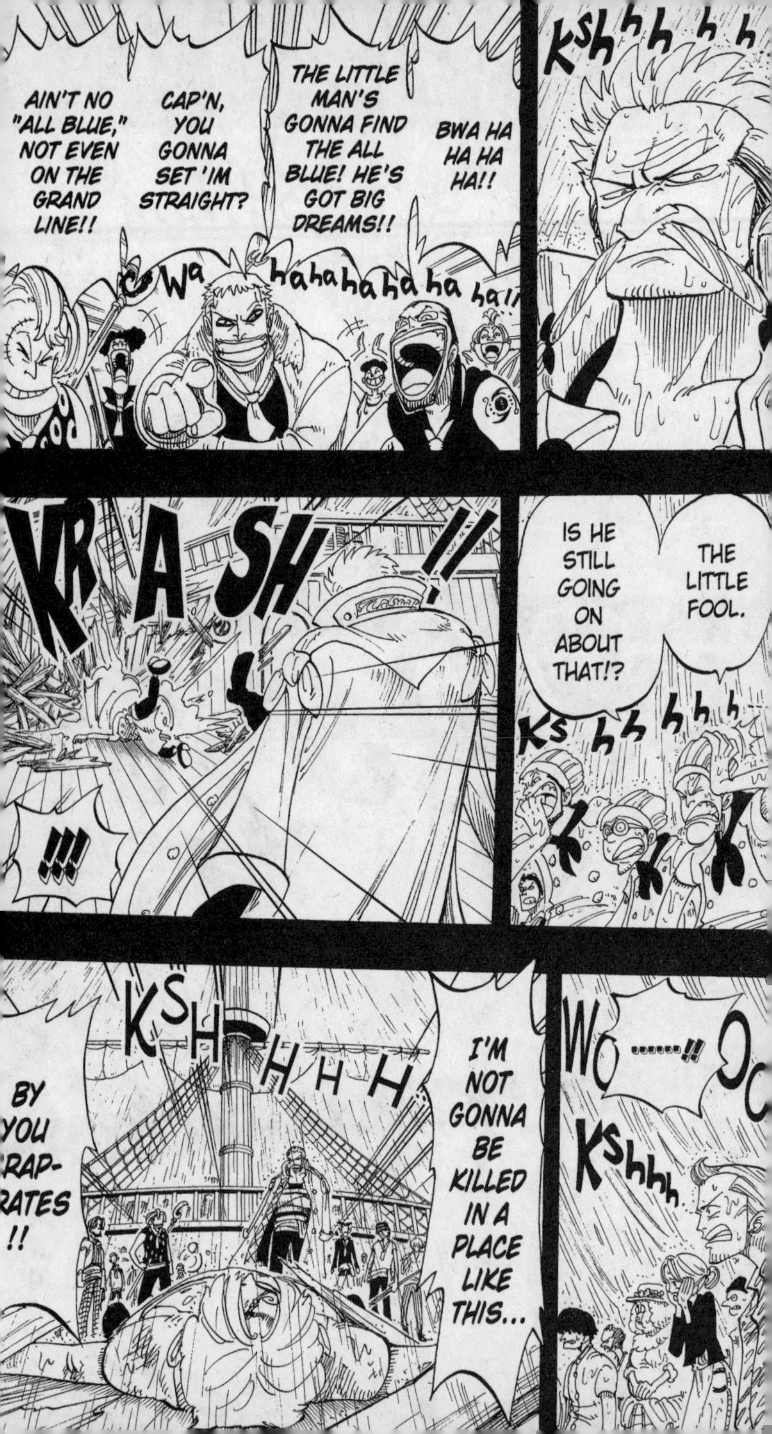
KSHHHHHH
BWA HA HA HA HA!!
THE LITTLE MAN'S GONNA FIND THE ALL BLUE! HE'S GOT BIG DREAMS!!
CAP'N, YOU GONNA SET 'IM STRAIGHT?
AIN'T NO "ALL BLUE," NOT EVEN ON THE GRAND LINE!!
WAHAHAHAHAHA HA HA!!
THE LITTLE FOOL.
IS HE STILL GOING ON ABOUT THAT!?
KSHHHHH
KRASH!!
!!!
WO......!! OO
KSHHH
I'M NOT GONNA BE KILLED IN A PLACE LIKE THIS...
KSHHHHH
BY YOU RAP- RATES !!

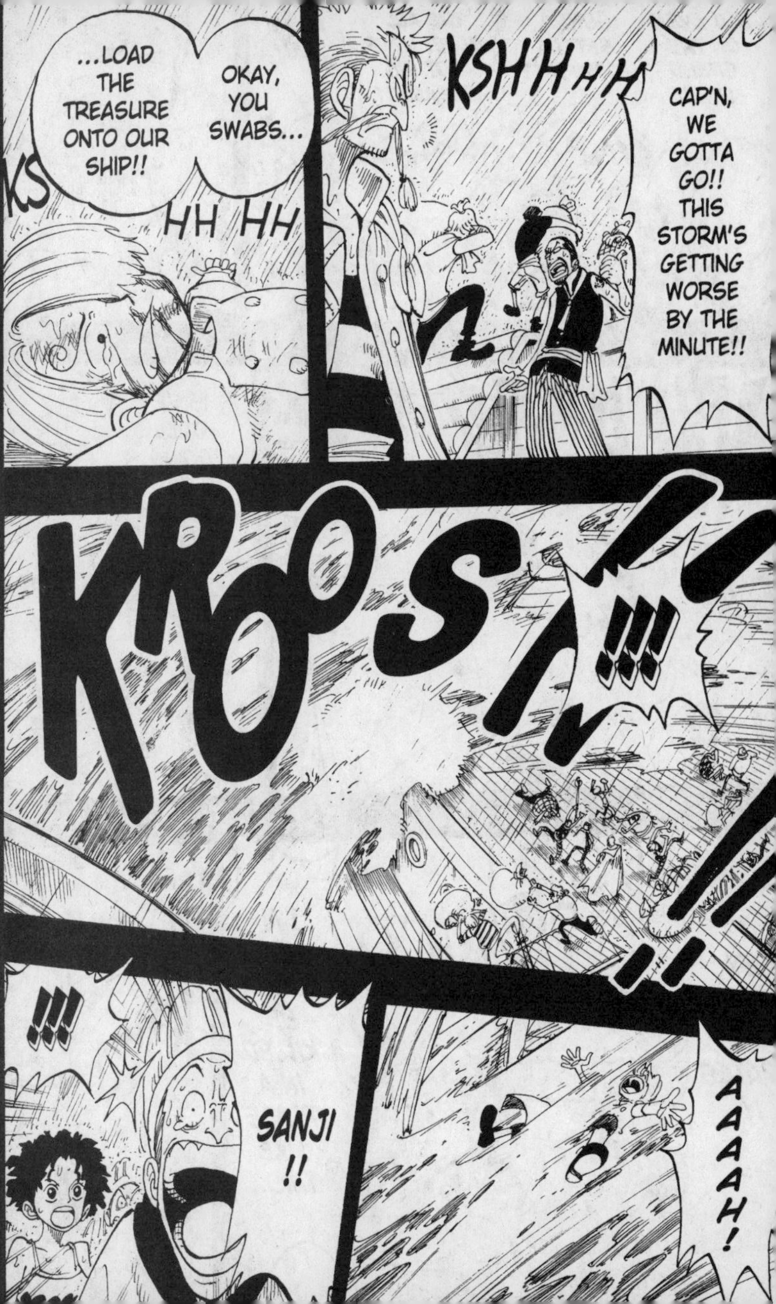

KSHHHHH
CAP'N, WE GOTTA GO!! THIS STORM'S GETTING WORSE BY THE MINUTE!!
OKAY, YOU SWABS...
...LOAD THE TREASURE ONTO OUR SHIP!!
KSHH HH HH
KROOSH!!!
AAAAAH!
SANJI!!

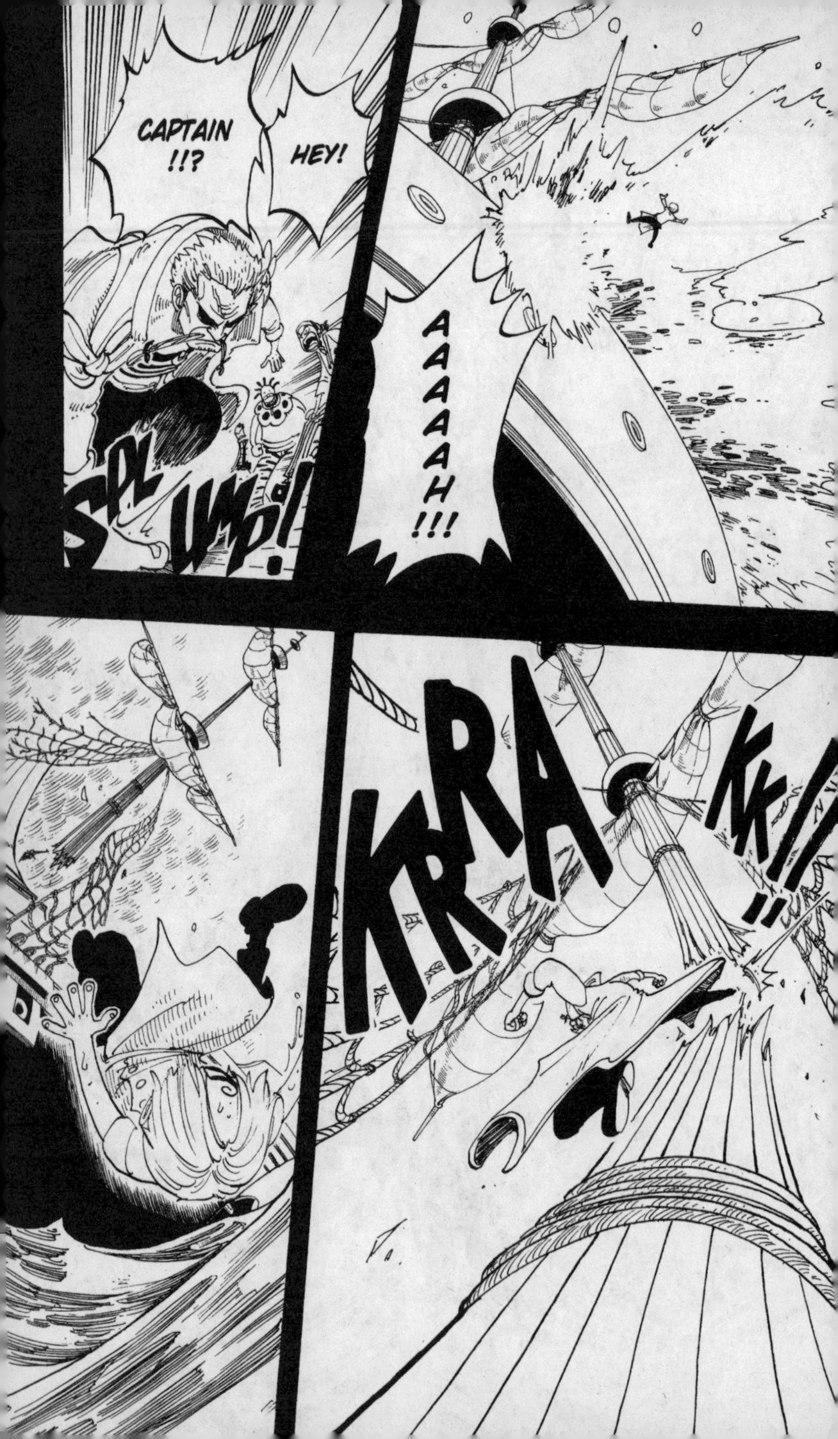
AAAAAAH!!!
HEY!
CAPTAIN!!?
SPLUMP!
KRRAKK!!

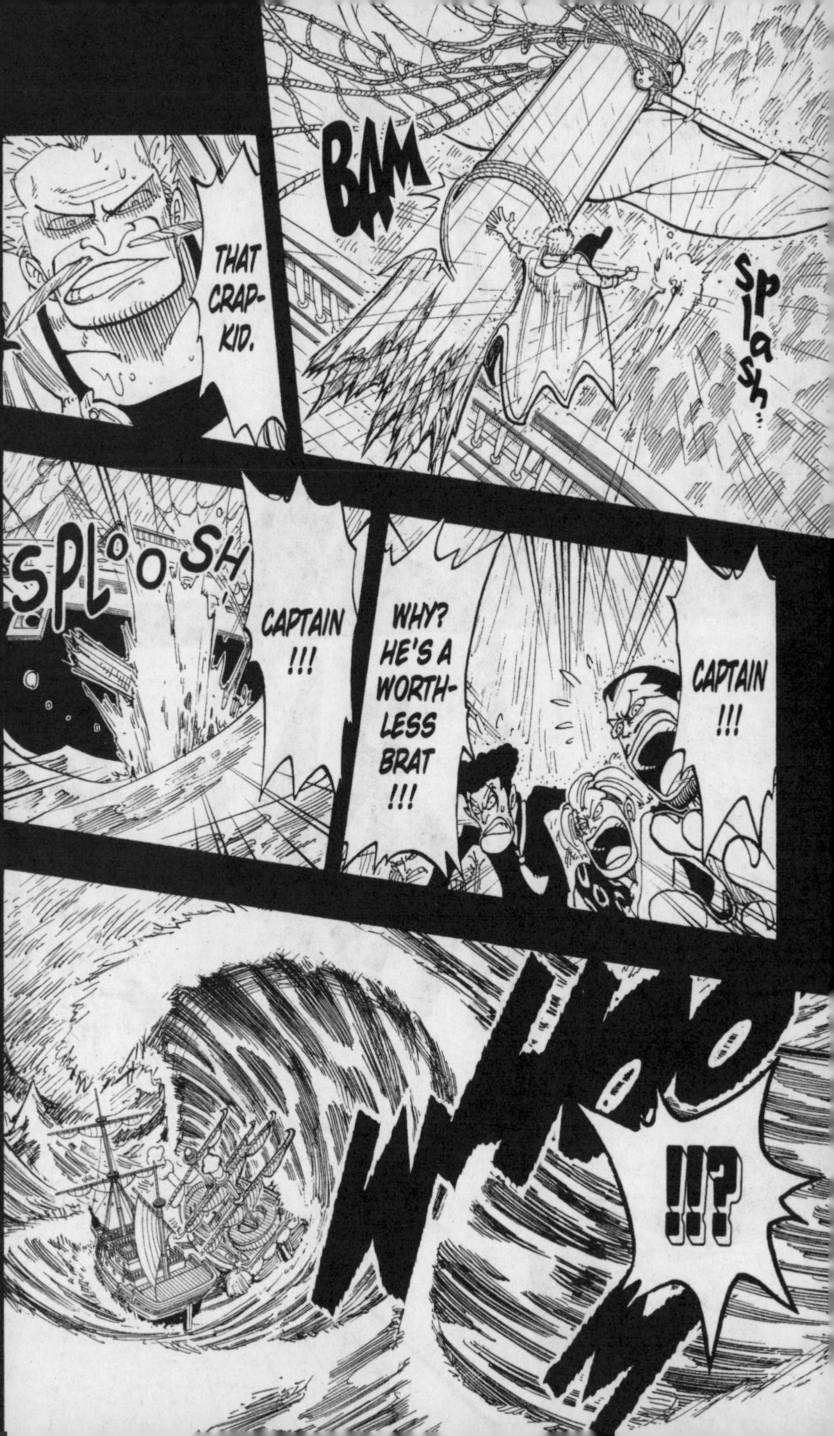
BAM
Splash...
THAT CRAP-KID.
CAPTAIN !!!
WHY? HE'S A WORTHLESS BRAT !!!
SPLOOSH
CAPTAIN !!!
!!?

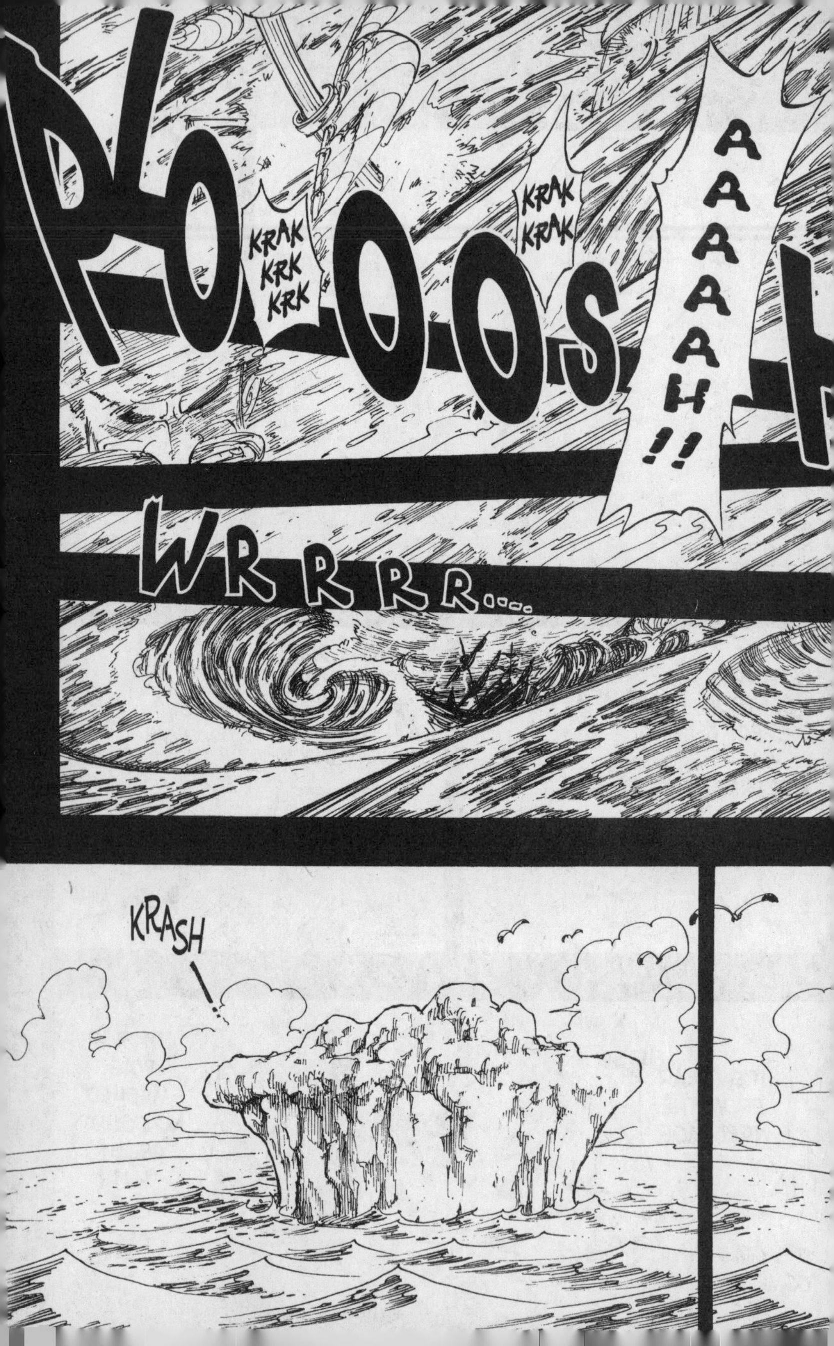
AAAAAH!!
KRAK KRAK
KRAK KRK KRK
PLOOOSH
WRRRR....
KRASH

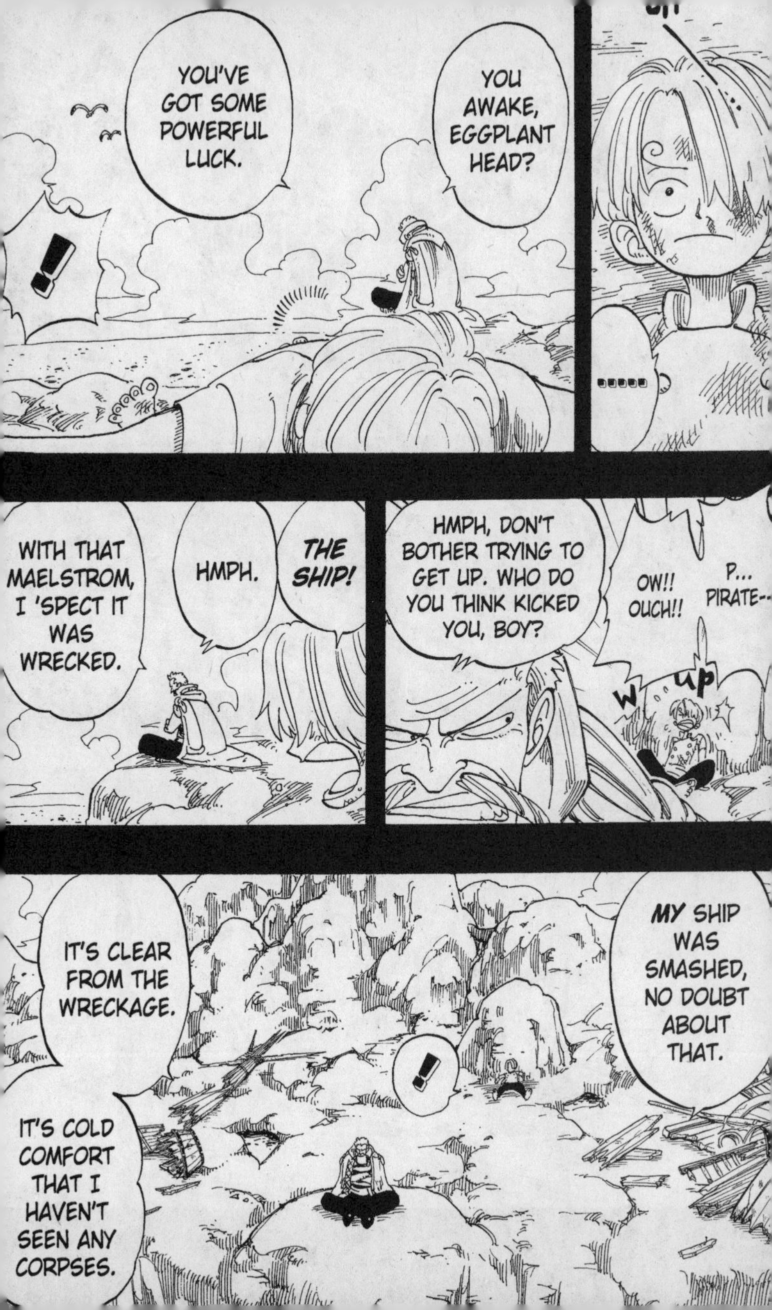
.....
YOU AWAKE, EGGPLANT HEAD?
YOU'VE GOT SOME POWERFUL LUCK.
!
P... PIRATE--
OW!! OUCH!!
W UP
HMPH, DON'T BOTHER TRYING TO GET UP. WHO DO YOU THINK KICKED YOU, BOY?
*THE SHIP!*
HMPH.
WITH THAT MAELSTROM, I 'SPECT IT WAS WRECKED.
***MY*** SHIP WAS SMASHED, NO DOUBT ABOUT THAT.
!
IT'S CLEAR FROM THE WRECKAGE.
IT'S COLD COMFORT THAT I HAVEN'T SEEN ANY CORPSES.

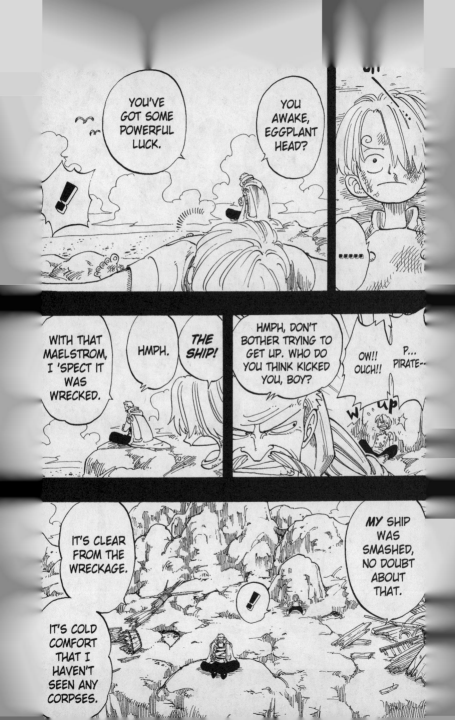

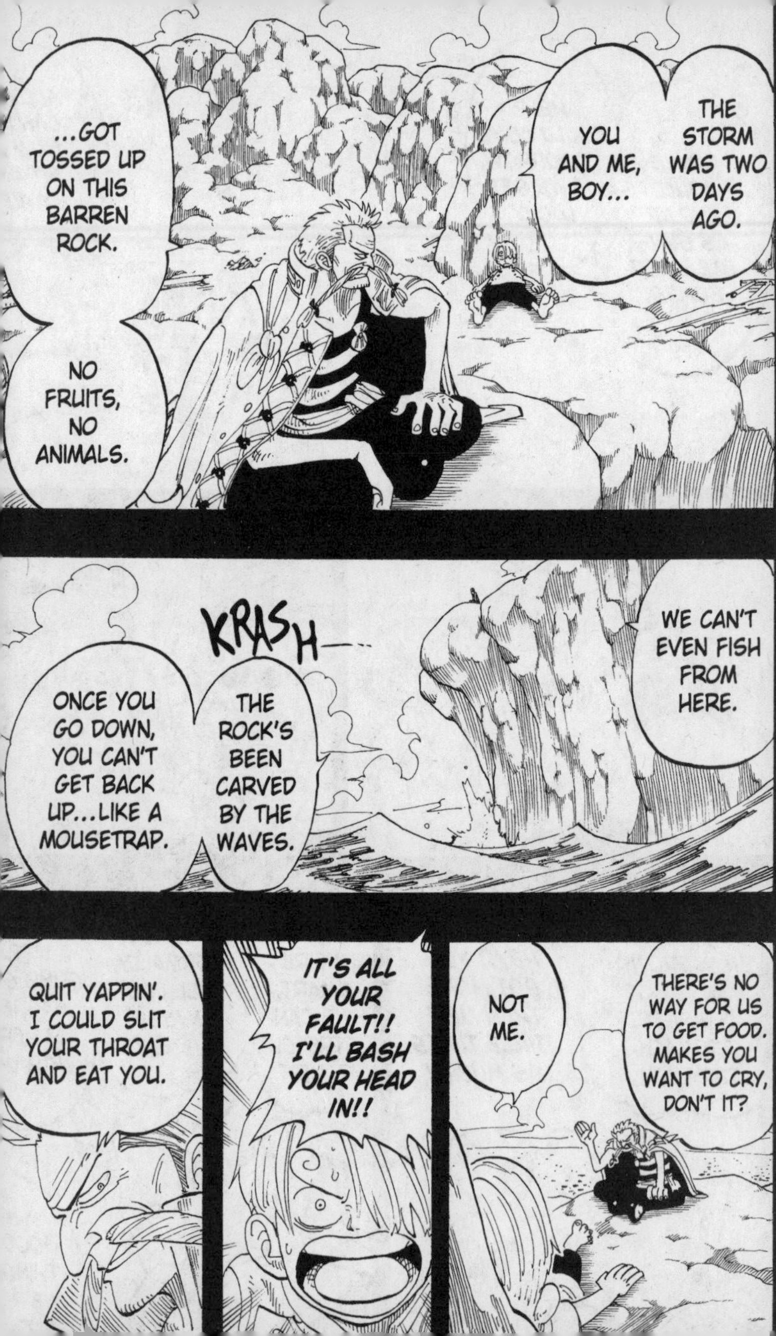
THE STORM WAS TWO DAYS AGO.
YOU AND ME, BOY...
...GOT TOSSED UP ON THIS BARREN ROCK.
NO FRUITS, NO ANIMALS.
WE CAN'T EVEN FISH FROM HERE.
KRASH
THE ROCK'S BEEN CARVED BY THE WAVES.
ONCE YOU GO DOWN, YOU CAN'T GET BACK UP...LIKE A MOUSETRAP.
THERE'S NO WAY FOR US TO GET FOOD. MAKES YOU WANT TO CRY, DON'T IT?
NOT ME.
IT'S ALL YOUR FAULT!! I'LL BASH YOUR HEAD IN!!
QUIT YAPPIN'. I COULD SLIT YOUR THROAT AND EAT YOU.

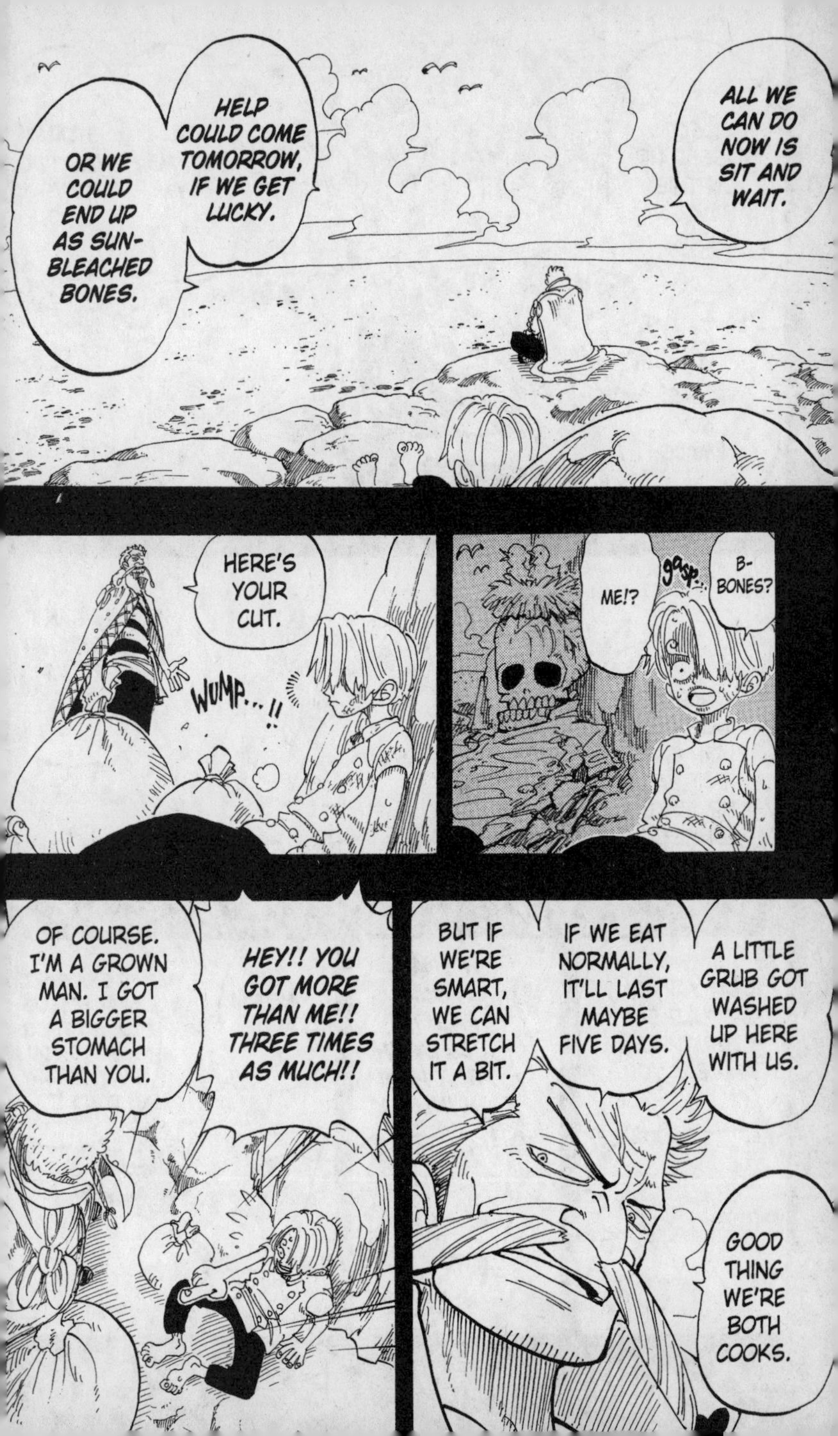
ALL WE CAN DO NOW IS SIT AND WAIT.
HELP COULD COME TOMORROW, IF WE GET LUCKY.
OR WE COULD END UP AS SUN-BLEACHED BONES.
B-BONES?
gasp..
ME!?
HERE'S YOUR CUT.
WUMP...!!
A LITTLE GRUB GOT WASHED UP HERE WITH US.
IF WE EAT NORMALLY, IT'LL LAST MAYBE FIVE DAYS.
BUT IF WE'RE SMART, WE CAN STRETCH IT A BIT.
GOOD THING WE'RE BOTH COOKS.
HEY!! YOU GOT MORE THAN ME!! THREE TIMES AS MUCH!!
OF COURSE. I'M A GROWN MAN. I GOT A BIGGER STOMACH THAN YOU.

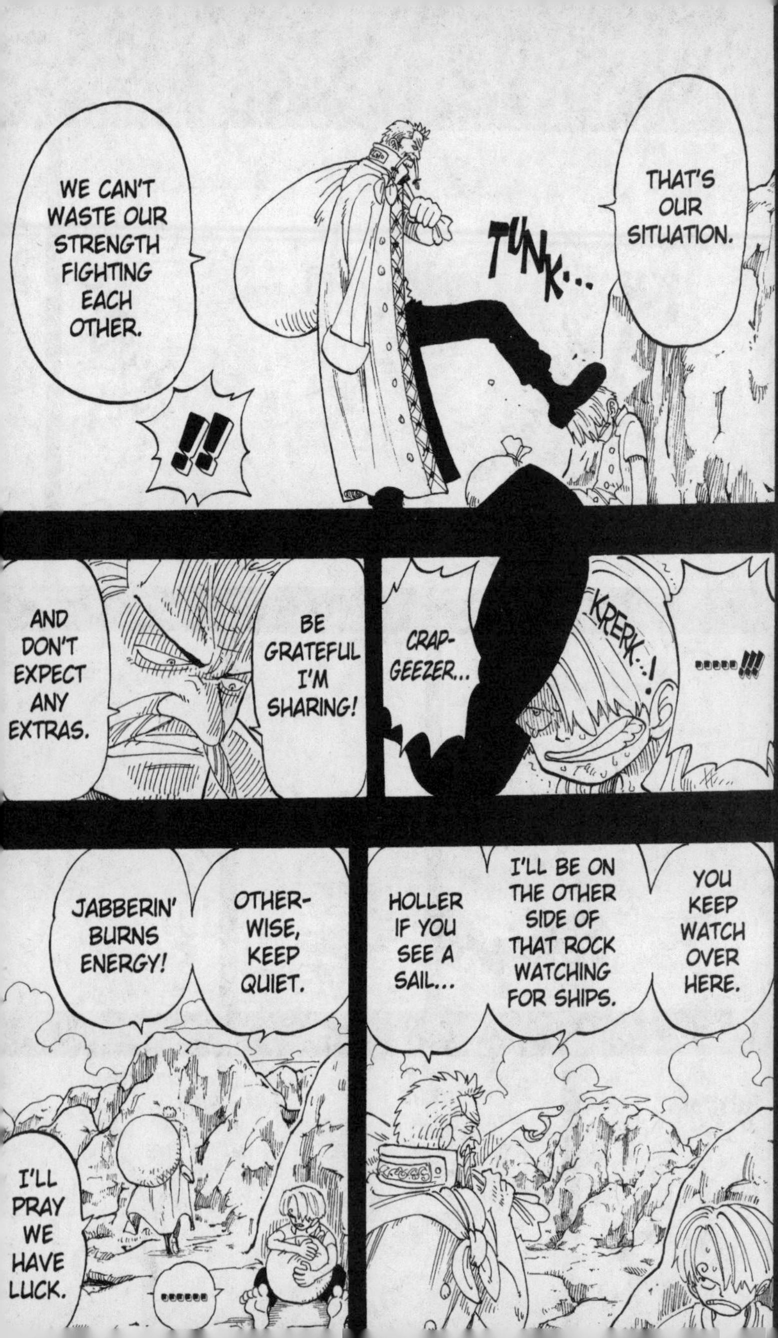
THAT'S OUR SITUATION.
TUNK...
WE CAN'T WASTE OUR STRENGTH FIGHTING EACH OTHER.
!!
......!!!
KRERK..!
CRAP-GEEZER...
BE GRATEFUL I'M SHARING!
AND DON'T EXPECT ANY EXTRAS.
YOU KEEP WATCH OVER HERE.
I'LL BE ON THE OTHER SIDE OF THAT ROCK WATCHING FOR SHIPS.
HOLLER IF YOU SEE A SAIL...
OTHER-WISE, KEEP QUIET.
JABBERIN' BURNS ENERGY!
......
I'LL PRAY WE HAVE LUCK.

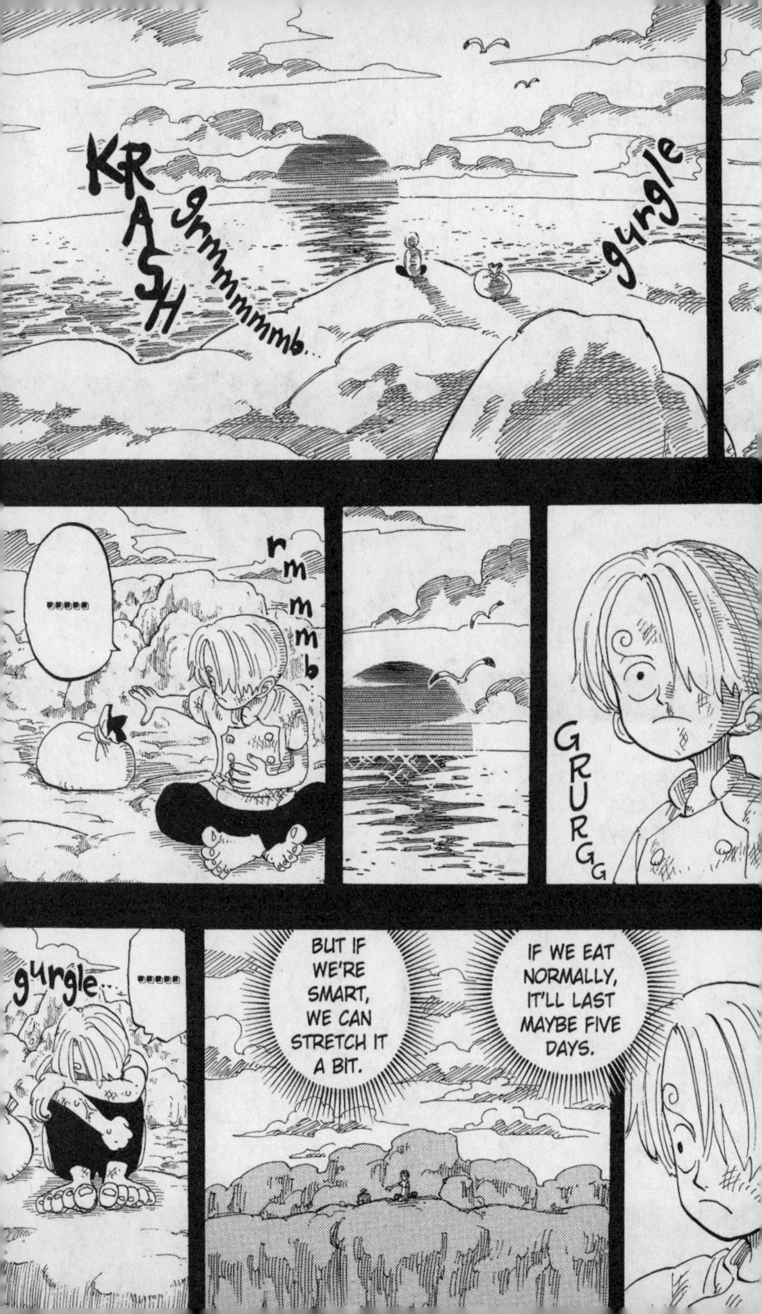
gurgle
KRASH
grmmmmmb...
GRURGG
rmmmb
.....
IF WE EAT NORMALLY, IT'LL LAST MAYBE FIVE DAYS.
BUT IF WE'RE SMART, WE CAN STRETCH IT A BIT.
.....
gurgle...

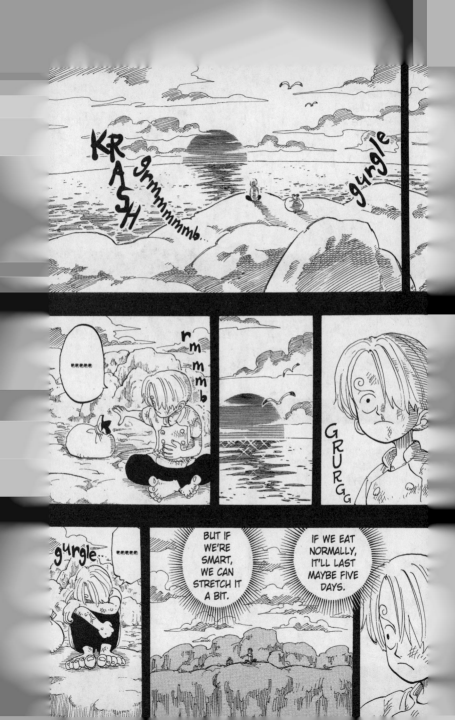

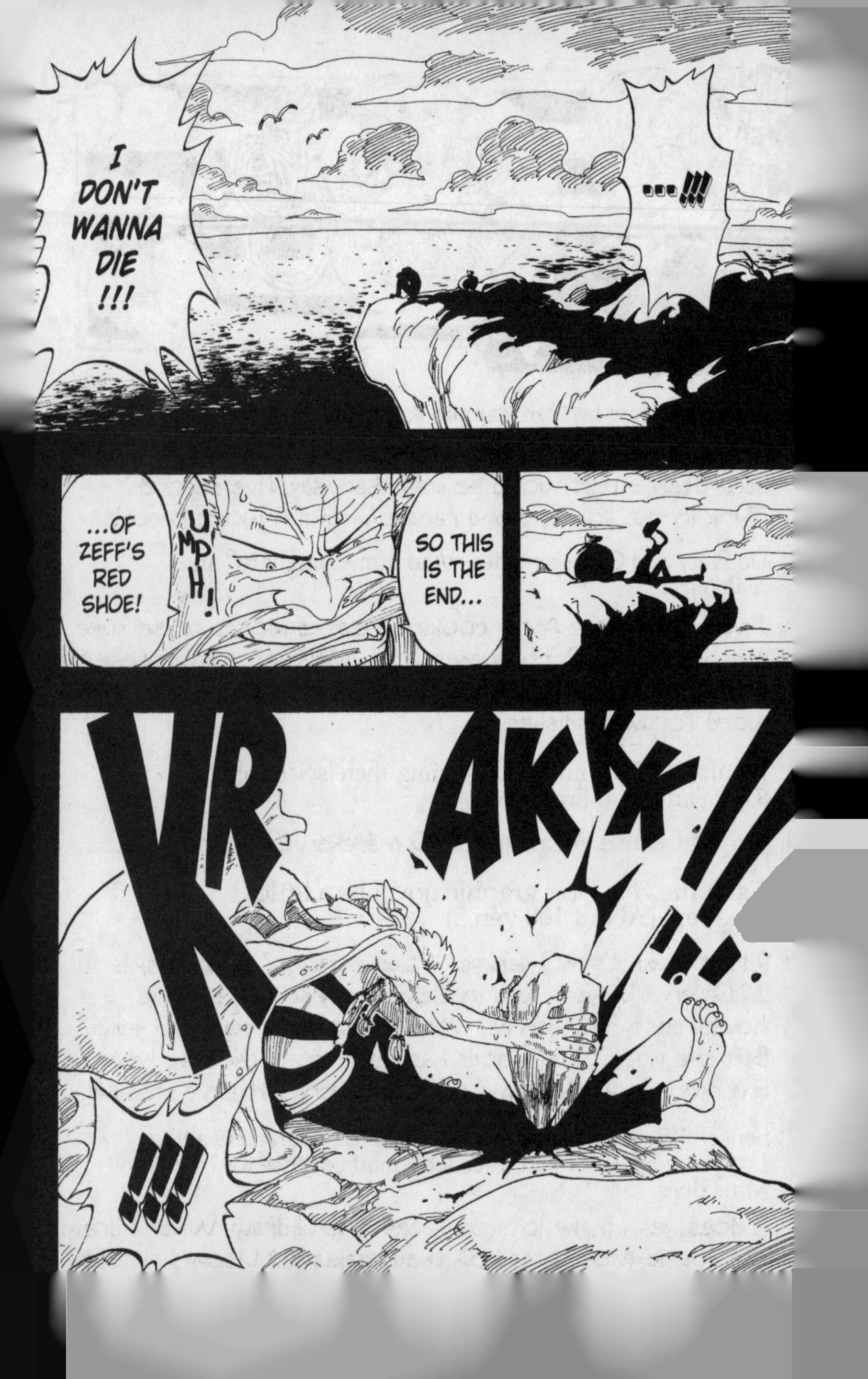
...!!!
I DON'T WANNA DIE !!!
SO THIS IS THE END...
UMPH!
...OF ZEFF'S RED SHOE!
KRAKK!!
!!!

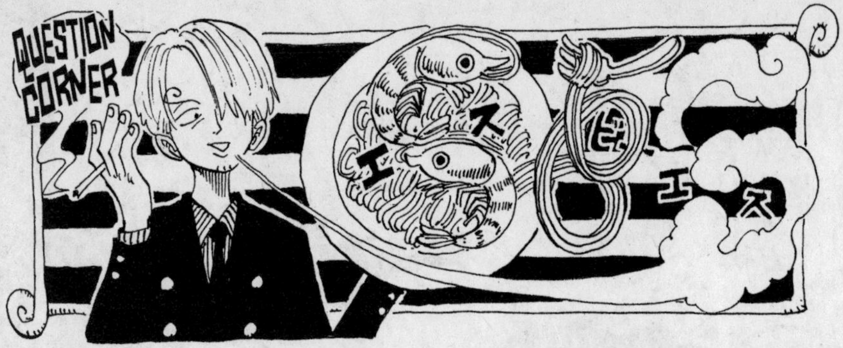
QUESTION CORNER

Q: Question. How fast can Captain Kuro run 100 meters?

A: To be honest, it's difficult to measure his speed accurately, but it would be less than, say, five seconds. Think in the four second range. Wow! A world record.

Q: Do Patty and Carne's names come from "*spa*ghe*tti*" and "*calzone*"?

A: Hmm! They come from cooking-related words to be sure, but not those. Patty comes from pâtissier, a pastry chef in charge of desserts. Carne comes directly from the Spanish word for meat dishes.

Q: If Luffy is 7,200 Funky Gum-Gums, then is Sanji about 8,500 Funky Ero-Ero?

A: No, not quite. More like 930 märchen Ero-Ero.

Q: Can't the *One Piece* graphic novel be a little cheaper? (About 100 yen...)

A: Right now it's 410 yen per volume, right? And *Jump* is 220 yen... When I was in elementary school, graphic novels cost 360 yen per volume and *Jump* cost 170 yen. But the price of all goods has risen, so it can't be helped. Everyone is in the same boat. 100 yen just isn't possible.

Q: Sensei! When you are drawing *One Piece* characters and Luffy is mad, does your face look mad or tense too? Tell me!! Mine does.

A: It does, yes. I make lots of faces when I draw. When I drew the double-page spread of the breakup of Usopp's pirate crew, my face got very tired. I was making a crying face the whole time I drew it, and my face started to cramp.

# Chapter 58:
# THE CRAP-GEEZER

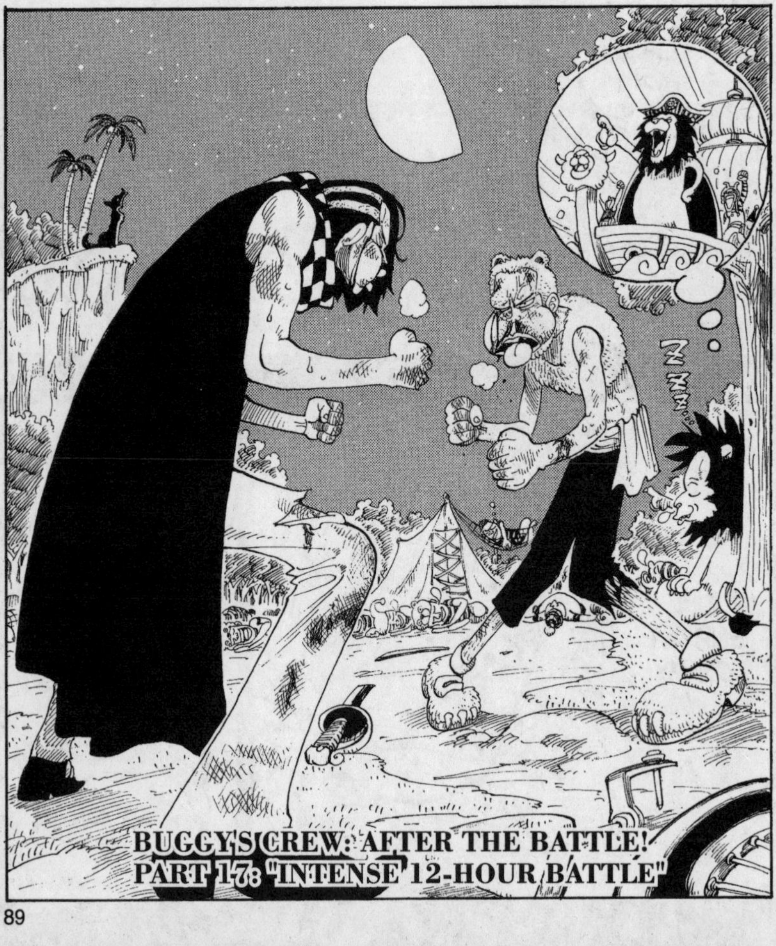

ZZ...
BUGGY'S CREW: AFTER THE BATTLE! PART 17: "INTENSE 12-HOUR BATTLE"

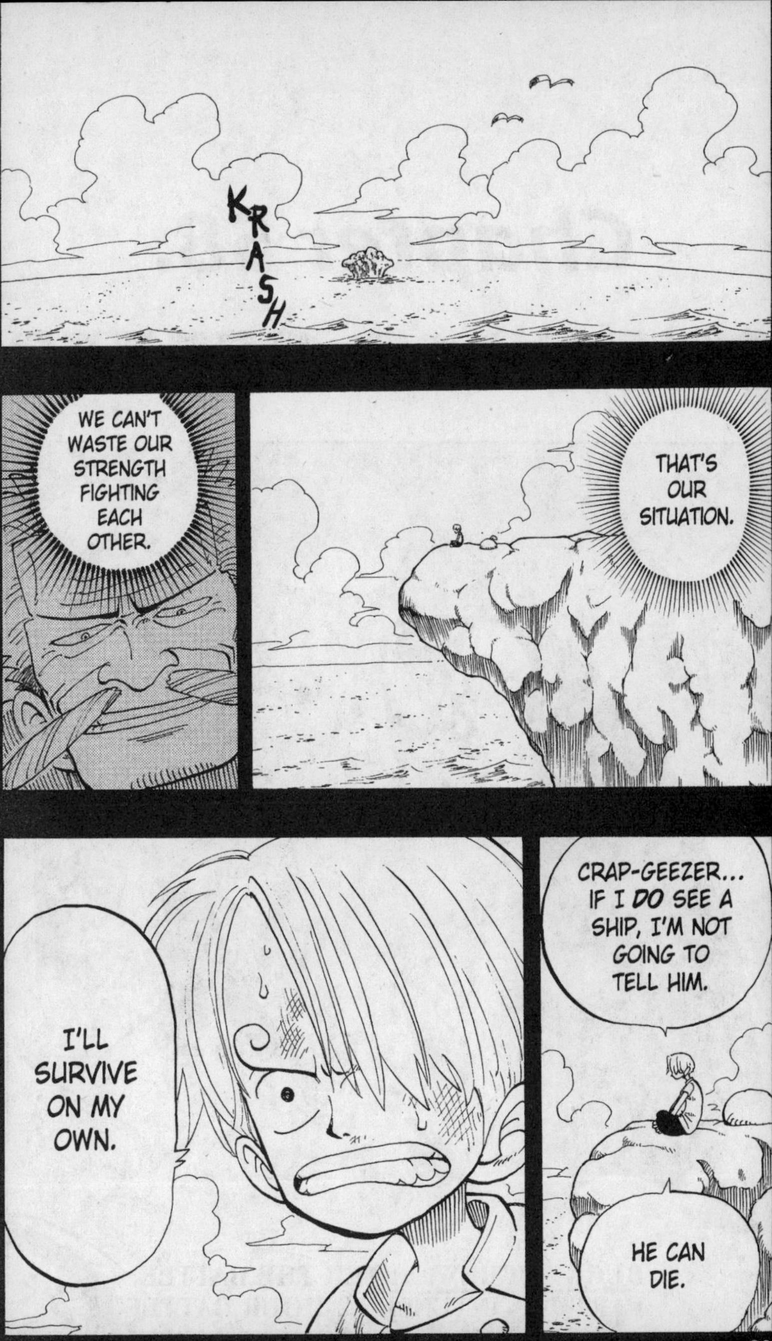
KRASH
THAT'S OUR SITUATION.
WE CAN'T WASTE OUR STRENGTH FIGHTING EACH OTHER.
CRAP-GEEZER... IF I *DO* SEE A SHIP, I'M NOT GOING TO TELL HIM.
HE CAN DIE.
I'LL SURVIVE ON MY OWN.

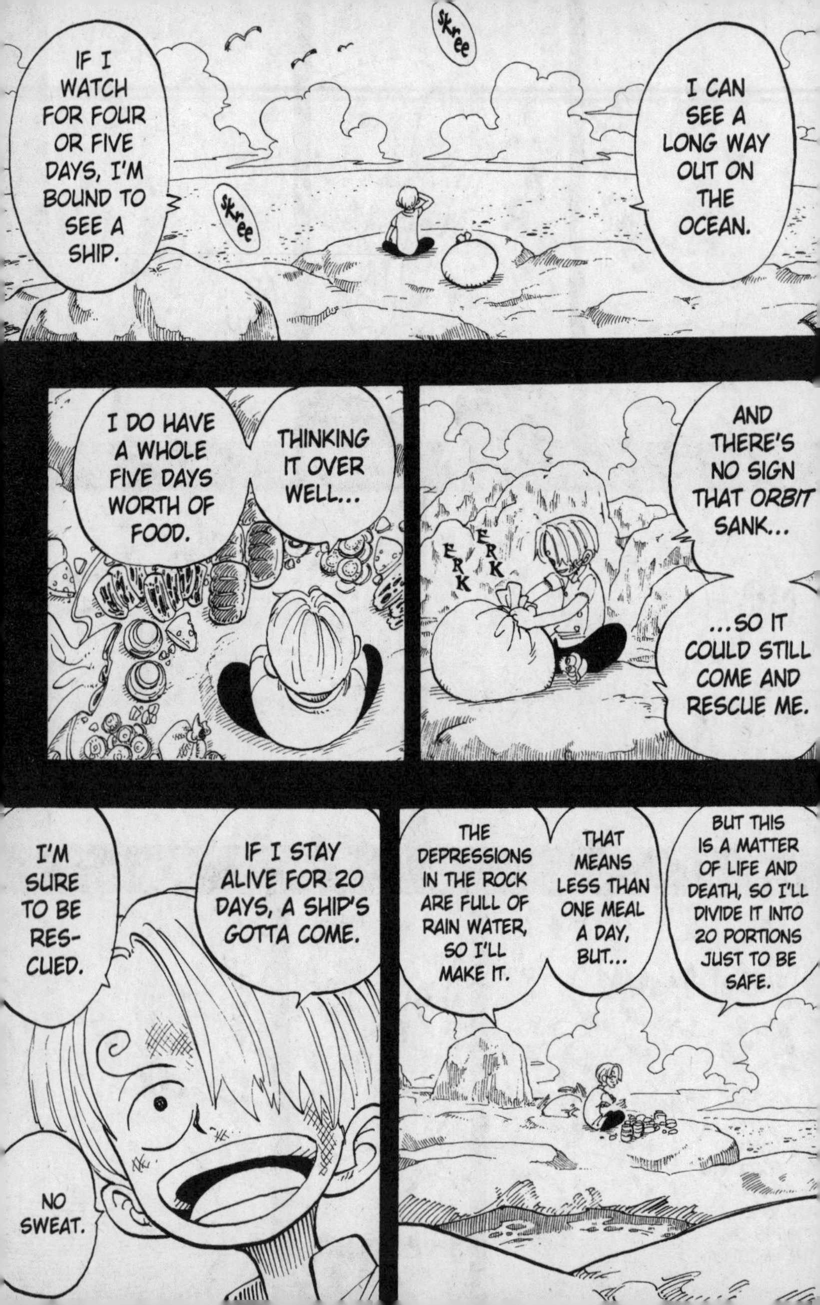
I CAN SEE A LONG WAY OUT ON THE OCEAN.
skree
IF I WATCH FOR FOUR OR FIVE DAYS, I'M BOUND TO SEE A SHIP.
skree
AND THERE'S NO SIGN THAT *ORBIT* SANK...
...SO IT COULD STILL COME AND RESCUE ME.
ERK
ERK
THINKING IT OVER WELL...
I DO HAVE A WHOLE FIVE DAYS WORTH OF FOOD.
BUT THIS IS A MATTER OF LIFE AND DEATH, SO I'LL DIVIDE IT INTO 20 PORTIONS JUST TO BE SAFE.
THAT MEANS LESS THAN ONE MEAL A DAY, BUT...
THE DEPRESSIONS IN THE ROCK ARE FULL OF RAIN WATER, SO I'LL MAKE IT.
IF I STAY ALIVE FOR 20 DAYS, A SHIP'S GOTTA COME.
I'M SURE TO BE RES-CUED.
NO SWEAT.

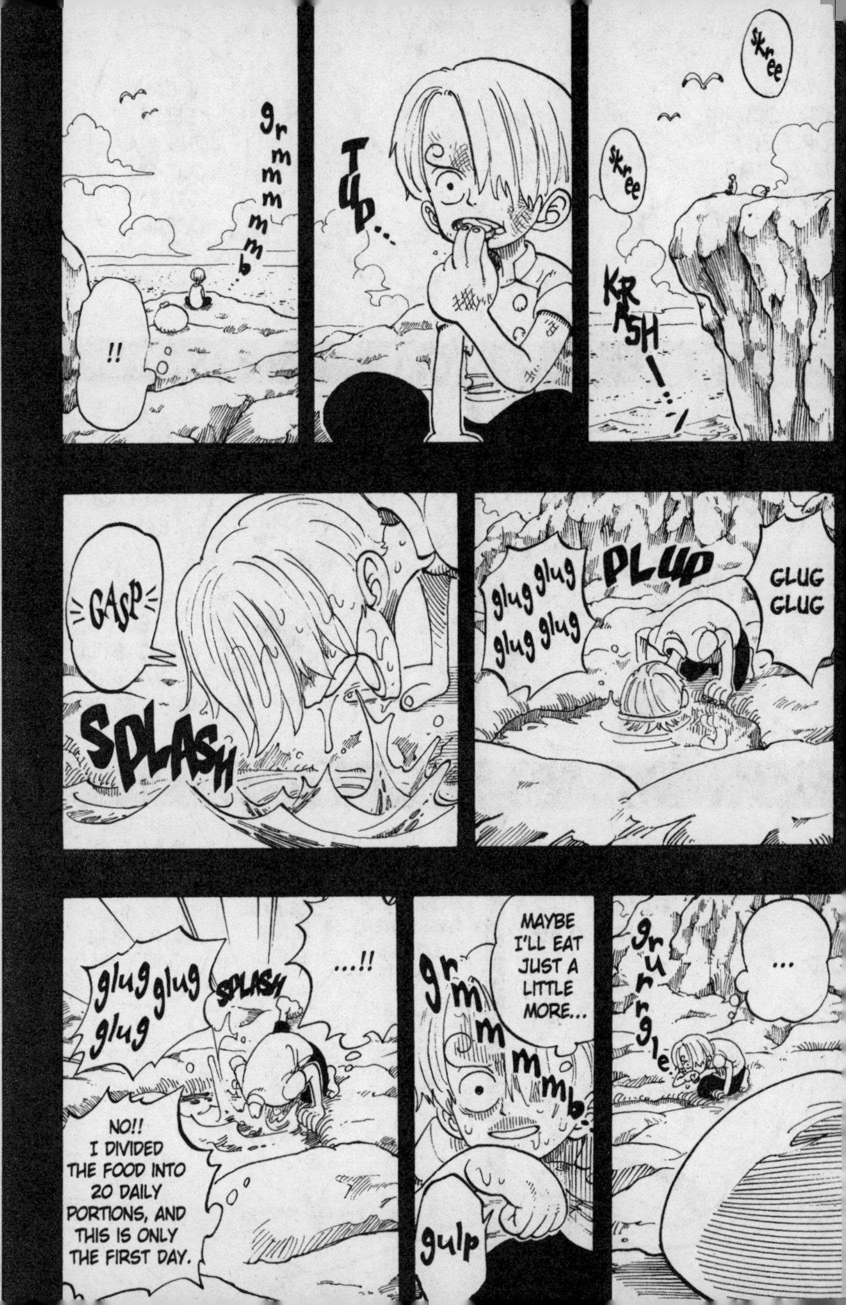
skree
skree
KRRSH...!
TUP...
grmmmmmb
!!
PLUP
glug glug glug glug
GLUG GLUG
GASP
SPLASH
grurrgle
...
MAYBE I'LL EAT JUST A LITTLE MORE...
grmmmmb
gulp
...!!
glug glug glug
SPLASH
NO!! I DIVIDED THE FOOD INTO 20 DAILY PORTIONS, AND THIS IS ONLY THE FIRST DAY.

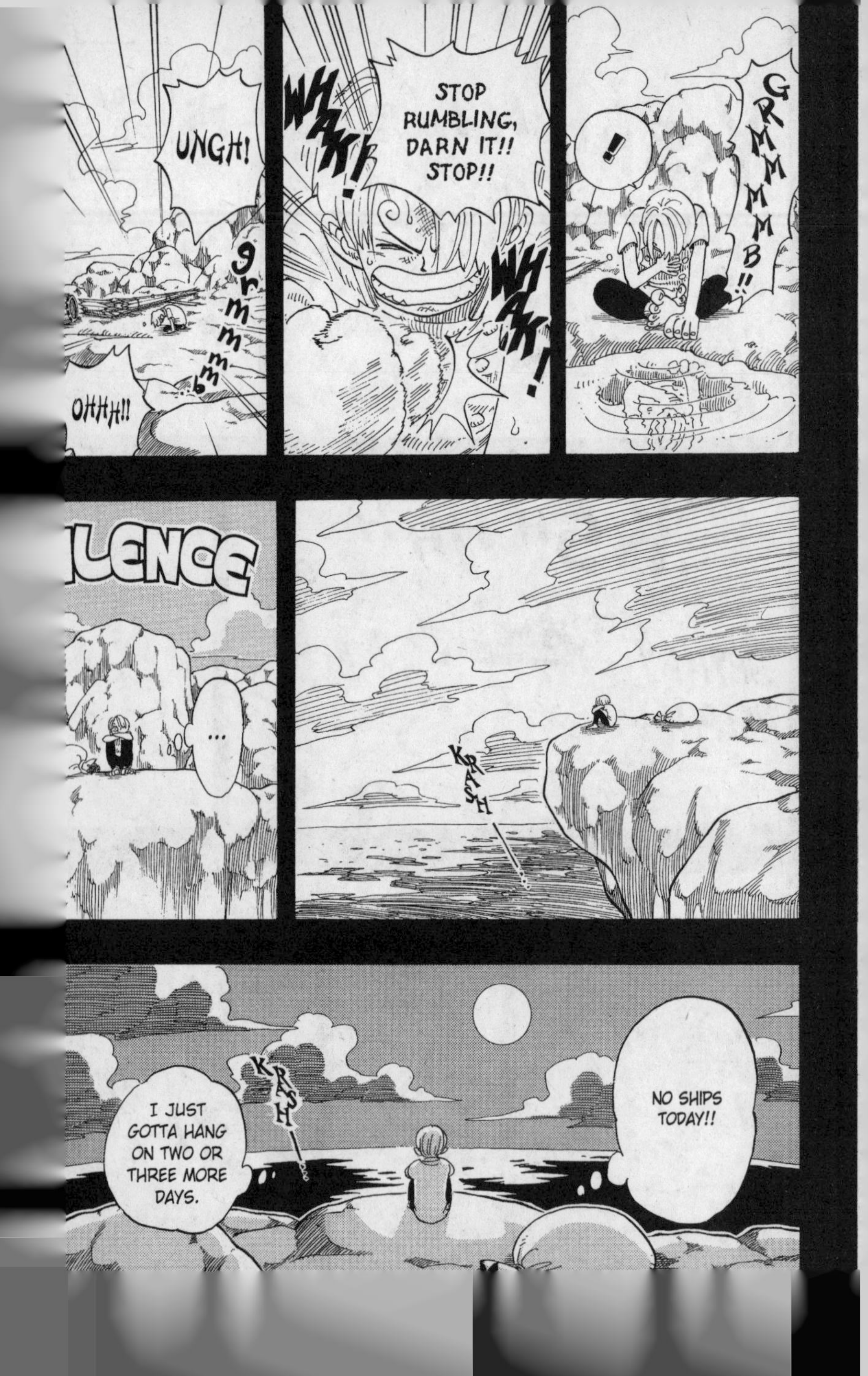
!
GRMMMMB!!
WHAK!
STOP RUMBLING, DARN IT!! STOP!!
WHAK!
UNGH!
grmmmmb
OHHH!!
KRASH
LENCE
...
NO SHIPS TODAY!!
KRASH
I JUST GOTTA HANG ON TWO OR THREE MORE DAYS.

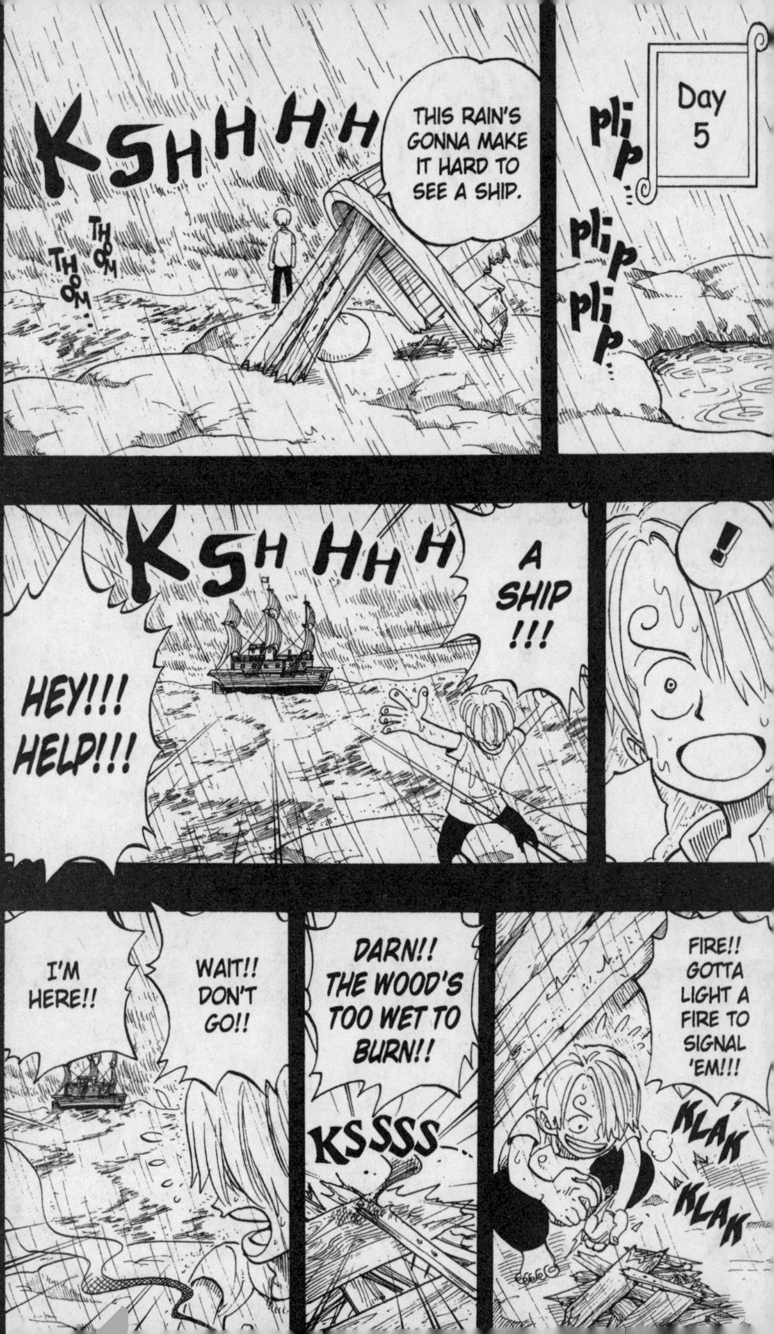
Day 5
plip plip plip plip
KSHHHHH
THIS RAIN'S GONNA MAKE IT HARD TO SEE A SHIP.
THOM THOM
!
KSHHHHH
A SHIP!!!
HEY!!! HELP!!!
FIRE!! GOTTA LIGHT A FIRE TO SIGNAL 'EM!!!
KLAK KLAK
DARN!! THE WOOD'S TOO WET TO BURN!!
KSSSS
WAIT!! DON'T GO!!
I'M HERE!!

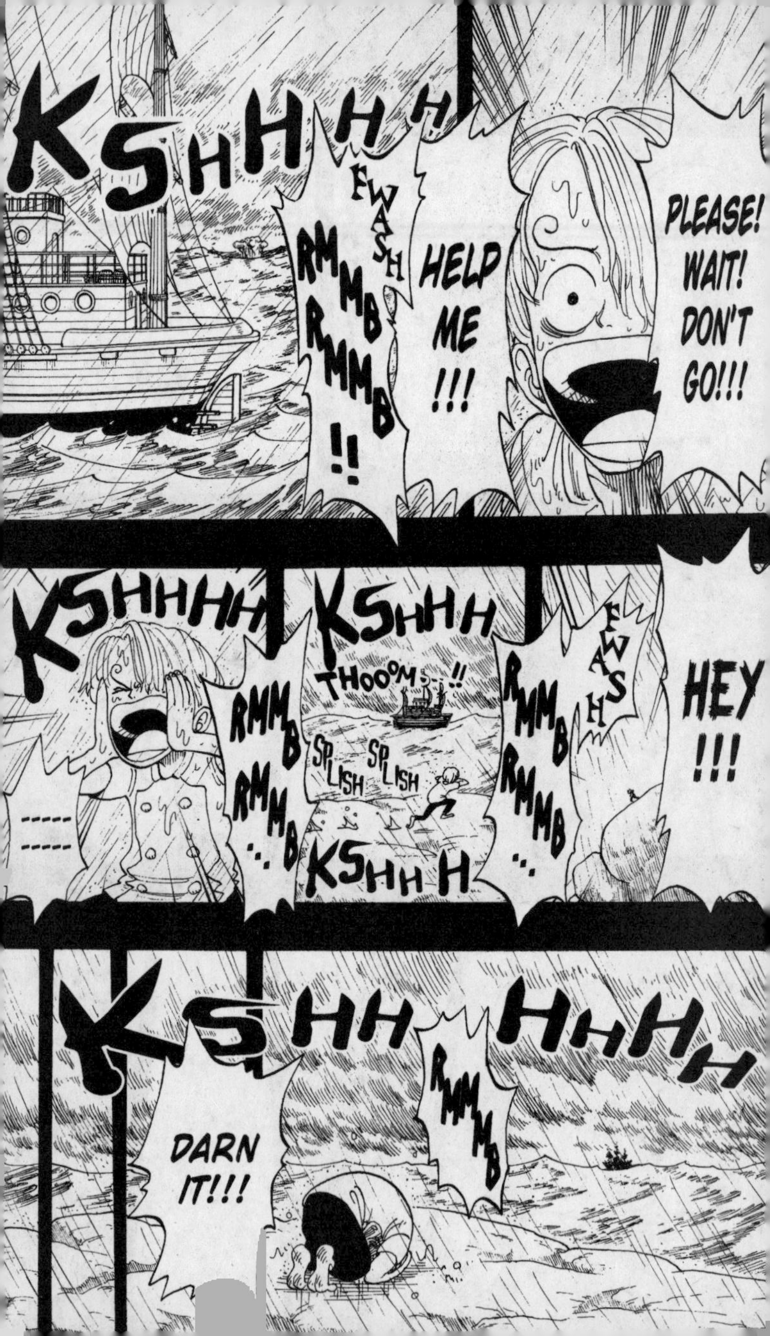
PLEASE! WAIT! DON'T GO!!!
HELP ME!!!
FWASH
RMMB RMMMB!!
KSHHHHH
HEY!!!
FWASH
RMMB RMMMB...
KSHHH
THOOOMS..!!
SPLISH SPLISH
KSHHH
RMMB RMMB...
KSHHHHH
-----
-----
KSHH HHHHH
RMMMB
DARN IT!!!

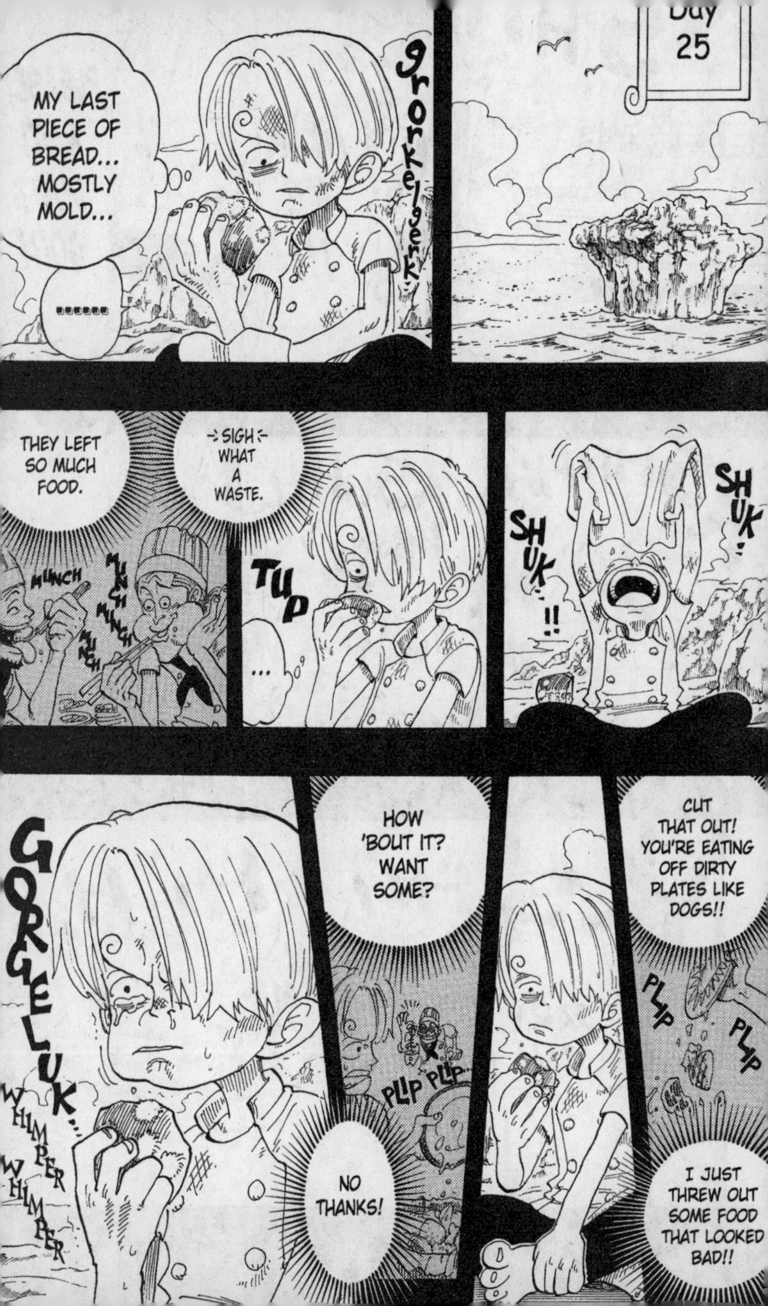
Day 25
grorkelserk
MY LAST PIECE OF BREAD... MOSTLY MOLD...
......
SHUK
SHUK!!
SIGH WHAT A WASTE.
TUP
...
THEY LEFT SO MUCH FOOD.
MUNCH
MUNCH MUNCH
MUNCH
CUT THAT OUT! YOU'RE EATING OFF DIRTY PLATES LIKE DOGS!!
PLIP
PLIP
I JUST THREW OUT SOME FOOD THAT LOOKED BAD!!
HOW 'BOUT IT? WANT SOME?
PLIP PLIP
NO THANKS!
GORGELUK...
WHIMPER
WHIMPER

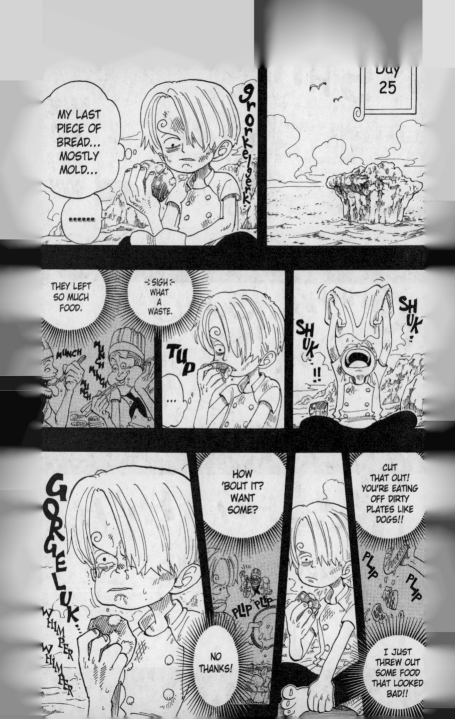

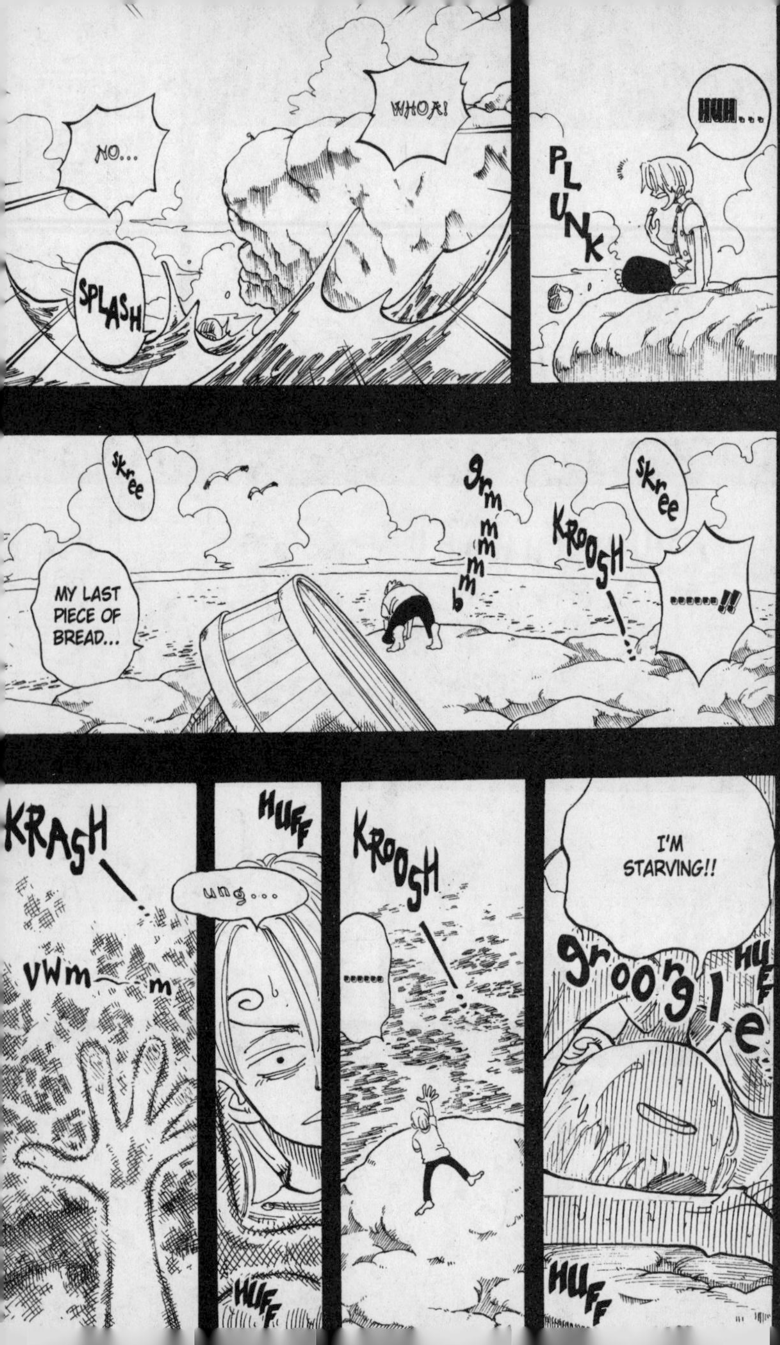
HUH...
PLUNK
WHOA!
NO...
SPLASH
skree
KROOSH
......!!
grmmmmmb
skree
MY LAST PIECE OF BREAD...
I'M STARVING!!
groogle
HUFF
HUFF
KROOSH
......
HUFF
ung...
HUFF
KRASH
vwm~m

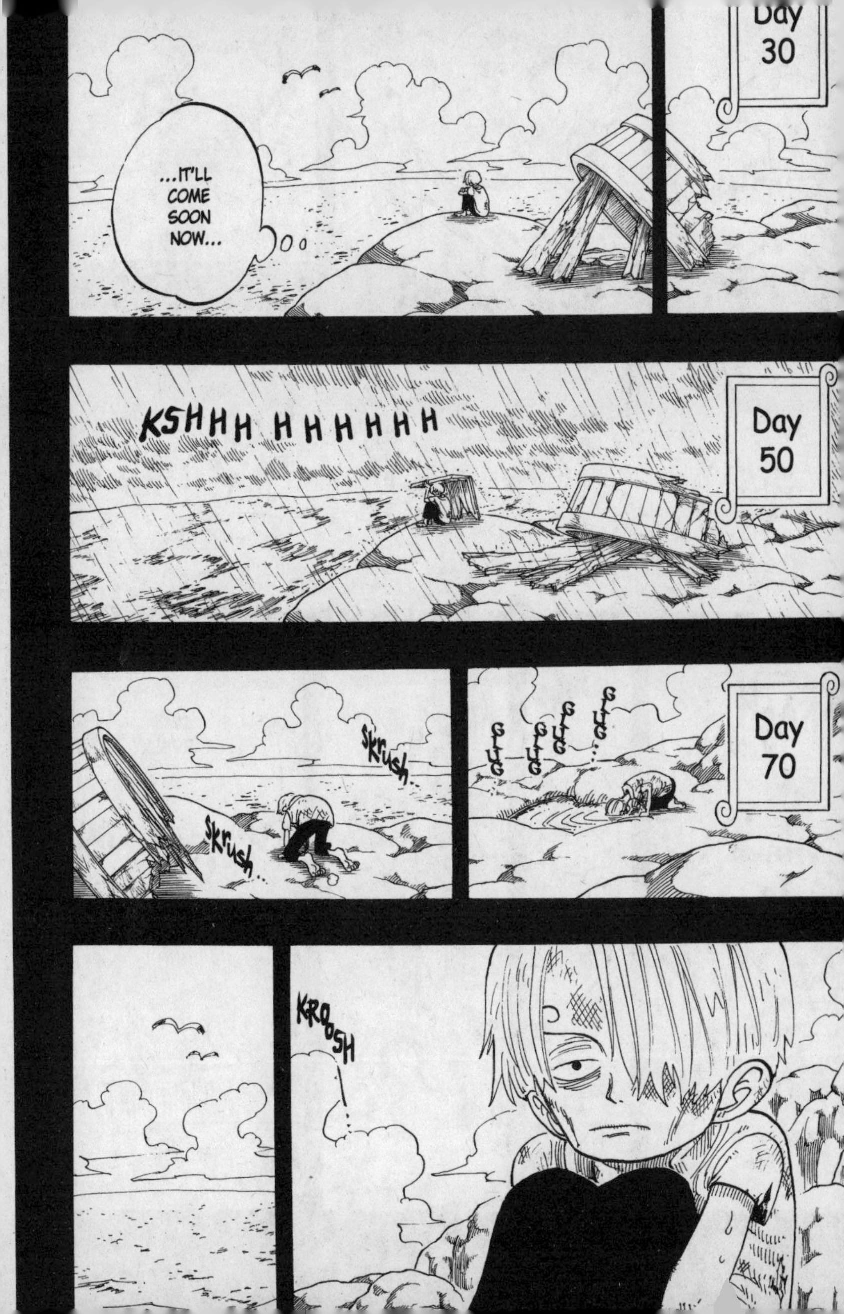
Day 30
...IT'LL COME SOON NOW...
Day 50
KSHHH HHHHHH
Day 70
GLUG GLUG GLUG GLUG...
SKRUSH...
SKRUSH...
KROOSH

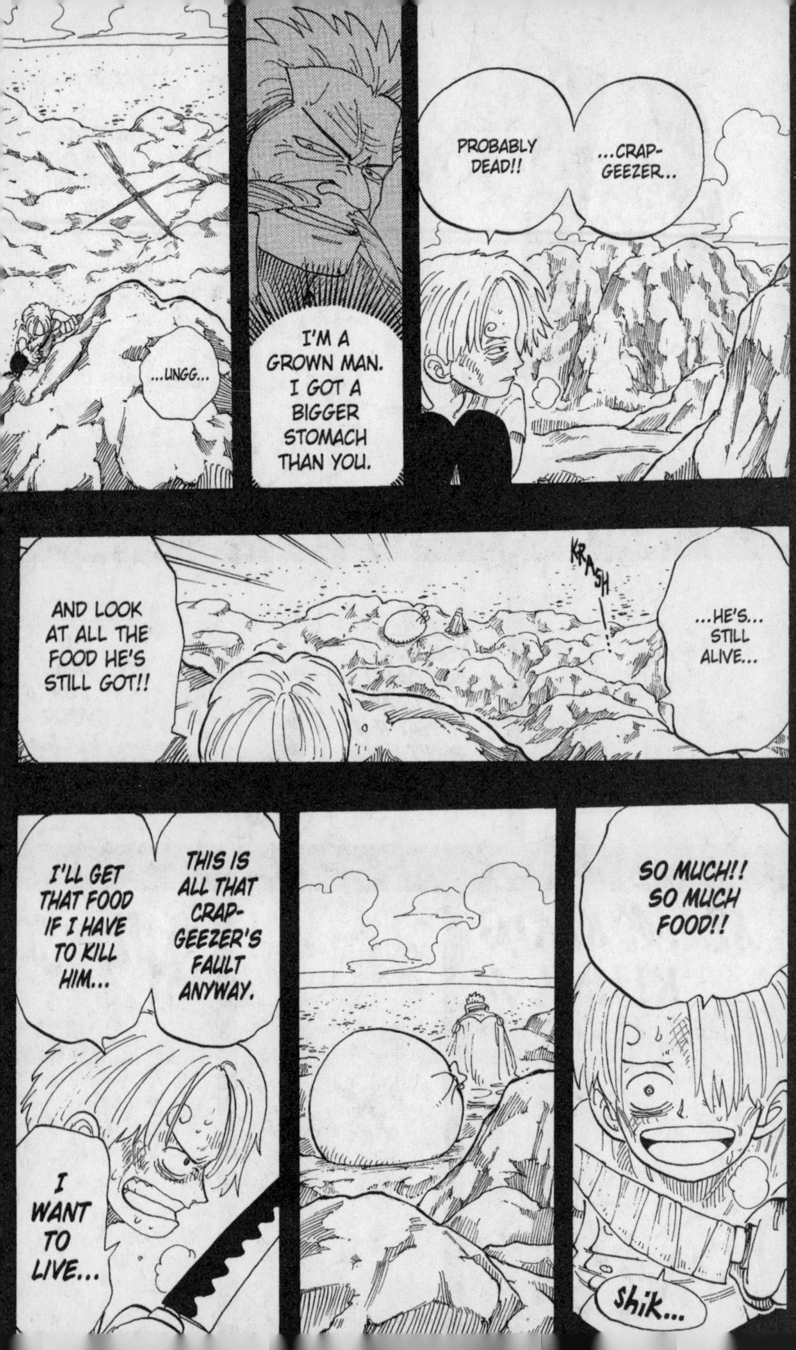
...CRAP-GEEZER...
PROBABLY DEAD!!
I'M A GROWN MAN. I GOT A BIGGER STOMACH THAN YOU.
...UNGG...
...HE'S... STILL ALIVE...
KRASH
AND LOOK AT ALL THE FOOD HE'S STILL GOT!!
SO MUCH!! SO MUCH FOOD!!
Shik...
THIS IS ALL THAT CRAP-GEEZER'S FAULT ANYWAY.
I'LL GET THAT FOOD IF I HAVE TO KILL HIM...
I WANT TO LIVE...

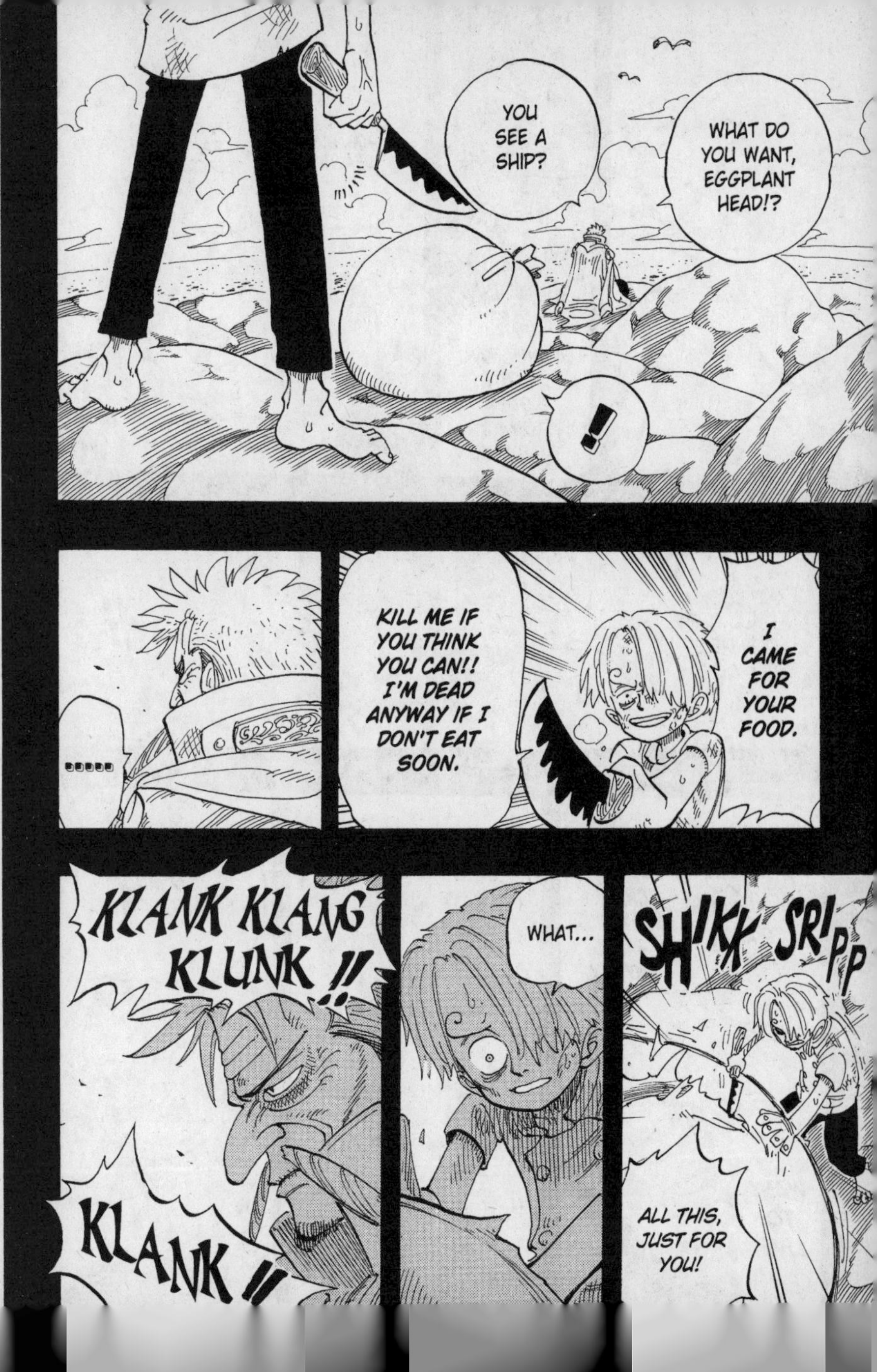
WHAT DO YOU WANT, EGGPLANT HEAD!?
YOU SEE A SHIP?
!
I CAME FOR YOUR FOOD.
KILL ME IF YOU THINK YOU CAN!! I'M DEAD ANYWAY IF I DON'T EAT SOON.
.....
SHIKK SRIPP
ALL THIS, JUST FOR YOU!
WHAT...
KLANK KLANG KLUNK!!
KLANK!!

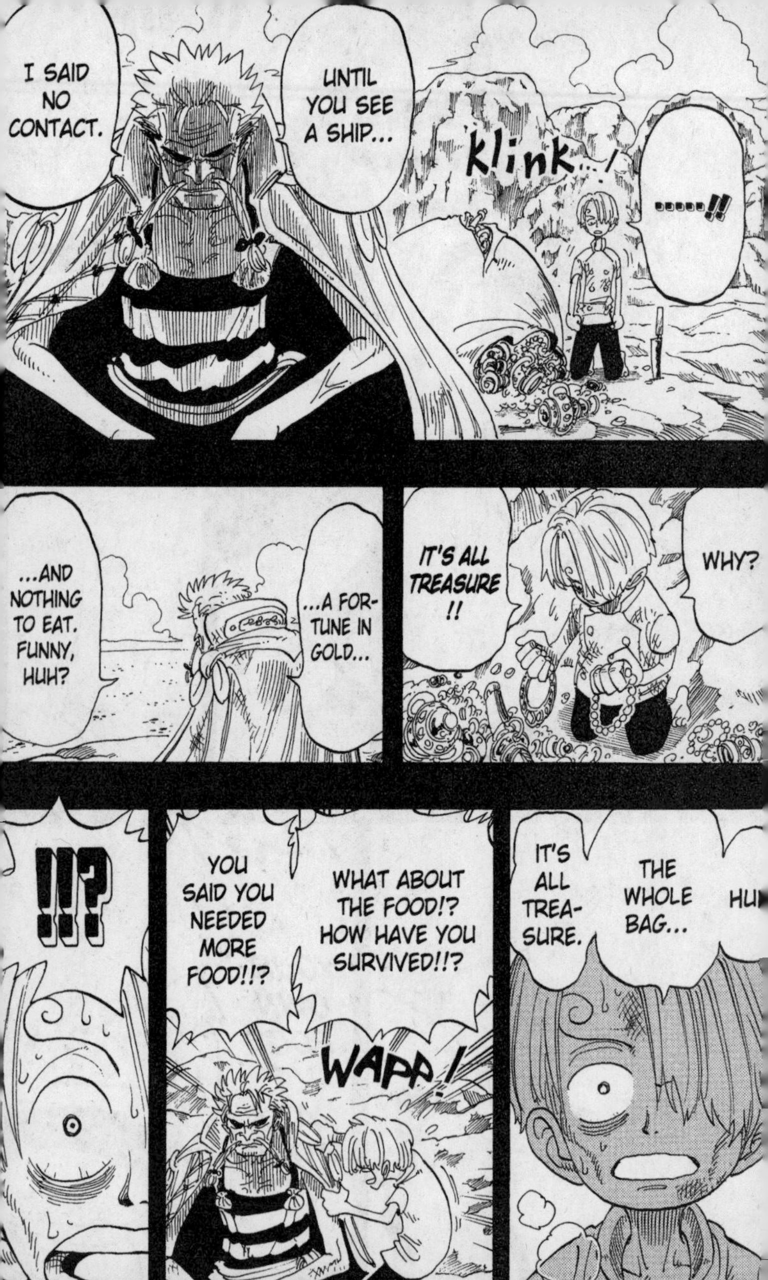
klink.../
......!!
UNTIL YOU SEE A SHIP...
I SAID NO CONTACT.
WHY?
IT'S ALL TREASURE !!
...A FOR-TUNE IN GOLD...
...AND NOTHING TO EAT. FUNNY, HUH?
HU
THE WHOLE BAG...
IT'S ALL TREA-SURE.
WHAT ABOUT THE FOOD!? HOW HAVE YOU SURVIVED!!?
YOU SAID YOU NEEDED MORE FOOD!!?
WAPP!
!!?

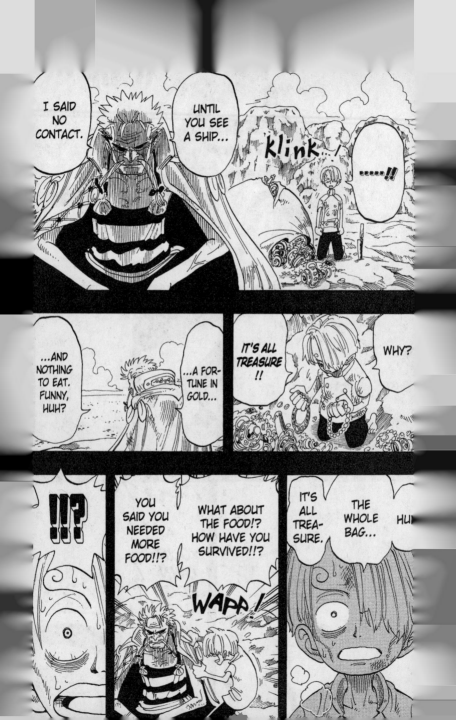

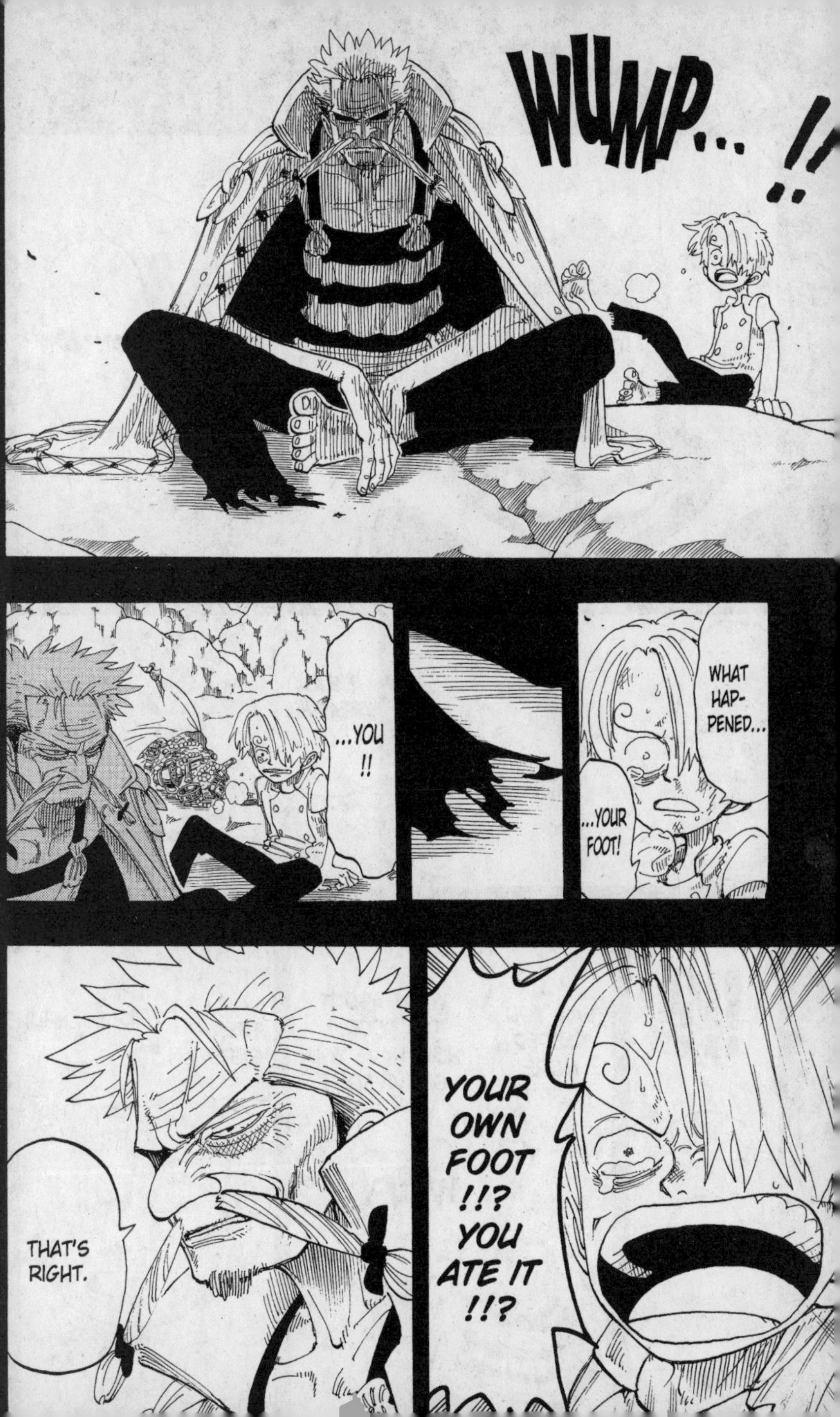
WUMP... !!
WHAT HAP-PENED...
...YOUR FOOT!
...YOU !!
YOUR OWN FOOT !!? YOU ATE IT !!?
THAT'S RIGHT.

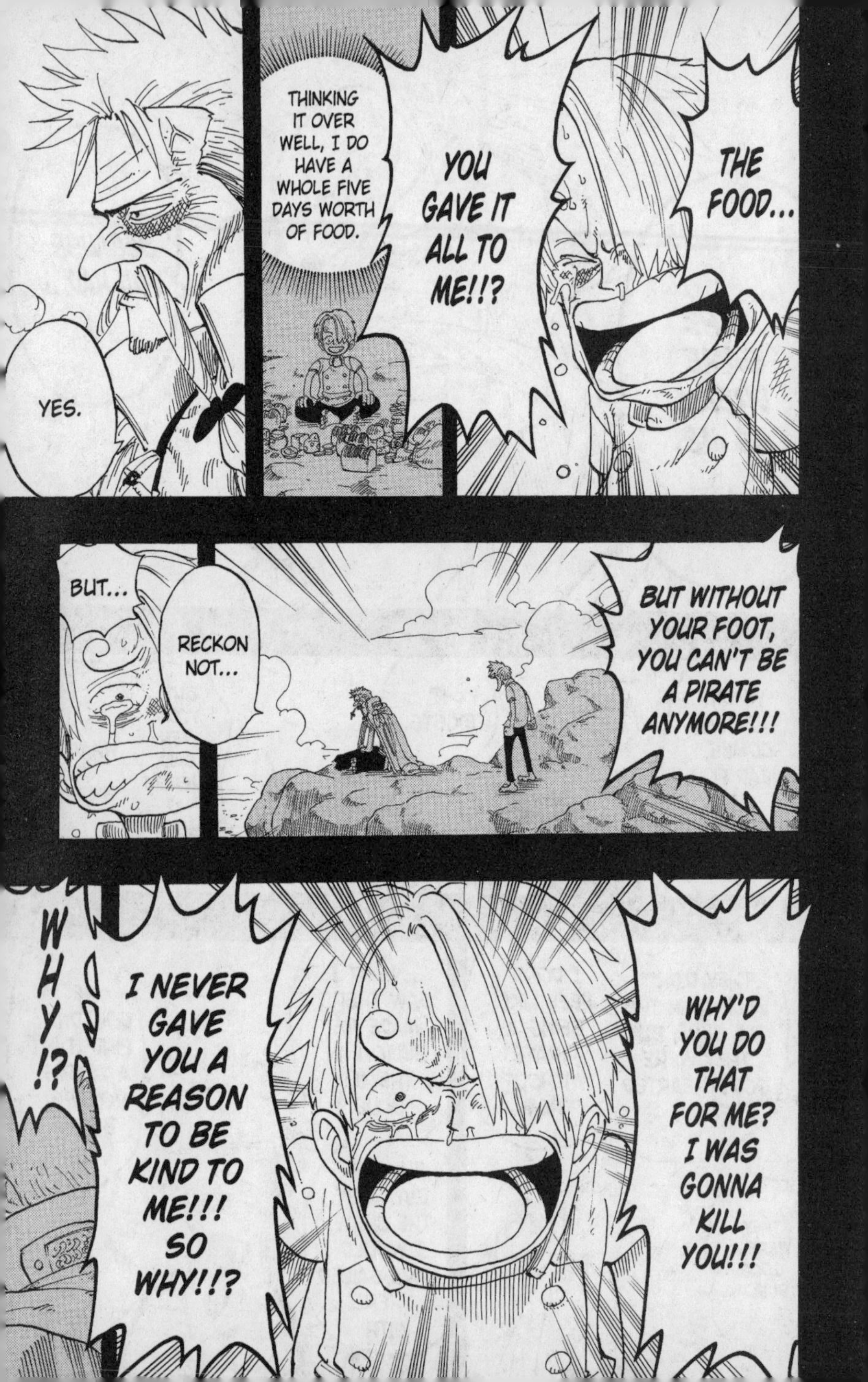
THE FOOD...
YOU GAVE IT ALL TO ME!!?
THINKING IT OVER WELL, I DO HAVE A WHOLE FIVE DAYS WORTH OF FOOD.
YES.
BUT WITHOUT YOUR FOOT, YOU CAN'T BE A PIRATE ANYMORE!!!
RECKON NOT...
BUT...
WHY'D YOU DO THAT FOR ME? I WAS GONNA KILL YOU!!!
I NEVER GAVE YOU A REASON TO BE KIND TO ME!!! SO WHY!!?
WHY!?

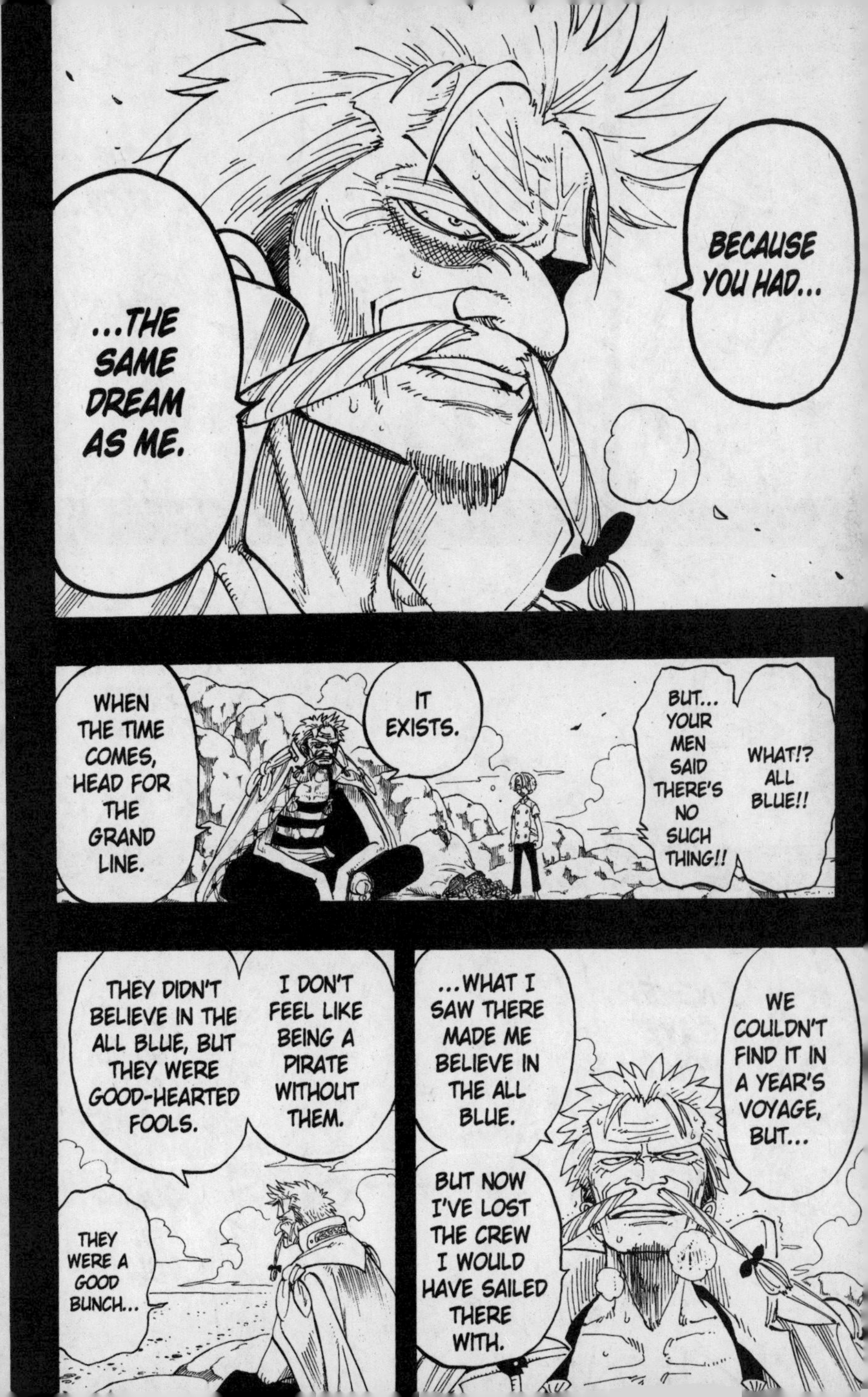
BECAUSE YOU HAD...
...THE SAME DREAM AS ME.
WHAT!? ALL BLUE!!
BUT... YOUR MEN SAID THERE'S NO SUCH THING!!
IT EXISTS.
WHEN THE TIME COMES, HEAD FOR THE GRAND LINE.
WE COULDN'T FIND IT IN A YEAR'S VOYAGE, BUT...
...WHAT I SAW THERE MADE ME BELIEVE IN THE ALL BLUE.
BUT NOW I'VE LOST THE CREW I WOULD HAVE SAILED THERE WITH.
I DON'T FEEL LIKE BEING A PIRATE WITHOUT THEM.
THEY DIDN'T BELIEVE IN THE ALL BLUE, BUT THEY WERE GOOD-HEARTED FOOLS.
THEY WERE A GOOD BUNCH...

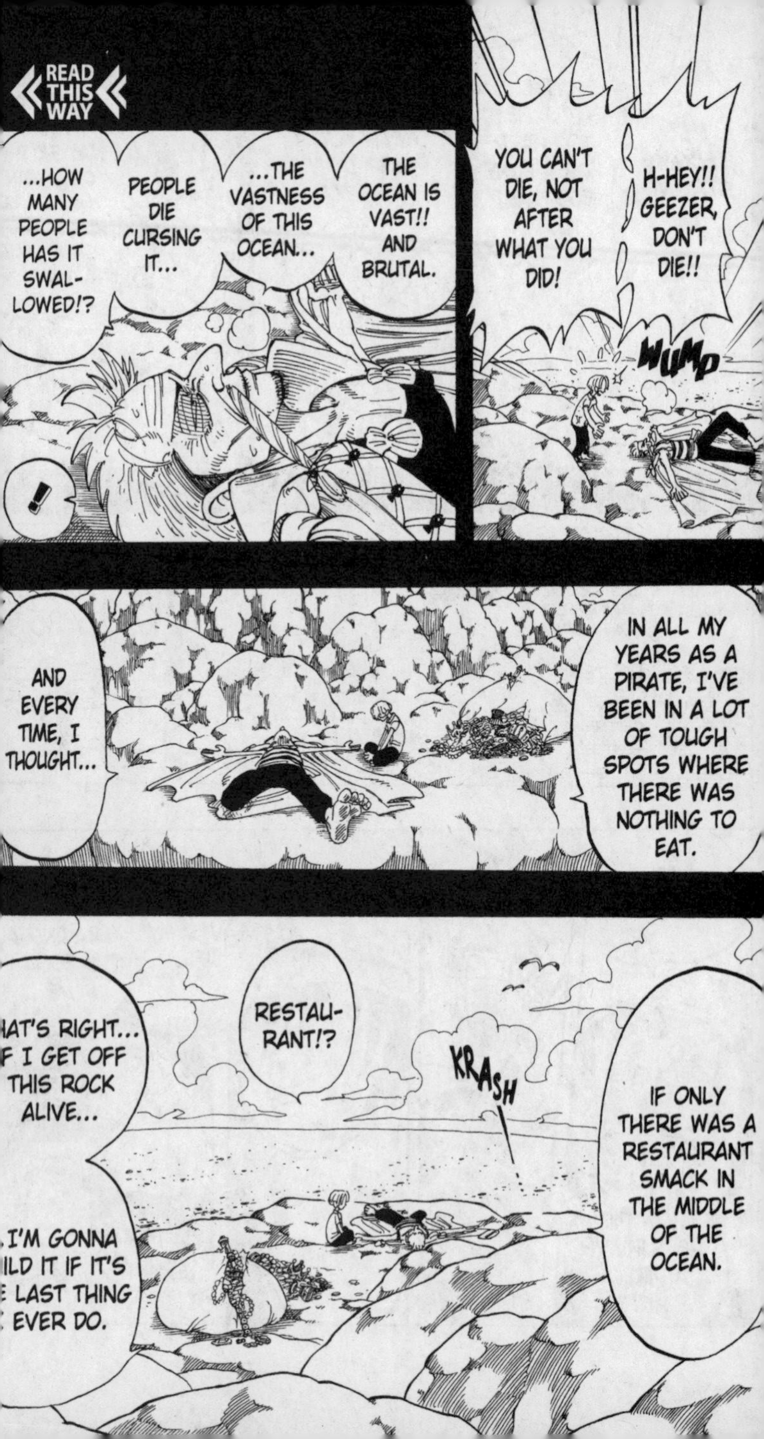
READ THIS WAY
H-HEY!! GEEZER, DON'T DIE!!
YOU CAN'T DIE, NOT AFTER WHAT YOU DID!
WUMP
THE OCEAN IS VAST!! AND BRUTAL.
...THE VASTNESS OF THIS OCEAN...
PEOPLE DIE CURSING IT...
...HOW MANY PEOPLE HAS IT SWALLOWED!?
!
IN ALL MY YEARS AS A PIRATE, I'VE BEEN IN A LOT OF TOUGH SPOTS WHERE THERE WAS NOTHING TO EAT.
AND EVERY TIME, I THOUGHT...
IF ONLY THERE WAS A RESTAURANT SMACK IN THE MIDDLE OF THE OCEAN.
KRASH
RESTAURANT!?
HAT'S RIGHT... F I GET OFF THIS ROCK ALIVE...
I'M GONNA ILD IT IF IT'S E LAST THING EVER DO.

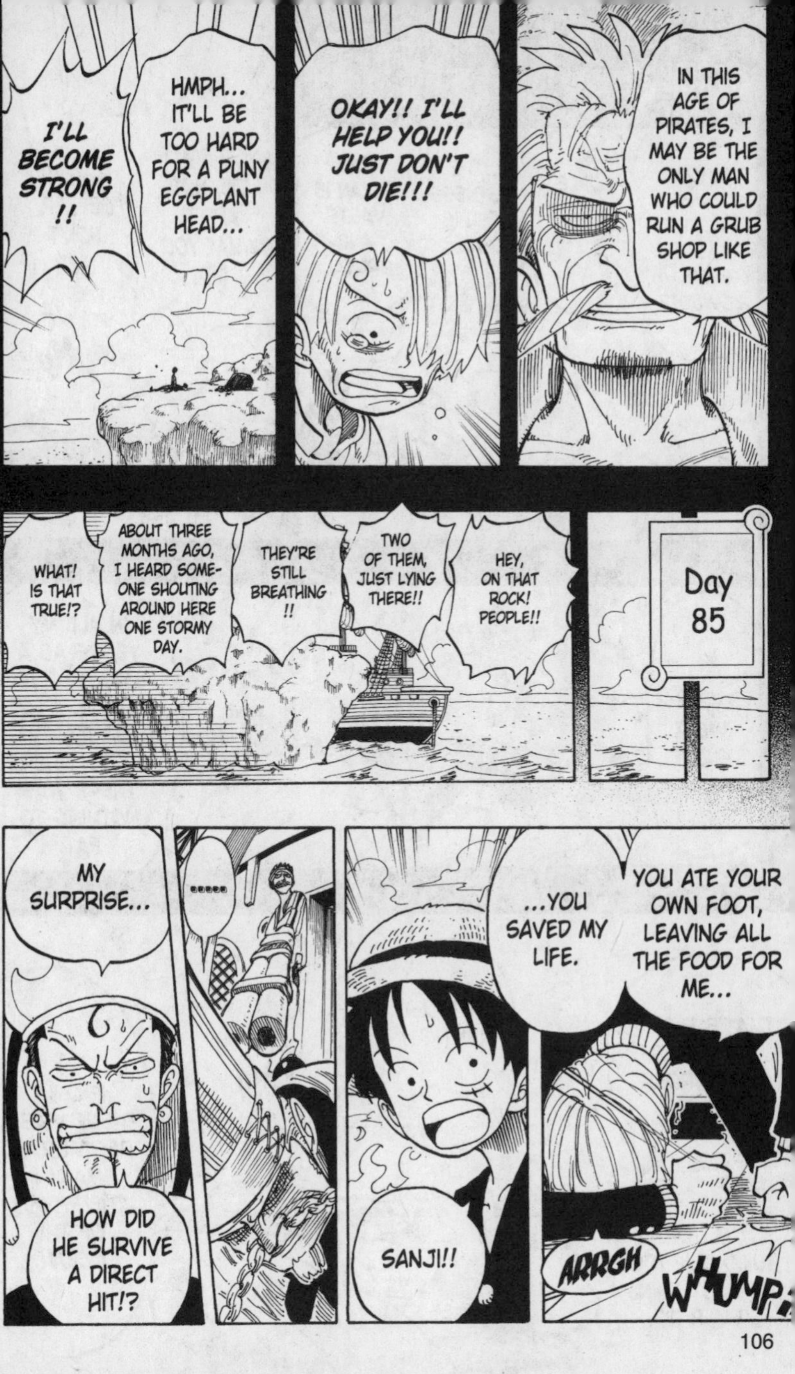

IN THIS AGE OF PIRATES, I MAY BE THE ONLY MAN WHO COULD RUN A GRUB SHOP LIKE THAT.
OKAY!! I'LL HELP YOU!! JUST DON'T DIE!!!
HMPH... IT'LL BE TOO HARD FOR A PUNY EGGPLANT HEAD...
I'LL BECOME STRONG !!
Day 85
HEY, ON THAT ROCK! PEOPLE!!
TWO OF THEM, JUST LYING THERE!!
THEY'RE STILL BREATHING !!
ABOUT THREE MONTHS AGO, I HEARD SOME-ONE SHOUTING AROUND HERE ONE STORMY DAY.
WHAT! IS THAT TRUE!?
YOU ATE YOUR OWN FOOT, LEAVING ALL THE FOOD FOR ME...
...YOU SAVED MY LIFE.
ARRGH
WHUMP!
SANJI!!
.....
MY SURPRISE...
HOW DID HE SURVIVE A DIRECT HIT!?

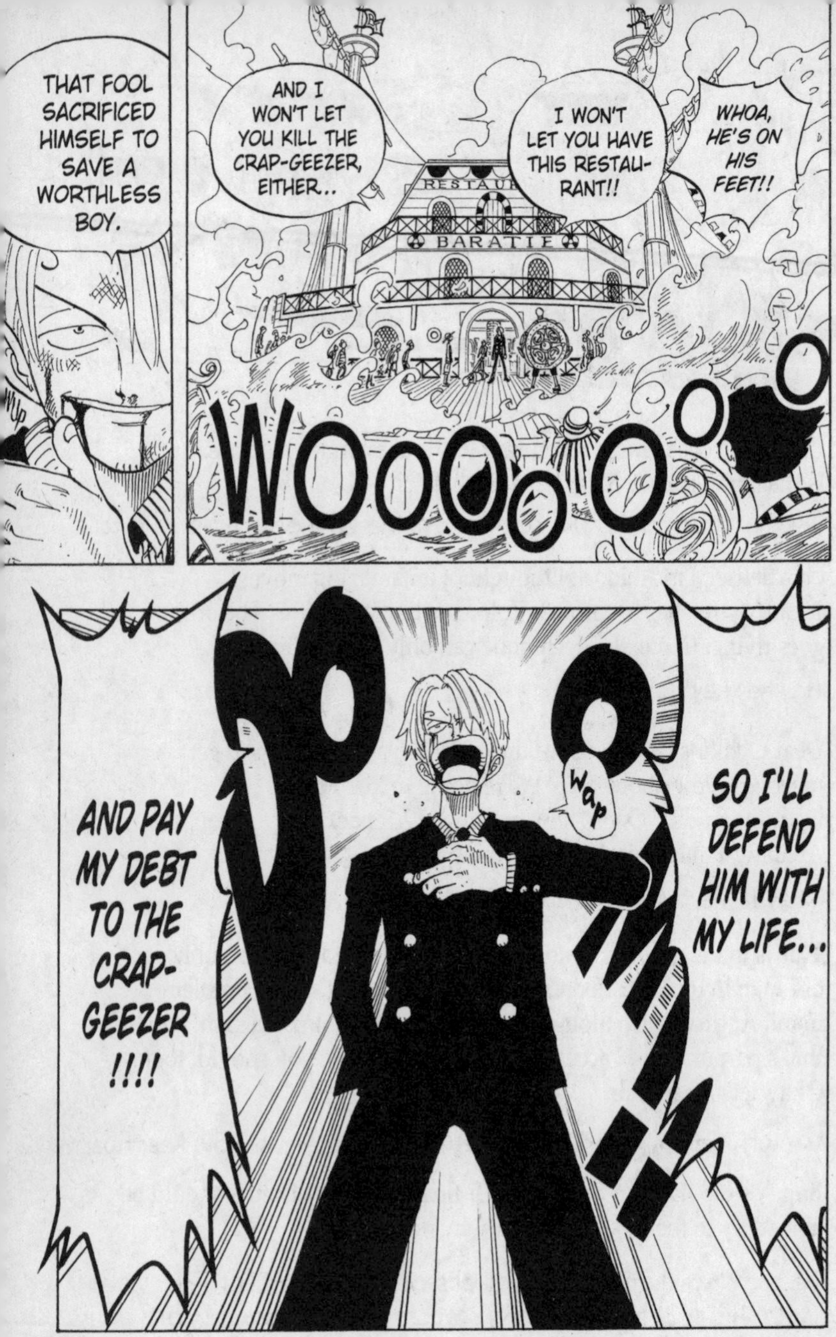
WHOA, HE'S ON HIS FEET!!
I WON'T LET YOU HAVE THIS RESTAU-RANT!!
AND I WON'T LET YOU KILL THE CRAP-GEEZER, EITHER...
RESTAU
BARATIE
WOOOOOOOO
THAT FOOL SACRIFICED HIMSELF TO SAVE A WORTHLESS BOY.
SO I'LL DEFEND HIM WITH MY LIFE...
Wap
AND PAY MY DEBT TO THE CRAP-GEEZER!!!!

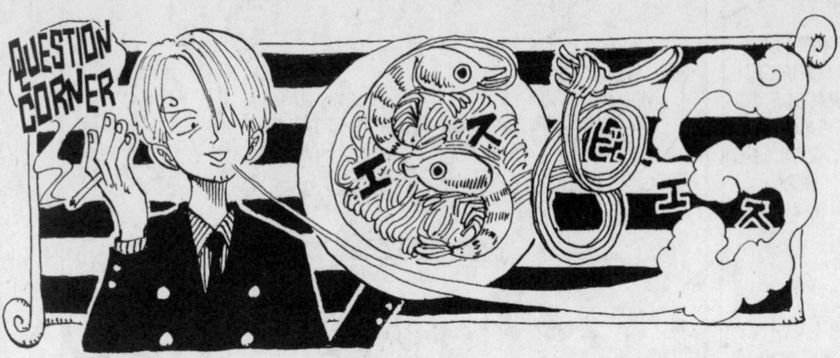
QUESTION CORNER

Q: Zeff of the oceangoing restaurant has braids under his nose. Is that a mustache? Nose hair? Fake hair?

A: They're "phony tails." The scientific name is "phonus bolognus tails."

Q: Oda Sensei, I'm Akinori! I thought of an amazing move! 1. Luffy stretches his arm. 2. Zolo cuts that arm off. 3. The arm goes flying. (Note: this technique can only be used twice!)

A: Hey hey hey...

Q: Dear Odakins ♡, I'm your fiancée. When are we going to get married? How about 11/1? We're going to kiss at the wedding, right!? Oooh, how exciting! ♡ Smack! ♡ Actually, I'm Namie Amuro's younger sister. ♡

A: Okay. I'll visit you in the hospital.

Q: This is to the guy who said that Zolo's sash made him look like an old man in the Question Corner in volume 4!! It's your problem, man!! At first, I also thought, "a cool guy like Zolo, in a sash?" but if that's part of Zolo, I accept it! Yes, I accept it!! So you should, too! Okay, let's be friends!

A: Wow! Friendship blossoming between my readers! How heartwarming.

Q: Buggy's top half can fly, right? (Or float, anyway.) Then it should be able to fly to the Grand Line. So why doesn't he?

A: He can't go that far. The powers of the Chop-Chop Fruit have limits. His body parts can only scatter up to a diameter of 200 Chop-Chops. Once this limit is exceeded, control is no longer possible.

# Chapter 59:
# SANJI'S DEBT

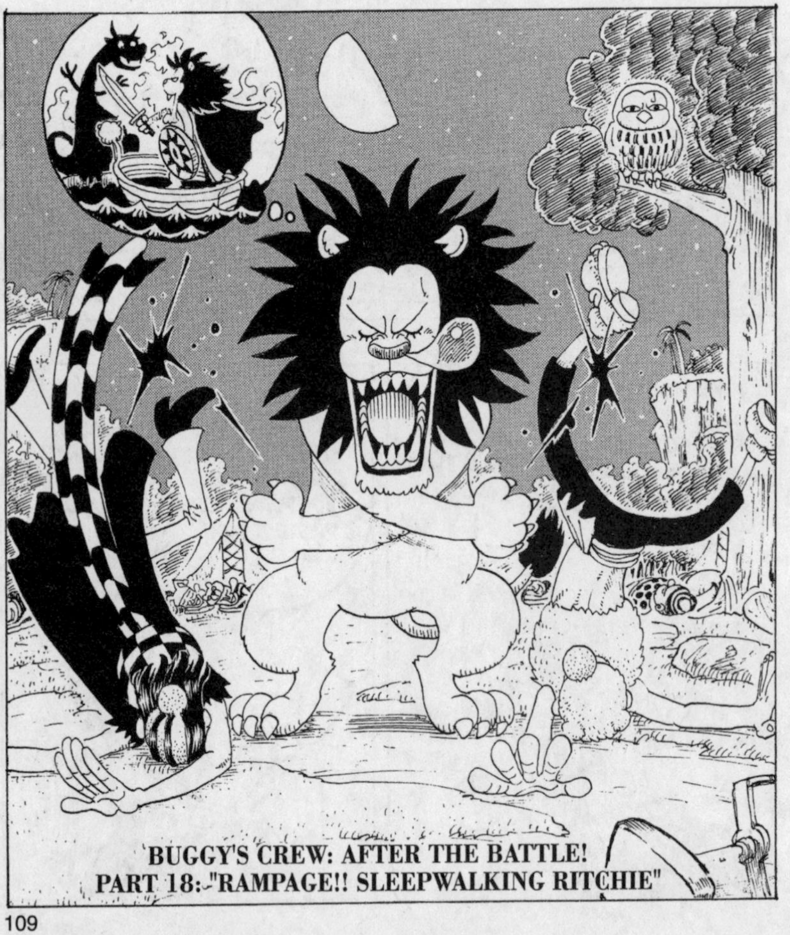
BUGGY'S CREW: AFTER THE BATTLE!
PART 18: "RAMPAGE!! SLEEPWALKING RITCHIE"

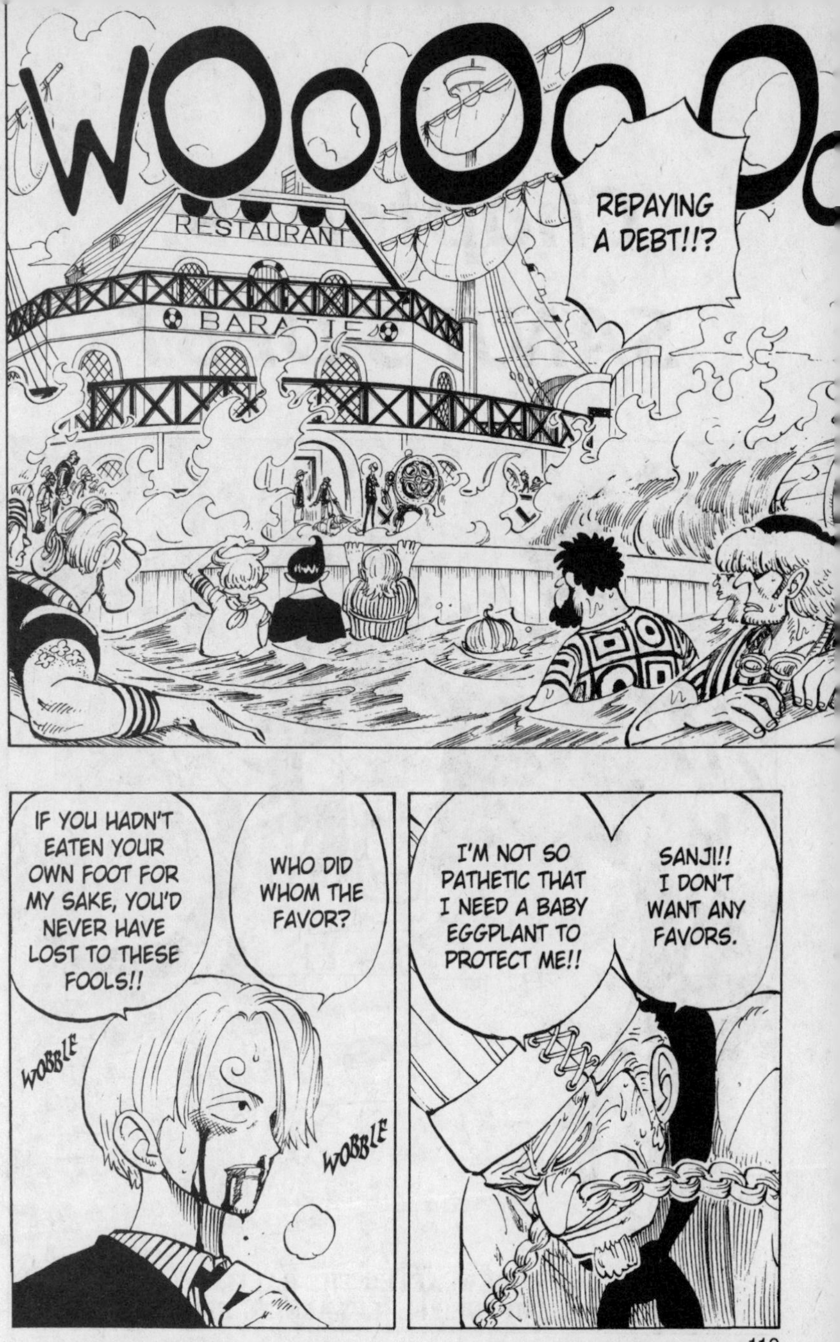
WOOOOO
RESTAURANT
BARATIE
REPAYING A DEBT!!?
SANJI!! I DON'T WANT ANY FAVORS.
I'M NOT SO PATHETIC THAT I NEED A BABY EGGPLANT TO PROTECT ME!!
WHO DID WHOM THE FAVOR?
IF YOU HADN'T EATEN YOUR OWN FOOT FOR MY SAKE, YOU'D NEVER HAVE LOST TO THESE FOOLS!!
WOBBLE
WOBBLE

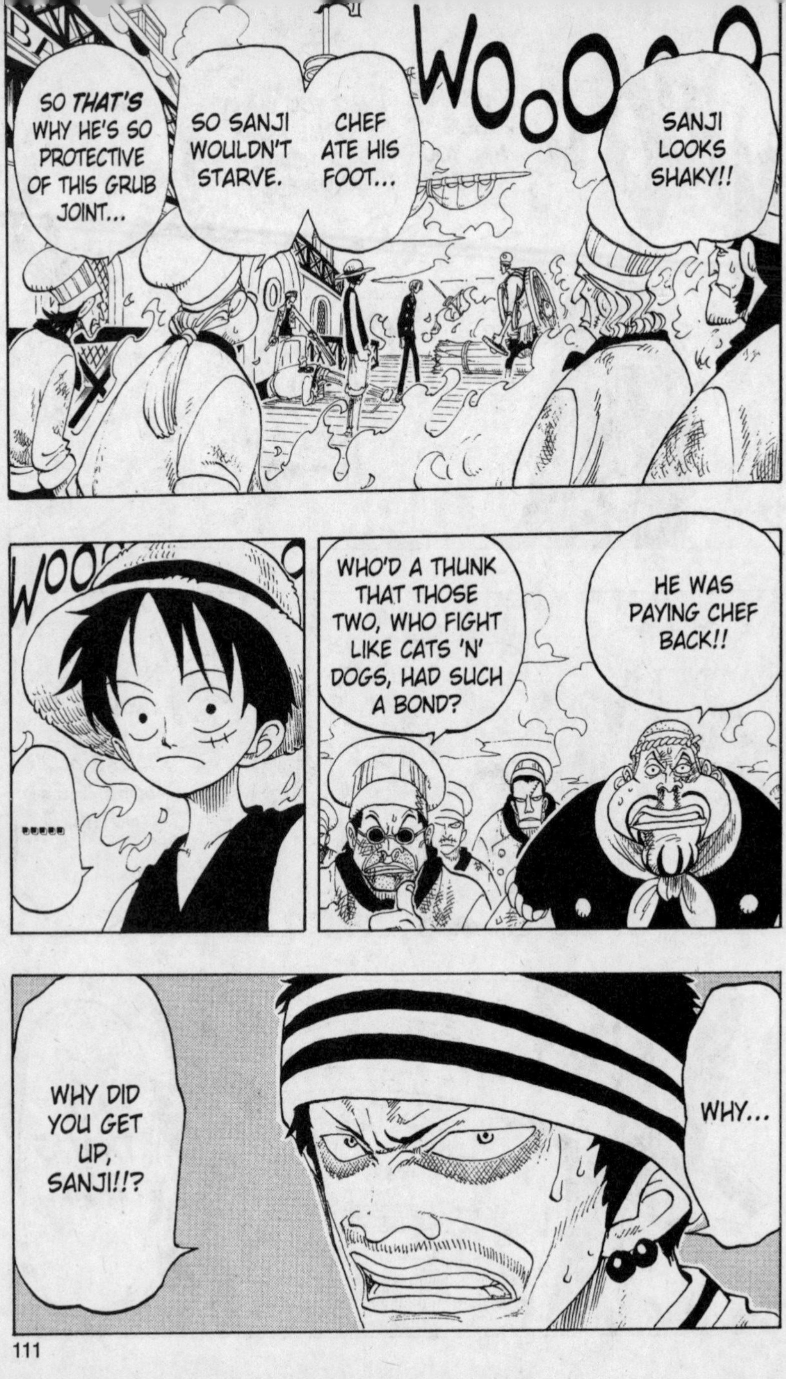

SANJI LOOKS SHAKY!!
WOOOOOO
CHEF ATE HIS FOOT...
SO SANJI WOULDN'T STARVE.
SO *THAT'S* WHY HE'S SO PROTECTIVE OF THIS GRUB JOINT...
HE WAS PAYING CHEF BACK!!
WHO'D A THUNK THAT THOSE TWO, WHO FIGHT LIKE CATS 'N' DOGS, HAD SUCH A BOND?
WOO
.....
WHY...
WHY DID YOU GET UP, SANJI!!?

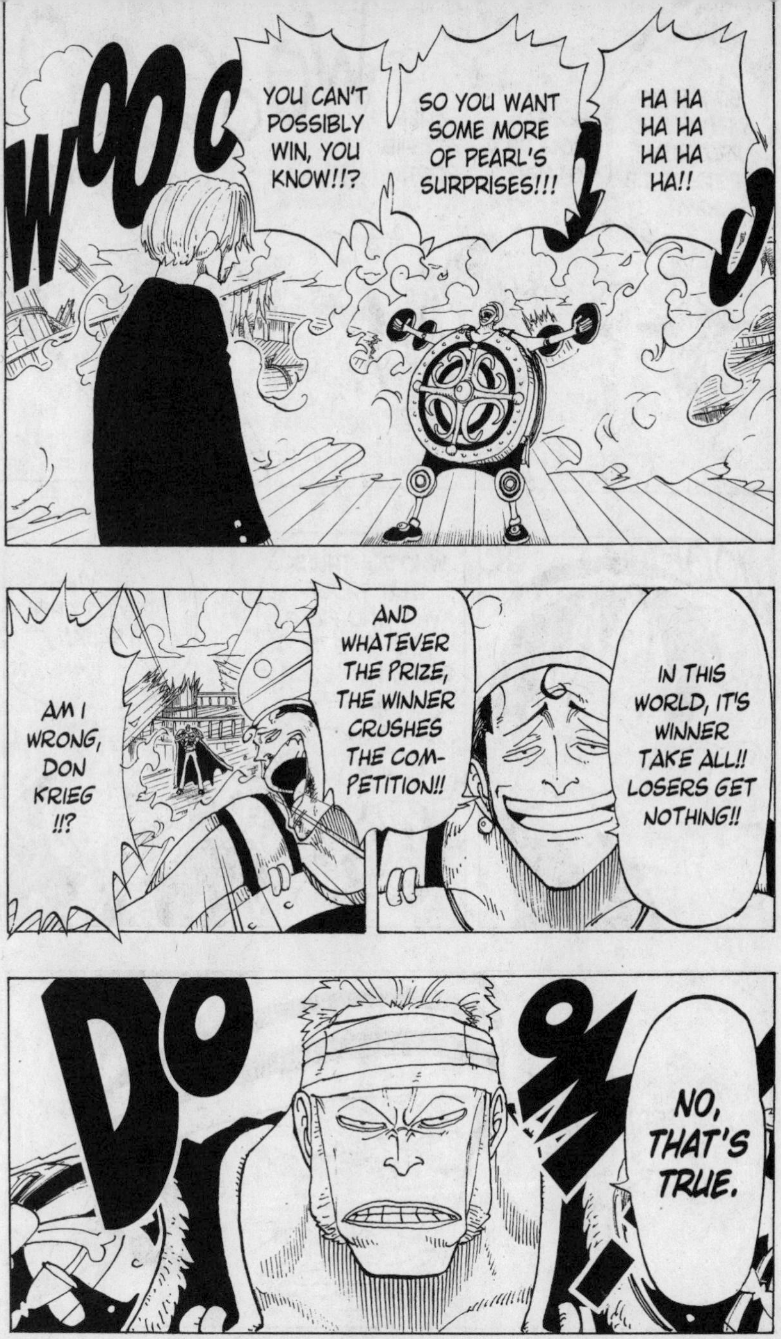
HA HA HA HA HA HA HA!!
SO YOU WANT SOME MORE OF PEARL'S SURPRISES!!!
YOU CAN'T POSSIBLY WIN, YOU KNOW!!?
IN THIS WORLD, IT'S WINNER TAKE ALL!! LOSERS GET NOTHING!!
AND WHATEVER THE PRIZE, THE WINNER CRUSHES THE COM-PETITION!!
AM I WRONG, DON KRIEG !!?
NO, THAT'S TRUE.

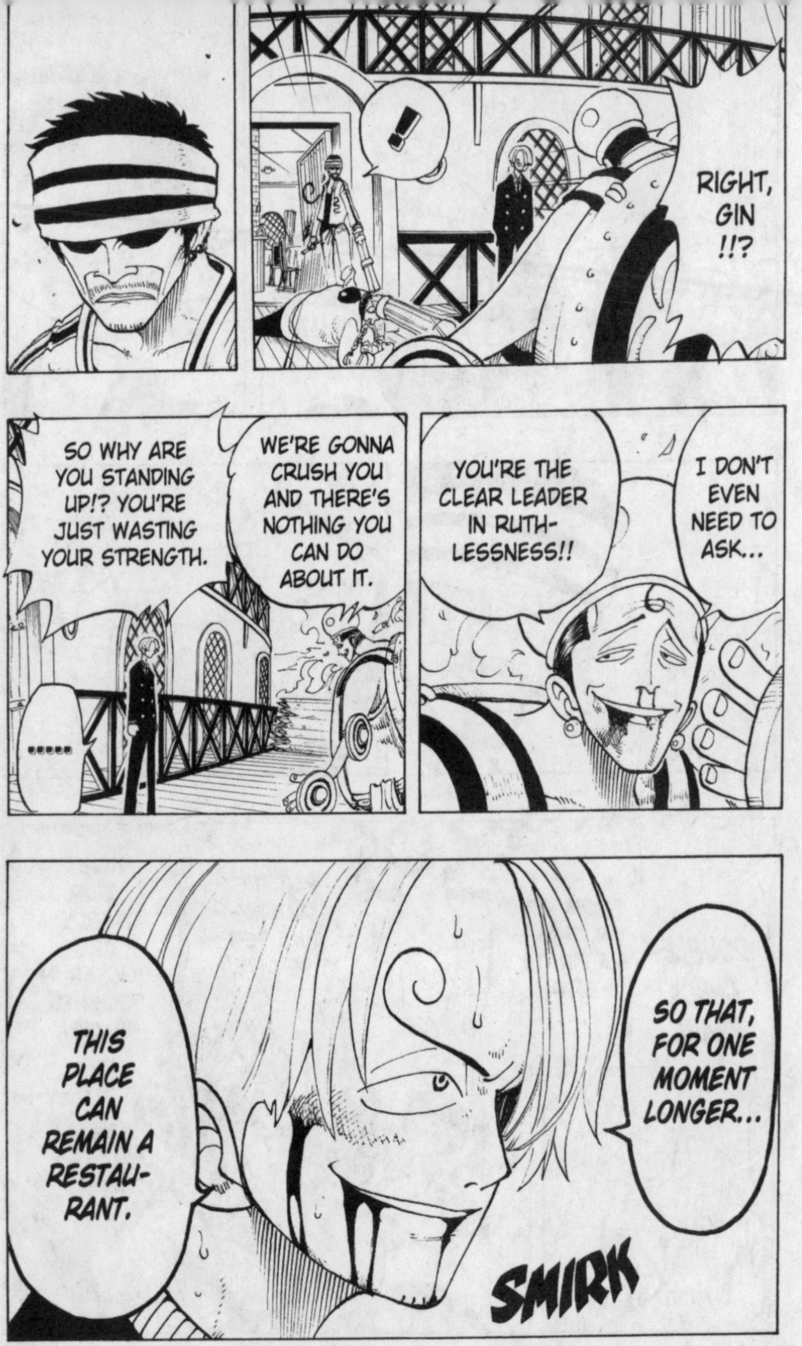
RIGHT, GIN !!?
!
I DON'T EVEN NEED TO ASK...
YOU'RE THE CLEAR LEADER IN RUTH-LESSNESS!!
WE'RE GONNA CRUSH YOU AND THERE'S NOTHING YOU CAN DO ABOUT IT.
SO WHY ARE YOU STANDING UP!? YOU'RE JUST WASTING YOUR STRENGTH.
.....
SO THAT, FOR ONE MOMENT LONGER...
THIS PLACE CAN REMAIN A RESTAU-RANT.
SMIRK

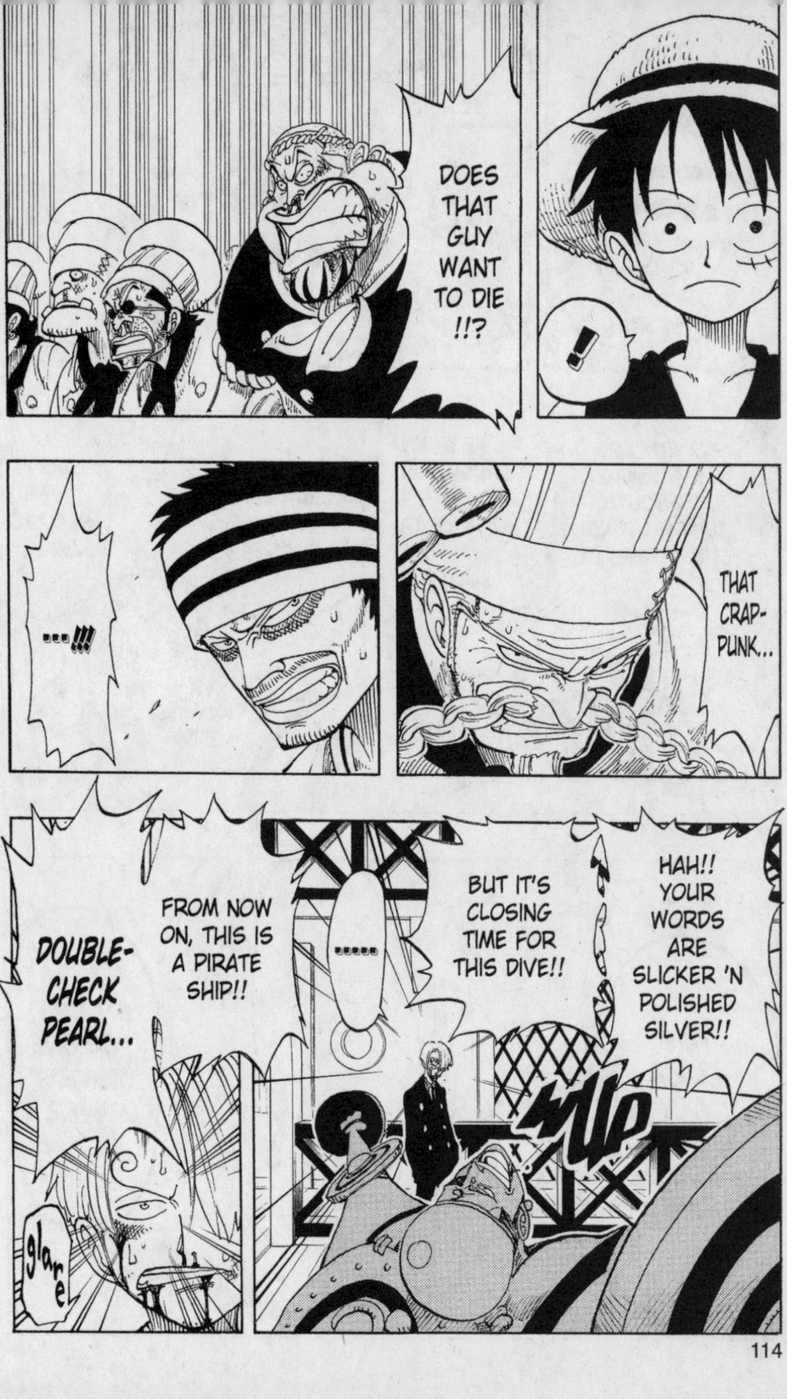
!
DOES THAT GUY WANT TO DIE !!?
THAT CRAP-PUNK...
...!!!
HAH!! YOUR WORDS ARE SLICKER 'N POLISHED SILVER!!
BUT IT'S CLOSING TIME FOR THIS DIVE!!
......
FROM NOW ON, THIS IS A PIRATE SHIP!!
WUP
DOUBLE-CHECK PEARL...
glare

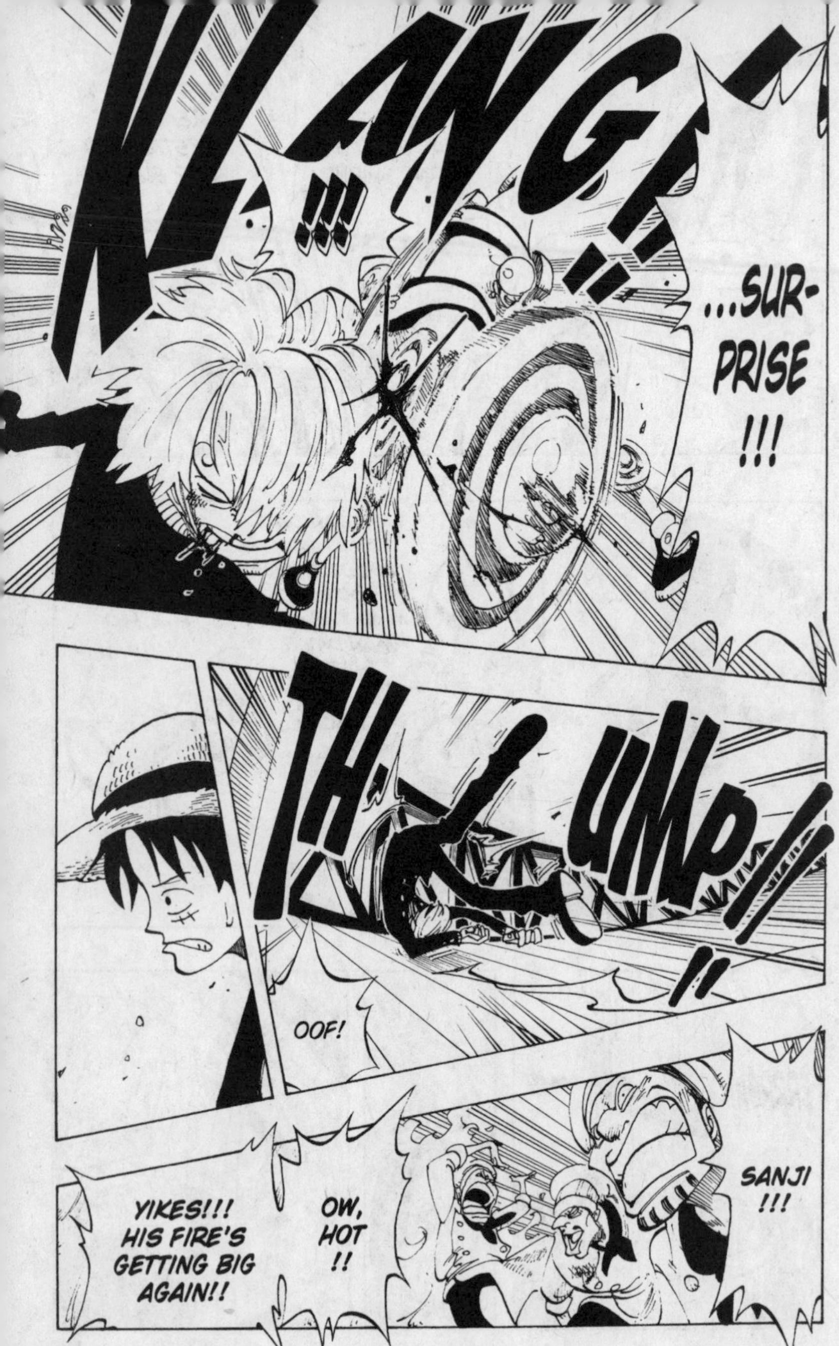
...SUR-
PRISE
!!!
KLANG!!!
THUMP!!
OOF!
SANJI
!!!
OW,
HOT
!!
YIKES!!!
HIS FIRE'S
GETTING BIG
AGAIN!!

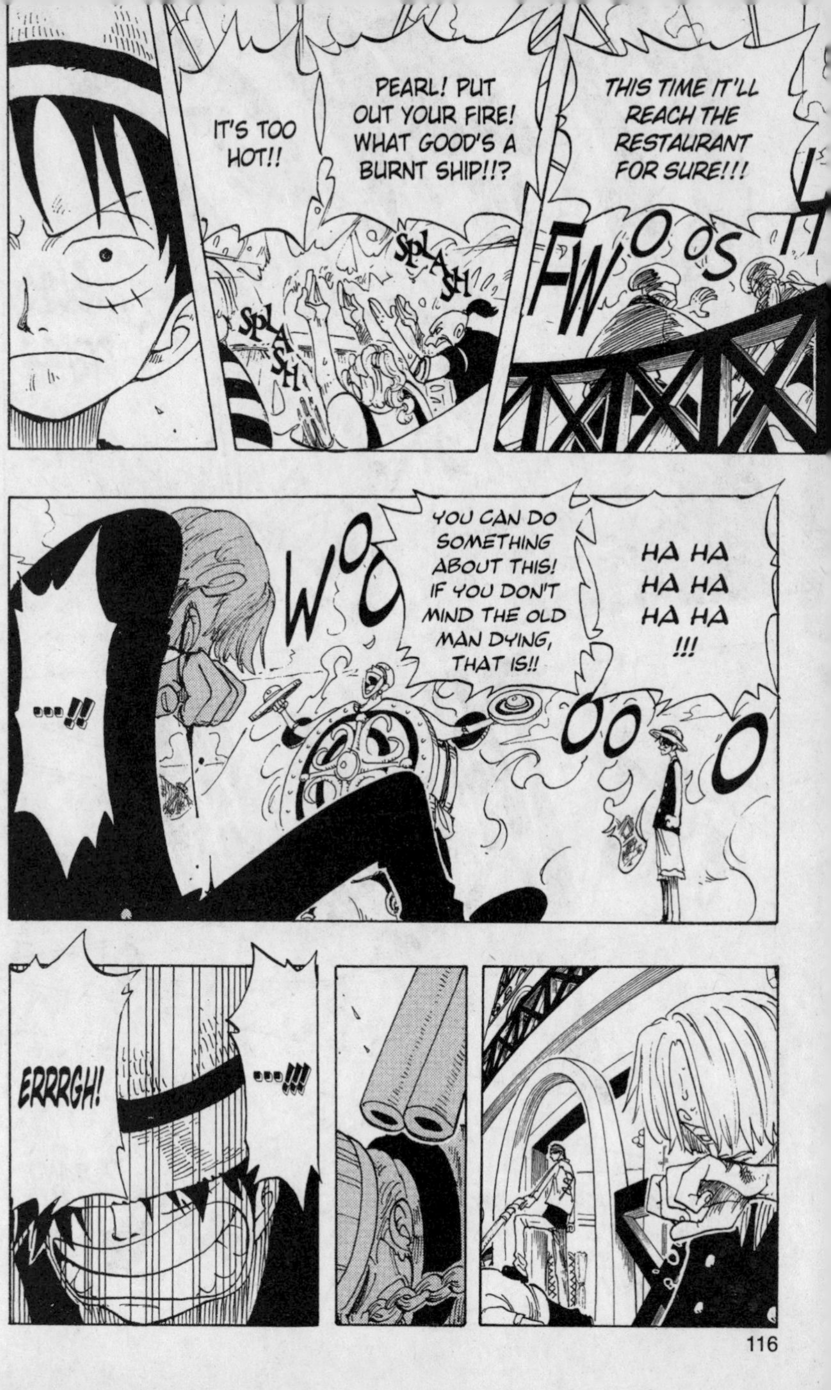

THIS TIME IT'LL REACH THE RESTAURANT FOR SURE!!!
FWOOSH
PEARL! PUT OUT YOUR FIRE! WHAT GOOD'S A BURNT SHIP!!?
SPLASH
IT'S TOO HOT!!
SPLASH
HA HA HA HA HA HA !!!
YOU CAN DO SOMETHING ABOUT THIS! IF YOU DON'T MIND THE OLD MAN DYING, THAT IS!!
WOOOOO
...!!
...!!!
ERRRGH!

READ THIS WAY

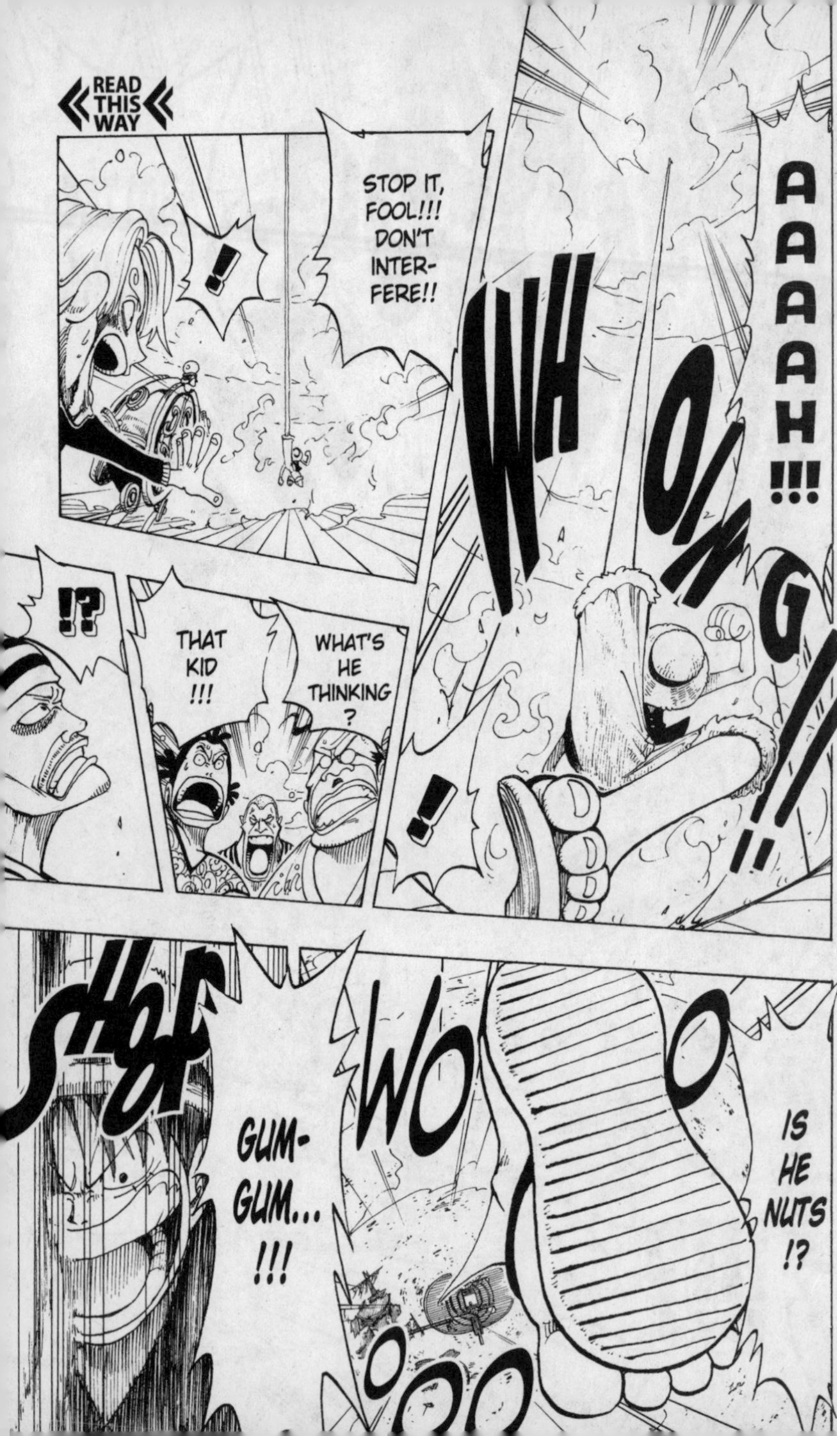
AAAAAH!!!
WHOOONG!!
!
!
STOP IT, FOOL!!! DON'T INTERFERE!!
WHAT'S HE THINKING?
THAT KID!!!
!?
IS HE NUTS!?
WOOOOO
SHOOF
GUM-GUM...!!!

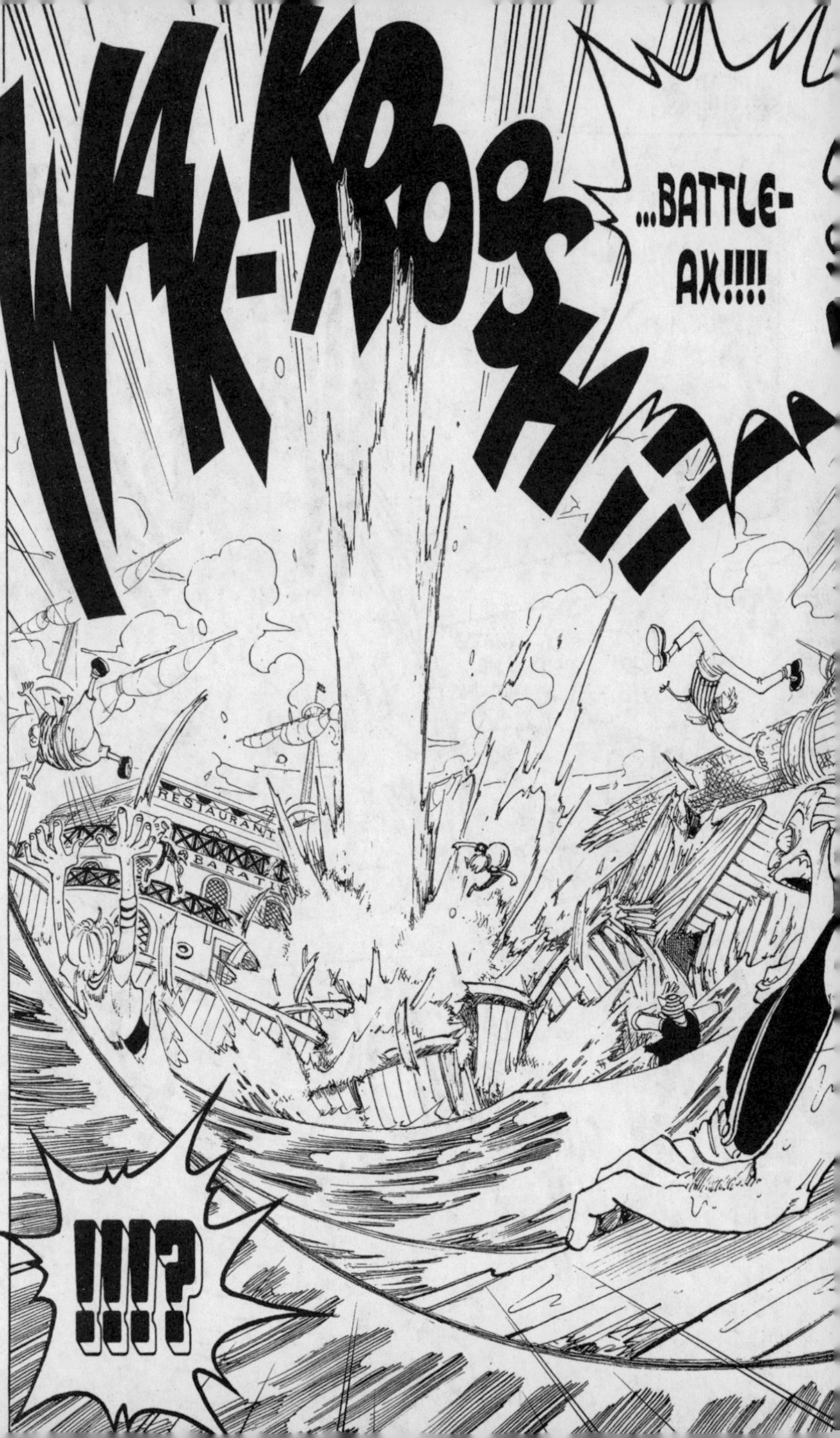
...BATTLE-
AX!!!!
KA-KROOOM!!
!!!?

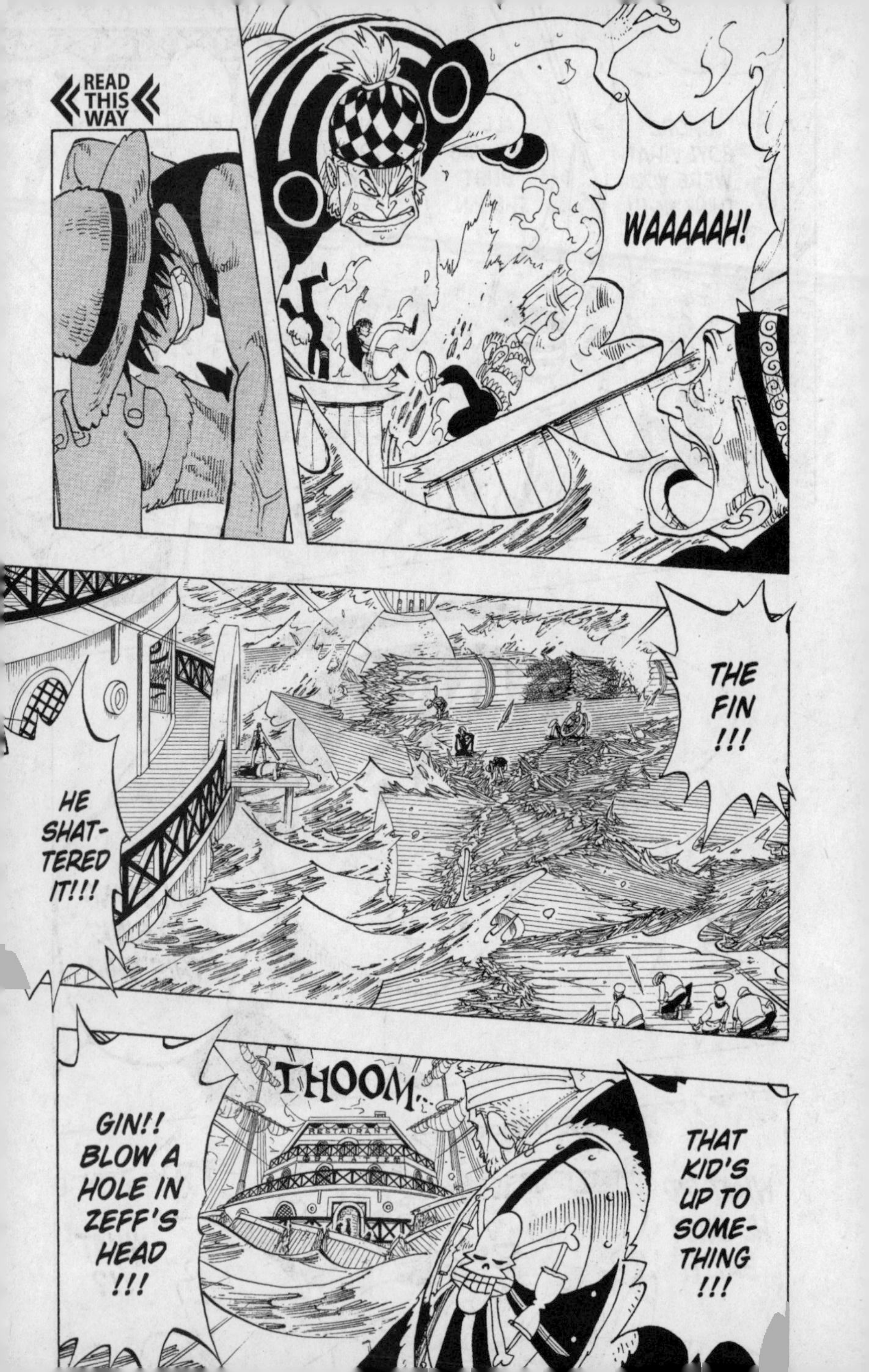
READ THIS WAY
WAAAAAH!
THE FIN !!!
HE SHAT-TERED IT!!!
THAT KID'S UP TO SOME-THING !!!
THOOM
GIN!! BLOW A HOLE IN ZEFF'S HEAD !!!

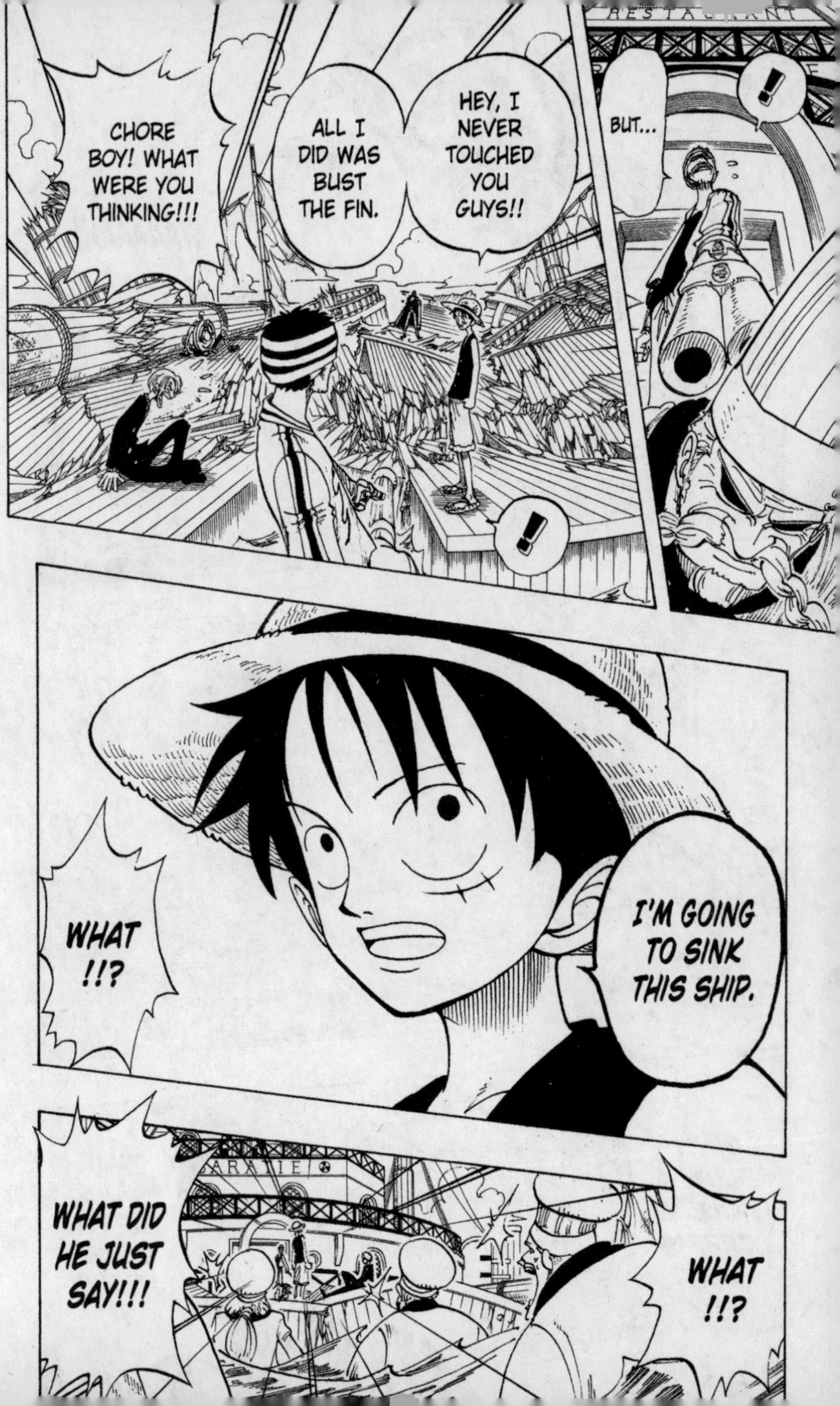
!
BUT...
HEY, I NEVER TOUCHED YOU GUYS!!
ALL I DID WAS BUST THE FIN.
CHORE BOY! WHAT WERE YOU THINKING!!!
!
I'M GOING TO SINK THIS SHIP.
WHAT !!?
WHAT !!?
WHAT DID HE JUST SAY!!!

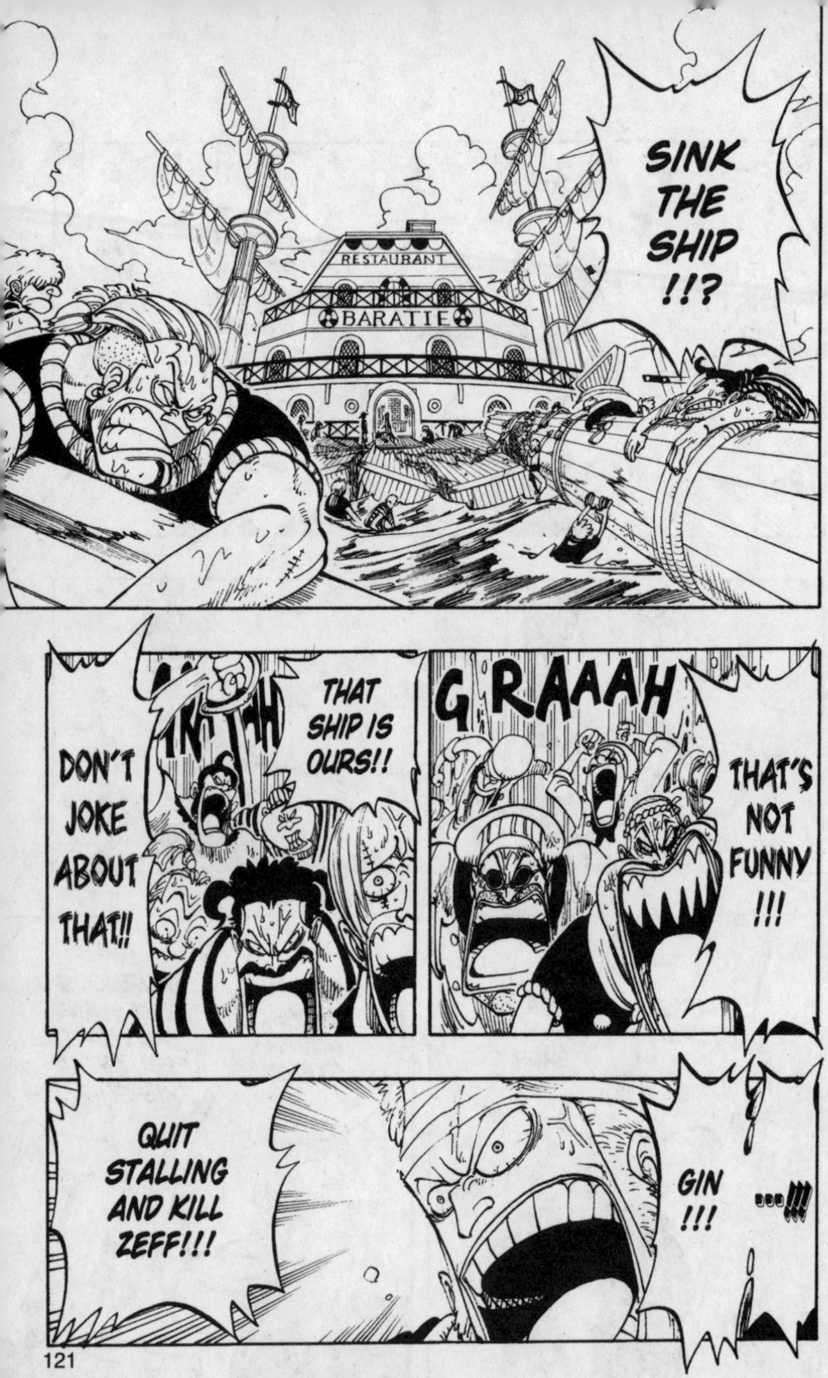
SINK THE SHIP !!?
GRAAAH
THAT'S NOT FUNNY !!!
THAT SHIP IS OURS!!
DON'T JOKE ABOUT THAT!!
...!!!
GIN !!!
QUIT STALLING AND KILL ZEFF!!!

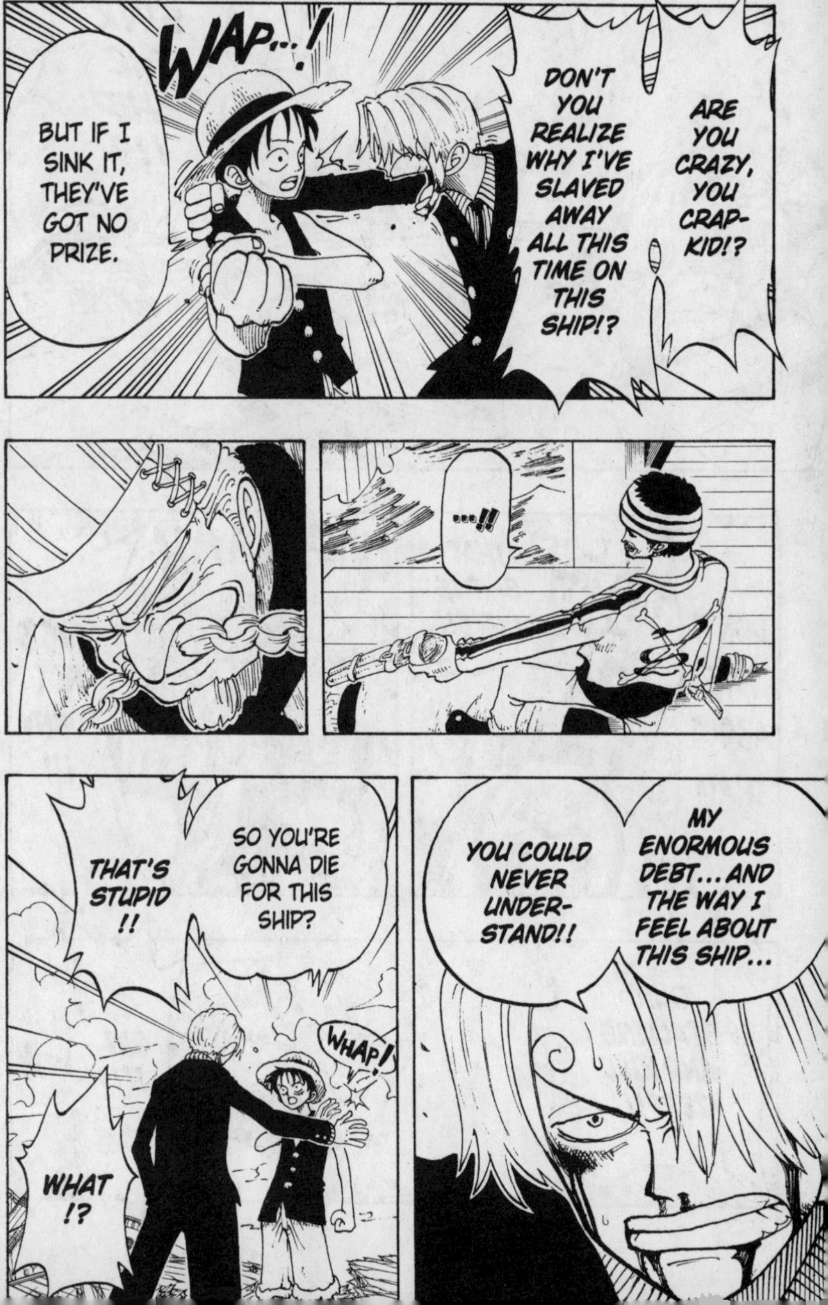
ARE YOU CRAZY, YOU CRAP-KID!?
DON'T YOU REALIZE WHY I'VE SLAVED AWAY ALL THIS TIME ON THIS SHIP!?
WAP...!
BUT IF I SINK IT, THEY'VE GOT NO PRIZE.
...!!
MY ENORMOUS DEBT... AND THE WAY I FEEL ABOUT THIS SHIP...
YOU COULD NEVER UNDER-STAND!!
SO YOU'RE GONNA DIE FOR THIS SHIP?
THAT'S STUPID !!
WHAP!
WHAT !?

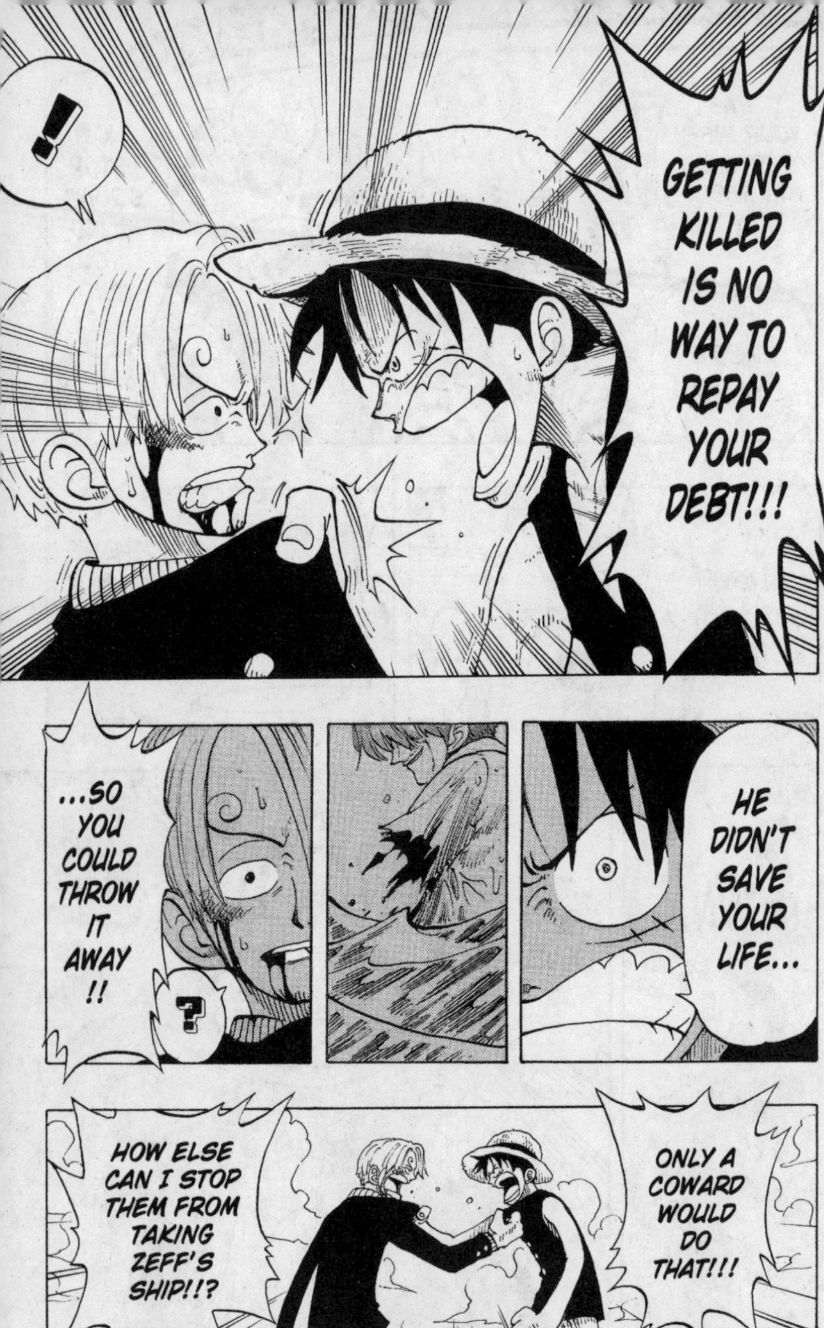
GETTING KILLED IS NO WAY TO REPAY YOUR DEBT!!!
!
HE DIDN'T SAVE YOUR LIFE...
...SO YOU COULD THROW IT AWAY!!
?
ONLY A COWARD WOULD DO THAT!!!
HOW ELSE CAN I STOP THEM FROM TAKING ZEFF'S SHIP!!?

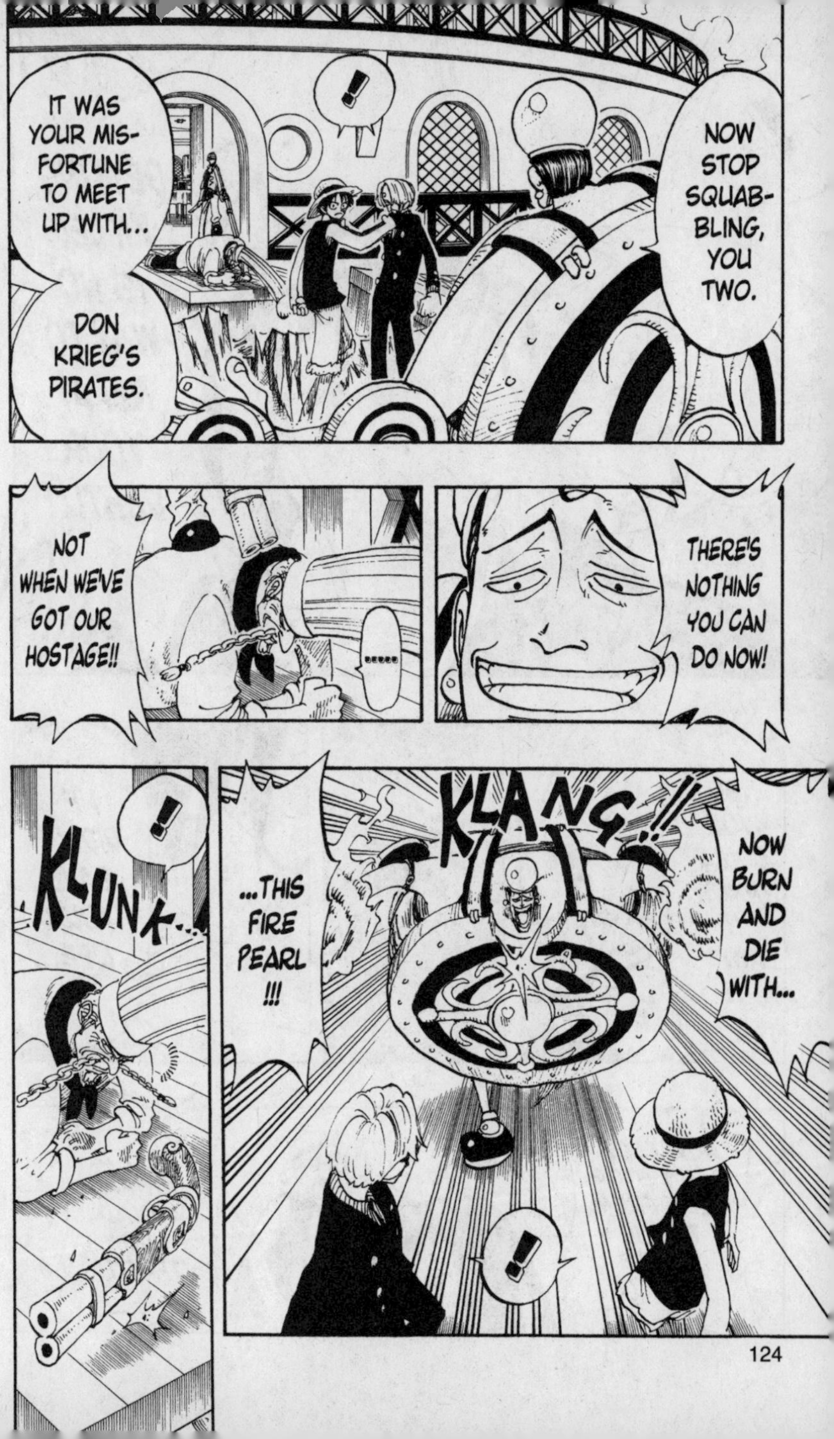
NOW STOP SQUAB-BLING, YOU TWO.
!
IT WAS YOUR MIS-FORTUNE TO MEET UP WITH...
DON KRIEG'S PIRATES.
THERE'S NOTHING YOU CAN DO NOW!
NOT WHEN WE'VE GOT OUR HOSTAGE!!
.....
KLANG!!
NOW BURN AND DIE WITH...
...THIS FIRE PEARL!!!
!
!
KLUNK...

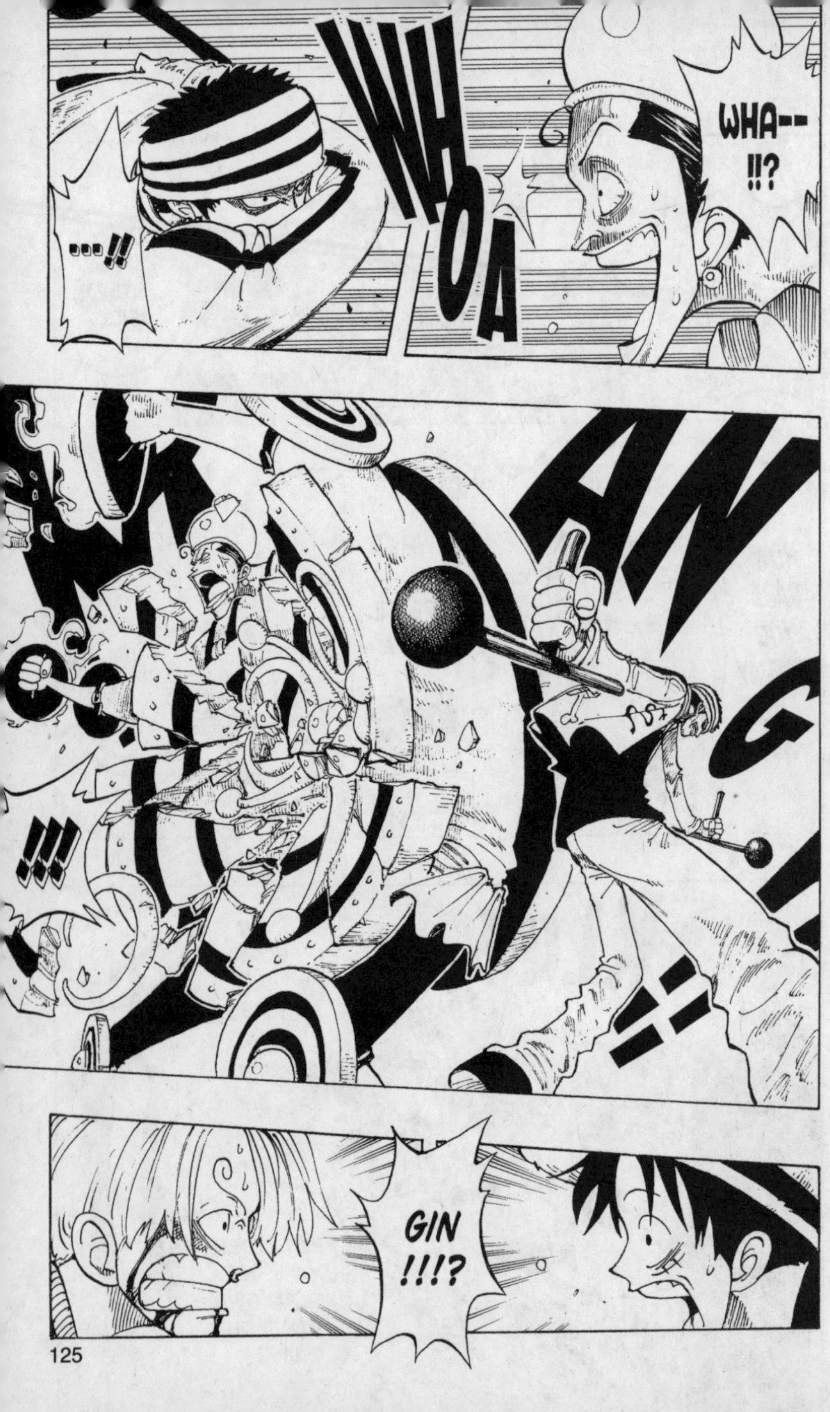
WHA-- !!?
WHOA
...!!
!!!!
!!
GIN !!!?

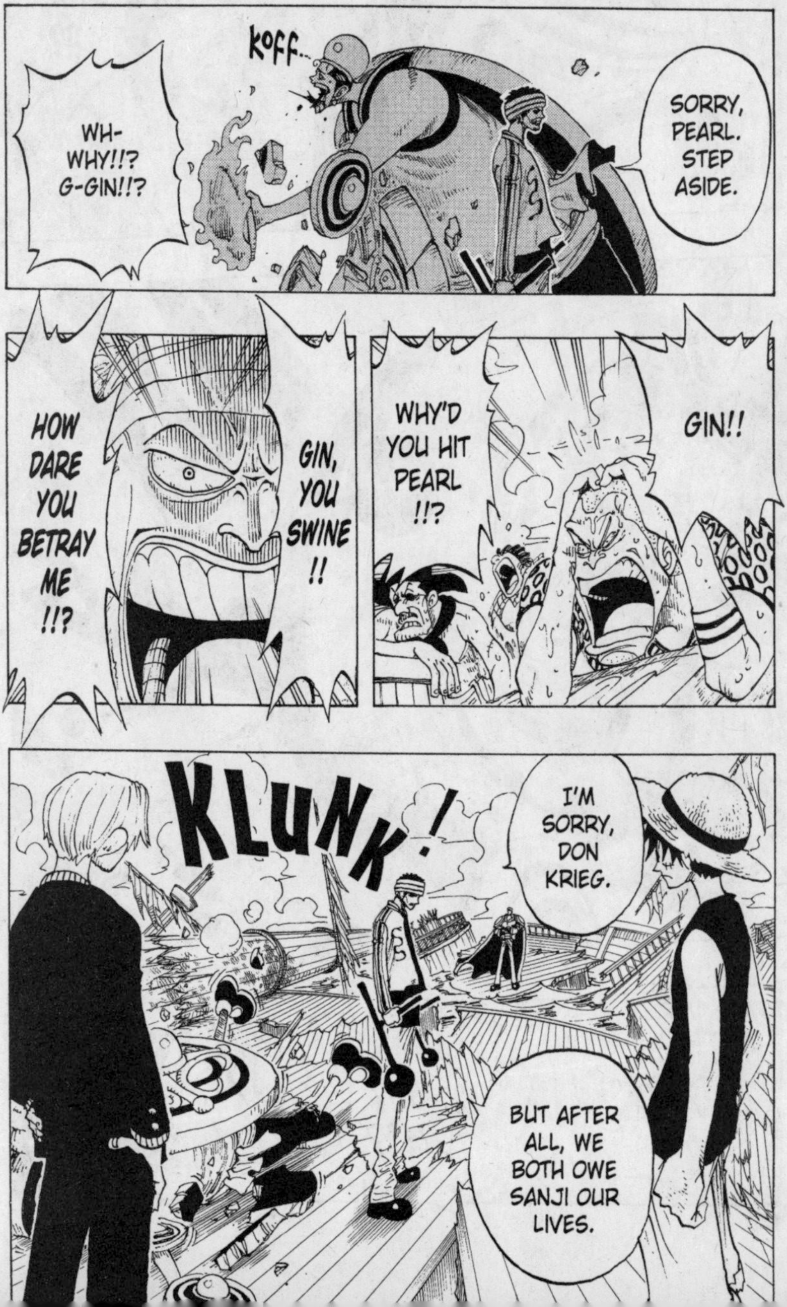
SORRY, PEARL. STEP ASIDE.
KOFF...
WH- WHY!!? G-GIN!!?
GIN!!
WHY'D YOU HIT PEARL !!?
GIN, YOU SWINE !!
HOW DARE YOU BETRAY ME !!?
I'M SORRY, DON KRIEG.
KLUNK!
BUT AFTER ALL, WE BOTH OWE SANJI OUR LIVES.

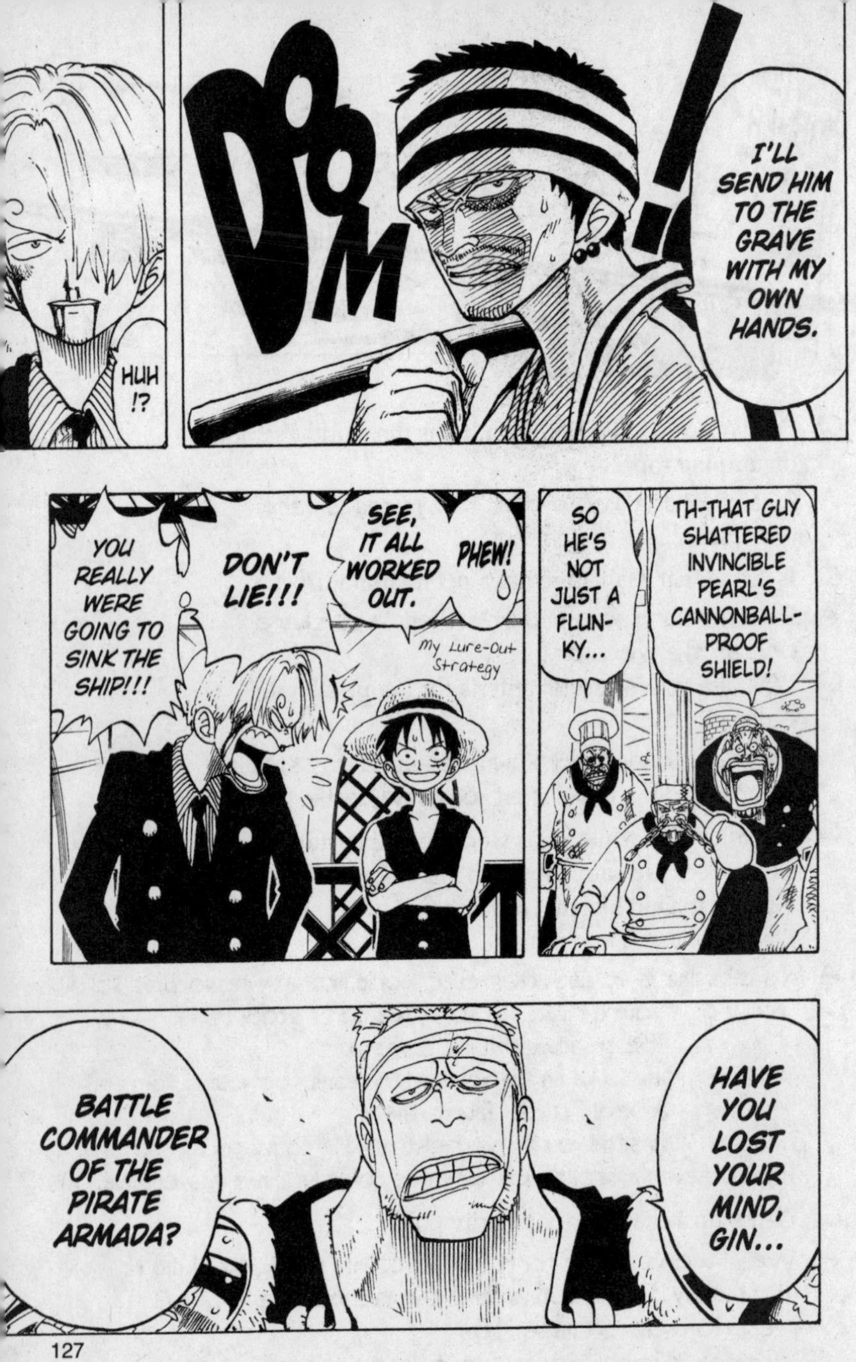
I'LL SEND HIM TO THE GRAVE WITH MY OWN HANDS.
DOOM!
HUH !?
TH-THAT GUY SHATTERED INVINCIBLE PEARL'S CANNONBALL-PROOF SHIELD!
SO HE'S NOT JUST A FLUN-KY...
PHEW!
SEE, IT ALL WORKED OUT.
My Lure-Out Strategy
DON'T LIE!!!
YOU REALLY WERE GOING TO SINK THE SHIP!!!
HAVE YOU LOST YOUR MIND, GIN...
BATTLE COMMANDER OF THE PIRATE ARMADA?

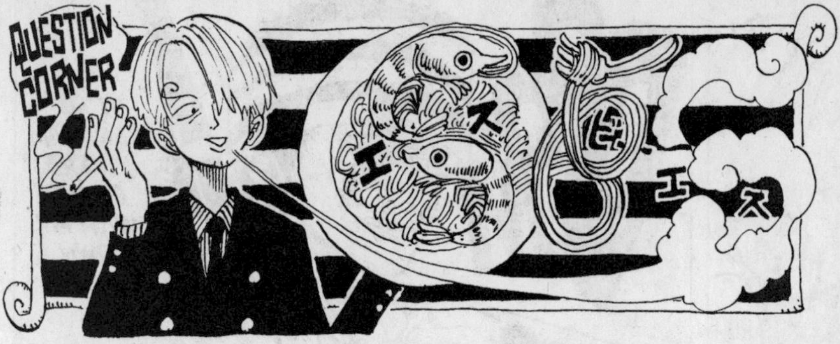
QUESTION CORNER

Q: Did you know that Koby's father is the world champion of jumping rope?

A: Really? I didn't know that. Koby's dad is very impressive...

Q: Is it true that Klahadore has a pet mammoth?

A: Really? I didn't know that either. Was there one at the mansion?

Q: What are your selection criteria for Usopp's Pirate Gallery?

A: Naturally, I consider skill, how interesting it is, style...but the most important thing is the spirit you convey in the postcard. Yeah.

Q: The other day while I was working at the fruit stand, this smart-aleck kid said, "You don't have Gum-Gum Fruit? What a dork." If a kid like that comes again, what should I say? Please tell me. (I'm serious.)

A: In a case like that, each character would probably respond as follows:

Makino: "You're right, I'm sorry we don't stock it." (Be an adult and let it pass.)

Shanks: "Ha ha ha ha ha!! You're ten years too young for a Devil Fruit!!" (Taunt him.)

Luffy: "I'll send you flying, right now." (No mercy.)

Try whichever approach you like--but don't hold me responsible.

Q: Please do a character popularity poll!!

A: Well, I won't be doing it in the comic book, but I did it in *Weekly Shonen Jump* and the results are in, so I'll present them on page 148.

(I think this poll was taken two or three weeks after *Chapter 49: Storm* came out.)

# Chapter 60: RESOLUTION

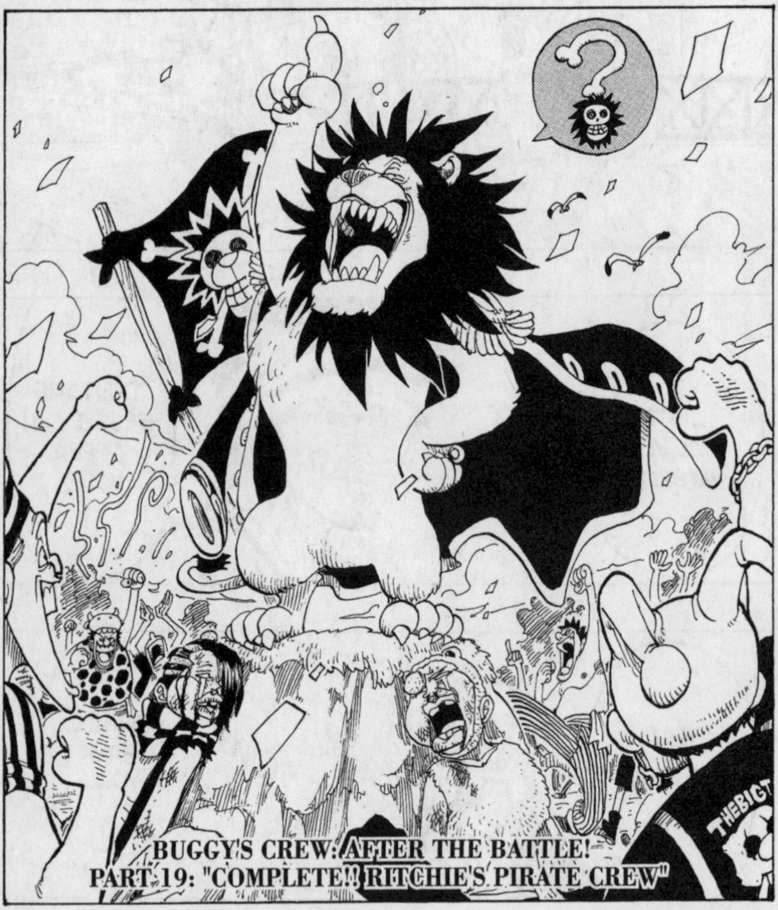
?
THEBIGT
BUGGY'S CREW: AFTER THE BATTLE!
PART 19: "COMPLETE!! RITCHIE'S PIRATE CREW"

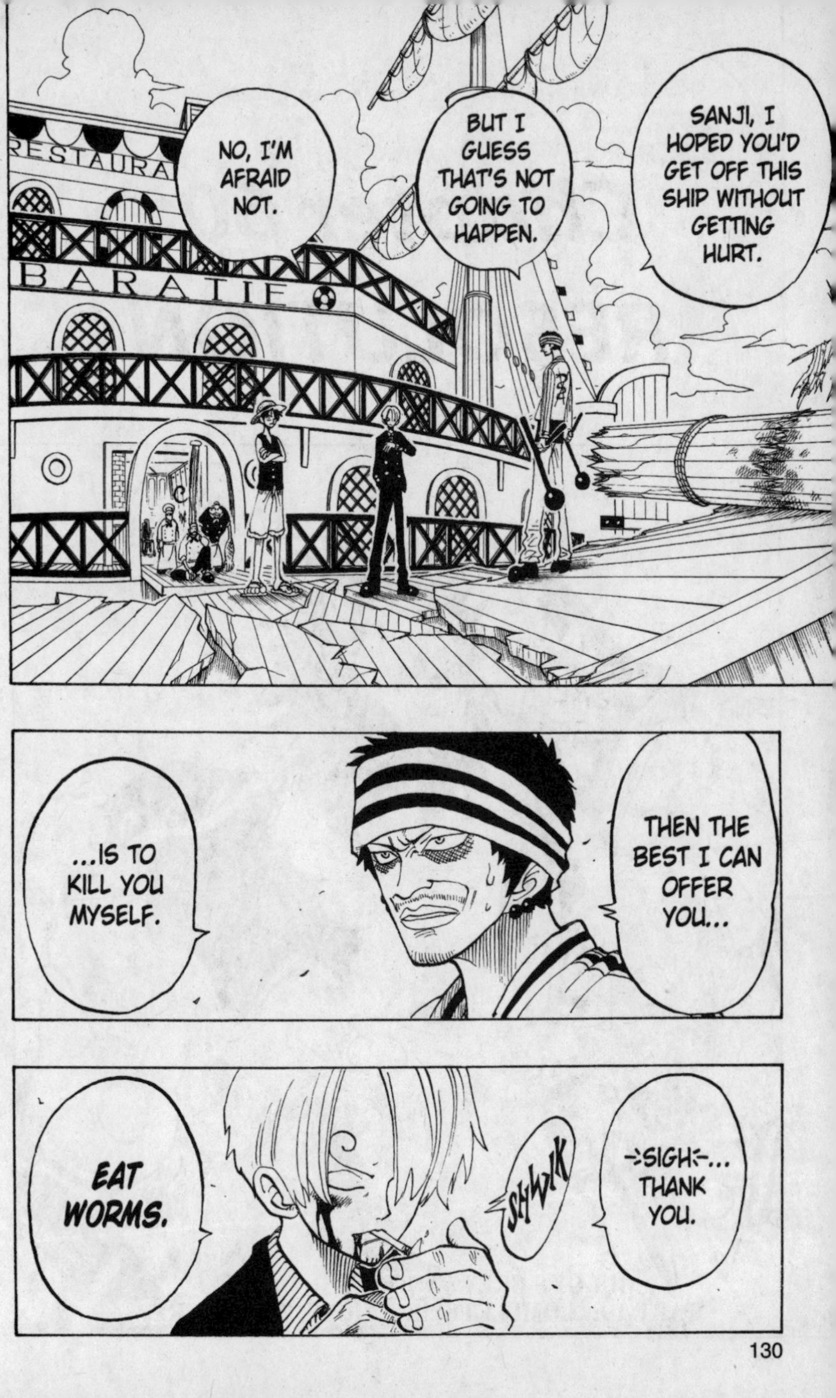
SANJI, I HOPED YOU'D GET OFF THIS SHIP WITHOUT GETTING HURT.
BUT I GUESS THAT'S NOT GOING TO HAPPEN.
NO, I'M AFRAID NOT.
RESTAURA
BARATIE
THEN THE BEST I CAN OFFER YOU...
...IS TO KILL YOU MYSELF.
-SIGH-... THANK YOU.
SHWIK
EAT WORMS.

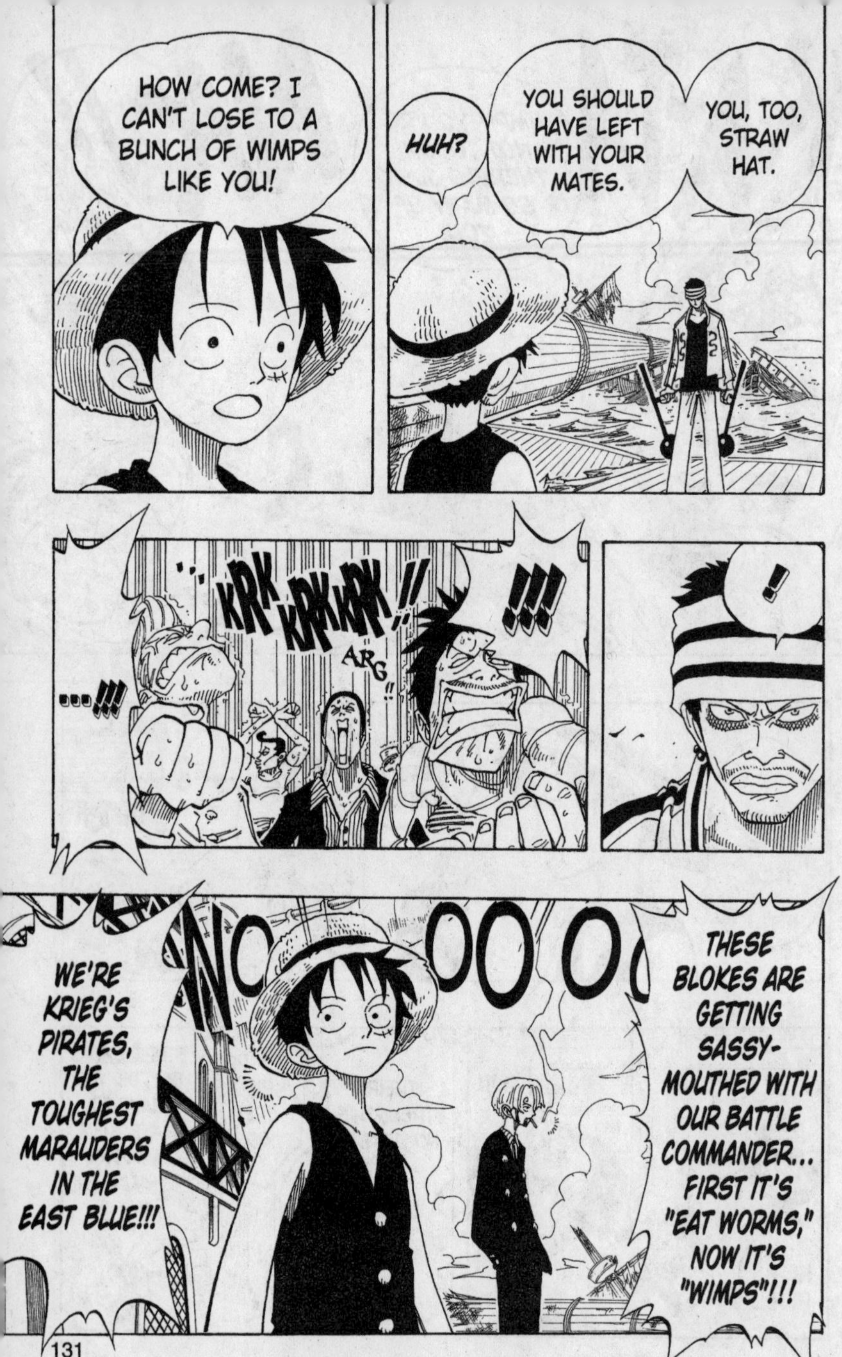

YOU, TOO, STRAW HAT.
YOU SHOULD HAVE LEFT WITH YOUR MATES.
HUH?
HOW COME? I CAN'T LOSE TO A BUNCH OF WIMPS LIKE YOU!
!
!!!
KRK KRKKRK!!
...
ARG!!
...!!!
NOOOOO
THESE BLOKES ARE GETTING SASSY-MOUTHED WITH OUR BATTLE COMMANDER... FIRST IT'S "EAT WORMS," NOW IT'S "WIMPS"!!!
WE'RE KRIEG'S PIRATES, THE TOUGHEST MARAUDERS IN THE EAST BLUE!!!

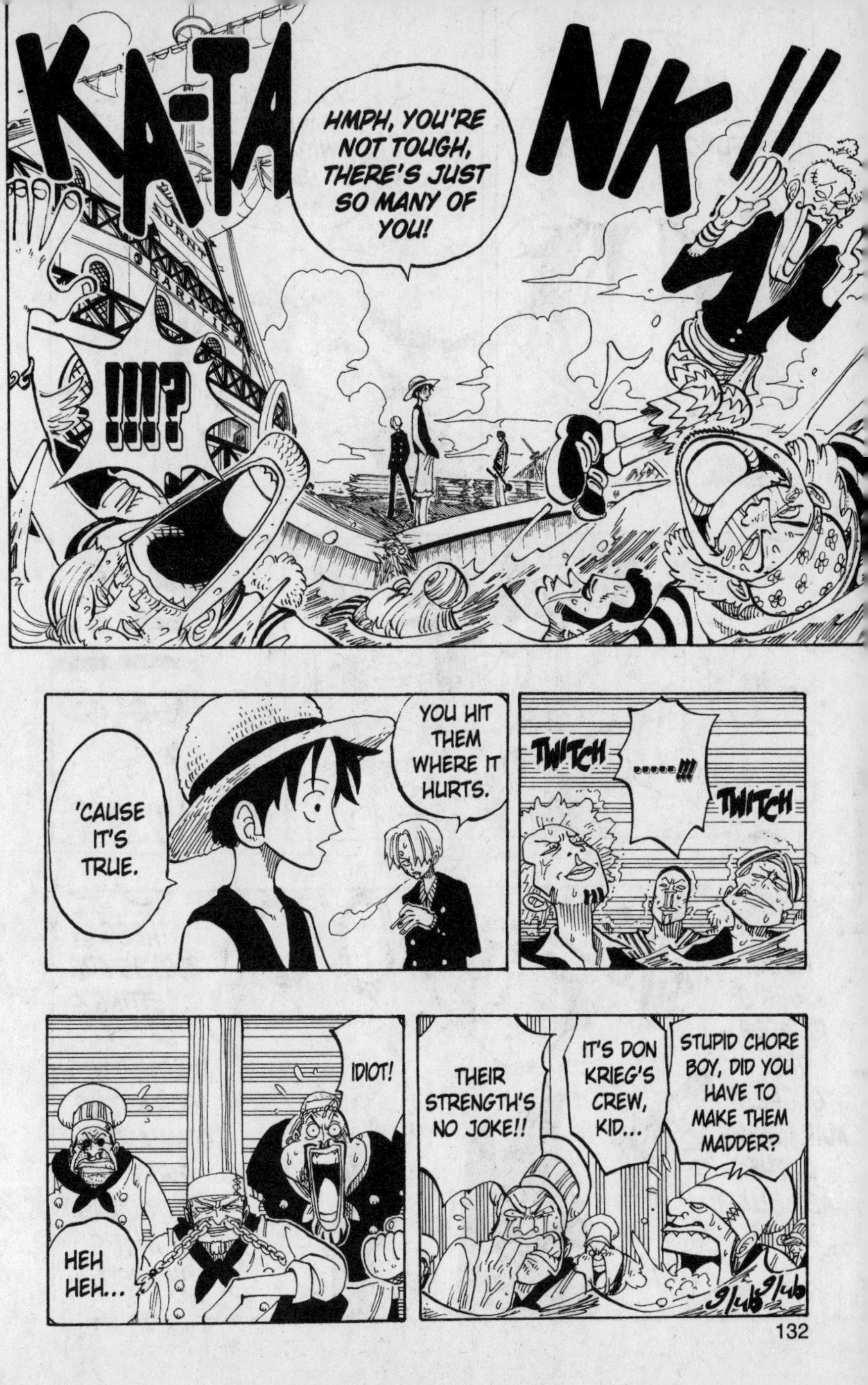
KA-TANK!!
HMPH, YOU'RE NOT TOUGH, THERE'S JUST SO MANY OF YOU!
!!!?
TWITCH
......!!!
TWITCH
YOU HIT THEM WHERE IT HURTS.
'CAUSE IT'S TRUE.
STUPID CHORE BOY, DID YOU HAVE TO MAKE THEM MADDER?
IT'S DON KRIEG'S CREW, KID...
THEIR STRENGTH'S NO JOKE!!
IDIOT!
HEH HEH...

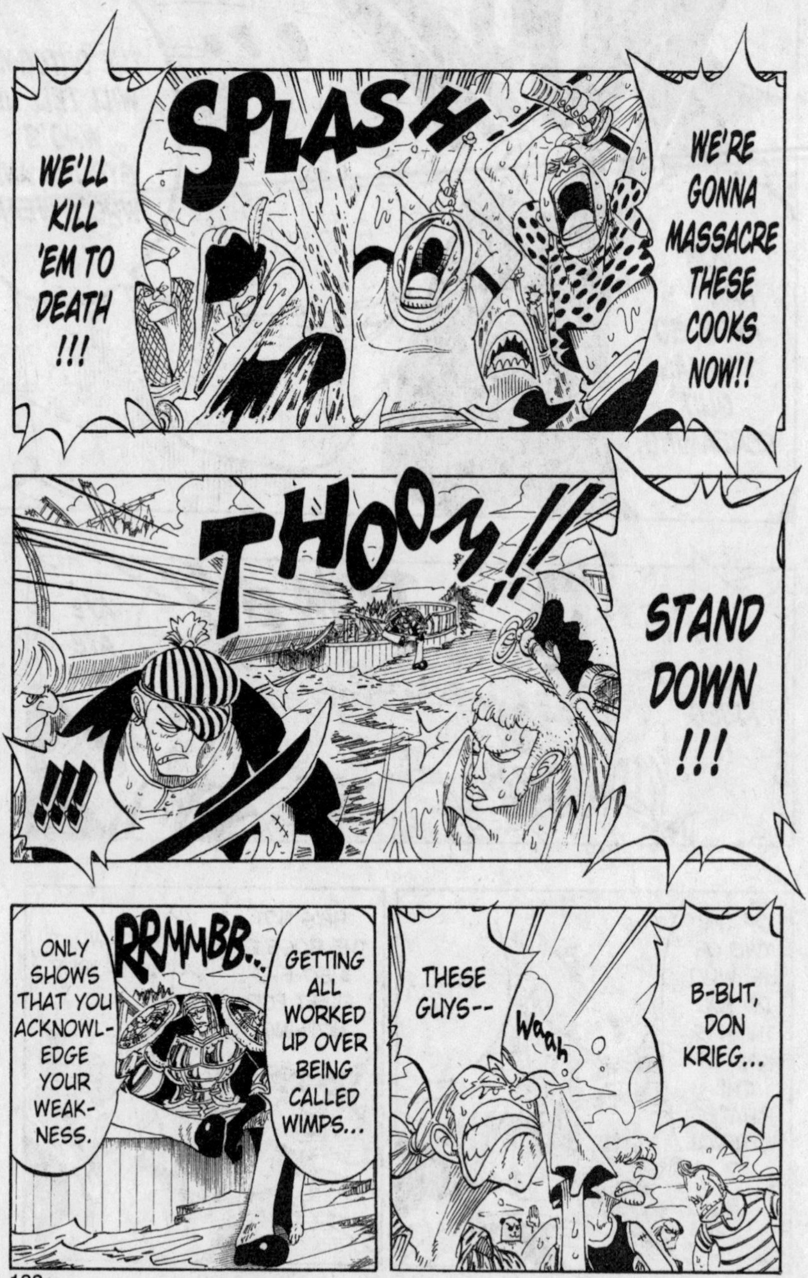

WE'RE GONNA MASSACRE THESE COOKS NOW!!
SPLASH
WE'LL KILL 'EM TO DEATH!!!
STAND DOWN!!!
THOOM!!
!!!
B-BUT, DON KRIEG...
Waah
THESE GUYS--
GETTING ALL WORKED UP OVER BEING CALLED WIMPS...
RRMMBB...
ONLY SHOWS THAT YOU ACKNOWL-EDGE YOUR WEAK-NESS.

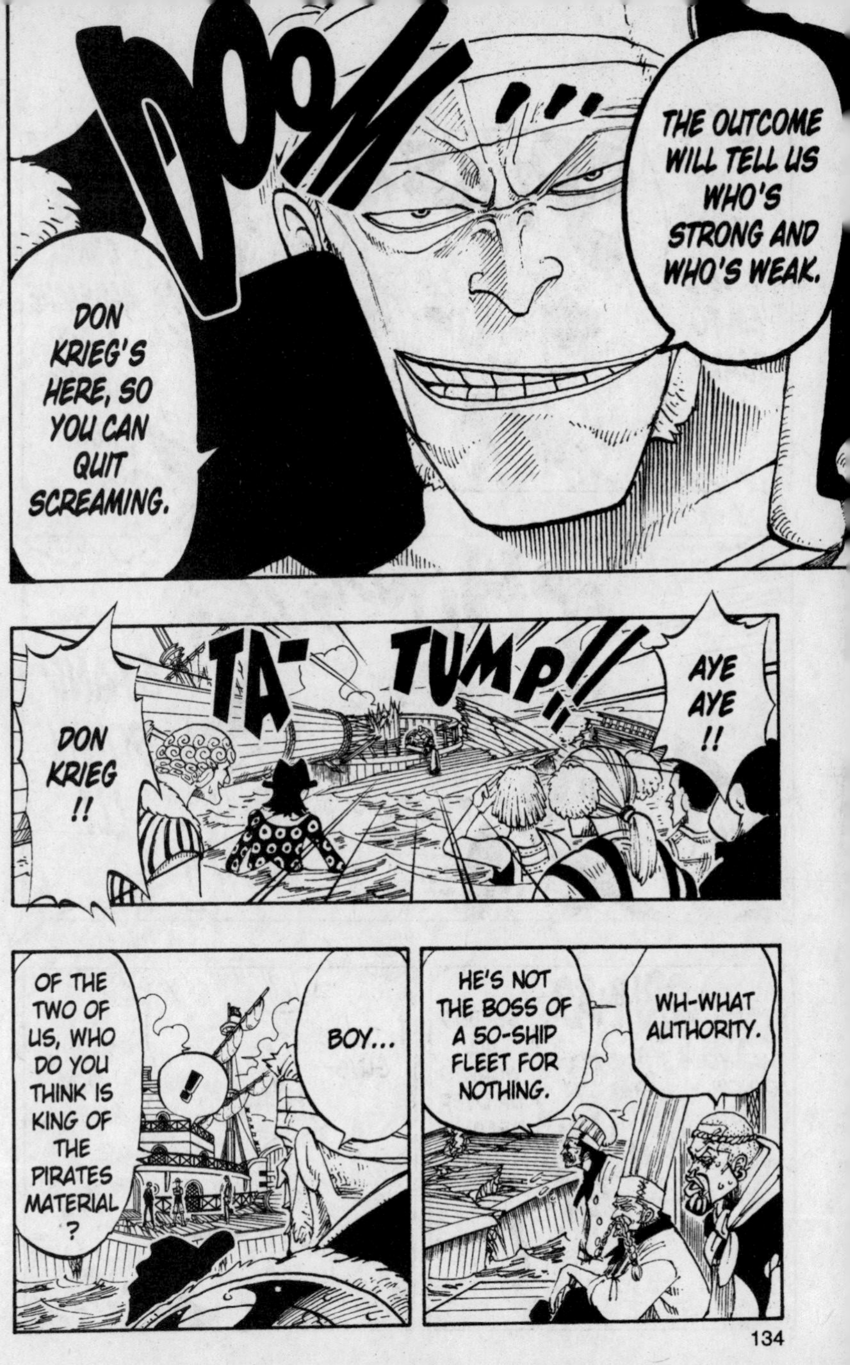
THE OUTCOME WILL TELL US WHO'S STRONG AND WHO'S WEAK.
DOOM
DON KRIEG'S HERE, SO YOU CAN QUIT SCREAMING.
AYE AYE !!
TA- TUMP!!
DON KRIEG !!
WH-WHAT AUTHORITY.
HE'S NOT THE BOSS OF A 50-SHIP FLEET FOR NOTHING.
BOY...
!
OF THE TWO OF US, WHO DO YOU THINK IS KING OF THE PIRATES MATERIAL ?

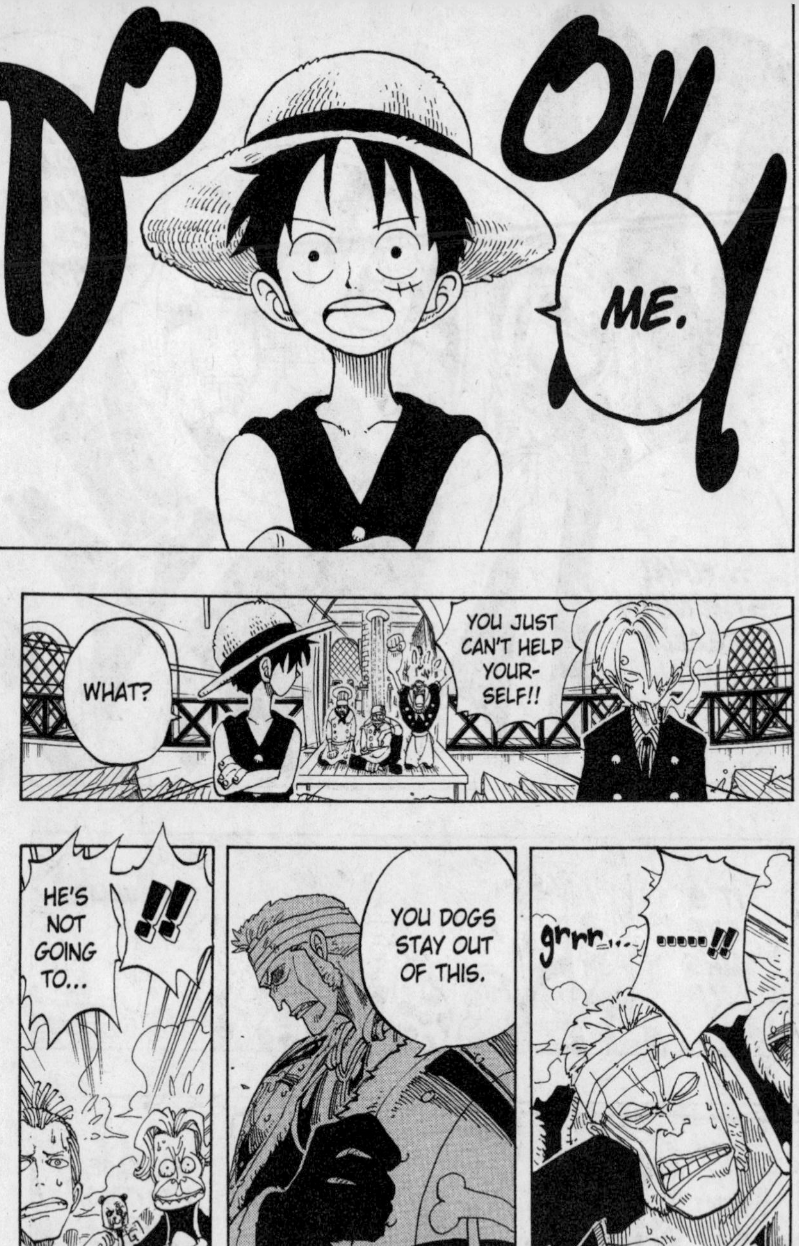
DOON
ME.
YOU JUST CAN'T HELP YOUR-SELF!!
WHAT?
......!!
grrr...
YOU DOGS STAY OUT OF THIS.
!!
HE'S NOT GOING TO...

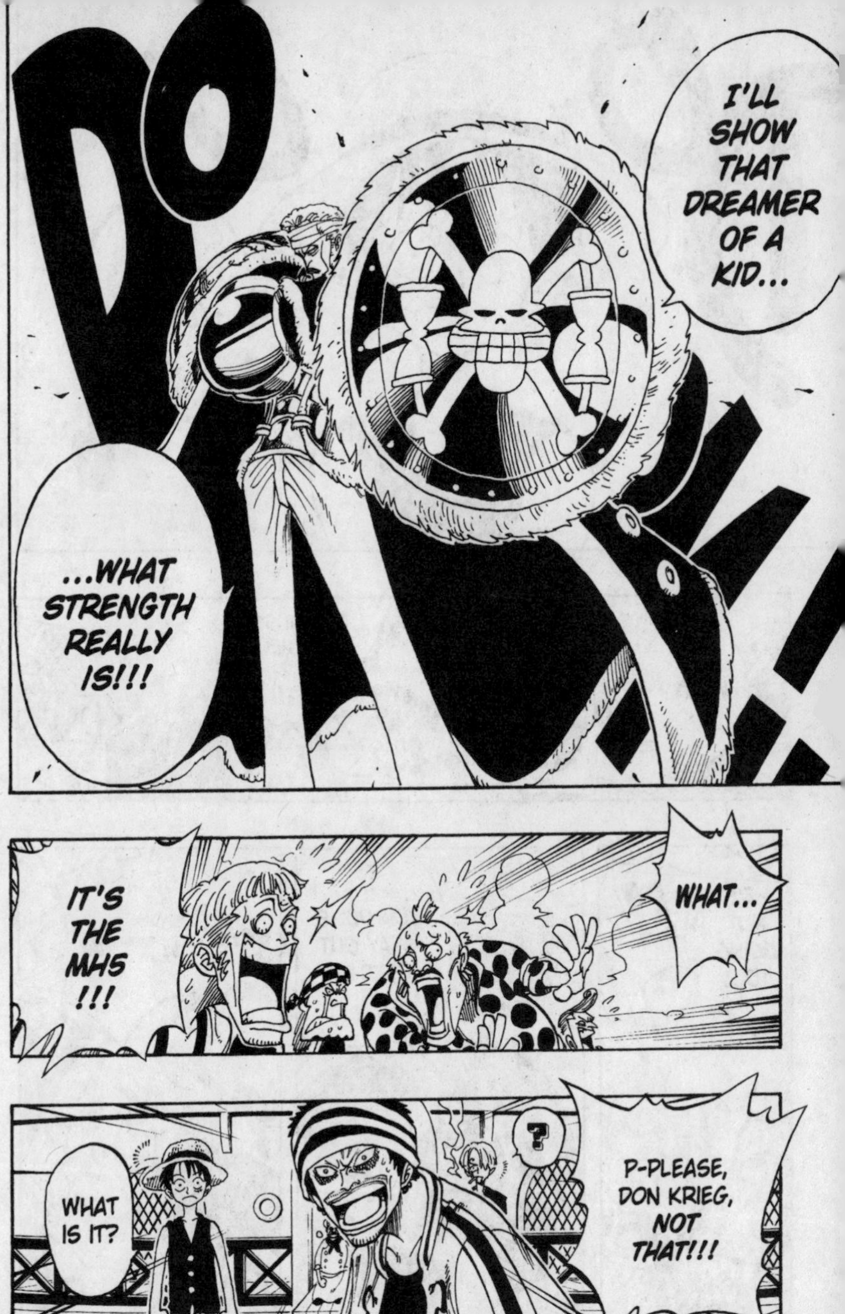
DO
I'LL SHOW THAT DREAMER OF A KID...
...WHAT STRENGTH REALLY IS!!!
WHAT...
IT'S THE MH5 !!!
P-PLEASE, DON KRIEG, NOT THAT!!!
?
WHAT IS IT?

READ THIS WAY

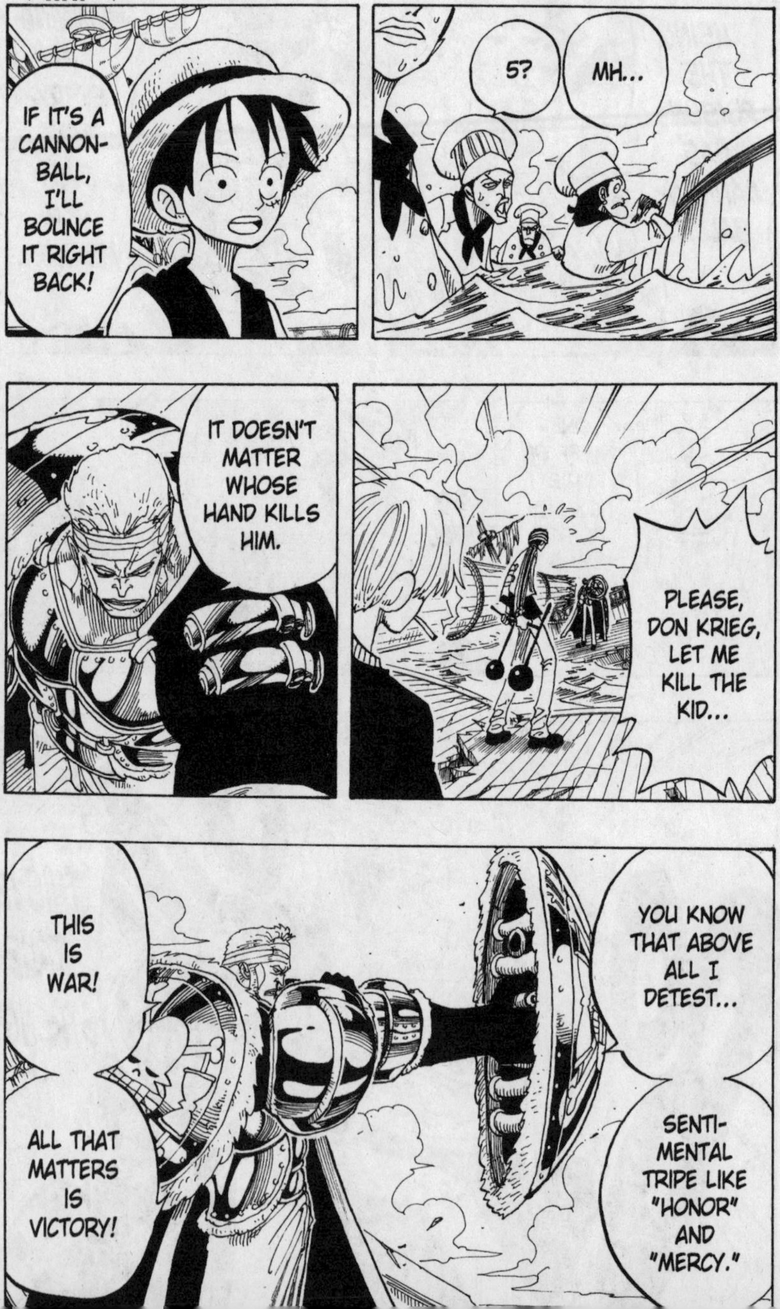
MH...
5?
IF IT'S A CANNON-BALL, I'LL BOUNCE IT RIGHT BACK!
PLEASE, DON KRIEG, LET ME KILL THE KID...
IT DOESN'T MATTER WHOSE HAND KILLS HIM.
YOU KNOW THAT ABOVE ALL I DETEST...
SENTI-MENTAL TRIPE LIKE "HONOR" AND "MERCY."
THIS IS WAR!
ALL THAT MATTERS IS VICTORY!

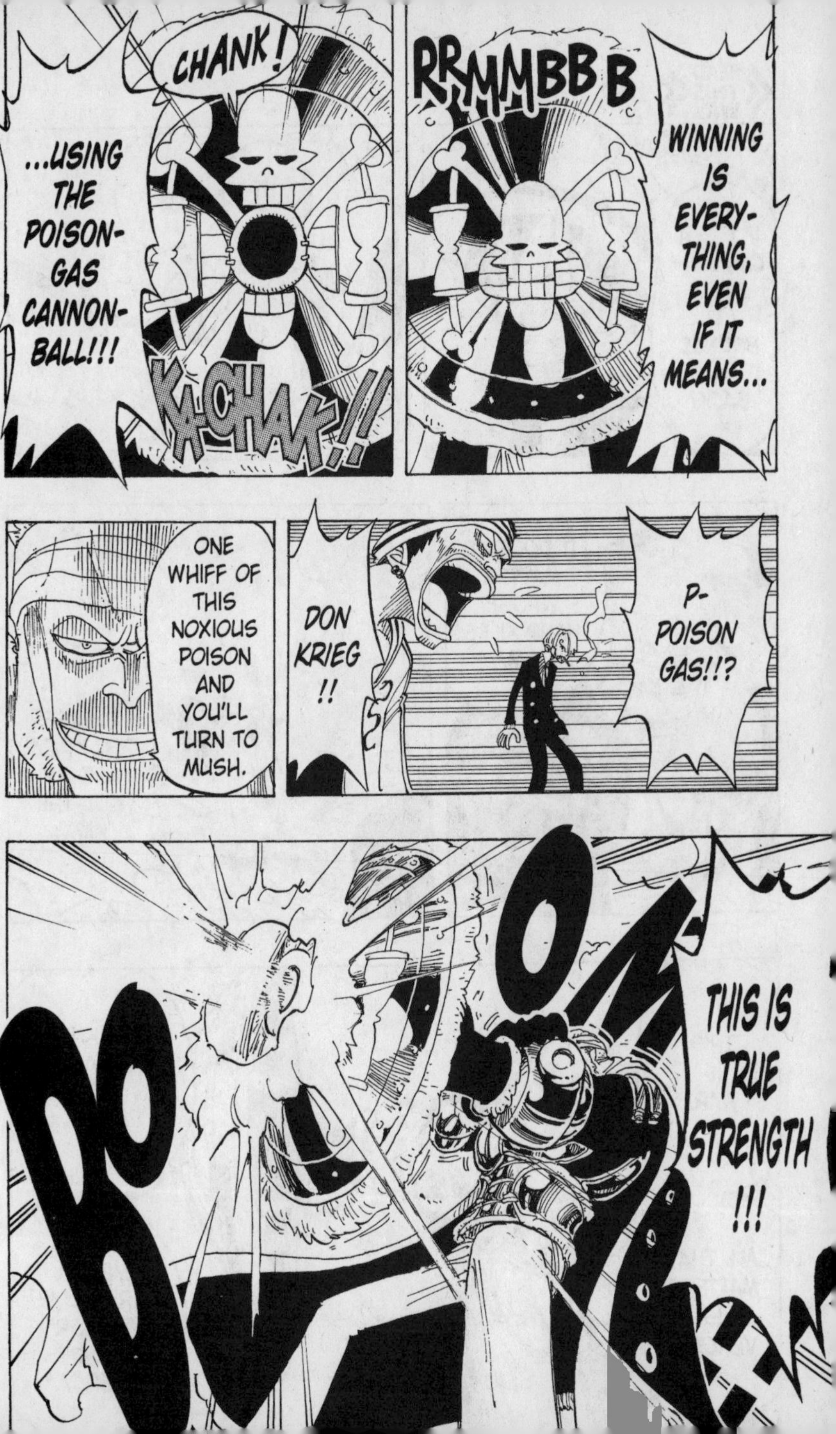
RRMMBB B
WINNING IS EVERYTHING, EVEN IF IT MEANS...
CHANK!
...USING THE POISON-GAS CANNONBALL!!!
KA-CHAK!!
P-POISON GAS!!?
DON KRIEG!!
ONE WHIFF OF THIS NOXIOUS POISON AND YOU'LL TURN TO MUSH.
THIS IS TRUE STRENGTH!!!
BOOM

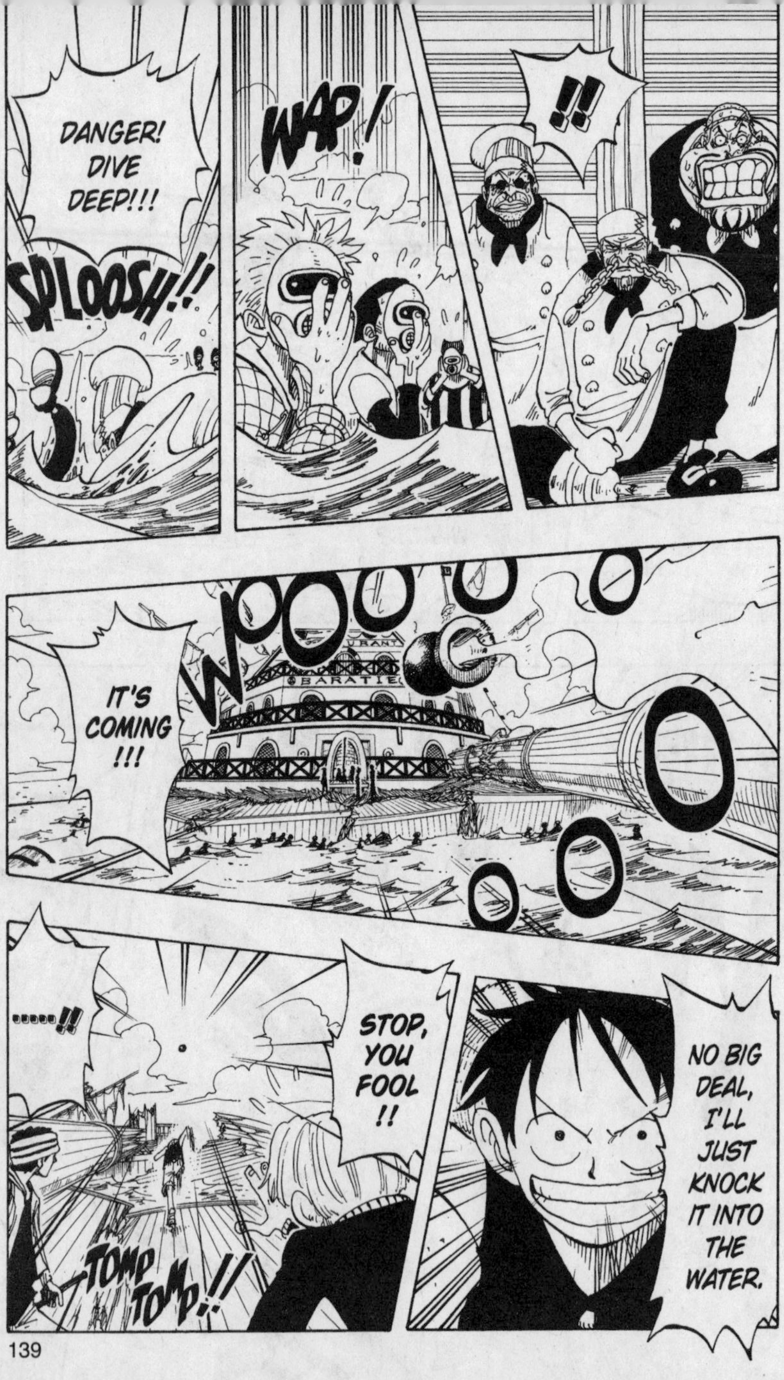
!!
WAP!
DANGER! DIVE DEEP!!!
SPLOOSH!!
IT'S COMING!!!
NO BIG DEAL, I'LL JUST KNOCK IT INTO THE WATER.
STOP, YOU FOOL!!
.....!!
TOMP TOMP!!

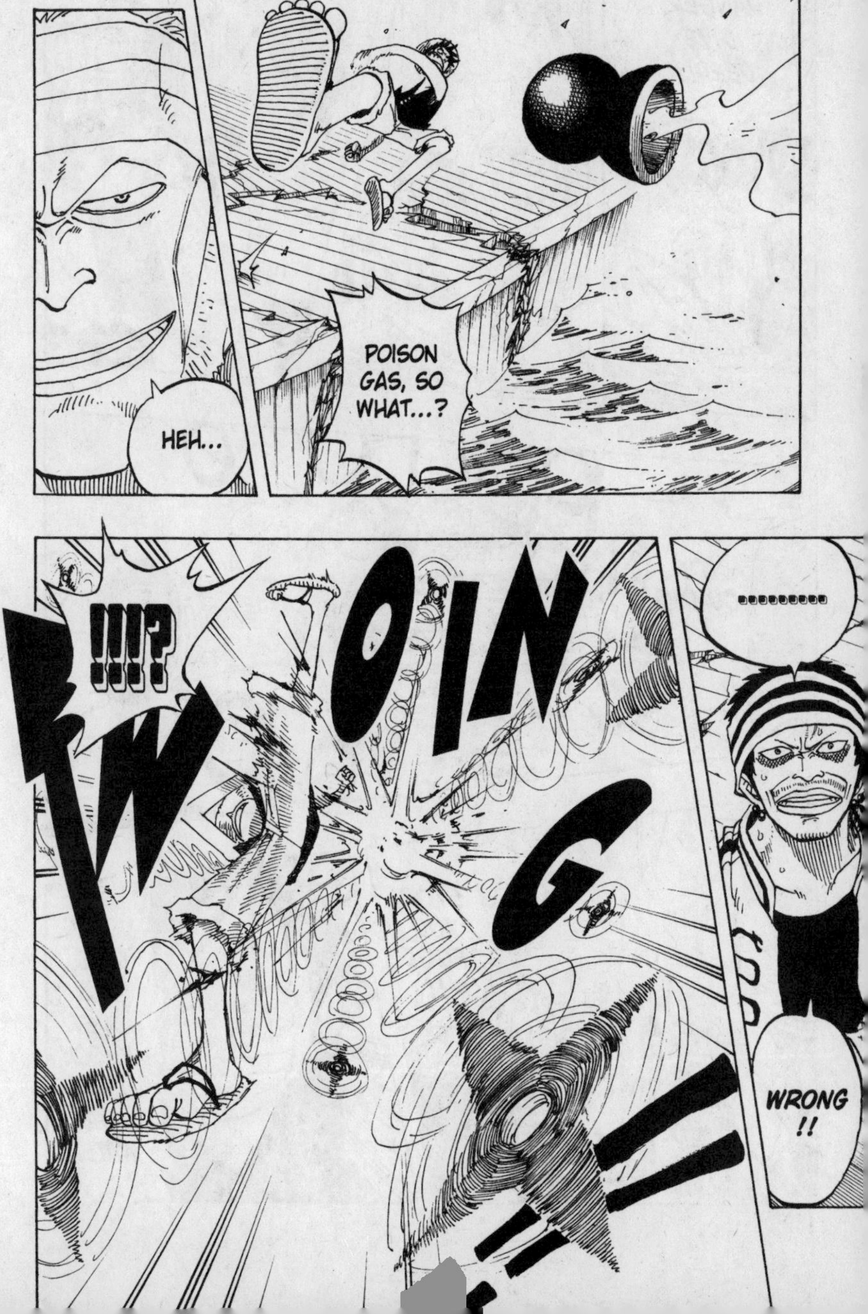
POISON GAS, SO WHAT...?
HEH...
.........
WRONG !!
!!!?
OING

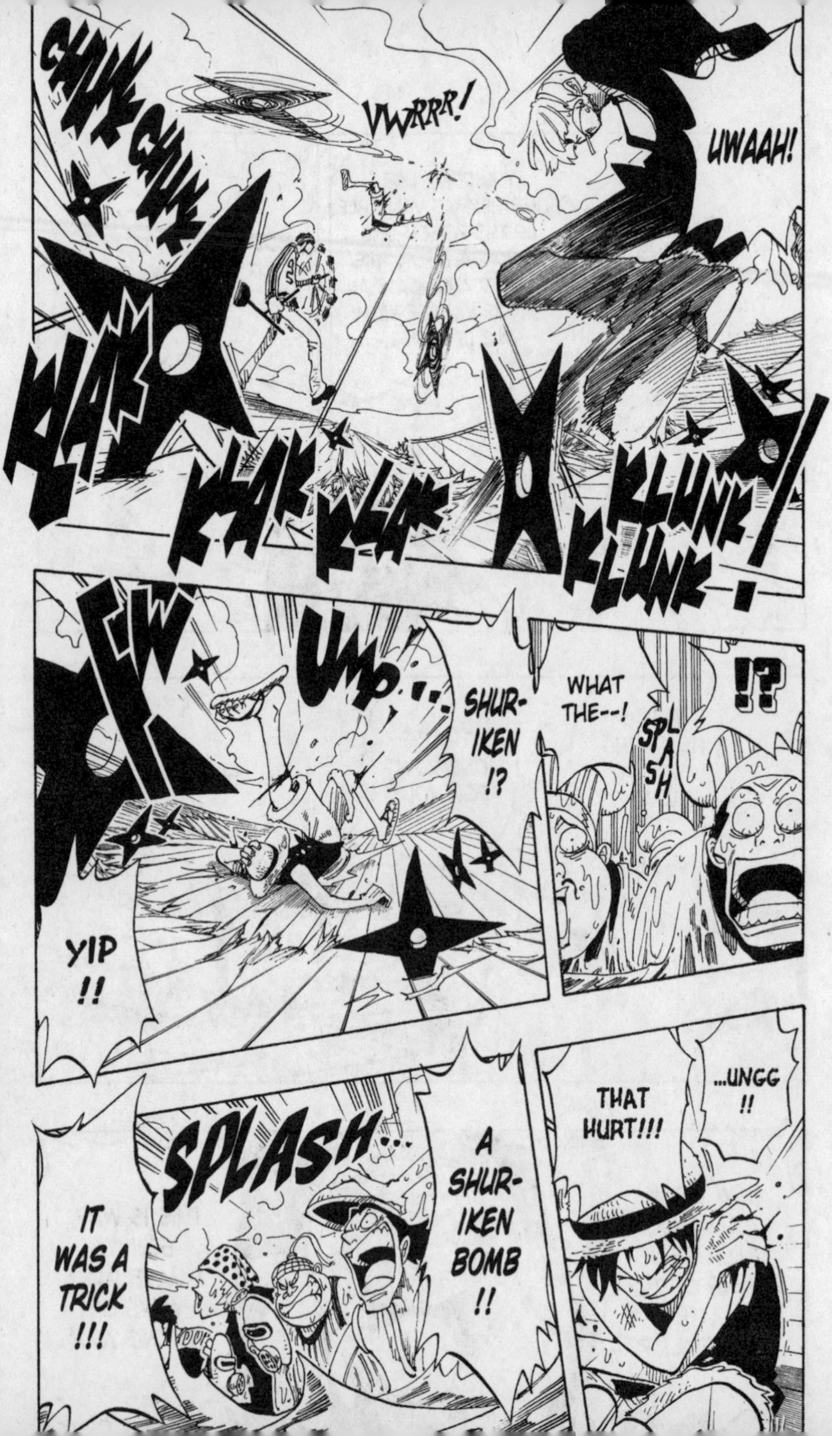
UWAAH!
VWRRR!
CHUNK CHUNK
KLUNK! KLUNK!
!?
SPLASH
WHAT THE--!
SHUR-IKEN !?
UMP...
YIP !!
...UNGG !!
THAT HURT!!!
A SHUR-IKEN BOMB !!
SPLASH...
IT WAS A TRICK !!!

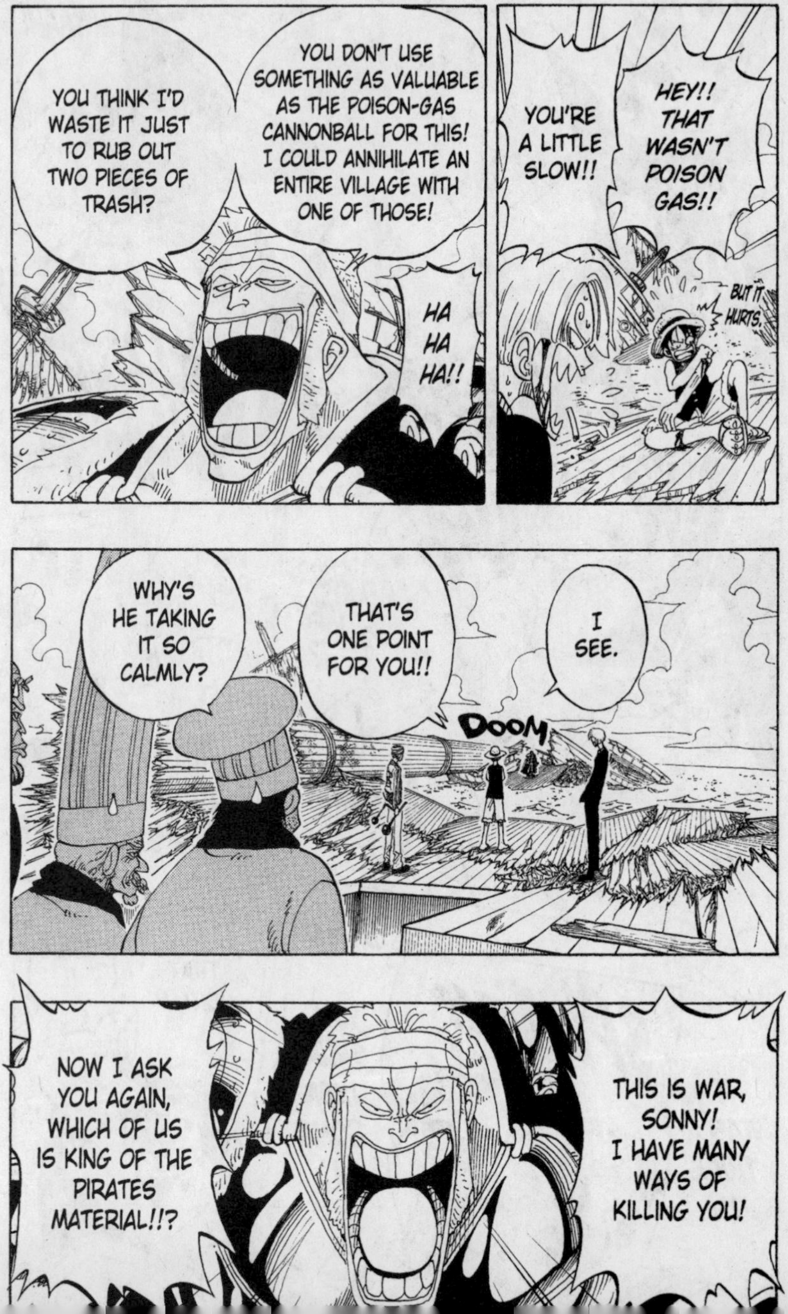
HEY!! THAT WASN'T POISON GAS!!
YOU'RE A LITTLE SLOW!!
BUT IT HURTS.
YOU DON'T USE SOMETHING AS VALUABLE AS THE POISON-GAS CANNONBALL FOR THIS! I COULD ANNIHILATE AN ENTIRE VILLAGE WITH ONE OF THOSE!
YOU THINK I'D WASTE IT JUST TO RUB OUT TWO PIECES OF TRASH?
HA HA HA!!
I SEE.
THAT'S ONE POINT FOR YOU!!
DOOM
WHY'S HE TAKING IT SO CALMLY?
THIS IS WAR, SONNY! I HAVE MANY WAYS OF KILLING YOU!
NOW I ASK YOU AGAIN, WHICH OF US IS KING OF THE PIRATES MATERIAL!!?

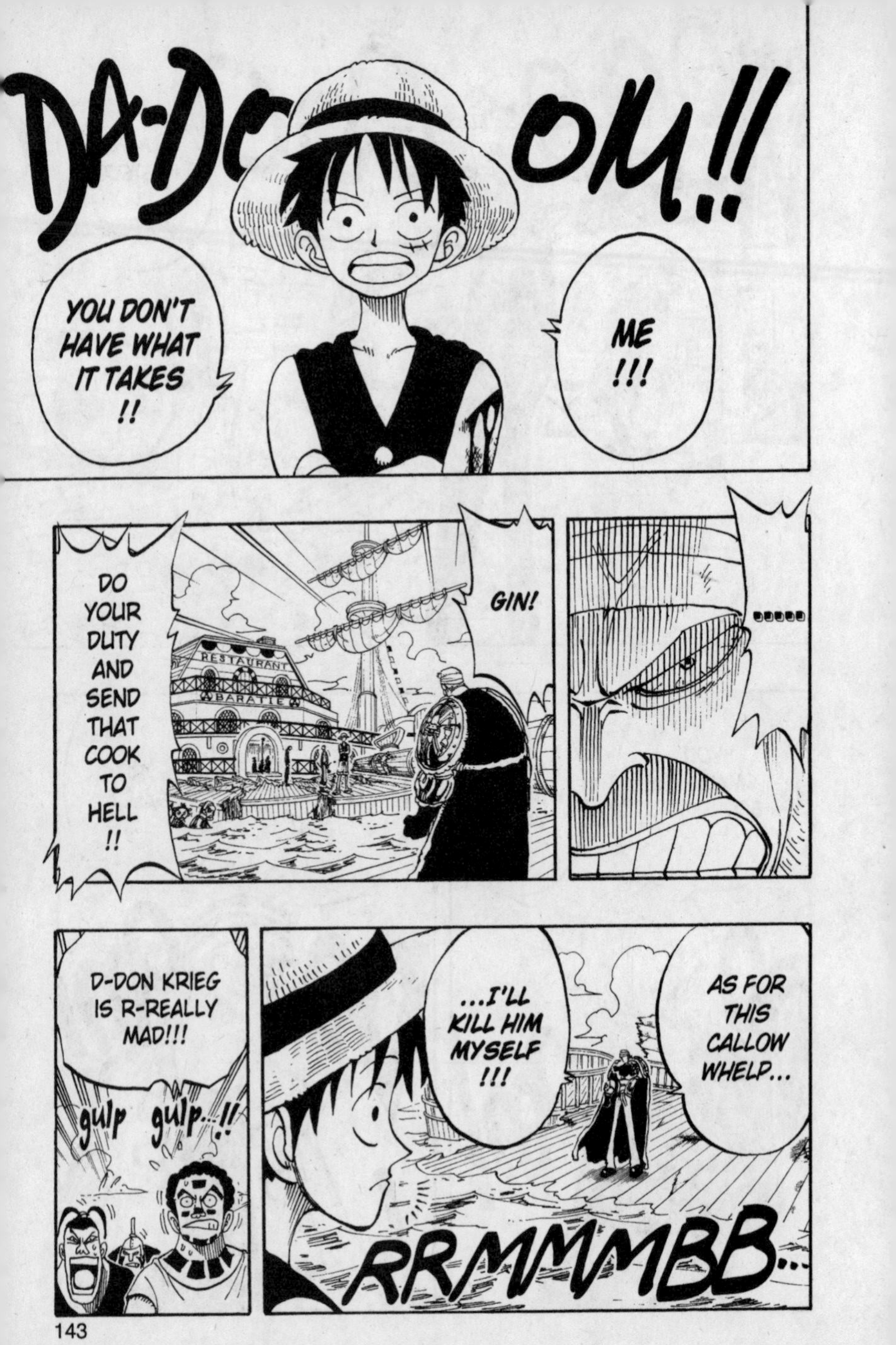
DA-DOOM!!
ME !!!
YOU DON'T HAVE WHAT IT TAKES !!
.....
GIN!
DO YOUR DUTY AND SEND THAT COOK TO HELL !!
RESTAURANT
BARATIE
AS FOR THIS CALLOW WHELP...
...I'LL KILL HIM MYSELF !!!
RRMMMMBB...
D-DON KRIEG IS R-REALLY MAD!!!
gulp gulp...!!

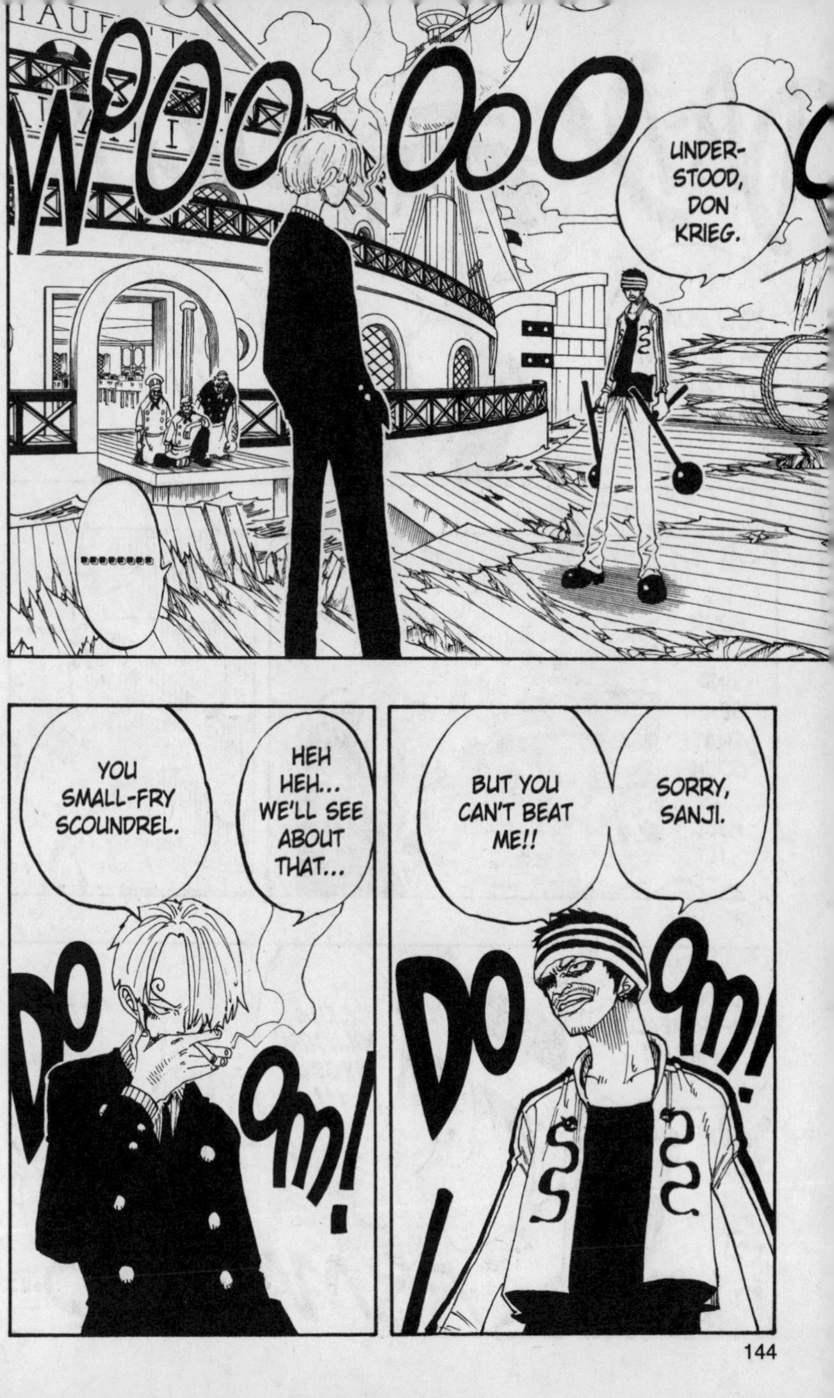
WOOOOOOO
UNDER-STOOD, DON KRIEG.
........
SORRY, SANJI.
BUT YOU CAN'T BEAT ME!!
DOOM!
HEH HEH... WE'LL SEE ABOUT THAT...
YOU SMALL-FRY SCOUNDREL.
DOOM!

READ THIS WAY

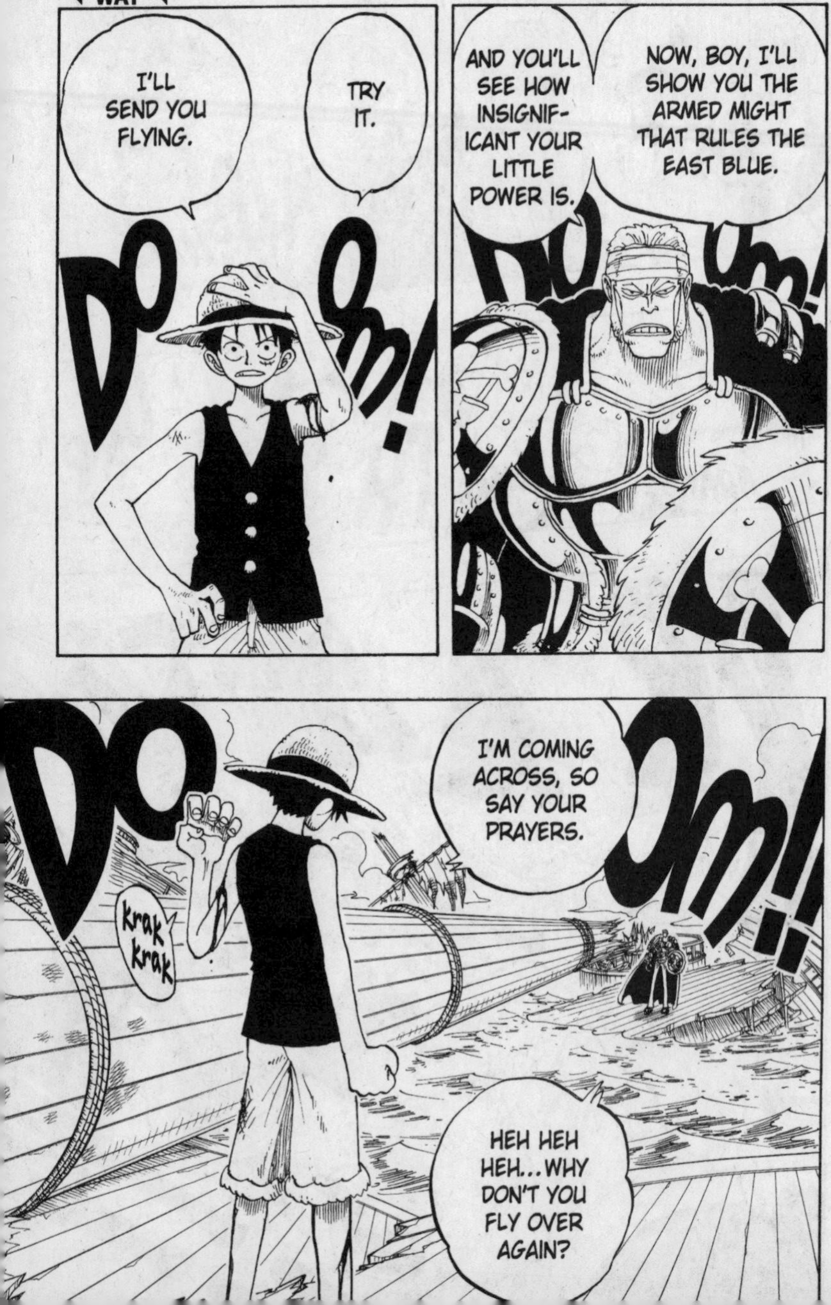
NOW, BOY, I'LL SHOW YOU THE ARMED MIGHT THAT RULES THE EAST BLUE.
AND YOU'LL SEE HOW INSIGNIF-ICANT YOUR LITTLE POWER IS.
DOOOM!
I'LL SEND YOU FLYING.
TRY IT.
DOOOM!
DOOOM!!
I'M COMING ACROSS, SO SAY YOUR PRAYERS.
krak krak
HEH HEH HEH...WHY DON'T YOU FLY OVER AGAIN?

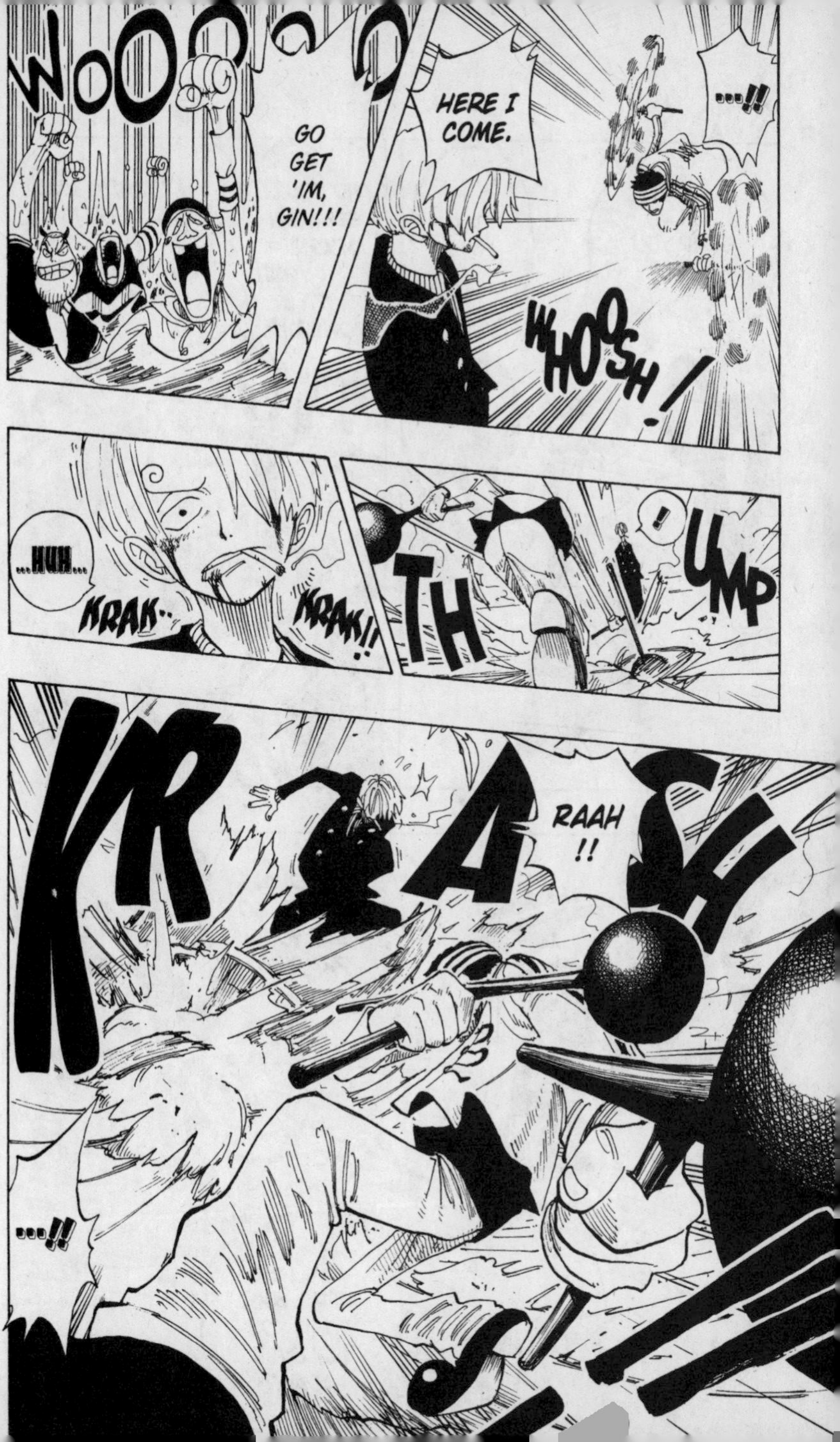

...!!
HERE I COME.
WHOOSH!
WOOOOO
GO GET 'IM, GIN!!!
!
THUMP
...HUH...
KRAK..
KRAK!!
KRASH
RAAH !!
...!!

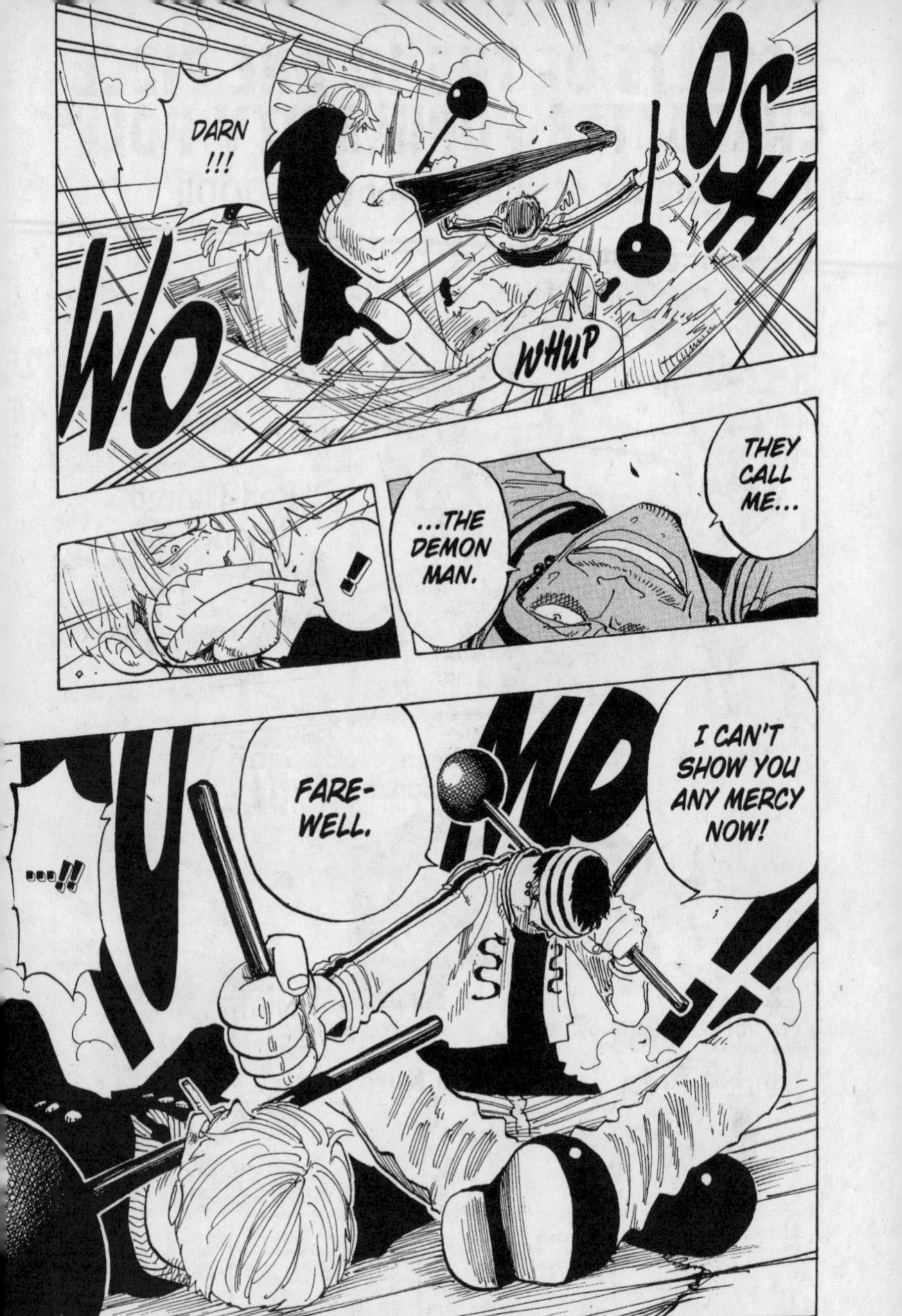
OSH
DARN !!!
WO
WHUP
THEY CALL ME...
...THE DEMON MAN.
!
I CAN'T SHOW YOU ANY MERCY NOW!
FARE-WELL.
...!!

# RESULTS OF THE 1st ONE PIECE CHARACTER POPULARITY POLL*

## Total number of submissions: 36,000!!

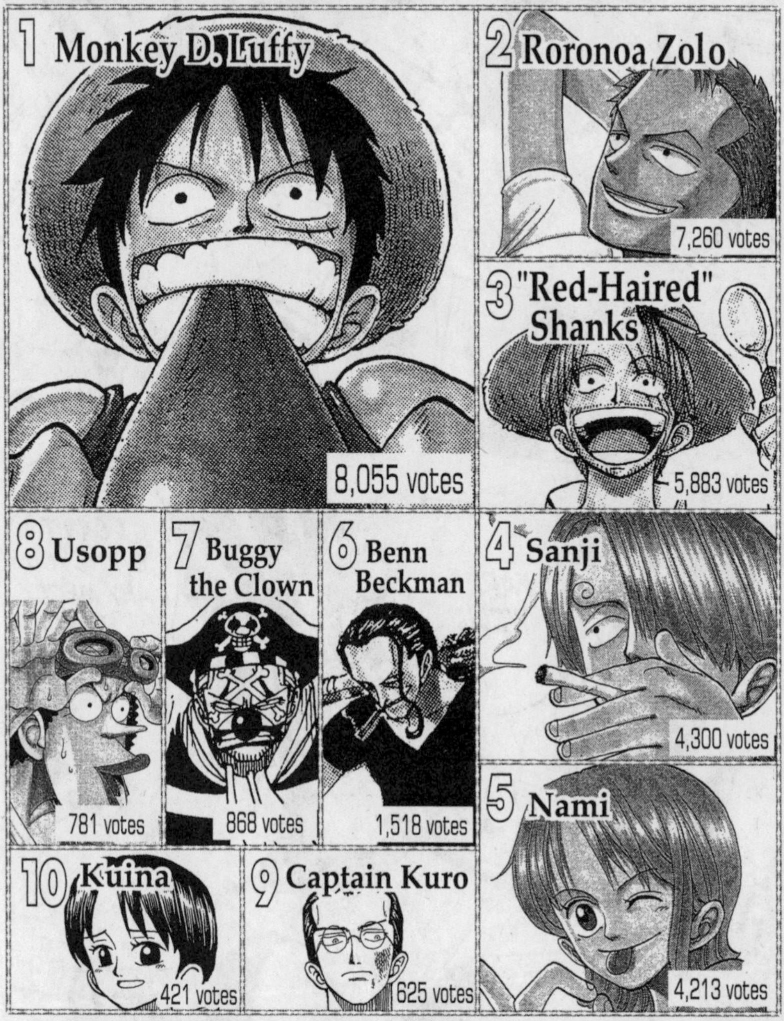

1 Monkey D. Luffy
8,055 votes
2 Roronoa Zolo
7,260 votes
3 "Red-Haired" Shanks
5,883 votes
4 Sanji
4,300 votes
5 Nami
4,213 votes
6 Benn Beckman
1,518 votes
7 Buggy the Clown
868 votes
8 Usopp
781 votes
9 Captain Kuro
625 votes
10 Kuina
421 votes


| | | | | | | | |
|---|---|---|---|---|---|---|---|
| 33rd place | Rabbit-snake | 26th place | Yasopp | 19th place | Django | 11th place | Gin |
| 33rd place | Pig-lion | 27th place | Patty | 20th place | Meowban brothers | 12th place | Makino |
| 35th place | Ganzak | 28th place | Yosaku | 21st place | Merry | 13th place | Gold Roger |
| 35th place | Rika | 29th place | Pepper | 22nd place | Zeff | 14th place | Mihawk |
| 35th place | Captain of the Naval base | 30th place | Mayor Boodle | 23rd place | Mohji | 15th place | Gaimon |
| | | 31st place | Master of the Near Sea | 24th place | Johnny | 16th place | Krieg |
| Many votes for others, too. | | 32nd place | Panda | 25th place | Cabaji | 17th place | Kaya |
| | | | | | | 18th place | Koby |

*Hey American **One Piece** fans! This popularity contest surveyed Japanese readers. Who is your favorite **One Piece** character? Let us know at:
One Piece c/o SHONEN JUMP, P.O. Box 77010, San Francisco, CA 94107

# Chapter 61: THE DEMON

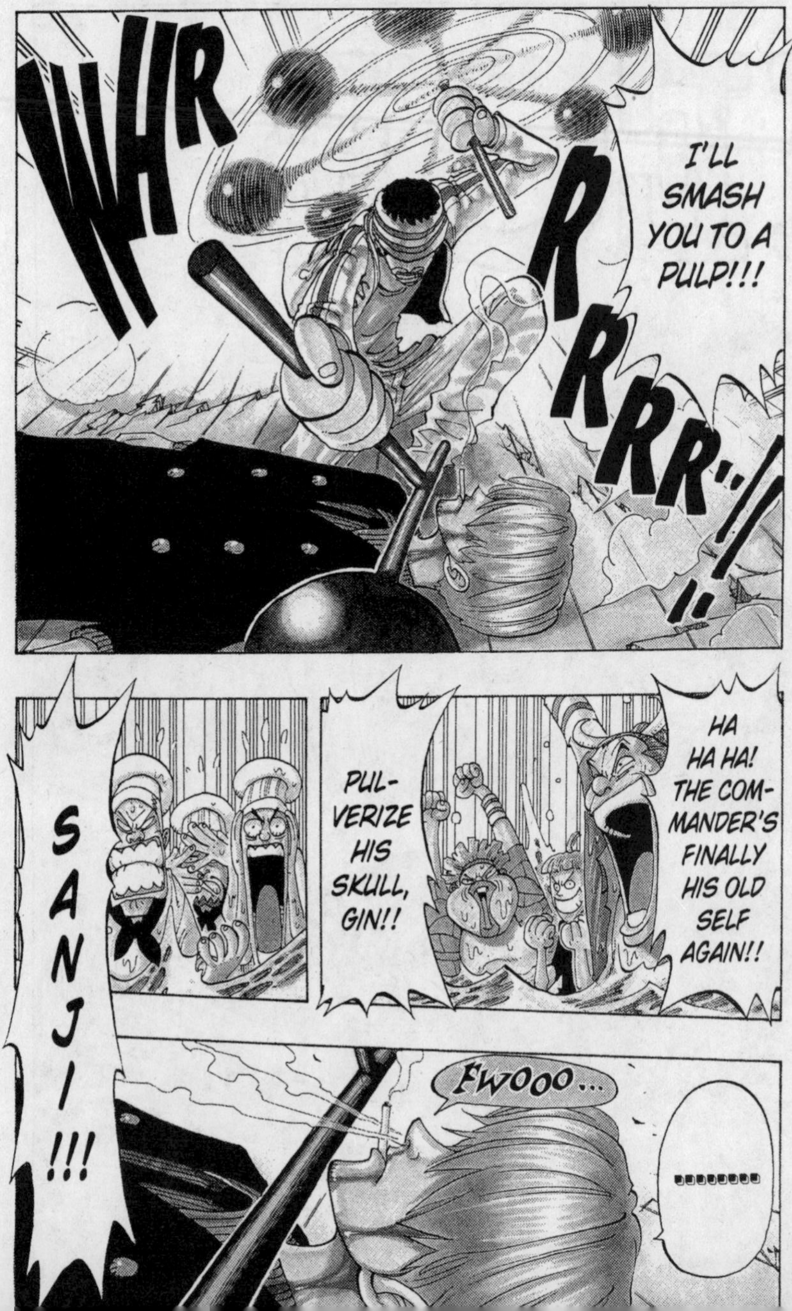
WHRRRRRR!!
I'LL SMASH YOU TO A PULP!!!
HA HA HA! THE COM-MANDER'S FINALLY HIS OLD SELF AGAIN!!
PUL-VERIZE HIS SKULL, GIN!!
SANJI!!!
FWOOO...
........

# Chapter 61: THE DEMON

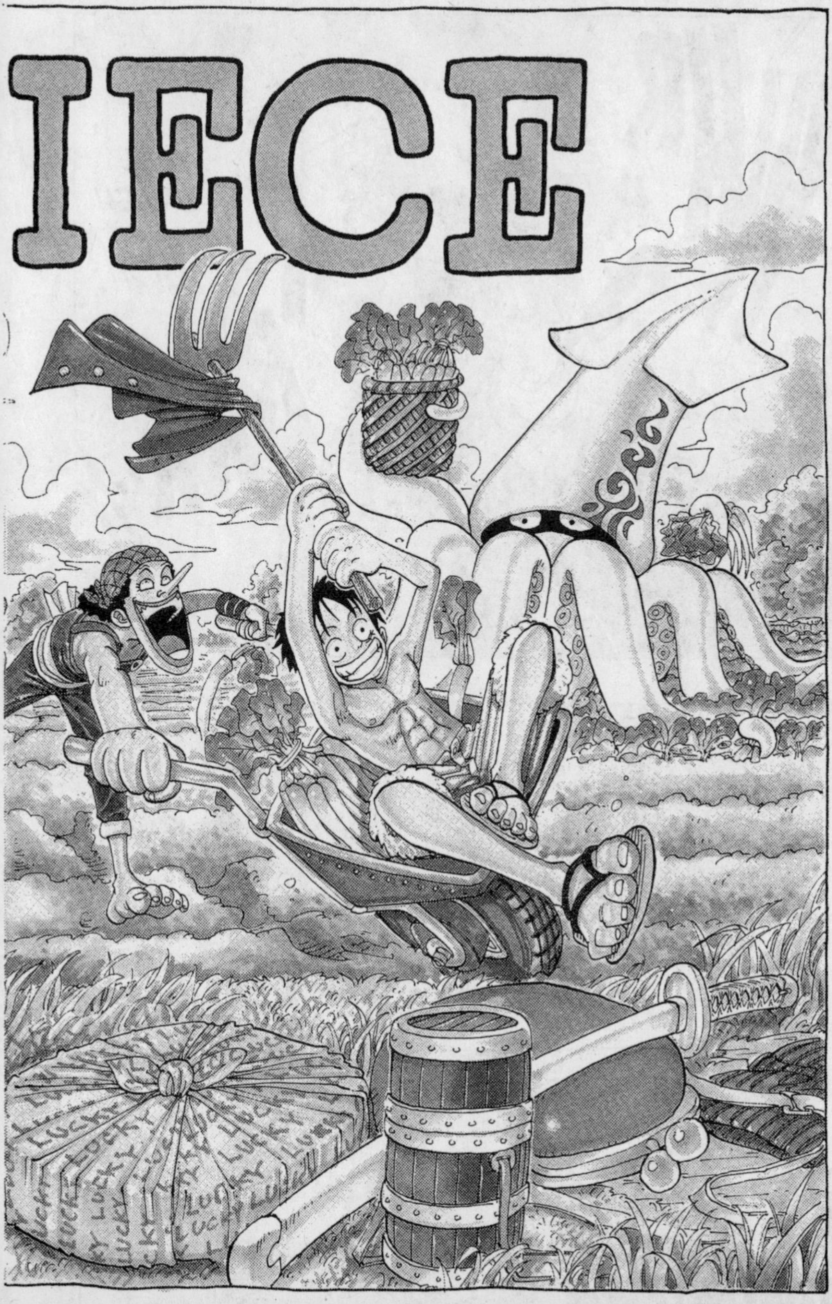
IECE

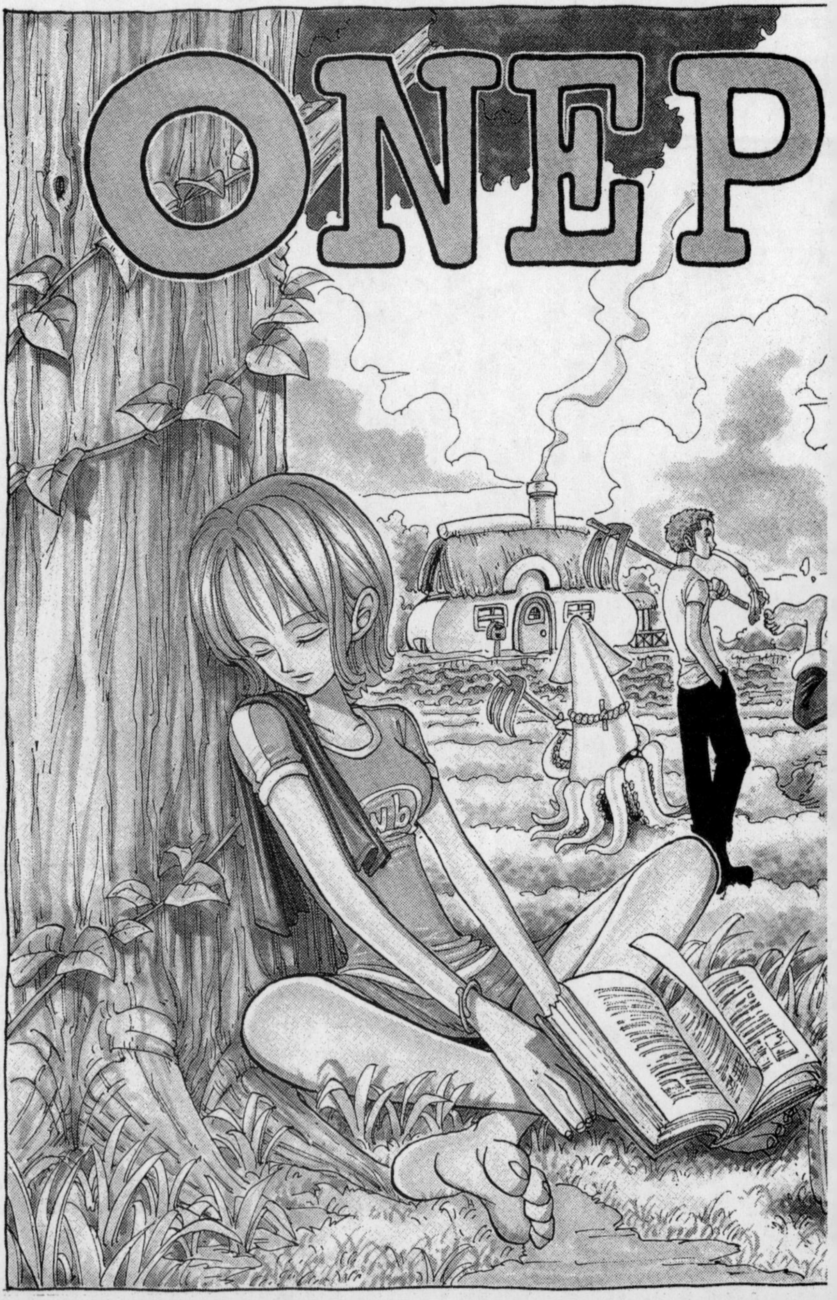
ONEP

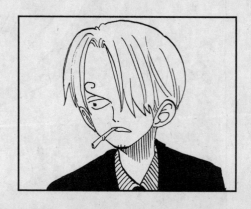

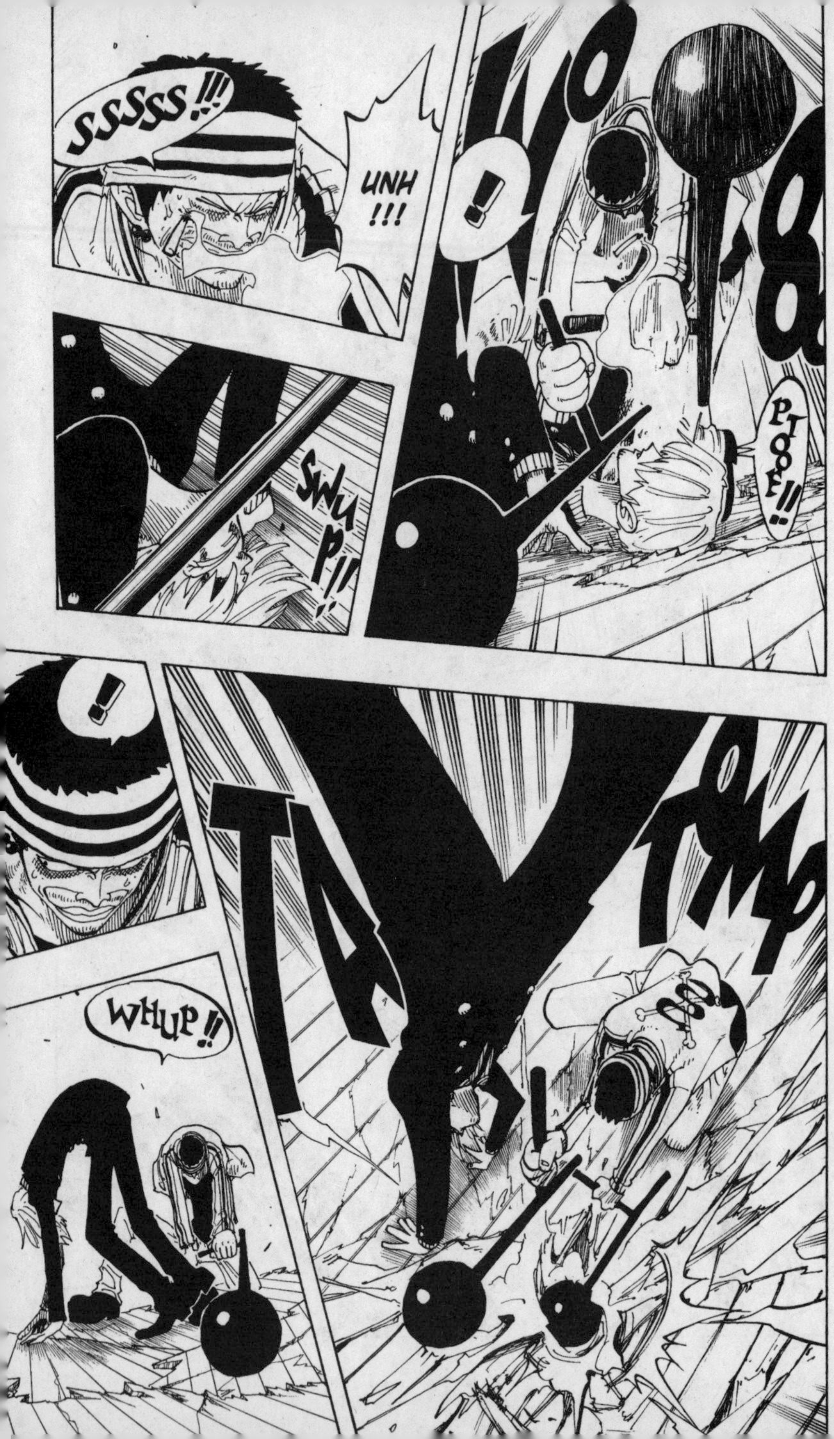
!
PTOOF!!
SSSSS!!!
UNH !!!
SWUP!!
!
WHUP!!

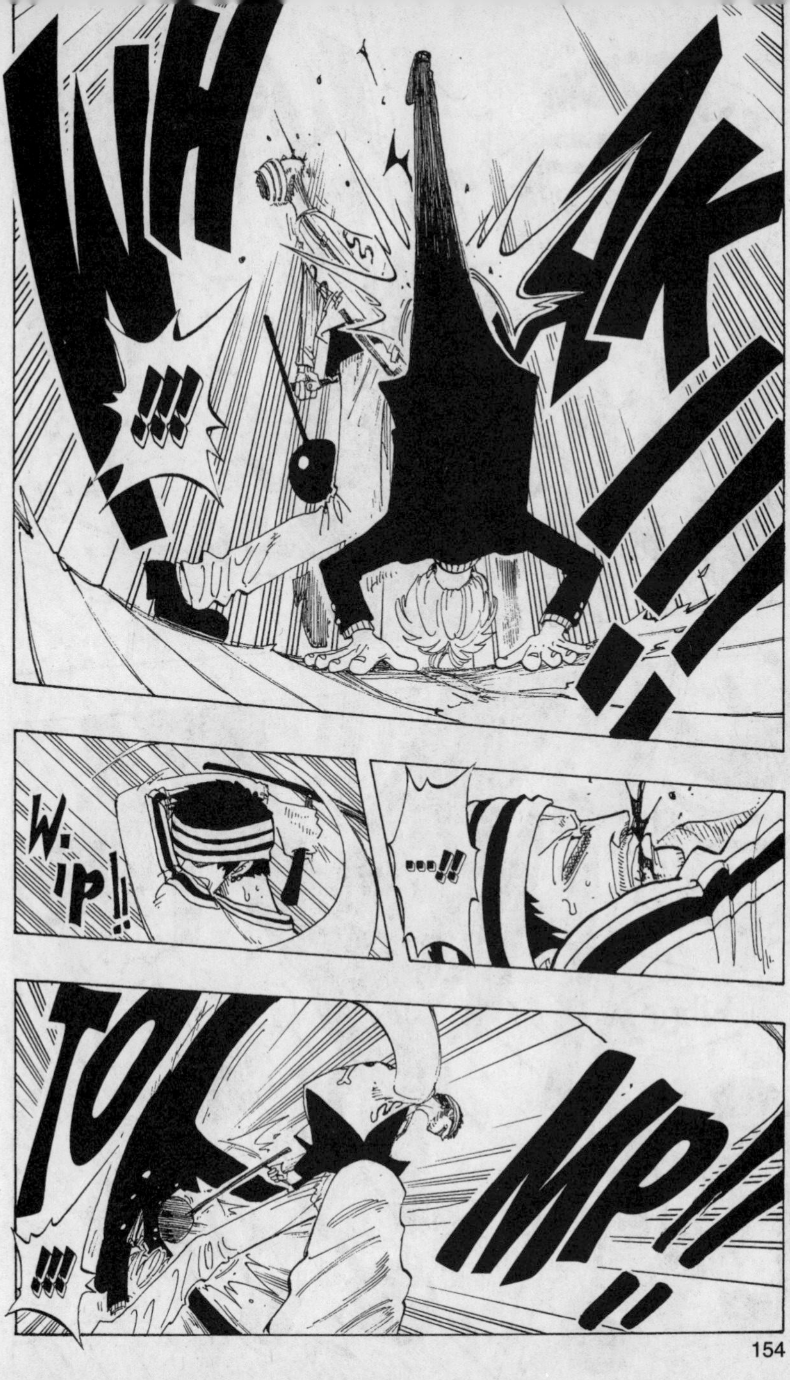
WHAK!!!
...!!
WHIP!!
THUMP!!

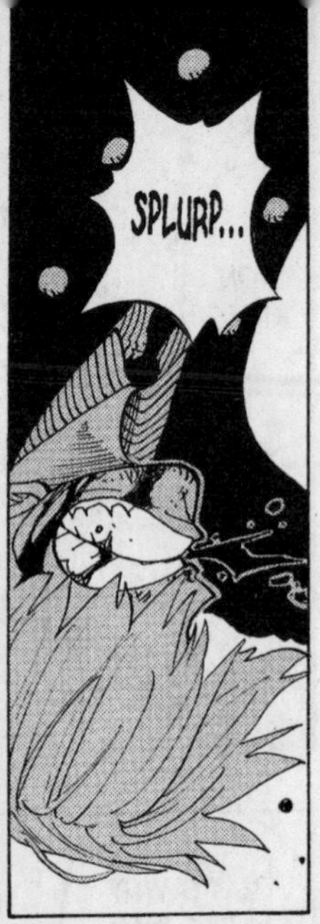
SPLURP...

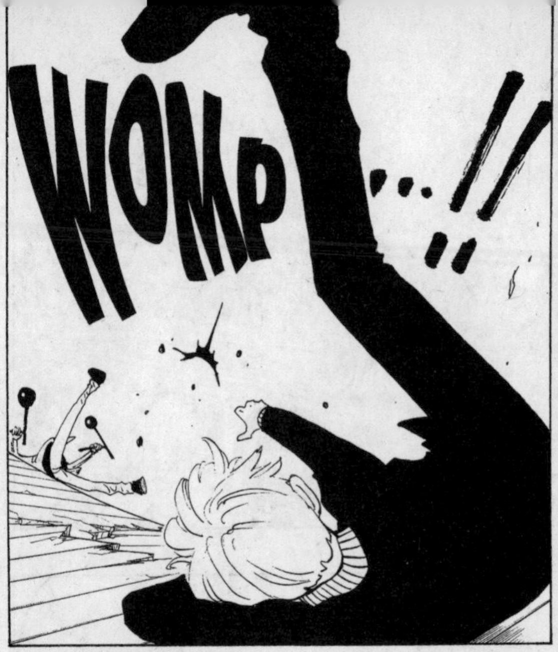
WOMP...!!

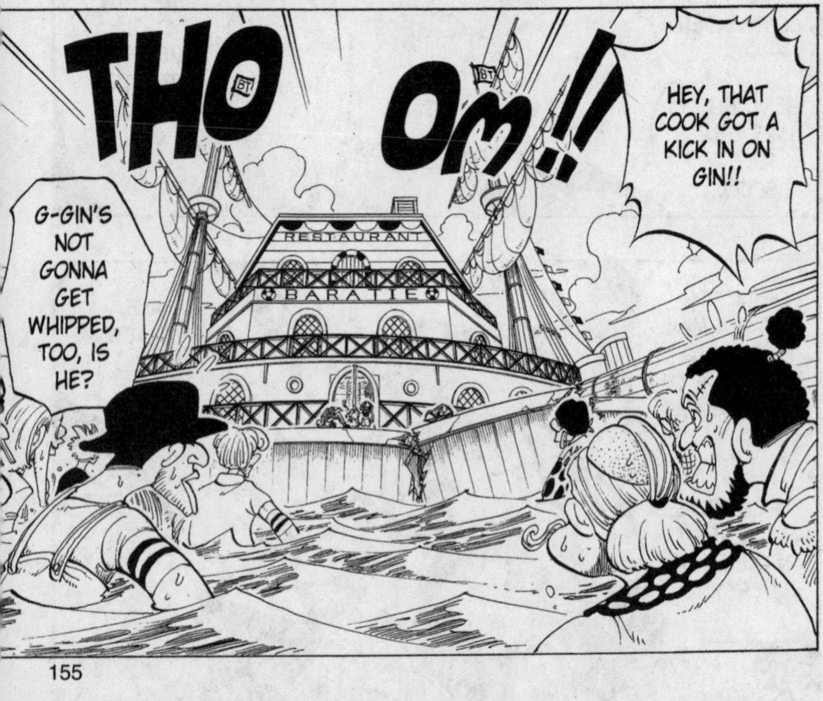
THOOM!!
RESTAURANT
BARATIE
HEY, THAT COOK GOT A KICK IN ON GIN!!
G-GIN'S NOT GONNA GET WHIPPED, TOO, IS HE?

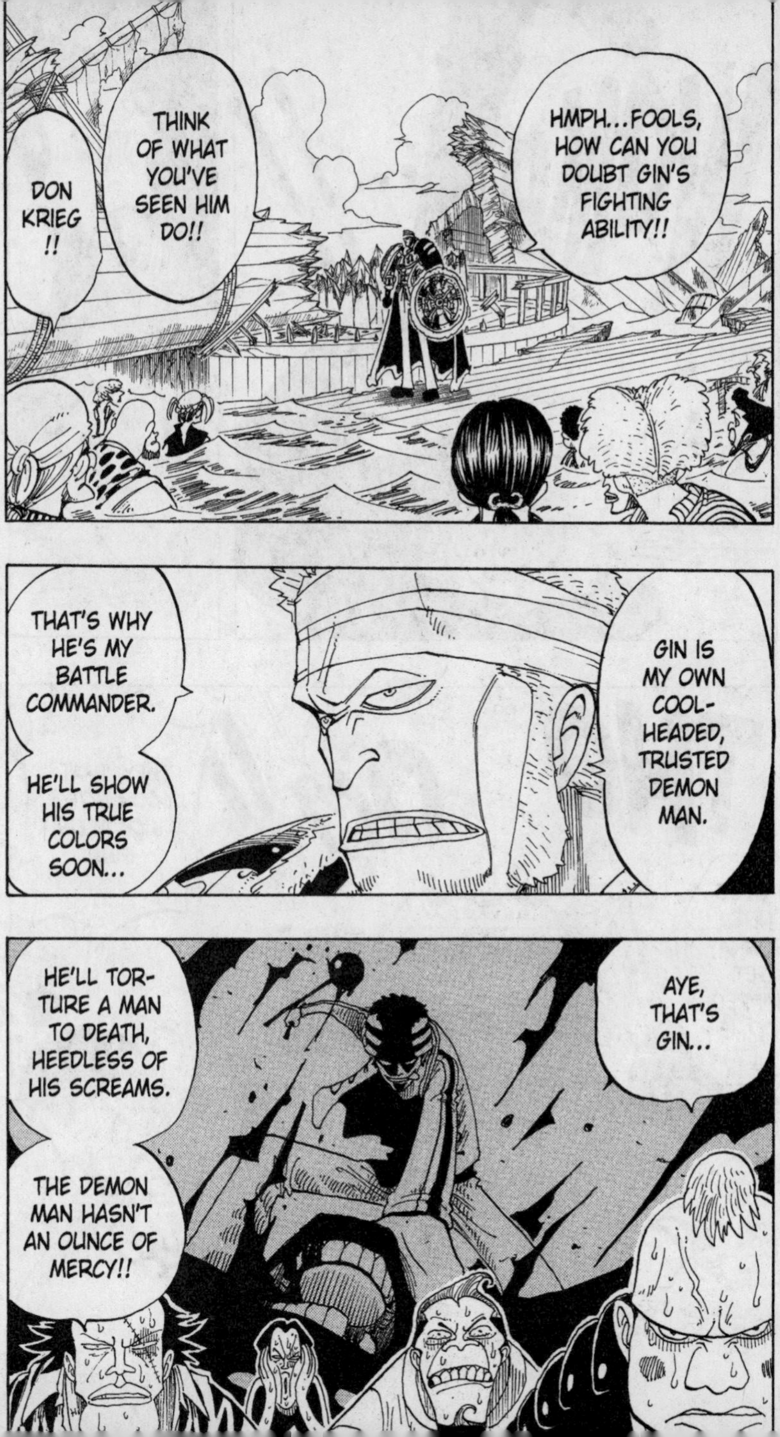
HMPH...FOOLS, HOW CAN YOU DOUBT GIN'S FIGHTING ABILITY!!
THINK OF WHAT YOU'VE SEEN HIM DO!!
DON KRIEG !!
GIN IS MY OWN COOL-HEADED, TRUSTED DEMON MAN.
THAT'S WHY HE'S MY BATTLE COMMANDER.
HE'LL SHOW HIS TRUE COLORS SOON...
AYE, THAT'S GIN...
HE'LL TORTURE A MAN TO DEATH, HEEDLESS OF HIS SCREAMS.
THE DEMON MAN HASN'T AN OUNCE OF MERCY!!

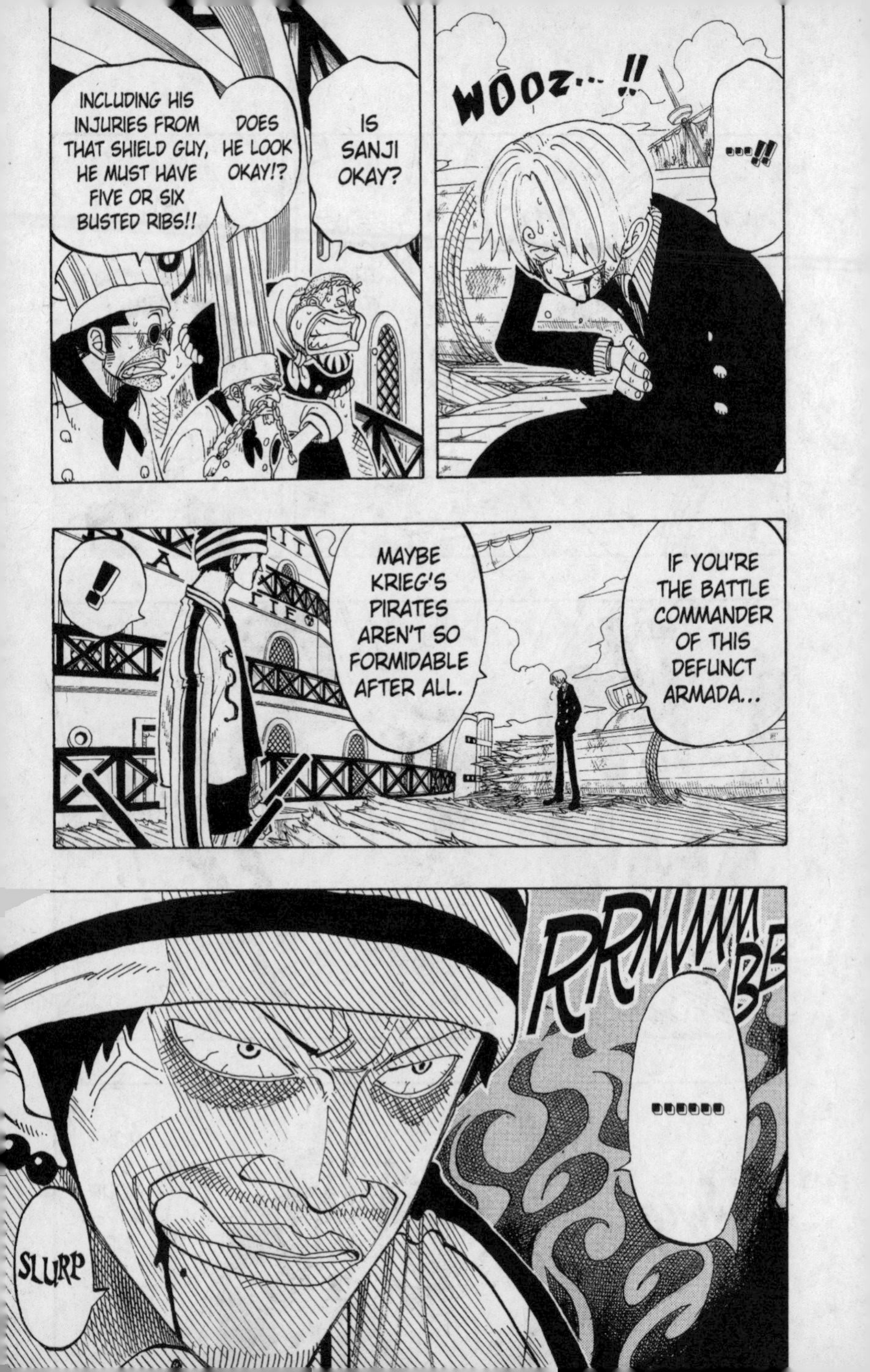
WOOZ...!!
...!!
IS SANJI OKAY?
DOES HE LOOK OKAY!?
INCLUDING HIS INJURIES FROM THAT SHIELD GUY, HE MUST HAVE FIVE OR SIX BUSTED RIBS!!
IF YOU'RE THE BATTLE COMMANDER OF THIS DEFUNCT ARMADA...
MAYBE KRIEG'S PIRATES AREN'T SO FORMIDABLE AFTER ALL.
!
RRMMBB
......
SLURP

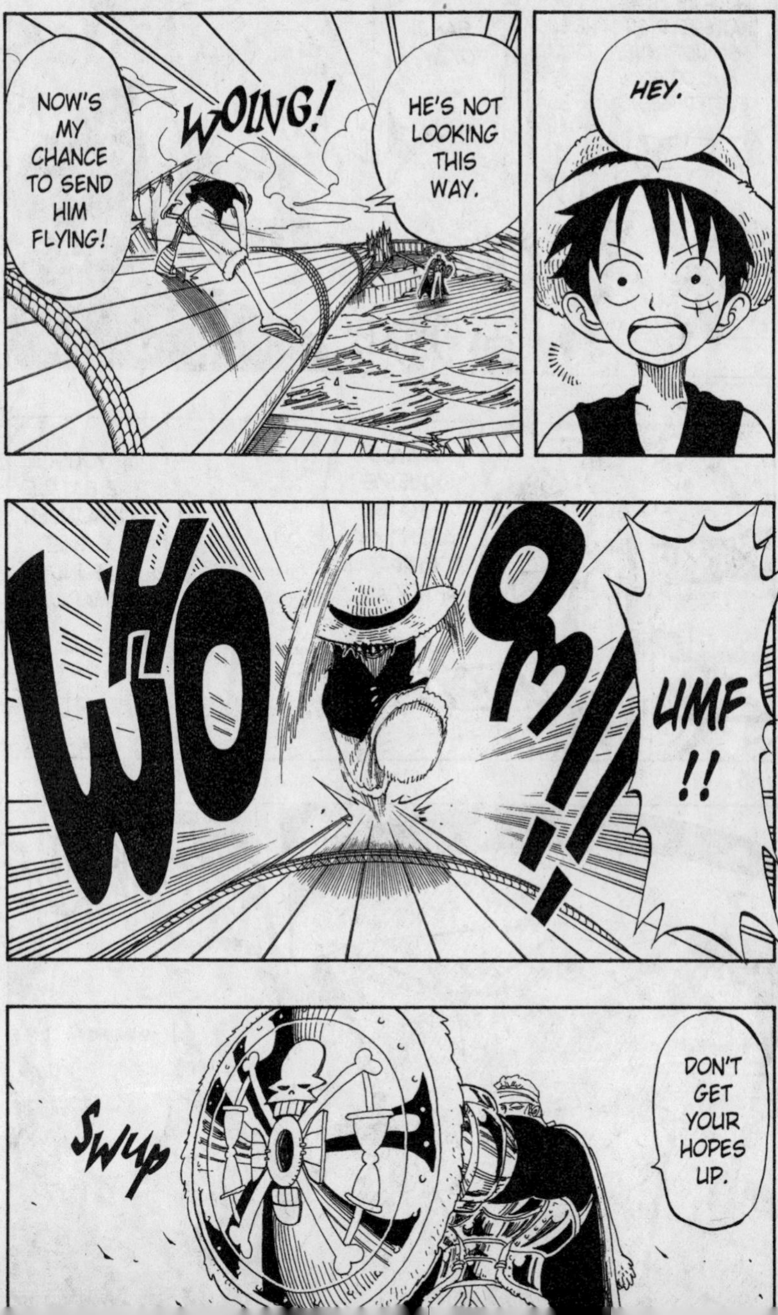
HEY.
HE'S NOT LOOKING THIS WAY.
WOING!
NOW'S MY CHANCE TO SEND HIM FLYING!
UMF !!
WOOM!!
DON'T GET YOUR HOPES UP.
SWUP

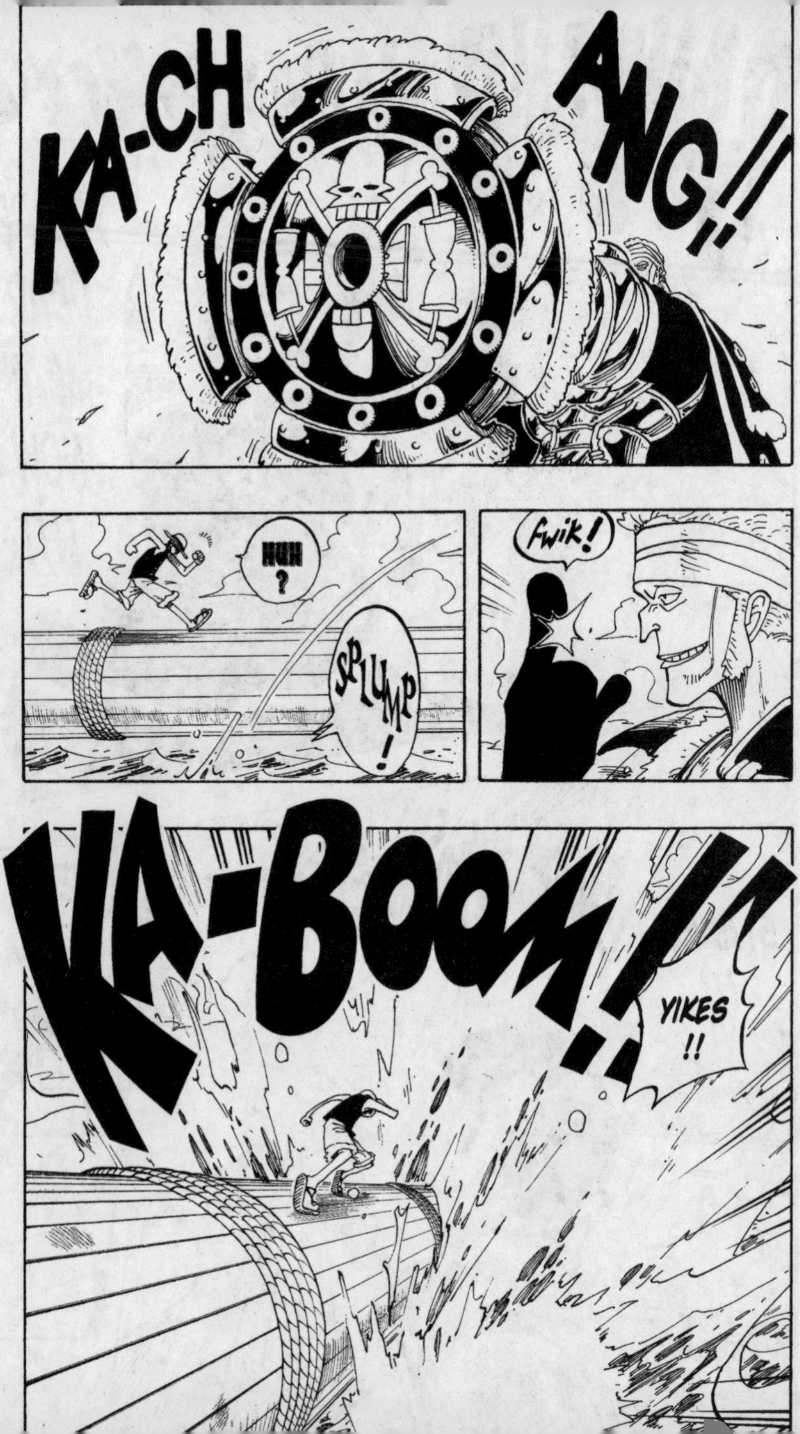
KA-CHANG!!
fwik!
HUH ?
SPLUMP !
KA-BOOM!!
YIKES !!

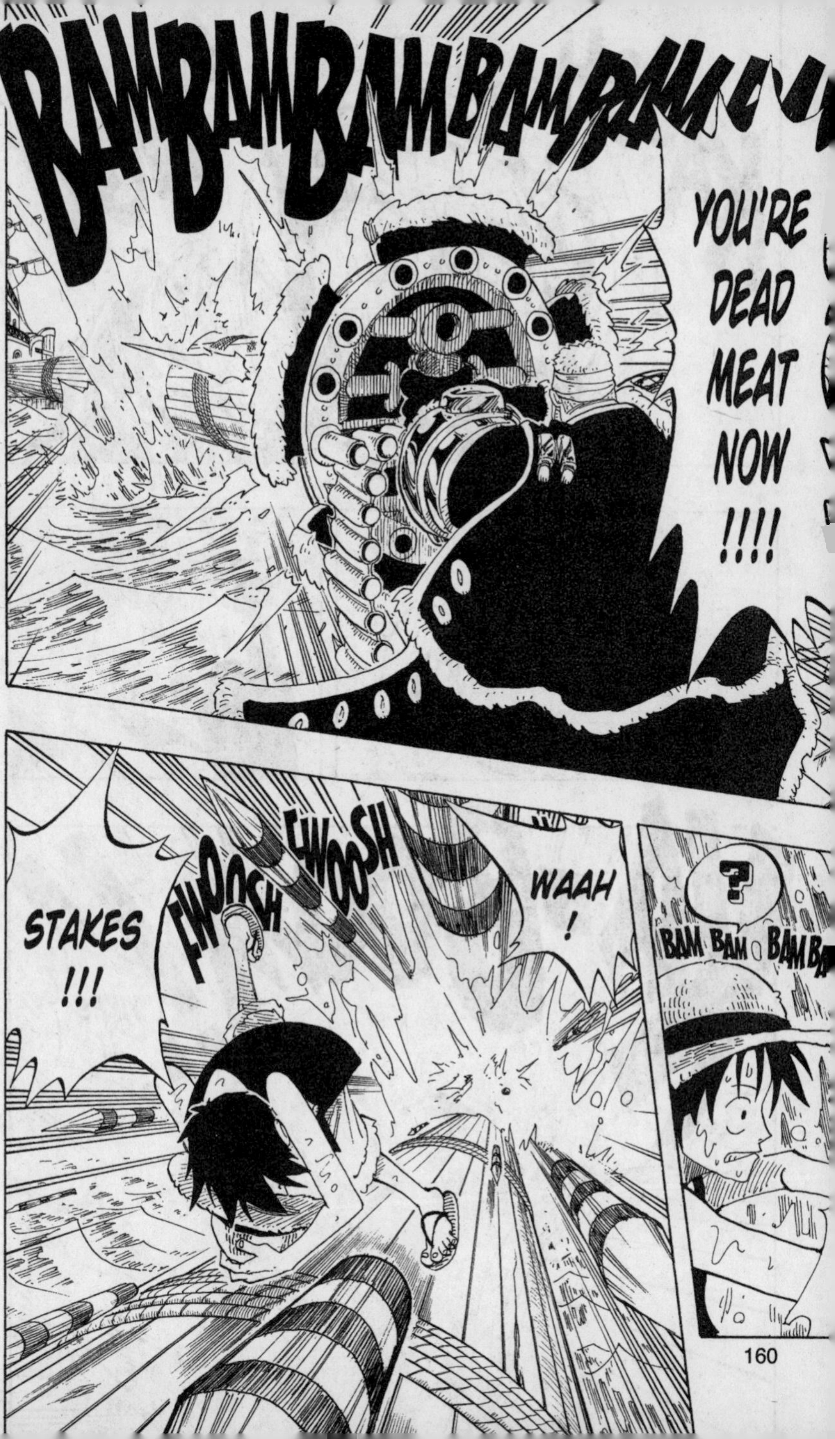

BAMBAMBAMBAMBAM
YOU'RE DEAD MEAT NOW!!!!
?
BAM BAM BAM
WAAH!
FWOOSH
FWOOSH
STAKES!!!

READ THIS WAY

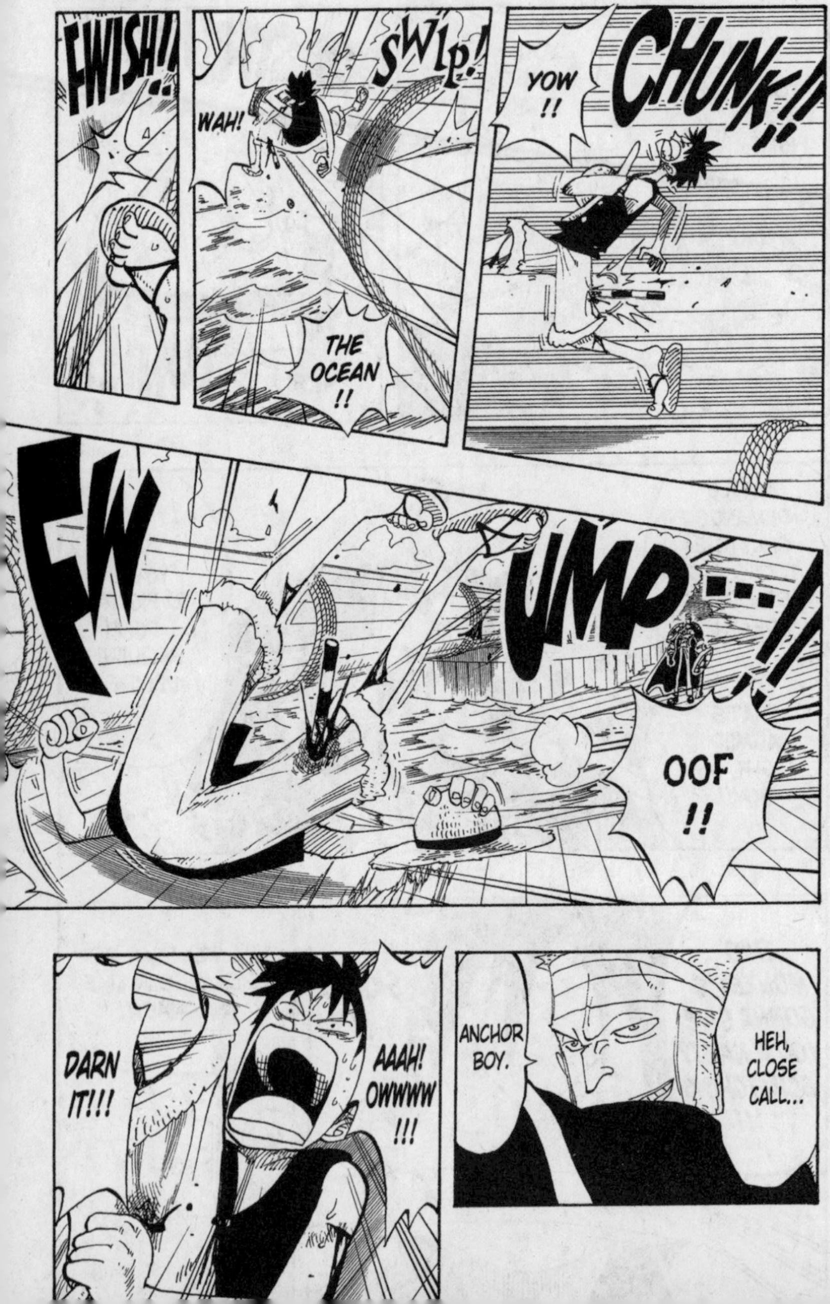

CHUNK!!
YOW!!
SWIP!
WAH!
THE OCEAN!!
FWISH!!
FWUMP...!!
OOF!!
HEH, CLOSE CALL...
ANCHOR BOY.
AAAH! OWWWW!!!
DARN IT!!!

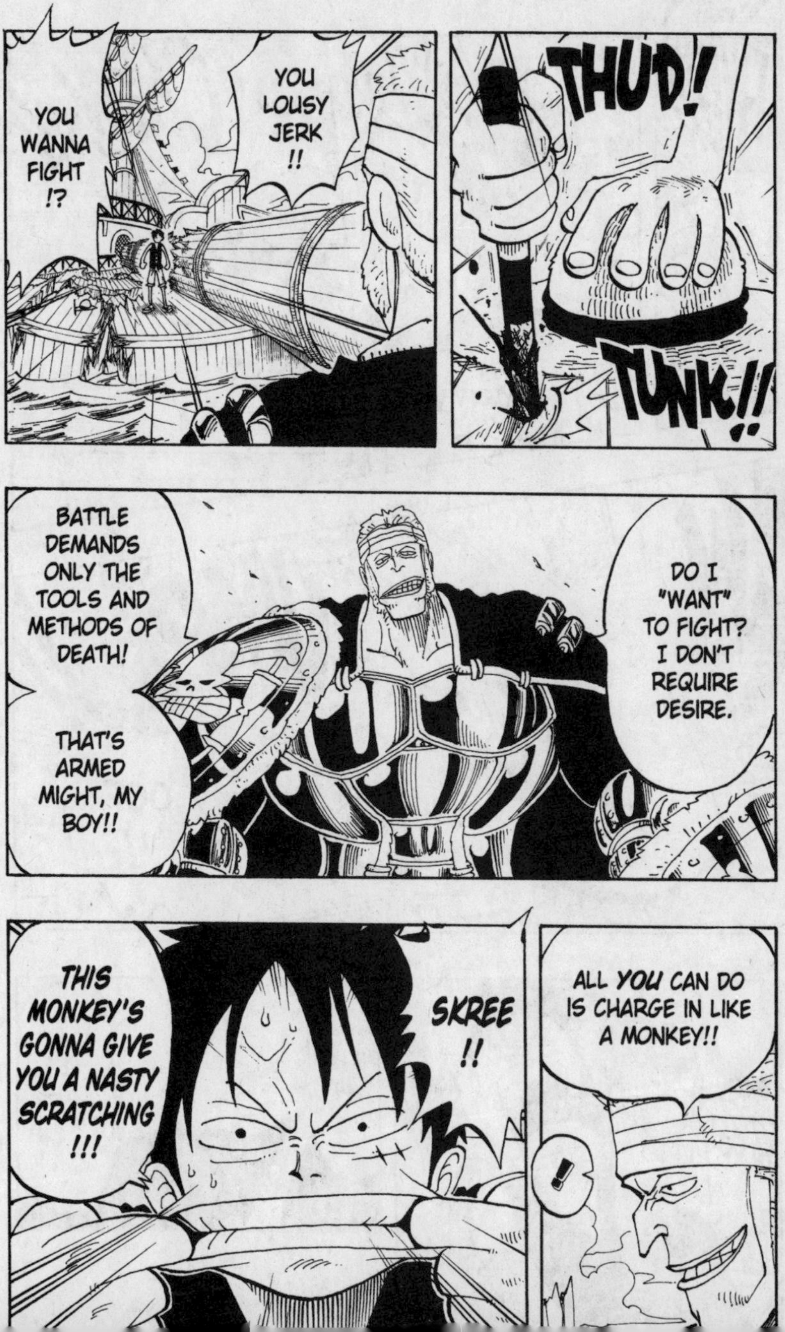
THUD!
TUNK!!
YOU LOUSY JERK!!
YOU WANNA FIGHT!?
DO I "WANT" TO FIGHT? I DON'T REQUIRE DESIRE.
BATTLE DEMANDS ONLY THE TOOLS AND METHODS OF DEATH!
THAT'S ARMED MIGHT, MY BOY!!
ALL YOU CAN DO IS CHARGE IN LIKE A MONKEY!!
!
SKREE!!
THIS MONKEY'S GONNA GIVE YOU A NASTY SCRATCHING!!!

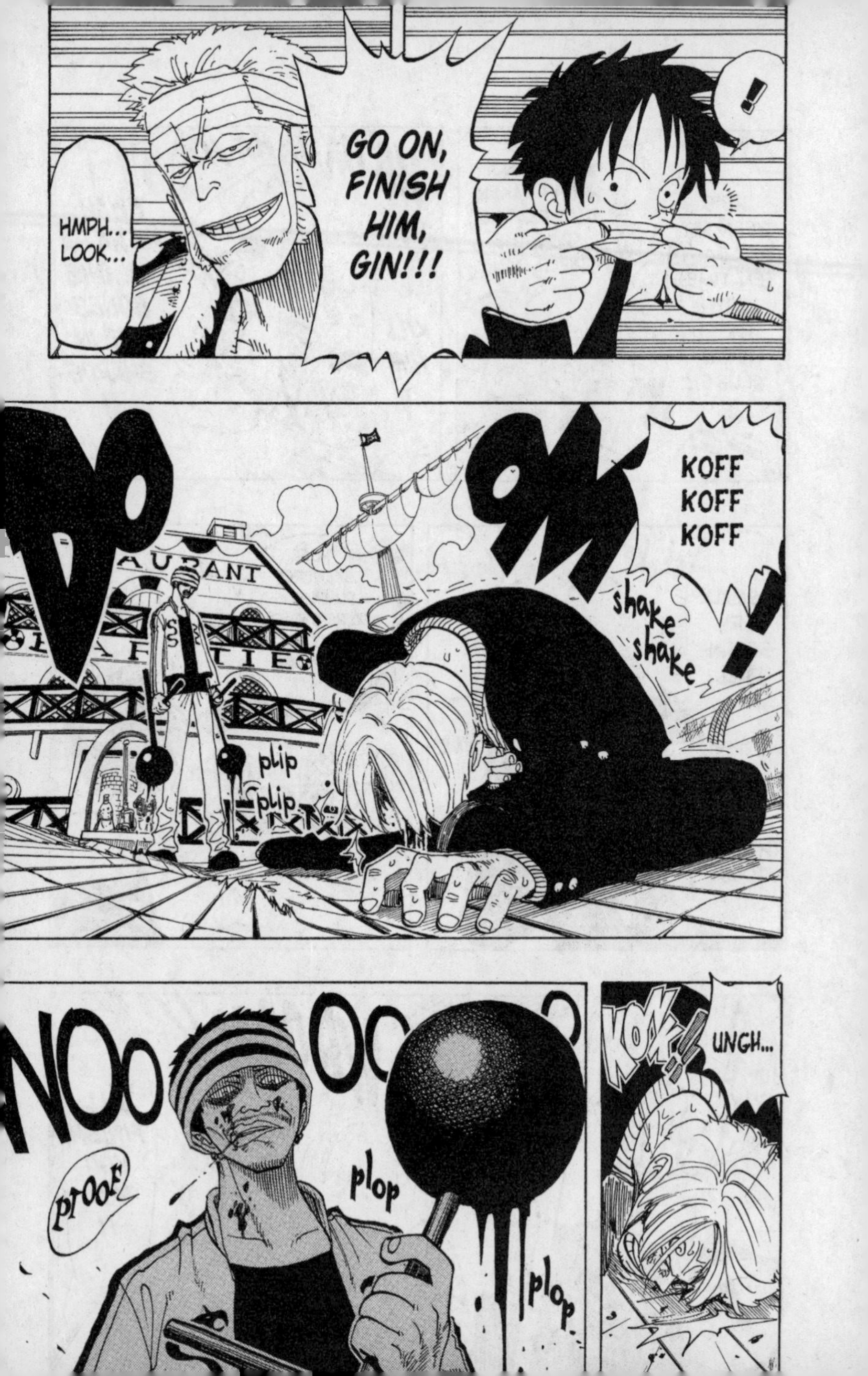
!
GO ON, FINISH HIM, GIN!!!
HMPH... LOOK...
KOFF KOFF KOFF
DOOM
shake shake
!
plip plip
KOK!!
UNGH...
NOOOO
ptoof
plop
plop

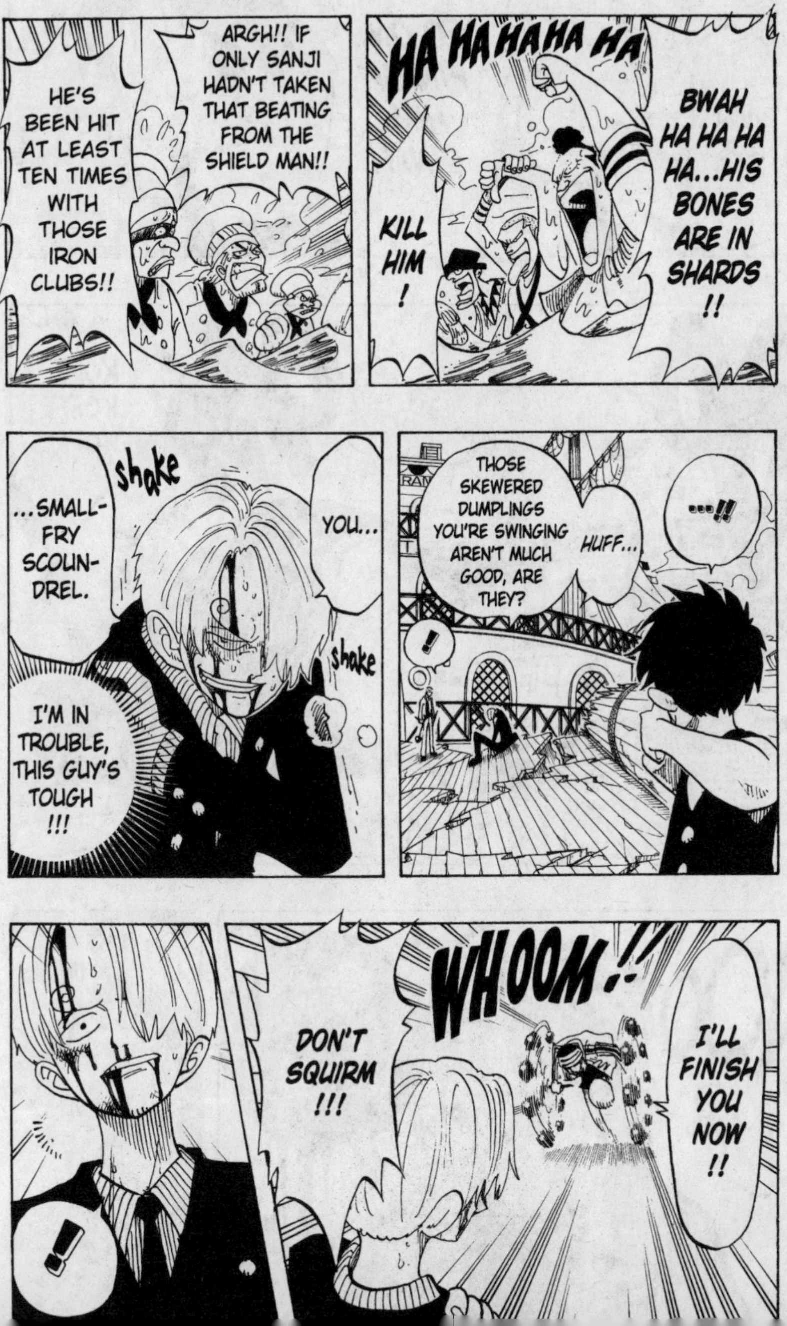
HA HA HAHA HA HA
BWAH HA HA HA HA...HIS BONES ARE IN SHARDS!!
KILL HIM!
ARGH!! IF ONLY SANJI HADN'T TAKEN THAT BEATING FROM THE SHIELD MAN!!
HE'S BEEN HIT AT LEAST TEN TIMES WITH THOSE IRON CLUBS!!
...!!
HUFF...
THOSE SKEWERED DUMPLINGS YOU'RE SWINGING AREN'T MUCH GOOD, ARE THEY?
!
YOU...
shake
...SMALL-FRY SCOUN-DREL.
shake
I'M IN TROUBLE, THIS GUY'S TOUGH!!!
WHOOM!!
I'LL FINISH YOU NOW!!
DON'T SQUIRM!!!
!

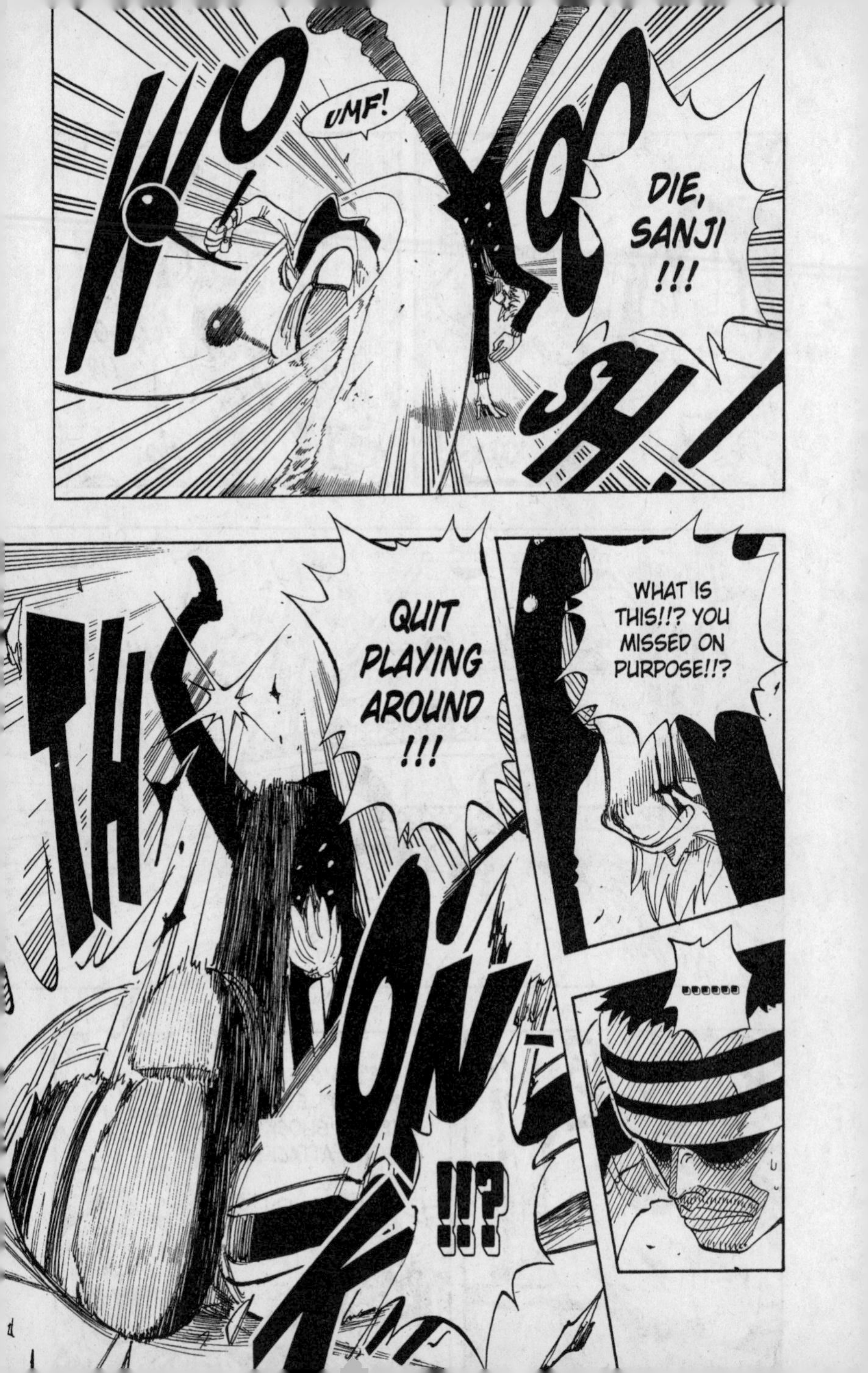
DIE, SANJI !!!
UMF!
WHAT IS THIS!!? YOU MISSED ON PURPOSE!!?
......
QUIT PLAYING AROUND !!!
!!?

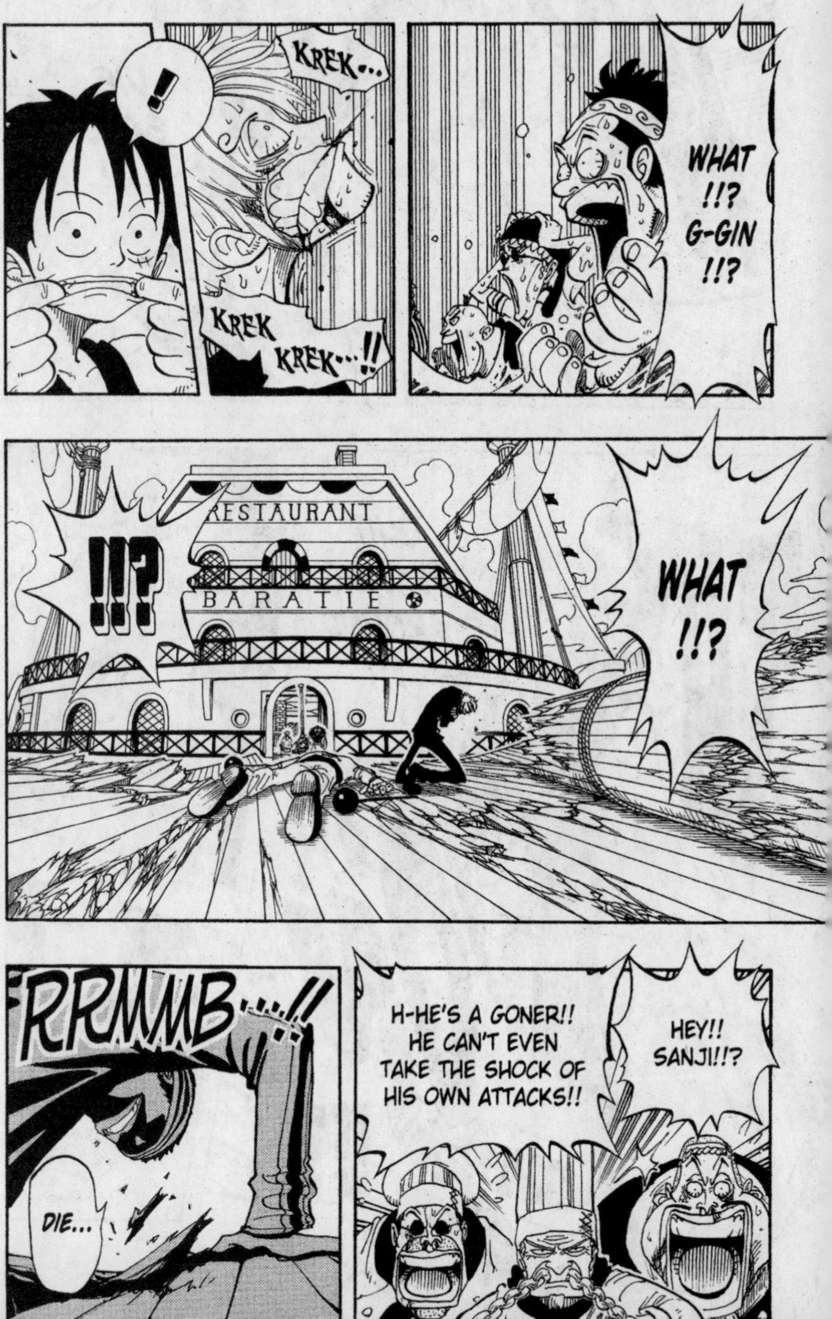
WHAT !!? G-GIN !!?
KREK...
!
KREK KREK...!!
WHAT !!?
!!?
HEY!! SANJI!!?
H-HE'S A GONER!! HE CAN'T EVEN TAKE THE SHOCK OF HIS OWN ATTACKS!!
RRMMB...!!
DIE...

READ THIS WAY

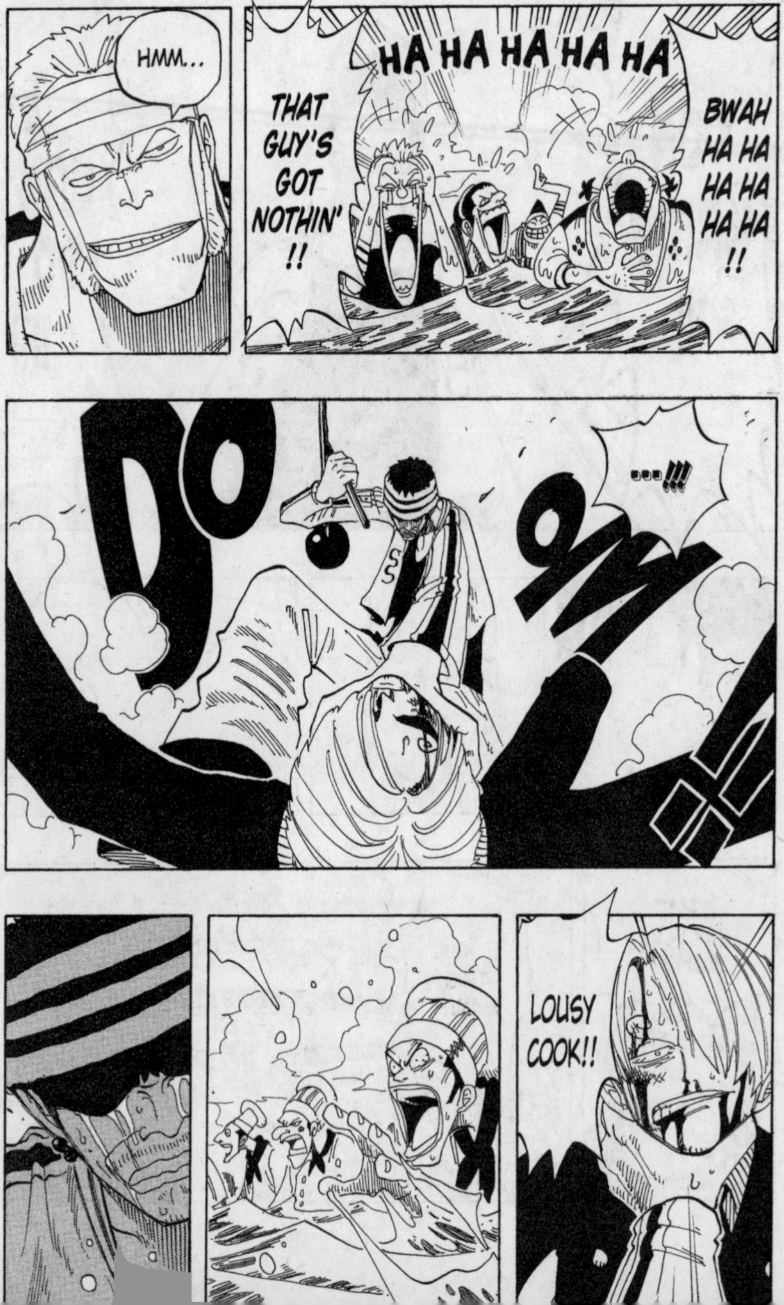
HA HA HA HA HA
BWAH HA HA HA HA HA HA!!
THAT GUY'S GOT NOTHIN'!!
HMM...
...!!!
DOOM!!
LOUSY COOK!!

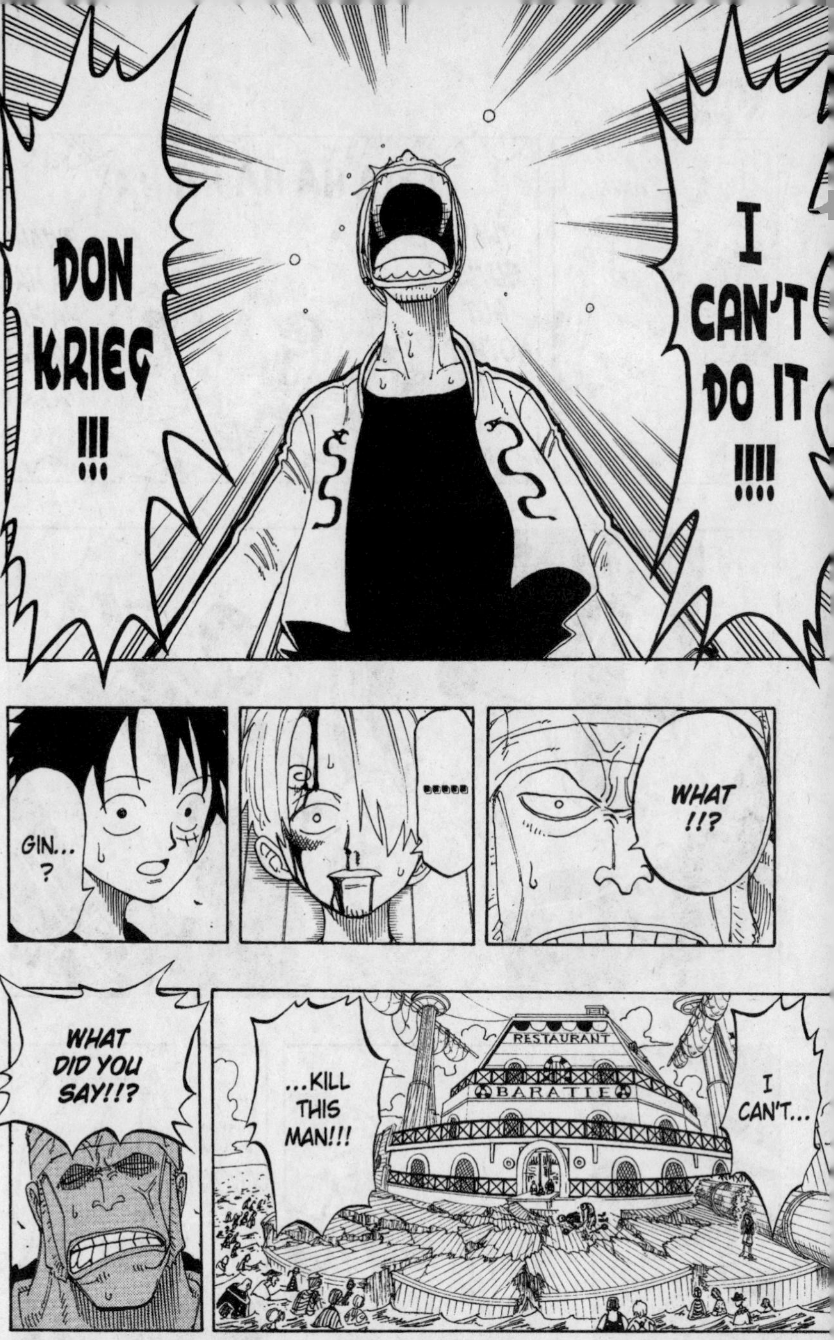
I CAN'T DO IT !!!!
DON KRIEG !!!
WHAT !!?
.....
GIN... ?
I CAN'T...
RESTAURANT
BARATIE
...KILL THIS MAN!!!
WHAT DID YOU SAY!!?

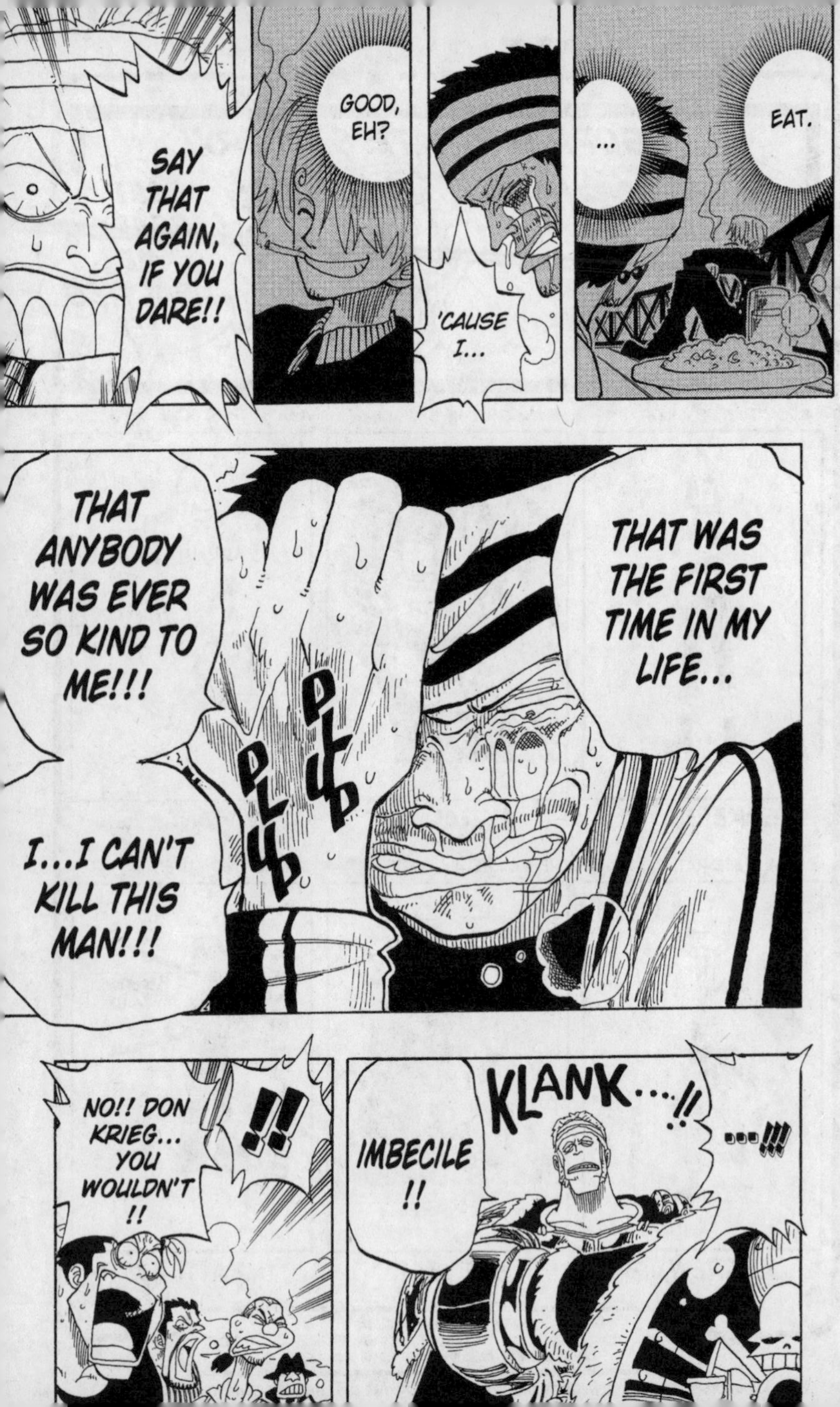
EAT.
...
'CAUSE I...
GOOD, EH?
SAY THAT AGAIN, IF YOU DARE!!
THAT WAS THE FIRST TIME IN MY LIFE...
THAT ANYBODY WAS EVER SO KIND TO ME!!!
PLUP PLUP
I...I CAN'T KILL THIS MAN!!!
KLANK....!!
...!!!
IMBECILE !!
!!
NO!! DON KRIEG... YOU WOULDN'T !!

# ONE PIECE

## USOPP'S PIRATE GALLERY!

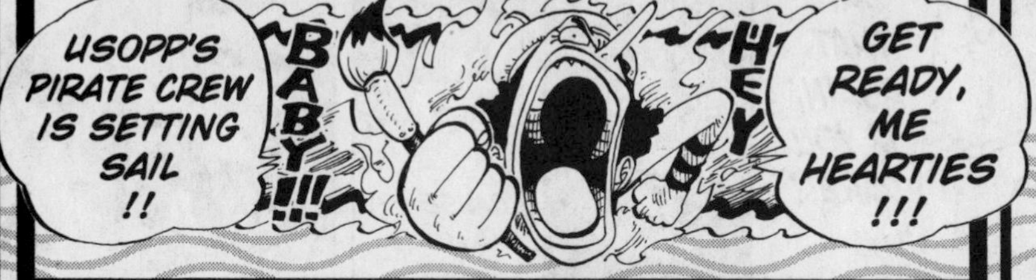

GET READY, ME HEARTIES!!!
HEY
BABY!!!
USOPP'S PIRATE CREW IS SETTING SAIL!!


A PORTRAIT OF VALOR.

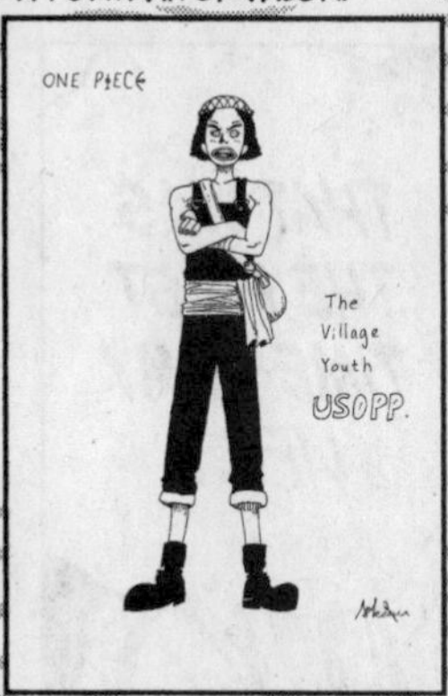

ONE PIECE
The Village Youth
USOPP.


SAKEENA, 17

HEY! SOMEONE'S MISSING!

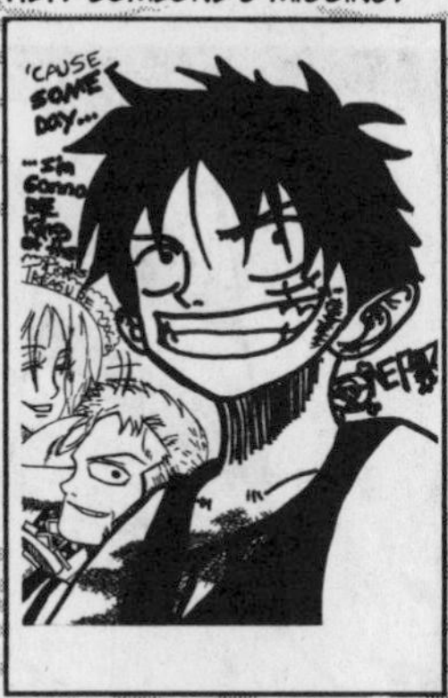

'CAUSE SOME DAY...


SARAH, 14

A SIGHT FOR SORE EYES...

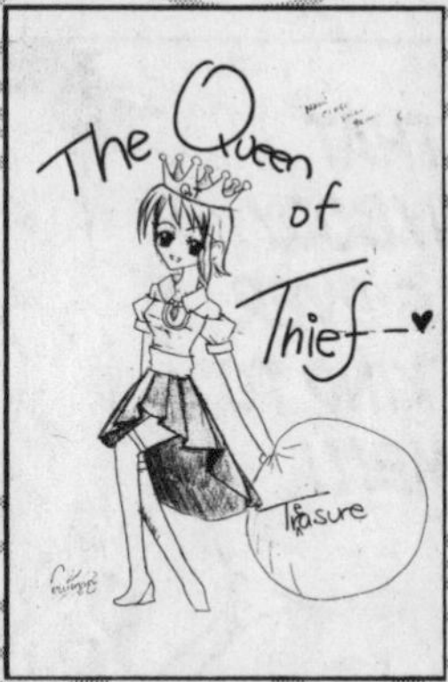

The Queen of Thief -♥
Treasure


VIVIANA, 15

...UM...NICE HAT...

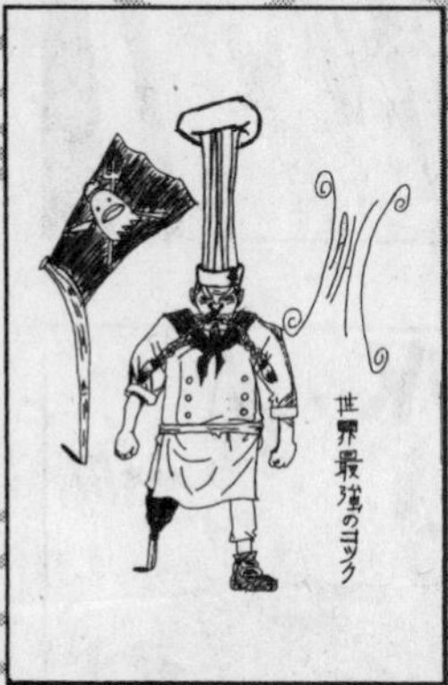

世界最強のコック


ANDREW, 13

THE GANG'S ALL HERE.

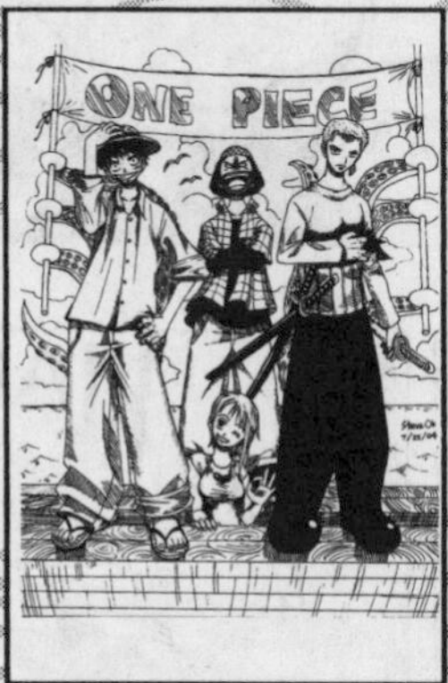

ONE PIECE


STEVE, 17

ZOLO'S...SO CUTE!

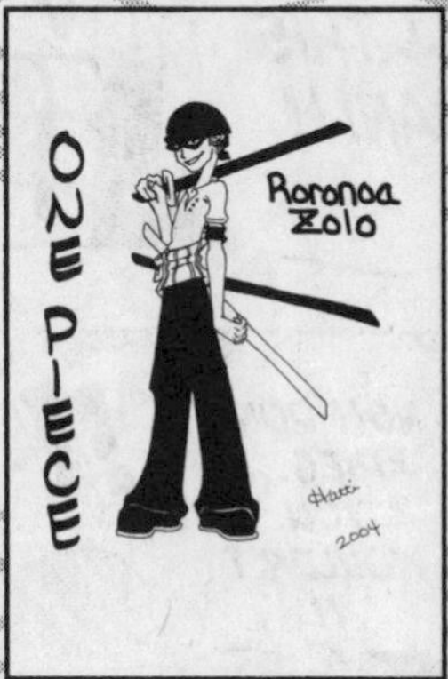

ONE PIECE
Roronoa Zolo
2004


HATTI, 19

SUBMIT YOUR FAN ART TO:
SHONEN JUMP C/O VIZ, LLC P.O. BOX 77010, SAN FRANCISCO, CA, 94107
REMEMBER TO INCLUDE YOUR NAME AND AGE!!

USOPP'S COMMENTS WERE TRANSMITTED THROUGH THE U.S. SHONEN JUMP TEAM–*EDITOR*

# Chapter 62: MH5

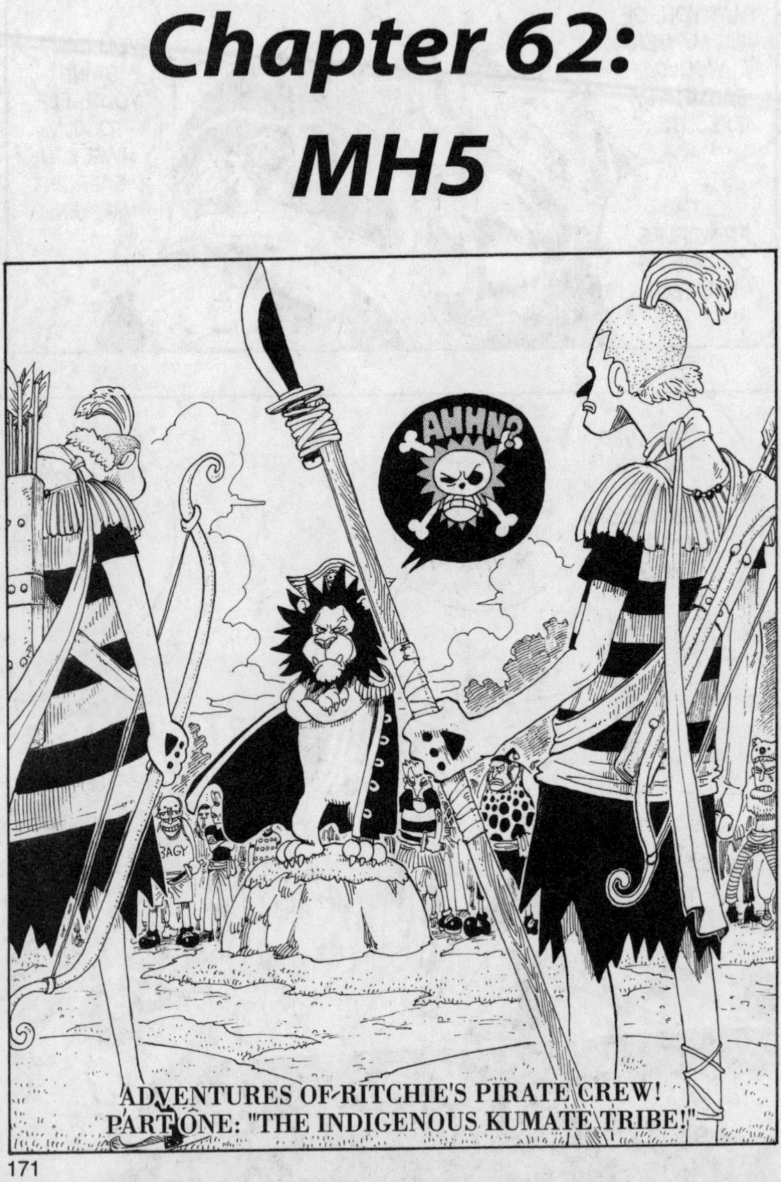
AHHN?
BAGY
ADVENTURES OF RITCHIE'S PIRATE CREW!
PART ONE: "THE INDIGENOUS KUMATE TRIBE!"

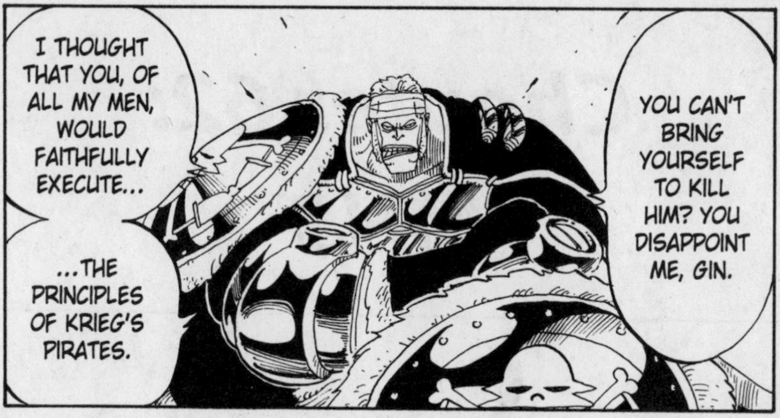
YOU CAN'T BRING YOURSELF TO KILL HIM? YOU DISAPPOINT ME, GIN.
I THOUGHT THAT YOU, OF ALL MY MEN, WOULD FAITHFULLY EXECUTE...
...THE PRINCIPLES OF KRIEG'S PIRATES.
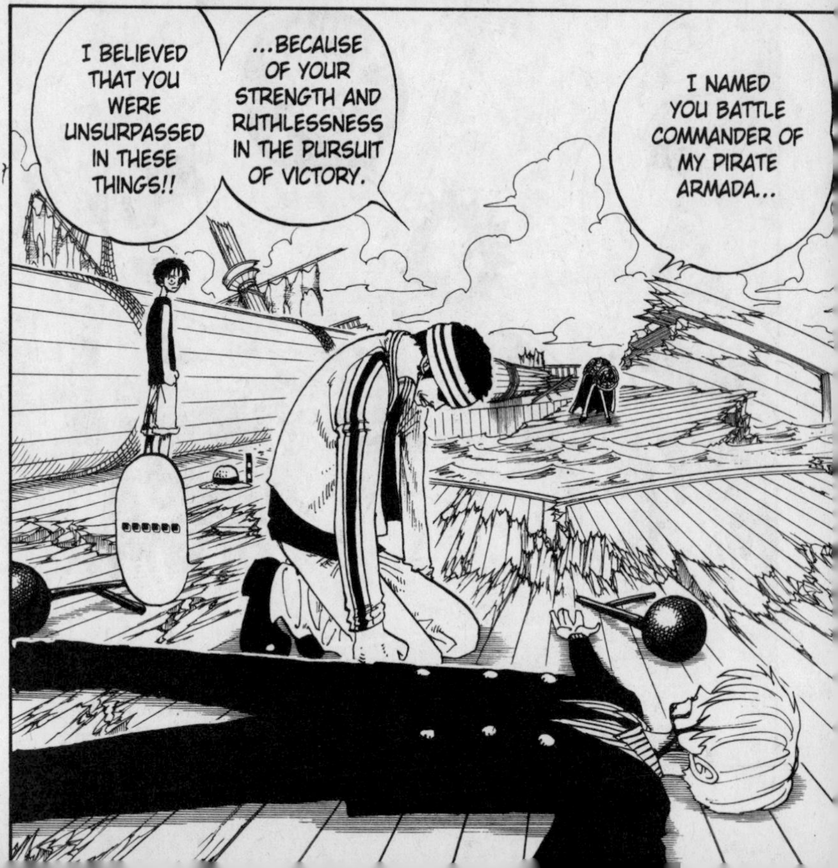
I NAMED YOU BATTLE COMMANDER OF MY PIRATE ARMADA...
...BECAUSE OF YOUR STRENGTH AND RUTHLESSNESS IN THE PURSUIT OF VICTORY.
I BELIEVED THAT YOU WERE UNSURPASSED IN THESE THINGS!!
......

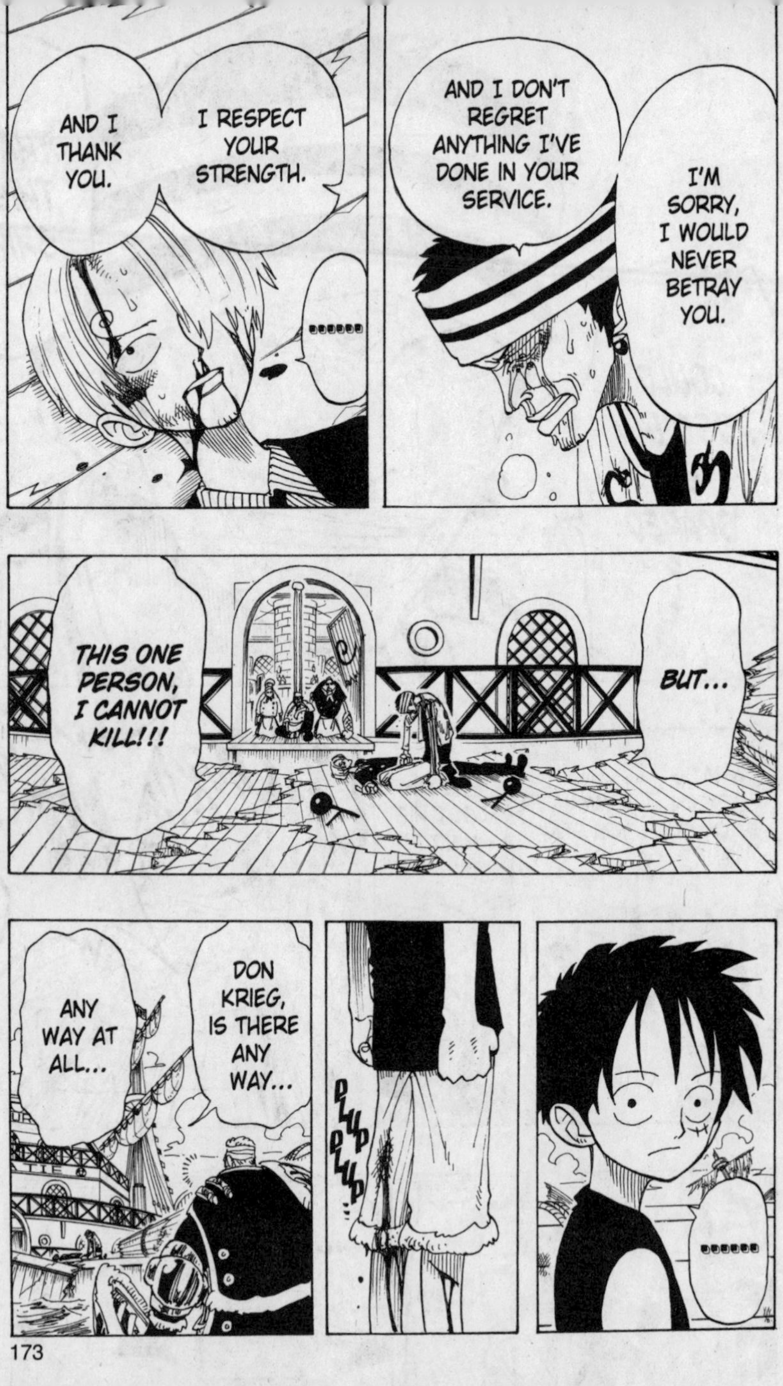
I'M SORRY, I WOULD NEVER BETRAY YOU.
AND I DON'T REGRET ANYTHING I'VE DONE IN YOUR SERVICE.
......
I RESPECT YOUR STRENGTH.
AND I THANK YOU.
BUT...
THIS ONE PERSON, I CANNOT KILL!!!
......
PLUP PLUP
DON KRIEG, IS THERE ANY WAY...
ANY WAY AT ALL...

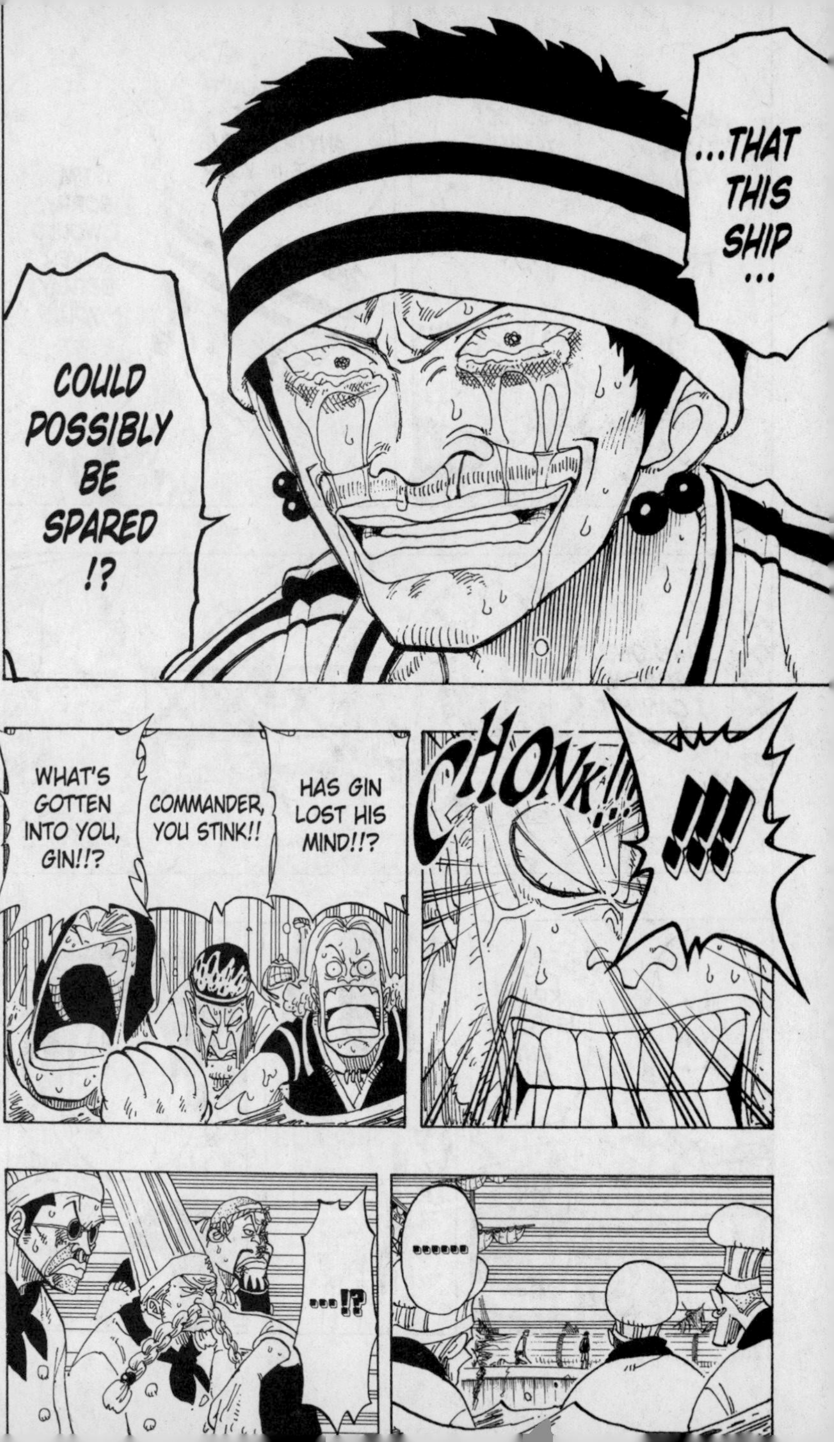
...THAT THIS SHIP...
COULD POSSIBLY BE SPARED!?
CHONK!!
!!!
HAS GIN LOST HIS MIND!!?
COMMANDER, YOU STINK!!
WHAT'S GOTTEN INTO YOU, GIN!!?
......
...!?

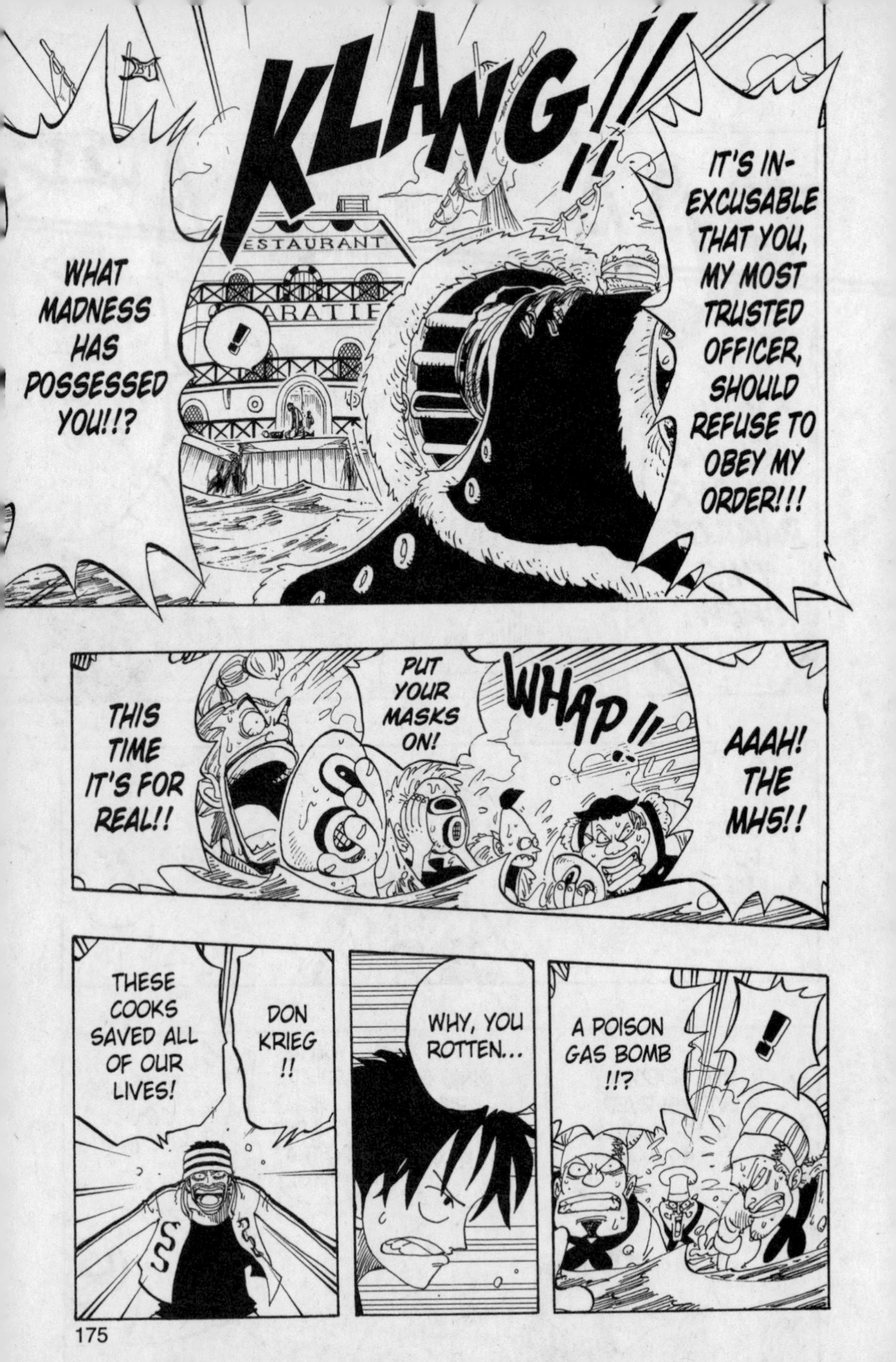

KLANG!!
IT'S IN-EXCUSABLE THAT YOU, MY MOST TRUSTED OFFICER, SHOULD REFUSE TO OBEY MY ORDER!!!
ESTAURANT
ARATIE
!
WHAT MADNESS HAS POSSESSED YOU!!?
AAAH! THE MH5!!
WHAP!!
PUT YOUR MASKS ON!
THIS TIME IT'S FOR REAL!!
!
A POISON GAS BOMB !!?
WHY, YOU ROTTEN...
DON KRIEG !!
THESE COOKS SAVED ALL OF OUR LIVES!

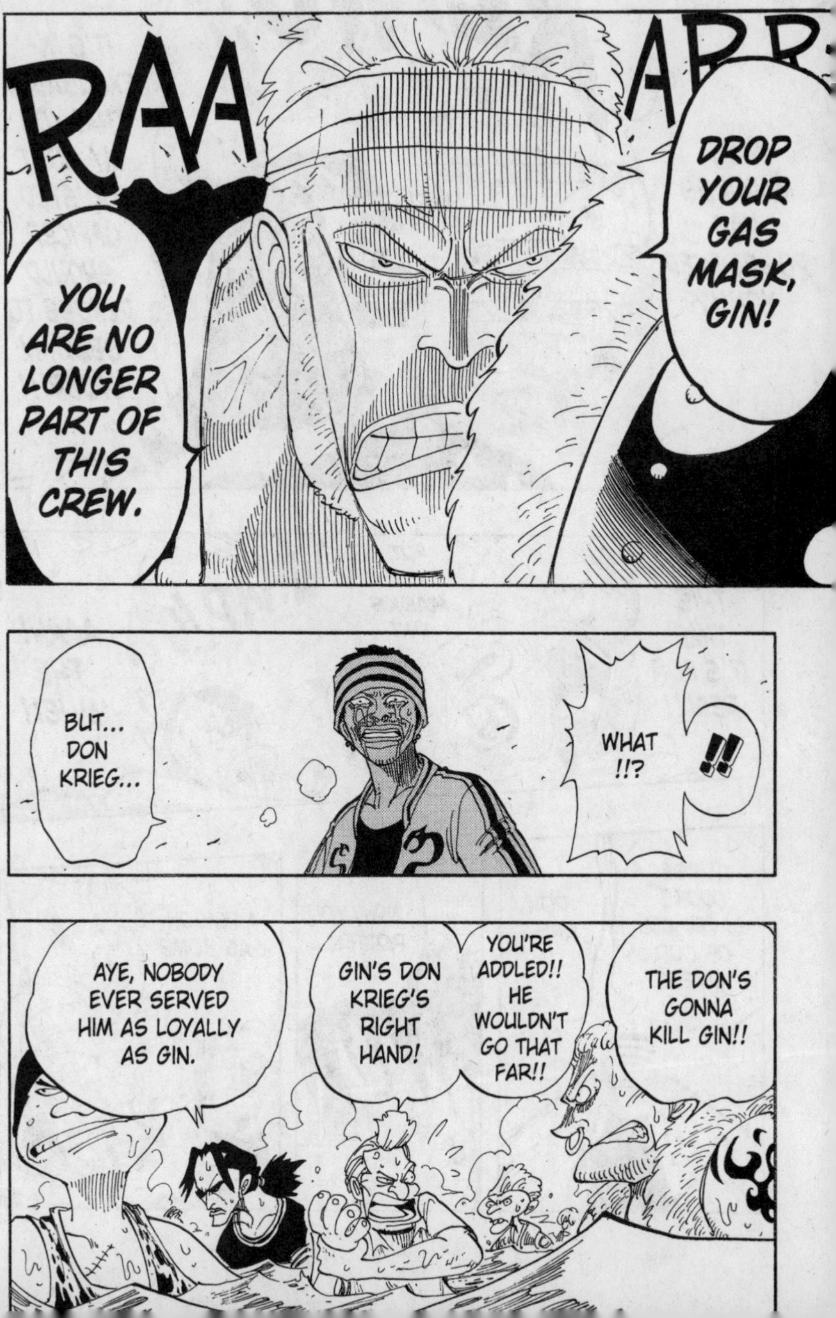
RAA ARR
DROP YOUR GAS MASK, GIN!
YOU ARE NO LONGER PART OF THIS CREW.
WHAT !!?
!!
BUT... DON KRIEG...
THE DON'S GONNA KILL GIN!!
YOU'RE ADDLED!! HE WOULDN'T GO THAT FAR!!
GIN'S DON KRIEG'S RIGHT HAND!
AYE, NOBODY EVER SERVED HIM AS LOYALLY AS GIN.

READ THIS WAY

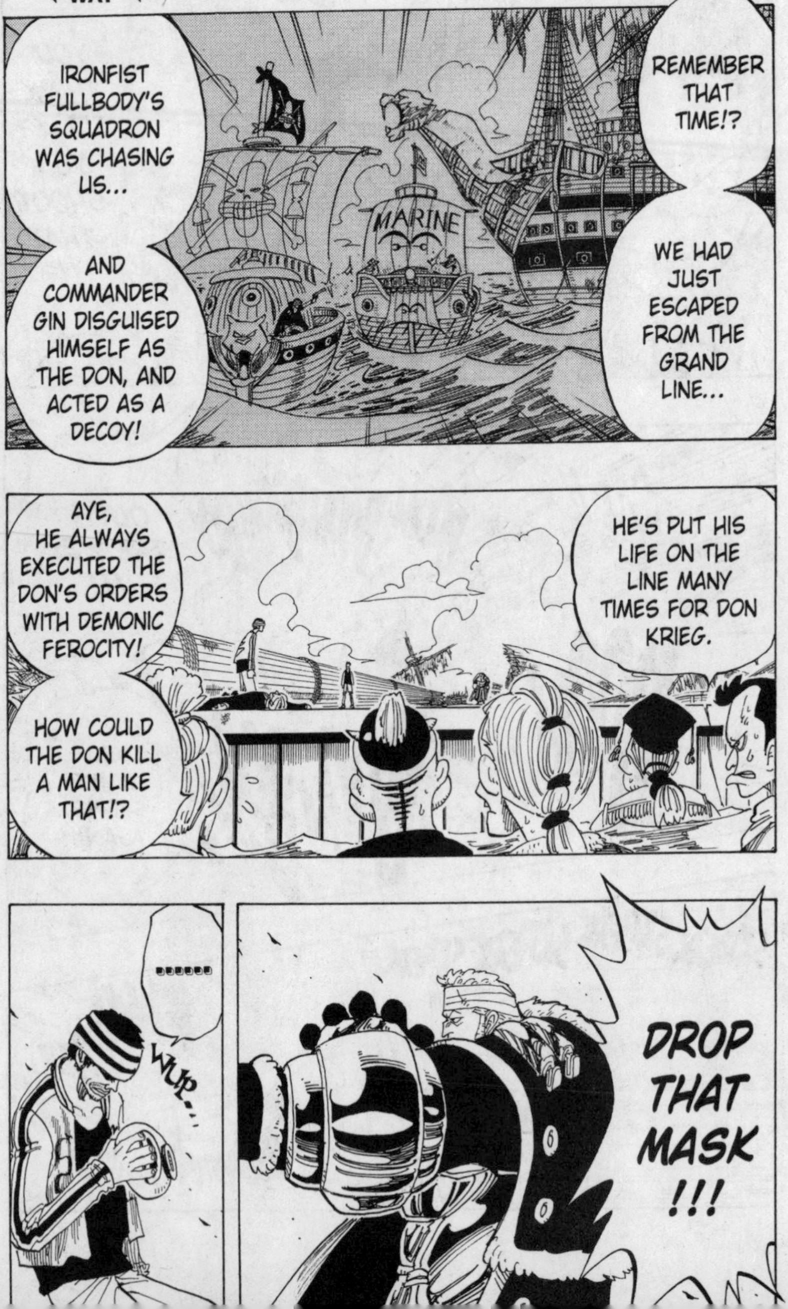
REMEMBER THAT TIME!?
WE HAD JUST ESCAPED FROM THE GRAND LINE...
MARINE
IRONFIST FULLBODY'S SQUADRON WAS CHASING US...
AND COMMANDER GIN DISGUISED HIMSELF AS THE DON, AND ACTED AS A DECOY!
HE'S PUT HIS LIFE ON THE LINE MANY TIMES FOR DON KRIEG.
AYE, HE ALWAYS EXECUTED THE DON'S ORDERS WITH DEMONIC FEROCITY!
HOW COULD THE DON KILL A MAN LIKE THAT!?
DROP THAT MASK!!!
......
WUP...

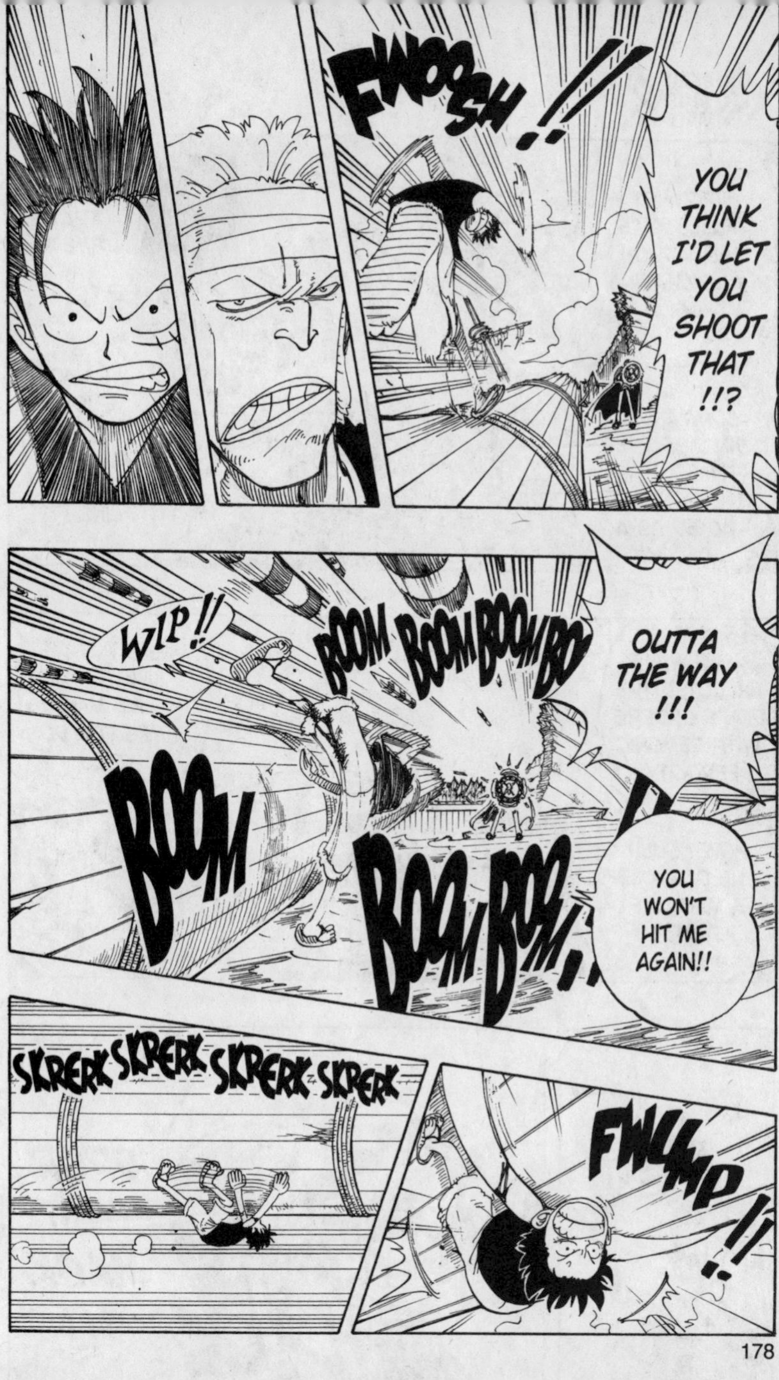
FWOOSH!!
YOU THINK I'D LET YOU SHOOT THAT!!?
OUTTA THE WAY!!!
BOOM BOOM BOOM BO
WLP!!
YOU WON'T HIT ME AGAIN!!
BOOM BOOM...!
BOOM
FWUMP!!
SKRERK SKRERK SKRERK SKRERK

READ THIS WAY

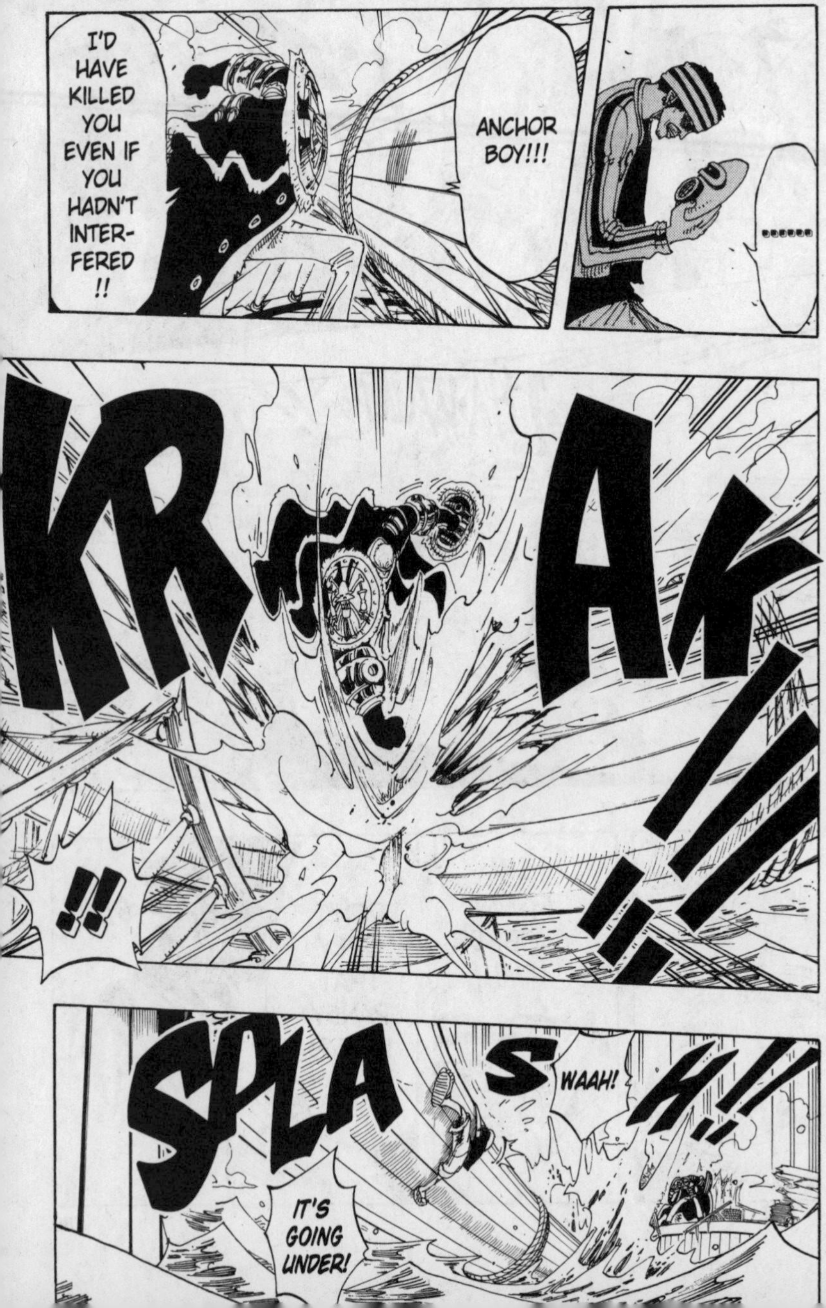
......
ANCHOR BOY!!!
I'D HAVE KILLED YOU EVEN IF YOU HADN'T INTER-FERED !!
KRAK!!!!
!!
SPLASH!!
WAAH!
IT'S GOING UNDER!

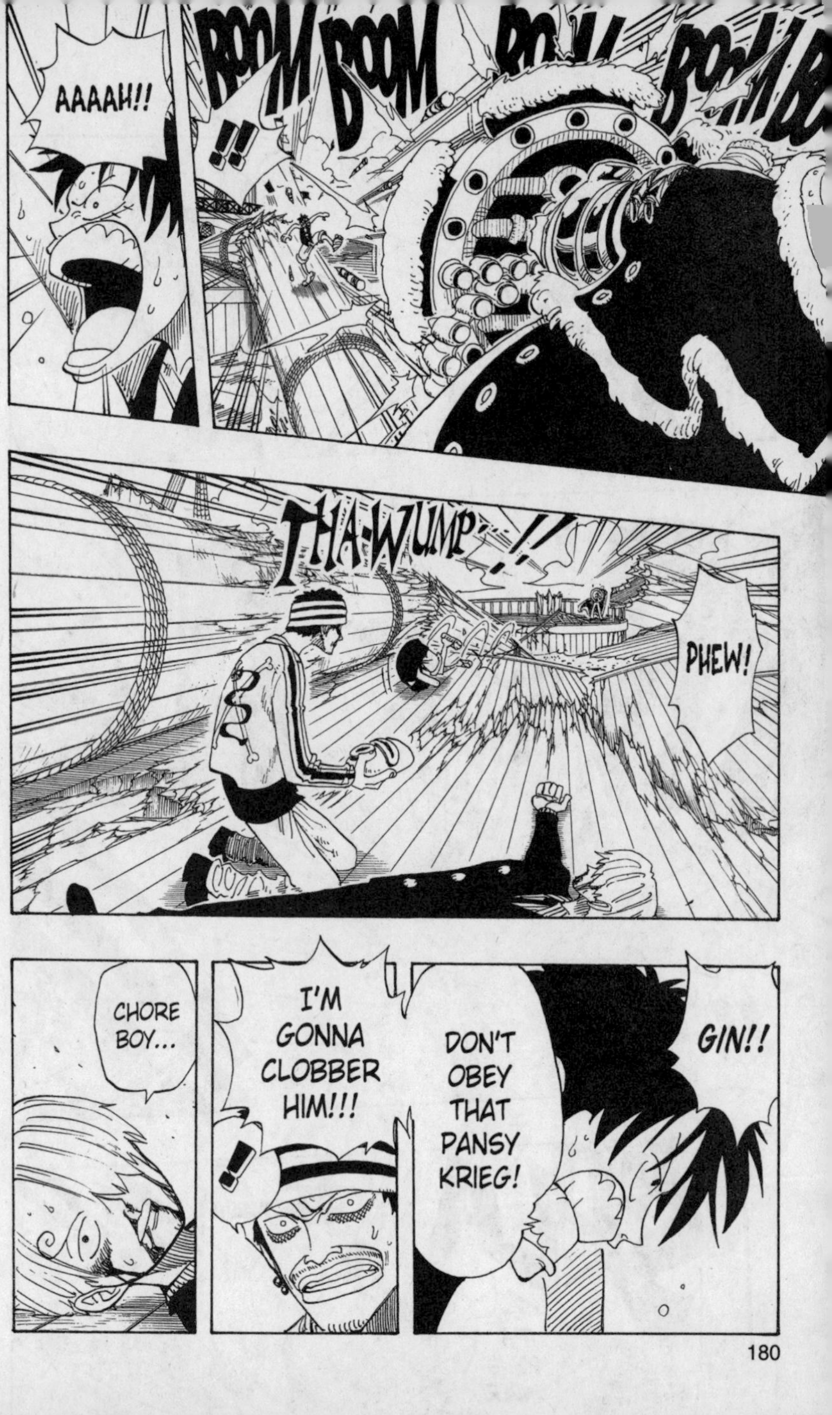
BOOM BOOM
!!
AAAAH!!
THA-WUMP!!
PHEW!
GIN!!
DON'T OBEY THAT PANSY KRIEG!
I'M GONNA CLOBBER HIM!!!
!
CHORE BOY...

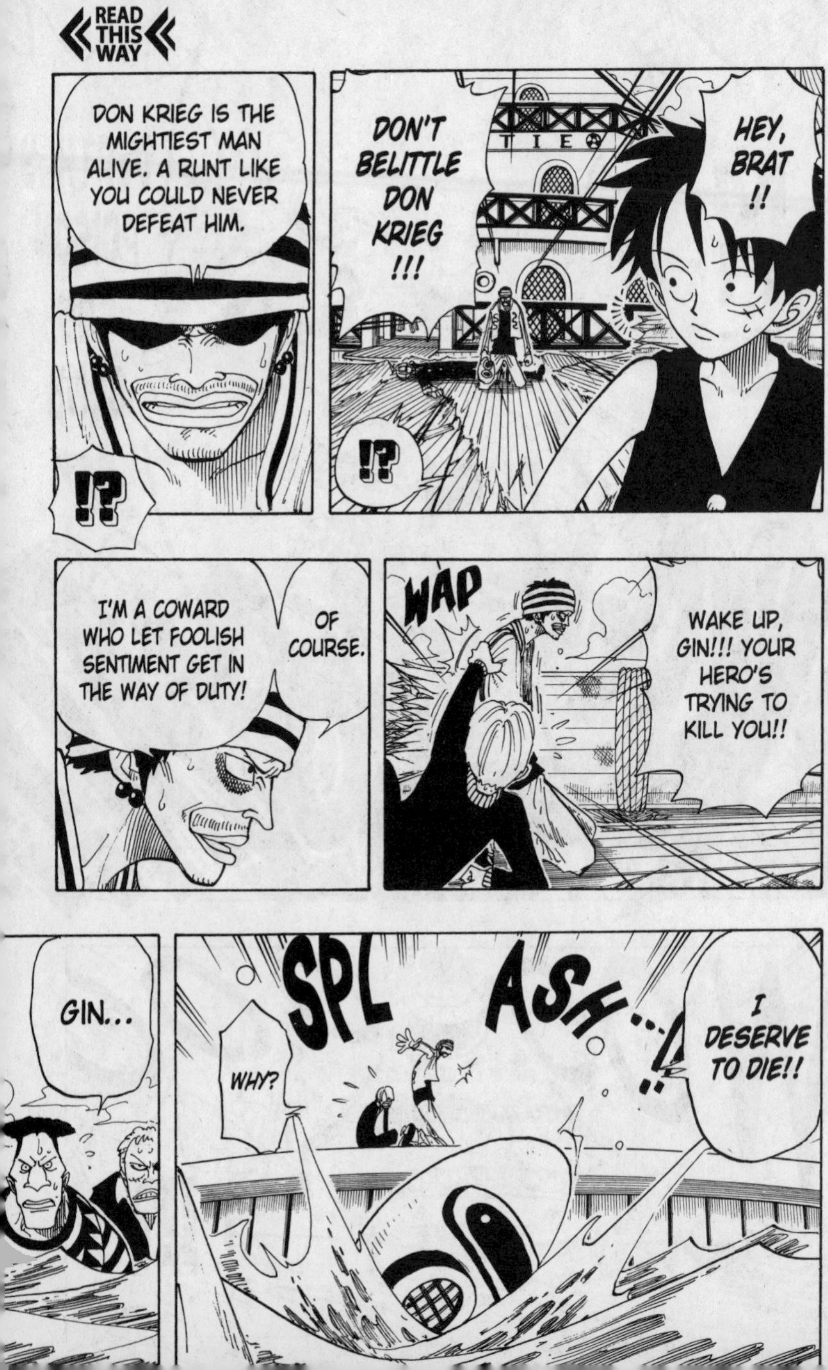
READ THIS WAY
HEY, BRAT !!
DON'T BELITTLE DON KRIEG !!!
!?
DON KRIEG IS THE MIGHTIEST MAN ALIVE. A RUNT LIKE YOU COULD NEVER DEFEAT HIM.
!?
WAP
WAKE UP, GIN!!! YOUR HERO'S TRYING TO KILL YOU!!
OF COURSE.
I'M A COWARD WHO LET FOOLISH SENTIMENT GET IN THE WAY OF DUTY!
I DESERVE TO DIE!!
SPLASH...!!
WHY?
GIN...

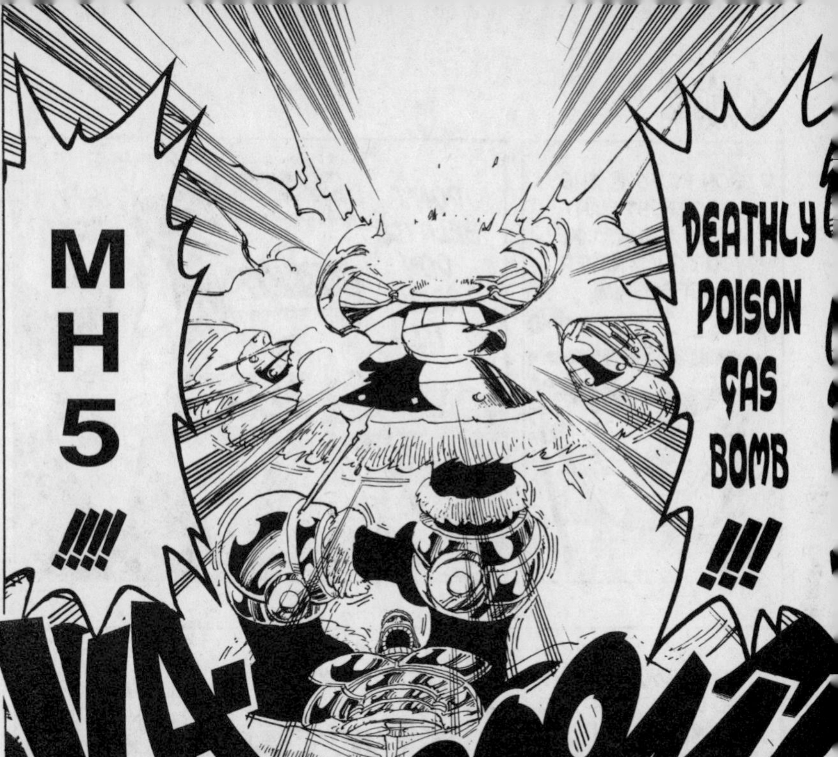
DEATHLY POISON GAS BOMB !!!
MH5 !!!!
KA-BOOM!!!

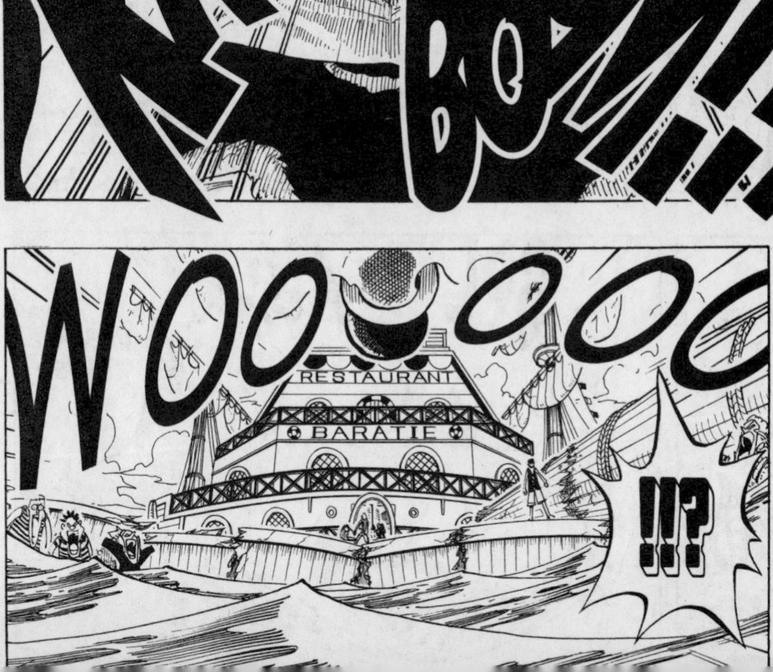
WOO-OOOO
RESTAURANT
BARATIE
!!?

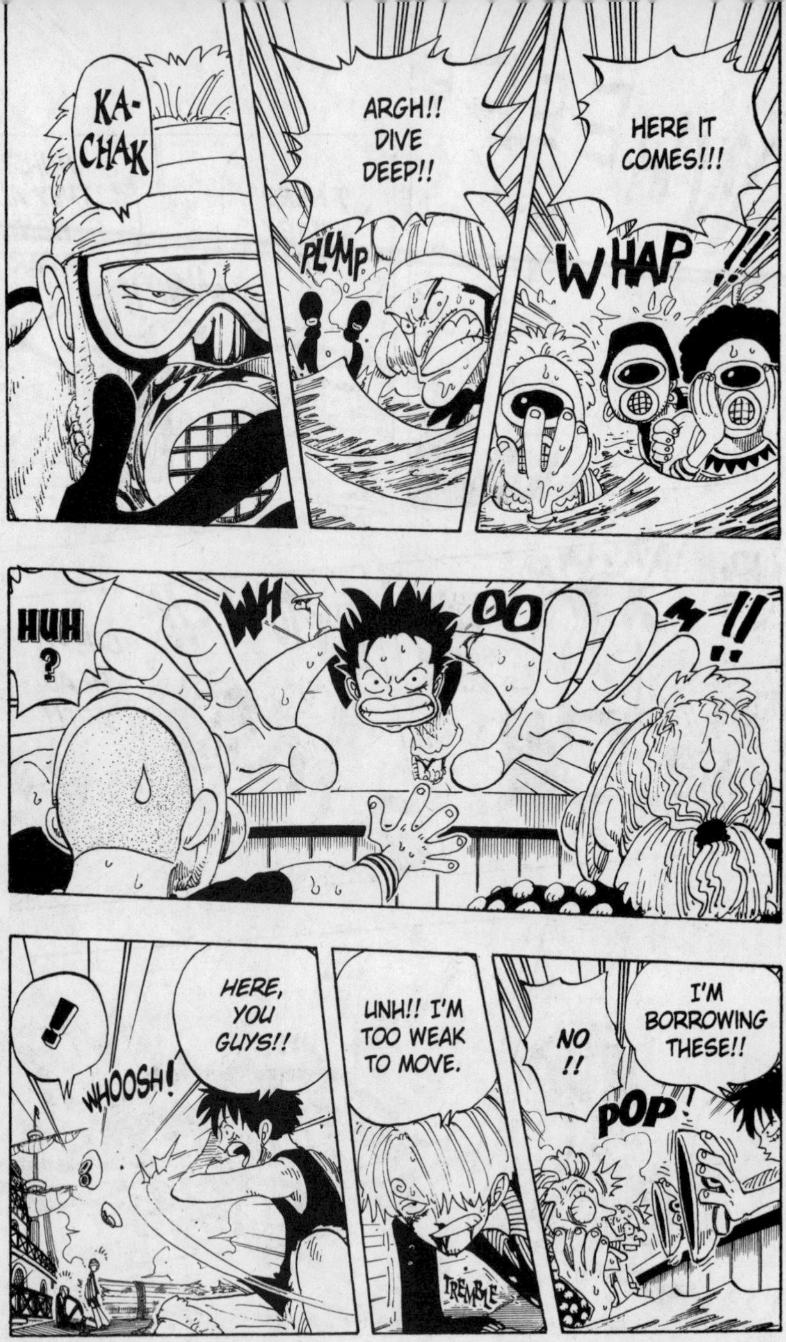
HERE IT COMES!!!
WHAP!!
ARGH!! DIVE DEEP!!
PLUMP
KA-CHAK
WHOOM!!
HUH ?
I'M BORROWING THESE!!
NO !!
POP!
UNH!! I'M TOO WEAK TO MOVE.
TREMBLE
HERE, YOU GUYS!!
!
WHOOSH!

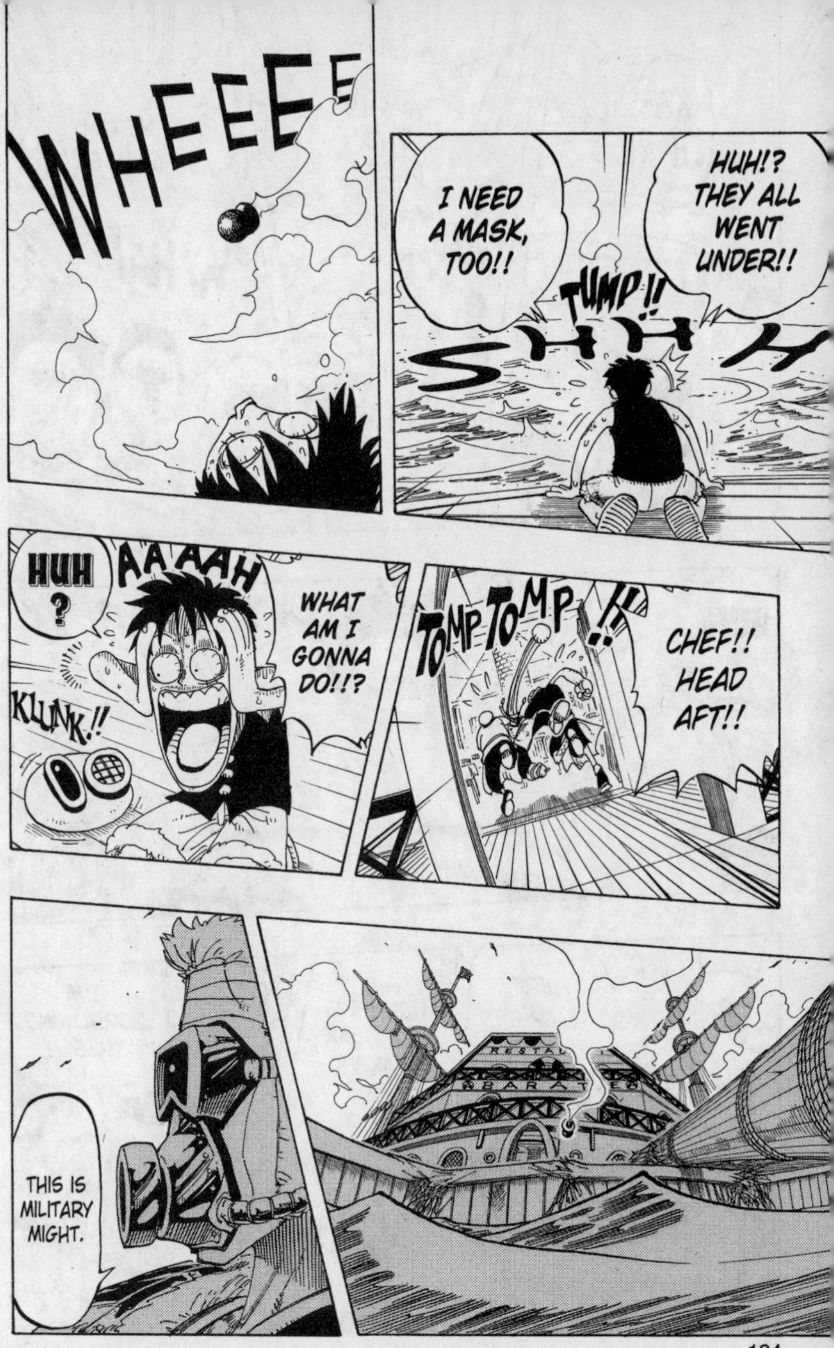
HUH!? THEY ALL WENT UNDER!!
I NEED A MASK, TOO!!
TUMP!!
SHHH
WHEEEE
CHEF!! HEAD AFT!!
TOMP TOMP!!
WHAT AM I GONNA DO!!?
AAAAH
HUH?
KLUNK!!
THIS IS MILITARY MIGHT.

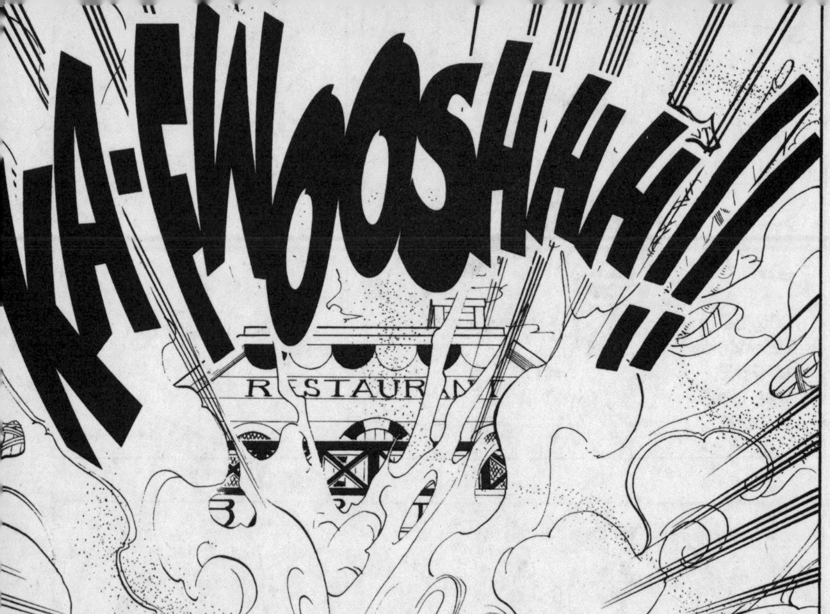
KA-FWOOSHHH!!!
!!!
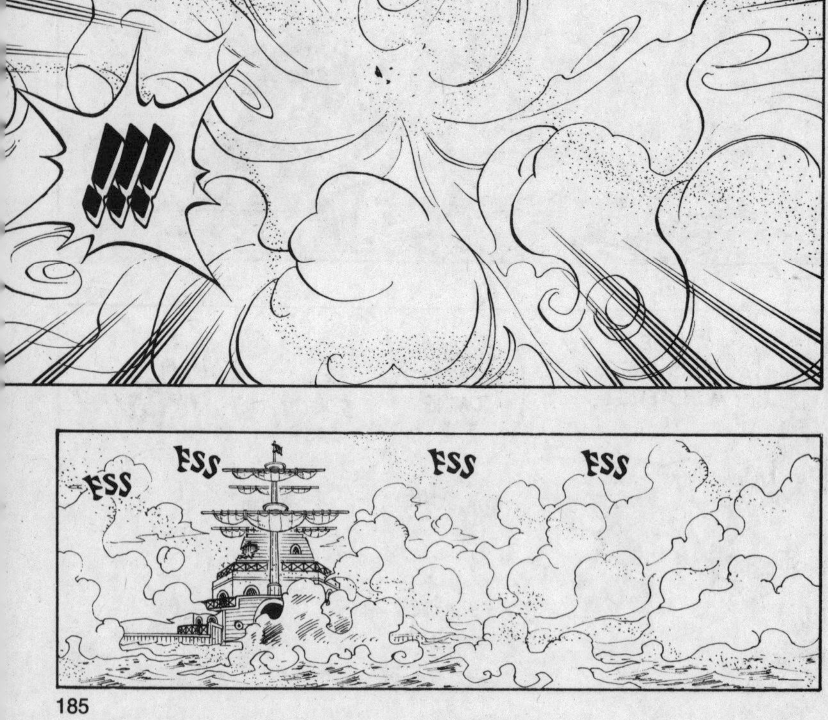
FSS
FSS
FSS
FSS

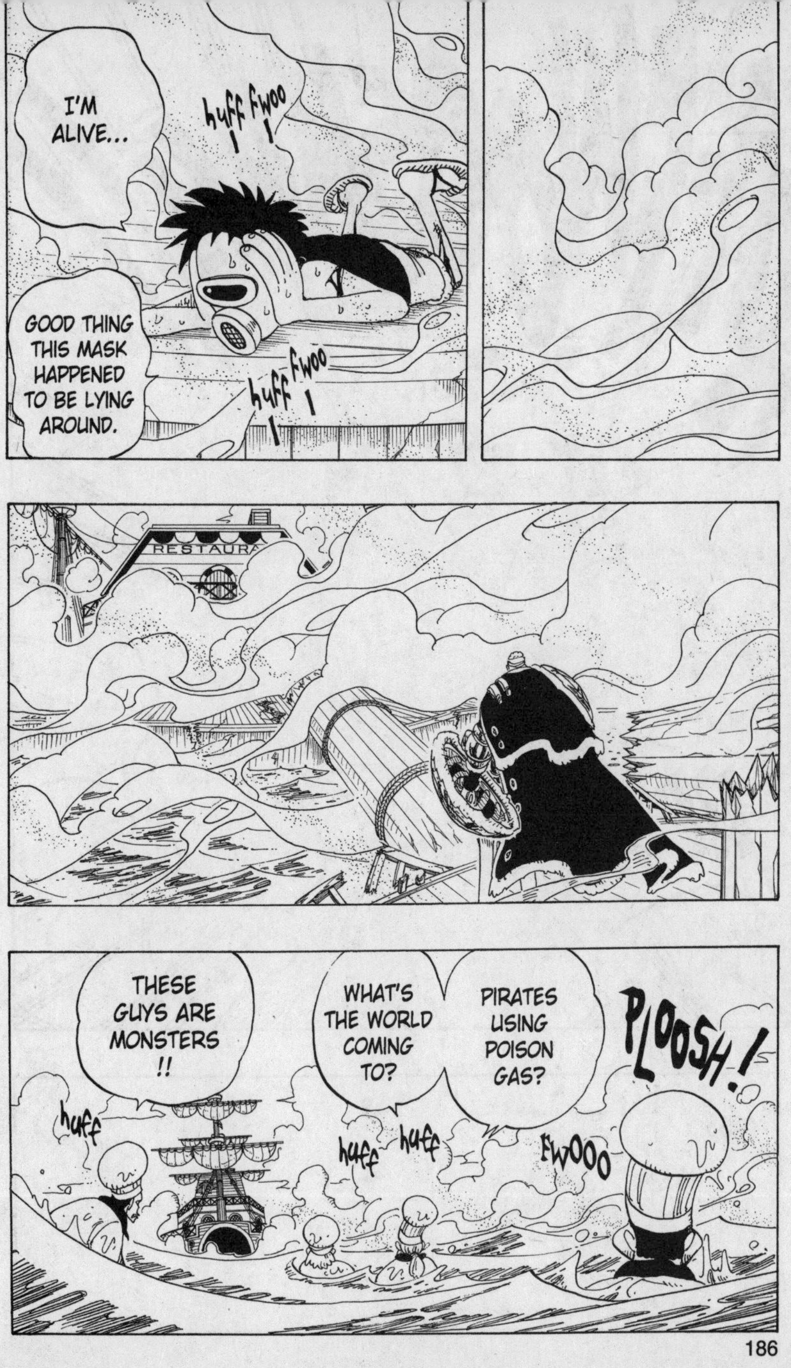
I'M ALIVE...
huff fwoo
GOOD THING THIS MASK HAPPENED TO BE LYING AROUND.
huff fwoo
RESTAURA
PLOOSH!
FWOOO
PIRATES USING POISON GAS?
huff
WHAT'S THE WORLD COMING TO?
huff
THESE GUYS ARE MONSTERS!!
huff

READ THIS WAY

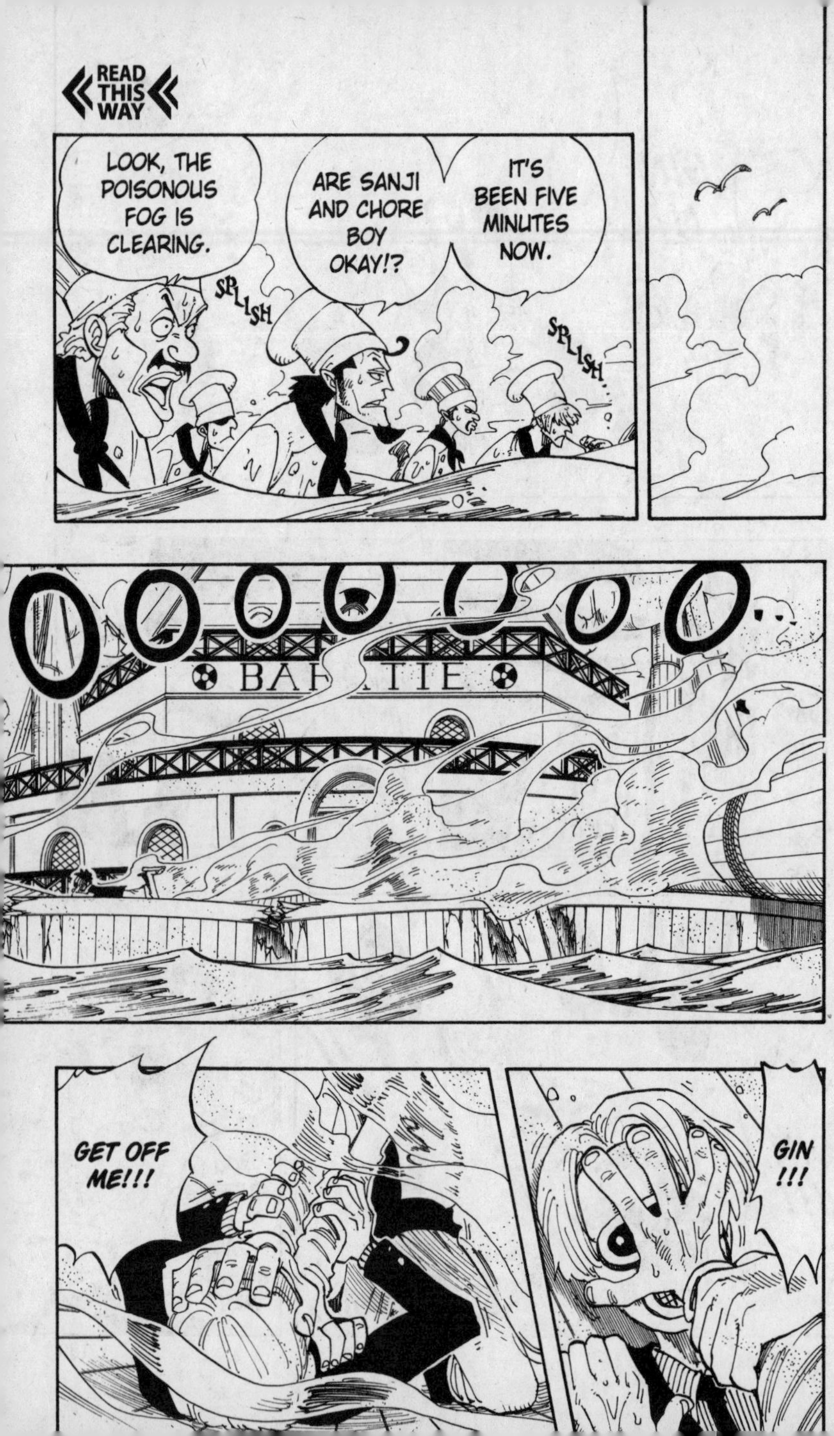

IT'S BEEN FIVE MINUTES NOW.
ARE SANJI AND CHORE BOY OKAY!?
LOOK, THE POISONOUS FOG IS CLEARING.
SPLISH
SPLISH...
GIN !!!
GET OFF ME!!!

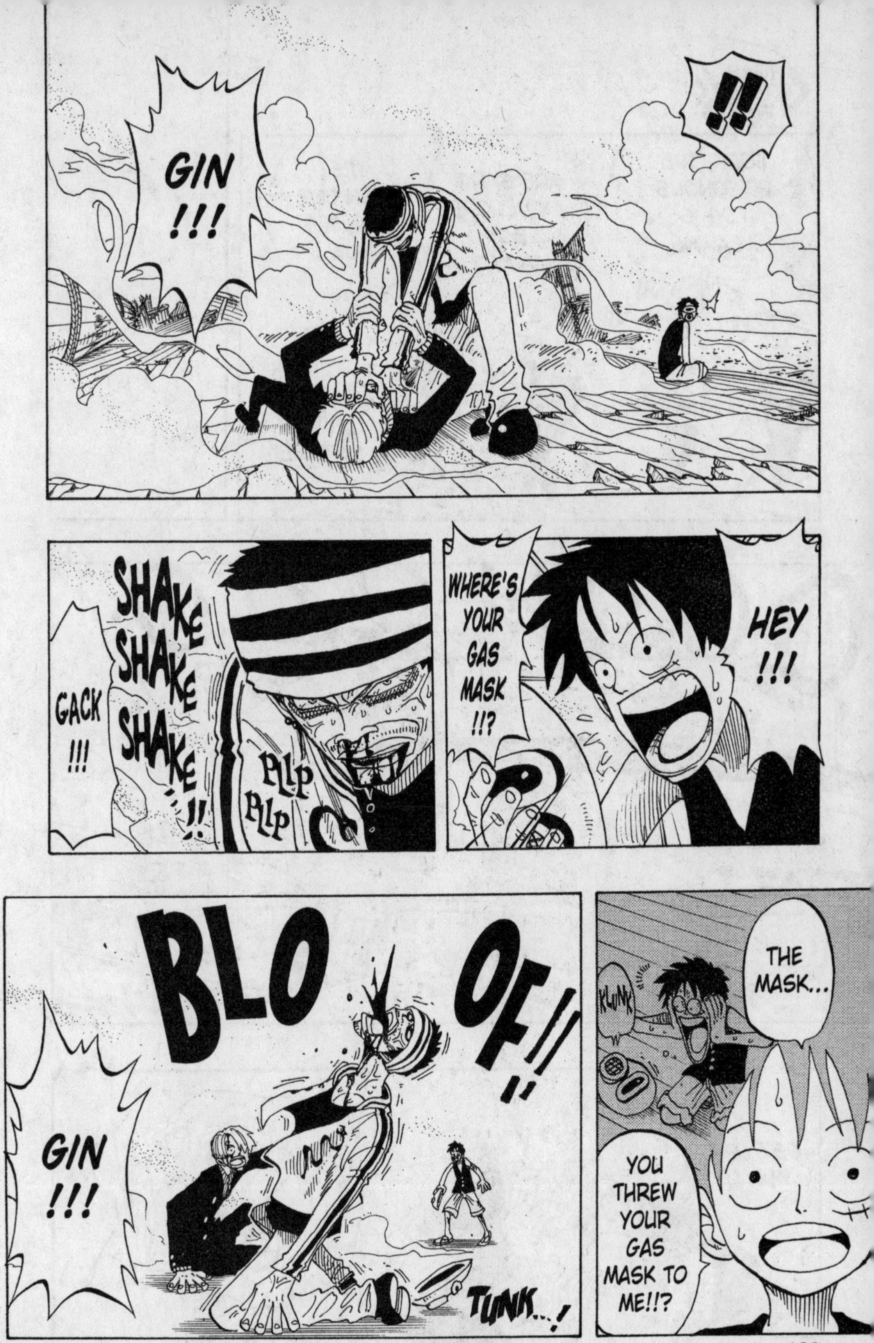
!!
GIN !!!
HEY !!!
WHERE'S YOUR GAS MASK !!?
SHAKE SHAKE SHAKE...!!
GACK !!!
PLIP PLIP
THE MASK...
KLUNK
YOU THREW YOUR GAS MASK TO ME!!?
BLOOF!!
GIN !!!
TUNK...!

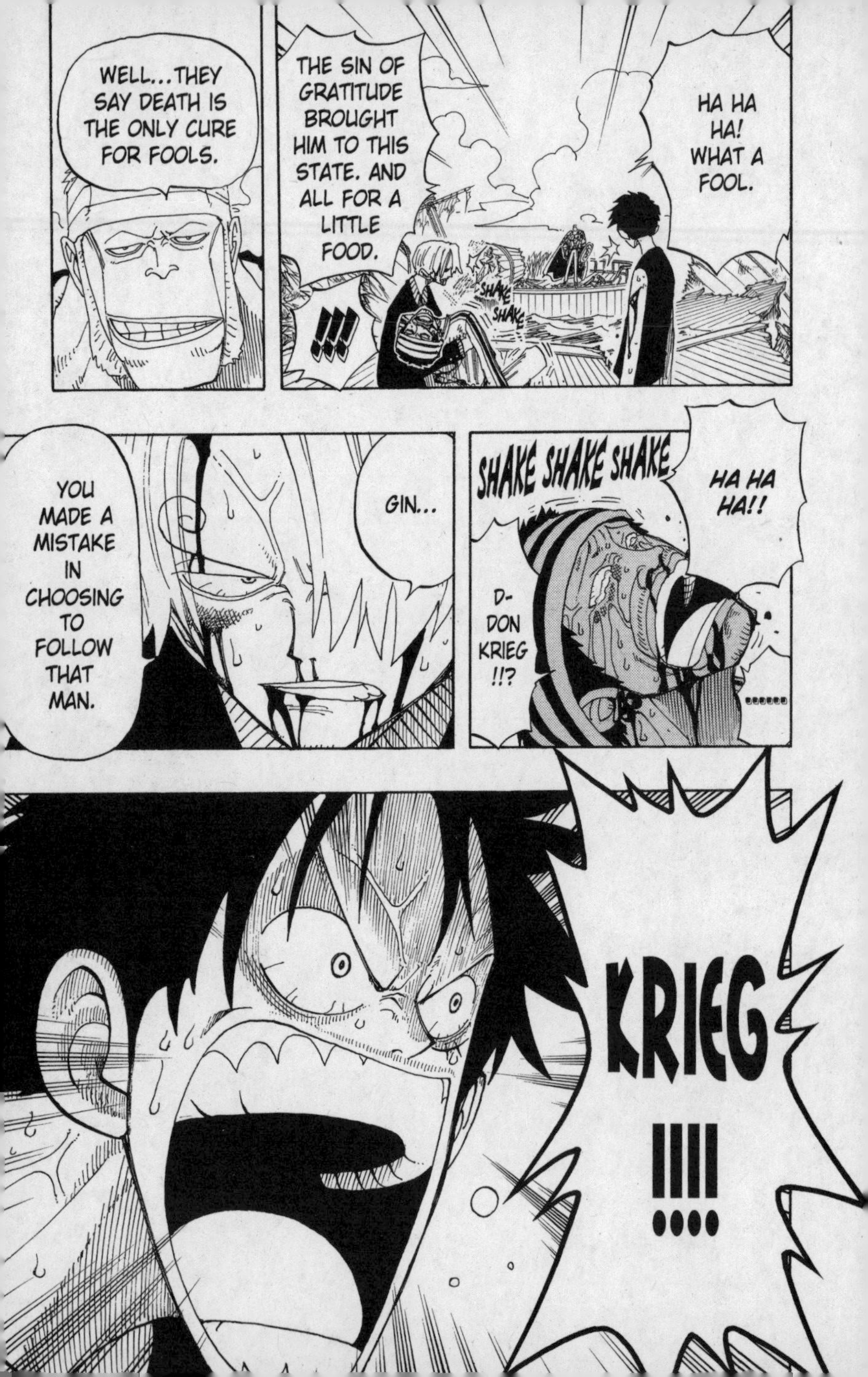
HA HA HA! WHAT A FOOL.
THE SIN OF GRATITUDE BROUGHT HIM TO THIS STATE. AND ALL FOR A LITTLE FOOD.
!!!
SHAKE SHAKE
WELL...THEY SAY DEATH IS THE ONLY CURE FOR FOOLS.
SHAKE SHAKE SHAKE
HA HA HA!!
D- DON KRIEG !!?
......
GIN...
YOU MADE A MISTAKE IN CHOOSING TO FOLLOW THAT MAN.
KRIEG !!!!....

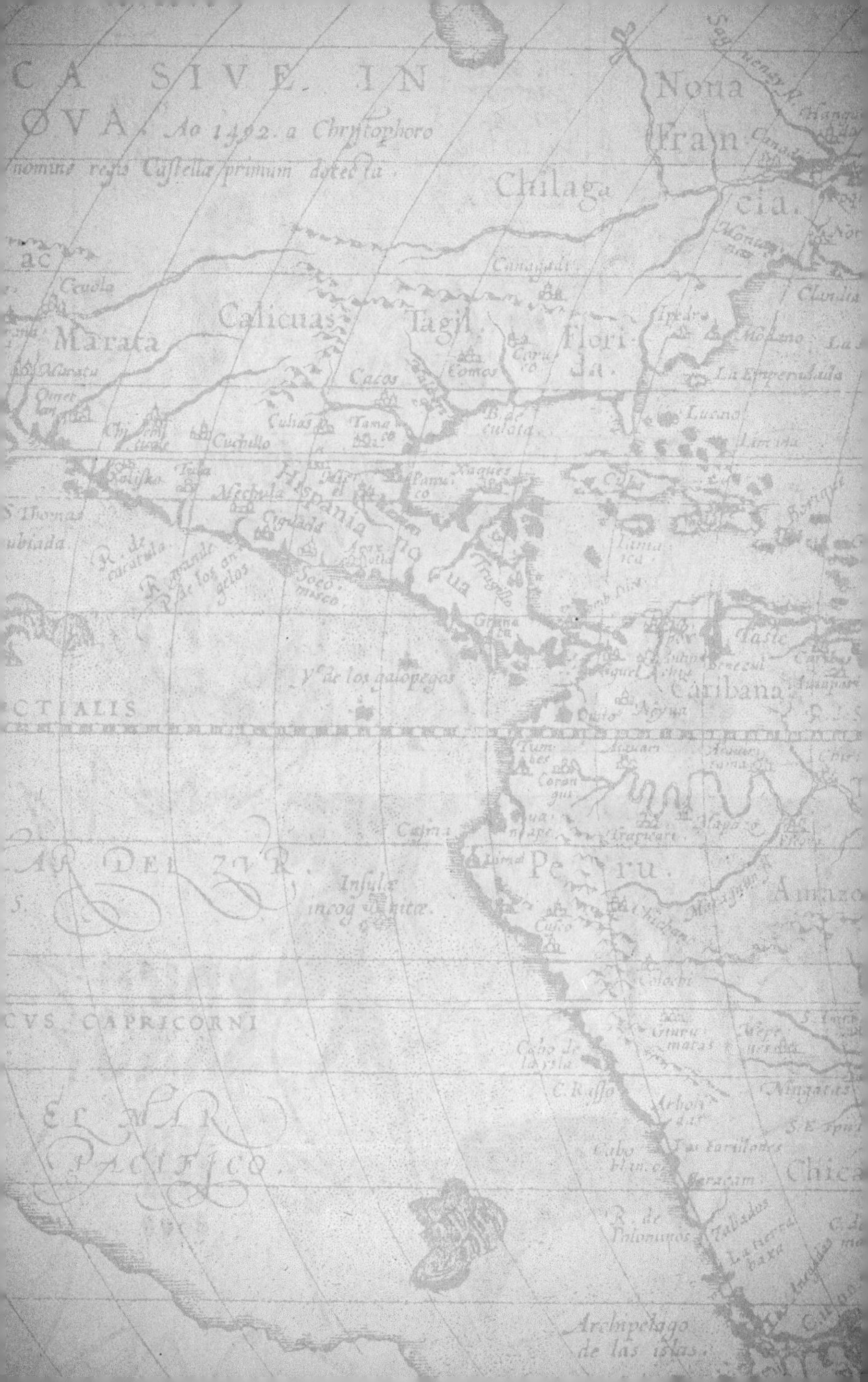

CA SIVE IN
QVA Ao 1492 a Chryftophoro
nomine regis Caftellæ primum detecta

Nona
Fran.
cia.

Chilaga

ac

Ccuola

Marata

Calicuas

Tagil

Flori

Miraçu

Comes

da

Omer

Caços

Mozino

La Empenuluita

Chi

Culias

Tama

B de

culata

Lucano

Cuchillo

Mercula

Clandia

Nor

La

S Thomas

ubiada

Mechula

Hyſpania

Cigdada

Soco

mico

noua

gua

Pann

co

Paques

Luina

Ld

Y de los galopegos

Grena

da

CTIALIS

Caſte

Caribana

Quito

Noyua

Tum

ber

Coron

guì

Pe ru

AR DEL ZVR

Cafma

Lima

Insulæ

incog nitæ

Cuſco

Amazo

CVS CAPRICORNI

Gturu

matas

Cabo de

ayfta

C Raffo

Arbol

Ningatas

EL MAR

PACIFICO

Cabo

Blanco

as tortillones

Chica

Palonuros

Talabos

La tierra

baxa

Archipelago

de las islas

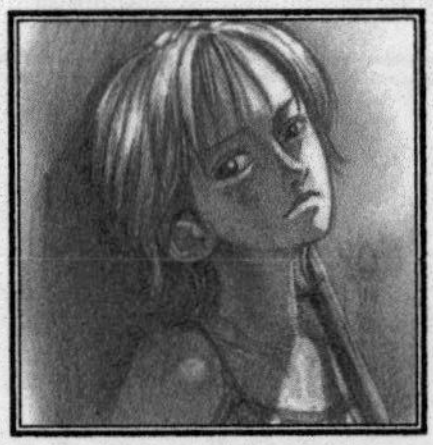

Here's a little story for you. Long, long ago, a really long time ago, rabbits were able to fly. The fact that we count rabbits in Japanese (ichiwa, niwa) the same way we count birds is a holdover from that time. Rabbits, flapping their big ears across the vast, clear skies of ancient times... Sounds like a horror story.

*–Eiichiro Oda, 1999*

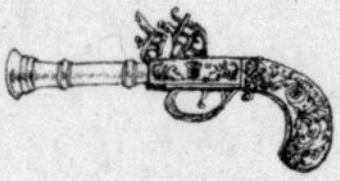

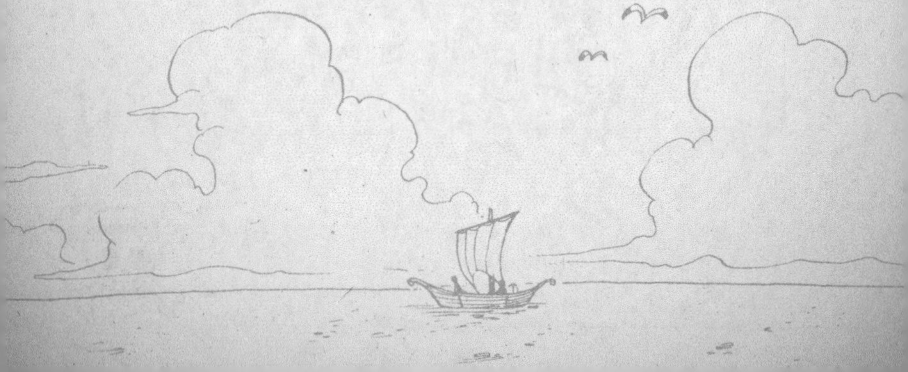

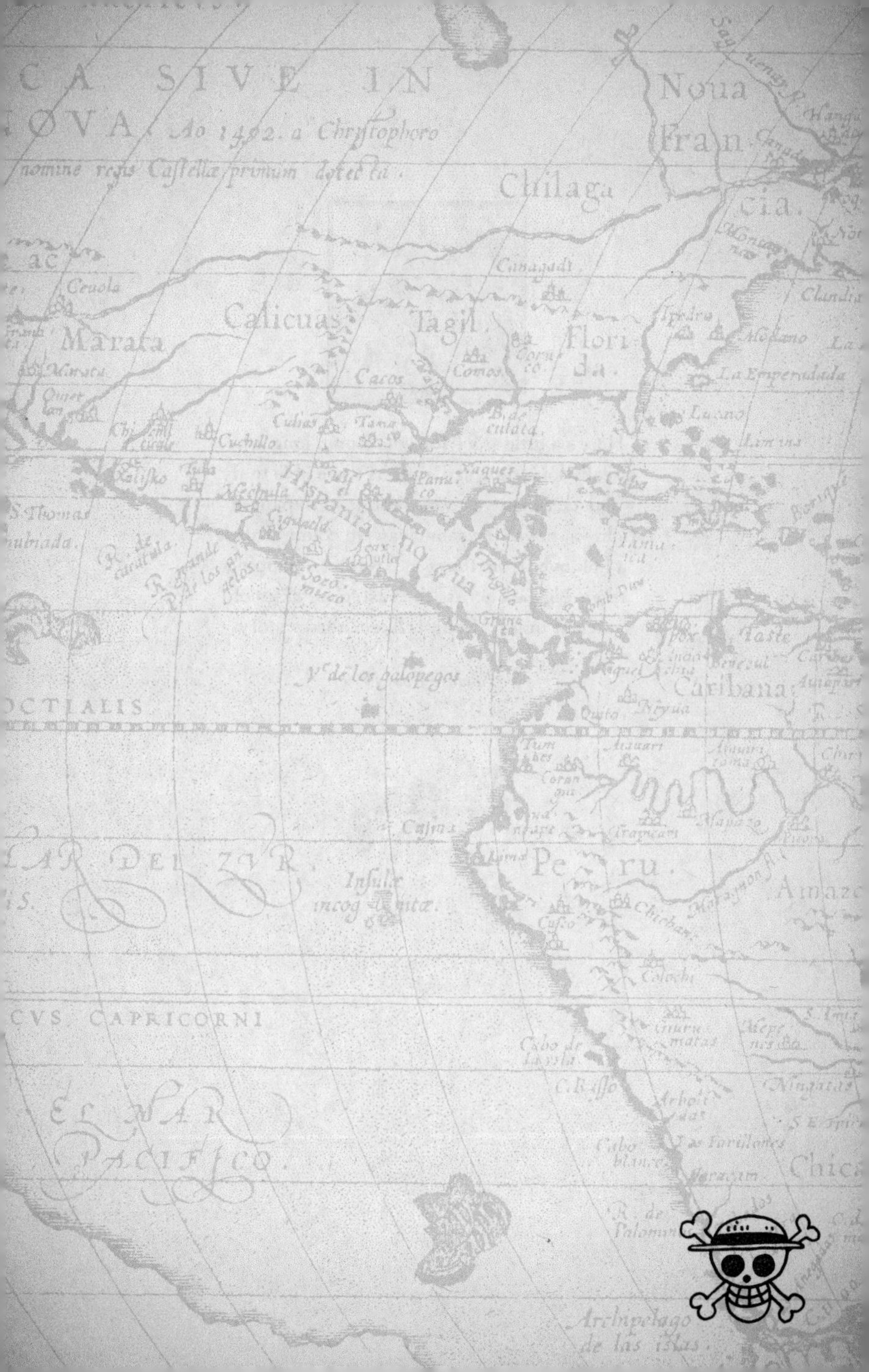

CA SIVE IN
NOVA. Ao 1492. a Christophoro
nomine regis Castella primum detecta.

Noua
Fran
cia.

Chilaga

Canagadi

...ac
Ceuola
Marata    Calicuas    Tagil.    Flori
Cacos    Corni    da.
Tana    co

Culiax    Tana    cutata    Lucano

Cuchillo

Hispania    Qua    Trugillo

ye de los galopegos    Caribana

OCTIALIS    Quito    Reyua

Tum
bes    Coron    qui

Cajras    Pe  ru.

LAR DEL ZVR    Insula
incognita.    Cusco    Amaze

Colochi

CVS CAPRICORNI

Cabo de
la isla

C.B.isso

EL MAR    Cabo
PACIFICO.    blanco    Chica

Archipelago
de las islas.

# Vol. 8

# I WON'T DIE

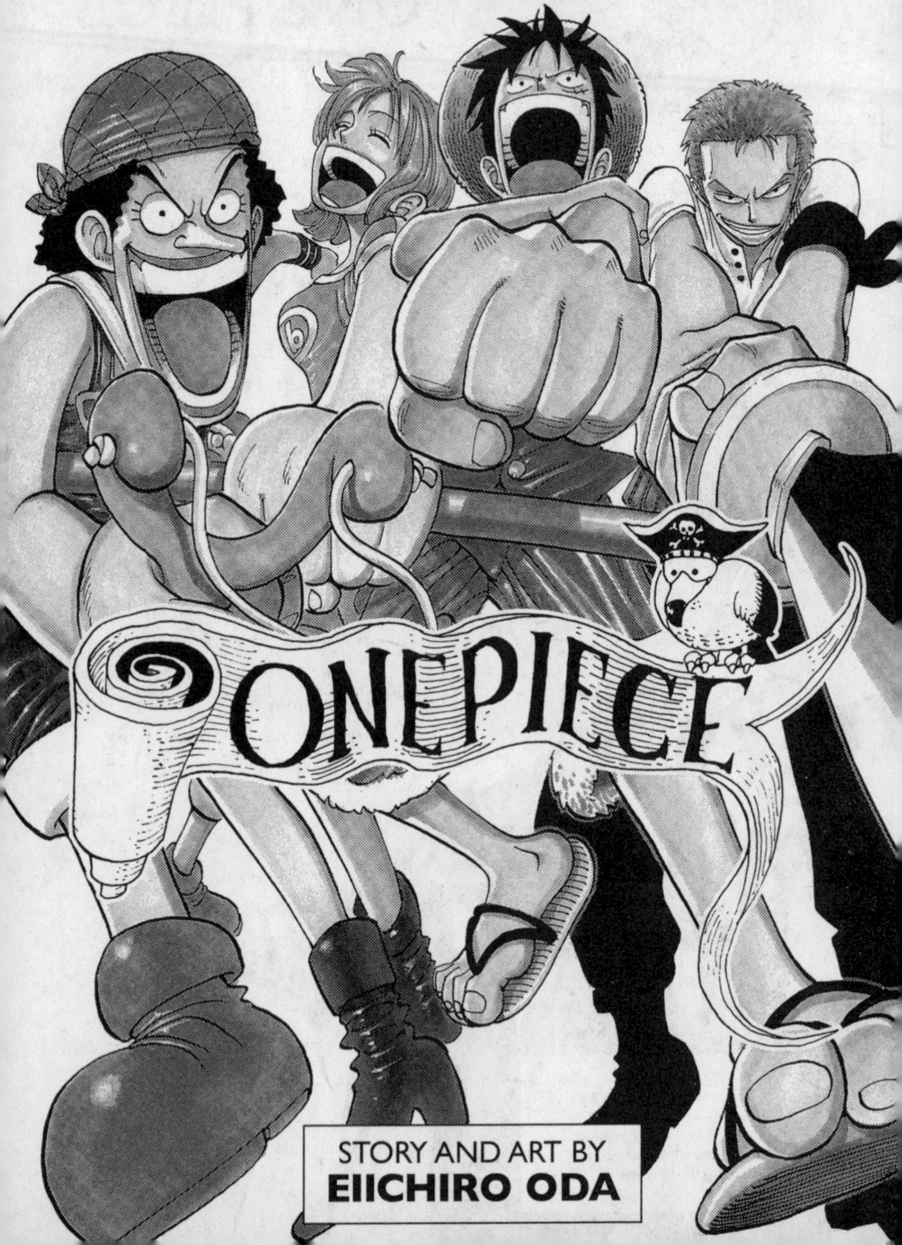
ONE PIECE
STORY AND ART BY
EIICHIRO ODA

# THE STORY OF
# ONE PIECE
## • VOLUME 8 •

Monkey D. Luffy started out as just a kid with a dream—and that dream was to become the greatest pirate in history! Stirred by the tales of pirate "Red-Haired" Shanks, Luffy vowed to become a pirate himself. That was before the enchanted Devil Fruit gave Luffy the power to stretch like rubber, at the cost of being unable to swim—a serious handicap for an aspiring sea dog. Undeterred, Luffy set out to sea and recruited some crewmates: master swordsman Zolo, treasure-hunting thief Nami and lying sharpshooter Usopp.

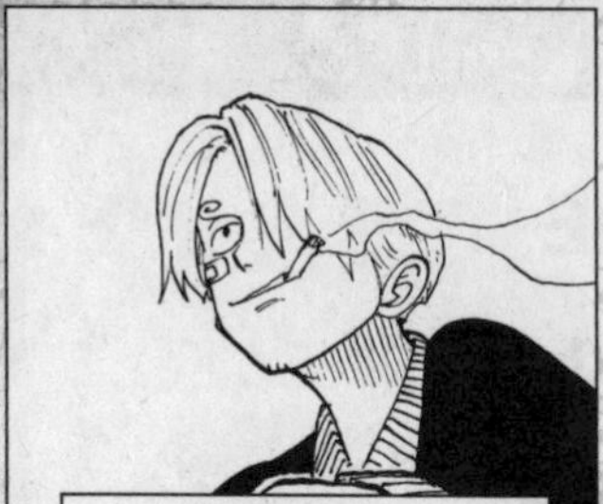

SANJI
A compassionate cook (and ladies' man) whose dream is to find the legendary sea, the "All Blue."

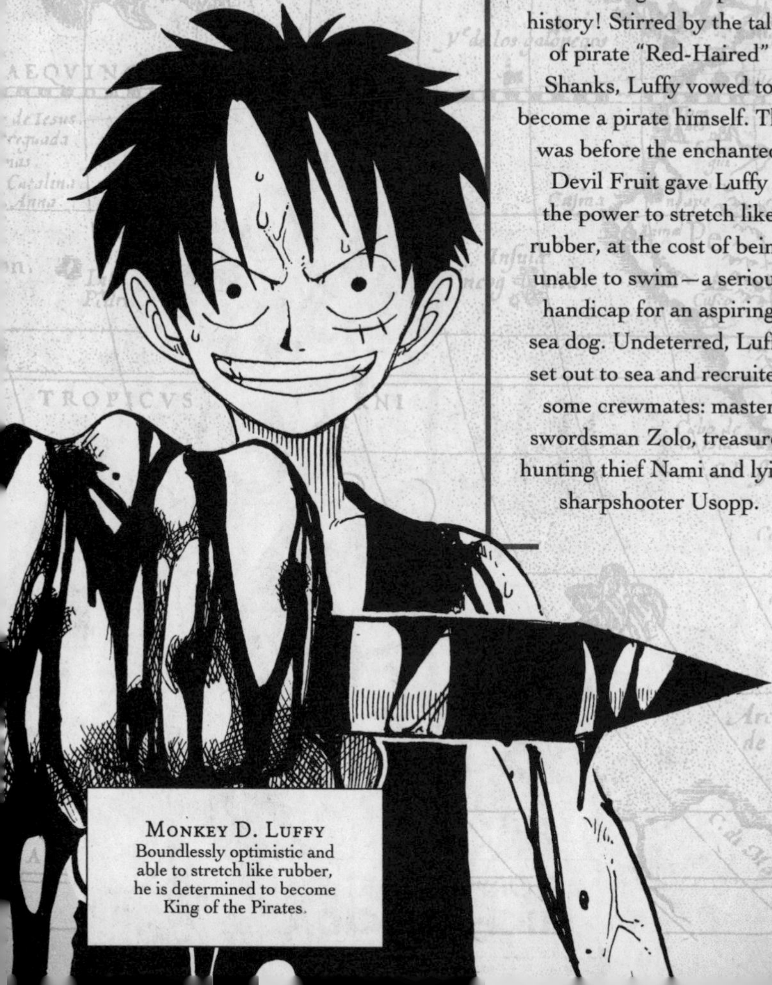

MONKEY D. LUFFY
Boundlessly optimistic and able to stretch like rubber, he is determined to become King of the Pirates.

Luffy and his crew visit the oceangoing restaurant Baratie, where they meet and befriend Sanji, the sous-chef. But the powerful and ruthless Don Krieg arrives with his pirates and declares that he wants Baratie for himself! So begins a battle royal for the restaurant ship. Sanji vows to defend the ship with his life, but when Chef Zeff is taken hostage, the situation turns desperate! Everyone wonders why Sanji is so determined to defend the ship, until he reveals a secret from the past: when Sanji was a young apprentice cook, he and Zeff (then known as the pirate "Red Shoes" Zeff) were swept overboard by a sudden storm and cast upon a rock in the ocean! Because Sanji shared Zeff's dream, the pirate gave the boy all the food he had and ate his own leg to survive.

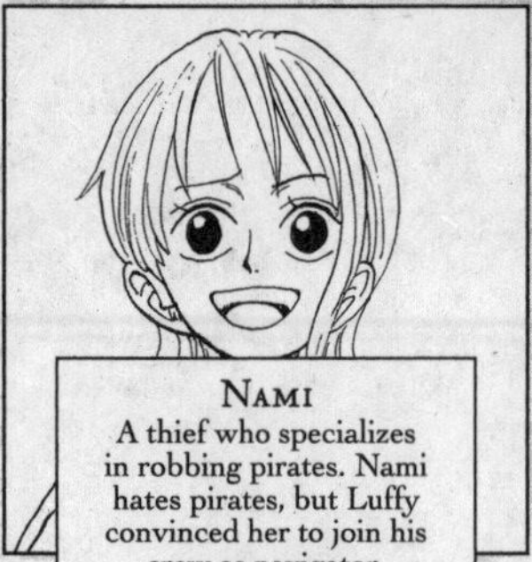

**Nami**
A thief who specializes in robbing pirates. Nami hates pirates, but Luffy convinced her to join his crew as navigator.

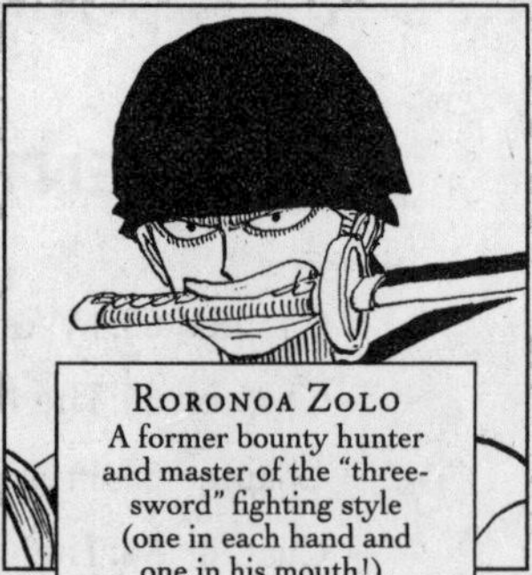

**Roronoa Zolo**
A former bounty hunter and master of the "three-sword" fighting style (one in each hand and one in his mouth!).

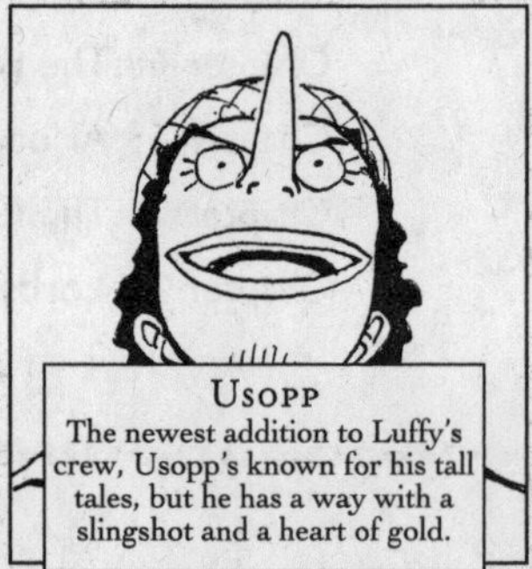

**Usopp**
The newest addition to Luffy's crew, Usopp's known for his tall tales, but he has a way with a slingshot and a heart of gold.

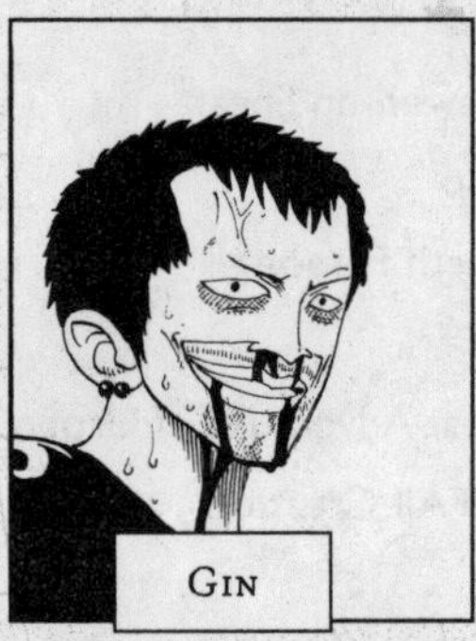

**Gin**

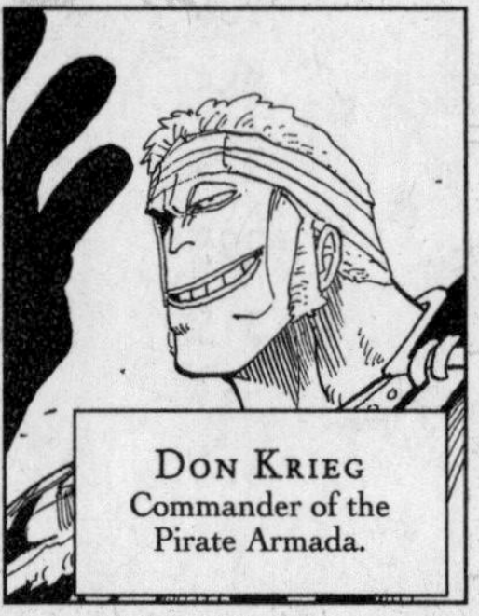

**Don Krieg**
Commander of the Pirate Armada.

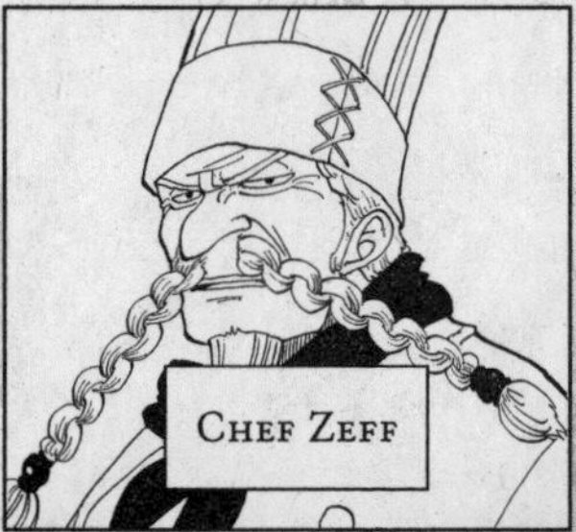

**Chef Zeff**

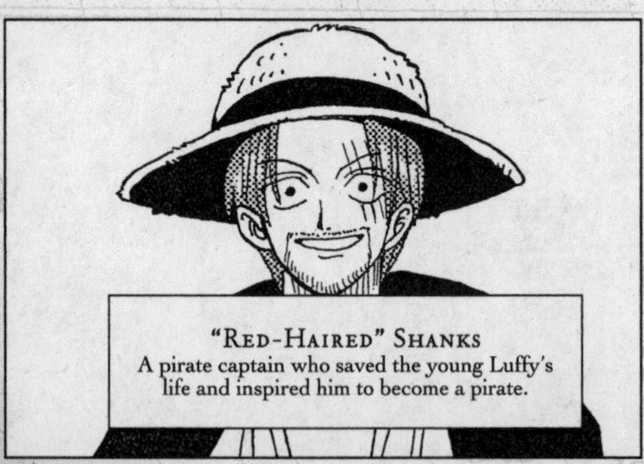

**"Red-Haired" Shanks**
A pirate captain who saved the young Luffy's life and inspired him to become a pirate.

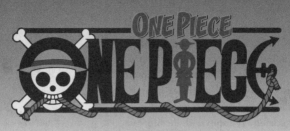

## Vol. 8
# I WON'T DIE

## CONTENTS

Chapter 63: I Won't Die     197

Chapter 64: The Mighty Battle Spear     216

Chapter 65: Prepared     235

Chapter 66: The Chewed-up Spear     255

Chapter 67: The Soup     275

Chapter 68: The Fourth Person     295

Chapter 69: Arlong Park     315

Chapter 70: The Great Adventure of Usopp the Man     337

Chapter 71: Lords of All Creation     359

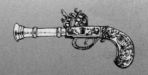

# Chapter 63:
# I WON'T DIE

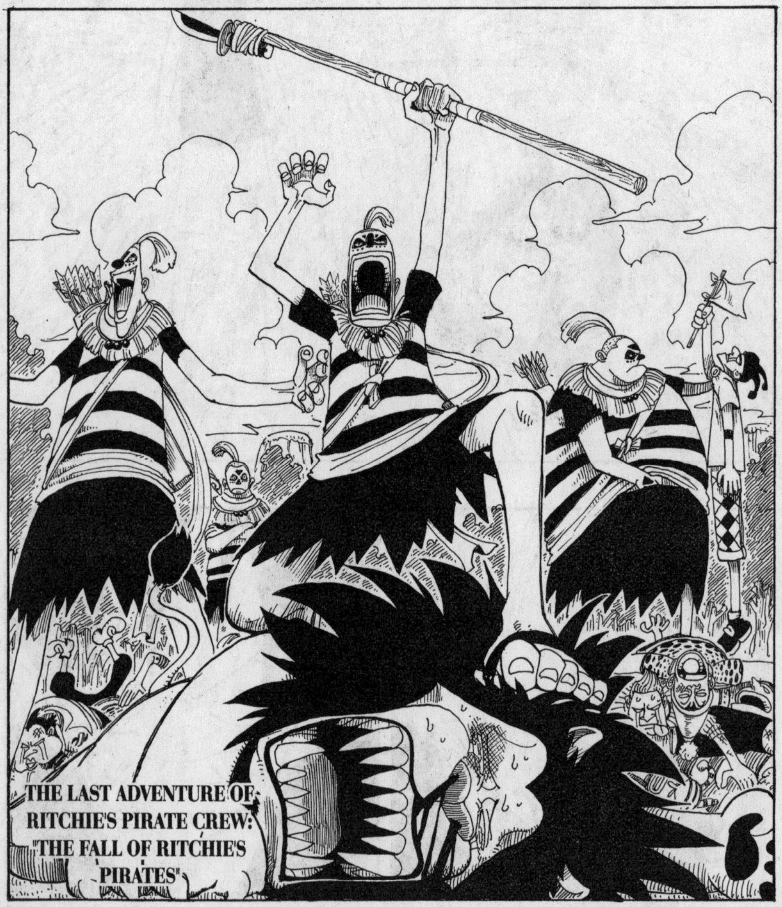
THE LAST ADVENTURE OF RITCHIE'S PIRATE CREW: "THE FALL OF RITCHIE'S PIRATES"

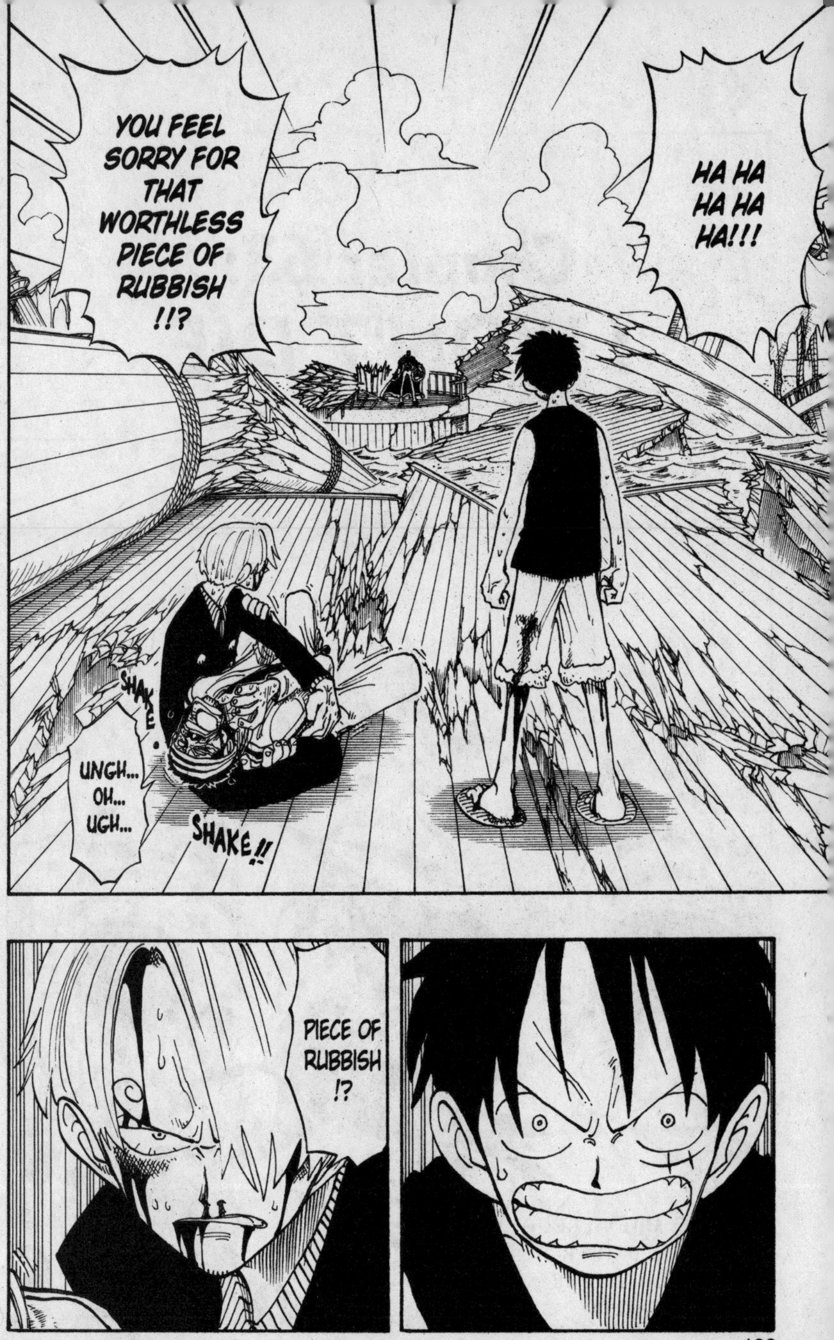
HA HA HA HA HA!!!
YOU FEEL SORRY FOR THAT WORTHLESS PIECE OF RUBBISH !!?
SHAKE
SHAKE!!
UNGH... OH... UGH...
PIECE OF RUBBISH !?

READ THIS WAY

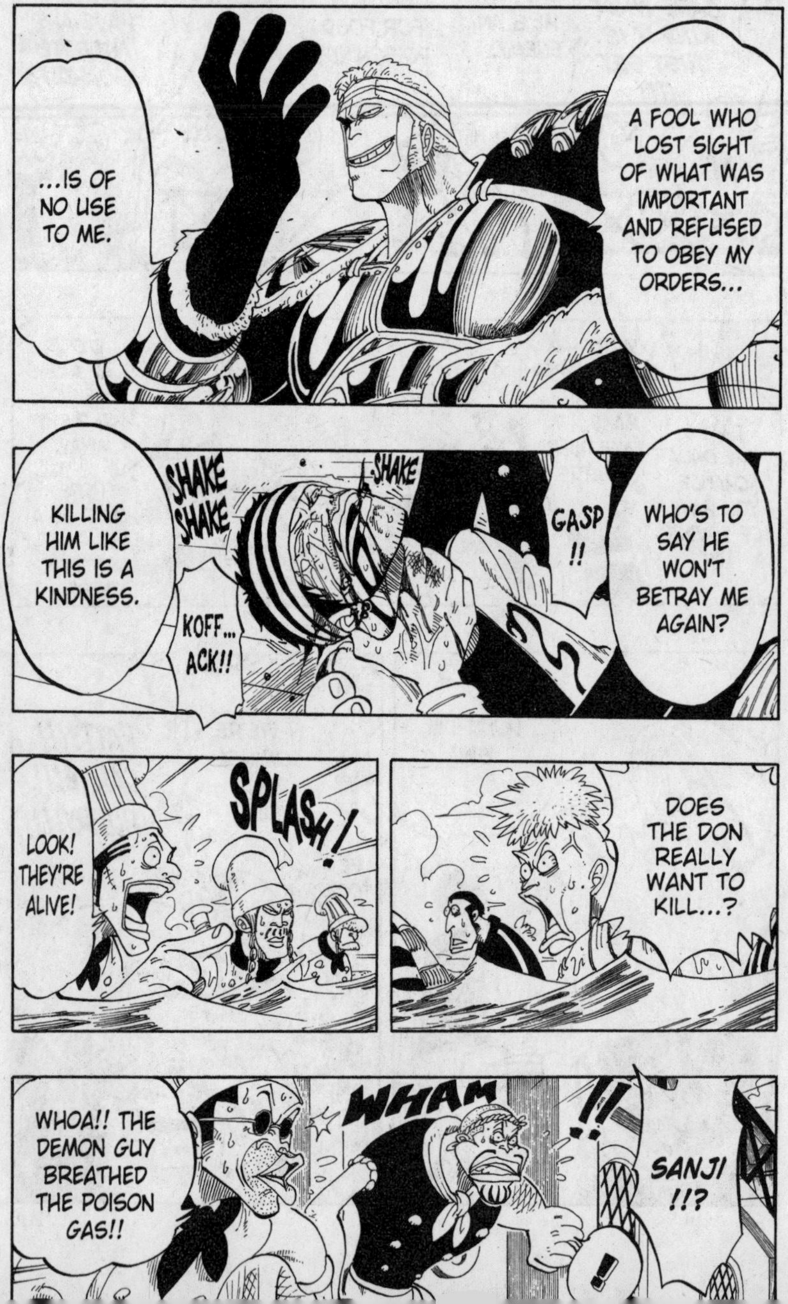
A FOOL WHO LOST SIGHT OF WHAT WAS IMPORTANT AND REFUSED TO OBEY MY ORDERS...
...IS OF NO USE TO ME.
WHO'S TO SAY HE WON'T BETRAY ME AGAIN?
GASP !!
SHAKE
SHAKE SHAKE
KOFF... ACK!!
KILLING HIM LIKE THIS IS A KINDNESS.
DOES THE DON REALLY WANT TO KILL...?
SPLASH!
LOOK! THEY'RE ALIVE!
SANJI !!?
!!
WHAM
WHOA!! THE DEMON GUY BREATHED THE POISON GAS!!
!

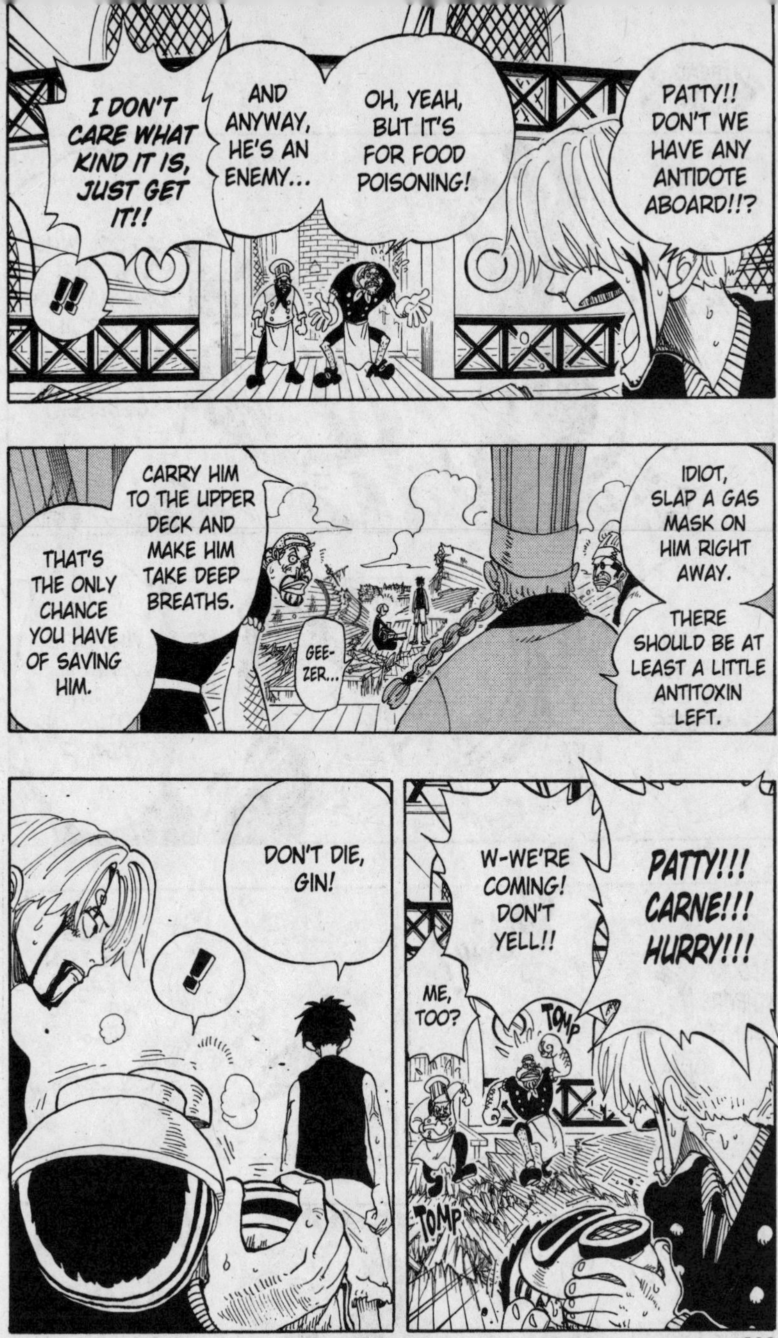
PATTY!! DON'T WE HAVE ANY ANTIDOTE ABOARD!!?
OH, YEAH, BUT IT'S FOR FOOD POISONING!
AND ANYWAY, HE'S AN ENEMY...
I DON'T CARE WHAT KIND IT IS, JUST GET IT!!
!!
IDIOT, SLAP A GAS MASK ON HIM RIGHT AWAY.
THERE SHOULD BE AT LEAST A LITTLE ANTITOXIN LEFT.
CARRY HIM TO THE UPPER DECK AND MAKE HIM TAKE DEEP BREATHS.
THAT'S THE ONLY CHANCE YOU HAVE OF SAVING HIM.
GEE-ZER...
PATTY!!! CARNE!!! HURRY!!!
W-WE'RE COMING! DON'T YELL!!
ME, TOO?
TOMP
TOMP
DON'T DIE, GIN!
!

READ THIS WAY

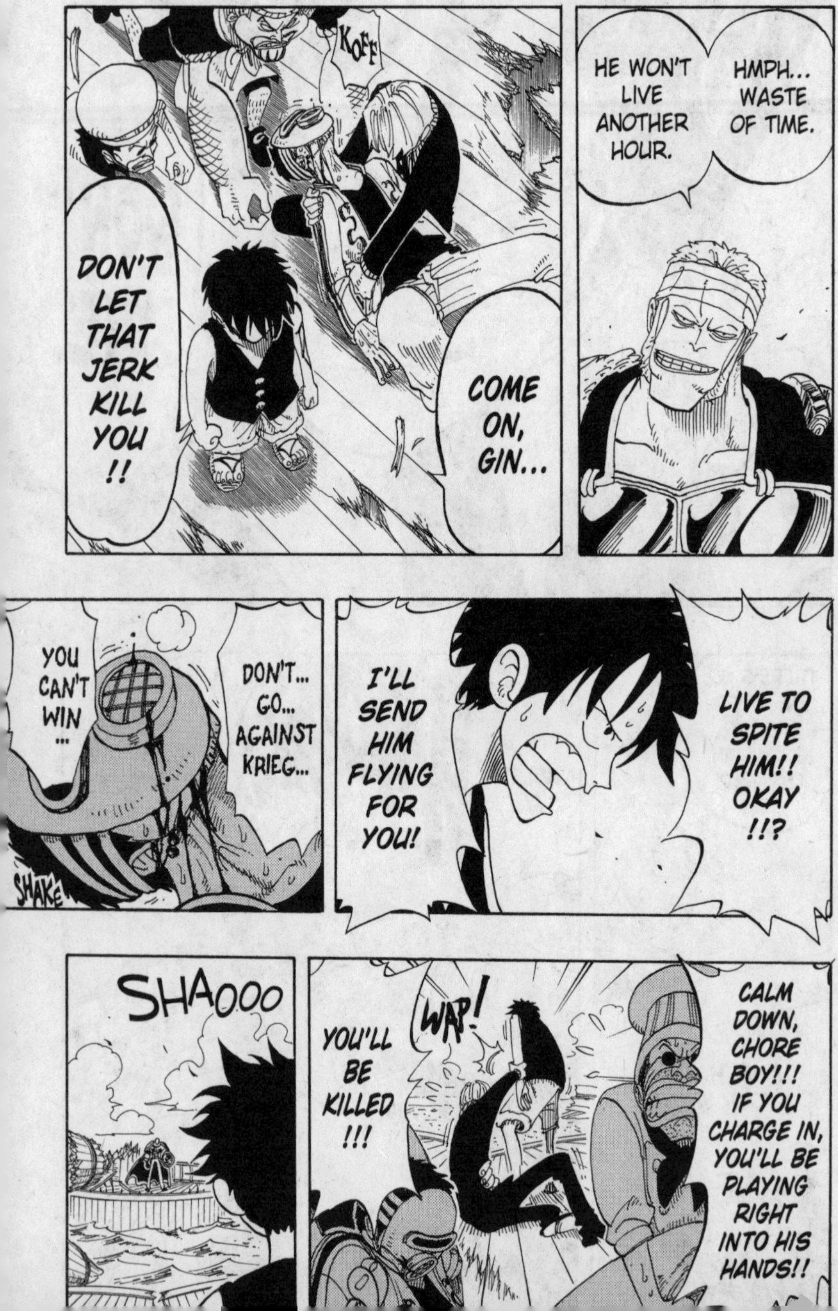
HMPH... WASTE OF TIME.
HE WON'T LIVE ANOTHER HOUR.
KOFF
COME ON, GIN...
DON'T LET THAT JERK KILL YOU!!
LIVE TO SPITE HIM!! OKAY!!?
I'LL SEND HIM FLYING FOR YOU!
DON'T... GO... AGAINST KRIEG...
YOU CAN'T WIN...
SHAKE
CALM DOWN, CHORE BOY!!! IF YOU CHARGE IN, YOU'LL BE PLAYING RIGHT INTO HIS HANDS!!
WAP!
YOU'LL BE KILLED!!!
SHAOOO

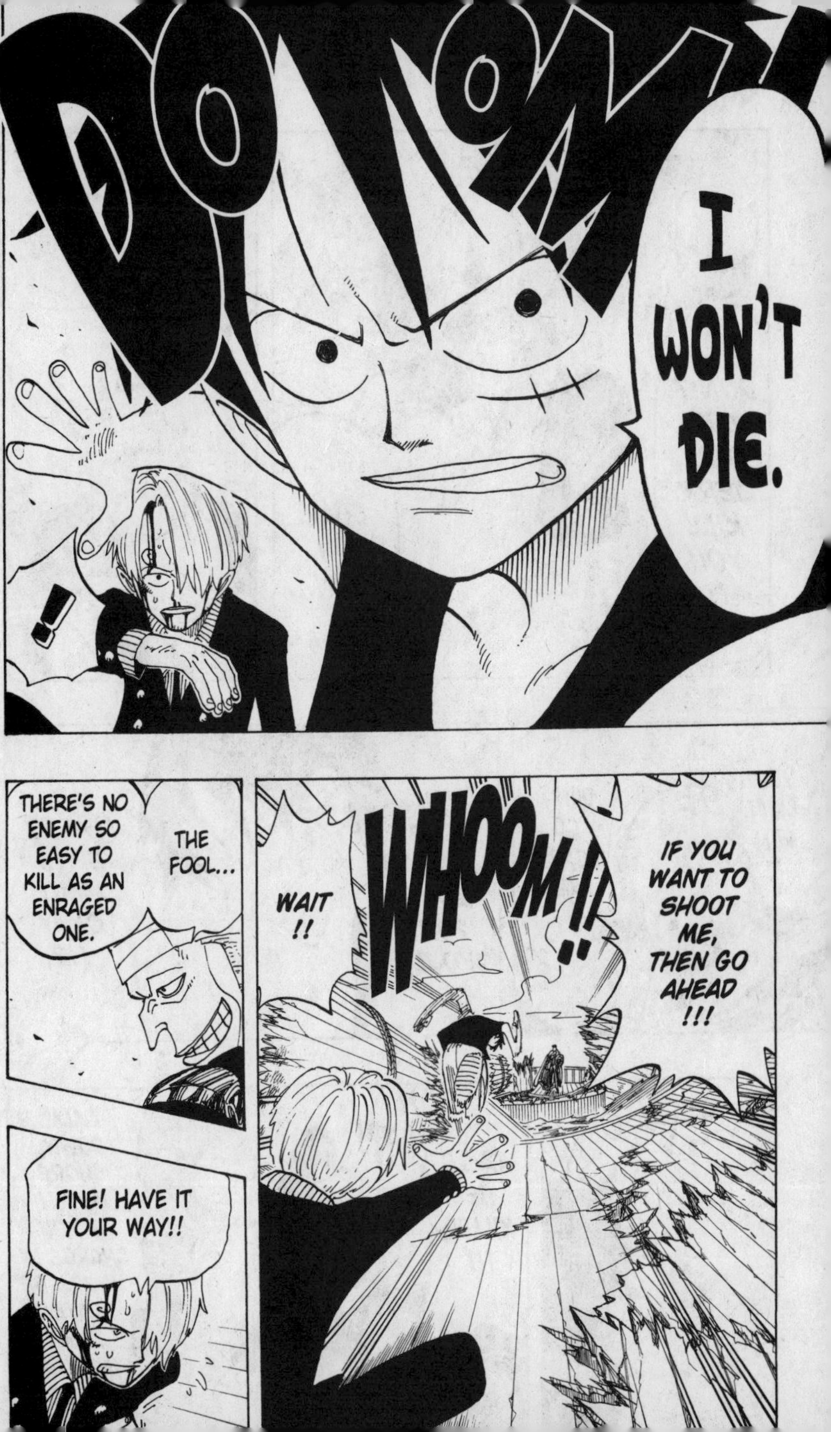
I WON'T DIE.
!
IF YOU WANT TO SHOOT ME, THEN GO AHEAD !!!
WHOOM !!
WAIT !!
THE FOOL...
THERE'S NO ENEMY SO EASY TO KILL AS AN ENRAGED ONE.
FINE! HAVE IT YOUR WAY!!

READ THIS WAY

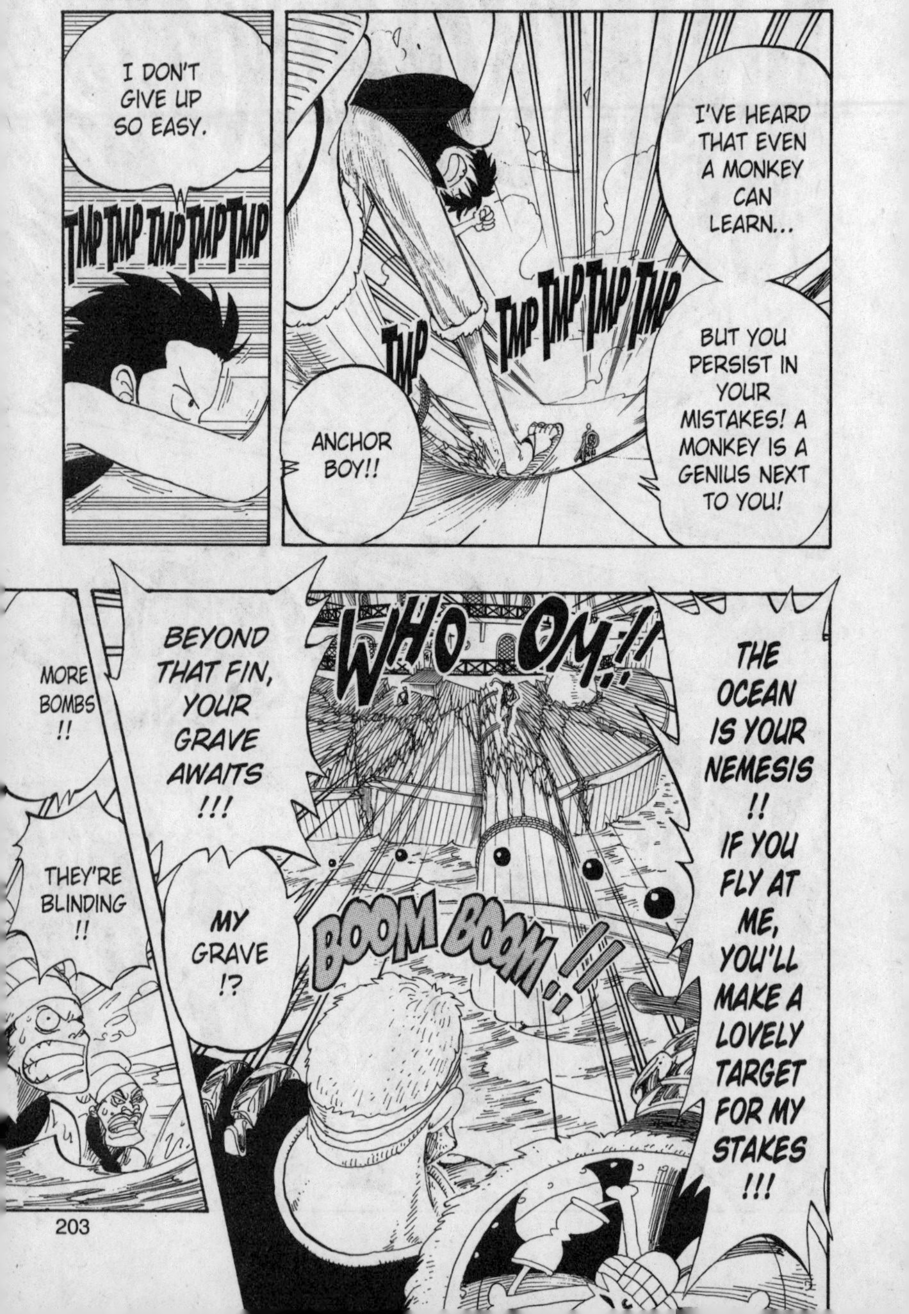

I'VE HEARD THAT EVEN A MONKEY CAN LEARN...
BUT YOU PERSIST IN YOUR MISTAKES! A MONKEY IS A GENIUS NEXT TO YOU!
TMP TMP TMP TMP TMP
ANCHOR BOY!!
I DON'T GIVE UP SO EASY.
TMP TMP TMP TMP TMP
WHO OM!!
THE OCEAN IS YOUR NEMESIS!! IF YOU FLY AT ME, YOU'LL MAKE A LOVELY TARGET FOR MY STAKES!!!
BEYOND THAT FIN, YOUR GRAVE AWAITS!!!
BOOM BOOM!!
MY GRAVE!?
MORE BOMBS!!
THEY'RE BLINDING!!

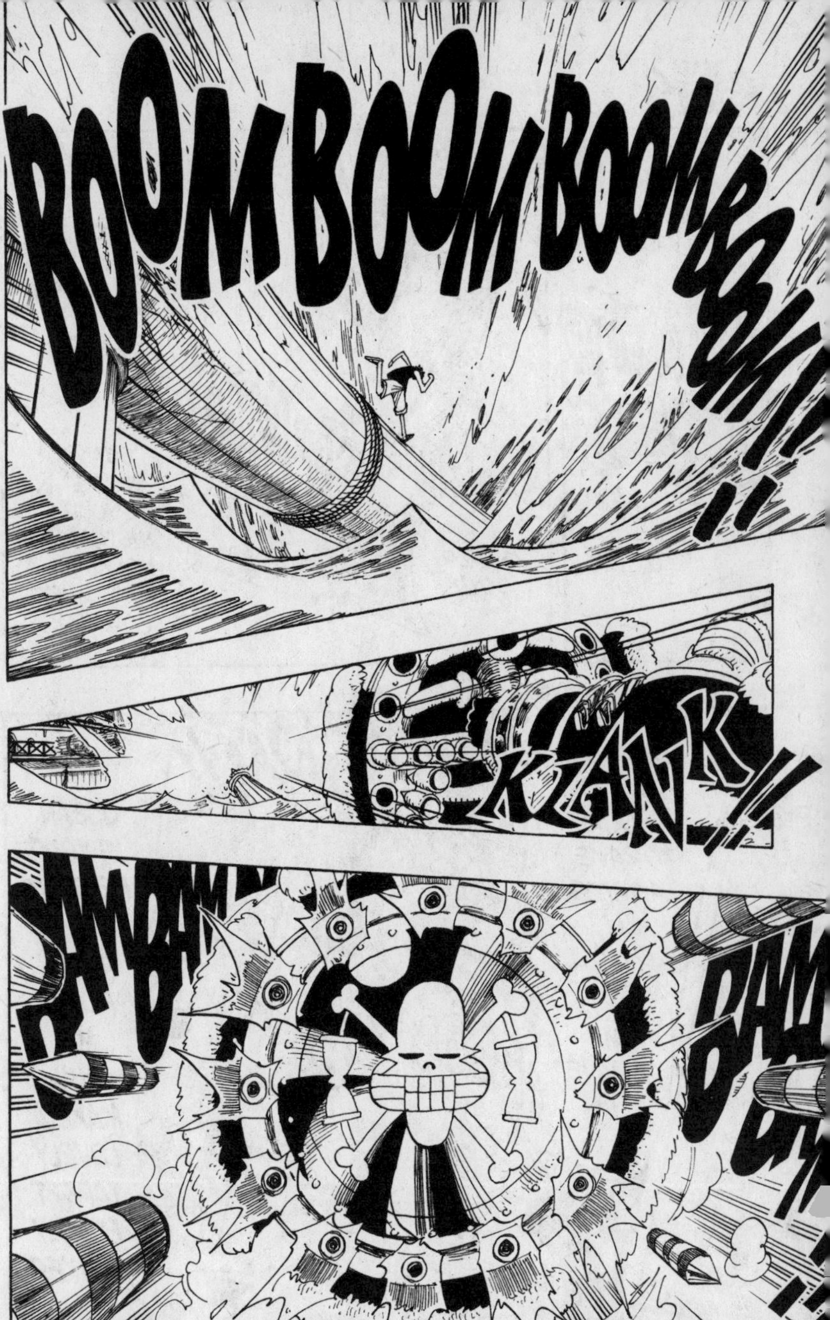
BOOM BOOM BOOM BOOM!!
KLANK!!
BAMBAM
BAMBAM!!

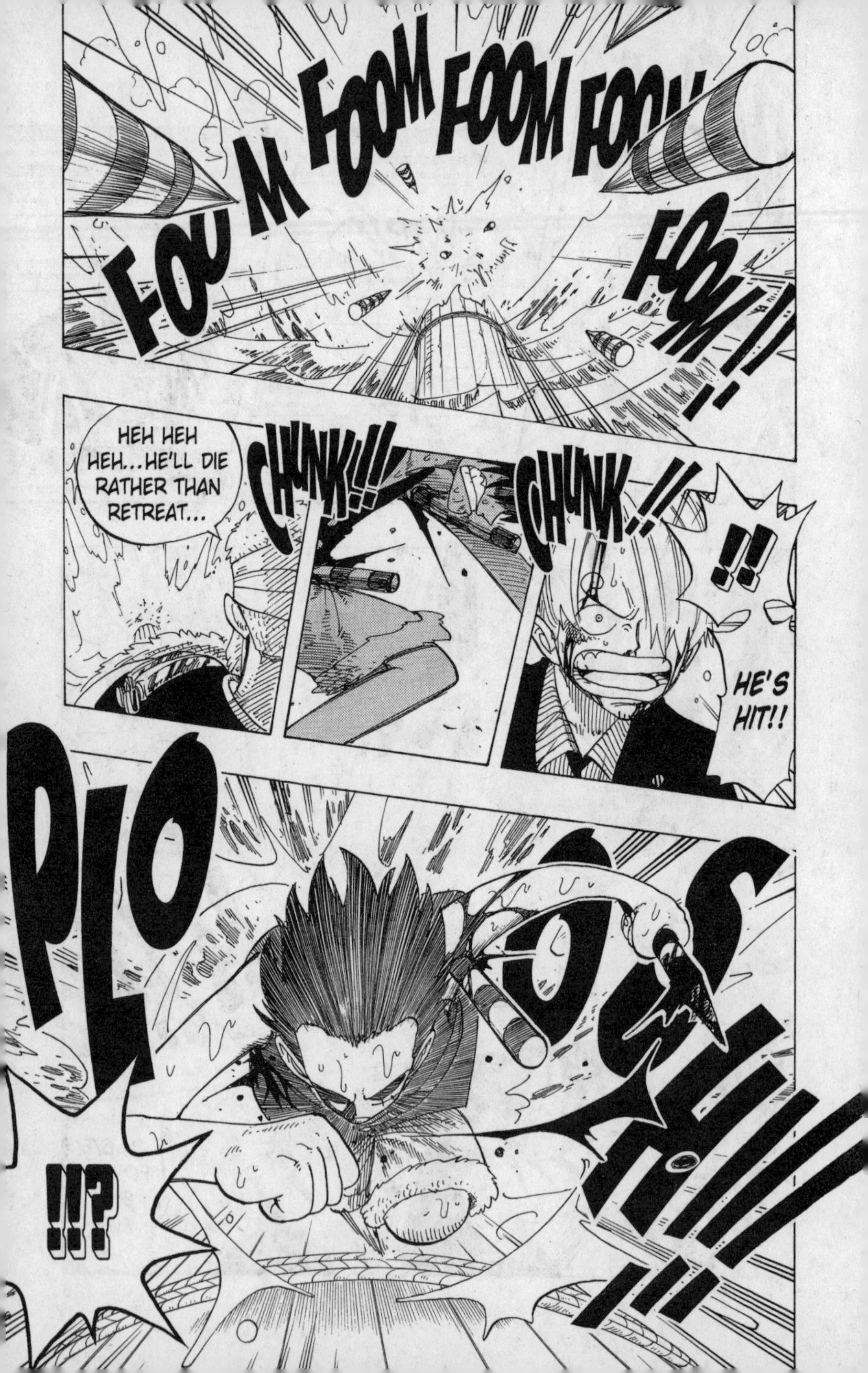

FOOM FOOM
FOOM!!
!!
HE'S HIT!!
CHUNK!!
CHUNK!!!
HEH HEH HEH...HE'LL DIE RATHER THAN RETREAT...
PLOOSH!!!
!!?

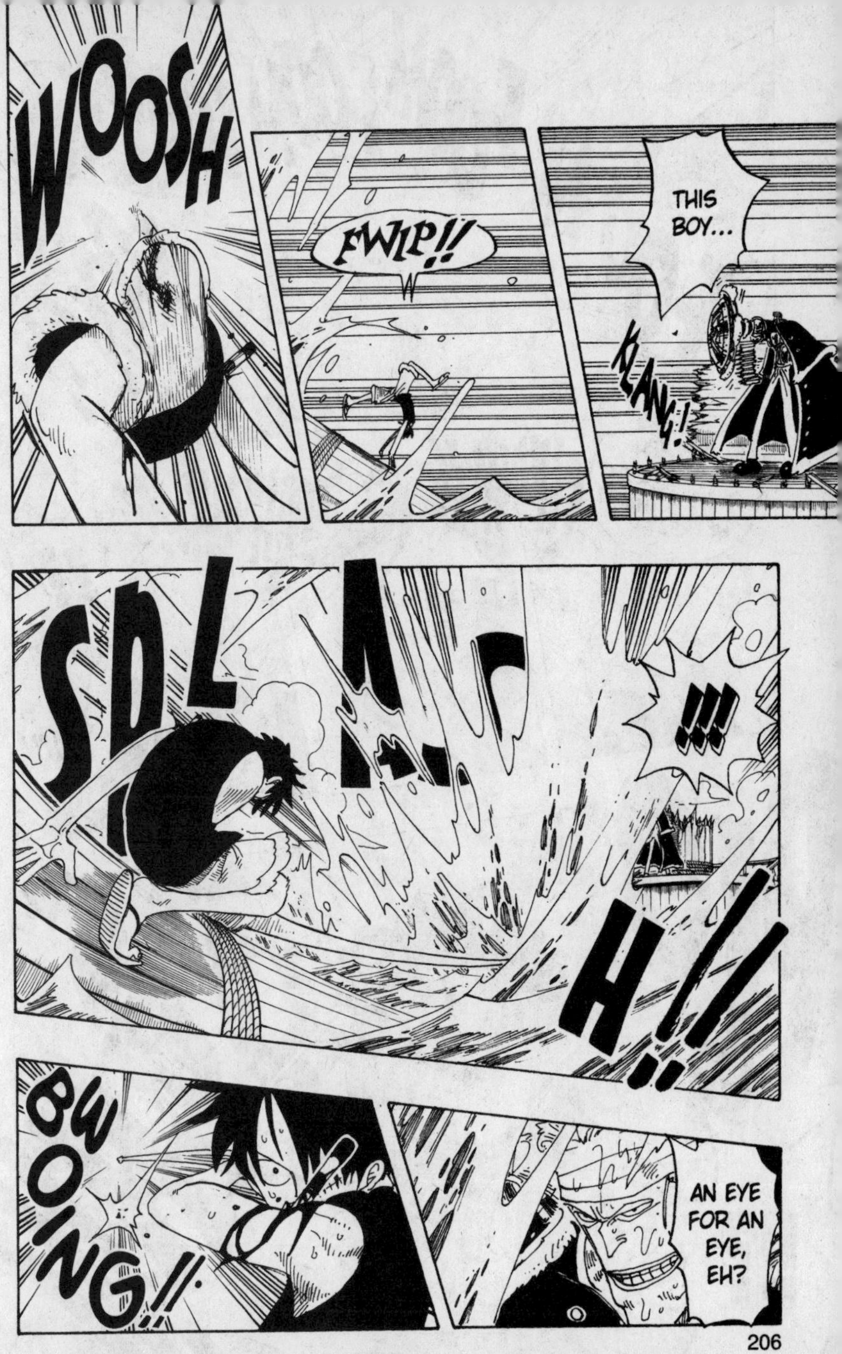
THIS BOY...
KLANG!
FWIP!!
WOOSH
!!!
SPLASH!!
AN EYE FOR AN EYE, EH?
BWOING!!

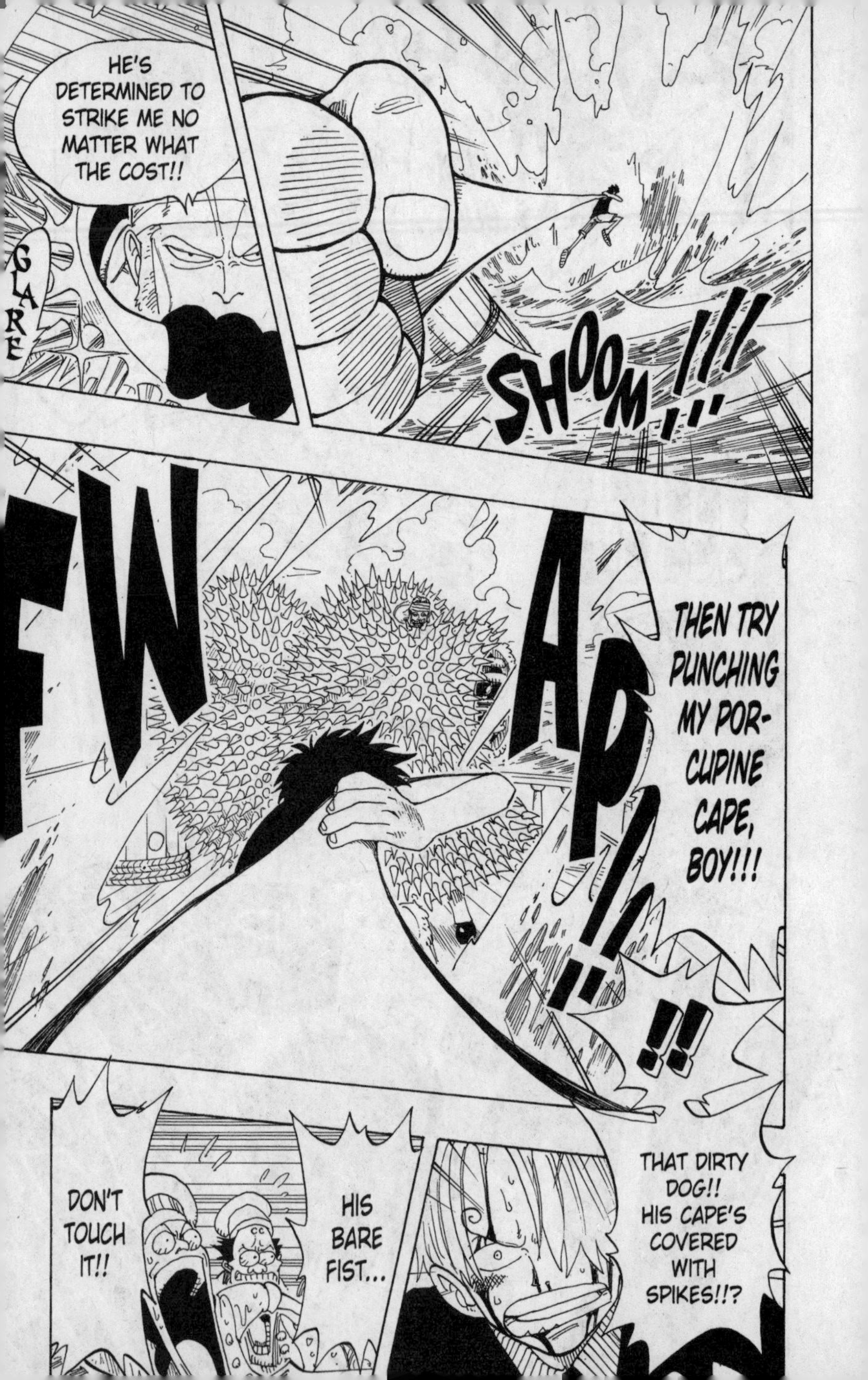

HE'S DETERMINED TO STRIKE ME NO MATTER WHAT THE COST!!
GLARE
SHOOM!!!
THEN TRY PUNCHING MY POR-CUPINE CAPE, BOY!!!
FWAP!!
THAT DIRTY DOG!! HIS CAPE'S COVERED WITH SPIKES!!?
HIS BARE FIST...
DON'T TOUCH IT!!

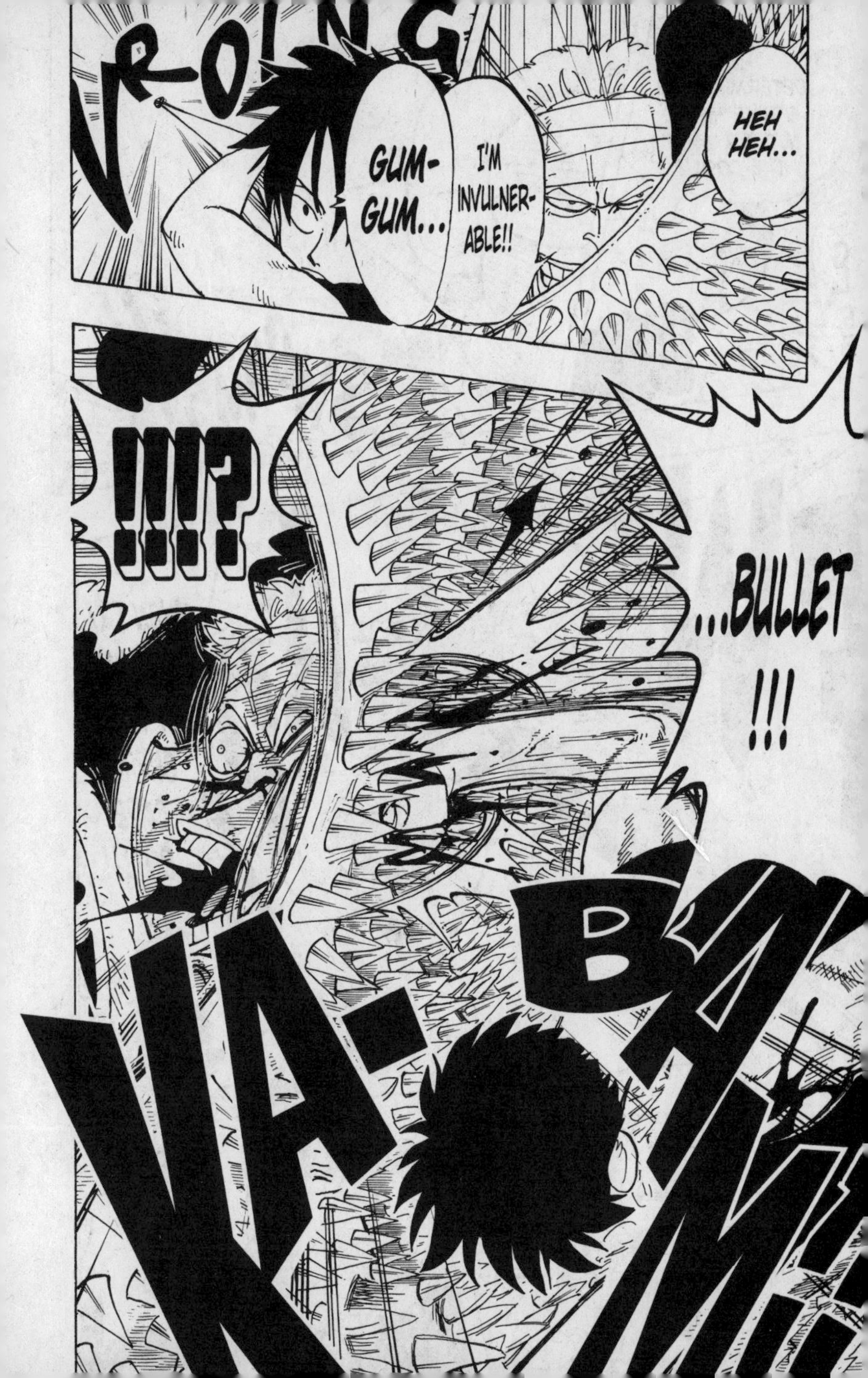
HEH HEH...
I'M INVULNERABLE!!
GUM-GUM...
VROING
...BULLET !!!
!!!?

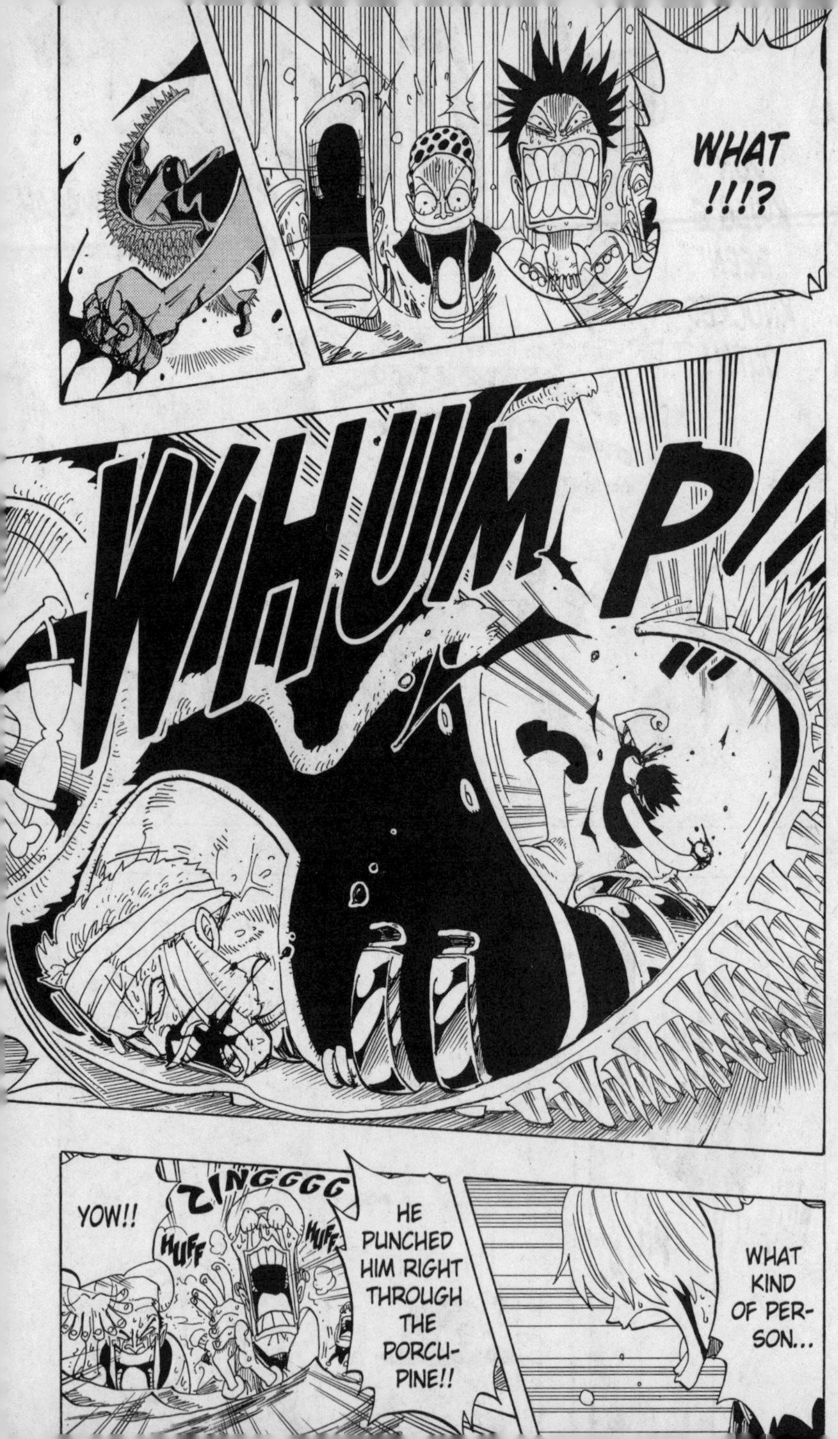
WHAT !!!?
WHUMP!!
WHAT KIND OF PER-SON...
HE PUNCHED HIM RIGHT THROUGH THE PORCU-PINE!!
ZINGGGG
HUFF
HUFF
YOW!!

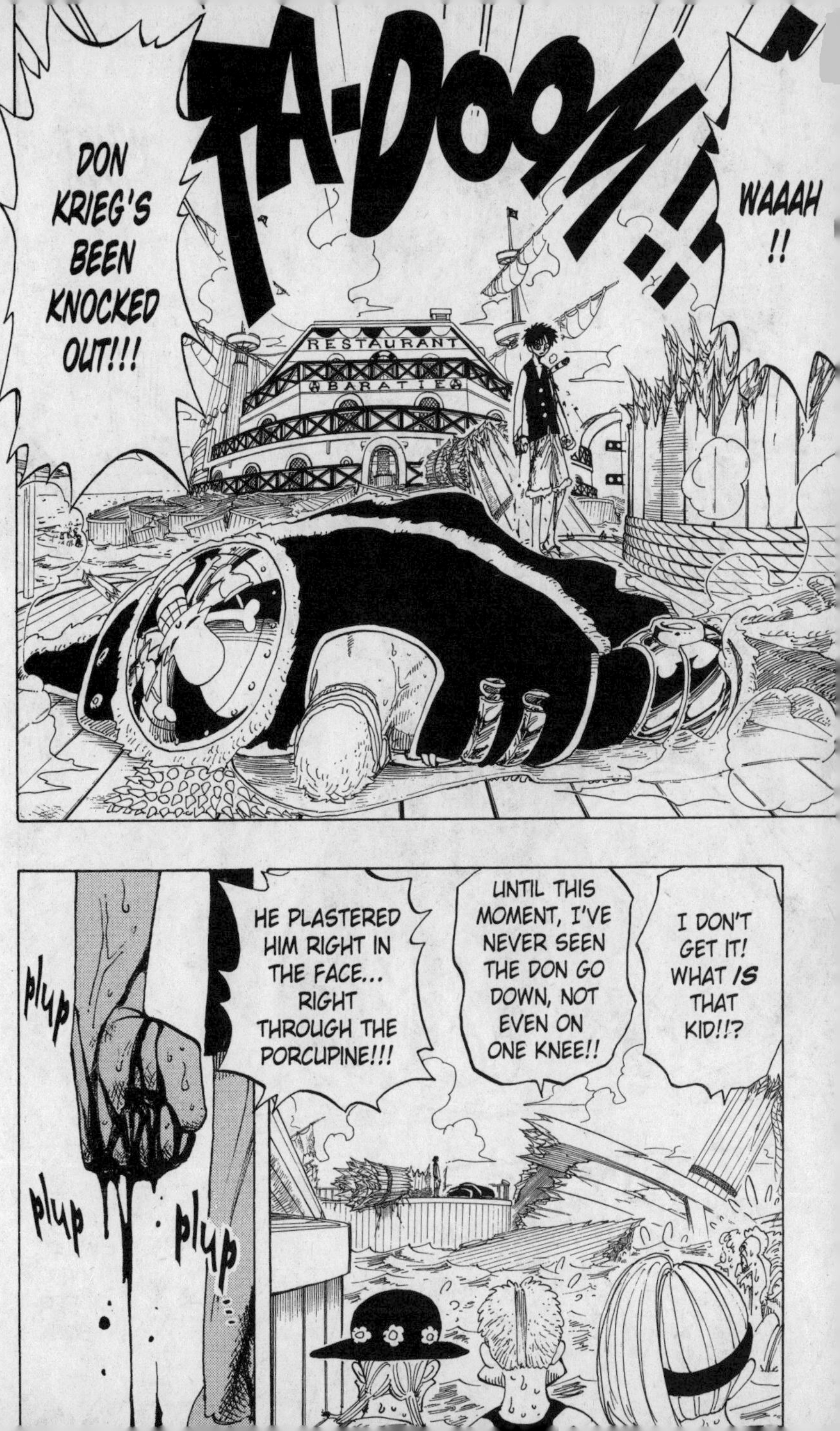
WAAAH !!
TA-DOOM!!
DON KRIEG'S BEEN KNOCKED OUT!!!
RESTAURANT BARATIE
I DON'T GET IT! WHAT *IS* THAT KID!!?
UNTIL THIS MOMENT, I'VE NEVER SEEN THE DON GO DOWN, NOT EVEN ON ONE KNEE!!
HE PLASTERED HIM RIGHT IN THE FACE... RIGHT THROUGH THE PORCUPINE!!!
plup
plup
plup

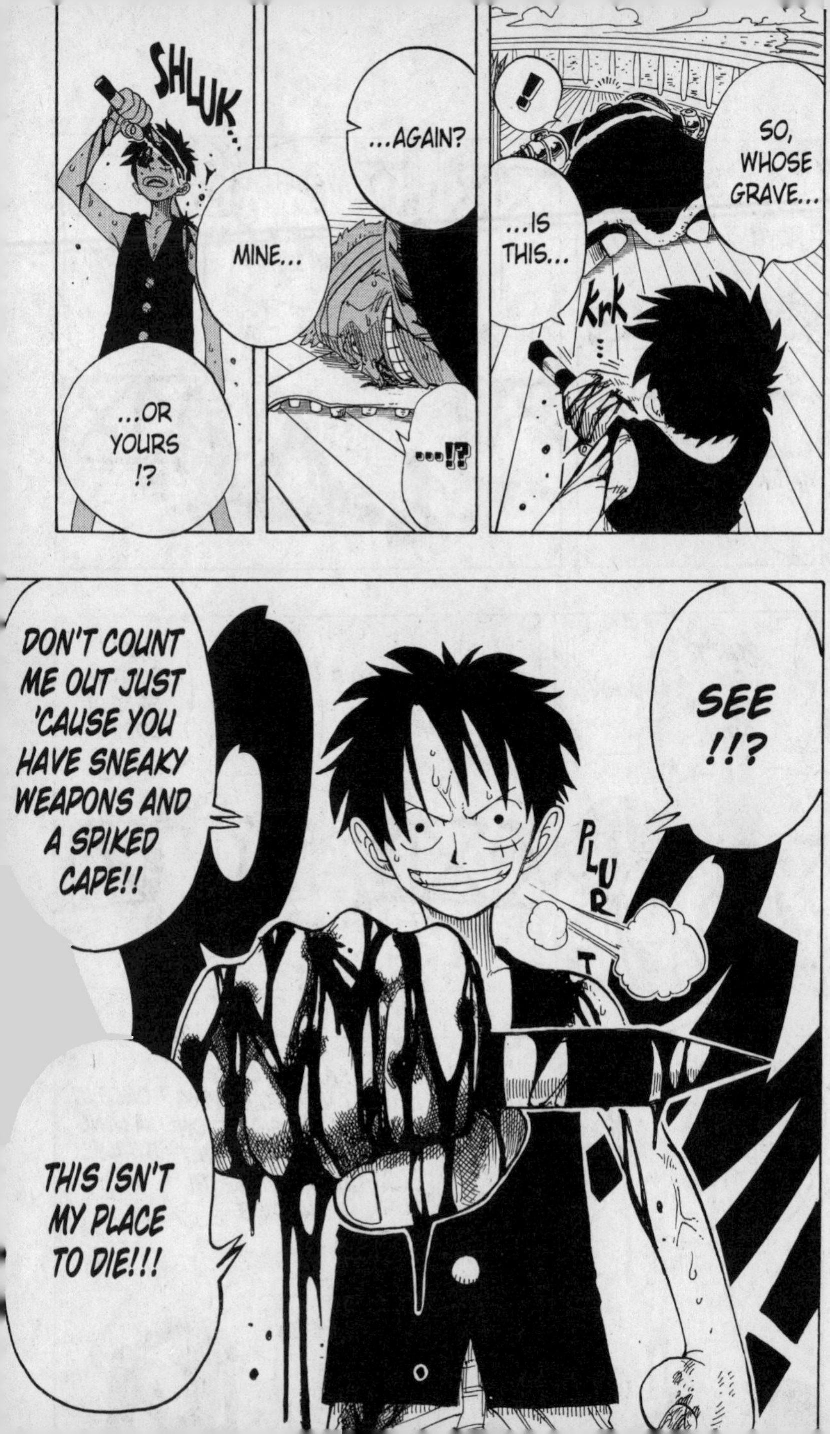
SO, WHOSE GRAVE...
!
...IS THIS...
KRK...
...AGAIN?
...!?
SHLUK...
MINE...
...OR YOURS !?
SEE !!?
PLURT
DON'T COUNT ME OUT JUST 'CAUSE YOU HAVE SNEAKY WEAPONS AND A SPIKED CAPE!!
THIS ISN'T MY PLACE TO DIE!!!

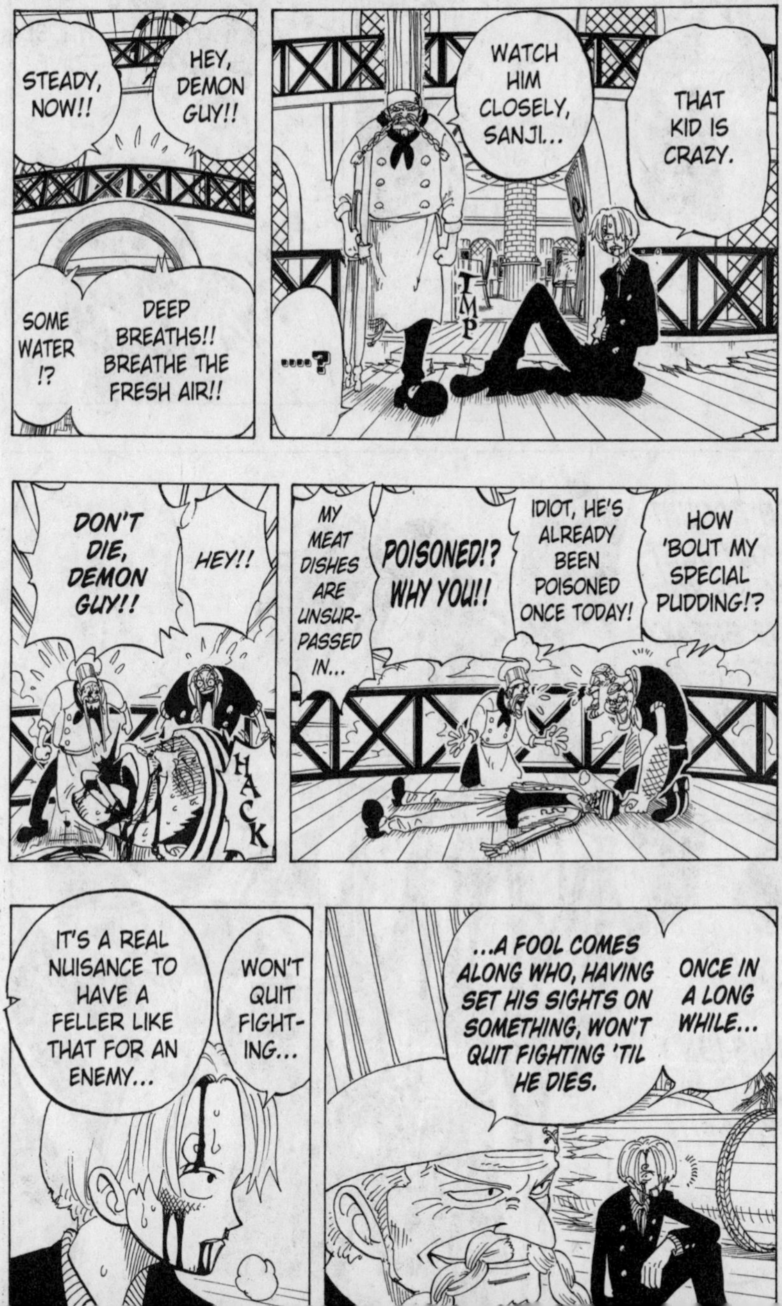
THAT KID IS CRAZY.
WATCH HIM CLOSELY, SANJI...
TMP
....?
HEY, DEMON GUY!!
STEADY, NOW!!
DEEP BREATHS!! BREATHE THE FRESH AIR!!
SOME WATER !?
HOW 'BOUT MY SPECIAL PUDDING!?
IDIOT, HE'S ALREADY BEEN POISONED ONCE TODAY!
POISONED!? WHY YOU!!
MY MEAT DISHES ARE UNSURPASSED IN...
HEY!!
DON'T DIE, DEMON GUY!!
HACK
ONCE IN A LONG WHILE...
...A FOOL COMES ALONG WHO, HAVING SET HIS SIGHTS ON SOMETHING, WON'T QUIT FIGHTING 'TIL HE DIES.
WON'T QUIT FIGHTING...
IT'S A REAL NUISANCE TO HAVE A FELLER LIKE THAT FOR AN ENEMY...

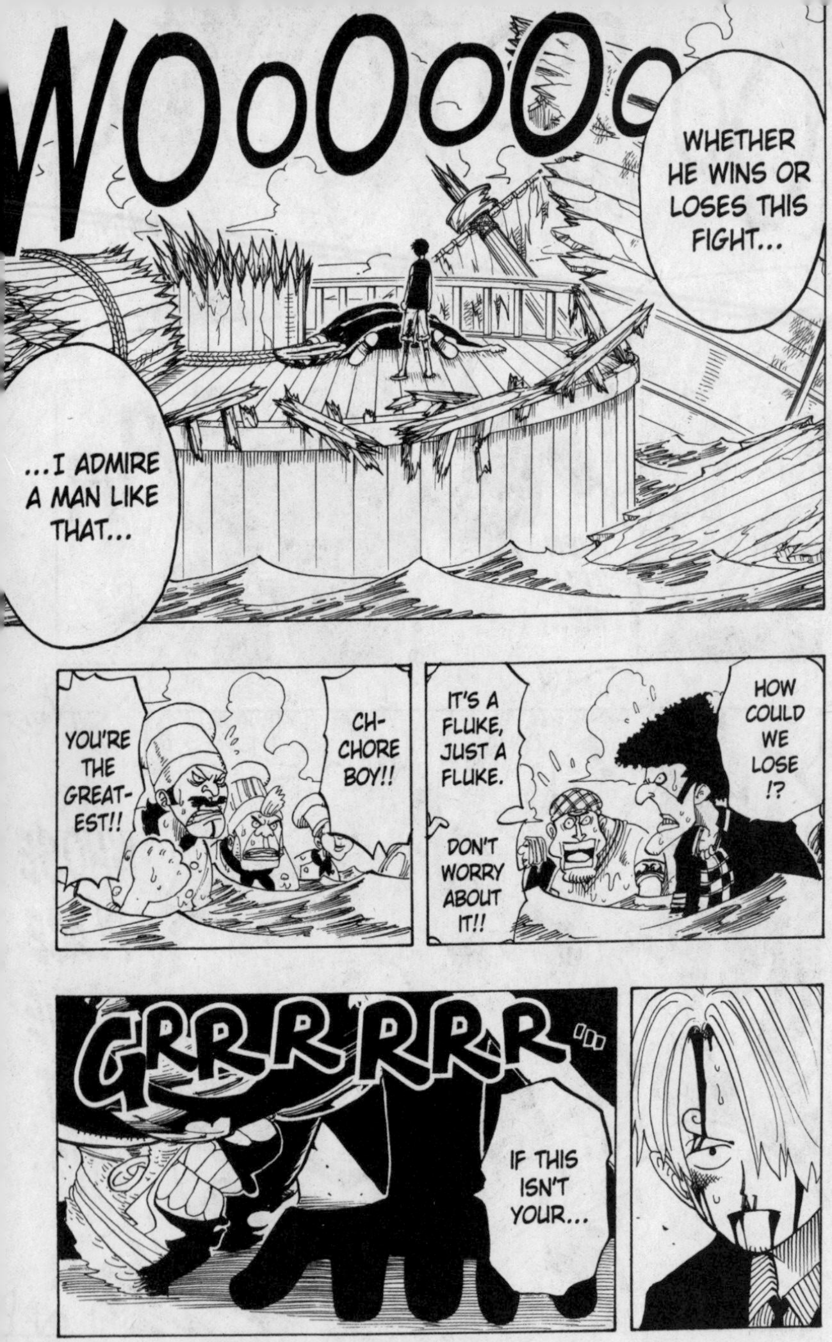
WOOOOOOO
WHETHER HE WINS OR LOSES THIS FIGHT...
...I ADMIRE A MAN LIKE THAT...
HOW COULD WE LOSE!?
IT'S A FLUKE, JUST A FLUKE.
DON'T WORRY ABOUT IT!!
CH-CHORE BOY!!
YOU'RE THE GREAT-EST!!
GRRRRRR
IF THIS ISN'T YOUR...

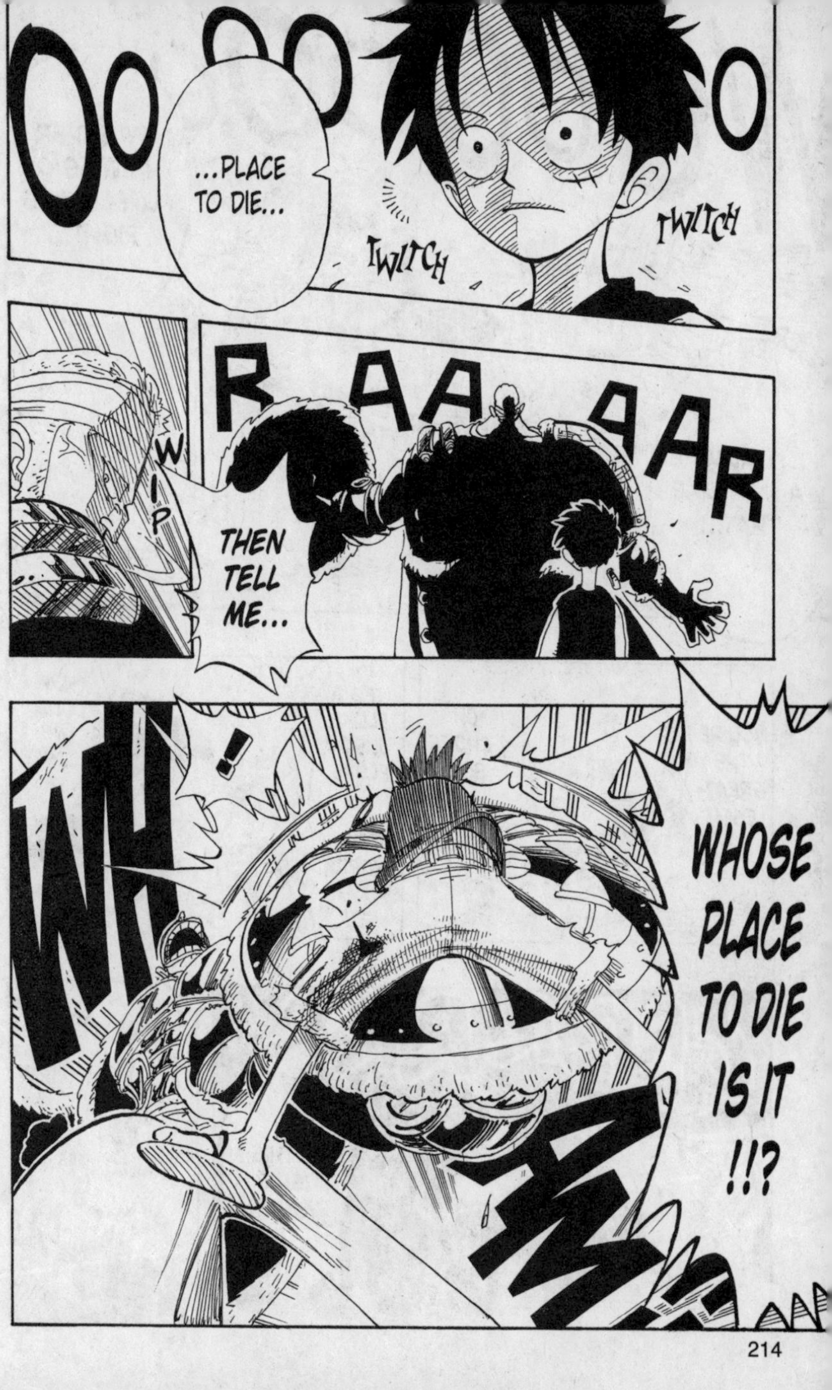
OOOOOO
...PLACE TO DIE...
TWITCH
TWITCH
RAAAAAR
THEN TELL ME...
WIP
WHOSE PLACE TO DIE IS IT !!?
!

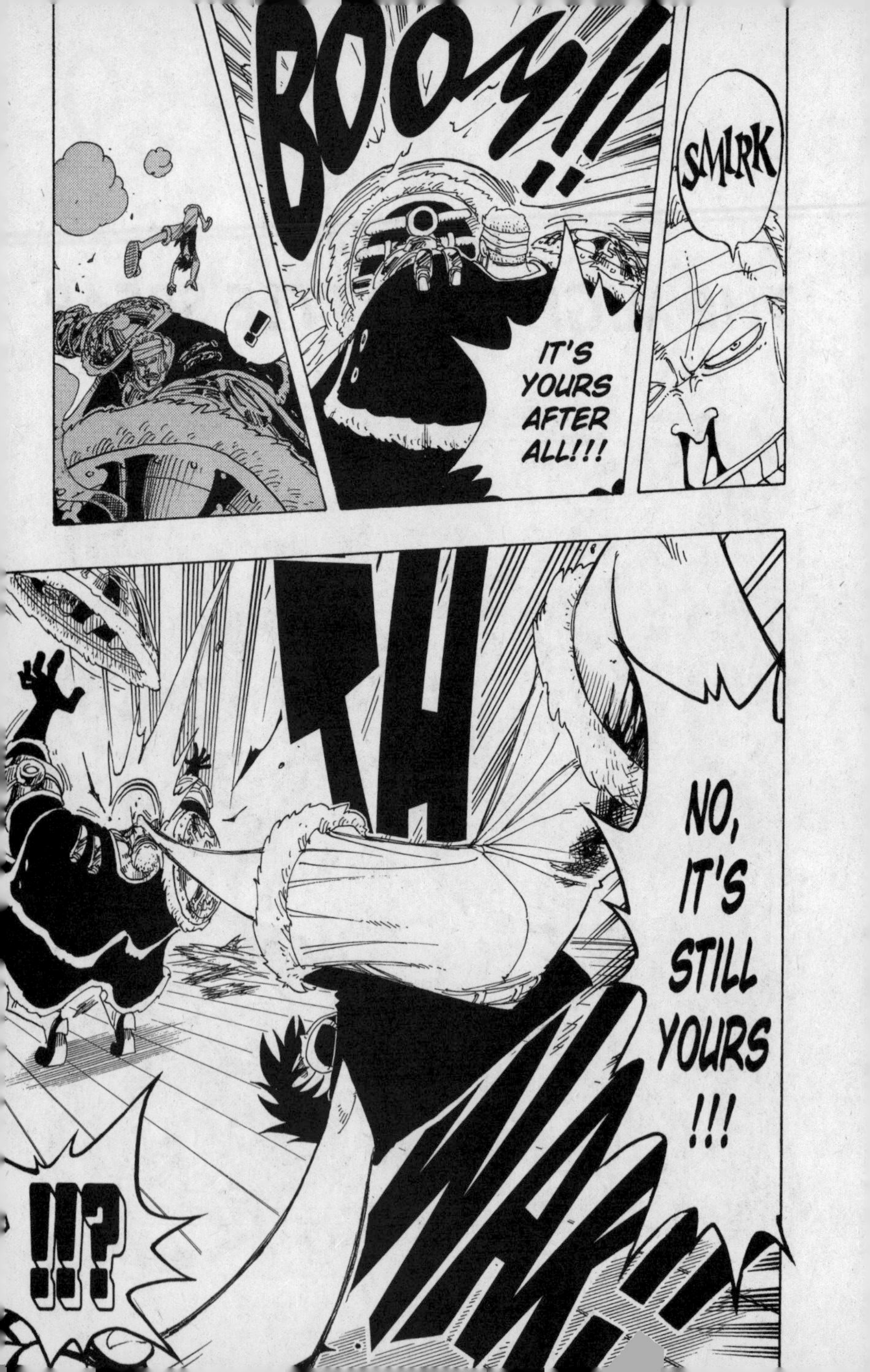
SMIRK
BOOM!!
IT'S YOURS AFTER ALL!!!
!
NO, IT'S STILL YOURS!!!
!!?

## Chapter 64:
# THE MIGHTY BATTLE SPEAR

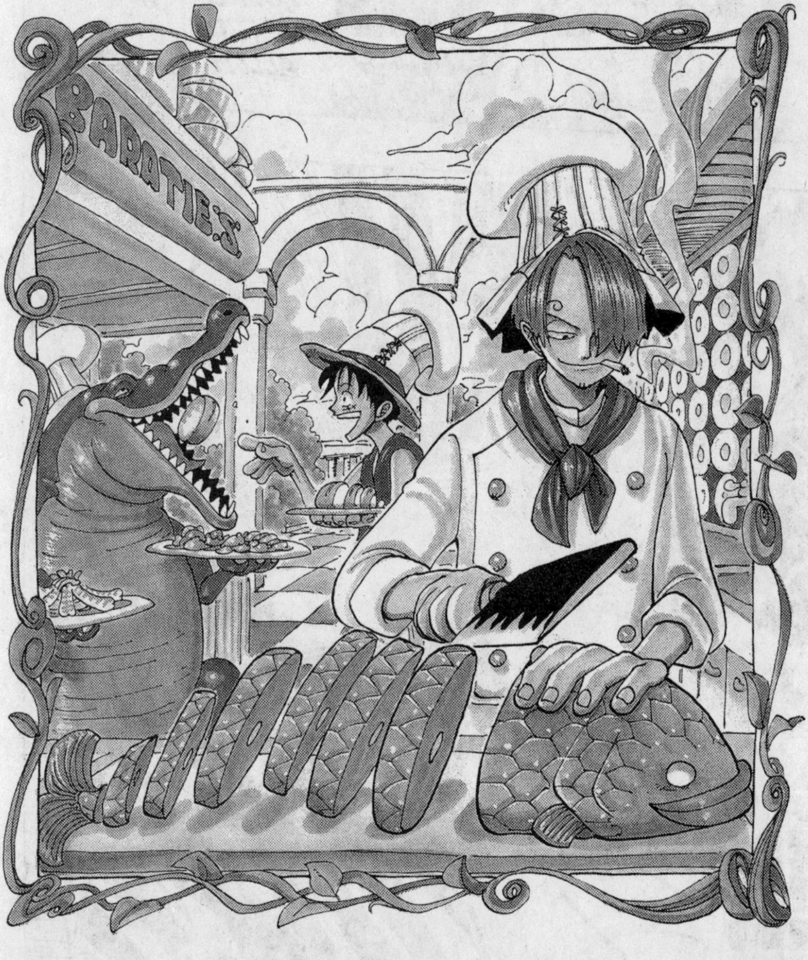
BARATIE'S

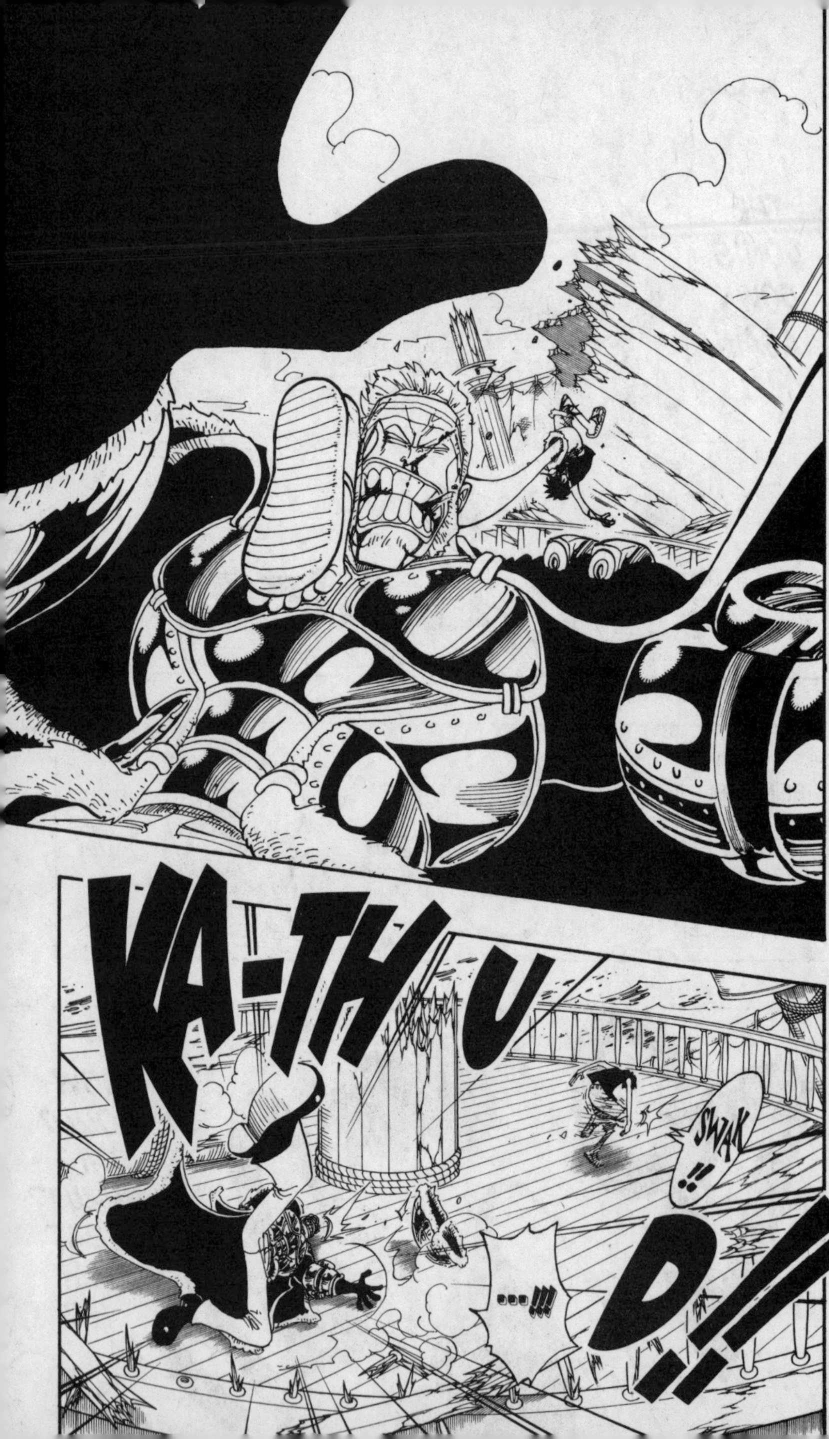
KA-THUD!!
SWAK!!
...!!!

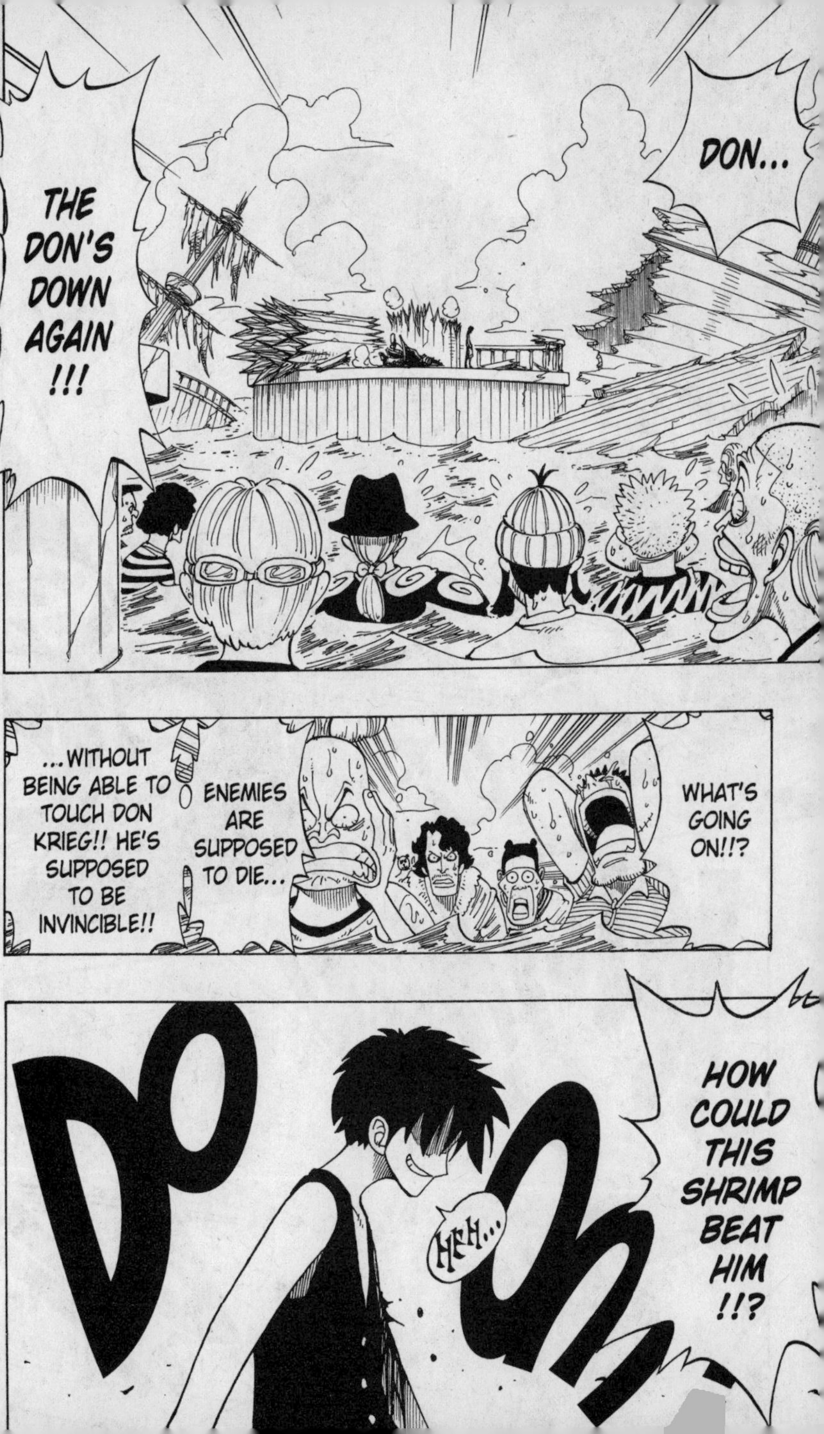
DON...
THE DON'S DOWN AGAIN !!!
WHAT'S GOING ON!!?
ENEMIES ARE SUPPOSED TO DIE...
...WITHOUT BEING ABLE TO TOUCH DON KRIEG!! HE'S SUPPOSED TO BE INVINCIBLE!!
HOW COULD THIS SHRIMP BEAT HIM!!?
HEH...

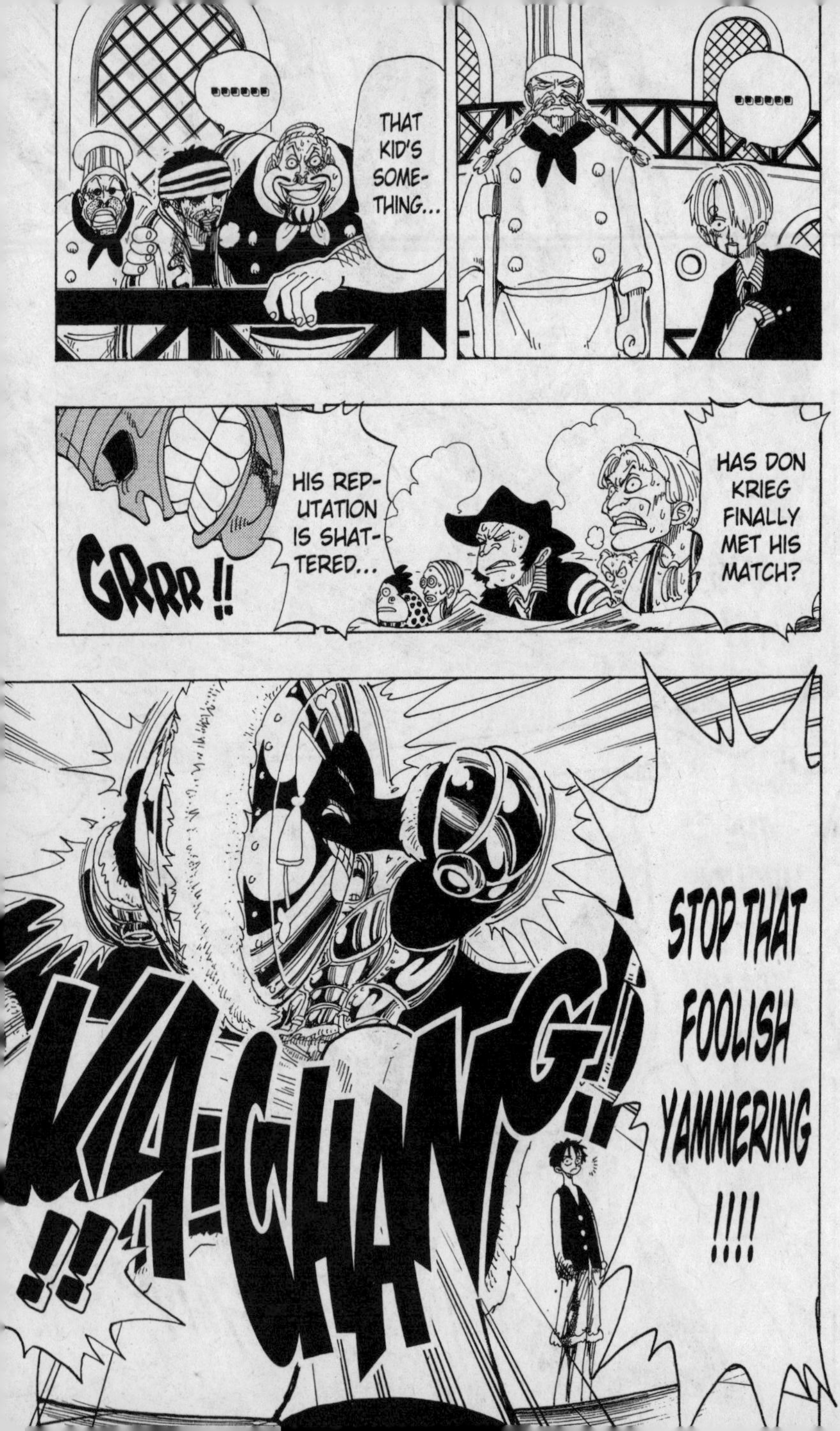
......
THAT KID'S SOMETHING...
......
HAS DON KRIEG FINALLY MET HIS MATCH?
HIS REPUTATION IS SHATTERED...
GRRR!!
STOP THAT FOOLISH YAMMERING!!!!
KA-CHANG!!

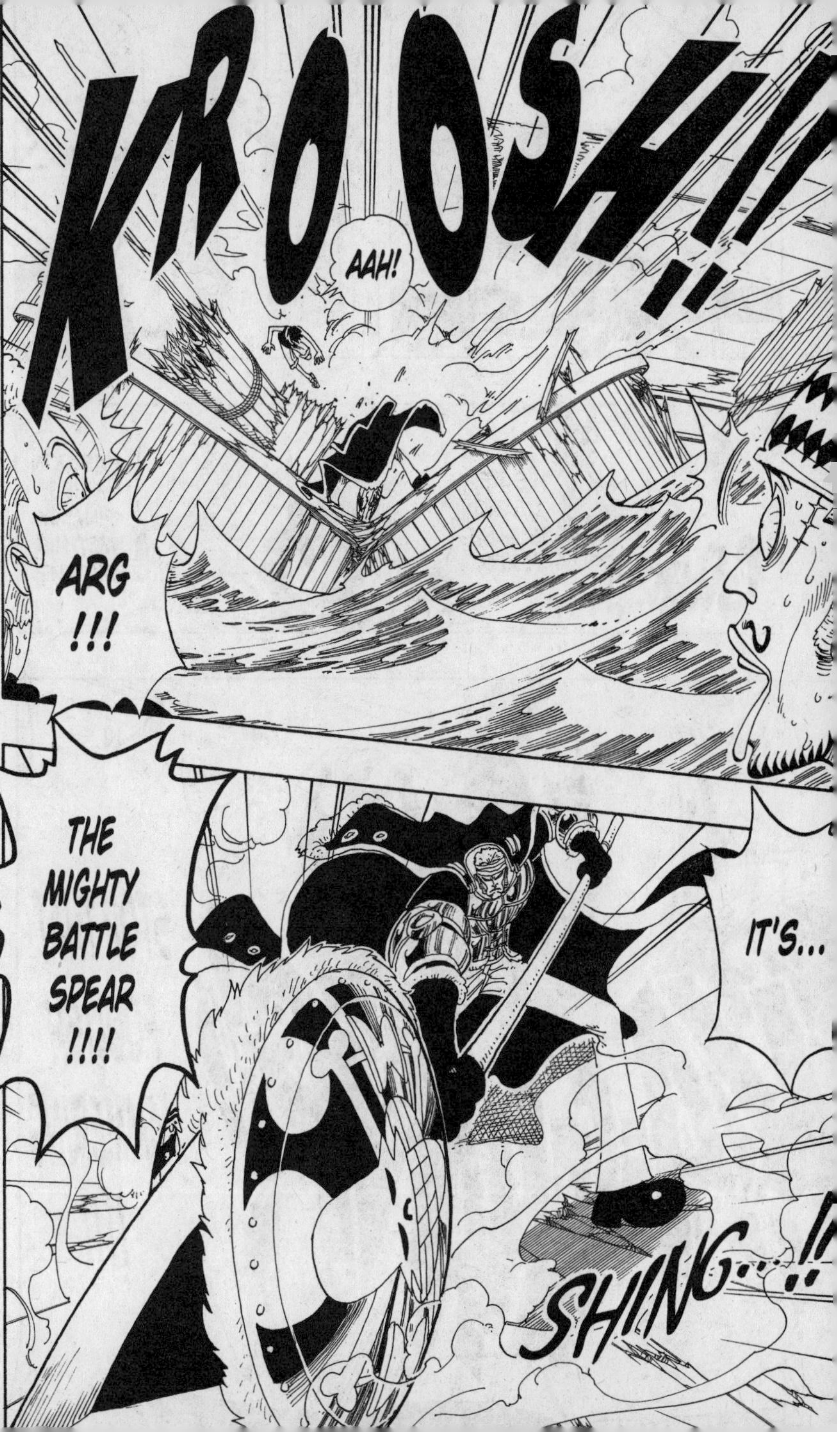

KROOSH!!
AAH!
ARG !!!
IT'S...
THE MIGHTY BATTLE SPEAR !!!!
SHING...!!

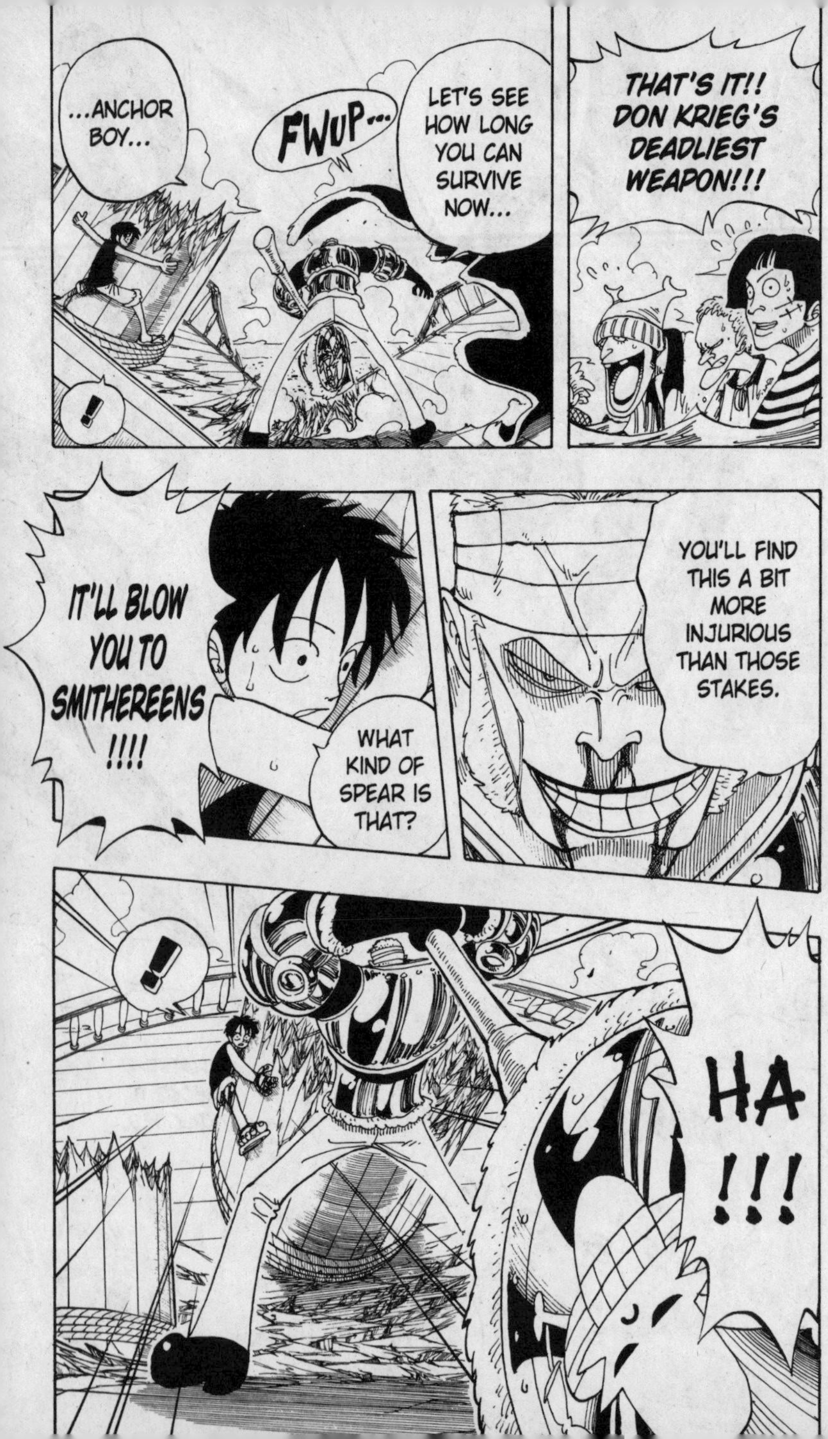
THAT'S IT!! DON KRIEG'S DEADLIEST WEAPON!!!
LET'S SEE HOW LONG YOU CAN SURVIVE NOW...
FWUP...
...ANCHOR BOY...
!
YOU'LL FIND THIS A BIT MORE INJURIOUS THAN THOSE STAKES.
WHAT KIND OF SPEAR IS THAT?
IT'LL BLOW YOU TO SMITHEREENS !!!!
HA !!!
!

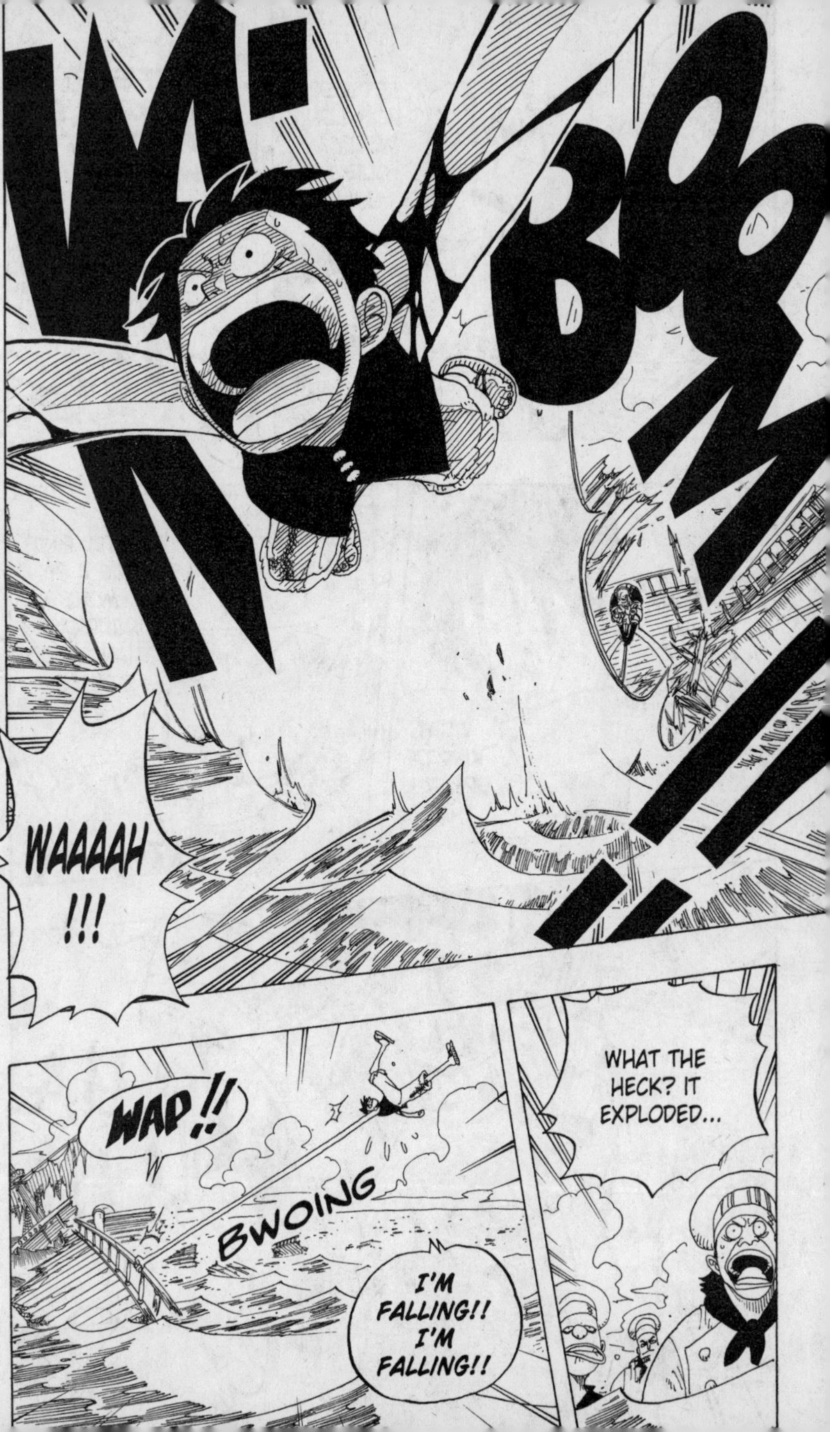
BOOM!!!
WAAAAH !!!
WHAT THE HECK? IT EXPLODED...
WAP!!
BWOING
I'M FALLING!! I'M FALLING!!

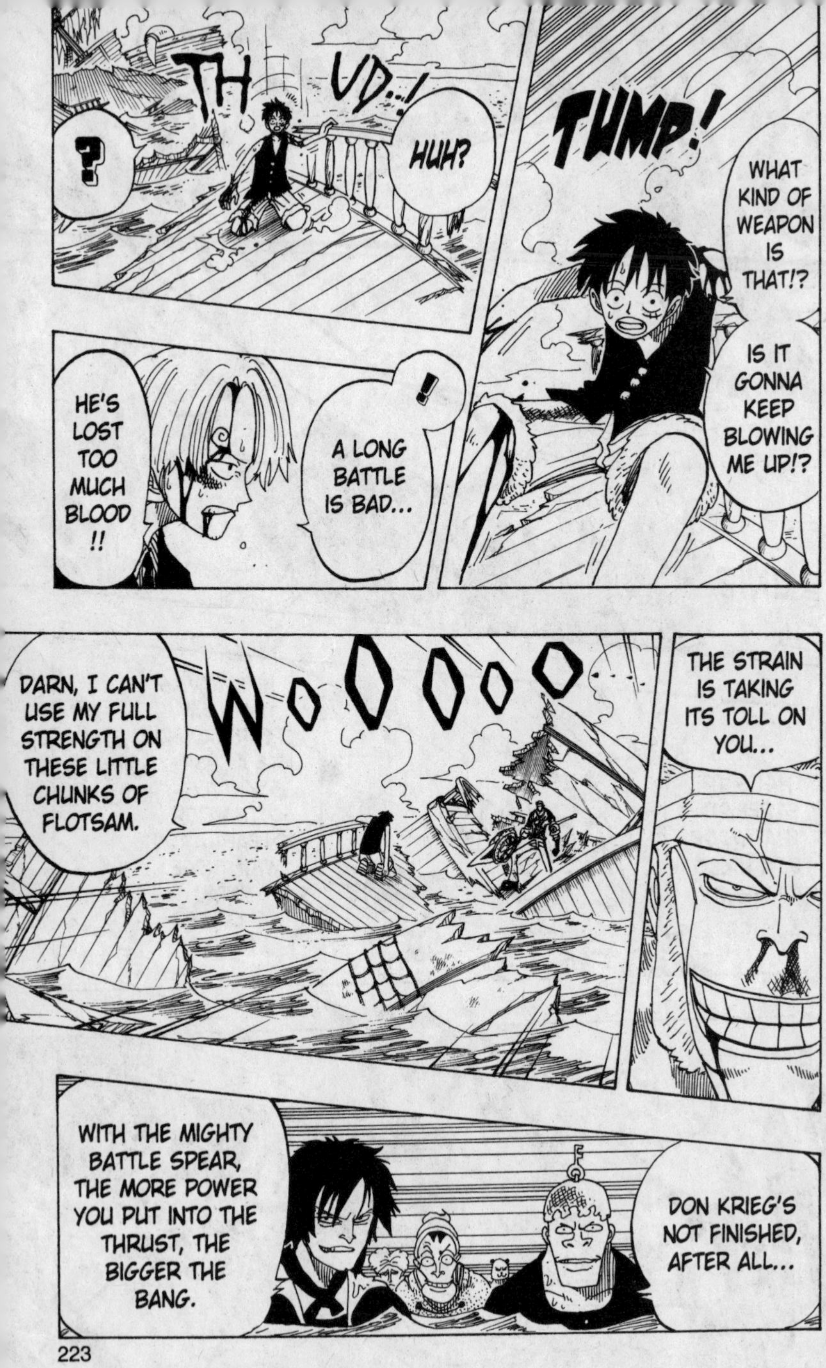
TUMP!
WHAT KIND OF WEAPON IS THAT!?
IS IT GONNA KEEP BLOWING ME UP!?
HUH?
THUD..!
?
!
A LONG BATTLE IS BAD...
HE'S LOST TOO MUCH BLOOD !!
THE STRAIN IS TAKING ITS TOLL ON YOU...
WOOOOO
...
DARN, I CAN'T USE MY FULL STRENGTH ON THESE LITTLE CHUNKS OF FLOTSAM.
DON KRIEG'S NOT FINISHED, AFTER ALL...
WITH THE MIGHTY BATTLE SPEAR, THE MORE POWER YOU PUT INTO THE THRUST, THE BIGGER THE BANG.

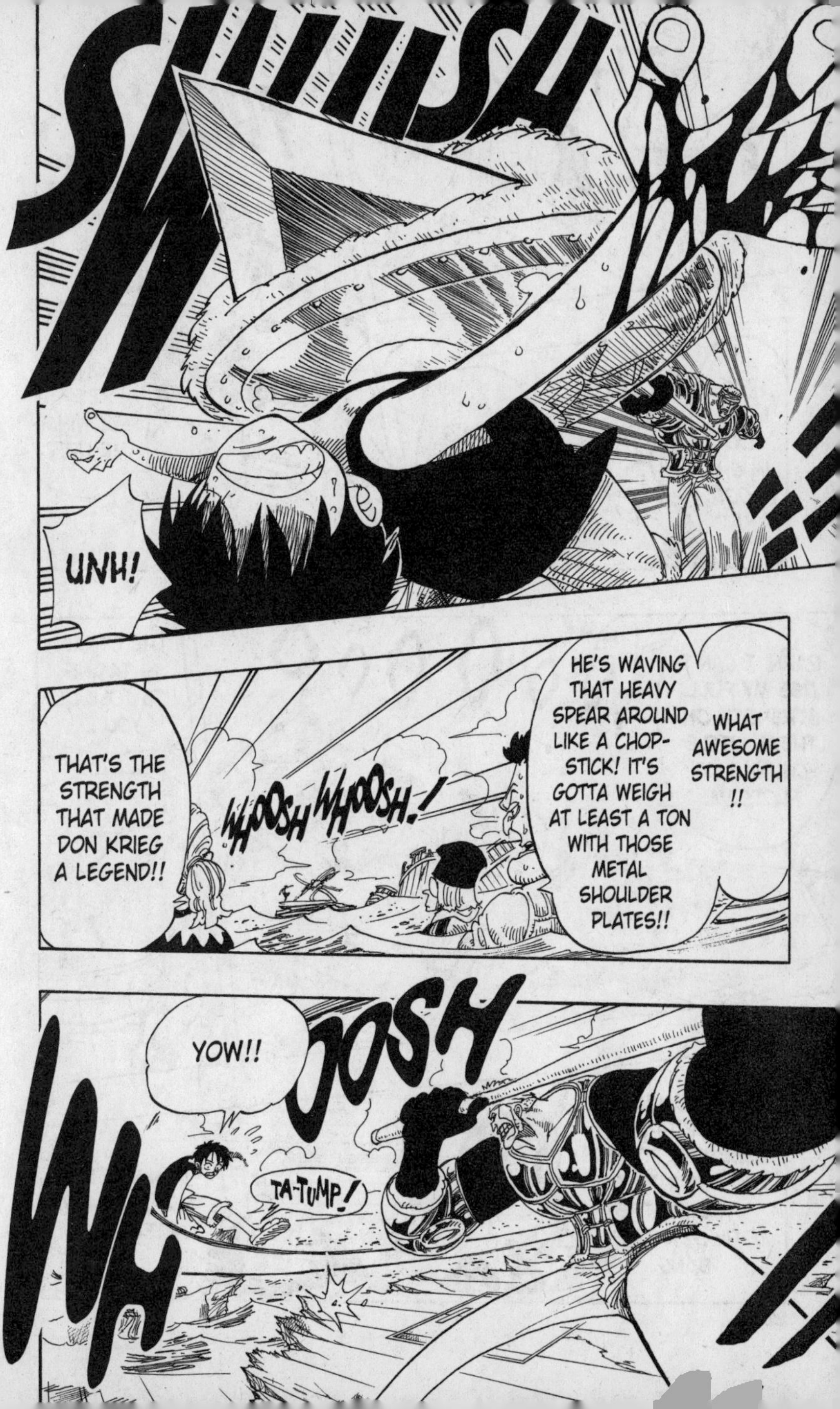
UNH!
WHAT AWESOME STRENGTH!!
HE'S WAVING THAT HEAVY SPEAR AROUND LIKE A CHOP-STICK! IT'S GOTTA WEIGH AT LEAST A TON WITH THOSE METAL SHOULDER PLATES!!
WHOOSH WHOOSH!
THAT'S THE STRENGTH THAT MADE DON KRIEG A LEGEND!!
WHOOSH
YOW!!
TA-TUMP!

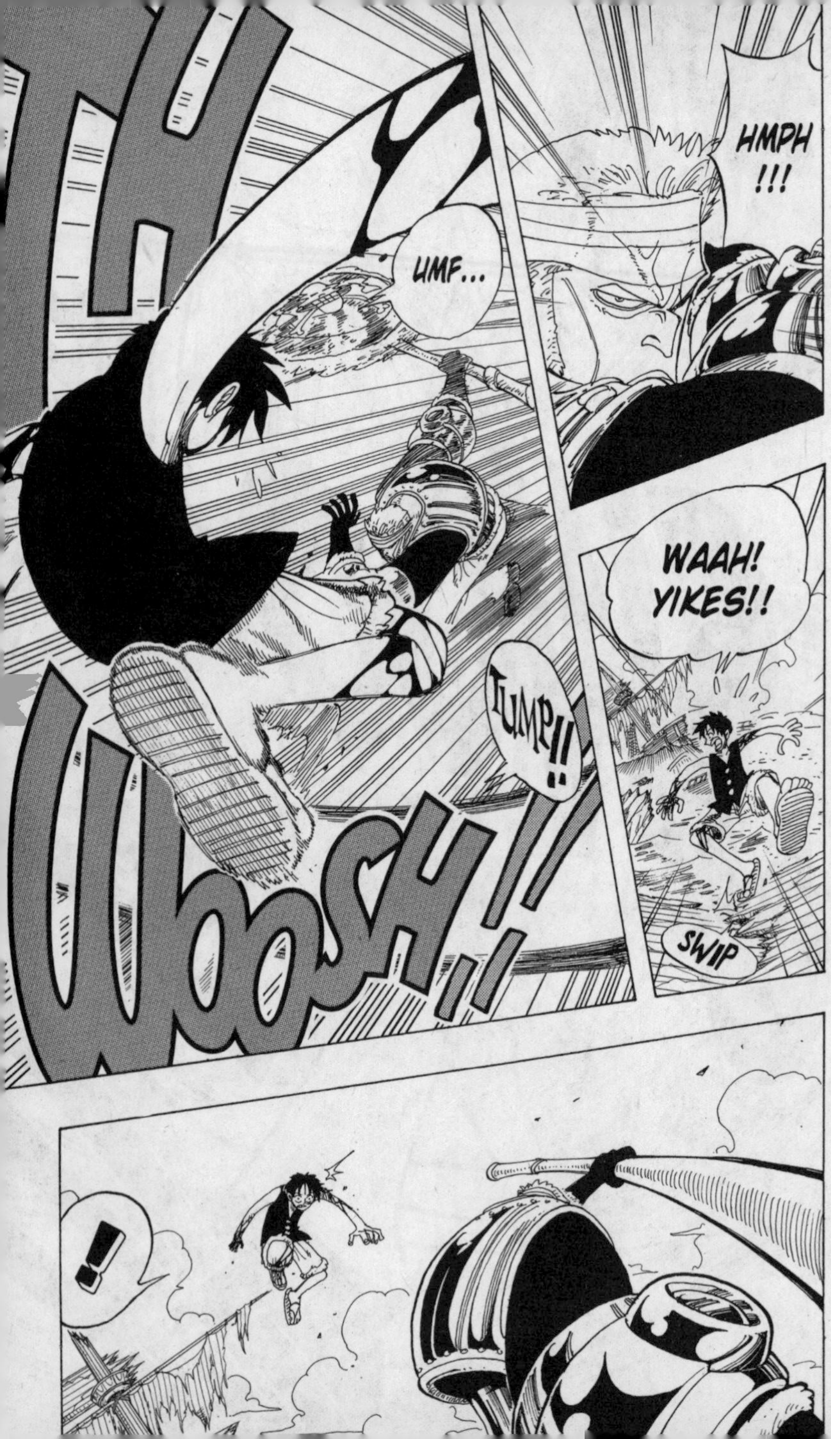
HMPH !!!
WAAH! YIKES!!
SWIP
UMF...
TUMP!!
WOOSH!!
!

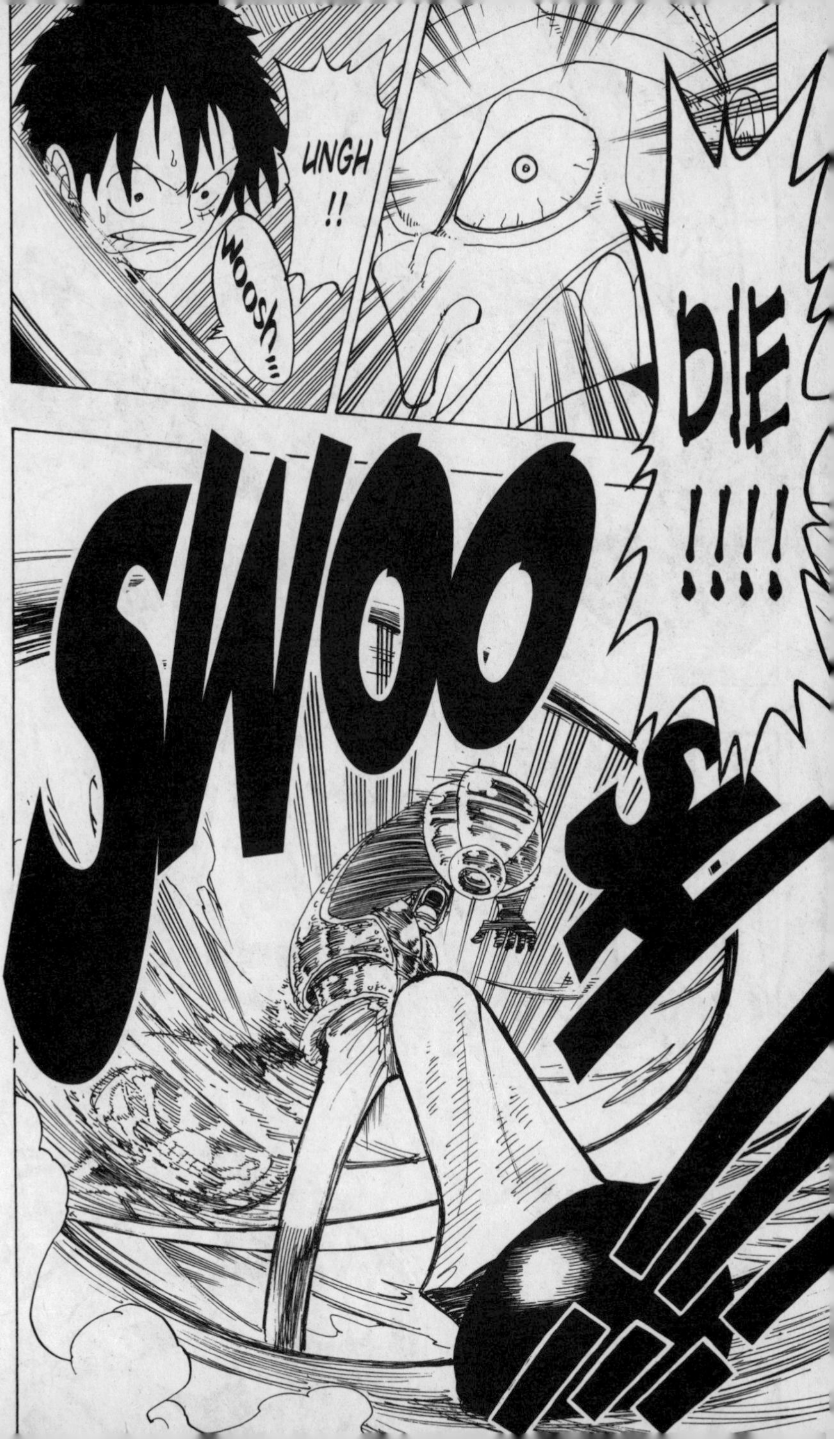

DIE!!!!
UNGH!!
Woosh!!!
SWOOSH

READ THIS WAY

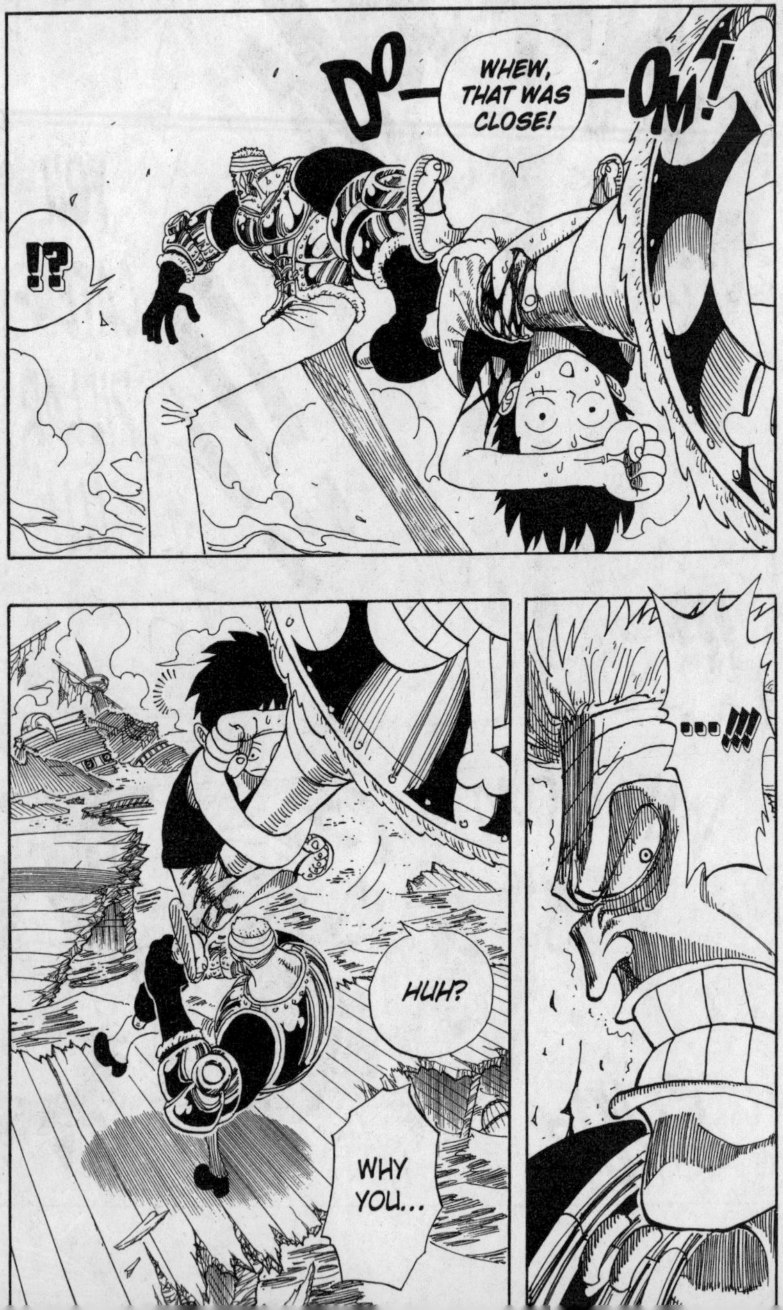

DO——OM!
WHEW, THAT WAS CLOSE!
!?
...!!!
HUH?
WHY YOU...

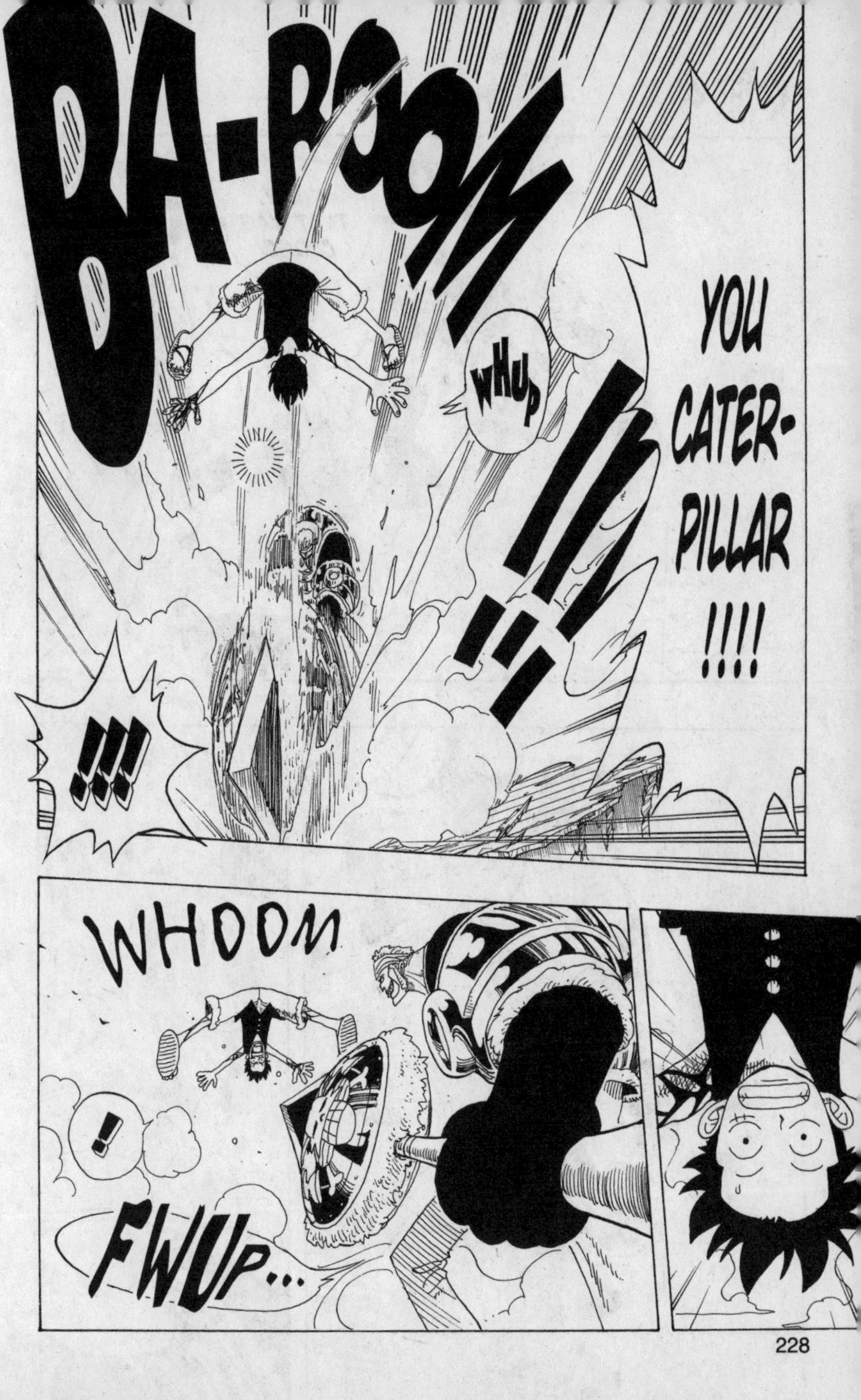
YOU CATER-PILLAR!!!!
WHUP
BA-BOOM
!!!!
WHOOM
!
FWUP...

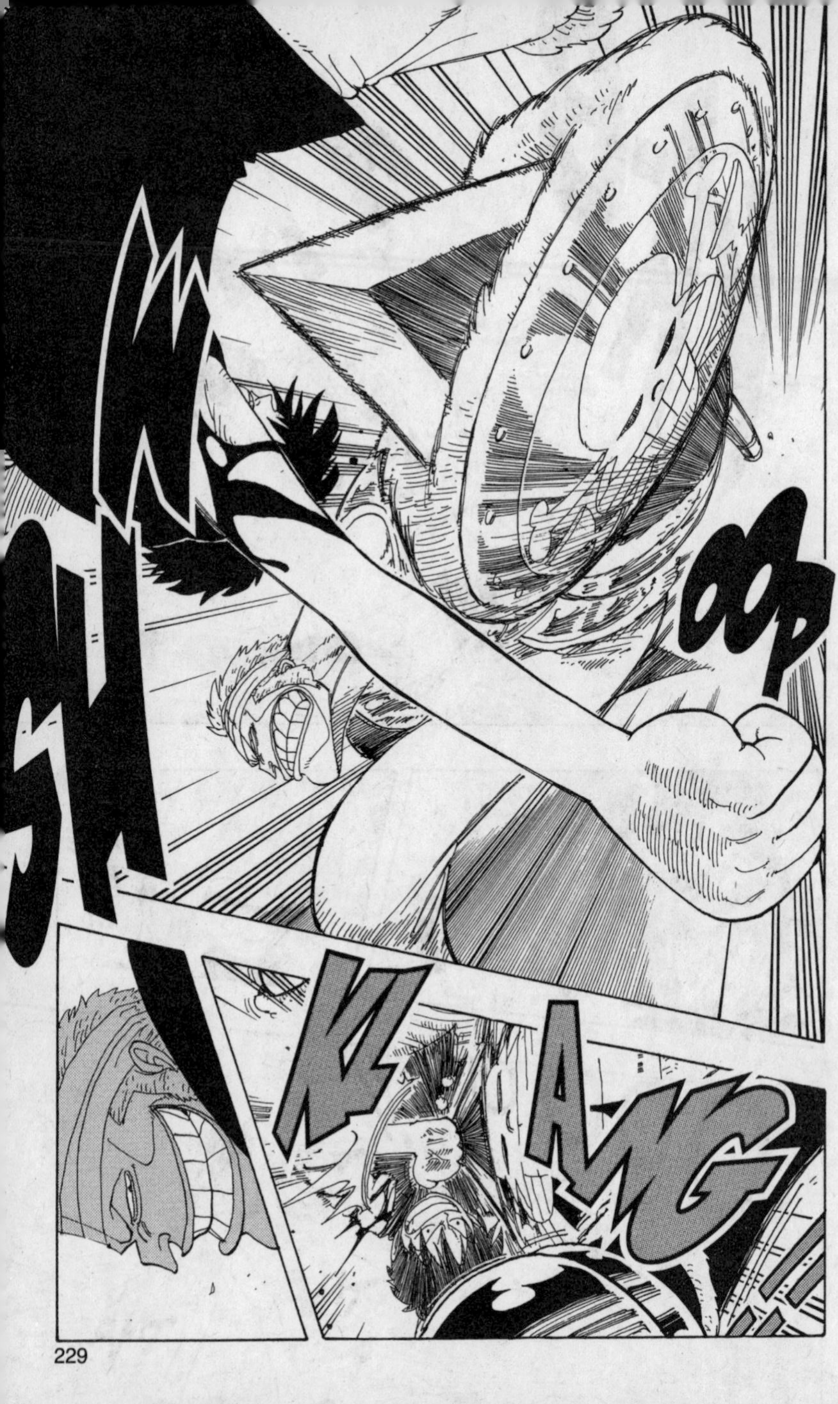
oop
KANG

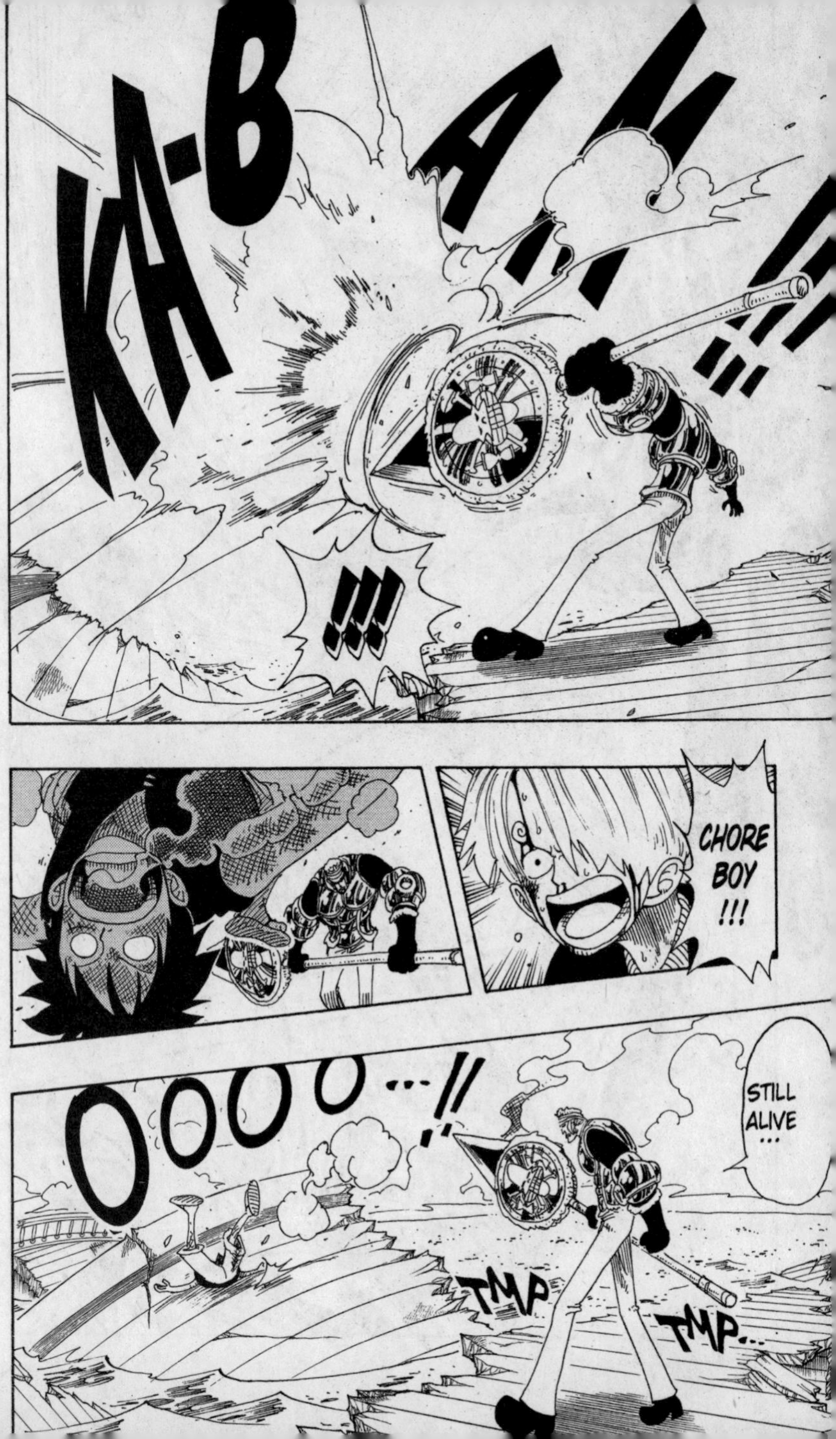
KA-BAM!!!
!!!
CHORE BOY !!!
STILL ALIVE ...
OOOO...!!
TMP
TMP...

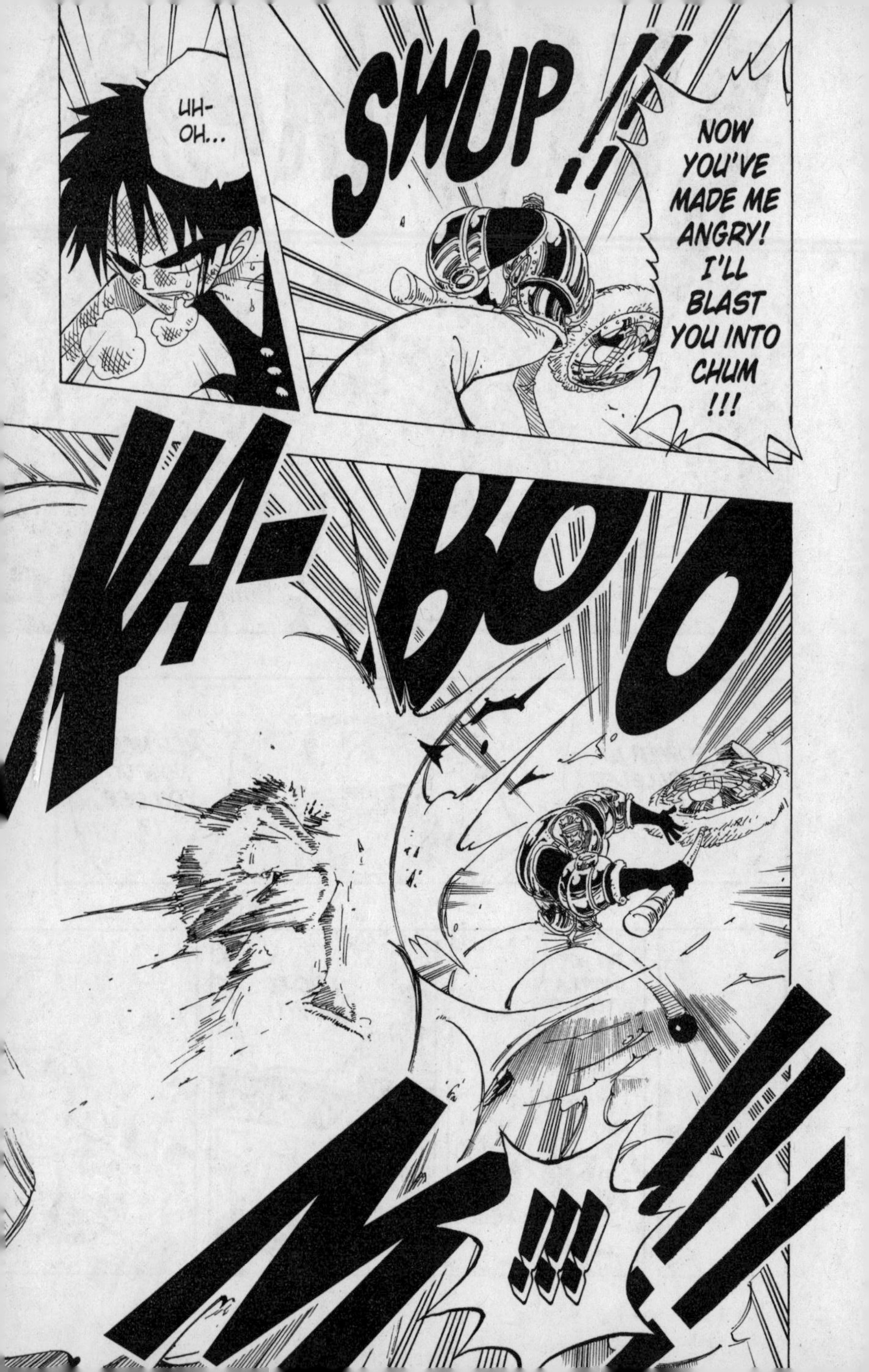
SWUP!!
NOW YOU'VE MADE ME ANGRY! I'LL BLAST YOU INTO CHUM!!!
UH-OH...
KA-BOOM!!!

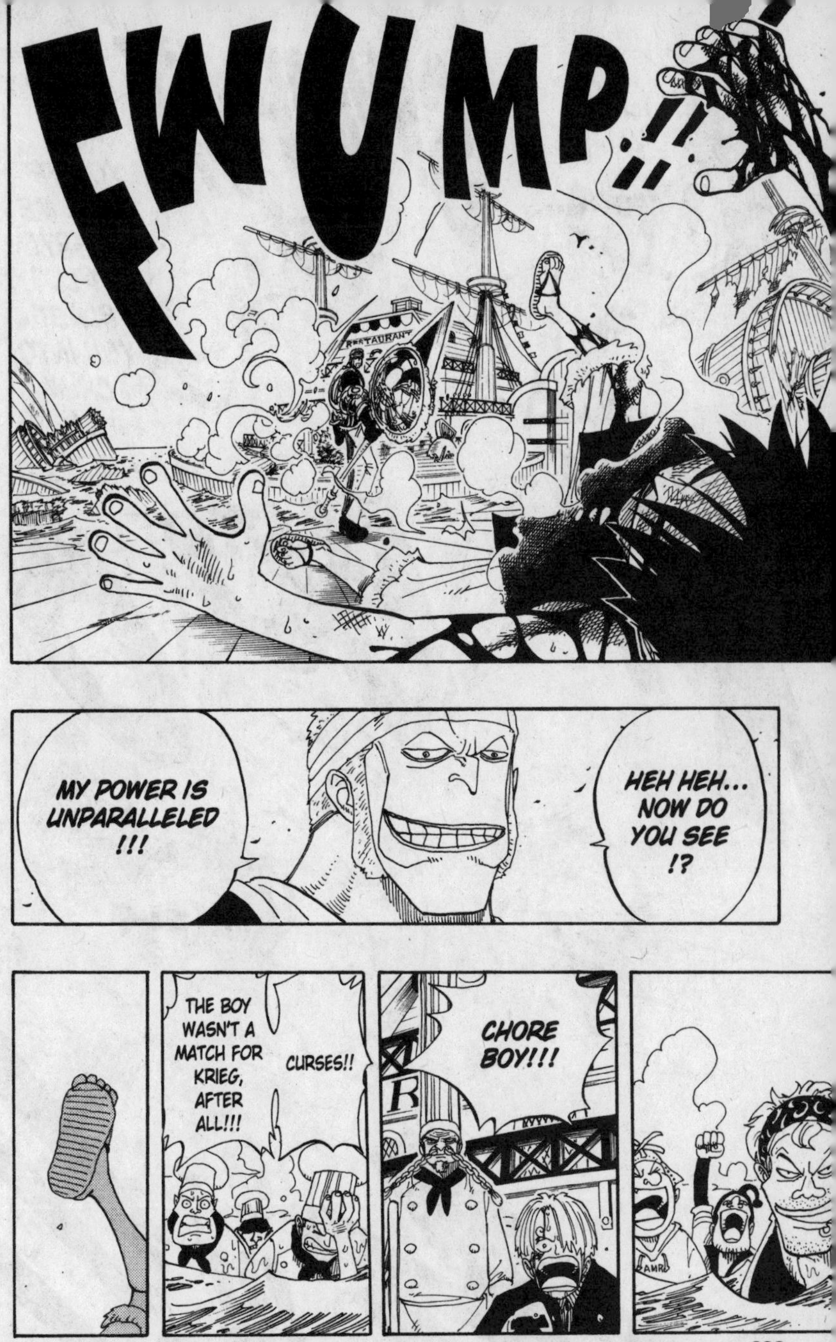
FWUMP!!
HEH HEH... NOW DO YOU SEE !?
MY POWER IS UNPARALLELED !!!
CHORE BOY!!!
CURSES!!
THE BOY WASN'T A MATCH FOR KRIEG, AFTER ALL!!!

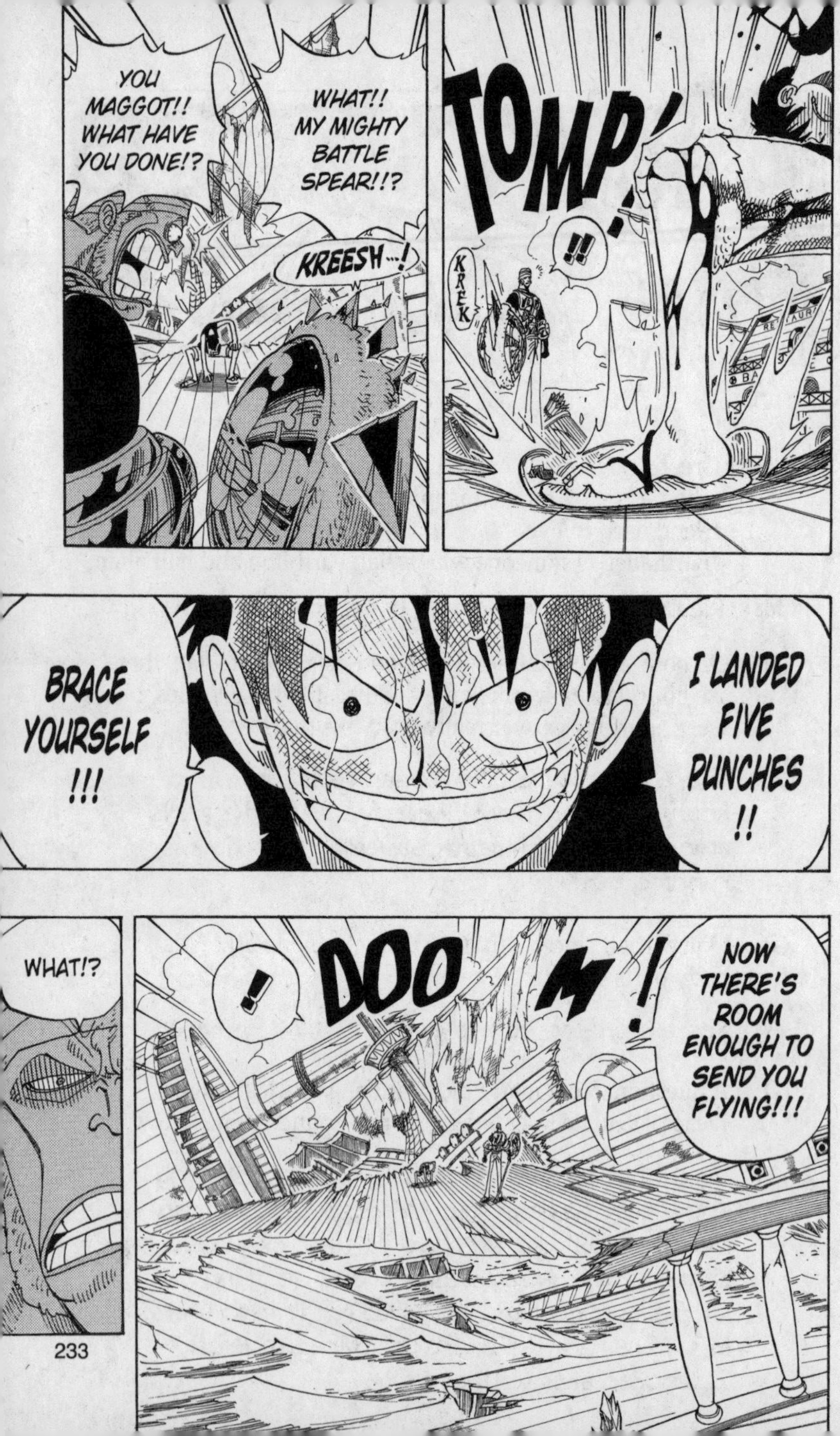
TOMP!
!!
KREK
WHAT!! MY MIGHTY BATTLE SPEAR!!?
YOU MAGGOT!! WHAT HAVE YOU DONE!?
KREESH...!
I LANDED FIVE PUNCHES!!
BRACE YOURSELF!!!
NOW THERE'S ROOM ENOUGH TO SEND YOU FLYING!!!
DOOM!
!
WHAT!?

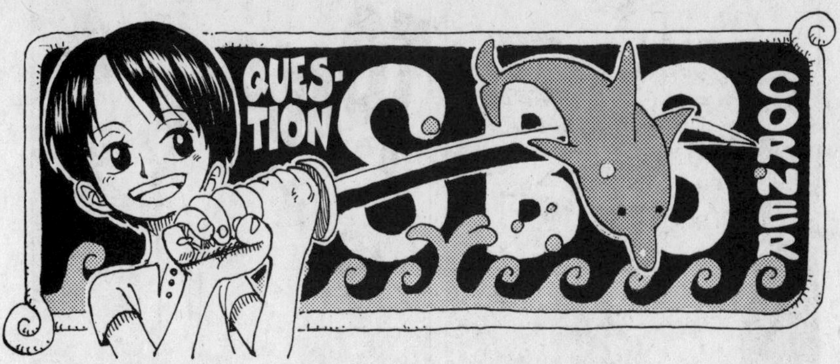
QUES-
TION
SBS
CORNER

**Reader:** Greetings. I am the earthalien living in the house where Usopp's father Yasopp's friend's brother's girlfriend used to live.
*Earthalien is someone who is half earthling and half alien.

**Oda:** Really? Question Corner is starting!! (Doom)

**Q:** On both sides of the skull on Don Krieg's pirate flag, there are hourglasses symbolizing the threat to his enemies, but were hourglasses ever really used like that?

**A:** There really were Jolly Roger flags with hourglasses on them. They symbolized the prey's appointment with death, basically: "Your time is running out!"

**Q:** Oda Sensei, since Luffy is a rubber man, do **all** of his body parts stretch?

**A:** Yes, everything stretches.

**Q:** A question. How many $g/cm^3$ is Sanji's kick strength? Please calculate to two decimal points and let me know.

**A:** To be frank, measurement is not possible. You know that game at the arcades where you can measure your kick strength? If, for example, Sanji did that, the whole machine would go flying out of the building. But if I had to put it into units, I'd say 21 bats--the energy required to break 21 wooden bats with one kick.

# Chapter 65: PREPARED

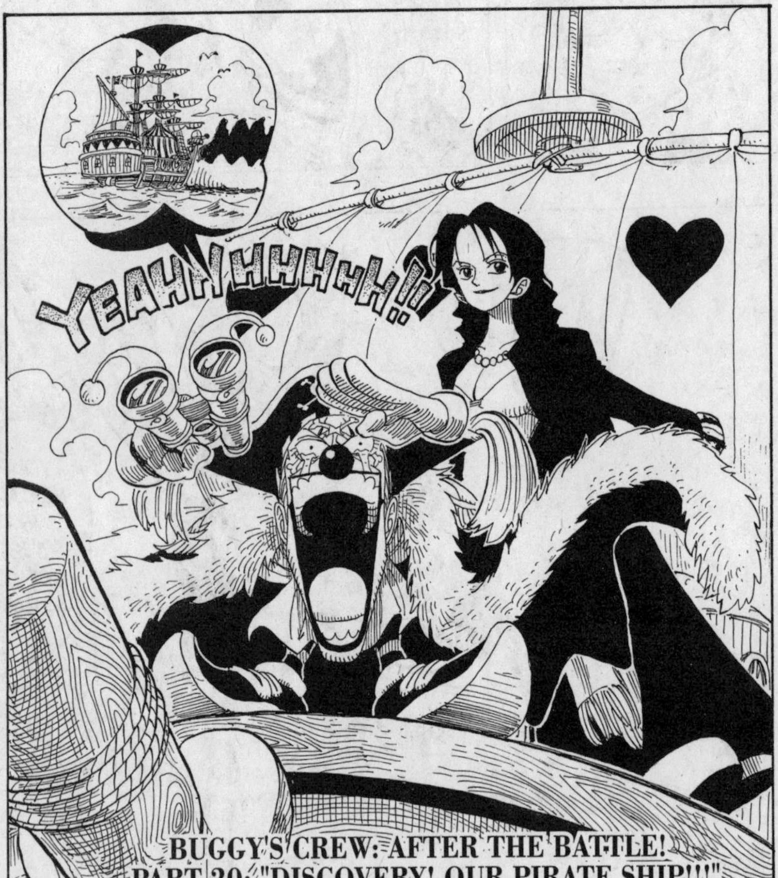
YEAHHHHHHH!!
BUGGY'S CREW: AFTER THE BATTLE!
PART 20: "DISCOVERY! OUR PIRATE SHIP!!!"

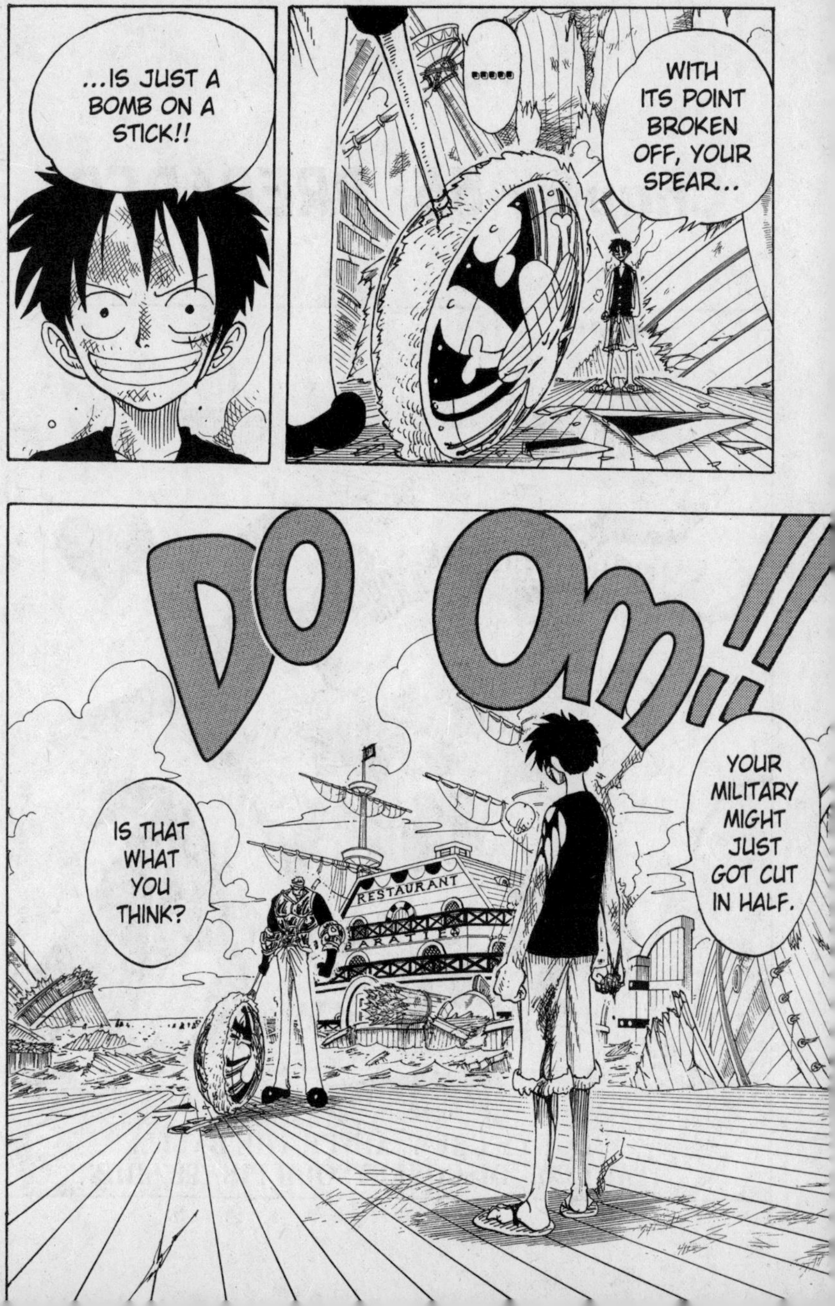
WITH ITS POINT BROKEN OFF, YOUR SPEAR...
......
...IS JUST A BOMB ON A STICK!!
DOOM!!
YOUR MILITARY MIGHT JUST GOT CUT IN HALF.
IS THAT WHAT YOU THINK?
RESTAURANT
BARATIE

READ THIS WAY

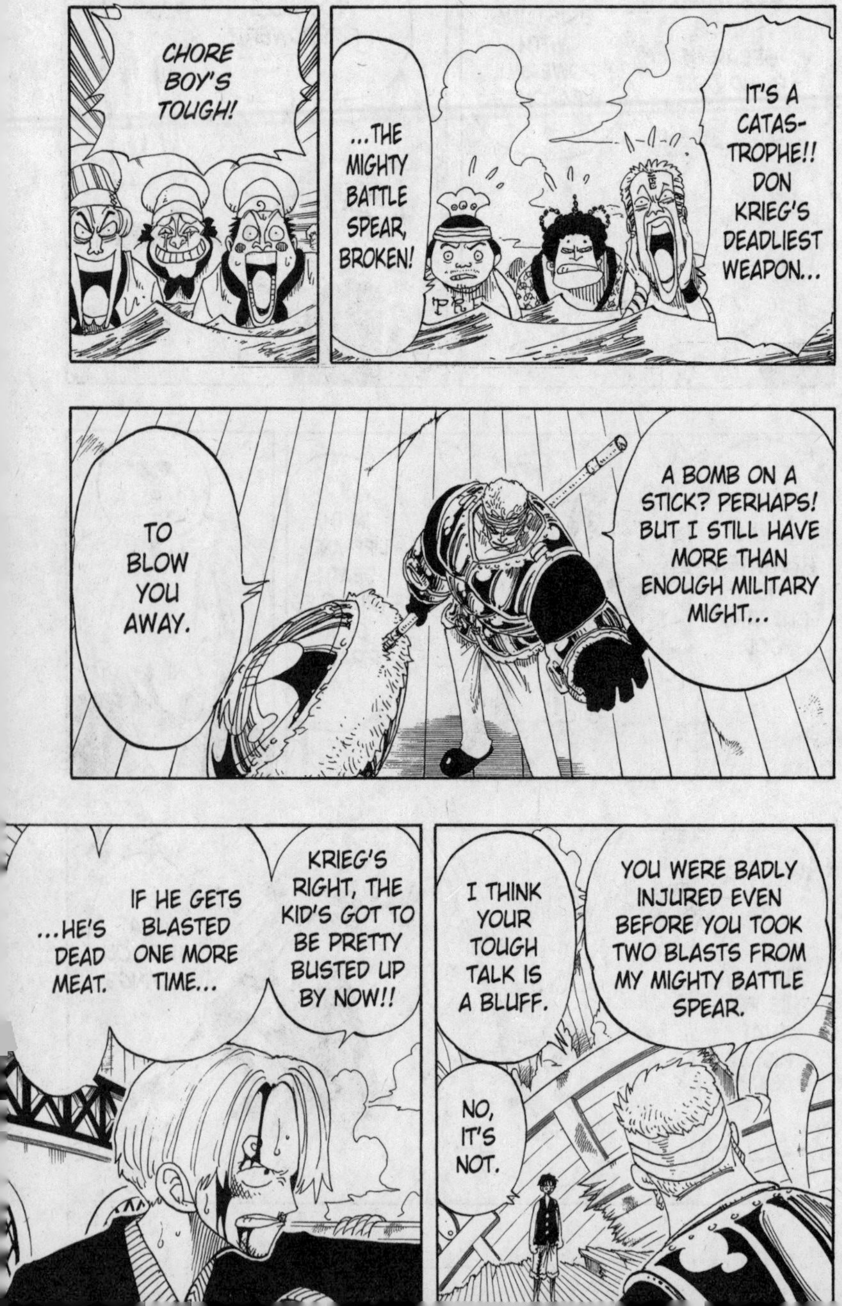

IT'S A CATASTROPHE!! DON KRIEG'S DEADLIEST WEAPON...
...THE MIGHTY BATTLE SPEAR, BROKEN!
CHORE BOY'S TOUGH!
A BOMB ON A STICK? PERHAPS! BUT I STILL HAVE MORE THAN ENOUGH MILITARY MIGHT...
TO BLOW YOU AWAY.
YOU WERE BADLY INJURED EVEN BEFORE YOU TOOK TWO BLASTS FROM MY MIGHTY BATTLE SPEAR.
I THINK YOUR TOUGH TALK IS A BLUFF.
NO, IT'S NOT.
KRIEG'S RIGHT, THE KID'S GOT TO BE PRETTY BUSTED UP BY NOW!!
IF HE GETS BLASTED ONE MORE TIME...
...HE'S DEAD MEAT.

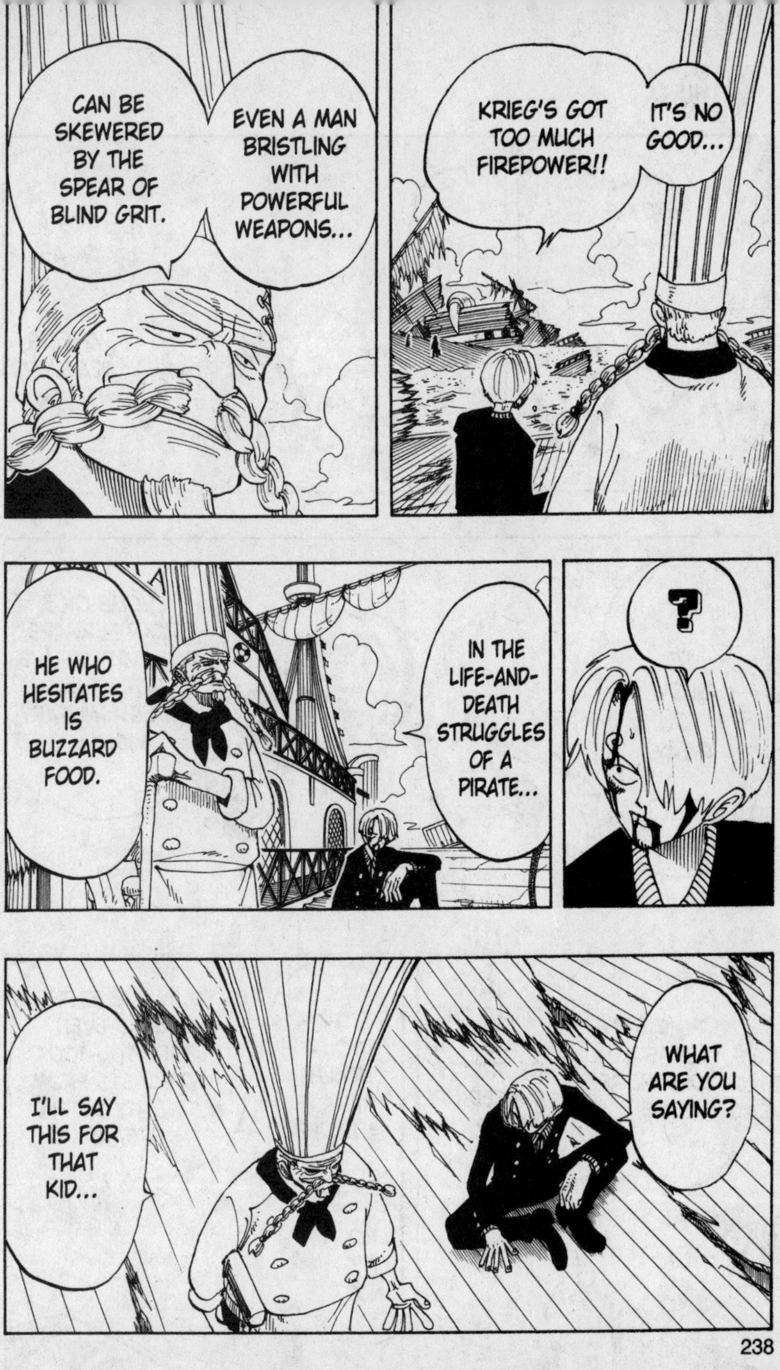
IT'S NO GOOD...
KRIEG'S GOT TOO MUCH FIREPOWER!!
EVEN A MAN BRISTLING WITH POWERFUL WEAPONS...
CAN BE SKEWERED BY THE SPEAR OF BLIND GRIT.
?
IN THE LIFE-AND-DEATH STRUGGLES OF A PIRATE...
HE WHO HESITATES IS BUZZARD FOOD.
WHAT ARE YOU SAYING?
I'LL SAY THIS FOR THAT KID...

READ THIS WAY

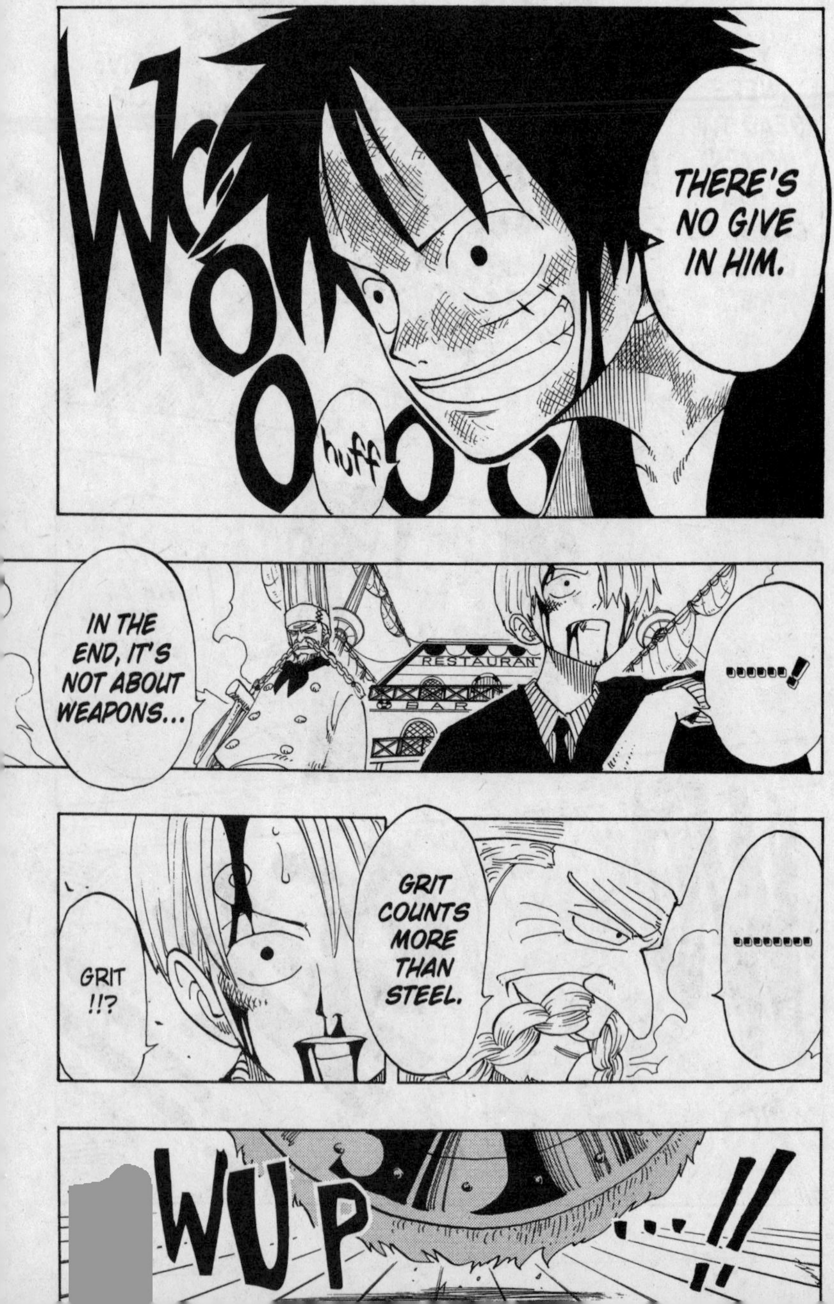
THERE'S NO GIVE IN HIM.
huff
......!
RESTAURAN
BAR
IN THE END, IT'S NOT ABOUT WEAPONS...
........
GRIT COUNTS MORE THAN STEEL.
GRIT !!?
WUP...!!

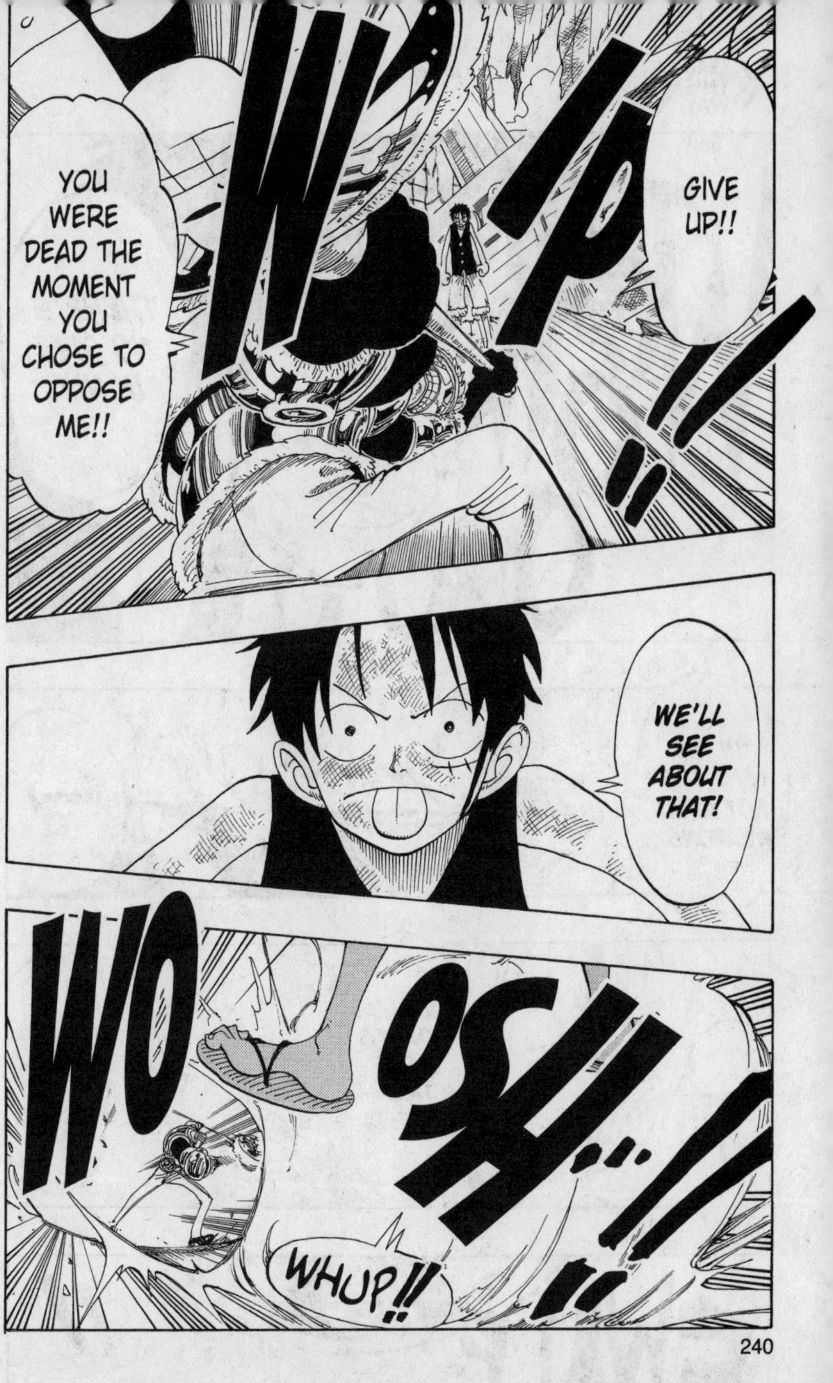
GIVE UP!!
WHAP!!
YOU WERE DEAD THE MOMENT YOU CHOSE TO OPPOSE ME!!
WE'LL SEE ABOUT THAT!
WOOSH!!
WHUP!!

READ THIS WAY

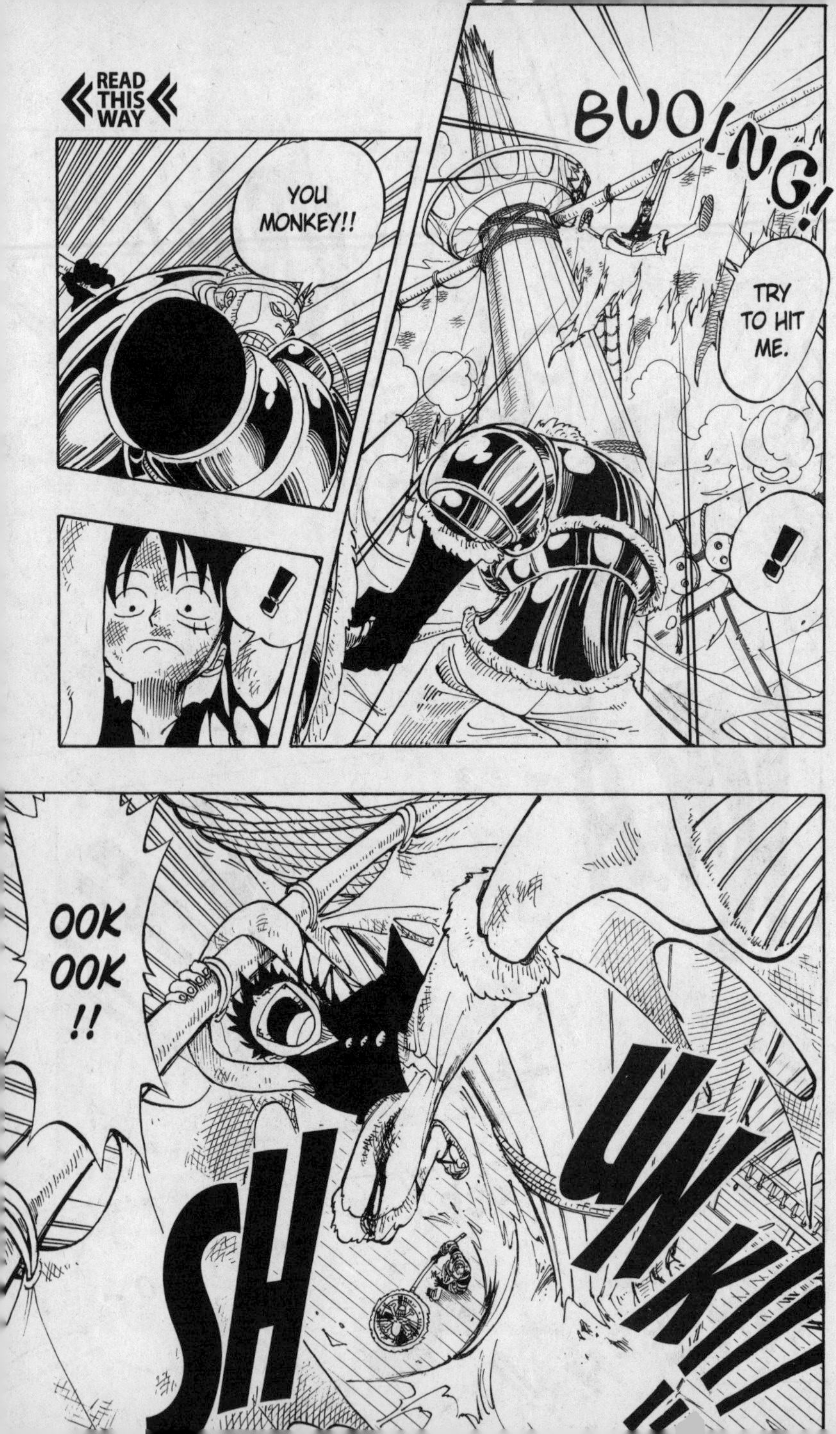
BWOING!
TRY TO HIT ME.
!
YOU MONKEY!!
!
UKI!!
OOK OOK !!
SH

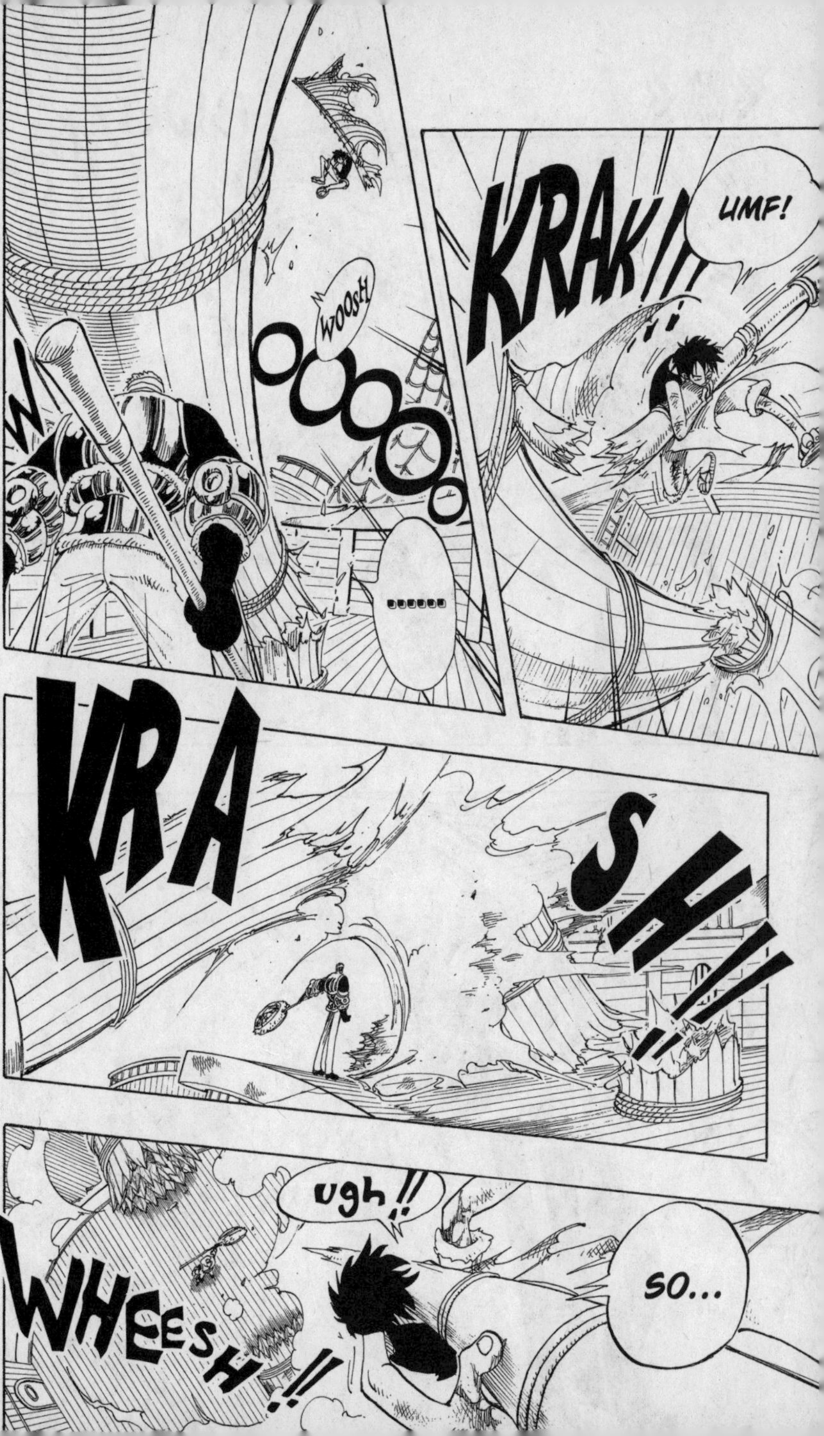
KRAK!!!
UMF!
WOOSH
......
KRASH!!
SO...
ugh!!
WHEESH!!

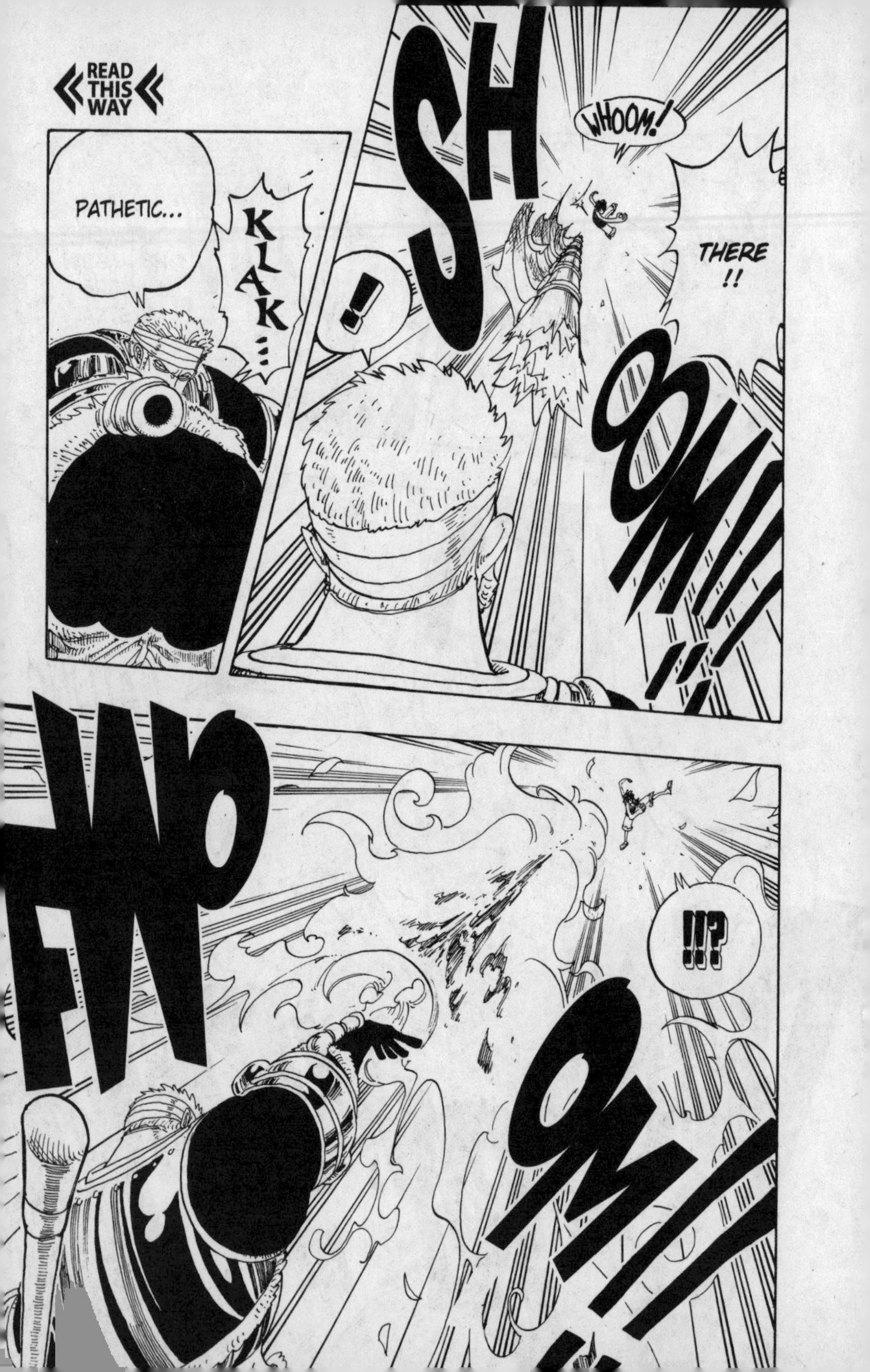
READ THIS WAY
WHOOM!
THERE !!
SHOOM!!
!
PATHETIC...
KLAK ...
!!?
FWOOM!!

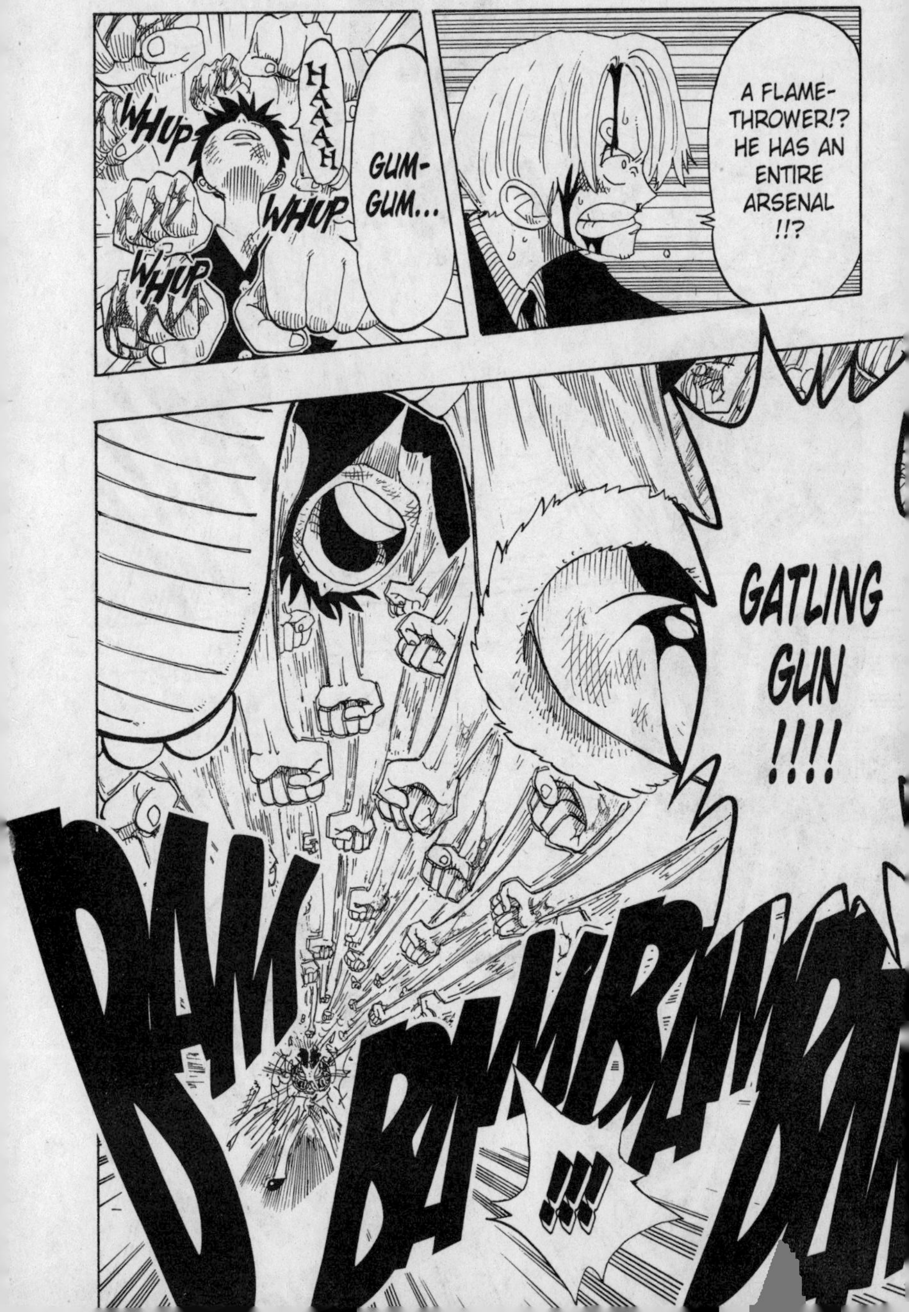
A FLAME-THROWER!? HE HAS AN ENTIRE ARSENAL!!?
HAAAAH
GUM-GUM...
WHUP
WHUP
WHUP
GATLING GUN!!!!

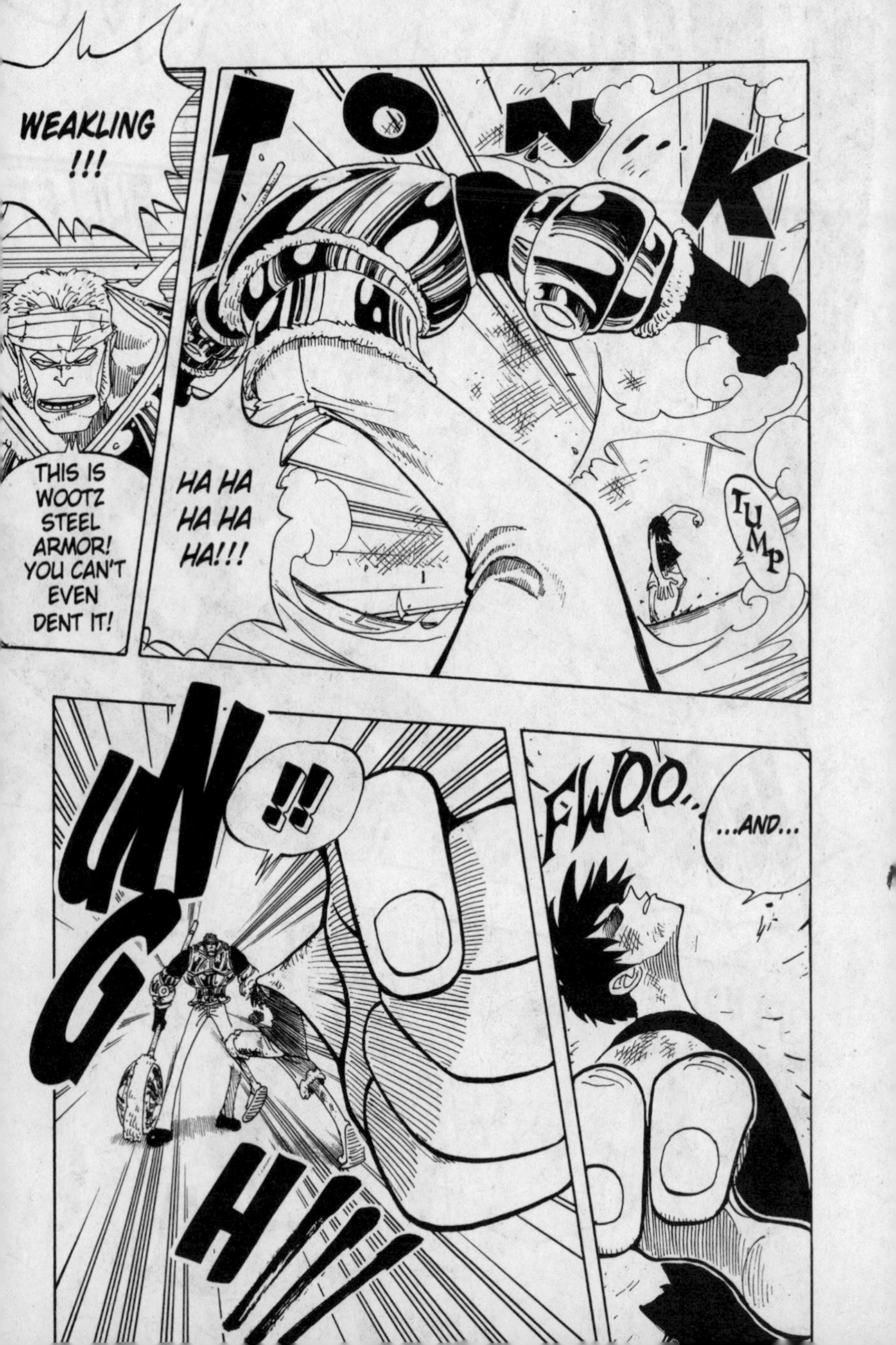
TONK
TUMP
HA HA HA HA HA!!!
WEAKLING !!!
THIS IS WOOTZ STEEL ARMOR! YOU CAN'T EVEN DENT IT!
FWOO...
...AND...
!!

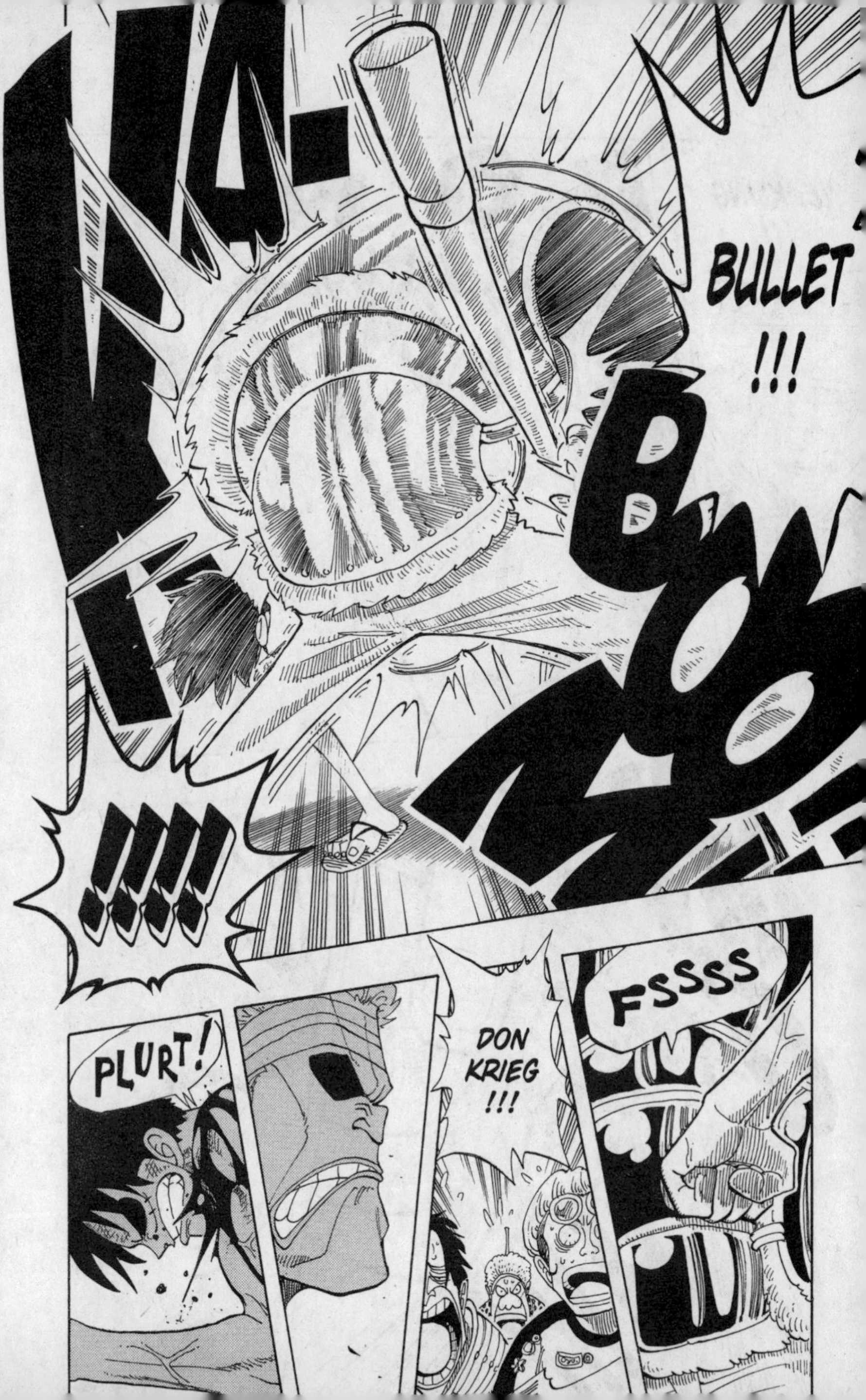
BULLET !!!
BOOM
FSSSS
DON KRIEG !!!
PLURT!

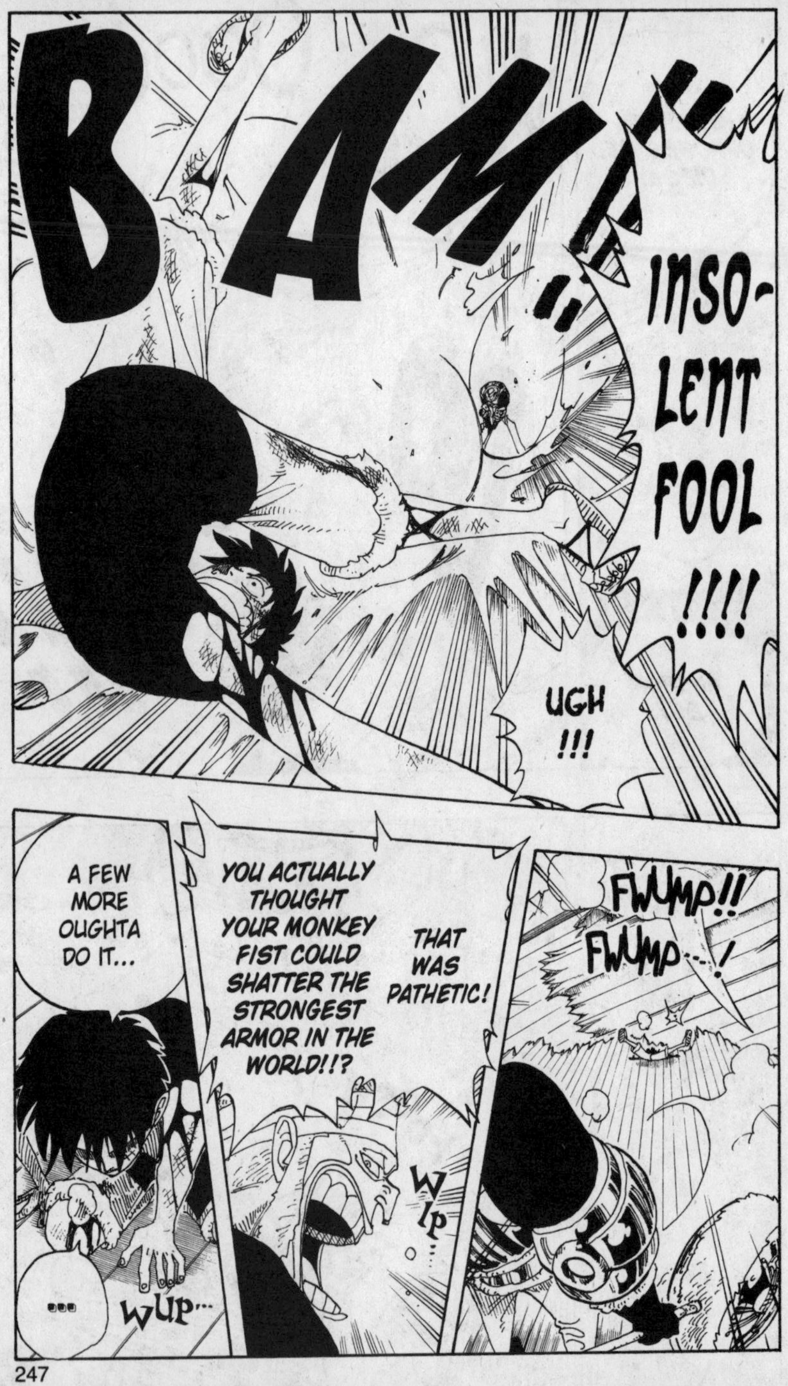
BAM
INSOLENT FOOL!!!!
UGH!!!
FWUMP!!
FWUMP...!
THAT WAS PATHETIC!
YOU ACTUALLY THOUGHT YOUR MONKEY FIST COULD SHATTER THE STRONGEST ARMOR IN THE WORLD!!?
WIP...
A FEW MORE OUGHTA DO IT...
...
WUP...

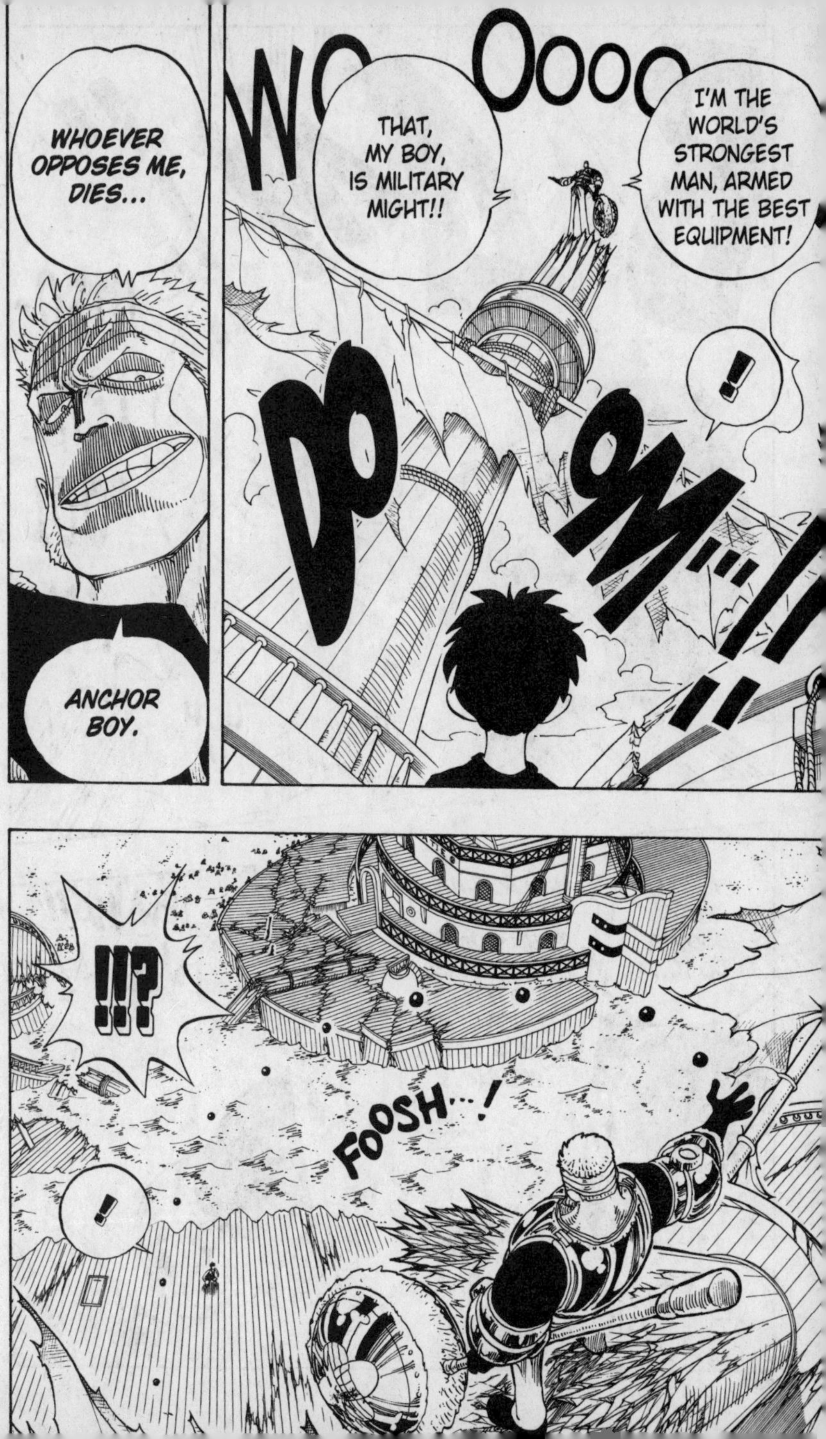
WOOOOO
I'M THE WORLD'S STRONGEST MAN, ARMED WITH THE BEST EQUIPMENT!
THAT, MY BOY, IS MILITARY MIGHT!!
!
DOOM!!
WHOEVER OPPOSES ME, DIES...
ANCHOR BOY.
!!?
FOOSH...!
!

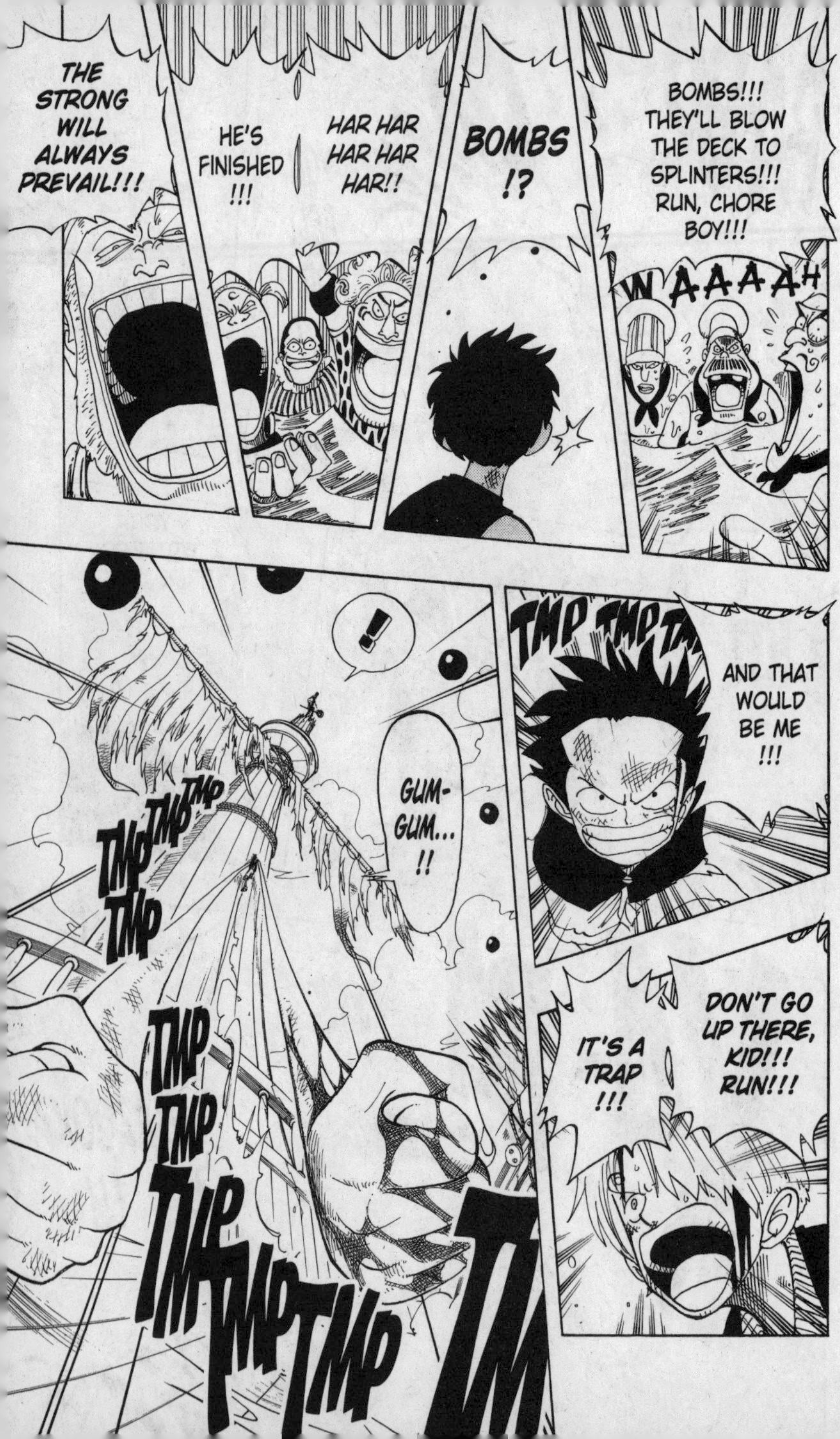
BOMBS!!! THEY'LL BLOW THE DECK TO SPLINTERS!!! RUN, CHORE BOY!!!
WAAAAH
BOMBS !?
HAR HAR HAR HAR HAR!!
HE'S FINISHED !!!
THE STRONG WILL ALWAYS PREVAIL!!!
TMP TMP TM
AND THAT WOULD BE ME !!!
DON'T GO UP THERE, KID!!! RUN!!!
IT'S A TRAP !!!
!
GUM-GUM... !!
TMP TMP TMP TMP
TMP TMP TMP TMP TMP TMP
TM

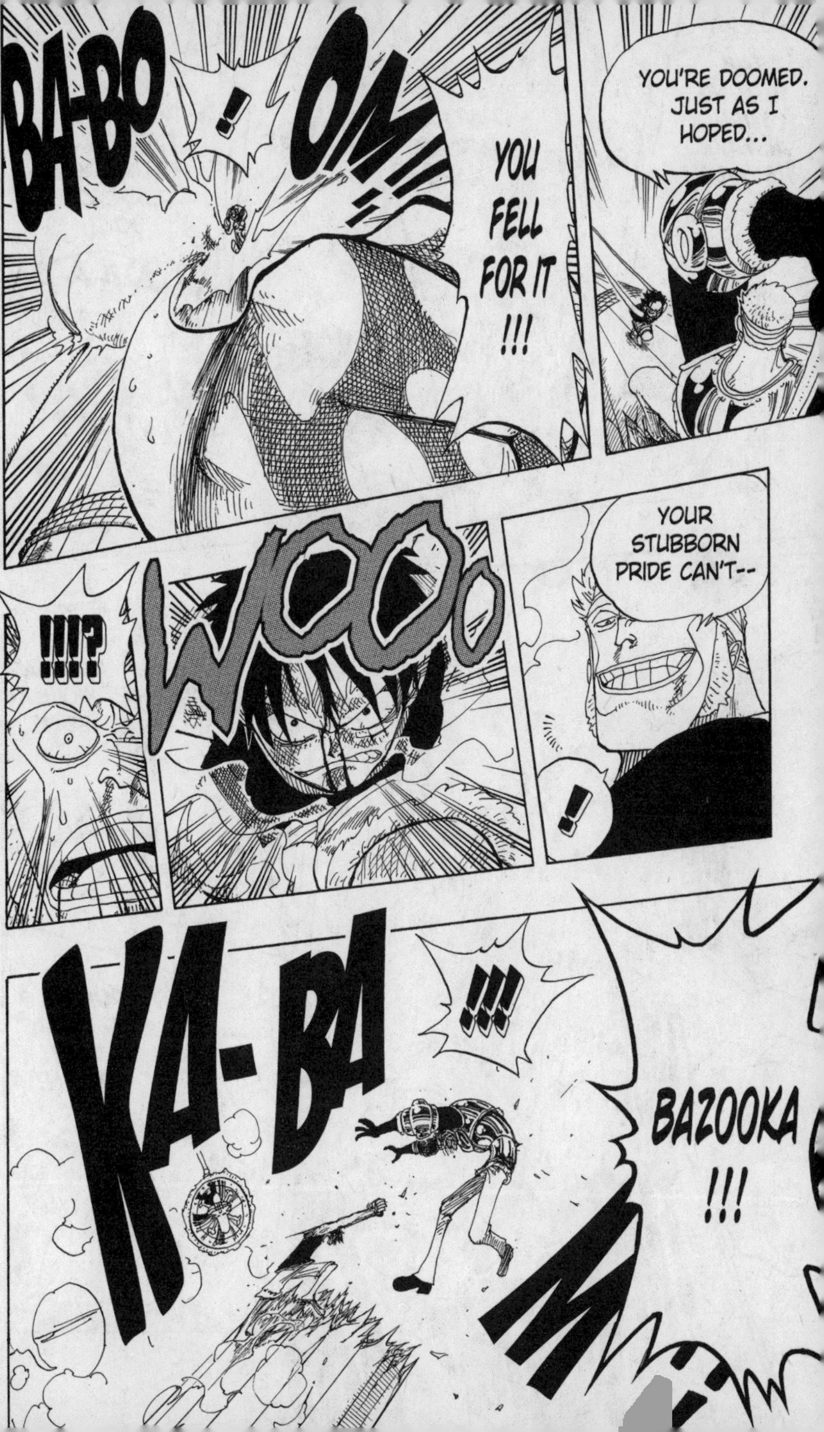
YOU'RE DOOMED. JUST AS I HOPED...
BA-BOOM!!
!
YOU FELL FOR IT !!!
YOUR STUBBORN PRIDE CAN'T--
!
WOOO
!!!?
BAZOOKA !!!
!!!
KA-BAM

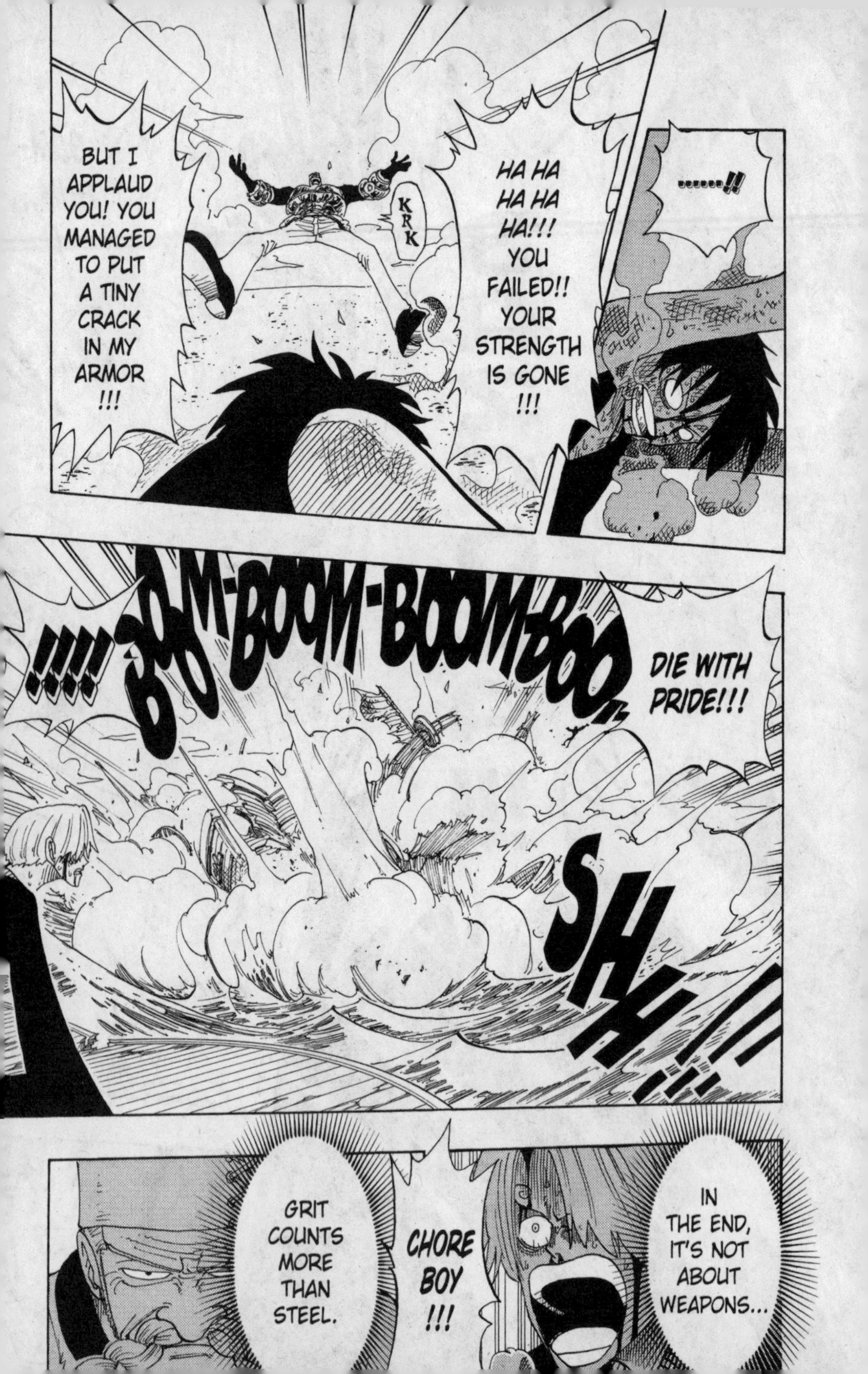
......!!
HA HA HA HA HA!!! YOU FAILED!! YOUR STRENGTH IS GONE!!!
KRK
BUT I APPLAUD YOU! YOU MANAGED TO PUT A TINY CRACK IN MY ARMOR!!!
DIE WITH PRIDE!!!
BOOM-BOOM-BOOM-BOO
!!!!
SH!!!!
IN THE END, IT'S NOT ABOUT WEAPONS...
CHORE BOY!!!
GRIT COUNTS MORE THAN STEEL.

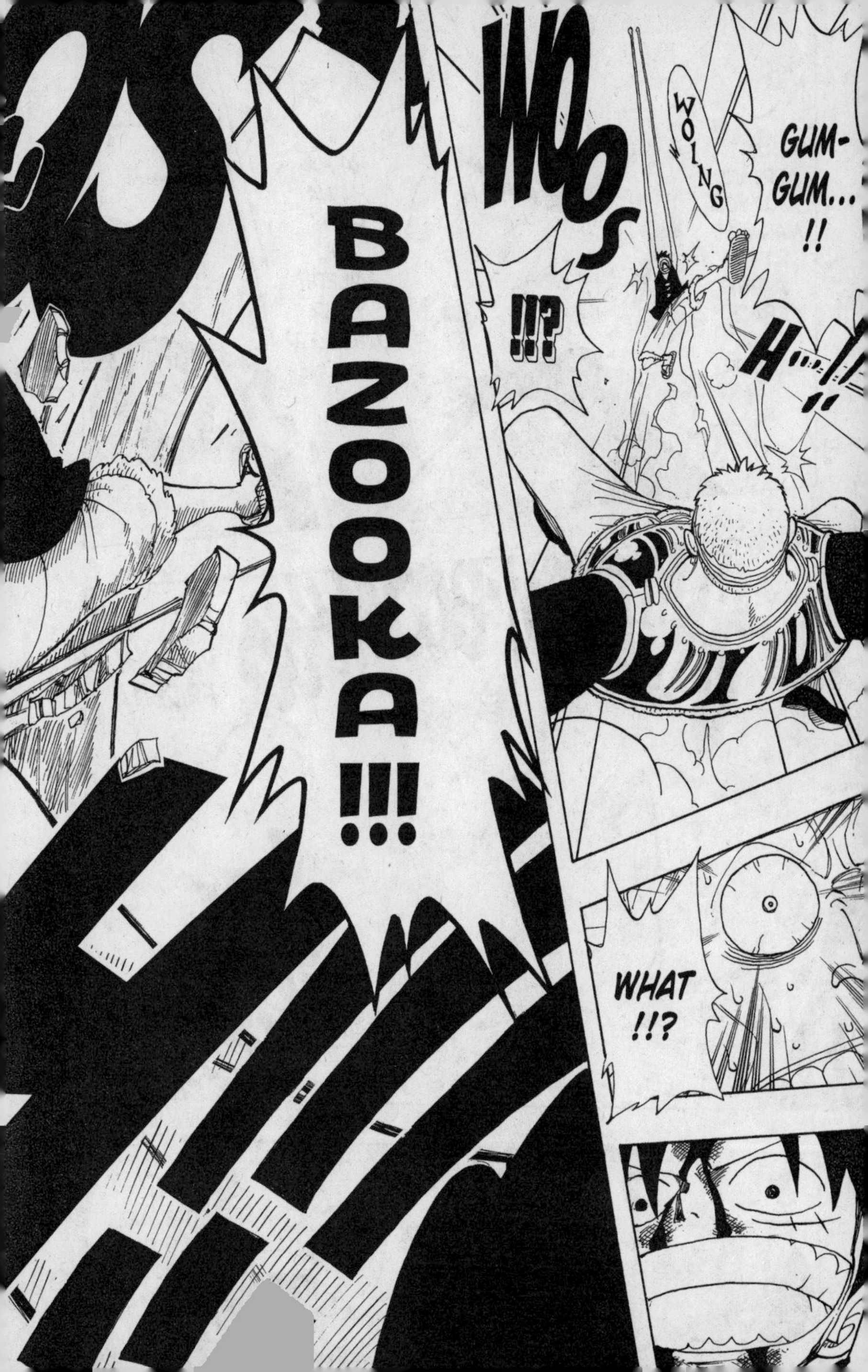
GUM-GUM...!!
WOING
H...!!
WOOSH
!!?
WHAT!!?
BAZOOKA!!!

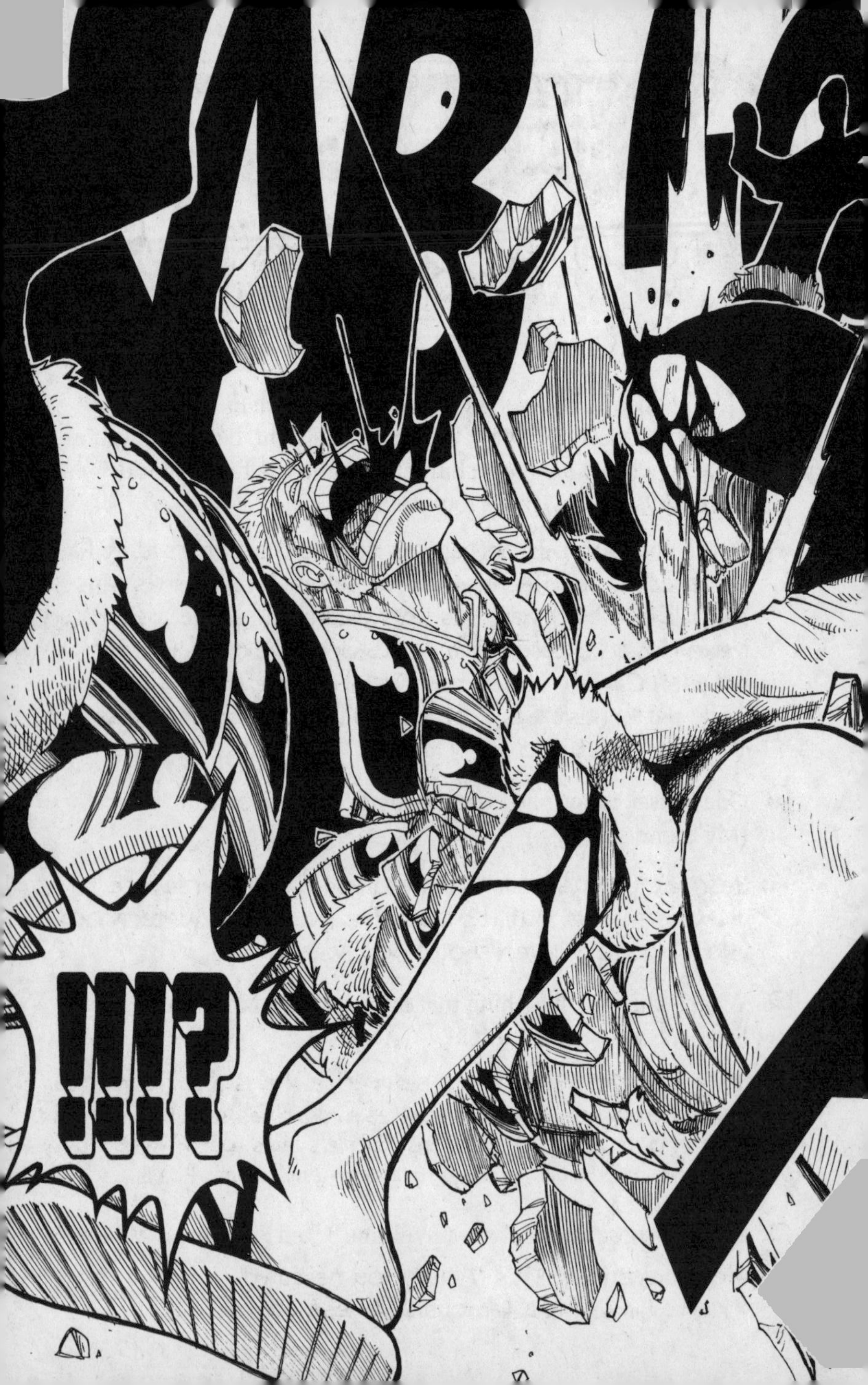
!!!?

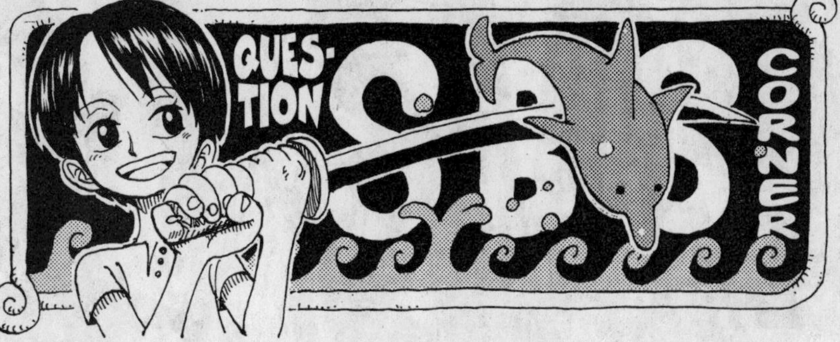
QUES-
TION
SBS
CORNER

Q: Hey, Ei-chan!! Have you been working on *One Piece* like you're supposed to? Draw your best!! All right, here's a question for you: which *One Piece* characters have the highest and lowest IQs?!! Okay, that's it for today.

A: I'll tell you, but this only applies to the characters that have appeared so far. The highest IQ belongs to Shanks' first mate, Benn Beckman--his unrivaled intelligence and brawn make him an excellent aid for Shanks. Next highest is probably Captain Kuro, then Nami. As for the characters with the lowest IQs, I can't decide who is number one--there are just too many idiots.

Q: Oda Sensei, is your house really made of cardboard? (My friend said it is.)

A: Yes. Yet through rain and wind and snow I persevere, drawing manga. But it's okay. The ink I use is waterproof!! (Note: Good children should not believe me!)

Q: What is the cape-like thing that Butchie of the Meowban Brothers wears? Is it a futon?

A: It's a **kotatsu-buton*, to be precise. He is a cat, after all.
*A kotatsu is a low, heated table that has a skirt-like quilt (futon or buton) that keeps people's legs warm when they sit at it. cats love to sleep under them on cold days.

Q: Is Luffy's pose on the cover of volume 3 Ken Shimura's* "Aiiin"?

A: Hey, you're right!! It's "Aiiin"!! You nailed it!!
*Ken Shimura is a famous Japanese comedian.

# Chapter 66:
# THE CHEWED-UP SPEAR

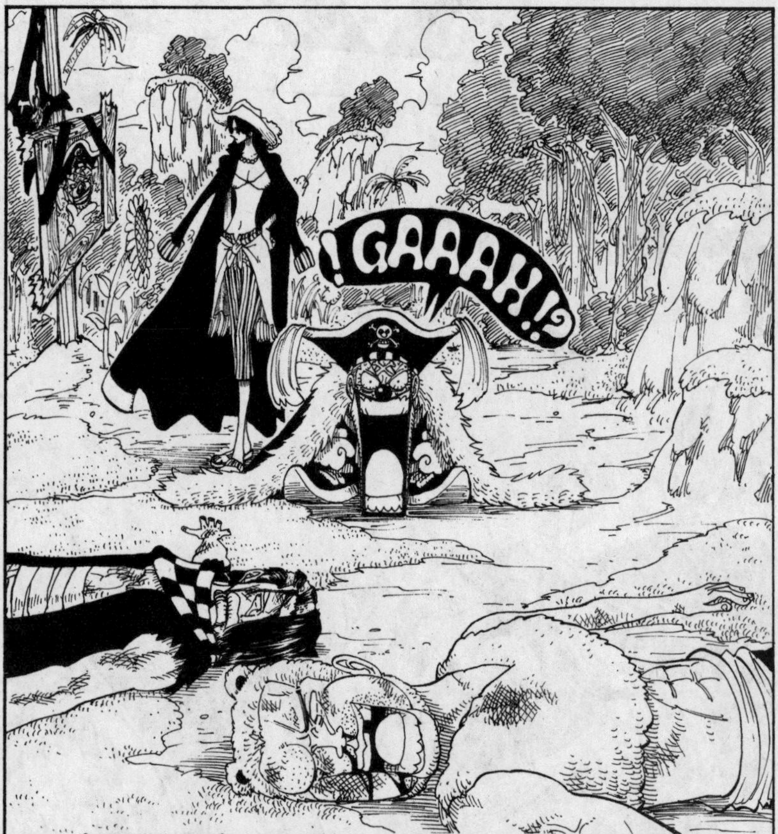
GAAAH!?
BUGGY'S CREW: AFTER THE BATTLE!
PART 21: "AN UNHAPPY REUNION"

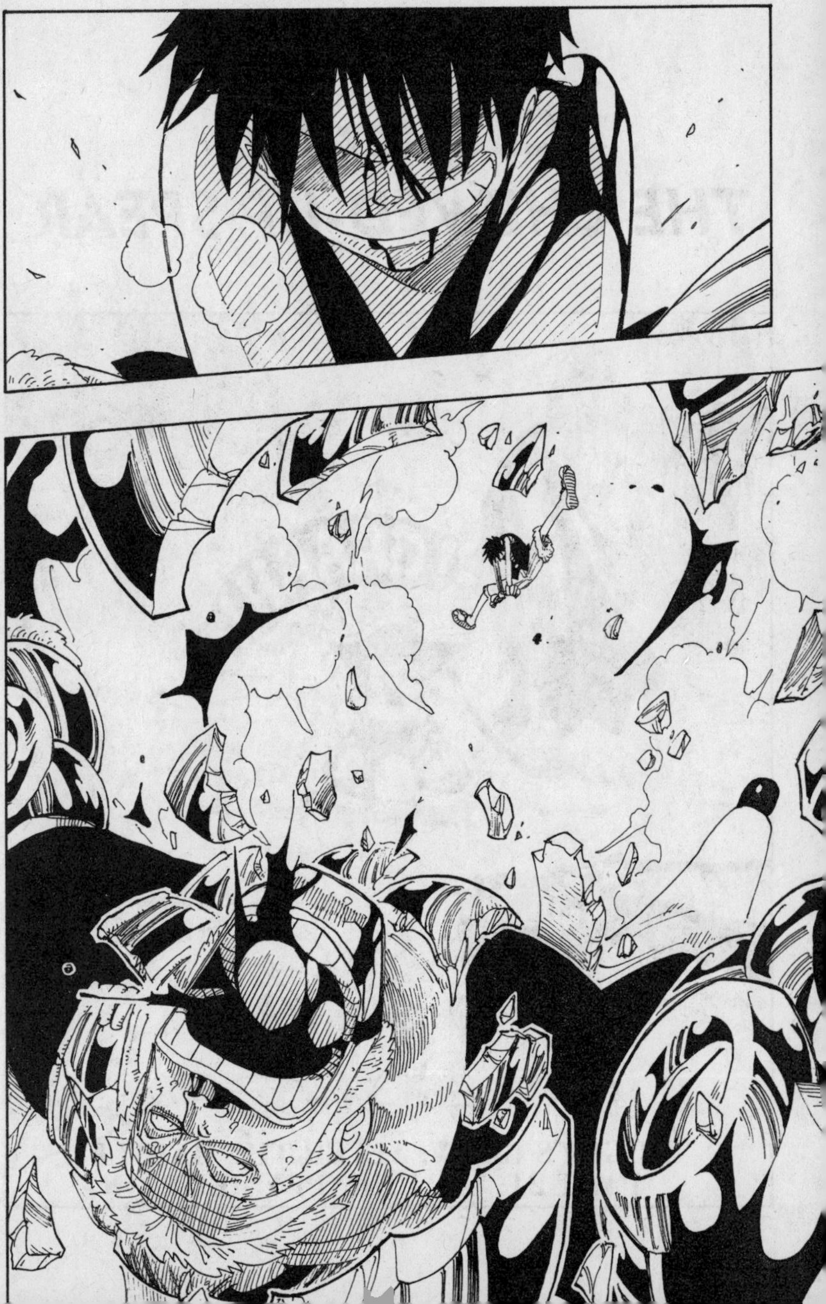

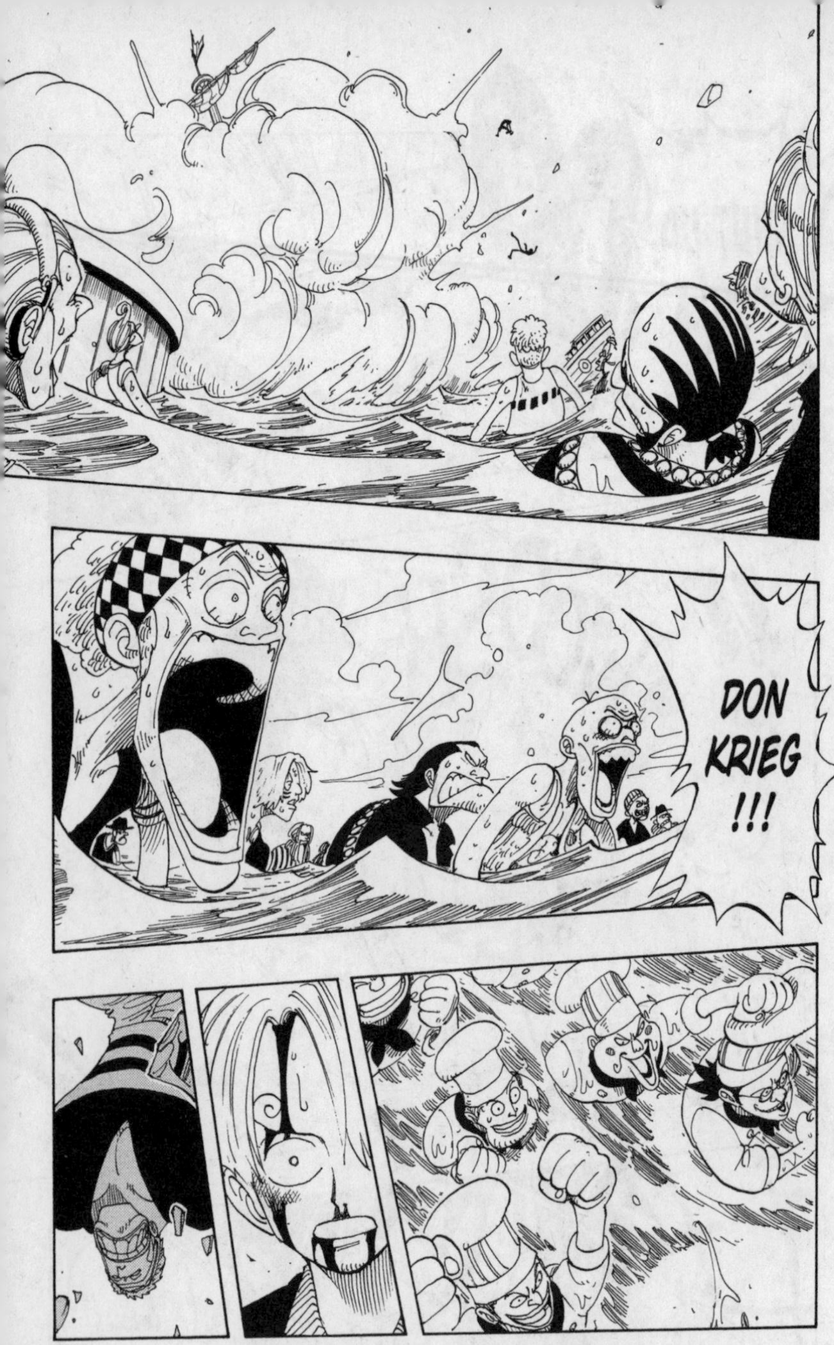
DON KRIEG !!!

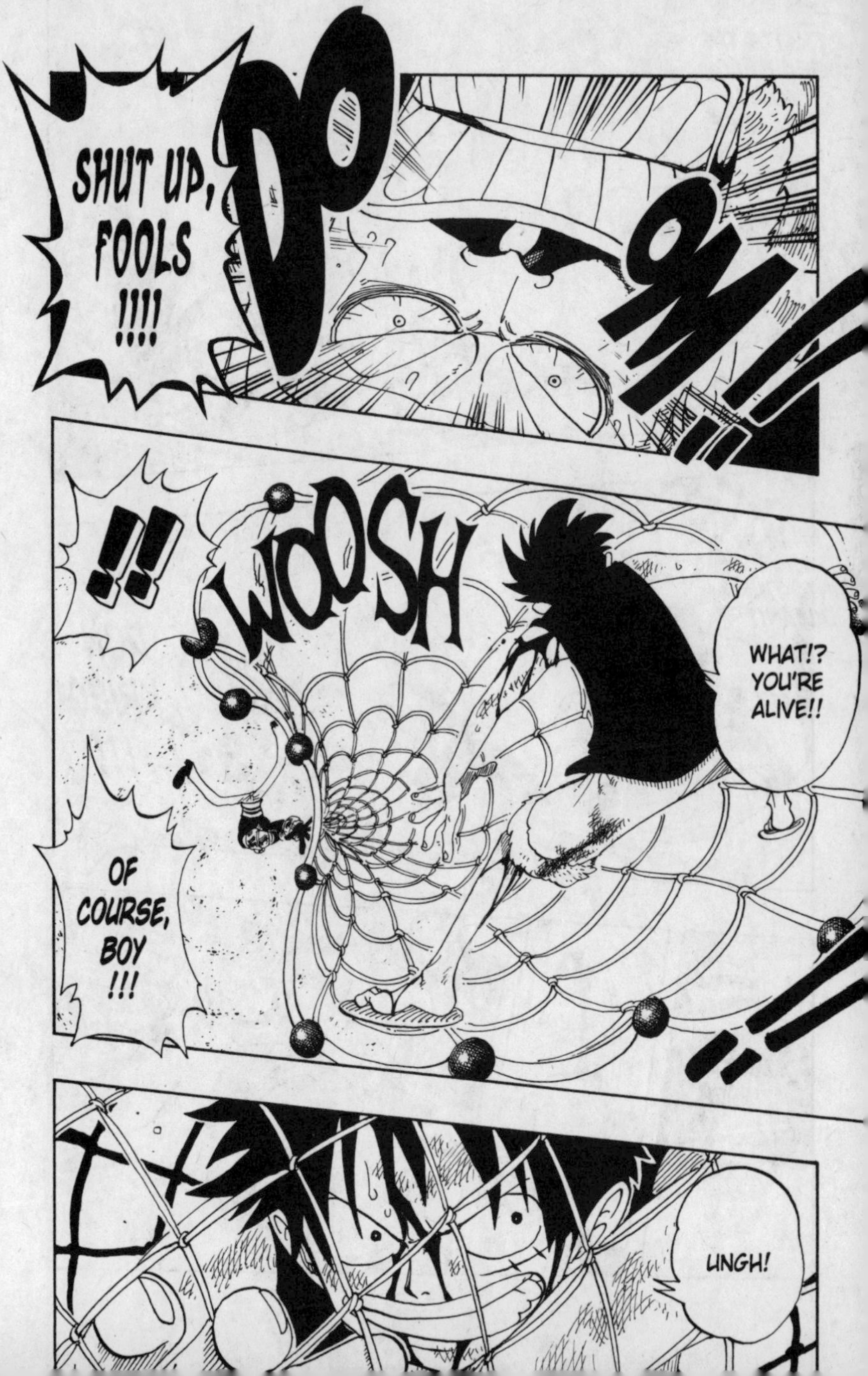
DOOM!!
SHUT UP, FOOLS!!!!
WHAT!? YOU'RE ALIVE!!
WOOSH
!!
OF COURSE, BOY!!!
UNGH!

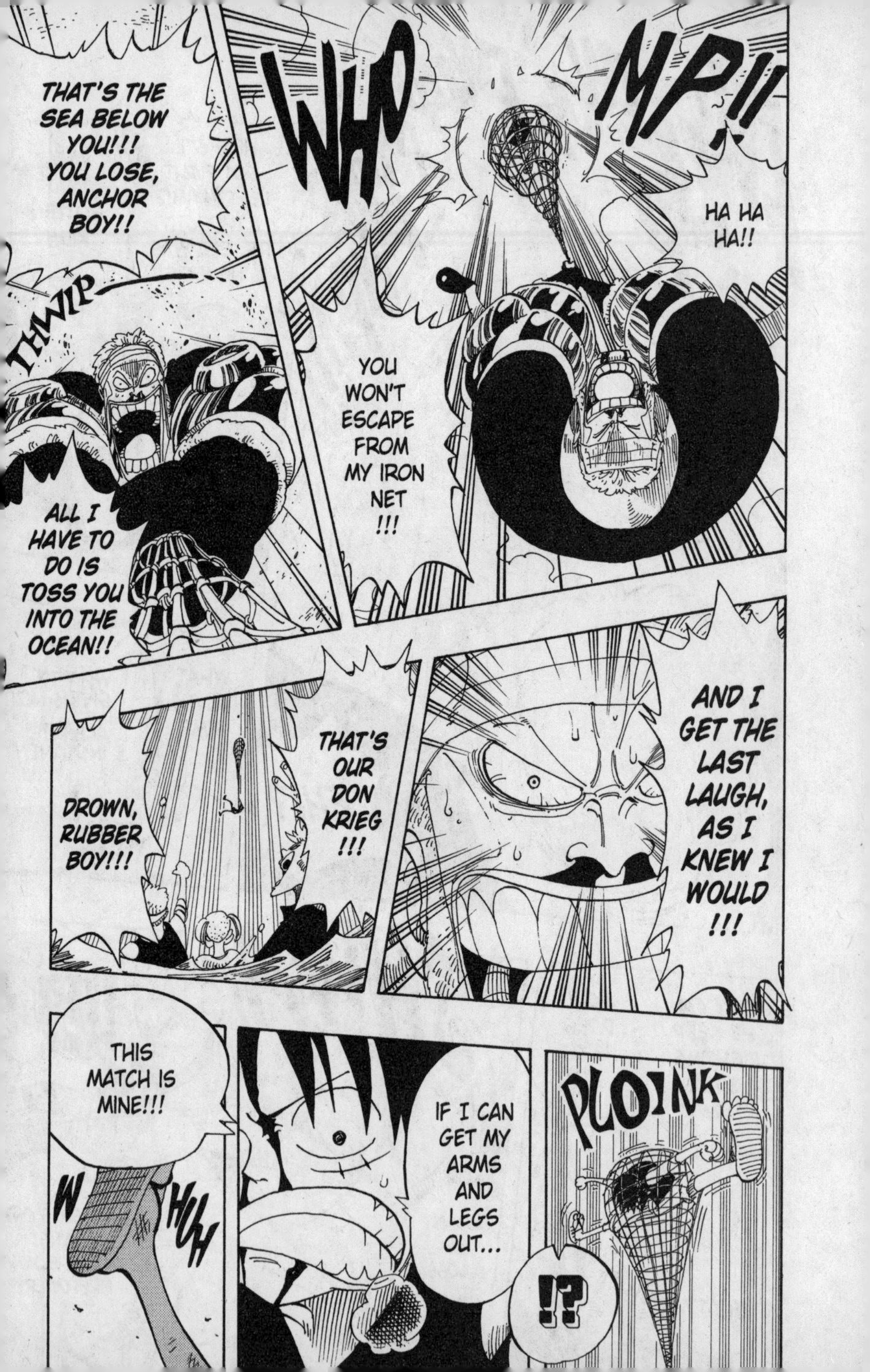
WHOMP!!
HA HA HA!!
YOU WON'T ESCAPE FROM MY IRON NET!!!
THAT'S THE SEA BELOW YOU!!! YOU LOSE, ANCHOR BOY!!
THWIP
ALL I HAVE TO DO IS TOSS YOU INTO THE OCEAN!!
AND I GET THE LAST LAUGH, AS I KNEW I WOULD!!!
THAT'S OUR DON KRIEG!!!
DROWN, RUBBER BOY!!!
PLOINK
!?
IF I CAN GET MY ARMS AND LEGS OUT...
THIS MATCH IS MINE!!!
WHUH

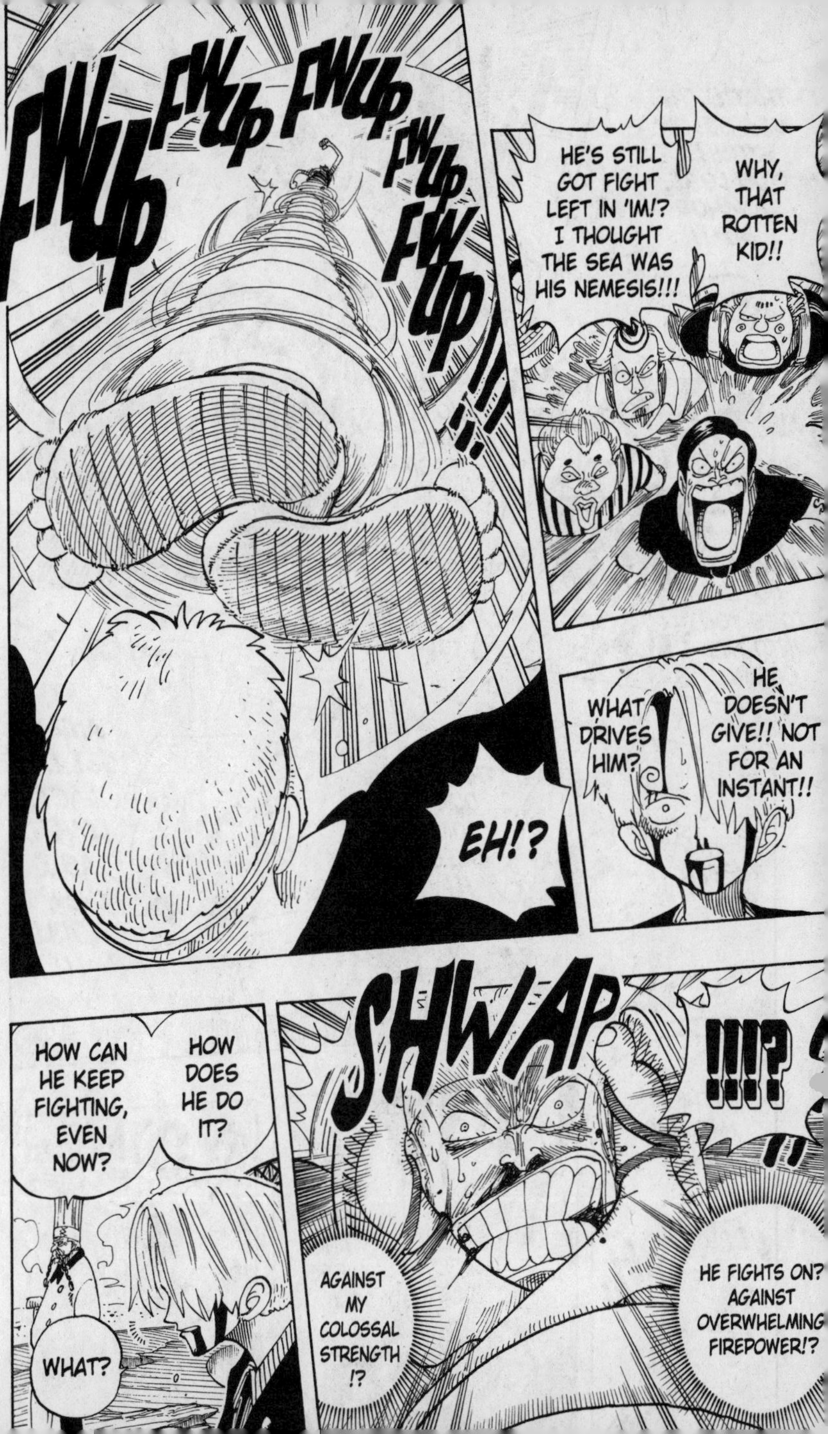
WHY, THAT ROTTEN KID!!
HE'S STILL GOT FIGHT LEFT IN 'IM!? I THOUGHT THE SEA WAS HIS NEMESIS!!!
HE DOESN'T GIVE!! NOT FOR AN INSTANT!!
WHAT DRIVES HIM?
FWUP FWUP FWUP FWUP FWUP!!!
EH!?
SHWAP
!!!?
HE FIGHTS ON? AGAINST OVERWHELMING FIREPOWER!?
AGAINST MY COLOSSAL STRENGTH!?
HOW DOES HE DO IT?
HOW CAN HE KEEP FIGHTING, EVEN NOW?
WHAT?

READ THIS WAY

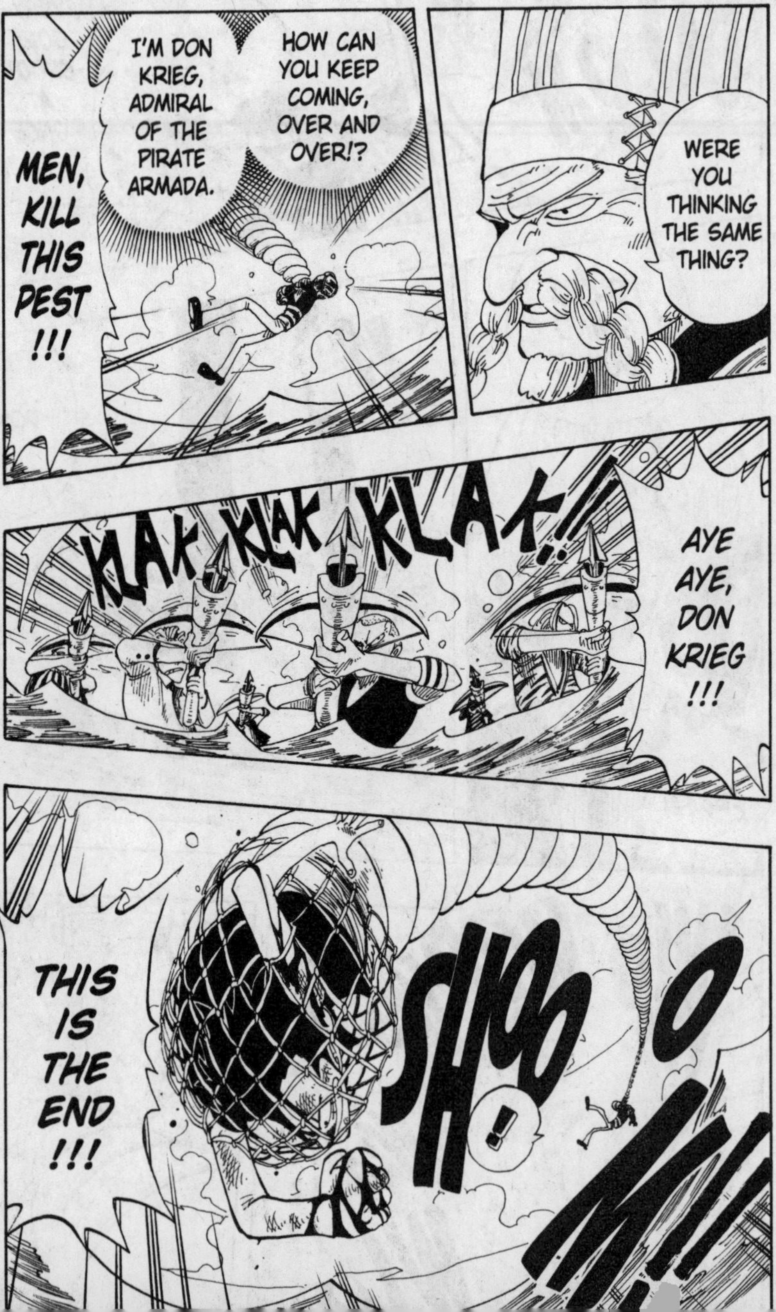

WERE YOU THINKING THE SAME THING?
HOW CAN YOU KEEP COMING, OVER AND OVER!?
I'M DON KRIEG, ADMIRAL OF THE PIRATE ARMADA.
MEN, KILL THIS PEST !!!
AYE AYE, DON KRIEG !!!
KLAK KLAK KLAK!!
SHOOOM!!
THIS IS THE END !!!

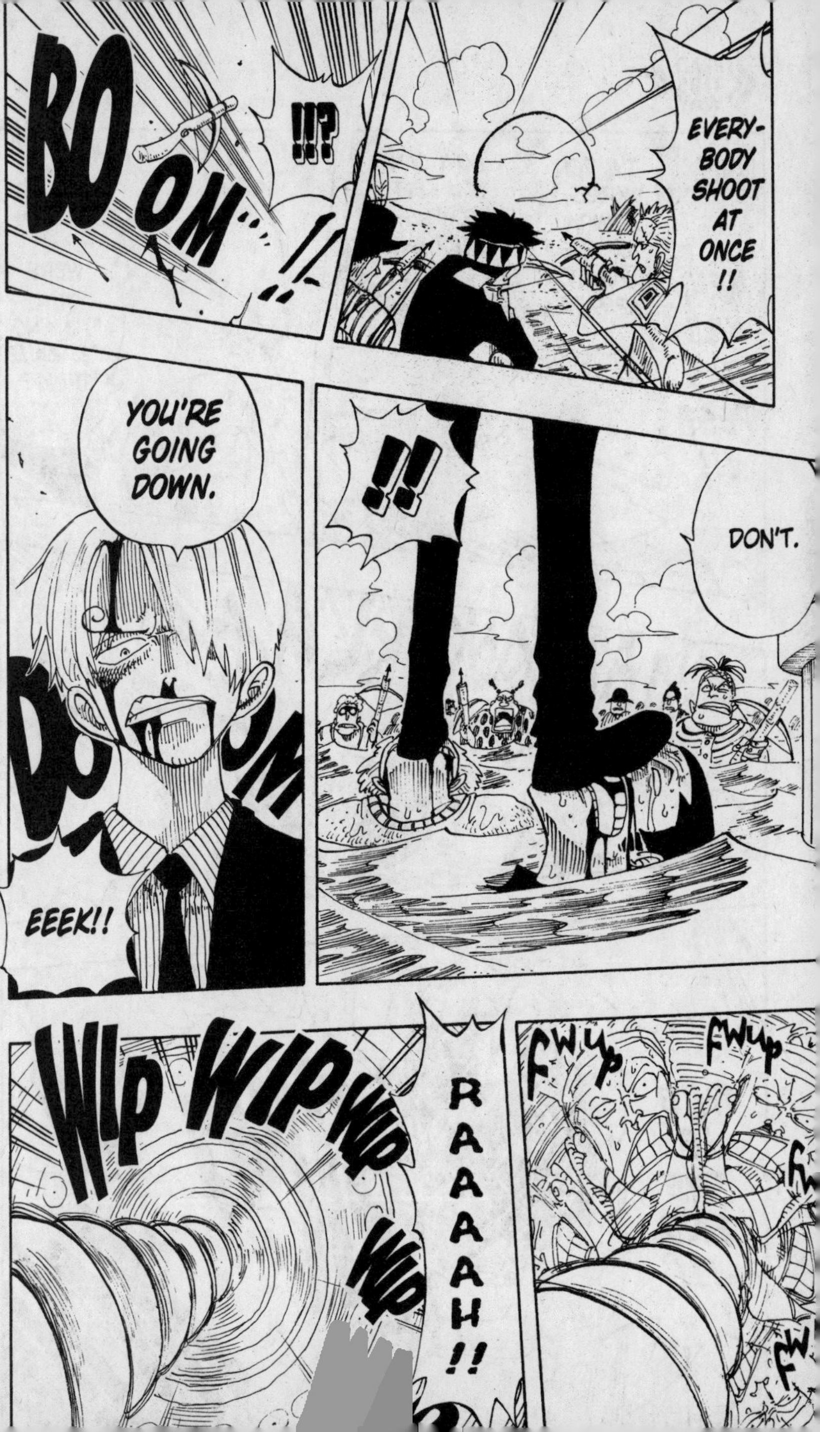
EVERY-BODY SHOOT AT ONCE !!
!!?
BOOM..!!
DON'T.
!!
YOU'RE GOING DOWN.
EEEK!!
fwup
fwup
RAAAAH!!
WIP
WIP
WIP
WIP

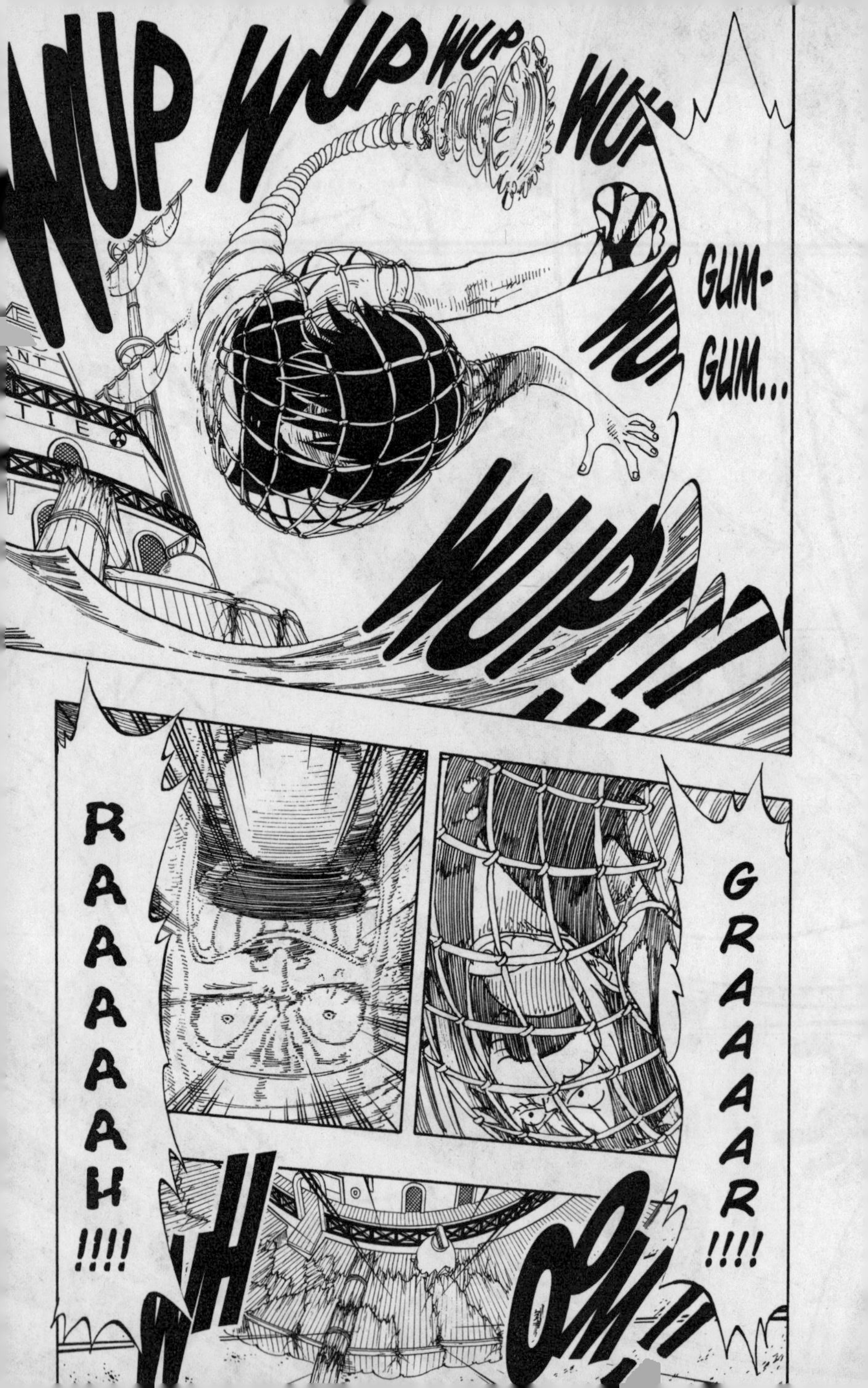

WUP
WUP
GUM-GUM...
WUP WUP WUP WUP
WUP!!!
GRAAAAAR!!!!
RAAAAAH!!!!
WHOOM!!

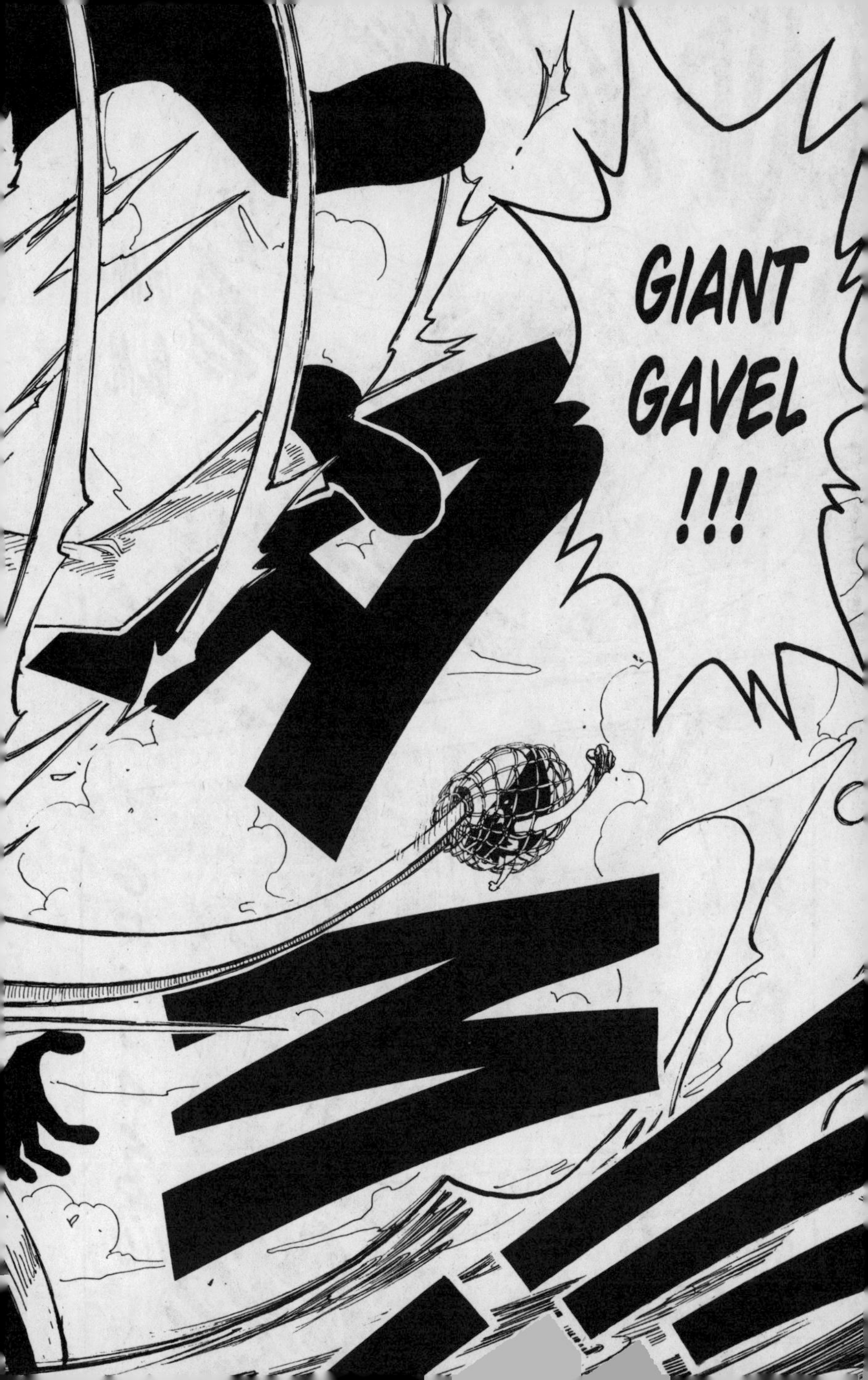
GIANT GAVEL !!!

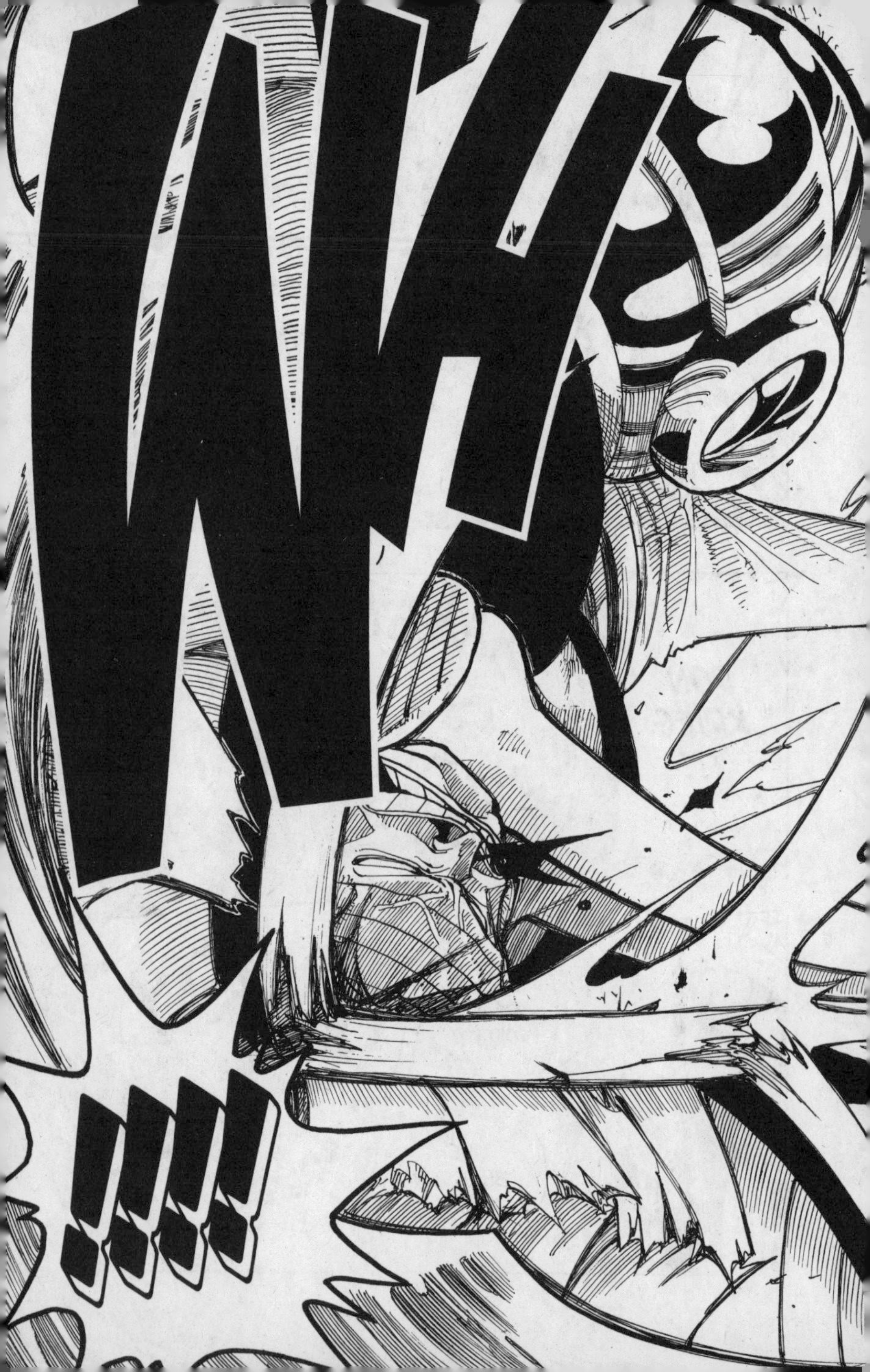

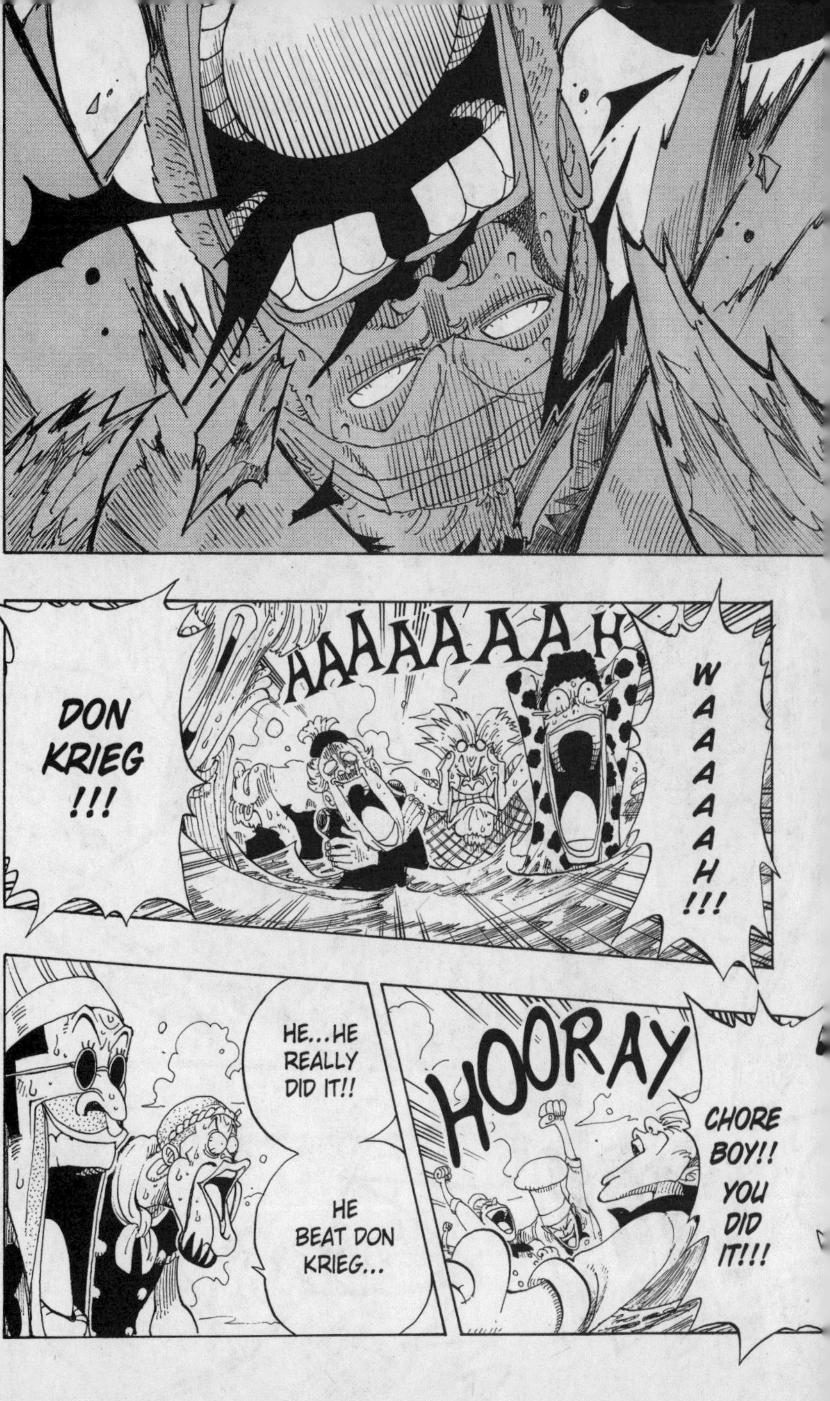
WAAAAAAH!!!
AAAAAAAAH
DON KRIEG!!!
CHORE BOY!! YOU DID IT!!!
HOORAY
HE...HE REALLY DID IT!!
HE BEAT DON KRIEG...

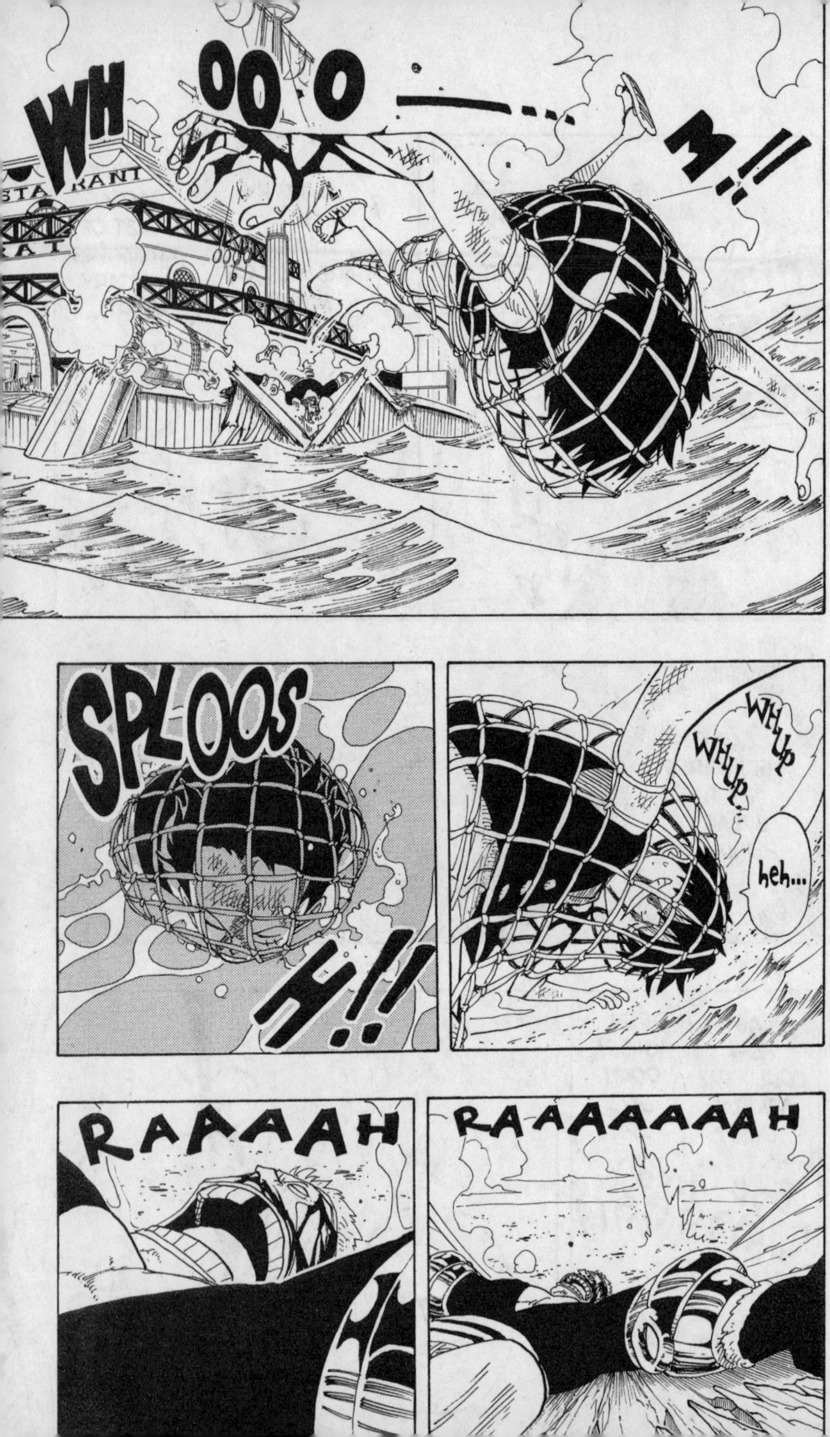
WHOOO——...M!!
WHUP WHUP...
heh...
SPLOOSH!!
RAAAAAAAH
RAAAAH

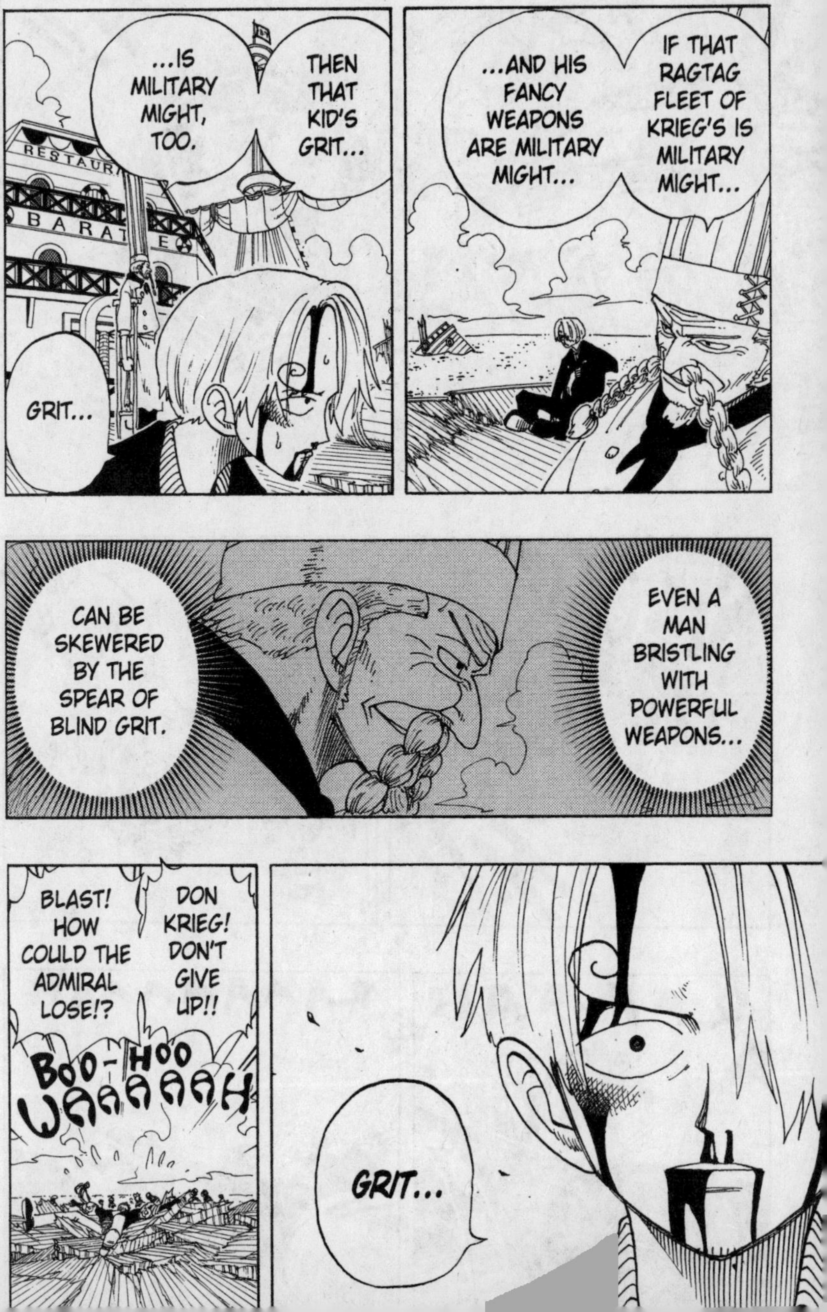
IF THAT RAGTAG FLEET OF KRIEG'S IS MILITARY MIGHT...
...AND HIS FANCY WEAPONS ARE MILITARY MIGHT...
THEN THAT KID'S GRIT...
...IS MILITARY MIGHT, TOO.
GRIT...
EVEN A MAN BRISTLING WITH POWERFUL WEAPONS...
CAN BE SKEWERED BY THE SPEAR OF BLIND GRIT.
GRIT...
DON KRIEG! DON'T GIVE UP!!
BLAST! HOW COULD THE ADMIRAL LOSE!?
BOO-HOO
WAAAAAAH

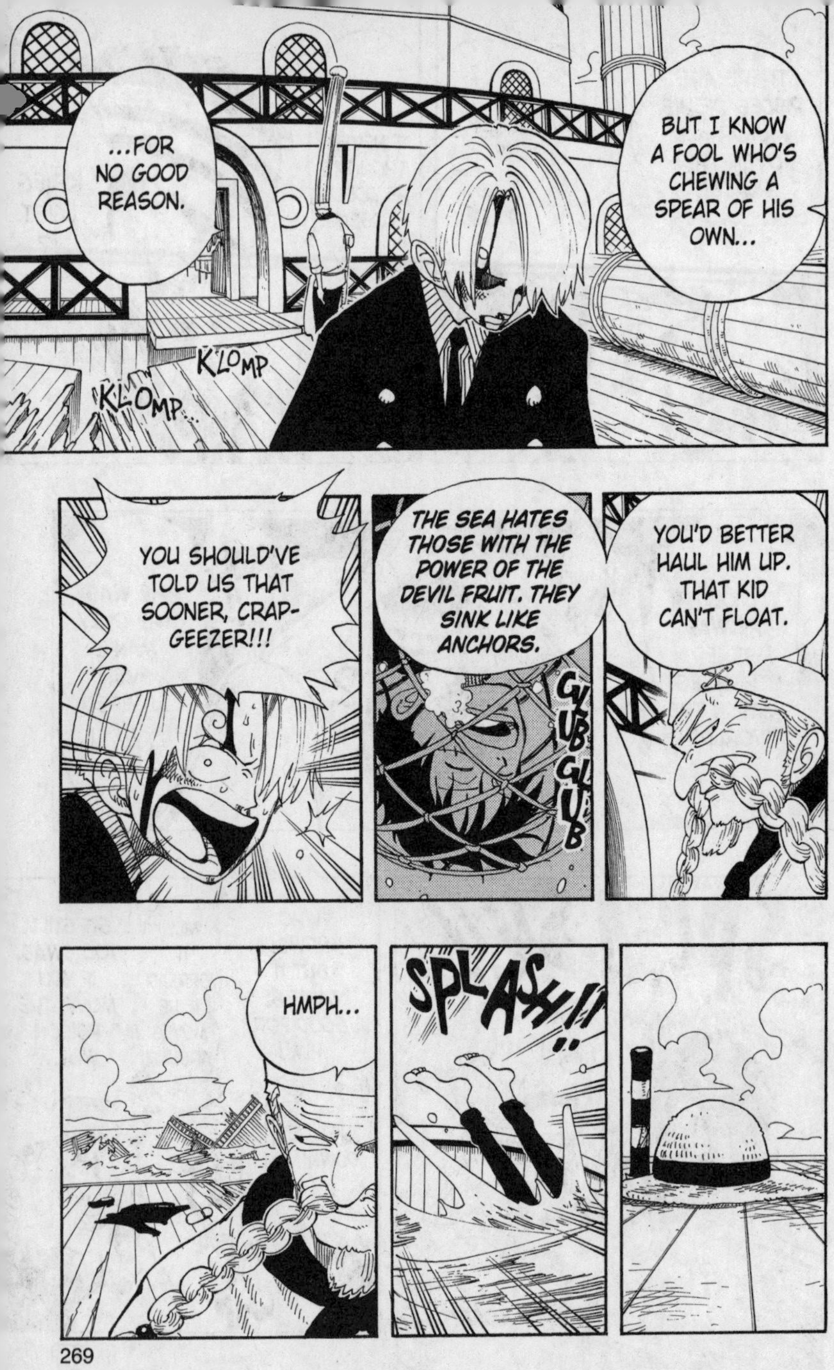
BUT I KNOW A FOOL WHO'S CHEWING A SPEAR OF HIS OWN...
...FOR NO GOOD REASON.
KLOMP
KLOMP...
YOU'D BETTER HAUL HIM UP. THAT KID CAN'T FLOAT.
THE SEA HATES THOSE WITH THE POWER OF THE DEVIL FRUIT. THEY SINK LIKE ANCHORS.
GLUB GLUB GLUB
YOU SHOULD'VE TOLD US THAT SOONER, CRAP-GEEZER!!!
SPLASH!!
HMPH...

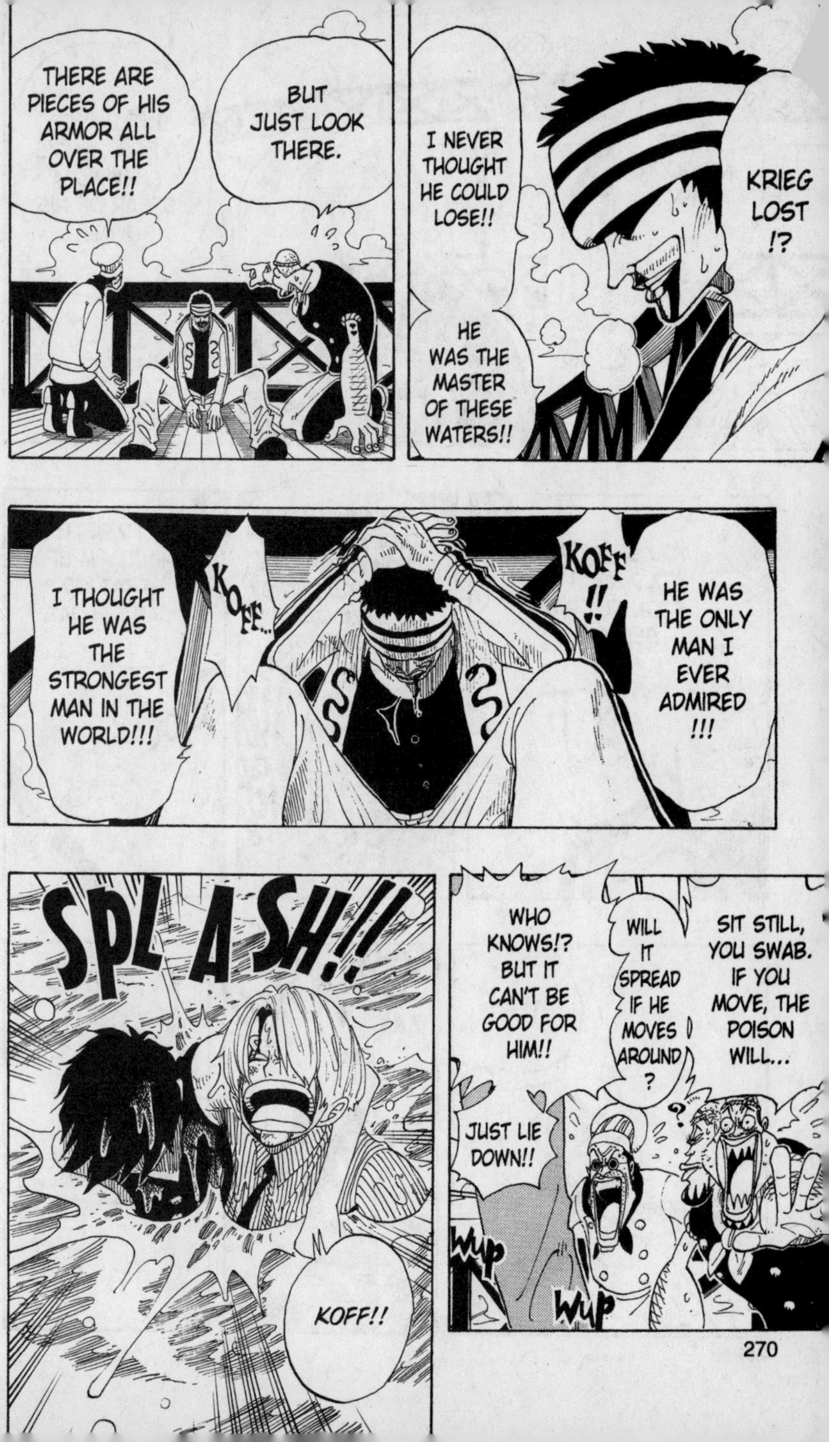
KRIEG LOST !?
I NEVER THOUGHT HE COULD LOSE!!
HE WAS THE MASTER OF THESE WATERS!!
BUT JUST LOOK THERE.
THERE ARE PIECES OF HIS ARMOR ALL OVER THE PLACE!!
KOFF !!
HE WAS THE ONLY MAN I EVER ADMIRED !!!
KOFF...
I THOUGHT HE WAS THE STRONGEST MAN IN THE WORLD!!!
SIT STILL, YOU SWAB. IF YOU MOVE, THE POISON WILL...
WILL IT SPREAD IF HE MOVES AROUND ?
WHO KNOWS!? BUT IT CAN'T BE GOOD FOR HIM!!
JUST LIE DOWN!!
WUP
WUP
SPLASH!!
KOFF!!

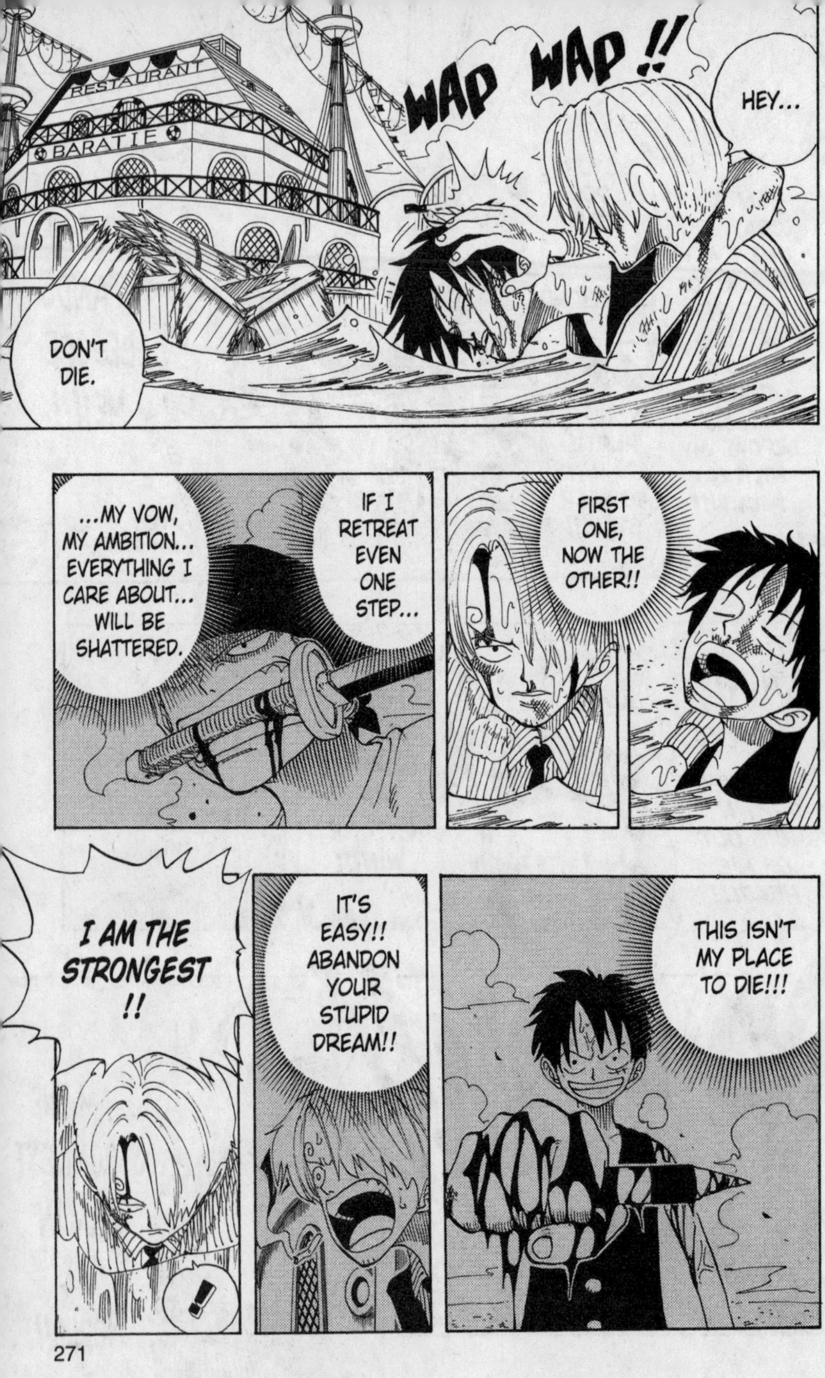
HEY...
WAP WAP!!
DON'T DIE.
FIRST ONE, NOW THE OTHER!!
IF I RETREAT EVEN ONE STEP...
...MY VOW, MY AMBITION... EVERYTHING I CARE ABOUT... WILL BE SHATTERED.
THIS ISN'T MY PLACE TO DIE!!!
IT'S EASY!! ABANDON YOUR STUPID DREAM!!
I AM THE STRONGEST!!
!

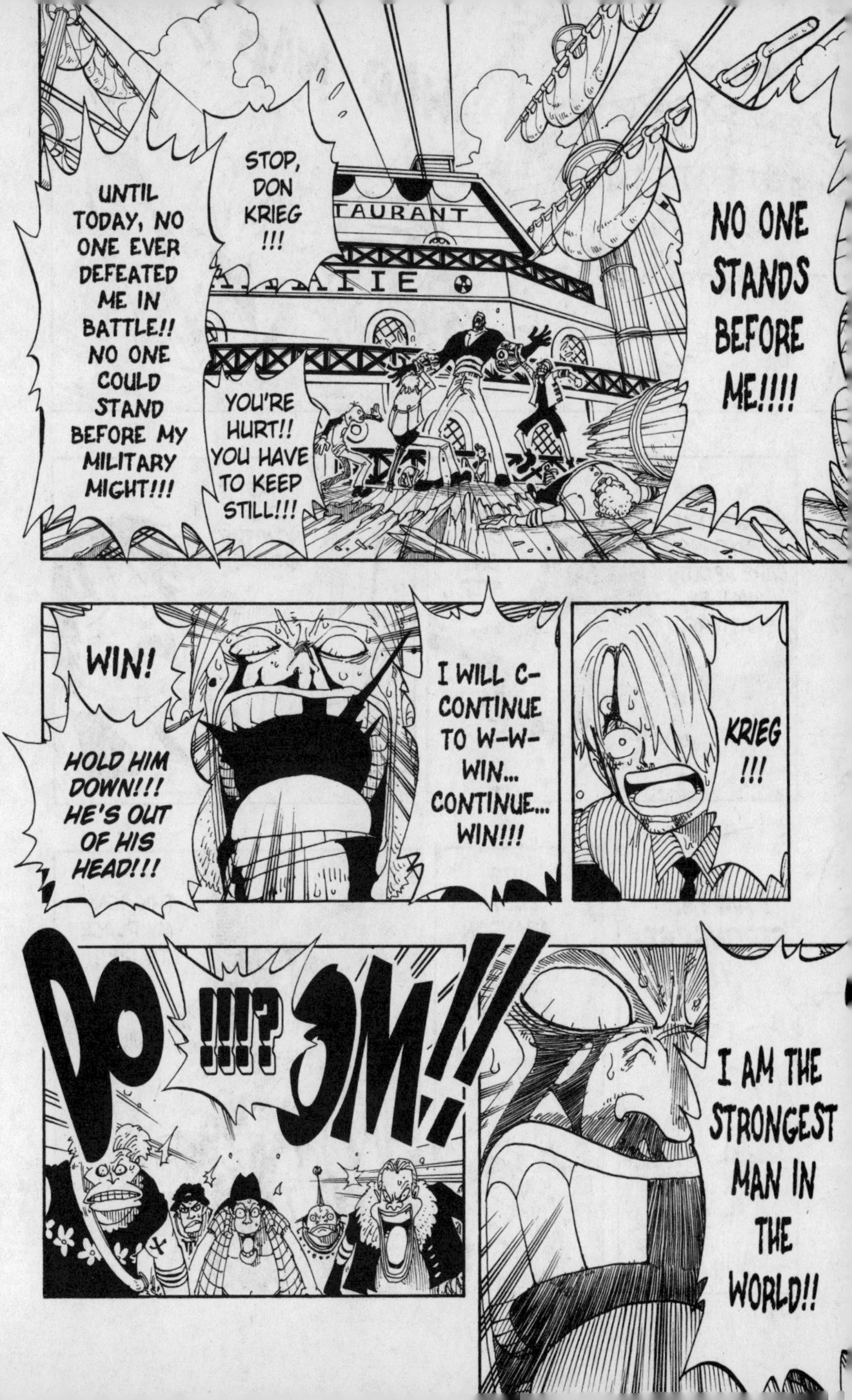
NO ONE STANDS BEFORE ME!!!!
STOP, DON KRIEG!!!
UNTIL TODAY, NO ONE EVER DEFEATED ME IN BATTLE!! NO ONE COULD STAND BEFORE MY MILITARY MIGHT!!!
YOU'RE HURT!! YOU HAVE TO KEEP STILL!!!
KRIEG!!!
I WILL C-CONTINUE TO W-W-WIN... CONTINUE... WIN!!!
WIN!
HOLD HIM DOWN!!! HE'S OUT OF HIS HEAD!!!
I AM THE STRONGEST MAN IN THE WORLD!!
DOOM!!
!!!?

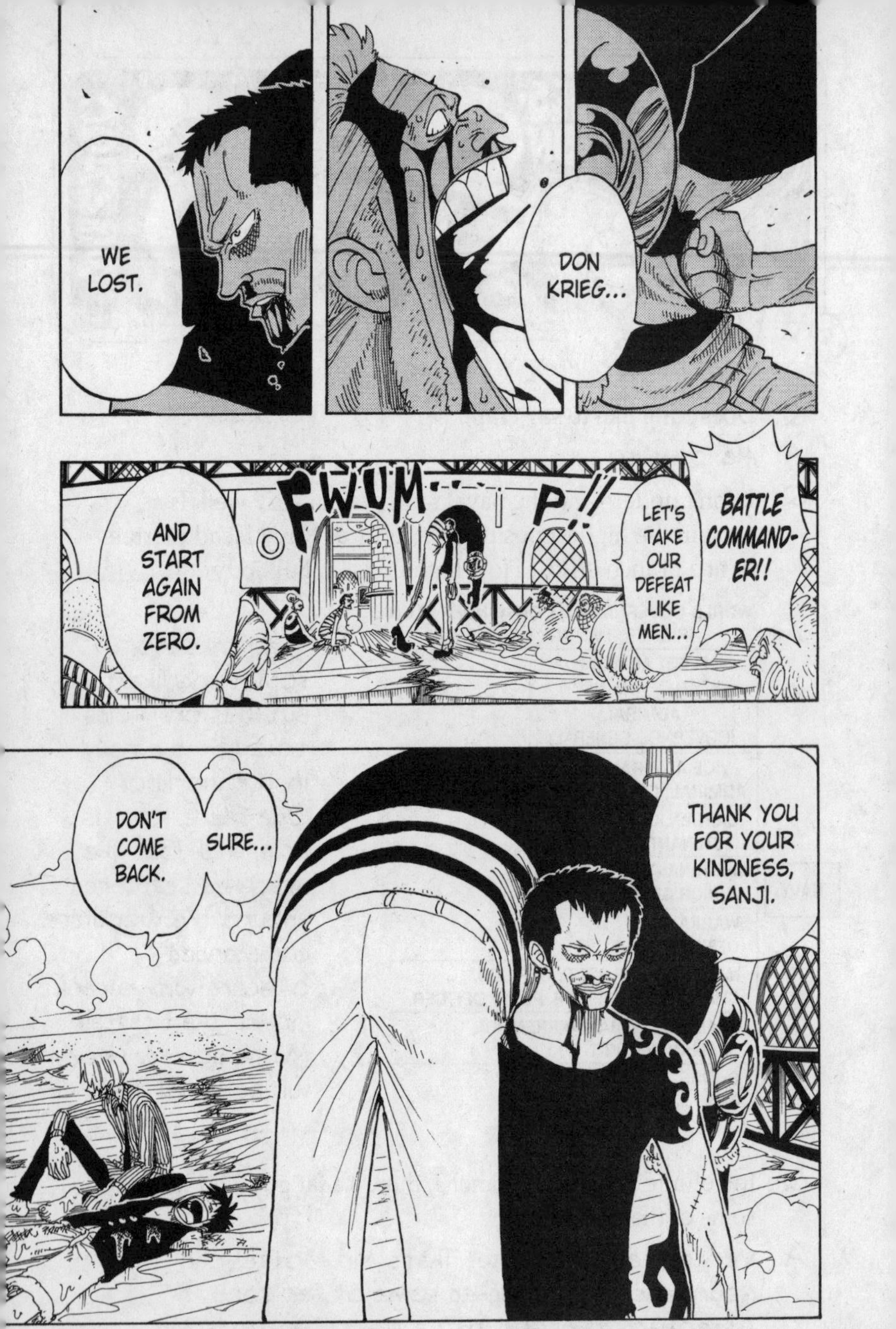
DON KRIEG...
WE LOST.
BATTLE COMMANDER!!
LET'S TAKE OUR DEFEAT LIKE MEN...
FWUMP!!
AND START AGAIN FROM ZERO.
THANK YOU FOR YOUR KINDNESS, SANJI.
SURE...
DON'T COME BACK.

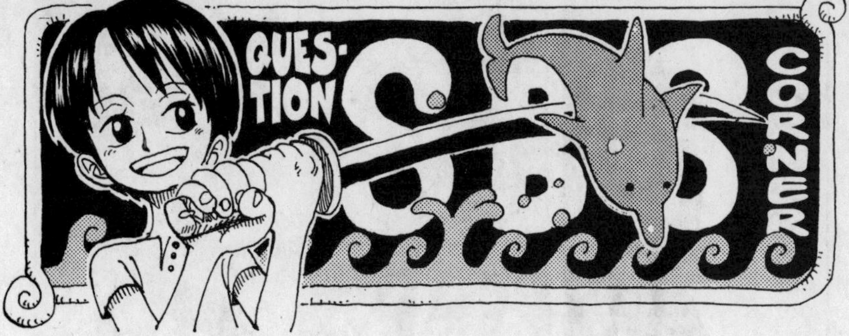
QUES-
TION
S.B.S.
CORNER

**Q:** Does Sanji like to say crap?

**A:** He loves to.

**Q:** I don't understand the naval rank system very well. Is a captain the highest position? Is Koby at Navy Headquarters or at a branch office? How high up is Lt. Fullbody?

**A:**

| | | |
|---|---|---|
| | (WORLD GOVERNMENT) COMMANDER IN CHIEF (HIGHER THAN ANY NAVAL RANK) | |
| NAVY | FLEET ADMIRAL (HEAD OF THE NAVY) | (COMMISSIONED NAVAL OFFICERS) |
| | ADMIRAL (GOVERNOR-GENERAL) | |
| | VICE ADMIRAL, REAR ADMIRAL, COMMODORE | |
| | CAPTAIN, COMMANDER, LIEUTENANT COMMANDER | |
| | LIEUTENANT, LIEUTENANT JUNIOR GRADE, ENSIGN | |
| | WARRANT OFFICER | |
| | MASTER CHIEF PETTY OFFICER, CHIEF PETTY OFFICER, PETTY OFFICER | |
| | SEAMAN, SEAMAN APPRENTICE, SEAMAN RECRUIT | |
| | CHORE BOY | |

The ranks work something like this, but this only holds true for the navy in the world of *One Piece*. Koby is at Branch 153. The branches scattered around the world are commanded by officers with a rank higher than captain. Maybe someday Koby will be an officer.

**Q:** In volume 5, page 159 panel 3, there's a fat guy. Did he steal some of that girl's food?

**A:** Very perceptive!! Wow!! That's Mr. Motzel, the gourmand. Yes, he filched some of her food. Afterward, they got into a fight. The girl is Mr. Motzel's daughter.

# Chapter 67: THE SOUP

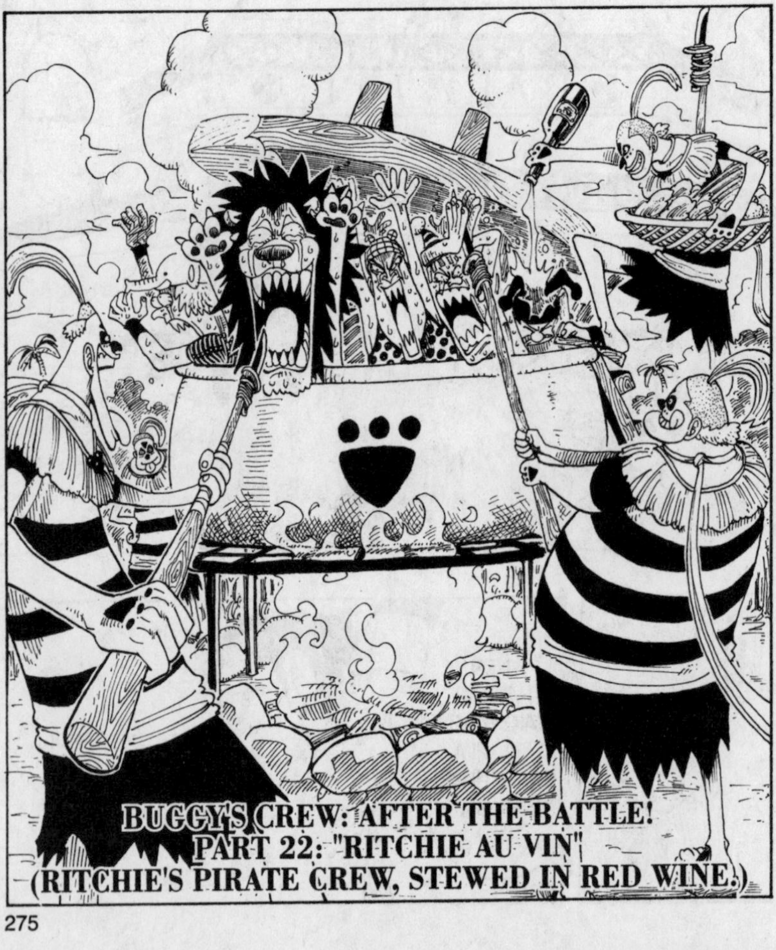
BUGGY'S CREW: AFTER THE BATTLE!
PART 22: "RITCHIE AU VIN"
(RITCHIE'S PIRATE CREW, STEWED IN RED WINE.)

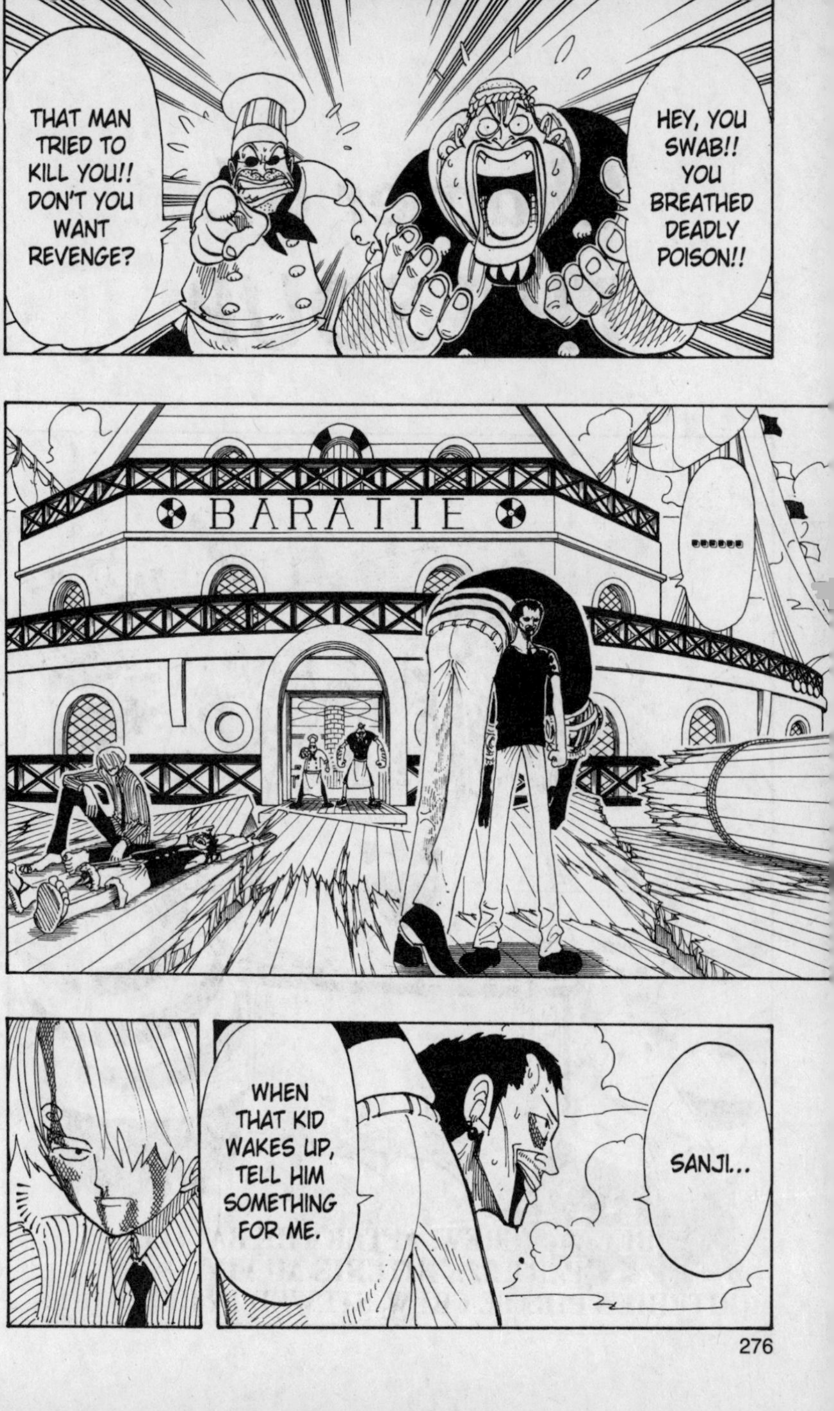
HEY, YOU SWAB!! YOU BREATHED DEADLY POISON!!
THAT MAN TRIED TO KILL YOU!! DON'T YOU WANT REVENGE?
BARATIE
......
SANJI...
WHEN THAT KID WAKES UP, TELL HIM SOMETHING FOR ME.

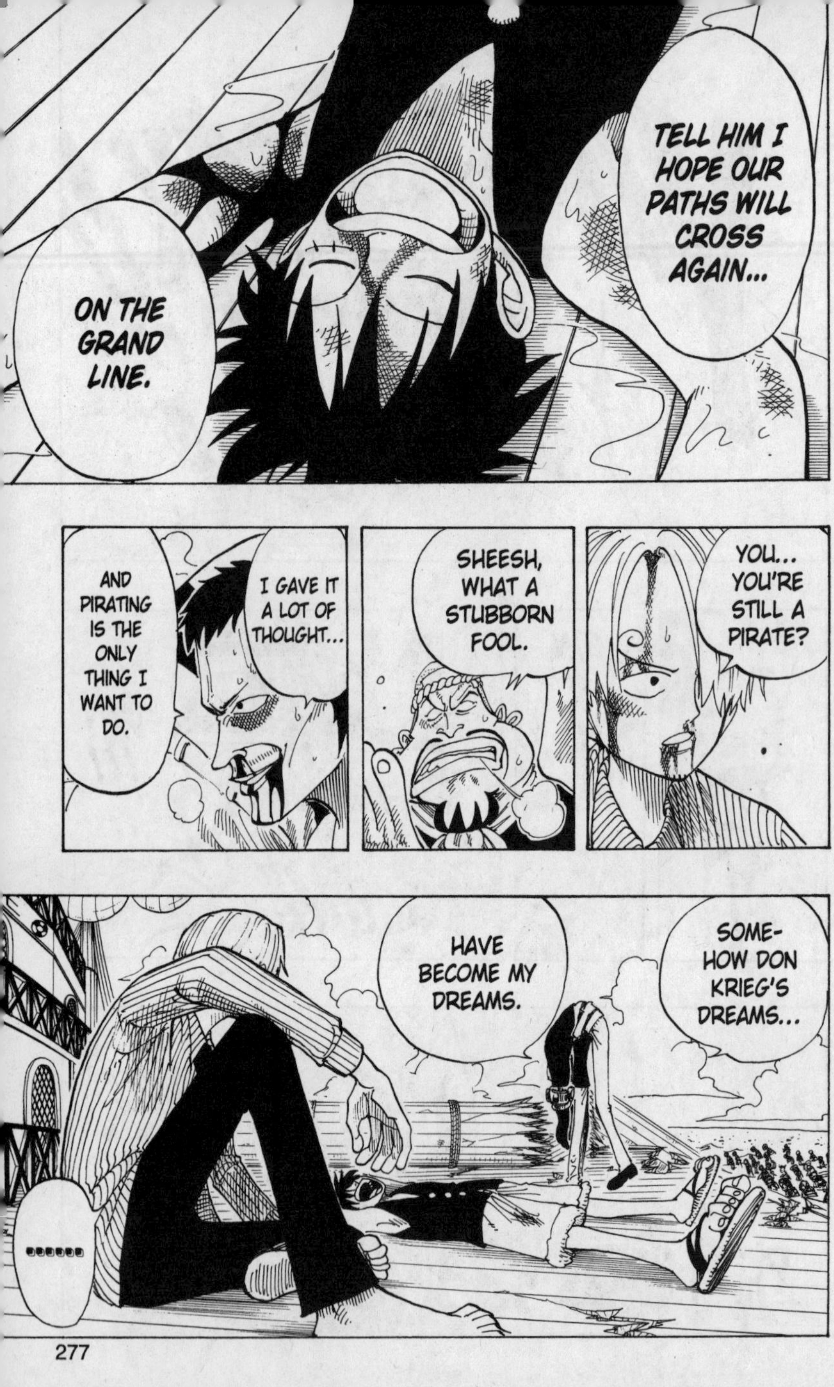
TELL HIM I HOPE OUR PATHS WILL CROSS AGAIN...
ON THE GRAND LINE.
YOU... YOU'RE STILL A PIRATE?
SHEESH, WHAT A STUBBORN FOOL.
I GAVE IT A LOT OF THOUGHT...
AND PIRATING IS THE ONLY THING I WANT TO DO.
SOME-HOW DON KRIEG'S DREAMS...
HAVE BECOME MY DREAMS.
......

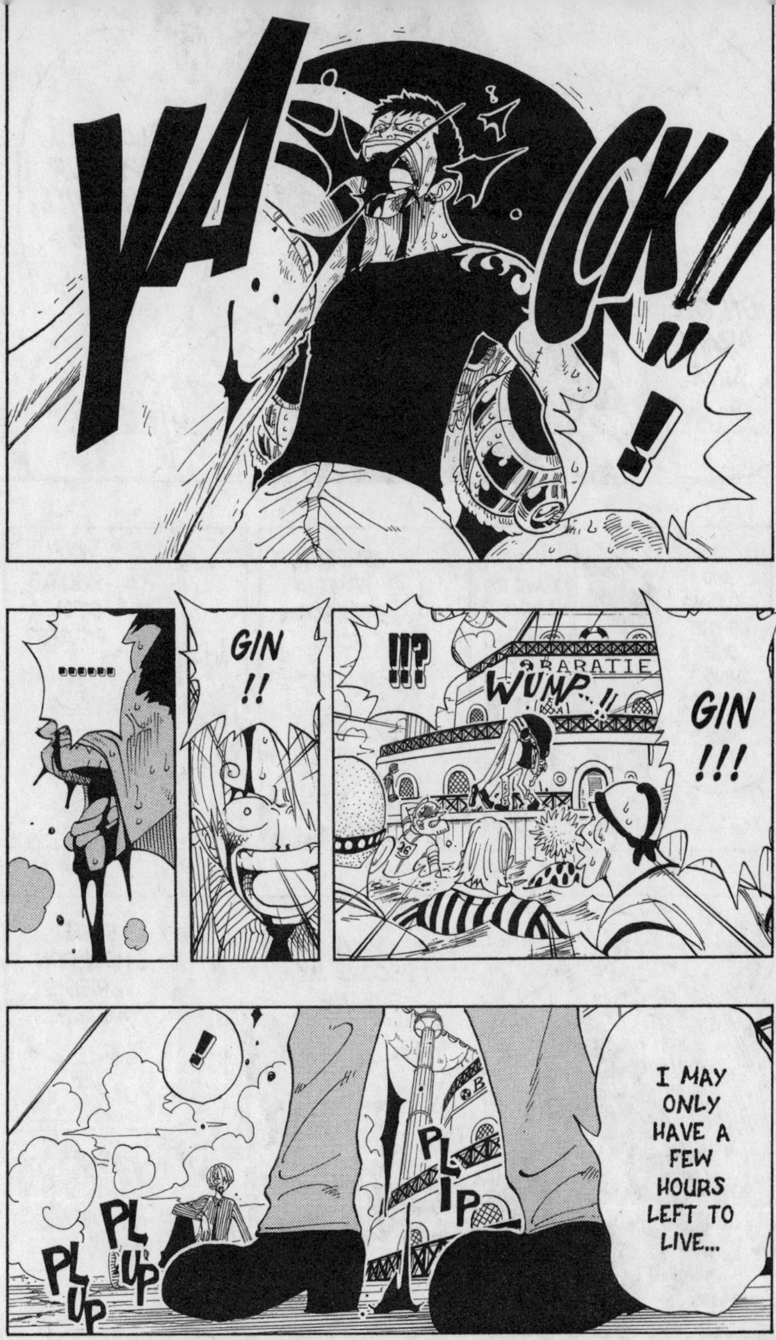
YA
CK!!
!
GIN!!!
!!?
WUMP..!!
GIN!!
......
I MAY ONLY HAVE A FEW HOURS LEFT TO LIVE...
PLIP
!
PLUP
PLUP

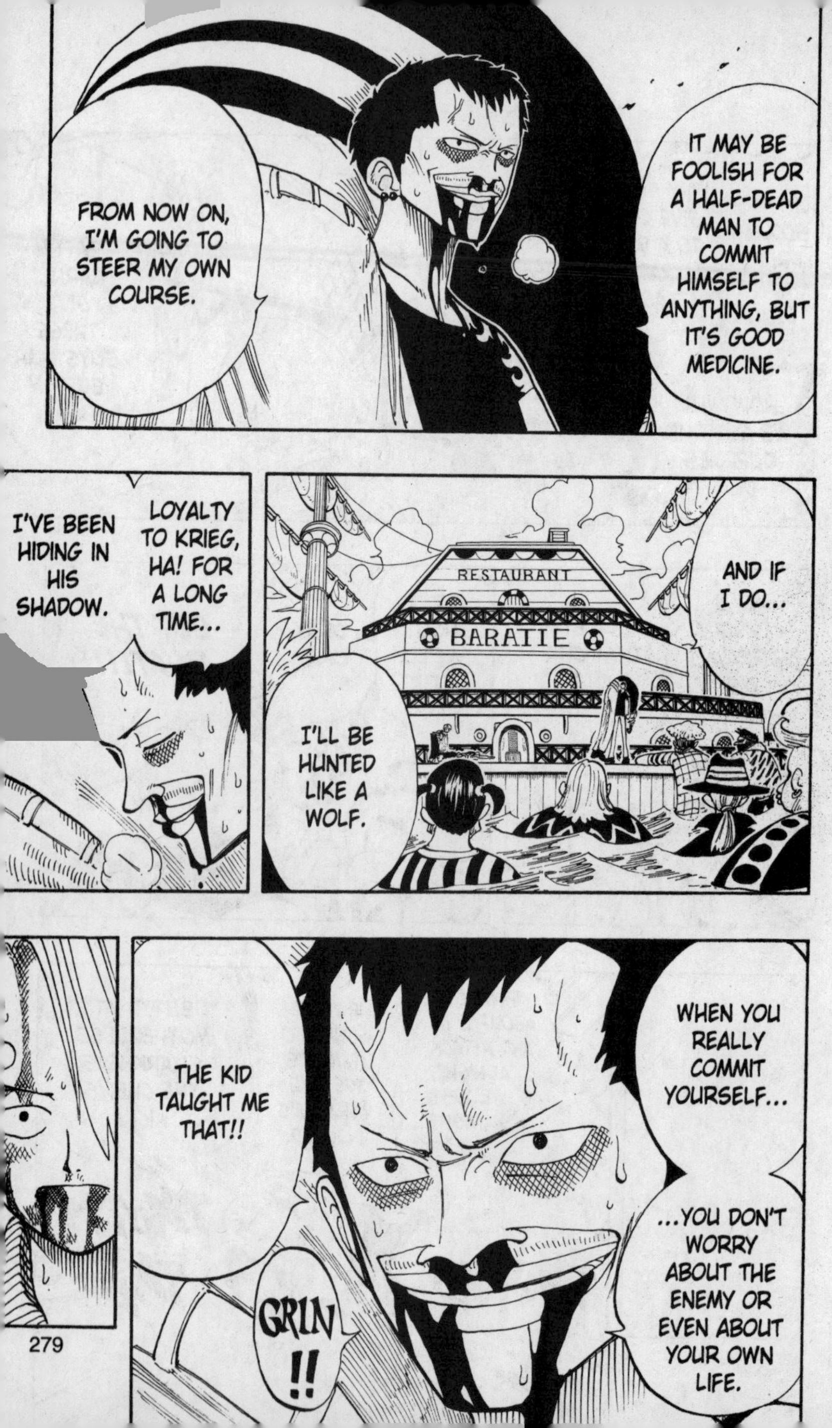
IT MAY BE FOOLISH FOR A HALF-DEAD MAN TO COMMIT HIMSELF TO ANYTHING, BUT IT'S GOOD MEDICINE.
FROM NOW ON, I'M GOING TO STEER MY OWN COURSE.
AND IF I DO...
I'LL BE HUNTED LIKE A WOLF.
RESTAURANT
BARATIE
LOYALTY TO KRIEG, HA! FOR A LONG TIME...
I'VE BEEN HIDING IN HIS SHADOW.
WHEN YOU REALLY COMMIT YOURSELF...
...YOU DON'T WORRY ABOUT THE ENEMY OR EVEN ABOUT YOUR OWN LIFE.
GRIN!!
THE KID TAUGHT ME THAT!!

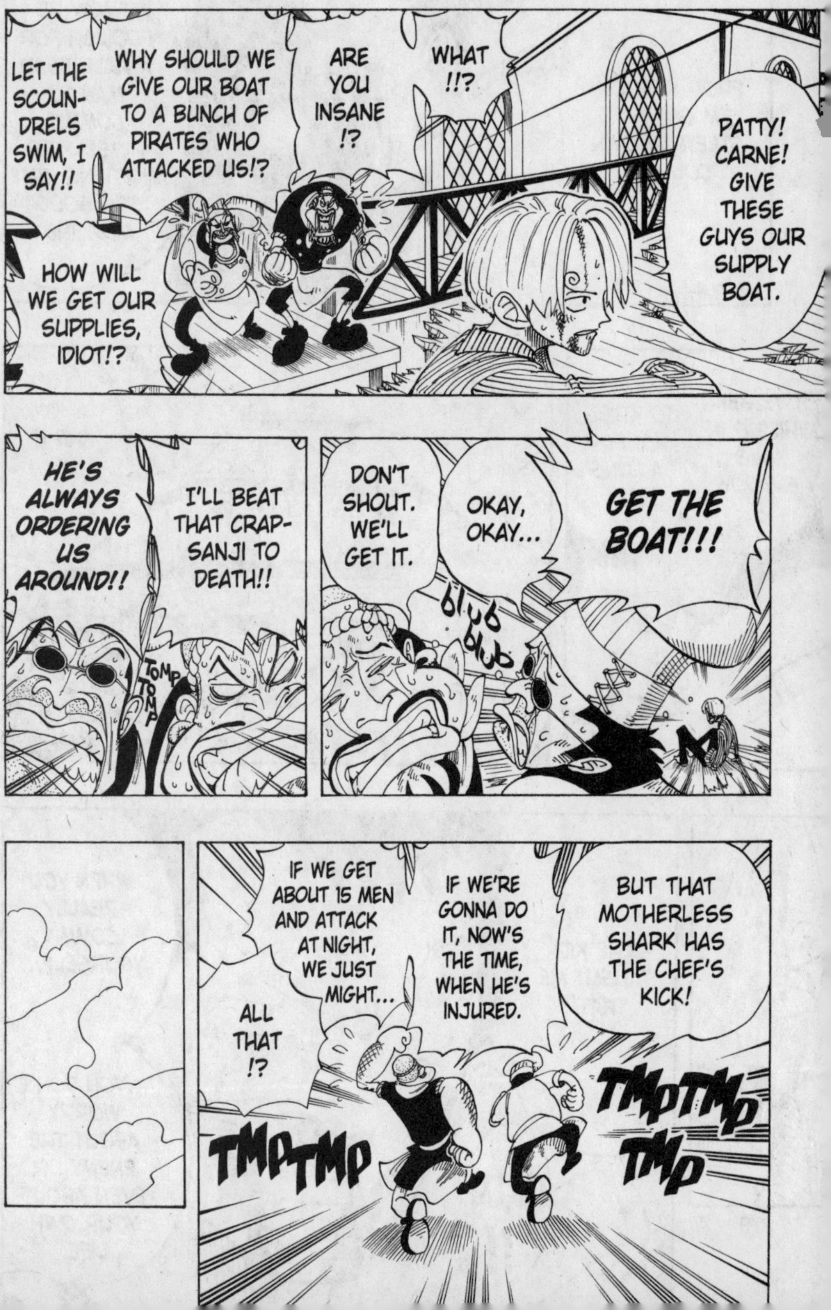
PATTY! CARNE! GIVE THESE GUYS OUR SUPPLY BOAT.
WHAT !!?
ARE YOU INSANE !?
WHY SHOULD WE GIVE OUR BOAT TO A BUNCH OF PIRATES WHO ATTACKED US!?
LET THE SCOUN-DRELS SWIM, I SAY!!
HOW WILL WE GET OUR SUPPLIES, IDIOT!?
GET THE BOAT!!!
OKAY, OKAY...
DON'T SHOUT. WE'LL GET IT.
blub blub
I'LL BEAT THAT CRAP-SANJI TO DEATH!!
TOMP TOMP
HE'S ALWAYS ORDERING US AROUND!!
BUT THAT MOTHERLESS SHARK HAS THE CHEF'S KICK!
IF WE'RE GONNA DO IT, NOW'S THE TIME, WHEN HE'S INJURED.
IF WE GET ABOUT 15 MEN AND ATTACK AT NIGHT, WE JUST MIGHT...
ALL THAT !?
TMPTMP TMP
TMPTMP

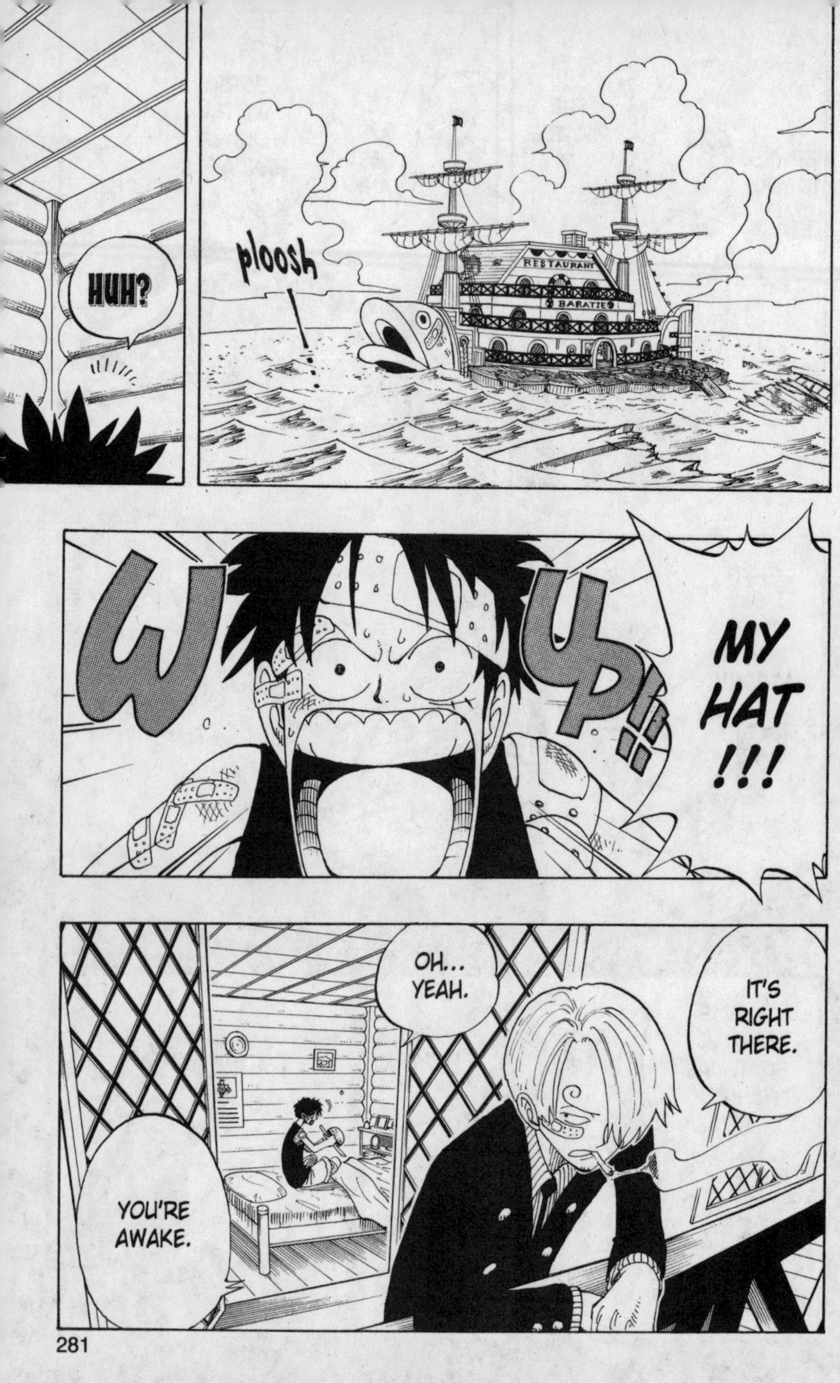
RESTAURANT
BARATIE
ploosh
HUH?
WUP!!
MY HAT!!!
IT'S RIGHT THERE.
OH... YEAH.
YOU'RE AWAKE.

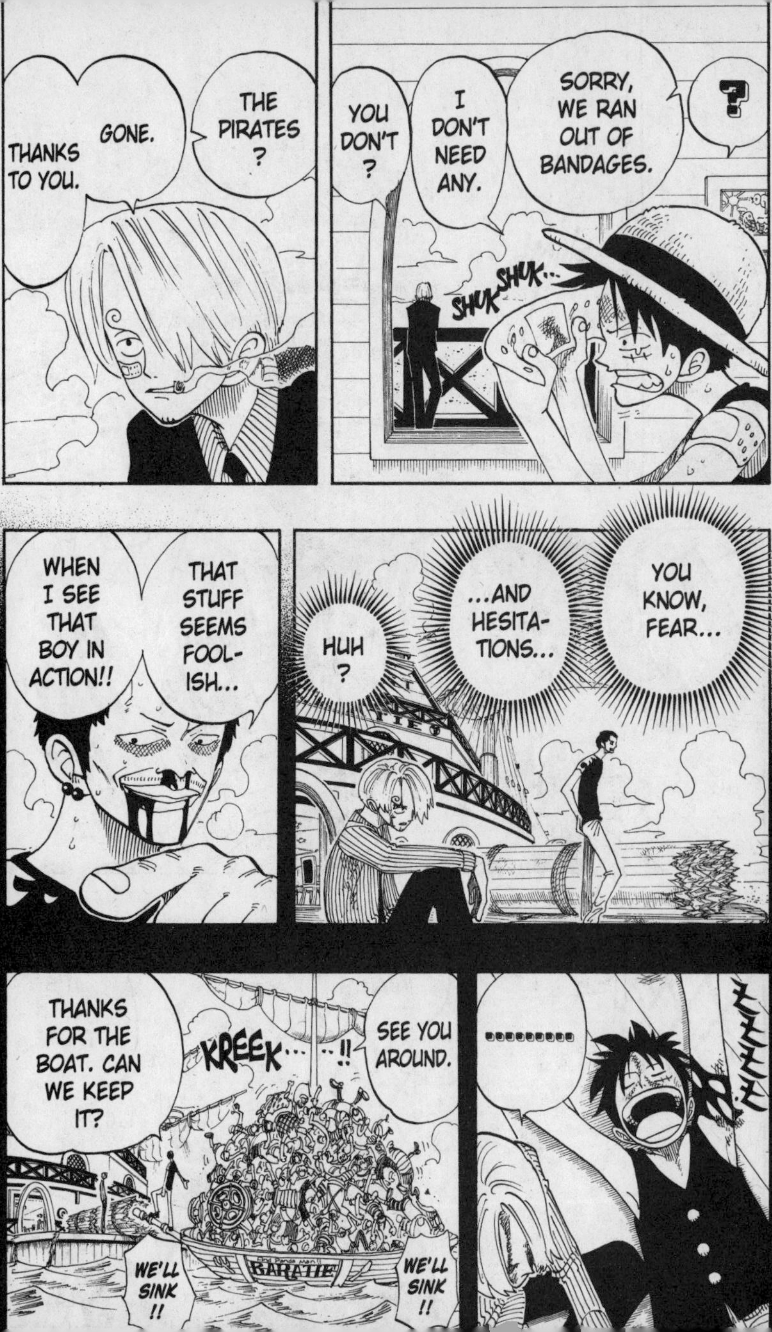
?
SORRY, WE RAN OUT OF BANDAGES.
I DON'T NEED ANY.
YOU DON'T ?
SHUK SHUK...
THE PIRATES ?
GONE.
THANKS TO YOU.
YOU KNOW, FEAR...
...AND HESITA-TIONS...
HUH ?
THAT STUFF SEEMS FOOL-ISH...
WHEN I SEE THAT BOY IN ACTION!!
ZZZZZ
........
SEE YOU AROUND.
KREEK...... !!
THANKS FOR THE BOAT. CAN WE KEEP IT?
WE'LL SINK !!
WE'LL SINK !!
BARATIE

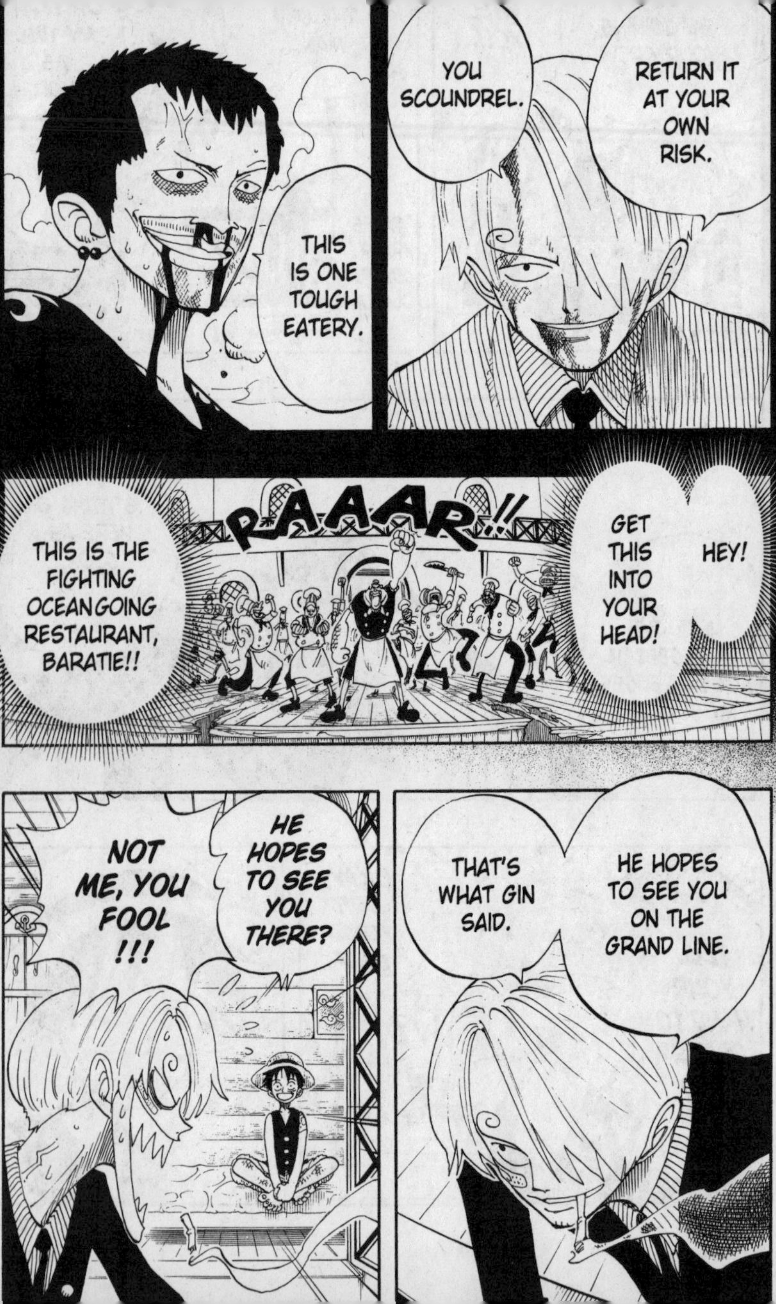
RETURN IT AT YOUR OWN RISK.
YOU SCOUNDREL.
THIS IS ONE TOUGH EATERY.
HEY!
GET THIS INTO YOUR HEAD!
RAAAR!!
THIS IS THE FIGHTING OCEANGOING RESTAURANT, BARATIE!!
HE HOPES TO SEE YOU ON THE GRAND LINE.
THAT'S WHAT GIN SAID.
HE HOPES TO SEE YOU THERE?
NOT ME, YOU FOOL!!!

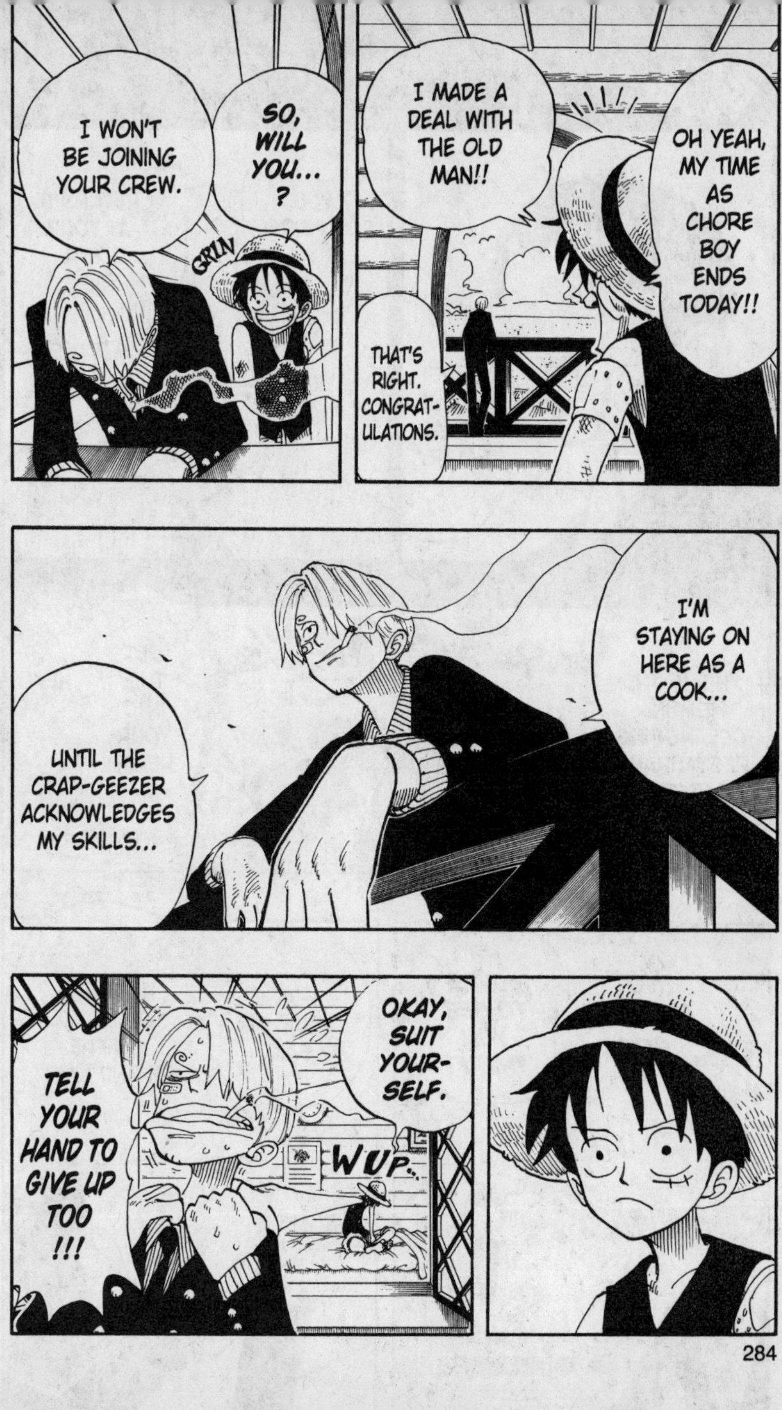
OH YEAH, MY TIME AS CHORE BOY ENDS TODAY!!
I MADE A DEAL WITH THE OLD MAN!!
THAT'S RIGHT. CONGRATULATIONS.
SO, WILL YOU... ?
GRIN
I WON'T BE JOINING YOUR CREW.
I'M STAYING ON HERE AS A COOK...
UNTIL THE CRAP-GEEZER ACKNOWLEDGES MY SKILLS...
OKAY, SUIT YOURSELF.
WUP..
TELL YOUR HAND TO GIVE UP TOO !!!

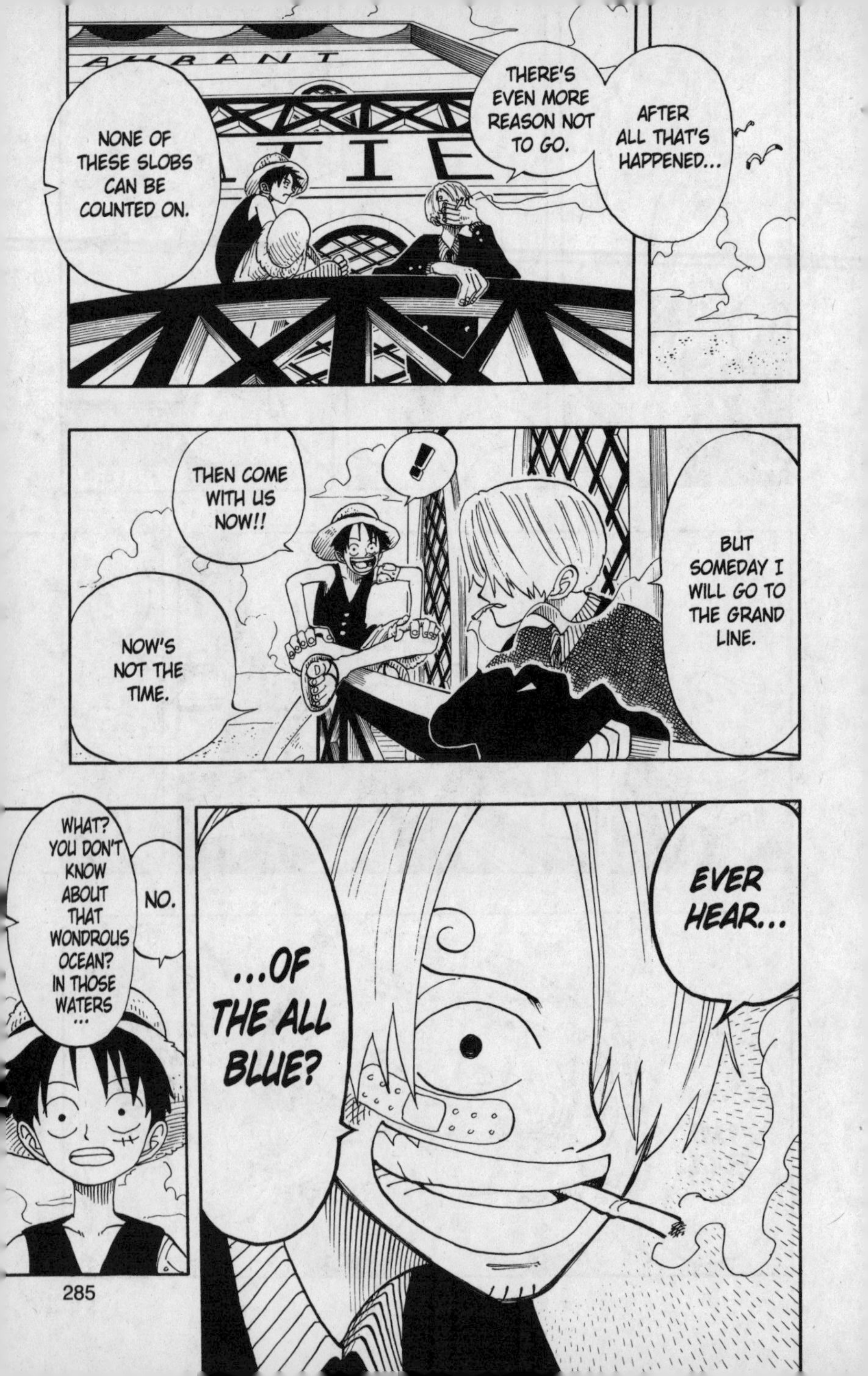
AFTER ALL THAT'S HAPPENED...
THERE'S EVEN MORE REASON NOT TO GO.
NONE OF THESE SLOBS CAN BE COUNTED ON.
BUT SOMEDAY I WILL GO TO THE GRAND LINE.
!
THEN COME WITH US NOW!!
NOW'S NOT THE TIME.
EVER HEAR...
...OF THE ALL BLUE?
NO.
WHAT? YOU DON'T KNOW ABOUT THAT WONDROUS OCEAN? IN THOSE WATERS ...

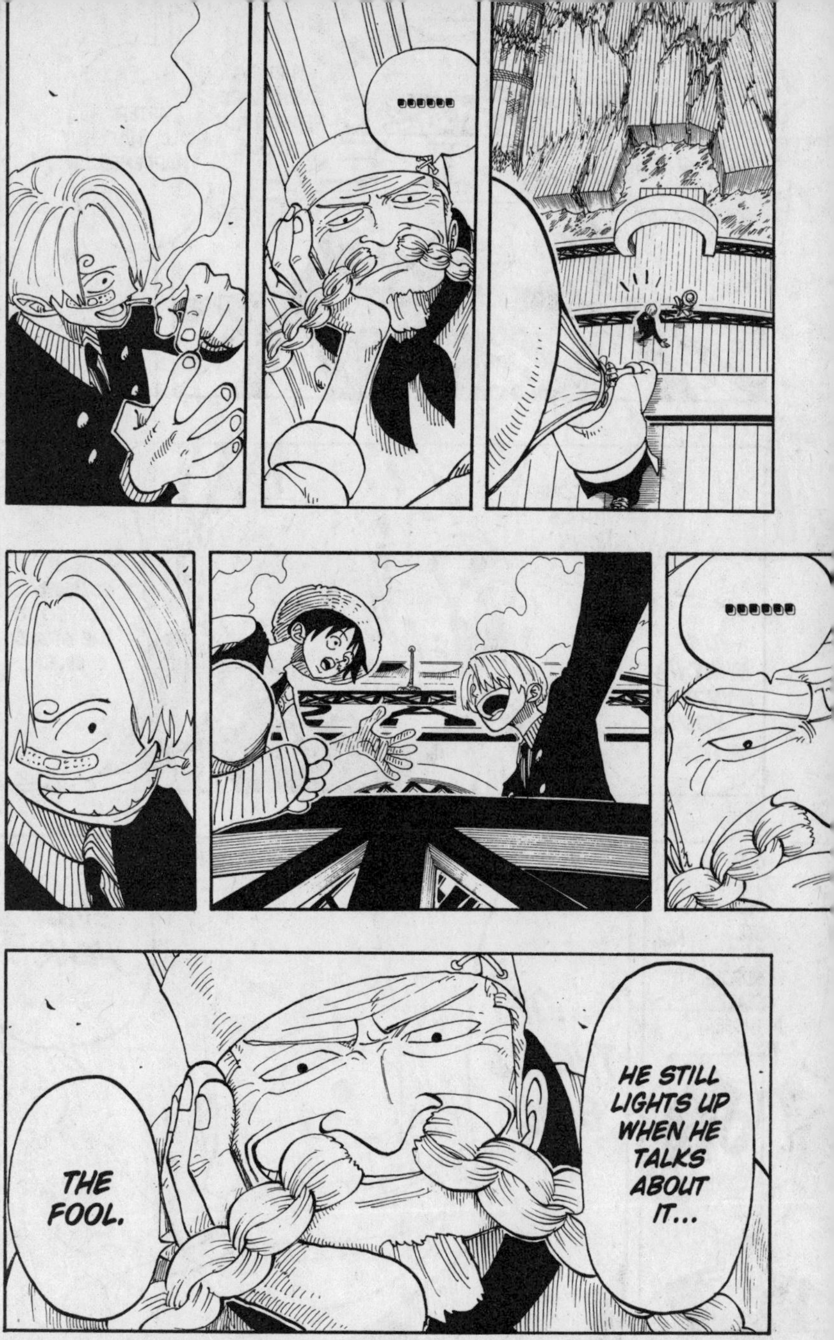
......
......
HE STILL LIGHTS UP WHEN HE TALKS ABOUT IT...
THE FOOL.

READ THIS WAY

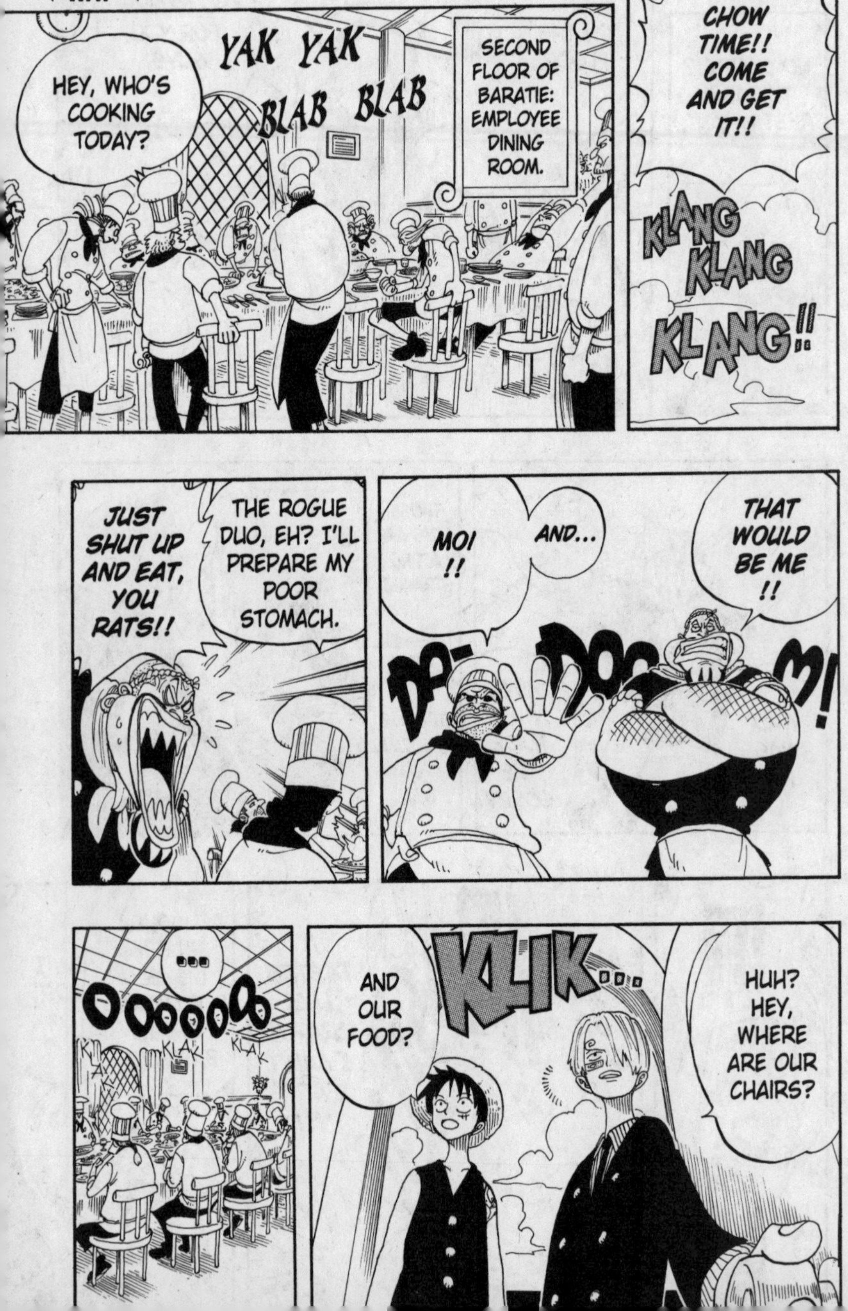
CHOW TIME!! COME AND GET IT!!
KLANG KLANG KLANG!!
SECOND FLOOR OF BARATIE: EMPLOYEE DINING ROOM.
YAK YAK
HEY, WHO'S COOKING TODAY?
BLAB BLAB
THAT WOULD BE ME!!
AND...
MOI!!
DA- DOO M!
THE ROGUE DUO, EH? I'LL PREPARE MY POOR STOMACH.
JUST SHUT UP AND EAT, YOU RATS!!
HUH? HEY, WHERE ARE OUR CHAIRS?
KLIK...
AND OUR FOOD?
...
OOOOOO
KLAK KLAK KLAK

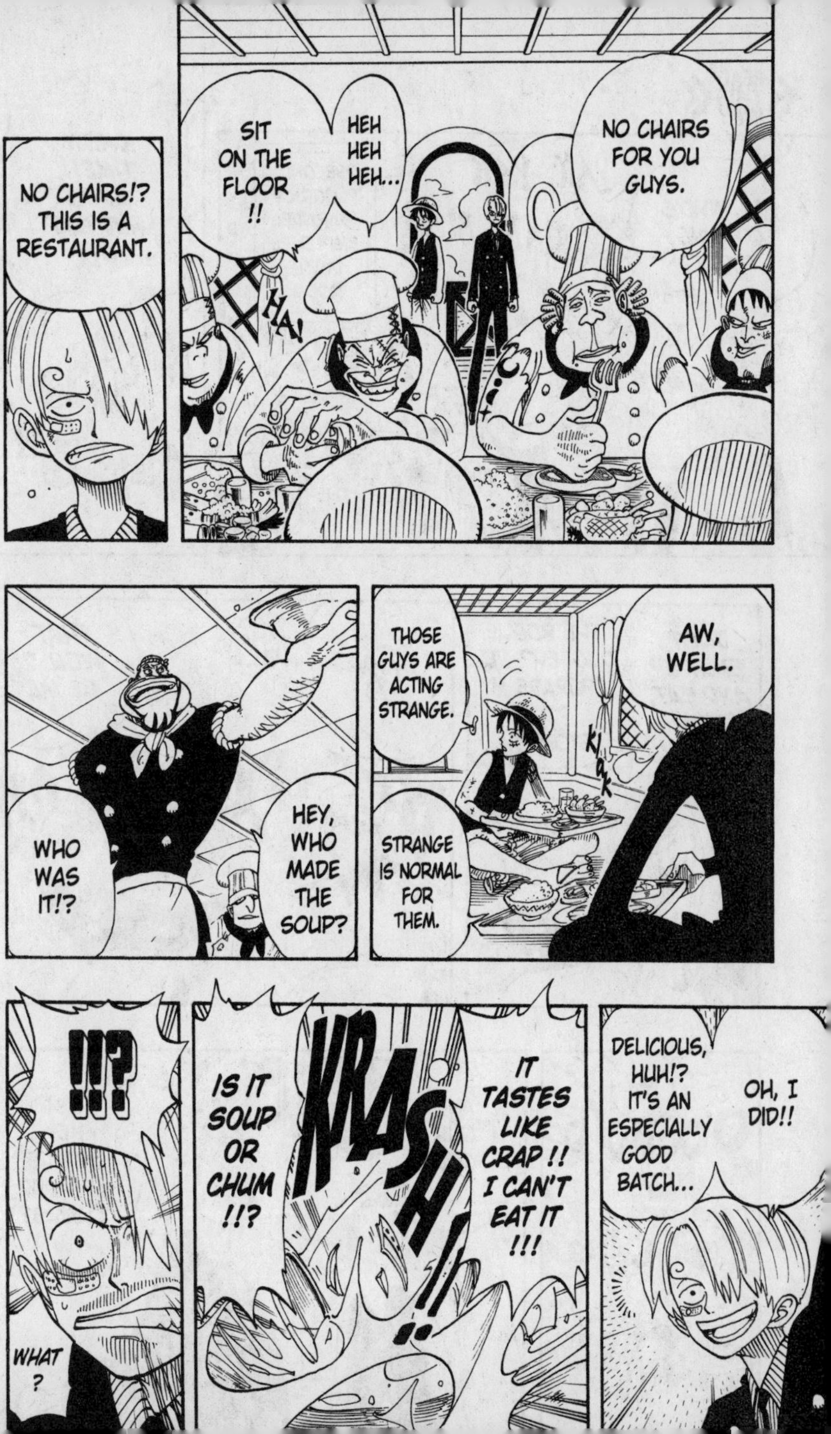
NO CHAIRS FOR YOU GUYS.
HEH HEH HEH...
SIT ON THE FLOOR !!
HA!
NO CHAIRS!? THIS IS A RESTAURANT.
AW, WELL.
THOSE GUYS ARE ACTING STRANGE.
KLAK
STRANGE IS NORMAL FOR THEM.
HEY, WHO MADE THE SOUP?
WHO WAS IT!?
OH, I DID!!
DELICIOUS, HUH!? IT'S AN ESPECIALLY GOOD BATCH...
IT TASTES LIKE CRAP !! I CAN'T EAT IT !!!
KRASH!!
IS IT SOUP OR CHUM !!?
!!?
WHAT ?

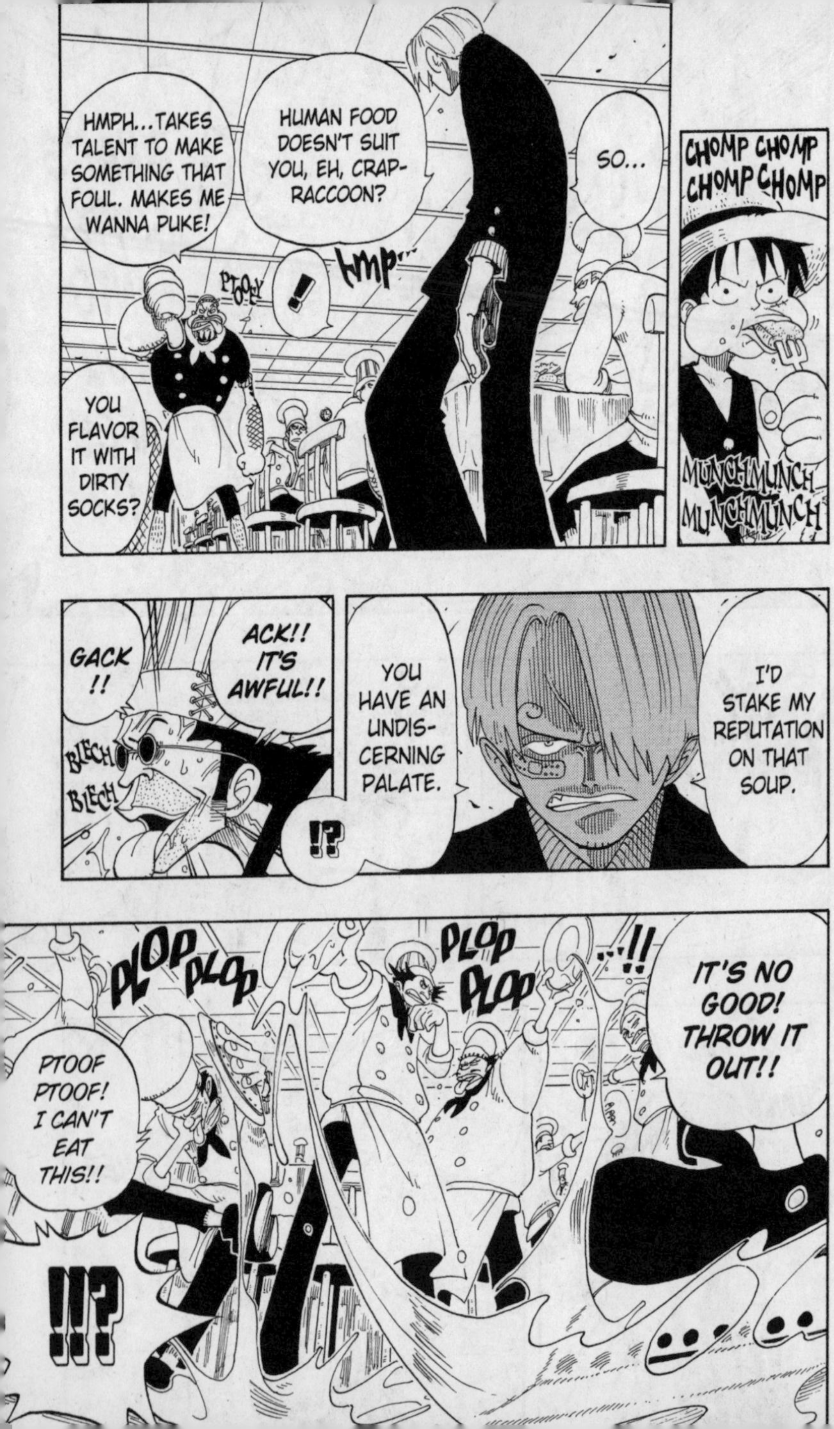
CHOMP CHOMP CHOMP CHOMP
MUNCHMUNCH MUNCHMUNCH
SO...
HUMAN FOOD DOESN'T SUIT YOU, EH, CRAP-RACCOON?
HMPH...TAKES TALENT TO MAKE SOMETHING THAT FOUL. MAKES ME WANNA PUKE!
HMP...
!
PTOOY
YOU FLAVOR IT WITH DIRTY SOCKS?
I'D STAKE MY REPUTATION ON THAT SOUP.
YOU HAVE AN UNDIS-CERNING PALATE.
!?
ACK!! IT'S AWFUL!!
GACK !!
BLECH BLECH
IT'S NO GOOD! THROW IT OUT!!
...!!
PLOP PLOP
PLOP PLOP
PTOOF PTOOF! I CAN'T EAT THIS!!
!!?

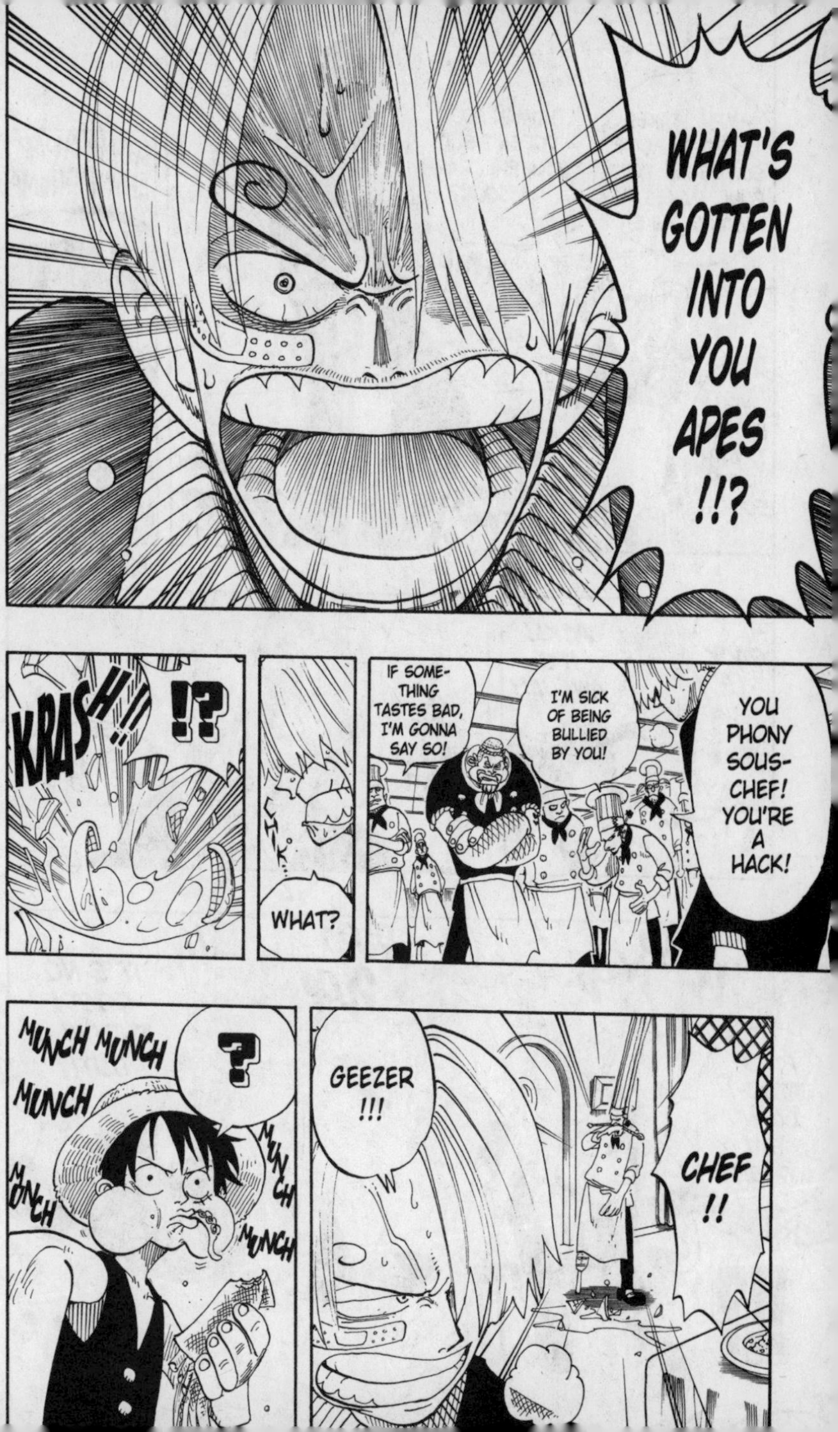
WHAT'S GOTTEN INTO YOU APES !!?
YOU PHONY SOUS-CHEF! YOU'RE A HACK!
I'M SICK OF BEING BULLIED BY YOU!
IF SOME-THING TASTES BAD, I'M GONNA SAY SO!
CHIK...
WHAT?
KRASH!!
!?
CHEF !!
GEEZER !!!
?
MUNCH MUNCH MUNCH
MUNCH MUNCH MUNCH

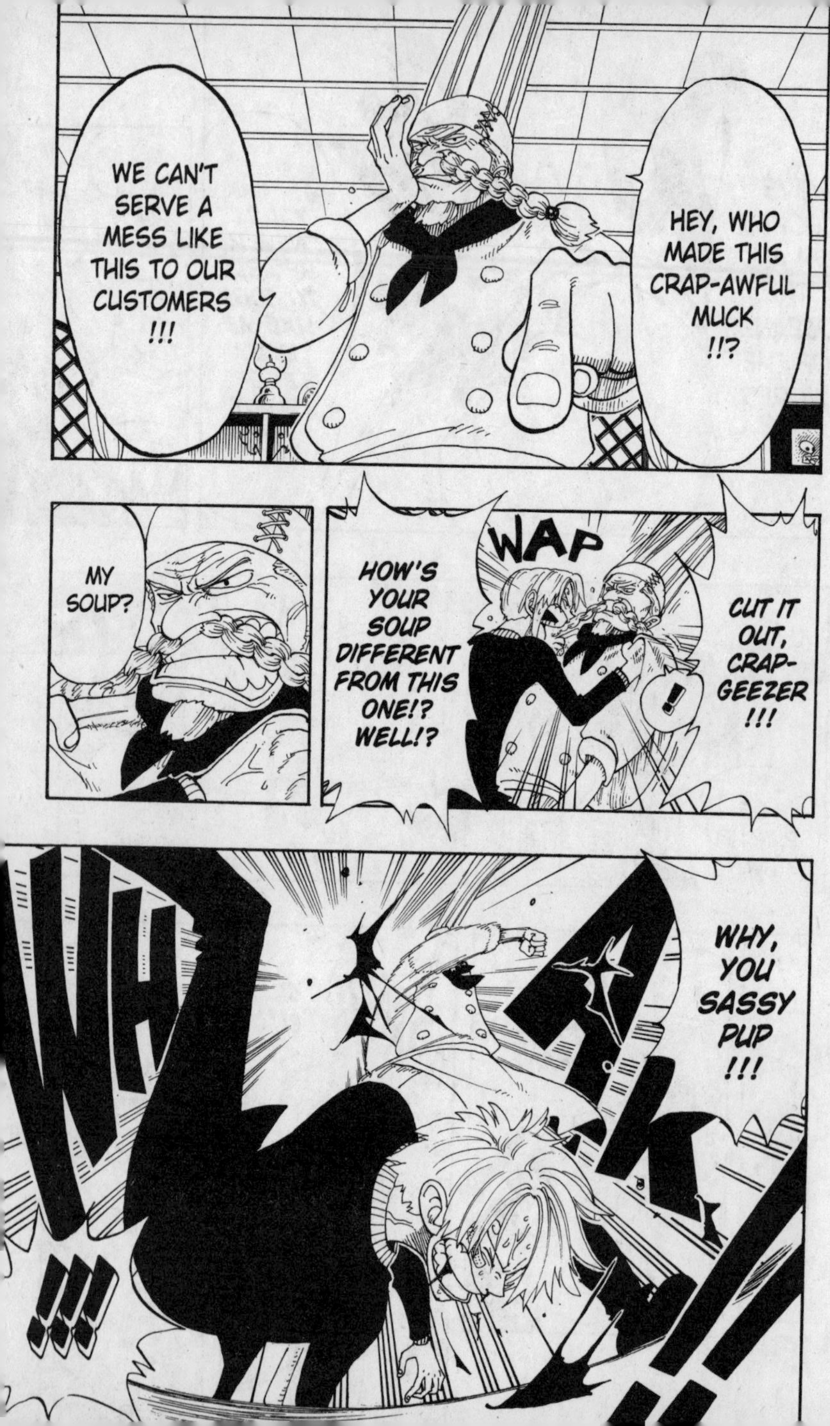
HEY, WHO MADE THIS CRAP-AWFUL MUCK !!?
WE CAN'T SERVE A MESS LIKE THIS TO OUR CUSTOMERS !!!
WAP
CUT IT OUT, CRAP-GEEZER !!!
HOW'S YOUR SOUP DIFFERENT FROM THIS ONE!? WELL!?
!
MY SOUP?
WHY, YOU SASSY PUP !!!
WHACK !!!!

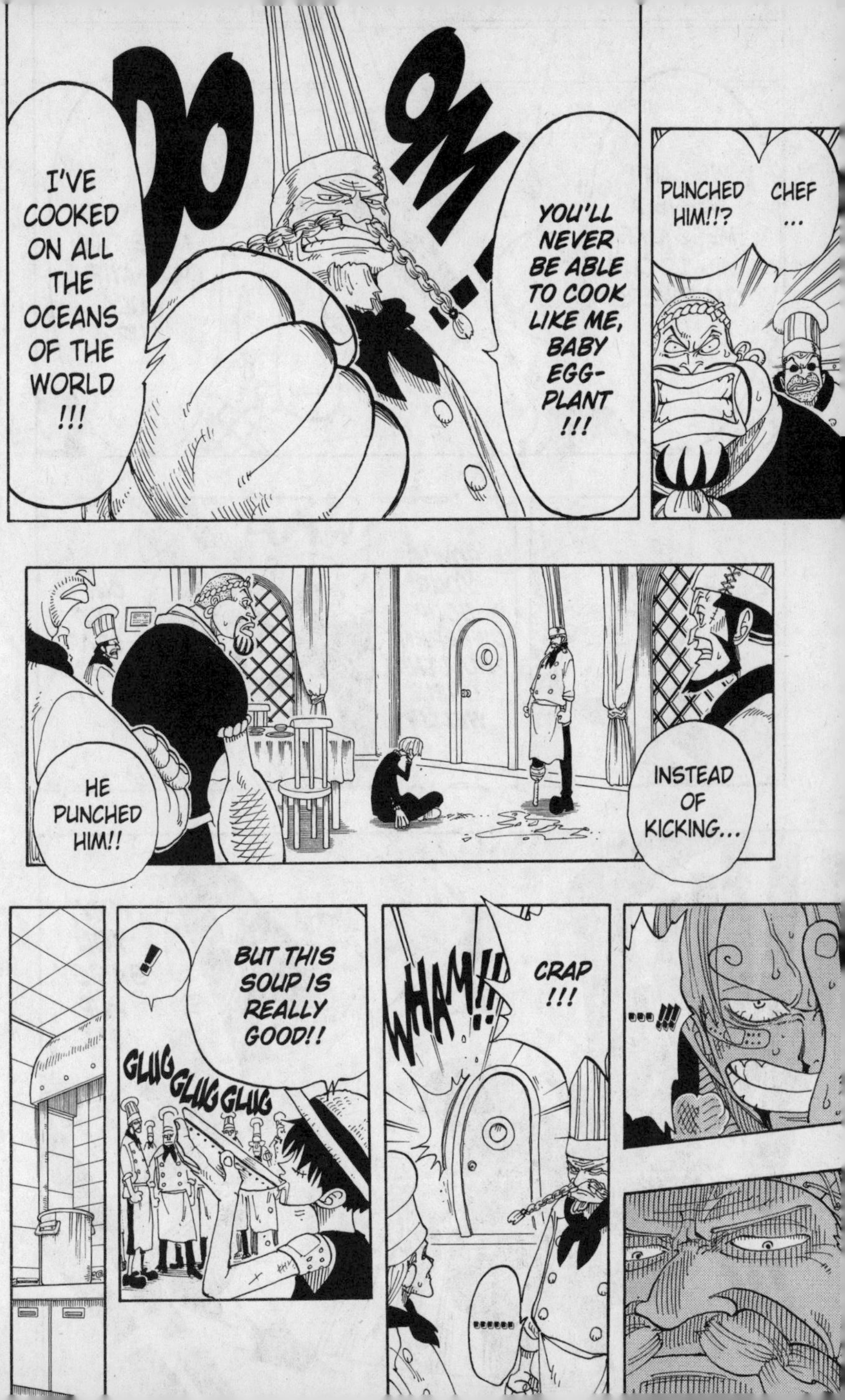
DOOM!!
CHEF ...
PUNCHED HIM!!?
YOU'LL NEVER BE ABLE TO COOK LIKE ME, BABY EGG-PLANT !!!
I'VE COOKED ON ALL THE OCEANS OF THE WORLD !!!
INSTEAD OF KICKING...
HE PUNCHED HIM!!
...!!!
CRAP !!!
WHAM!!
......
BUT THIS SOUP IS REALLY GOOD!!
!
GLUG GLUG GLUG

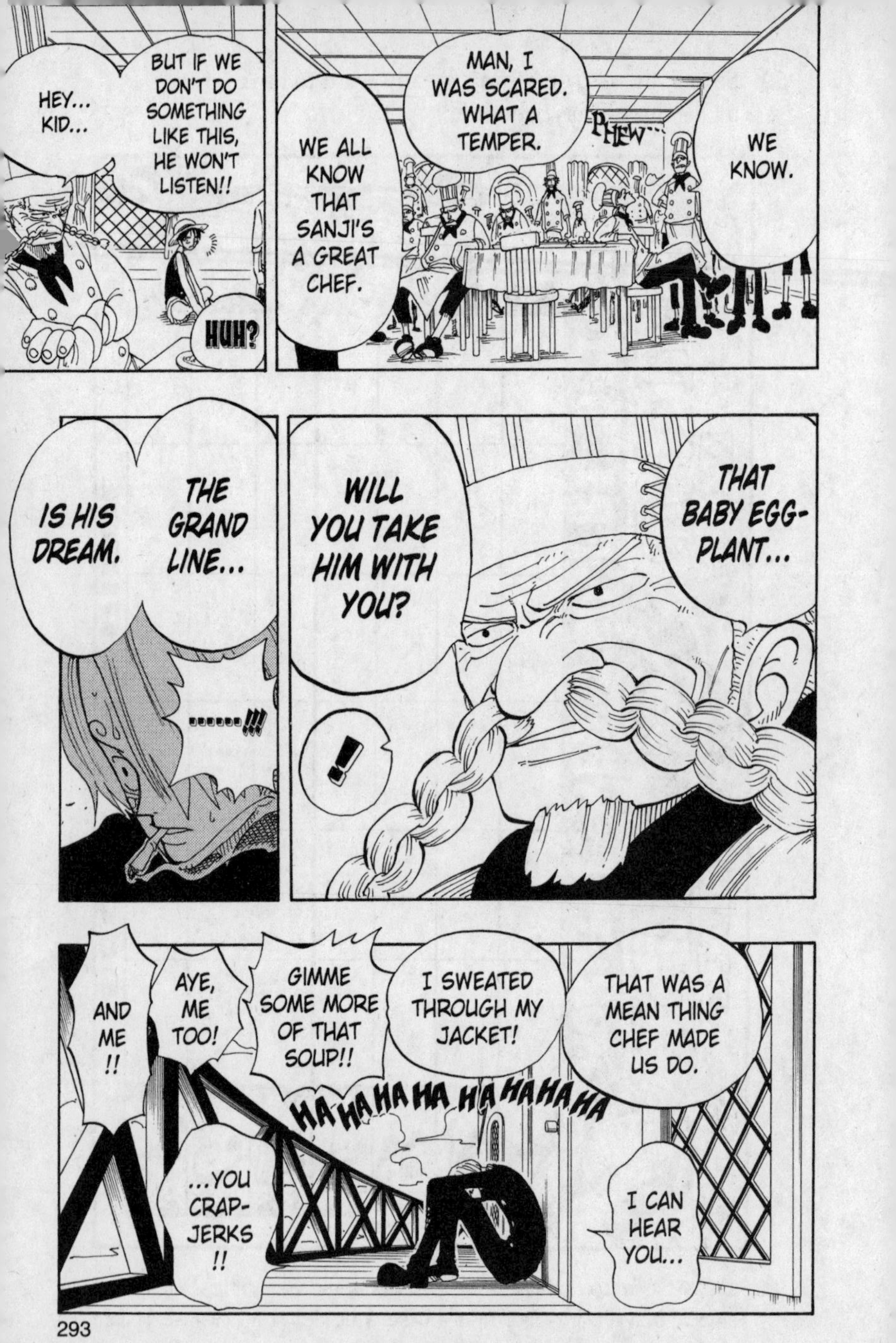
WE KNOW.
MAN, I WAS SCARED. WHAT A TEMPER.
PHEW...
WE ALL KNOW THAT SANJI'S A GREAT CHEF.
BUT IF WE DON'T DO SOMETHING LIKE THIS, HE WON'T LISTEN!!
HEY... KID...
HUH?
THAT BABY EGG-PLANT...
WILL YOU TAKE HIM WITH YOU?
!
THE GRAND LINE...
IS HIS DREAM.
......!!!
THAT WAS A MEAN THING CHEF MADE US DO.
I SWEATED THROUGH MY JACKET!
GIMME SOME MORE OF THAT SOUP!!
AYE, ME TOO!
AND ME !!
HA HA HA HA HA HA HA HA HA HA
I CAN HEAR YOU...
...YOU CRAP-JERKS !!

Q: Sensei, there's something I really want to have--a *One Piece* Class Schedule!!

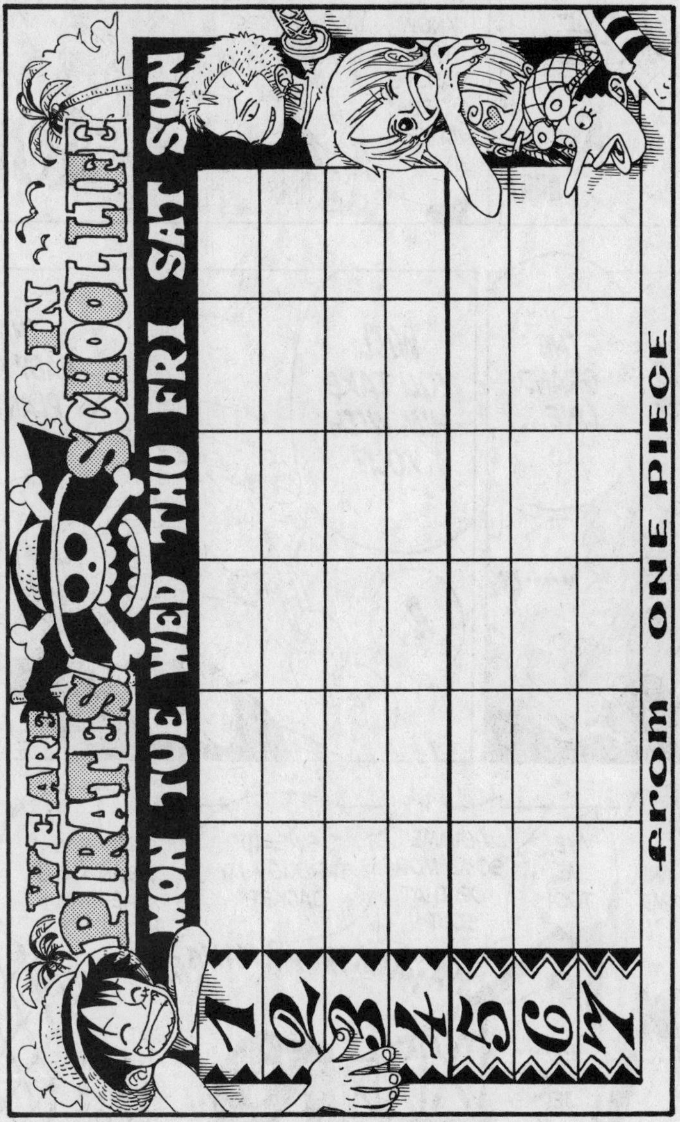
WE ARE PIRATES! IN SCHOOL LIFE
MON TUE WED THU FRI SAT SUN
1
2
3
4
5
6
7
from ONE PIECE

A: Class Schedule...ahhh...that brings back memories! How about something like this!? Use a copier to enlarge it or shrink it, and use it however you like!! Are there schools with seven periods? I drew it that way, just in case.

# Chapter 68:
# THE FOURTH PERSON

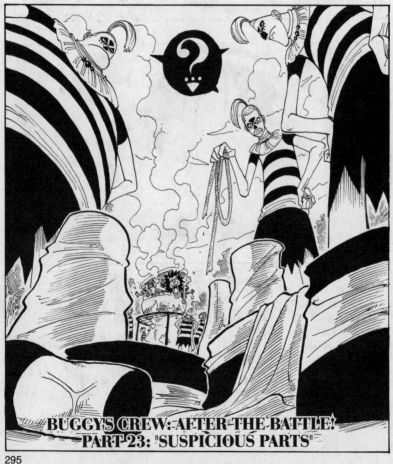

BUGGY'S CREW: AFTER THE BATTLE!
PART 23: "SUSPICIOUS PARTS"

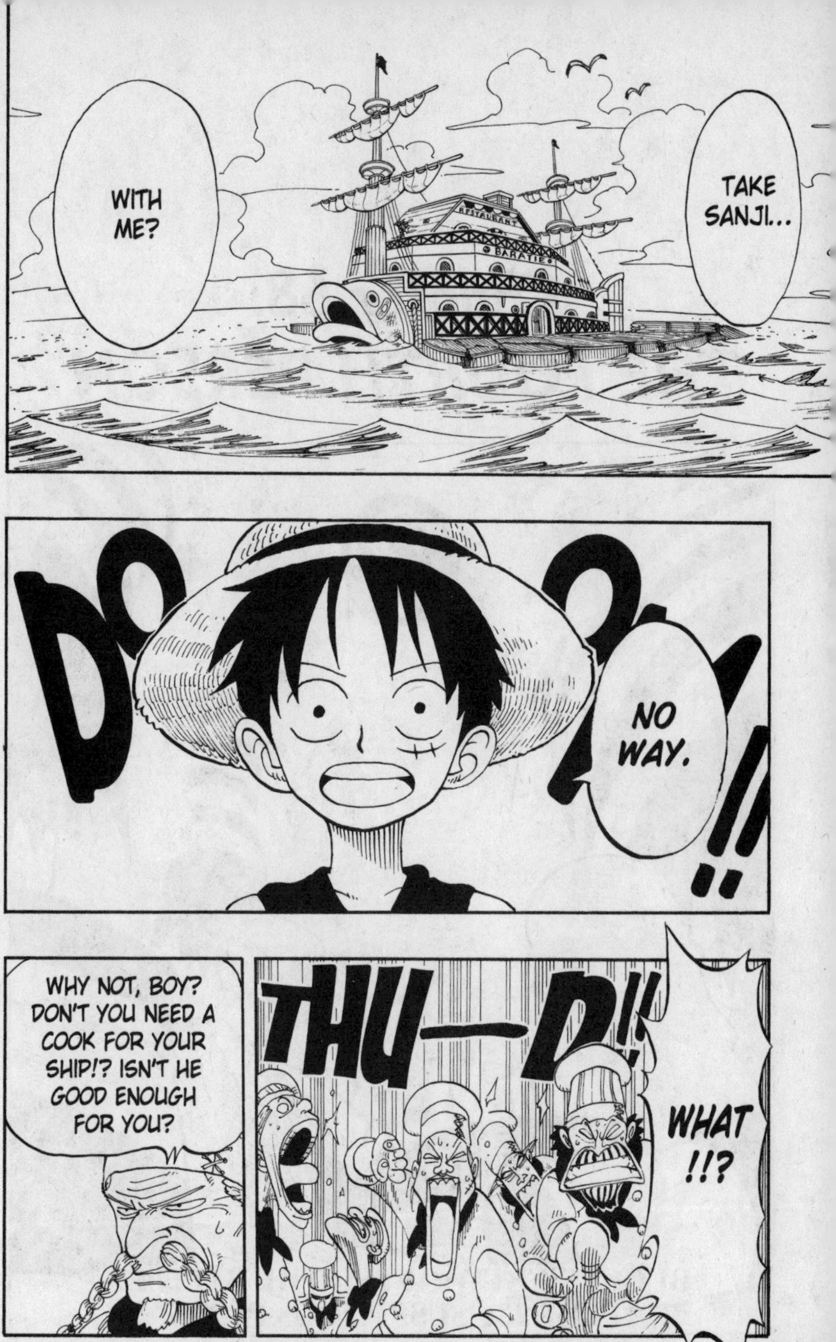
TAKE SANJI...
WITH ME?
BARATIE
NO WAY.
THU—D!!
WHAT!!?
WHY NOT, BOY? DON'T YOU NEED A COOK FOR YOUR SHIP!? ISN'T HE GOOD ENOUGH FOR YOU?

READ THIS WAY

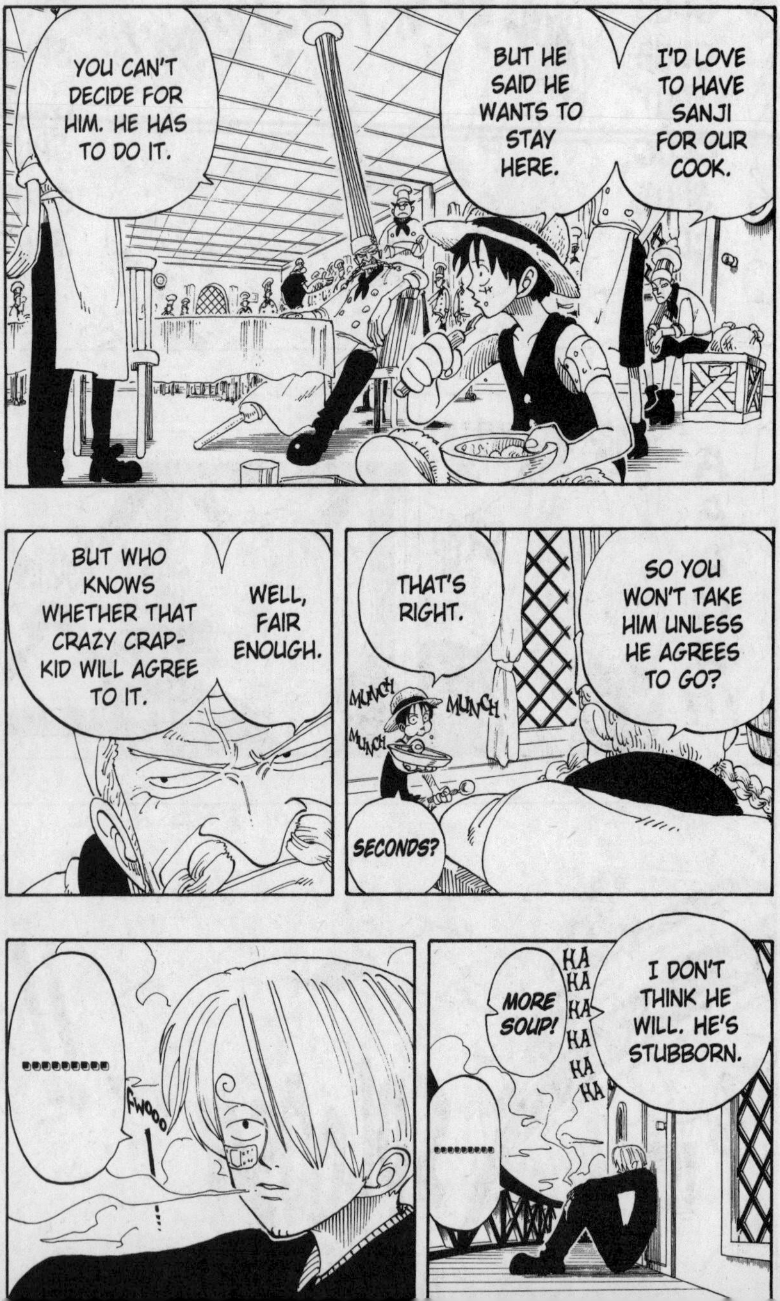
I'D LOVE TO HAVE SANJI FOR OUR COOK.
BUT HE SAID HE WANTS TO STAY HERE.
YOU CAN'T DECIDE FOR HIM. HE HAS TO DO IT.
SO YOU WON'T TAKE HIM UNLESS HE AGREES TO GO?
THAT'S RIGHT.
MUNCH MUNCH MUNCH
SECONDS?
WELL, FAIR ENOUGH.
BUT WHO KNOWS WHETHER THAT CRAZY CRAP-KID WILL AGREE TO IT.
I DON'T THINK HE WILL. HE'S STUBBORN.
HA HA HA HA HA HA HA
MORE SOUP!
.........
.........
FWOOO

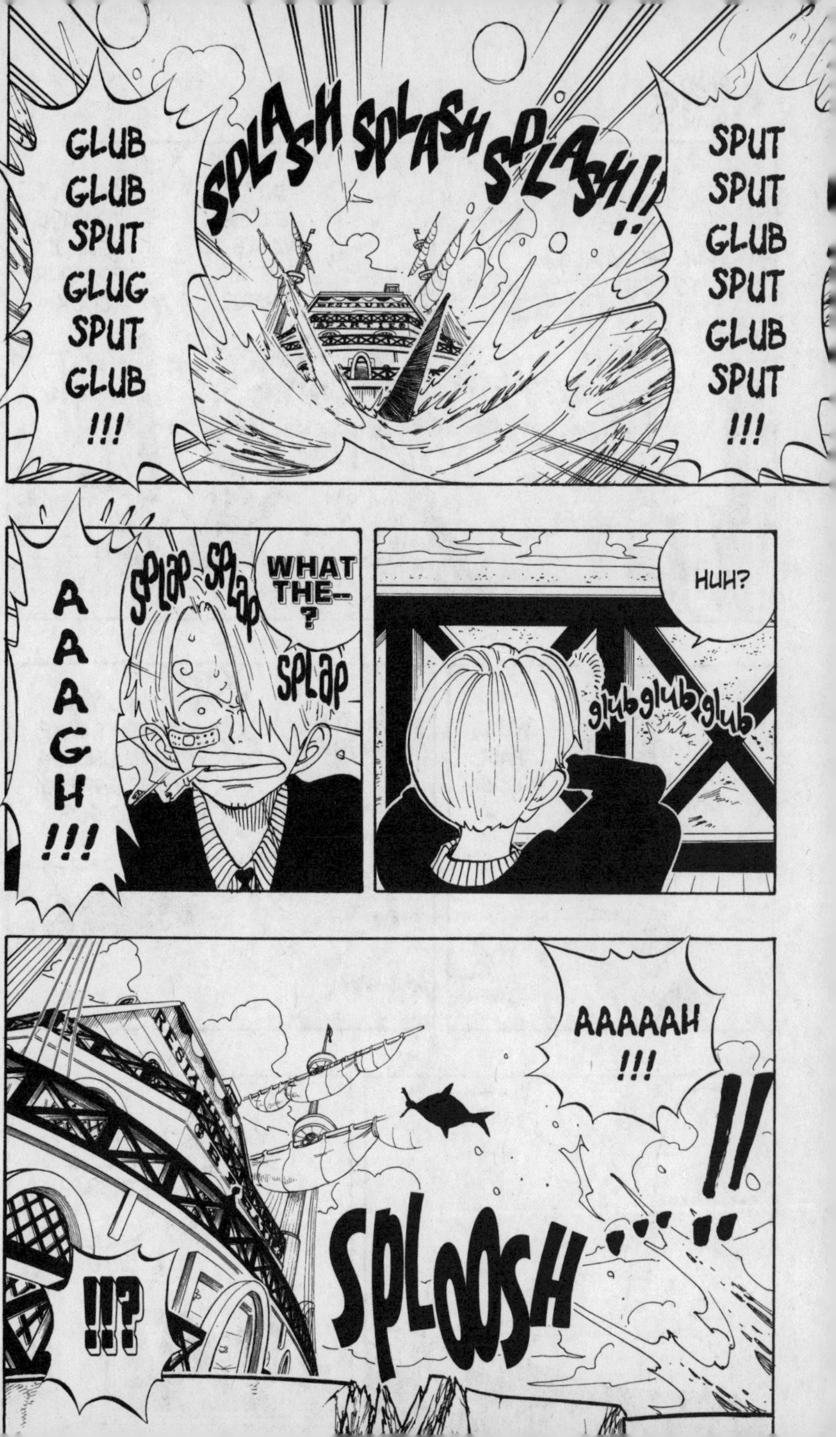
SPUT SPUT GLUB SPUT GLUB SPUT !!!
SPLASH SPLASH SPLASH!!
GLUB GLUB SPUT GLUG SPUT GLUB !!!
HUH?
glubglub glub
WHAT THE--?
SPLAP SPLAP
SPLAP
AAAAGH!!!
AAAAAH !!!
SPLOOSH..!!
!!?

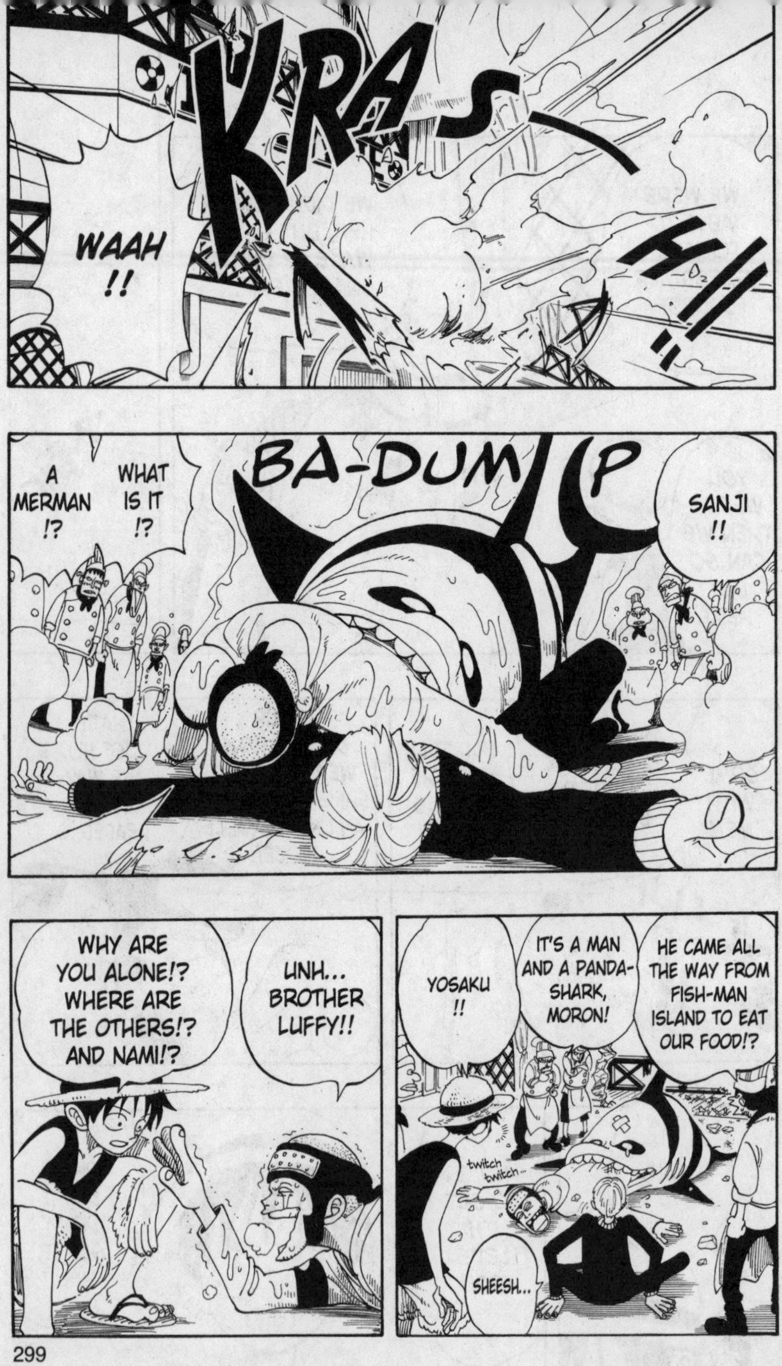
KRASH!!
WAAH !!
BA-DUMP
SANJI !!
WHAT IS IT !?
A MERMAN !?
HE CAME ALL THE WAY FROM FISH-MAN ISLAND TO EAT OUR FOOD!?
IT'S A MAN AND A PANDA-SHARK, MORON!
YOSAKU !!
twitch twitch...
SHEESH...
UNH... BROTHER LUFFY!!
WHY ARE YOU ALONE!? WHERE ARE THE OTHERS!? AND NAMI!?

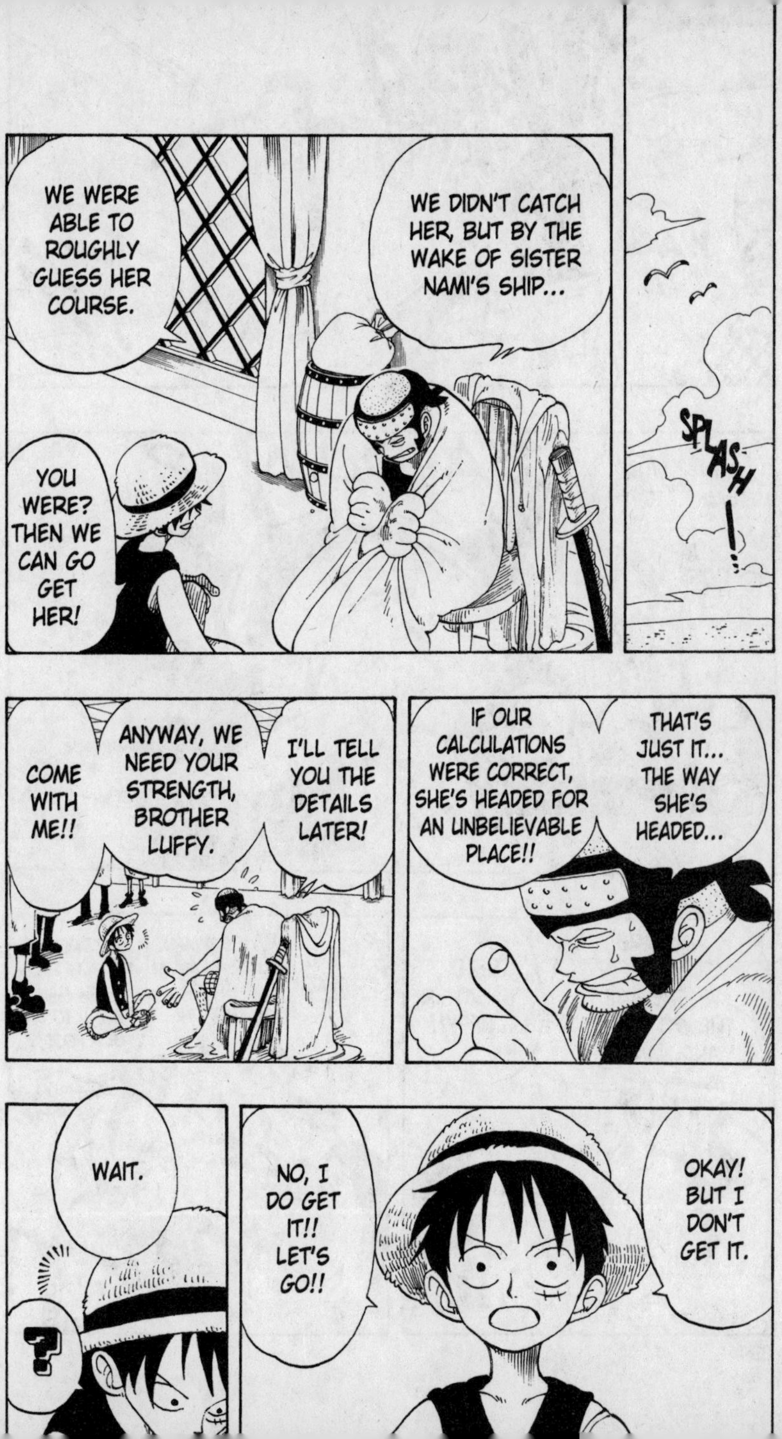
SPLASH!
WE DIDN'T CATCH HER, BUT BY THE WAKE OF SISTER NAMI'S SHIP...
WE WERE ABLE TO ROUGHLY GUESS HER COURSE.
YOU WERE? THEN WE CAN GO GET HER!
THAT'S JUST IT... THE WAY SHE'S HEADED...
IF OUR CALCULATIONS WERE CORRECT, SHE'S HEADED FOR AN UNBELIEVABLE PLACE!!
I'LL TELL YOU THE DETAILS LATER!
ANYWAY, WE NEED YOUR STRENGTH, BROTHER LUFFY.
COME WITH ME!!
OKAY! BUT I DON'T GET IT.
NO, I DO GET IT!! LET'S GO!!
WAIT.
?

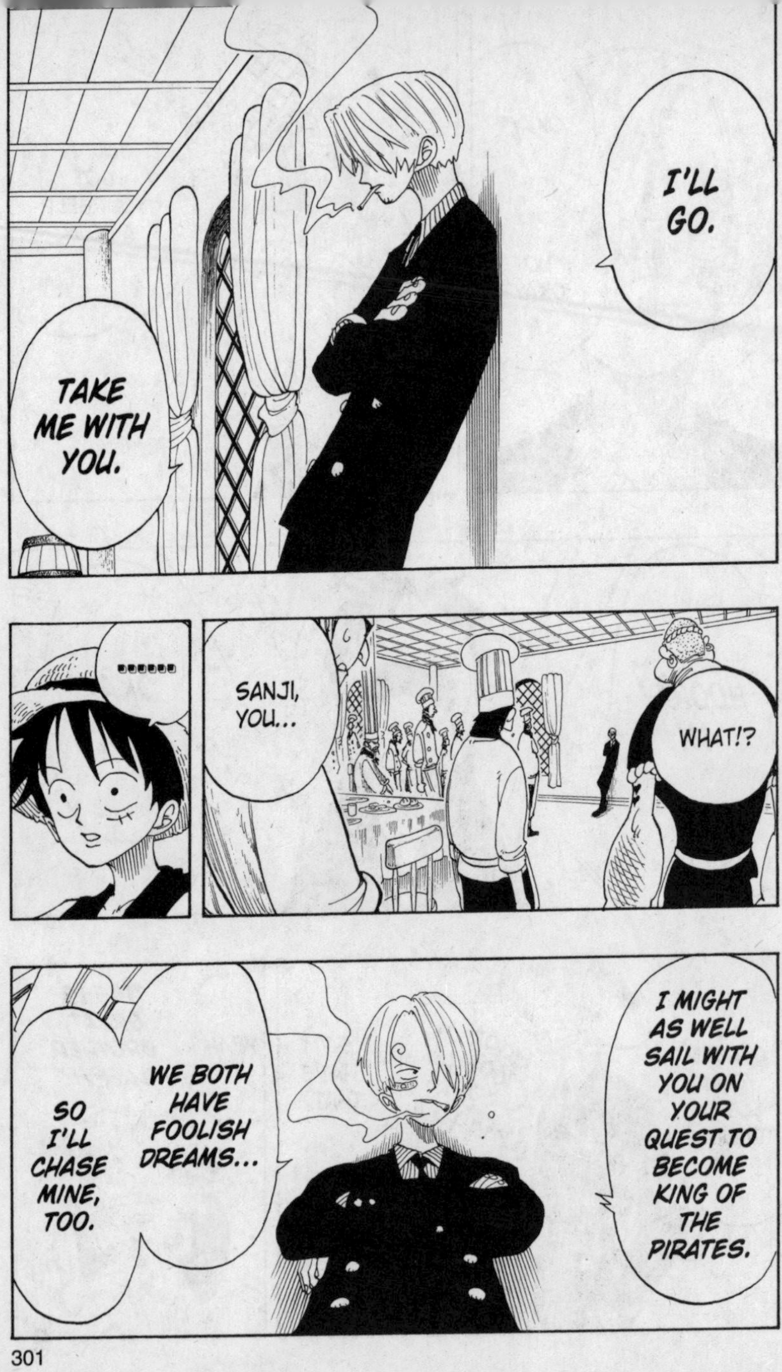
I'LL GO.
TAKE ME WITH YOU.
WHAT!?
SANJI, YOU...
......
I MIGHT AS WELL SAIL WITH YOU ON YOUR QUEST TO BECOME KING OF THE PIRATES.
WE BOTH HAVE FOOLISH DREAMS...
SO I'LL CHASE MINE, TOO.

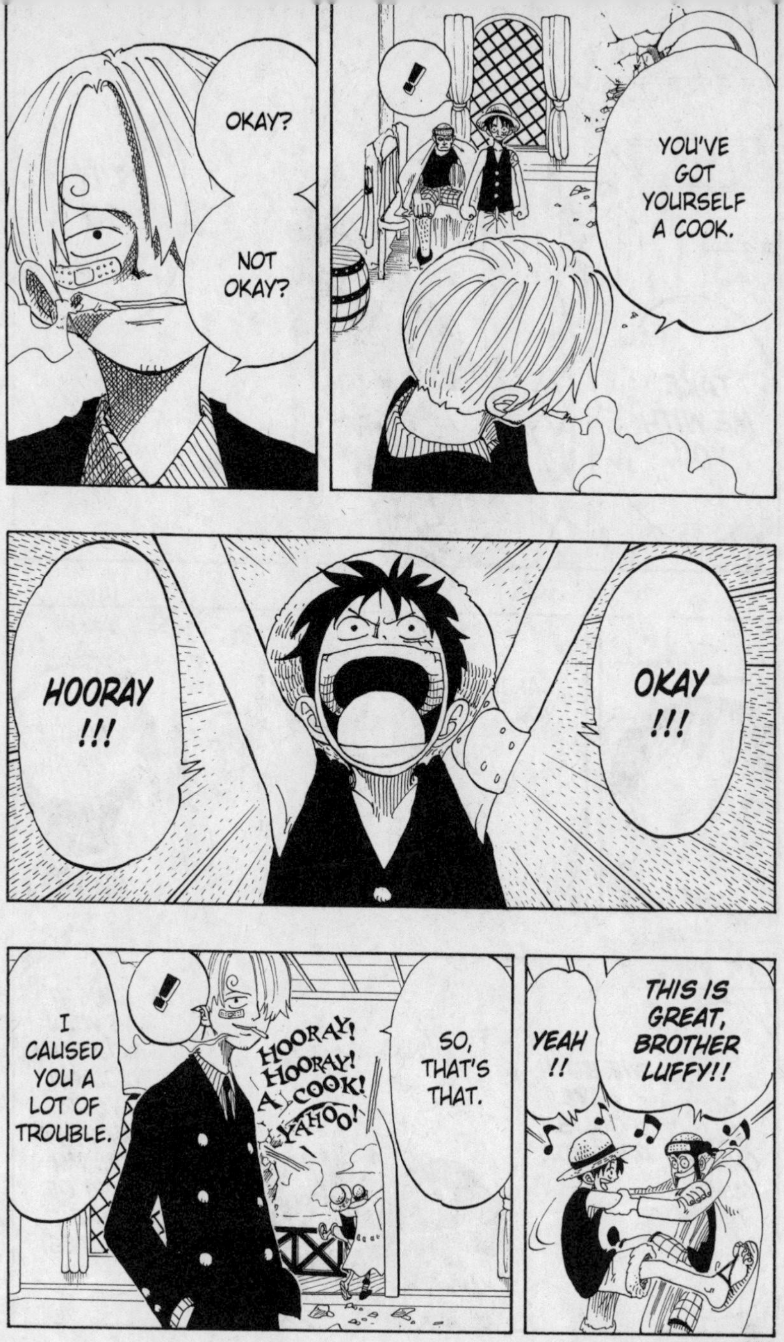
YOU'VE GOT YOURSELF A COOK.
!
OKAY?
NOT OKAY?
OKAY !!!
HOORAY !!!
THIS IS GREAT, BROTHER LUFFY!!
YEAH !!
SO, THAT'S THAT.
HOORAY! HOORAY! A COOK! YAHOO!
!
I CAUSED YOU A LOT OF TROUBLE.

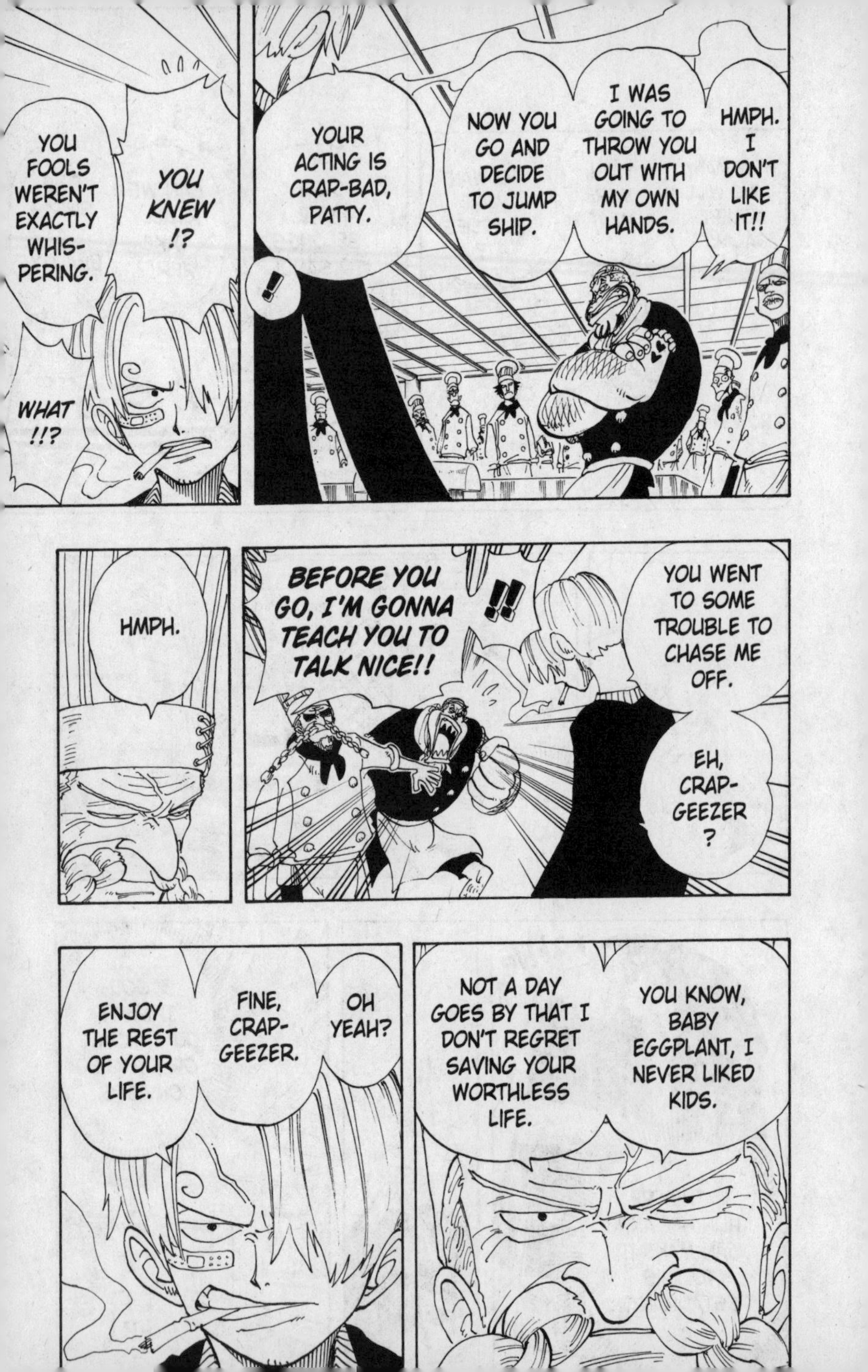
HMPH. I DON'T LIKE IT!!
I WAS GOING TO THROW YOU OUT WITH MY OWN HANDS.
NOW YOU GO AND DECIDE TO JUMP SHIP.
YOUR ACTING IS CRAP-BAD, PATTY.
!
YOU KNEW !?
YOU FOOLS WEREN'T EXACTLY WHIS-PERING.
WHAT !!?
YOU WENT TO SOME TROUBLE TO CHASE ME OFF.
EH, CRAP-GEEZER ?
!!
BEFORE YOU GO, I'M GONNA TEACH YOU TO TALK NICE!!
HMPH.
YOU KNOW, BABY EGGPLANT, I NEVER LIKED KIDS.
NOT A DAY GOES BY THAT I DON'T REGRET SAVING YOUR WORTHLESS LIFE.
OH YEAH?
FINE, CRAP-GEEZER.
ENJOY THE REST OF YOUR LIFE.

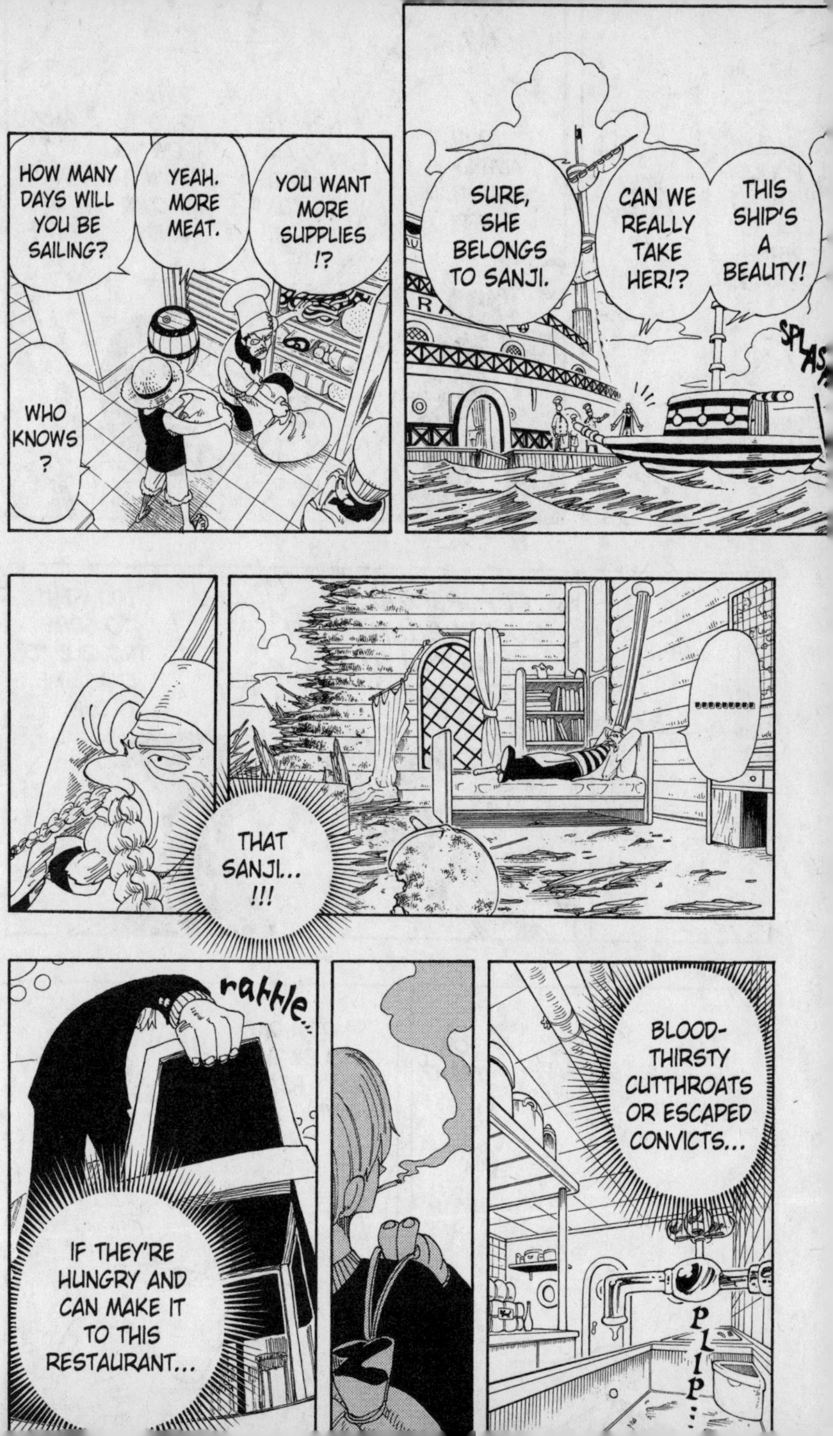
THIS SHIP'S A BEAUTY!
CAN WE REALLY TAKE HER!?
SURE, SHE BELONGS TO SANJI.
SPLASH
YOU WANT MORE SUPPLIES !?
YEAH. MORE MEAT.
HOW MANY DAYS WILL YOU BE SAILING?
WHO KNOWS ?
........
THAT SANJI... !!!
BLOOD-THIRSTY CUTTHROATS OR ESCAPED CONVICTS...
PLIP...
rattle...
IF THEY'RE HUNGRY AND CAN MAKE IT TO THIS RESTAURANT...

READ THIS WAY

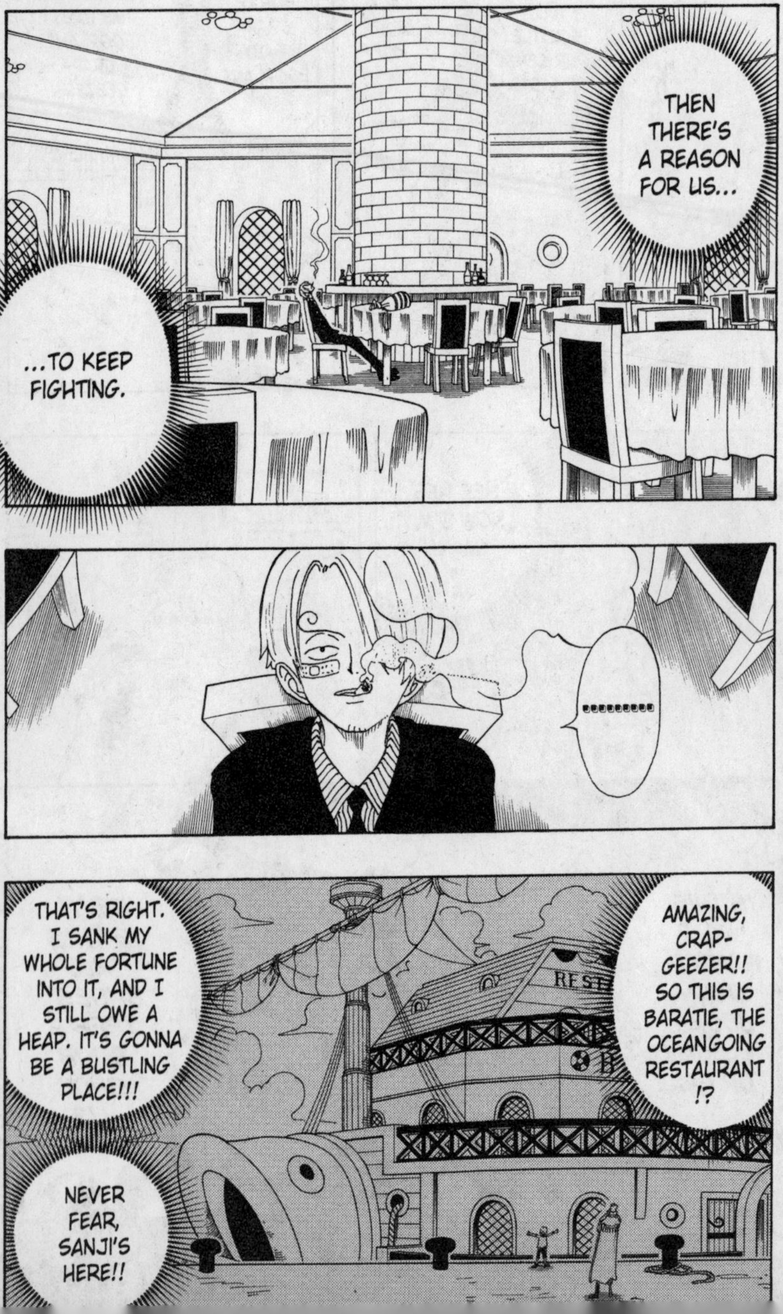
THEN THERE'S A REASON FOR US...
...TO KEEP FIGHTING.
.........
AMAZING, CRAP-GEEZER!! SO THIS IS BARATIE, THE OCEANGOING RESTAURANT!?
THAT'S RIGHT. I SANK MY WHOLE FORTUNE INTO IT, AND I STILL OWE A HEAP. IT'S GONNA BE A BUSTLING PLACE!!!
NEVER FEAR, SANJI'S HERE!!

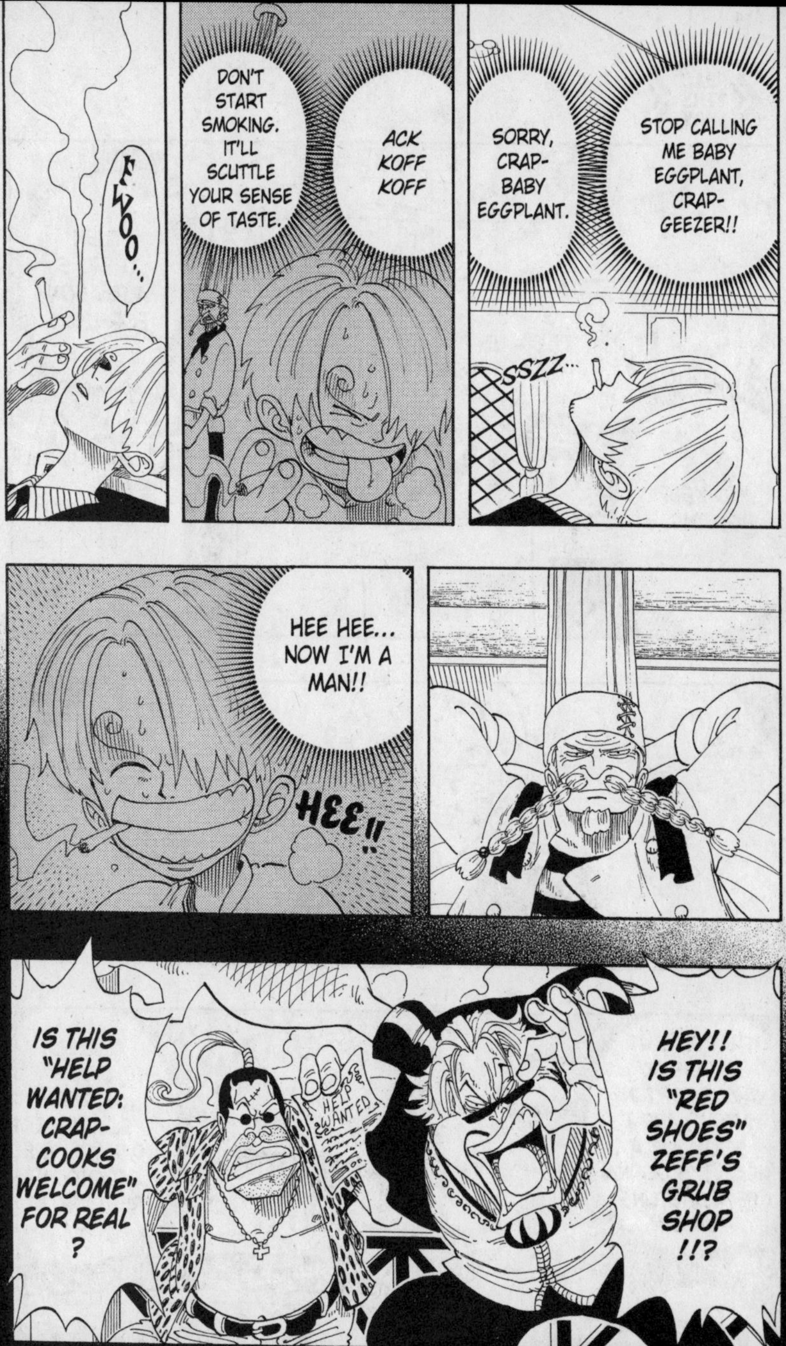
STOP CALLING ME BABY EGGPLANT, CRAP-GEEZER!!
SORRY, CRAP-BABY EGGPLANT.
SSZZ...
ACK KOFF KOFF
DON'T START SMOKING. IT'LL SCUTTLE YOUR SENSE OF TASTE.
FWOO...
HEE HEE... NOW I'M A MAN!!
HEE!!
HEY!! IS THIS "RED SHOES" ZEFF'S GRUB SHOP !!?
IS THIS "HELP WANTED: CRAP-COOKS WELCOME" FOR REAL ?
HELP WANTED

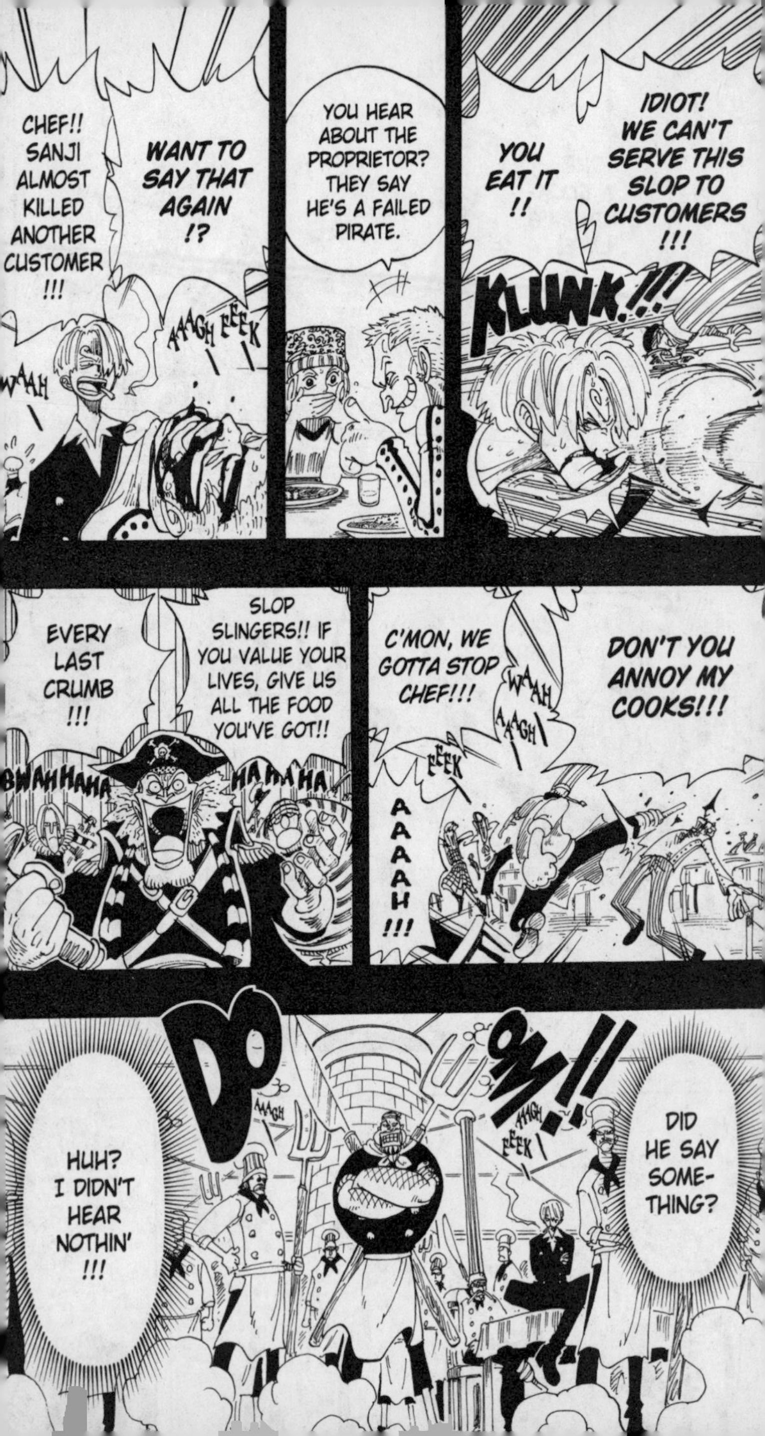
IDIOT! WE CAN'T SERVE THIS SLOP TO CUSTOMERS!!!
YOU EAT IT!!
KLUNK!!!
YOU HEAR ABOUT THE PROPRIETOR? THEY SAY HE'S A FAILED PIRATE.
WANT TO SAY THAT AGAIN!?
CHEF!! SANJI ALMOST KILLED ANOTHER CUSTOMER!!!
EEEK
AAAGH
WAAH
DON'T YOU ANNOY MY COOKS!!!
C'MON, WE GOTTA STOP CHEF!!!
WAAAH
AAAGH
EEEK
AAAAAH!!!
SLOP SLINGERS!! IF YOU VALUE YOUR LIVES, GIVE US ALL THE FOOD YOU'VE GOT!!
EVERY LAST CRUMB!!!
HAHAHA
BWAHHAHA
DID HE SAY SOMETHING?
DOOM!!
AAAGH
EEEK
AAAGH
HUH? I DIDN'T HEAR NOTHIN'!!!

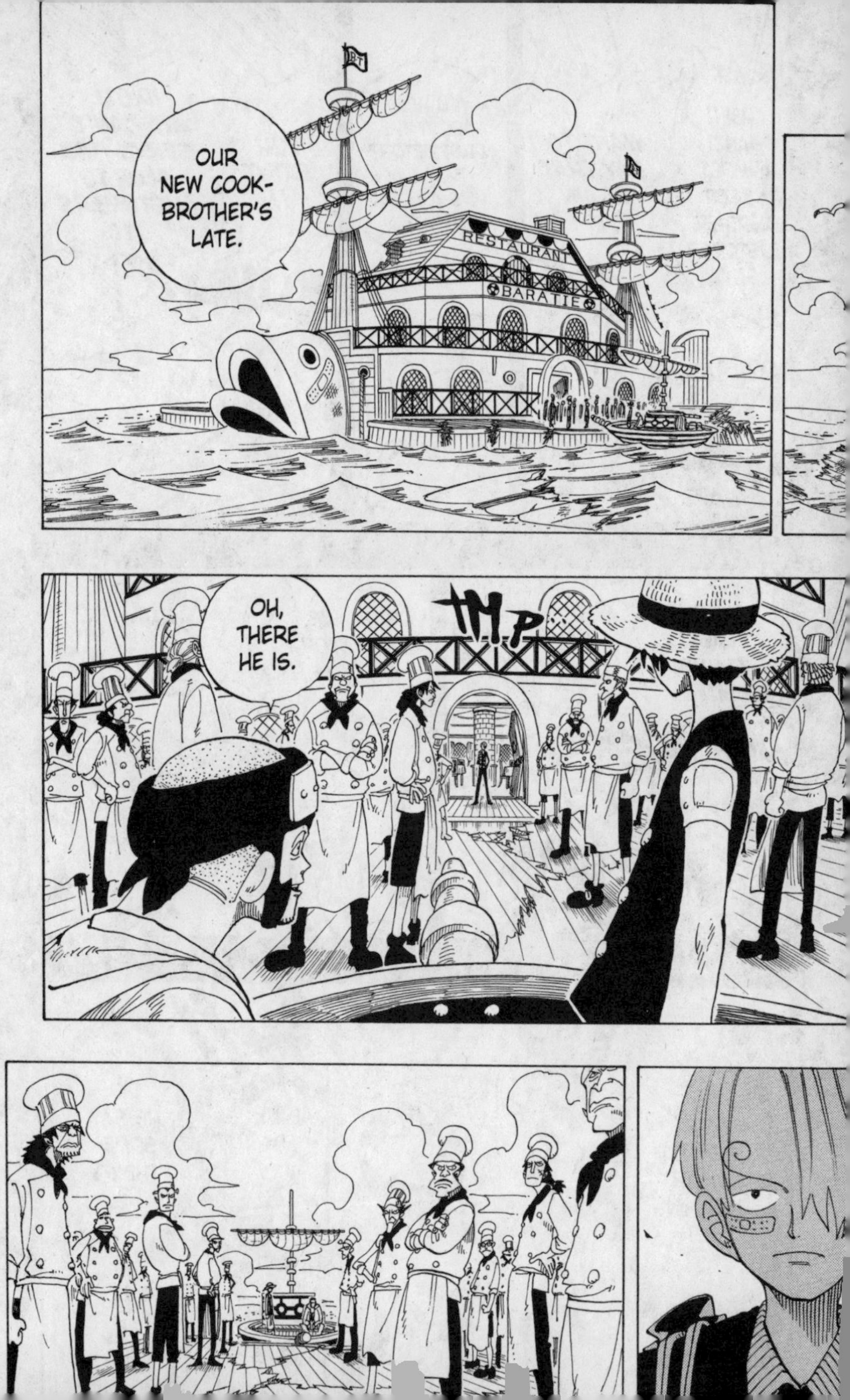
OUR NEW COOK-BROTHER'S LATE.
TMP
OH, THERE HE IS.

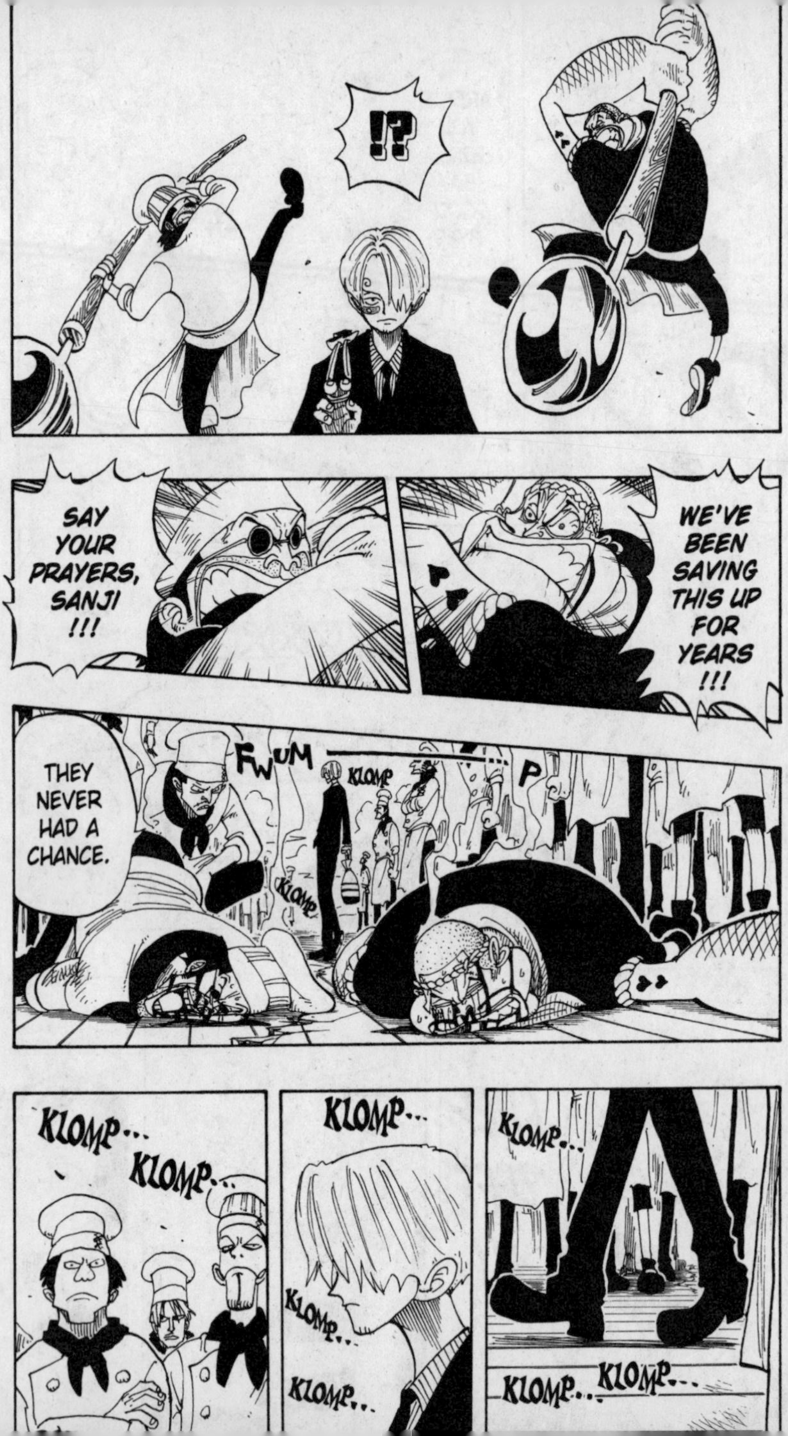
!?
WE'VE BEEN SAVING THIS UP FOR YEARS !!!
SAY YOUR PRAYERS, SANJI !!!
FWUM...P
KLOMP
THEY NEVER HAD A CHANCE.
KLOMP
KLOMP...
KLOMP... KLOMP...
KLOMP...
KLOMP...
KLOMP...
KLOMP...
KLOMP...

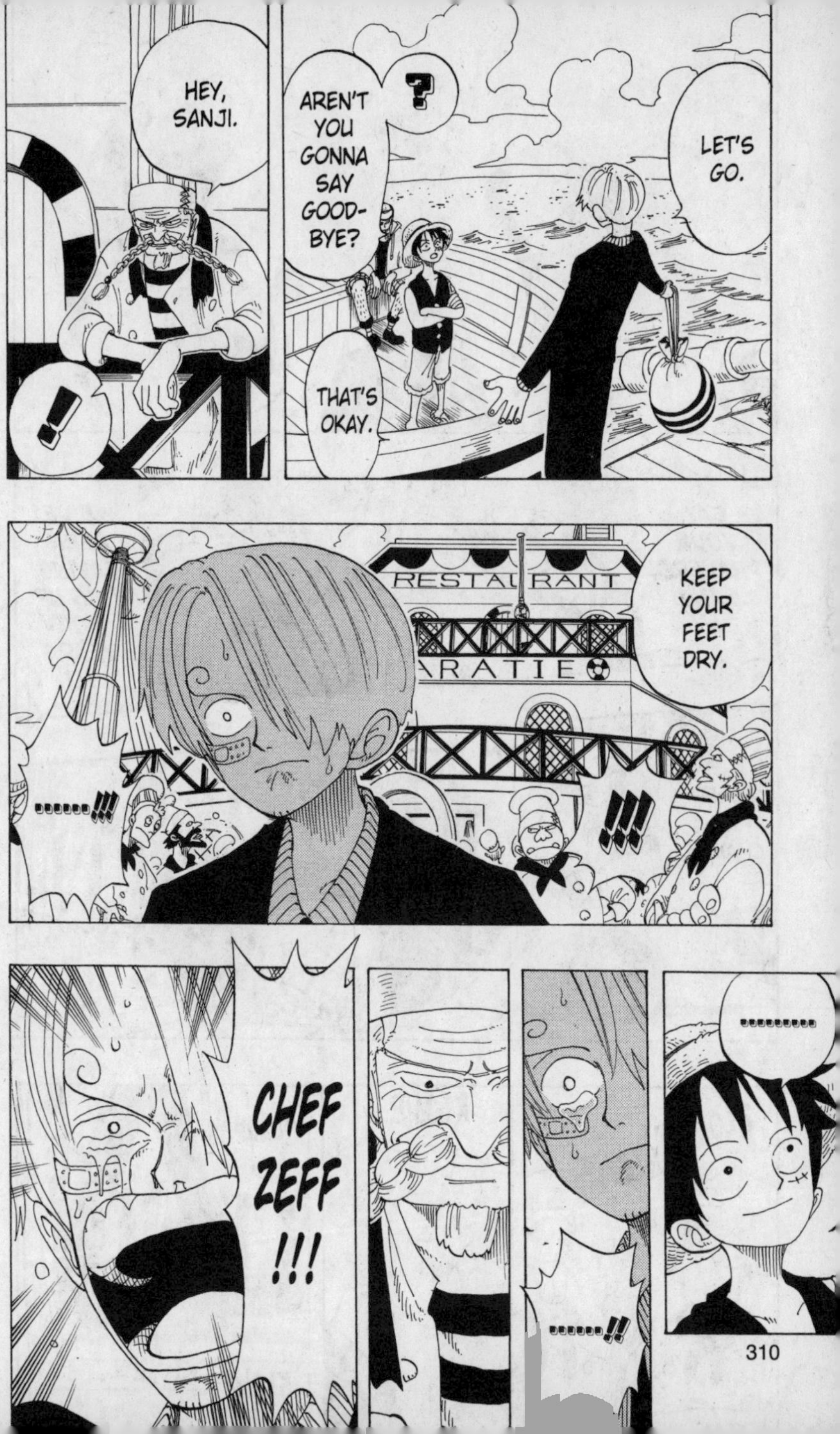
LET'S GO.
?
AREN'T YOU GONNA SAY GOOD-BYE?
THAT'S OKAY.
HEY, SANJI.
!
KEEP YOUR FEET DRY.
RESTAURANT
ARATIE
!!!
......!!!
.........
......!!
CHEF ZEFF!!!

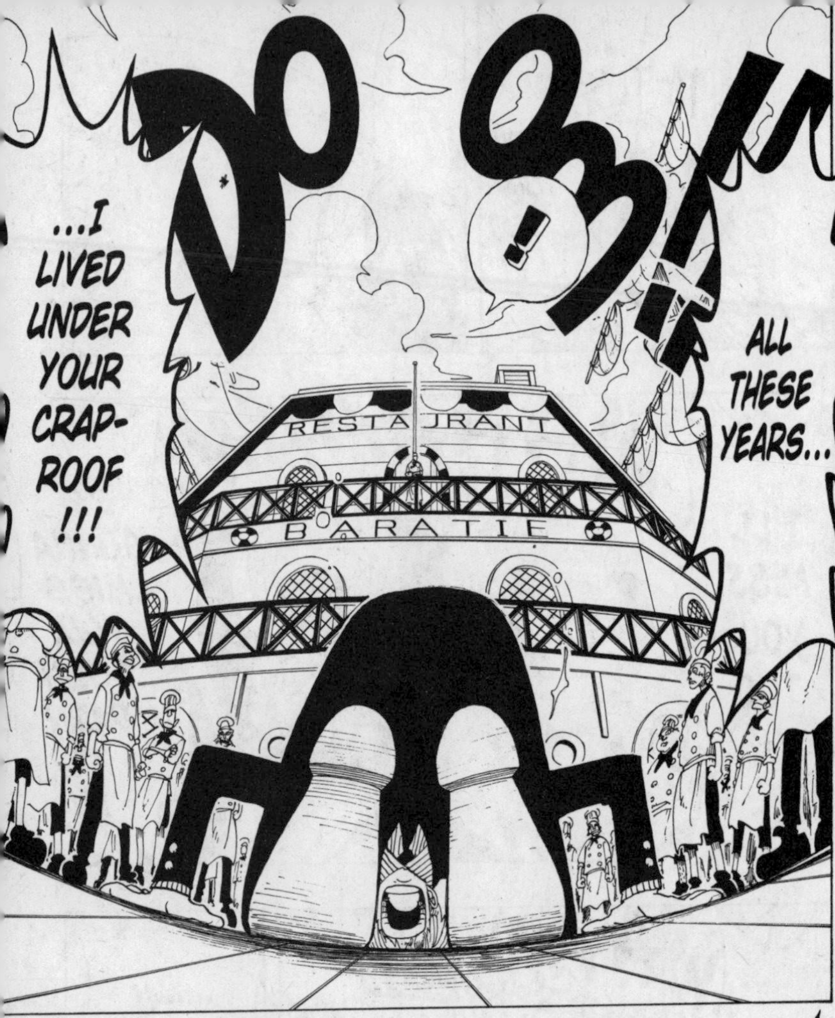
DOOM!!
ALL THESE YEARS...
...I LIVED UNDER YOUR CRAP-ROOF!!!
RESTAURANT
BARATIE
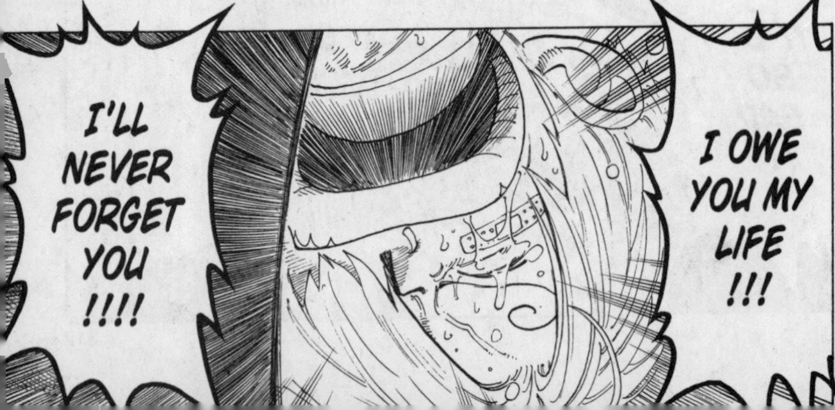
I OWE YOU MY LIFE!!!
I'LL NEVER FORGET YOU!!!!

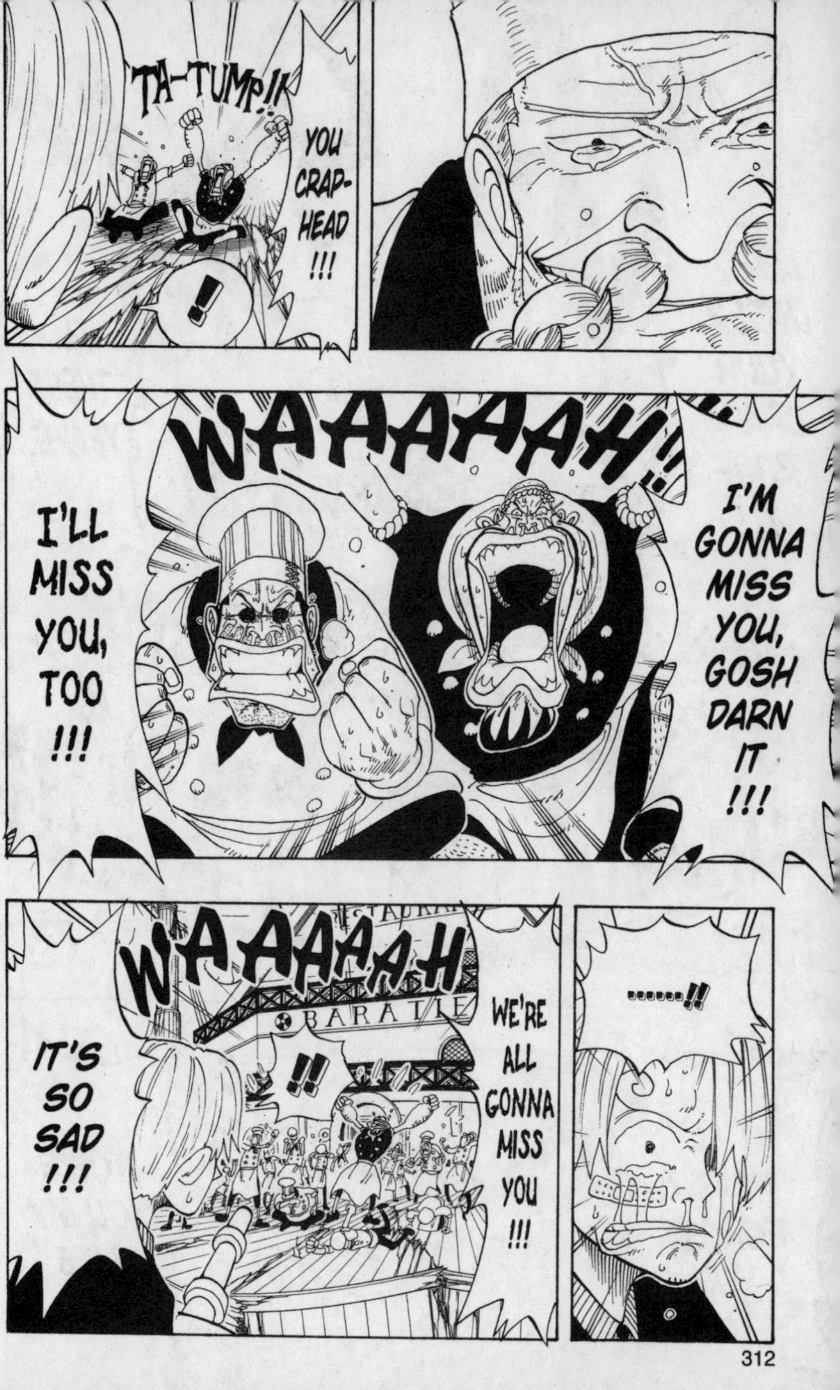
TA-TUMP!!
YOU CRAP-HEAD !!!
!
WAAAAAH!!
I'M GONNA MISS YOU, GOSH DARN IT !!!
I'LL MISS YOU, TOO !!!
......!!
WAAAAAH
BARATIE
WE'RE ALL GONNA MISS YOU !!!
!!
IT'S SO SAD !!!

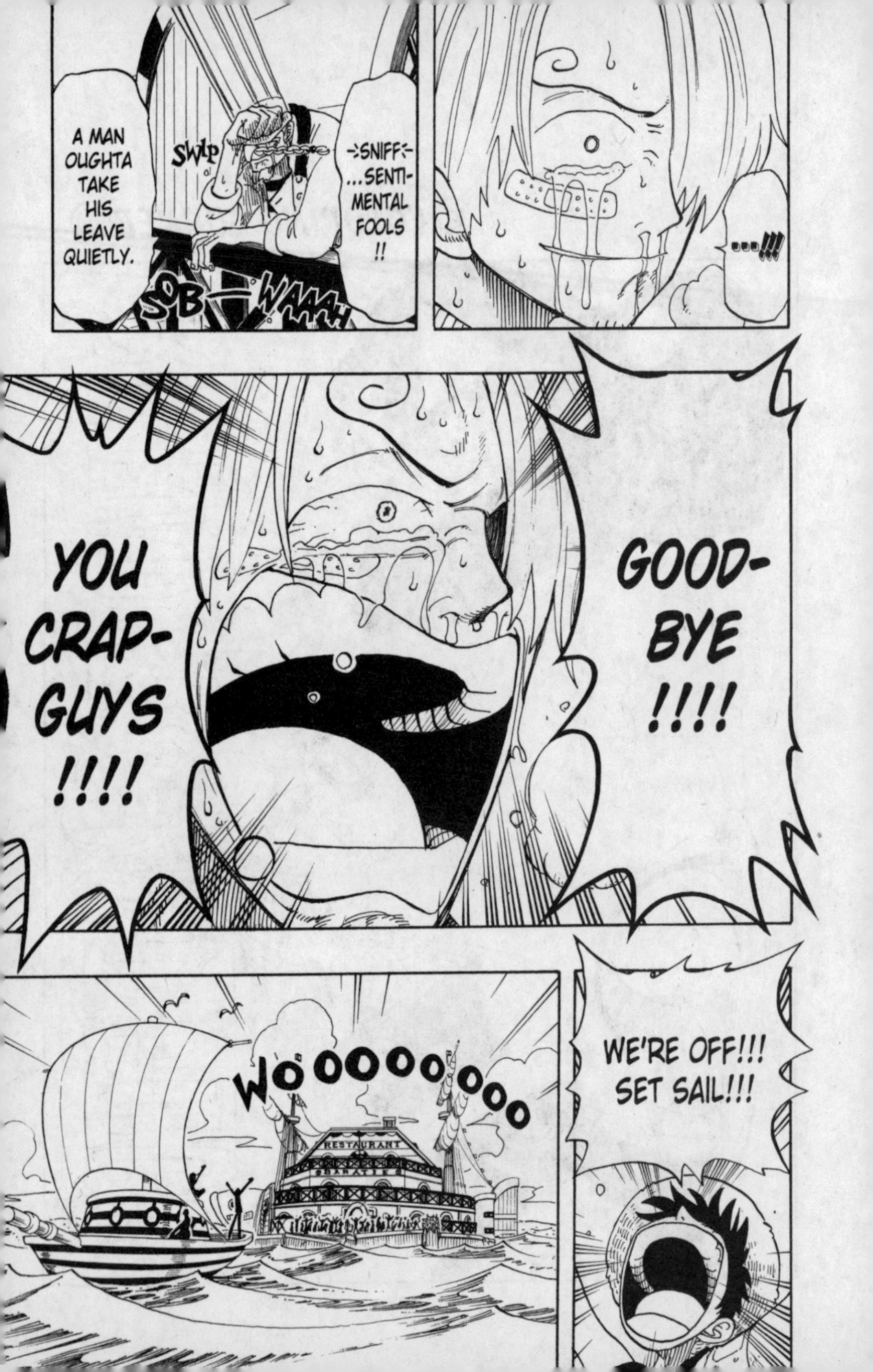
...!!!
-SNIFF- ...SENTI-MENTAL FOOLS !!
A MAN OUGHTA TAKE HIS LEAVE QUIETLY.
SWIP
SOB WAAAH
GOOD-BYE !!!!
YOU CRAP-GUYS !!!!
WE'RE OFF!!! SET SAIL!!!
WOOOOOOOO
RESTAURANT BARATIE

## ◎COLORING CORNER◎

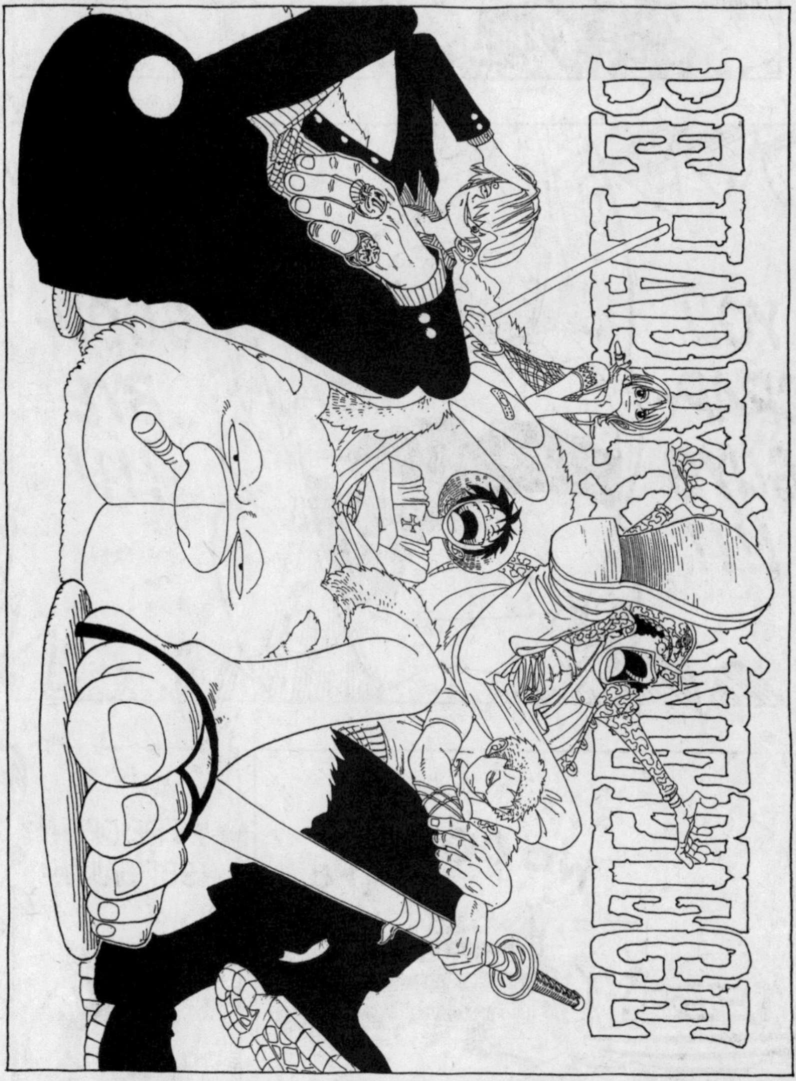

# Chapter 69:
# ARLONG PARK

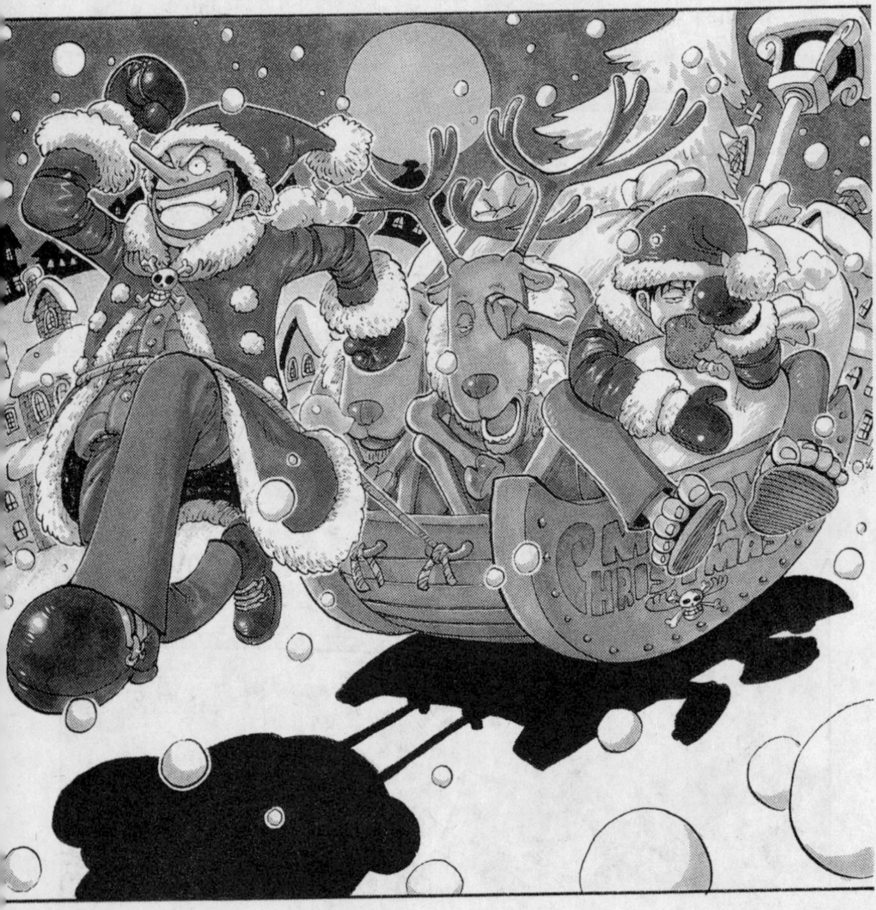
MERRY CHRISTMAS

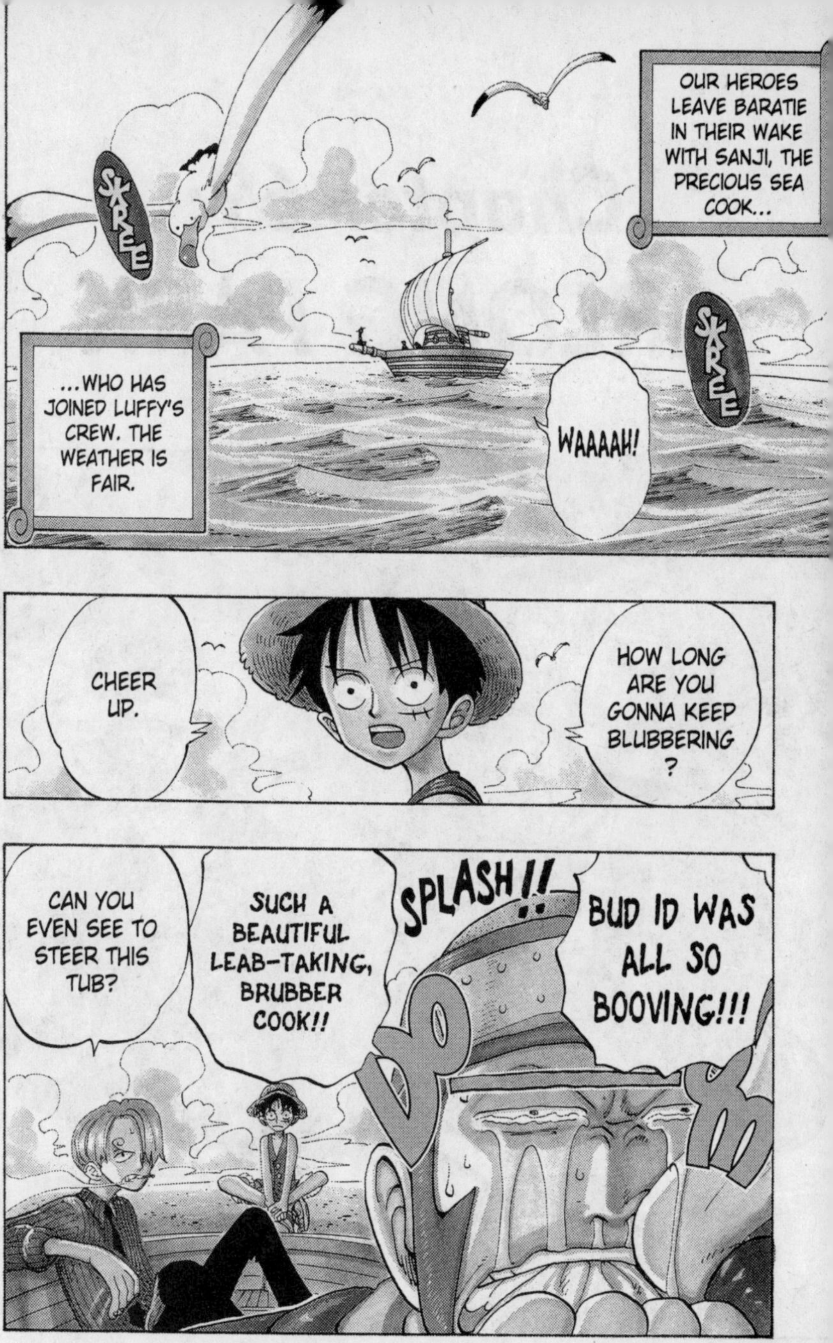
OUR HEROES LEAVE BARATIE IN THEIR WAKE WITH SANJI, THE PRECIOUS SEA COOK...
SKREE
WAAAAH!
SKREE
...WHO HAS JOINED LUFFY'S CREW. THE WEATHER IS FAIR.
HOW LONG ARE YOU GONNA KEEP BLUBBERING ?
CHEER UP.
BUD ID WAS ALL SO BOOVING!!!
SPLASH!!
SUCH A BEAUTIFUL LEAB-TAKING, BRUBBER COOK!!
CAN YOU EVEN SEE TO STEER THIS TUB?

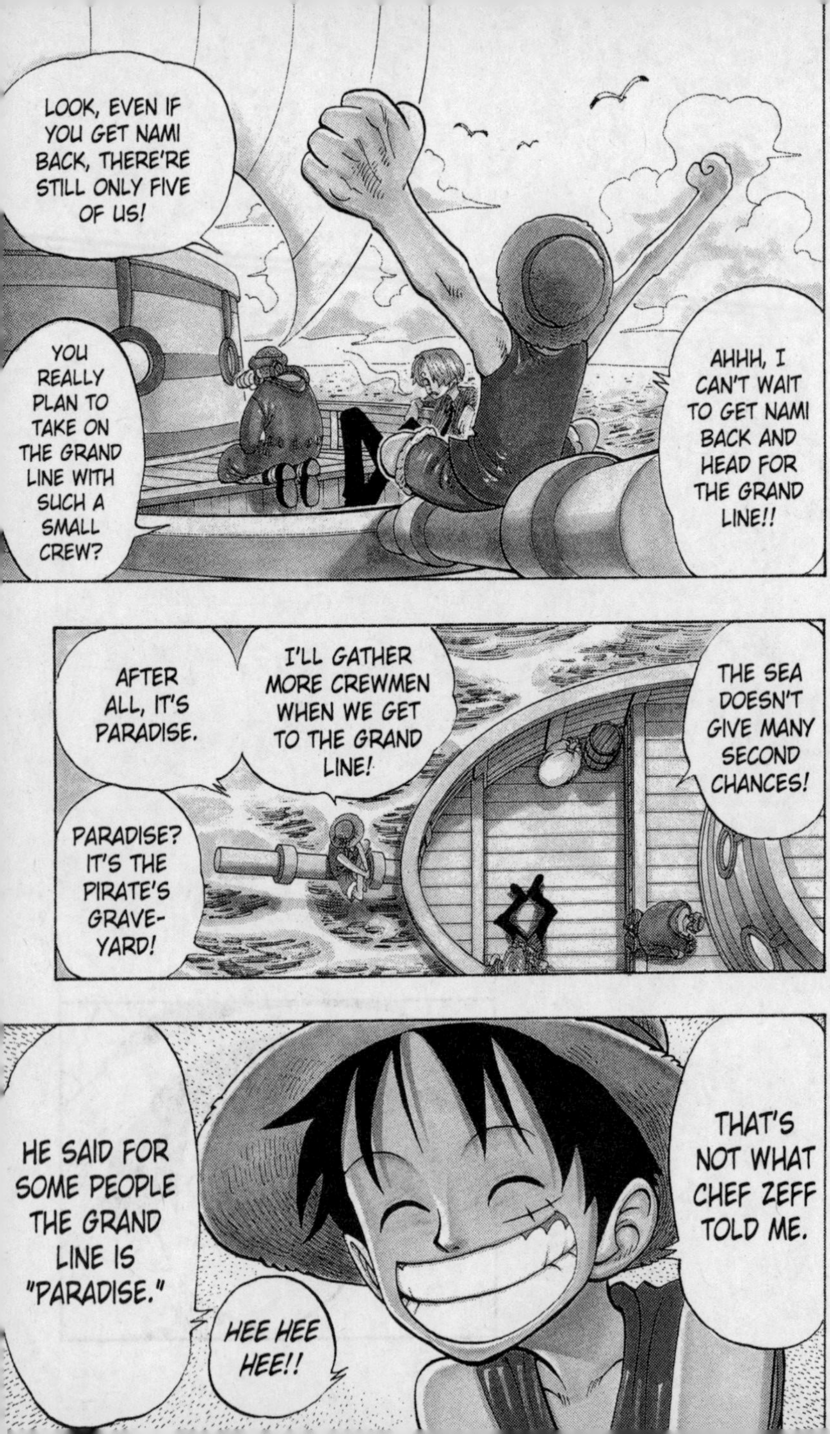
AHHH, I CAN'T WAIT TO GET NAMI BACK AND HEAD FOR THE GRAND LINE!!
LOOK, EVEN IF YOU GET NAMI BACK, THERE'RE STILL ONLY FIVE OF US!
YOU REALLY PLAN TO TAKE ON THE GRAND LINE WITH SUCH A SMALL CREW?
THE SEA DOESN'T GIVE MANY SECOND CHANCES!
I'LL GATHER MORE CREWMEN WHEN WE GET TO THE GRAND LINE!
AFTER ALL, IT'S PARADISE.
PARADISE? IT'S THE PIRATE'S GRAVE-YARD!
THAT'S NOT WHAT CHEF ZEFF TOLD ME.
HE SAID FOR SOME PEOPLE THE GRAND LINE IS "PARADISE."
HEE HEE HEE!!

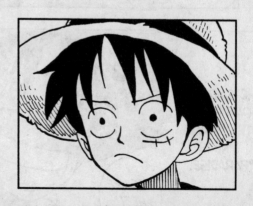

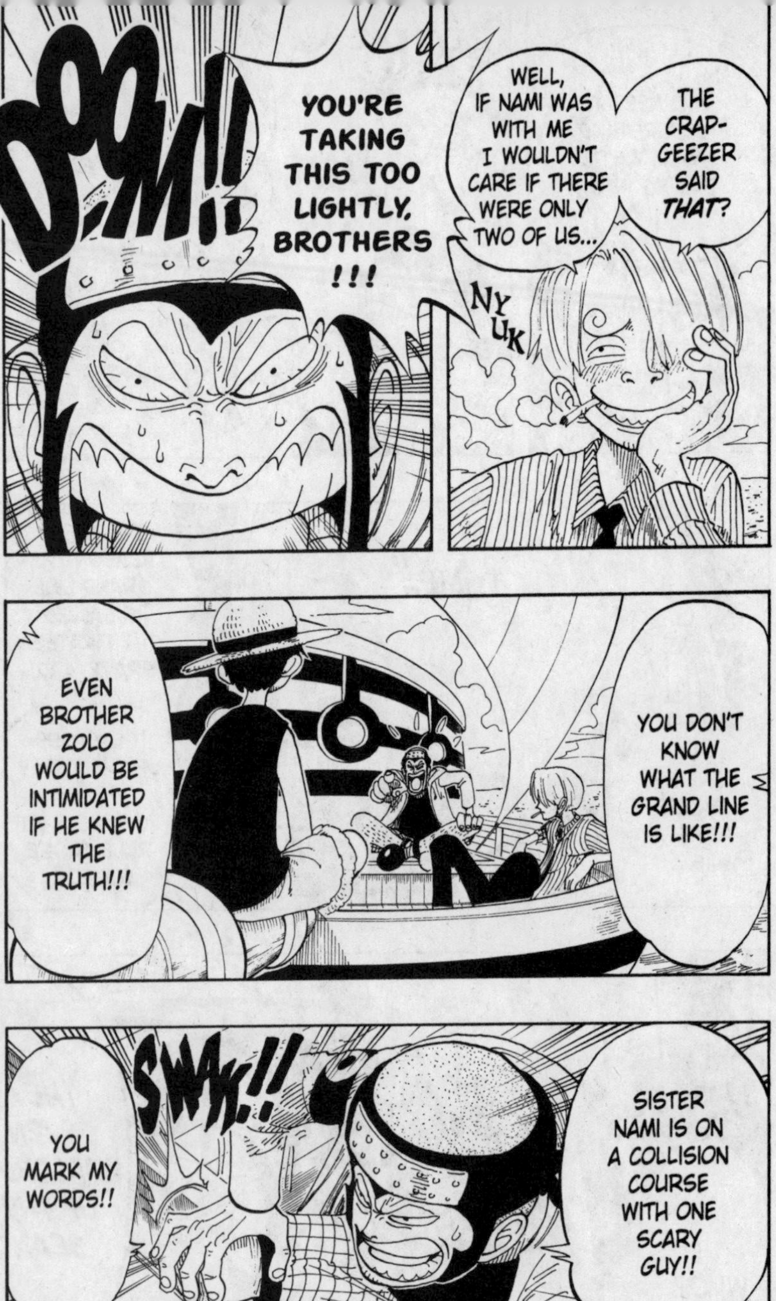
THE CRAP-GEEZER SAID *THAT*?
WELL, IF NAMI WAS WITH ME I WOULDN'T CARE IF THERE WERE ONLY TWO OF US...
NYUK
DOOM!!
YOU'RE TAKING THIS TOO LIGHTLY, BROTHERS!!!
YOU DON'T KNOW WHAT THE GRAND LINE IS LIKE!!!
EVEN BROTHER ZOLO WOULD BE INTIMIDATED IF HE KNEW THE TRUTH!!!
SISTER NAMI IS ON A COLLISION COURSE WITH ONE SCARY GUY!!
SWAK!!
YOU MARK MY WORDS!!

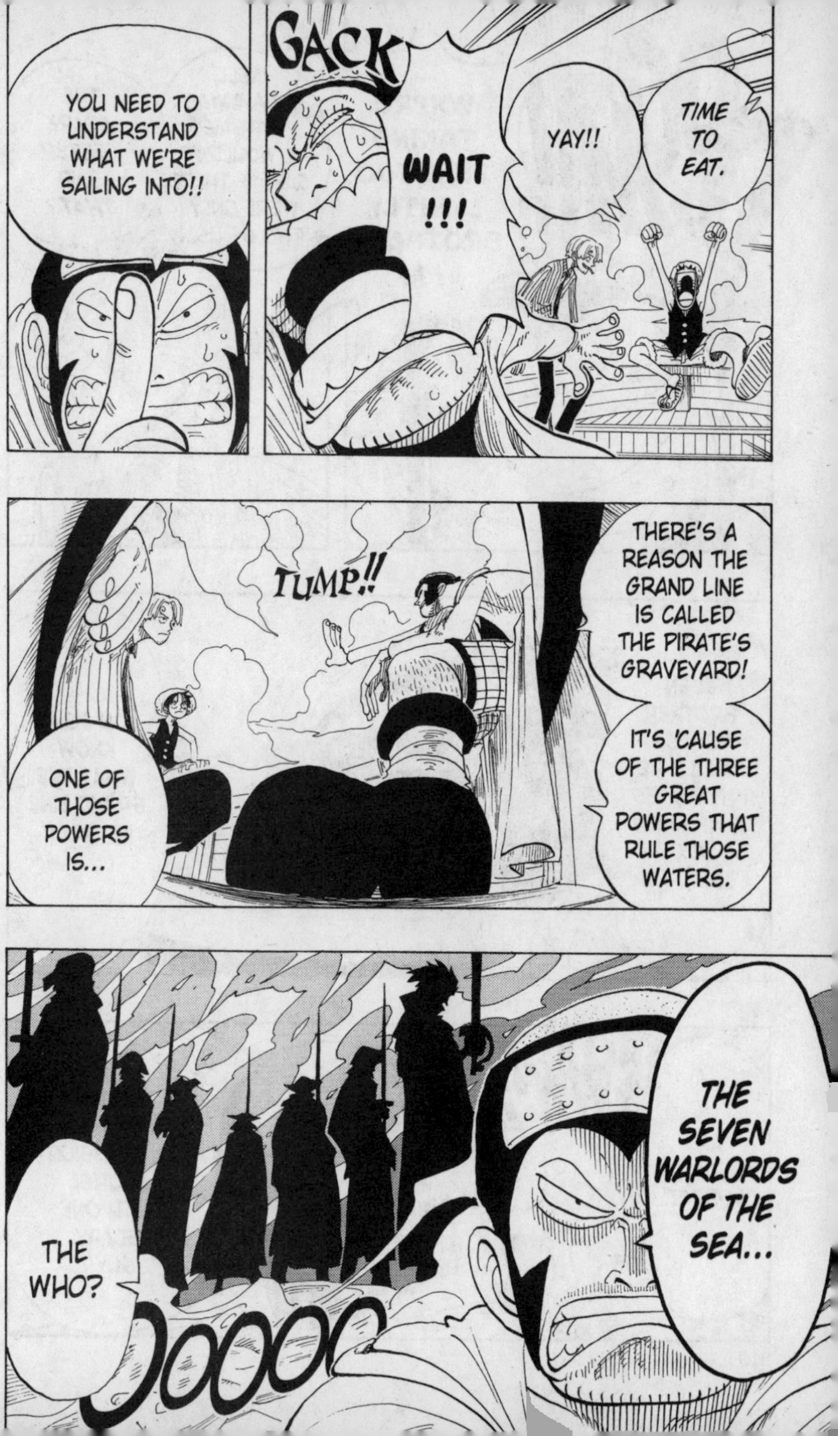
TIME TO EAT.
YAY!!
GACK
WAIT!!!
YOU NEED TO UNDERSTAND WHAT WE'RE SAILING INTO!!
THERE'S A REASON THE GRAND LINE IS CALLED THE PIRATE'S GRAVEYARD!
TUMP!!
IT'S 'CAUSE OF THE THREE GREAT POWERS THAT RULE THOSE WATERS.
ONE OF THOSE POWERS IS...
THE SEVEN WARLORDS OF THE SEA...
THE WHO?

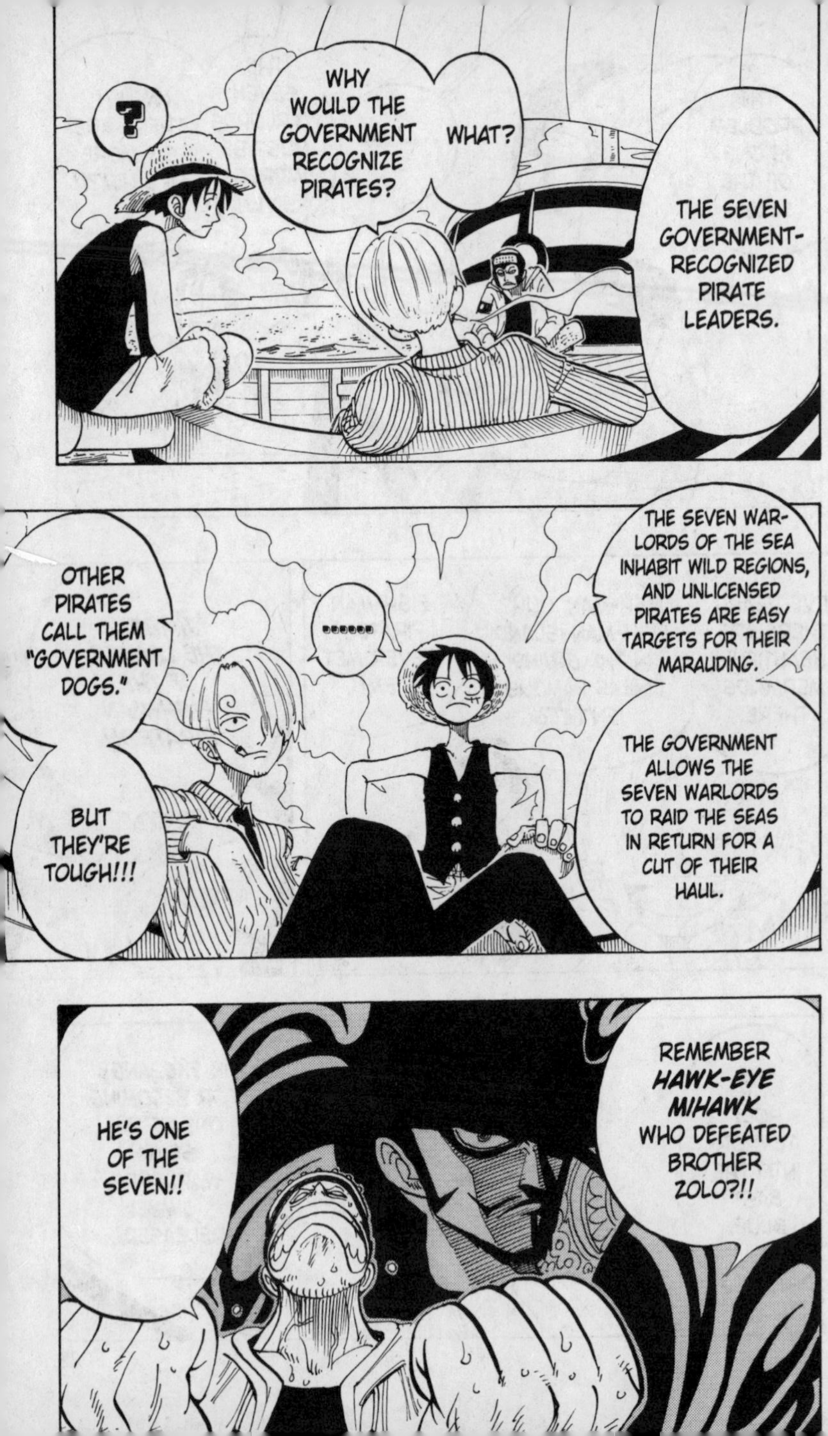
THE SEVEN GOVERNMENT-RECOGNIZED PIRATE LEADERS.
WHAT?
WHY WOULD THE GOVERNMENT RECOGNIZE PIRATES?
?
THE SEVEN WAR-LORDS OF THE SEA INHABIT WILD REGIONS, AND UNLICENSED PIRATES ARE EASY TARGETS FOR THEIR MARAUDING.
THE GOVERNMENT ALLOWS THE SEVEN WARLORDS TO RAID THE SEAS IN RETURN FOR A CUT OF THEIR HAUL.
......
OTHER PIRATES CALL THEM "GOVERNMENT DOGS."
BUT THEY'RE TOUGH!!!
REMEMBER *HAWK-EYE MIHAWK* WHO DEFEATED BROTHER ZOLO?!!
HE'S ONE OF THE SEVEN!!

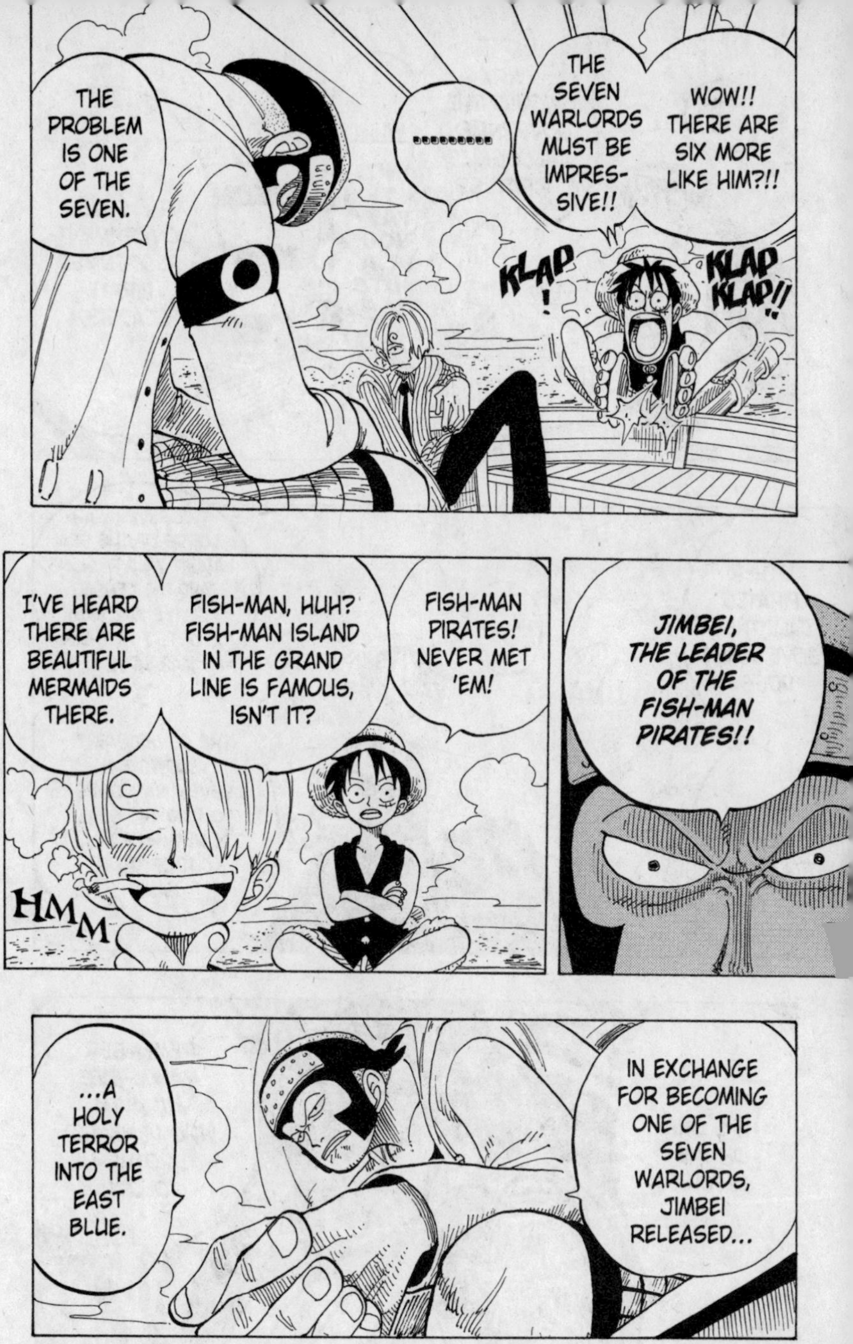
WOW!! THERE ARE SIX MORE LIKE HIM?!!
THE SEVEN WARLORDS MUST BE IMPRES-SIVE!!
KLAP KLAP!!
KLAP!
.........
THE PROBLEM IS ONE OF THE SEVEN.
JIMBEI, THE LEADER OF THE FISH-MAN PIRATES!!
FISH-MAN PIRATES! NEVER MET 'EM!
FISH-MAN, HUH? FISH-MAN ISLAND IN THE GRAND LINE IS FAMOUS, ISN'T IT?
I'VE HEARD THERE ARE BEAUTIFUL MERMAIDS THERE.
HMM
IN EXCHANGE FOR BECOMING ONE OF THE SEVEN WARLORDS, JIMBEI RELEASED...
...A HOLY TERROR INTO THE EAST BLUE.

READ THIS WAY

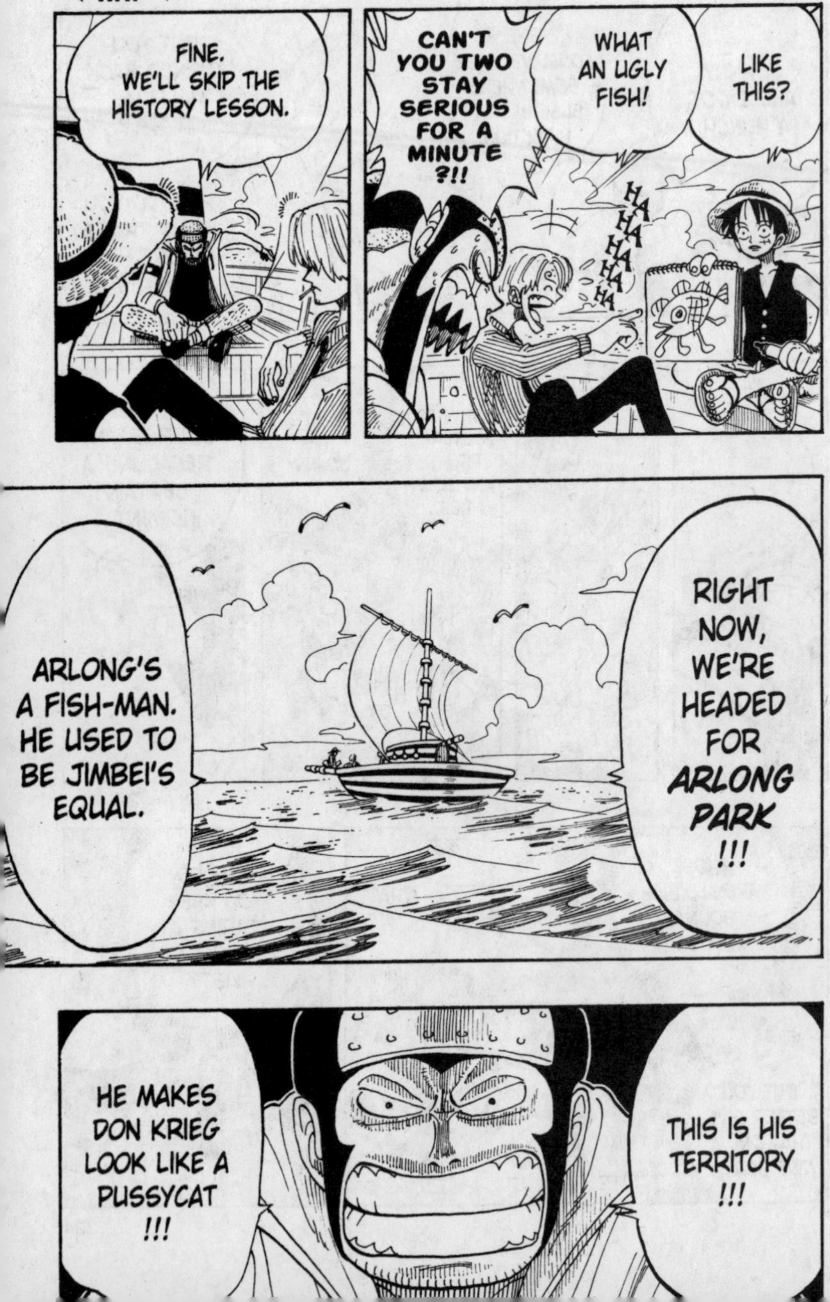
LIKE THIS?
WHAT AN UGLY FISH!
HA HA HA HA HA HA
CAN'T YOU TWO STAY SERIOUS FOR A MINUTE ?!!
FINE. WE'LL SKIP THE HISTORY LESSON.
RIGHT NOW, WE'RE HEADED FOR ARLONG PARK !!!
ARLONG'S A FISH-MAN. HE USED TO BE JIMBEI'S EQUAL.
THIS IS HIS TERRITORY !!!
HE MAKES DON KRIEG LOOK LIKE A PUSSYCAT !!!

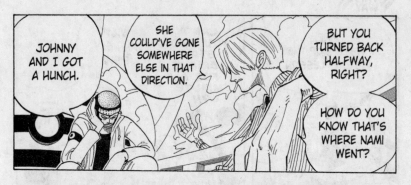

BUT YOU TURNED BACK HALFWAY, RIGHT?
HOW DO YOU KNOW THAT'S WHERE NAMI WENT?
SHE COULD'VE GONE SOMEWHERE ELSE IN THAT DIRECTION.
JOHNNY AND I GOT A HUNCH.
GIVEN HER COURSE, AND RECALLING A CERTAIN INCIDENT...
WHAT'S THIS, JOHNNY ?
WANTED POSTERS... PIRATES AND BOUNTIES...
KRUSH!!!
WHY DO YOU KEEP STARING AT THAT BOUNTY LIST?
WHAT?
NO REASON.
THOSE ARE ALL BIG-BOUNTY PIRATES...
...BUT YOU'D BETTER GIVE THAT ONE A WIDE BERTH.

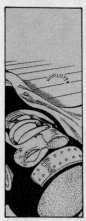

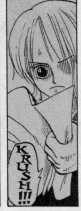

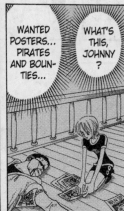

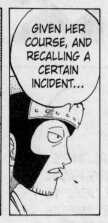

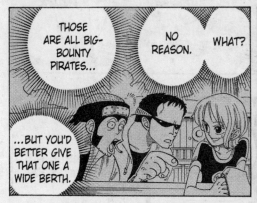

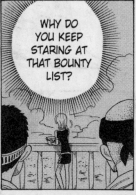

READ THIS WAY

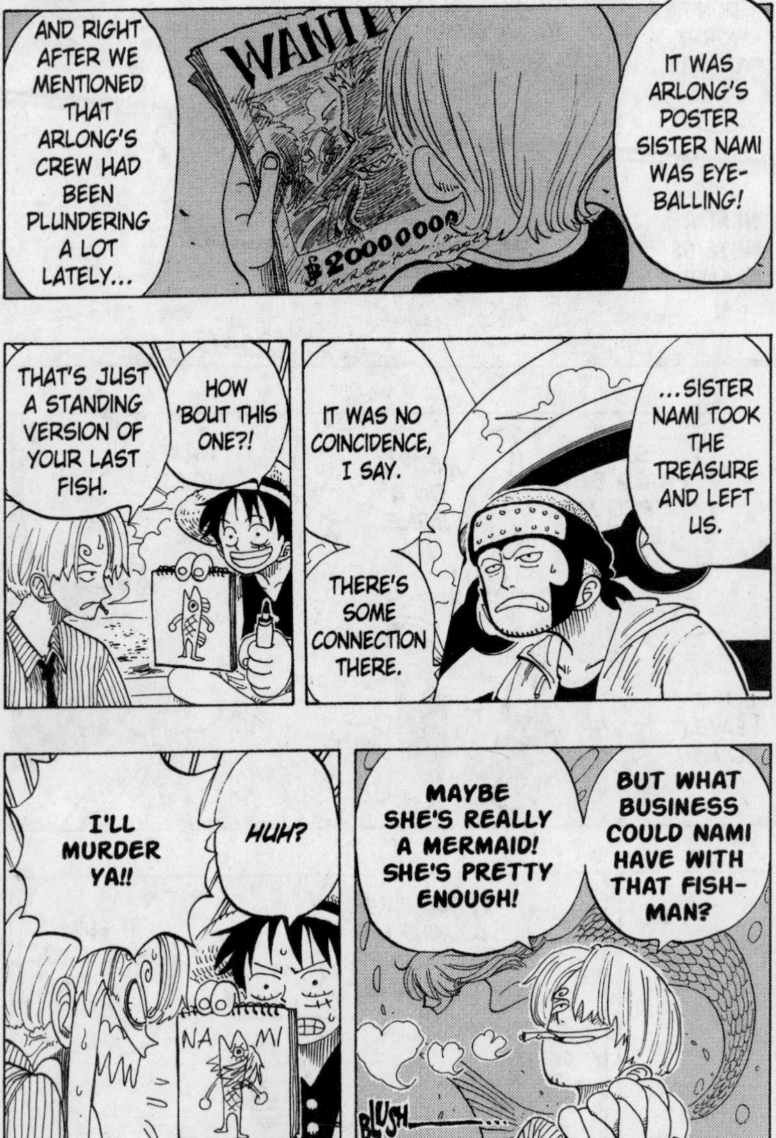
IT WAS ARLONG'S POSTER SISTER NAMI WAS EYE-BALLING!
WANTE
ß20000000
AND RIGHT AFTER WE MENTIONED THAT ARLONG'S CREW HAD BEEN PLUNDERING A LOT LATELY...
...SISTER NAMI TOOK THE TREASURE AND LEFT US.
IT WAS NO COINCIDENCE, I SAY.
THERE'S SOME CONNECTION THERE.
HOW 'BOUT THIS ONE?!
THAT'S JUST A STANDING VERSION OF YOUR LAST FISH.
BUT WHAT BUSINESS COULD NAMI HAVE WITH THAT FISH-MAN?
MAYBE SHE'S REALLY A MERMAID! SHE'S PRETTY ENOUGH!
BLUSH
HUH?
I'LL MURDER YA!!
NA MI

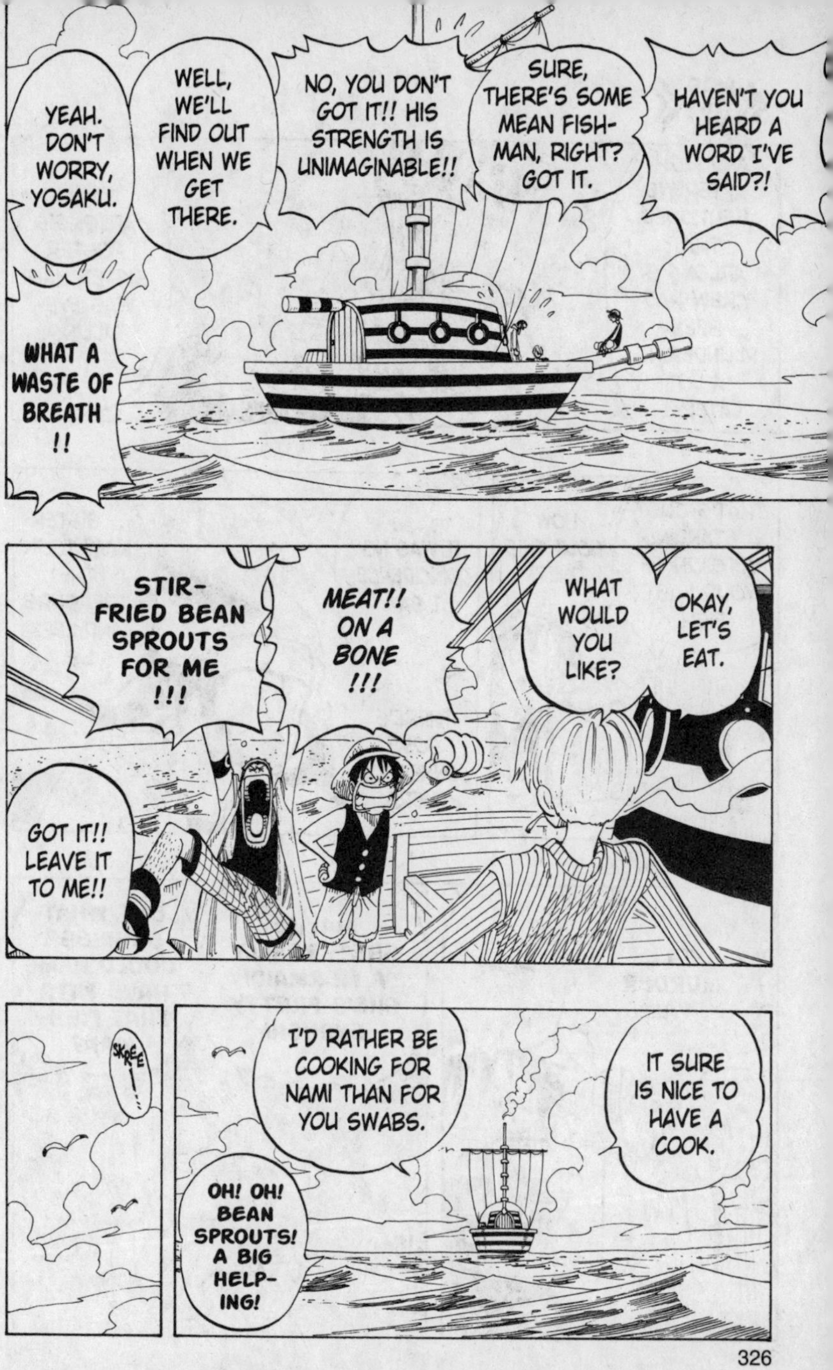
HAVEN'T YOU HEARD A WORD I'VE SAID?!
SURE, THERE'S SOME MEAN FISH-MAN, RIGHT? GOT IT.
NO, YOU DON'T GOT IT!! HIS STRENGTH IS UNIMAGINABLE!!
WELL, WE'LL FIND OUT WHEN WE GET THERE.
YEAH. DON'T WORRY, YOSAKU.
WHAT A WASTE OF BREATH !!
OKAY, LET'S EAT.
WHAT WOULD YOU LIKE?
MEAT!! ON A BONE !!!
STIR-FRIED BEAN SPROUTS FOR ME !!!
GOT IT!! LEAVE IT TO ME!!
IT SURE IS NICE TO HAVE A COOK.
I'D RATHER BE COOKING FOR NAMI THAN FOR YOU SWABS.
OH! OH! BEAN SPROUTS! A BIG HELPING!
SKREE...

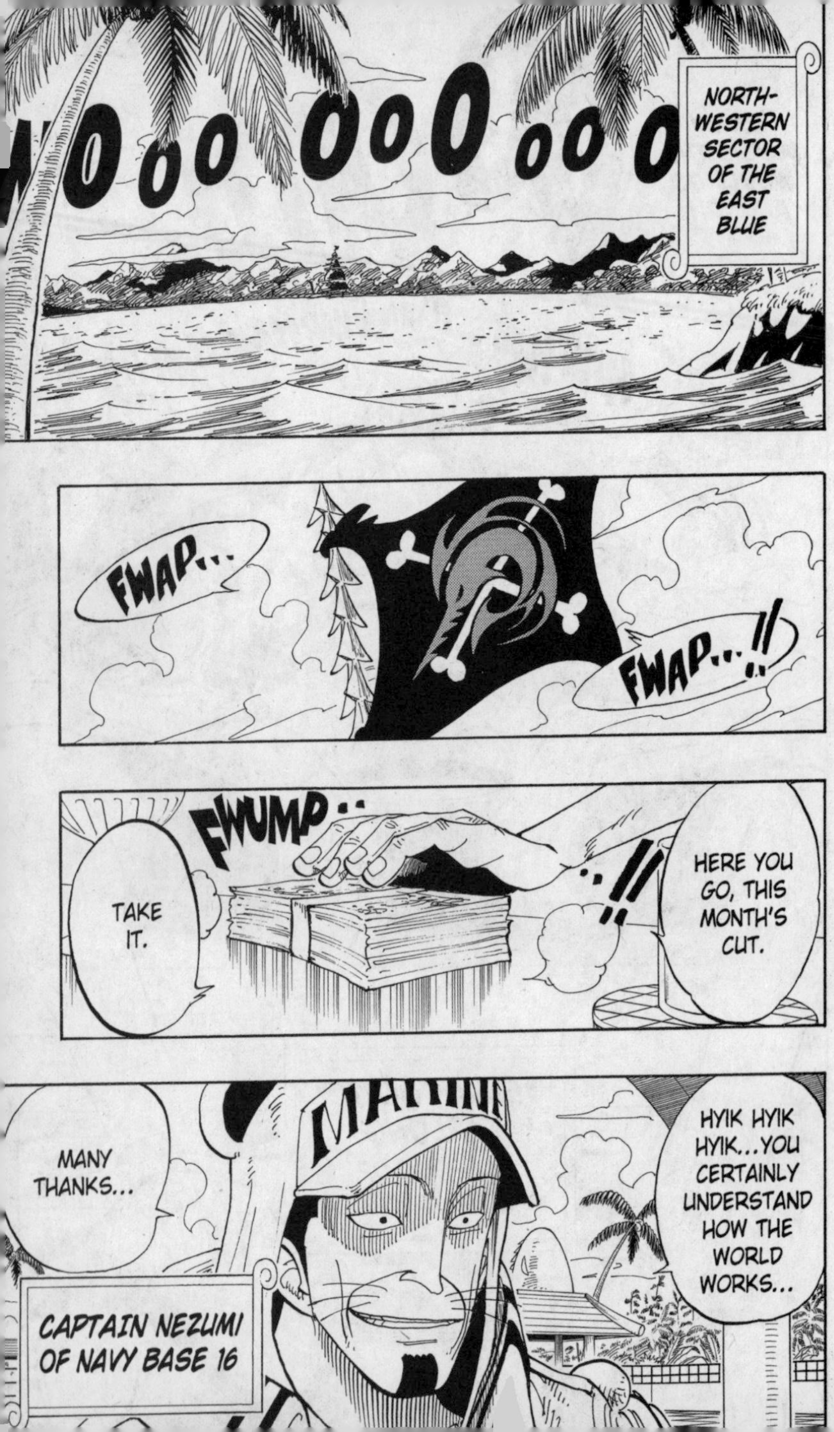
NORTH-WESTERN SECTOR OF THE EAST BLUE
FWAP...!!
FWAP...
HERE YOU GO, THIS MONTH'S CUT.
FWUMP..!!
TAKE IT.
HYIK HYIK HYIK...YOU CERTAINLY UNDERSTAND HOW THE WORLD WORKS...
MANY THANKS...
MARINE
CAPTAIN NEZUMI OF NAVY BASE 16

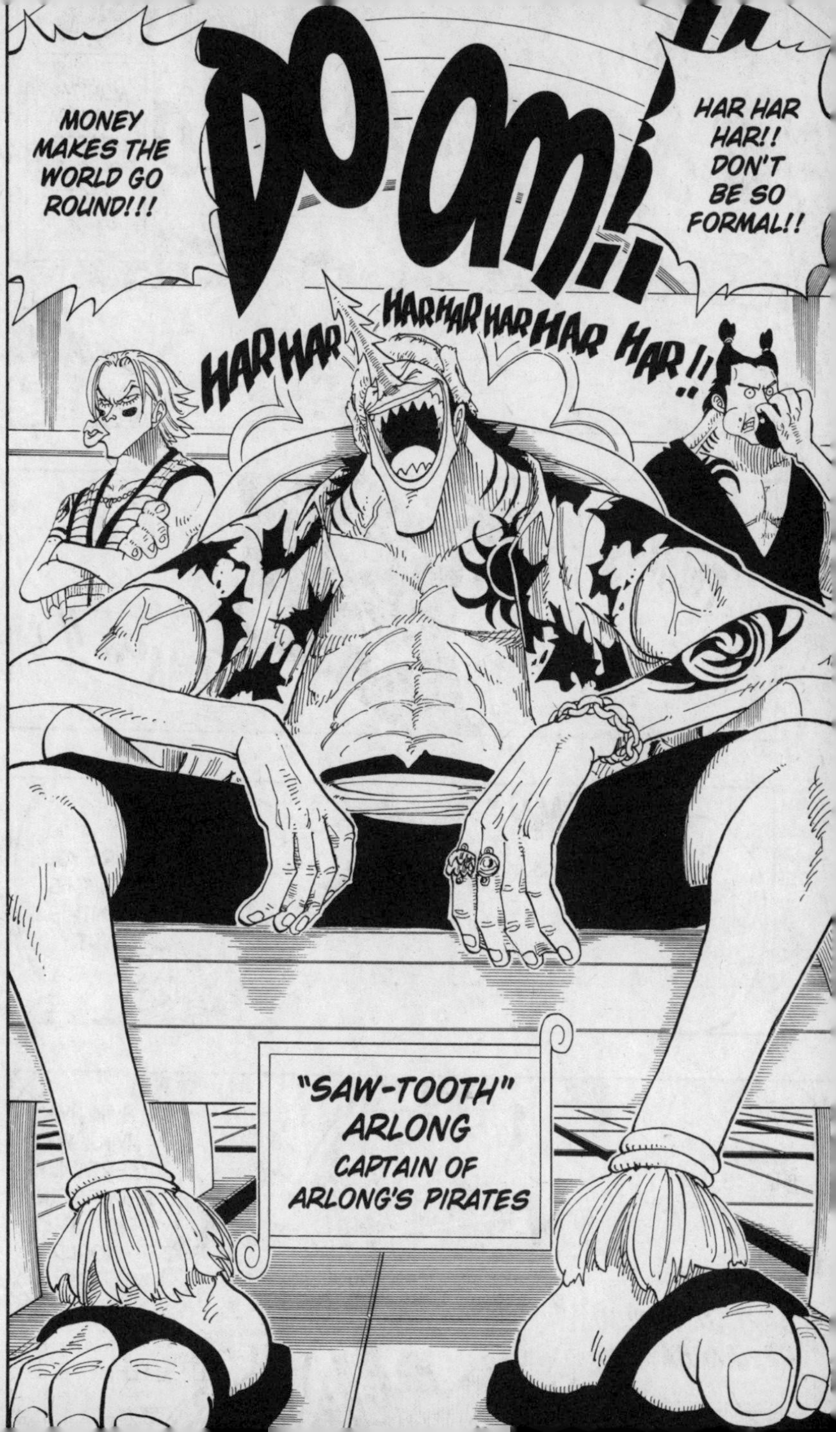
HAR HAR HAR!! DON'T BE SO FORMAL!!
DOOM!!
MONEY MAKES THE WORLD GO ROUND!!!
HAR HAR HAR HAR HAR HAR HAR!!
"SAW-TOOTH" ARLONG
CAPTAIN OF ARLONG'S PIRATES

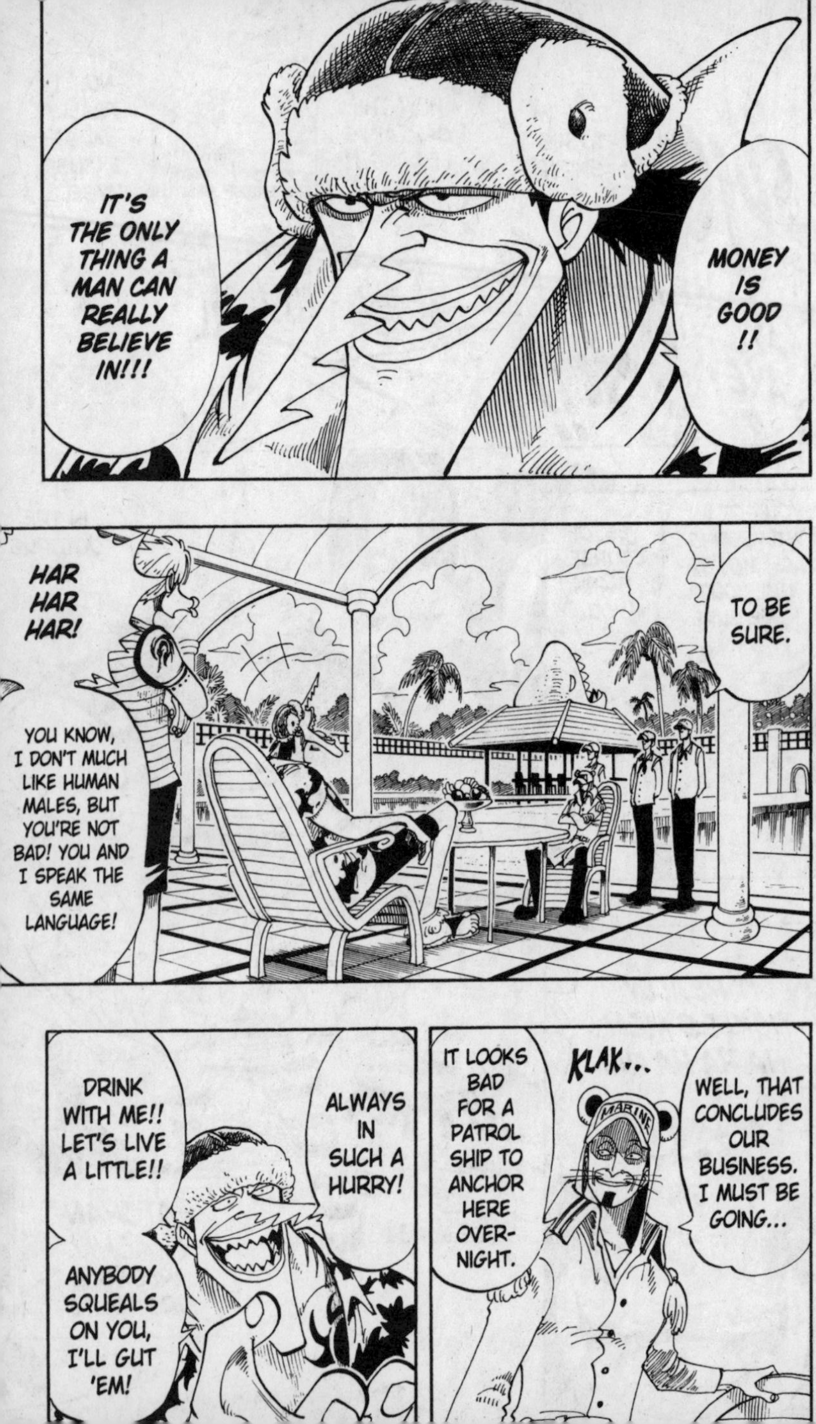
MONEY IS GOOD !!
IT'S THE ONLY THING A MAN CAN REALLY BELIEVE IN!!!
TO BE SURE.
HAR HAR HAR!
YOU KNOW, I DON'T MUCH LIKE HUMAN MALES, BUT YOU'RE NOT BAD! YOU AND I SPEAK THE SAME LANGUAGE!
WELL, THAT CONCLUDES OUR BUSINESS. I MUST BE GOING...
KLAK...
IT LOOKS BAD FOR A PATROL SHIP TO ANCHOR HERE OVER-NIGHT.
MARINE
ALWAYS IN SUCH A HURRY!
DRINK WITH ME!! LET'S LIVE A LITTLE!!
ANYBODY SQUEALS ON YOU, I'LL GUT 'EM!

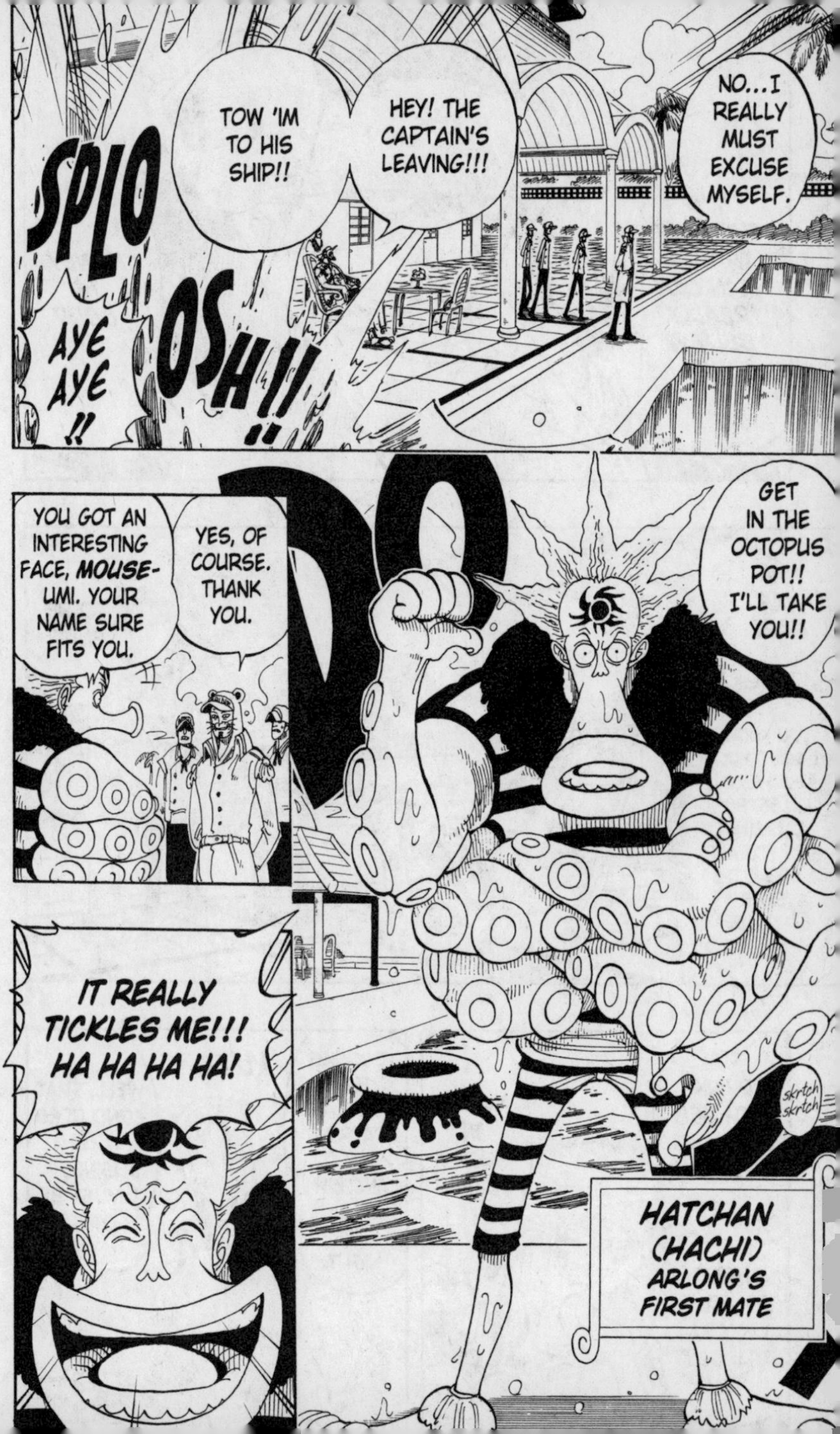
NO...I REALLY MUST EXCUSE MYSELF.
HEY! THE CAPTAIN'S LEAVING!!!
TOW 'IM TO HIS SHIP!!
SPLOOSH!!
AYE AYE!!
GET IN THE OCTOPUS POT!! I'LL TAKE YOU!!
skrtch skrtch
HATCHAN (HACHI) ARLONG'S FIRST MATE
YES, OF COURSE. THANK YOU.
YOU GOT AN INTERESTING FACE, MOUSE-UMI. YOUR NAME SURE FITS YOU.
IT REALLY TICKLES ME!!! HA HA HA HA!

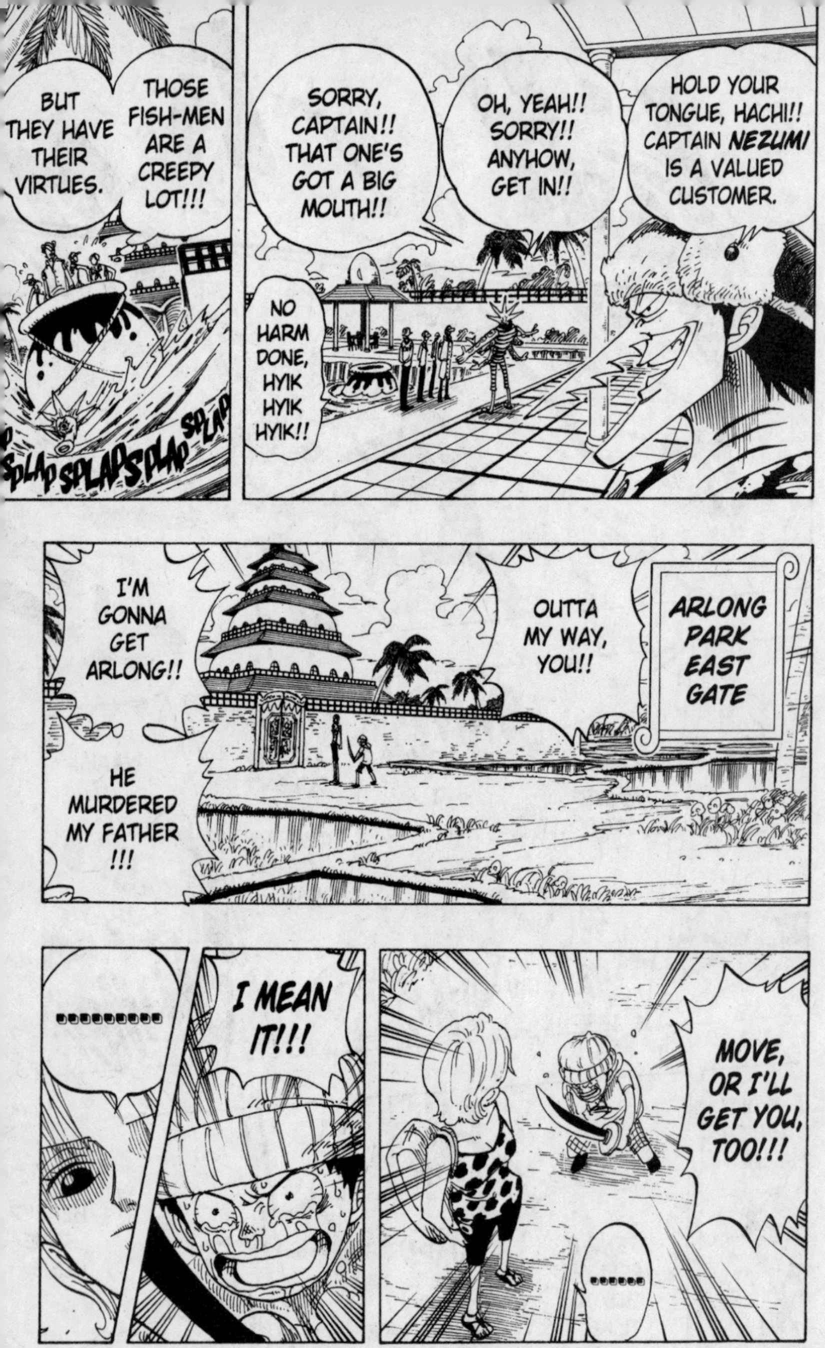
HOLD YOUR TONGUE, HACHI!! CAPTAIN NEZUMI IS A VALUED CUSTOMER.
OH, YEAH!! SORRY!! ANYHOW, GET IN!!
SORRY, CAPTAIN!! THAT ONE'S GOT A BIG MOUTH!!
NO HARM DONE, HYIK HYIK HYIK!!
THOSE FISH-MEN ARE A CREEPY LOT!!!
BUT THEY HAVE THEIR VIRTUES.
SPLAP SPLAP SPLAP SPLAP
ARLONG PARK EAST GATE
OUTTA MY WAY, YOU!!
I'M GONNA GET ARLONG!!
HE MURDERED MY FATHER!!!
MOVE, OR I'LL GET YOU, TOO!!!
......
I MEAN IT!!!
.........

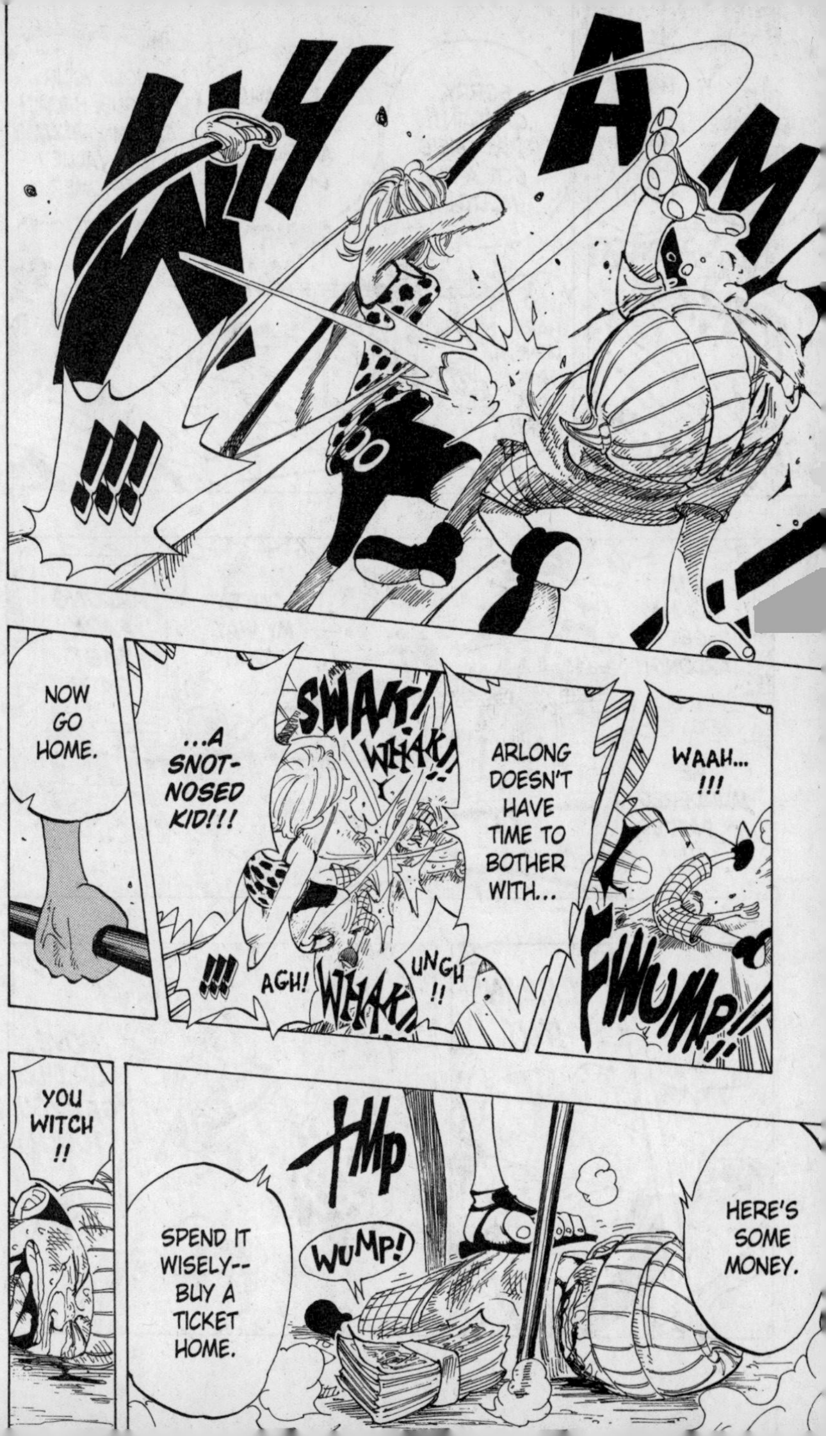
WHAM!!
!!!
WAAH... !!!
FWUMP!!
ARLONG DOESN'T HAVE TIME TO BOTHER WITH...
SWAK!
WHAK!!
...A SNOT-NOSED KID!!!
UNGH !!
WHAK!!
AGH!
!!!
NOW GO HOME.
HERE'S SOME MONEY.
HMP
WUMP!
SPEND IT WISELY-- BUY A TICKET HOME.
YOU WITCH !!

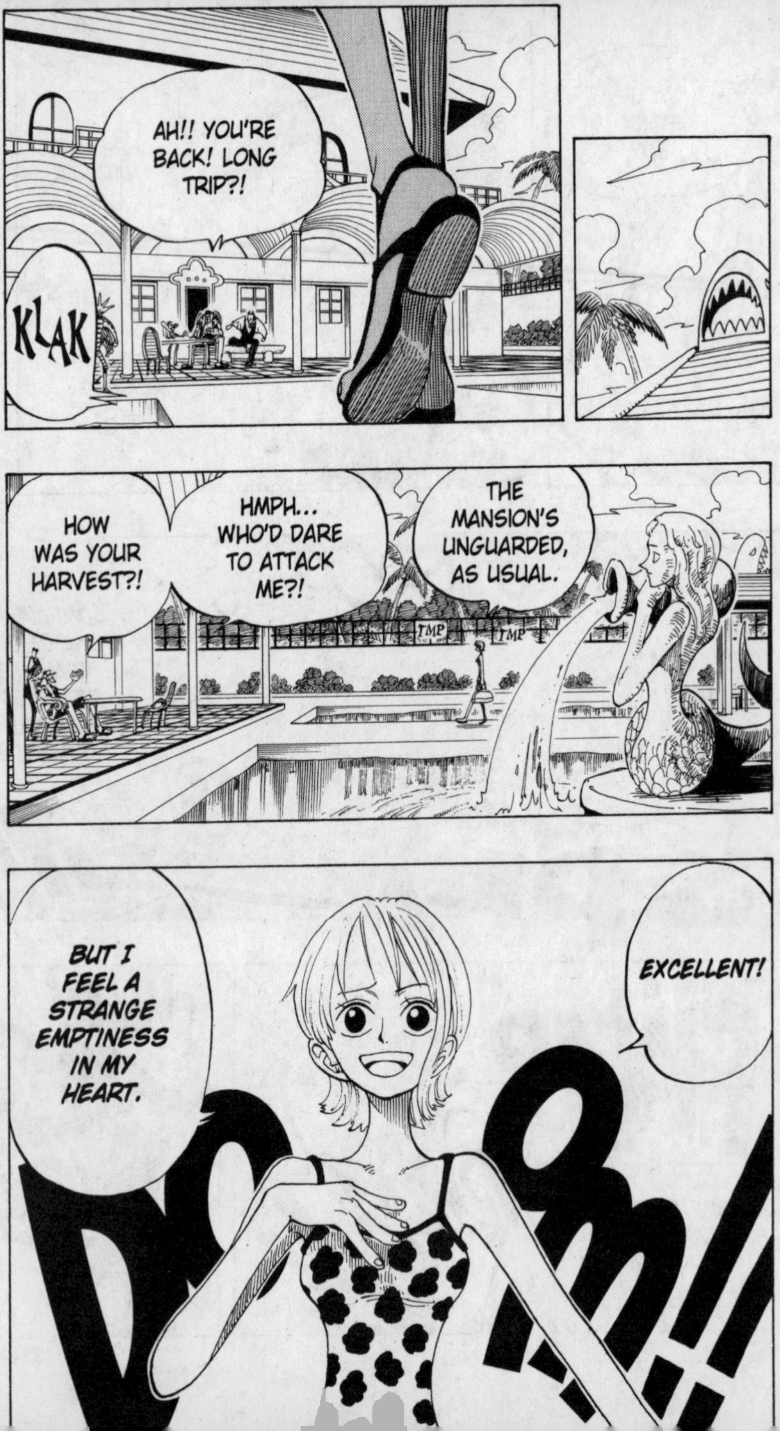
AH!! YOU'RE BACK! LONG TRIP?!
KLAK
THE MANSION'S UNGUARDED, AS USUAL.
TMP
TMP
HMPH... WHO'D DARE TO ATTACK ME?!
HOW WAS YOUR HARVEST?!
EXCELLENT!
BUT I FEEL A STRANGE EMPTINESS IN MY HEART.
DOOM!!

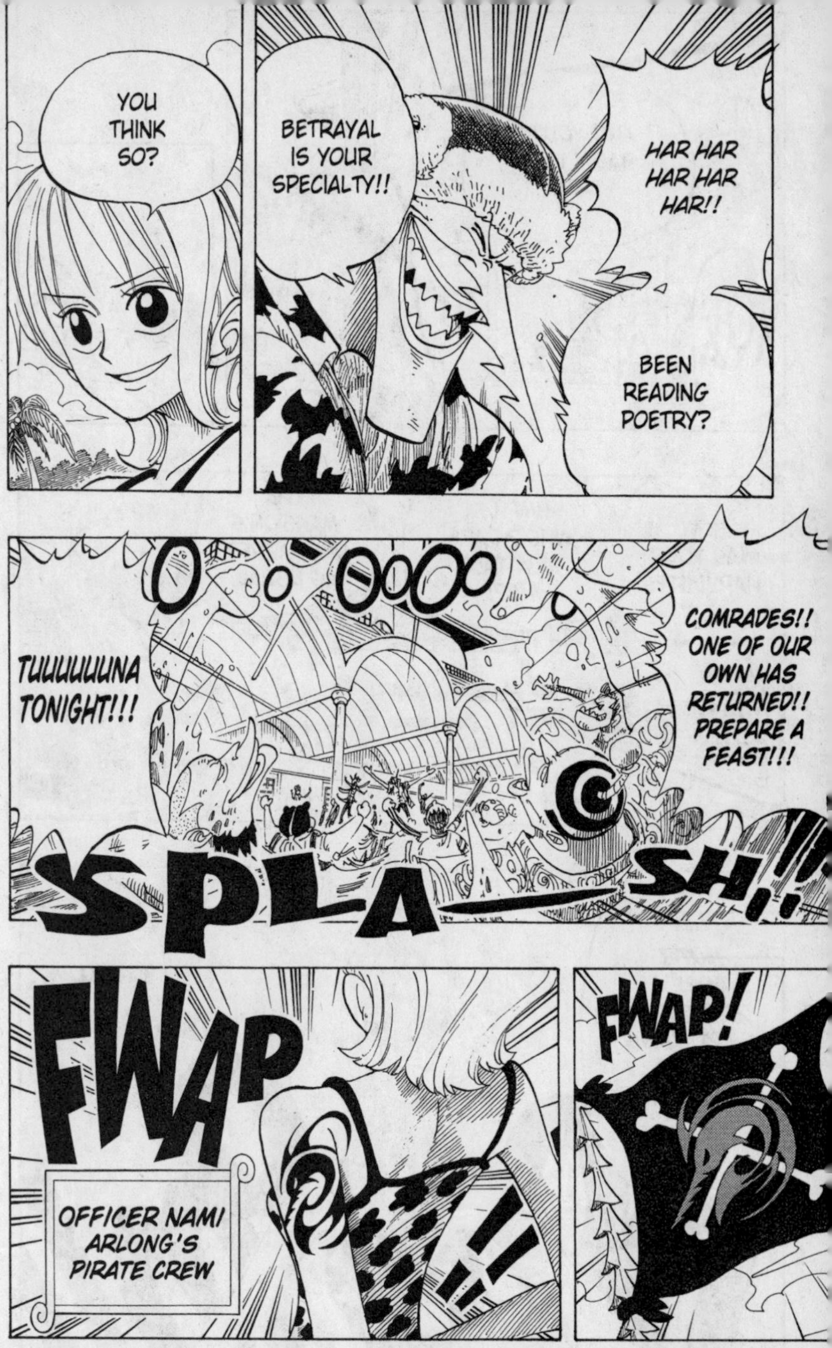
HAR HAR HAR HAR HAR!!
BEEN READING POETRY?
BETRAYAL IS YOUR SPECIALTY!!
YOU THINK SO?
COMRADES!! ONE OF OUR OWN HAS RETURNED!! PREPARE A FEAST!!!
OOOOOOO
TUUUUUUNA TONIGHT!!!
SPLA—SH!!!
FWAP!
FWAP
OFFICER NAMI ARLONG'S PIRATE CREW

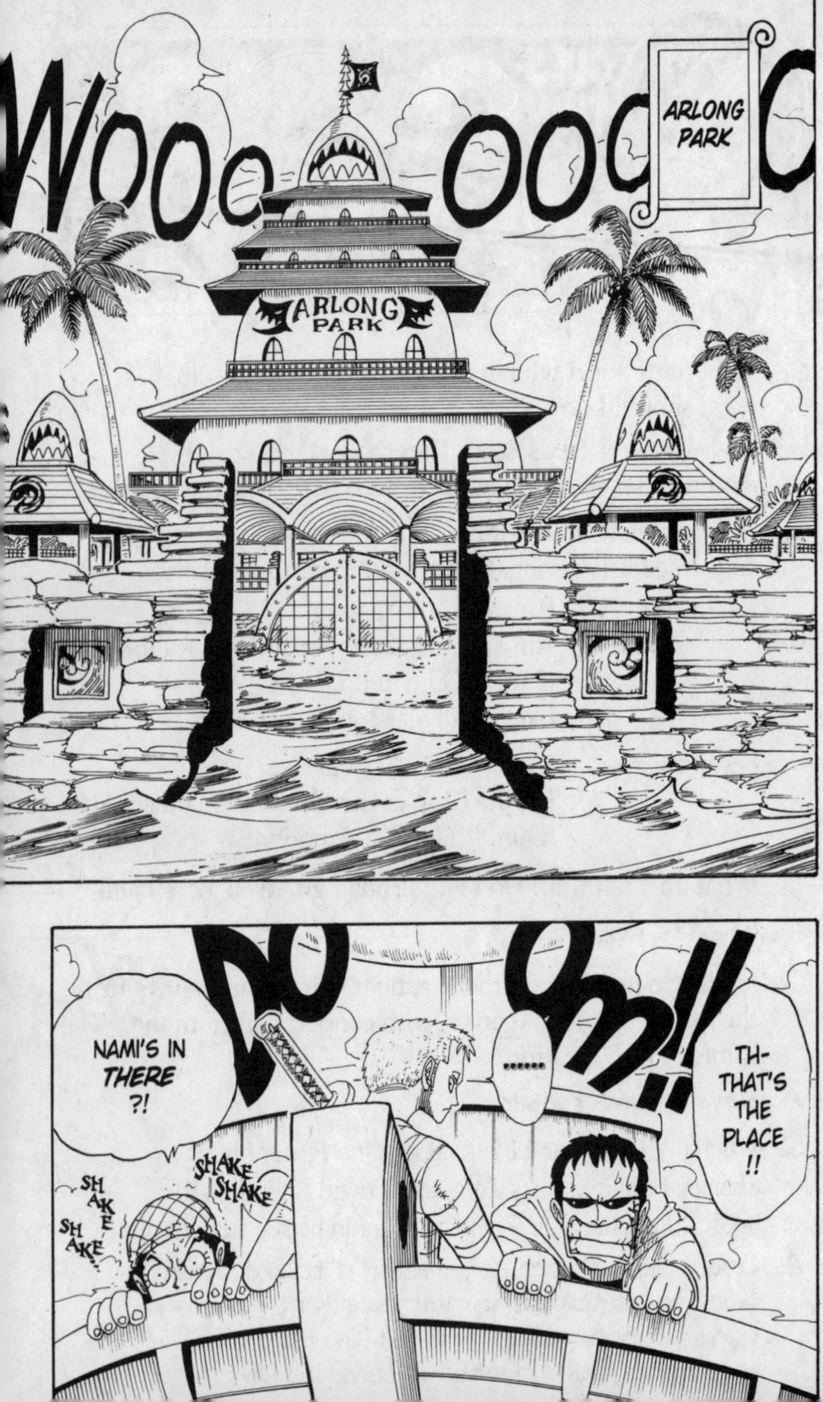
ARLONG PARK
WOOO OOOO
ARLONG PARK
TH-THAT'S THE PLACE!!
DO OM!!
......
NAMI'S IN THERE?!
SHAKE SHAKE
SHAKE SHAKE...

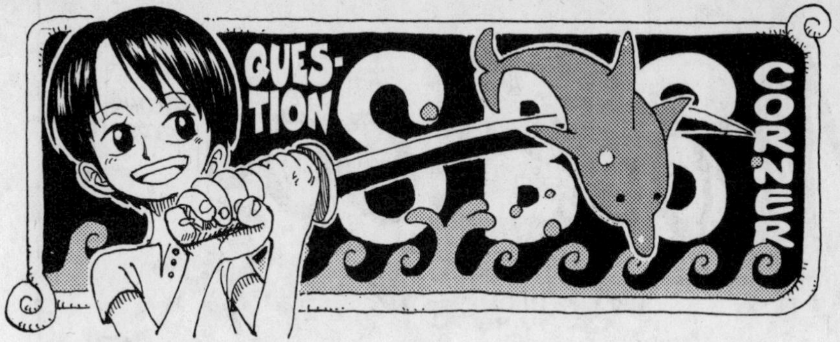
QUES-
TION
SBS
CORNER

Q: To become a **girl** who is as cool and strong as Zolo, what should I do?

A: Hmm...a girl? Let's see... First of all, do squats!! And eat sardines to strengthen your mental powers!!

Q: Oda Sensei, hello, or rather, *ni hao*!! I used my whole brain to compose Luffy's song. Please read it, dance, and cry!

First verse: Gum$^{\times 3}$ Gum Ya-a-ay
Am I a Gum-Gum Person, or a Rubber Man?
Gum$^{\times 3}$ Gum Yahoo
Lalalalaa Lalaa Lalalalaa Oooh

Second verse: Gum$^{\times 3}$ Gum Stretch
I'm the King of the Pirates, I'm amazing!!
(Gum$^{\times 3}$ Gum)$^{\times 2}$ Amooon

What do you think? Do I win? Shall I go? Well, here I go!!

A: Yay!! Yes, go!! Go far!!

Q: Is Luffy natural or synthetic rubber? This is an inquiry from the Meteorological Agency (with cooperation from the Ministry of Education).

A: Natural ~~dumb~~ rubber.

Q: When my friends and I talk about *One Piece*, I like Shanks, Friend S. likes Zolo, and Friend I. likes Luffy, but R. likes Buggy and Django. Should he see a doctor?

A: One would have to be seriously ill to like those two. Please tell him to rest quietly at home and drink plenty of liquids. And tell him that if he perseveres, good things will come to him...

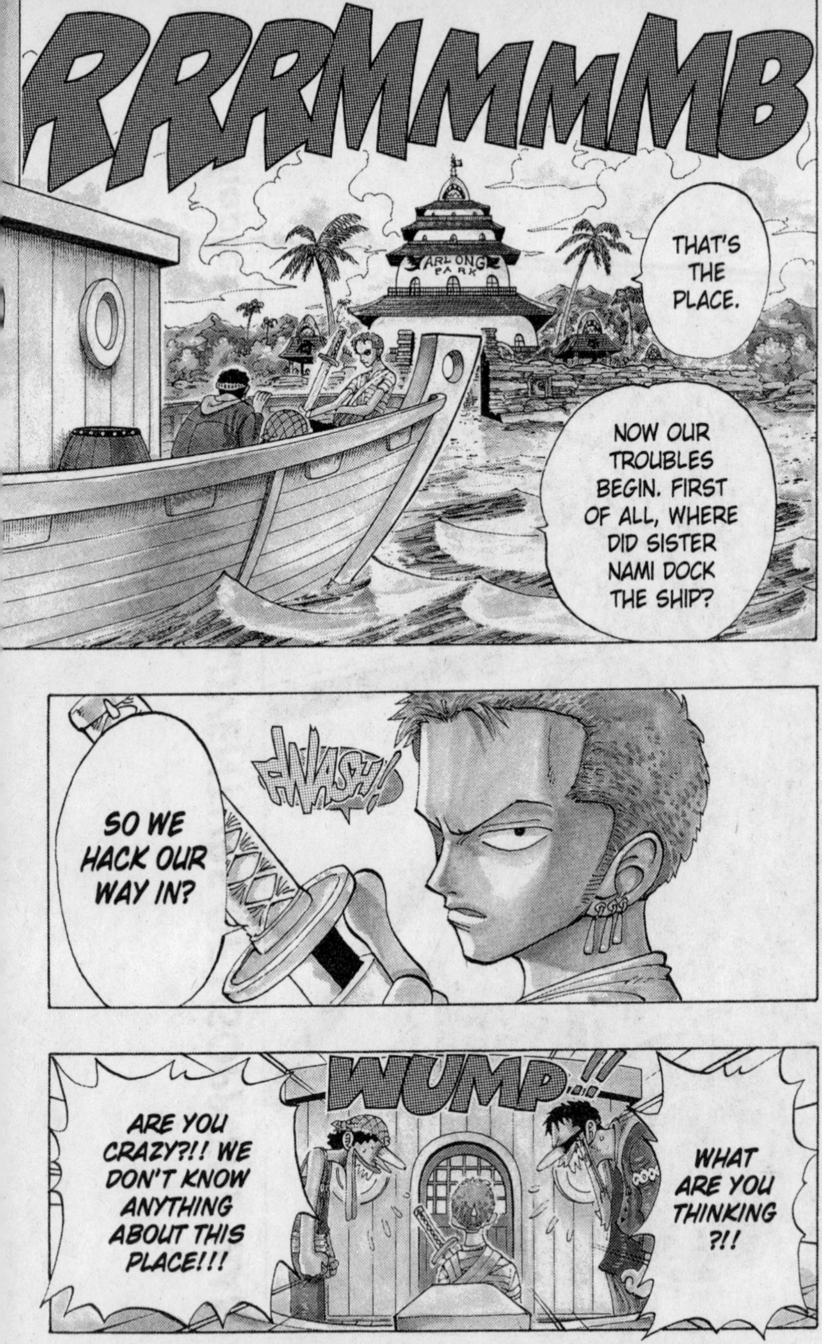
RRRMMMMMB
ARLONG PARK
THAT'S THE PLACE.
NOW OUR TROUBLES BEGIN. FIRST OF ALL, WHERE DID SISTER NAMI DOCK THE SHIP?
FWASH!
SO WE HACK OUR WAY IN?
WUMP!!
WHAT ARE YOU THINKING ?!!
ARE YOU CRAZY?!! WE DON'T KNOW ANYTHING ABOUT THIS PLACE!!!

## Chapter 70: THE GREAT ADVENTURE OF USOPP THE MAN

# Chapter 70: THE GREAT ADVENTURE OF USOPP THE MAN

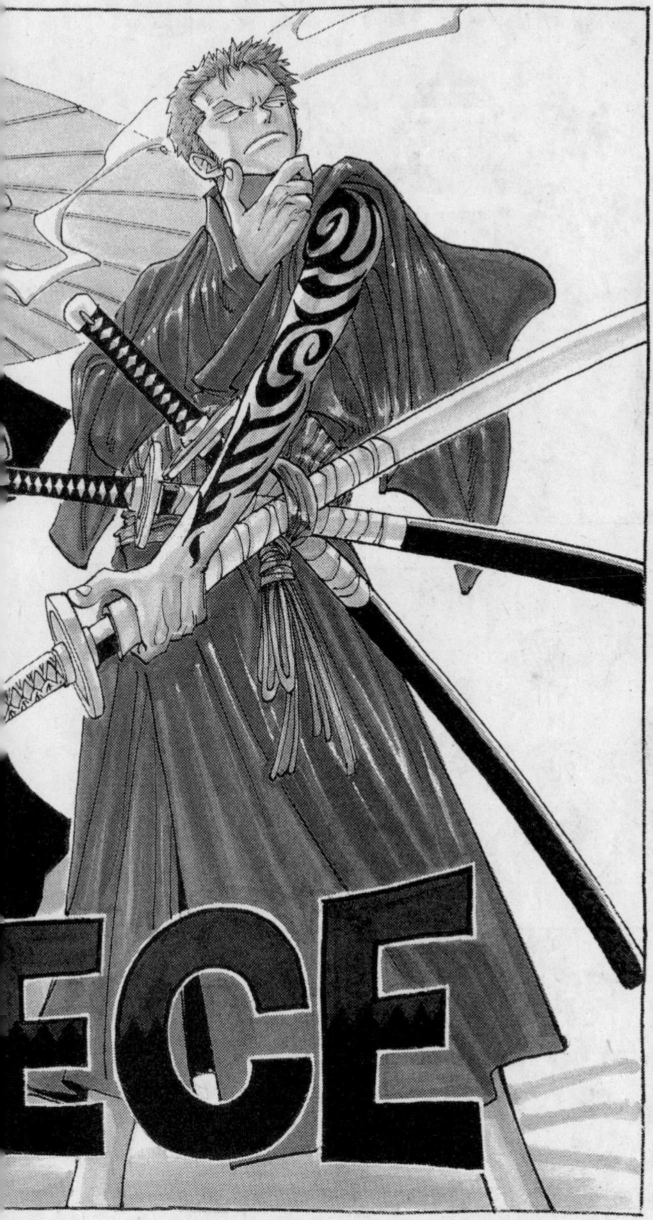
ECE

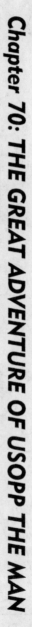

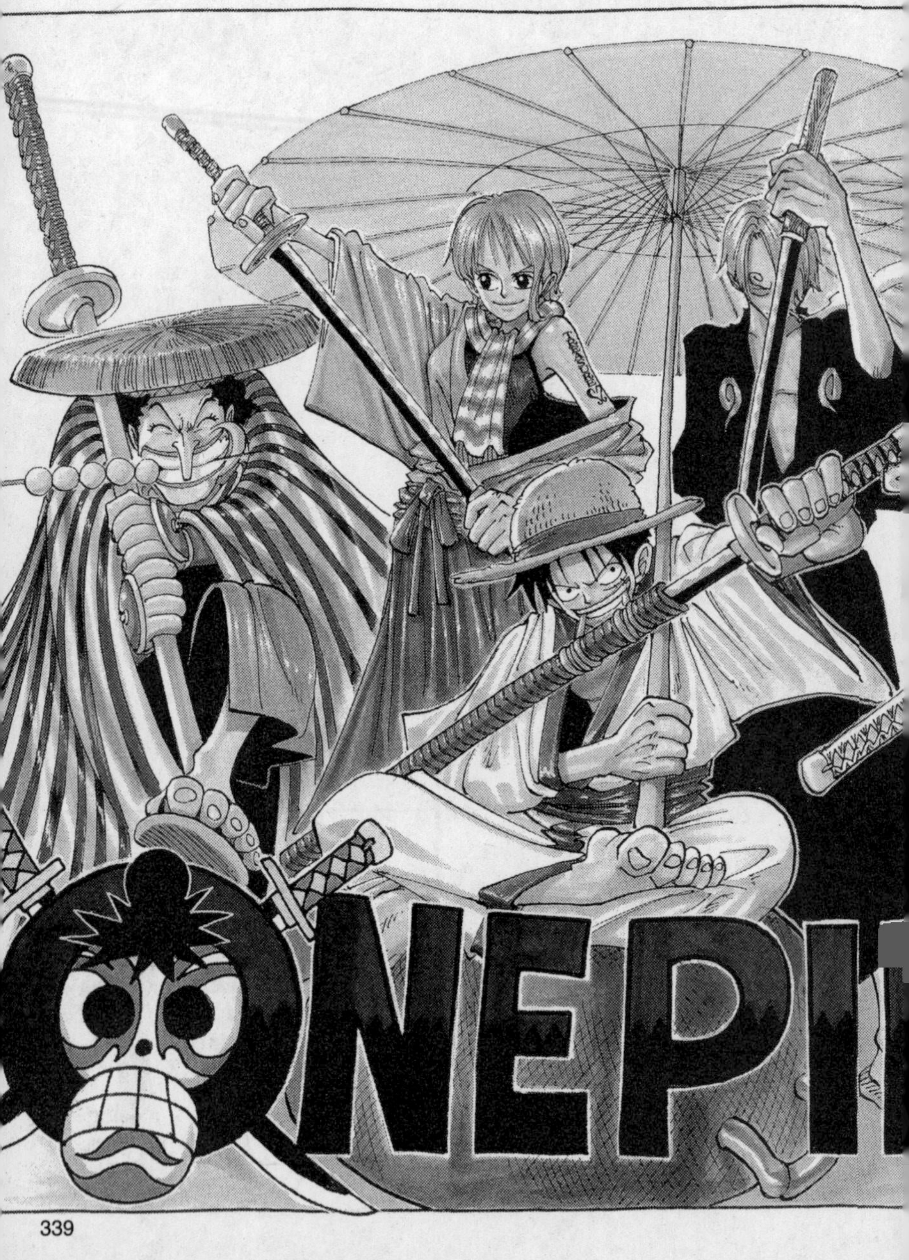
ONEPI

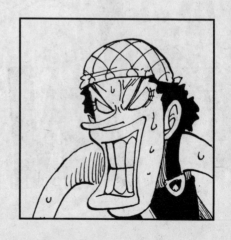

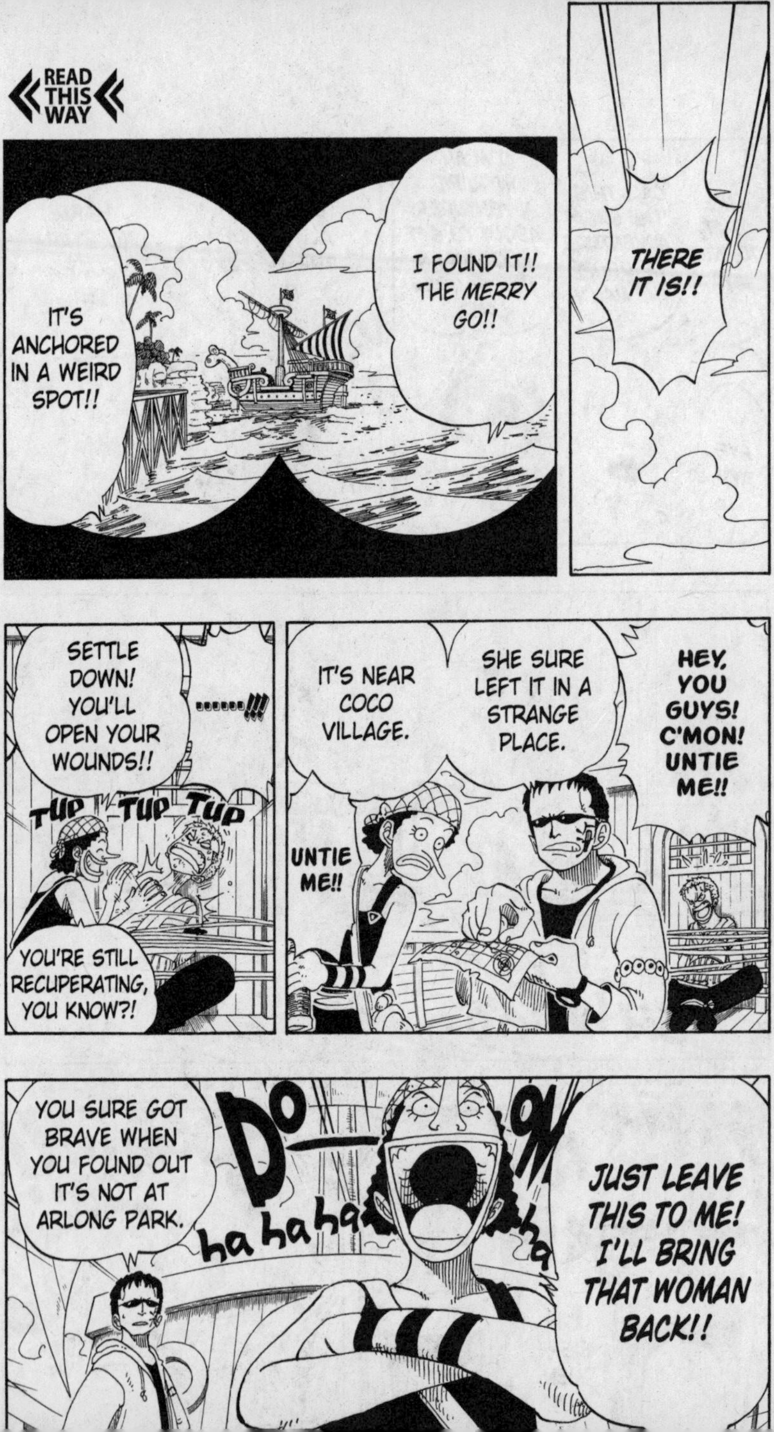
READ THIS WAY
THERE IT IS!!
I FOUND IT!! THE MERRY GO!!
IT'S ANCHORED IN A WEIRD SPOT!!
HEY, YOU GUYS! C'MON! UNTIE ME!!
SHE SURE LEFT IT IN A STRANGE PLACE.
IT'S NEAR COCO VILLAGE.
UNTIE ME!!
......!!!
SETTLE DOWN! YOU'LL OPEN YOUR WOUNDS!!
TUP TUP TUP
YOU'RE STILL RECUPERATING, YOU KNOW?!
JUST LEAVE THIS TO ME! I'LL BRING THAT WOMAN BACK!!
DO—OM
ha ha ha ha
YOU SURE GOT BRAVE WHEN YOU FOUND OUT IT'S NOT AT ARLONG PARK.

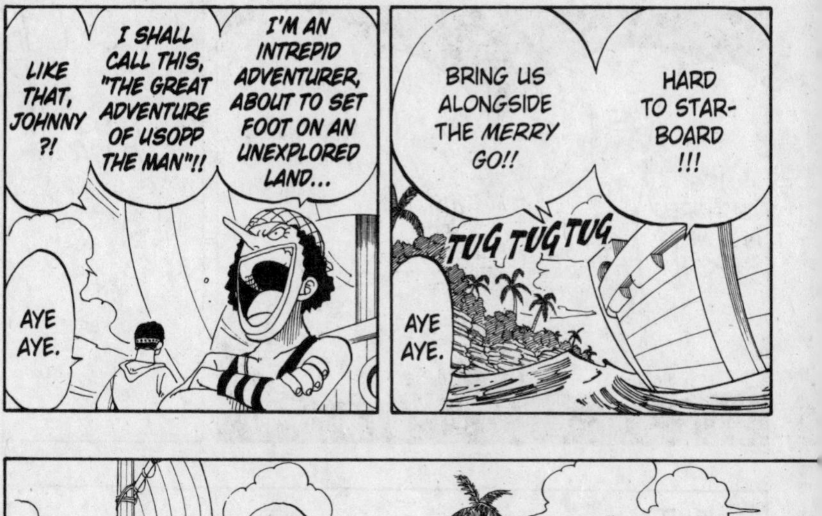
HARD TO STAR-BOARD!!!
BRING US ALONGSIDE THE MERRY GO!!
TUG TUG TUG
AYE AYE.
I'M AN INTREPID ADVENTURER, ABOUT TO SET FOOT ON AN UNEXPLORED LAND...
I SHALL CALL THIS, "THE GREAT ADVENTURE OF USOPP THE MAN"!!
LIKE THAT, JOHNNY?!
AYE AYE.
?
SHWOOO...

UNLIKE THE INFAMOUS SWASTIKA OF NAZI GERMANY, THE BUDDHIST *MANJI* IS DEPICTED AS A SQUARE (RATHER THAN DIAMOND SHAPE), AND CAN POINT EITHER CLOCKWISE OR COUNTER-CLOCKWISE. AN ANCIENT SYMBOL, THE *MANJI* CAN BE SEEN ON THE CHEST, PALMS AND FEET OF BUDDHA, REPRESENTING GOOD LUCK. YOU'LL ALSO SEE IT ON THE BELLY OF THE FISHY BAD-BOY BELOW.

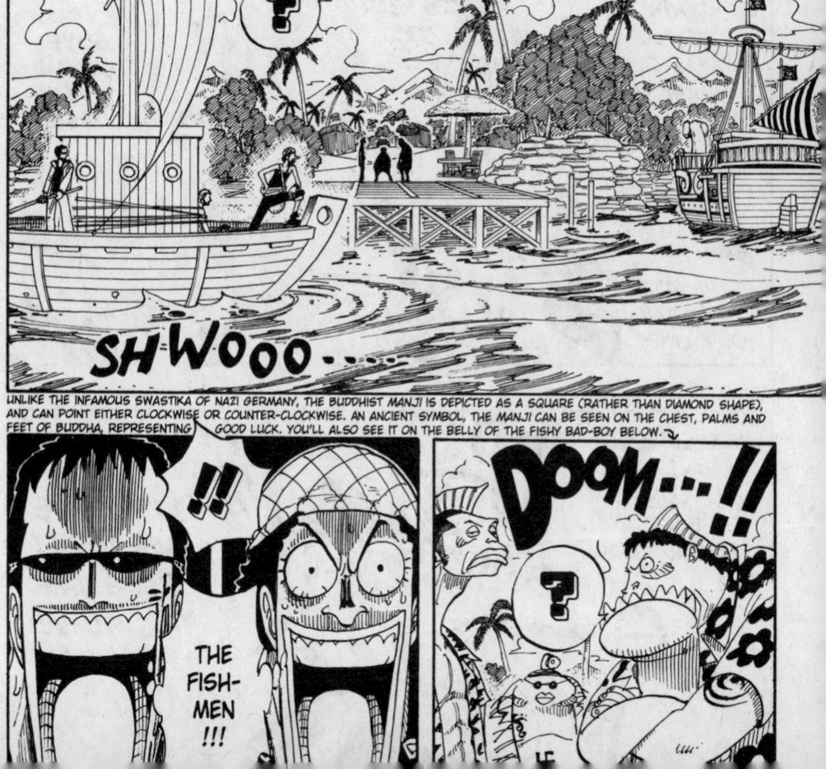
DOOM...!!
?
!!
THE FISH-MEN!!!

READ THIS WAY

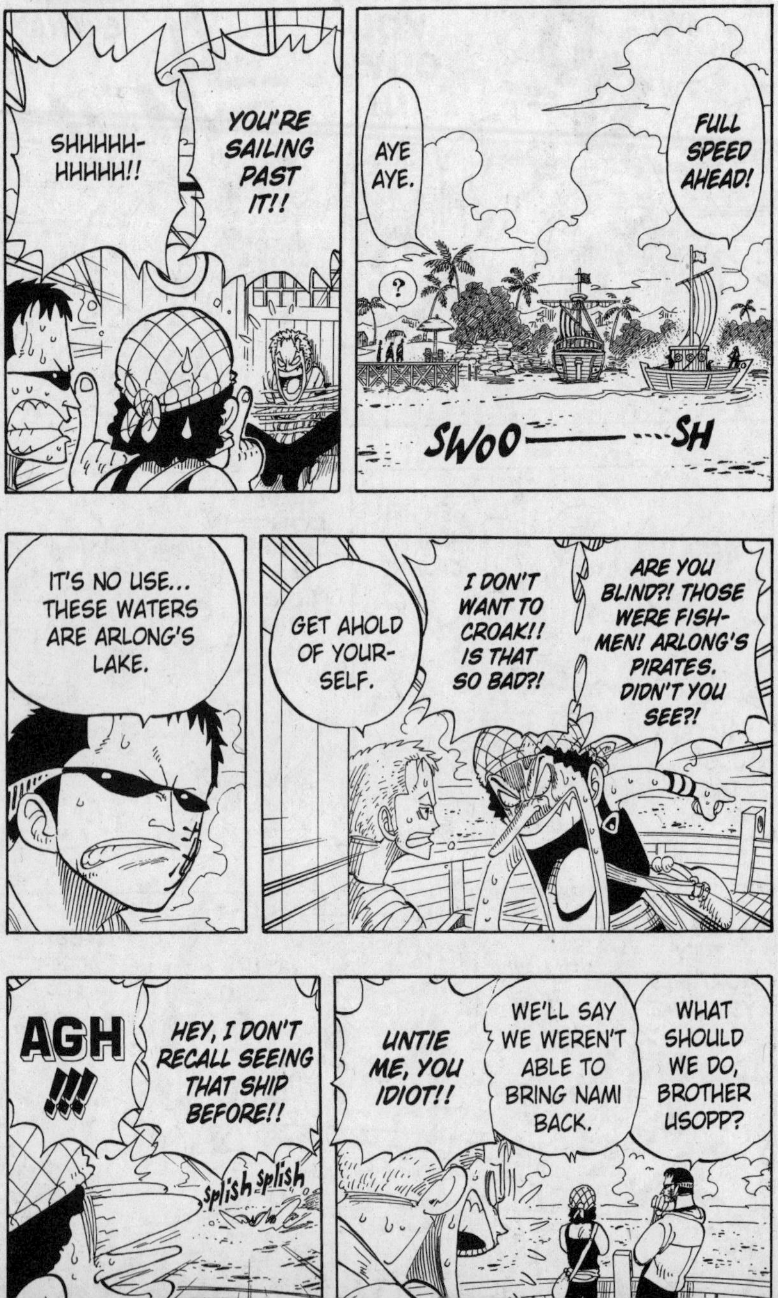
FULL SPEED AHEAD!
AYE AYE.
?
SWOO———SH
YOU'RE SAILING PAST IT!!
SHHHHH-HHHHH!!
ARE YOU BLIND?! THOSE WERE FISH-MEN! ARLONG'S PIRATES. DIDN'T YOU SEE?!
I DON'T WANT TO CROAK!! IS THAT SO BAD?!
GET AHOLD OF YOUR-SELF.
IT'S NO USE... THESE WATERS ARE ARLONG'S LAKE.
WHAT SHOULD WE DO, BROTHER USOPP?
WE'LL SAY WE WEREN'T ABLE TO BRING NAMI BACK.
UNTIE ME, YOU IDIOT!!
HEY, I DON'T RECALL SEEING THAT SHIP BEFORE!!
AGH!!!
splish splish

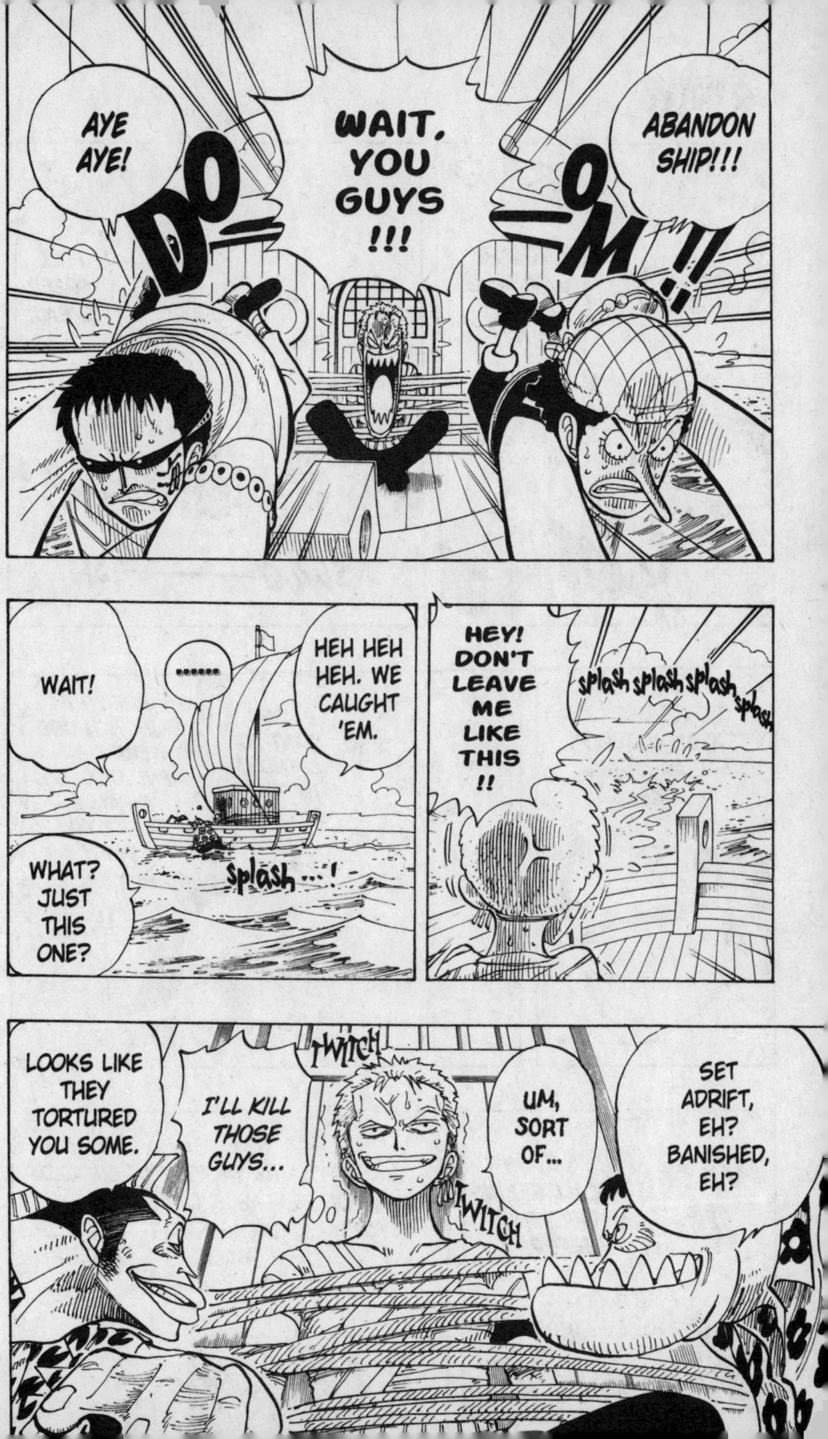
ABANDON SHIP!!!
WAIT, YOU GUYS!!!
AYE AYE!
DO—OM!!
HEY! DON'T LEAVE ME LIKE THIS!!
splash splash splash splash
HEH HEH HEH. WE CAUGHT 'EM.
......
WAIT!
splash...!
WHAT? JUST THIS ONE?
SET ADRIFT, EH? BANISHED, EH?
UM, SORT OF...
TWITCH
I'LL KILL THOSE GUYS...
TWITCH
LOOKS LIKE THEY TORTURED YOU SOME.

READ THIS WAY

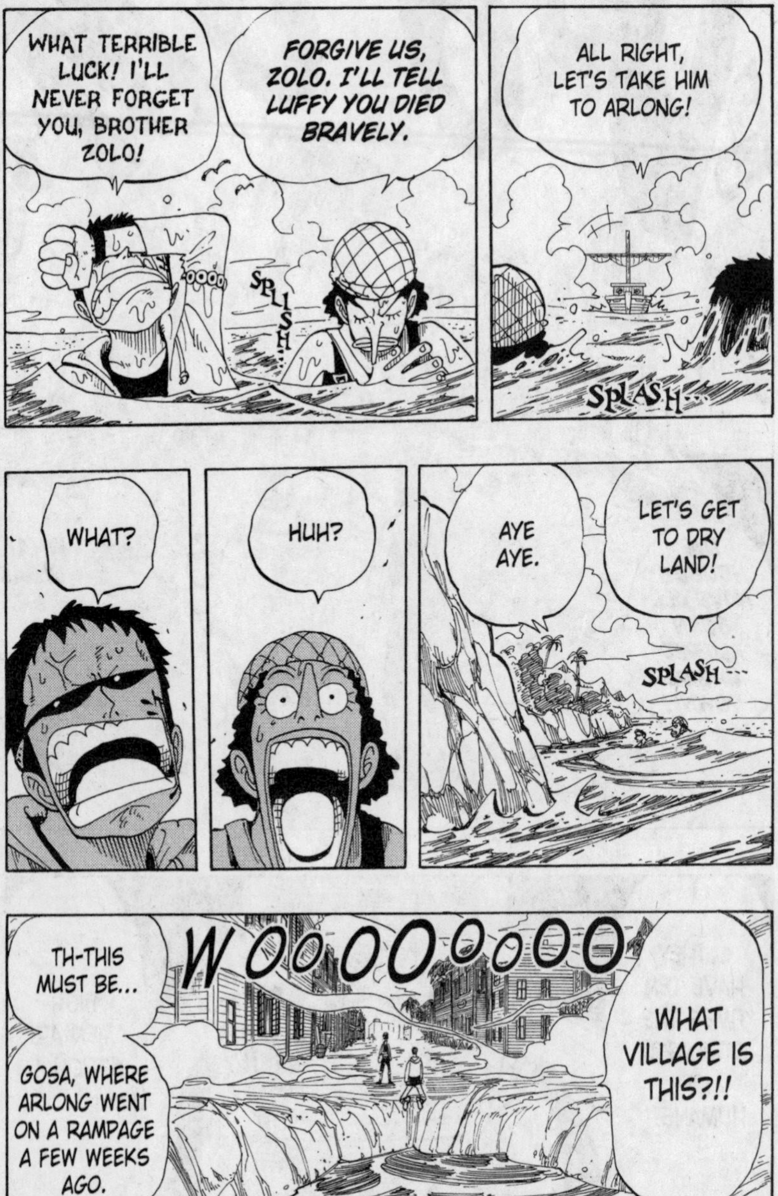
ALL RIGHT, LET'S TAKE HIM TO ARLONG!
SPLASH...
FORGIVE US, ZOLO. I'LL TELL LUFFY YOU DIED BRAVELY.
WHAT TERRIBLE LUCK! I'LL NEVER FORGET YOU, BROTHER ZOLO!
SPLISH...
LET'S GET TO DRY LAND!
AYE AYE.
SPLASH...
HUH?
WHAT?
WHAT VILLAGE IS THIS?!!
WOOOOOOOOO
TH-THIS MUST BE...
GOSA, WHERE ARLONG WENT ON A RAMPAGE A FEW WEEKS AGO.

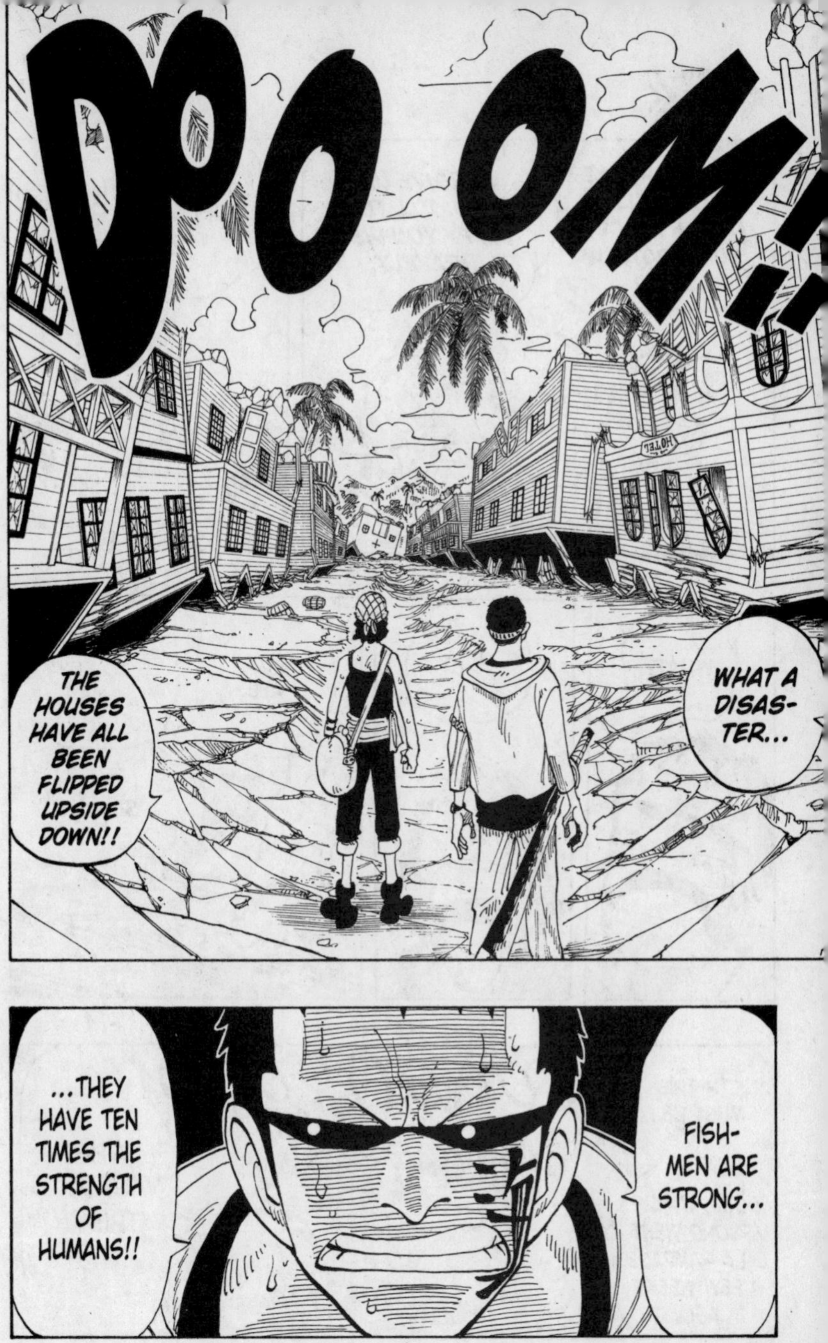
DOOOM!!
WHAT A DISASTER...
THE HOUSES HAVE ALL BEEN FLIPPED UPSIDE DOWN!!
FISH-MEN ARE STRONG...
...THEY HAVE TEN TIMES THE STRENGTH OF HUMANS!!

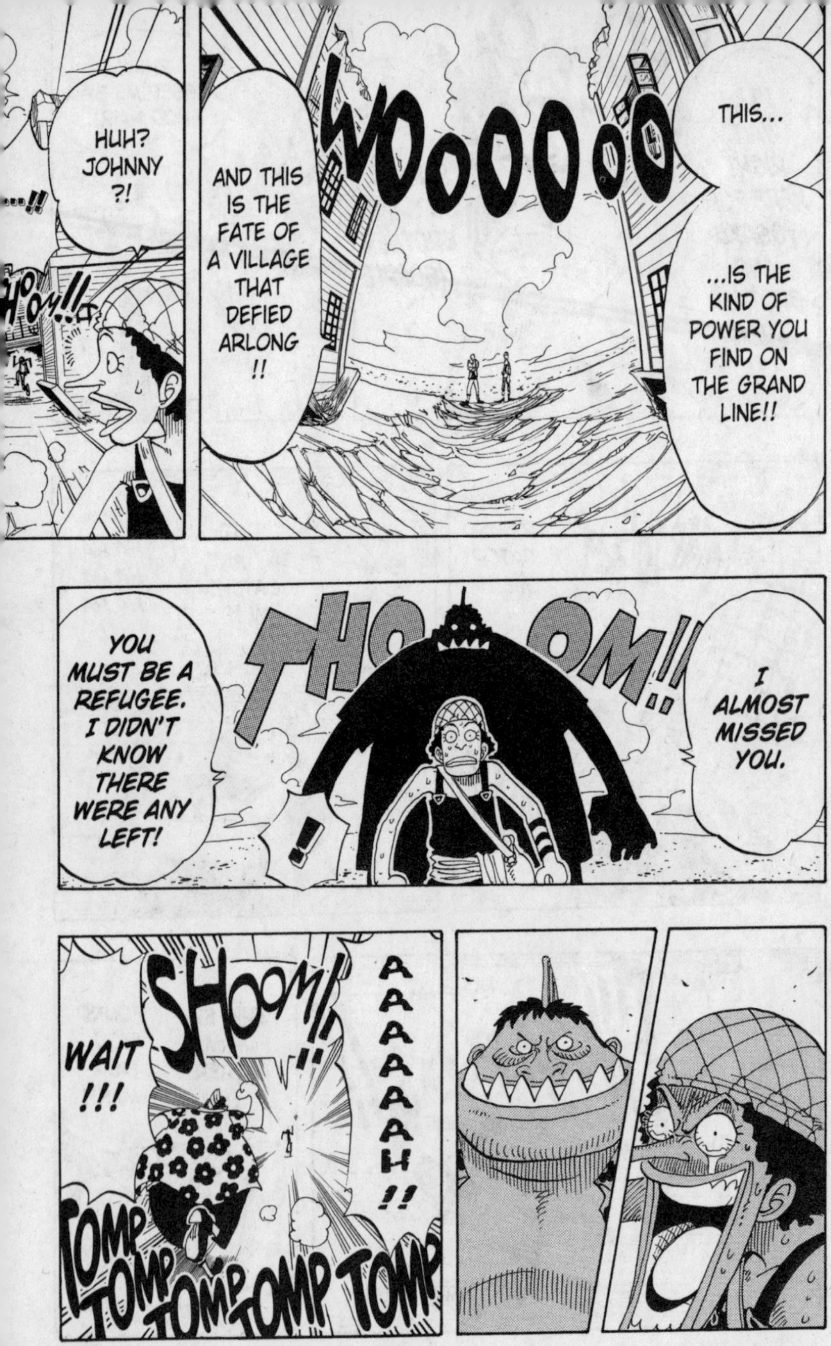
THIS...
...IS THE KIND OF POWER YOU FIND ON THE GRAND LINE!!
WOOOOOO
AND THIS IS THE FATE OF A VILLAGE THAT DEFIED ARLONG !!
HUH? JOHNNY ?!
...!!
I ALMOST MISSED YOU.
THOOM!!
YOU MUST BE A REFUGEE. I DIDN'T KNOW THERE WERE ANY LEFT!
!
AAAAAAAH !!
SHOOM!!
WAIT !!!
TOMP TOMP TOMP TOMP TOMP

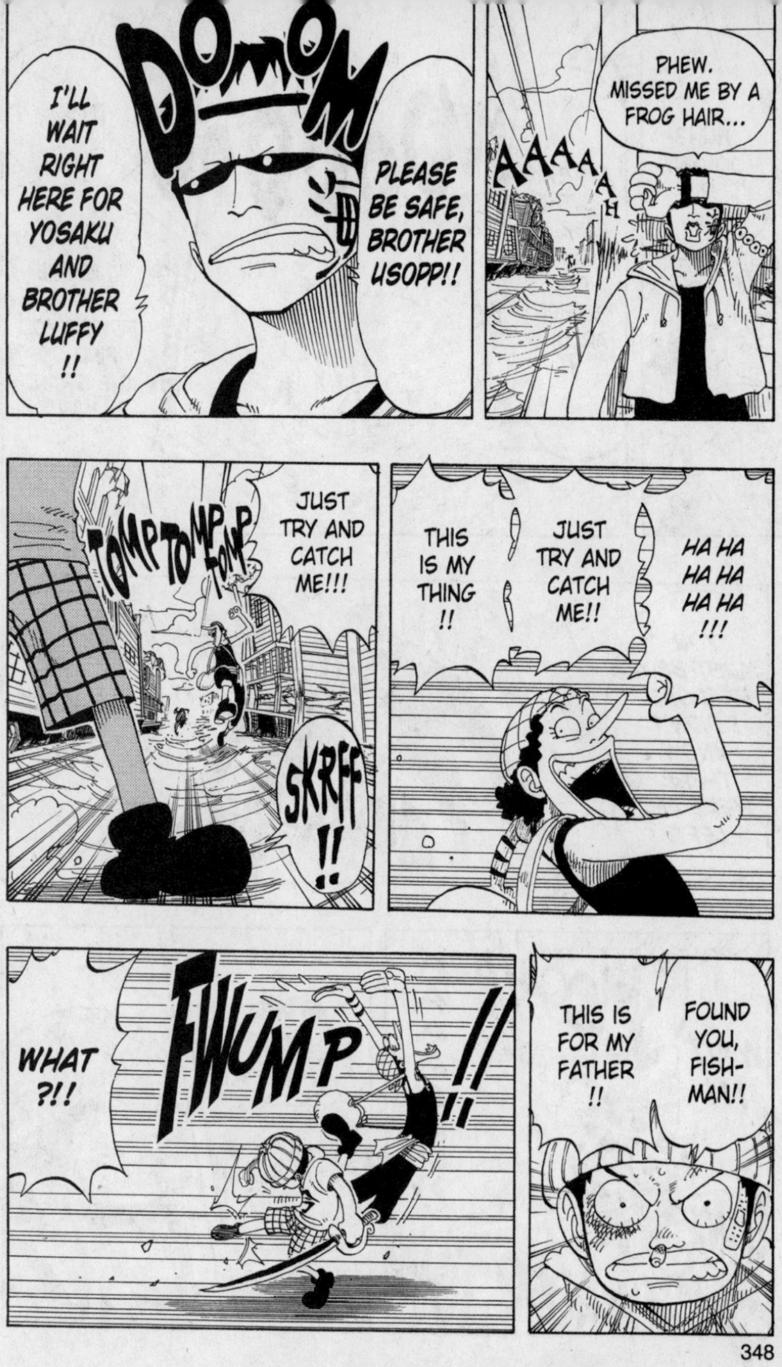
PHEW. MISSED ME BY A FROG HAIR...
AAAAAAH
DOMON
PLEASE BE SAFE, BROTHER USOPP!!
I'LL WAIT RIGHT HERE FOR YOSAKU AND BROTHER LUFFY !!
HA HA HA HA HA HA !!!
JUST TRY AND CATCH ME!!
THIS IS MY THING !!
JUST TRY AND CATCH ME!!!
TOMPTOMPTOMP
SKRFF !!
FOUND YOU, FISH-MAN!!
THIS IS FOR MY FATHER !!
FWUMP !!
WHAT ?!!

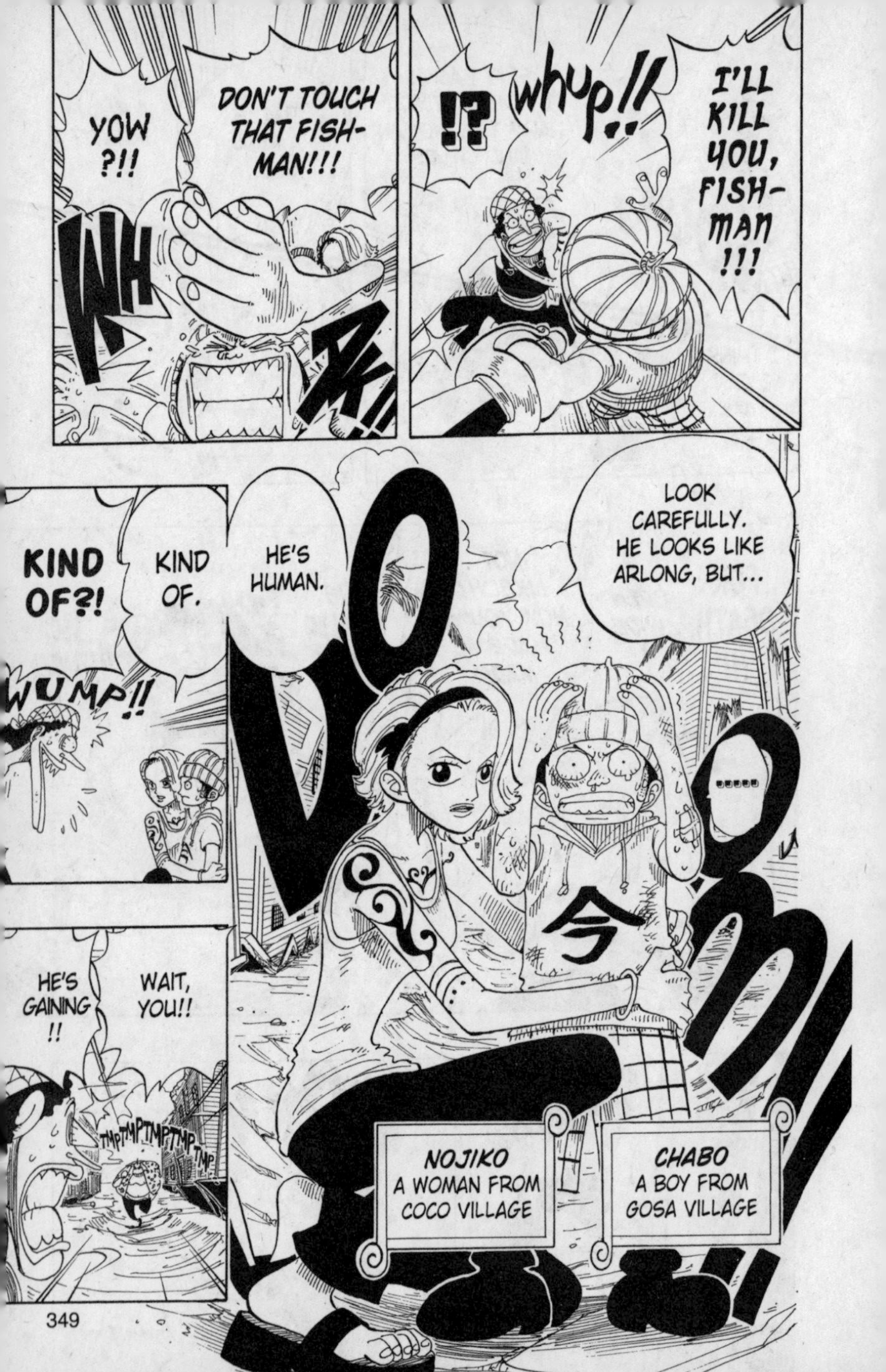
I'LL KILL YOU, FISH-MAN!!!
WHUP!!
!?
DON'T TOUCH THAT FISH-MAN!!!
YOW?!!
WHAK!!
LOOK CAREFULLY. HE LOOKS LIKE ARLONG, BUT...
HE'S HUMAN.
DOOM!!
.....
NOJIKO
A WOMAN FROM COCO VILLAGE
CHABO
A BOY FROM GOSA VILLAGE
KIND OF.
KIND OF?!
WUMP!!
WAIT, YOU!!
HE'S GAINING!!
TMPTMPTMPTMPTMP

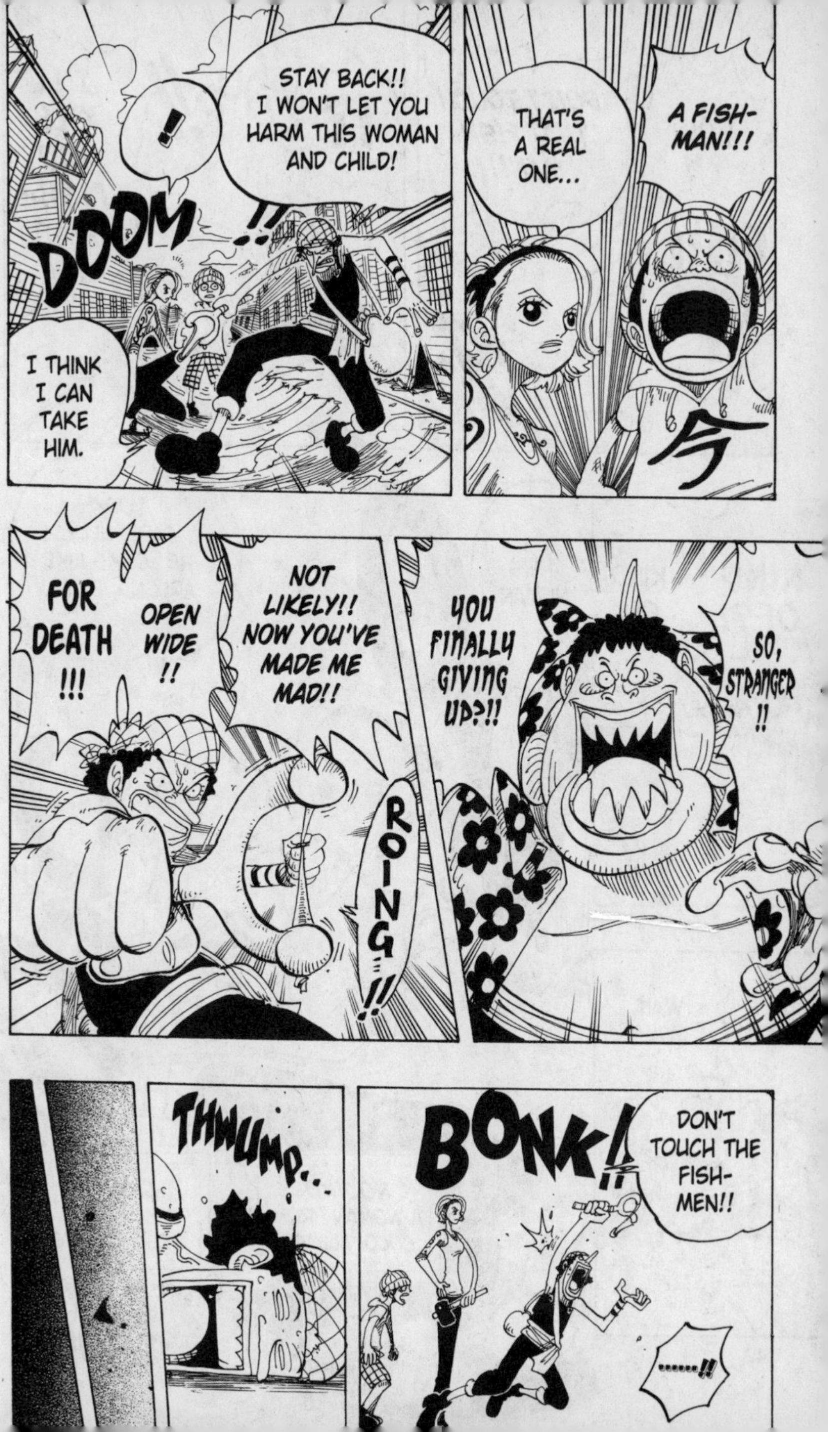
A FISH-MAN!!!
THAT'S A REAL ONE...
STAY BACK!! I WON'T LET YOU HARM THIS WOMAN AND CHILD!
!
DOOM!!
I THINK I CAN TAKE HIM.
SO, STRANGER!!
YOU FINALLY GIVING UP?!!
NOT LIKELY!! NOW YOU'VE MADE ME MAD!!
OPEN WIDE!!
FOR DEATH!!!
ROING..!!
DON'T TOUCH THE FISH-MEN!!
BONK!!
......!!
THWUMP...

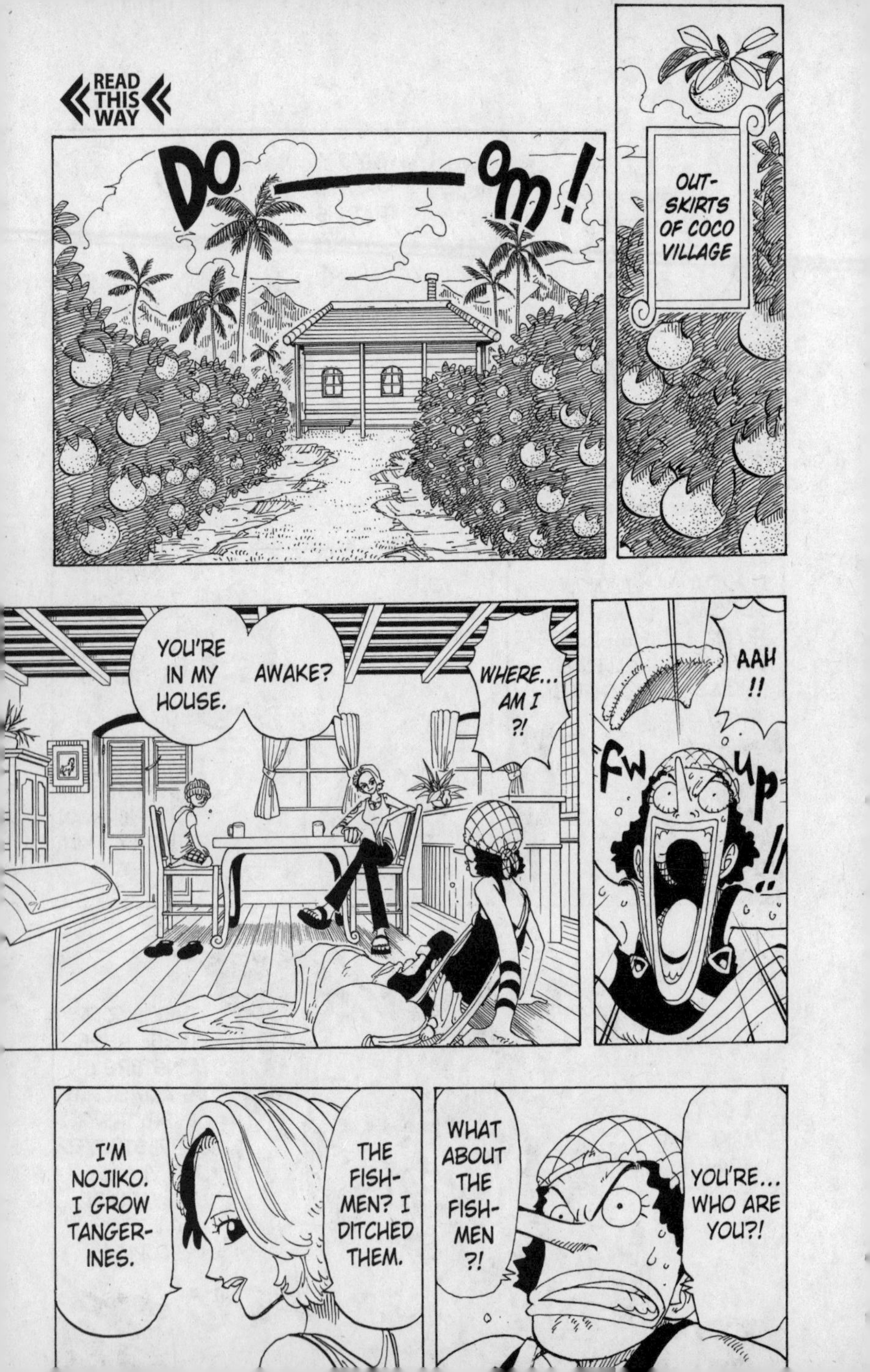

READ THIS WAY
OUT-SKIRTS OF COCO VILLAGE
DO—om!
AAH!!
Fwup!!
WHERE... AM I?!
AWAKE?
YOU'RE IN MY HOUSE.
YOU'RE... WHO ARE YOU?!
WHAT ABOUT THE FISH-MEN?!
THE FISH-MEN? I DITCHED THEM.
I'M NOJIKO. I GROW TANGER-INES.

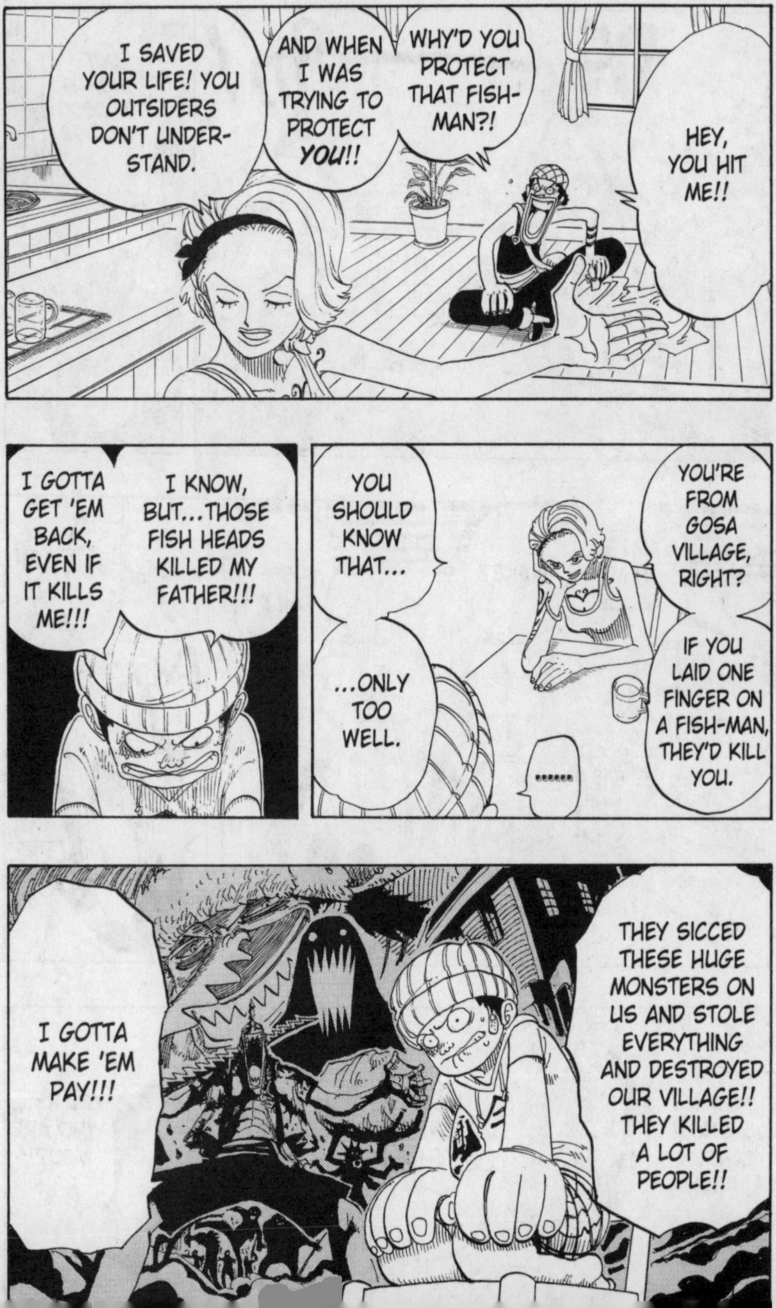
HEY, YOU HIT ME!!
WHY'D YOU PROTECT THAT FISH-MAN?!
AND WHEN I WAS TRYING TO PROTECT *YOU*!!
I SAVED YOUR LIFE! YOU OUTSIDERS DON'T UNDERSTAND.
YOU'RE FROM GOSA VILLAGE, RIGHT?
IF YOU LAID ONE FINGER ON A FISH-MAN, THEY'D KILL YOU.
......
YOU SHOULD KNOW THAT...
...ONLY TOO WELL.
I KNOW, BUT...THOSE FISH HEADS KILLED MY FATHER!!!
I GOTTA GET 'EM BACK, EVEN IF IT KILLS ME!!!
THEY SICCED THESE HUGE MONSTERS ON US AND STOLE EVERYTHING AND DESTROYED OUR VILLAGE!! THEY KILLED A LOT OF PEOPLE!!
I GOTTA MAKE 'EM PAY!!!

READ THIS WAY

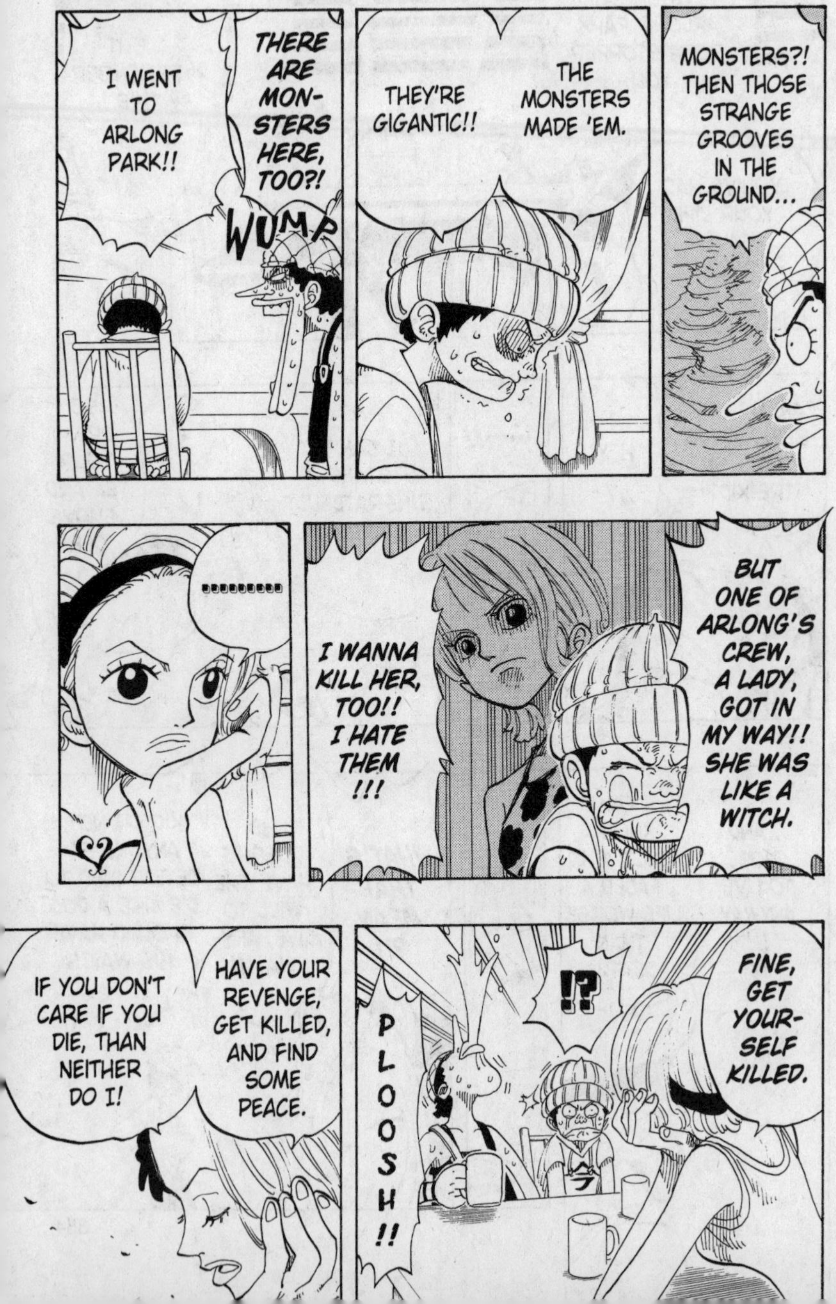
MONSTERS?! THEN THOSE STRANGE GROOVES IN THE GROUND...
THE MONSTERS MADE 'EM.
THEY'RE GIGANTIC!!
THERE ARE MONSTERS HERE, TOO?!
I WENT TO ARLONG PARK!!
WUMP
BUT ONE OF ARLONG'S CREW, A LADY, GOT IN MY WAY!! SHE WAS LIKE A WITCH.
I WANNA KILL HER, TOO!! I HATE THEM!!!
.........
FINE, GET YOURSELF KILLED.
!?
PLOOSH!!
HAVE YOUR REVENGE, GET KILLED, AND FIND SOME PEACE.
IF YOU DON'T CARE IF YOU DIE, THAN NEITHER DO I!

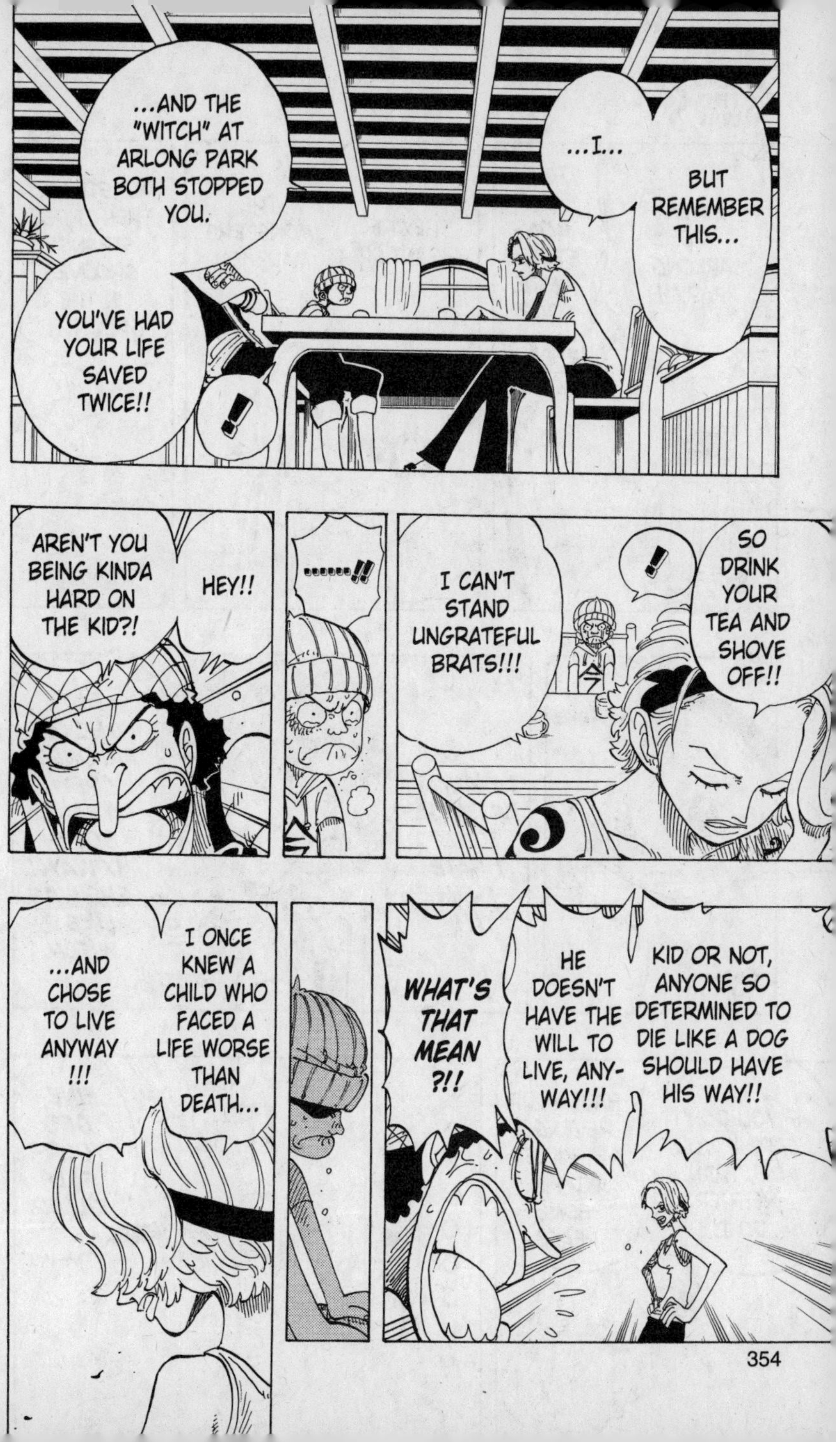
...I...
BUT REMEMBER THIS...
...AND THE "WITCH" AT ARLONG PARK BOTH STOPPED YOU.
YOU'VE HAD YOUR LIFE SAVED TWICE!!
!
SO DRINK YOUR TEA AND SHOVE OFF!!
!
I CAN'T STAND UNGRATEFUL BRATS!!!
......!!
HEY!!
AREN'T YOU BEING KINDA HARD ON THE KID?!
KID OR NOT, ANYONE SO DETERMINED TO DIE LIKE A DOG SHOULD HAVE HIS WAY!!
HE DOESN'T HAVE THE WILL TO LIVE, ANY-WAY!!!
WHAT'S THAT MEAN?!!
I ONCE KNEW A CHILD WHO FACED A LIFE WORSE THAN DEATH...
...AND CHOSE TO LIVE ANYWAY!!!

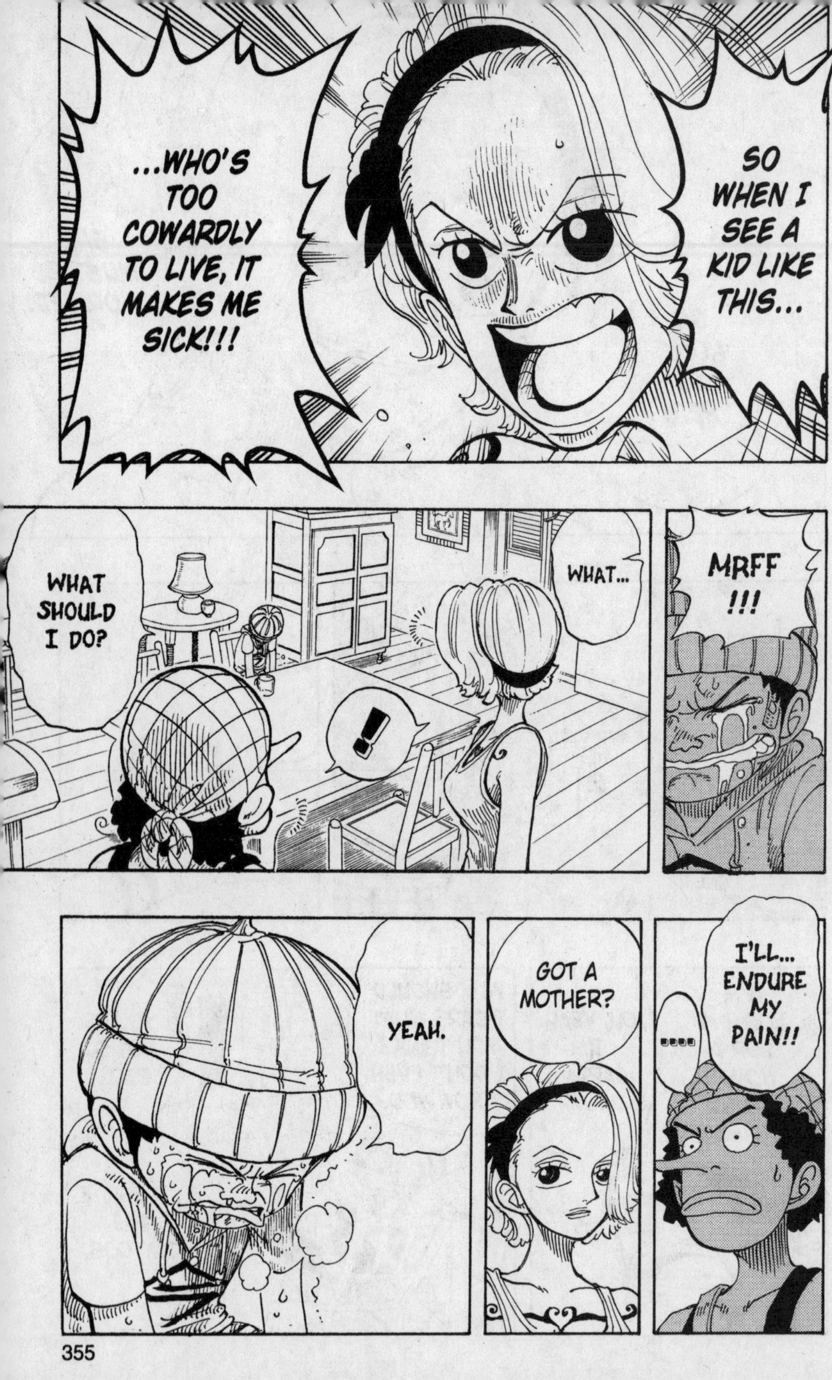
SO WHEN I SEE A KID LIKE THIS...
...WHO'S TOO COWARDLY TO LIVE, IT MAKES ME SICK!!!
MRFF !!!
WHAT...
WHAT SHOULD I DO?
!
I'LL... ENDURE MY PAIN!!
....
GOT A MOTHER?
YEAH.

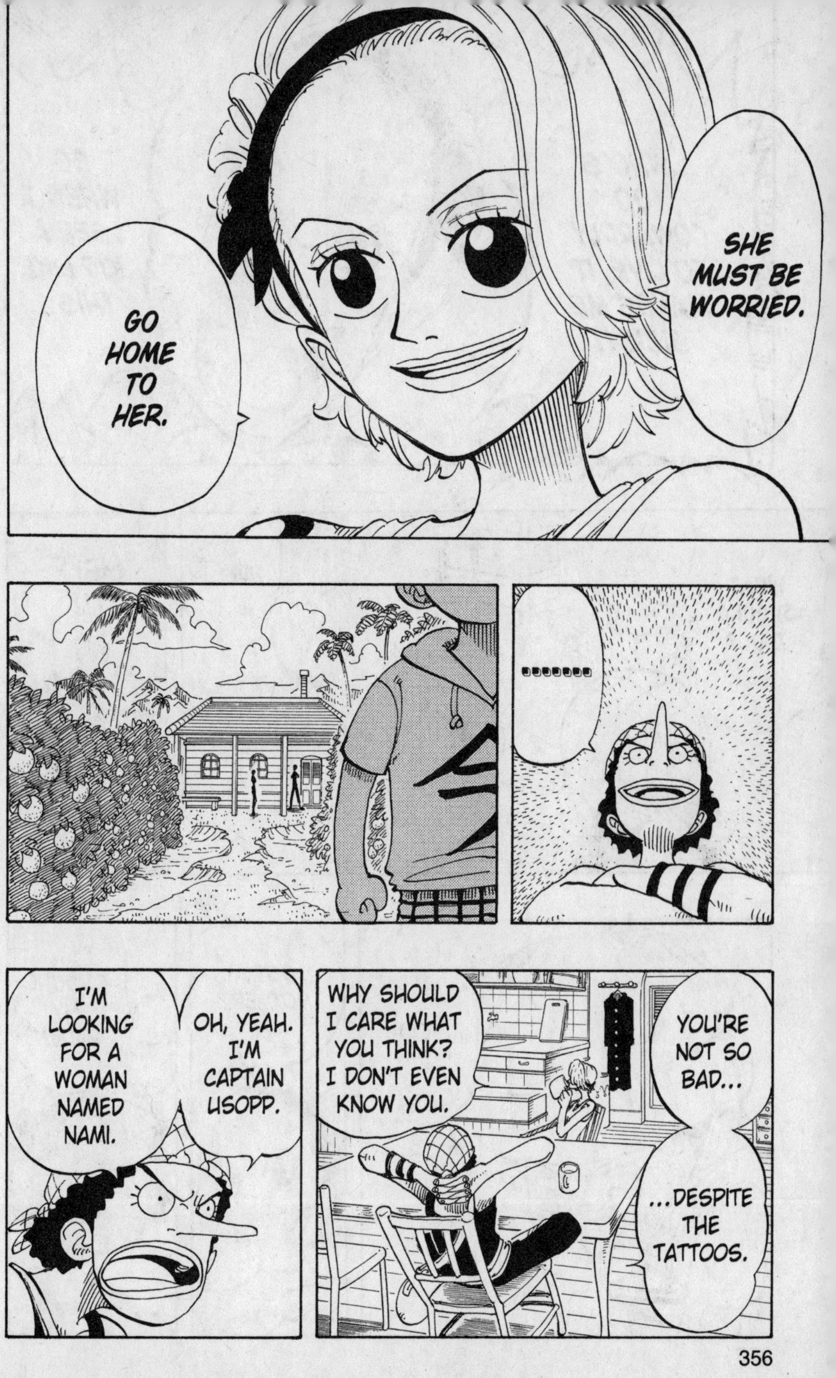
SHE MUST BE WORRIED.
GO HOME TO HER.
.......
YOU'RE NOT SO BAD...
...DESPITE THE TATTOOS.
WHY SHOULD I CARE WHAT YOU THINK? I DON'T EVEN KNOW YOU.
OH, YEAH. I'M CAPTAIN USOPP.
I'M LOOKING FOR A WOMAN NAMED NAMI.

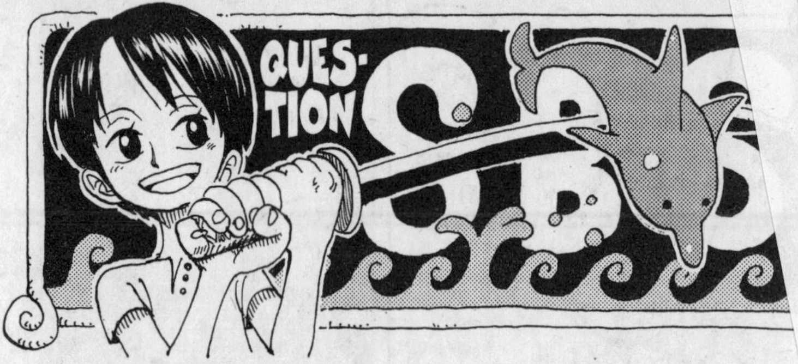
QUES-
TION
SBS

Q: What does the D in Monkey D. Luffy stand for? Is it Donburi (a bowl of rice with topping)? Daibutsu (a statue of the Great Buddha)? What?! I gotta know!!

A: I get this question all the time.
But I can't answer it...yet. For now, don't worry about it. Just read it as "D."

Q: What's the relationship between pirates and rum? In books, pirates and rum are inseparable.

A: Not just pirates and rum, but all seafarers and rum. The short story is that rum was cheap, so the British navy in pirate times switched from brandy to rum fo the sailors' grog rations, which led to hard-drinking mariners being associated with rum. By the way, the reason there was so much alcohol aboard the ships was that on long sea voyages, water would go bad.

Q: The other night, I met an inhabitant of the planet Gum-Gum. I asked him how long his arms stretched, and he said, "705 Poison Gum-Gums." How long is 705 Poison Gum-Gums?

A: You met a Gum-Gummian!! Amazing!! And lucky!! A "Poison Gum-Gum" is a unit equal to ten Gum-Gum So that's 7,050 Gum-Gums!! We're talking cosmic distances!! But be warned--of all the races in the universe, the Gum-Gummians are the most likely to say ridiculous things.

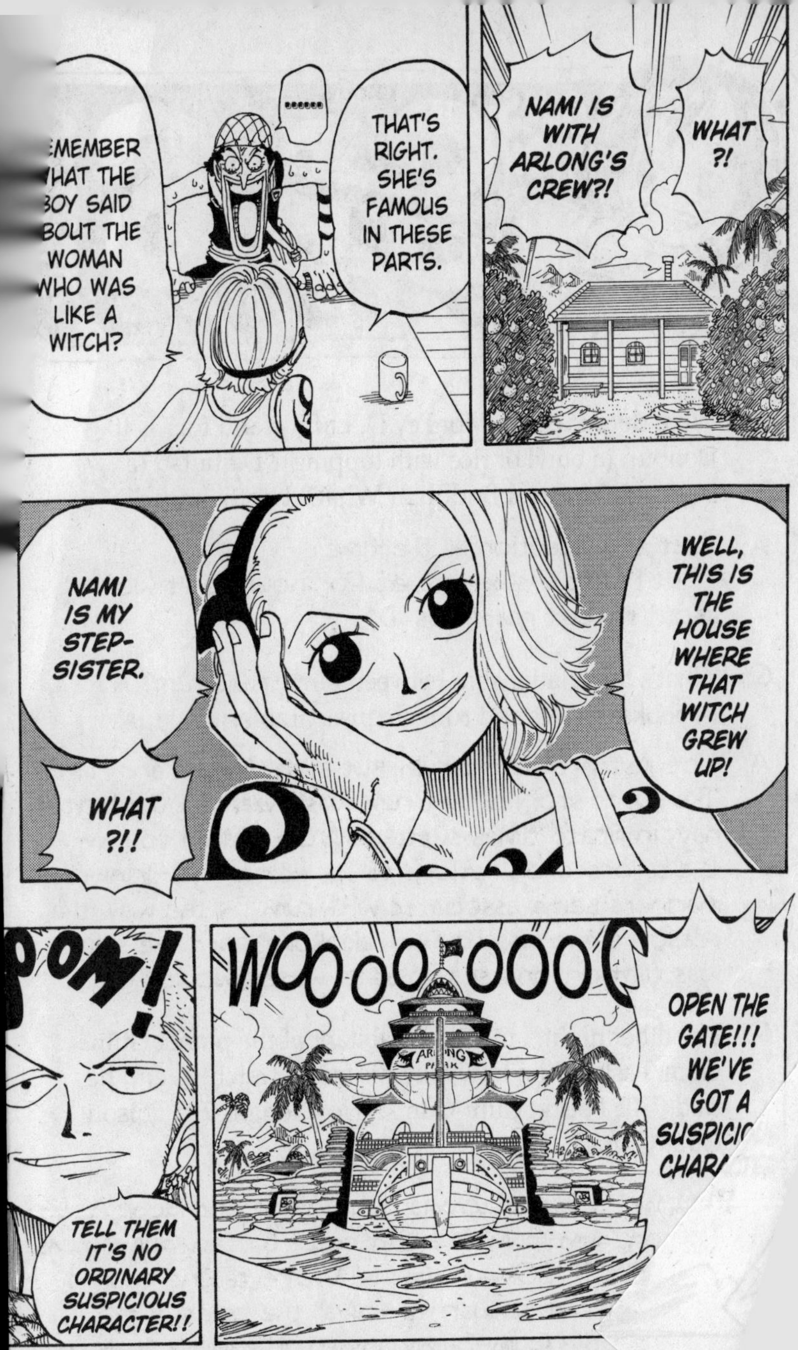
WHAT?!
NAMI IS WITH ARLONG'S CREW?!
THAT'S RIGHT. SHE'S FAMOUS IN THESE PARTS.
......
EMEMBER HAT THE BOY SAID BOUT THE WOMAN WHO WAS LIKE A WITCH?
WELL, THIS IS THE HOUSE WHERE THAT WITCH GREW UP!
NAMI IS MY STEP-SISTER.
WHAT?!!
OPEN THE GATE!!! WE'VE GOT A SUSPICIO CHARA
WOOOOOOOO
OOM!
TELL THEM IT'S NO ORDINARY SUSPICIOUS CHARACTER!!

# Chapter 71:
# LORDS OF ALL CREATION

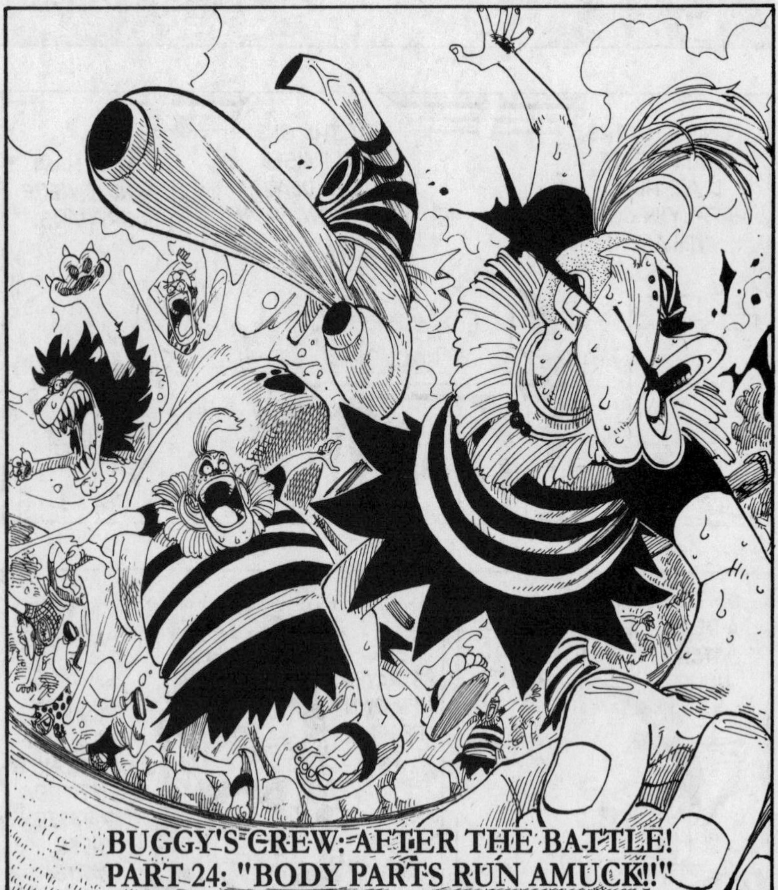
BUGGY'S CREW: AFTER THE BATTLE!
PART 24: "BODY PARTS RUN AMUCK!!"

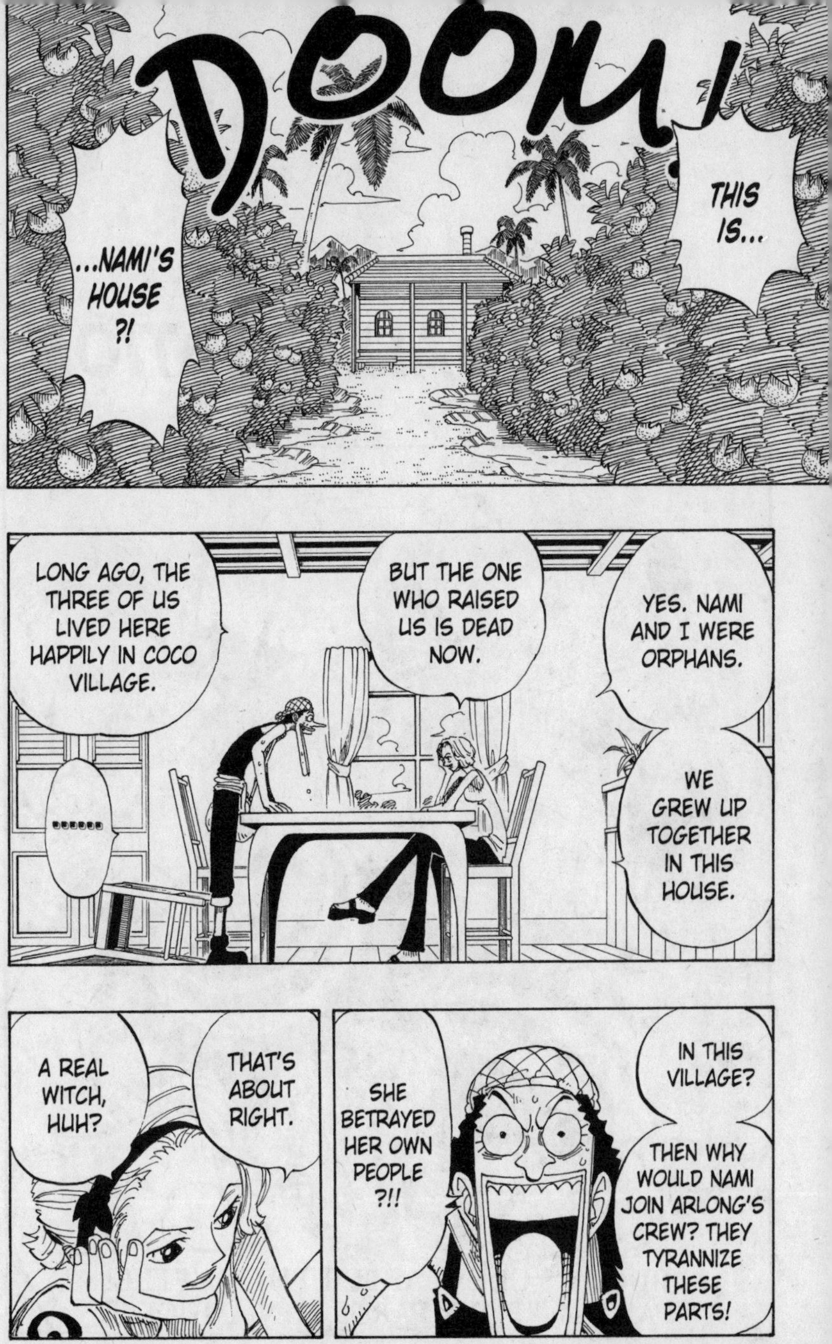
DOOM!
THIS IS...
...NAMI'S HOUSE ?!
YES. NAMI AND I WERE ORPHANS.
WE GREW UP TOGETHER IN THIS HOUSE.
BUT THE ONE WHO RAISED US IS DEAD NOW.
LONG AGO, THE THREE OF US LIVED HERE HAPPILY IN COCO VILLAGE.
.....
IN THIS VILLAGE?
THEN WHY WOULD NAMI JOIN ARLONG'S CREW? THEY TYRANNIZE THESE PARTS!
SHE BETRAYED HER OWN PEOPLE ?!!
THAT'S ABOUT RIGHT.
A REAL WITCH, HUH?

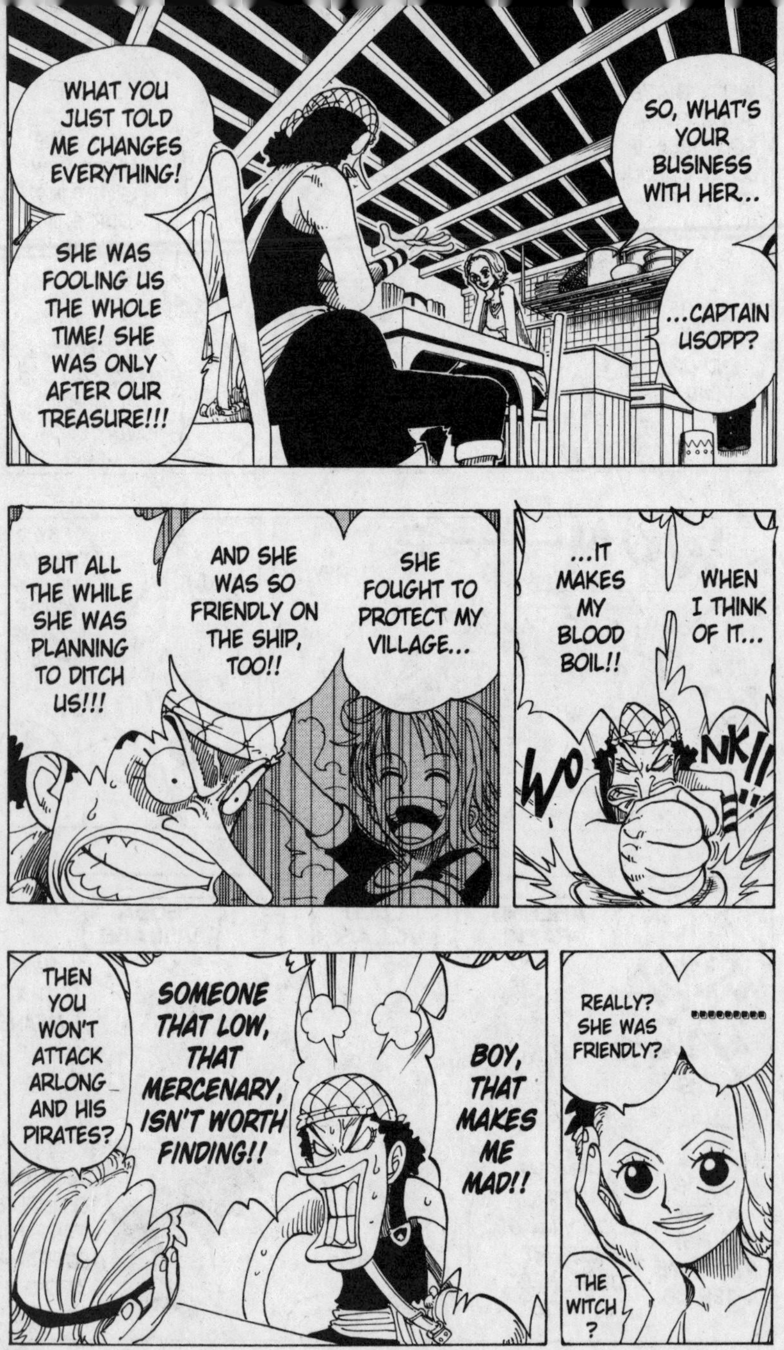
SO, WHAT'S YOUR BUSINESS WITH HER...
...CAPTAIN USOPP?
WHAT YOU JUST TOLD ME CHANGES EVERYTHING!
SHE WAS FOOLING US THE WHOLE TIME! SHE WAS ONLY AFTER OUR TREASURE!!!
WHEN I THINK OF IT...
...IT MAKES MY BLOOD BOIL!!
WO NK!!
SHE FOUGHT TO PROTECT MY VILLAGE...
AND SHE WAS SO FRIENDLY ON THE SHIP, TOO!!
BUT ALL THE WHILE SHE WAS PLANNING TO DITCH US!!!
.........
REALLY? SHE WAS FRIENDLY?
THE WITCH?
BOY, THAT MAKES ME MAD!!
SOMEONE THAT LOW, THAT MERCENARY, ISN'T WORTH FINDING!!
THEN YOU WON'T ATTACK ARLONG AND HIS PIRATES?

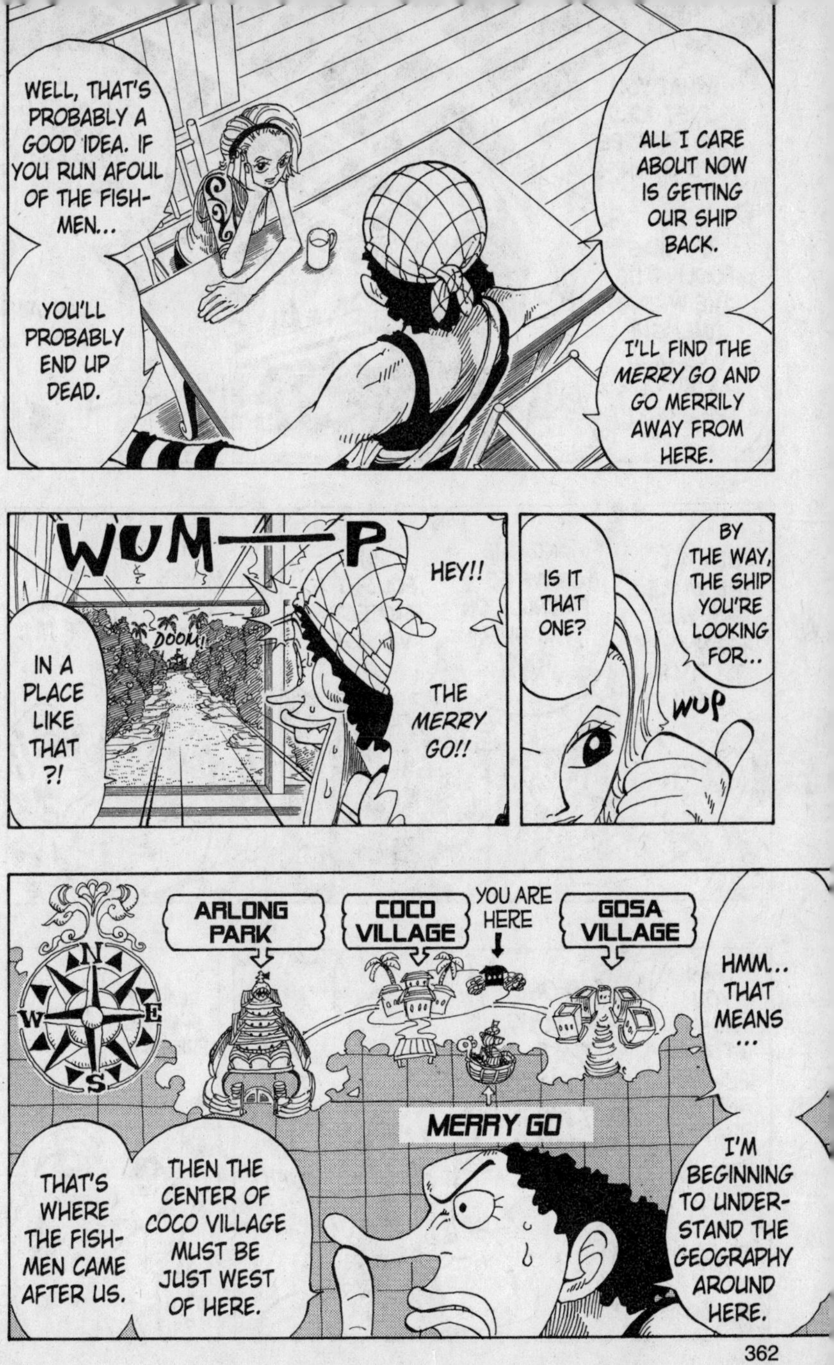
ALL I CARE ABOUT NOW IS GETTING OUR SHIP BACK.
I'LL FIND THE MERRY GO AND GO MERRILY AWAY FROM HERE.
WELL, THAT'S PROBABLY A GOOD IDEA. IF YOU RUN AFOUL OF THE FISH-MEN...
YOU'LL PROBABLY END UP DEAD.
BY THE WAY, THE SHIP YOU'RE LOOKING FOR...
IS IT THAT ONE?
WUP
WUM—P
HEY!!
THE MERRY GO!!
DOOM!
IN A PLACE LIKE THAT ?!
HMM... THAT MEANS...
GOSA VILLAGE
YOU ARE HERE
COCO VILLAGE
ARLONG PARK
N
E
W
S
MERRY GO
I'M BEGINNING TO UNDER-STAND THE GEOGRAPHY AROUND HERE.
THEN THE CENTER OF COCO VILLAGE MUST BE JUST WEST OF HERE.
THAT'S WHERE THE FISH-MEN CAME AFTER US.

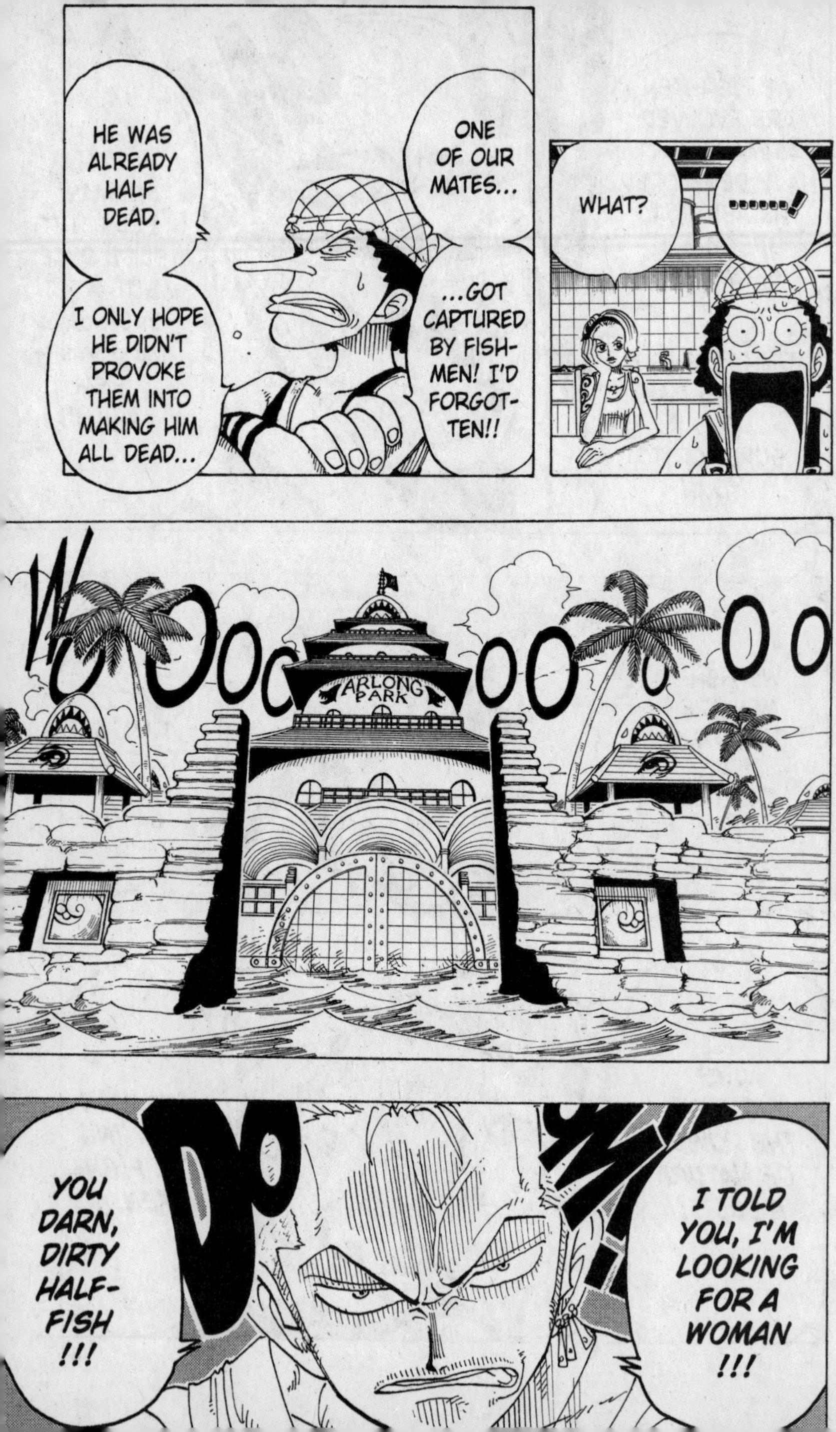
......!
WHAT?
ONE OF OUR MATES...
...GOT CAPTURED BY FISH-MEN! I'D FORGOT-TEN!!
HE WAS ALREADY HALF DEAD.
I ONLY HOPE HE DIDN'T PROVOKE THEM INTO MAKING HIM ALL DEAD...
WOOOOOOOOOO
ARLONG PARK
I TOLD YOU, I'M LOOKING FOR A WOMAN !!!
YOU DARN, DIRTY HALF-FISH !!!

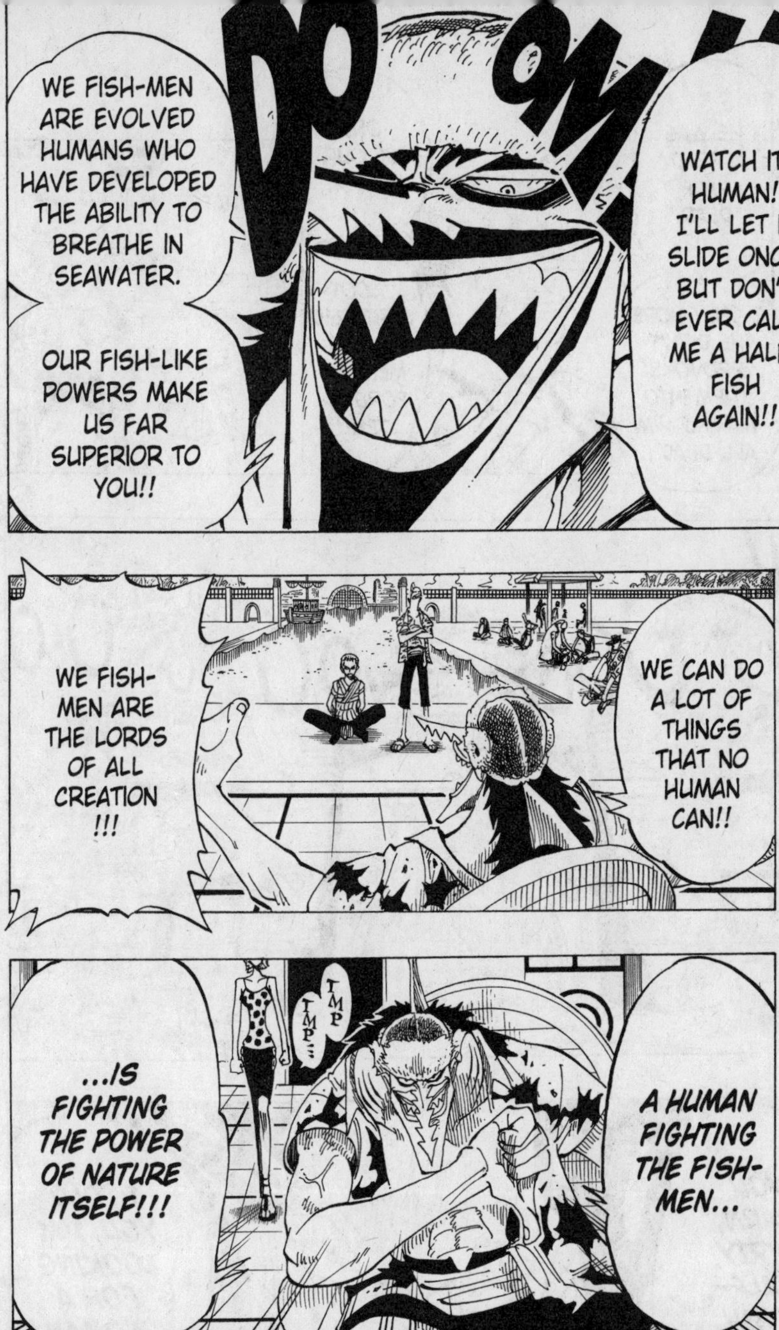
DOOM
WATCH IT, HUMAN! I'LL LET IT SLIDE ONCE, BUT DON'T EVER CALL ME A HALF-FISH AGAIN!!
WE FISH-MEN ARE EVOLVED HUMANS WHO HAVE DEVELOPED THE ABILITY TO BREATHE IN SEAWATER.
OUR FISH-LIKE POWERS MAKE US FAR SUPERIOR TO YOU!!
WE CAN DO A LOT OF THINGS THAT NO HUMAN CAN!!
WE FISH-MEN ARE THE LORDS OF ALL CREATION !!!
A HUMAN FIGHTING THE FISH-MEN...
TMP TMP...
...IS FIGHTING THE POWER OF NATURE ITSELF!!!

READ THIS WAY

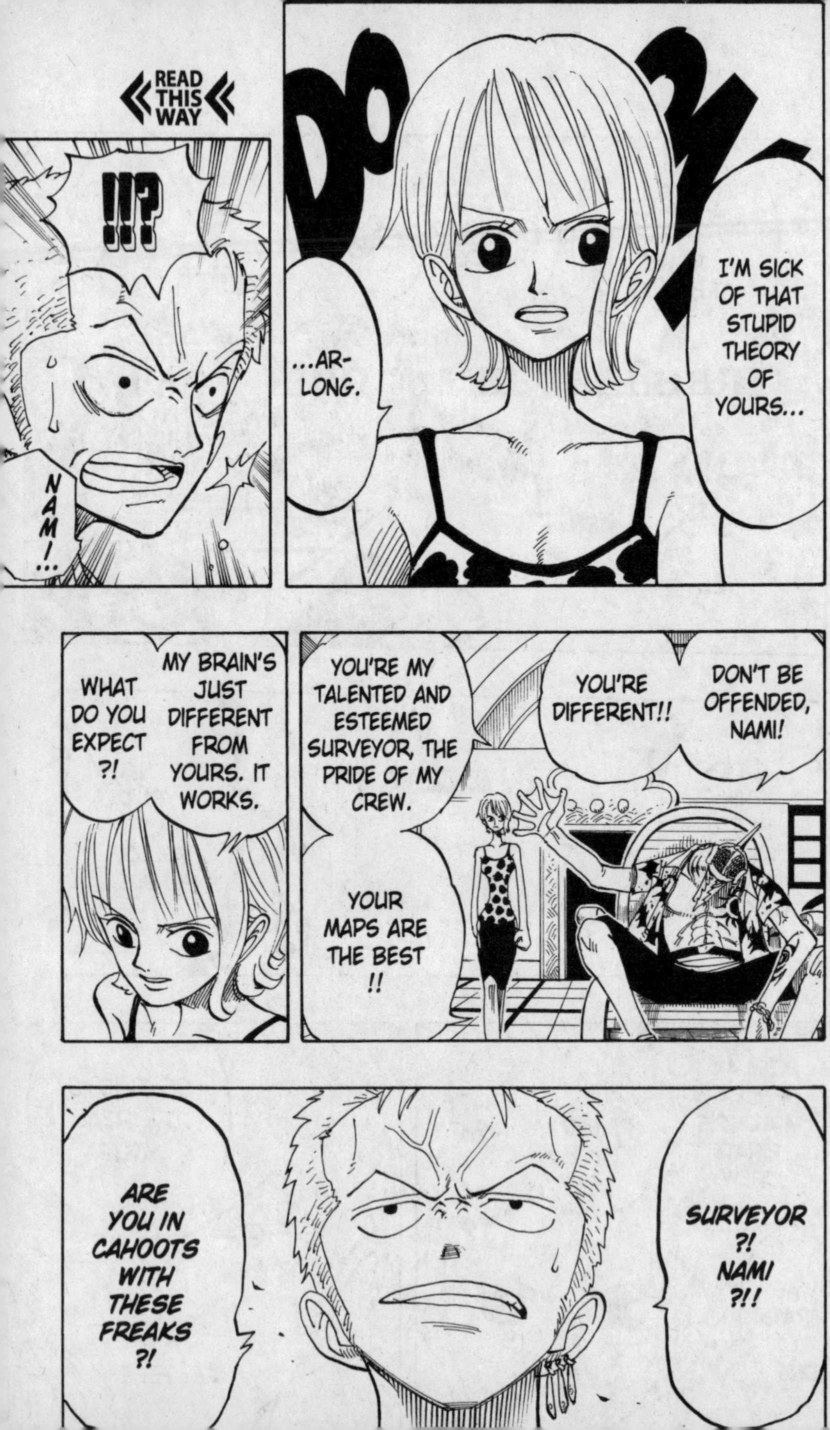
I'M SICK OF THAT STUPID THEORY OF YOURS...
...AR-LONG.
!!?
NAMI...!
DON'T BE OFFENDED, NAMI!
YOU'RE DIFFERENT!!
YOU'RE MY TALENTED AND ESTEEMED SURVEYOR, THE PRIDE OF MY CREW.
YOUR MAPS ARE THE BEST!!
MY BRAIN'S JUST DIFFERENT FROM YOURS. IT WORKS.
WHAT DO YOU EXPECT?!
SURVEYOR?! NAMI?!!
ARE YOU IN CAHOOTS WITH THESE FREAKS?!

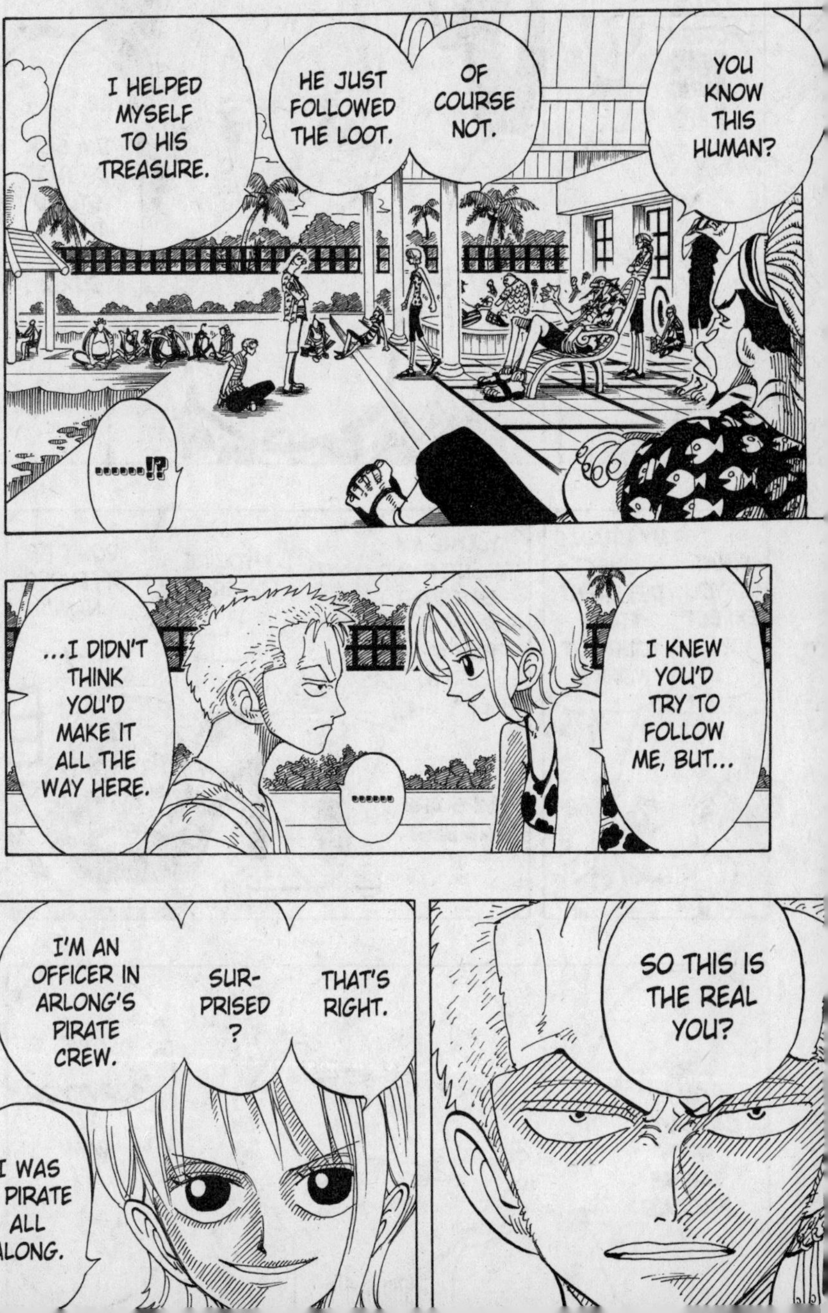
YOU KNOW THIS HUMAN?
OF COURSE NOT.
HE JUST FOLLOWED THE LOOT.
I HELPED MYSELF TO HIS TREASURE.
......!?
I KNEW YOU'D TRY TO FOLLOW ME, BUT...
......
...I DIDN'T THINK YOU'D MAKE IT ALL THE WAY HERE.
SO THIS IS THE REAL YOU?
THAT'S RIGHT.
SUR-PRISED?
I'M AN OFFICER IN ARLONG'S PIRATE CREW.
I WAS A PIRATE ALL ALONG.

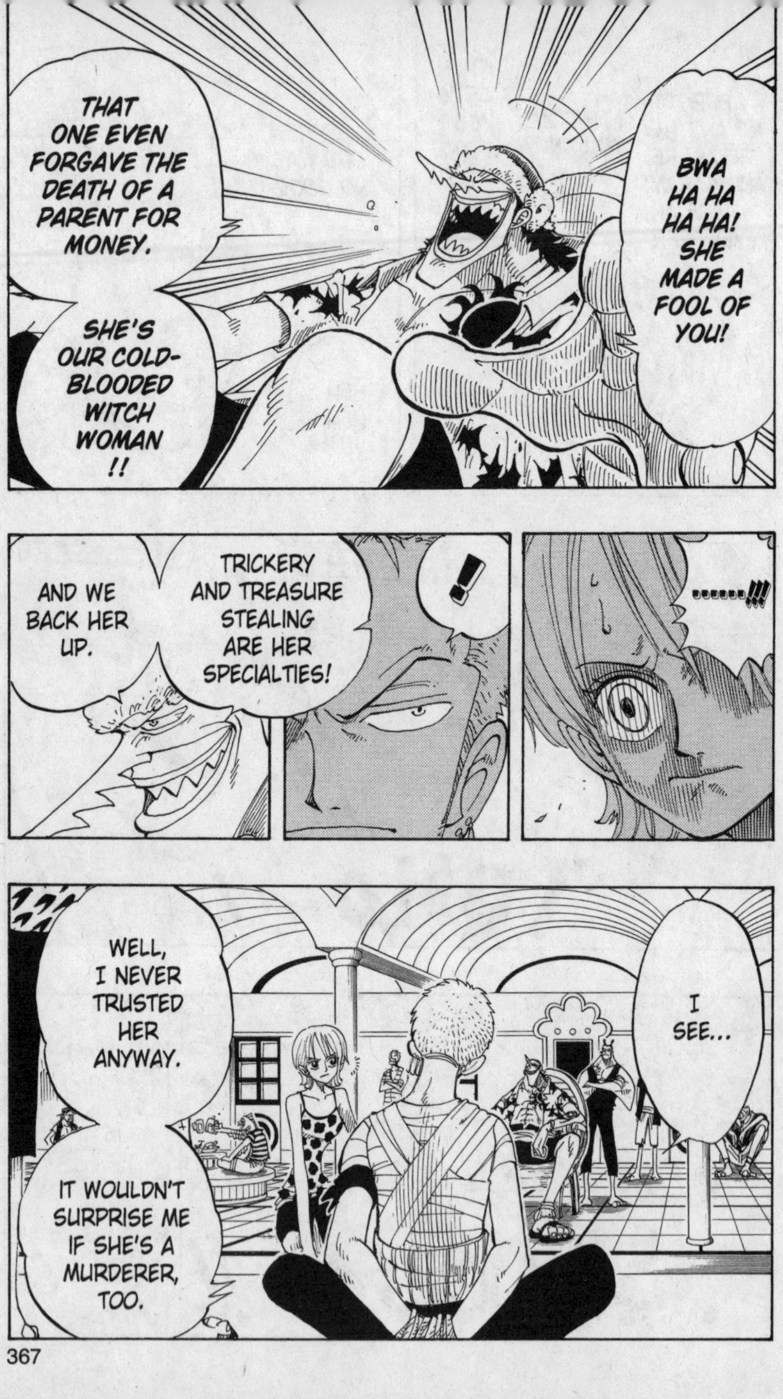
BWA HA HA HA HA! SHE MADE A FOOL OF YOU!
THAT ONE EVEN FORGAVE THE DEATH OF A PARENT FOR MONEY.
SHE'S OUR COLD-BLOODED WITCH WOMAN !!
......!!!
!
TRICKERY AND TREASURE STEALING ARE HER SPECIALTIES!
AND WE BACK HER UP.
I SEE...
WELL, I NEVER TRUSTED HER ANYWAY.
IT WOULDN'T SURPRISE ME IF SHE'S A MURDERER, TOO.

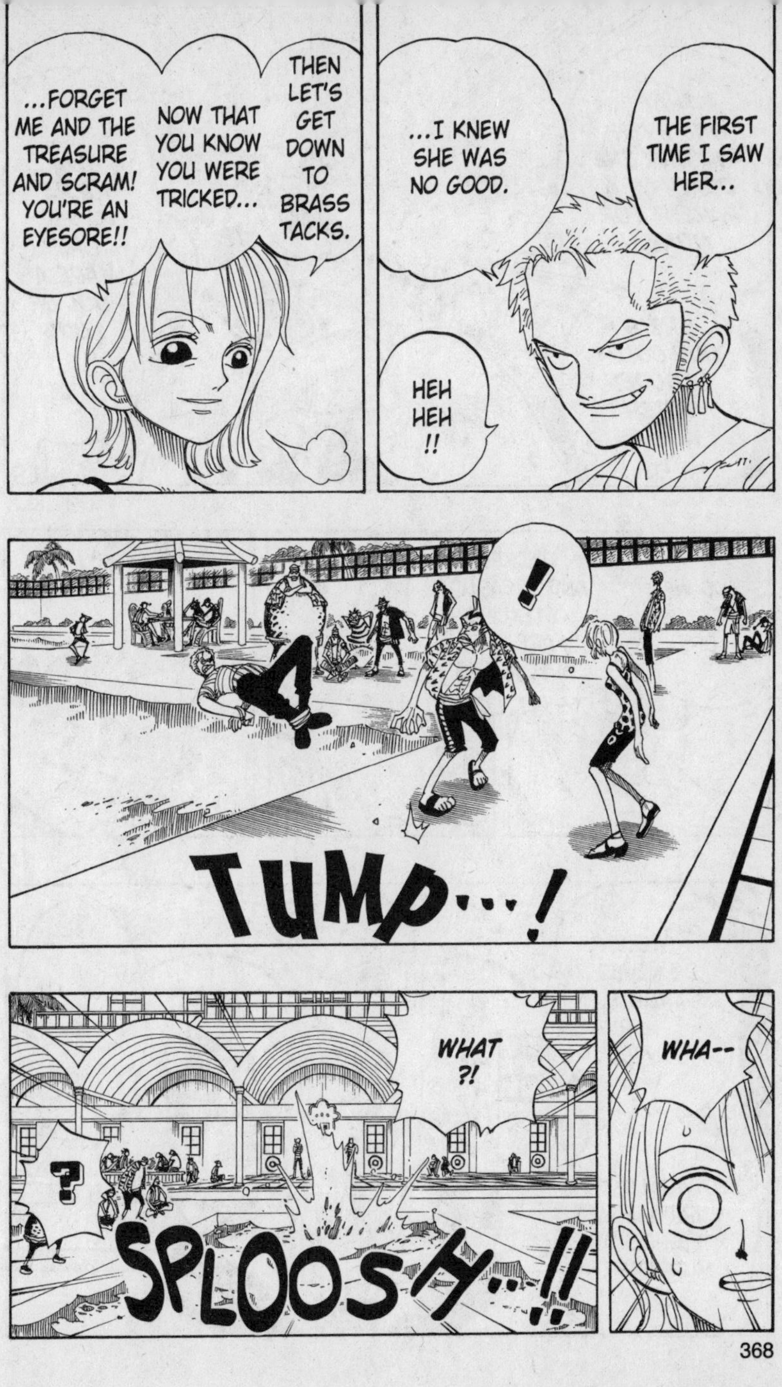
THE FIRST TIME I SAW HER..
...I KNEW SHE WAS NO GOOD.
HEH HEH !!
THEN LET'S GET DOWN TO BRASS TACKS.
NOW THAT YOU KNOW YOU WERE TRICKED...
...FORGET ME AND THE TREASURE AND SCRAM! YOU'RE AN EYESORE!!
!
TUMP...!
WHA--
WHAT ?!
?
SPLOOSH..!!

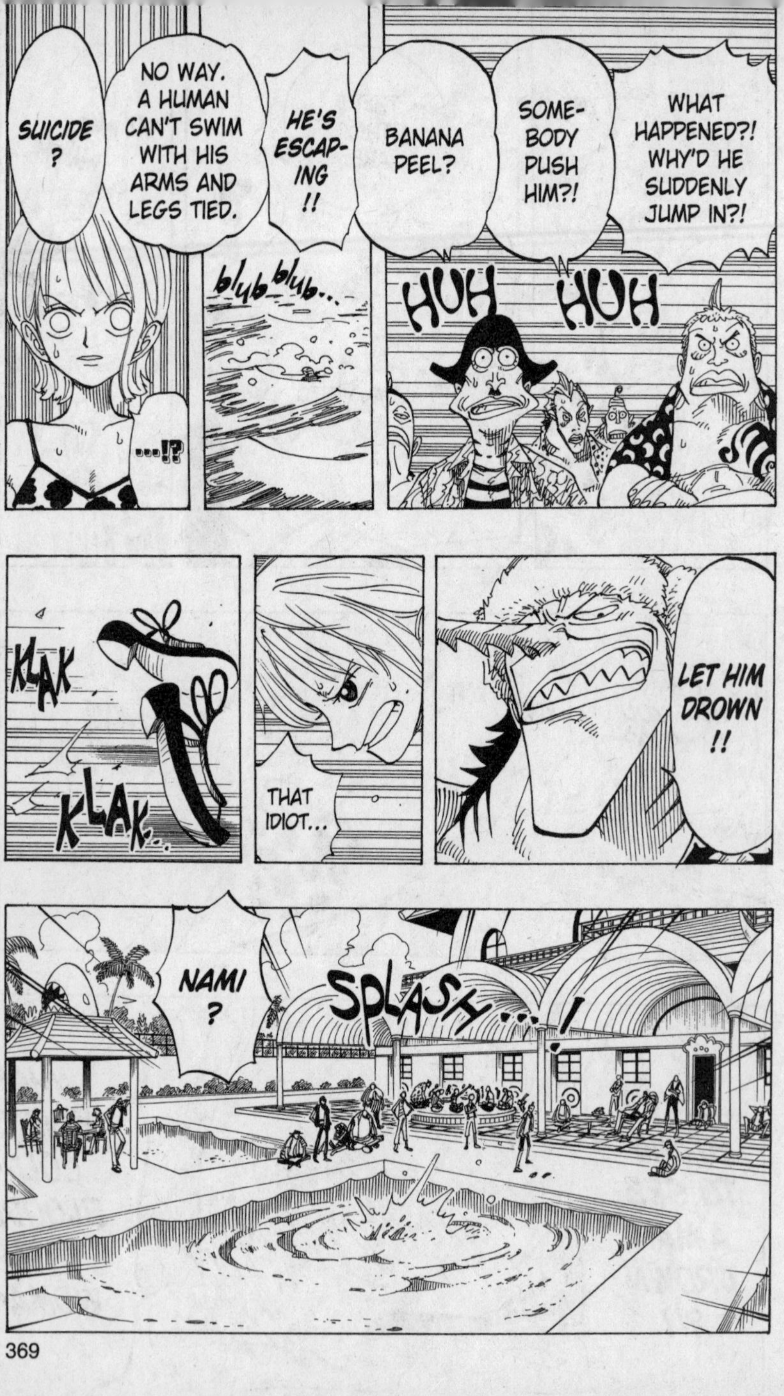
WHAT HAPPENED?! WHY'D HE SUDDENLY JUMP IN?!
SOME-BODY PUSH HIM?!
BANANA PEEL?
HUH HUH
HE'S ESCAP-ING !!
blub blub...
NO WAY. A HUMAN CAN'T SWIM WITH HIS ARMS AND LEGS TIED.
SUICIDE ?
...!?
LET HIM DROWN !!
THAT IDIOT...
KLAK KLAK..
NAMI ?
SPLASH...!

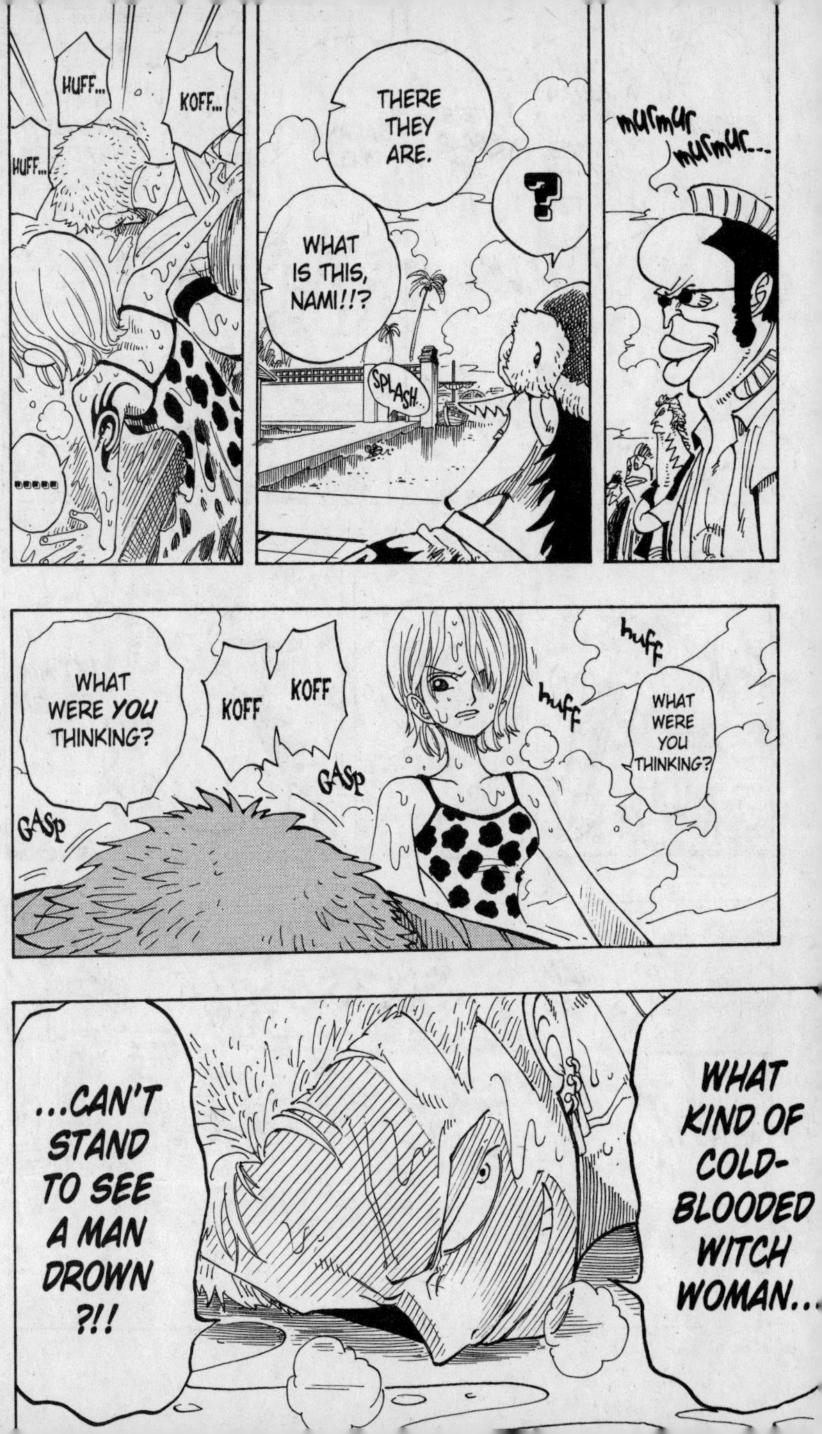
MURMUR MURMUR...
THERE THEY ARE.
?
WHAT IS THIS, NAMI!!?
SPLASH...
KOFF...
HUFF...
HUFF...
......
HUFF
HUFF
WHAT WERE YOU THINKING?
KOFF
KOFF
GASP
WHAT WERE YOU THINKING?
GASP
WHAT KIND OF COLD-BLOODED WITCH WOMAN...
...CAN'T STAND TO SEE A MAN DROWN?!!

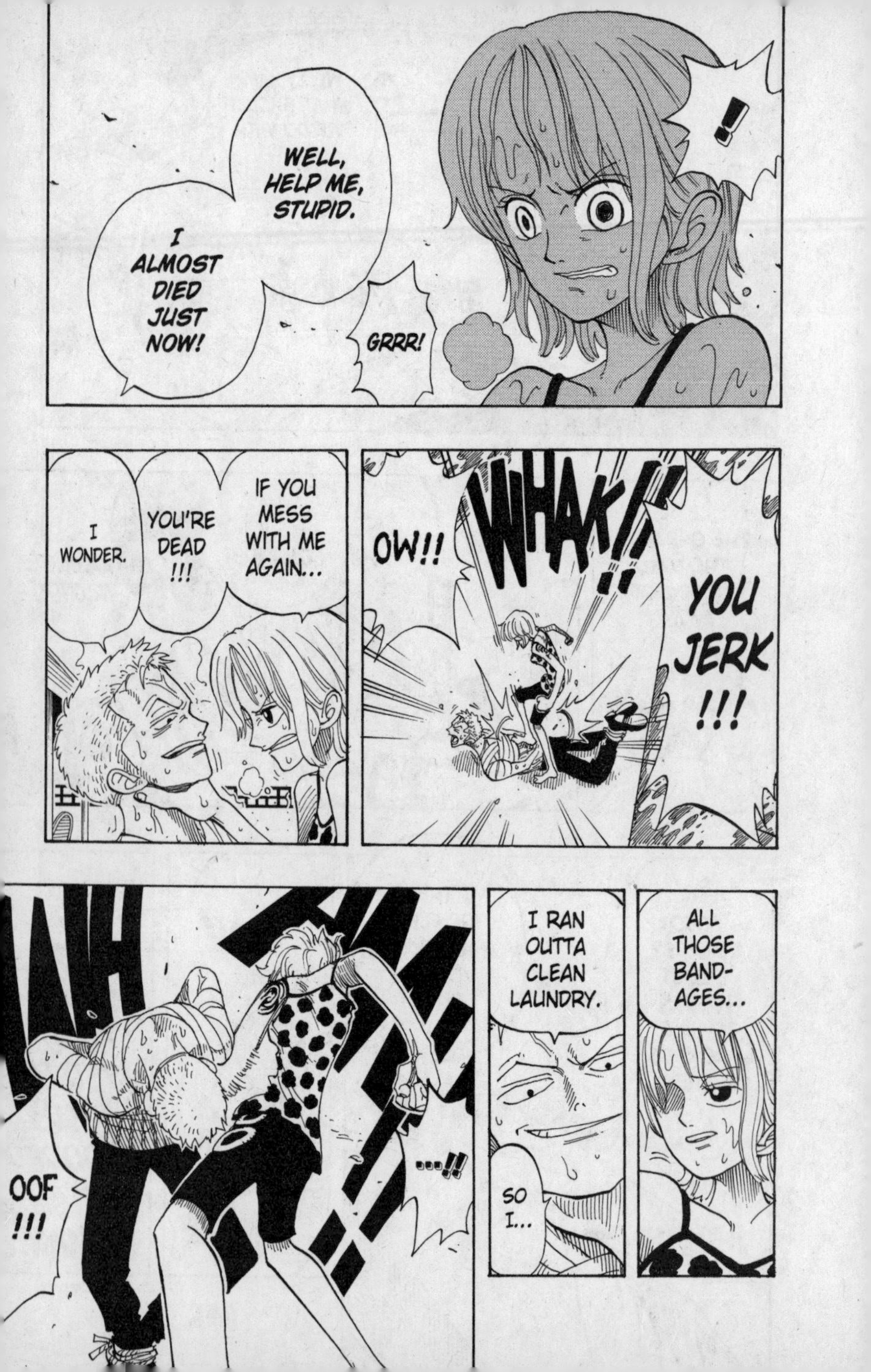
!
WELL, HELP ME, STUPID.
I ALMOST DIED JUST NOW!
GRRR!
WHAK!!
YOU JERK!!!
OW!!
IF YOU MESS WITH ME AGAIN...
YOU'RE DEAD!!!
I WONDER.
ALL THOSE BAND-AGES...
I RAN OUTTA CLEAN LAUNDRY.
SO I...
...!!
OOF!!!

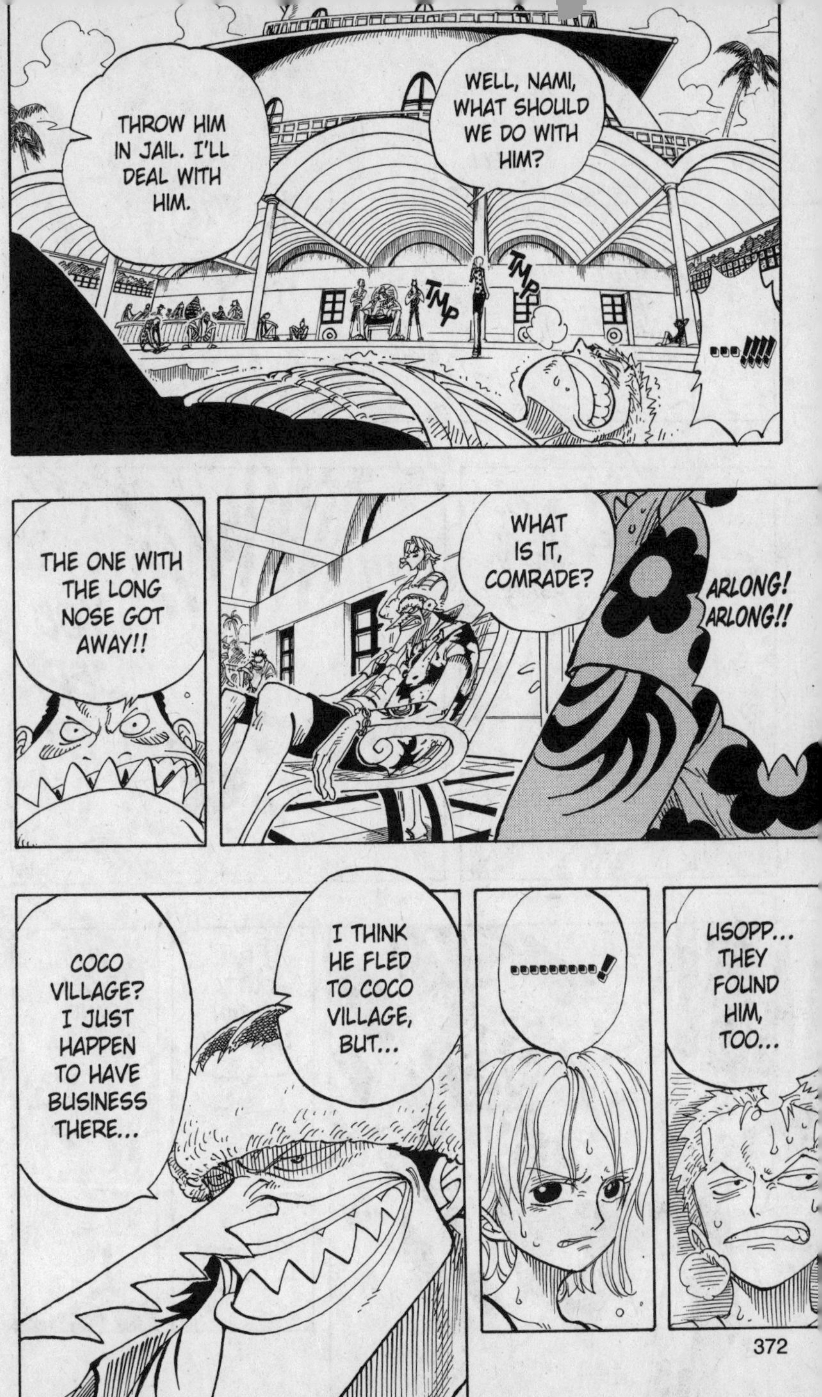
WELL, NAMI, WHAT SHOULD WE DO WITH HIM?
THROW HIM IN JAIL. I'LL DEAL WITH HIM.
TMP
TMP
...!!!!
ARLONG! ARLONG!!
WHAT IS IT, COMRADE?
THE ONE WITH THE LONG NOSE GOT AWAY!!
USOPP... THEY FOUND HIM, TOO...
..........!
I THINK HE FLED TO COCO VILLAGE, BUT...
COCO VILLAGE? I JUST HAPPEN TO HAVE BUSINESS THERE...

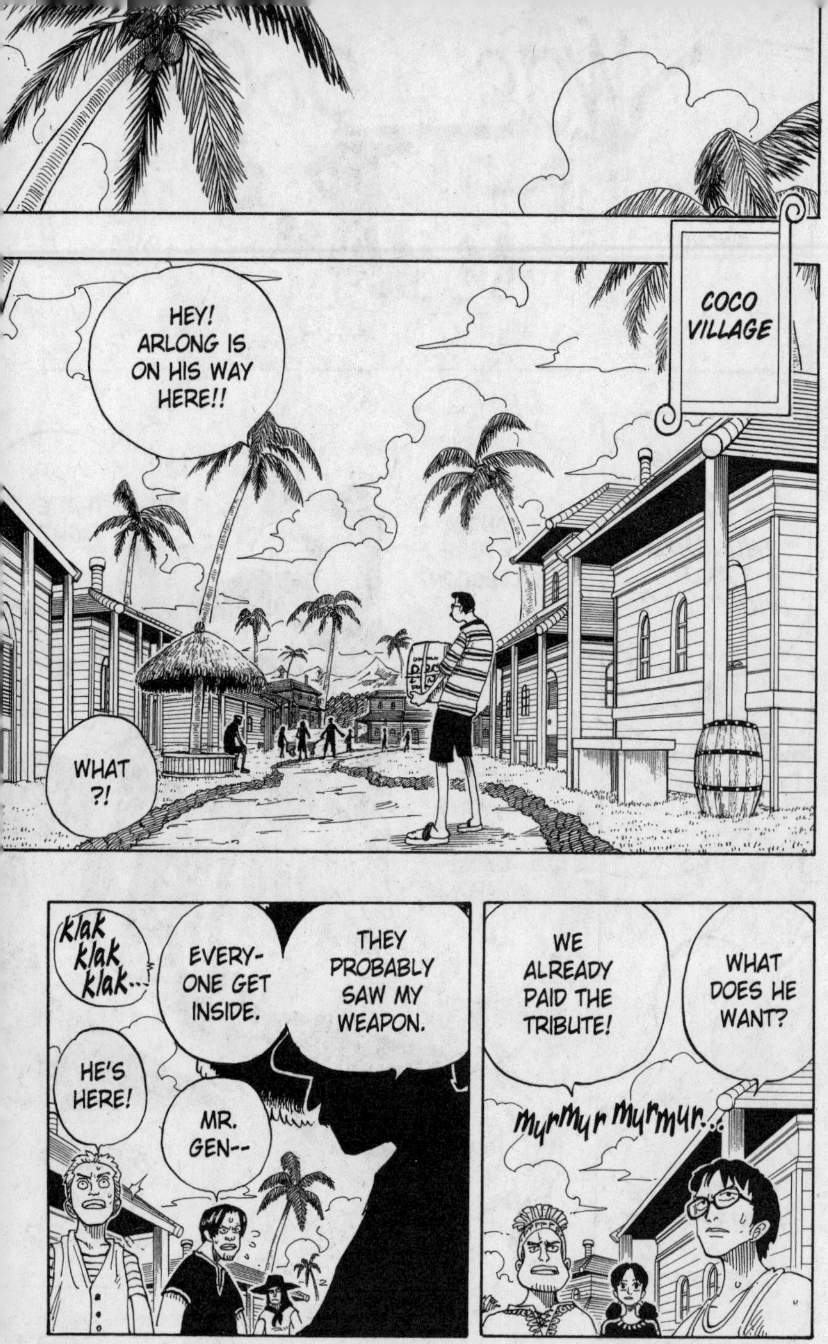
COCO VILLAGE
HEY! ARLONG IS ON HIS WAY HERE!!
WHAT ?!
WHAT DOES HE WANT?
WE ALREADY PAID THE TRIBUTE!
murmur murmur...
THEY PROBABLY SAW MY WEAPON.
EVERY-ONE GET INSIDE.
klak klak klak...
MR. GEN--
HE'S HERE!

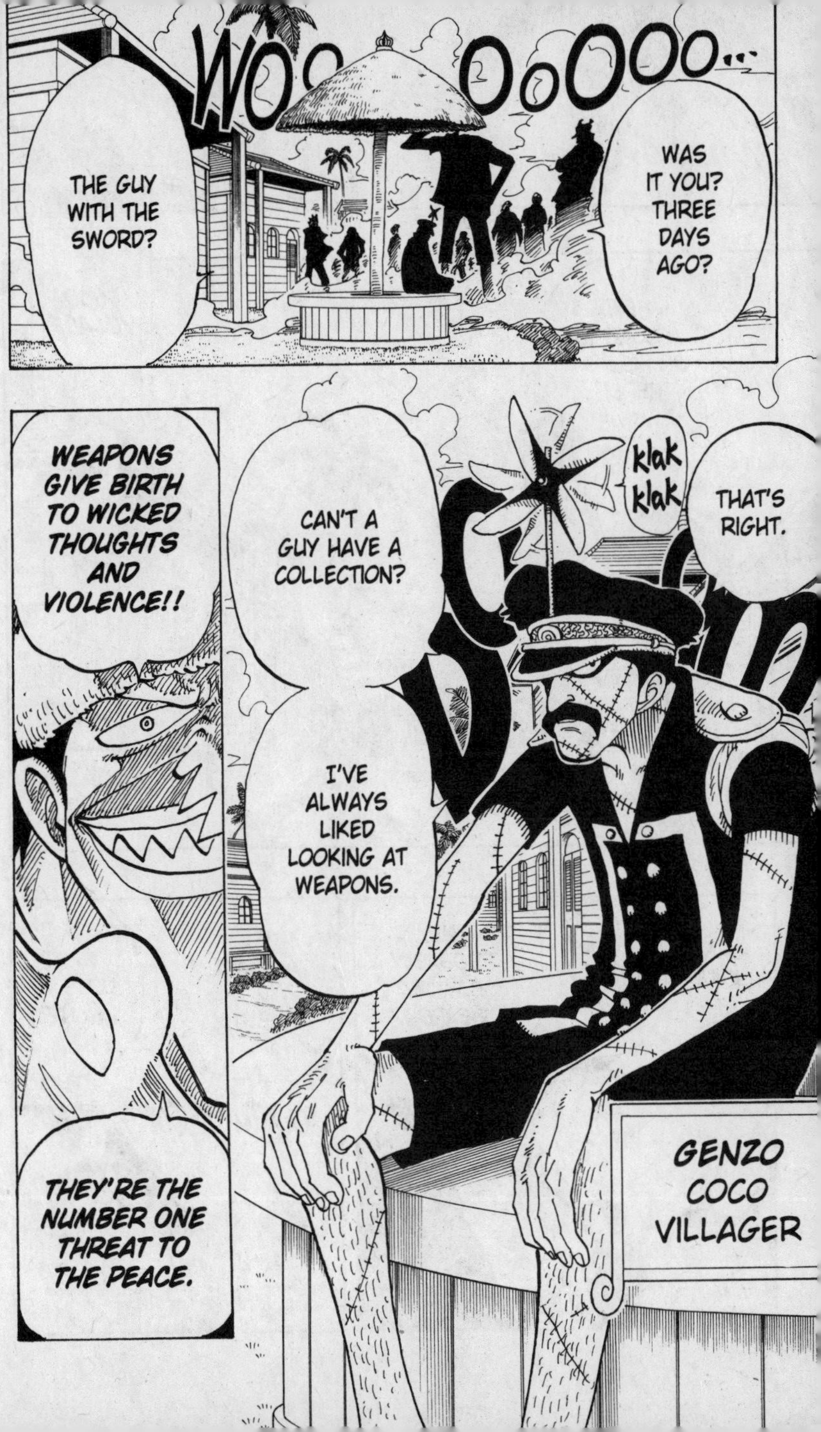
WO OoOOO...
WAS IT YOU? THREE DAYS AGO?
THE GUY WITH THE SWORD?
THAT'S RIGHT.
klak klak
CAN'T A GUY HAVE A COLLECTION?
I'VE ALWAYS LIKED LOOKING AT WEAPONS.
GENZO COCO VILLAGER
WEAPONS GIVE BIRTH TO WICKED THOUGHTS AND VIOLENCE!!
THEY'RE THE NUMBER ONE THREAT TO THE PEACE.

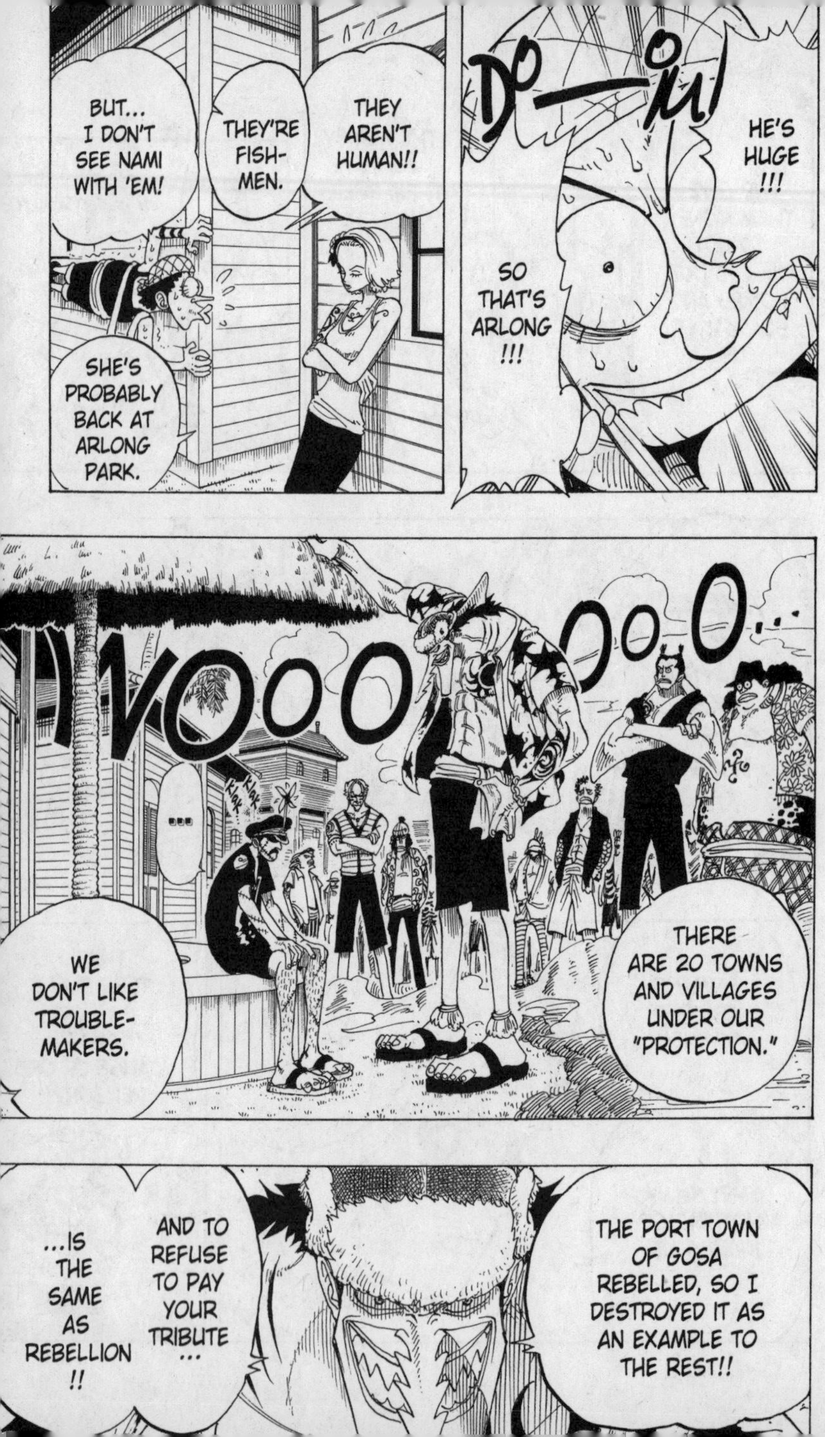
DO—OM
HE'S HUGE!!!
SO THAT'S ARLONG!!!
THEY AREN'T HUMAN!!
THEY'RE FISH-MEN.
BUT... I DON'T SEE NAMI WITH 'EM!
SHE'S PROBABLY BACK AT ARLONG PARK.
WOOOOOO-O...
THERE ARE 20 TOWNS AND VILLAGES UNDER OUR "PROTECTION."
Klak klak
...
WE DON'T LIKE TROUBLE-MAKERS.
THE PORT TOWN OF GOSA REBELLED, SO I DESTROYED IT AS AN EXAMPLE TO THE REST!!
AND TO REFUSE TO PAY YOUR TRIBUTE...
...IS THE SAME AS REBELLION!!

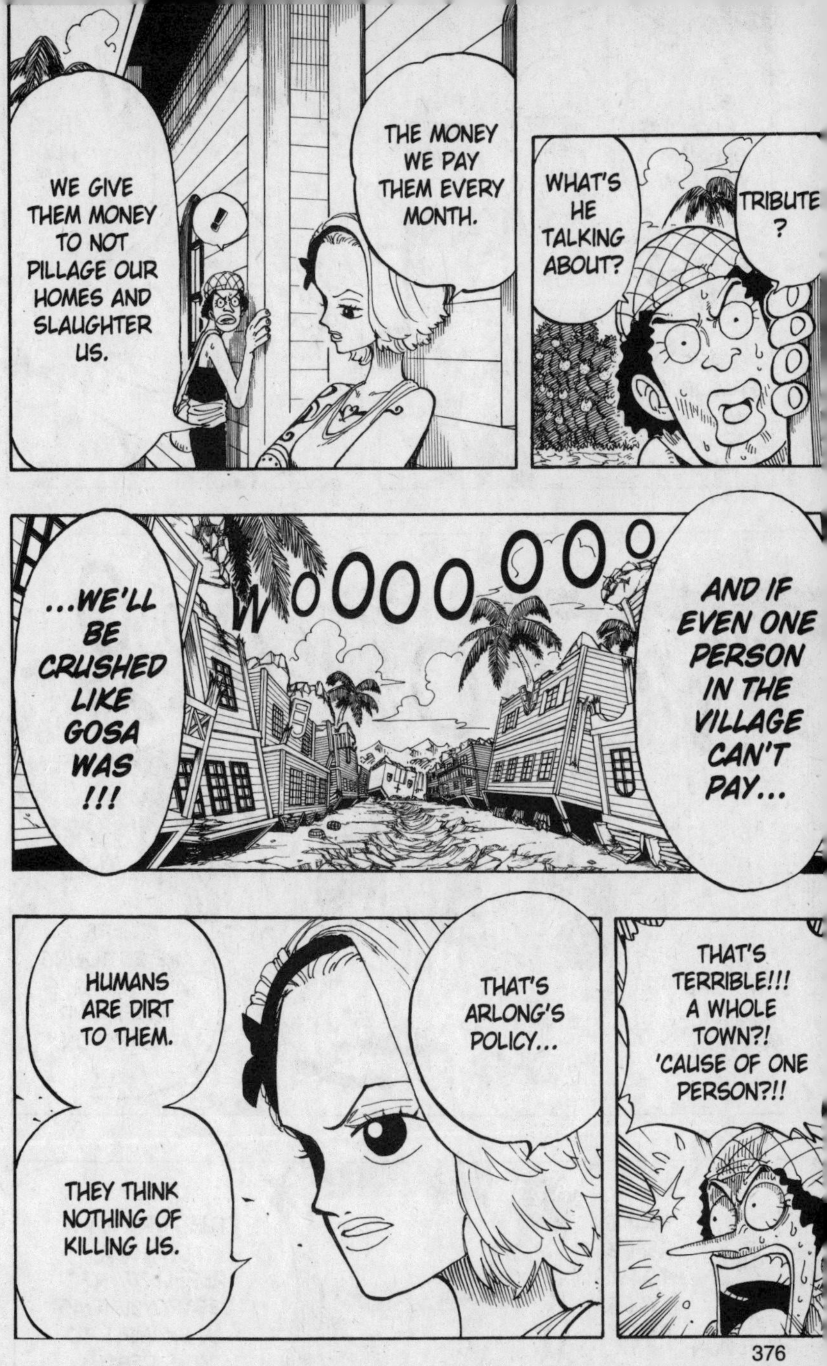
TRIBUTE?
WHAT'S HE TALKING ABOUT?
THE MONEY WE PAY THEM EVERY MONTH.
!
WE GIVE THEM MONEY TO NOT PILLAGE OUR HOMES AND SLAUGHTER US.
AND IF EVEN ONE PERSON IN THE VILLAGE CAN'T PAY...
WOOOOOOOO
...WE'LL BE CRUSHED LIKE GOSA WAS!!!
THAT'S TERRIBLE!!! A WHOLE TOWN?! 'CAUSE OF ONE PERSON?!!
THAT'S ARLONG'S POLICY...
HUMANS ARE DIRT TO THEM.
THEY THINK NOTHING OF KILLING US.

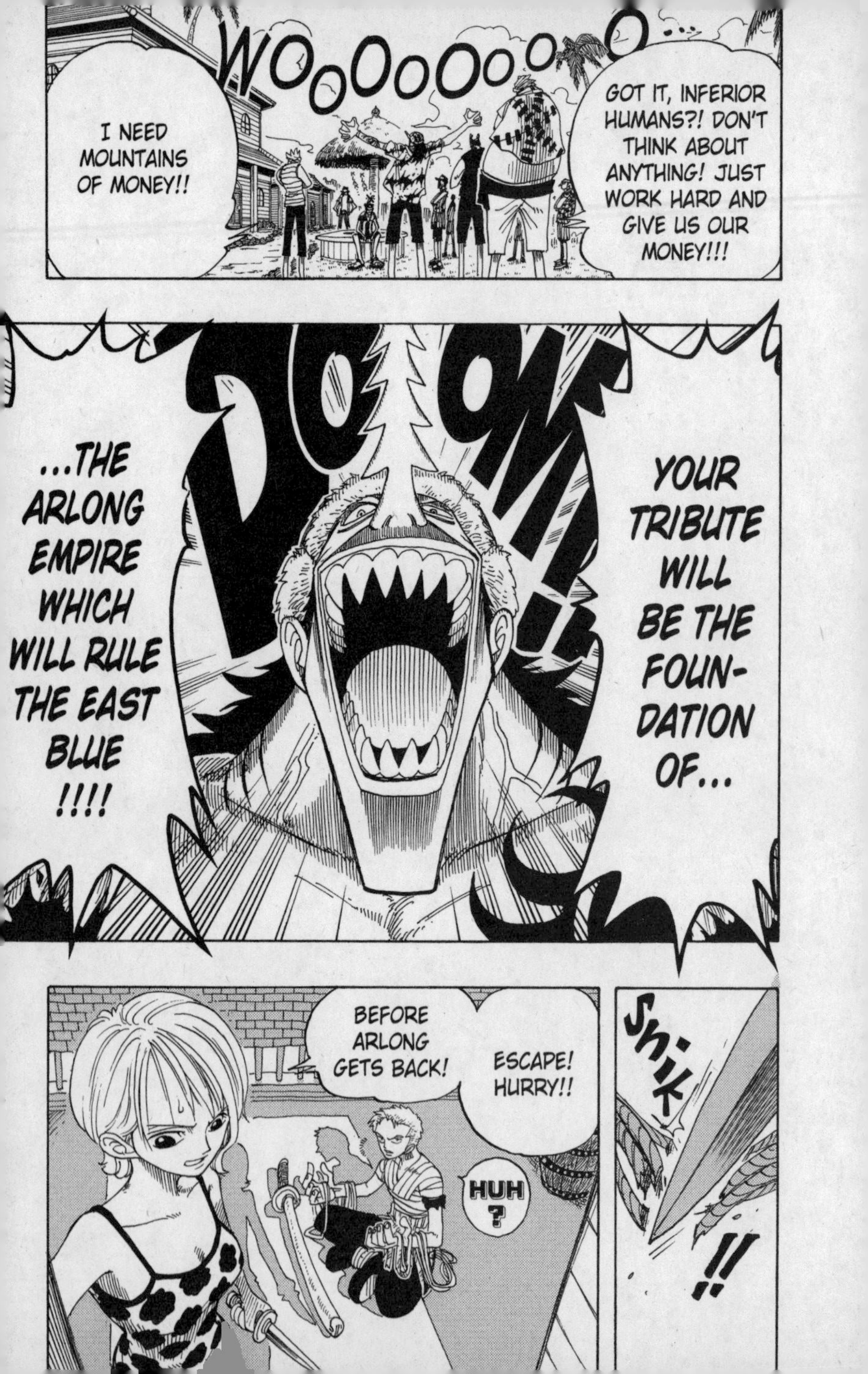
WOOOOOOOO
GOT IT, INFERIOR HUMANS?! DON'T THINK ABOUT ANYTHING! JUST WORK HARD AND GIVE US OUR MONEY!!!
I NEED MOUNTAINS OF MONEY!!
DOOM!!
YOUR TRIBUTE WILL BE THE FOUN-DATION OF...
...THE ARLONG EMPIRE WHICH WILL RULE THE EAST BLUE !!!!
SNIK
!!
ESCAPE! HURRY!!
BEFORE ARLONG GETS BACK!
HUH ?

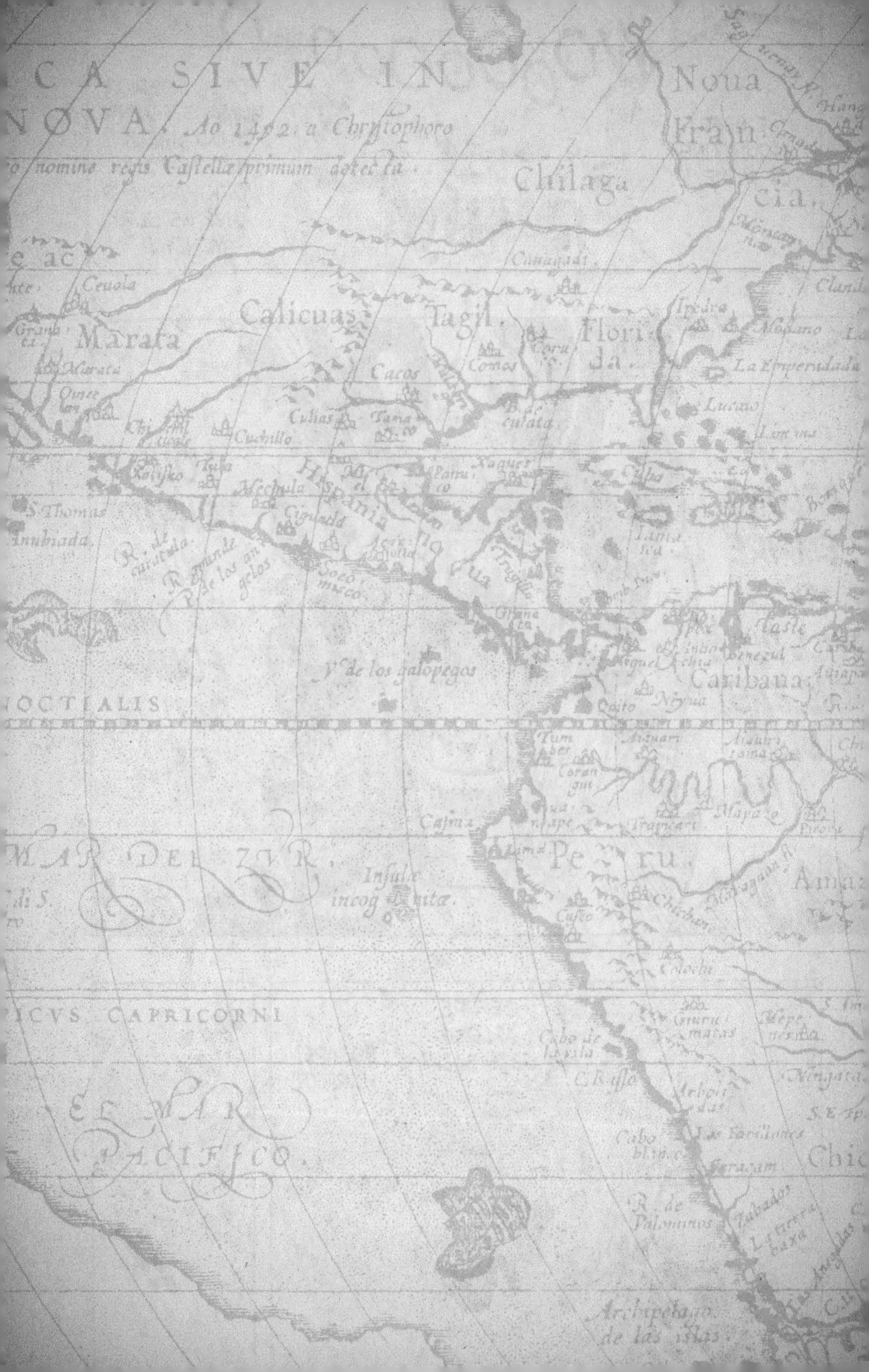

CA SIVE IN Noua
NOVA. Ao 1492. a Christophoro Fran
o nomine regis Castelle primum detecta. cia.
Chilaga
e ac
Ceuola Cumagad. Clanda
Gran Indra Mopano
el Marata Calicuas Tagil Flori
Mirata Cacos Coru da La Emperidada
Quiet Chi Culias Tana B. Lucaio
Cuchillo culata Somons
Loryko Haquer Cuba
Mechula Hispania Patru
S.Thomas Cigueld
Anubiada R. del Agu nia
Grande Soco Trinta
P. de los an marco
gelos Grana
V. de los galopegos Caste
benezul Carib
OCTIALIS Caribana
Quito Nouua
Tum
ber Aruari Aratu
Coran lana
gui
ape Trapicari Maya
Casina
MAR DEL ZVR Pe ru Ama
di S. Infule Achiche
incog nita Moiaganaf
Cusio
du Colochi
ICVS CAPRICORNI
Gnuru
matas mesta
Cabo de
la isla
C.Basso Arboi S.E.
das
Cabo de las Forcilanes
ELMAR blines Chic
PACIFICO S arazim
R. de Sabador
Palomnos L. tierra
baxa
Archipelago.
de las islas

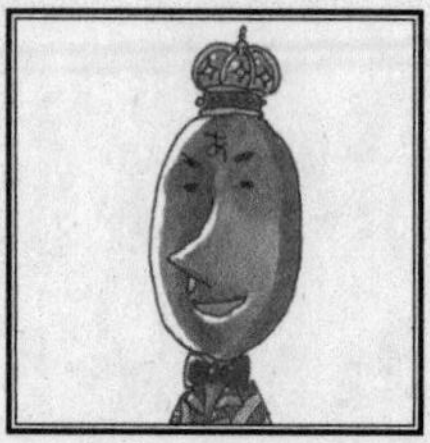

Um... Right now, it's the seventh month of the year 1999, going by the western calendar. It's the month that Brother Nostra[damus] predicted would see "the destruction of the world by the great king of Anglemois." And so the world governments have taken the opportunity to put the great king of Anglemois on the most wanted list. His royal mug appears above. 🡅 His punishment: "Confinement until the eighth month." If you should find him, please refrain from using any rolling savate or piledriver attack moves. (Signed, the world governments.)

*–Eiichiro Oda, 1999*

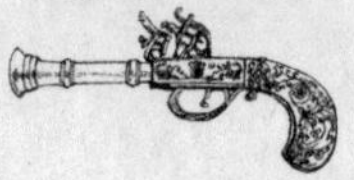

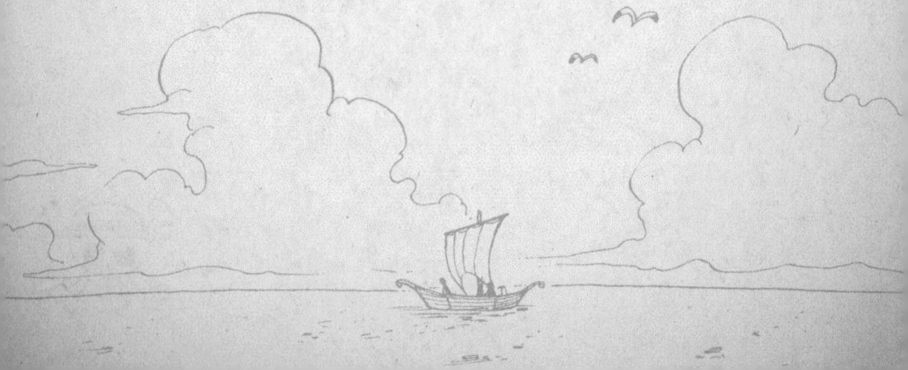

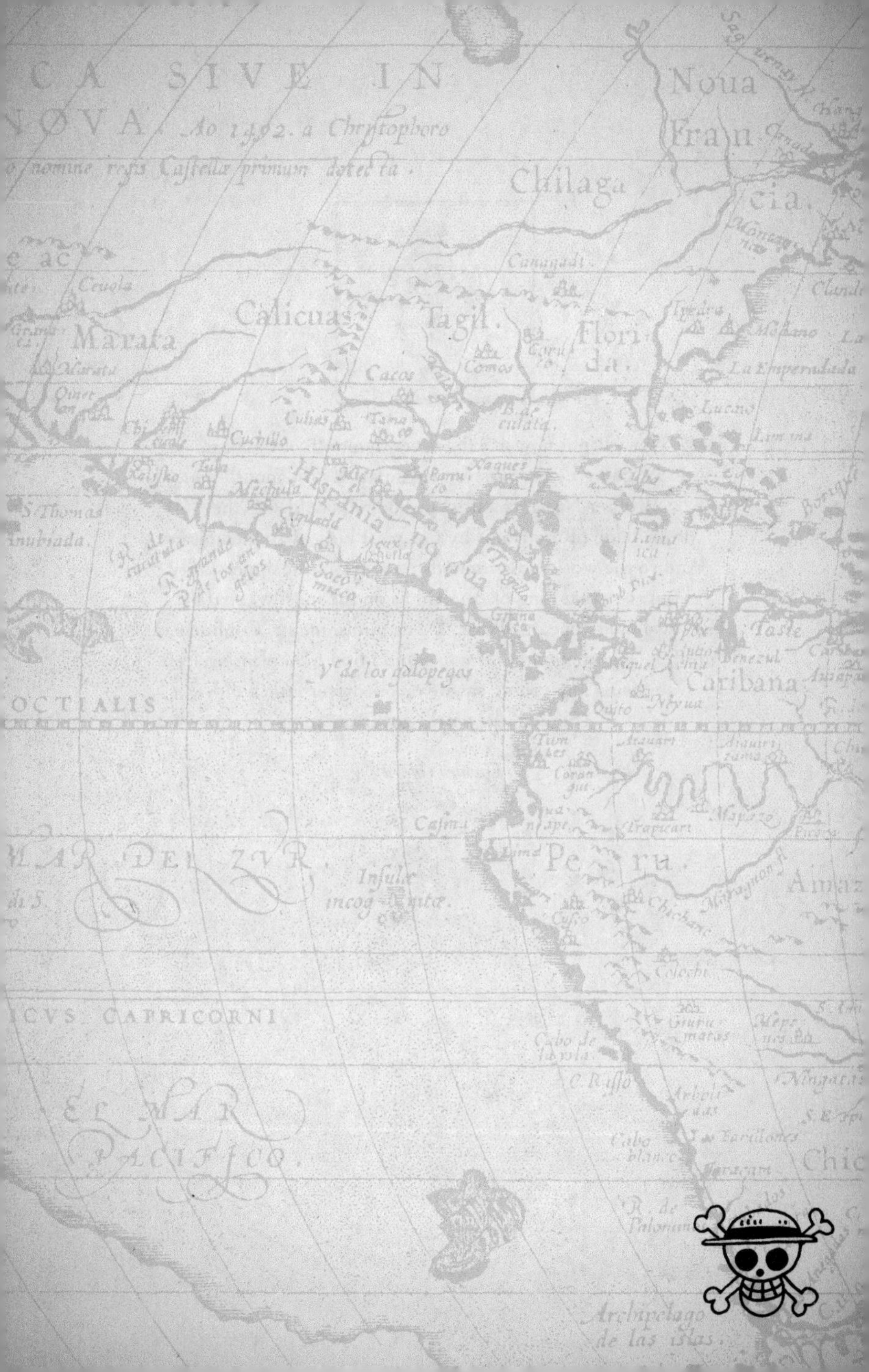

CA SIVE IN
NOVA *Ao 1492. a Chryſtophoro*
o nomine regis Caſtellæ primum detecta.

Noua
Fran
cia.

Chilaga

e ac
Ceuola
Canigadi
Clande

Marata
Calicuas
Tagil.
Flori
da.
Iſpiria
Mechano La

Xarata
Cacos
Ecarsi
La Emperaduda

Quet
Comos
Lucuo
Lim ina

Chi
Cutillo
Culias
Tana
culata.
B. de

Mechula
Hispania
Cuba
Borgi

S. Thomas
Quedl
Iſola
Parui
co
Naques

inuciada
R. de
cucul ata
R. grande
de los
arlos
Soco
maca
ua

Tiguta

Sacb
Giena
Faste

Benezul

yſle de los galopegos
Miquel
Caribana

OCTIALIS
Quito
Nbyua

Tum
bes
Azuan
Atauiri
tama

Corar
gus

Casma
Tropicart
Mayeza

MAR DEL ZVR
Pe ru.
Amaz

di S.
Inſulæ
incognita.
Chicha
Maragnon

Cuſco

Colechi

ICVS CAPRICORNI
Giuria
matas
Mepe
ucuada

Cabo de
ſauia

C. Ruſſo
Arbola
das
Nongaça

EL MAR
PACIFICO.
Cabo
blanco
Paricones

Veracan
Chic

R. de
Palomon

Archipelago
de las islas

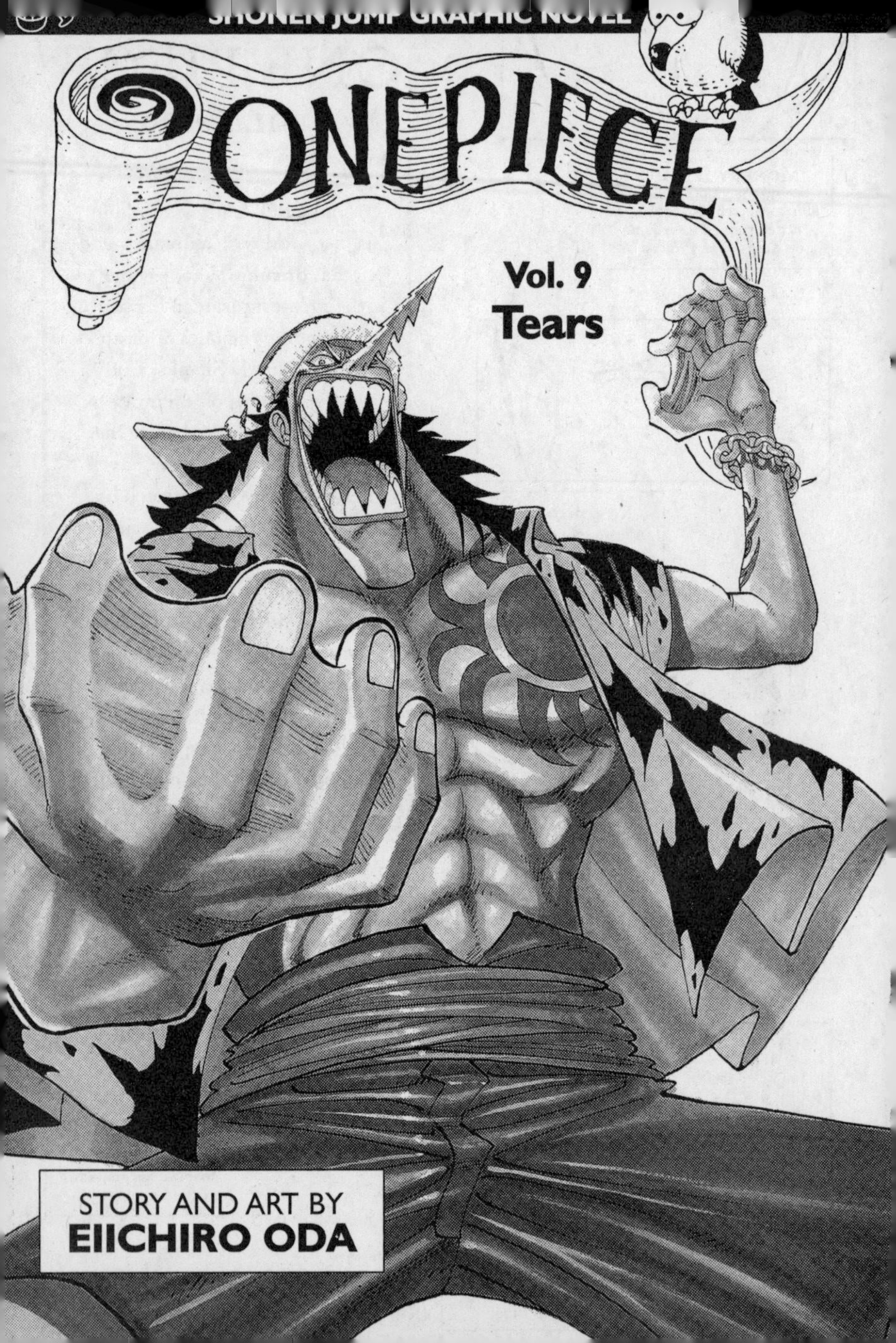
SHONEN JUMP GRAPHIC NOVEL
ONE PIECE
Vol. 9
Tears
STORY AND ART BY
EIICHIRO ODA

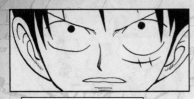

# THE STORY OF
# ONE PIECE
## · VOLUME 9·

### MONKEY D. LUFFY
Boundlessly optimistic and able to stretch like rubber, he is determined to become King of the Pirates.

Monkey D. Luffy started out as just a kid with a dream—and that dream was to become the greatest pirate in history! Stirred by the tales of pirate "Red-Haired" Shanks, Luffy vowed to become a pirate himself. That was before the enchanted Devil Fruit gave Luffy the power to stretch like rubber, at the cost of being unable to swim—a serious handicap for an aspiring sea dog. Undeterred, Luffy set out to sea and recruited some crewmates: master swordsman Zolo, treasure-hunting thief Nami, lying sharpshooter Usopp and the sous-chef Sanji.

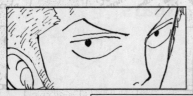

### RORONOA ZOLO
A former bounty hunter and master of the "three-sword" fighting style.

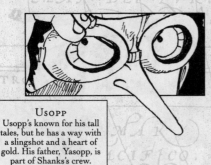

### USOPP
Usopp's known for his tall tales, but he has a way with a slingshot and a heart of gold. His father, Yasopp, is part of Shanks's crew.

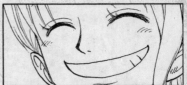

### NAMI
A thief who specializes in robbing pirates. Nami hates pirates, but Luffy convinced her to join his crew as navigator

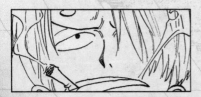

### SANJI
A compassionate cook (and ladies' man) whose dream is to find the legendary sea, the "All Blue."

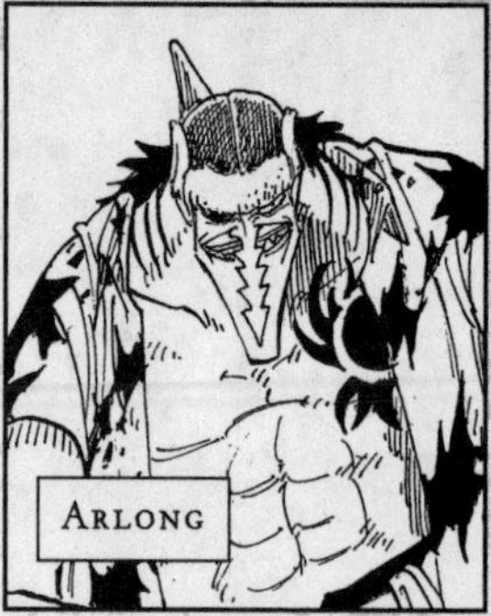
Arlong

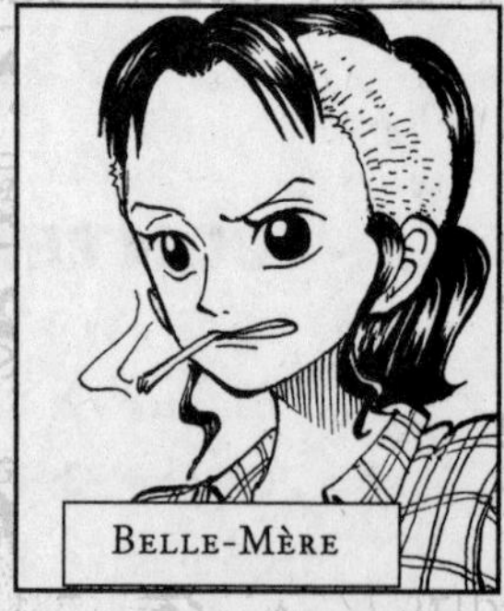
Belle-Mère

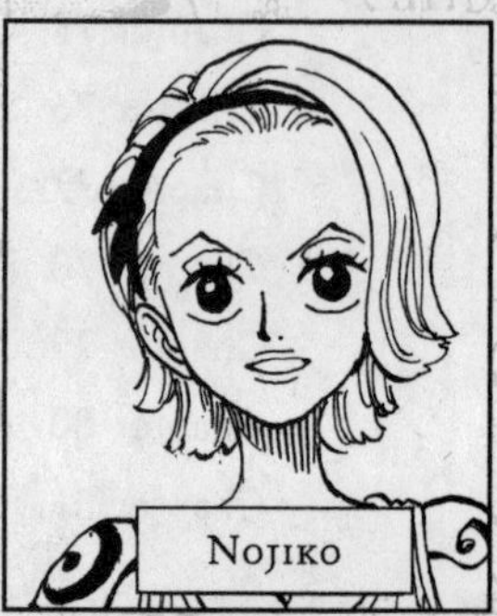
Nojiko

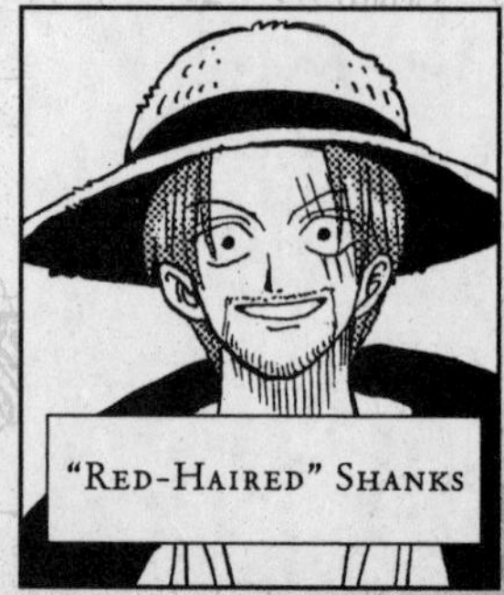
"Red-Haired" Shanks

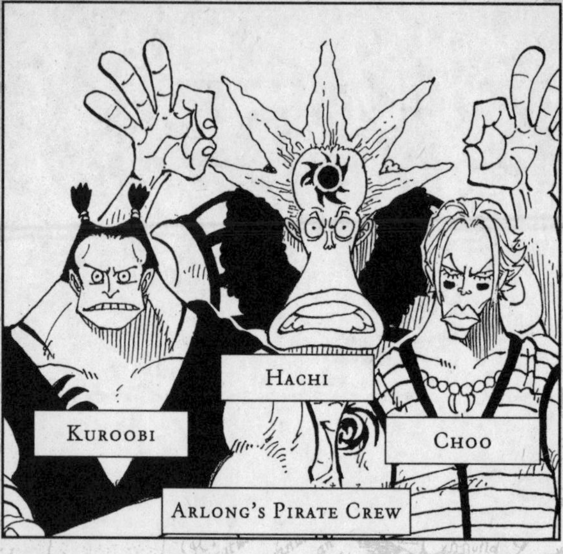
Hachi
Kuroobi
Choo
Arlong's Pirate Crew

While working off the damage he caused aboard the oceangoing restaurant Baratie, Luffy meets Sanji the sea cook and asks him to join his crew. But Sanji, for reasons only he knows, refuses to leave the restaurant ship. Before that mystery can be solved, Don Krieg and his pirates try to capture the Baratie, triggering a ferocious battle. In the end, Luffy and Krieg face off, and Luffy proves that courage is sometimes more than a match for overwhelming firepower. After the battle, Luffy again asks Sanji to sail with him, and once more Sanji refuses, until Chef Zeff and his fighting cooks conspire to convince Sanji that he should follow his dream. Touched by their extremely tough brand of love, Sanji says a tearful goodbye and sets off with Luffy! Meanwhile, Zolo and Usopp sail ahead in pursuit of Nami and arrive at an island ruled by the Fish-Man warlord, "Saw-Tooth" Arlong. Scarcely have they arrived when, to their shock, they find Nami—consorting with the pirates!!

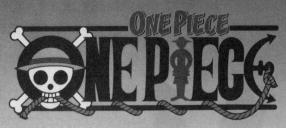

# Vol. 9
# TEARS

## CONTENTS

Chapter 72: Proper Living                              385

Chapter 73: Monsters of the Grand Line                 405

Chapter 74: Business                                   425

Chapter 75: Of Maps and Fish-Men                       445

Chapter 76: Sleep                                      465

Chapter 77: The First Step Toward a Dream              485

Chapter 78: Belle-Mère                                 505

Chapter 79: To Live                                    525

Chapter 80: A Thief Is a Thief                         545

Chapter 81: Tears                                      565

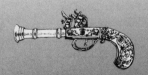

# Chapter 72:
# PROPER LIVING

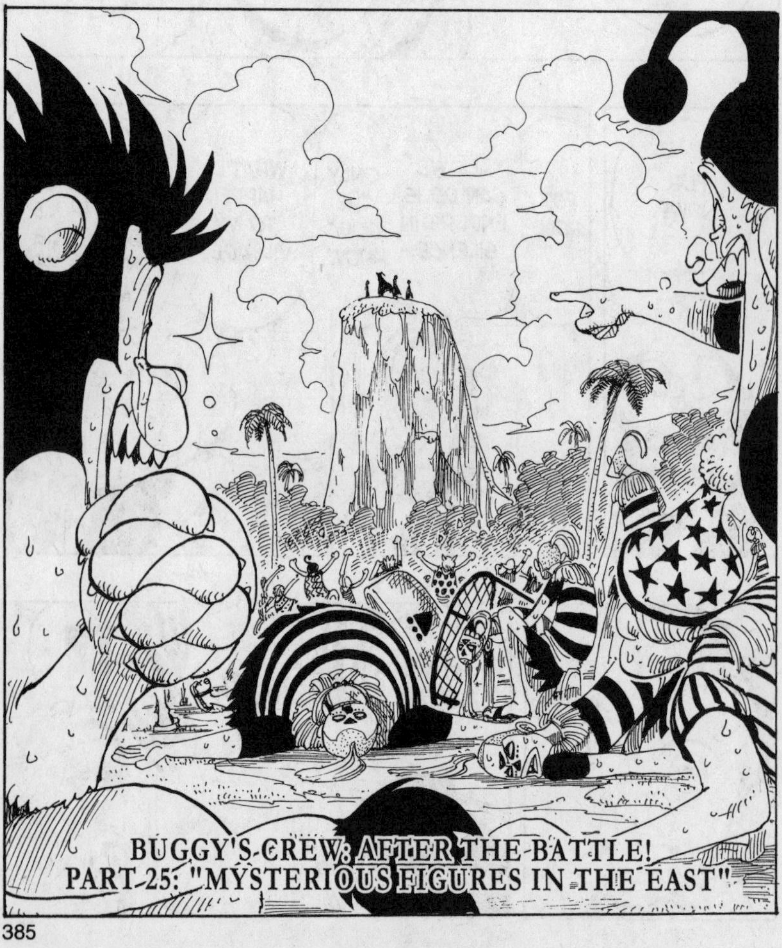
BUGGY'S CREW: AFTER THE BATTLE!
PART 25: "MYSTERIOUS FIGURES IN THE EAST"

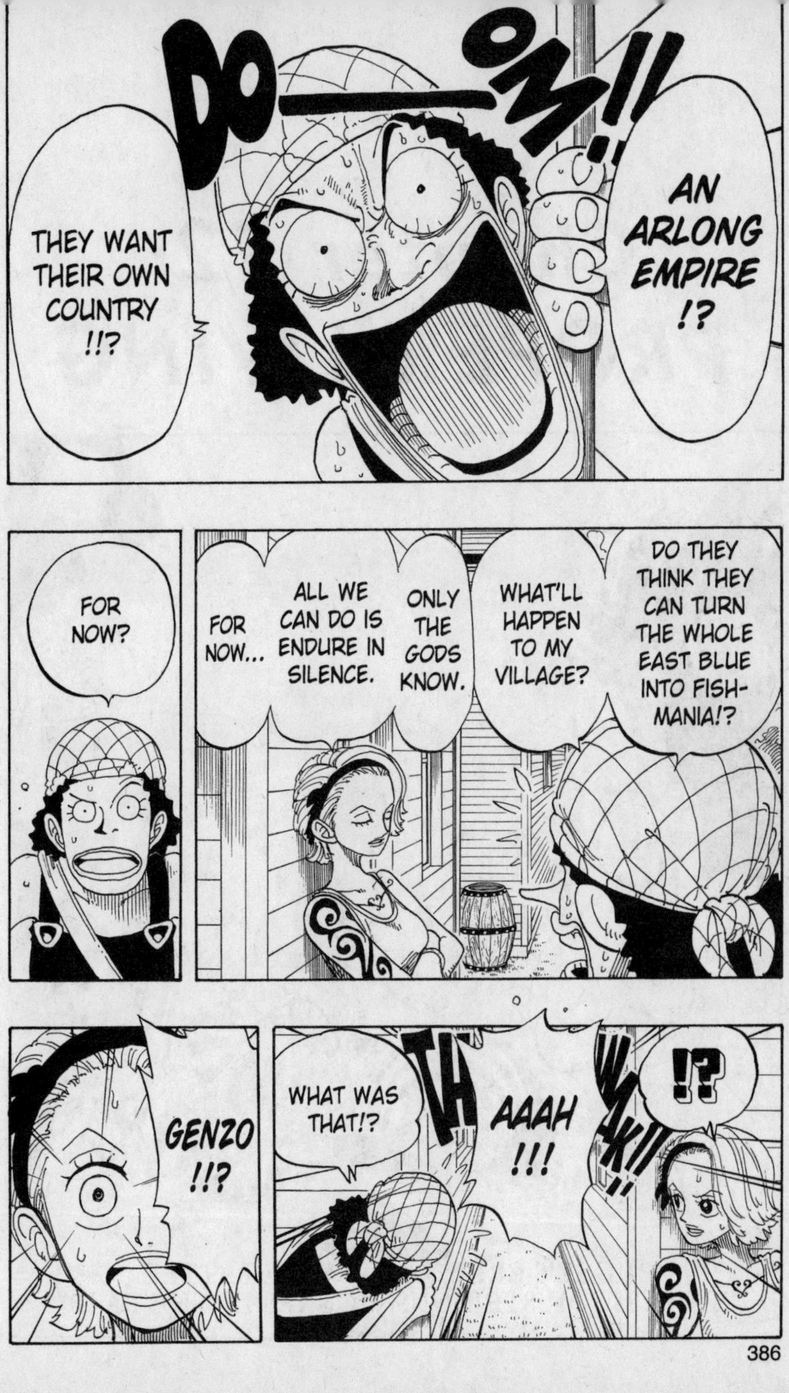

DO—OM!!
AN ARLONG EMPIRE!?
THEY WANT THEIR OWN COUNTRY!!?
DO THEY THINK THEY CAN TURN THE WHOLE EAST BLUE INTO FISH-MANIA!?
WHAT'LL HAPPEN TO MY VILLAGE?
ONLY THE GODS KNOW.
ALL WE CAN DO IS ENDURE IN SILENCE.
FOR NOW...
FOR NOW?
!?
TH
WAK!!
AAAH!!!
WHAT WAS THAT!?
GENZO!!?

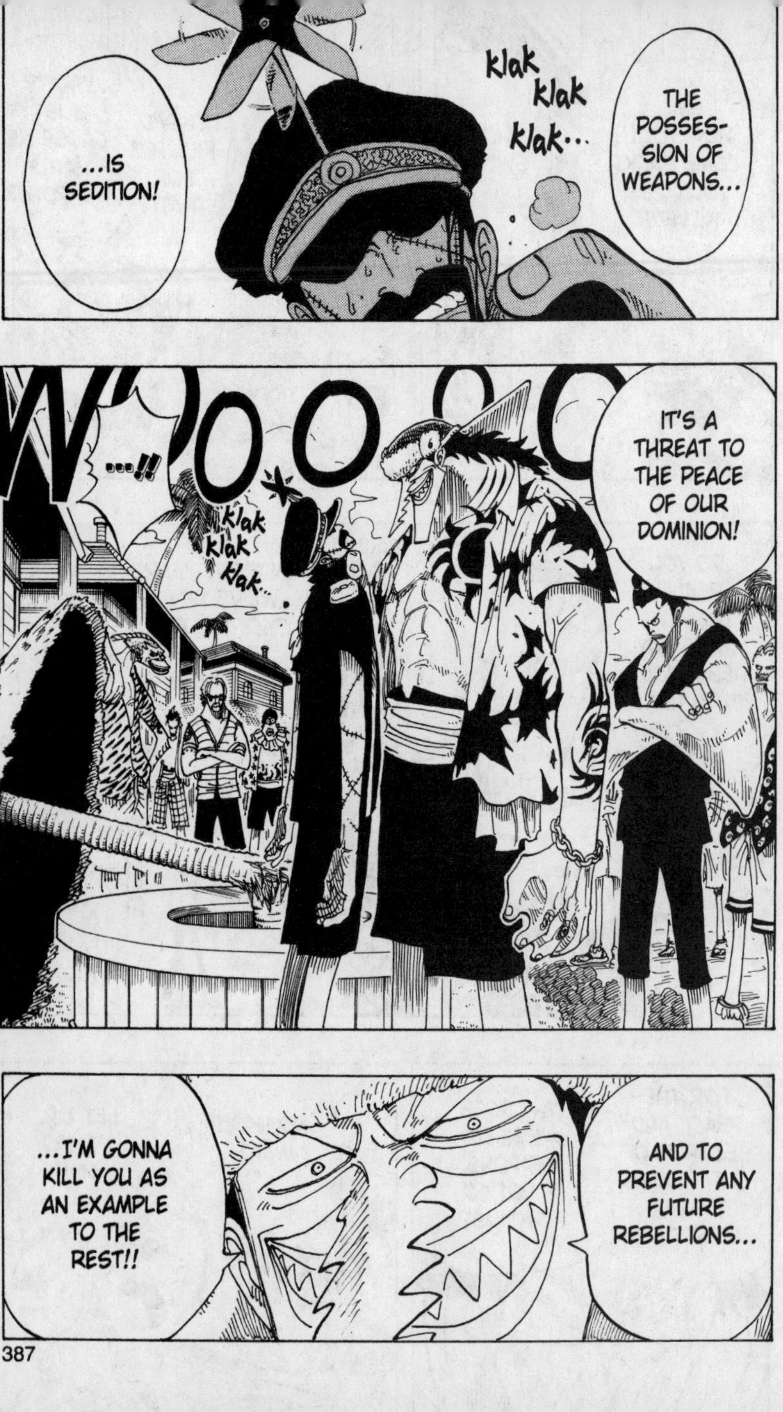
THE POSSES-SION OF WEAPONS...
klak klak klak...
...IS SEDITION!
IT'S A THREAT TO THE PEACE OF OUR DOMINION!
WOOOO
...!!
klak klak klak...
AND TO PREVENT ANY FUTURE REBELLIONS...
...I'M GONNA KILL YOU AS AN EXAMPLE TO THE REST!!

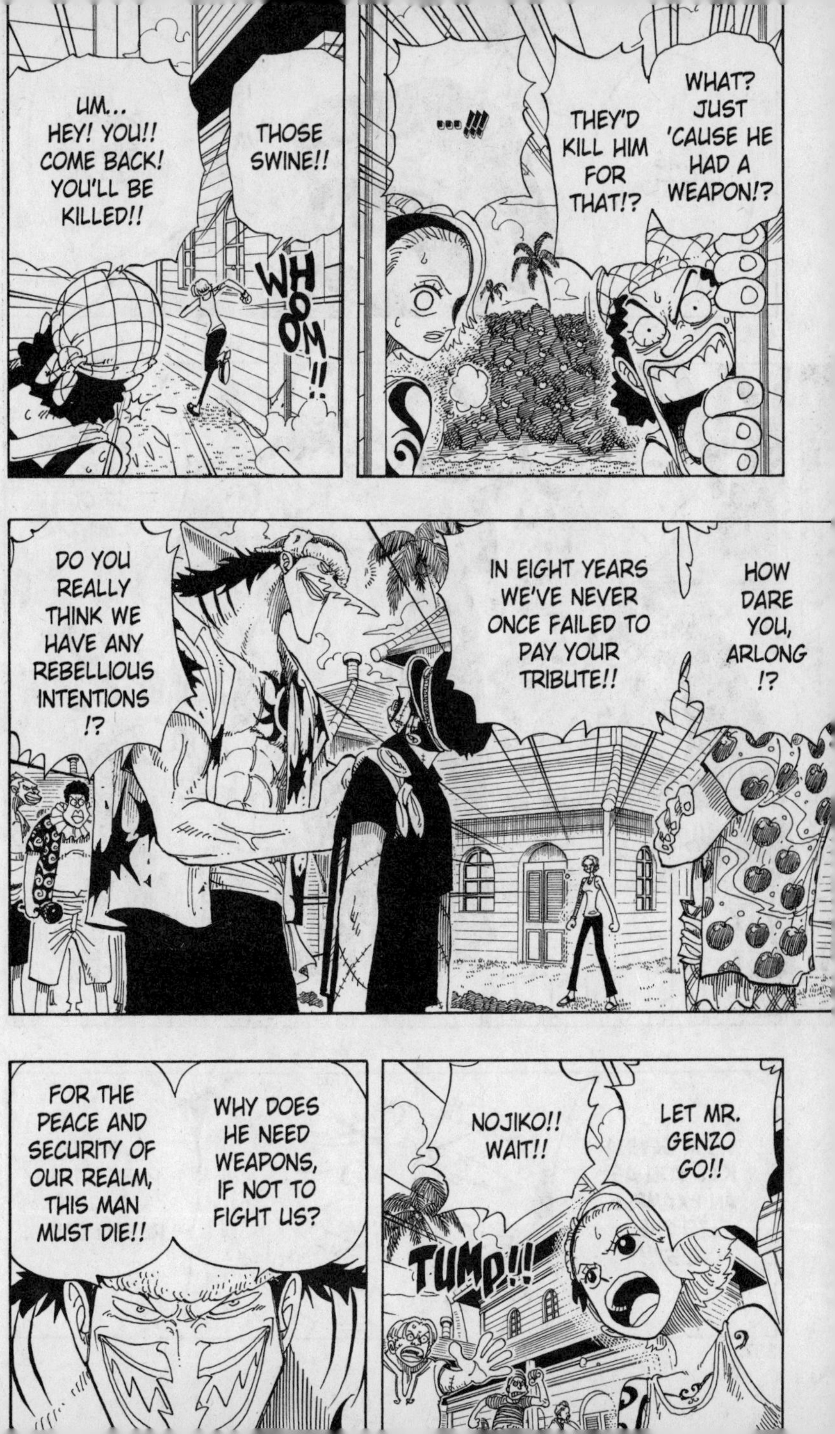
WHAT? JUST 'CAUSE HE HAD A WEAPON!?
THEY'D KILL HIM FOR THAT!?
...!!!
THOSE SWINE!!
WHOOM!!
UM... HEY! YOU!! COME BACK! YOU'LL BE KILLED!!
HOW DARE YOU, ARLONG !?
IN EIGHT YEARS WE'VE NEVER ONCE FAILED TO PAY YOUR TRIBUTE!!
DO YOU REALLY THINK WE HAVE ANY REBELLIOUS INTENTIONS !?
LET MR. GENZO GO!!
NOJIKO!! WAIT!!
TUMP!!!
WHY DOES HE NEED WEAPONS, IF NOT TO FIGHT US?
FOR THE PEACE AND SECURITY OF OUR REALM, THIS MAN MUST DIE!!

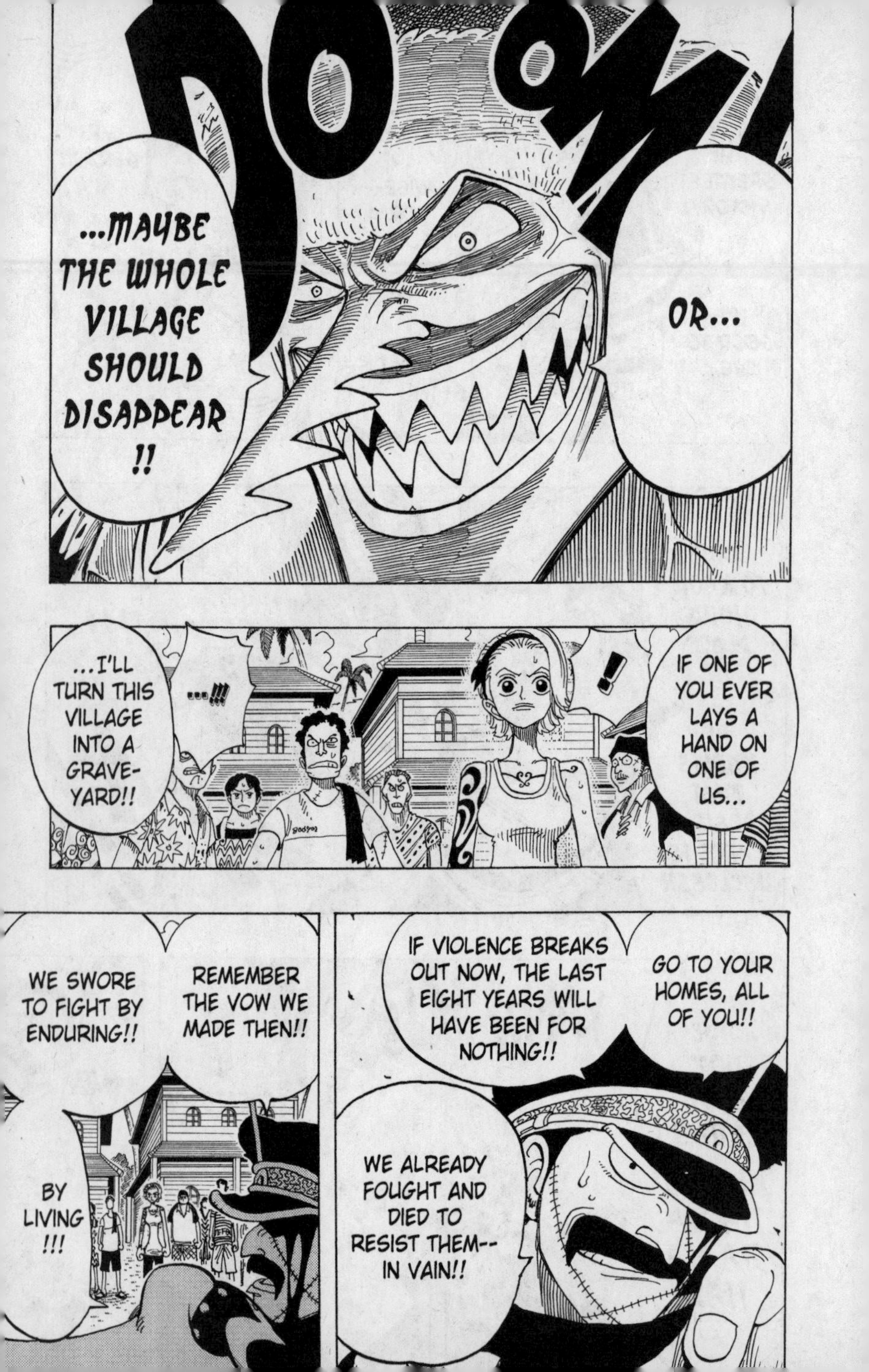
DOOM!
OR...
...MAYBE THE WHOLE VILLAGE SHOULD DISAPPEAR!!
IF ONE OF YOU EVER LAYS A HAND ON ONE OF US...
!
...!!!
...I'LL TURN THIS VILLAGE INTO A GRAVE-YARD!!
GO TO YOUR HOMES, ALL OF YOU!!
IF VIOLENCE BREAKS OUT NOW, THE LAST EIGHT YEARS WILL HAVE BEEN FOR NOTHING!!
WE ALREADY FOUGHT AND DIED TO RESIST THEM-- IN VAIN!!
REMEMBER THE VOW WE MADE THEN!!
WE SWORE TO FIGHT BY ENDURING!!
BY LIVING!!!

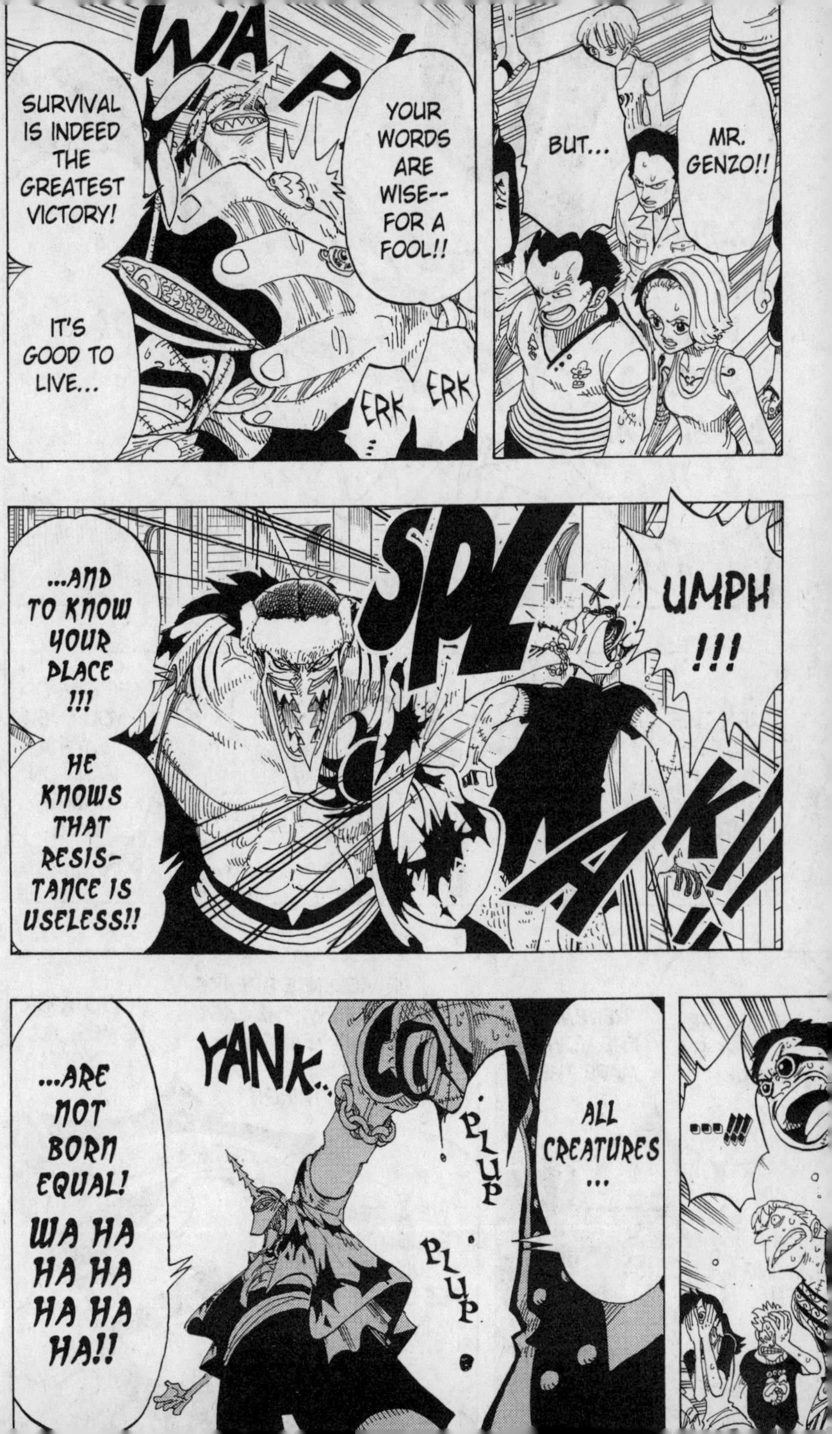
MR. GENZO!!
BUT...
YOUR WORDS ARE WISE-- FOR A FOOL!!
WAP
ERK
ERK
SURVIVAL IS INDEED THE GREATEST VICTORY!
IT'S GOOD TO LIVE...
UMPH !!!
SPL
AK!!
...AND TO KNOW YOUR PLACE !!!
HE KNOWS THAT RESIS- TANCE IS USELESS!!
...!!!
ALL CREATURES ...
PLUP
PLUP
YANK...
...ARE NOT BORN EQUAL!
WA HA HA HA HA HA HA HA HA!!

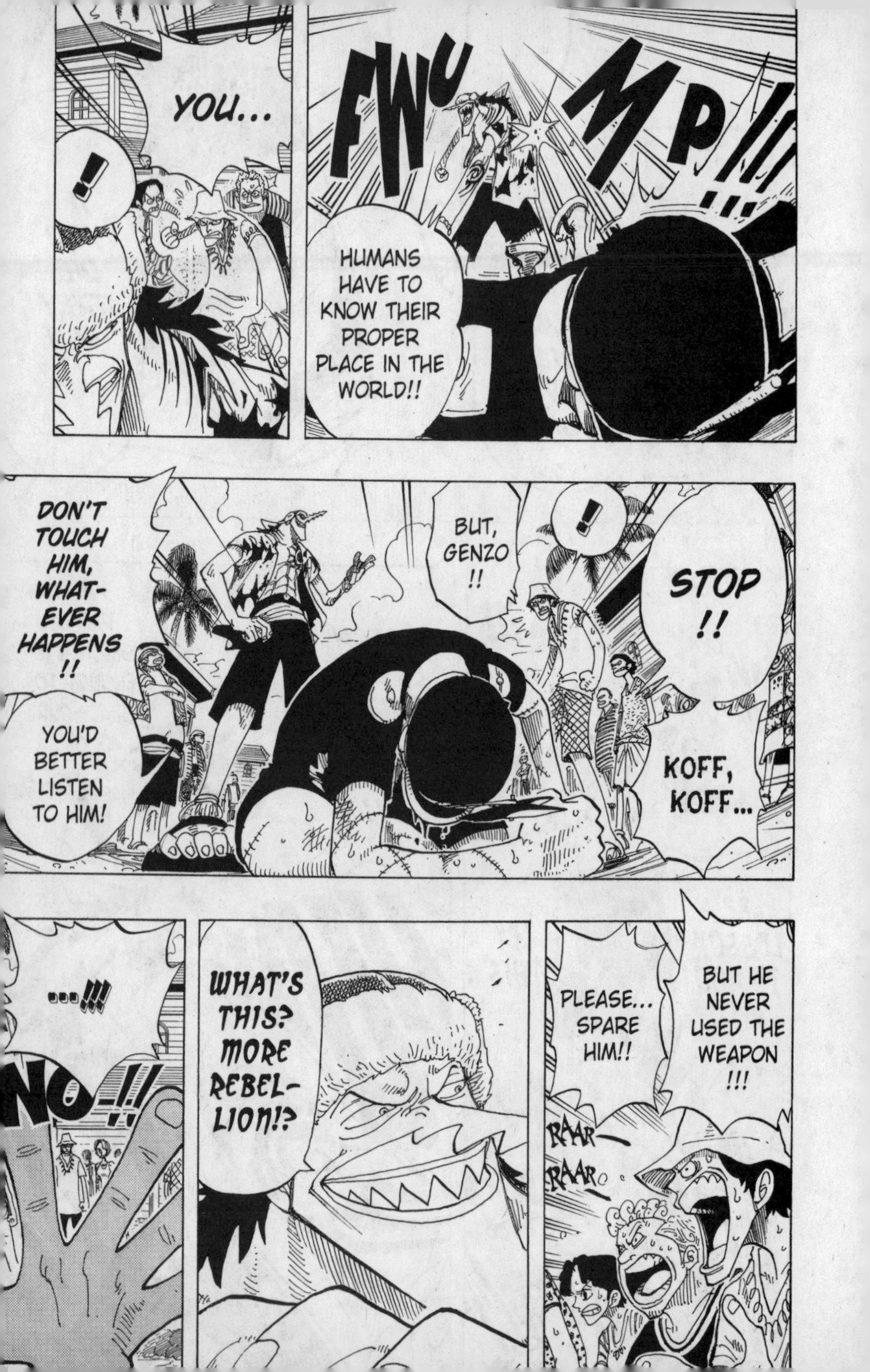
FWUMP!!!
HUMANS HAVE TO KNOW THEIR PROPER PLACE IN THE WORLD!!
YOU...
!
STOP!!
KOFF, KOFF...
!
BUT, GENZO!!
DON'T TOUCH HIM, WHATEVER HAPPENS!!
YOU'D BETTER LISTEN TO HIM!
BUT HE NEVER USED THE WEAPON!!!
PLEASE... SPARE HIM!!
RAAR— RAAR
WHAT'S THIS? MORE REBELLION!?
...!!!
NO-!!

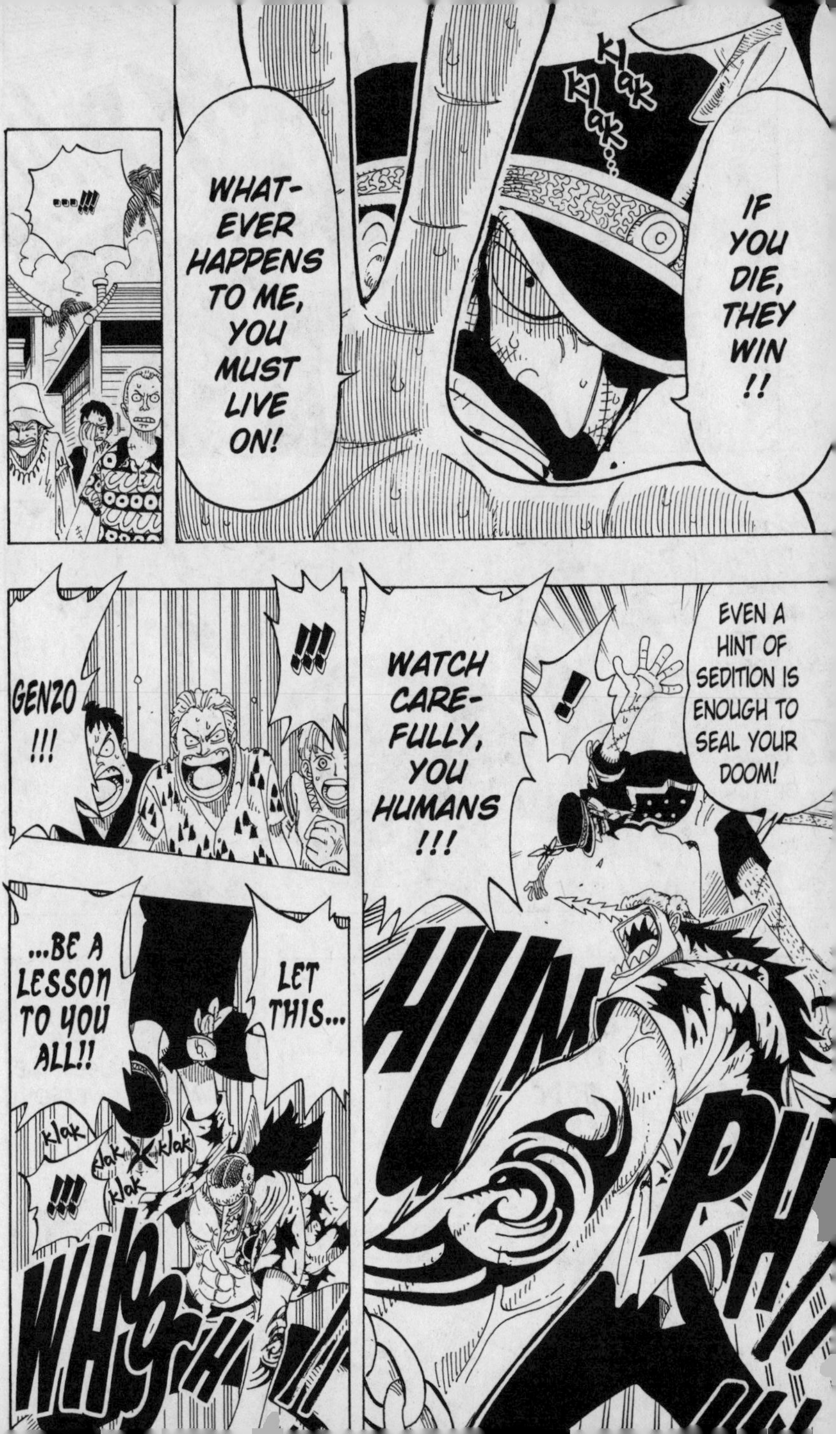

klak klak klak...
IF YOU DIE, THEY WIN!!
WHAT-EVER HAPPENS TO ME, YOU MUST LIVE ON!
...!!!
EVEN A HINT OF SEDITION IS ENOUGH TO SEAL YOUR DOOM!
WATCH CARE-FULLY, YOU HUMANS!!!
!
!!!
GENZO!!!
LET THIS...
...BE A LESSON TO YOU ALL!!
klak klak klak klak
!!!

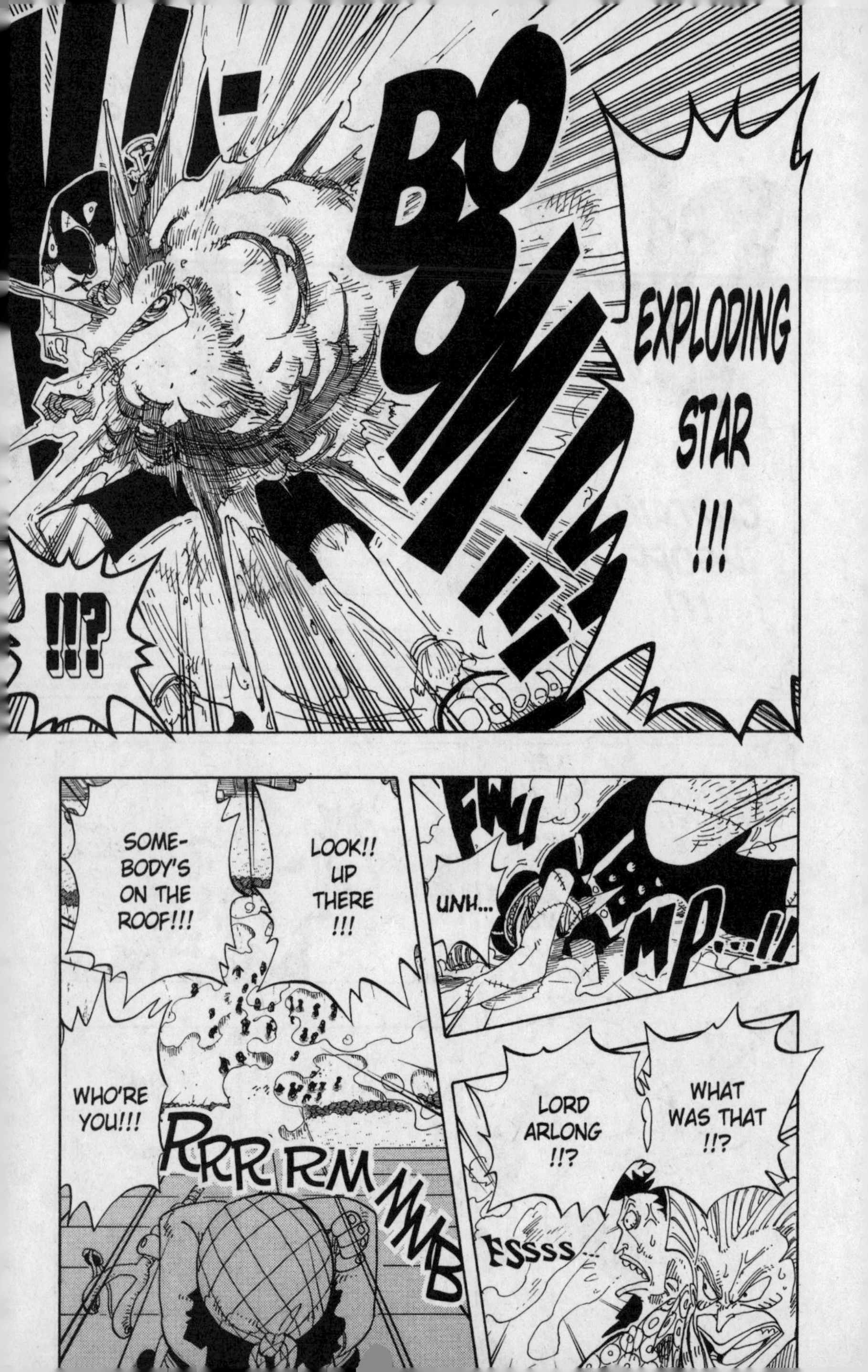
EXPLODING STAR !!!
BOOM!!!
!!?
UNH...
FWUMP..!!
WHAT WAS THAT !!?
LORD ARLONG !!?
FSSSS...
LOOK!! UP THERE !!!
SOME-BODY'S ON THE ROOF!!!
WHO'RE YOU!!!
RRRR RMMMB

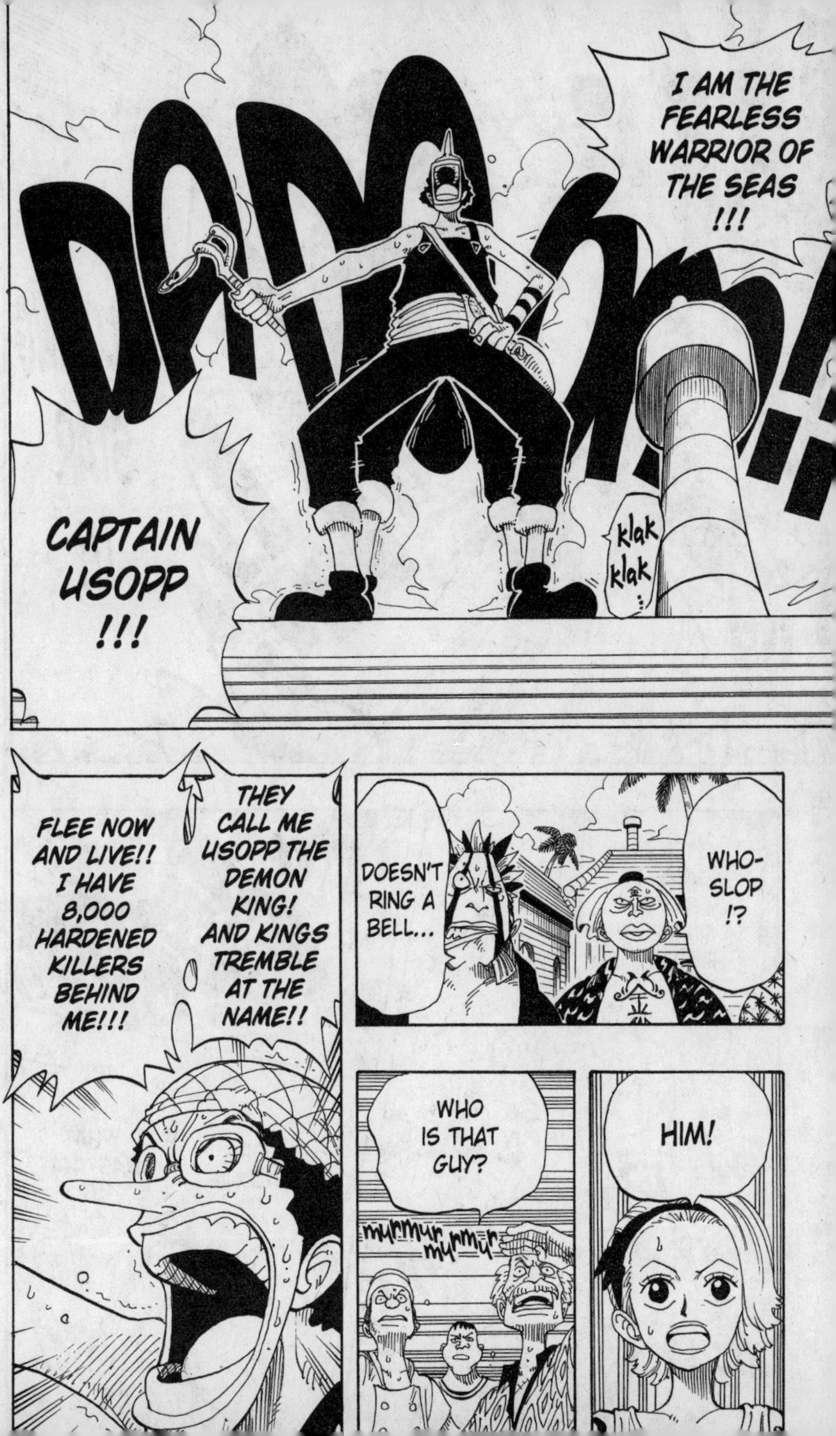
I AM THE FEARLESS WARRIOR OF THE SEAS !!!
CAPTAIN USOPP !!!
klak klak
WHO-SLOP !?
DOESN'T RING A BELL...
HIM!
WHO IS THAT GUY?
murmur murmur
THEY CALL ME USOPP THE DEMON KING! AND KINGS TREMBLE AT THE NAME!!
FLEE NOW AND LIVE!! I HAVE 8,000 HARDENED KILLERS BEHIND ME!!!

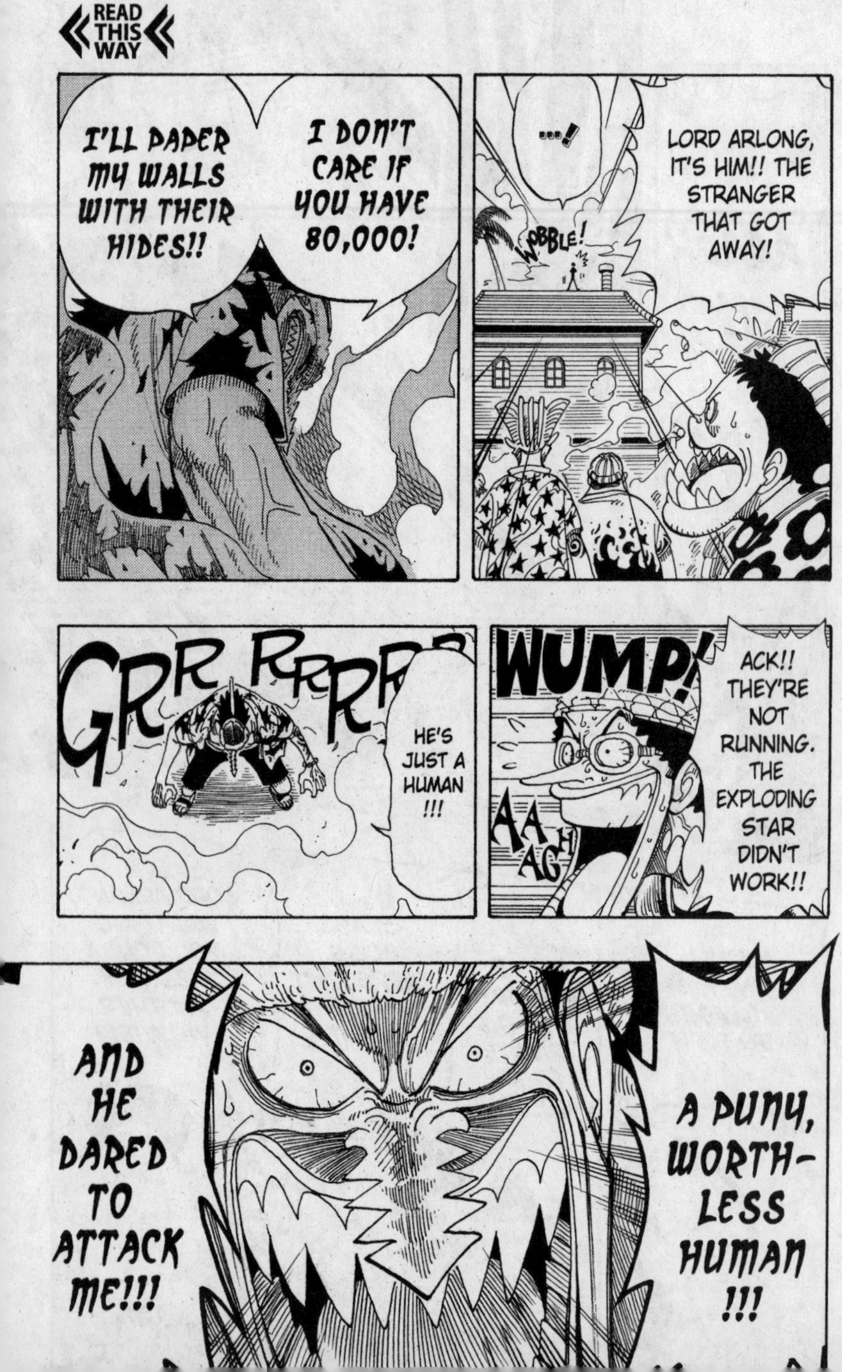
READ THIS WAY
...!
LORD ARLONG, IT'S HIM!! THE STRANGER THAT GOT AWAY!
WOBBLE!
I DON'T CARE IF YOU HAVE 80,000!
I'LL PAPER MY WALLS WITH THEIR HIDES!!
WUMP!
ACK!! THEY'RE NOT RUNNING. THE EXPLODING STAR DIDN'T WORK!!
AAAGH
GRRRRRRR
HE'S JUST A HUMAN !!!
A PUNY, WORTHLESS HUMAN !!!
AND HE DARED TO ATTACK ME!!!

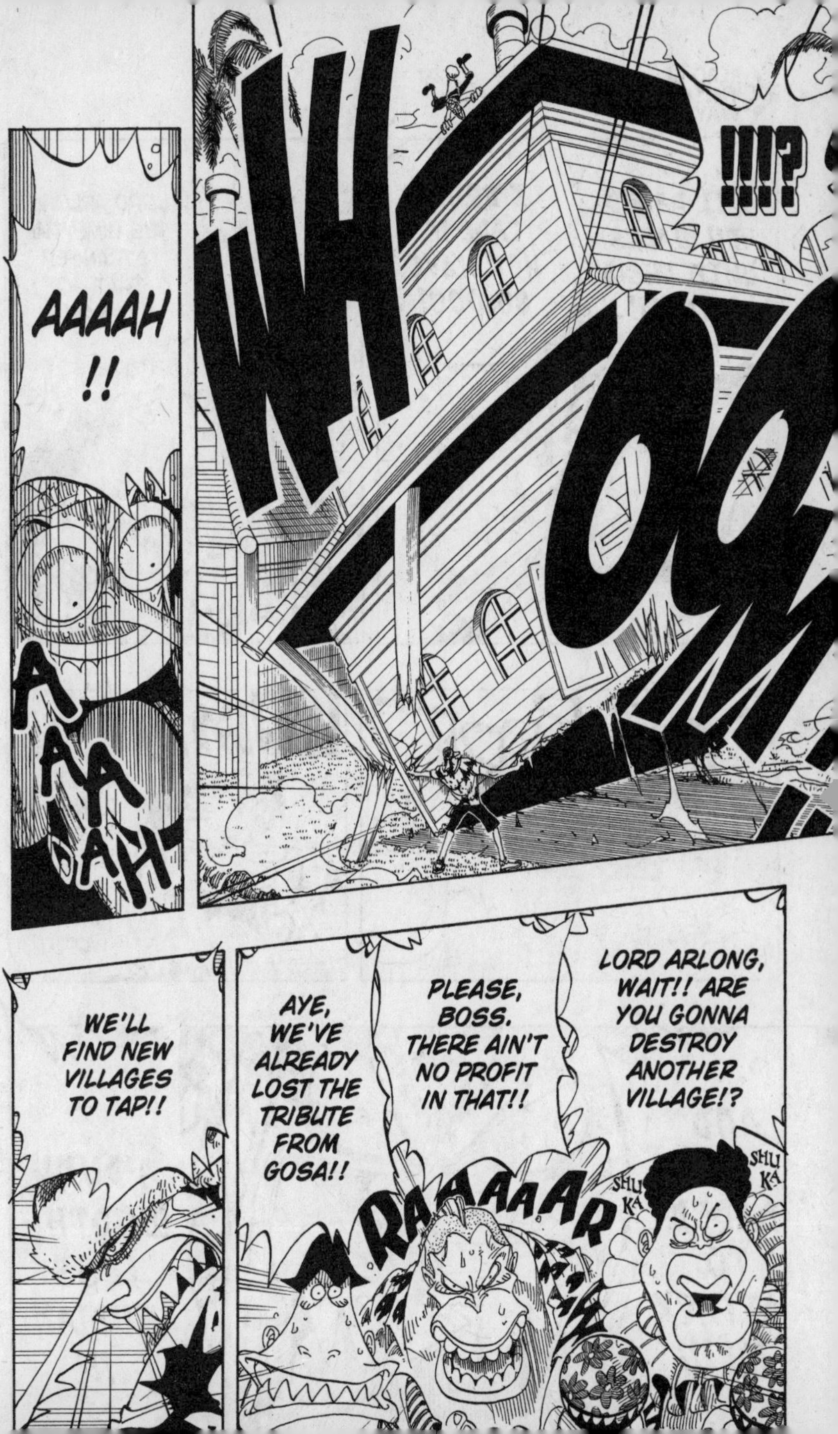

WHOOM
!!!?
AAAAH !!
AAAAH
LORD ARLONG, WAIT!! ARE YOU GONNA DESTROY ANOTHER VILLAGE!?
PLEASE, BOSS. THERE AIN'T NO PROFIT IN THAT!!
AYE, WE'VE ALREADY LOST THE TRIBUTE FROM GOSA!!
SHUKA
SHUKA
RAAAAAR
WE'LL FIND NEW VILLAGES TO TAP!!

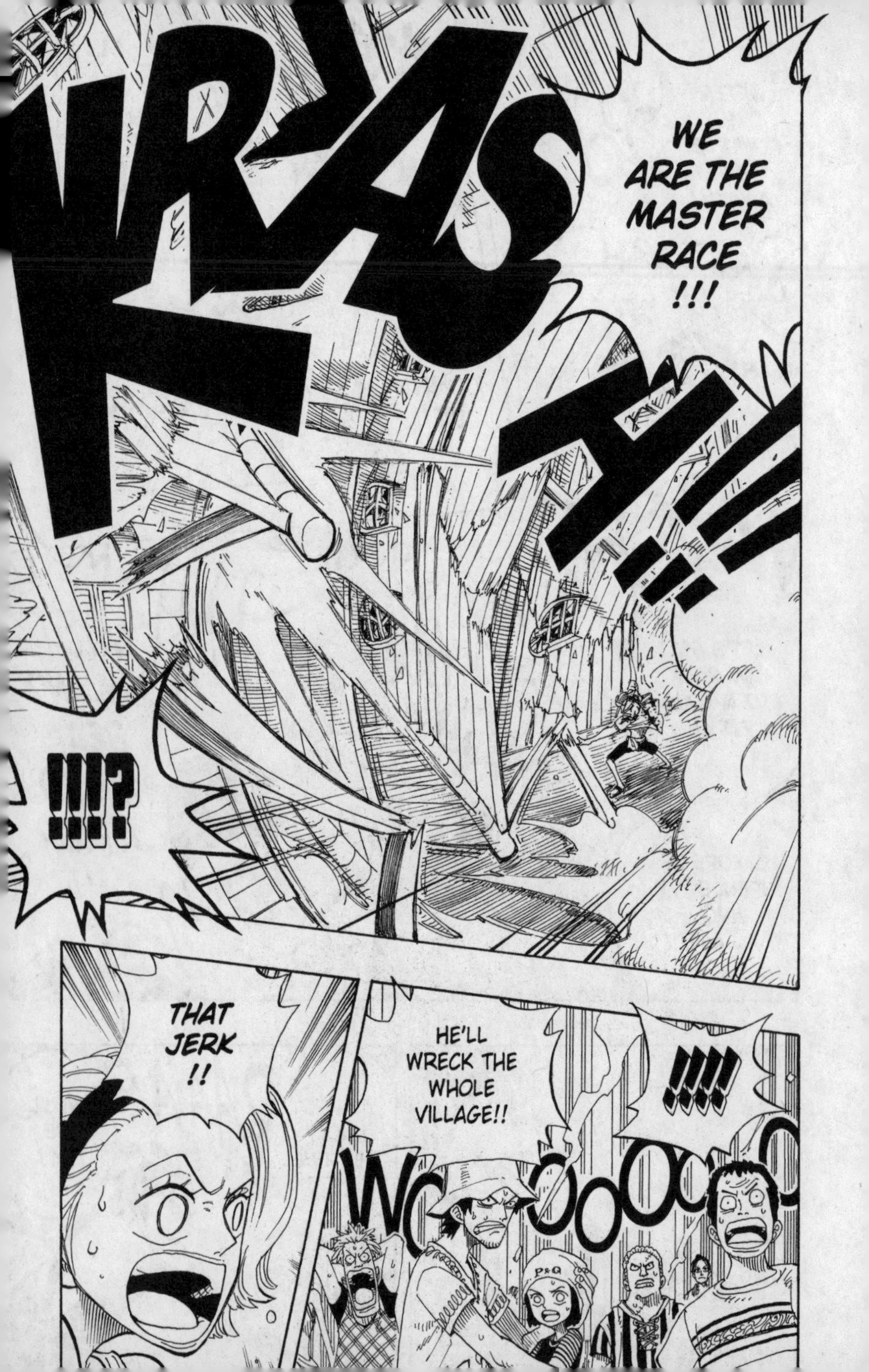
WE ARE THE MASTER RACE!!!
KRASH!!!
!!!?
!!!!
WOOOOOO
HE'LL WRECK THE WHOLE VILLAGE!!
THAT JERK!!

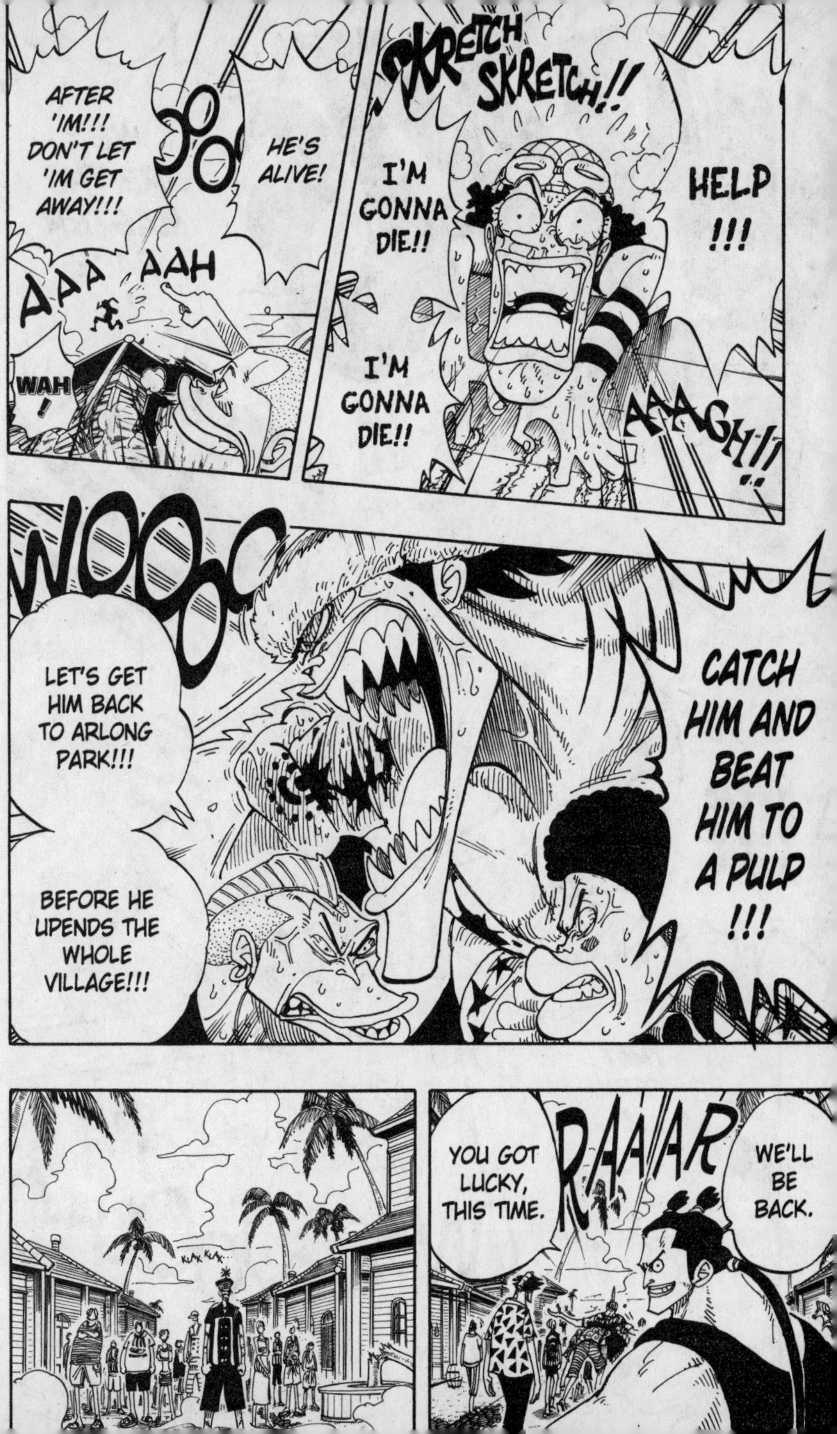
SKRETCH SKRETCH!!
HELP !!!
I'M GONNA DIE!!
I'M GONNA DIE!!
AAAGH!!
HE'S ALIVE!
AFTER 'IM!!! DON'T LET 'IM GET AWAY!!!
AAA AAH
WAH!
CATCH HIM AND BEAT HIM TO A PULP !!!
WOOO
LET'S GET HIM BACK TO ARLONG PARK!!!
BEFORE HE UPENDS THE WHOLE VILLAGE!!!
WE'LL BE BACK.
RAAAR
YOU GOT LUCKY, THIS TIME.

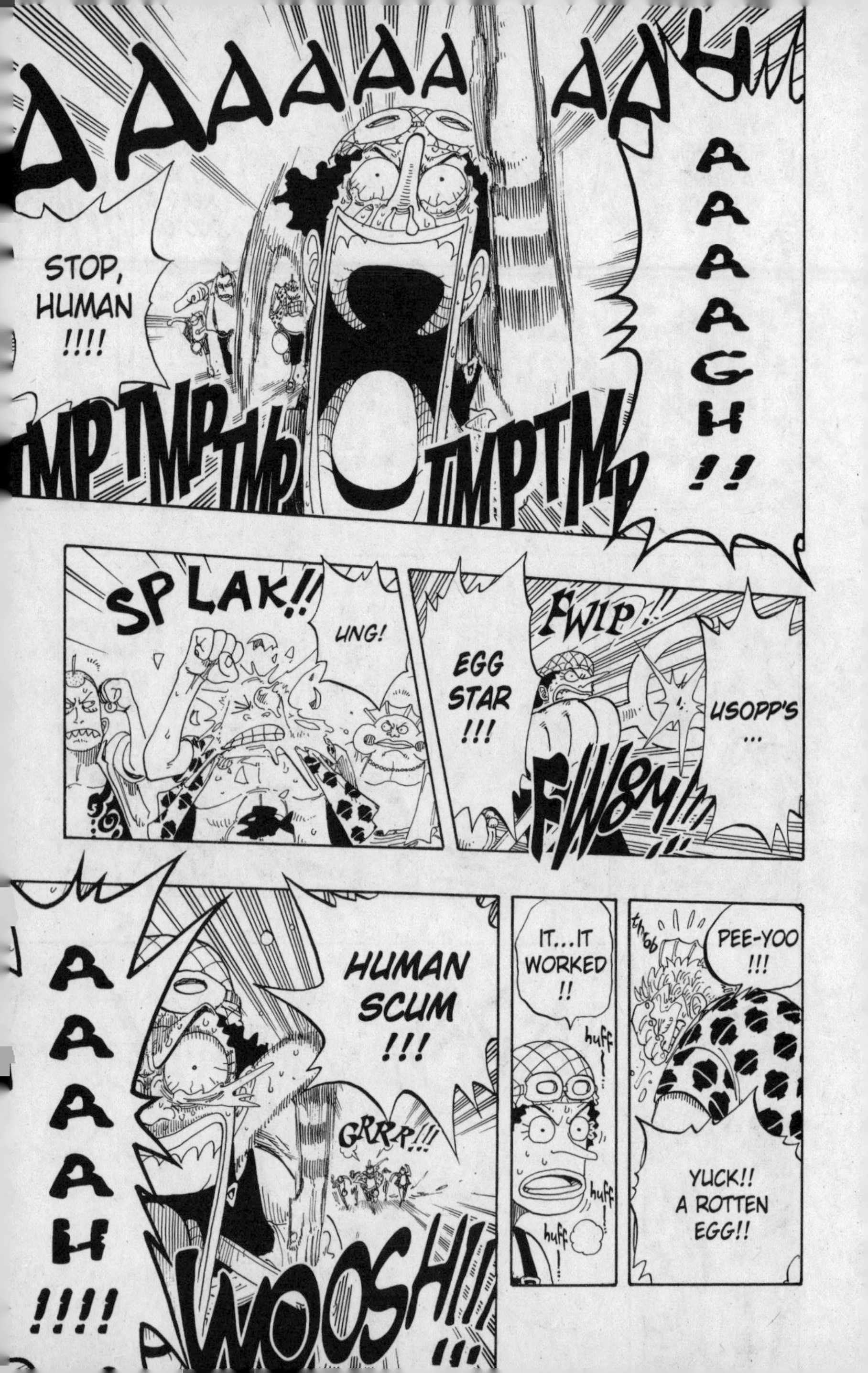
AAAAAAAA
AAAAGH!!
STOP, HUMAN!!!!
TMP TMP TMP TMP TMP
USOPP'S ...
EGG STAR!!!
FWIP!!
FWOOM!!
SPLAK!!
UNG!
PEE-YOO!!!
YUCK!! A ROTTEN EGG!!
IT...IT WORKED!!
huff
huff
huff
HUMAN SCUM!!!
AAAAAH!!!!
GRRR!!!
WOOSH!!!

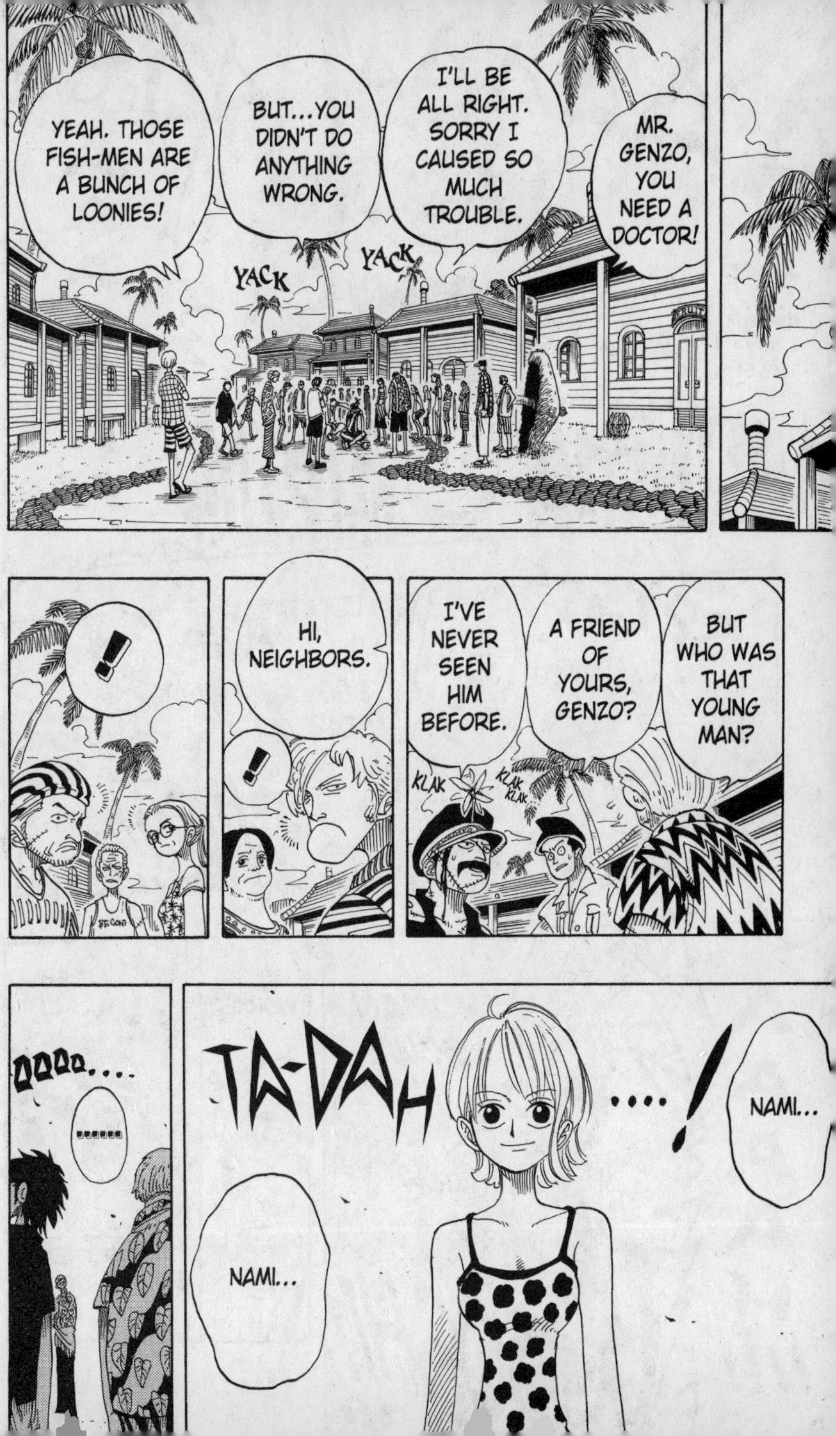
MR. GENZO, YOU NEED A DOCTOR!
I'LL BE ALL RIGHT. SORRY I CAUSED SO MUCH TROUBLE.
YACK
BUT...YOU DIDN'T DO ANYTHING WRONG.
YACK
YEAH. THOSE FISH-MEN ARE A BUNCH OF LOONIES!
BUT WHO WAS THAT YOUNG MAN?
A FRIEND OF YOURS, GENZO?
I'VE NEVER SEEN HIM BEFORE.
KLAK KLAK
KLAK
HI, NEIGHBORS.
!
!
NAMI...
....!
TA-DAH
NAMI...
QQQQ....
......

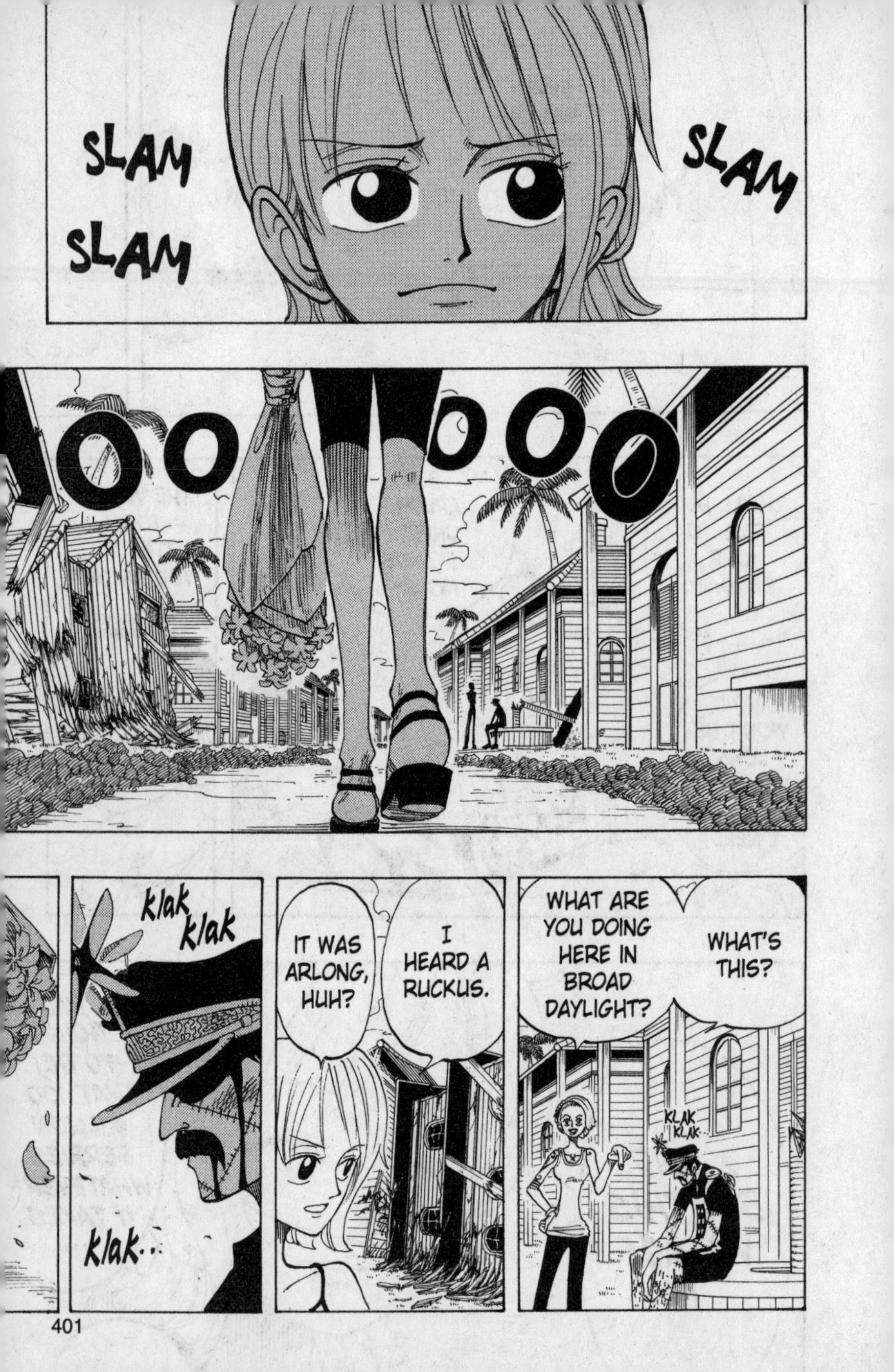
SLAM
SLAM
SLAM
DOOO
OO
WHAT'S THIS?
WHAT ARE YOU DOING HERE IN BROAD DAYLIGHT?
KLAK KLAK
I HEARD A RUCKUS.
IT WAS ARLONG, HUH?
klak klak
klak..

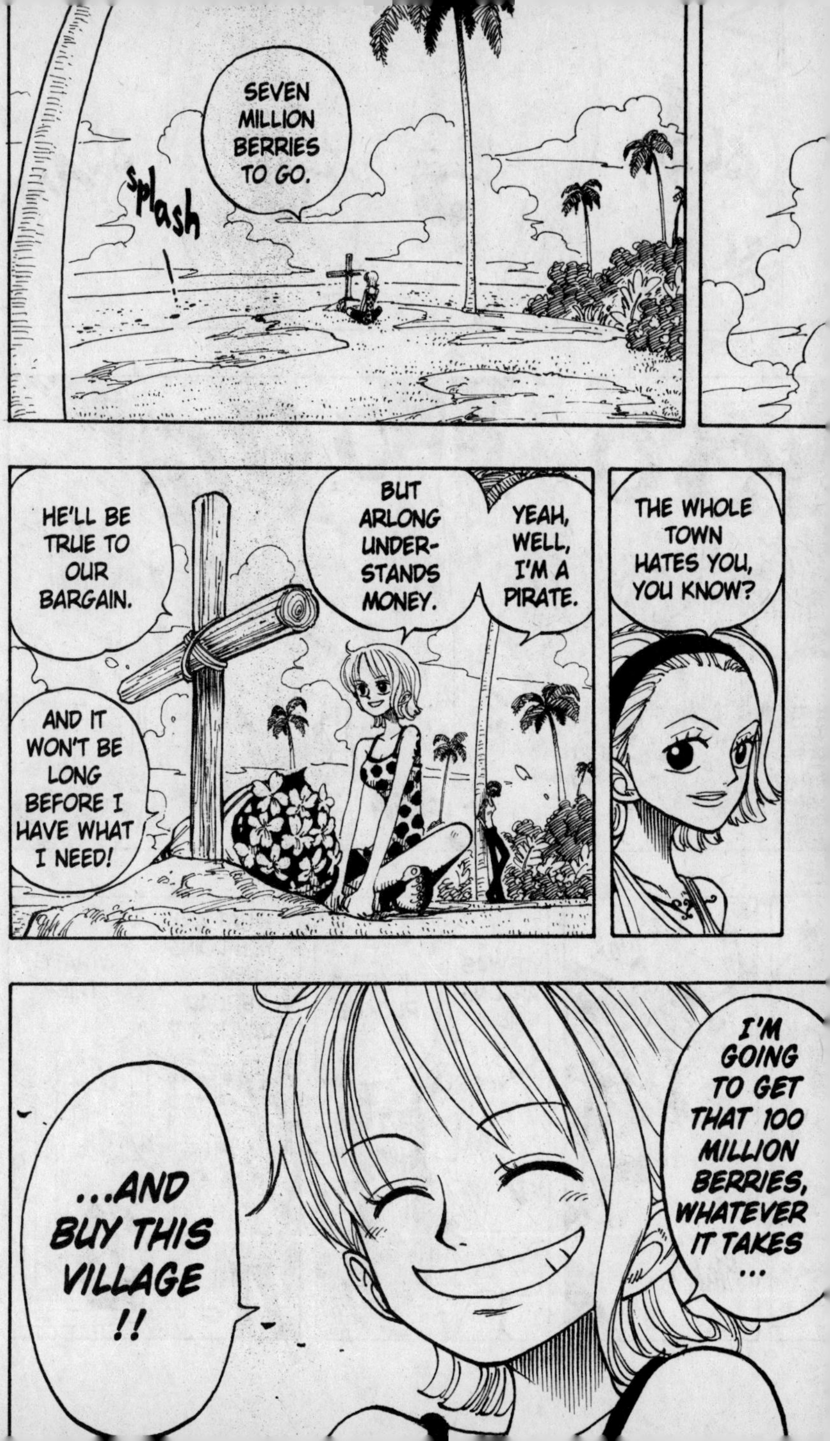
SEVEN MILLION BERRIES TO GO.
Splash
THE WHOLE TOWN HATES YOU, YOU KNOW?
YEAH, WELL, I'M A PIRATE.
BUT ARLONG UNDER-STANDS MONEY.
HE'LL BE TRUE TO OUR BARGAIN.
AND IT WON'T BE LONG BEFORE I HAVE WHAT I NEED!
I'M GOING TO GET THAT 100 MILLION BERRIES, WHATEVER IT TAKES ...
...AND BUY THIS VILLAGE !!

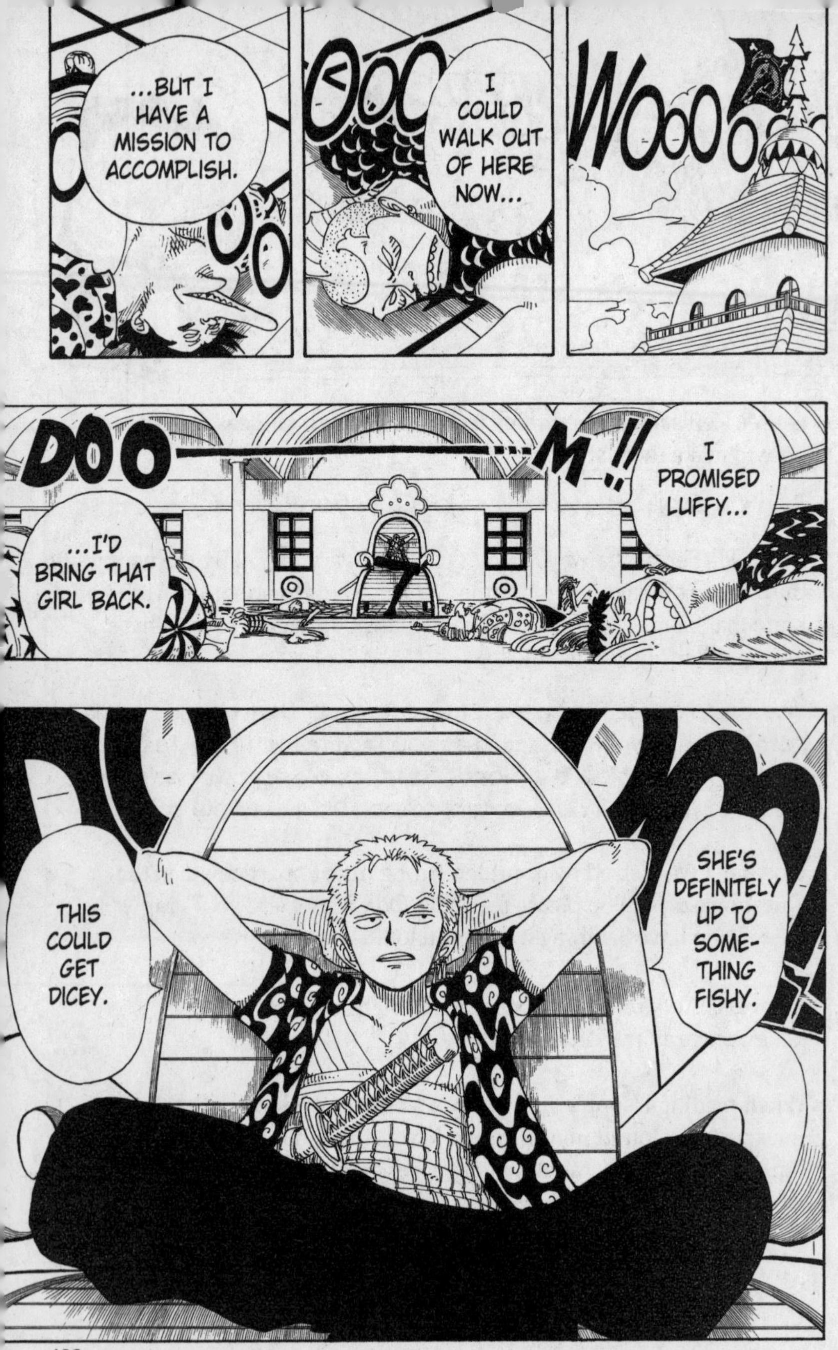
WOOOOO
OOO
I COULD WALK OUT OF HERE NOW...
...BUT I HAVE A MISSION TO ACCOMPLISH.
DOO———M!!
I PROMISED LUFFY...
...I'D BRING THAT GIRL BACK.
SHE'S DEFINITELY UP TO SOME-THING FISHY.
THIS COULD GET DICEY.

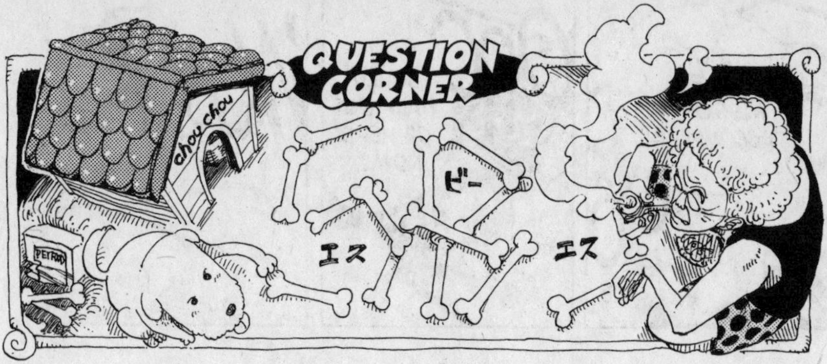
QUESTION CORNER
chou chou
エス
ビー
エス

**Q:** Sensei, Zeff's mustache-braids won't stop growing! Please tell me how to make them stop.

**A:** Don't worry!! Sit back and enjoy Question Corner!!

**Q:** Dear Oda Sensei, I always enjoy *One Piece* very much! By the way, in the third panel on page 18 of volume 7, there seems to be some writing on the knife that Sanji is holding, but I can't make out what it says. What's written there? Please tell me!!

**A:** You couldn't read it because I wrote it so that no one could read it. Still, I'm impressed that you spotted it. I'll confess. I did in fact write **Fist of the North Star**. It's a great manga that I was crazy about in elementary school. Do you know it?

**Q:** One day I was seized by a sudden strong urge to participate in the Question Corner!! So please read this. Oda Sensei, are you "crap"-crazy? You have Sanji say it an awful lot!!

**A:** Heavens! What a filthy, nasty word! I'm embarrassed to even read it!! Please stop!!

**Q:** When reading Usopp's tale, Merry's words moved me so that I unexpectedly found myself crying like a strong man (even though I'm a girl). The tears ran down my cheeks and got in my mouth. Know what they tasted like?

**A:** Eyes cream?

**Q:** I heard that Sanji's favorite snack is cake.

**A:** It is?

# Chapter 73:
# MONSTERS OF THE GRAND LINE

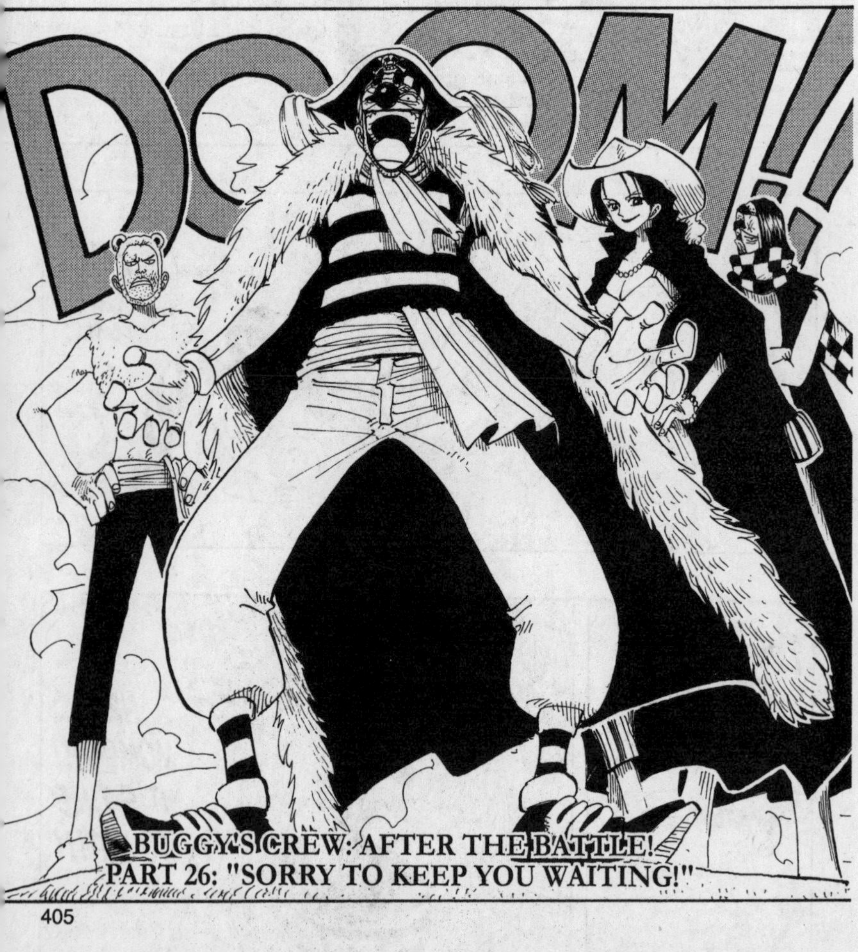
DOOM!!
BUGGY'S CREW: AFTER THE BATTLE!
PART 26: "SORRY TO KEEP YOU WAITING!"

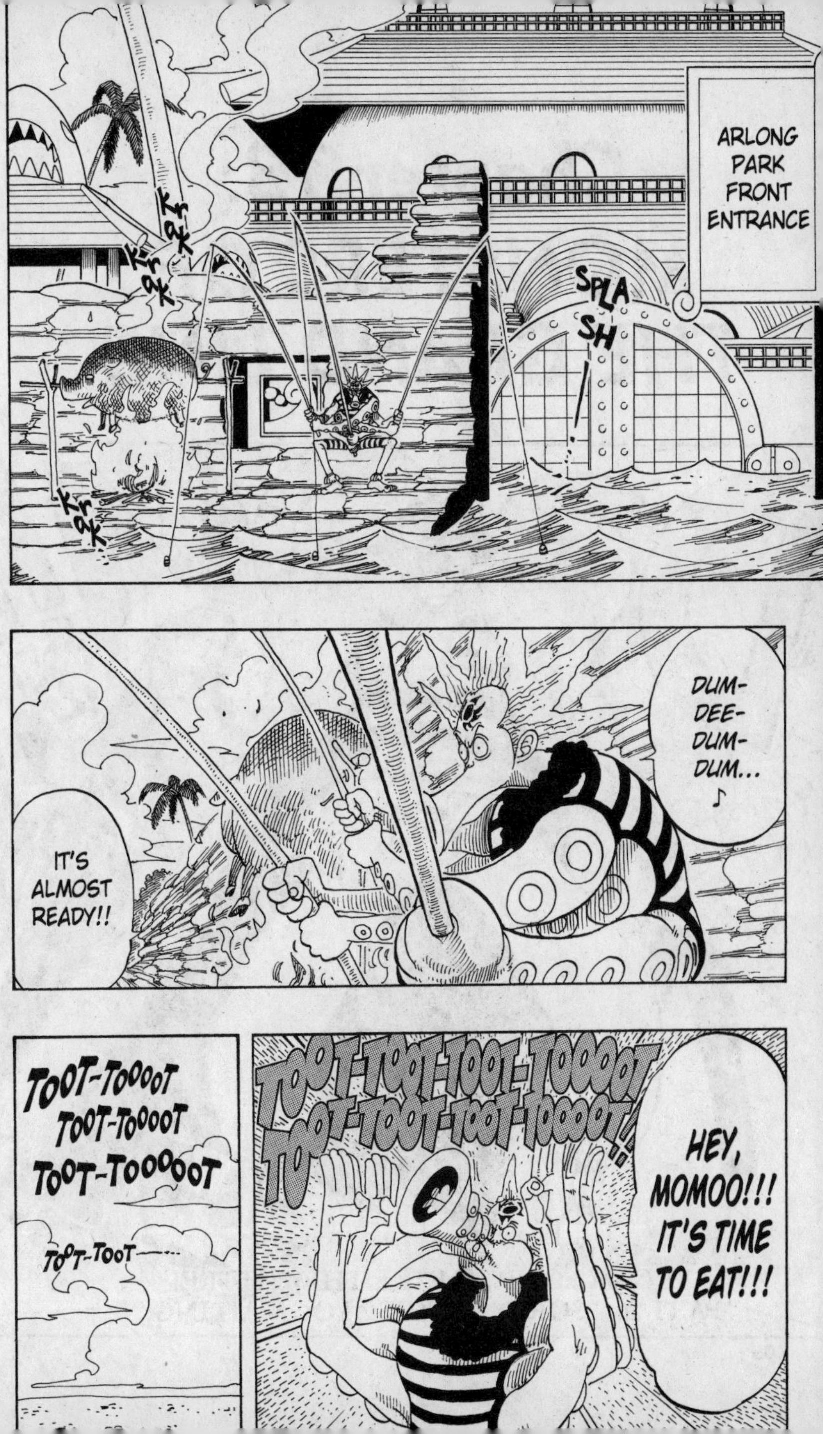
ARLONG PARK FRONT ENTRANCE
SPLASH
krak
krak
krak
DUM-DEE-DUM-DUM... ♪
IT'S ALMOST READY!!
HEY, MOMOO!!! IT'S TIME TO EAT!!!
TOOT-TOOT-TOOT-TOOOOT
TOOT-TOOT-TOOT-TOOOOT!!
TOOT-TOOOOT
TOOT-TOOOOT
TOOT-TOOOOOT
TOOT-TOOT----

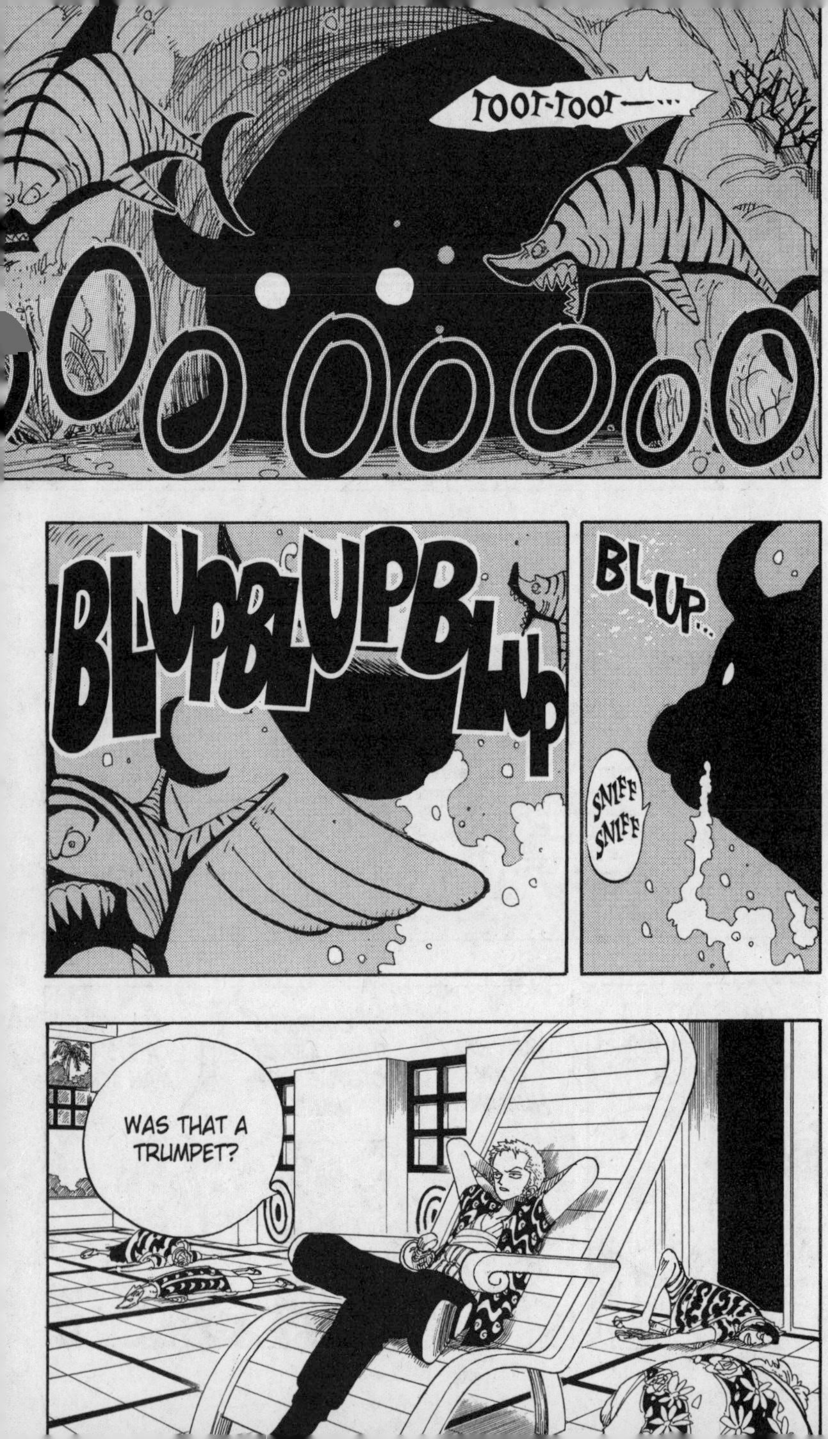
TOOT-TOOT—...
OOOOOOOO
BLUP...
SNIFF SNIFF
BLUPBLUPBLUP
WAS THAT A TRUMPET?

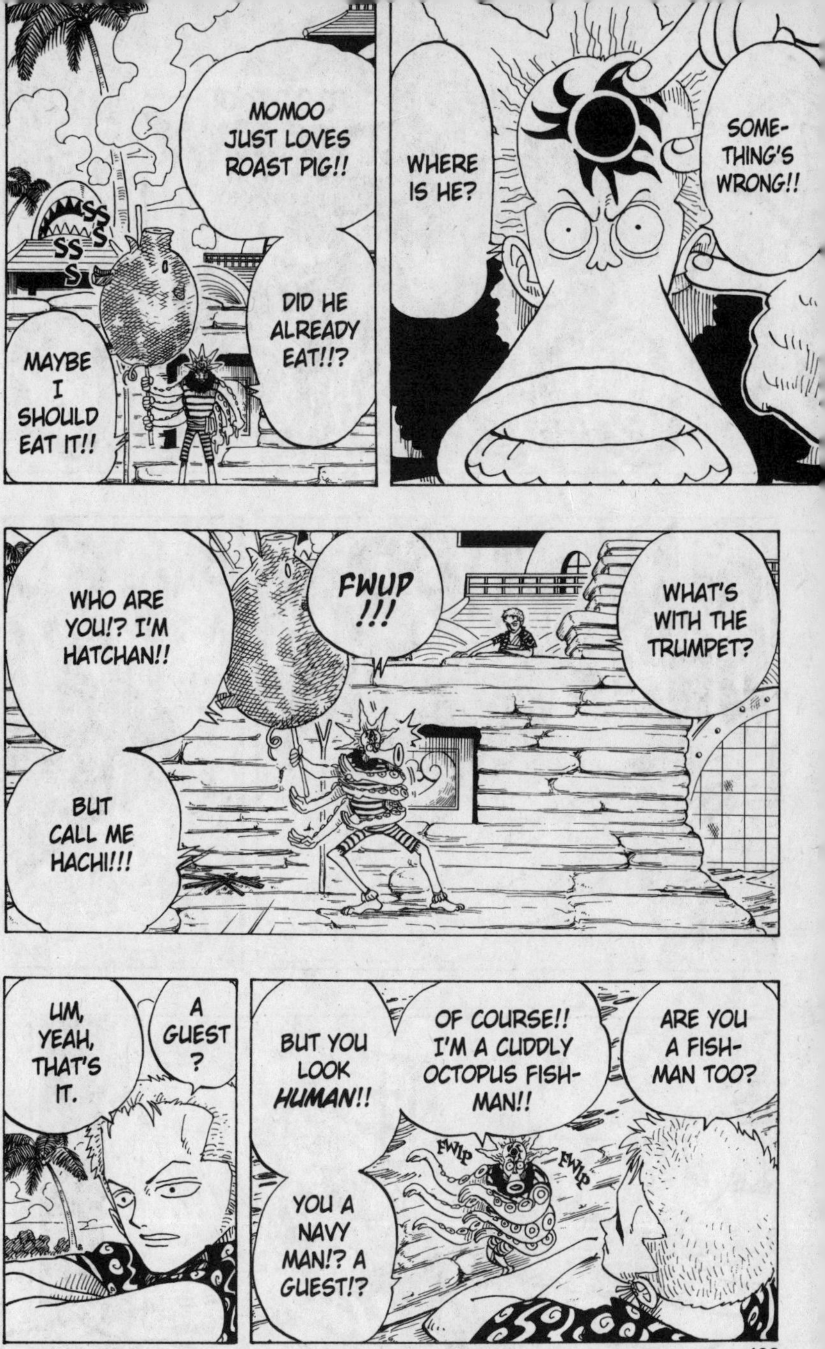
SOME-THING'S WRONG!!
WHERE IS HE?
MOMOO JUST LOVES ROAST PIG!!
DID HE ALREADY EAT!!?
SSSS
MAYBE I SHOULD EAT IT!!
WHAT'S WITH THE TRUMPET?
FWUP!!!
WHO ARE YOU!? I'M HATCHAN!!
BUT CALL ME HACHI!!!
ARE YOU A FISH-MAN TOO?
OF COURSE!! I'M A CUDDLY OCTOPUS FISH-MAN!!
FWIP FWIP
BUT YOU LOOK **HUMAN**!!
YOU A NAVY MAN!? A GUEST!?
A GUEST?
UM, YEAH, THAT'S IT.

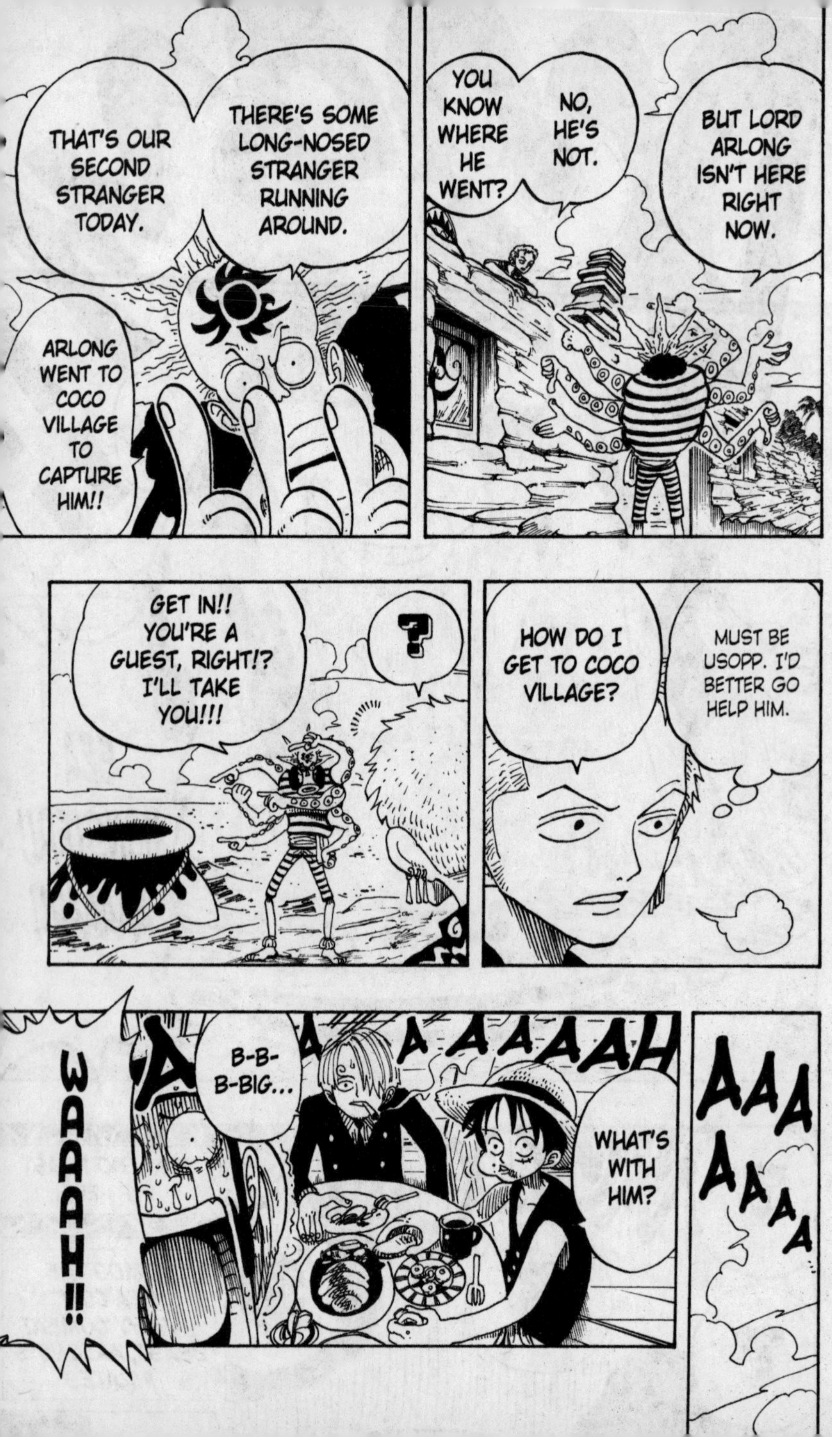
BUT LORD ARLONG ISN'T HERE RIGHT NOW.
NO, HE'S NOT.
YOU KNOW WHERE HE WENT?
THERE'S SOME LONG-NOSED STRANGER RUNNING AROUND.
THAT'S OUR SECOND STRANGER TODAY.
ARLONG WENT TO COCO VILLAGE TO CAPTURE HIM!!
MUST BE USOPP. I'D BETTER GO HELP HIM.
HOW DO I GET TO COCO VILLAGE?
?
GET IN!! YOU'RE A GUEST, RIGHT!? I'LL TAKE YOU!!!
AAAAAAA
AAAAAAH
WHAT'S WITH HIM?
B-B-B-BIG...
WAAAAH!!

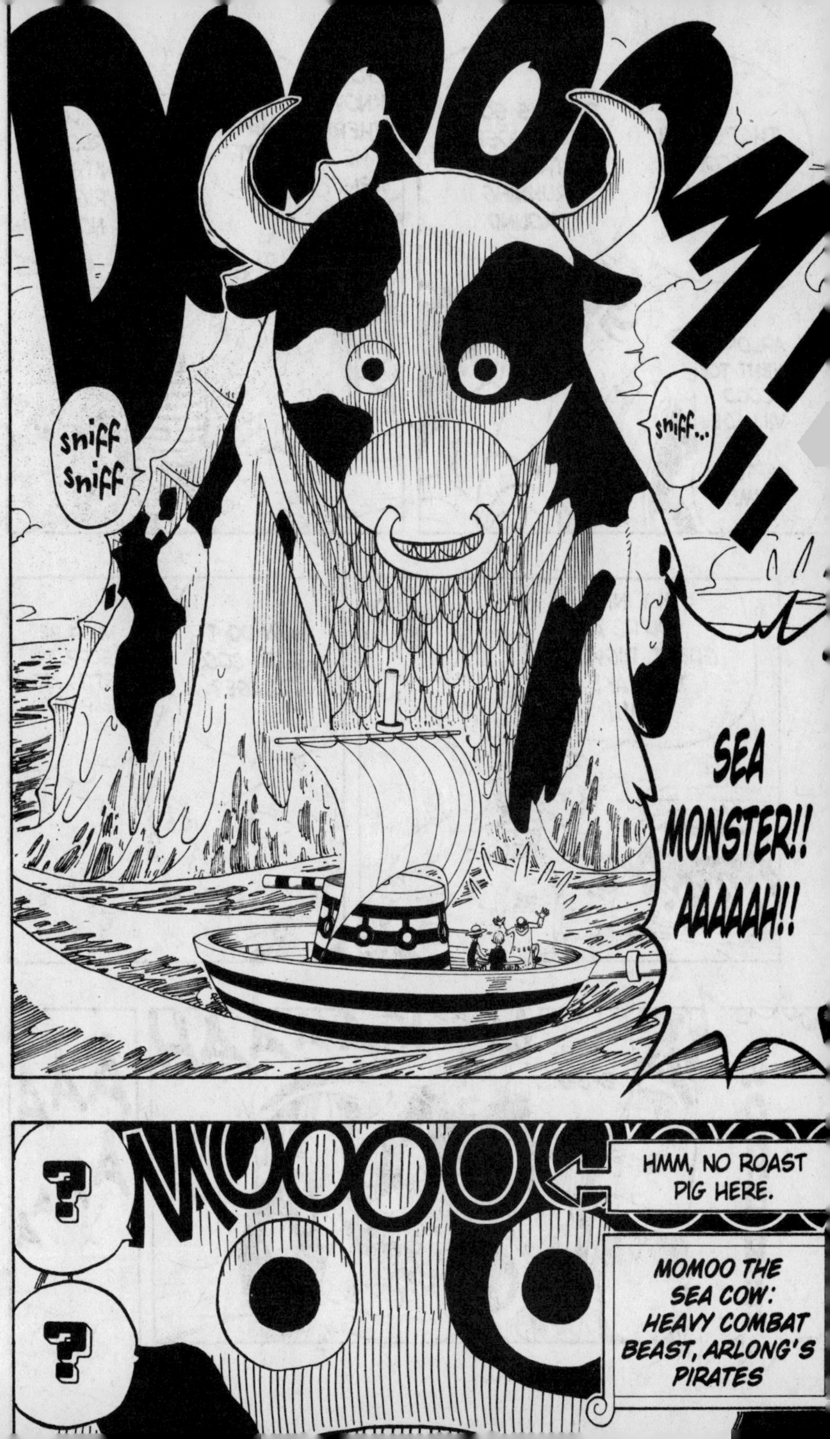
DOOOOM!!!!
sniff...
sniff sniff
SEA MONSTER!! AAAAAH!!
HMM, NO ROAST PIG HERE.
MOMOO THE SEA COW: HEAVY COMBAT BEAST, ARLONG'S PIRATES
MOOOO
?
?

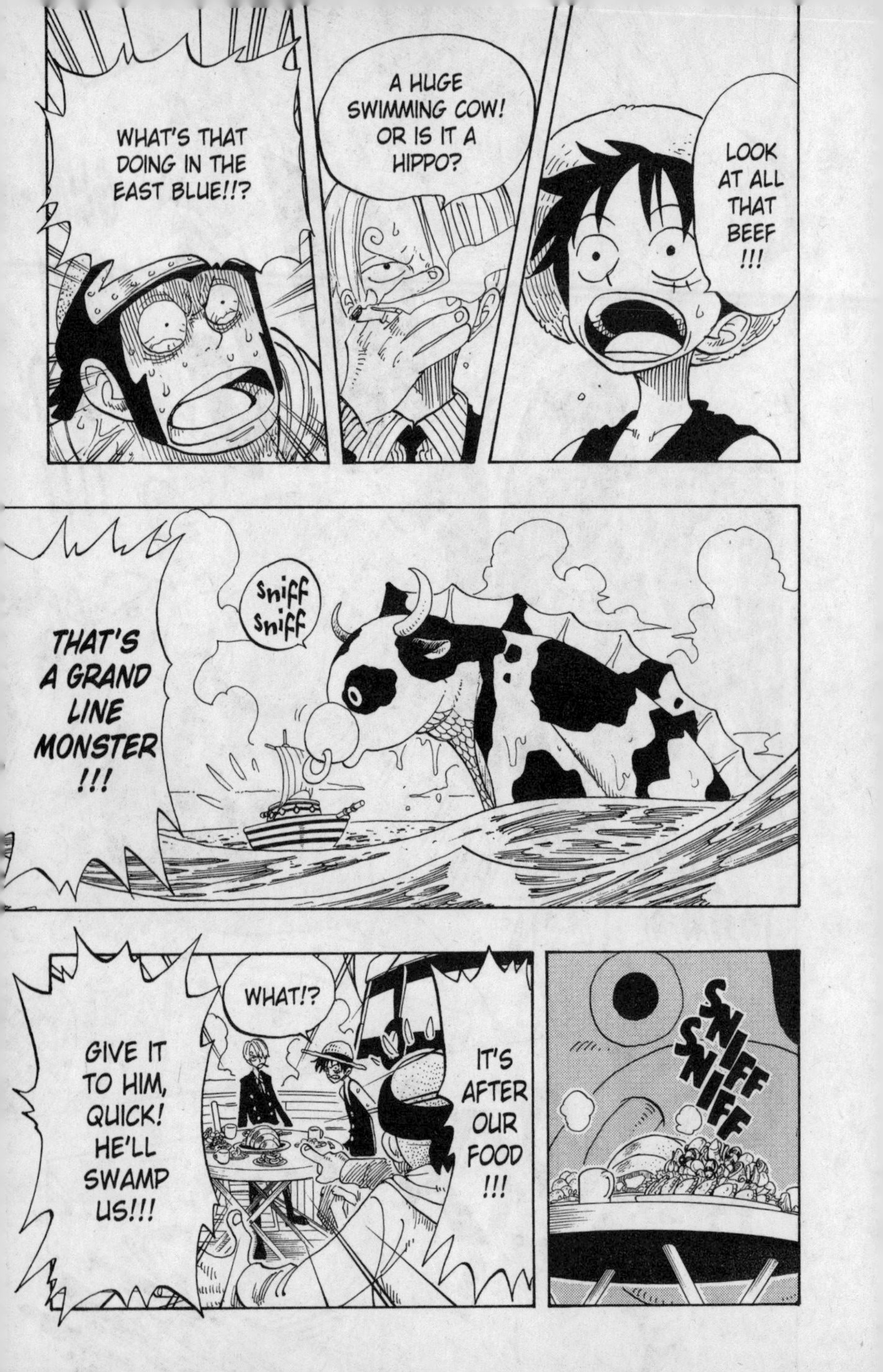
LOOK AT ALL THAT BEEF!!!
A HUGE SWIMMING COW! OR IS IT A HIPPO?
WHAT'S THAT DOING IN THE EAST BLUE!!?
sniff sniff
THAT'S A GRAND LINE MONSTER!!!
SNIFF SNIFF
IT'S AFTER OUR FOOD!!!
WHAT!?
GIVE IT TO HIM, QUICK! HE'LL SWAMP US!!!

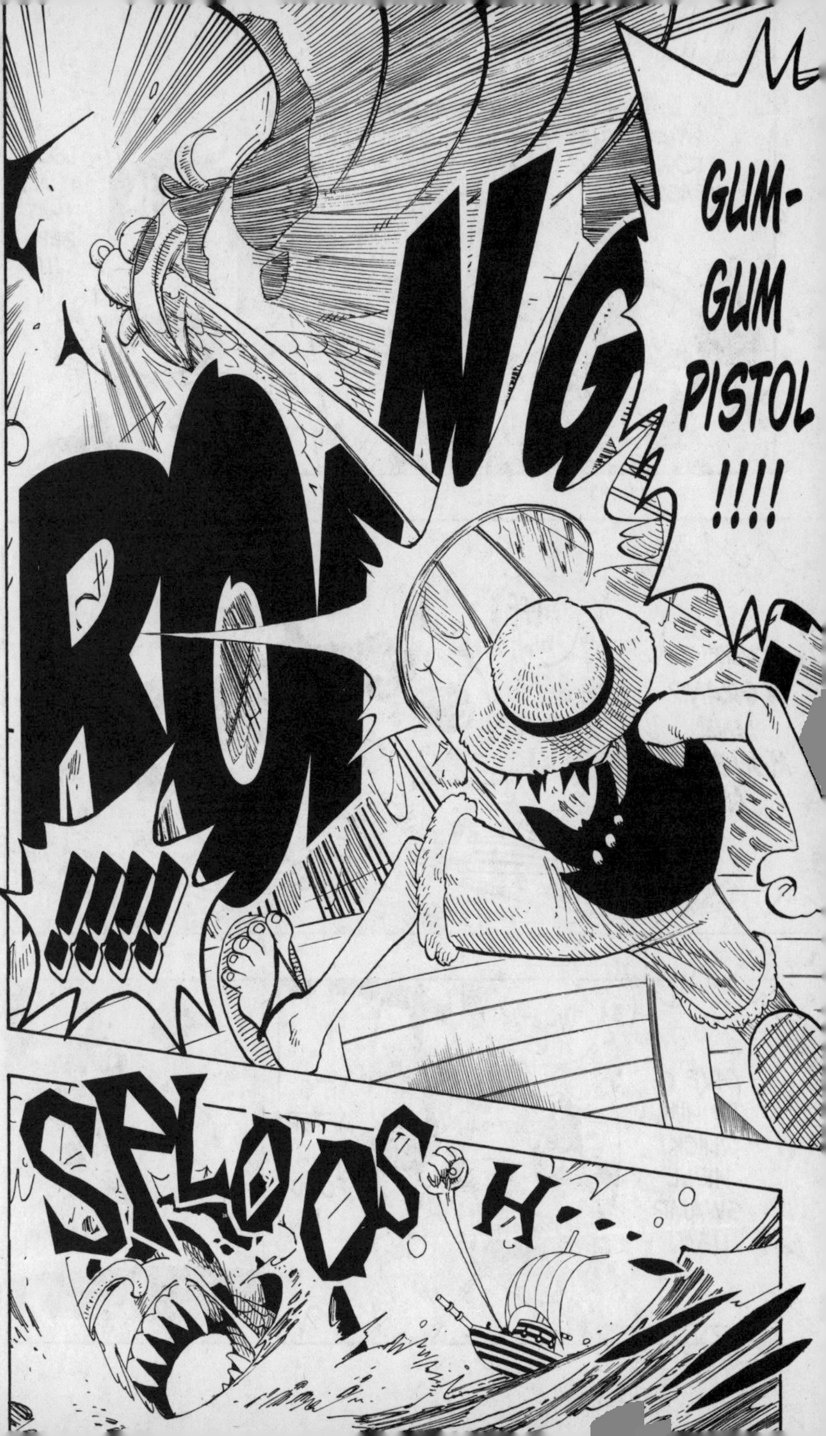
GUM-GUM PISTOL!!!!
SPLOOSH

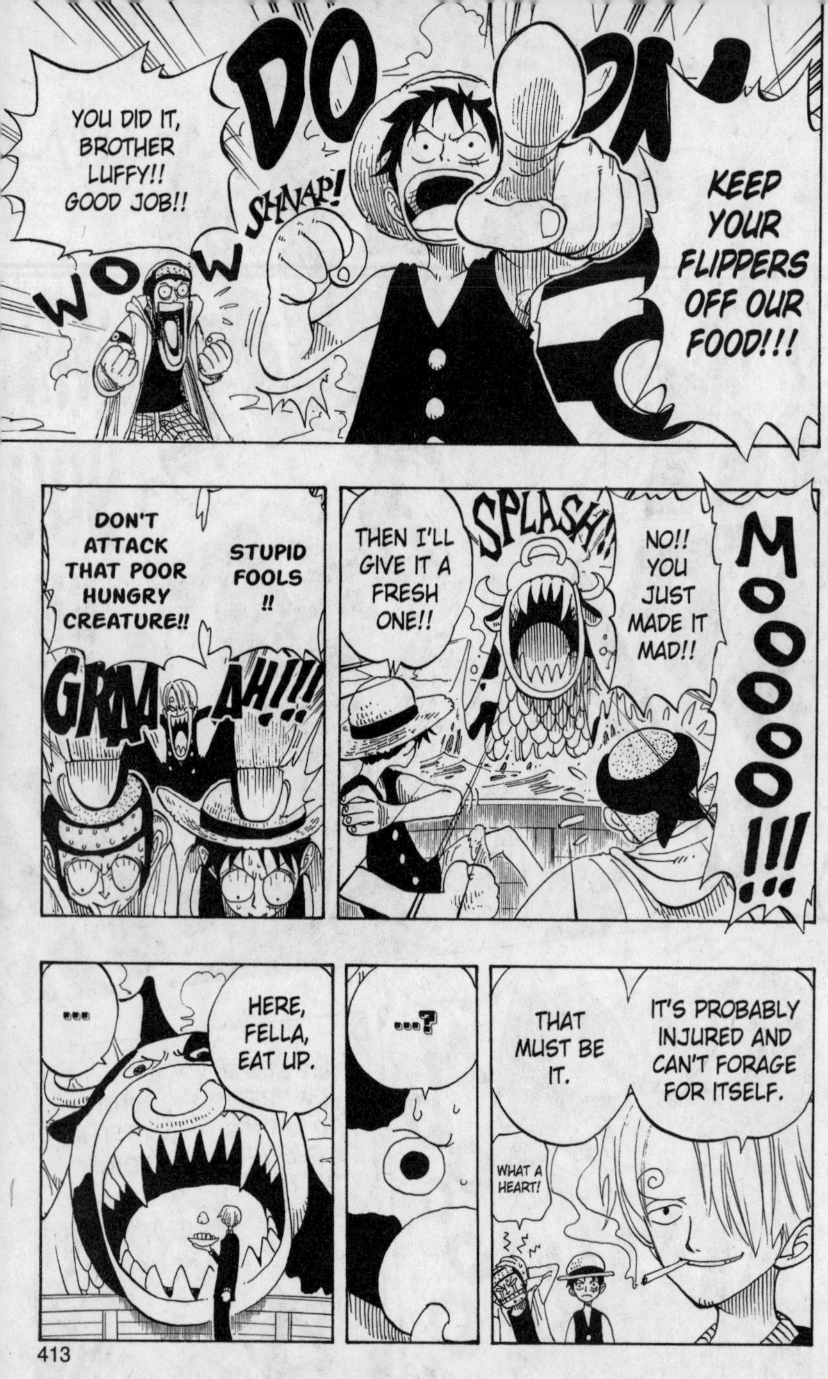
KEEP YOUR FLIPPERS OFF OUR FOOD!!!
DO
SHNAP!
YOU DID IT, BROTHER LUFFY!! GOOD JOB!!
WOW
MOOOOOO!!!
NO!! YOU JUST MADE IT MAD!!
SPLASH!!
THEN I'LL GIVE IT A FRESH ONE!!
STUPID FOOLS!!
DON'T ATTACK THAT POOR HUNGRY CREATURE!!
GRAA...AH!!!
IT'S PROBABLY INJURED AND CAN'T FORAGE FOR ITSELF.
THAT MUST BE IT.
WHAT A HEART!
...?
HERE, FELLA, EAT UP.
...

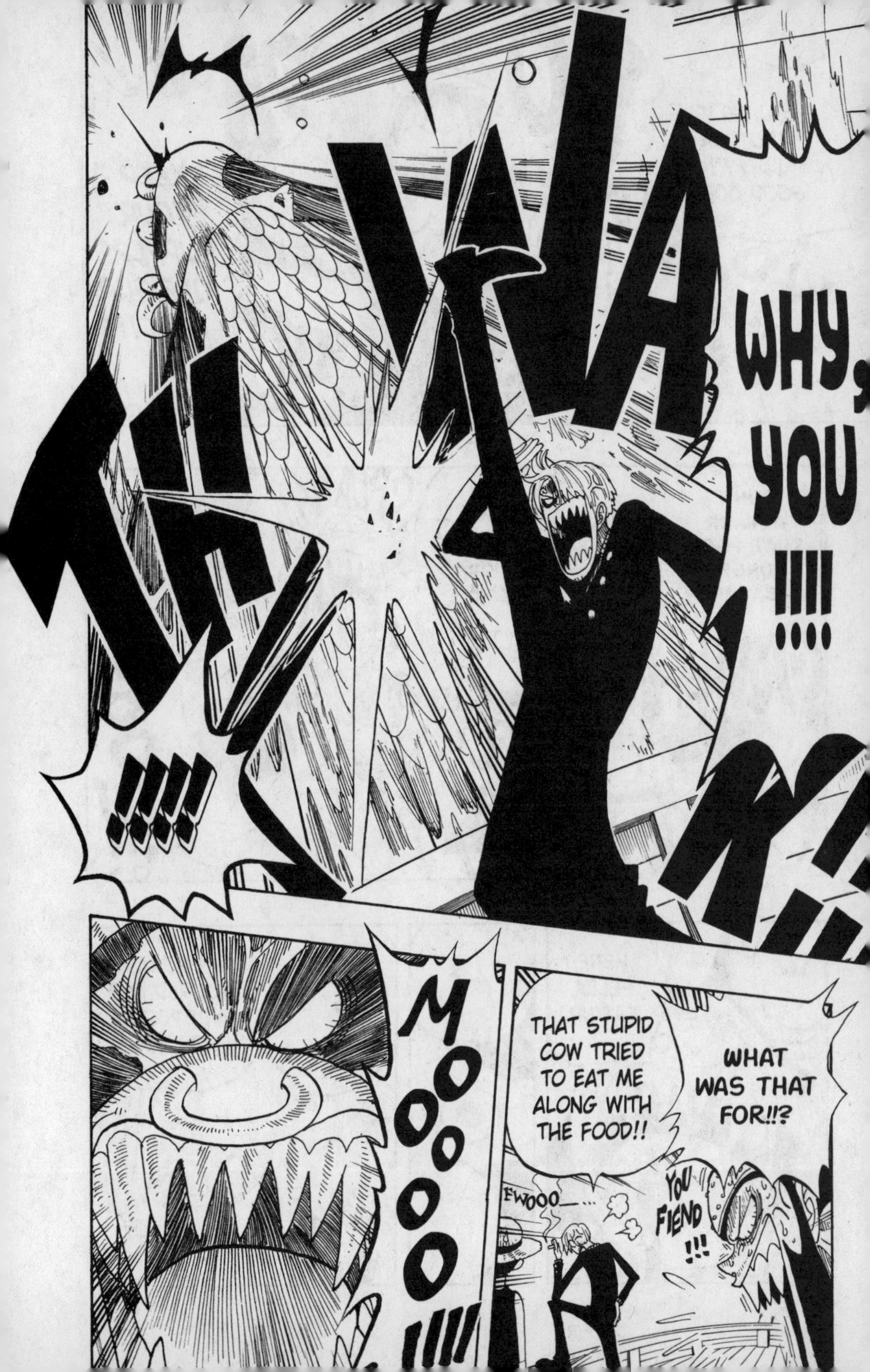
WHY, YOU!!!!
THWAK!!!!
WHAT WAS THAT FOR!!?
THAT STUPID COW TRIED TO EAT ME ALONG WITH THE FOOD!!
YOU FIEND!!!
FWOOO_...
MOOOOOOO!!!!

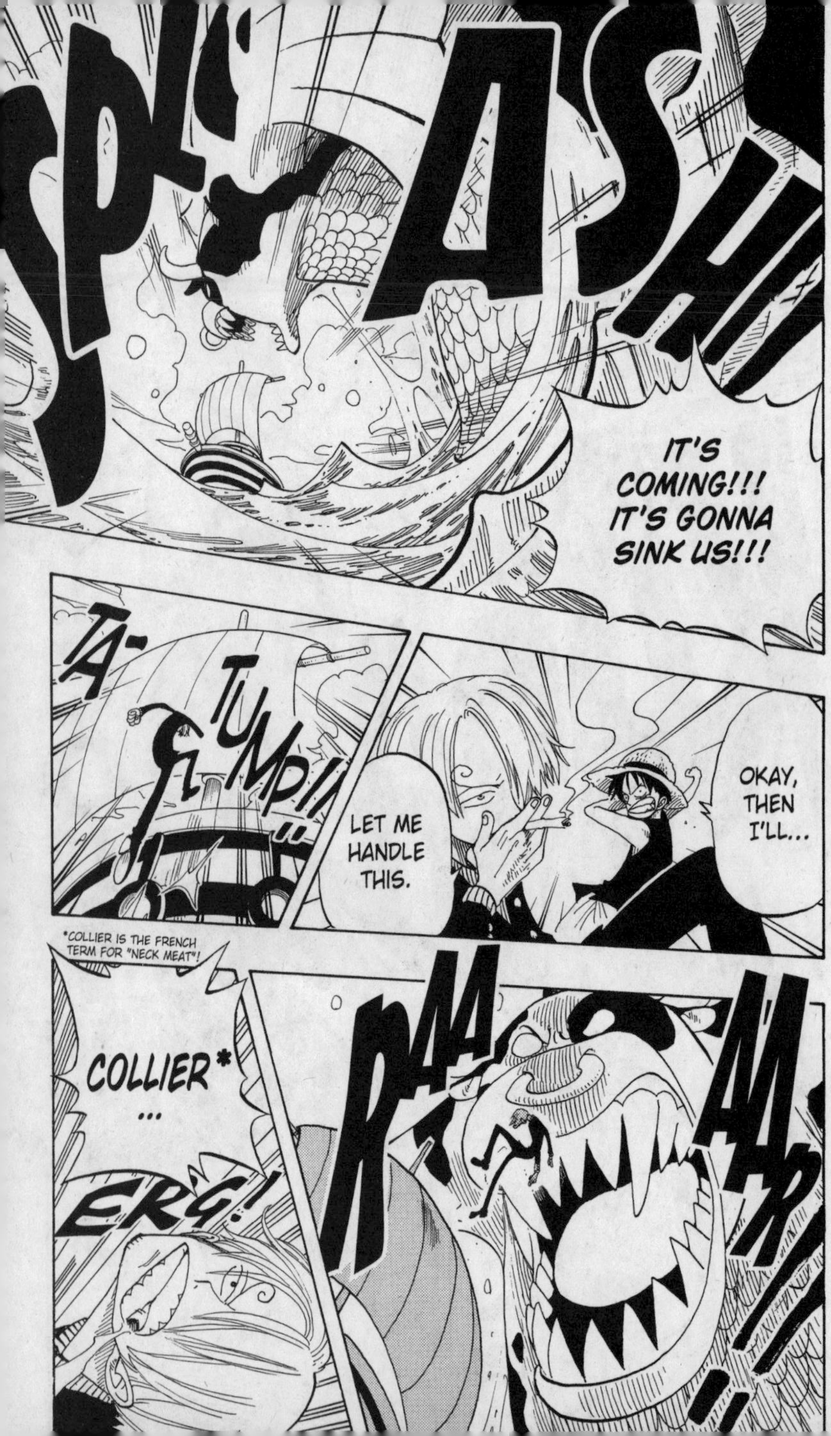
SPLASH
IT'S COMING!!! IT'S GONNA SINK US!!!
OKAY, THEN I'LL...
LET ME HANDLE THIS.
TA-TUMP!!
RAAAAR!!
COLLIER* ...
ERG!
*COLLIER IS THE FRENCH TERM FOR "NECK MEAT"!

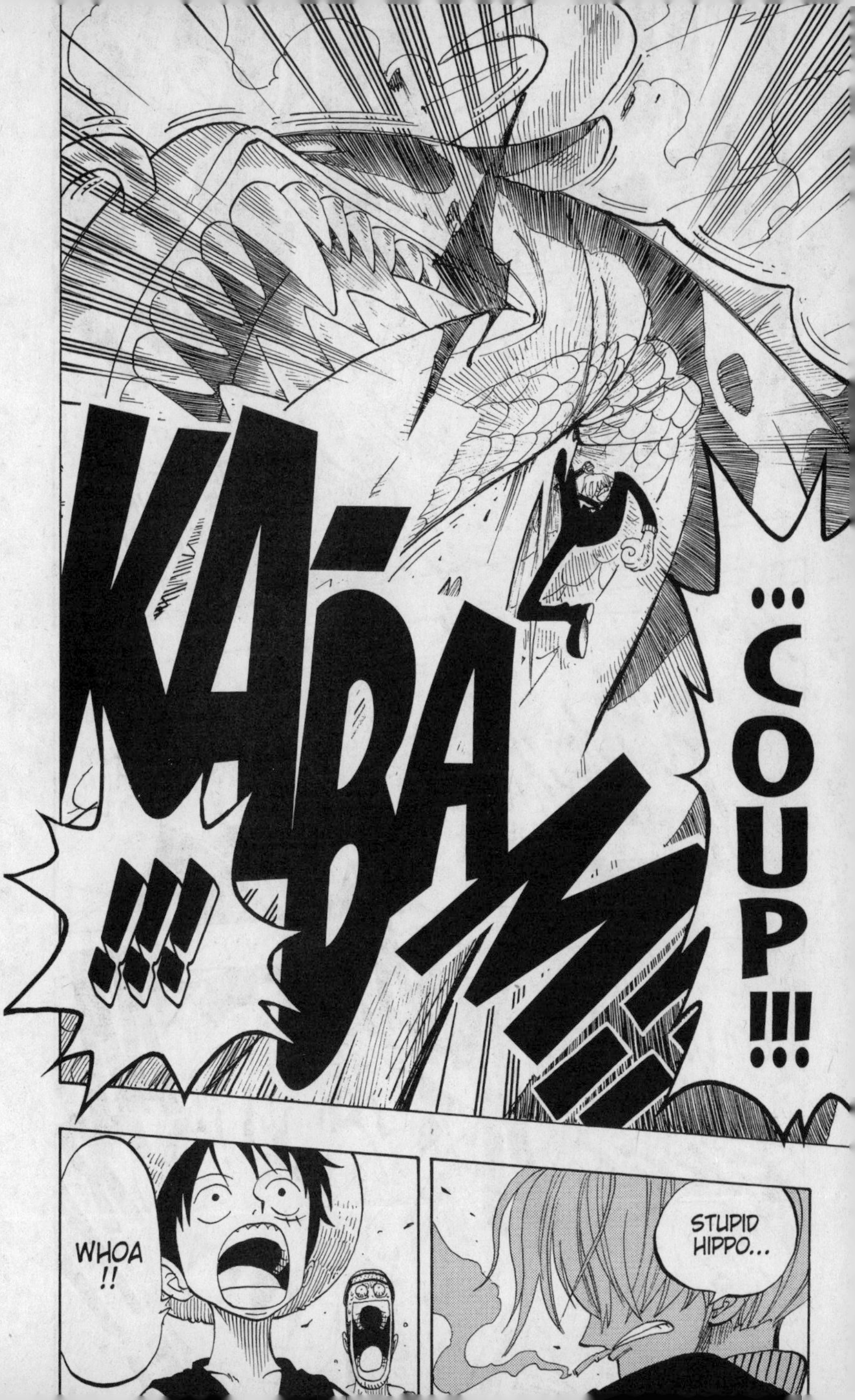
...COUP!!!
KABAM!!!
STUPID HIPPO...
WHOA !!

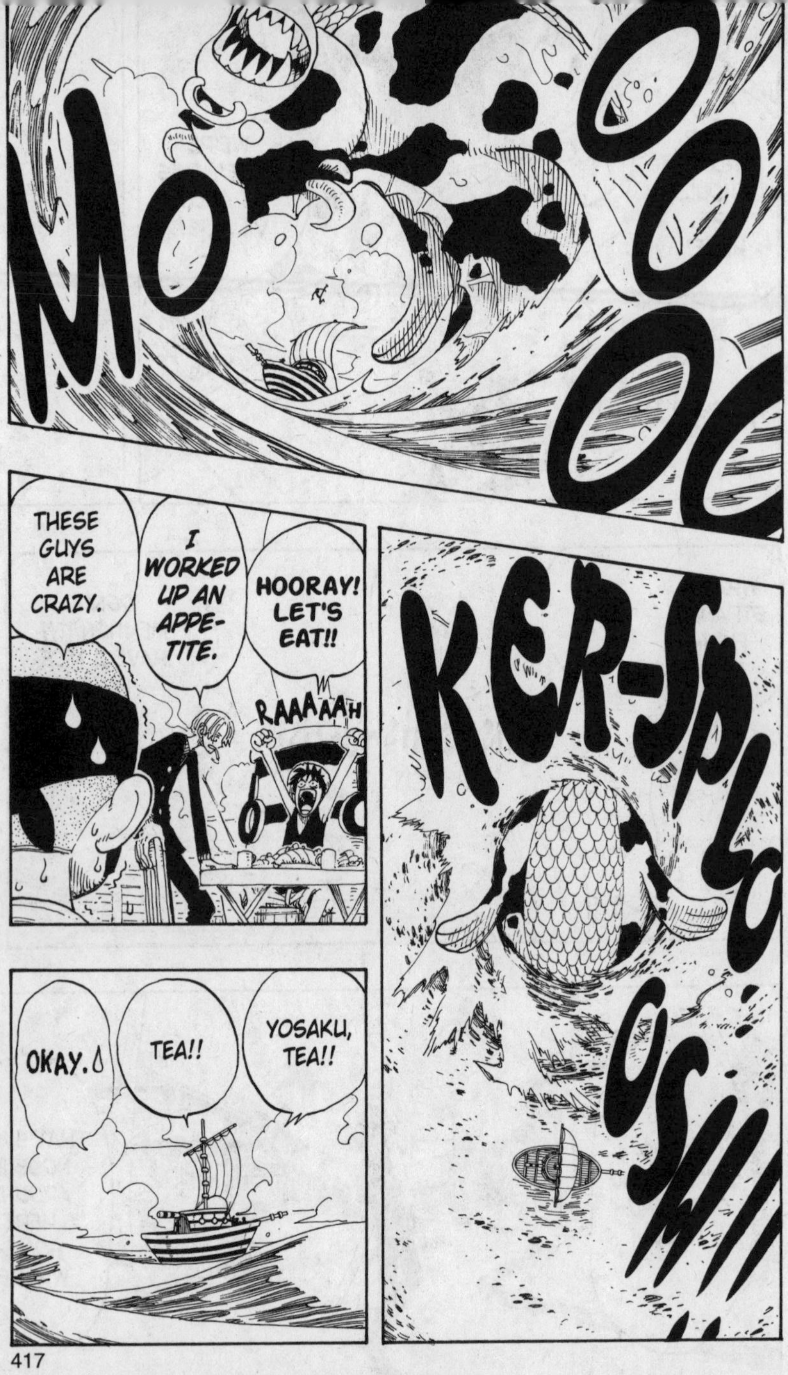

MOOOOO
KER-SPLOOSH!!!
HOORAY! LET'S EAT!!
RAAAAAH
I WORKED UP AN APPE-TITE.
THESE GUYS ARE CRAZY.
YOSAKU, TEA!!
TEA!!
OKAY.

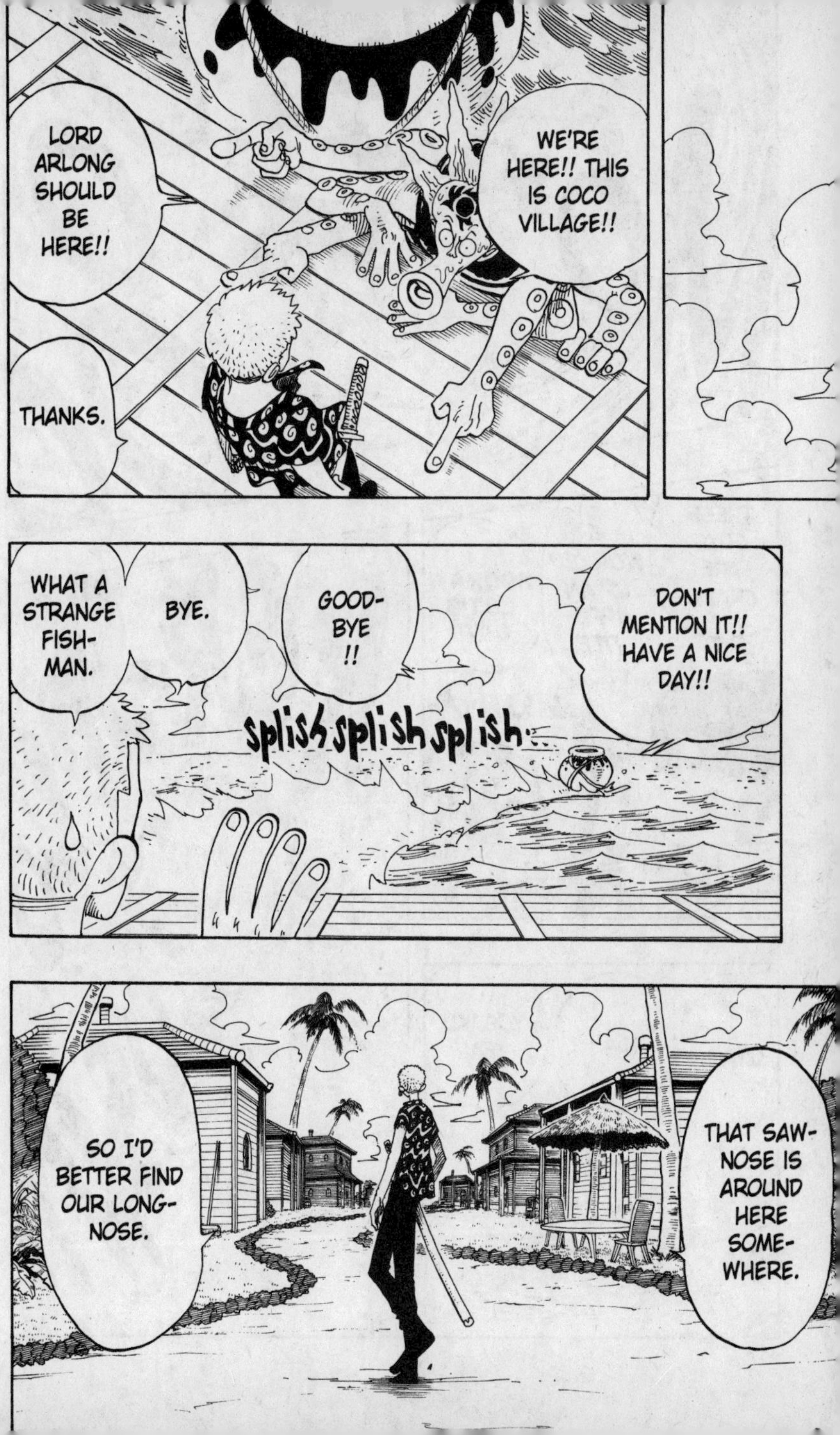
WE'RE HERE!! THIS IS COCO VILLAGE!!
LORD ARLONG SHOULD BE HERE!!
THANKS.
DON'T MENTION IT!! HAVE A NICE DAY!!
GOOD-BYE !!
splish splish splish
BYE.
WHAT A STRANGE FISH-MAN.
THAT SAW-NOSE IS AROUND HERE SOME-WHERE.
SO I'D BETTER FIND OUR LONG-NOSE.

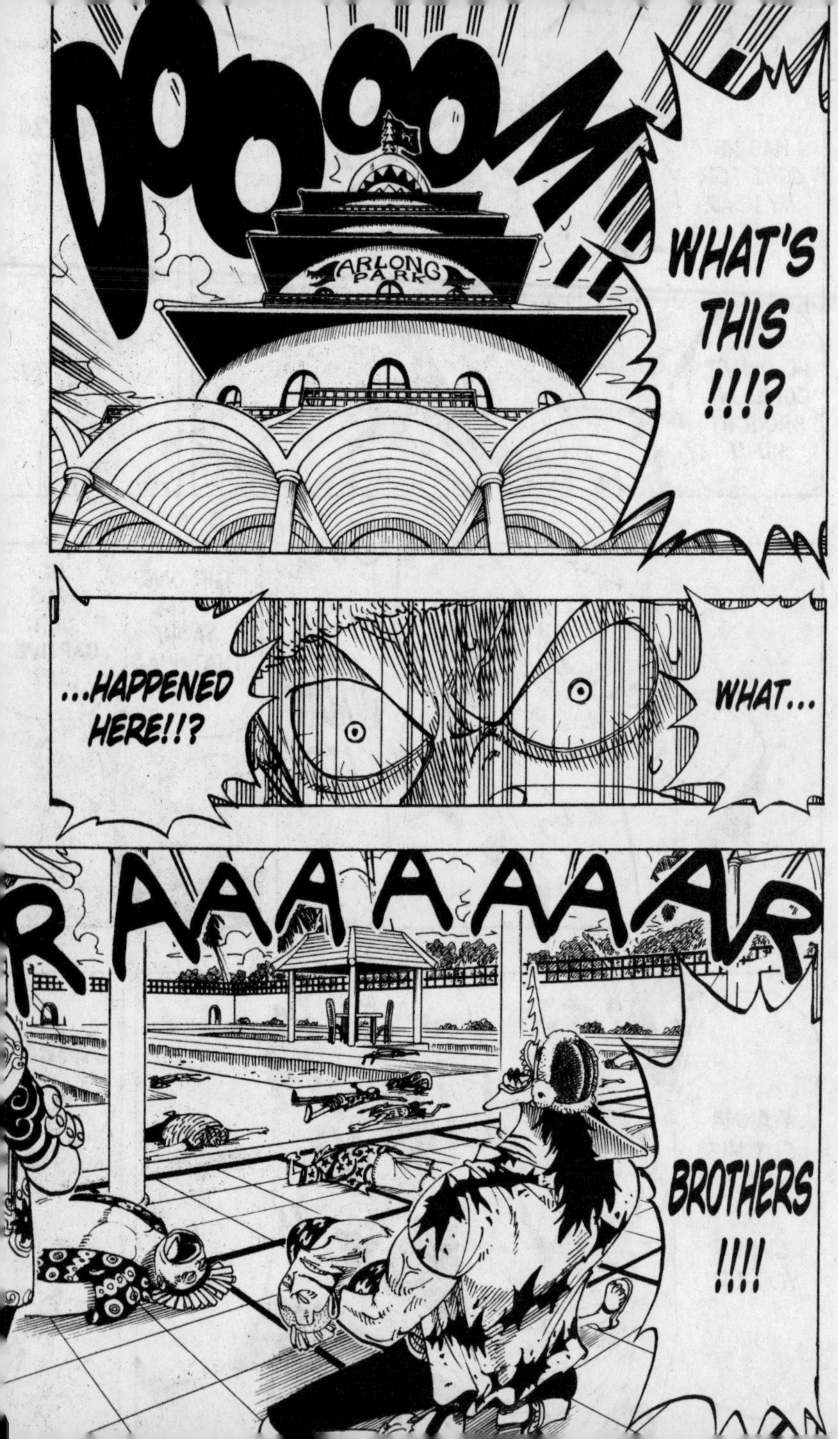
DOOOOM!!
WHAT'S THIS!!!?
WHAT...
...HAPPENED HERE!!?
RAAAAAAAR
BROTHERS!!!!

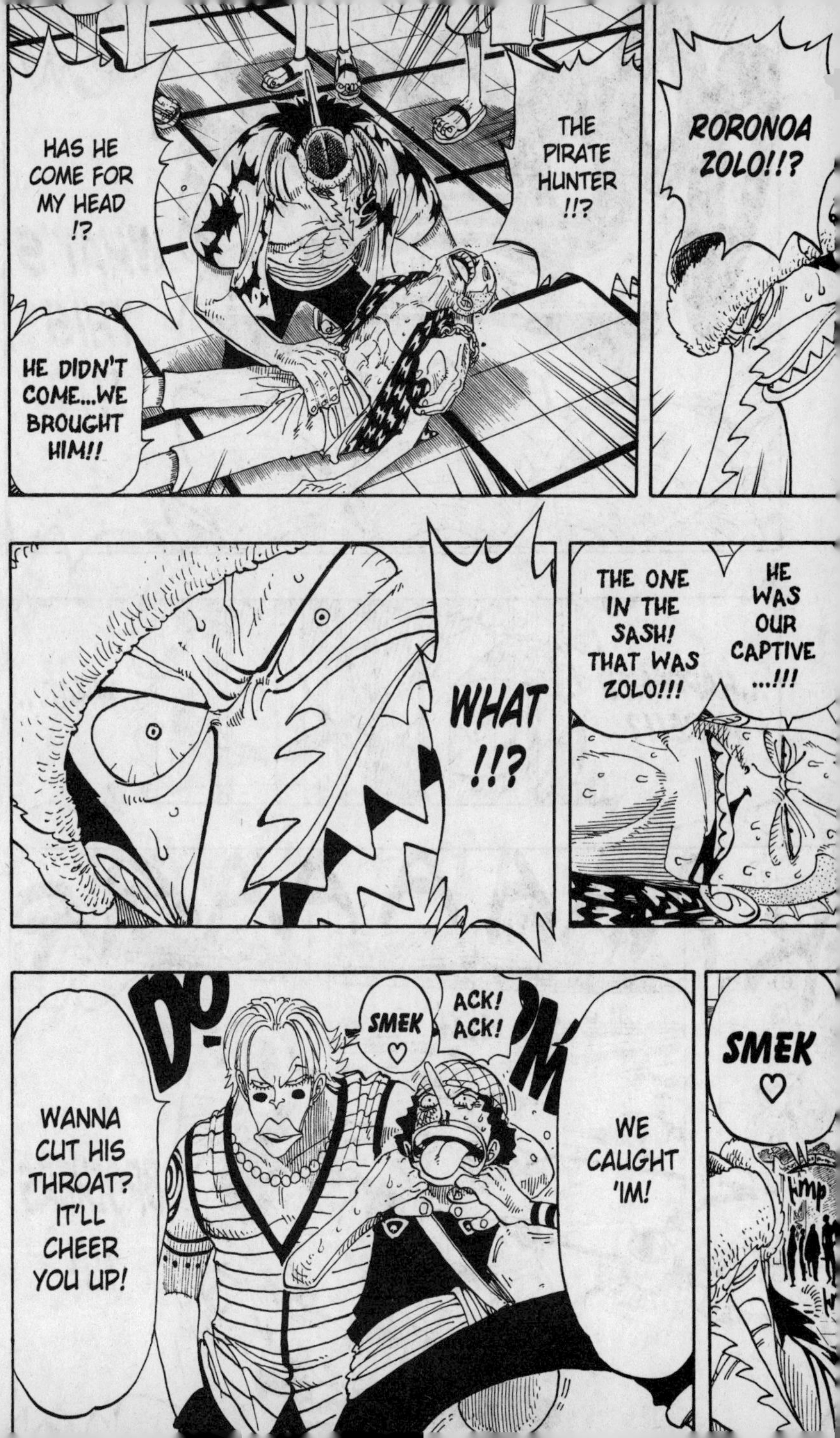
RORONOA ZOLO!!?
THE PIRATE HUNTER !!?
HAS HE COME FOR MY HEAD !?
HE DIDN'T COME...WE BROUGHT HIM!!
HE WAS OUR CAPTIVE ...!!!
THE ONE IN THE SASH! THAT WAS ZOLO!!!
WHAT !!?
SMEK ♡
WE CAUGHT 'IM!
ACK! ACK!
SMEK ♡
WANNA CUT HIS THROAT? IT'LL CHEER YOU UP!

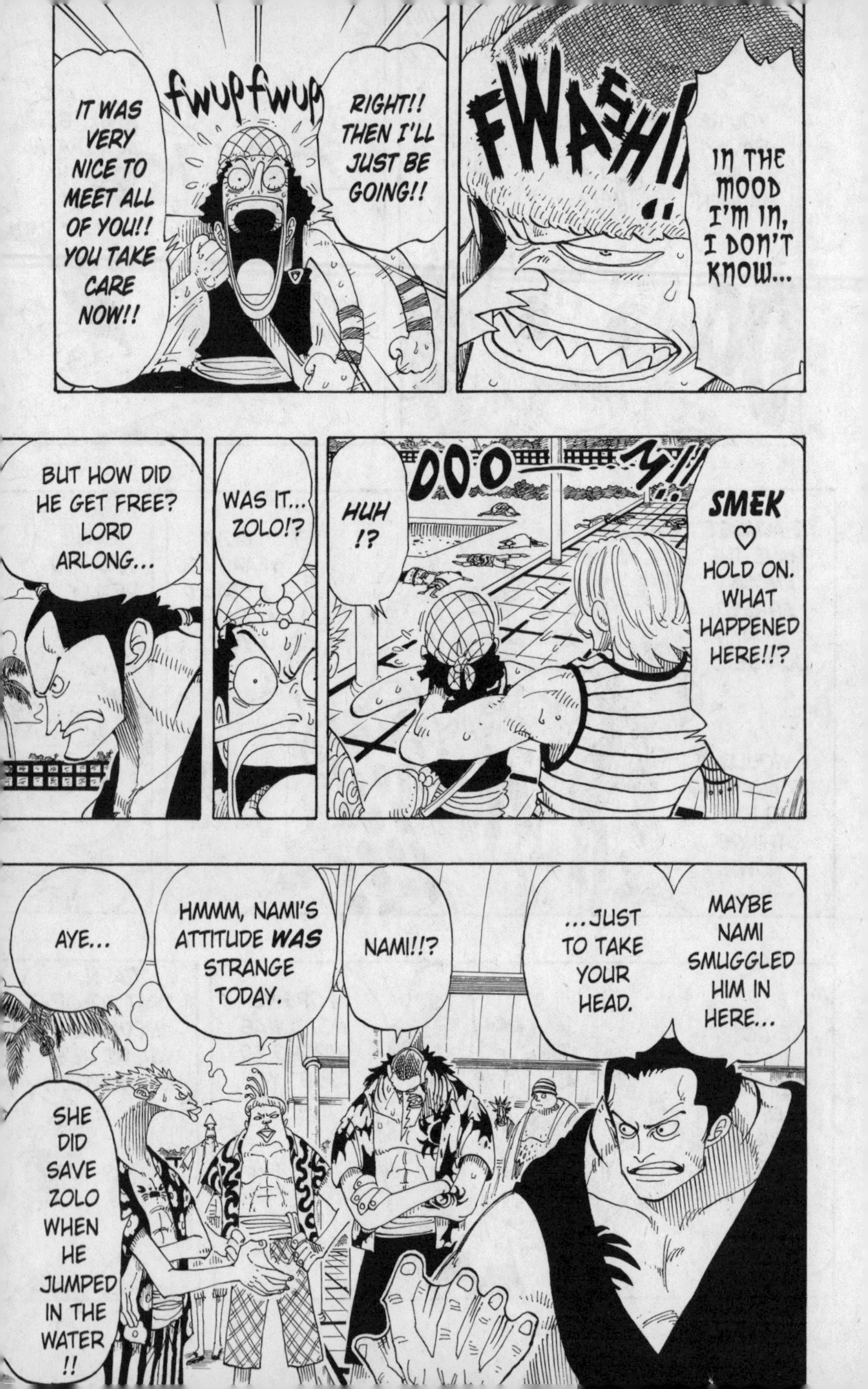

FWASH!!
IN THE MOOD I'M IN, I DON'T KNOW...
RIGHT!! THEN I'LL JUST BE GOING!!
fwupfwup
IT WAS VERY NICE TO MEET ALL OF YOU!! YOU TAKE CARE NOW!!
SMEK ♡ HOLD ON. WHAT HAPPENED HERE!!?
DOO—M!!
HUH!?
WAS IT... ZOLO!?
BUT HOW DID HE GET FREE? LORD ARLONG...
MAYBE NAMI SMUGGLED HIM IN HERE...
...JUST TO TAKE YOUR HEAD.
NAMI!!?
HMMM, NAMI'S ATTITUDE WAS STRANGE TODAY.
AYE...
SHE DID SAVE ZOLO WHEN HE JUMPED IN THE WATER!!

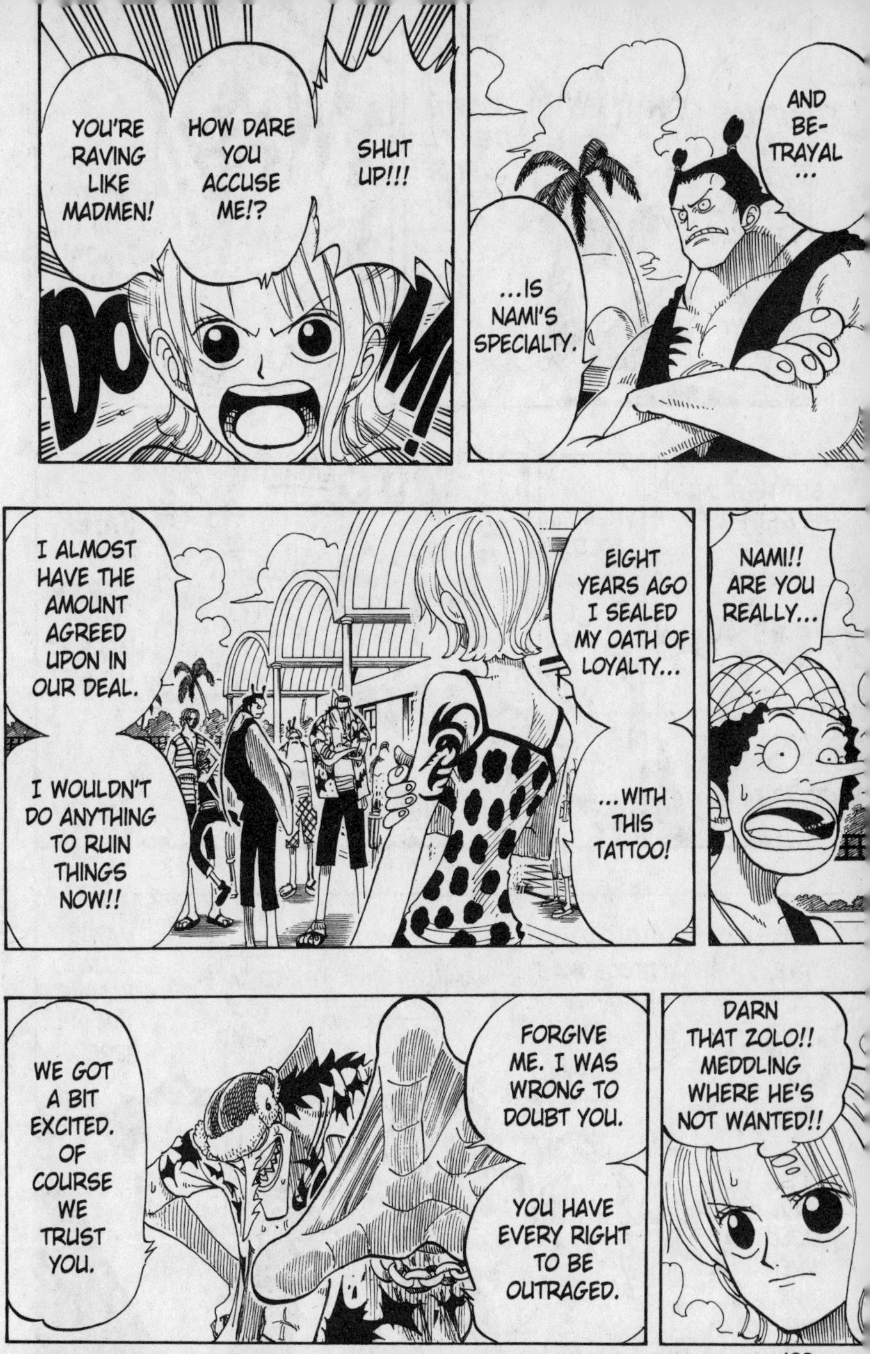
AND BE-TRAYAL...
...IS NAMI'S SPECIALTY.
SHUT UP!!!
HOW DARE YOU ACCUSE ME!?
YOU'RE RAVING LIKE MADMEN!
DOM!
NAMI!! ARE YOU REALLY...
EIGHT YEARS AGO I SEALED MY OATH OF LOYALTY...
...WITH THIS TATTOO!
I ALMOST HAVE THE AMOUNT AGREED UPON IN OUR DEAL.
I WOULDN'T DO ANYTHING TO RUIN THINGS NOW!!
DARN THAT ZOLO!! MEDDLING WHERE HE'S NOT WANTED!!
FORGIVE ME. I WAS WRONG TO DOUBT YOU.
YOU HAVE EVERY RIGHT TO BE OUTRAGED.
WE GOT A BIT EXCITED. OF COURSE WE TRUST YOU.

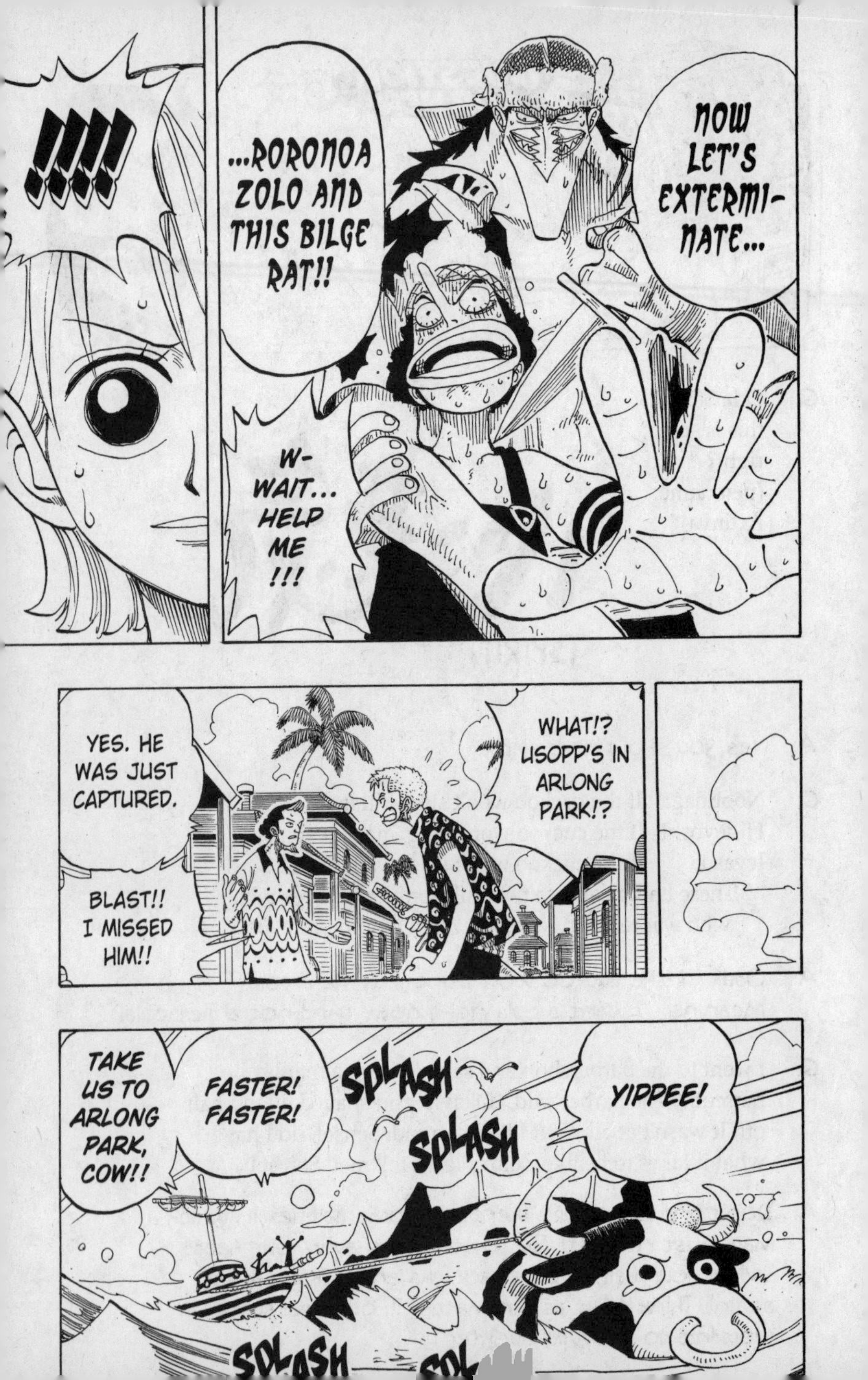
NOW LET'S EXTERMI-NATE...
...RORONOA ZOLO AND THIS BILGE RAT!!
W-WAIT... HELP ME!!!
!!!!
WHAT!? USOPP'S IN ARLONG PARK!?
YES. HE WAS JUST CAPTURED.
BLAST!! I MISSED HIM!!
YIPPEE!
SPLASH
SPLASH
FASTER! FASTER!
TAKE US TO ARLONG PARK, COW!!
SPLASH

QUESTION CORNER
chou chou
PETROL
エス
ビー
エス

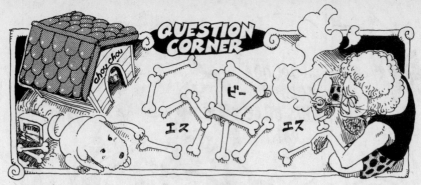

Q: Oda Sensei, this is spirit, right? (pen name: Arunya)

心意気

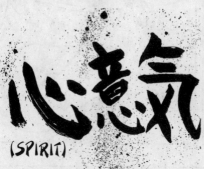

(SPIRIT)

A: Yes, you show true spirit.

Q: Nobunaga: If the cuckoo won't sing, kill it.
Hideyoshi: If the cuckoo won't sing, make it sing.
Ieyasu: If the cuckoo won't sing, wait until it does.
^ These haiku capture the philosophies of three men who wanted to rule Japan. What would yours be?

A: Oda: If the cuckoo won't sing, buy me a cola.
Meaning: "I want a cola right now." (And not a diet cola.)

Q: I went to the barbershop and said, "I want a manly haircut!!" The barber said, "Okay!!" and shaved all my hair off. It wasn't at all what I had in mind. Sensei, do I have what it takes to be like Zolo? Please tell me!! Sob sob.

A: Don't cry!! Stand up!! There are some battles in which a man must retreat!! So what if he shaved your head!! When your hair grows back, challenge that barber again!! Think of it as a rematch!! Though personally, I wouldn't do it. (Wild laughter)

# Chapter 74: BUSINESS

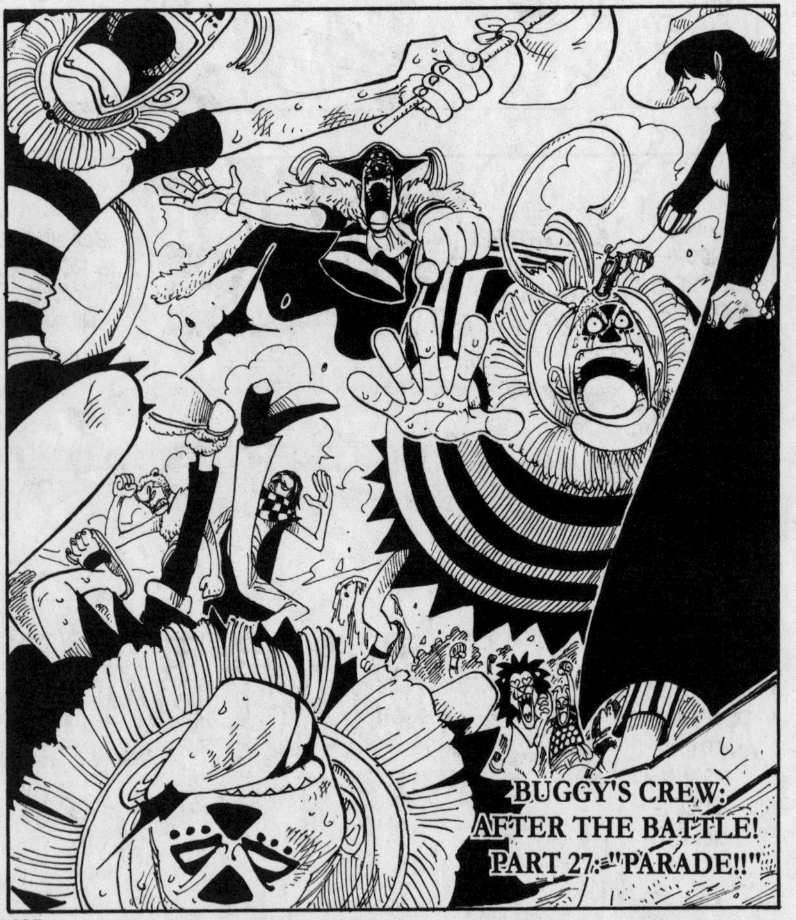
BUGGY'S CREW: AFTER THE BATTLE! PART 27: "PARADE!!"

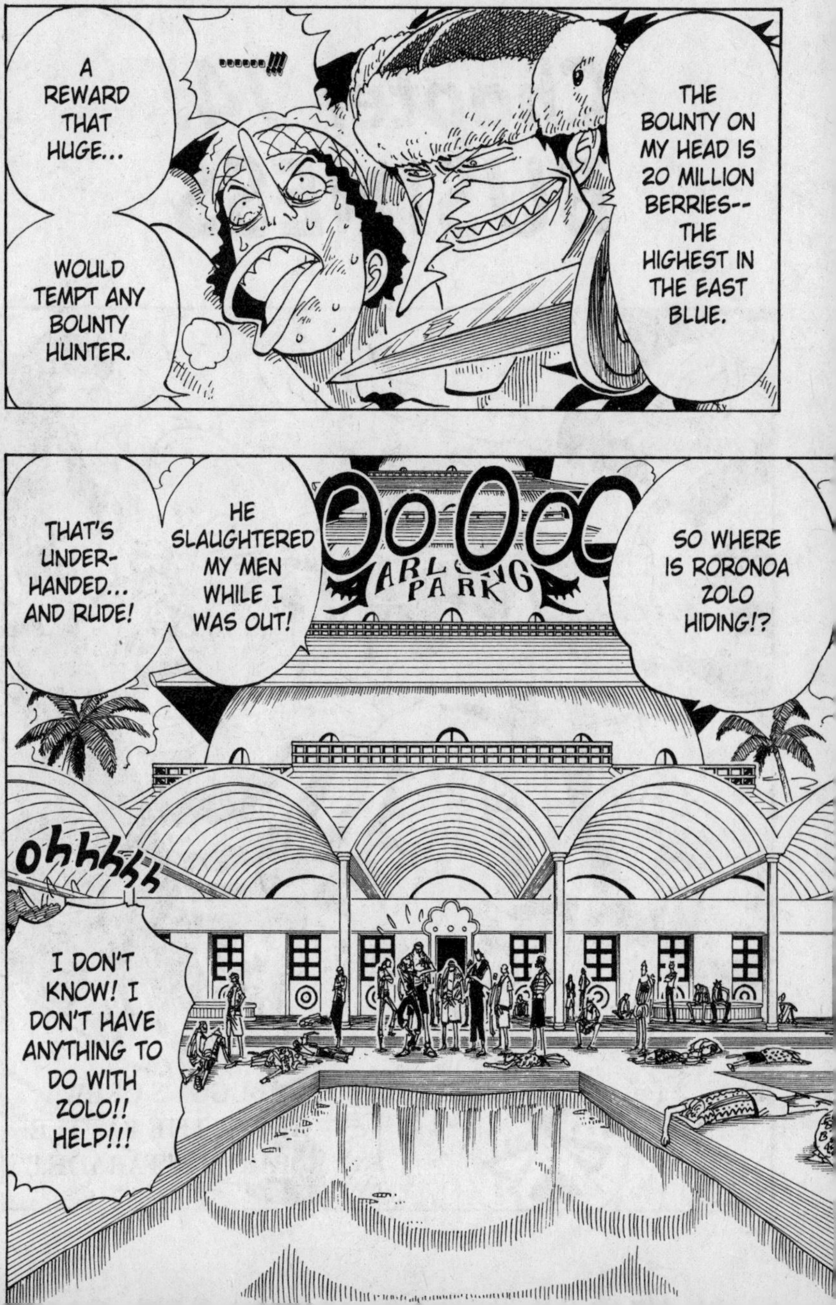
THE BOUNTY ON MY HEAD IS 20 MILLION BERRIES-- THE HIGHEST IN THE EAST BLUE.
......!!!
A REWARD THAT HUGE...
WOULD TEMPT ANY BOUNTY HUNTER.
SO WHERE IS RORONOA ZOLO HIDING!?
HE SLAUGHTERED MY MEN WHILE I WAS OUT!
THAT'S UNDER-HANDED... AND RUDE!
OHHHHH
I DON'T KNOW! I DON'T HAVE ANYTHING TO DO WITH ZOLO!! HELP!!!

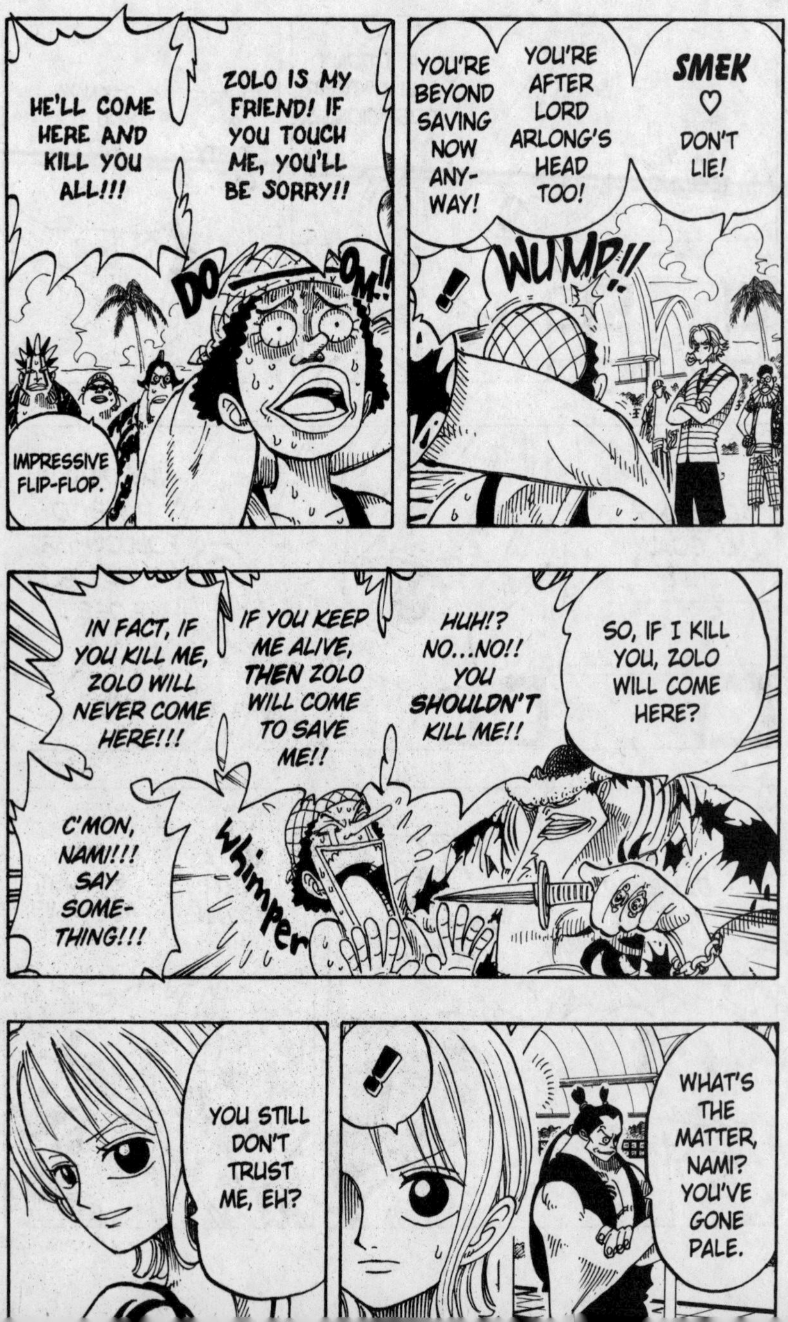
SMEK ♡ DON'T LIE!
YOU'RE AFTER LORD ARLONG'S HEAD TOO!
YOU'RE BEYOND SAVING NOW ANY-WAY!
WUMP!!
!
ZOLO IS MY FRIEND! IF YOU TOUCH ME, YOU'LL BE SORRY!!
HE'LL COME HERE AND KILL YOU ALL!!!
DOOM!!
IMPRESSIVE FLIP-FLOP.
SO, IF I KILL YOU, ZOLO WILL COME HERE?
HUH!? NO...NO!! YOU SHOULDN'T KILL ME!!
IF YOU KEEP ME ALIVE, THEN ZOLO WILL COME TO SAVE ME!!
IN FACT, IF YOU KILL ME, ZOLO WILL NEVER COME HERE!!!
whimper
C'MON, NAMI!!! SAY SOME-THING!!!
WHAT'S THE MATTER, NAMI? YOU'VE GONE PALE.
!
YOU STILL DON'T TRUST ME, EH?

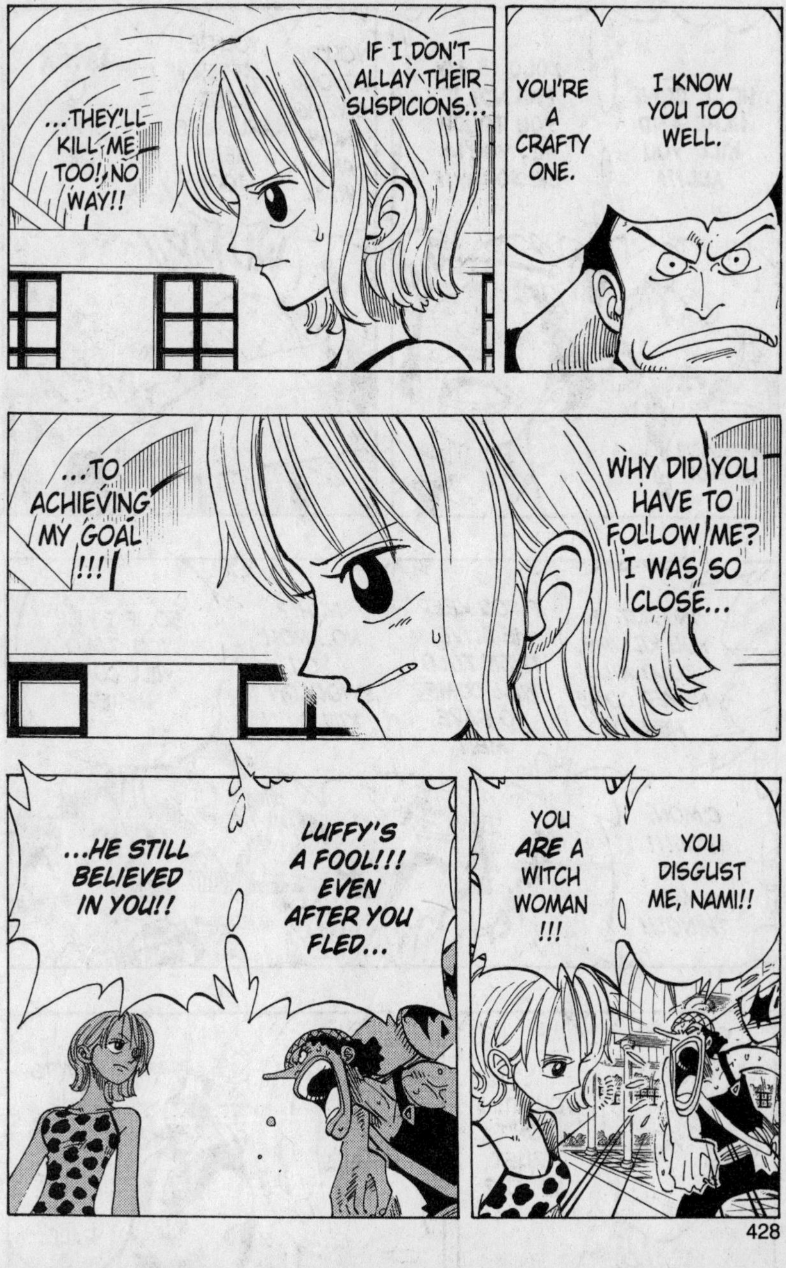

I KNOW YOU TOO WELL.
YOU'RE A CRAFTY ONE.
IF I DON'T ALLAY THEIR SUSPICIONS...
...THEY'LL KILL ME TOO!! NO WAY!!
WHY DID YOU HAVE TO FOLLOW ME? I WAS SO CLOSE...
...TO ACHIEVING MY GOAL!!!
YOU DISGUST ME, NAMI!!
YOU ARE A WITCH WOMAN!!!
LUFFY'S A FOOL!!! EVEN AFTER YOU FLED...
...HE STILL BELIEVED IN YOU!!

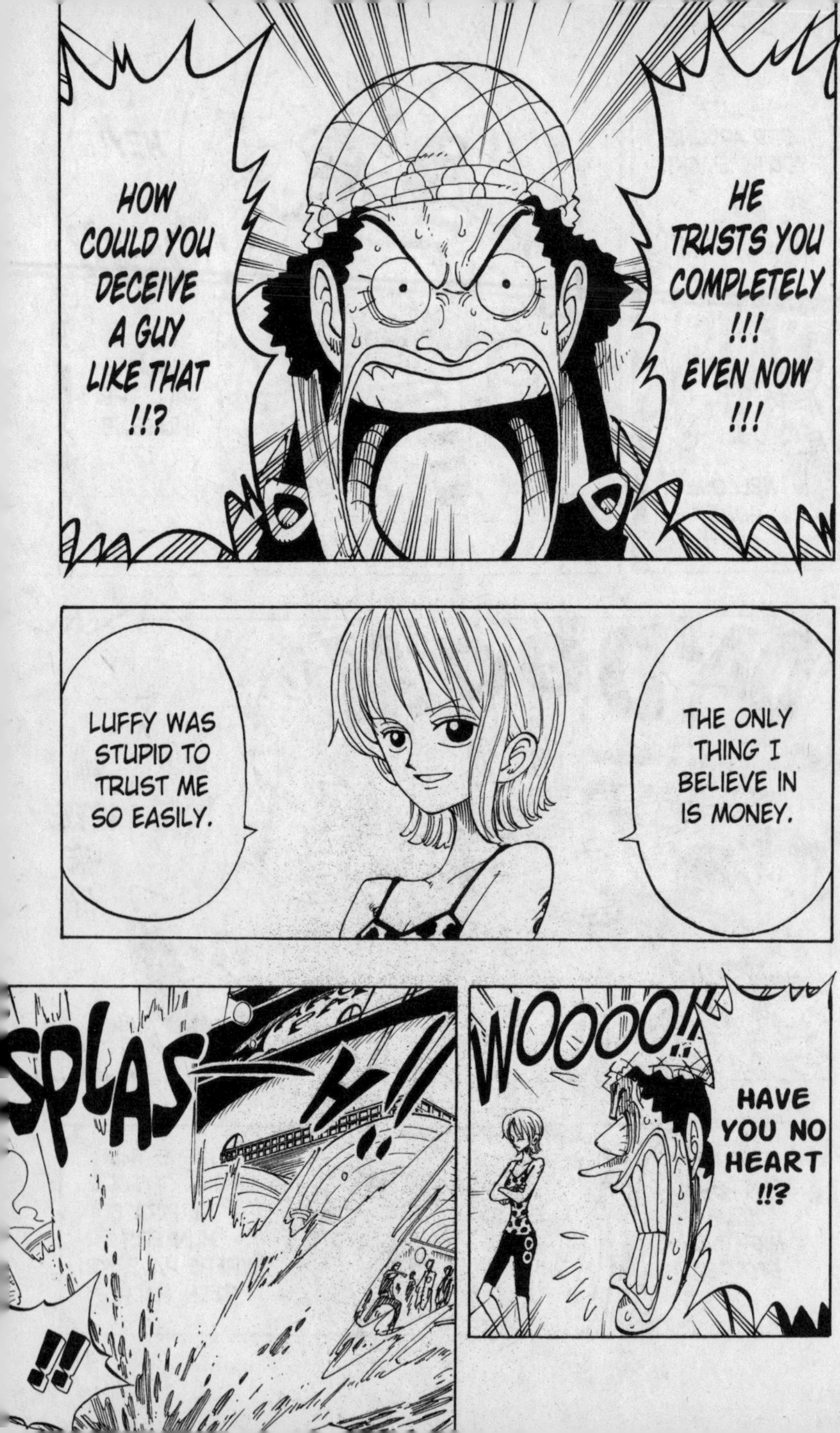
HE TRUSTS YOU COMPLETELY!!! EVEN NOW!!!
HOW COULD YOU DECEIVE A GUY LIKE THAT!!?
THE ONLY THING I BELIEVE IN IS MONEY.
LUFFY WAS STUPID TO TRUST ME SO EASILY.
WOOOO!!
HAVE YOU NO HEART!!?
SPLASH!!

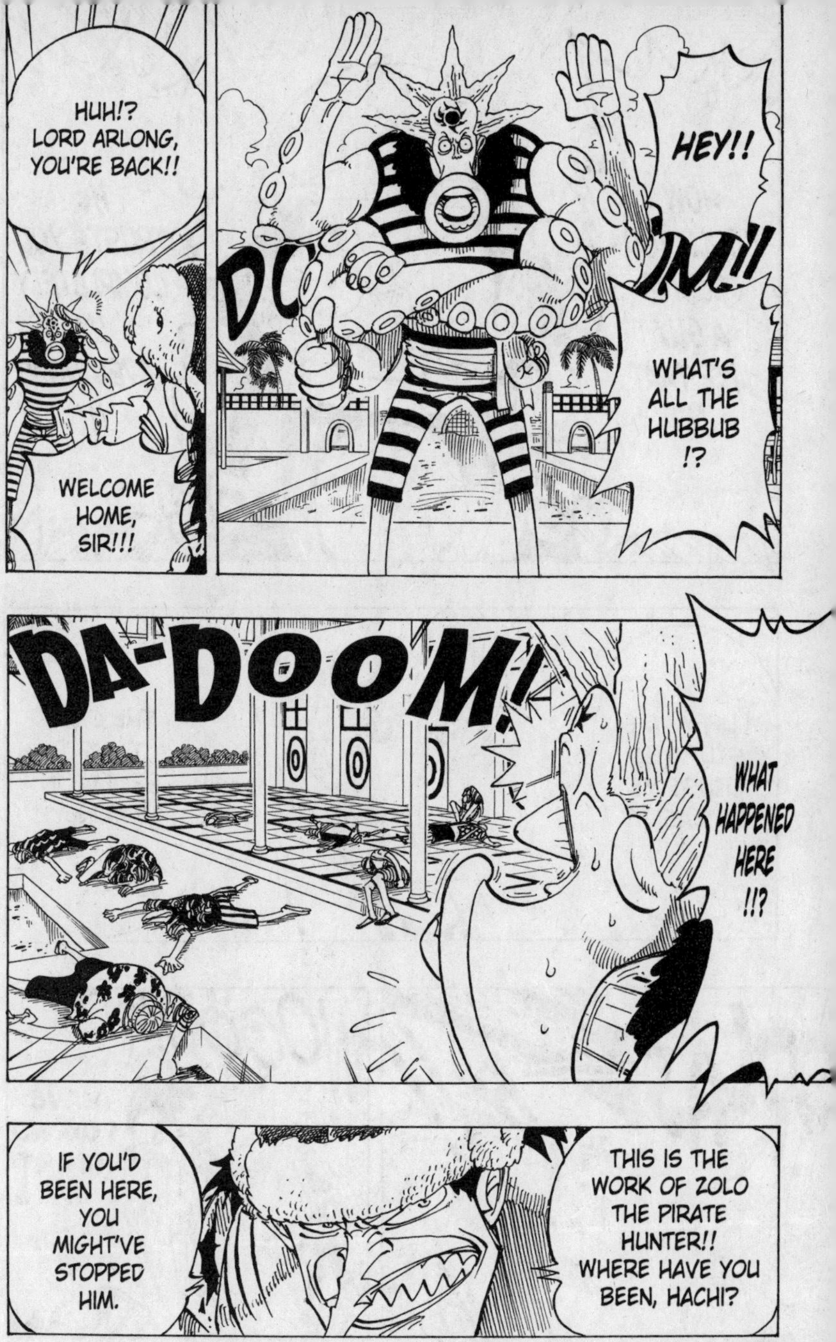
HEY!!
DO
M!!
WHAT'S ALL THE HUBBUB !?
HUH!? LORD ARLONG, YOU'RE BACK!!
WELCOME HOME, SIR!!!
DA-DOOM!
WHAT HAPPENED HERE !!?
THIS IS THE WORK OF ZOLO THE PIRATE HUNTER!! WHERE HAVE YOU BEEN, HACHI?
IF YOU'D BEEN HERE, YOU MIGHT'VE STOPPED HIM.

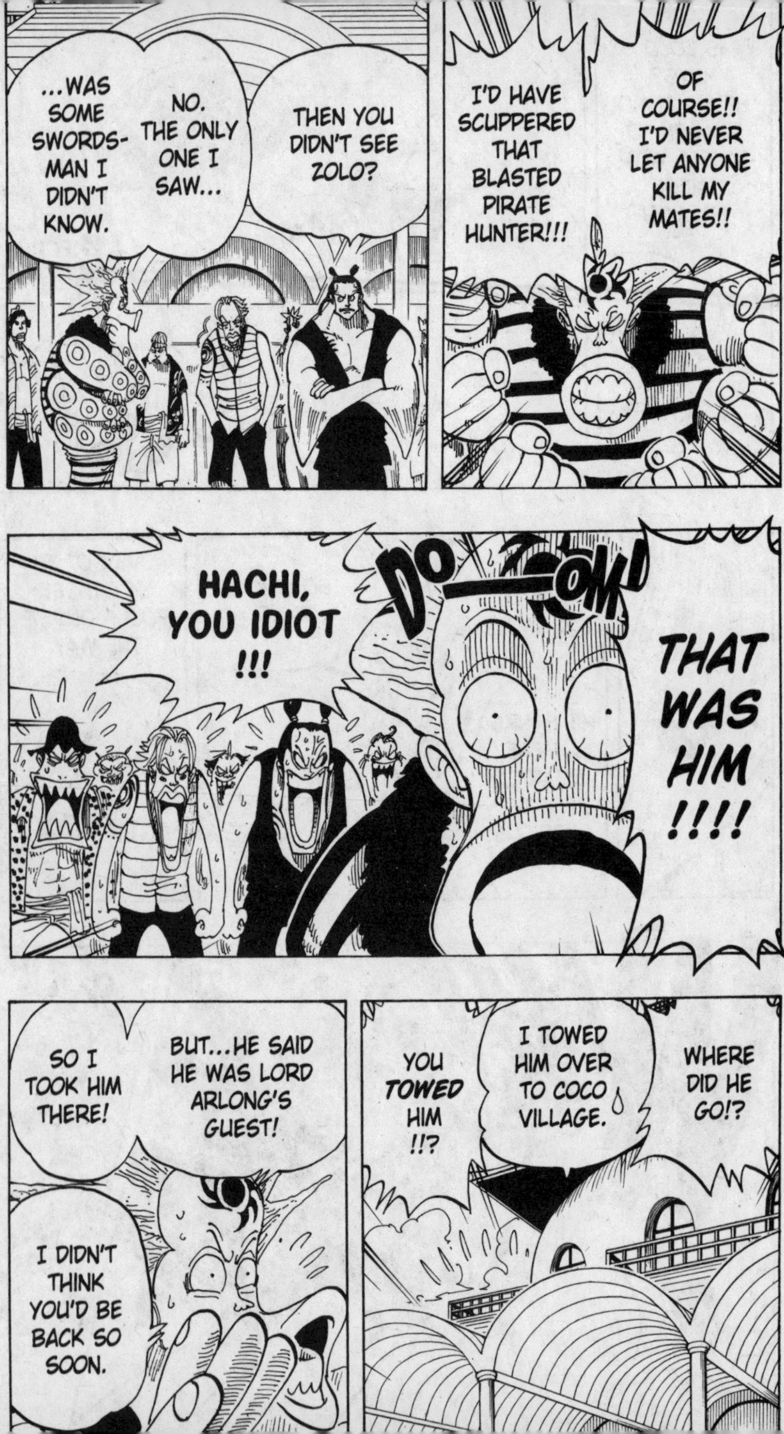
OF COURSE!! I'D NEVER LET ANYONE KILL MY MATES!!
I'D HAVE SCUPPERED THAT BLASTED PIRATE HUNTER!!!
THEN YOU DIDN'T SEE ZOLO?
NO. THE ONLY ONE I SAW...
...WAS SOME SWORDSMAN I DIDN'T KNOW.
THAT WAS HIM!!!!
DO—OM!
HACHI, YOU IDIOT!!!
WHERE DID HE GO!?
I TOWED HIM OVER TO COCO VILLAGE.
YOU TOWED HIM!!?
BUT...HE SAID HE WAS LORD ARLONG'S GUEST!
SO I TOOK HIM THERE!
I DIDN'T THINK YOU'D BE BACK SO SOON.

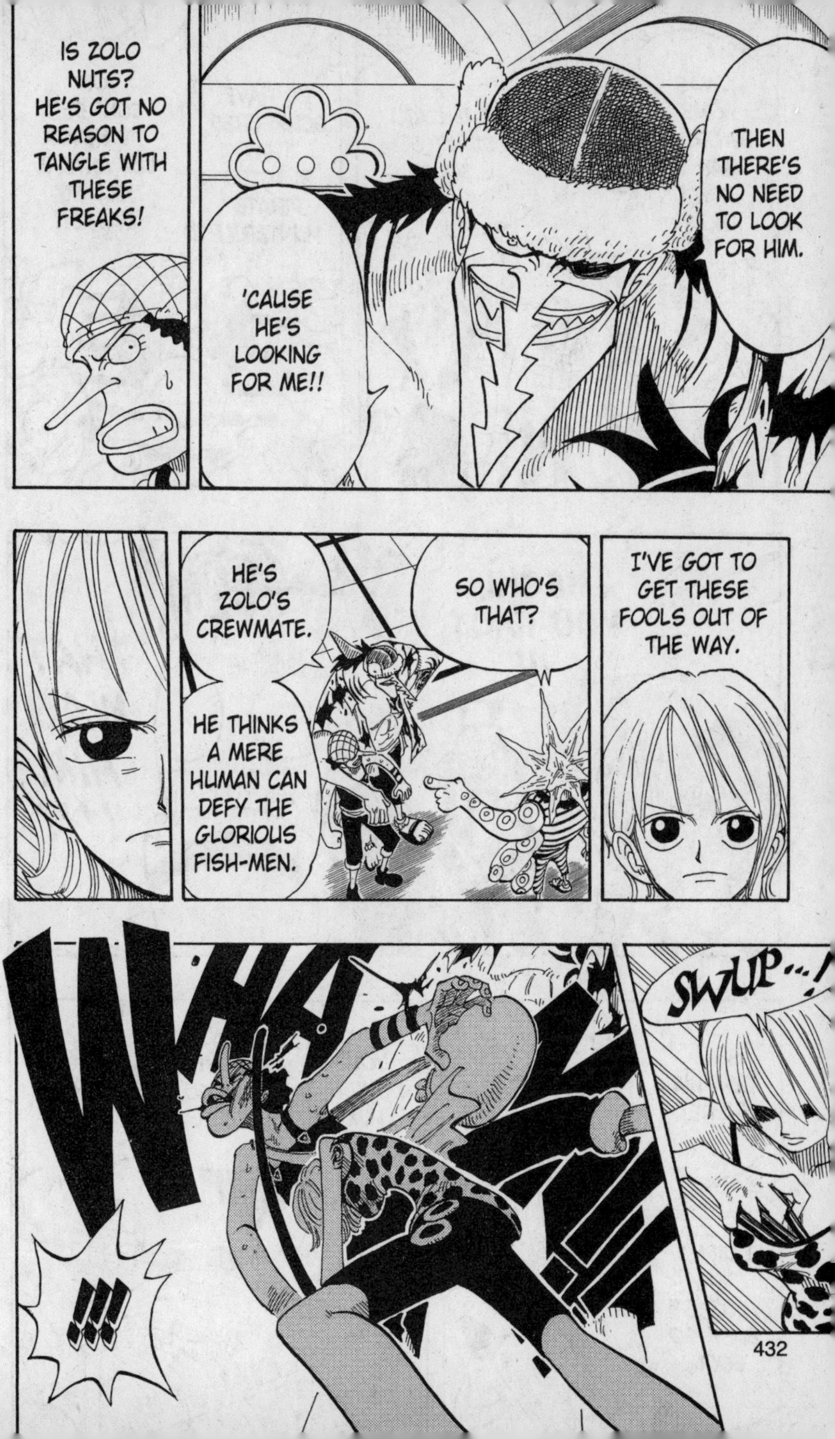
THEN THERE'S NO NEED TO LOOK FOR HIM.
'CAUSE HE'S LOOKING FOR ME!!
IS ZOLO NUTS? HE'S GOT NO REASON TO TANGLE WITH THESE FREAKS!
I'VE GOT TO GET THESE FOOLS OUT OF THE WAY.
SO WHO'S THAT?
HE'S ZOLO'S CREWMATE.
HE THINKS A MERE HUMAN CAN DEFY THE GLORIOUS FISH-MEN.
SWUP...!
WHA
!!!

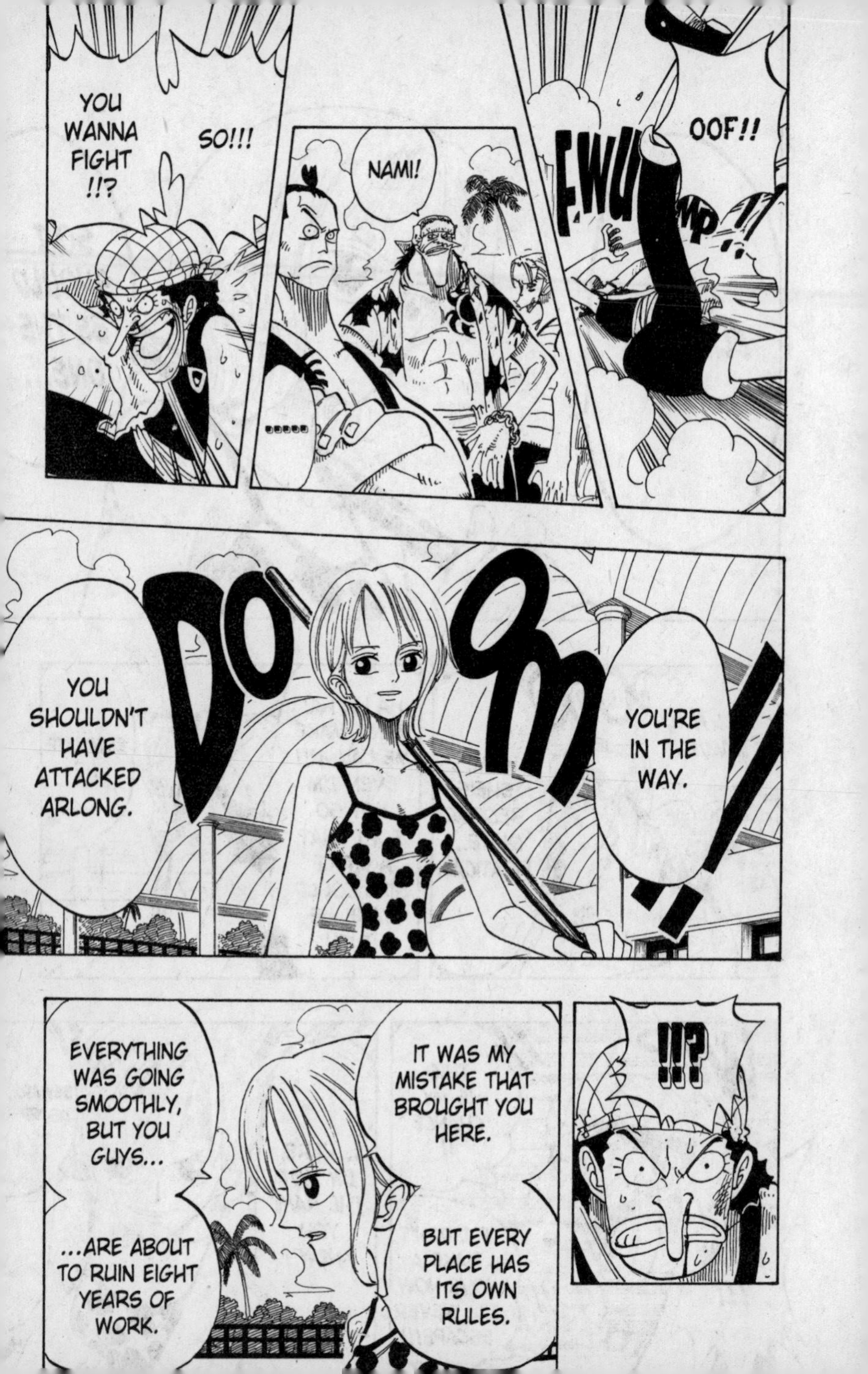
OOF!!
F.WUMP!!
NAMI!
.....
SO!!!
YOU WANNA FIGHT !!?
YOU'RE IN THE WAY.
DOOM!!
YOU SHOULDN'T HAVE ATTACKED ARLONG.
!!?
IT WAS MY MISTAKE THAT BROUGHT YOU HERE.
BUT EVERY PLACE HAS ITS OWN RULES.
EVERYTHING WAS GOING SMOOTHLY, BUT YOU GUYS...
...ARE ABOUT TO RUIN EIGHT YEARS OF WORK.

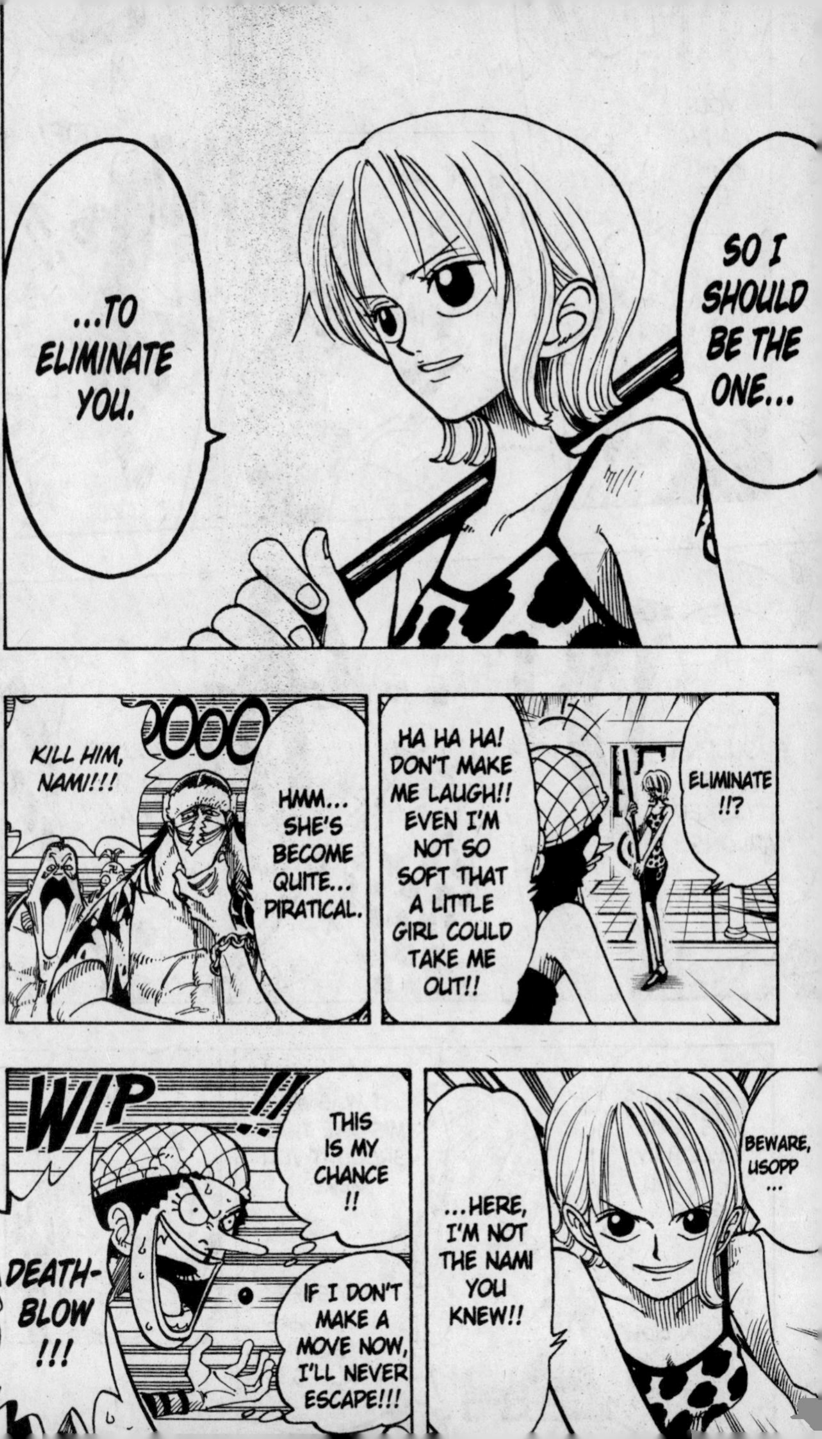
SO I SHOULD BE THE ONE...
...TO ELIMINATE YOU.
ELIMINATE!!?
HA HA HA! DON'T MAKE ME LAUGH!! EVEN I'M NOT SO SOFT THAT A LITTLE GIRL COULD TAKE ME OUT!!
HMM... SHE'S BECOME QUITE... PIRATICAL.
KILL HIM, NAMI!!!
BEWARE, USOPP...
...HERE, I'M NOT THE NAMI YOU KNEW!!
THIS IS MY CHANCE!!
IF I DON'T MAKE A MOVE NOW, I'LL NEVER ESCAPE!!!
WIP!!
DEATH-BLOW!!!

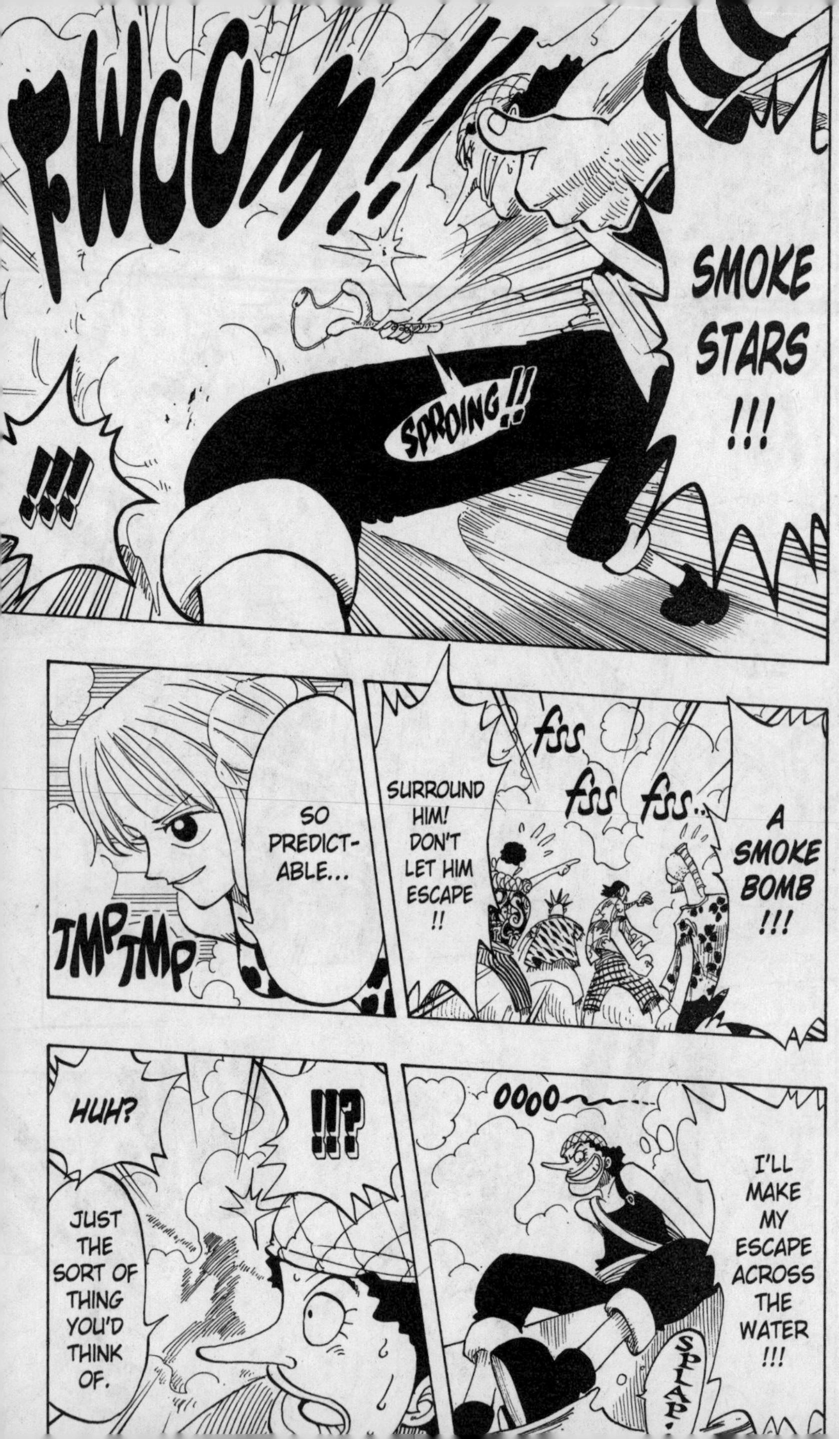
SMOKE STARS !!!
FWOOM!!
SPROING!!
!!!!
fss
fss fss...
A SMOKE BOMB !!!
SURROUND HIM! DON'T LET HIM ESCAPE !!
SO PREDICT-ABLE...
TMP TMP
OOOO~
I'LL MAKE MY ESCAPE ACROSS THE WATER !!!
SPLAP
HUH?
!!?
JUST THE SORT OF THING YOU'D THINK OF.

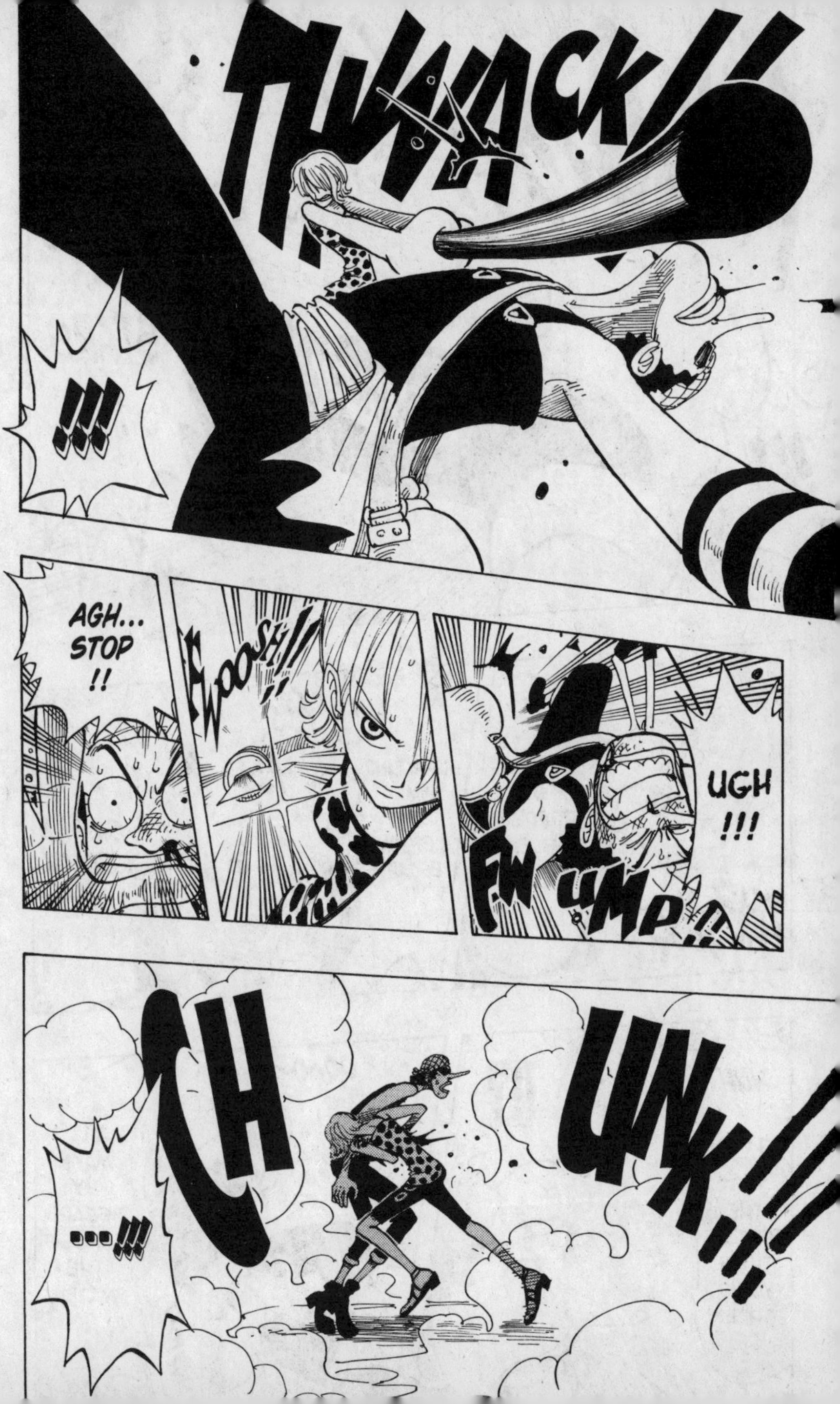
THWACK!!
!!!
UGH !!!
FWUMP!!
FWOOSH!!
AGH... STOP !!
CHUNK!!!
...!!!

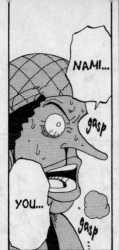

NAMI...

*gasp*

YOU...

*gasp*

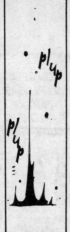

plup

plup

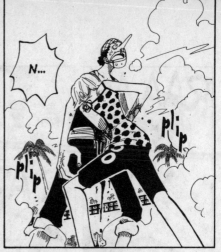

N...

plip

plip

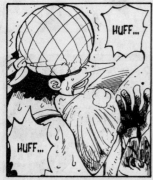

HUFF...

HUFF...

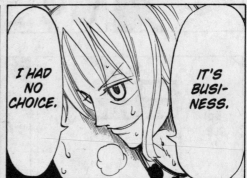

I HAD NO CHOICE.

IT'S BUSINESS.

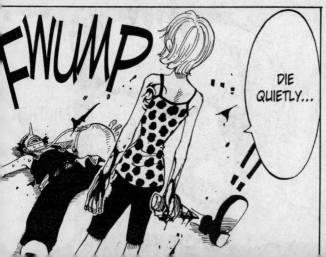

FWUMP

DIE QUIETLY...

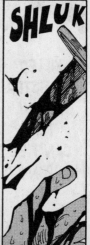

SHLUK

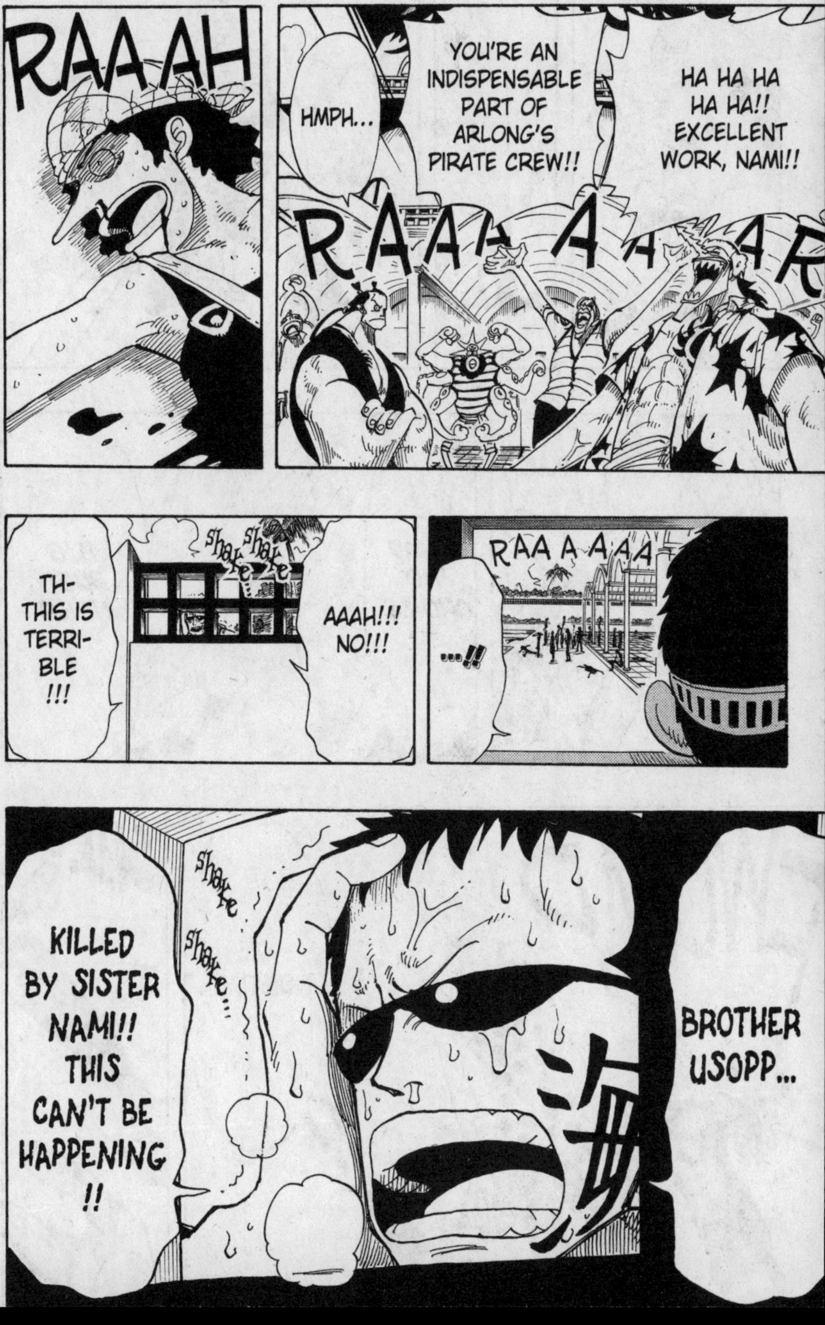
HA HA HA HA HA!! EXCELLENT WORK, NAMI!!
YOU'RE AN INDISPENSABLE PART OF ARLONG'S PIRATE CREW!!
HMPH...
RAAAAAAAR
RAAAH
RAAAAAA
...!!
AAAH!!! NO!!!
shake shake
TH- THIS IS TERRIBLE!!!
BROTHER USOPP...
shake shake...
KILLED BY SISTER NAMI!! THIS CAN'T BE HAPPENING!!

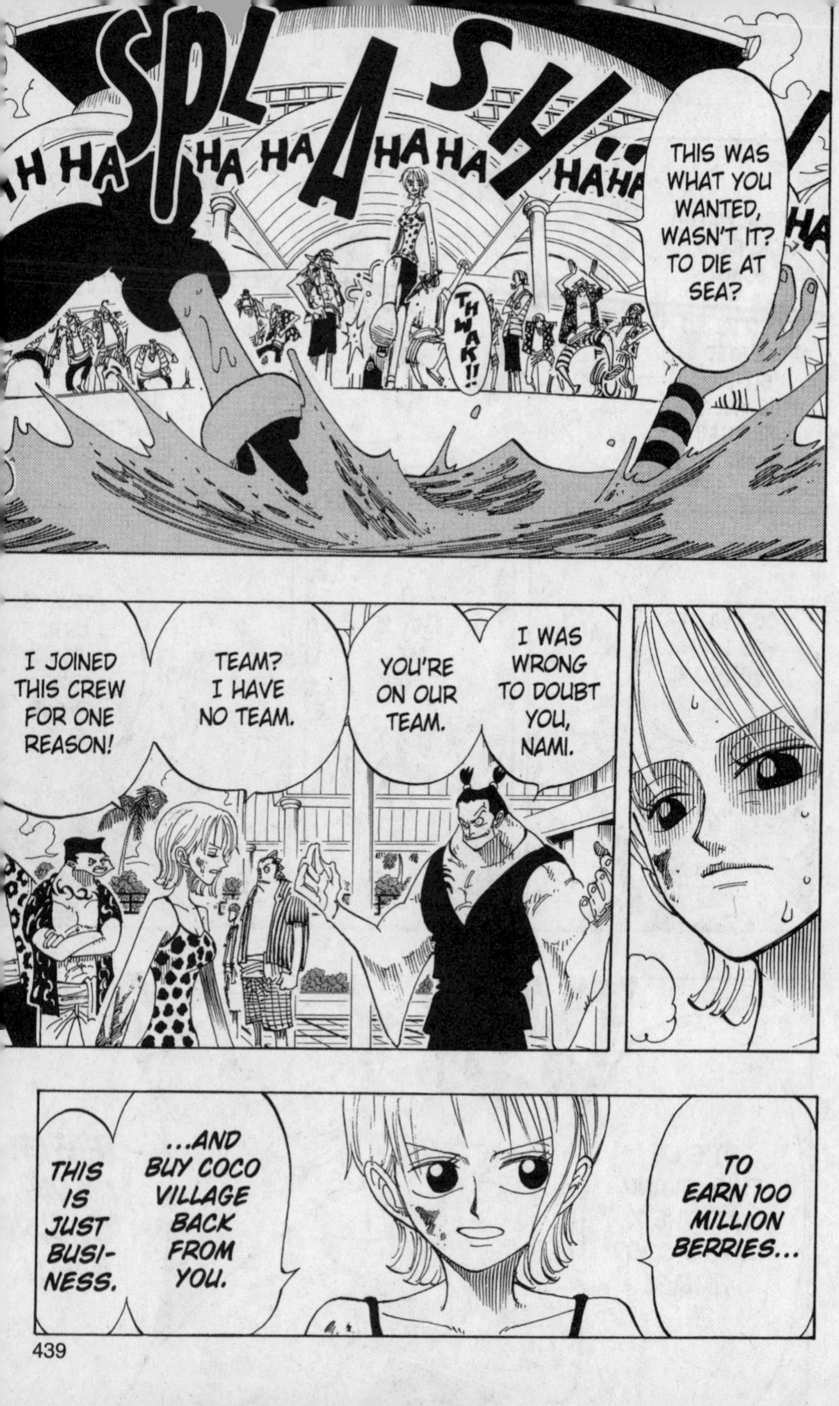
THIS WAS WHAT YOU WANTED, WASN'T IT? TO DIE AT SEA?
SPLASH
HA HA HA HA HA HA HA HA HA
THWAK!!
I WAS WRONG TO DOUBT YOU, NAMI.
YOU'RE ON OUR TEAM.
TEAM? I HAVE NO TEAM.
I JOINED THIS CREW FOR ONE REASON!
TO EARN 100 MILLION BERRIES...
...AND BUY COCO VILLAGE BACK FROM YOU.
THIS IS JUST BUSINESS.

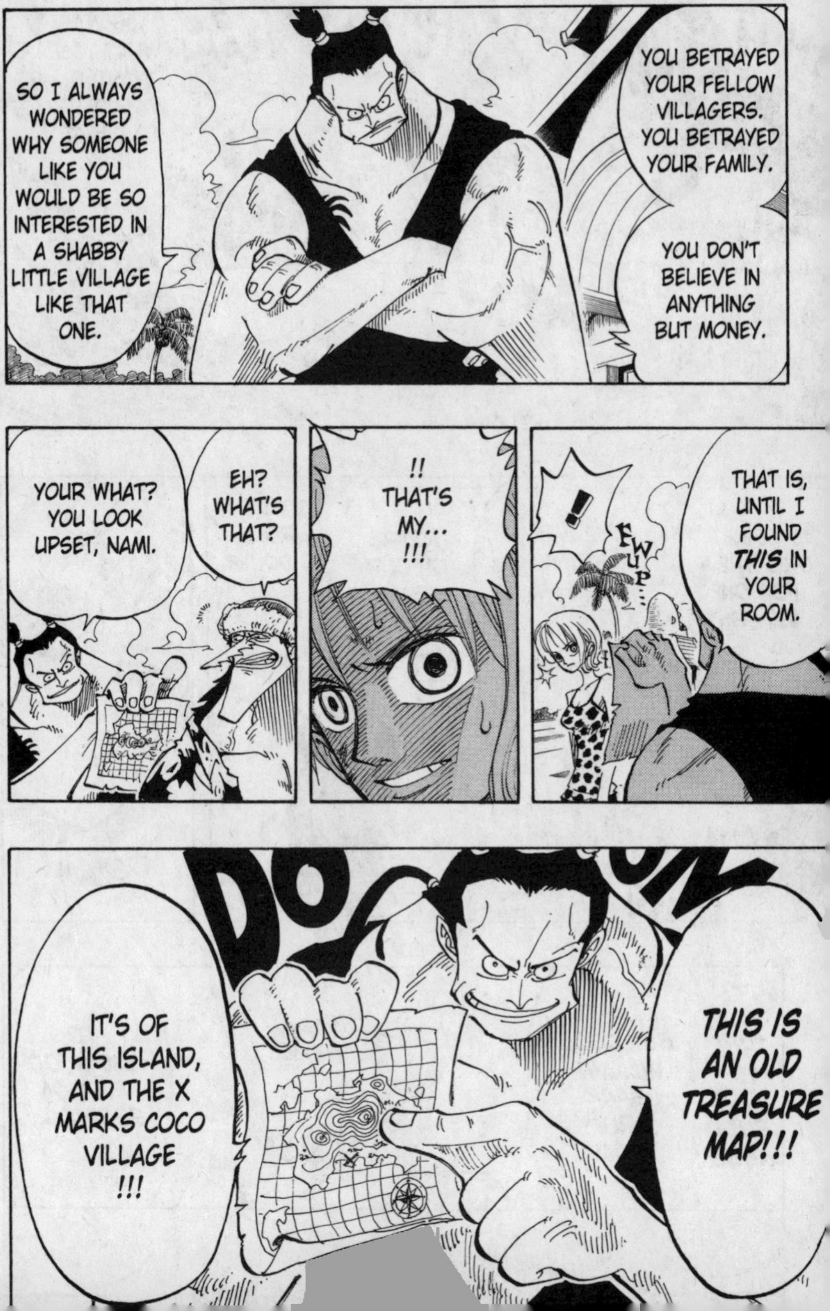
YOU BETRAYED YOUR FELLOW VILLAGERS. YOU BETRAYED YOUR FAMILY.
YOU DON'T BELIEVE IN ANYTHING BUT MONEY.
SO I ALWAYS WONDERED WHY SOMEONE LIKE YOU WOULD BE SO INTERESTED IN A SHABBY LITTLE VILLAGE LIKE THAT ONE.
THAT IS, UNTIL I FOUND *THIS* IN YOUR ROOM.
!
FWUP
!! THAT'S MY... !!!
EH? WHAT'S THAT?
YOUR WHAT? YOU LOOK UPSET, NAMI.
THIS IS AN OLD TREASURE MAP!!!
IT'S OF THIS ISLAND, AND THE X MARKS COCO VILLAGE !!!

READ THIS WAY

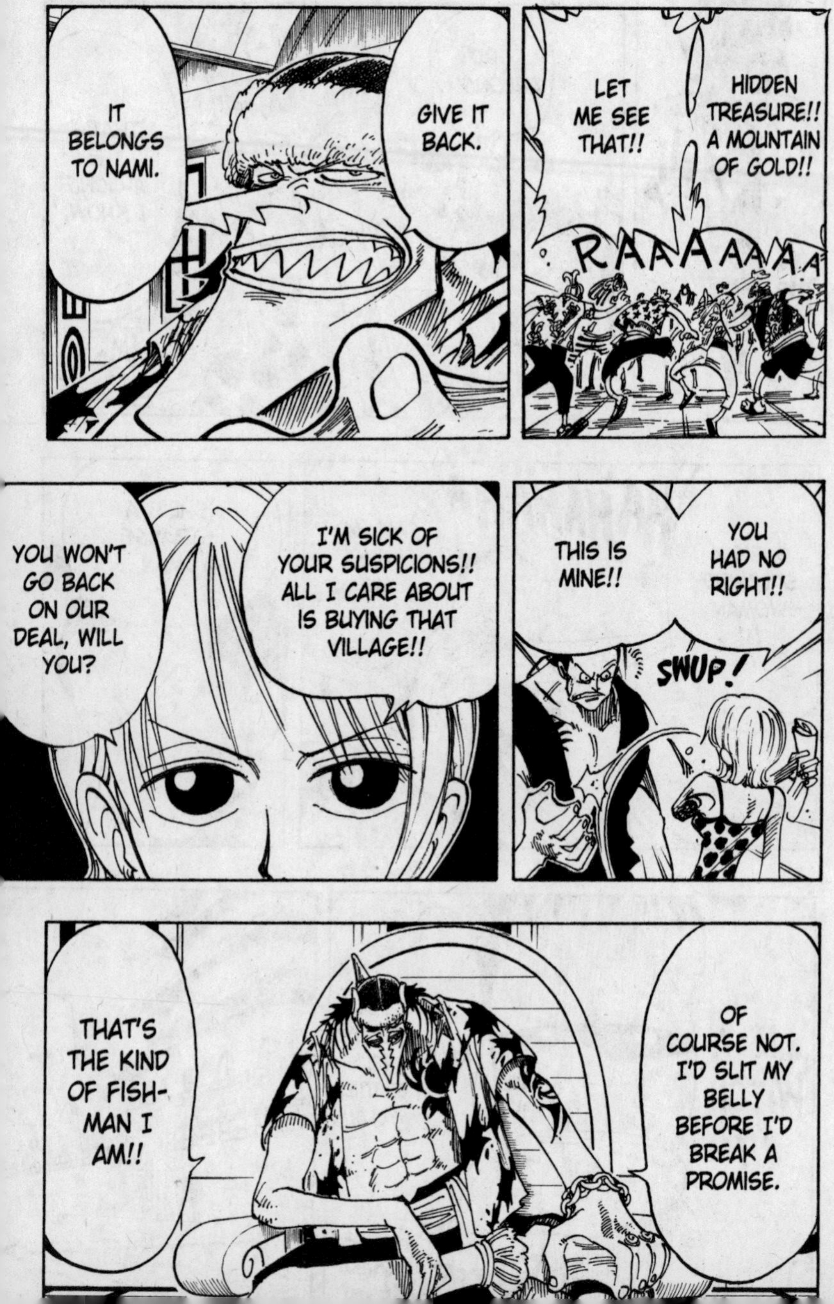
HIDDEN TREASURE!! A MOUNTAIN OF GOLD!!
LET ME SEE THAT!!
RAAAAAAAA
GIVE IT BACK.
IT BELONGS TO NAMI.
YOU HAD NO RIGHT!!
THIS IS MINE!!
SWUP!
I'M SICK OF YOUR SUSPICIONS!! ALL I CARE ABOUT IS BUYING THAT VILLAGE!!
YOU WON'T GO BACK ON OUR DEAL, WILL YOU?
OF COURSE NOT. I'D SLIT MY BELLY BEFORE I'D BREAK A PROMISE.
THAT'S THE KIND OF FISH-MAN I AM!!

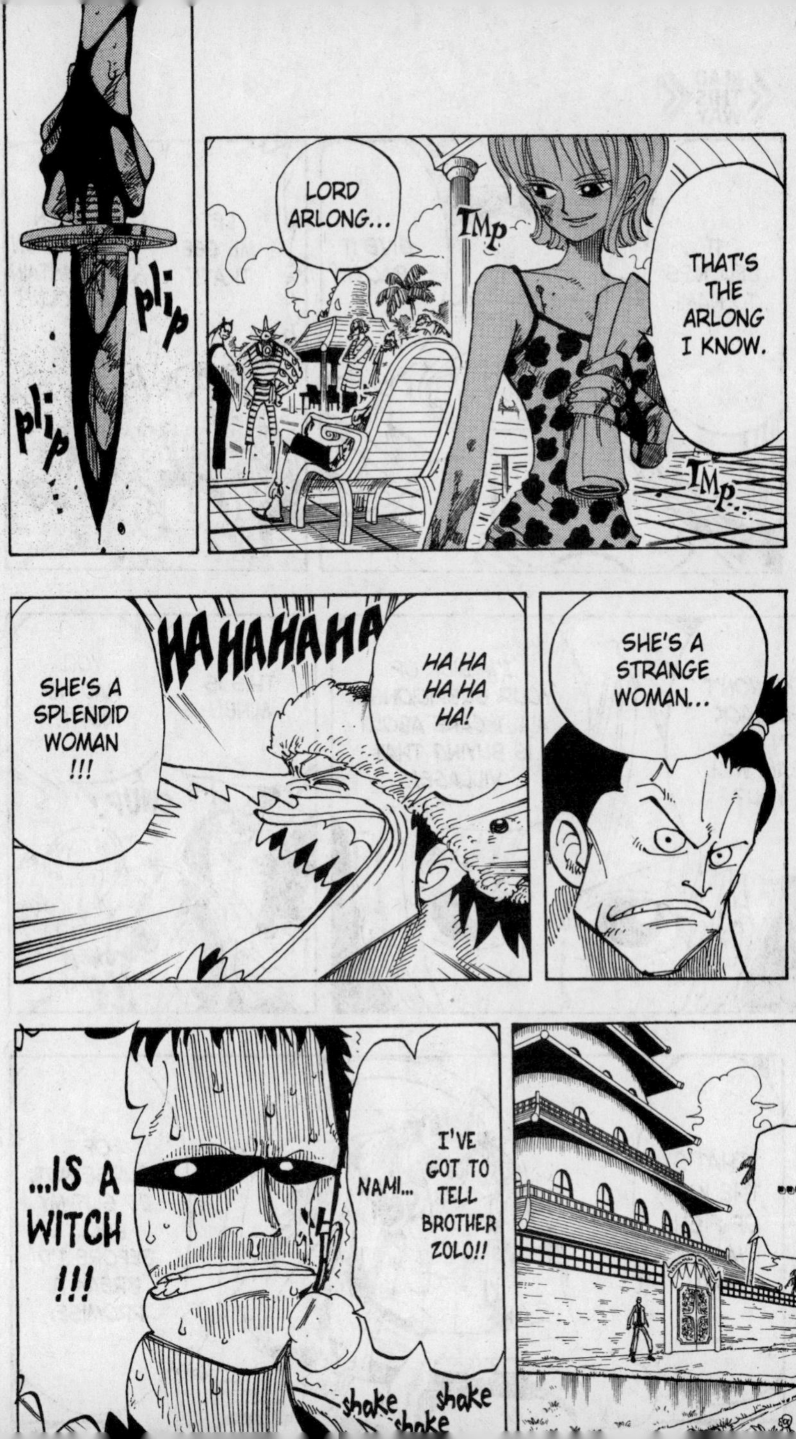
THAT'S THE ARLONG I KNOW.
TMp...
TMp
LORD ARLONG...
plip
plip...
SHE'S A STRANGE WOMAN...
HA HA HA HA HA!
HAHAHAHA
SHE'S A SPLENDID WOMAN !!!
...
I'VE GOT TO TELL BROTHER ZOLO!!
NAMI...
...IS A WITCH !!!
shake
shake
shake

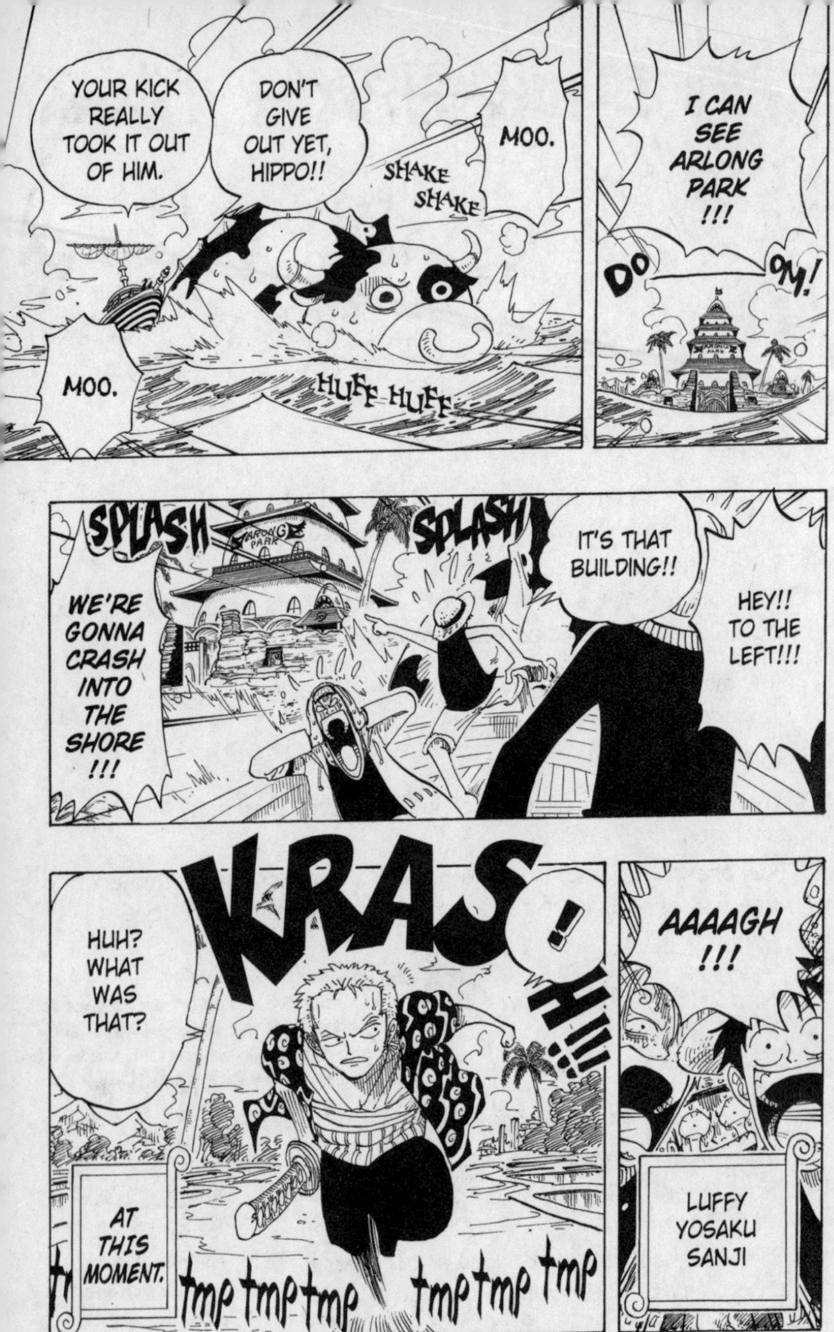
I CAN SEE ARLONG PARK!!!
DOOM!
MOO.
SHAKE SHAKE
DON'T GIVE OUT YET, HIPPO!!
YOUR KICK REALLY TOOK IT OUT OF HIM.
MOO.
HUFF HUFF
HEY!! TO THE LEFT!!!
IT'S THAT BUILDING!!
SPLASH
SPLASH
WE'RE GONNA CRASH INTO THE SHORE!!!
AAAAGH!!!
LUFFY YOSAKU SANJI
KRASH!!!!
HUH? WHAT WAS THAT?
AT THIS MOMENT.
tmp tmp tmp tmp tmp tmp tmp tmp

QUESTION CORNER
chou chou

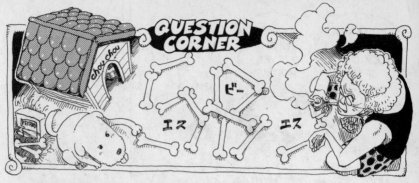

Q: **That's the kind of Sanji I like.**

A: What kind?

Q: Oda Sensei!! It's terrible!! My friend has caught the dreaded "I'll Die without a Snack" disease. What will cure it!? Hurry or he'll die!!

A: Don't panic!! Get a firm grip on yourself!! It'll be okay!! Keep your cool!! Calm down!! Good. Next question?

Q: How many fat-fats is Alvida's fatness? Whizzzzz. Crack! Agh!

A: Oh please, get outta here.

Q: What do you call the pistols used in **One Piece**? They don't look like matchlocks.

A: They are flintlocks. Flint is a rock that makes a spark when it strikes metal. Think of it as one step above a matchlock.

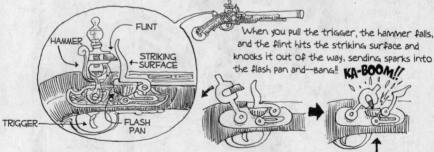

FLINT
HAMMER
STRIKING SURFACE
TRIGGER
FLASH PAN
When you pull the trigger, the hammer falls, and the flint hits the striking surface and knocks it out of the way, sending sparks into the flash pan and--bang!!
KA-BOOM!!

A flintlock had to be reloaded after every shot, so pirates sometimes carried 5 or 6 of them. However, in the world of **One Piece** some have been modified to fire repeatedly. Scary, huh?

Sparks ignite the gunpowder, and the bullet shoots off with a bang.

# Chapter 75: OF MAPS AND FISH-MEN

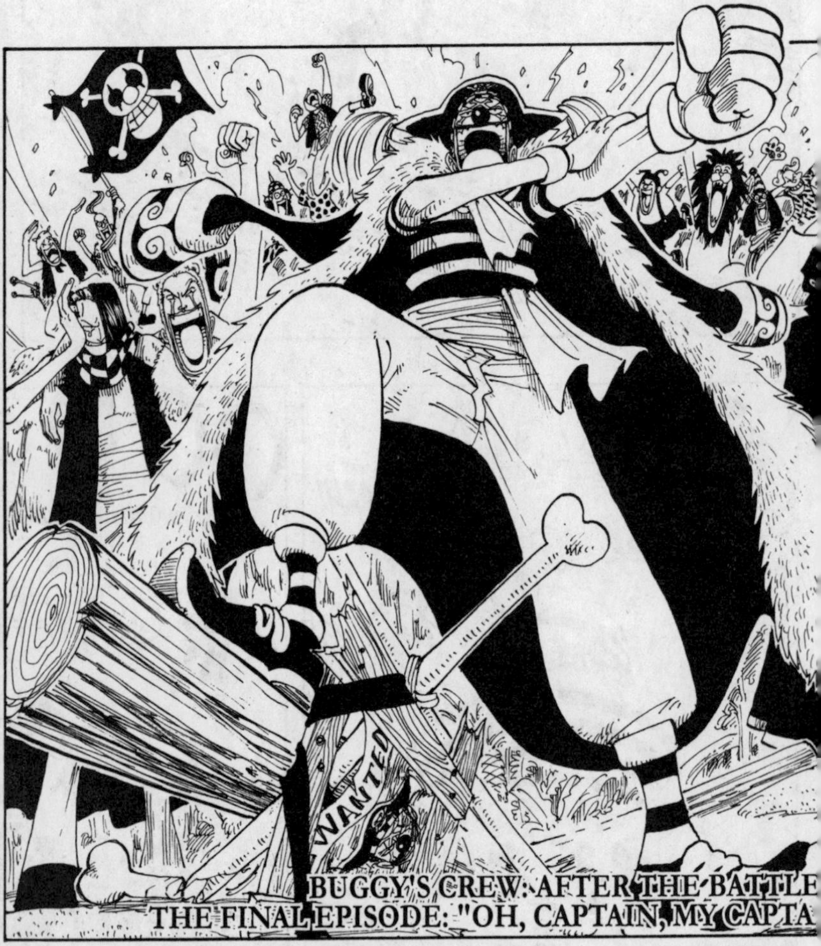
WANTED
BUGGY'S CREW: AFTER THE BATTLE
THE FINAL EPISODE: "OH, CAPTAIN, MY CAPTA

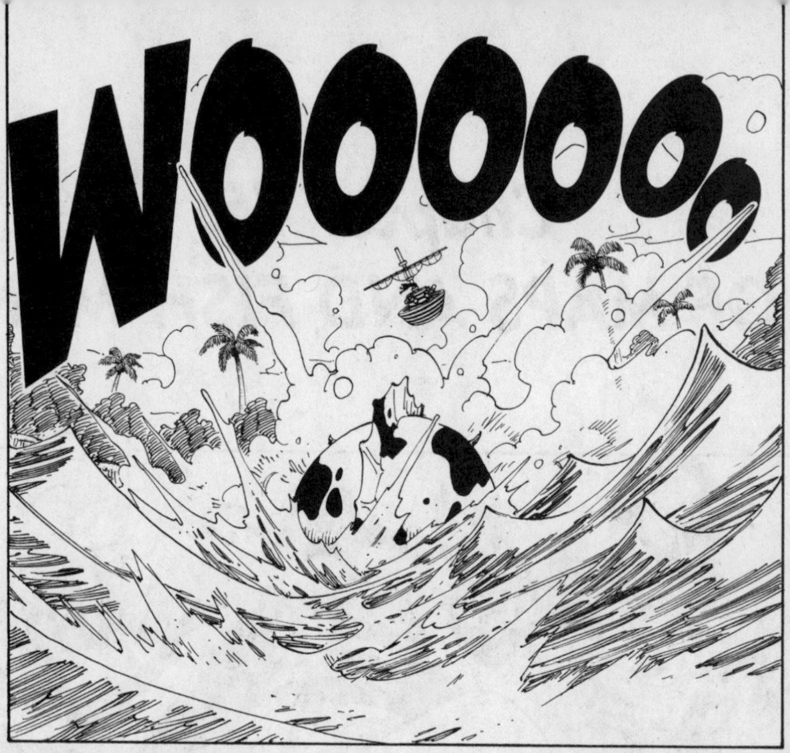
WOOOOOO

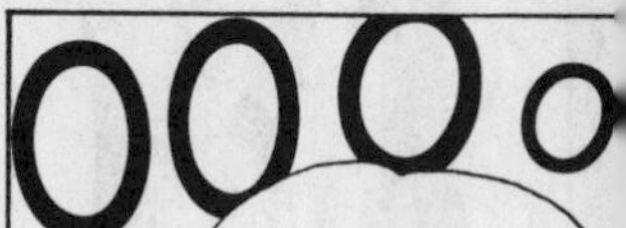
OOOO
WHAT WAS THAT!? I HEARD A LOUD NOISE COMING FROM THE PORT!!

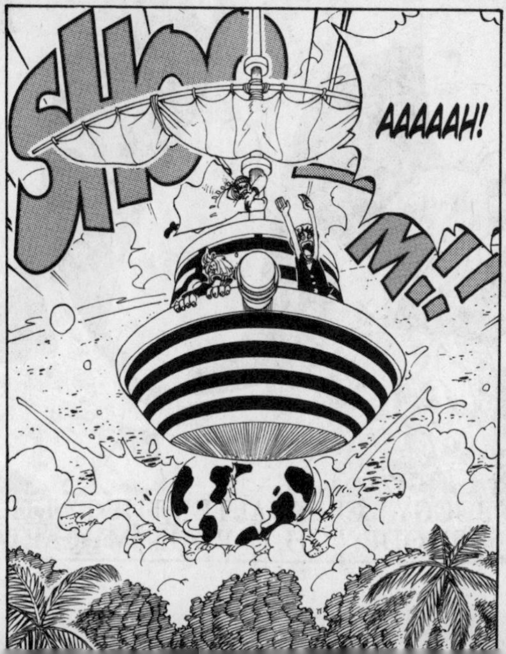
SHOOM!!
AAAAAH!

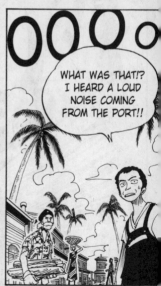

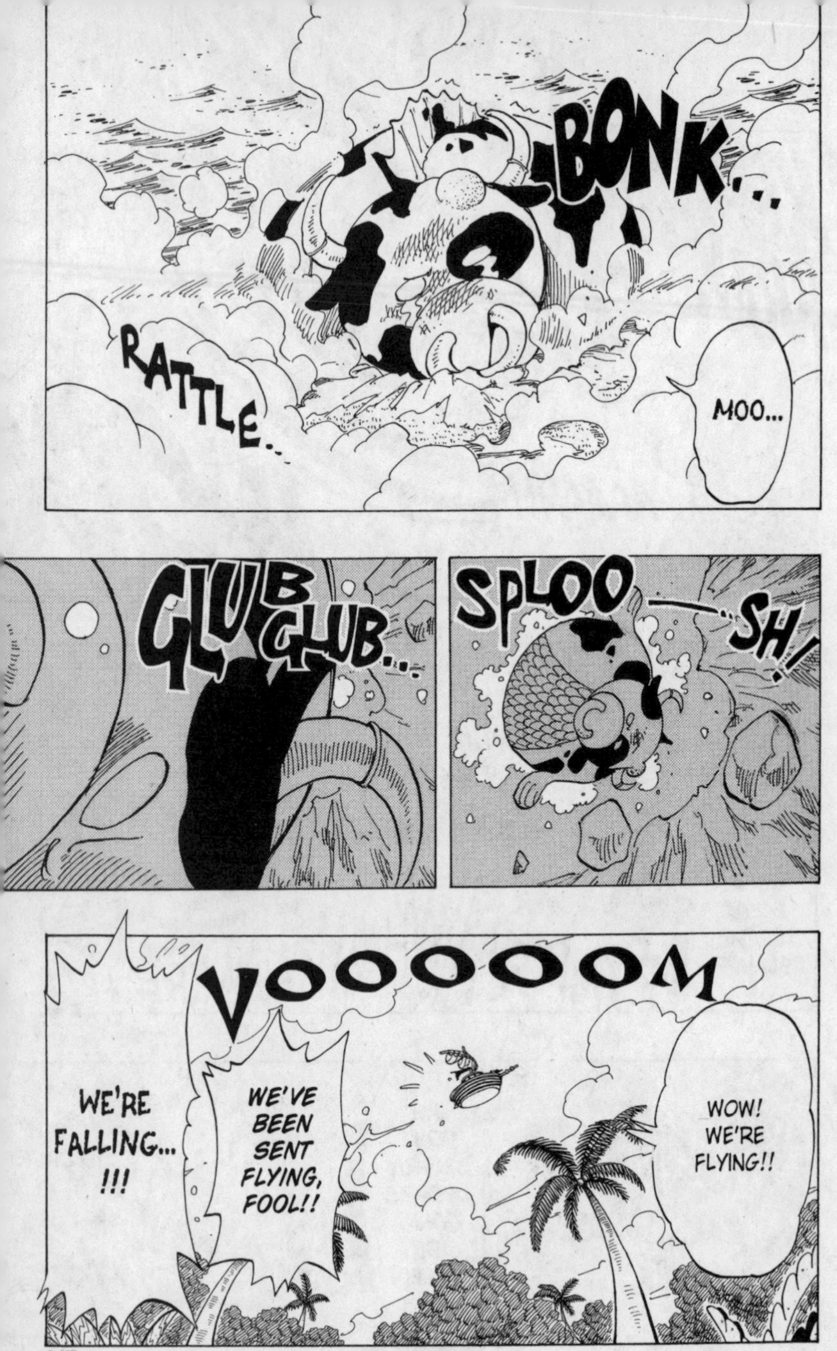
BONK...
MOO...
RATTLE...
SPLOO---SH!
GLUB GLUB...
VOOOOOM
WOW! WE'RE FLYING!!
WE'VE BEEN SENT FLYING, FOOL!!
WE'RE FALLING... !!!

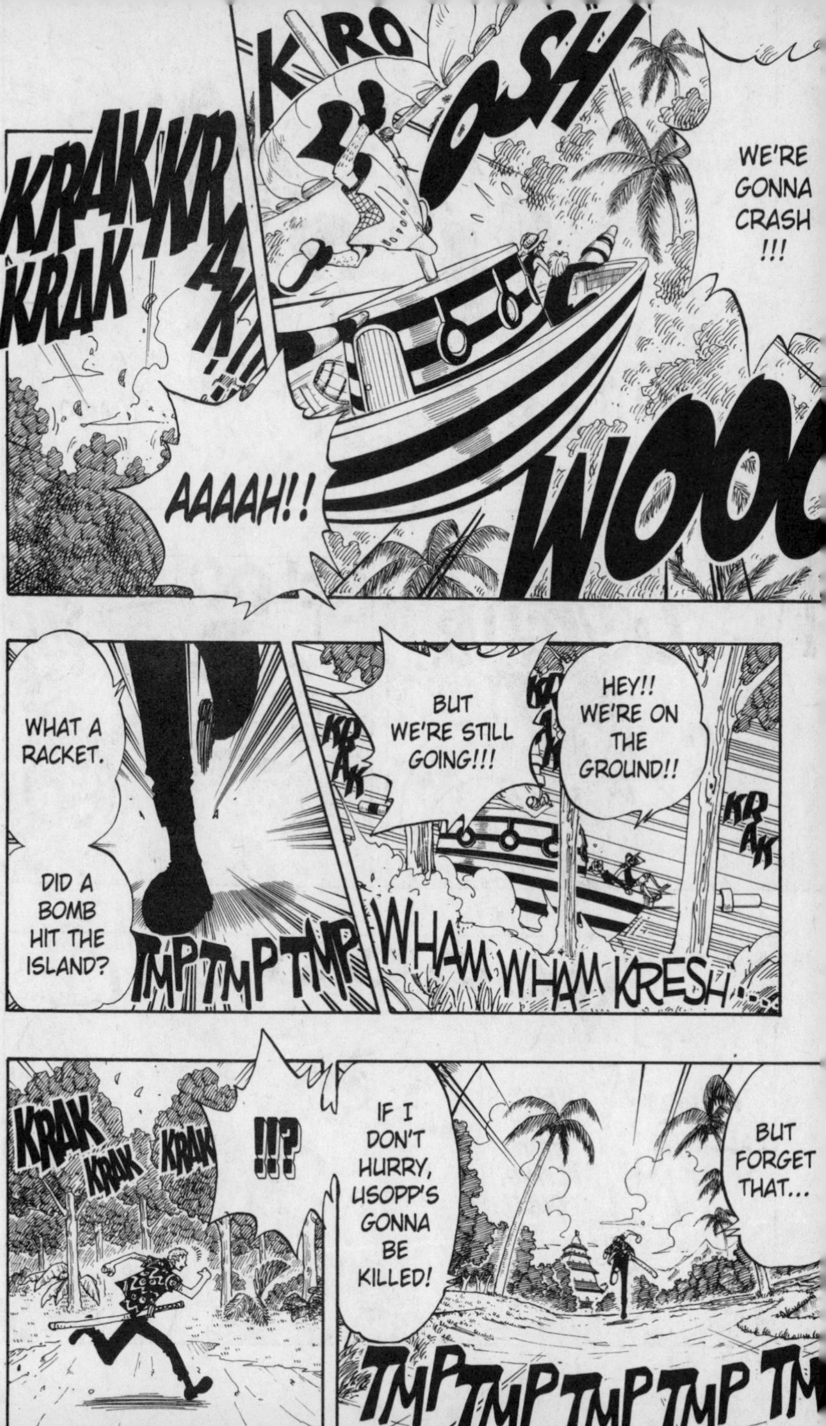
WE'RE GONNA CRASH !!!
WOOO
KROOSH
KRAKKRAKK!!
KRAK KRAK
AAAAH!!
HEY!! WE'RE ON THE GROUND!!
KRAK
BUT WE'RE STILL GOING!!!
KRAK
WHAM WHAM KRESH...
WHAT A RACKET.
DID A BOMB HIT THE ISLAND?
TMP TMP TMP
BUT FORGET THAT...
IF I DON'T HURRY, USOPP'S GONNA BE KILLED!
TMP TMP TMP TMP TM
!!?
KRAK KRAK KRAK

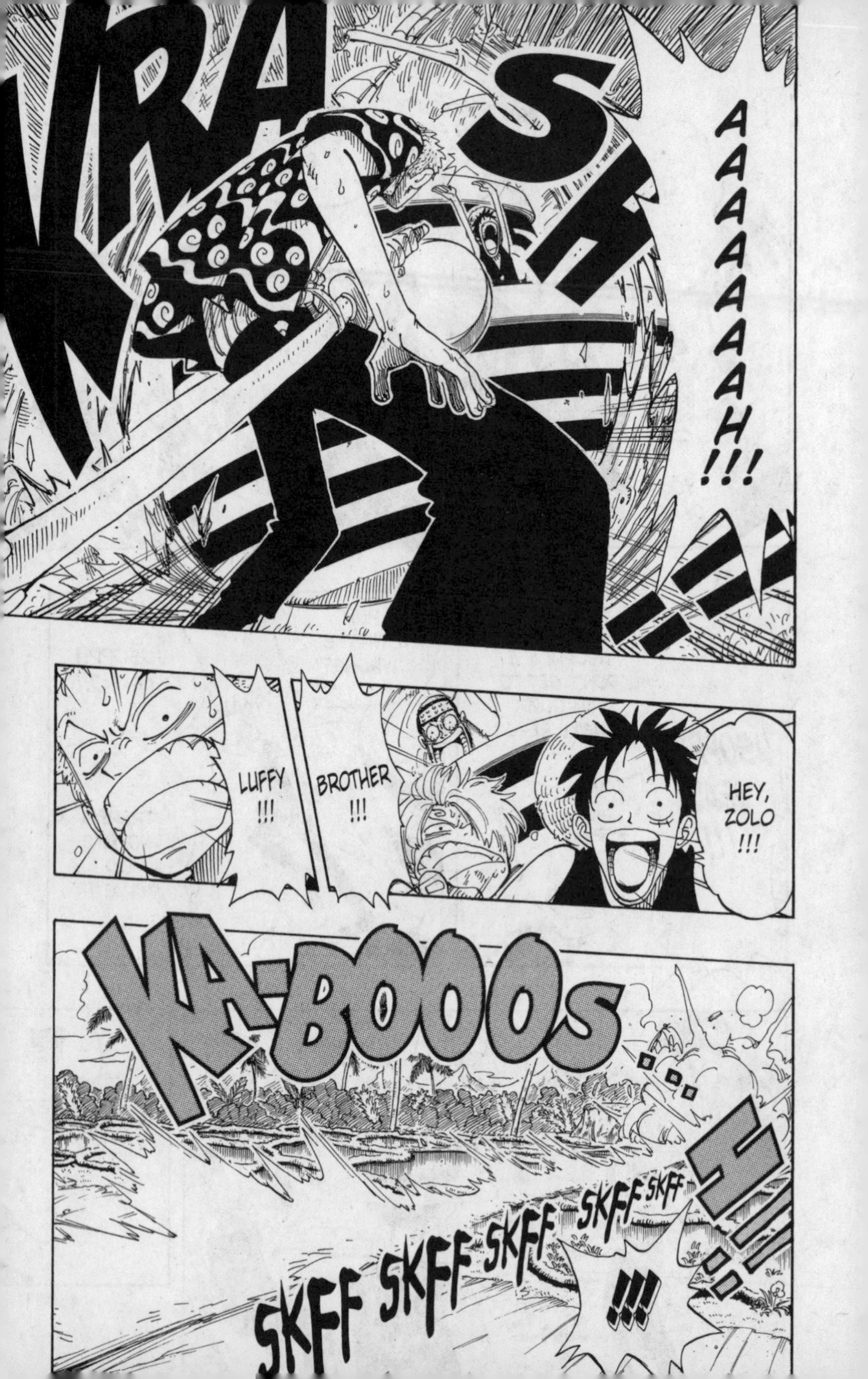
AAAAAAAAH!!!
HEY, ZOLO!!!
BROTHER!!!
LUFFY!!!
KA-BOOOSH!!
SKFF SKFF SKFF SKFF SKFF SKFF
!!!

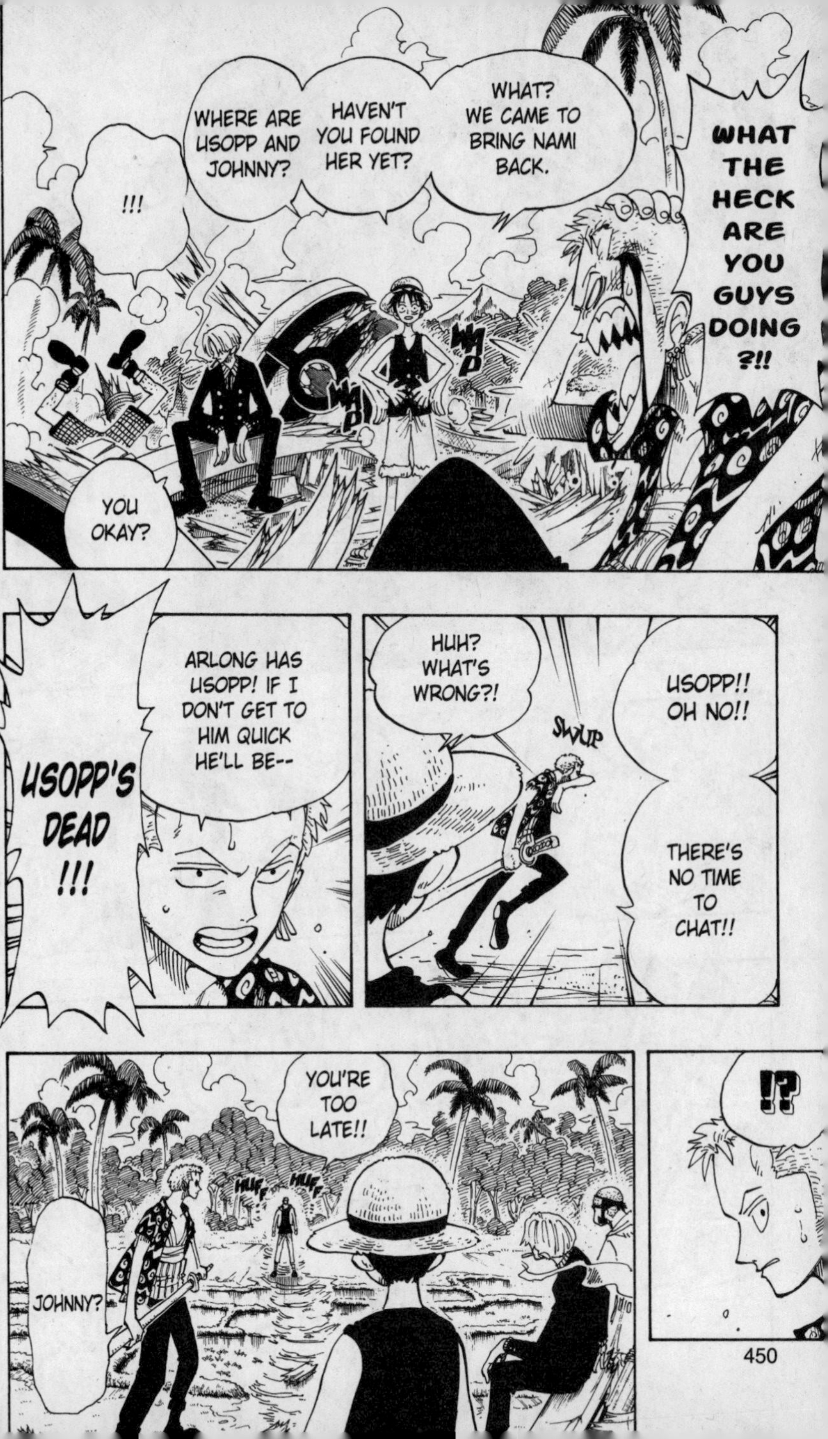
WHAT THE HECK ARE YOU GUYS DOING ?!!
WHAT? WE CAME TO BRING NAMI BACK.
HAVEN'T YOU FOUND HER YET?
WHERE ARE USOPP AND JOHNNY?
!!!
YOU OKAY?
USOPP!! OH NO!!
HUH? WHAT'S WRONG?!
SWUP
THERE'S NO TIME TO CHAT!!
ARLONG HAS USOPP! IF I DON'T GET TO HIM QUICK HE'LL BE--
USOPP'S DEAD !!!
!?
YOU'RE TOO LATE!!
HUFF
HUFF
JOHNNY?

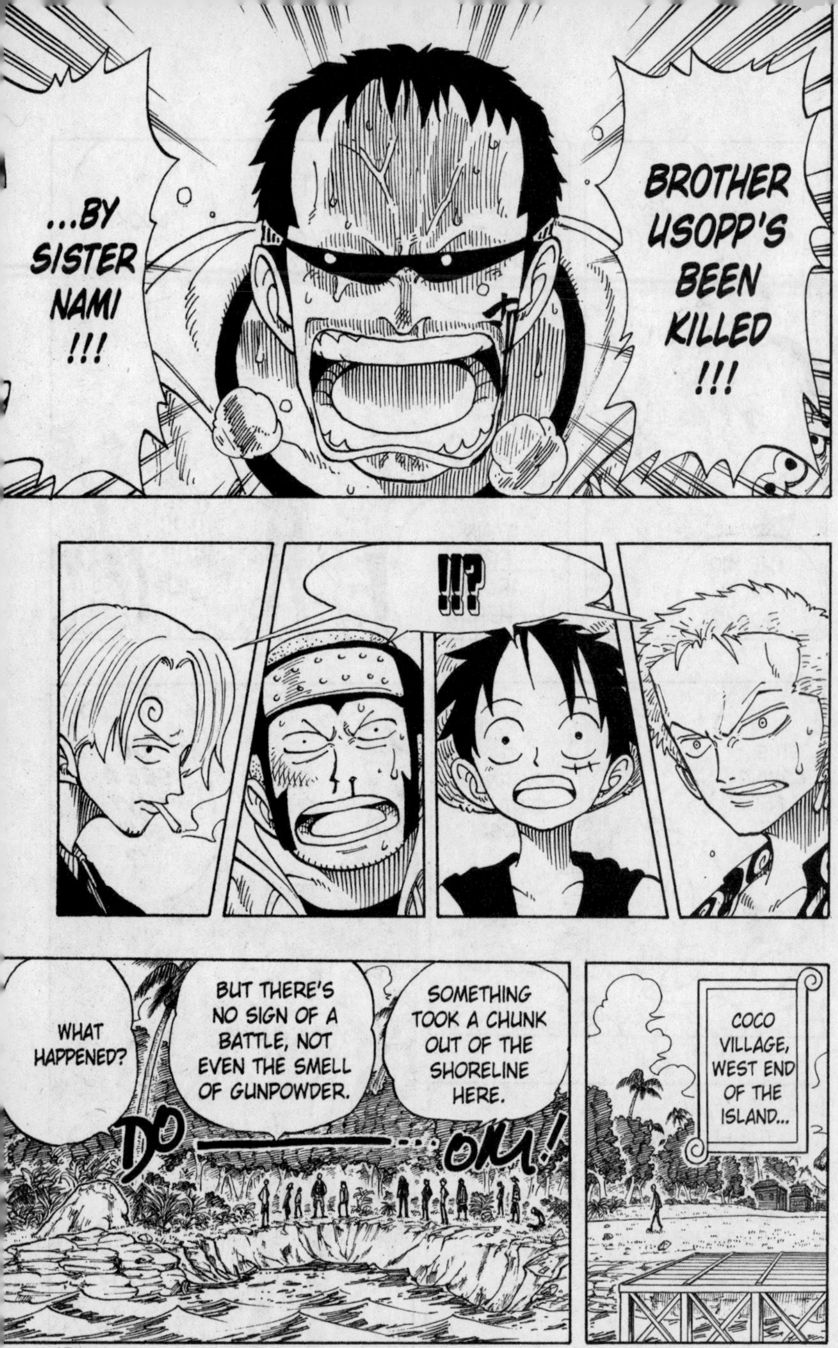
BROTHER USOPP'S BEEN KILLED !!!
...BY SISTER NAMI !!!
!!?
COCO VILLAGE, WEST END OF THE ISLAND...
SOMETHING TOOK A CHUNK OUT OF THE SHORELINE HERE.
BUT THERE'S NO SIGN OF A BATTLE, NOT EVEN THE SMELL OF GUNPOWDER.
WHAT HAPPENED?
DO———OM!

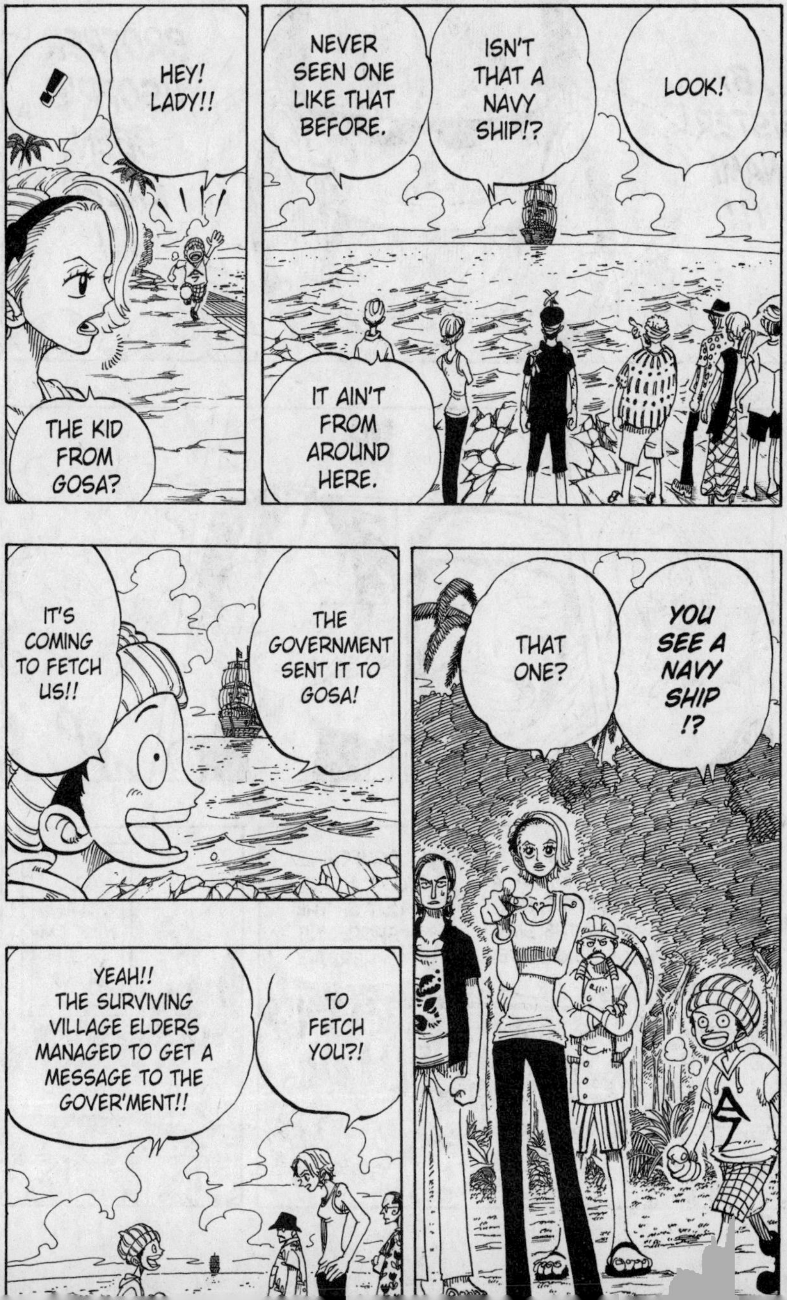
LOOK!
ISN'T THAT A NAVY SHIP!?
NEVER SEEN ONE LIKE THAT BEFORE.
IT AIN'T FROM AROUND HERE.
HEY! LADY!!
!
THE KID FROM GOSA?
YOU SEE A NAVY SHIP!?
THAT ONE?
THE GOVERNMENT SENT IT TO GOSA!
IT'S COMING TO FETCH US!!
TO FETCH YOU?!
YEAH!! THE SURVIVING VILLAGE ELDERS MANAGED TO GET A MESSAGE TO THE GOVER'MENT!!

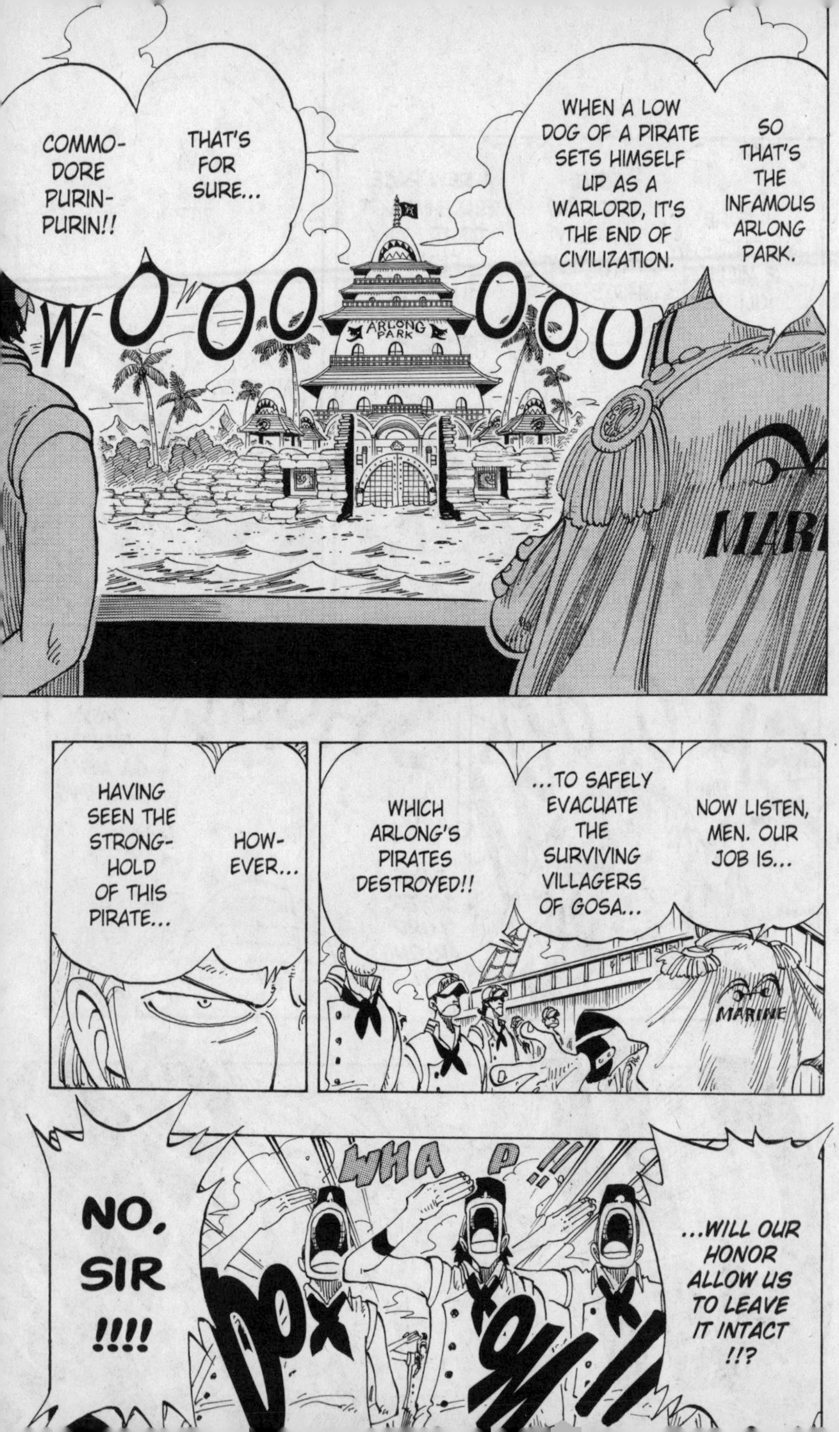
SO THAT'S THE INFAMOUS ARLONG PARK.
WHEN A LOW DOG OF A PIRATE SETS HIMSELF UP AS A WARLORD, IT'S THE END OF CIVILIZATION.
THAT'S FOR SURE...
COMMODORE PURIN-PURIN!!
WOOOOOOO
ARLONG PARK
MARI
NOW LISTEN, MEN. OUR JOB IS...
...TO SAFELY EVACUATE THE SURVIVING VILLAGERS OF GOSA...
WHICH ARLONG'S PIRATES DESTROYED!!
MARINE
HOW-EVER...
HAVING SEEN THE STRONGHOLD OF THIS PIRATE...
...WILL OUR HONOR ALLOW US TO LEAVE IT INTACT!!?
WHAP!!!
NO, SIR!!!!

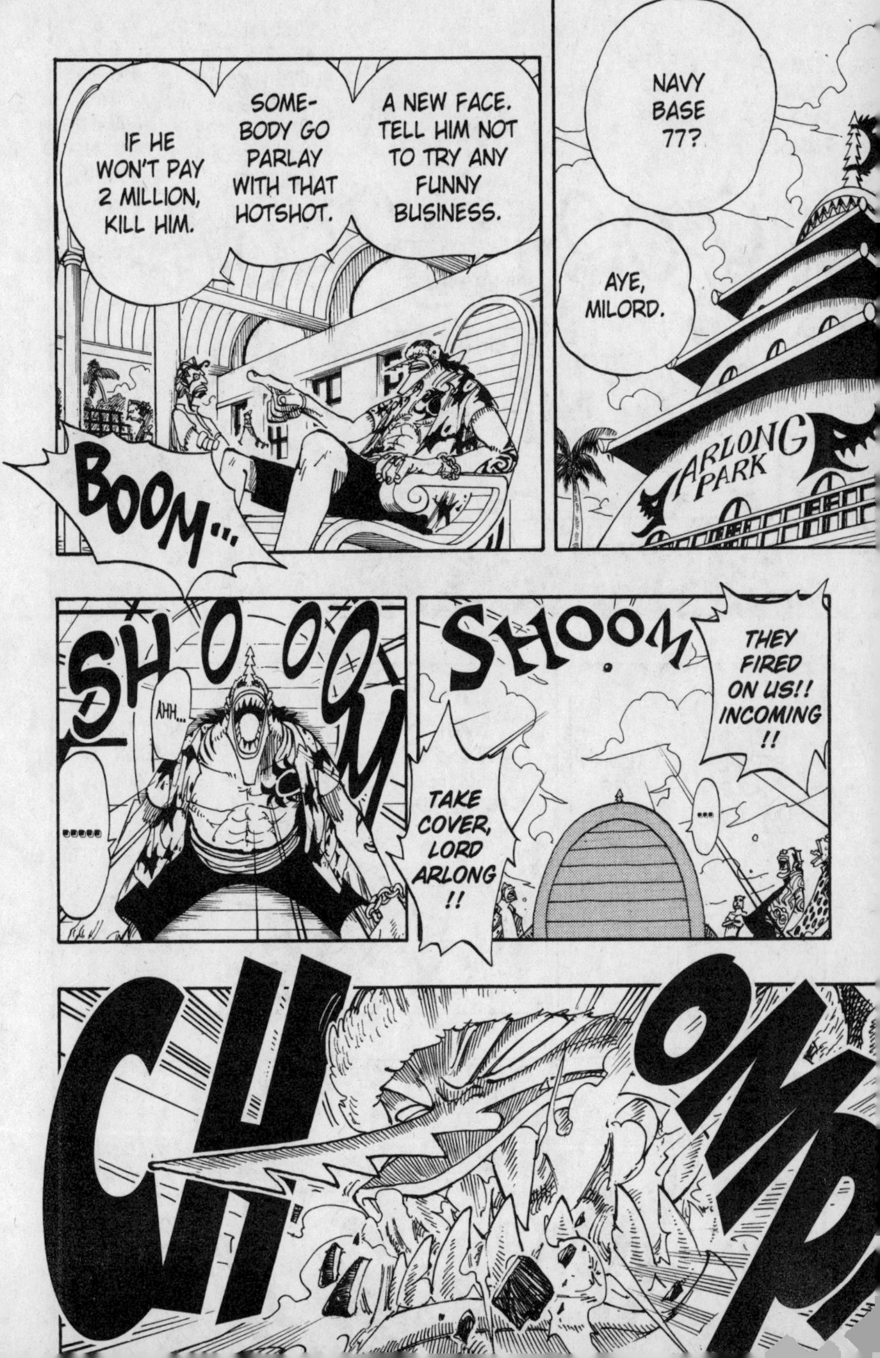
NAVY BASE 77?
AYE, MILORD.
ARLONG PARK
A NEW FACE. TELL HIM NOT TO TRY ANY FUNNY BUSINESS.
SOME-BODY GO PARLAY WITH THAT HOTSHOT.
IF HE WON'T PAY 2 MILLION, KILL HIM.
BOOM...
THEY FIRED ON US!! INCOMING!!
SHOOM
...
TAKE COVER, LORD ARLONG!!
SHOOOM
AHH...
.....
CHOMP

READ THIS WAY

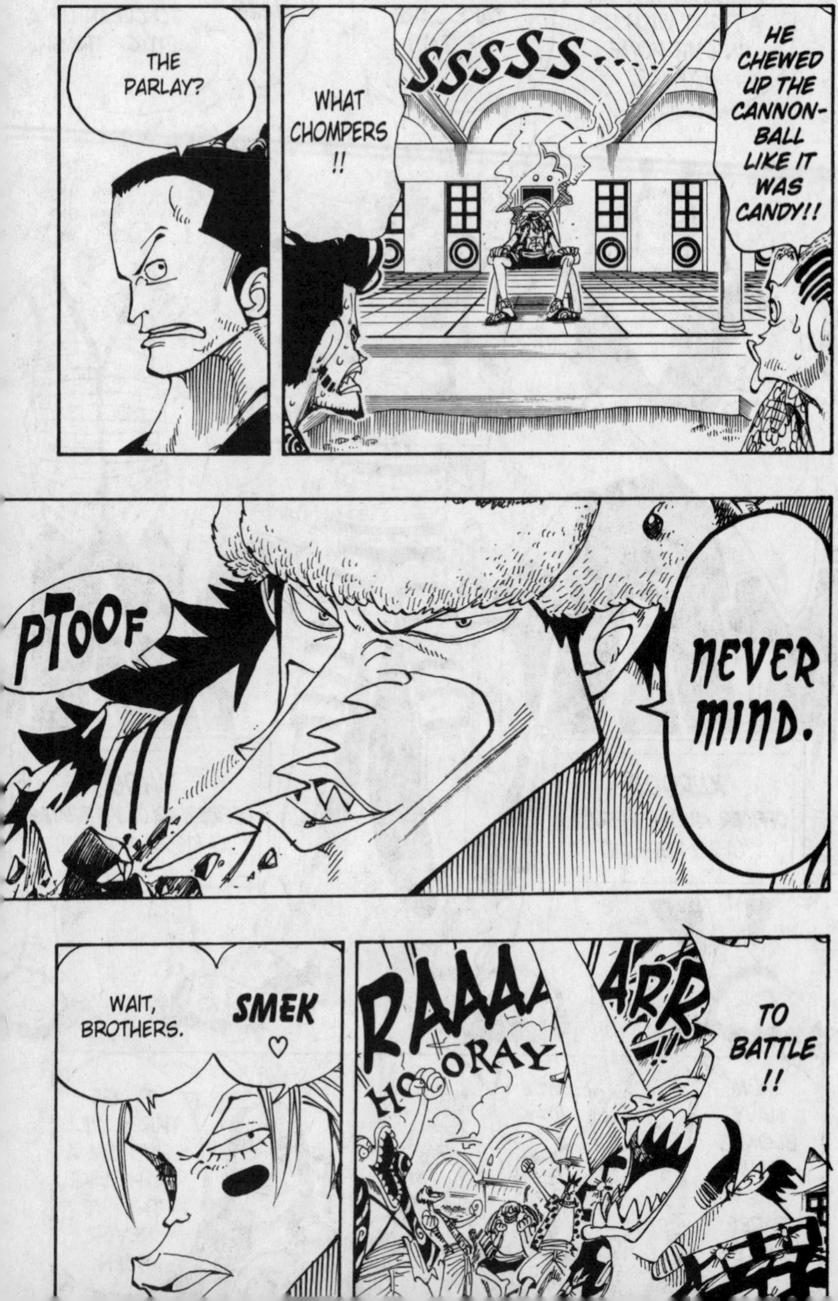

HE CHEWED UP THE CANNON-BALL LIKE IT WAS CANDY!!
SSSSS...
WHAT CHOMPERS !!
THE PARLAY?
NEVER MIND.
PTOOF
TO BATTLE !!
RAAAARR
HOORAY
SMEK
WAIT, BROTHERS.

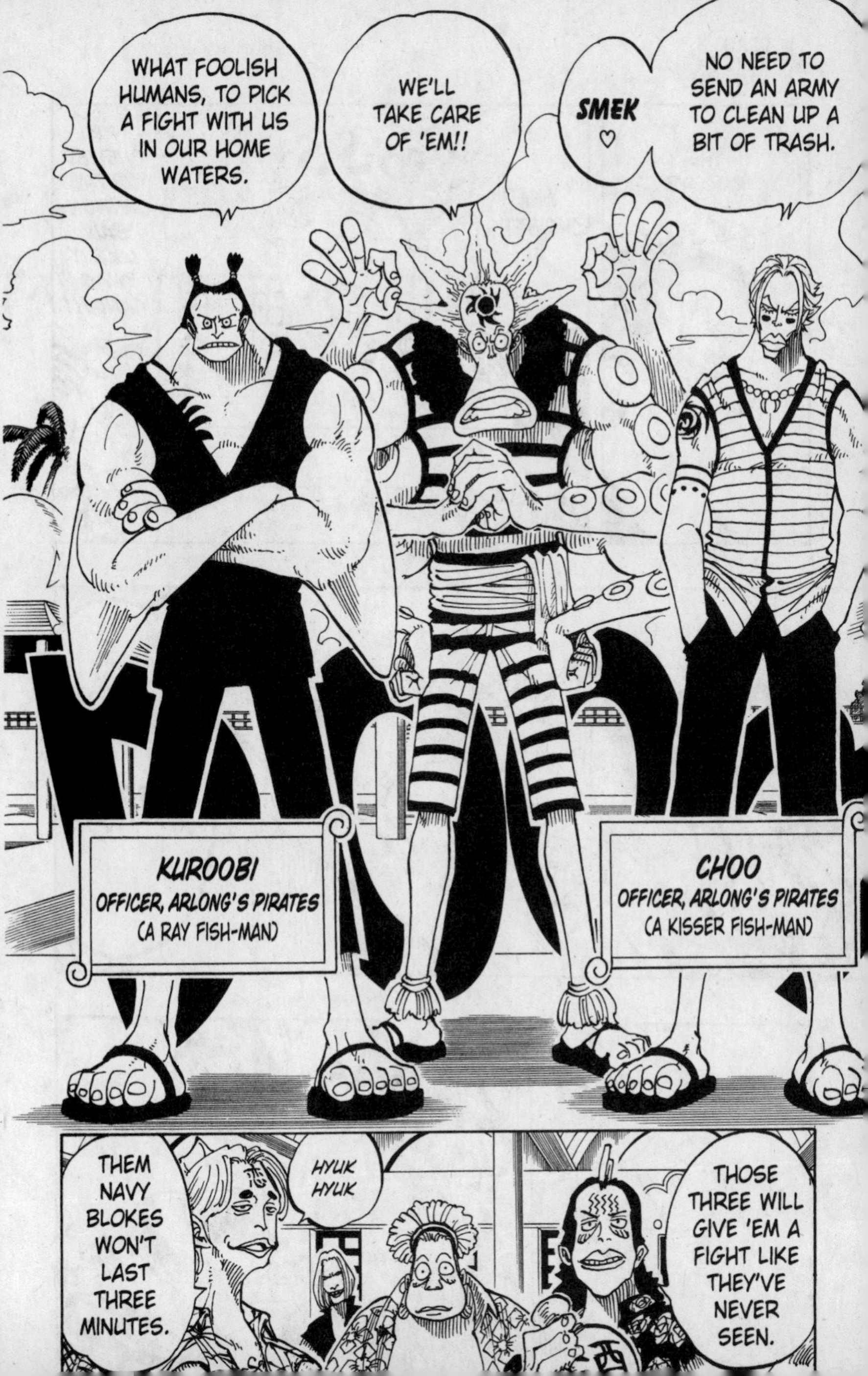
NO NEED TO SEND AN ARMY TO CLEAN UP A BIT OF TRASH.
SMEK ♡
WE'LL TAKE CARE OF 'EM!!
WHAT FOOLISH HUMANS, TO PICK A FIGHT WITH US IN OUR HOME WATERS.
CHOO
OFFICER, ARLONG'S PIRATES
(A KISSER FISH-MAN)
KUROOBI
OFFICER, ARLONG'S PIRATES
(A RAY FISH-MAN)
THOSE THREE WILL GIVE 'EM A FIGHT LIKE THEY'VE NEVER SEEN.
HYUK HYUK
THEM NAVY BLOKES WON'T LAST THREE MINUTES.

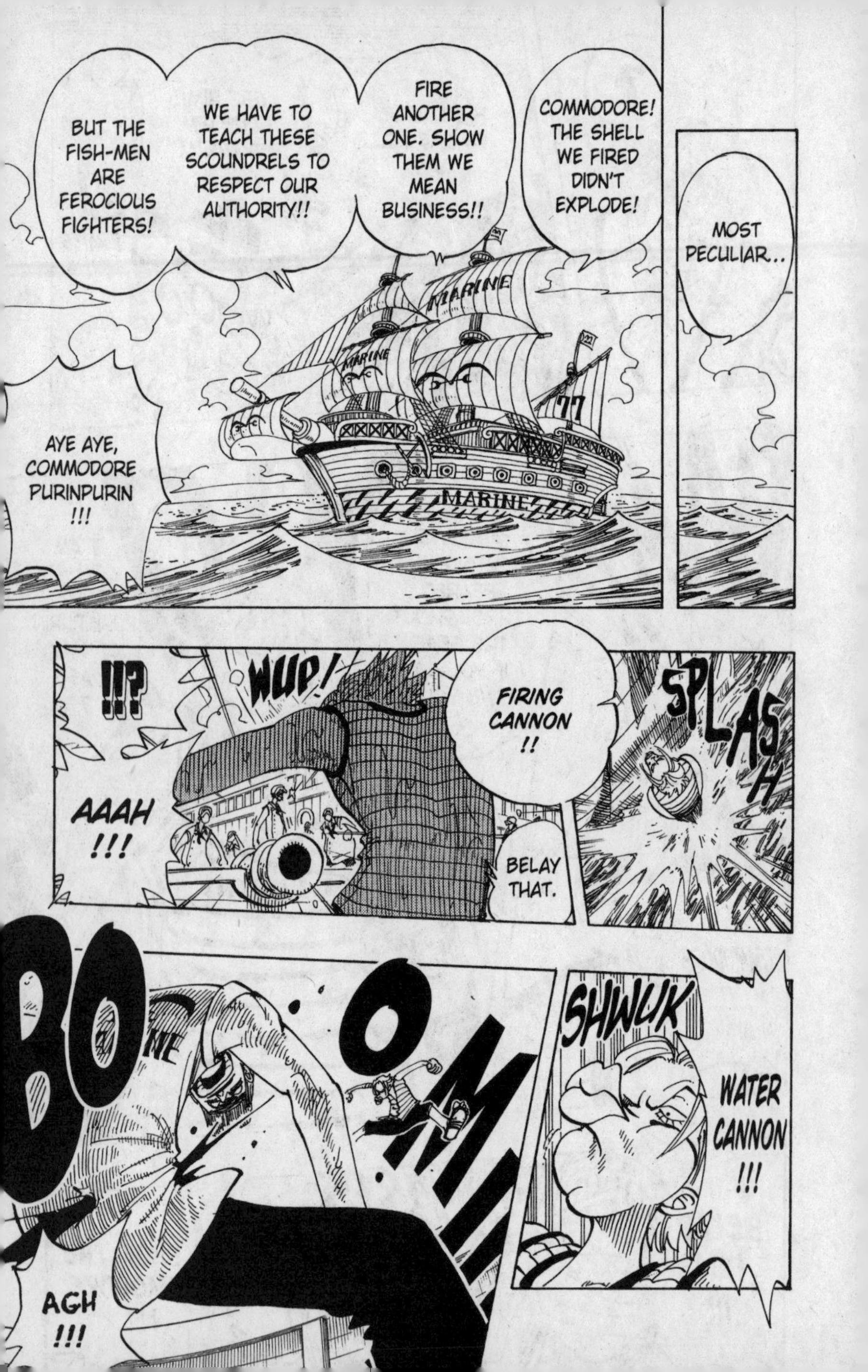

MOST PECULIAR...
COMMODORE! THE SHELL WE FIRED DIDN'T EXPLODE!
FIRE ANOTHER ONE. SHOW THEM WE MEAN BUSINESS!!
WE HAVE TO TEACH THESE SCOUNDRELS TO RESPECT OUR AUTHORITY!!
BUT THE FISH-MEN ARE FEROCIOUS FIGHTERS!
MARINE
MARINE
77
MARINE
AYE AYE, COMMODORE PURINPURIN!!!
SPLASH
FIRING CANNON!!
BELAY THAT.
WUP!
!!?
AAAH!!!
SHWUK
WATER CANNON!!!
BOOM
AGH!!!

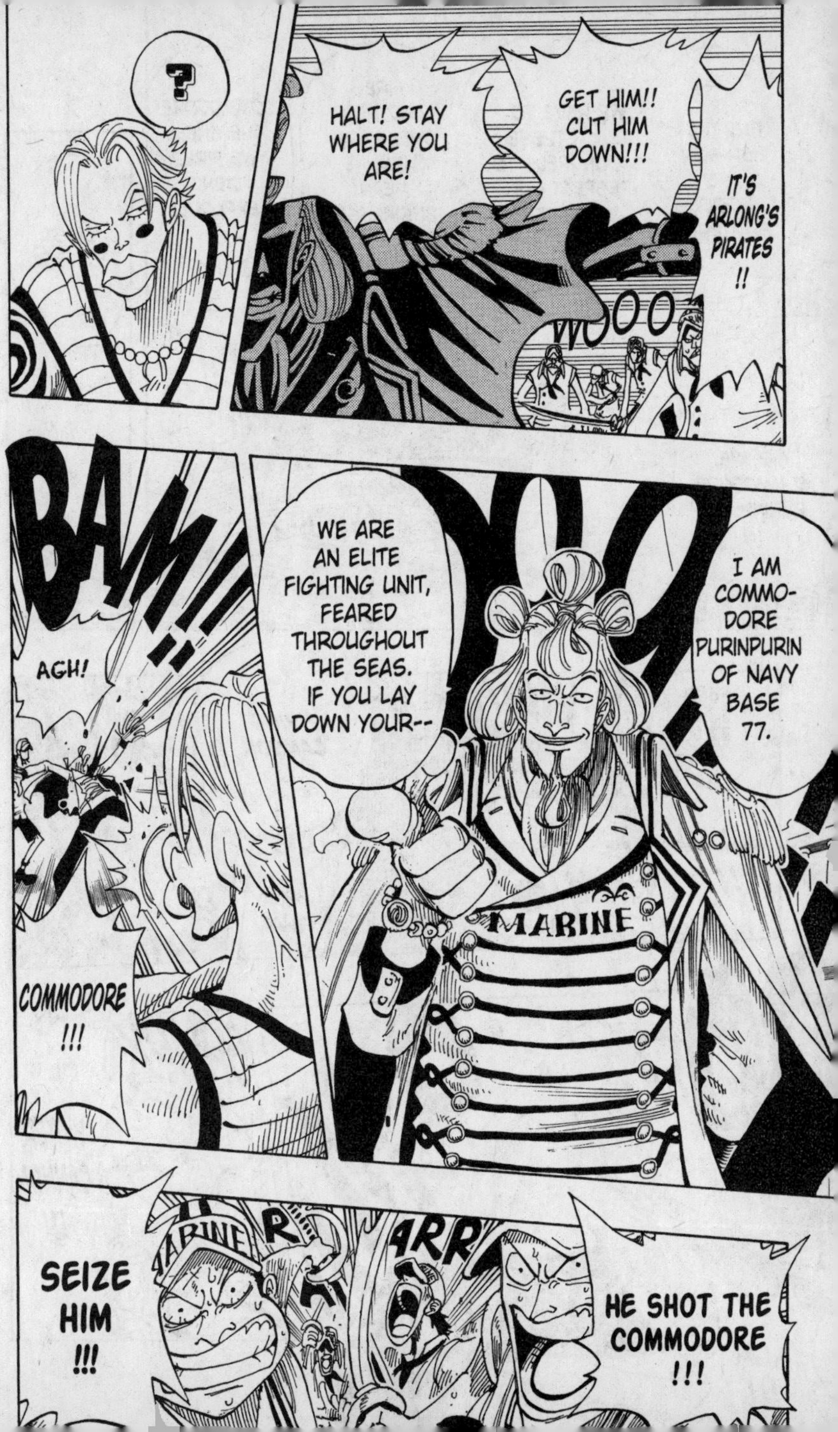
IT'S ARLONG'S PIRATES !!
GET HIM!! CUT HIM DOWN!!!
HALT! STAY WHERE YOU ARE!
WOOO
?
I AM COMMODORE PURINPURIN OF NAVY BASE 77.
MARINE
WE ARE AN ELITE FIGHTING UNIT, FEARED THROUGHOUT THE SEAS. IF YOU LAY DOWN YOUR--
BAM!!
AGH!
COMMODORE !!!
HE SHOT THE COMMODORE !!!
ARR
R
SEIZE HIM !!!

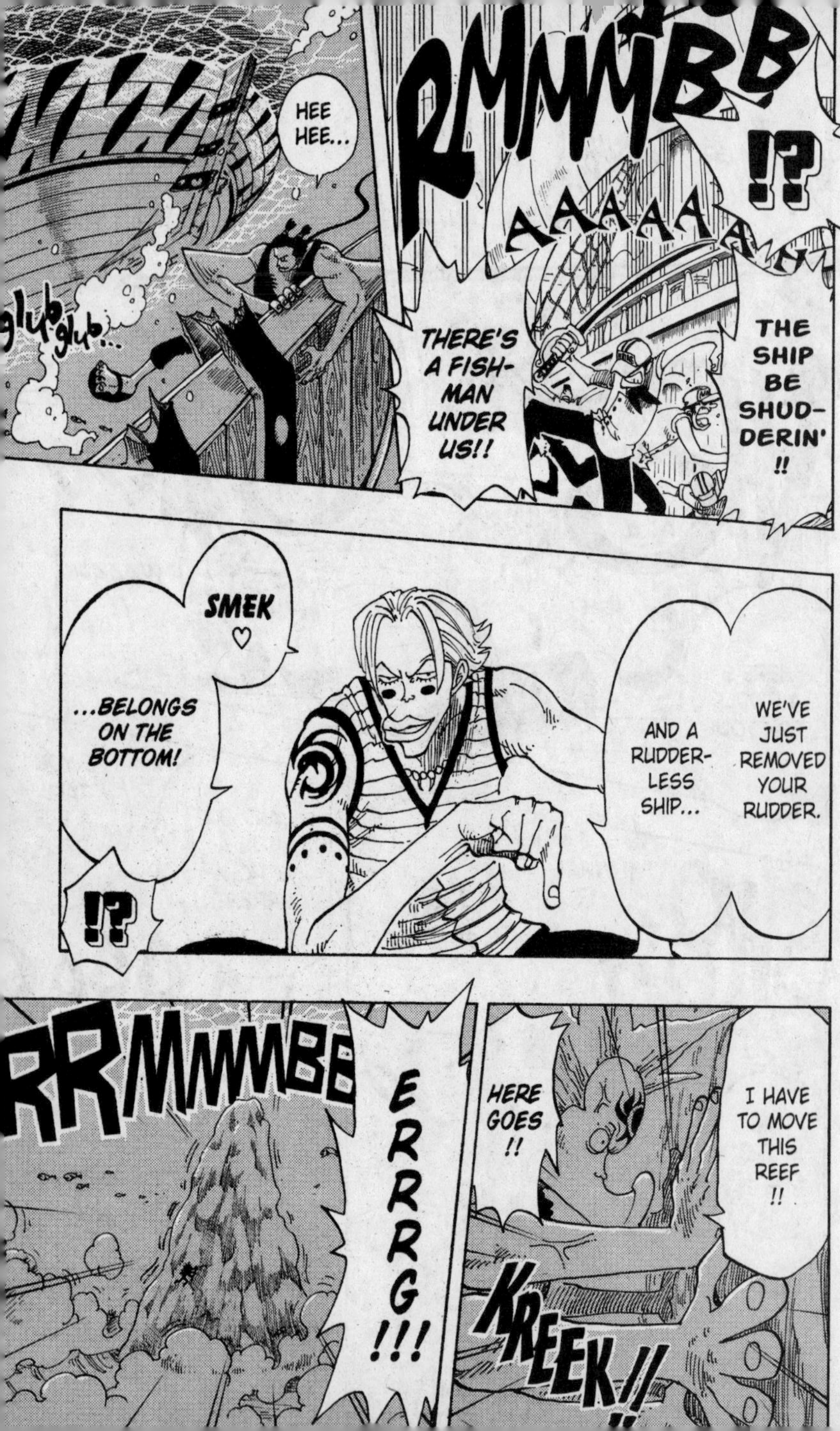

RMMMBB
!?
AAAAAA
THE SHIP BE SHUDDERIN'!!
THERE'S A FISHMAN UNDER US!!
HEE HEE...
glub glub...
WE'VE JUST REMOVED YOUR RUDDER.
AND A RUDDERLESS SHIP...
...BELONGS ON THE BOTTOM!
SMEK ♡
!?
I HAVE TO MOVE THIS REEF!!
HERE GOES!!
KREEK!!
ERRRG!!!
RRMMMBB

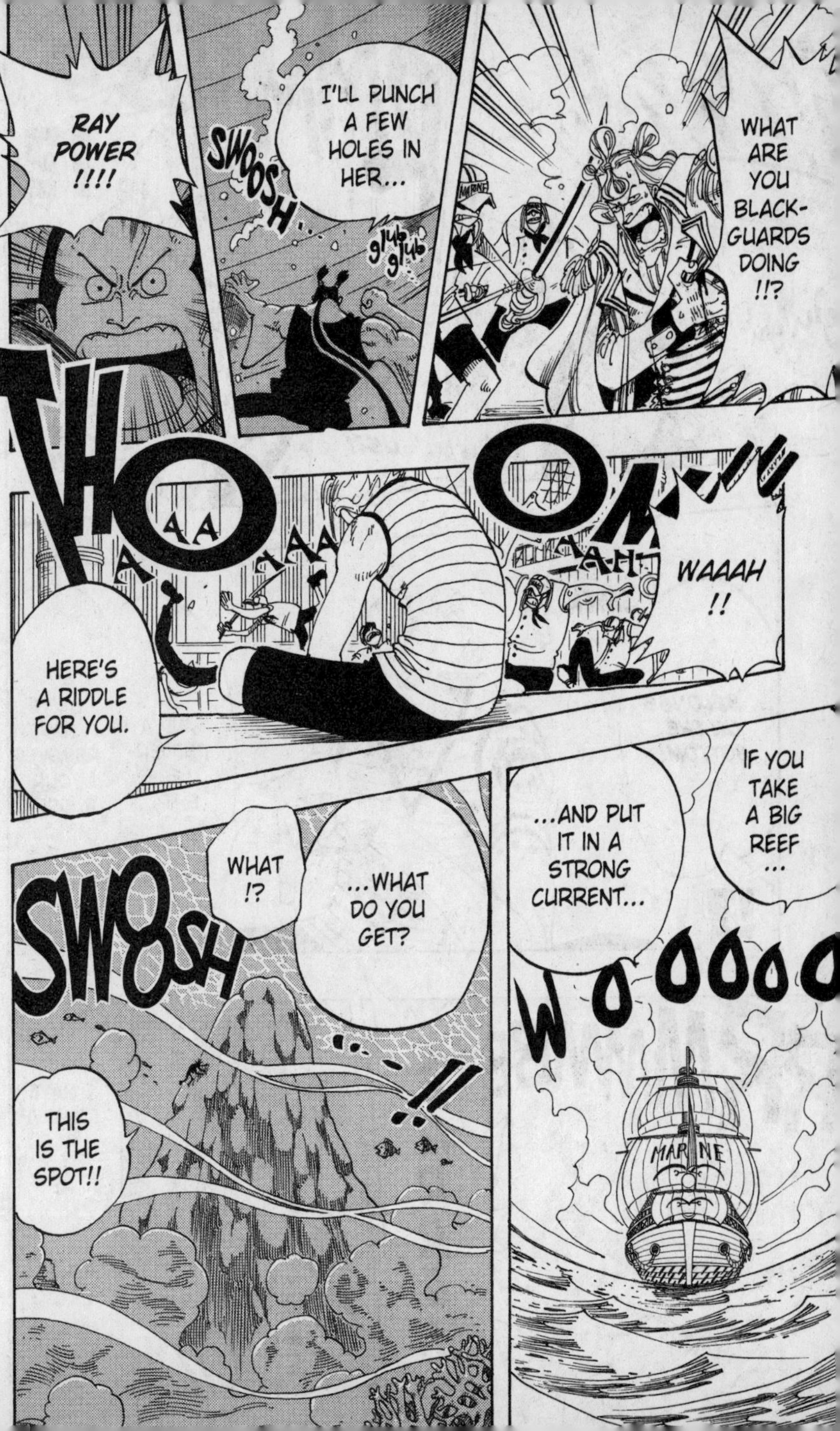
WHAT ARE YOU BLACK-GUARDS DOING !!?
I'LL PUNCH A FEW HOLES IN HER...
SWOOSH
glub glub
RAY POWER !!!!
VHOOM
WAAAH !!
HERE'S A RIDDLE FOR YOU.
IF YOU TAKE A BIG REEF...
...AND PUT IT IN A STRONG CURRENT...
WOOOOO
...WHAT DO YOU GET?
WHAT !?
SWOSH
..-..!!
THIS IS THE SPOT!!

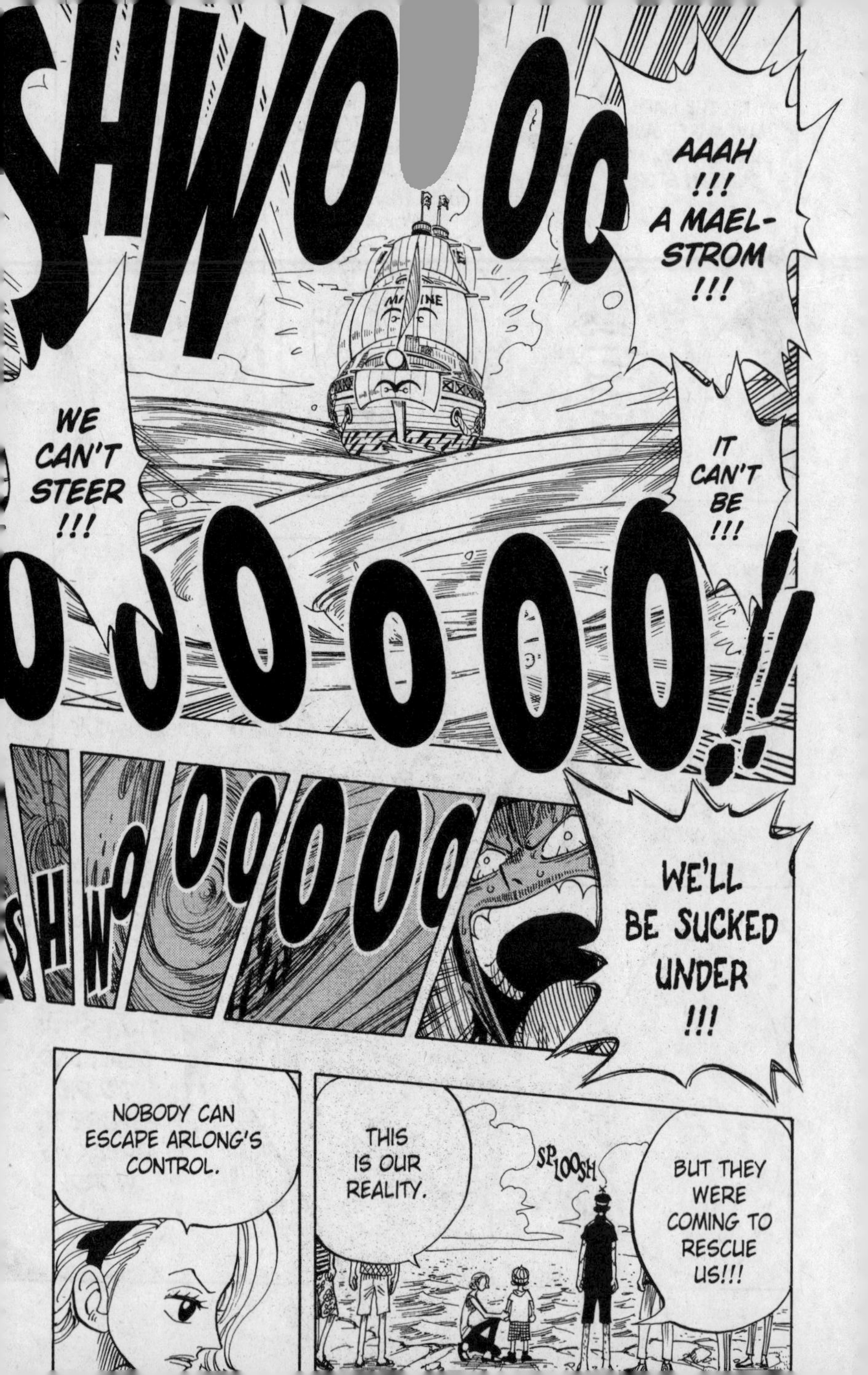
SHWOOOOOOOOOO!!
AAAH!!! A MAELSTROM!!!
WE CAN'T STEER!!!
IT CAN'T BE!!!
SHWOOOOOO
WE'LL BE SUCKED UNDER!!!
SPLOOSH
BUT THEY WERE COMING TO RESCUE US!!!
THIS IS OUR REALITY.
NOBODY CAN ESCAPE ARLONG'S CONTROL.

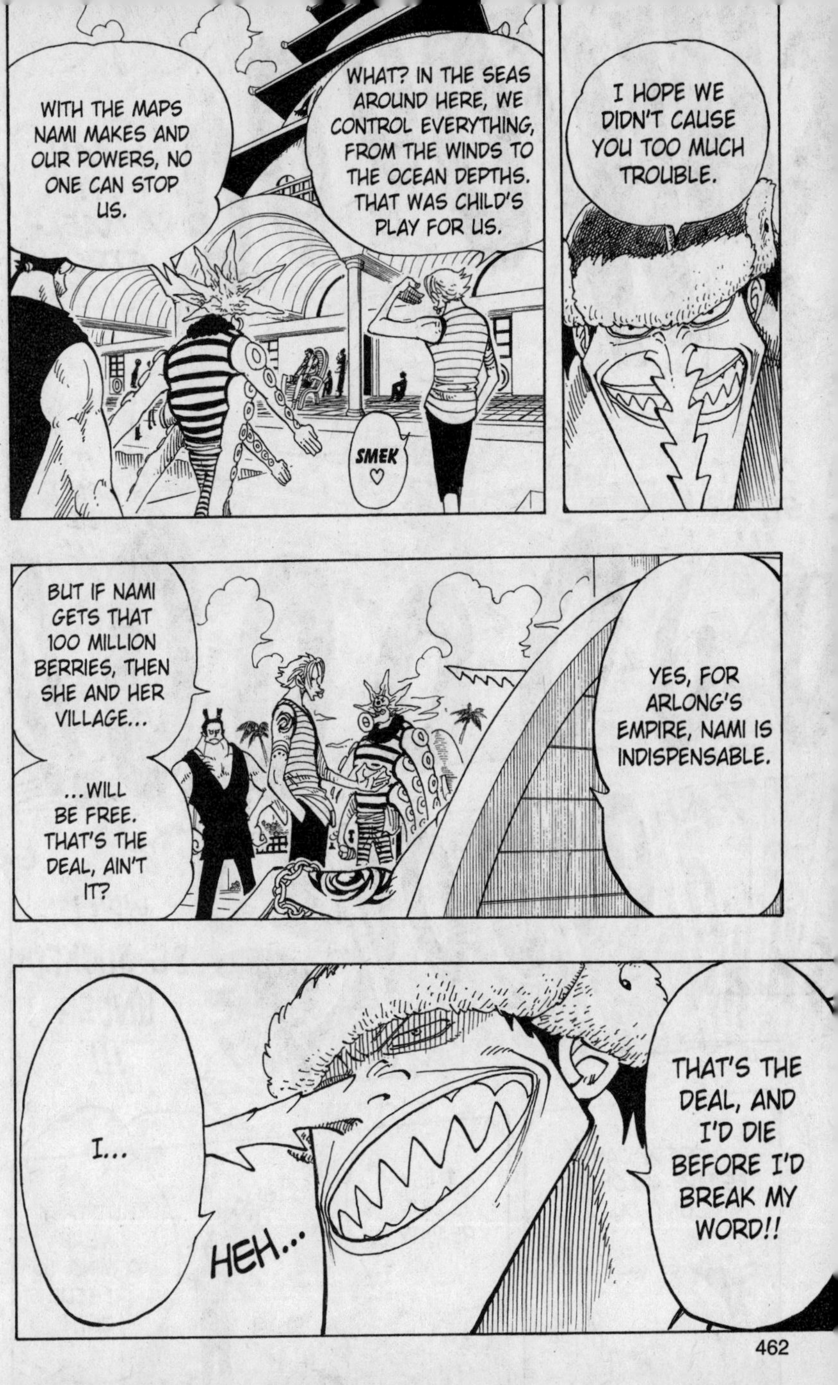
I HOPE WE DIDN'T CAUSE YOU TOO MUCH TROUBLE.
WHAT? IN THE SEAS AROUND HERE, WE CONTROL EVERYTHING, FROM THE WINDS TO THE OCEAN DEPTHS. THAT WAS CHILD'S PLAY FOR US.
WITH THE MAPS NAMI MAKES AND OUR POWERS, NO ONE CAN STOP US.
SMEK ♡
YES, FOR ARLONG'S EMPIRE, NAMI IS INDISPENSABLE.
BUT IF NAMI GETS THAT 100 MILLION BERRIES, THEN SHE AND HER VILLAGE...
...WILL BE FREE. THAT'S THE DEAL, AIN'T IT?
THAT'S THE DEAL, AND I'D DIE BEFORE I'D BREAK MY WORD!!
HEH...
I...

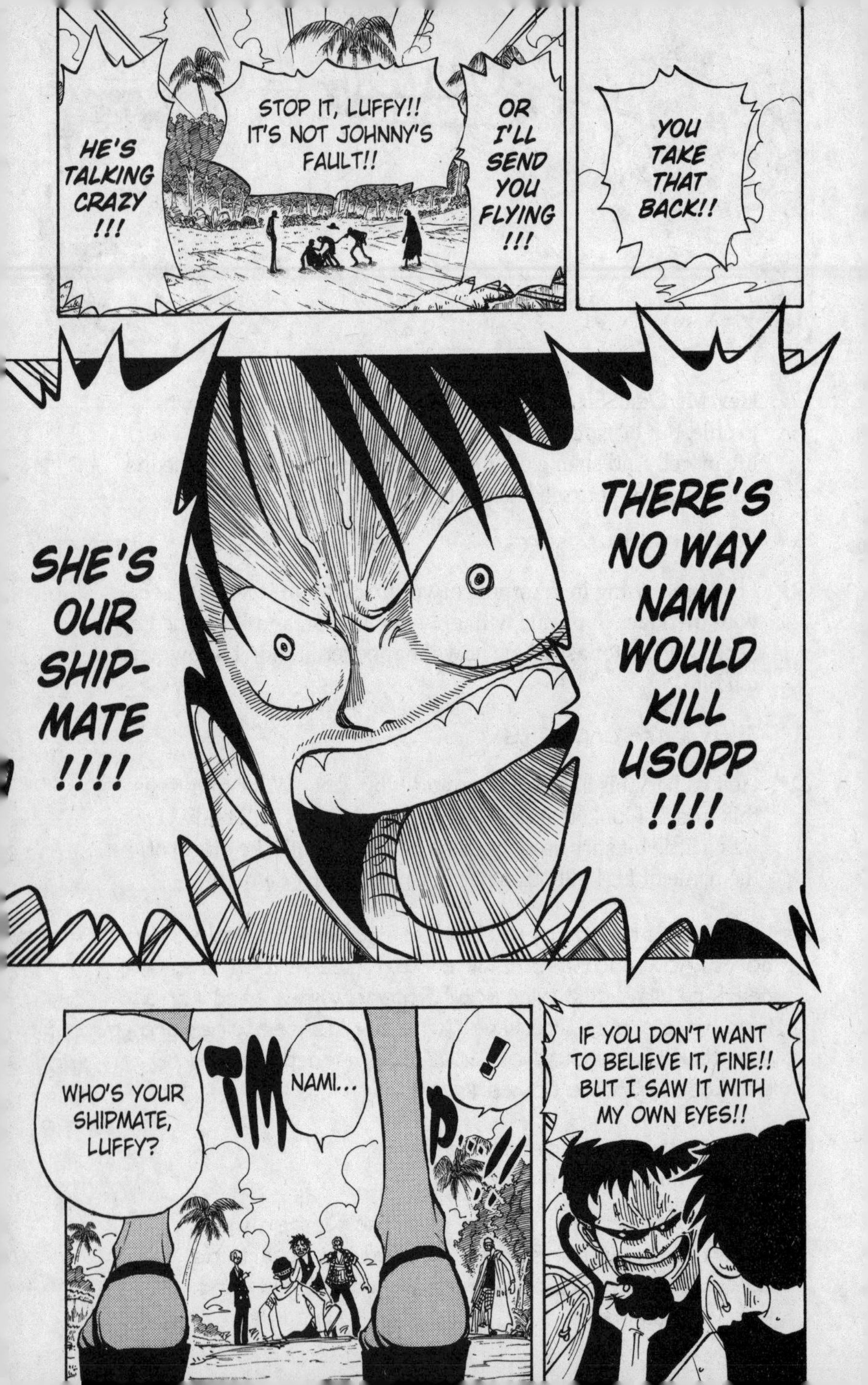
YOU TAKE THAT BACK!!
OR I'LL SEND YOU FLYING!!!
STOP IT, LUFFY!! IT'S NOT JOHNNY'S FAULT!!
HE'S TALKING CRAZY!!!
THERE'S NO WAY NAMI WOULD KILL USOPP!!!!
SHE'S OUR SHIPMATE!!!!
IF YOU DON'T WANT TO BELIEVE IT, FINE!! BUT I SAW IT WITH MY OWN EYES!!
!
NAMI...
TMP!!!
WHO'S YOUR SHIPMATE, LUFFY?

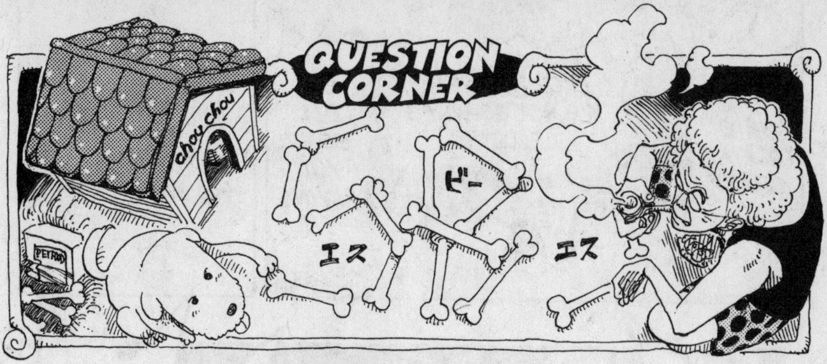
QUESTION CORNER
chou chou
PETMO
ビー
エス
エス

Q: Hey, Mr. Oda!! Sit down!! I know you want to see your own profile, but be careful!! You could break your neck! Value your life more!! And shame on you for having to be told by someone younger than yourself!! Repent!! Dismissed!!

A: You're right...I'm sorry.

Q: I tried that thing in your note of volume 7 about trying to see your own face in profile with only one mirror, and I sprained my neck. The doctor asked me how it happened. I didn't know what to tell him.

A: Then you're one of **us**.

Q: Hello. I had this bottle of wine and I thought, "What country is this from?" I looked at the label and it said, "dry, full body." I was a little bit surprised, but also pleased. That's the origin of the name of Lt. Fullbody's name, isn't it? Don't deny it.

A: I won't, that's exactly it! I don't drink much alcohol, so I don't know a lot about wine, but it seems that the depth of flavor is called body! Strong wines aged for a long time are said to have "full" body. Lighter wines are said to have "medium" or "light" body. And that's where Lt. Fullbody's name comes from!

Q: Where was Gin hiding that weapon?
Was it "down there" or what?

A: What?! Are you insinuating that the weapon was hidden between Gin's legs?! He wouldn't do a thing like that. Gin's fans are gonna be mad at you--and he's very popular.

# Chapter 76: SLEEP

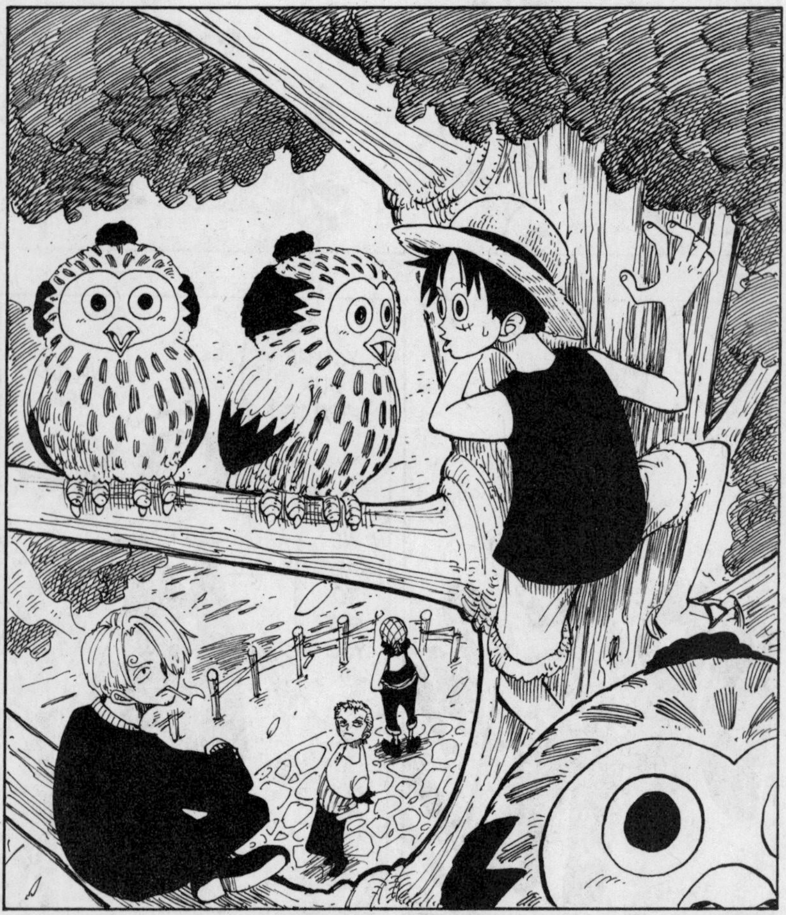

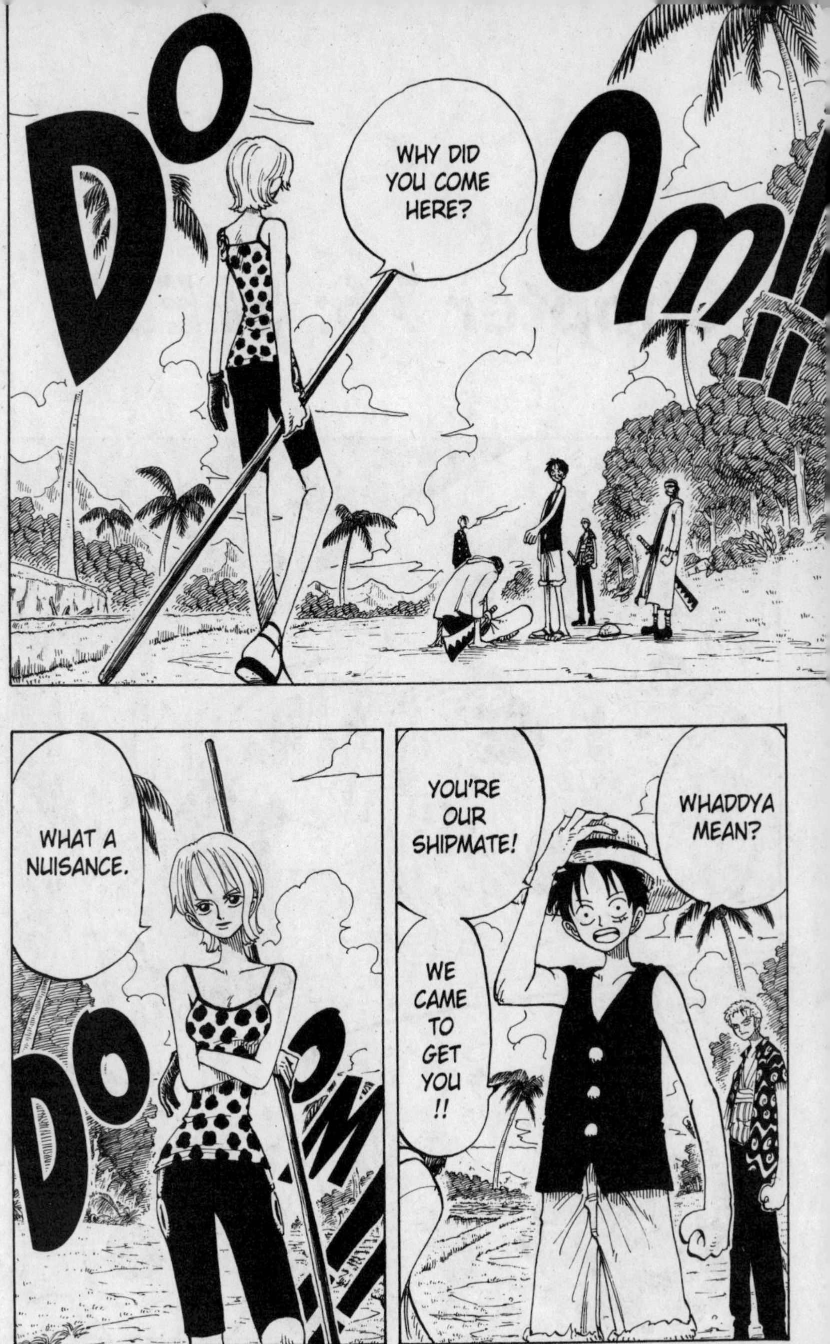
DOOM!!
WHY DID YOU COME HERE?
WHADDYA MEAN?
YOU'RE OUR SHIPMATE!
WE CAME TO GET YOU!!
WHAT A NUISANCE.
DOOM!!

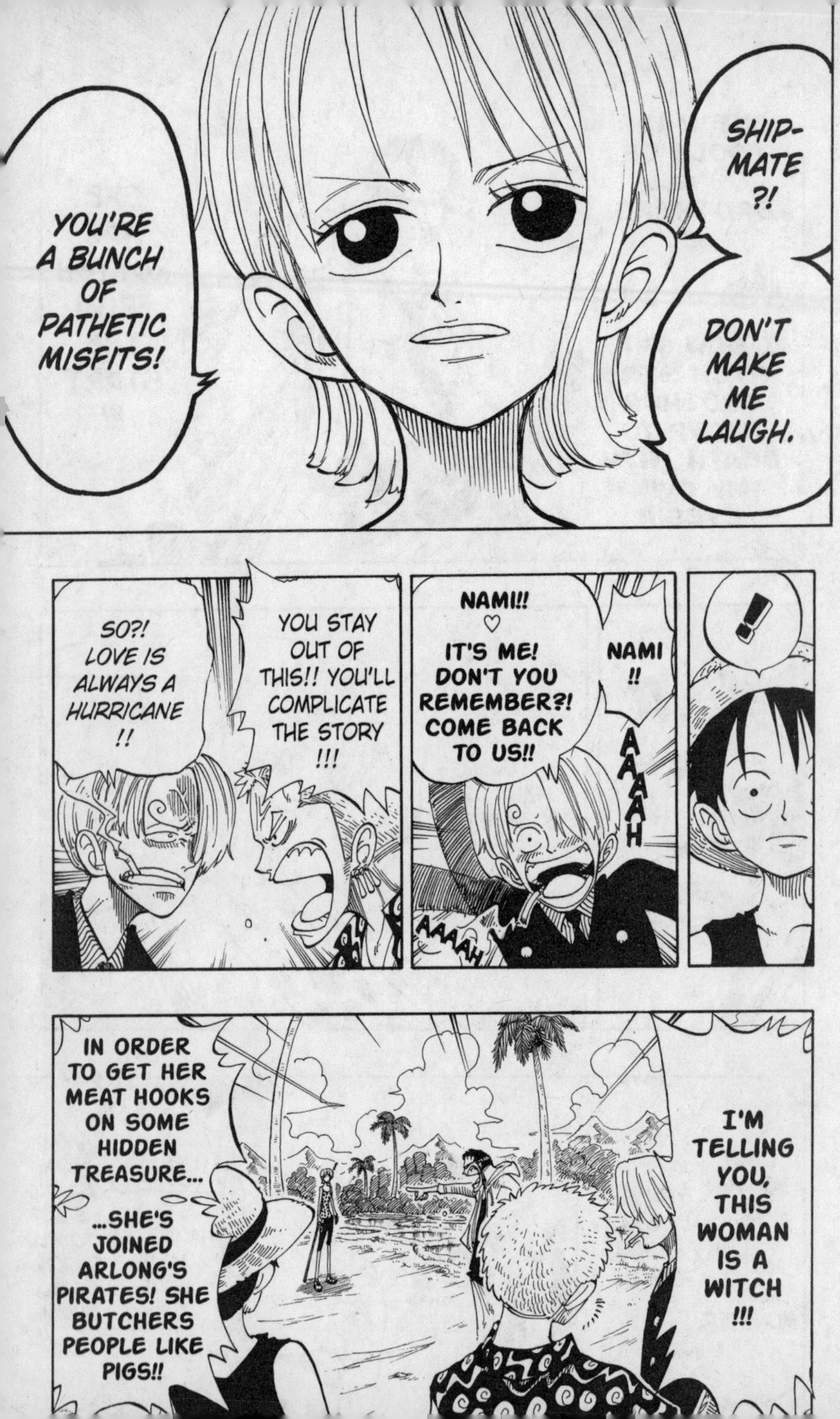

SHIP-MATE ?!
DON'T MAKE ME LAUGH.
YOU'RE A BUNCH OF PATHETIC MISFITS!
!
NAMI !!
AAAAH
NAMI!! ♡
IT'S ME! DON'T YOU REMEMBER?! COME BACK TO US!!
AAAAH
YOU STAY OUT OF THIS!! YOU'LL COMPLICATE THE STORY !!!
SO?! LOVE IS ALWAYS A HURRICANE !!
I'M TELLING YOU, THIS WOMAN IS A WITCH !!!
IN ORDER TO GET HER MEAT HOOKS ON SOME HIDDEN TREASURE...
...SHE'S JOINED ARLONG'S PIRATES! SHE BUTCHERS PEOPLE LIKE PIGS!!

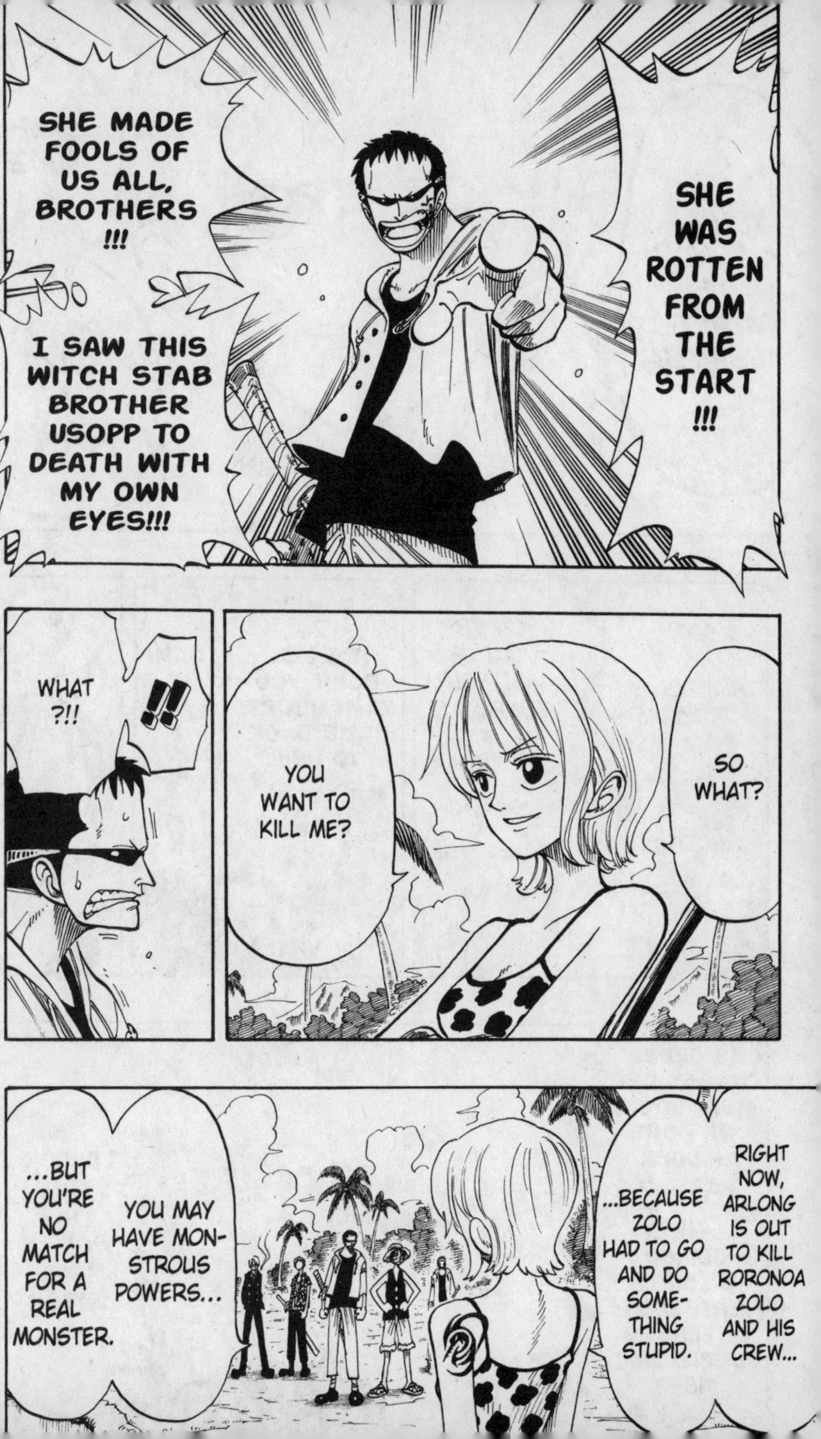
SHE WAS ROTTEN FROM THE START!!!
SHE MADE FOOLS OF US ALL, BROTHERS!!!
I SAW THIS WITCH STAB BROTHER USOPP TO DEATH WITH MY OWN EYES!!!
SO WHAT?
YOU WANT TO KILL ME?
!!
WHAT?!!
RIGHT NOW, ARLONG IS OUT TO KILL RORONOA ZOLO AND HIS CREW...
...BECAUSE ZOLO HAD TO GO AND DO SOMETHING STUPID.
YOU MAY HAVE MONSTROUS POWERS...
...BUT YOU'RE NO MATCH FOR A REAL MONSTER.

READ THIS WAY

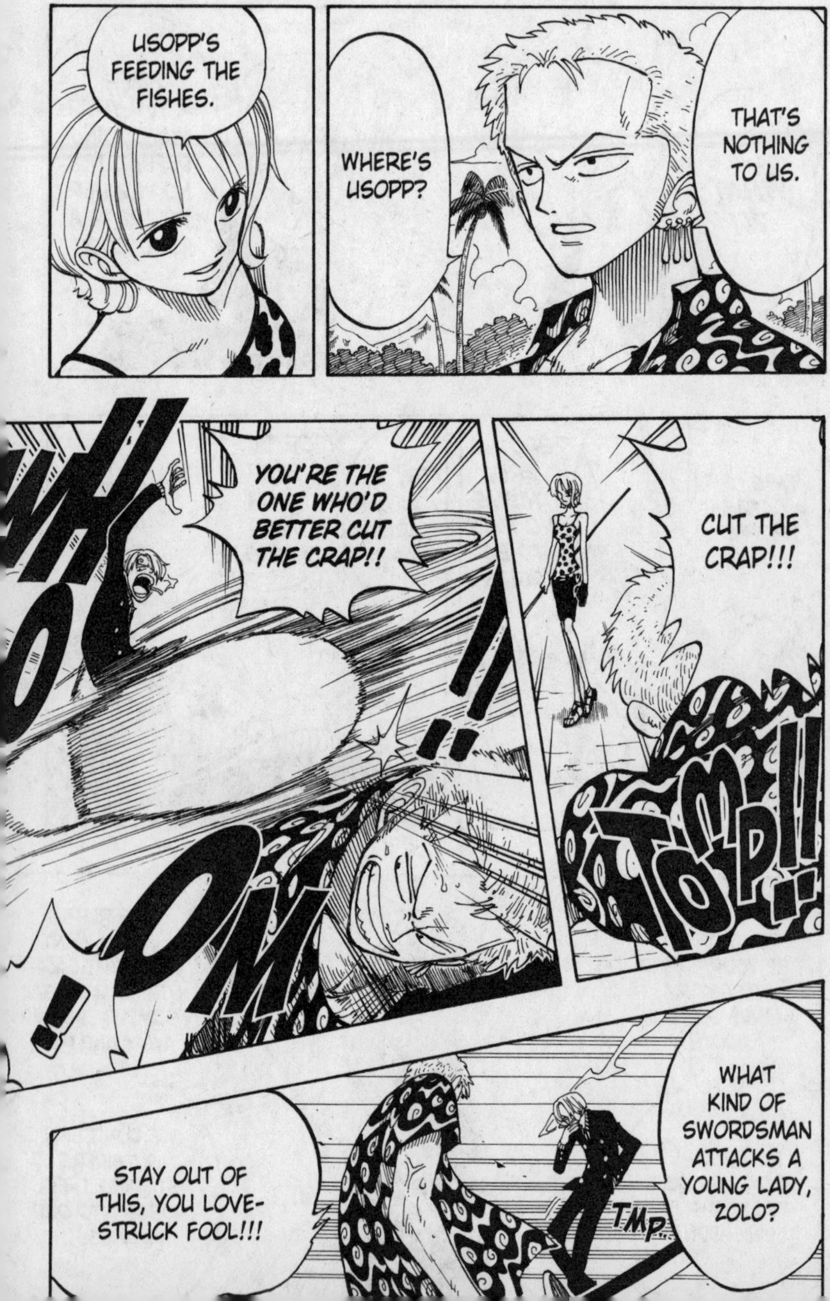
THAT'S NOTHING TO US.
WHERE'S USOPP?
USOPP'S FEEDING THE FISHES.
CUT THE CRAP!!!
TOMP!!
YOU'RE THE ONE WHO'D BETTER CUT THE CRAP!!
WHOOM!!
WHAT KIND OF SWORDSMAN ATTACKS A YOUNG LADY, ZOLO?
TMP
STAY OUT OF THIS, YOU LOVE-STRUCK FOOL!!!

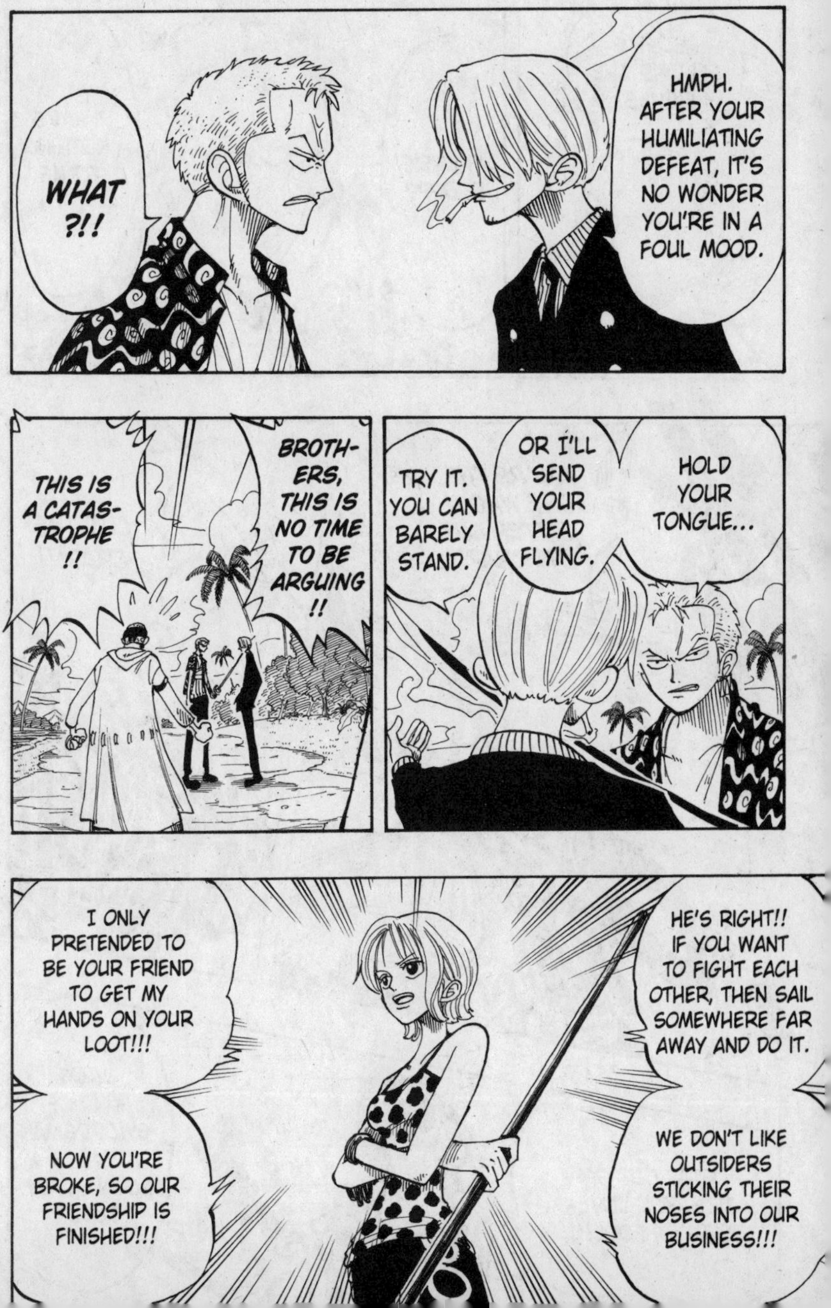
HMPH. AFTER YOUR HUMILIATING DEFEAT, IT'S NO WONDER YOU'RE IN A FOUL MOOD.
WHAT ?!!
HOLD YOUR TONGUE...
OR I'LL SEND YOUR HEAD FLYING.
TRY IT. YOU CAN BARELY STAND.
BROTH-ERS, THIS IS NO TIME TO BE ARGUING !!
THIS IS A CATAS-TROPHE !!
HE'S RIGHT!! IF YOU WANT TO FIGHT EACH OTHER, THEN SAIL SOMEWHERE FAR AWAY AND DO IT.
WE DON'T LIKE OUTSIDERS STICKING THEIR NOSES INTO OUR BUSINESS!!!
I ONLY PRETENDED TO BE YOUR FRIEND TO GET MY HANDS ON YOUR LOOT!!!
NOW YOU'RE BROKE, SO OUR FRIENDSHIP IS FINISHED!!!

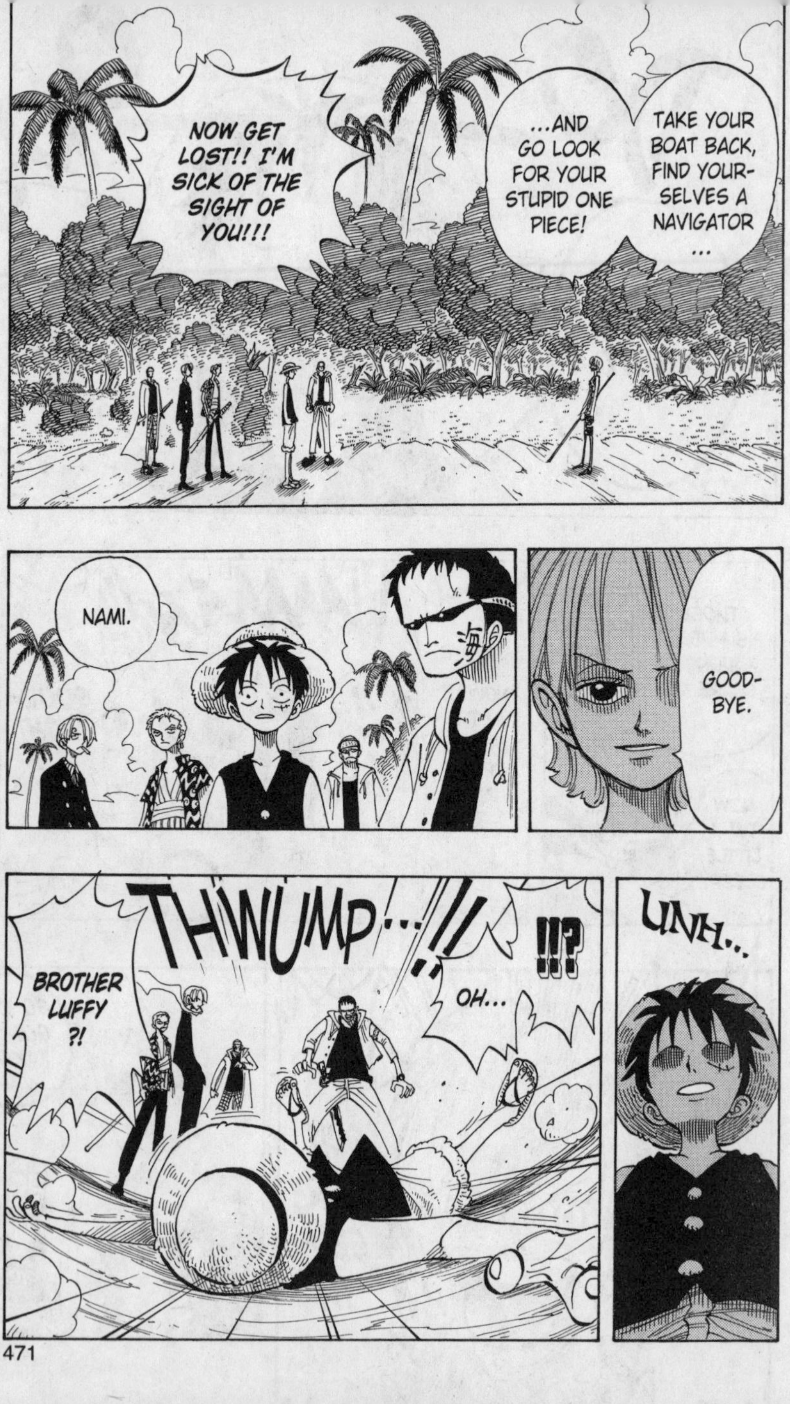
TAKE YOUR BOAT BACK, FIND YOURSELVES A NAVIGATOR ...
...AND GO LOOK FOR YOUR STUPID ONE PIECE!
NOW GET LOST!! I'M SICK OF THE SIGHT OF YOU!!!
GOOD-BYE.
NAMI.
UNH...
THWUMP...!!
!!?
OH...
BROTHER LUFFY ?!

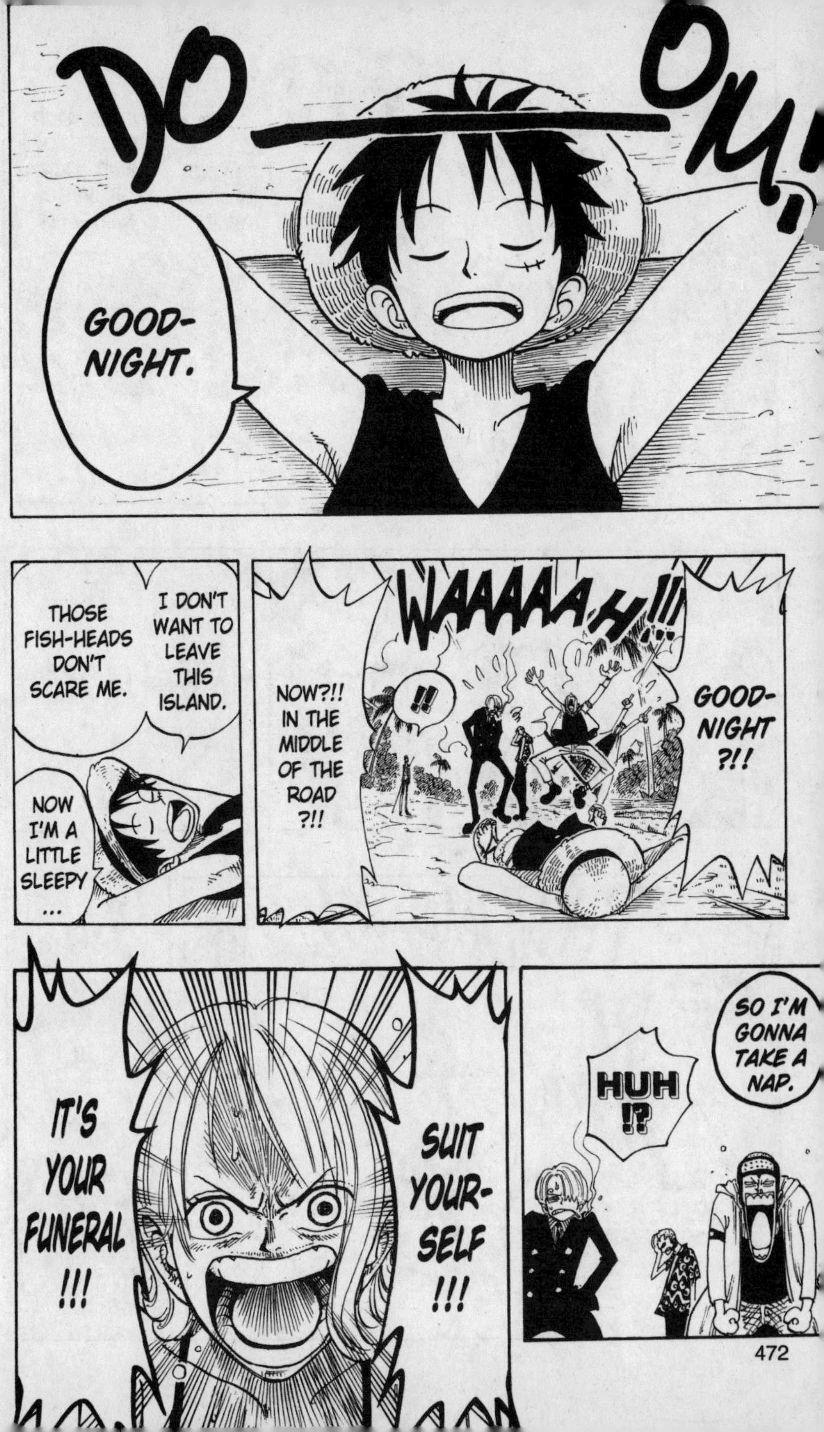
DO-OM!
GOOD-NIGHT.
WAAAAA-H!!!
GOOD-NIGHT?!!
!!
NOW?!! IN THE MIDDLE OF THE ROAD?!!
I DON'T WANT TO LEAVE THIS ISLAND.
THOSE FISH-HEADS DON'T SCARE ME.
NOW I'M A LITTLE SLEEPY...
SO I'M GONNA TAKE A NAP.
HUH!?
SUIT YOURSELF!!!
IT'S YOUR FUNERAL!!!

READ THIS WAY

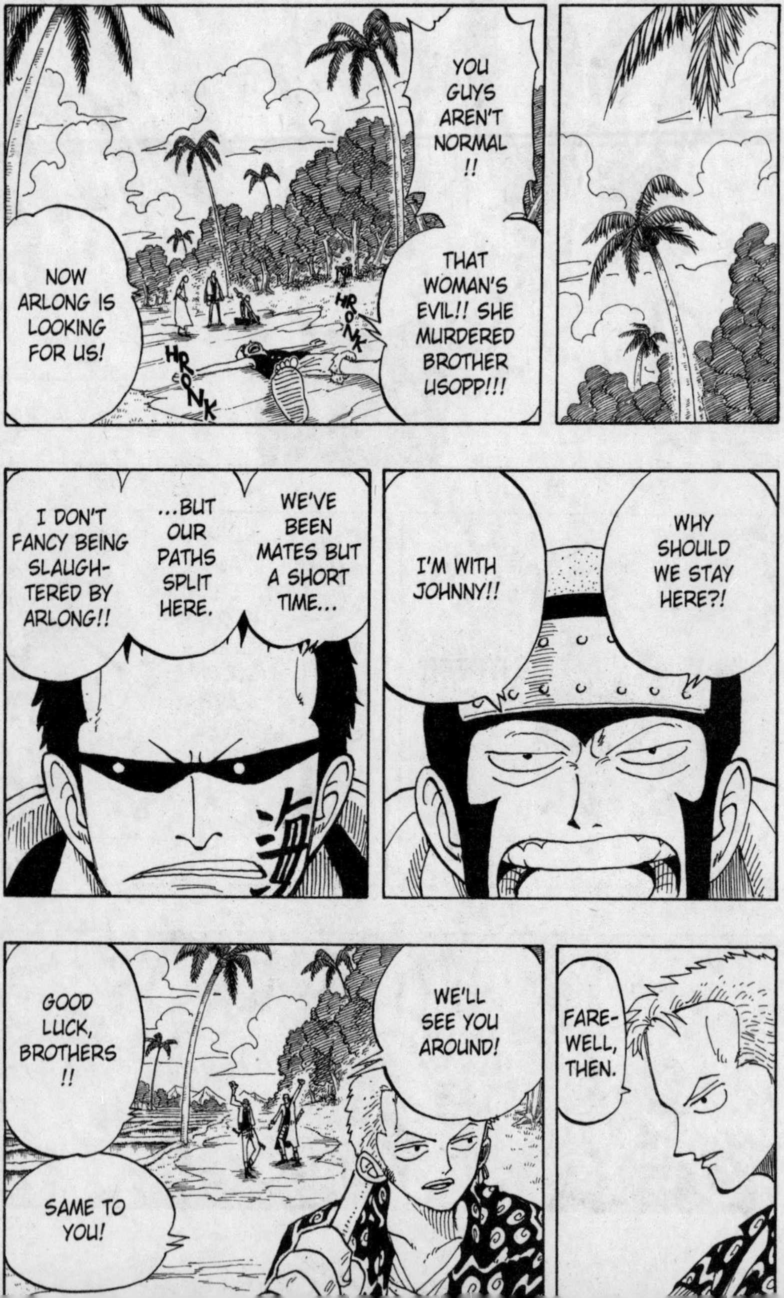
YOU GUYS AREN'T NORMAL!!
THAT WOMAN'S EVIL!! SHE MURDERED BROTHER USOPP!!!
HRONK
HRONK
NOW ARLONG IS LOOKING FOR US!
WHY SHOULD WE STAY HERE?!
I'M WITH JOHNNY!!
WE'VE BEEN MATES BUT A SHORT TIME...
...BUT OUR PATHS SPLIT HERE.
I DON'T FANCY BEING SLAUGH-TERED BY ARLONG!!
FARE-WELL, THEN.
WE'LL SEE YOU AROUND!
GOOD LUCK, BROTHERS!!
SAME TO YOU!

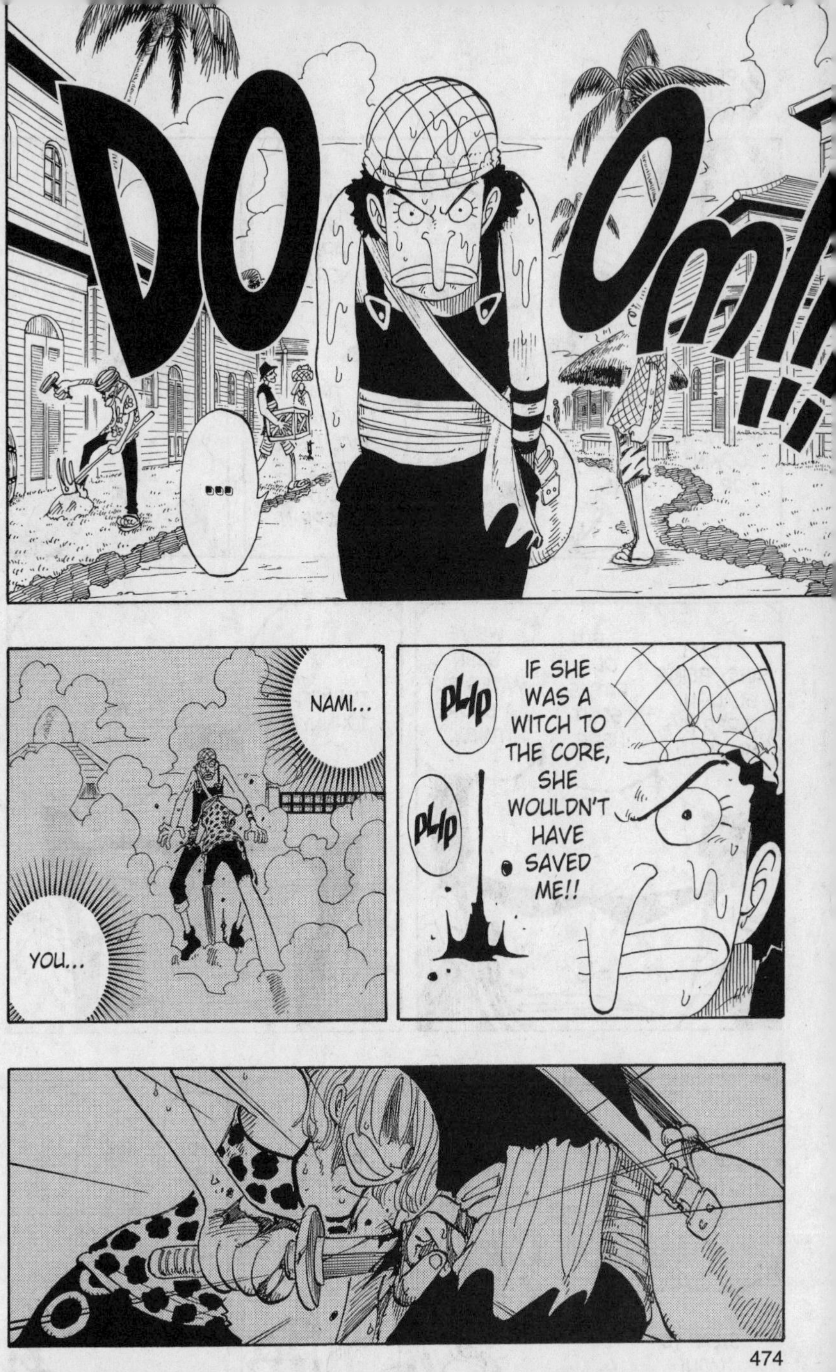
DOOM!!!
...
PLIP
PLIP
IF SHE WAS A WITCH TO THE CORE, SHE WOULDN'T HAVE SAVED ME!!
NAMI...
YOU...

READ THIS WAY

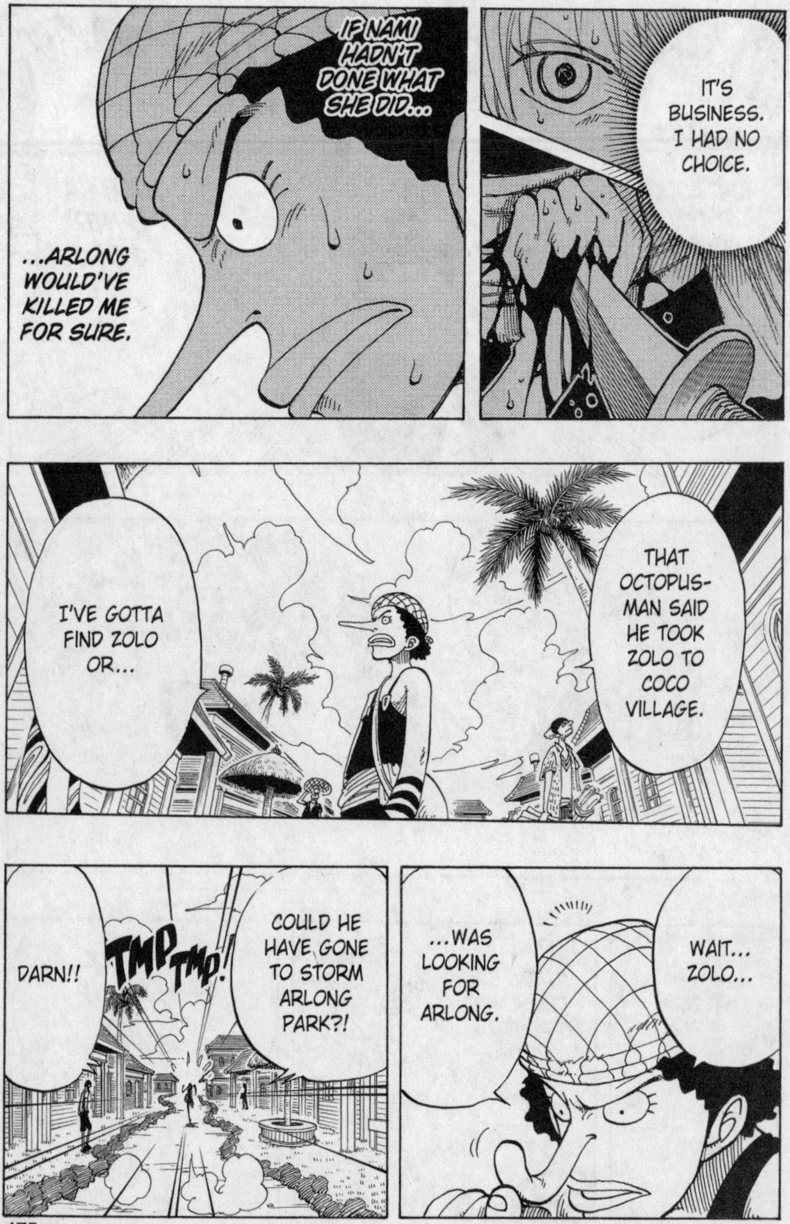
IT'S BUSINESS. I HAD NO CHOICE.
IF NAMI HADN'T DONE WHAT SHE DID...
...ARLONG WOULD'VE KILLED ME FOR SURE.
THAT OCTOPUS-MAN SAID HE TOOK ZOLO TO COCO VILLAGE.
I'VE GOTTA FIND ZOLO OR...
WAIT... ZOLO...
...WAS LOOKING FOR ARLONG.
COULD HE HAVE GONE TO STORM ARLONG PARK?!
TMP TMP!
DARN!!

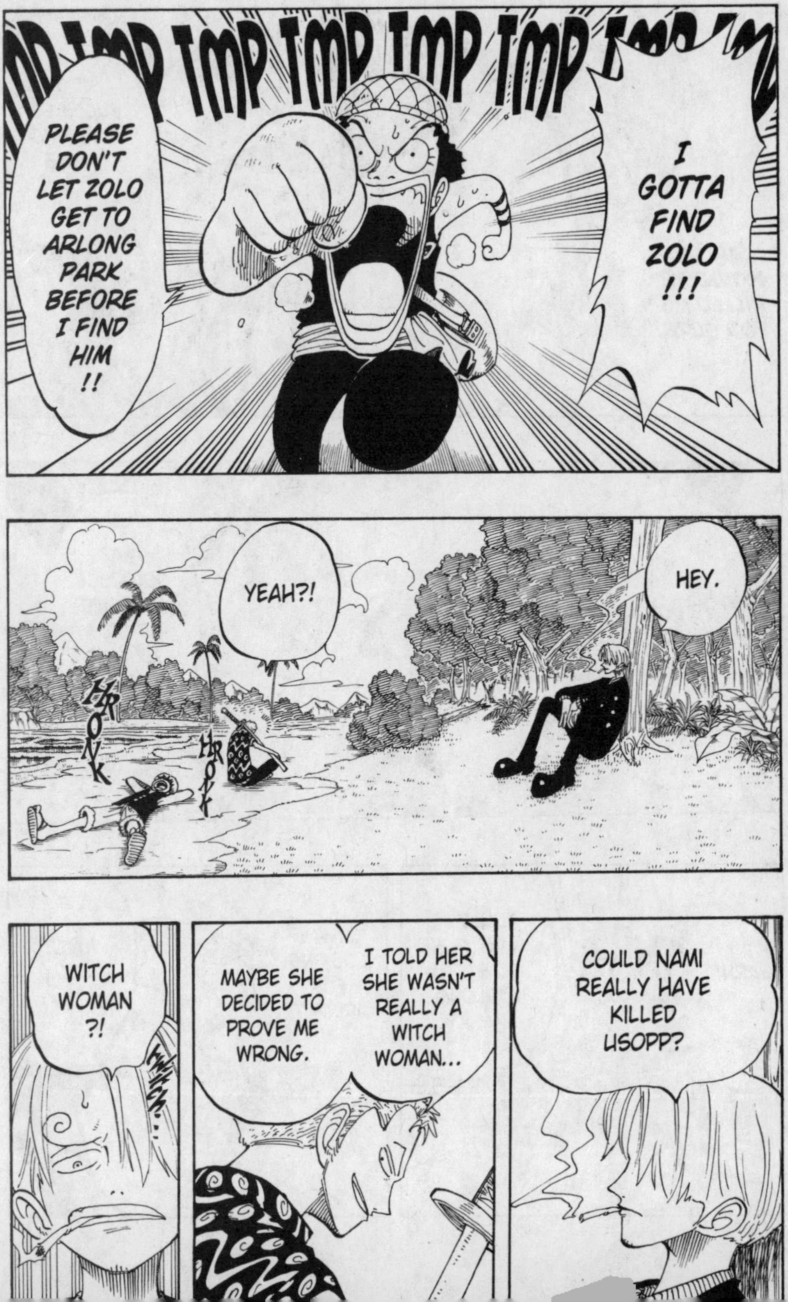
TMP TMP TMP TMP TMP TMP
I GOTTA FIND ZOLO !!!
PLEASE DON'T LET ZOLO GET TO ARLONG PARK BEFORE I FIND HIM !!
HEY.
YEAH?!
HRONK
HRONK
COULD NAMI REALLY HAVE KILLED USOPP?
I TOLD HER SHE WASN'T REALLY A WITCH WOMAN...
MAYBE SHE DECIDED TO PROVE ME WRONG.
WITCH WOMAN ?!

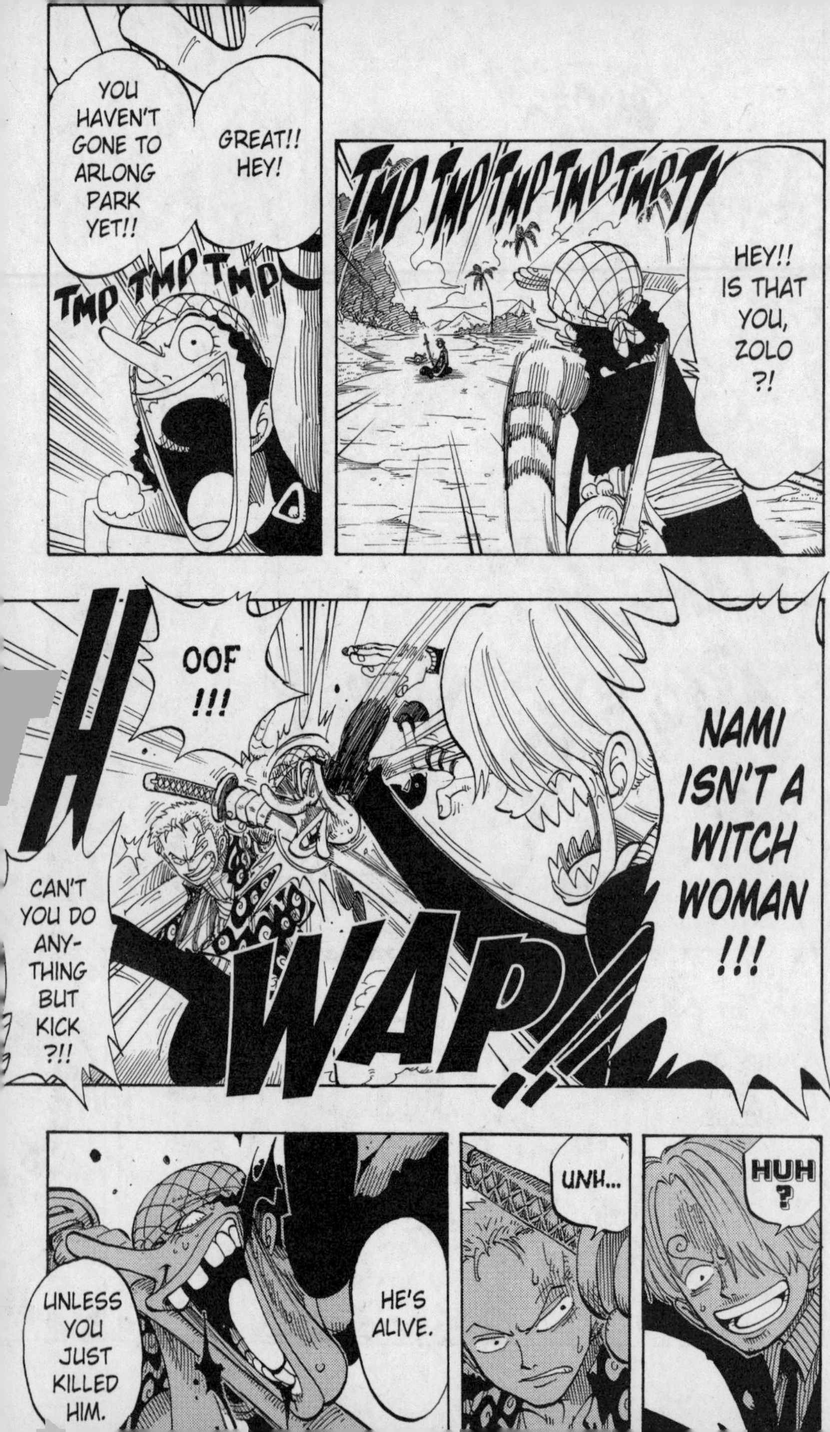
TMP TMP TMP TMP TMP T!
HEY!! IS THAT YOU, ZOLO ?!
GREAT!! HEY!
YOU HAVEN'T GONE TO ARLONG PARK YET!!
TMP TMP TMP
NAMI ISN'T A WITCH WOMAN !!!
OOF !!!
H
WAP!!
CAN'T YOU DO ANY-THING BUT KICK ?!!
HUH ?
UNH...
HE'S ALIVE.
UNLESS YOU JUST KILLED HIM.

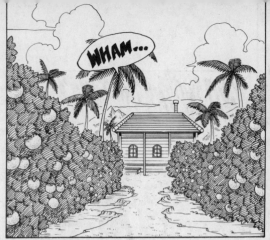

WHAM...

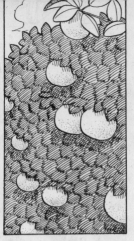

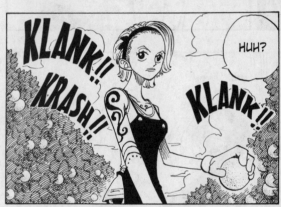

KLANK!!

KRASH!!

KLANK!!

HUH?

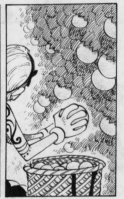

WRECKING THE HOUSE AGAIN, NAMI?

WHAT'S WRONG?

OH NO.

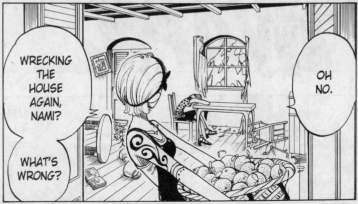

KREEK...

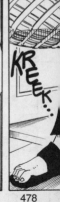

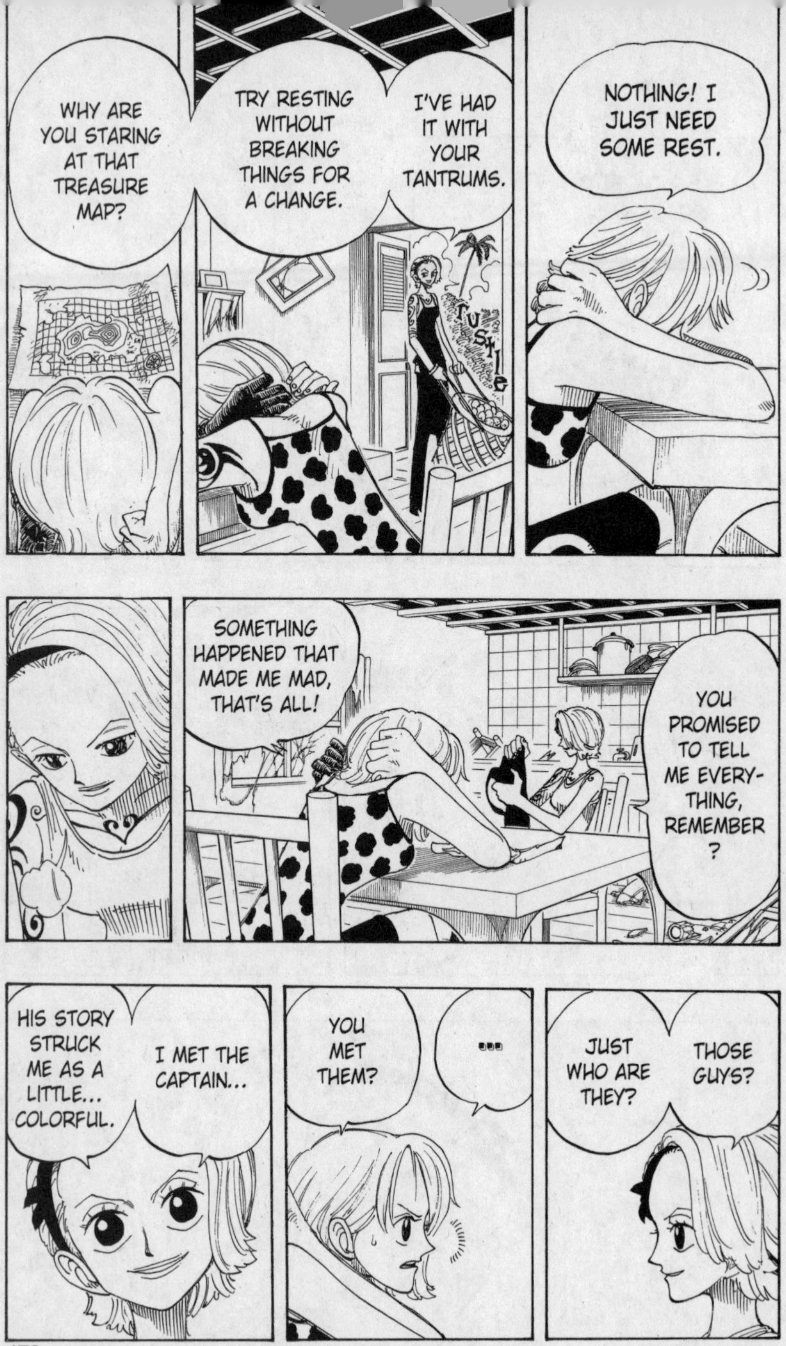
NOTHING! I JUST NEED SOME REST.
I'VE HAD IT WITH YOUR TANTRUMS.
TRY RESTING WITHOUT BREAKING THINGS FOR A CHANGE.
RUSTLE
WHY ARE YOU STARING AT THAT TREASURE MAP?
YOU PROMISED TO TELL ME EVERY-THING, REMEMBER?
SOMETHING HAPPENED THAT MADE ME MAD, THAT'S ALL!
THOSE GUYS?
JUST WHO ARE THEY?
...
YOU MET THEM?
I MET THE CAPTAIN...
HIS STORY STRUCK ME AS A LITTLE... COLORFUL.

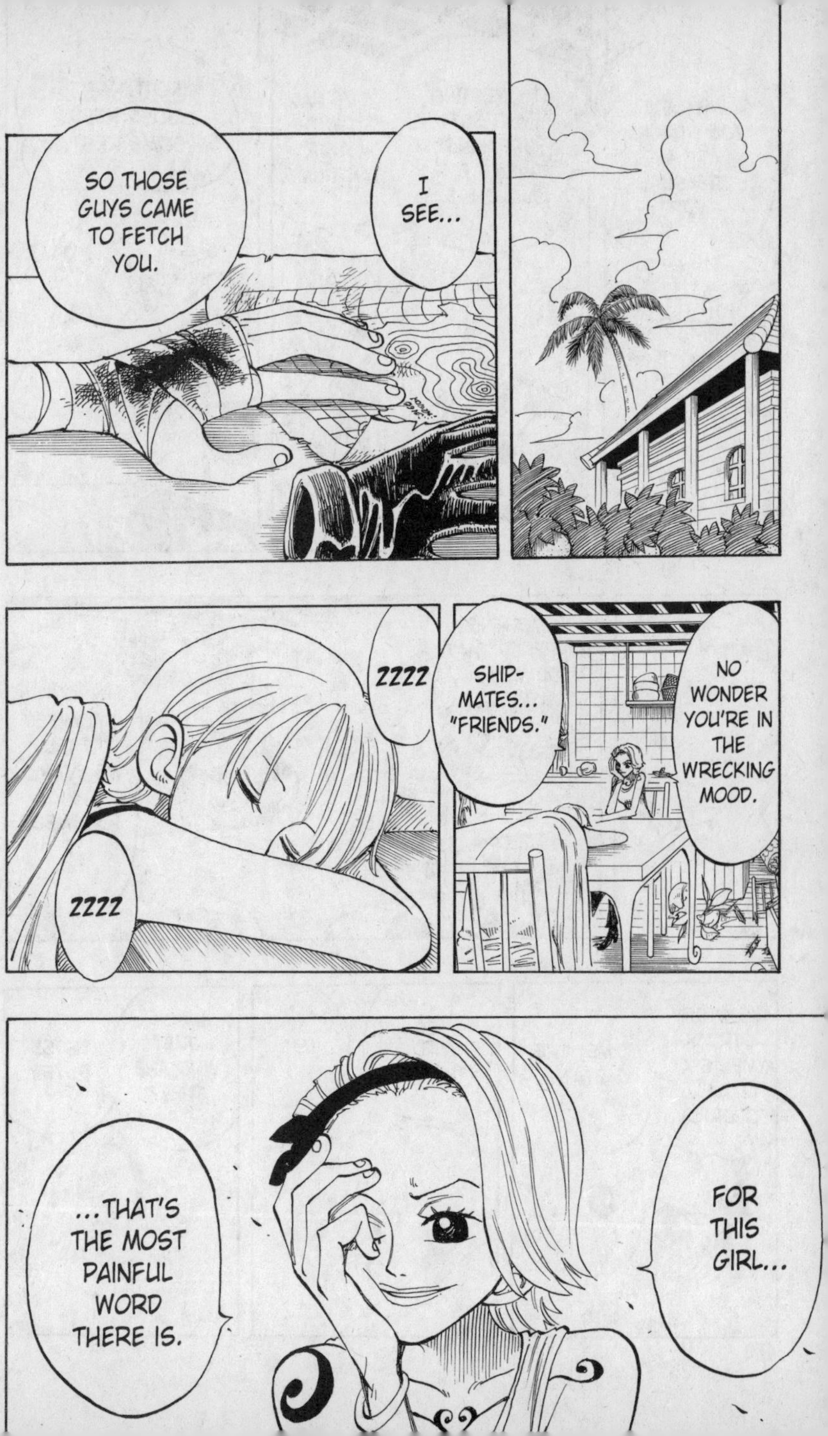
I SEE...
SO THOSE GUYS CAME TO FETCH YOU.
NO WONDER YOU'RE IN THE WRECKING MOOD.
SHIP-MATES... "FRIENDS."
ZZZZ
ZZZZ
FOR THIS GIRL...
...THAT'S THE MOST PAINFUL WORD THERE IS.

READ THIS WAY

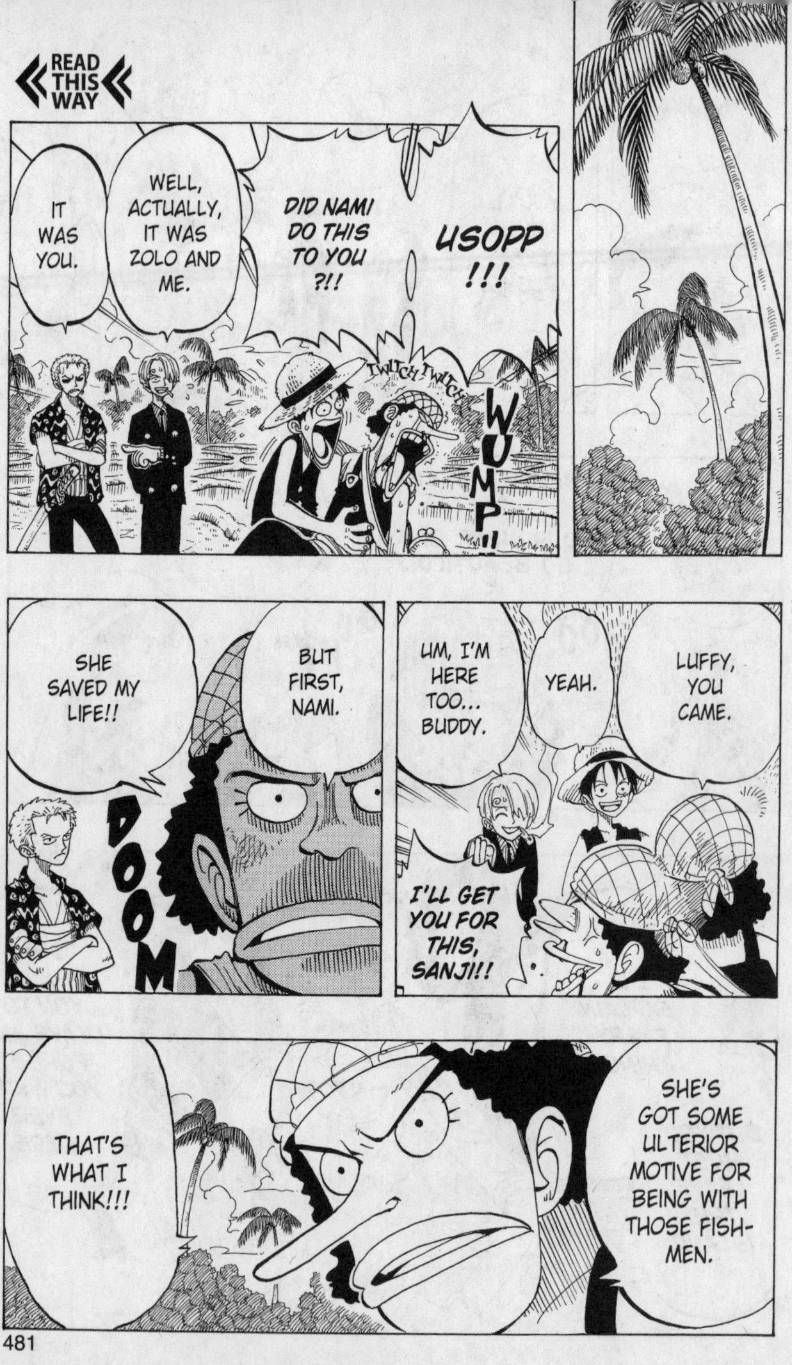
USOPP !!!
DID NAMI DO THIS TO YOU ?!!
WELL, ACTUALLY, IT WAS ZOLO AND ME.
IT WAS YOU.
TWITCH TWITCH
WUMP!!
LUFFY, YOU CAME.
YEAH.
UM, I'M HERE TOO... BUDDY.
I'LL GET YOU FOR THIS, SANJI!!
BUT FIRST, NAMI.
SHE SAVED MY LIFE!!
DOOM
SHE'S GOT SOME ULTERIOR MOTIVE FOR BEING WITH THOSE FISH-MEN.
THAT'S WHAT I THINK!!!

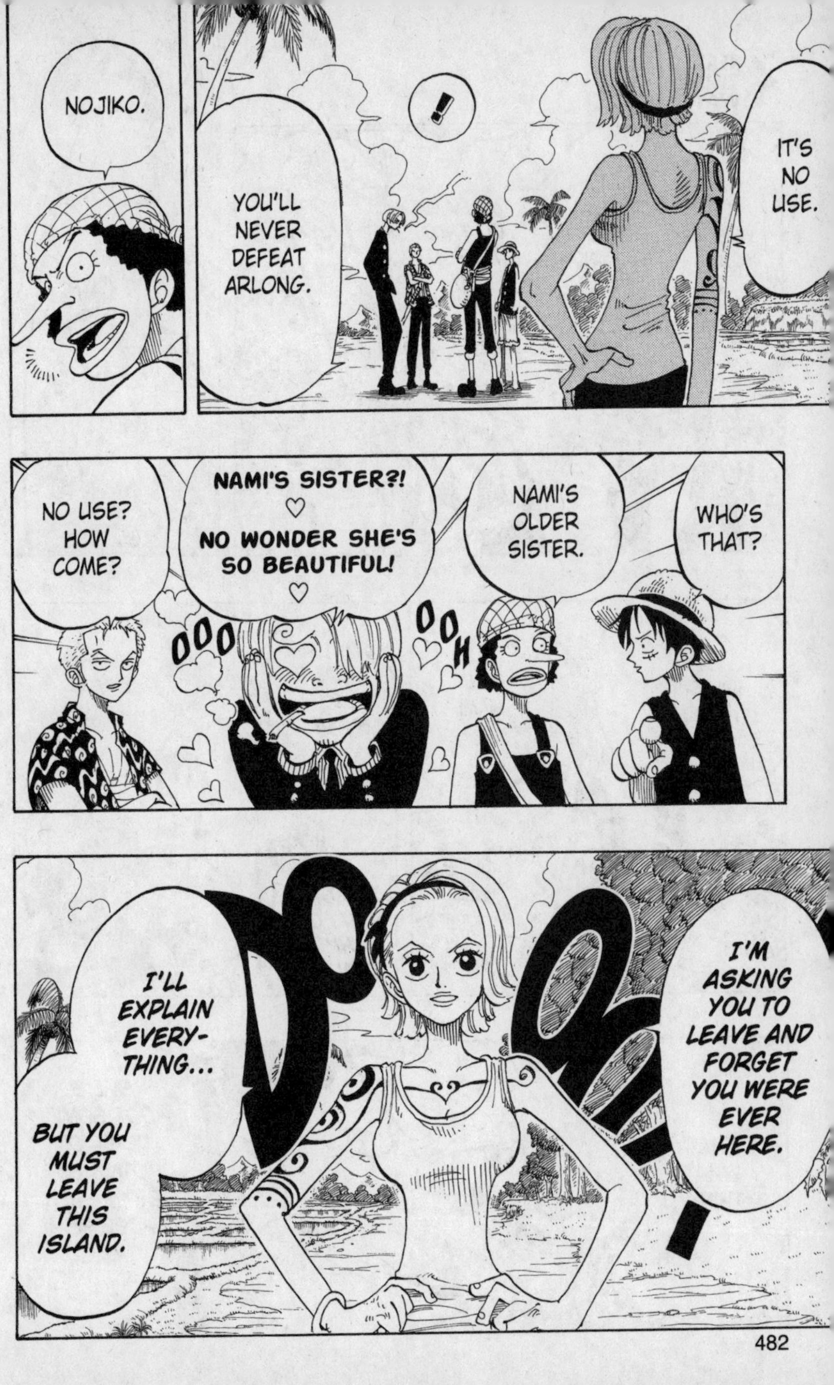
IT'S NO USE.
!
YOU'LL NEVER DEFEAT ARLONG.
NOJIKO.
WHO'S THAT?
NAMI'S OLDER SISTER.
NAMI'S SISTER?! ♡ NO WONDER SHE'S SO BEAUTIFUL! ♡
NO USE? HOW COME?
I'M ASKING YOU TO LEAVE AND FORGET YOU WERE EVER HERE.
I'LL EXPLAIN EVERY-THING...
BUT YOU MUST LEAVE THIS ISLAND.

READ THIS WAY

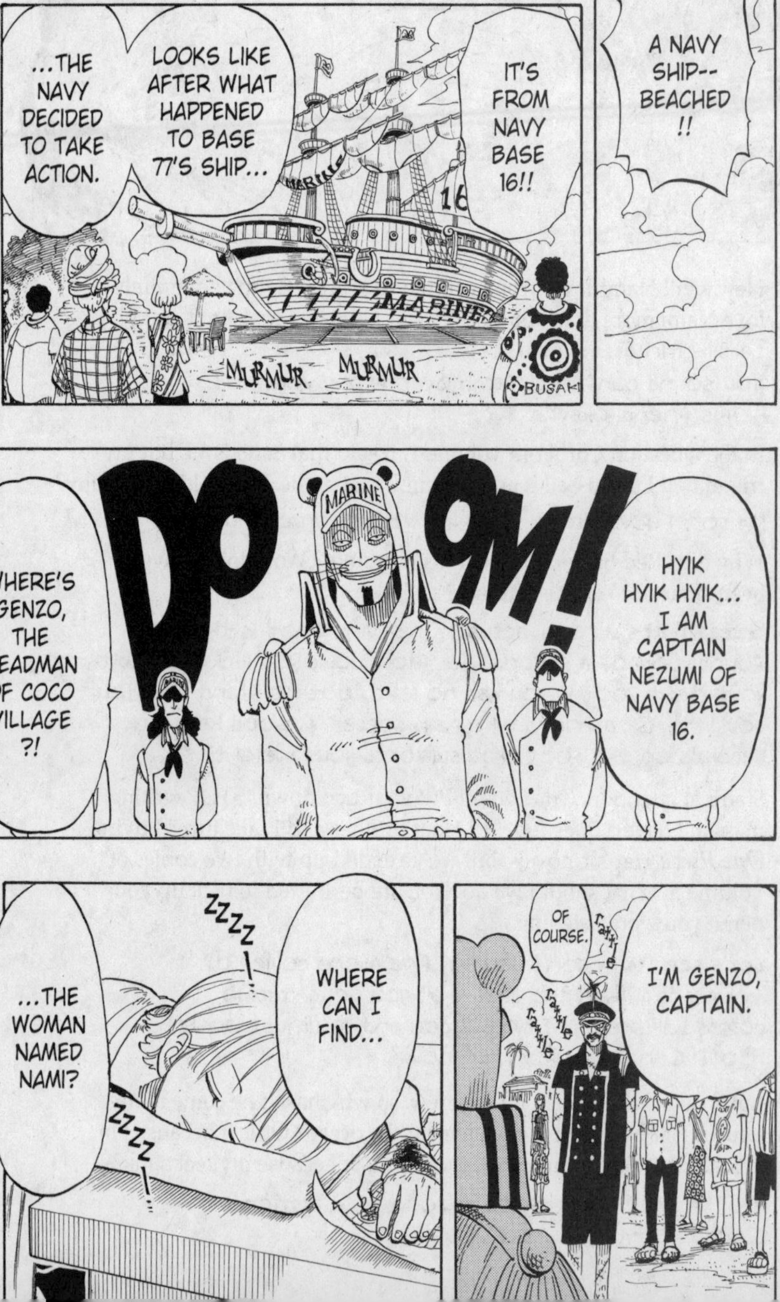
A NAVY SHIP-- BEACHED!!
IT'S FROM NAVY BASE 16!!
LOOKS LIKE AFTER WHAT HAPPENED TO BASE 77'S SHIP...
...THE NAVY DECIDED TO TAKE ACTION.
MARINE
MARINE
16
MURMUR
MURMUR
BUSAKI
HYIK HYIK HYIK... I AM CAPTAIN NEZUMI OF NAVY BASE 16.
DOOM!
MARINE
WHERE'S GENZO, THE HEADMAN OF COCO VILLAGE ?!
I'M GENZO, CAPTAIN.
rattle
OF COURSE.
rattle rattle
WHERE CAN I FIND...
ZZZZ
...THE WOMAN NAMED NAMI?
ZZZZ

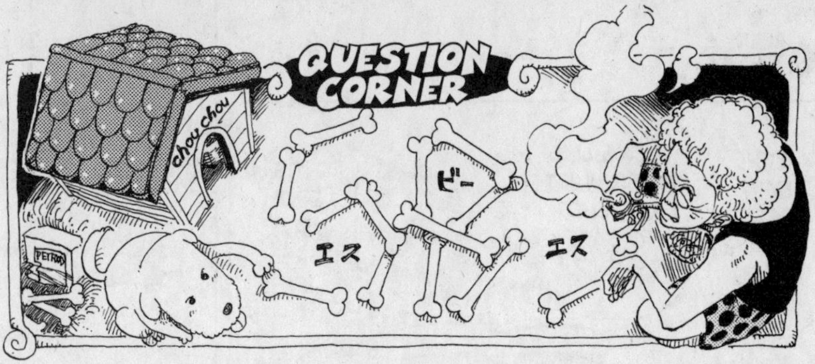
QUESTION CORNER
chou chou
ビー
エス
エス

Q: Hey, you!! Nami-lover from volume 7!! Wanna fight?! I definitely love Nami more than you do! (x100) But I like you too! Am I crazy? Let's be friends.

A: You sound confused. Nami-lover from volume 7, be his friend, okay?

Q: In the Question Corner in volume 7, it said that Sanji is 19, but my friend and I discussed it and we think that's a lie. How old is he really?

A: I'm sorry if you think it's a lie, but it's true. True, I tell you!!

Q: Why did "Red-Shoes" Zeff" eat his right foot? Wouldn't it have been smarter to eat his left foot?

A: Bzzz. That's wrong, actually. The plant foot is the foundation of a strong kick. How could you kick a ball with your right foot if you had no left foot to stand on? You couldn't! Ask a friend who plays soccer. A good hard kick depends on the foot that supports your weight!!

Q: Stand at attention, Oda Sensei! Put your pen down! STOP writing manga! I have a question. My older brother and I take turns buying *One Piece* graphic novels, but we've ended up with two copies of volume 5. What should we do? You are permitted to pick up your pen if you were listening.

A: Let's see...Why don't you buy five more copies of volume 5? Then the fact that you bought two copies will seem like no big deal and you'll just laugh it off! Can I pick up my pen now?

Q: Luffy needs a musician for his crew, so why hasn't he come to my house? Is it because I don't live near the ocean? Or is it because I'm actually an alien from outer space? Or is it because my feet stink?

A: It's the feet. Well, that's it for the Question Corner--until the next volume!!

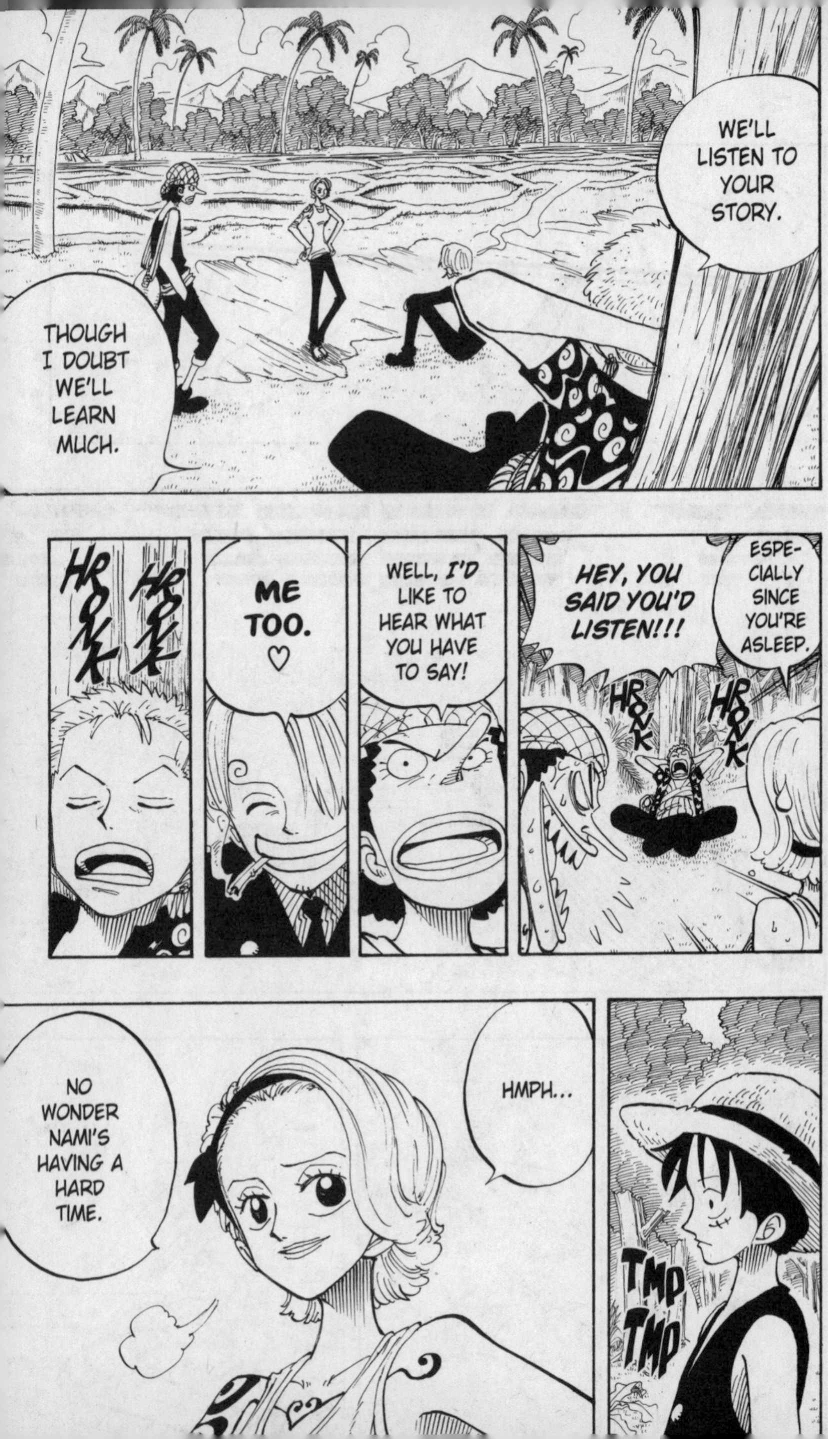
WE'LL LISTEN TO YOUR STORY.
THOUGH I DOUBT WE'LL LEARN MUCH.
ESPE-CIALLY SINCE YOU'RE ASLEEP.
HEY, YOU SAID YOU'D LISTEN!!!
HRONK
HRONK
WELL, I'D LIKE TO HEAR WHAT YOU HAVE TO SAY!
ME TOO. ♡
HRONK
HRONK
TMP TMP
HMPH...
NO WONDER NAMI'S HAVING A HARD TIME.

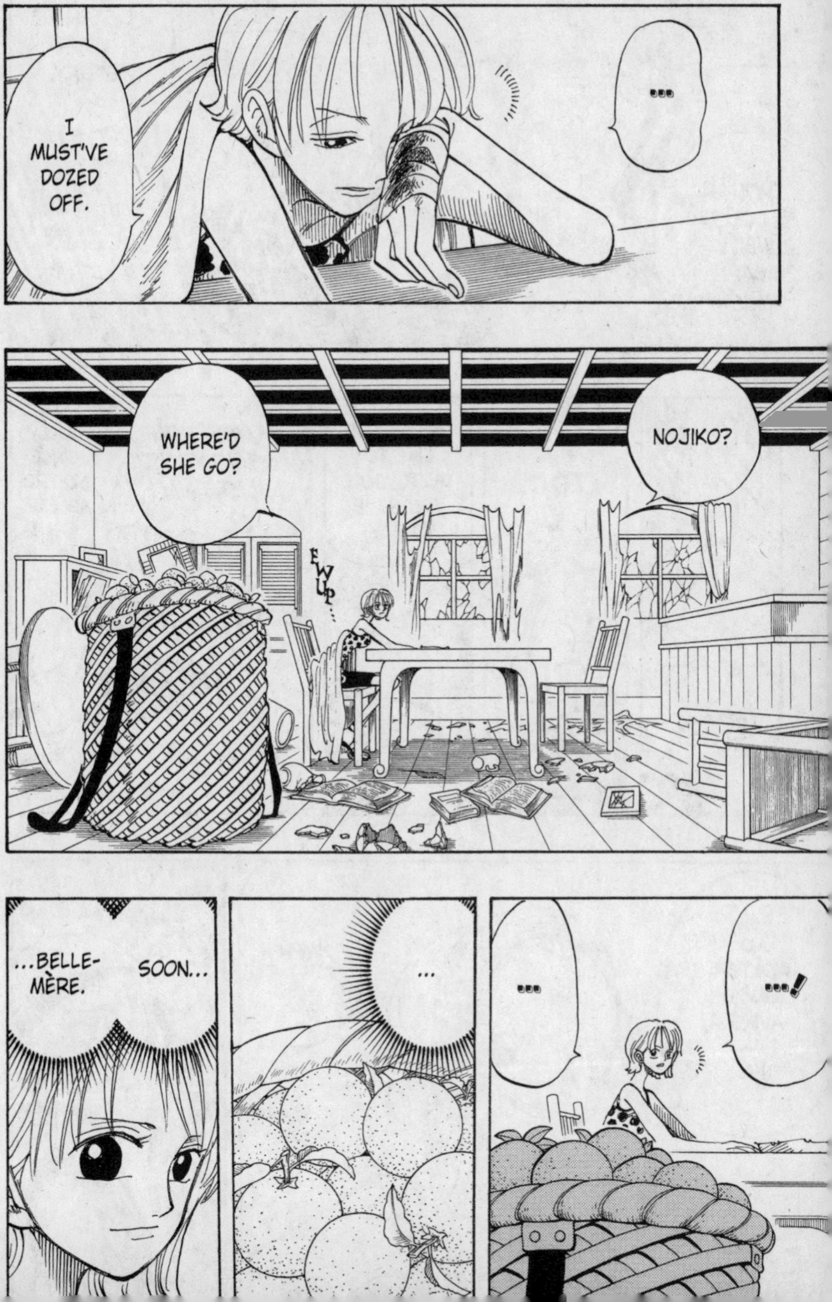
...
I MUST'VE DOZED OFF.
NOJIKO?
WHERE'D SHE GO?
FWUP
...!
...
...
SOON...
...BELLE-MÈRE.

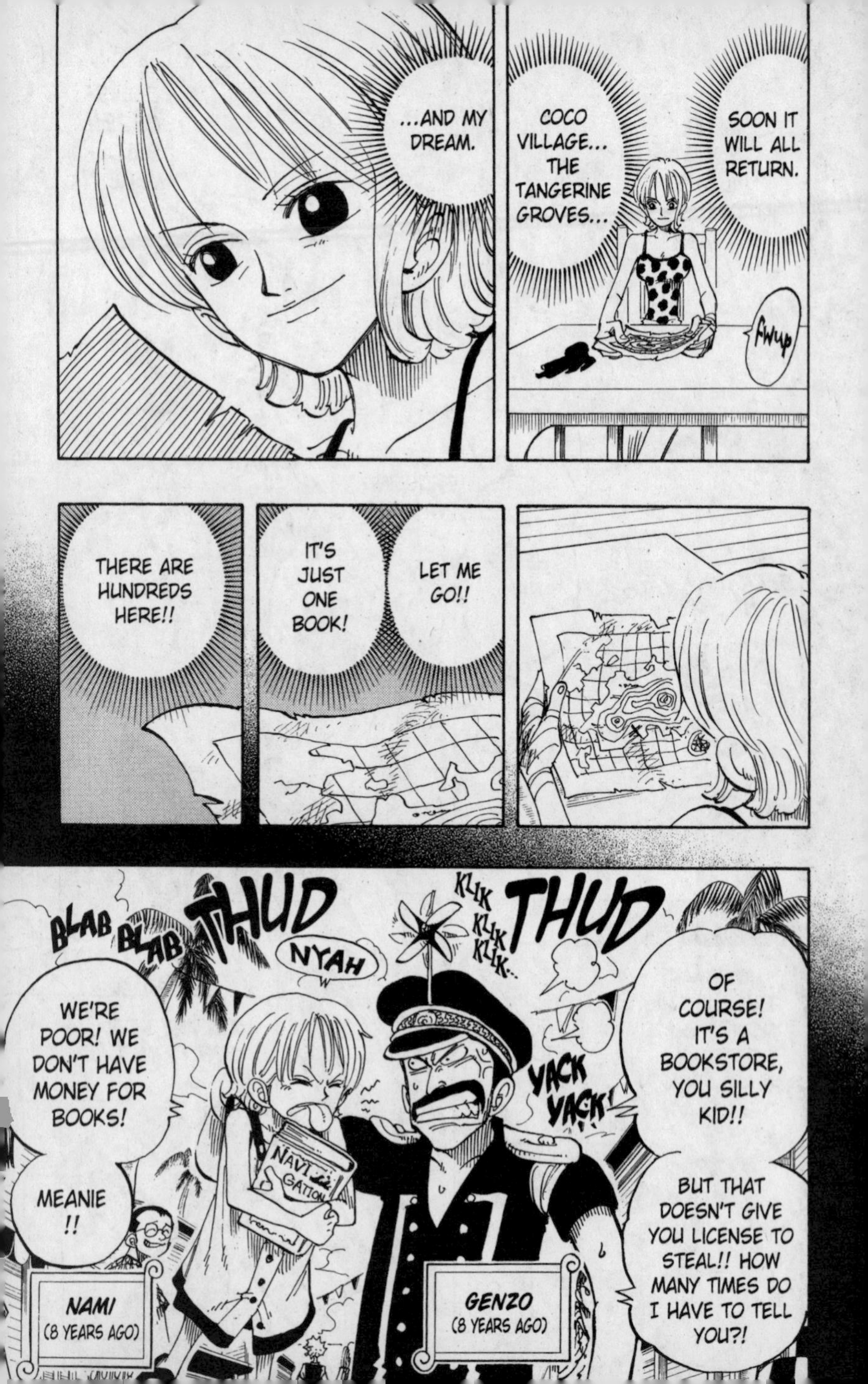
SOON IT WILL ALL RETURN.
COCO VILLAGE... THE TANGERINE GROVES...
fwup
...AND MY DREAM.
LET ME GO!!
IT'S JUST ONE BOOK!
THERE ARE HUNDREDS HERE!!
THUD
KLIK KLIK KLIK..
OF COURSE! IT'S A BOOKSTORE, YOU SILLY KID!!
YACK YACK
BUT THAT DOESN'T GIVE YOU LICENSE TO STEAL!! HOW MANY TIMES DO I HAVE TO TELL YOU?!
GENZO
(8 YEARS AGO)
NYAH
THUD
BLAB BLAB
WE'RE POOR! WE DON'T HAVE MONEY FOR BOOKS!
NAVI GATION
MEANIE !!
NAMI
(8 YEARS AGO)

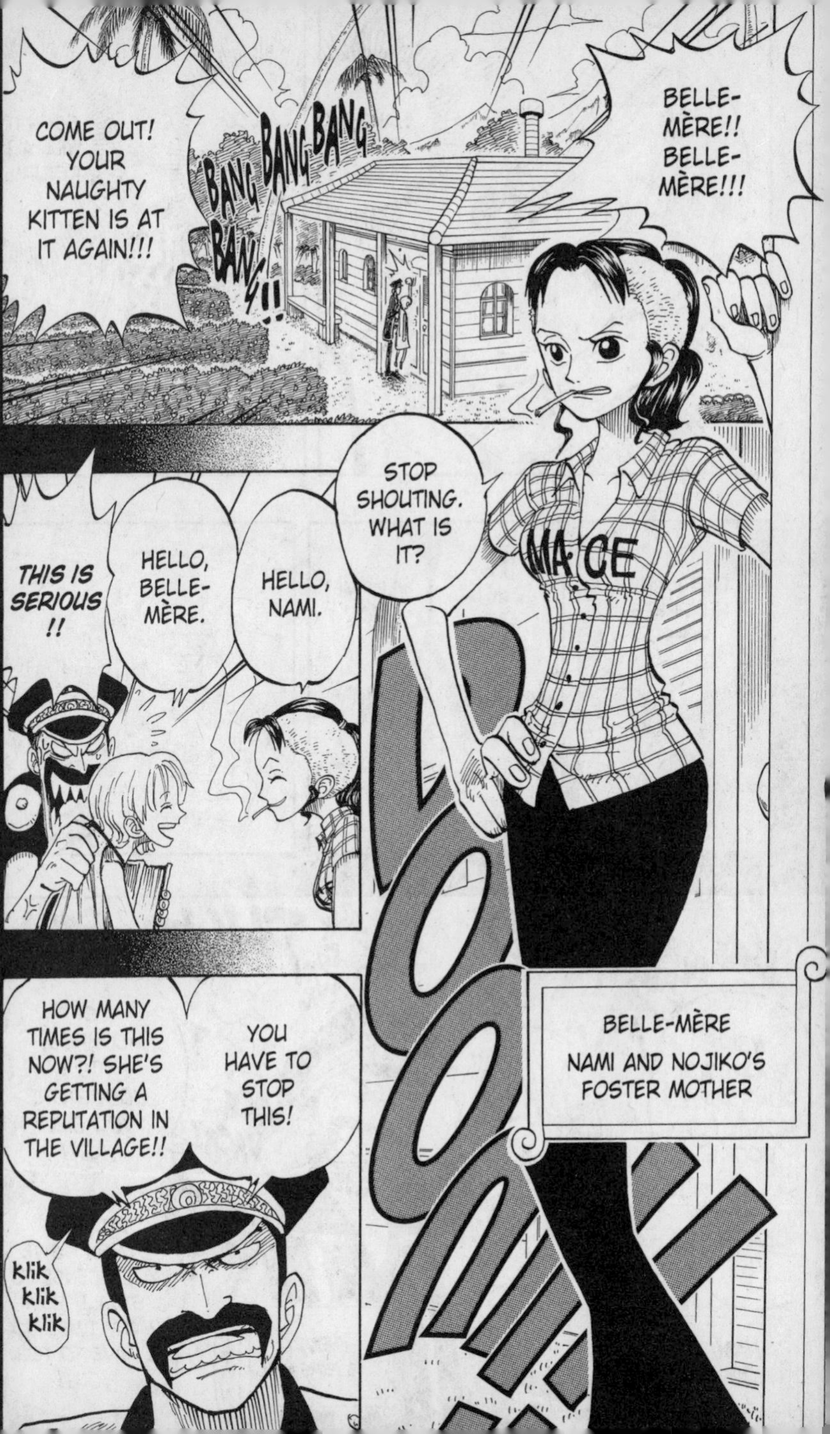
BELLE-MÈRE!! BELLE-MÈRE!!!
BANG BANG BANG BANG!!
COME OUT! YOUR NAUGHTY KITTEN IS AT IT AGAIN!!!
STOP SHOUTING. WHAT IS IT?
BELLE-MÈRE
NAMI AND NOJIKO'S FOSTER MOTHER
HELLO, NAMI.
HELLO, BELLE-MÈRE.
THIS IS SERIOUS!!
YOU HAVE TO STOP THIS!
HOW MANY TIMES IS THIS NOW?! SHE'S GETTING A REPUTATION IN THE VILLAGE!!
klik klik klik

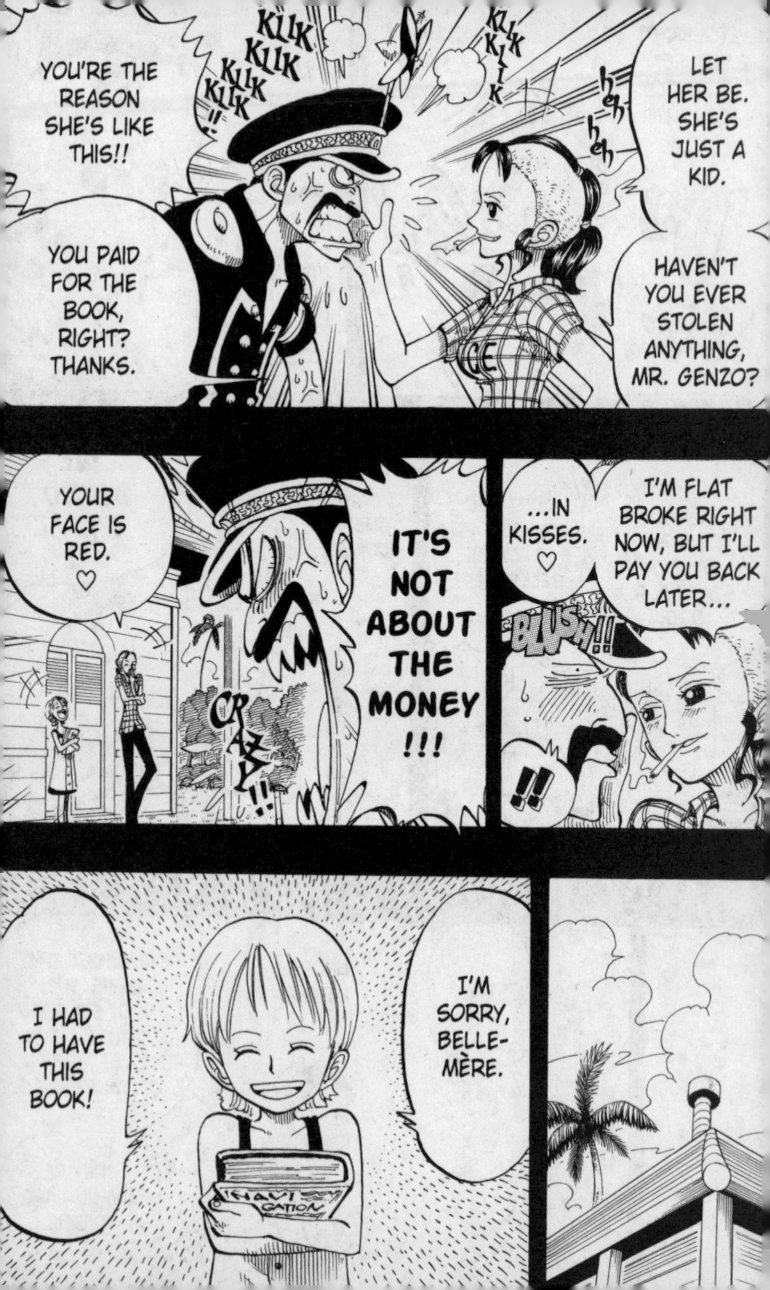
LET HER BE. SHE'S JUST A KID.
heh heh heh
KLIK KLIK KLIK KLIK!!
YOU'RE THE REASON SHE'S LIKE THIS!!
HAVEN'T YOU EVER STOLEN ANYTHING, MR. GENZO?
YOU PAID FOR THE BOOK, RIGHT? THANKS.
I'M FLAT BROKE RIGHT NOW, BUT I'LL PAY YOU BACK LATER...
...IN KISSES. ♡
BLUSH!!
!!
IT'S NOT ABOUT THE MONEY!!!
YOUR FACE IS RED. ♡
CRAZY!!
I'M SORRY, BELLE-MÈRE.
I HAD TO HAVE THIS BOOK!
NAVIGATION

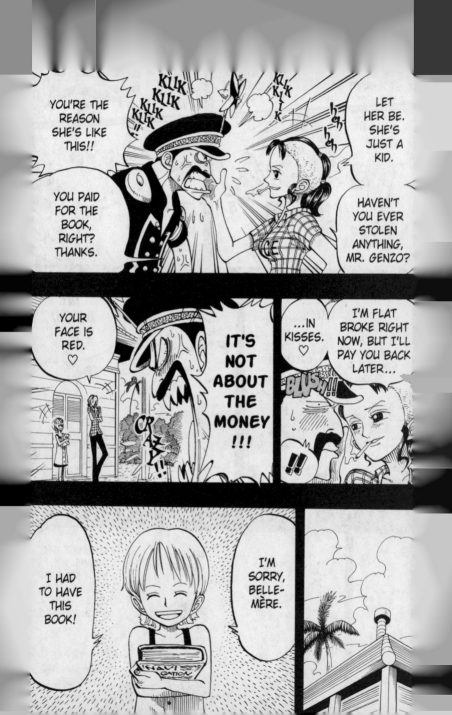

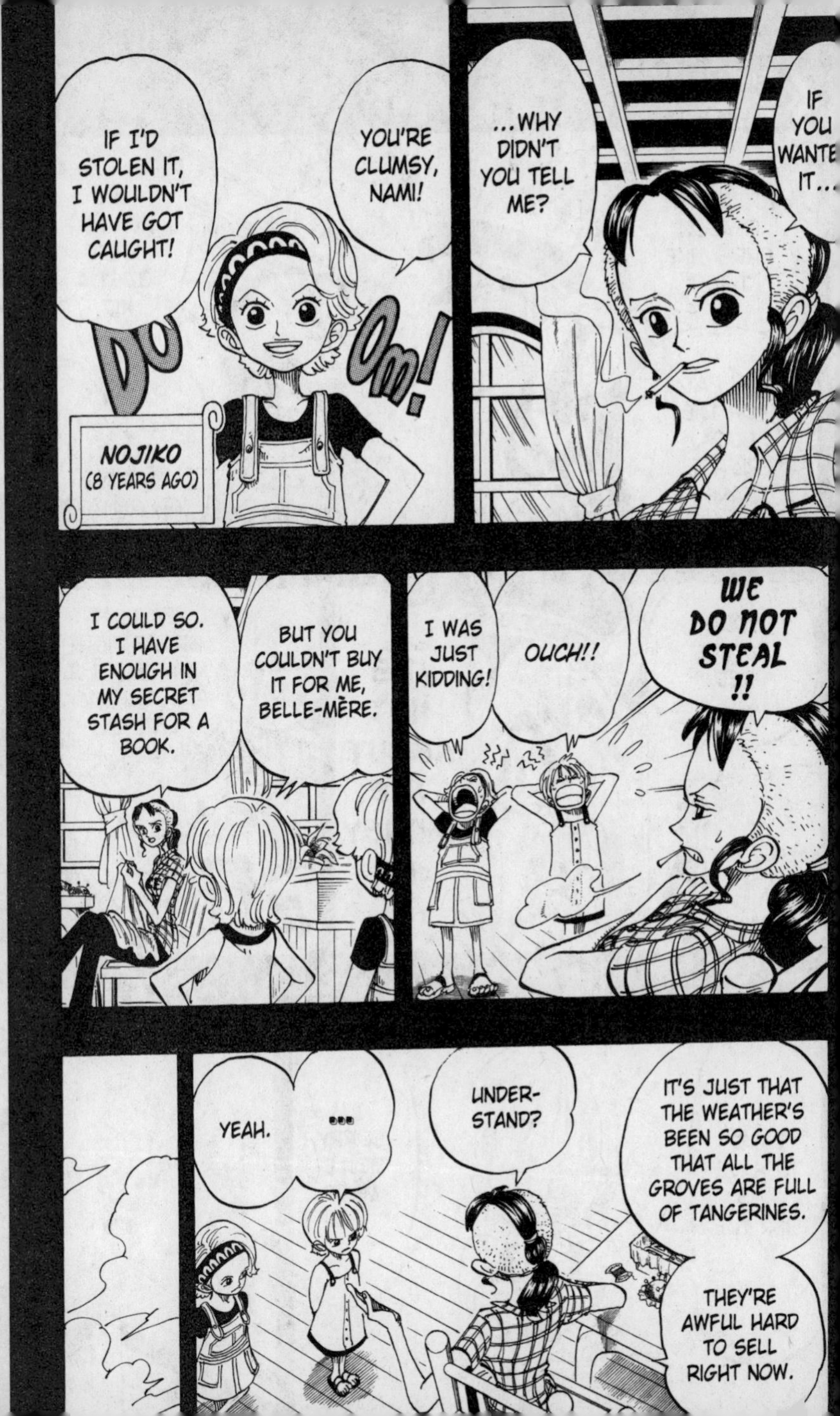
IF YOU WANTE IT…
…WHY DIDN'T YOU TELL ME?
YOU'RE CLUMSY, NAMI!
IF I'D STOLEN IT, I WOULDN'T HAVE GOT CAUGHT!
DOOM!
NOJIKO (8 YEARS AGO)
WE DO NOT STEAL!!
OUCH!!
I WAS JUST KIDDING!
BUT YOU COULDN'T BUY IT FOR ME, BELLE-MÈRE.
I COULD SO. I HAVE ENOUGH IN MY SECRET STASH FOR A BOOK.
IT'S JUST THAT THE WEATHER'S BEEN SO GOOD THAT ALL THE GROVES ARE FULL OF TANGERINES.
THEY'RE AWFUL HARD TO SELL RIGHT NOW.
UNDER-STAND?
…
YEAH.

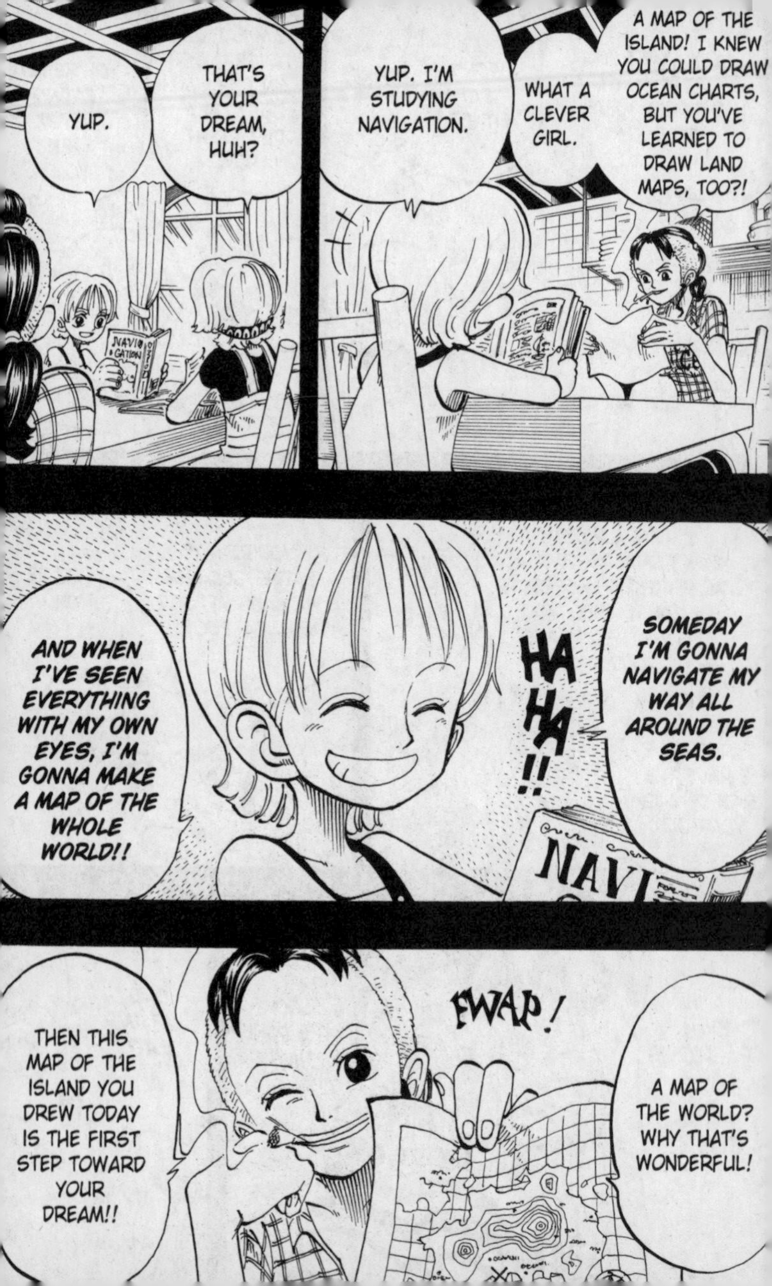
A MAP OF THE ISLAND! I KNEW YOU COULD DRAW OCEAN CHARTS, BUT YOU'VE LEARNED TO DRAW LAND MAPS, TOO?!
WHAT A CLEVER GIRL.
YUP. I'M STUDYING NAVIGATION.
THAT'S YOUR DREAM, HUH?
YUP.
NAVIGATION
SOMEDAY I'M GONNA NAVIGATE MY WAY ALL AROUND THE SEAS.
HA HA!!
AND WHEN I'VE SEEN EVERYTHING WITH MY OWN EYES, I'M GONNA MAKE A MAP OF THE WHOLE WORLD!!
NAVI
A MAP OF THE WORLD? WHY THAT'S WONDERFUL!
FWAP!
THEN THIS MAP OF THE ISLAND YOU DREW TODAY IS THE FIRST STEP TOWARD YOUR DREAM!!

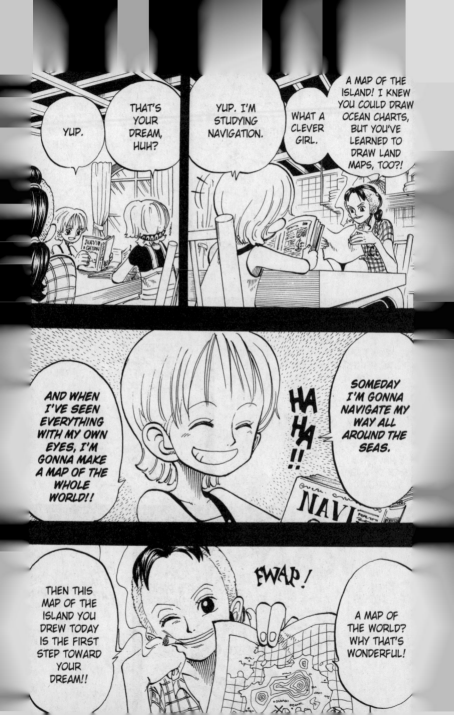

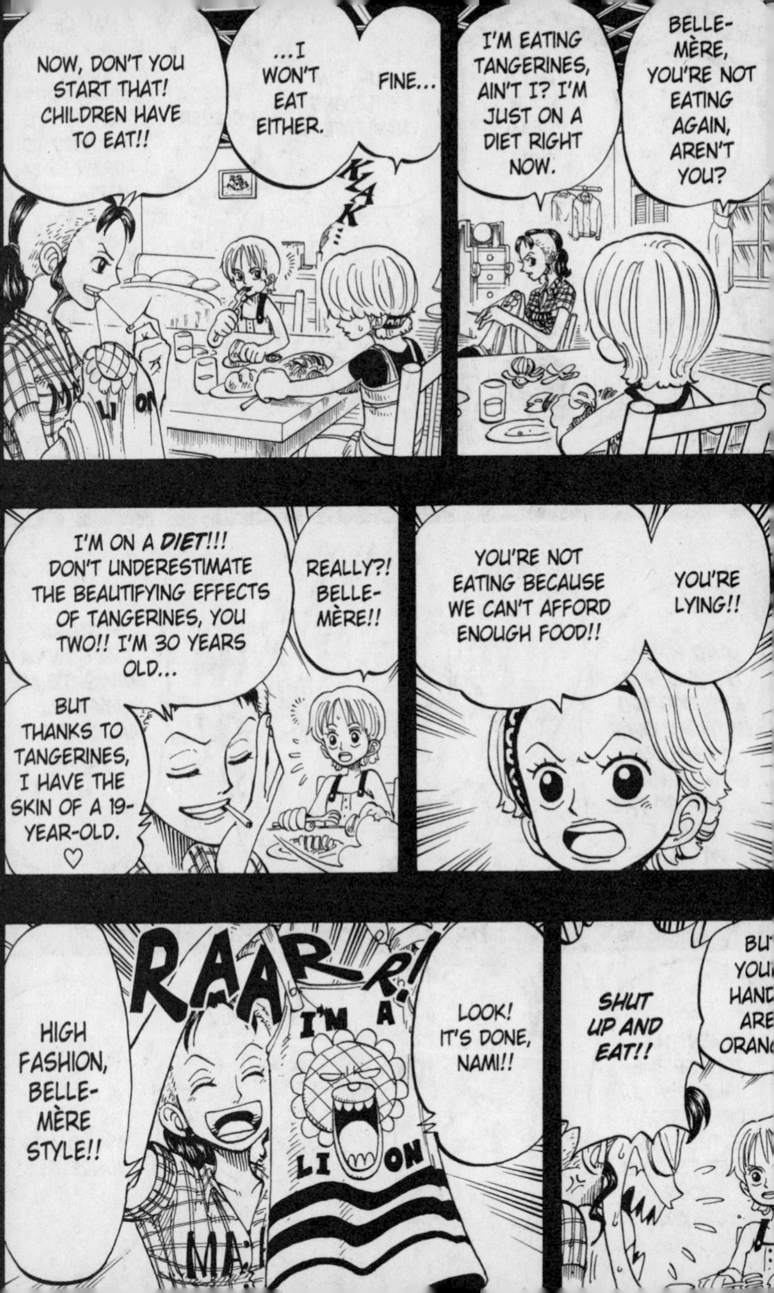
BELLE-MÈRE, YOU'RE NOT EATING AGAIN, AREN'T YOU?
I'M EATING TANGERINES, AIN'T I? I'M JUST ON A DIET RIGHT NOW.
FINE...
...I WON'T EAT EITHER.
NOW, DON'T YOU START THAT! CHILDREN HAVE TO EAT!!
KLAK...
YOU'RE LYING!!
YOU'RE NOT EATING BECAUSE WE CAN'T AFFORD ENOUGH FOOD!!
REALLY?! BELLE-MÈRE!!
I'M ON A *DIET*!!! DON'T UNDERESTIMATE THE BEAUTIFYING EFFECTS OF TANGERINES, YOU TWO!! I'M 30 YEARS OLD...
BUT THANKS TO TANGERINES, I HAVE THE SKIN OF A 19-YEAR-OLD. ♡
BUT YOU HAND ARE ORANG
SHUT UP AND EAT!!
LOOK! IT'S DONE, NAMI!!
RAARR!
I'M A
LI ON
HIGH FASHION, BELLE-MÈRE STYLE!!

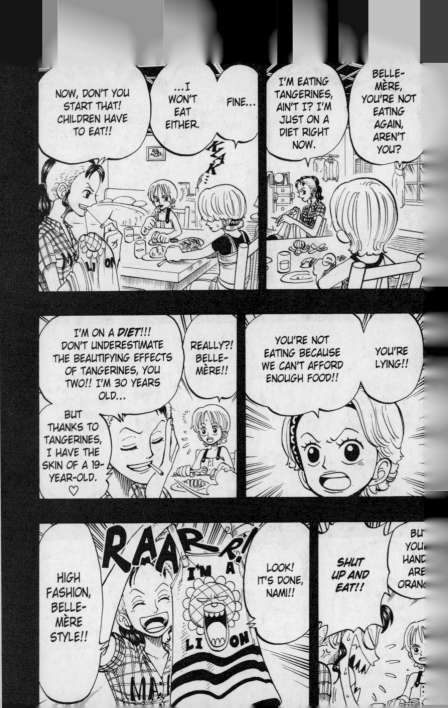

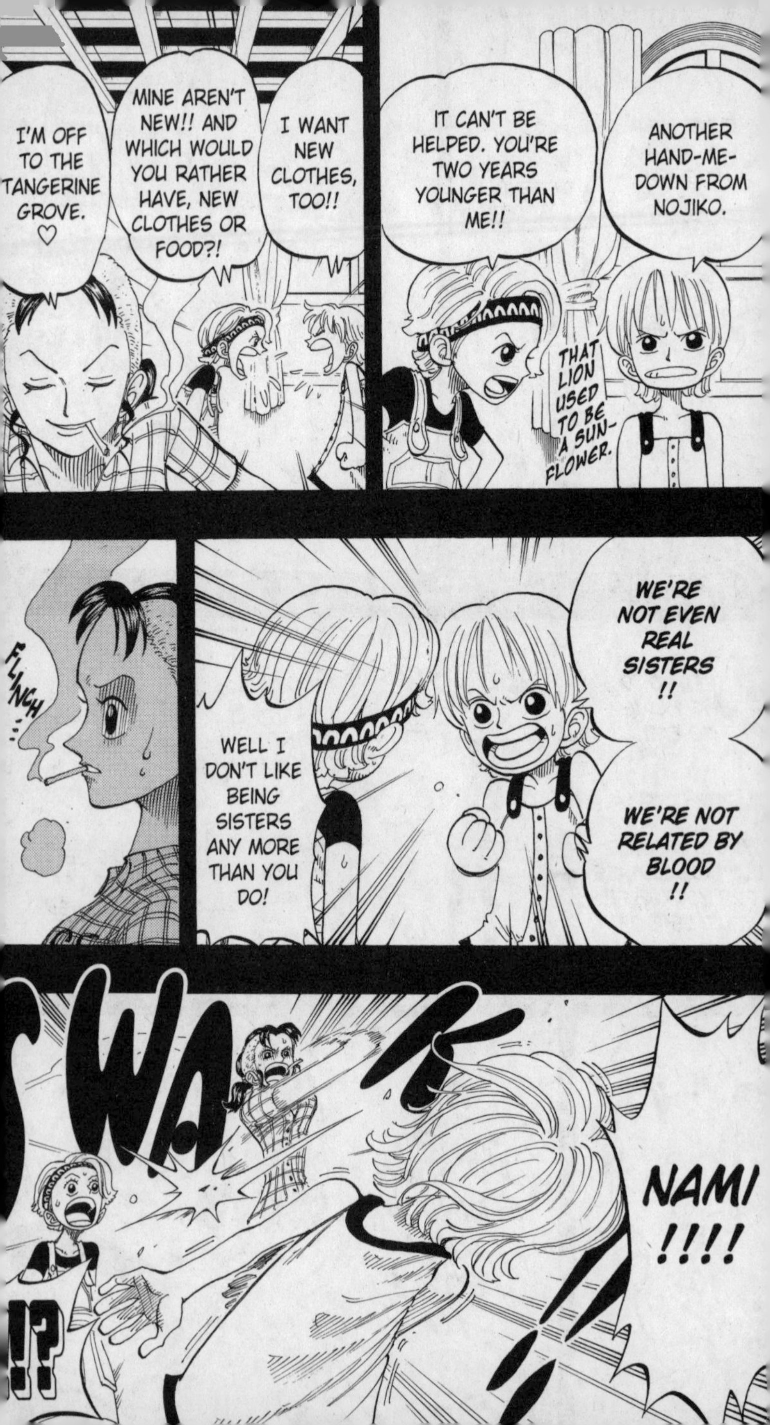
ANOTHER HAND-ME-DOWN FROM NOJIKO.
IT CAN'T BE HELPED. YOU'RE TWO YEARS YOUNGER THAN ME!!
THAT LION USED TO BE A SUN-FLOWER.
I WANT NEW CLOTHES, TOO!!
MINE AREN'T NEW!! AND WHICH WOULD YOU RATHER HAVE, NEW CLOTHES OR FOOD?!
I'M OFF TO THE TANGERINE GROVE. ♡
WE'RE NOT EVEN REAL SISTERS !!
WE'RE NOT RELATED BY BLOOD !!
WELL I DON'T LIKE BEING SISTERS ANY MORE THAN YOU DO!
FLINCH
NAMI !!!!
WAK
!?

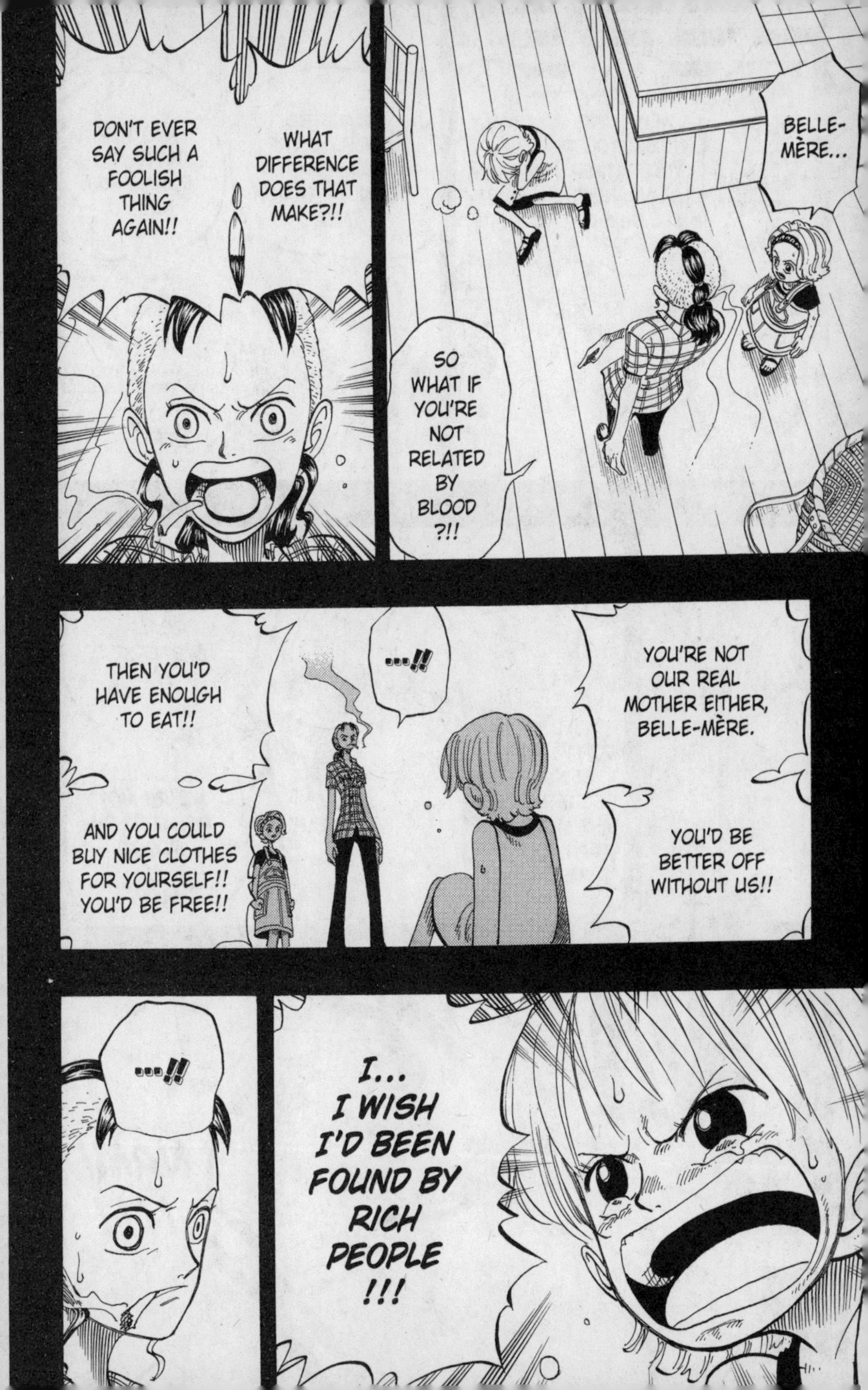
BELLE-MÈRE...
SO WHAT IF YOU'RE NOT RELATED BY BLOOD?!!
WHAT DIFFERENCE DOES THAT MAKE?!!
DON'T EVER SAY SUCH A FOOLISH THING AGAIN!!
YOU'RE NOT OUR REAL MOTHER EITHER, BELLE-MÈRE.
YOU'D BE BETTER OFF WITHOUT US!!
...!!
THEN YOU'D HAVE ENOUGH TO EAT!!
AND YOU COULD BUY NICE CLOTHES FOR YOURSELF!! YOU'D BE FREE!!
I... I WISH I'D BEEN FOUND BY RICH PEOPLE!!!
...!!

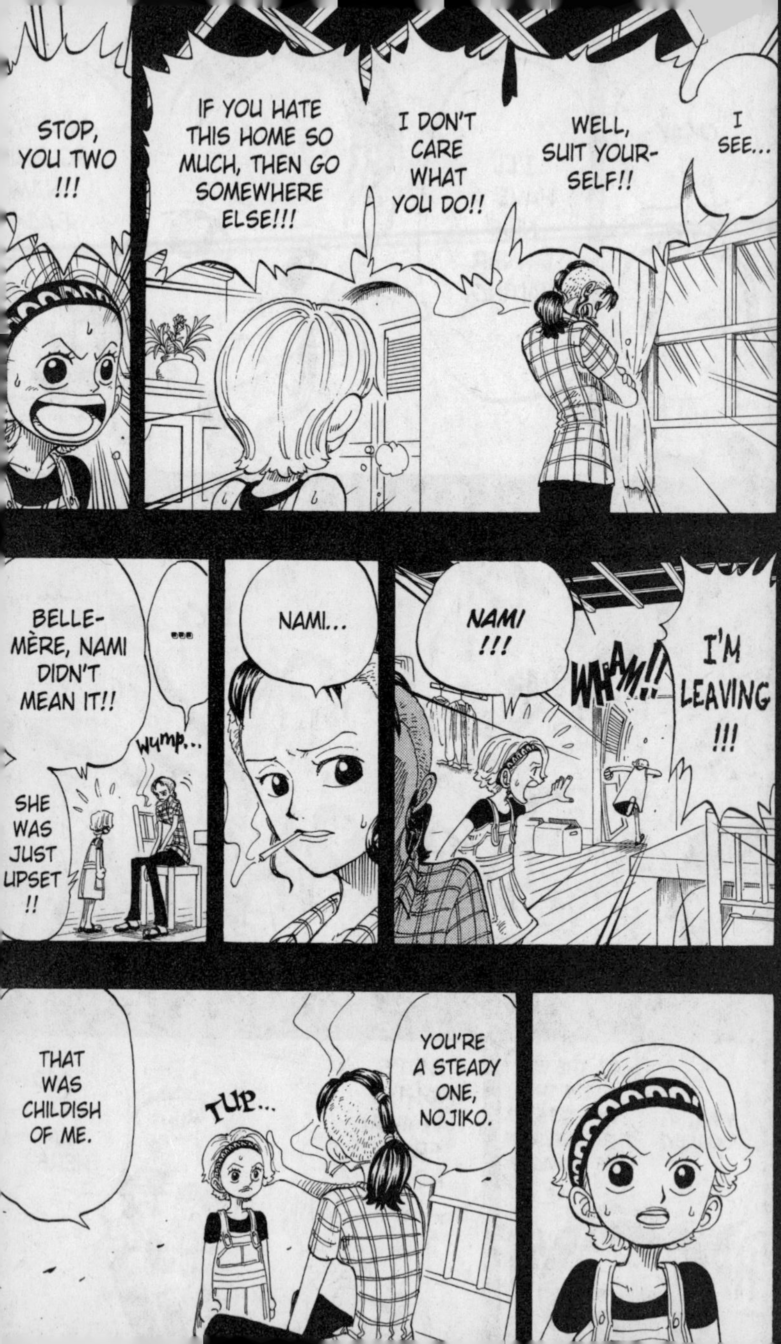
I SEE...
WELL, SUIT YOURSELF!!
I DON'T CARE WHAT YOU DO!!
IF YOU HATE THIS HOME SO MUCH, THEN GO SOMEWHERE ELSE!!!
STOP, YOU TWO!!!
I'M LEAVING!!!
WHAM!!
NAMI!!!
NAMI...
...
BELLE-MÈRE, NAMI DIDN'T MEAN IT!!
SHE WAS JUST UPSET!!
wump...
YOU'RE A STEADY ONE, NOJIKO.
TUP...
THAT WAS CHILDISH OF ME.

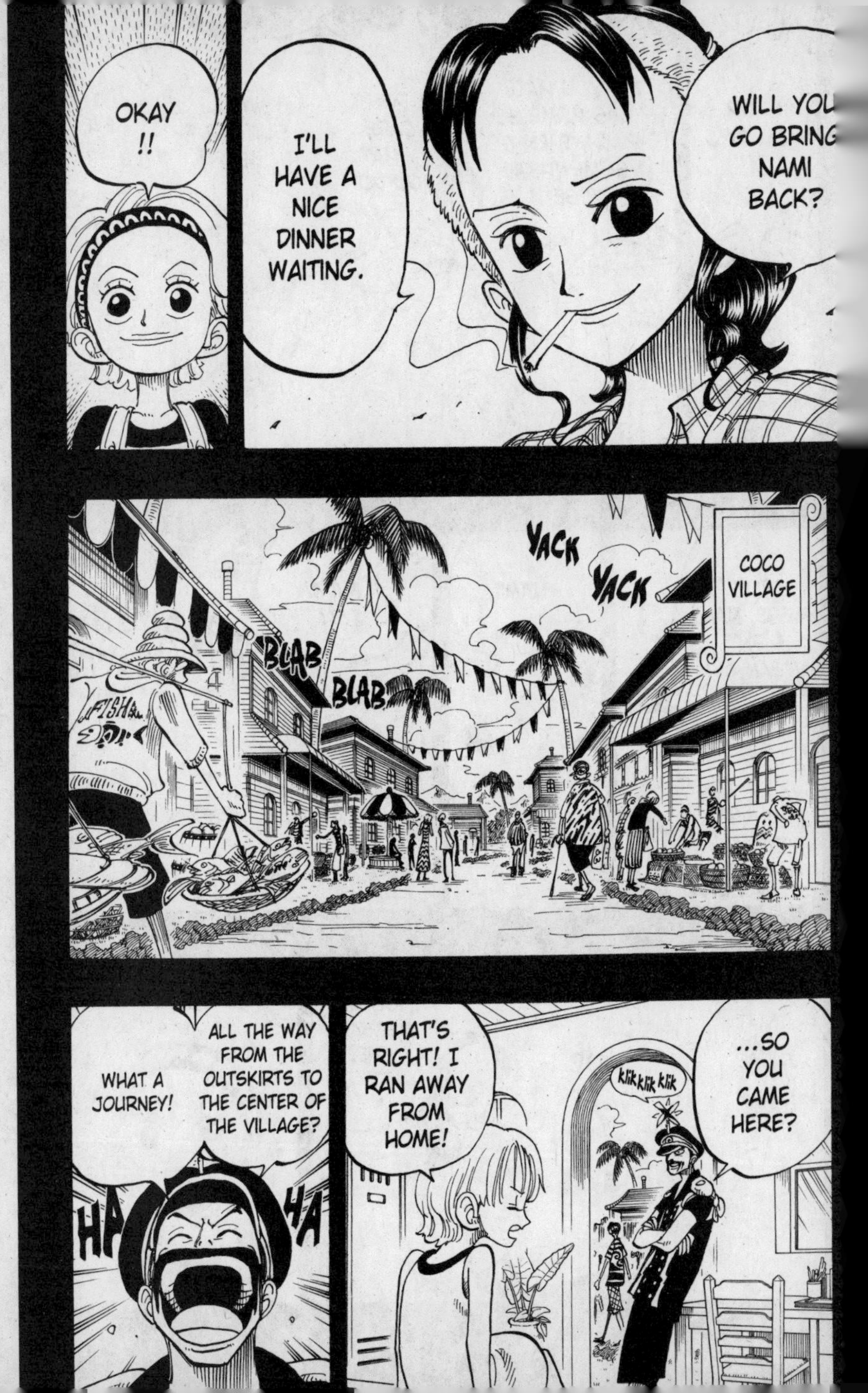
WILL YOU GO BRING NAMI BACK?
I'LL HAVE A NICE DINNER WAITING.
OKAY !!
COCO VILLAGE
YACK
YACK
BLAB
BLAB
...SO YOU CAME HERE?
klik klik klik
THAT'S RIGHT! I RAN AWAY FROM HOME!
ALL THE WAY FROM THE OUTSKIRTS TO THE CENTER OF THE VILLAGE?
WHAT A JOURNEY!
HA

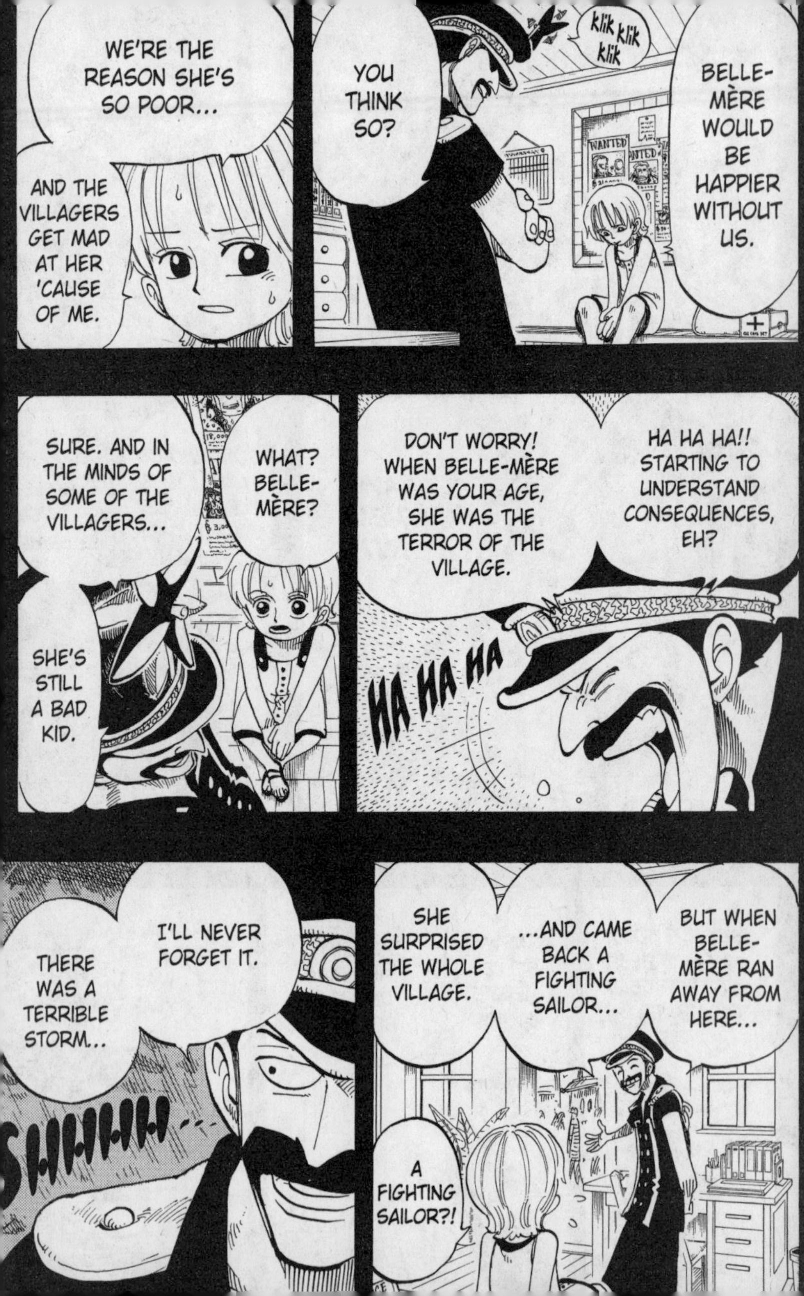
klik klik klik
BELLE-MÈRE WOULD BE HAPPIER WITHOUT US.
YOU THINK SO?
WE'RE THE REASON SHE'S SO POOR...
AND THE VILLAGERS GET MAD AT HER 'CAUSE OF ME.
HA HA HA!! STARTING TO UNDERSTAND CONSEQUENCES, EH?
DON'T WORRY! WHEN BELLE-MÈRE WAS YOUR AGE, SHE WAS THE TERROR OF THE VILLAGE.
HA HA HA
WHAT? BELLE-MÈRE?
SURE. AND IN THE MINDS OF SOME OF THE VILLAGERS...
SHE'S STILL A BAD KID.
BUT WHEN BELLE-MÈRE RAN AWAY FROM HERE...
...AND CAME BACK A FIGHTING SAILOR...
SHE SURPRISED THE WHOLE VILLAGE.
A FIGHTING SAILOR?!
I'LL NEVER FORGET IT.
THERE WAS A TERRIBLE STORM...

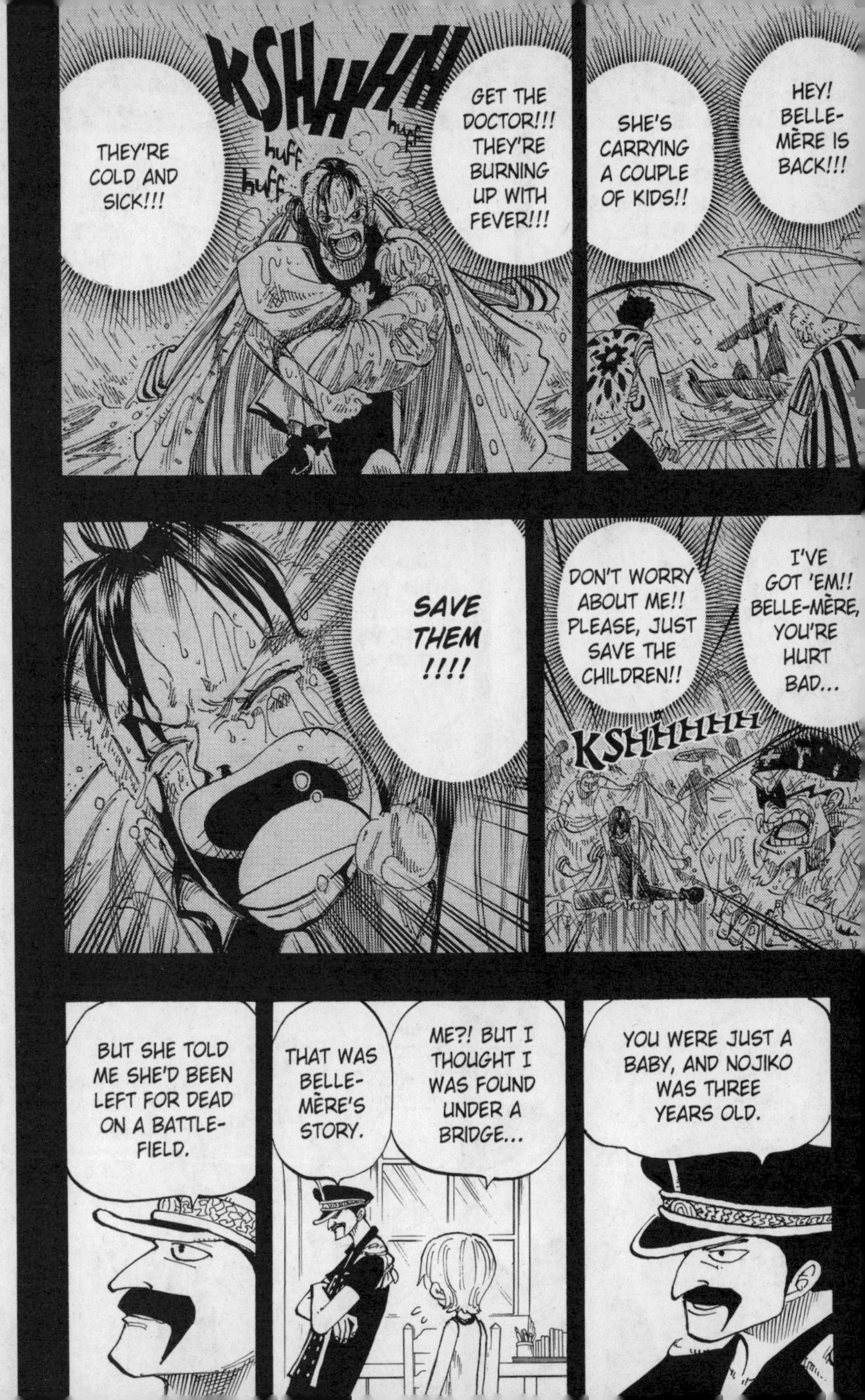
HEY! BELLE-MÈRE IS BACK!!!
SHE'S CARRYING A COUPLE OF KIDS!!
KSHHHH
GET THE DOCTOR!!! THEY'RE BURNING UP WITH FEVER!!!
huff huff huff
THEY'RE COLD AND SICK!!!
I'VE GOT 'EM!! BELLE-MÈRE, YOU'RE HURT BAD...
DON'T WORRY ABOUT ME!! PLEASE, JUST SAVE THE CHILDREN!!
KSHHHHH
SAVE THEM !!!!
YOU WERE JUST A BABY, AND NOJIKO WAS THREE YEARS OLD.
ME?! BUT I THOUGHT I WAS FOUND UNDER A BRIDGE...
THAT WAS BELLE-MÈRE'S STORY.
BUT SHE TOLD ME SHE'D BEEN LEFT FOR DEAD ON A BATTLE-FIELD.

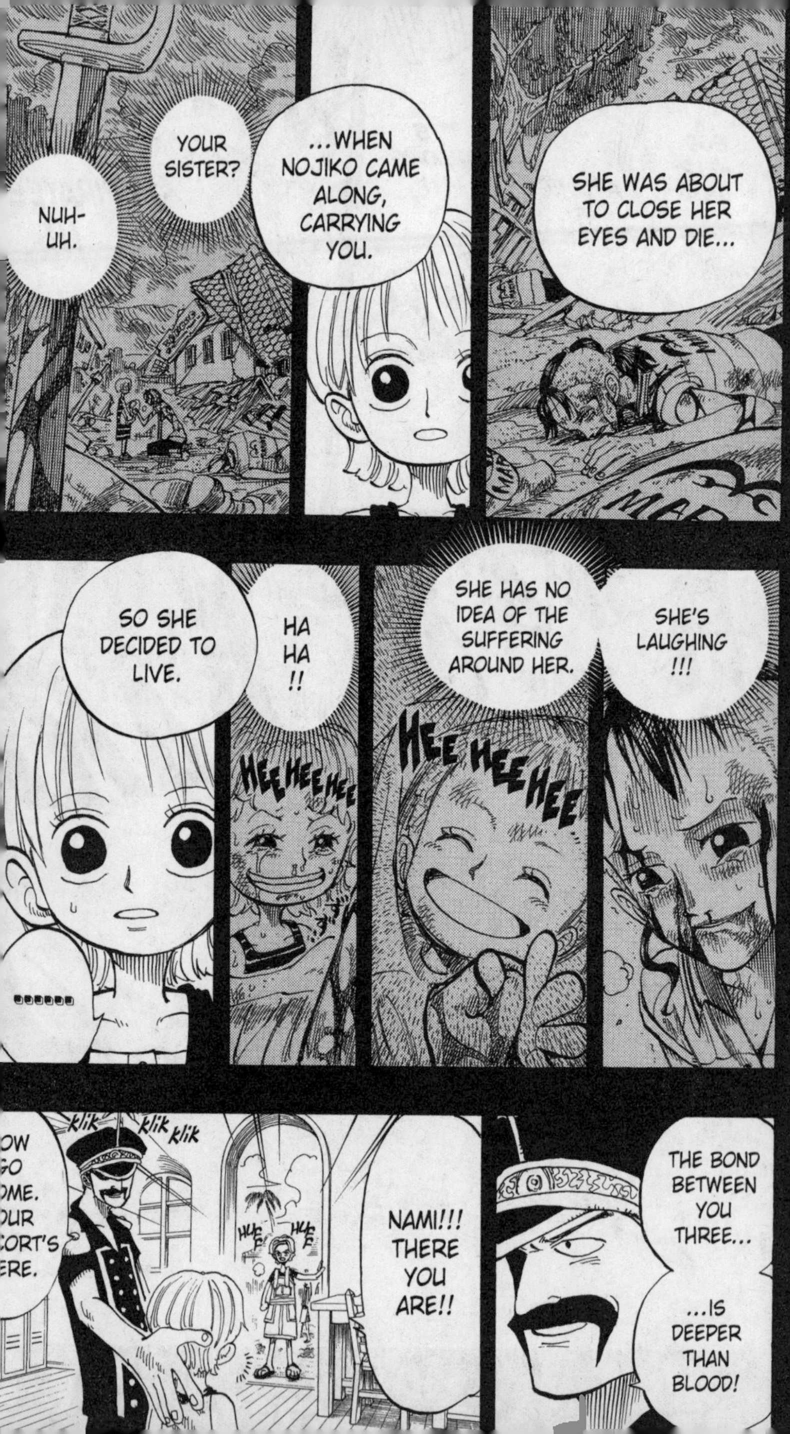
SHE WAS ABOUT TO CLOSE HER EYES AND DIE...
...WHEN NOJIKO CAME ALONG, CARRYING YOU.
YOUR SISTER?
NUH-UH.
SHE'S LAUGHING !!!
SHE HAS NO IDEA OF THE SUFFERING AROUND HER.
HEE HEE HEE HEE
HA HA !!
HEE HEE HEE
SO SHE DECIDED TO LIVE.
THE BOND BETWEEN YOU THREE...
...IS DEEPER THAN BLOOD!
NAMI!!! THERE YOU ARE!!
HUF HUF
klik klik klik

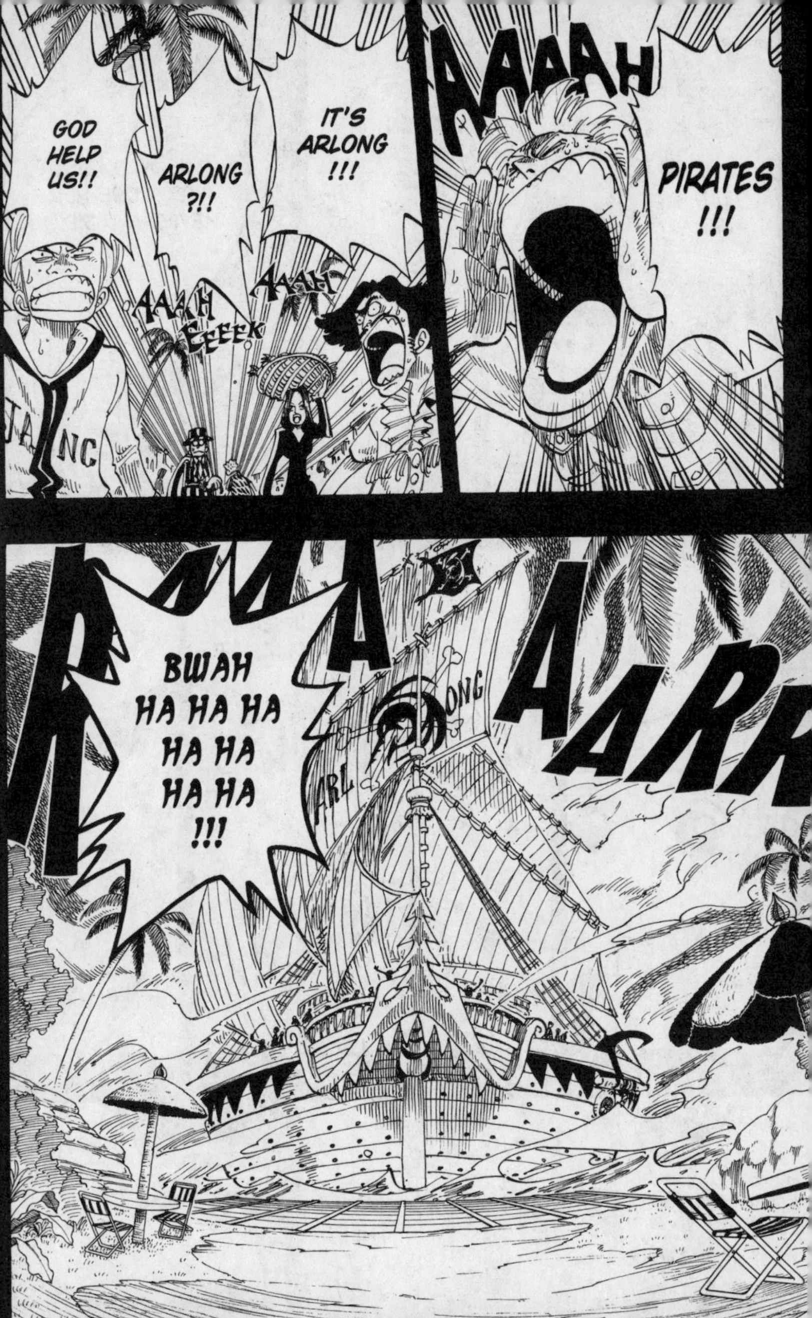
AAAAH
PIRATES!!!
IT'S ARLONG!!!
AAAH
ARLONG?!!
AAAH
EEEEK
GOD HELP US!!
AARR
AAAAA
BWAH HA HA HA HA HA HA HA HA!!!

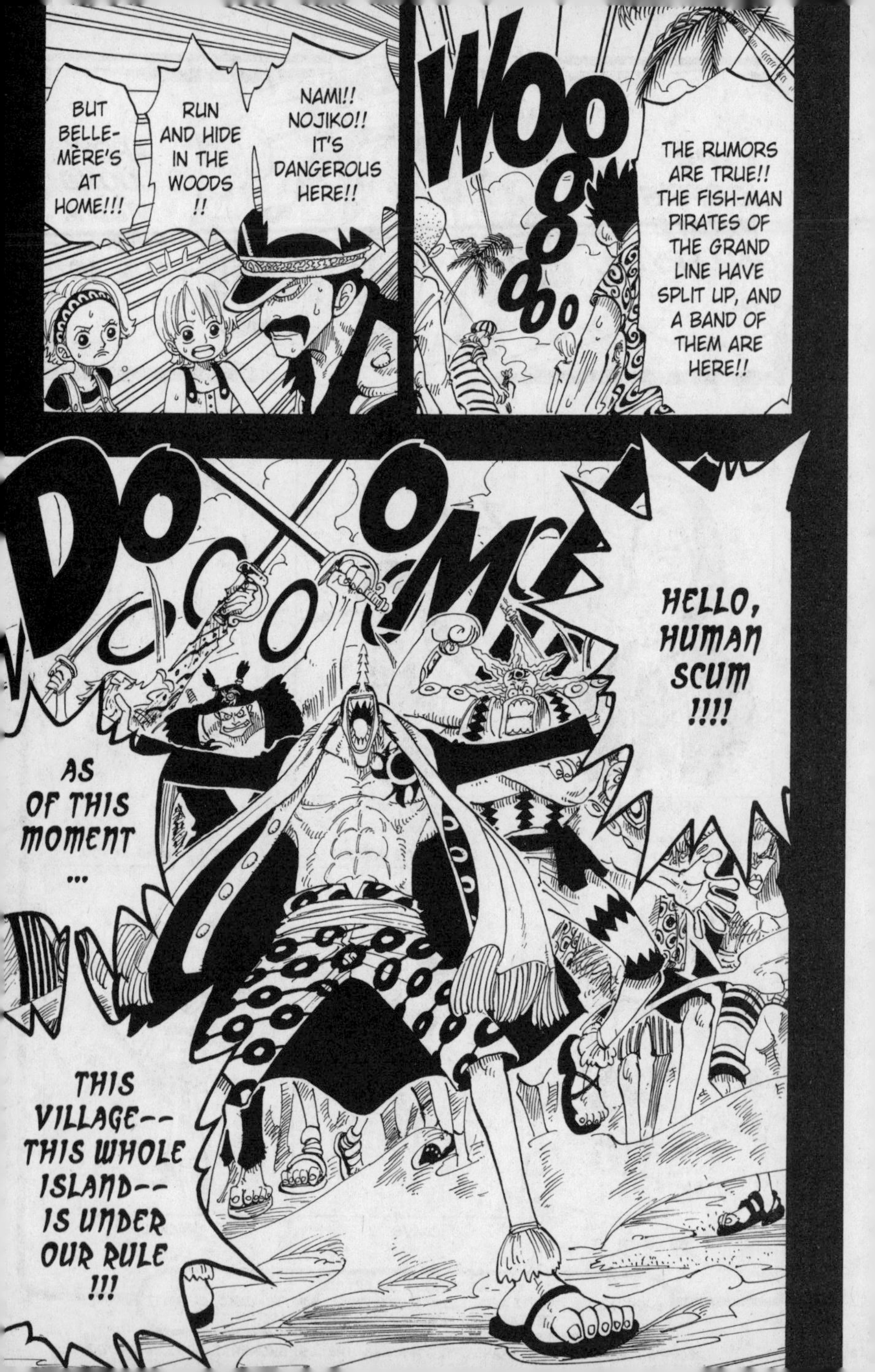
WOOOOOOO
THE RUMORS ARE TRUE!! THE FISH-MAN PIRATES OF THE GRAND LINE HAVE SPLIT UP, AND A BAND OF THEM ARE HERE!!
NAMI!! NOJIKO!! IT'S DANGEROUS HERE!!
RUN AND HIDE IN THE WOODS !!
BUT BELLE-MÈRE'S AT HOME!!!
DOOOOOM
HELLO, HUMAN SCUM !!!!
AS OF THIS MOMENT ...
THIS VILLAGE-- THIS WHOLE ISLAND-- IS UNDER OUR RULE !!!

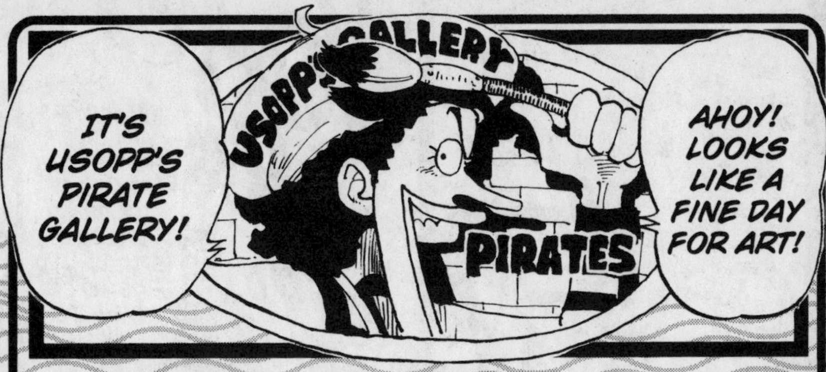
USOPP'S GALLERY
PIRATES
AHOY! LOOKS LIKE A FINE DAY FOR ART!
IT'S USOPP'S PIRATE GALLERY!

*ONE PIECE* HEARTTHROB, SANJI.

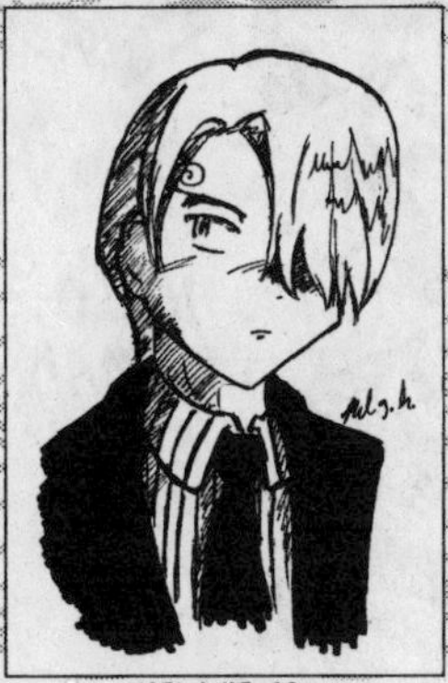

MELANIE, 18

ARRRR!

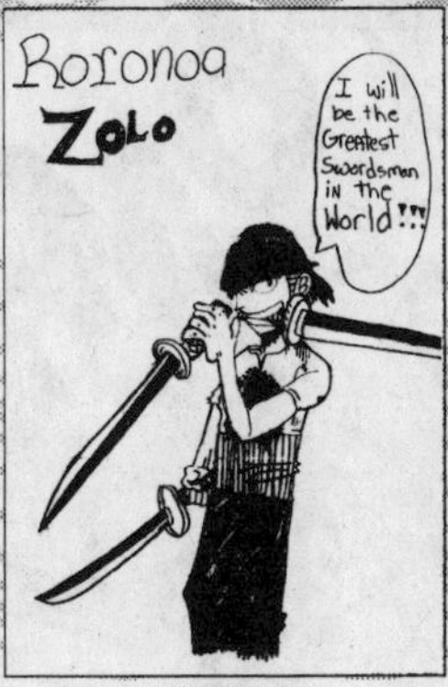
Roronoa
ZOLO
I will be the Greatest Swordsman in the World!!!

ANDY, 14

THE WORLD'S BEST NAVIGATOR.

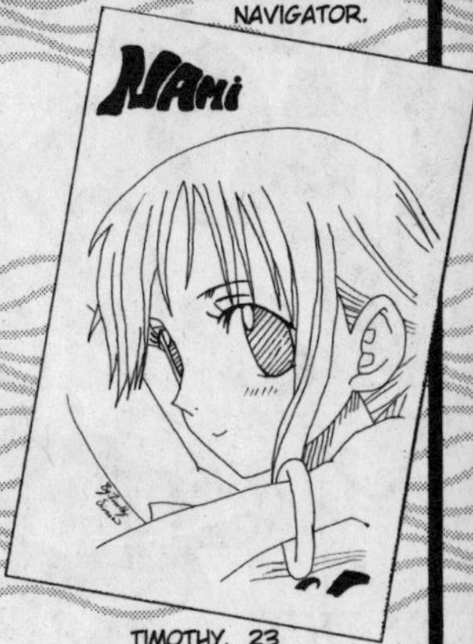
NAMi

TIMOTHY, 23

WHO'S THE TOUGHEST PIRATE HERE?

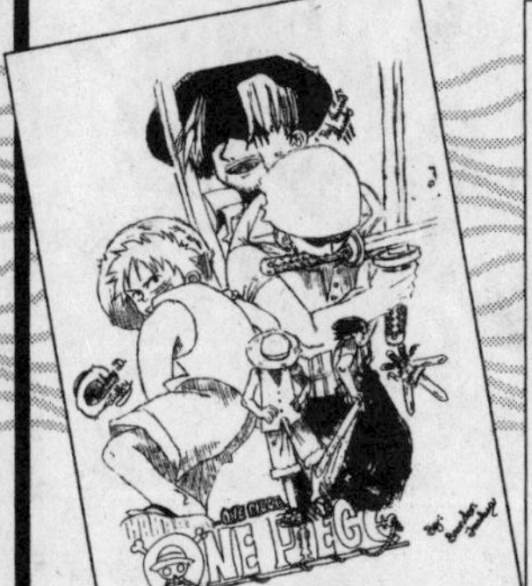
ONE PIECE

BRANDON, 13

UH-OH! IT'S MOMOO!

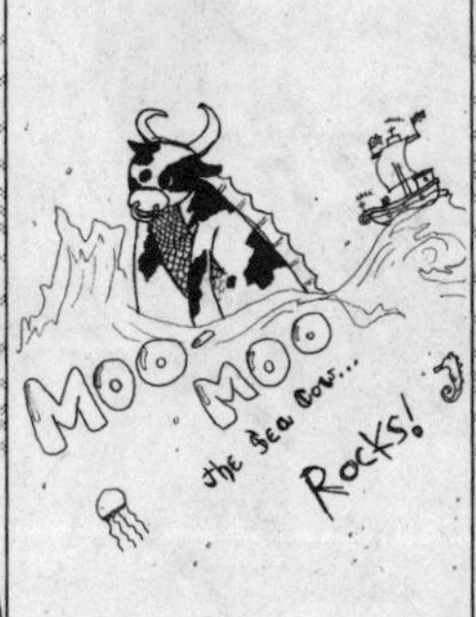
MOO MOO
the Sea Cow...
ROCKS!

CLAVE, 13

HERE'S WINKING AT YOU.

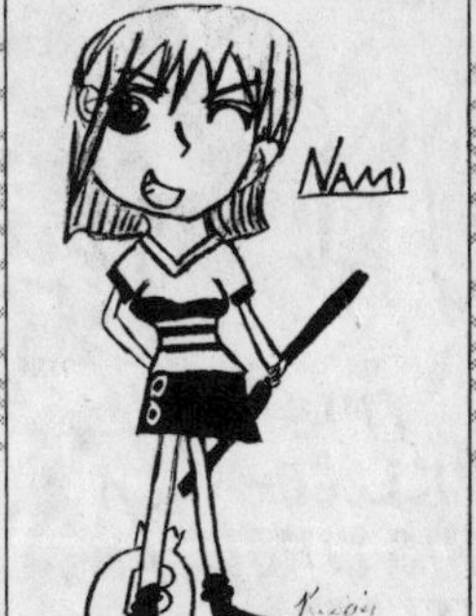
NAMI

RACHEL, 13

SUBMIT YOUR FAN ART TO:
SHONEN JUMP C/O VIZ MEDIA, LLC P.O. BOX 77010, SAN FRANCISCO, CA, 94107
REMEMBER TO INCLUDE YOUR NAME AND AGE!!

USOPP'S COMMENTS WERE TRANSMITTED THROUGH THE U.S. SHONEN JUMP TEAM—*EDITOR*

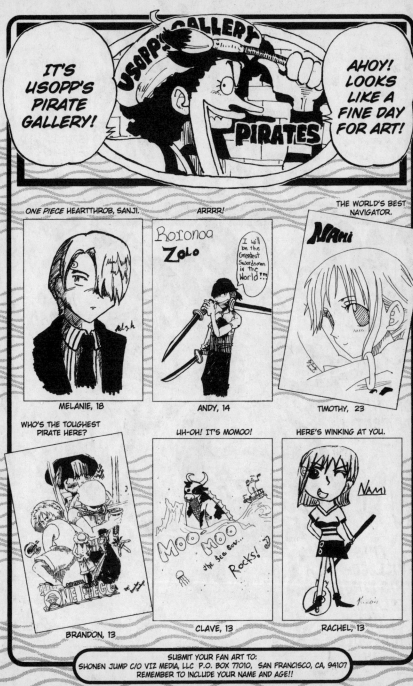

# Chapter 78: Belle-Mère

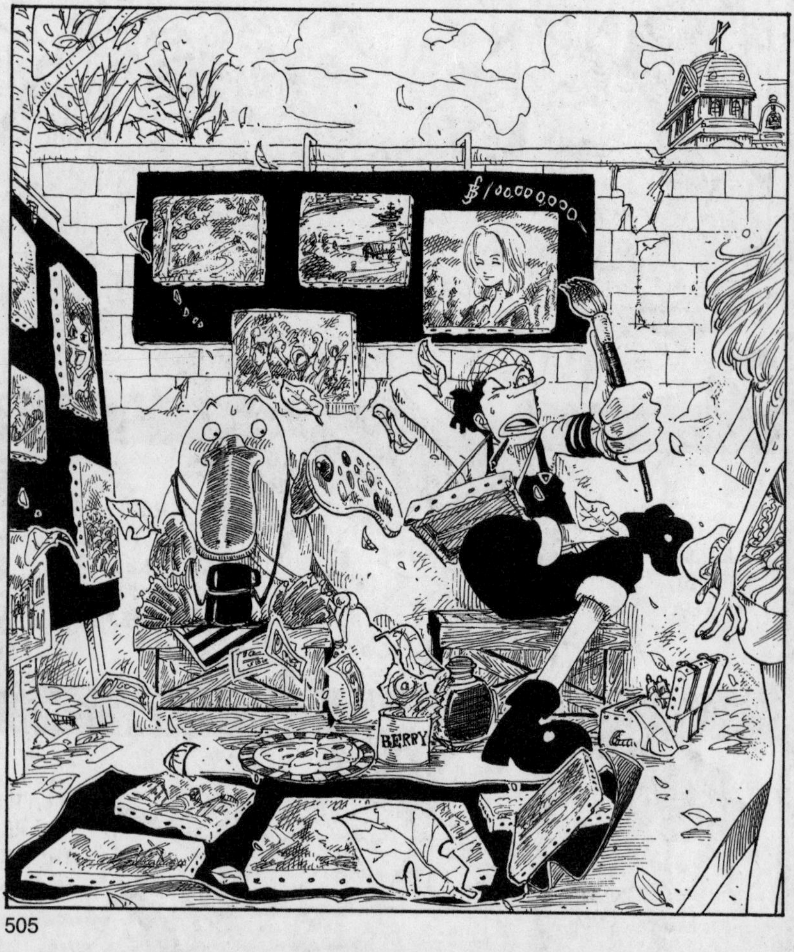

BERRY

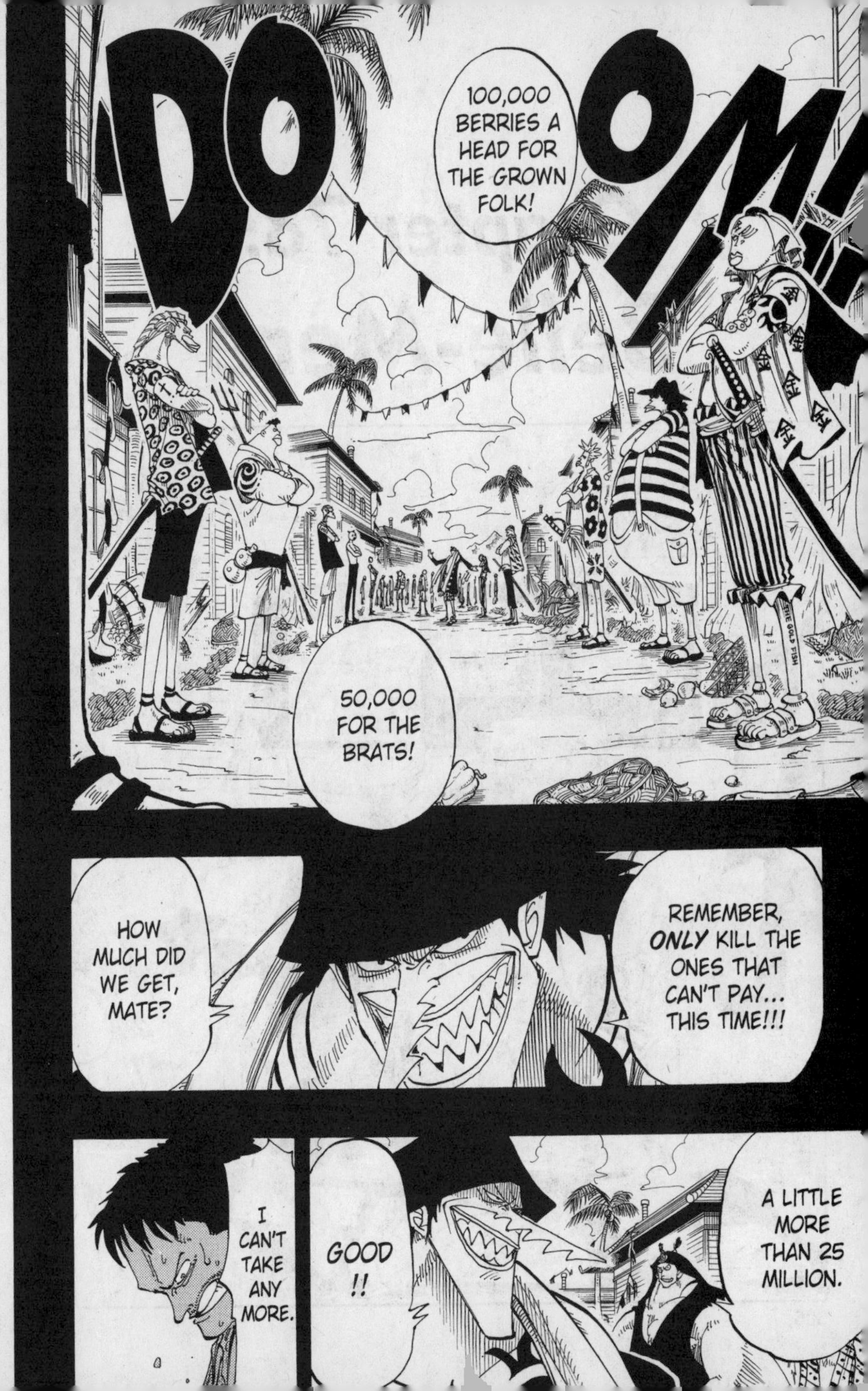
DO-OM!!
100,000 BERRIES A HEAD FOR THE GROWN FOLK!
50,000 FOR THE BRATS!
REMEMBER, *ONLY* KILL THE ONES THAT CAN'T PAY... THIS TIME!!!
HOW MUCH DID WE GET, MATE?
A LITTLE MORE THAN 25 MILLION.
GOOD!!
I CAN'T TAKE ANY MORE.

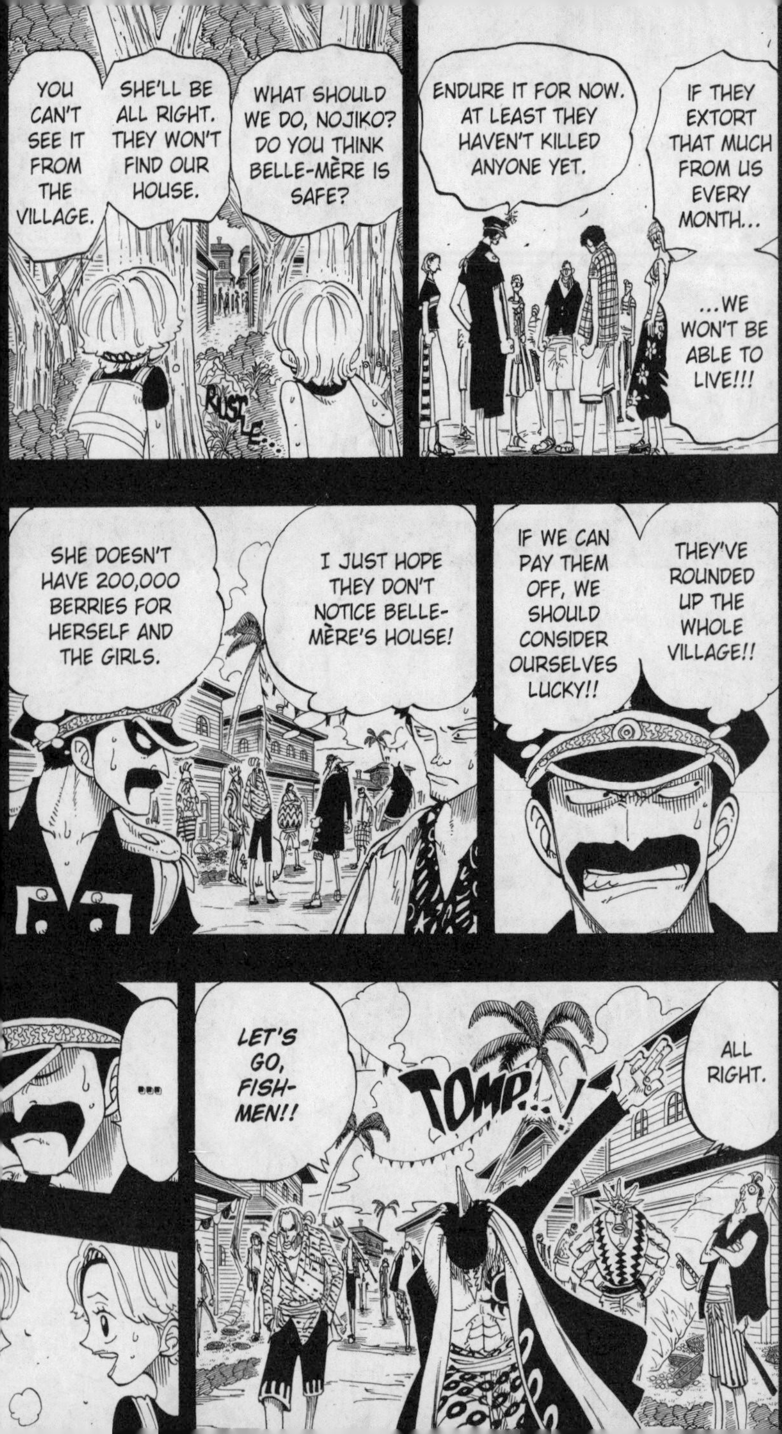
IF THEY EXTORT THAT MUCH FROM US EVERY MONTH...
...WE WON'T BE ABLE TO LIVE!!!
ENDURE IT FOR NOW. AT LEAST THEY HAVEN'T KILLED ANYONE YET.
WHAT SHOULD WE DO, NOJIKO? DO YOU THINK BELLE-MÈRE IS SAFE?
SHE'LL BE ALL RIGHT. THEY WON'T FIND OUR HOUSE.
YOU CAN'T SEE IT FROM THE VILLAGE.
RUSTLE...
THEY'VE ROUNDED UP THE WHOLE VILLAGE!!
IF WE CAN PAY THEM OFF, WE SHOULD CONSIDER OURSELVES LUCKY!!
I JUST HOPE THEY DON'T NOTICE BELLE-MÈRE'S HOUSE!
SHE DOESN'T HAVE 200,000 BERRIES FOR HERSELF AND THE GIRLS.
ALL RIGHT.
TOMP...!
LET'S GO, FISH-MEN!!
...

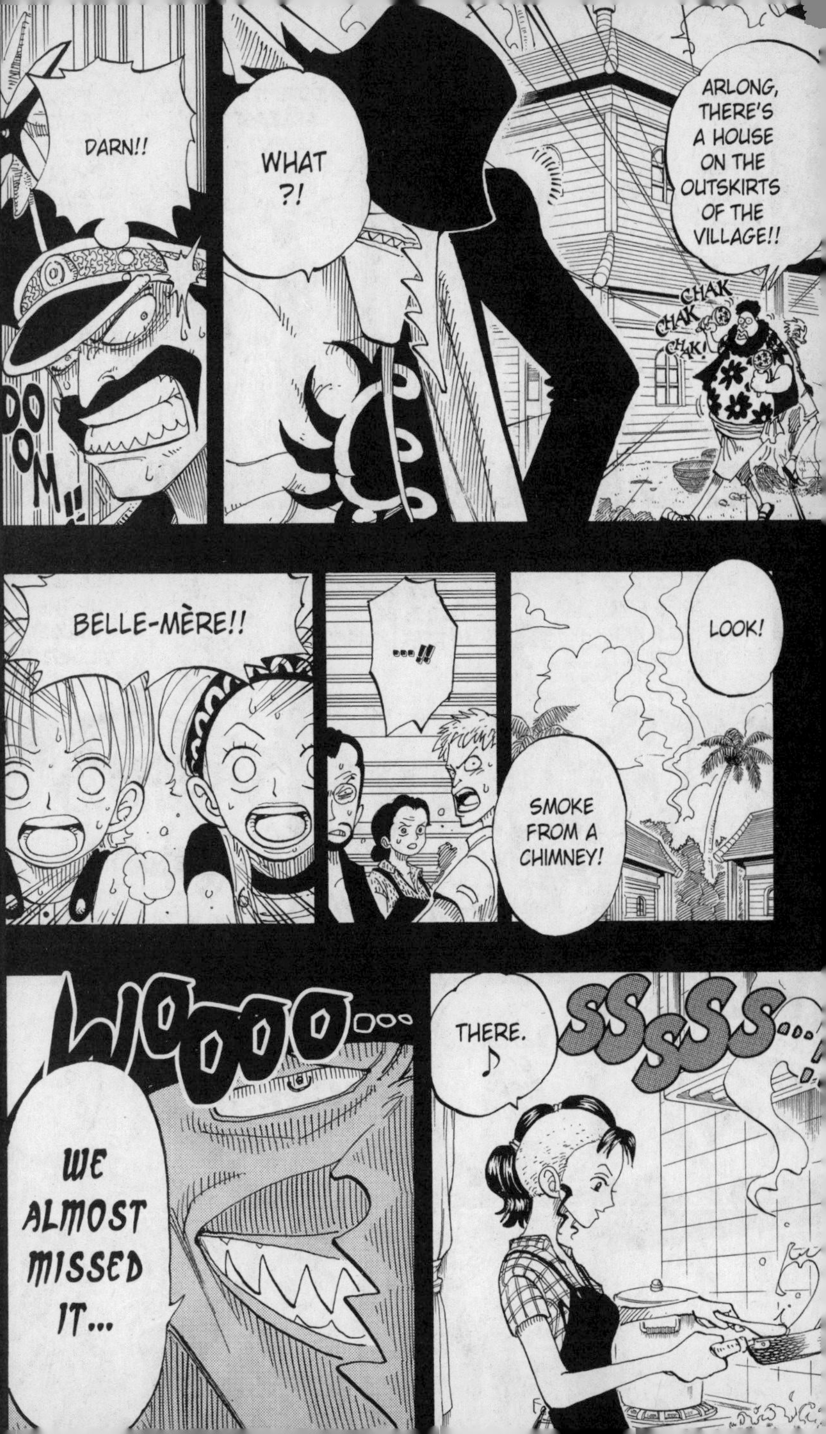
ARLONG, THERE'S A HOUSE ON THE OUTSKIRTS OF THE VILLAGE!!
CHAK CHAK CHAK!
WHAT ?!
DARN!!
LOOK!
SMOKE FROM A CHIMNEY!
...!!
BELLE-MÈRE!!
THERE. ♪
SSSSS...
WOOOOO...
WE ALMOST MISSED IT...

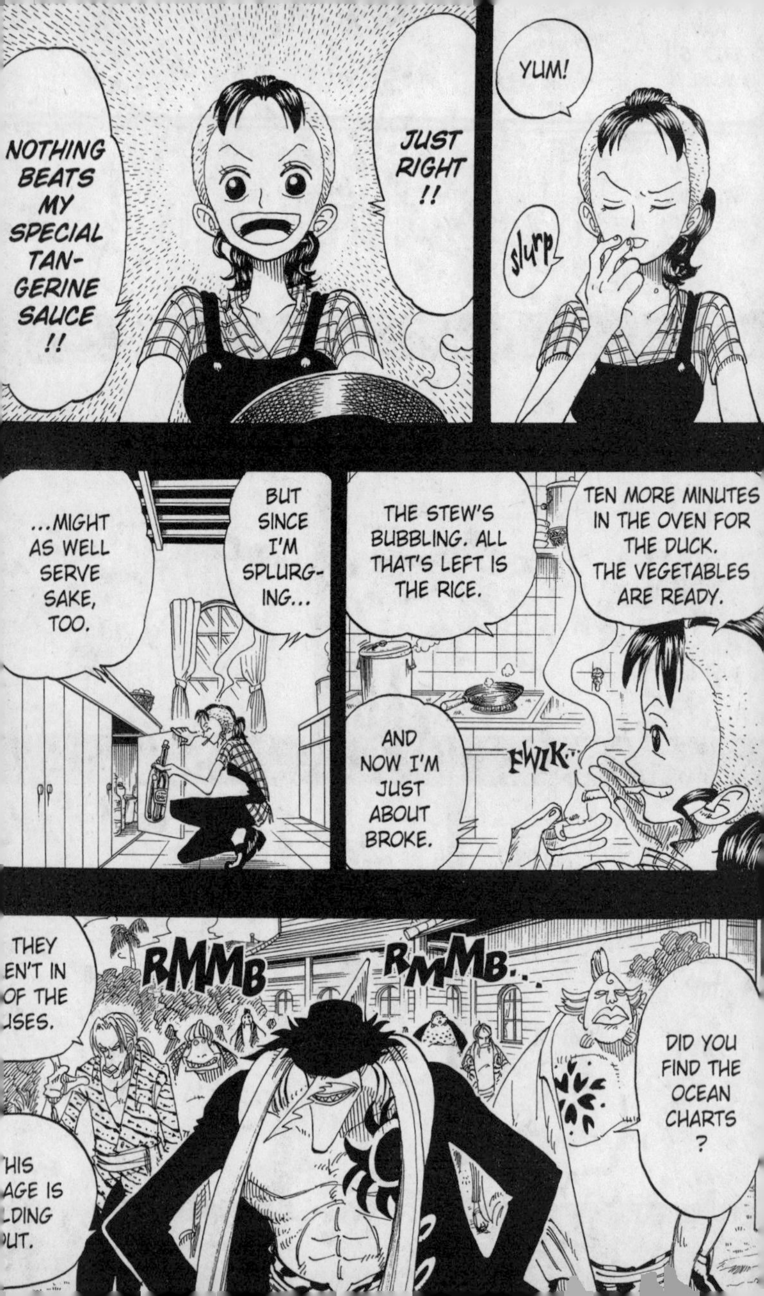
YUM!
slurp
JUST RIGHT!!
NOTHING BEATS MY SPECIAL TAN-GERINE SAUCE!!
TEN MORE MINUTES IN THE OVEN FOR THE DUCK. THE VEGETABLES ARE READY.
THE STEW'S BUBBLING. ALL THAT'S LEFT IS THE RICE.
FWIK
AND NOW I'M JUST ABOUT BROKE.
BUT SINCE I'M SPLURG-ING...
...MIGHT AS WELL SERVE SAKE, TOO.
RMMB RMMB...
DID YOU FIND THE OCEAN CHARTS?
THEY EN'T IN OF THE USES.
HIS AGE IS LDING UT.

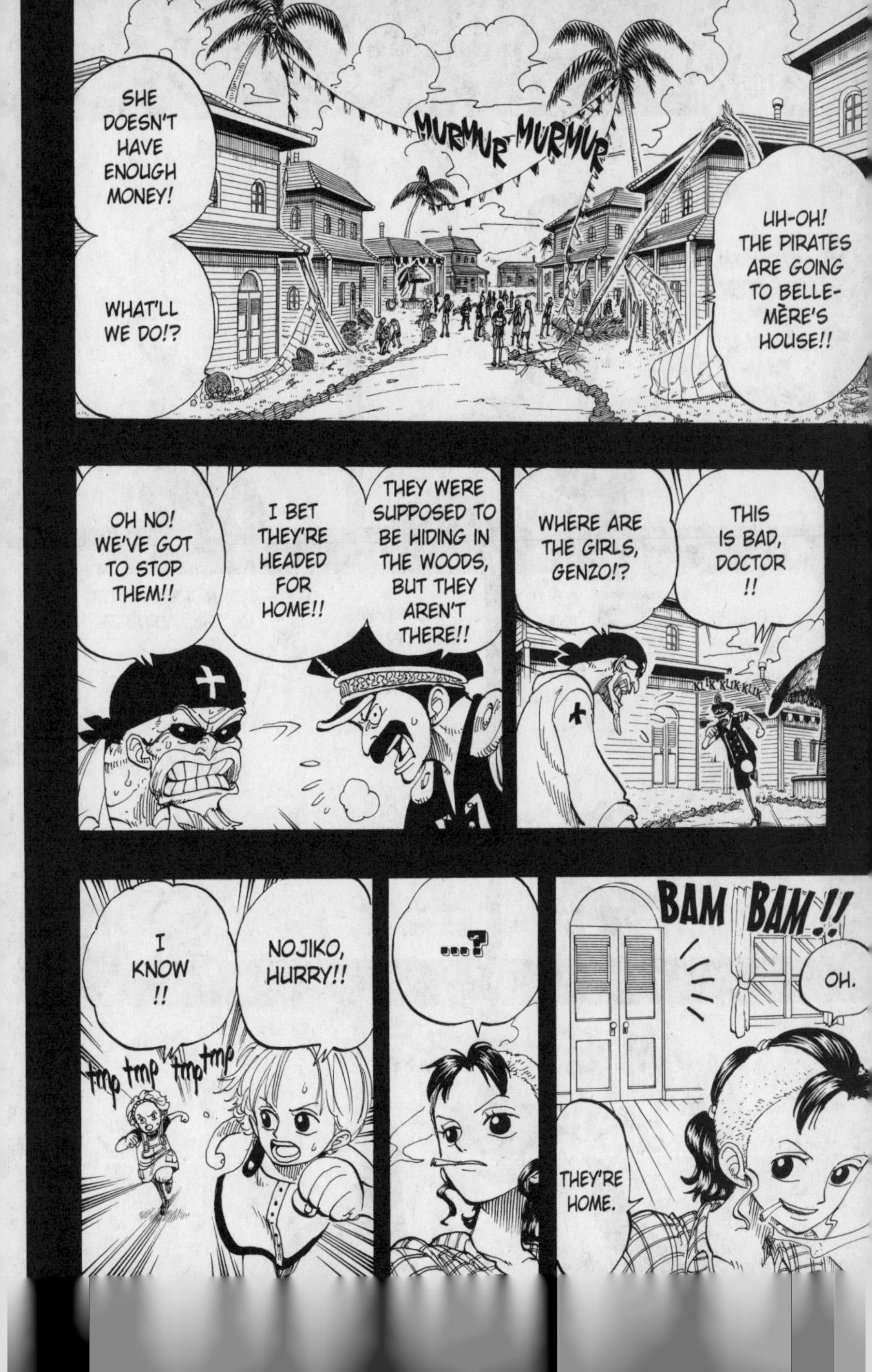
MURMUR MURMUR
UH-OH! THE PIRATES ARE GOING TO BELLE-MÈRE'S HOUSE!!
SHE DOESN'T HAVE ENOUGH MONEY!
WHAT'LL WE DO!?
THIS IS BAD, DOCTOR!!
WHERE ARE THE GIRLS, GENZO!?
KLIK KLIK KLIK
THEY WERE SUPPOSED TO BE HIDING IN THE WOODS, BUT THEY AREN'T THERE!!
I BET THEY'RE HEADED FOR HOME!!
OH NO! WE'VE GOT TO STOP THEM!!
BAM BAM!!
OH.
THEY'RE HOME.
...?
NOJIKO, HURRY!!
I KNOW!!
tmp tmp tmp tmp

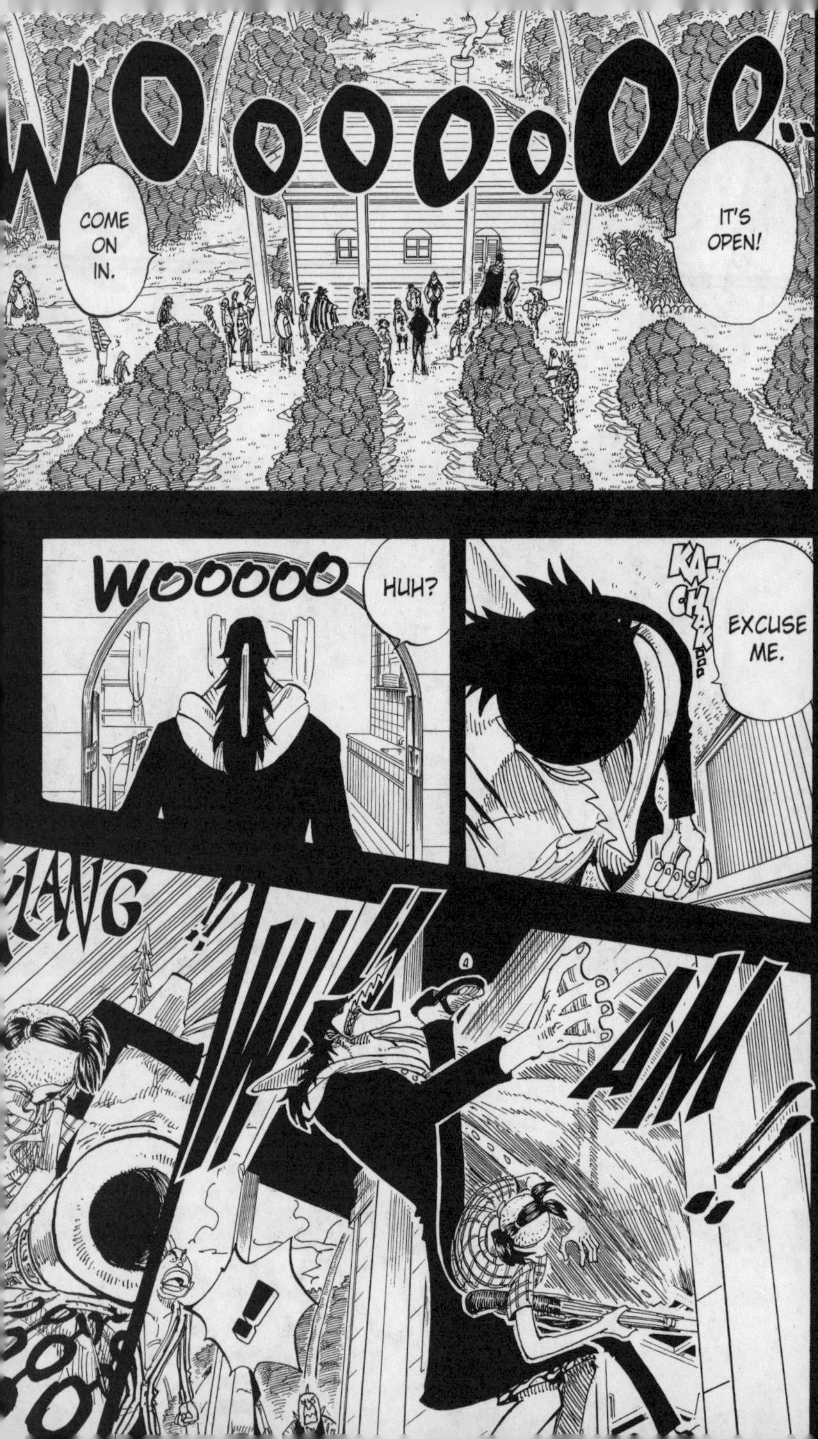
WOOOOOOO..
IT'S OPEN!
COME ON IN.
KA-CHAK...
EXCUSE ME.
WOOOOO
HUH?
WHAM!!

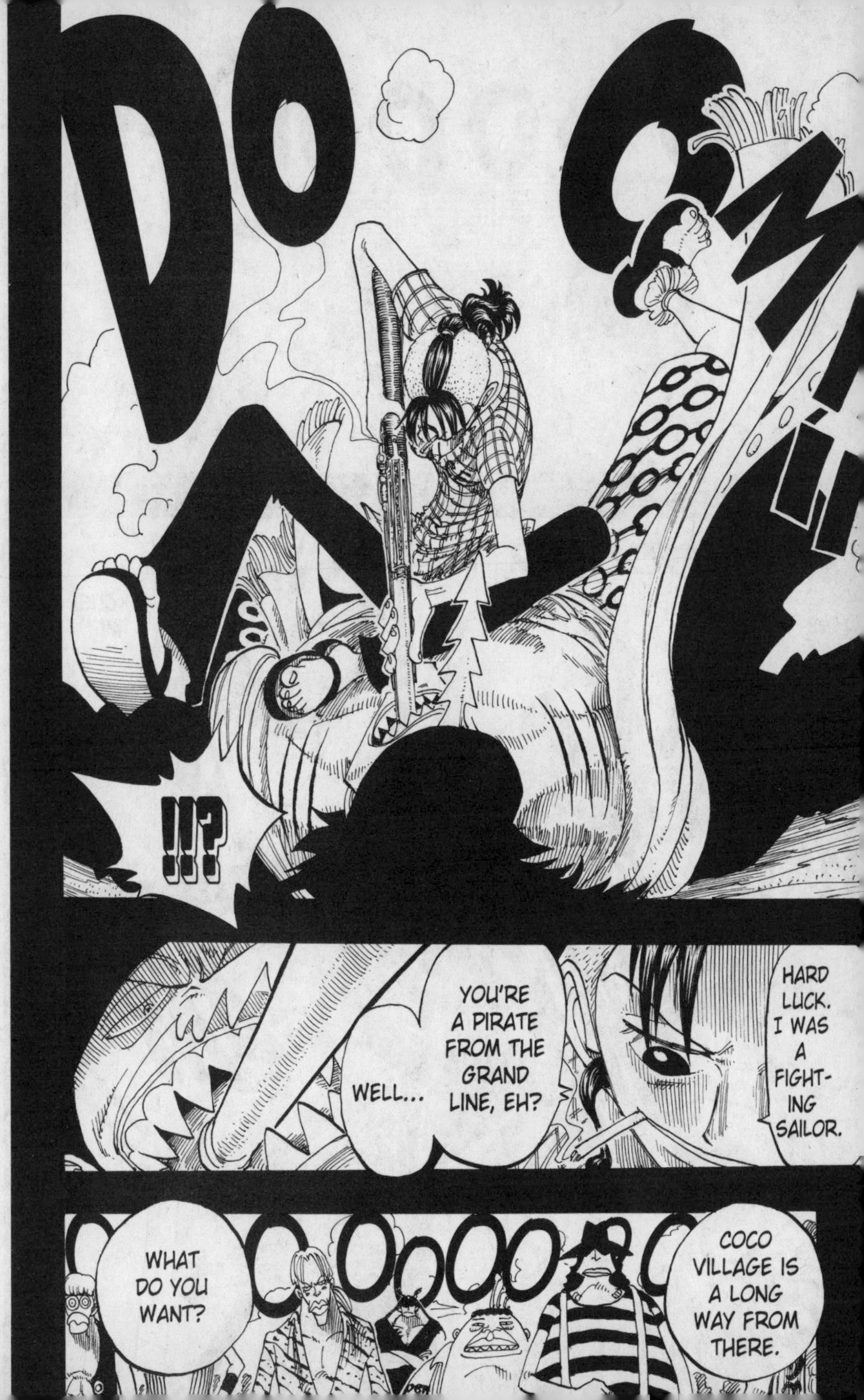
DOOM!!
!!?
HARD LUCK. I WAS A FIGHTING SAILOR.
WELL... YOU'RE A PIRATE FROM THE GRAND LINE, EH?
COCO VILLAGE IS A LONG WAY FROM THERE.
OOOOOOO
WHAT DO YOU WANT?

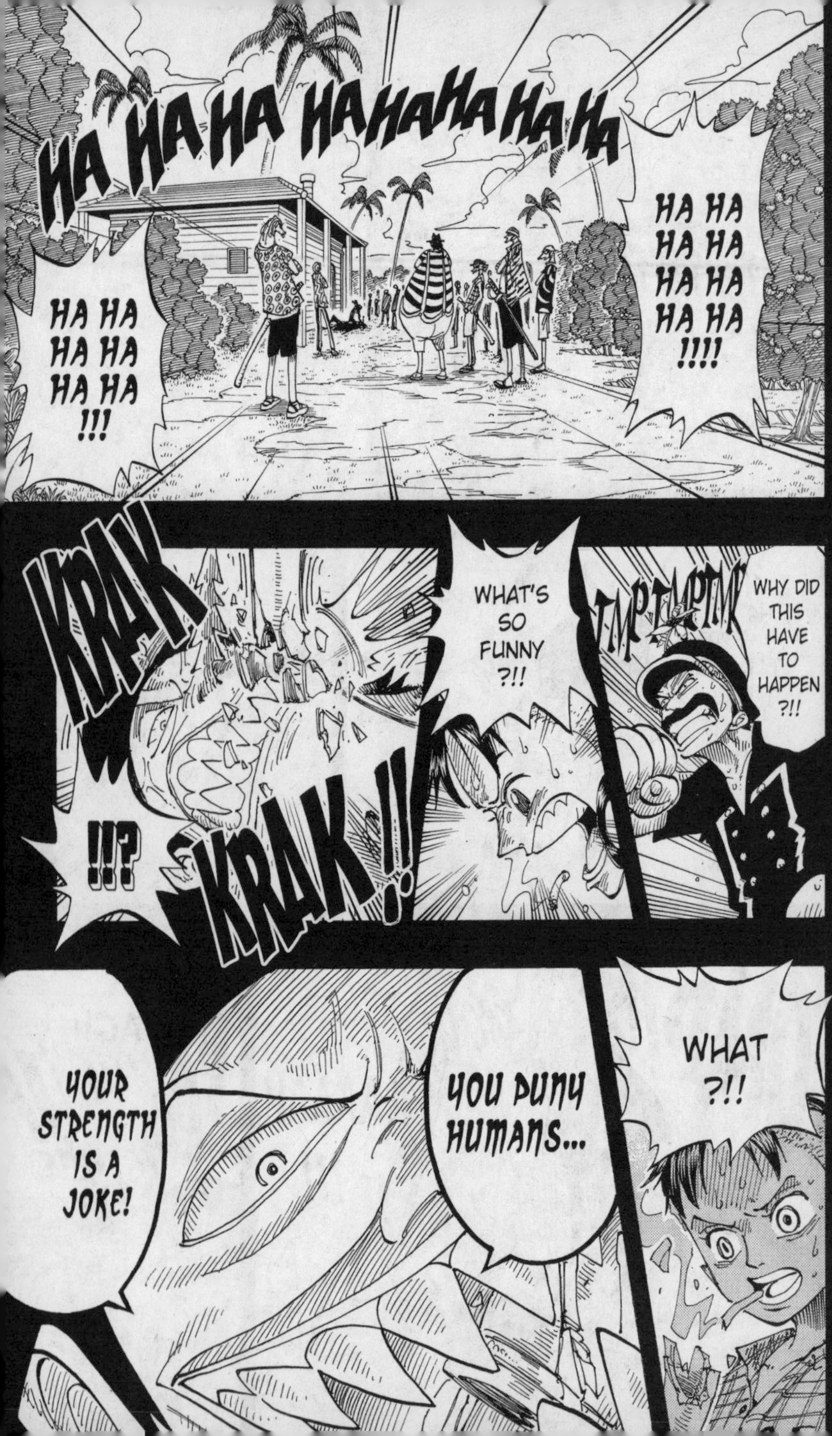
HA HA HA HAHAHAHAHA
HA HA HA HA HA HA HA HA !!!!
HA HA HA HA HA HA !!!
WHY DID THIS HAVE TO HAPPEN ?!!
TMP TMP TMP
WHAT'S SO FUNNY ?!!
KRAK
!!?
KRAK !!
WHAT ?!!
YOU PUNY HUMANS...
YOUR STRENGTH IS A JOKE!

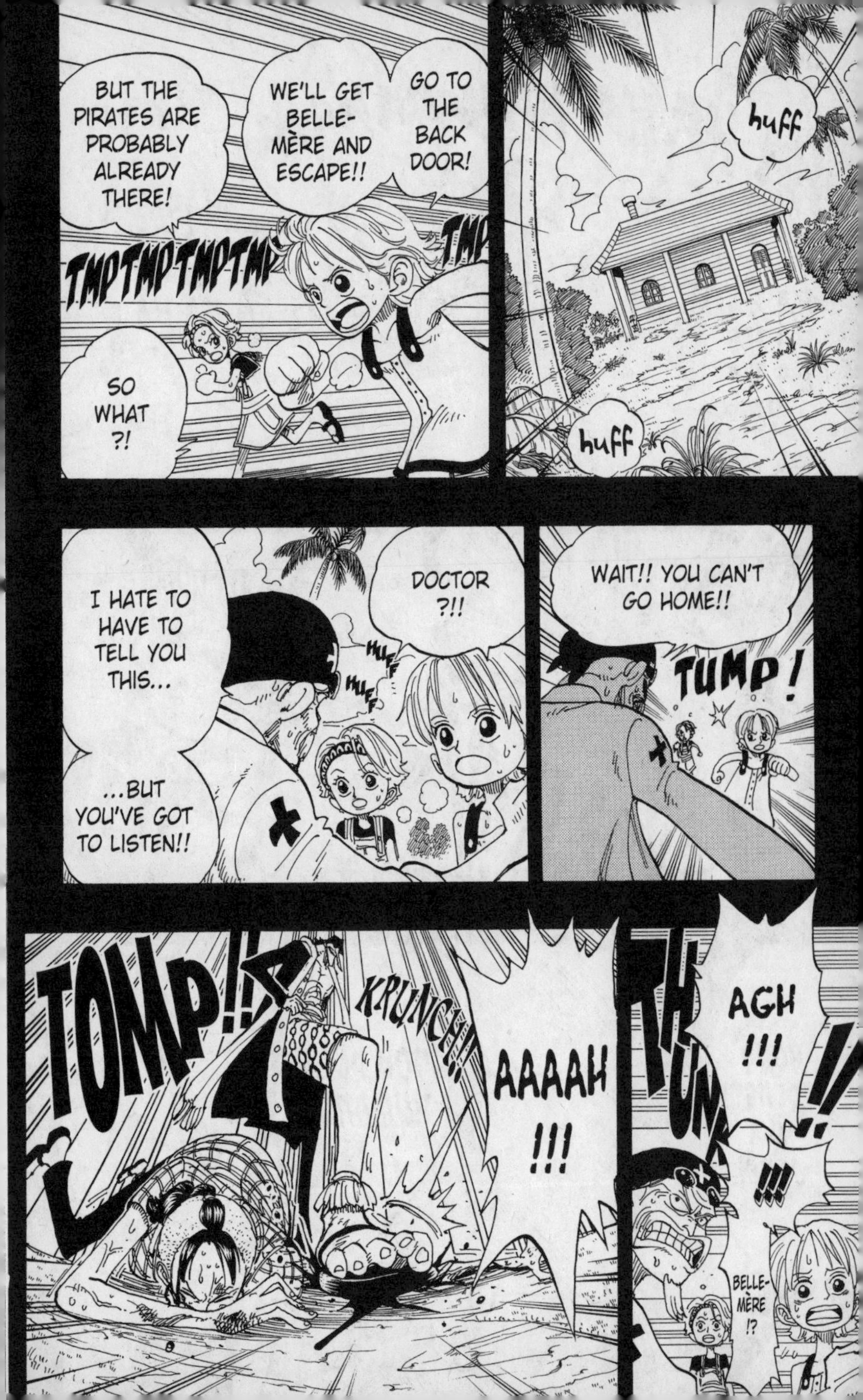
huff
huff
GO TO THE BACK DOOR!
WE'LL GET BELLE-MÈRE AND ESCAPE!!
TMP
BUT THE PIRATES ARE PROBABLY ALREADY THERE!
TMPTMPTMPTMP
SO WHAT?!
WAIT!! YOU CAN'T GO HOME!!
TUMP!
DOCTOR?!!
HUFF
HUFF
I HATE TO HAVE TO TELL YOU THIS...
...BUT YOU'VE GOT TO LISTEN!!
AGH!!!
THUNK!!
BELLE-MÈRE!?
AAAAH!!!
KRUNCH!!!
TOMP!!!

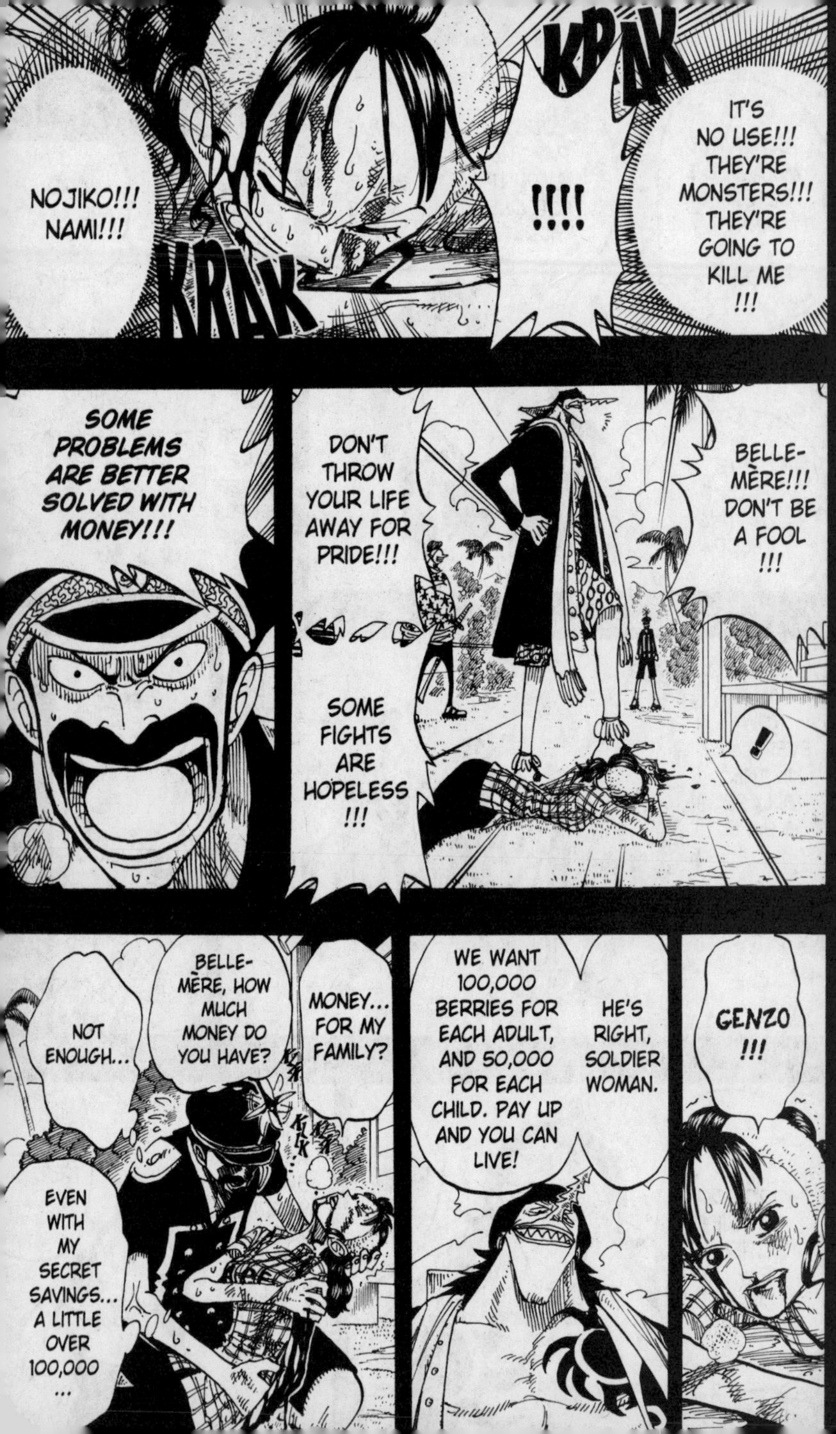
KRAK
IT'S NO USE!!! THEY'RE MONSTERS!!! THEY'RE GOING TO KILL ME !!!
!!!!
NOJIKO!!! NAMI!!!
KRAK
BELLE-MÈRE!!! DON'T BE A FOOL !!!
DON'T THROW YOUR LIFE AWAY FOR PRIDE!!!
!
SOME FIGHTS ARE HOPELESS !!!
SOME PROBLEMS ARE BETTER SOLVED WITH MONEY!!!
GENZO !!!
HE'S RIGHT, SOLDIER WOMAN.
WE WANT 100,000 BERRIES FOR EACH ADULT, AND 50,000 FOR EACH CHILD. PAY UP AND YOU CAN LIVE!
MONEY... FOR MY FAMILY?
BELLE-MÈRE, HOW MUCH MONEY DO YOU HAVE?
NOT ENOUGH...
EVEN WITH MY SECRET SAVINGS... A LITTLE OVER 100,000 ...

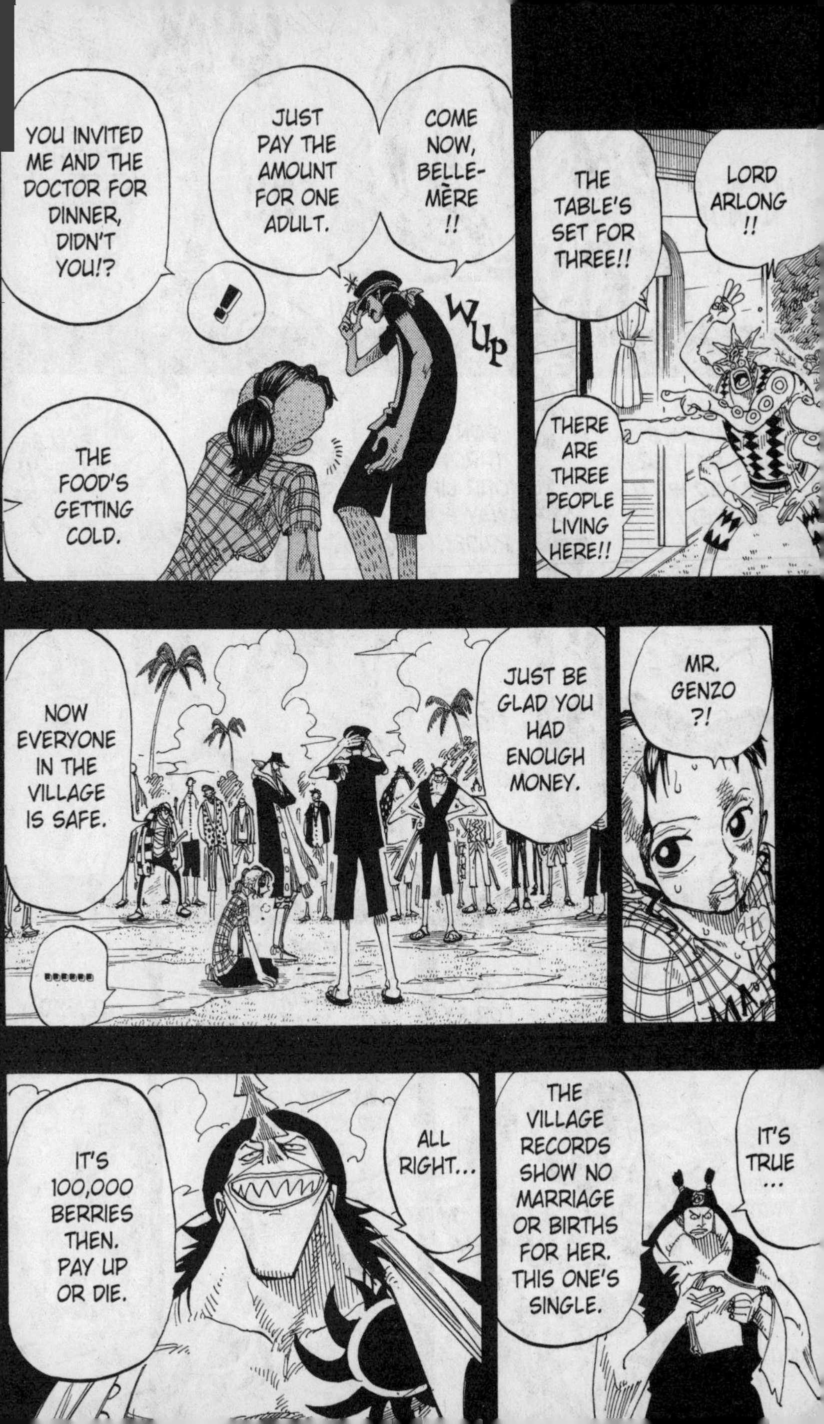
LORD ARLONG !!
THE TABLE'S SET FOR THREE!!
THERE ARE THREE PEOPLE LIVING HERE!!
COME NOW, BELLE-MÈRE !!
JUST PAY THE AMOUNT FOR ONE ADULT.
!
WUP
YOU INVITED ME AND THE DOCTOR FOR DINNER, DIDN'T YOU!?
THE FOOD'S GETTING COLD.
MR. GENZO ?!
JUST BE GLAD YOU HAD ENOUGH MONEY.
NOW EVERYONE IN THE VILLAGE IS SAFE.
......
IT'S TRUE ...
THE VILLAGE RECORDS SHOW NO MARRIAGE OR BIRTHS FOR HER. THIS ONE'S SINGLE.
ALL RIGHT...
IT'S 100,000 BERRIES THEN. PAY UP OR DIE.

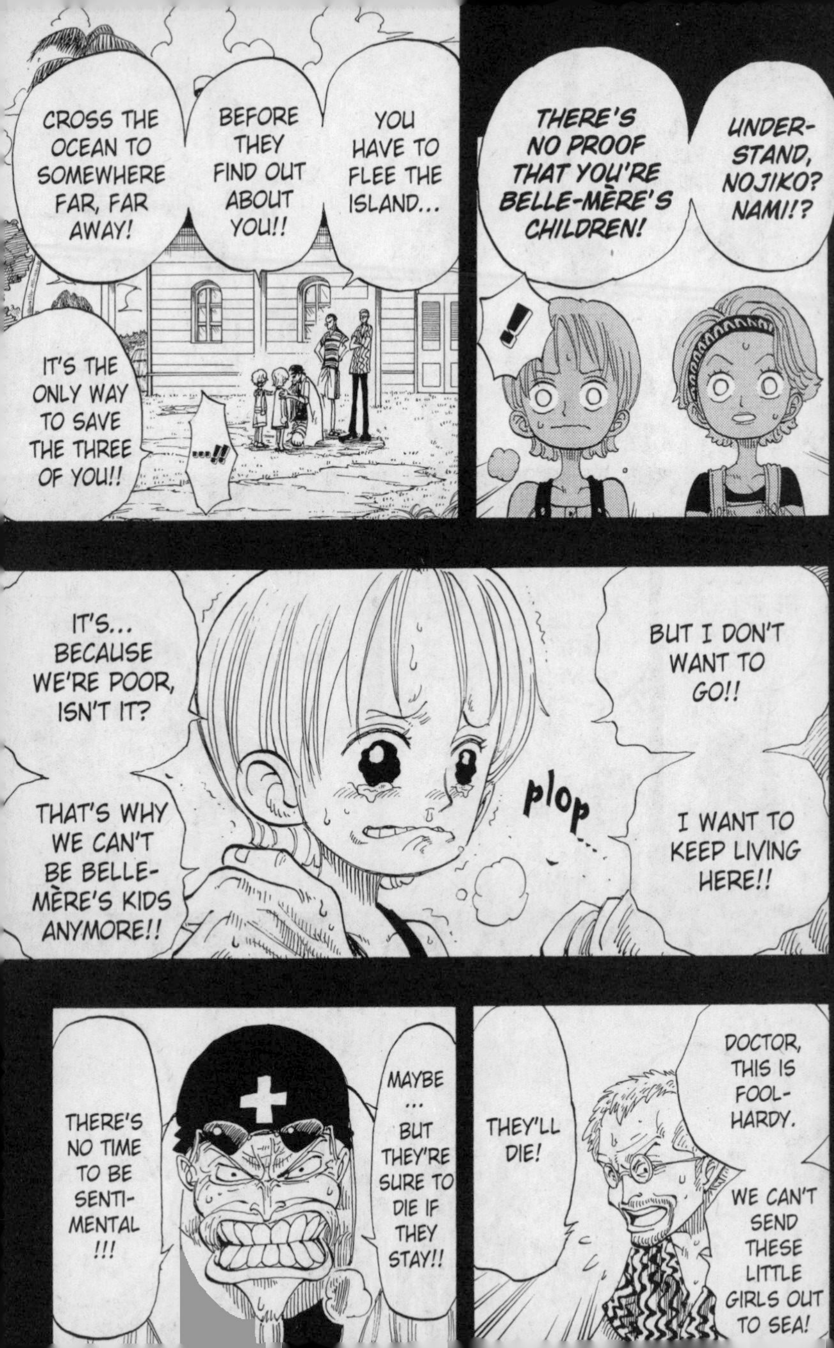
UNDER-STAND, NOJIKO? NAMI!?
THERE'S NO PROOF THAT YOU'RE BELLE-MÈRE'S CHILDREN!
!
YOU HAVE TO FLEE THE ISLAND...
BEFORE THEY FIND OUT ABOUT YOU!!
CROSS THE OCEAN TO SOMEWHERE FAR, FAR AWAY!
IT'S THE ONLY WAY TO SAVE THE THREE OF YOU!!
...!!
BUT I DON'T WANT TO GO!!
I WANT TO KEEP LIVING HERE!!
plop...
IT'S... BECAUSE WE'RE POOR, ISN'T IT?
THAT'S WHY WE CAN'T BE BELLE-MÈRE'S KIDS ANYMORE!!
DOCTOR, THIS IS FOOL-HARDY.
WE CAN'T SEND THESE LITTLE GIRLS OUT TO SEA!
THEY'LL DIE!
MAYBE... BUT THEY'RE SURE TO DIE IF THEY STAY!!
THERE'S NO TIME TO BE SENTI-MENTAL!!!

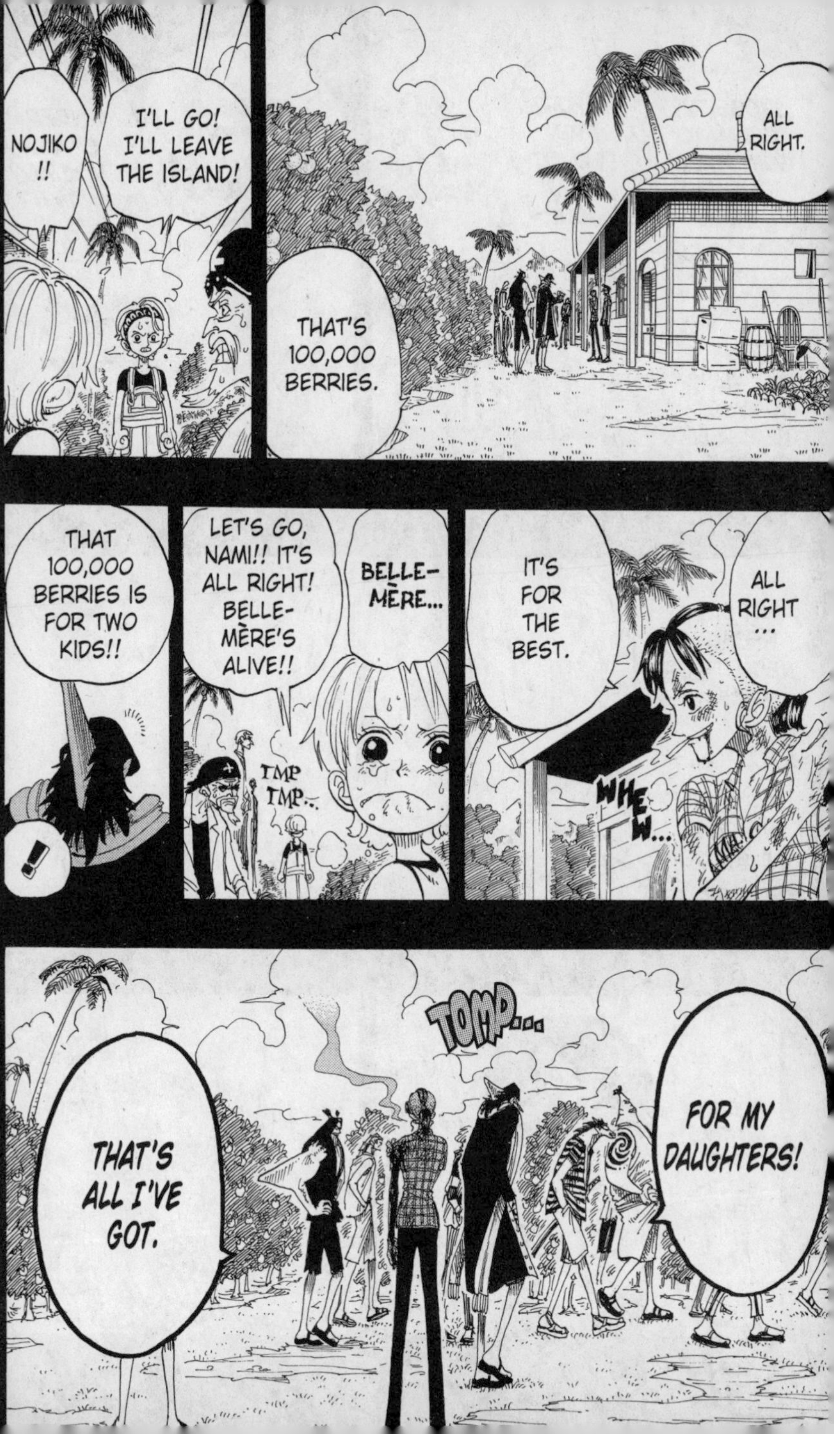
ALL RIGHT.
THAT'S 100,000 BERRIES.
I'LL GO! I'LL LEAVE THE ISLAND!
NOJIKO!!
ALL RIGHT...
IT'S FOR THE BEST.
WHEW...
BELLE-MÈRE...
LET'S GO, NAMI!! IT'S ALL RIGHT! BELLE-MÈRE'S ALIVE!!
TMP TMP...
THAT 100,000 BERRIES IS FOR TWO KIDS!!
!
TOMP...
FOR MY DAUGHTERS!
THAT'S ALL I'VE GOT.

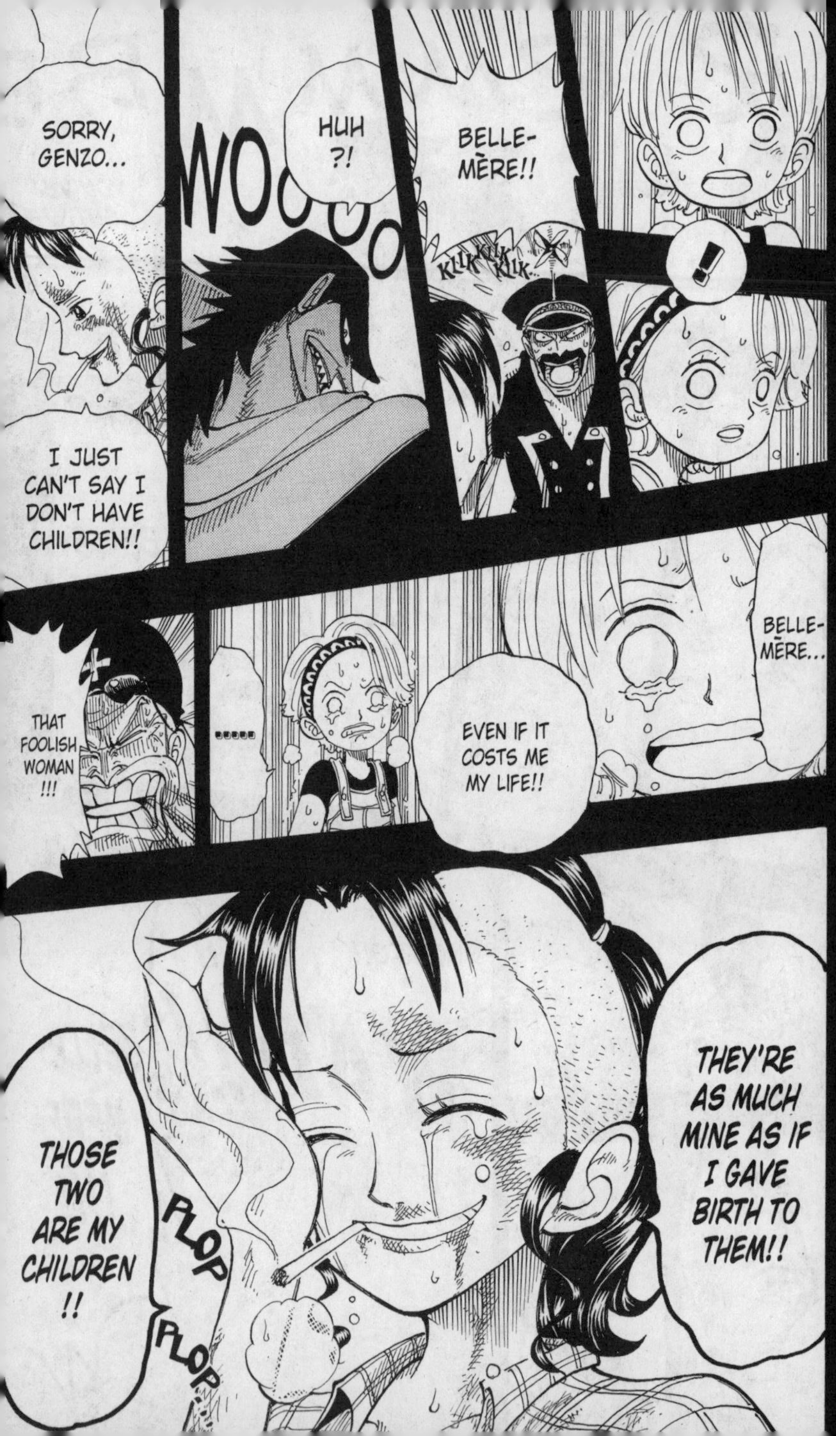
!
BELLE-MÈRE!!
KLIK KLIK KLIK
HUH ?!
WOOOOO
SORRY, GENZO...
I JUST CAN'T SAY I DON'T HAVE CHILDREN!!
BELLE-MÈRE...
EVEN IF IT COSTS ME MY LIFE!!
......
THAT FOOLISH WOMAN !!!
THEY'RE AS MUCH MINE AS IF I GAVE BIRTH TO THEM!!
THOSE TWO ARE MY CHILDREN !!
PLOP
PLOP

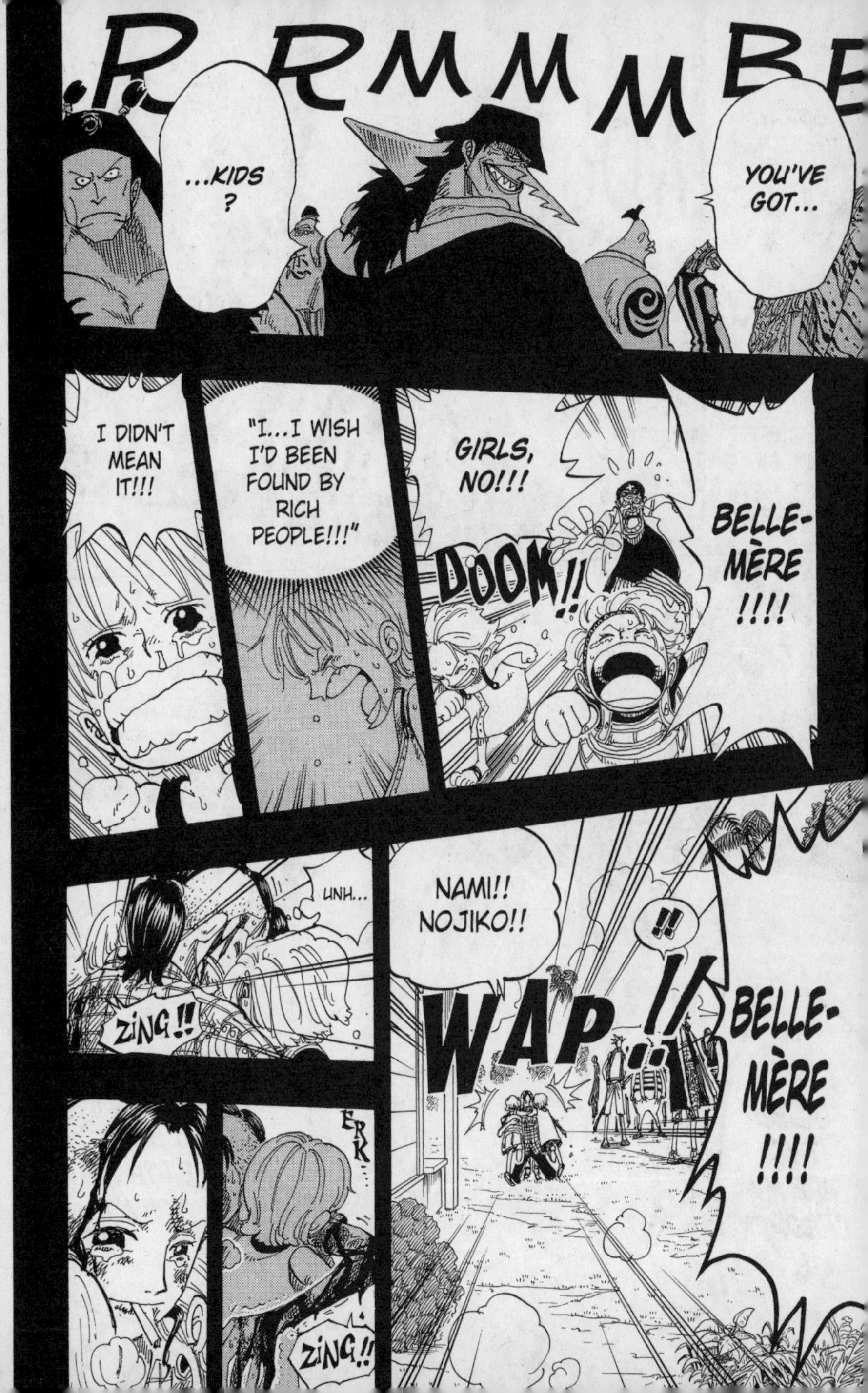
RRMMMBE
YOU'VE GOT...
...KIDS ?
GIRLS, NO!!!
DOOM!!
BELLE-MÈRE!!!!
"I...I WISH I'D BEEN FOUND BY RICH PEOPLE!!!"
I DIDN'T MEAN IT!!!
BELLE-MÈRE!!!!
!!
NAMI!! NOJIKO!!
WAP!!
UNH...
ZING!!
ERK...
ZING!!

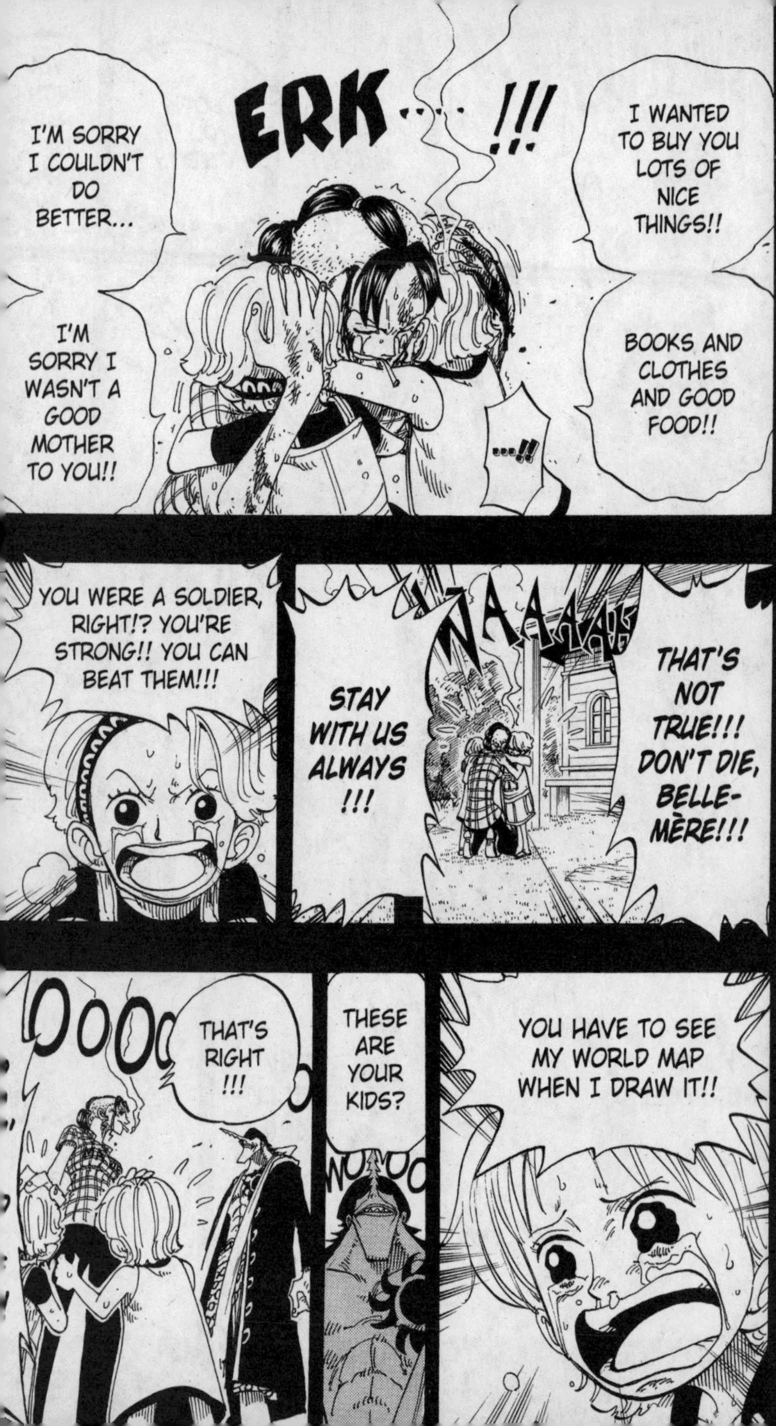
I WANTED TO BUY YOU LOTS OF NICE THINGS!!
ERK.....!!!
I'M SORRY I COULDN'T DO BETTER...
BOOKS AND CLOTHES AND GOOD FOOD!!
...!!
I'M SORRY I WASN'T A GOOD MOTHER TO YOU!!
THAT'S NOT TRUE!!! DON'T DIE, BELLE-MÈRE!!!
STAY WITH US ALWAYS!!!
YOU WERE A SOLDIER, RIGHT!? YOU'RE STRONG!! YOU CAN BEAT THEM!!!
YOU HAVE TO SEE MY WORLD MAP WHEN I DRAW IT!!
THESE ARE YOUR KIDS?
THAT'S RIGHT!!!

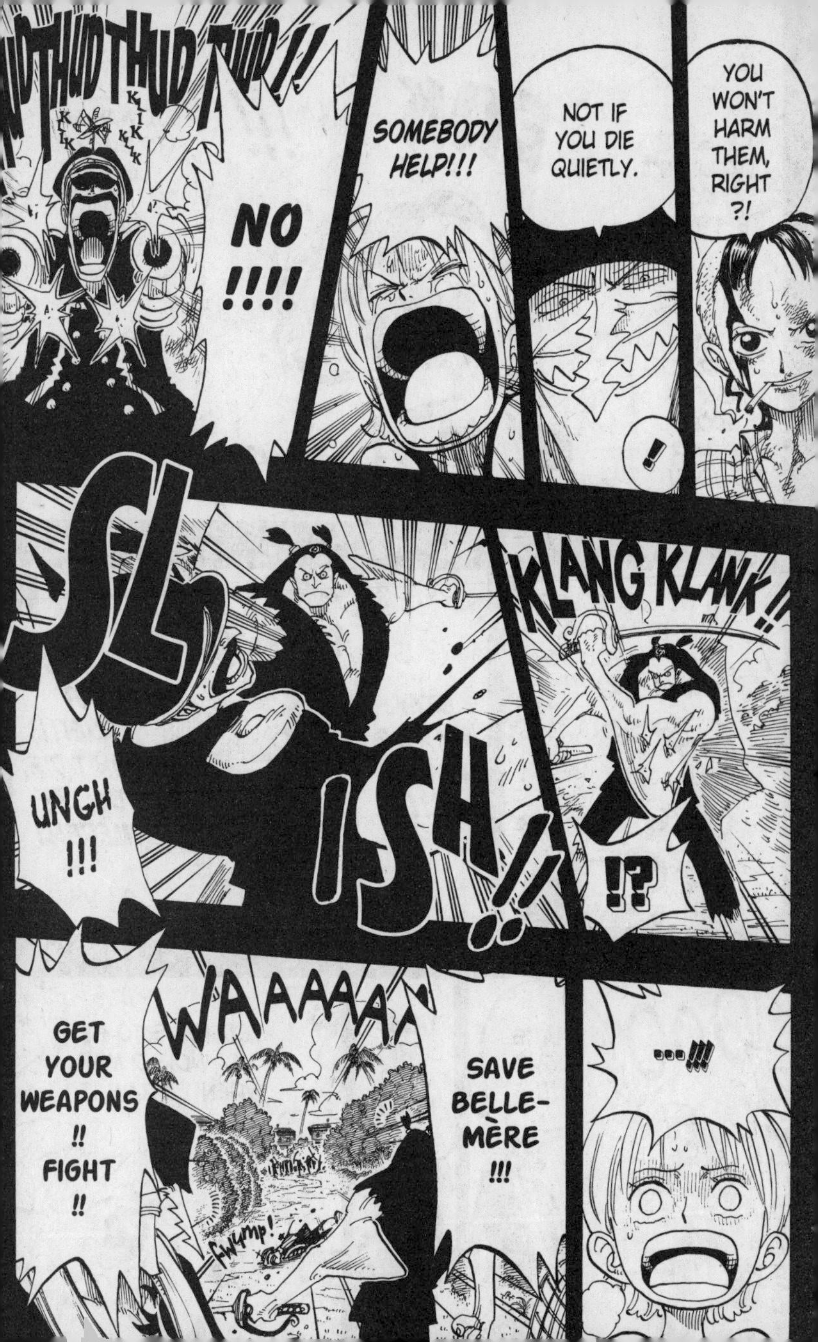
YOU WON'T HARM THEM, RIGHT ?!
NOT IF YOU DIE QUIETLY.
!
SOMEBODY HELP!!!
NO !!!!
UD THUD THUD THUD!!
KLIK KLIK KLIK
KLANG KLANK!!
!?
SLISH!!
UNGH !!!
...!!!
SAVE BELLE-MÈRE !!!
WAAAAAA
fwump!
GET YOUR WEAPONS !! FIGHT !!

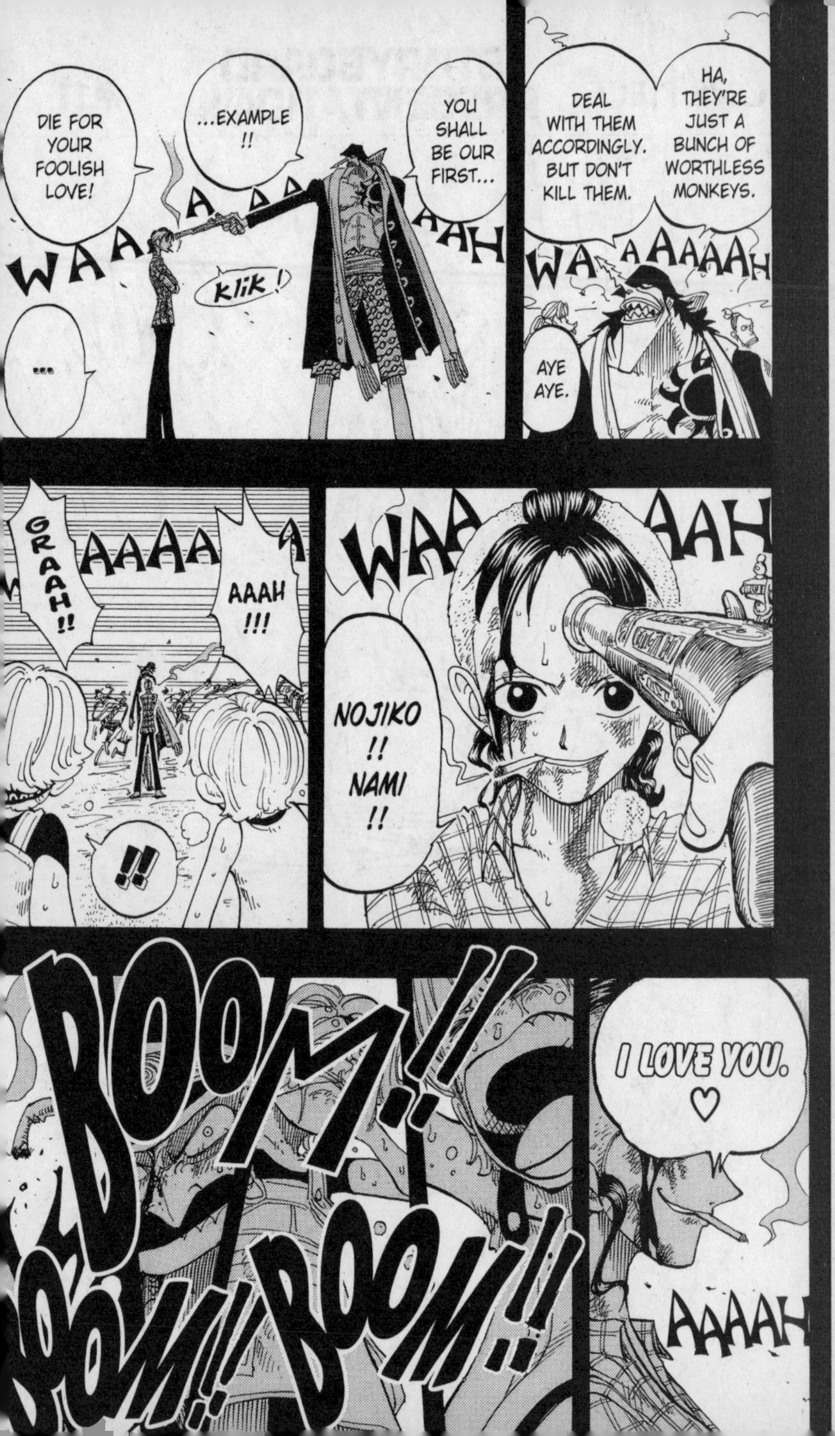
HA, THEY'RE JUST A BUNCH OF WORTHLESS MONKEYS.
DEAL WITH THEM ACCORDINGLY. BUT DON'T KILL THEM.
WAAAAAAH
AYE AYE.
YOU SHALL BE OUR FIRST...
...EXAMPLE !!
DIE FOR YOUR FOOLISH LOVE!
WAAAAAAAH
klik!
...
WAA AAH
NOJIKO !! NAMI !!
GRAAAH!!
AAAAA
AAAH !!!
!!
I LOVE YOU. ♥
AAAAH
BOOM!!
BOOM!!
BOOM!!

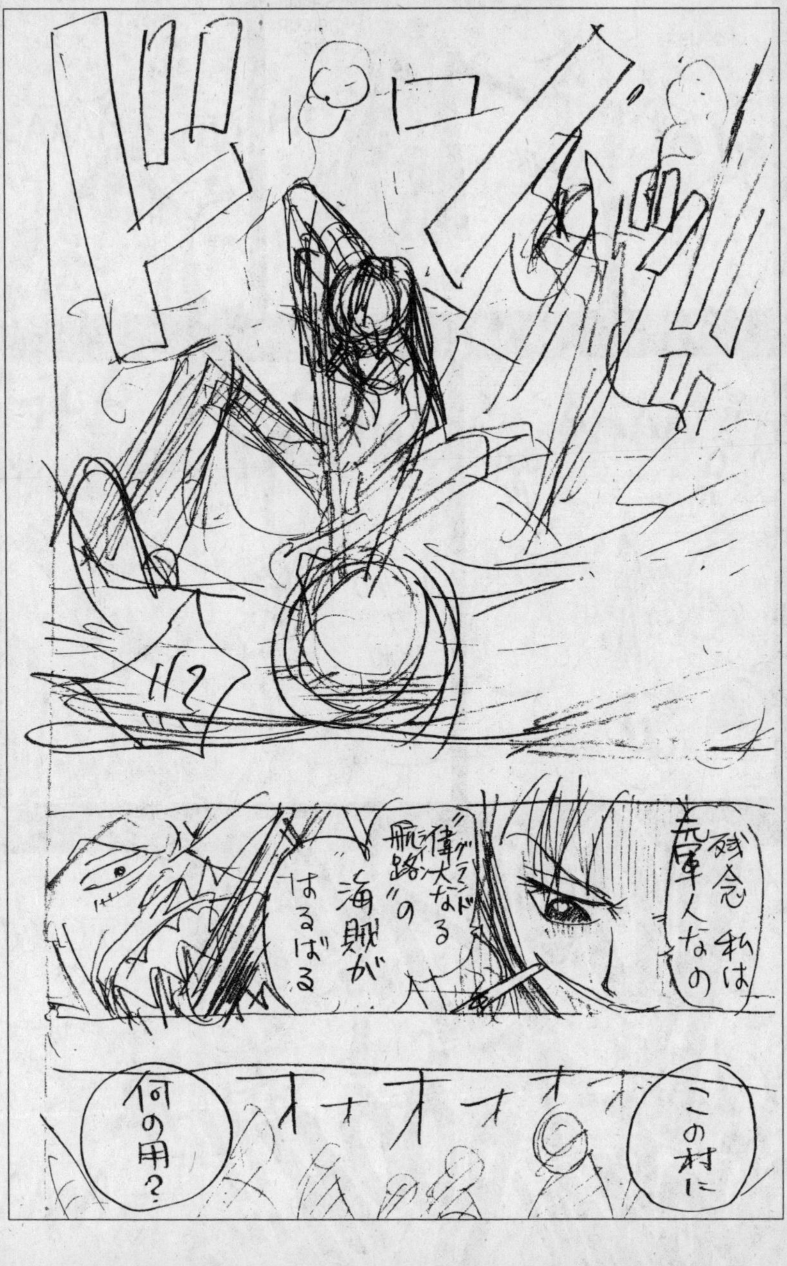
残念 私は
海軍人なの
“偉大なる航路(グランドライン)”の海賊がはるばる
この村に
オオオオオ
何の用?

# Chapter 79: TO LIVE

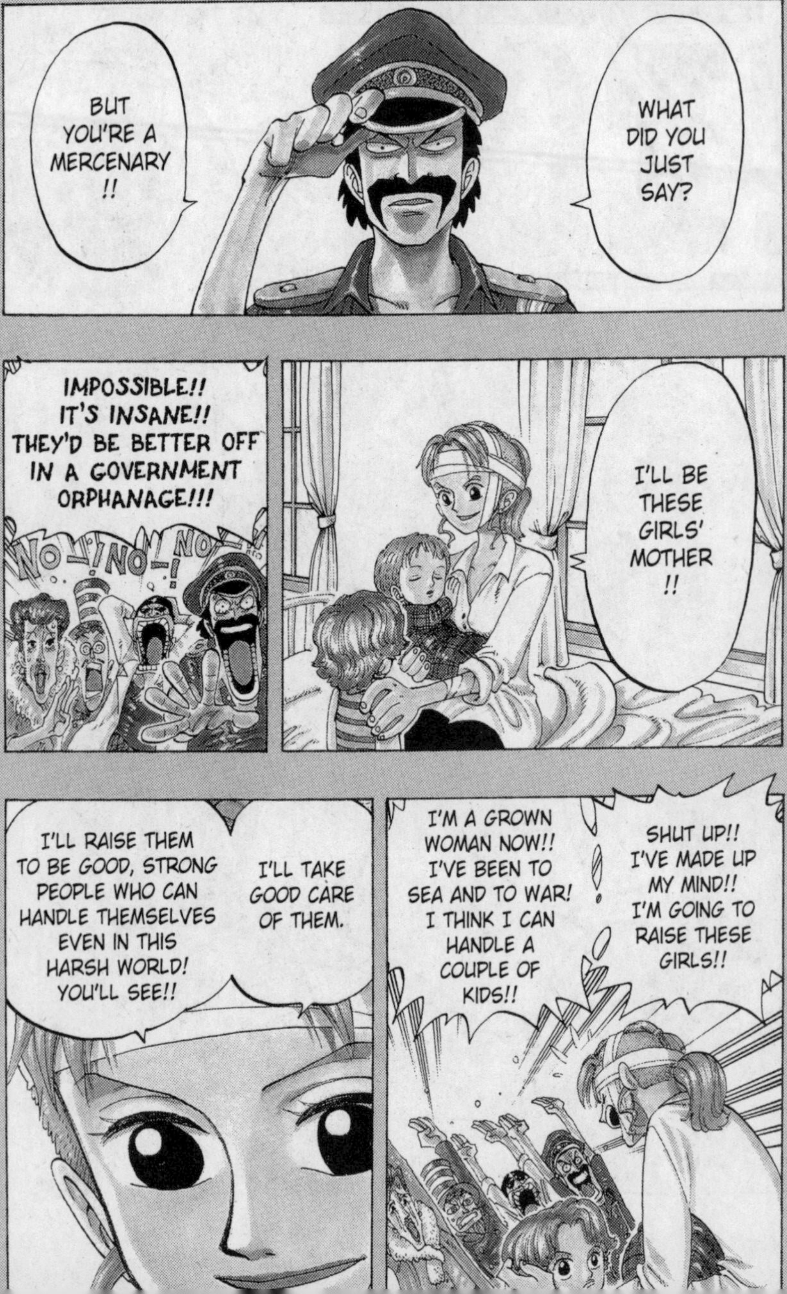
WHAT DID YOU JUST SAY?
BUT YOU'RE A MERCENARY !!
I'LL BE THESE GIRLS' MOTHER !!
IMPOSSIBLE!! IT'S INSANE!! THEY'D BE BETTER OFF IN A GOVERNMENT ORPHANAGE!!!
NO--!! NO--!! NO--!!
SHUT UP!! I'VE MADE UP MY MIND!! I'M GOING TO RAISE THESE GIRLS!!
I'M A GROWN WOMAN NOW!! I'VE BEEN TO SEA AND TO WAR! I THINK I CAN HANDLE A COUPLE OF KIDS!!
I'LL TAKE GOOD CARE OF THEM.
I'LL RAISE THEM TO BE GOOD, STRONG PEOPLE WHO CAN HANDLE THEMSELVES EVEN IN THIS HARSH WORLD! YOU'LL SEE!!

# Chapter 79: TO LIVE

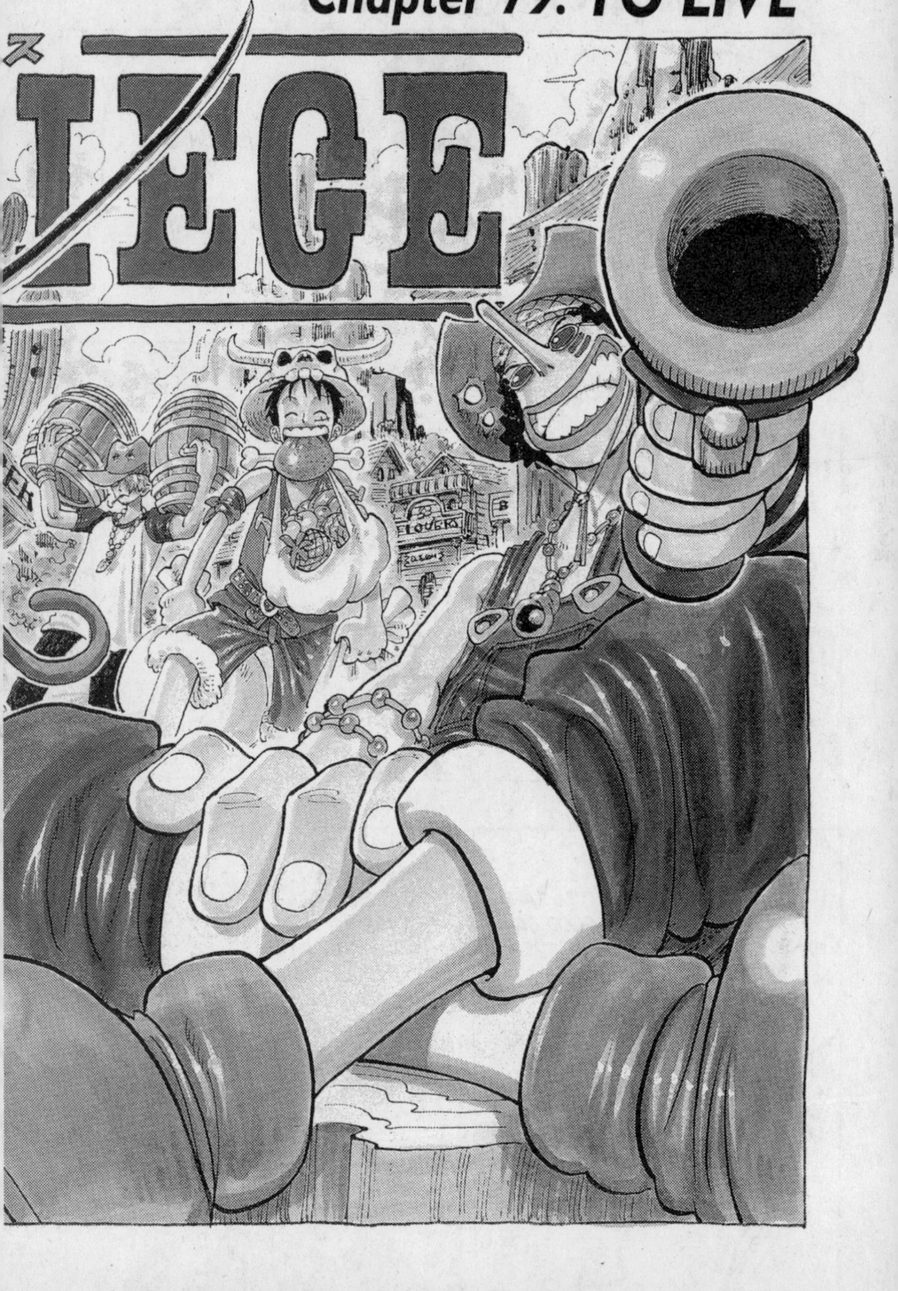
LEGE

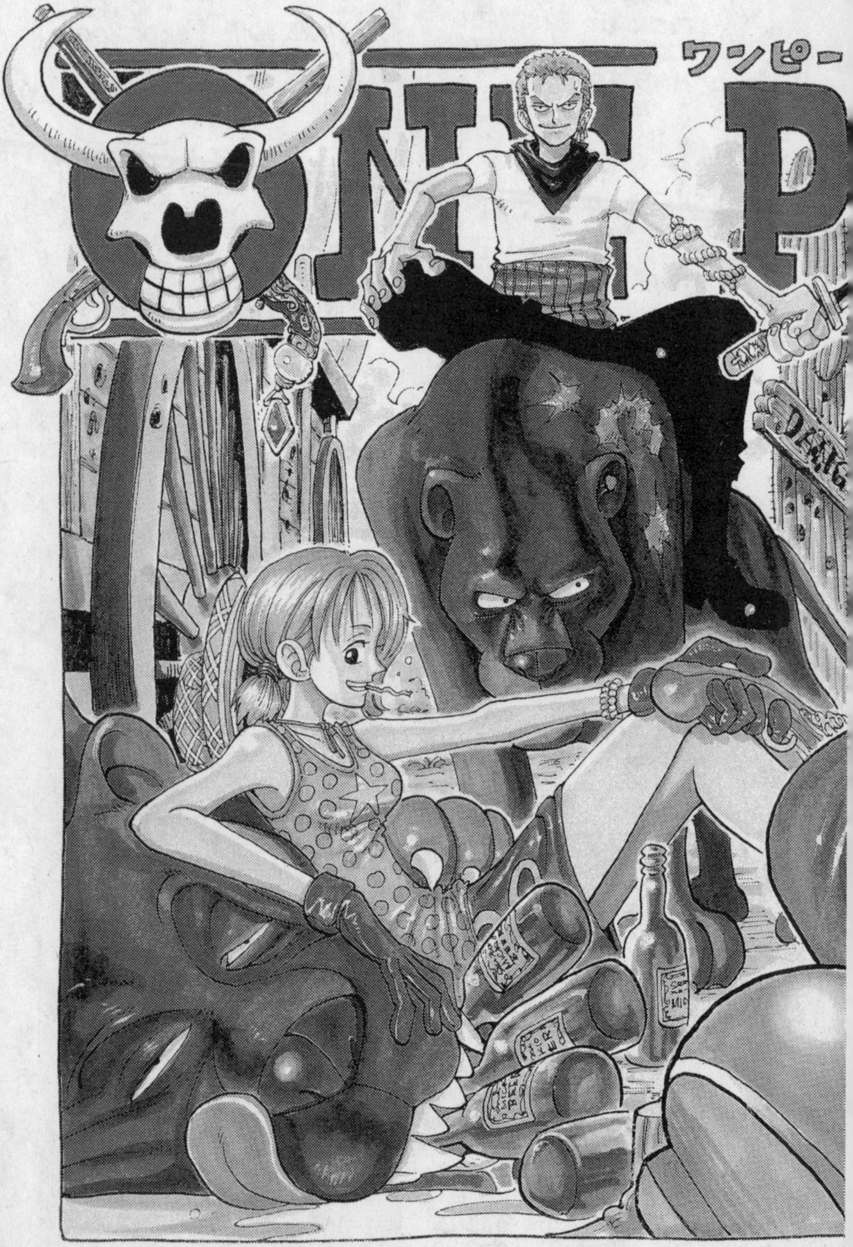
ワンピー

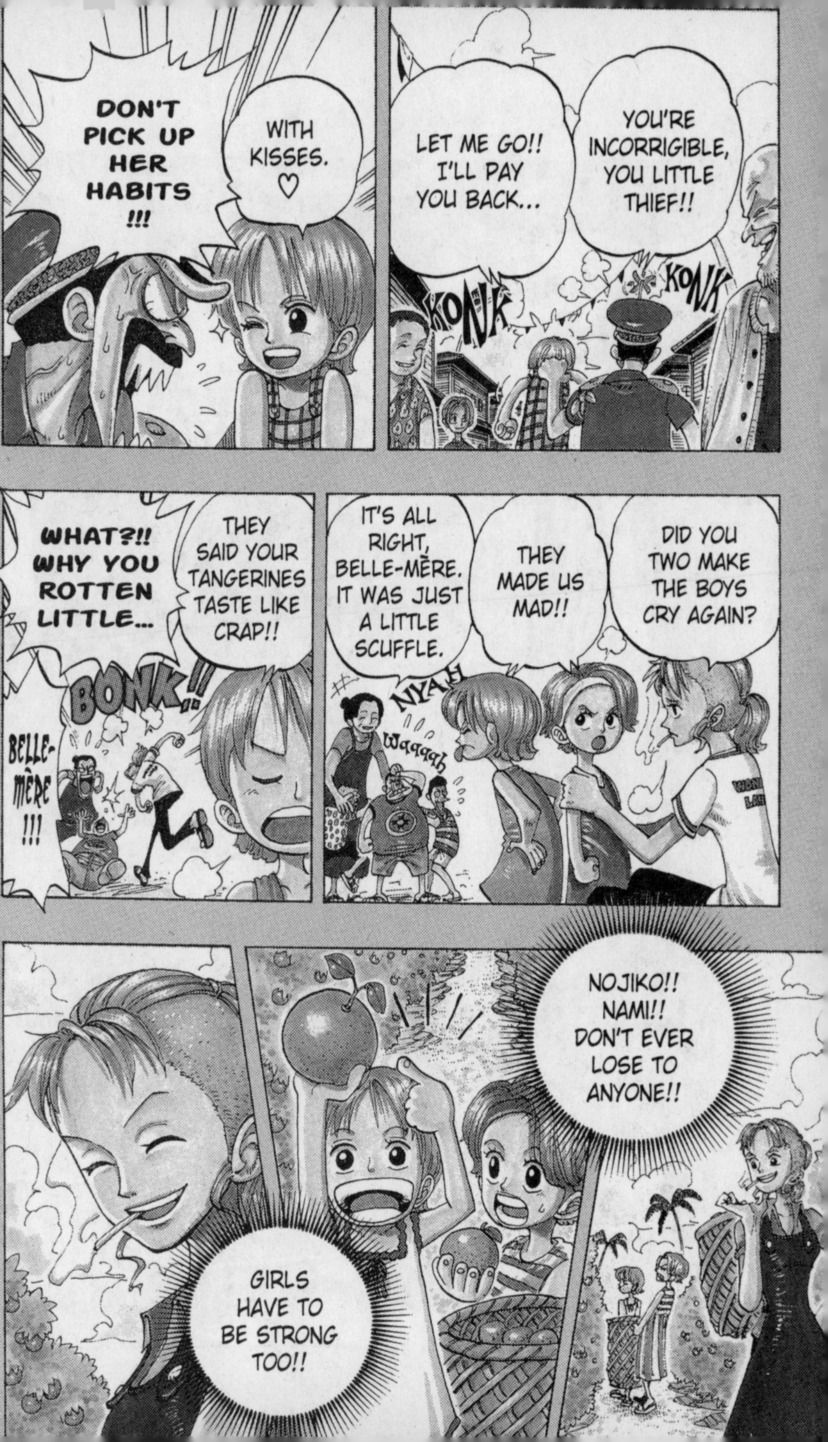
YOU'RE INCORRIGIBLE, YOU LITTLE THIEF!!
LET ME GO!! I'LL PAY YOU BACK...
KONK
KONK
WITH KISSES. ♡
DON'T PICK UP HER HABITS!!!
DID YOU TWO MAKE THE BOYS CRY AGAIN?
THEY MADE US MAD!!
IT'S ALL RIGHT, BELLE-MÈRE. IT WAS JUST A LITTLE SCUFFLE.
NYAH
Waaaah
THEY SAID YOUR TANGERINES TASTE LIKE CRAP!!
WHAT?!! WHY YOU ROTTEN LITTLE...
BONK!!
BELLE-MÈRE!!!
NOJIKO!! NAMI!! DON'T EVER LOSE TO ANYONE!!
GIRLS HAVE TO BE STRONG TOO!!

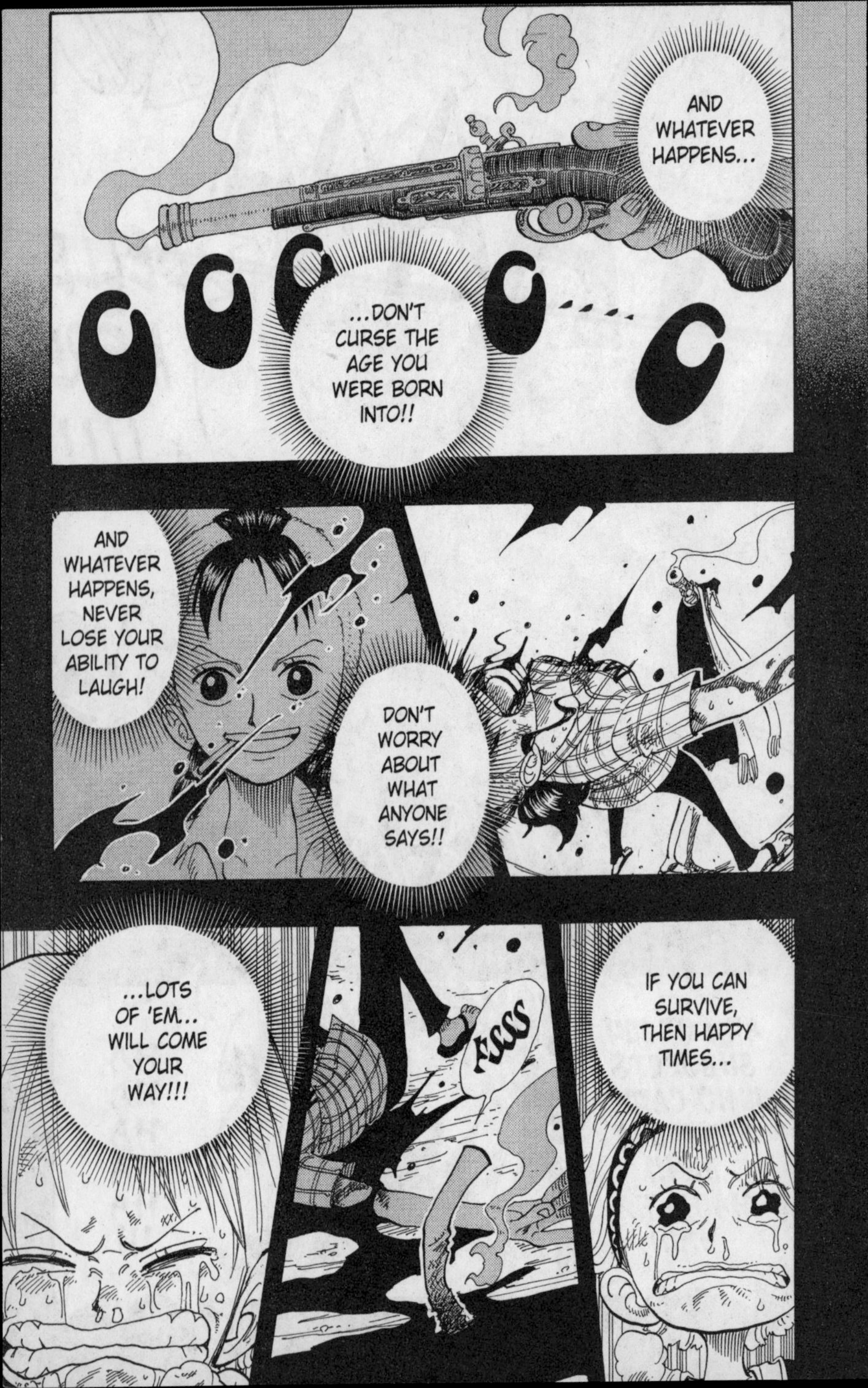
AND WHATEVER HAPPENS...
...DON'T CURSE THE AGE YOU WERE BORN INTO!!
DON'T WORRY ABOUT WHAT ANYONE SAYS!!
AND WHATEVER HAPPENS, NEVER LOSE YOUR ABILITY TO LAUGH!
IF YOU CAN SURVIVE, THEN HAPPY TIMES...
FSSS
...LOTS OF 'EM... WILL COME YOUR WAY!!!

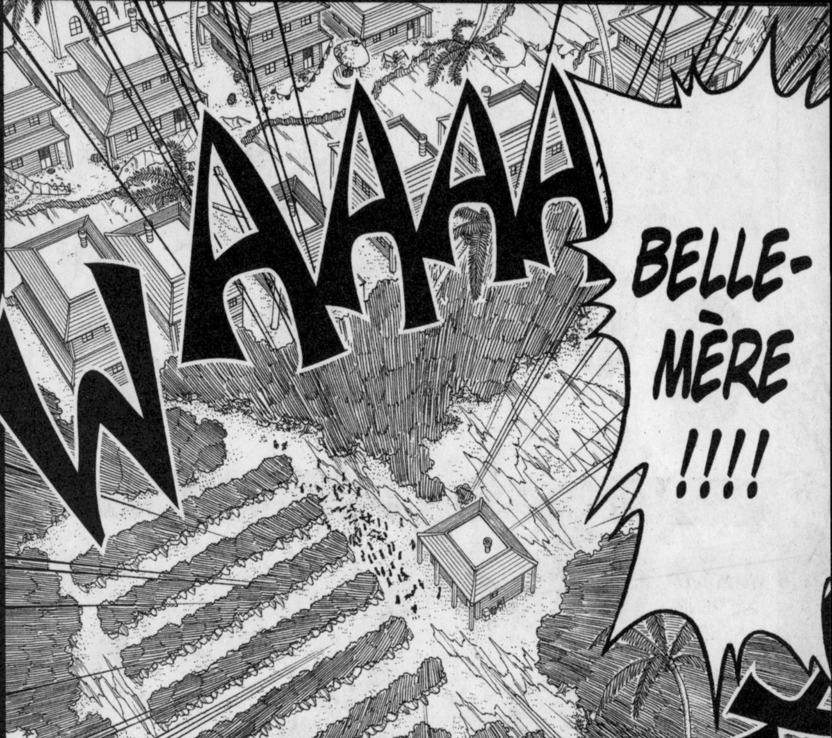
WAAAA
BELLE-MÈRE!!!!

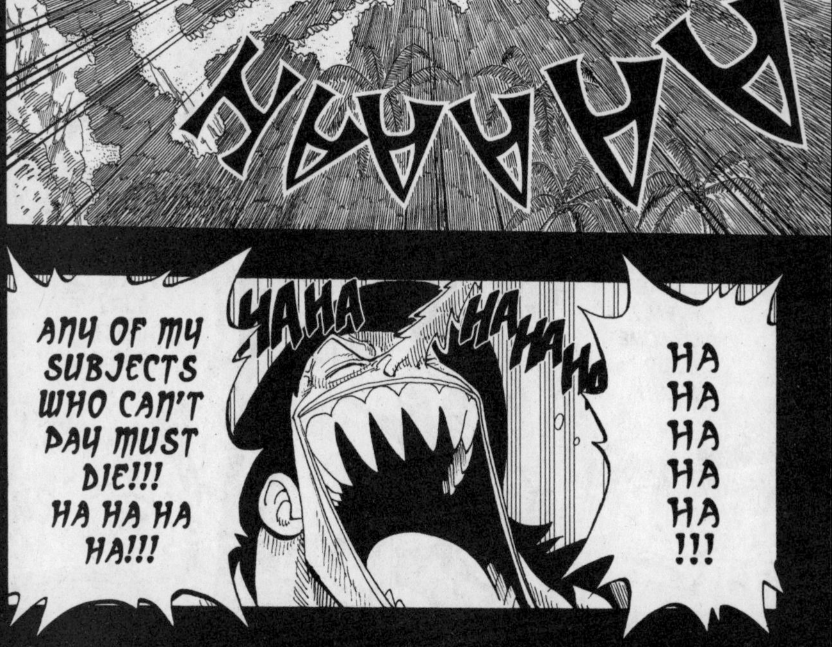
HA HA HA HA HA !!!
HAHA
HAHAHAHO
ANY OF MY SUBJECTS WHO CAN'T PAY MUST DIE!!! HA HA HA HA!!!

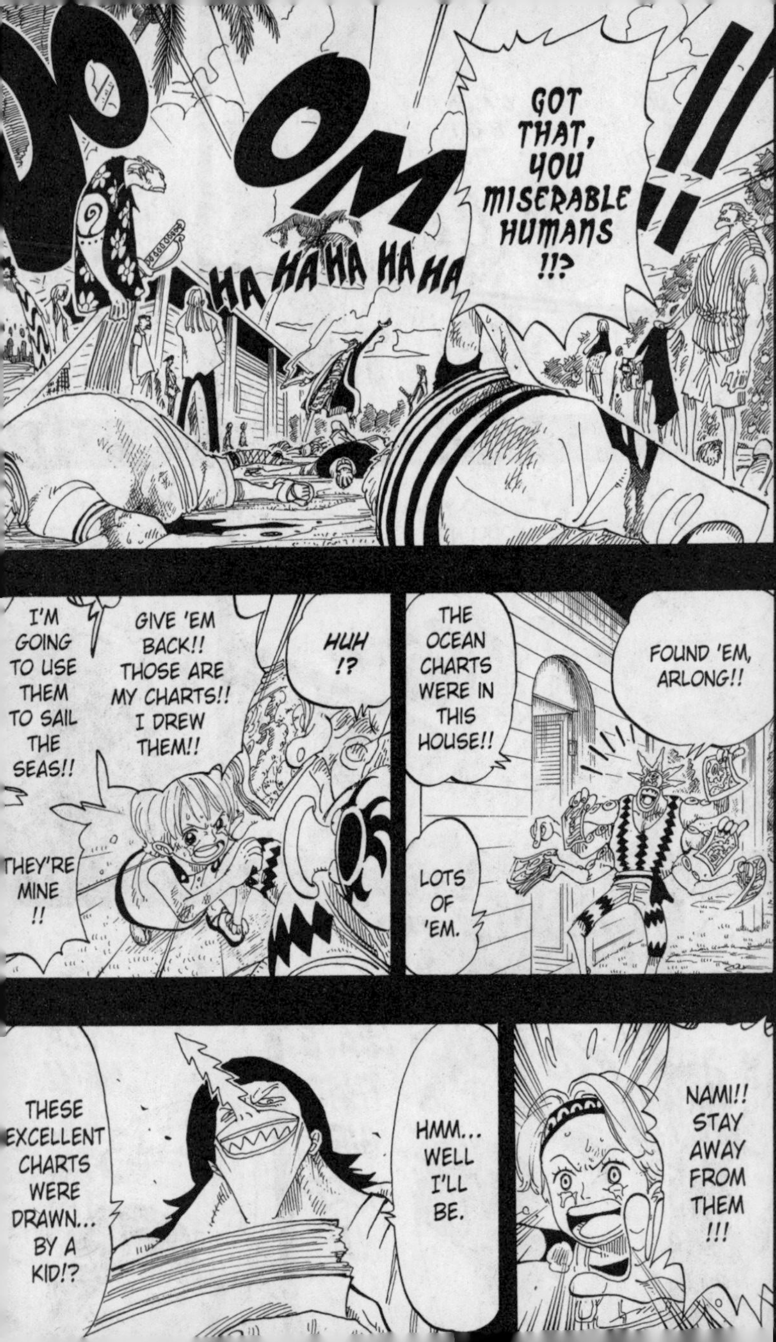
GOT THAT, YOU MISERABLE HUMANS !!?
HA HA HA HA HA HA
FOUND 'EM, ARLONG!!
THE OCEAN CHARTS WERE IN THIS HOUSE!!
LOTS OF 'EM.
HUH !?
GIVE 'EM BACK!! THOSE ARE MY CHARTS!! I DREW THEM!!
I'M GOING TO USE THEM TO SAIL THE SEAS!!
THEY'RE MINE !!
NAMI!! STAY AWAY FROM THEM !!!
HMM... WELL I'LL BE.
THESE EXCELLENT CHARTS WERE DRAWN... BY A KID!?

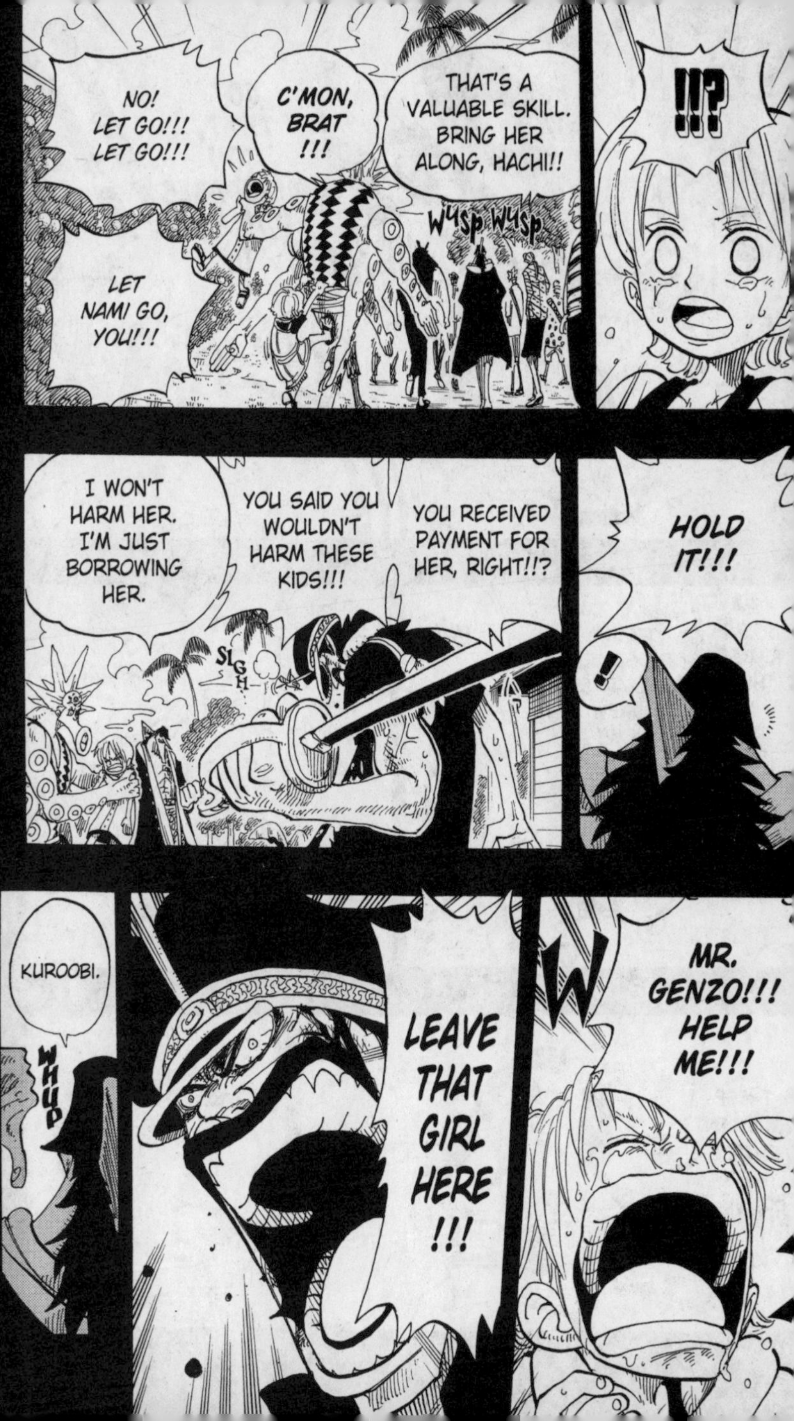
!!?
THAT'S A VALUABLE SKILL. BRING HER ALONG, HACHI!!
C'MON, BRAT !!!
NO! LET GO!!! LET GO!!!
WUSP WUSP
LET NAMI GO, YOU!!!
HOLD IT!!!
!
YOU RECEIVED PAYMENT FOR HER, RIGHT!!?
YOU SAID YOU WOULDN'T HARM THESE KIDS!!!
I WON'T HARM HER. I'M JUST BORROWING HER.
SIGH
MR. GENZO!!! HELP ME!!!
W
LEAVE THAT GIRL HERE!!!
KUROOBI.
WHUP

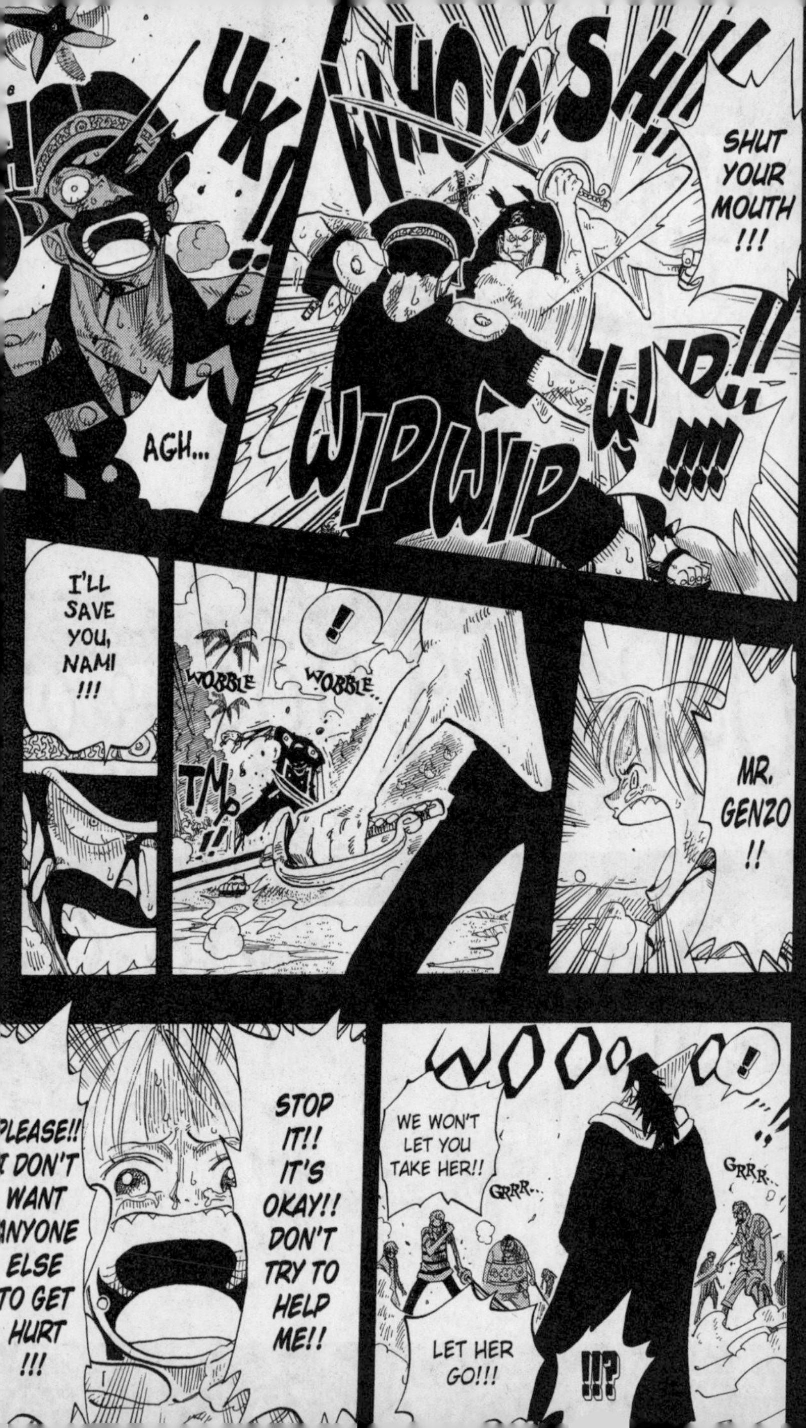
WHOOSH!!
SHUT YOUR MOUTH!!!
WUD!!!!!!
WIP WIP
UK!!
AGH...
MR. GENZO!!
!
WOBBLE WOBBLE
TMP!!
I'LL SAVE YOU, NAMI!!!
WOOOO!
WE WON'T LET YOU TAKE HER!!
GRRR...
GRRR...
LET HER GO!!!
!!?
STOP IT!! IT'S OKAY!! DON'T TRY TO HELP ME!!
PLEASE!! I DON'T WANT ANYONE ELSE TO GET HURT!!!

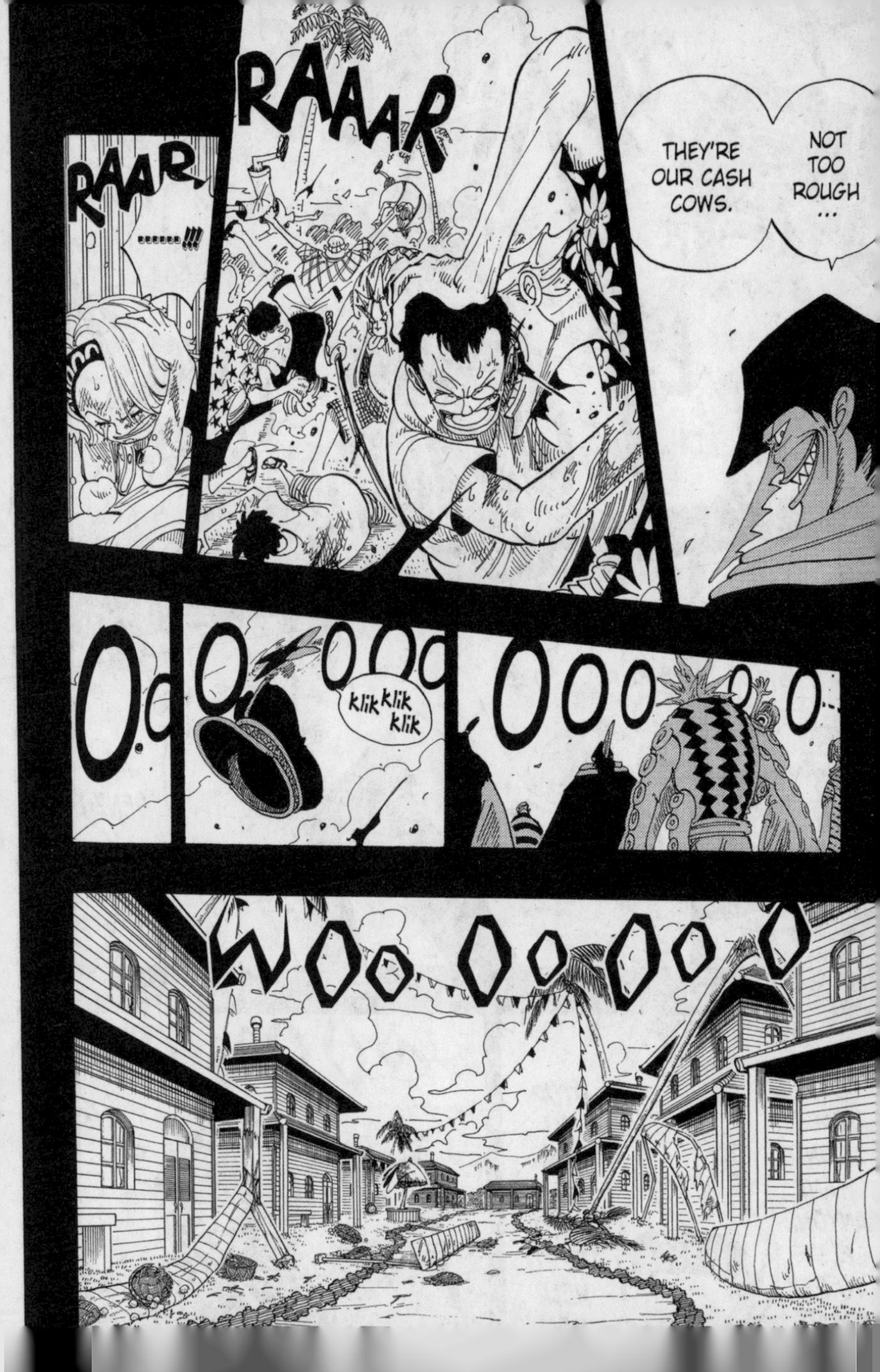
NOT TOO ROUGH ...
THEY'RE OUR CASH COWS.
RAAAR
RAAR
......!!!
OOOO...
OOOO
klik klik klik
OO
WOOOOOOO

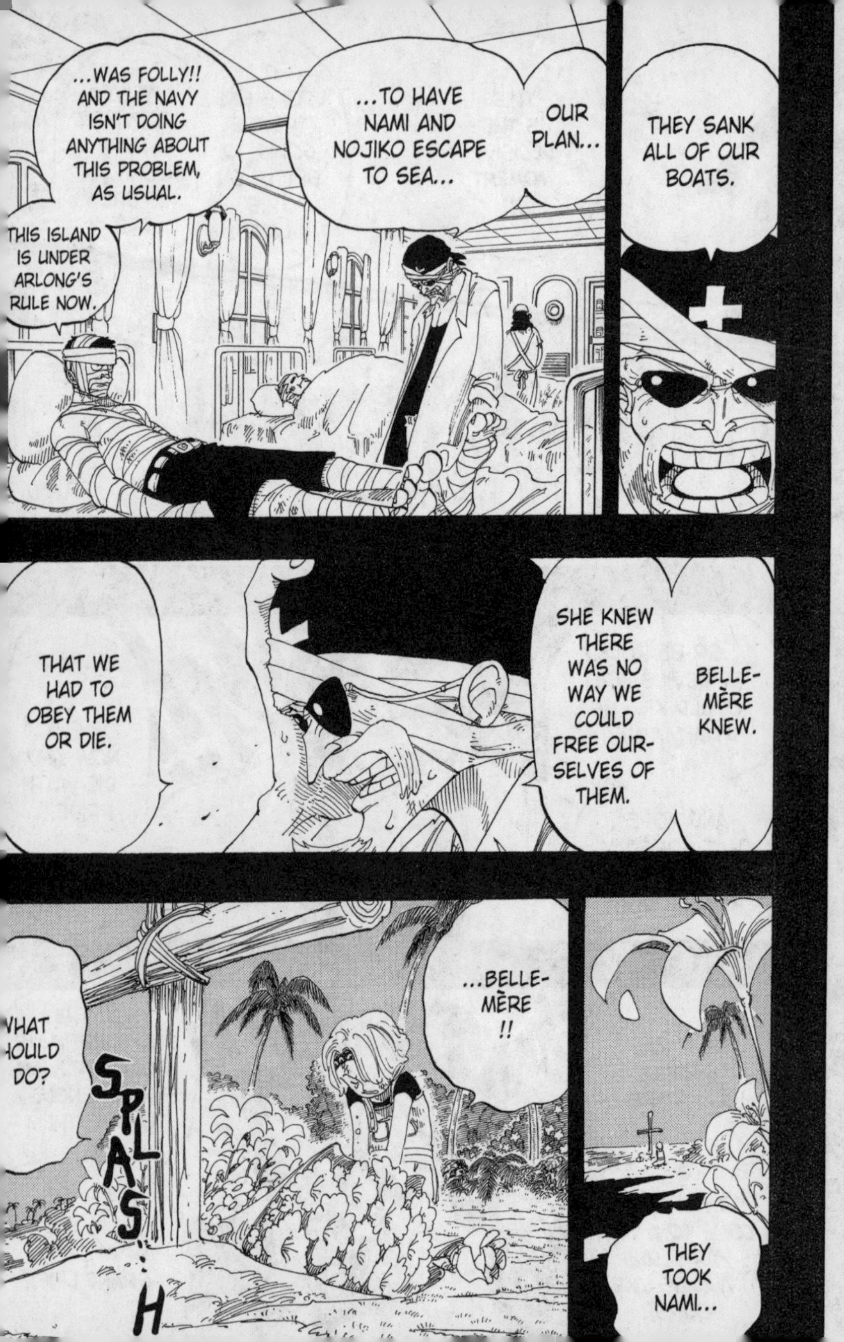
THEY SANK ALL OF OUR BOATS.
OUR PLAN...
...TO HAVE NAMI AND NOJIKO ESCAPE TO SEA...
...WAS FOLLY!! AND THE NAVY ISN'T DOING ANYTHING ABOUT THIS PROBLEM, AS USUAL.
THIS ISLAND IS UNDER ARLONG'S RULE NOW.
BELLE-MÈRE KNEW.
SHE KNEW THERE WAS NO WAY WE COULD FREE OURSELVES OF THEM.
THAT WE HAD TO OBEY THEM OR DIE.
THEY TOOK NAMI...
...BELLE-MÈRE !!
SPLASH
WHAT HOULD DO?

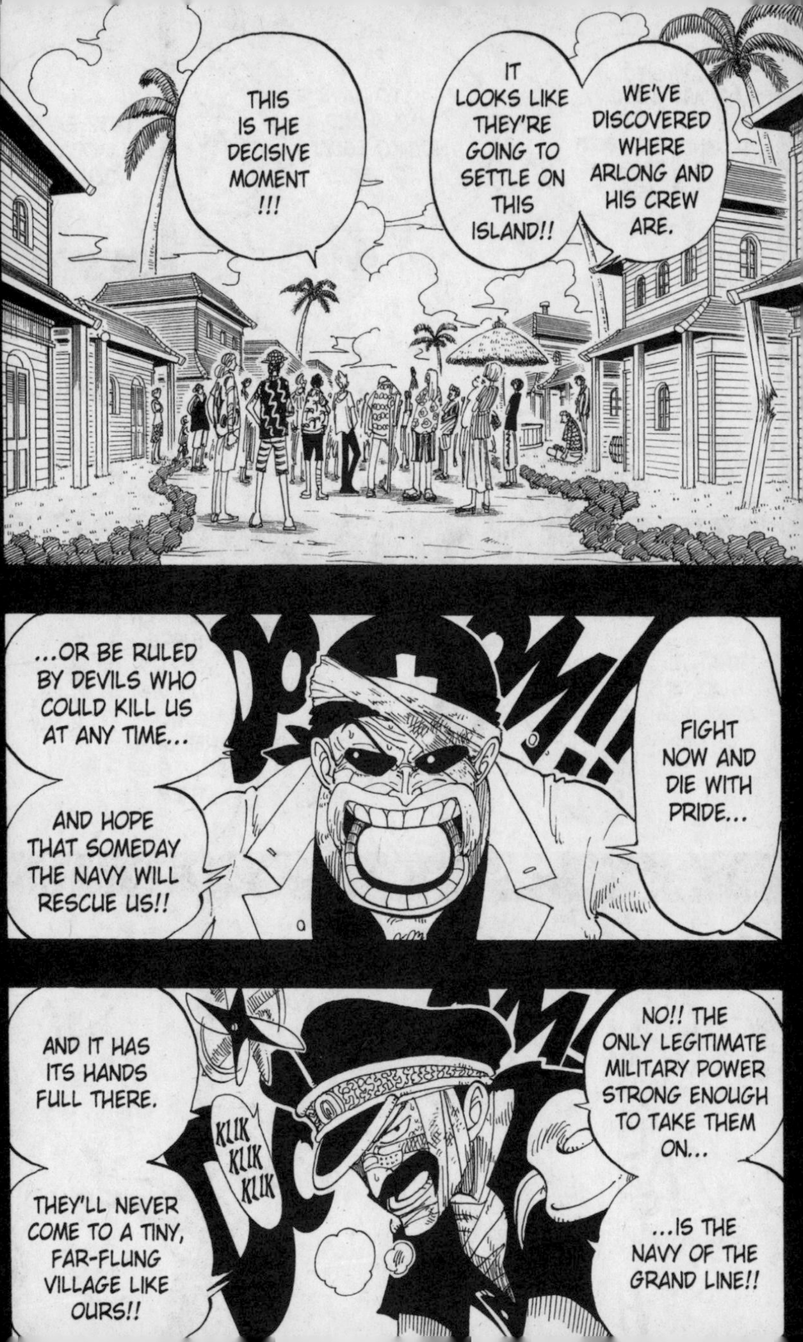
WE'VE DISCOVERED WHERE ARLONG AND HIS CREW ARE.
IT LOOKS LIKE THEY'RE GOING TO SETTLE ON THIS ISLAND!!
THIS IS THE DECISIVE MOMENT!!!
FIGHT NOW AND DIE WITH PRIDE...
...OR BE RULED BY DEVILS WHO COULD KILL US AT ANY TIME...
AND HOPE THAT SOMEDAY THE NAVY WILL RESCUE US!!
NO!! THE ONLY LEGITIMATE MILITARY POWER STRONG ENOUGH TO TAKE THEM ON...
...IS THE NAVY OF THE GRAND LINE!!
AND IT HAS ITS HANDS FULL THERE.
KLIK KLIK KLIK
THEY'LL NEVER COME TO A TINY, FAR-FLUNG VILLAGE LIKE OURS!!

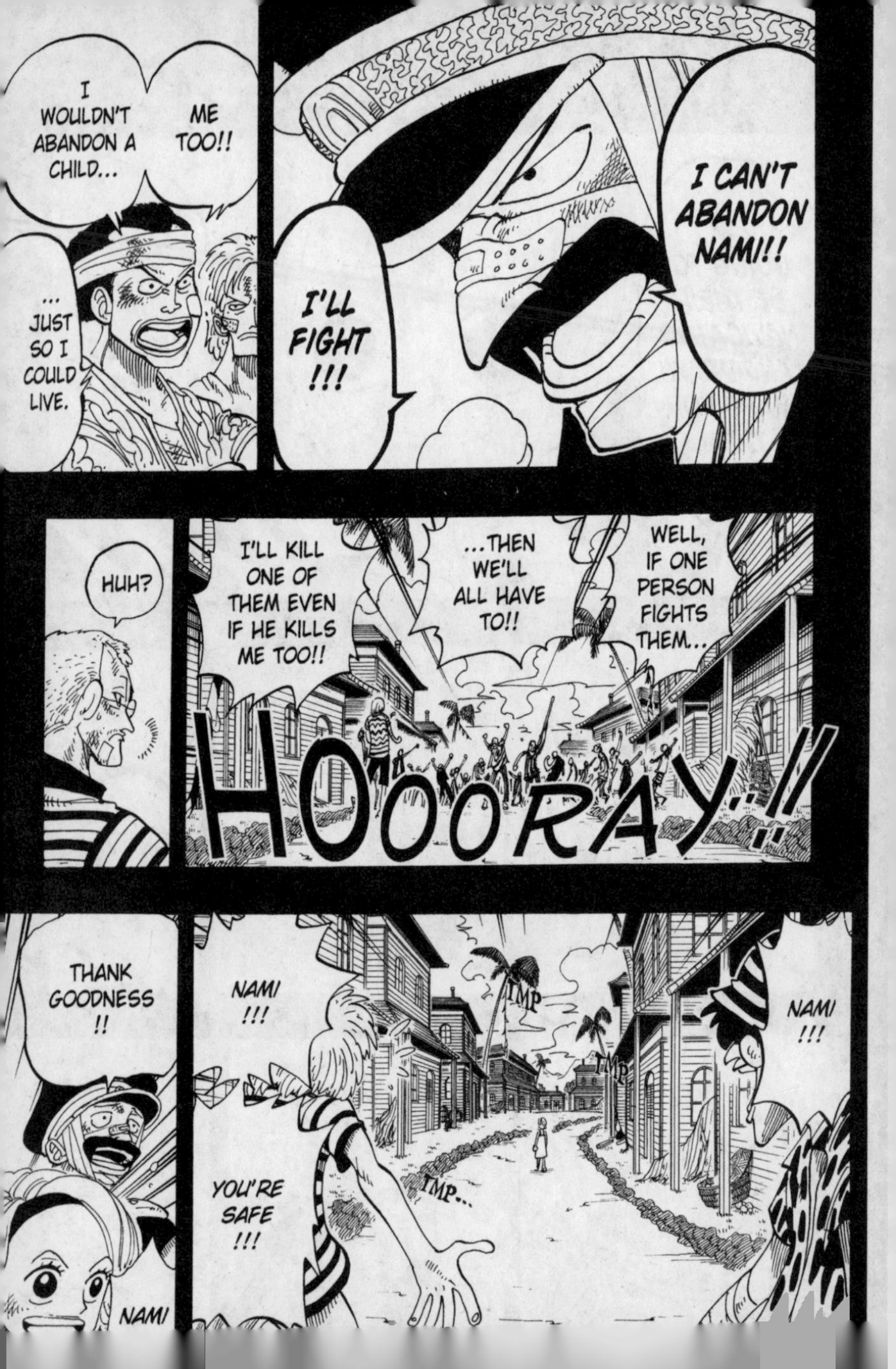
I CAN'T ABANDON NAMI!!
I'LL FIGHT!!!
ME TOO!!
I WOULDN'T ABANDON A CHILD...
... JUST SO I COULD LIVE.
WELL, IF ONE PERSON FIGHTS THEM...
...THEN WE'LL ALL HAVE TO!!
I'LL KILL ONE OF THEM EVEN IF HE KILLS ME TOO!!
HOOORAY..!!
HUH?
NAMI!!!
TMP
TMP
NAMI!!!
TMP..
YOU'RE SAFE!!!
THANK GOODNESS!!
NAMI

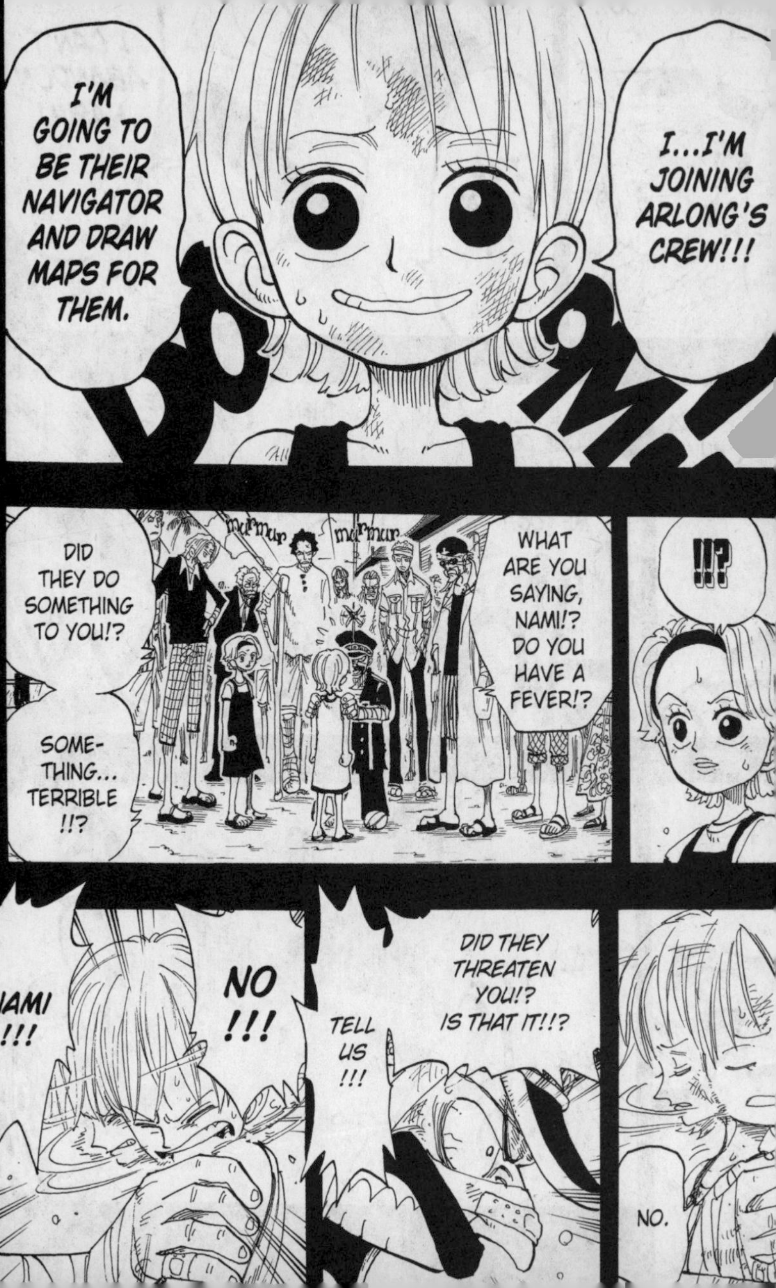
I...I'M JOINING ARLONG'S CREW!!!
I'M GOING TO BE THEIR NAVIGATOR AND DRAW MAPS FOR THEM.
!!?
WHAT ARE YOU SAYING, NAMI!? DO YOU HAVE A FEVER!?
murmur
murmur
DID THEY DO SOMETHING TO YOU!?
SOME-THING... TERRIBLE !!?
NO.
DID THEY THREATEN YOU!? IS THAT IT!!?
TELL US !!!
NO !!!
NAMI !!!

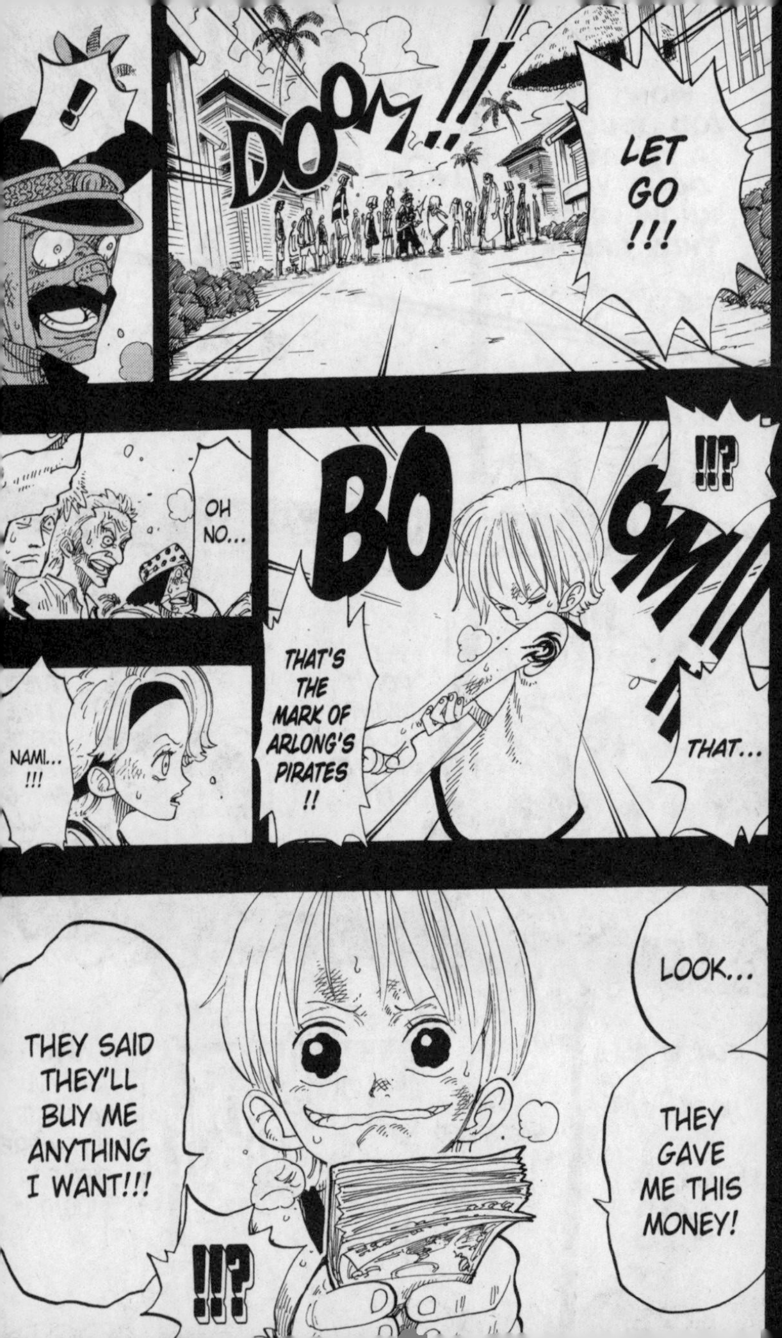
LET GO!!!
DOOM!!
!
!!?
BOOM!!
THAT...
THAT'S THE MARK OF ARLONG'S PIRATES!!
OH NO...
NAMI...!!!
LOOK...
THEY GAVE ME THIS MONEY!
THEY SAID THEY'LL BUY ME ANYTHING I WANT!!!
!!?

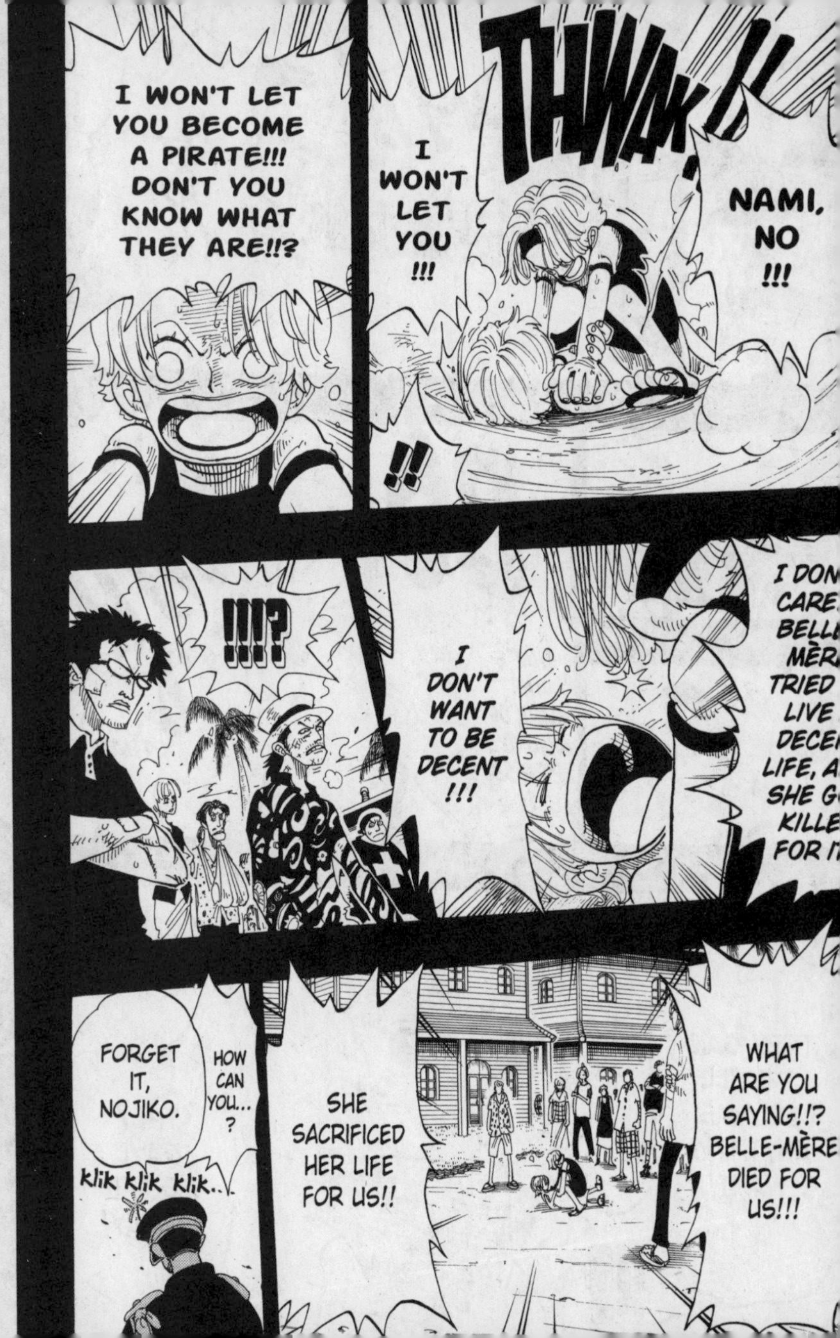
THWAK!!
NAMI, NO!!!
I WON'T LET YOU!!!
!!
I WON'T LET YOU BECOME A PIRATE!!! DON'T YOU KNOW WHAT THEY ARE!!?
I DON CARE. BELL MÈR TRIED LIVE DECE LIFE, A SHE G KILLE FOR I
I DON'T WANT TO BE DECENT!!!
!!!?
WHAT ARE YOU SAYING!!? BELLE-MÈRE DIED FOR US!!!
SHE SACRIFICED HER LIFE FOR US!!
HOW CAN YOU...?
FORGET IT, NOJIKO.
klik klik klik..

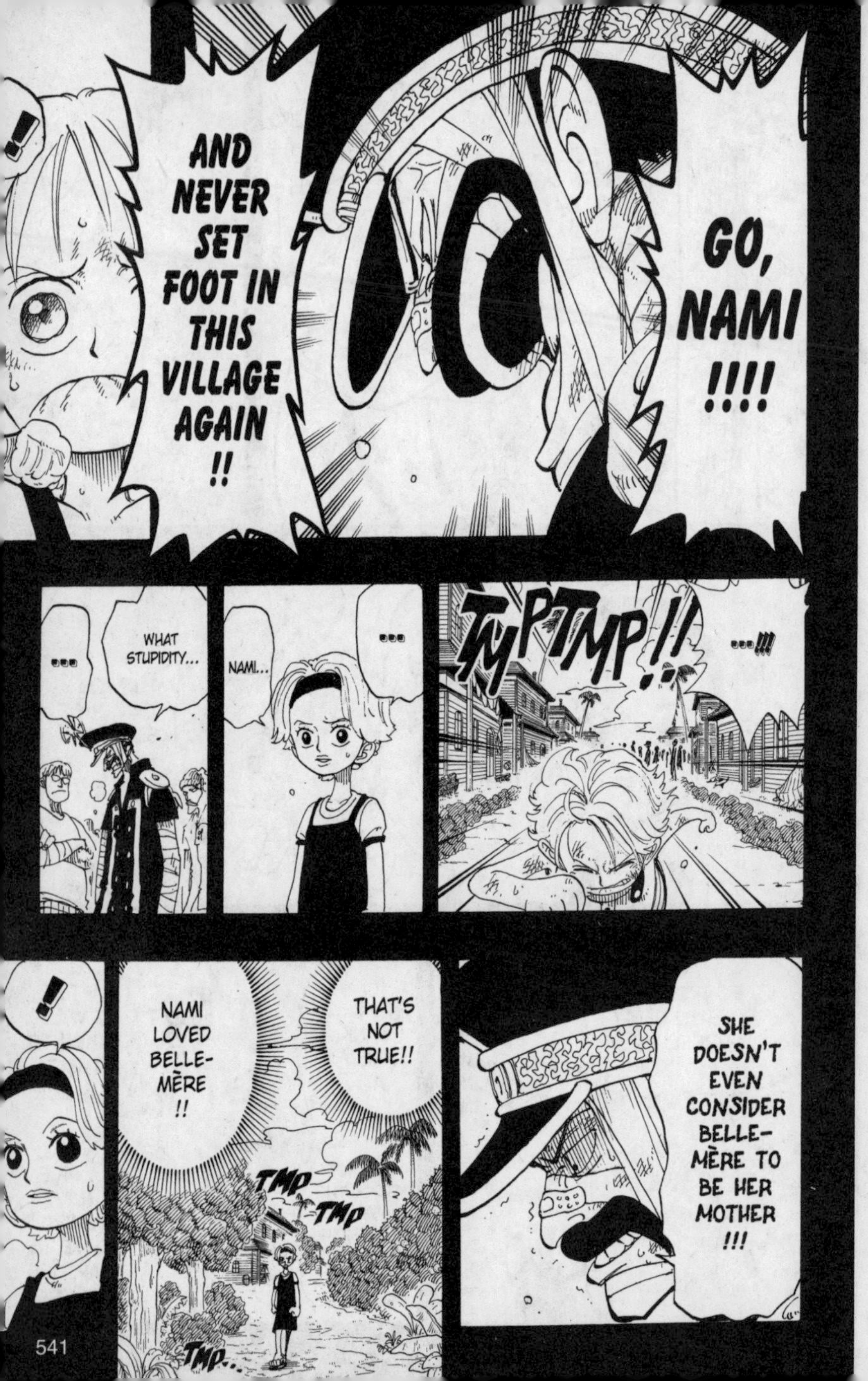
GO, NAMI !!!!
AND NEVER SET FOOT IN THIS VILLAGE AGAIN !!
!
TMPTMP !!
...!!!
...
NAMI...
WHAT STUPIDITY...
...
SHE DOESN'T EVEN CONSIDER BELLE-MÈRE TO BE HER MOTHER !!!
THAT'S NOT TRUE!!
NAMI LOVED BELLE-MÈRE !!
TMP
TMP
TMP...
!

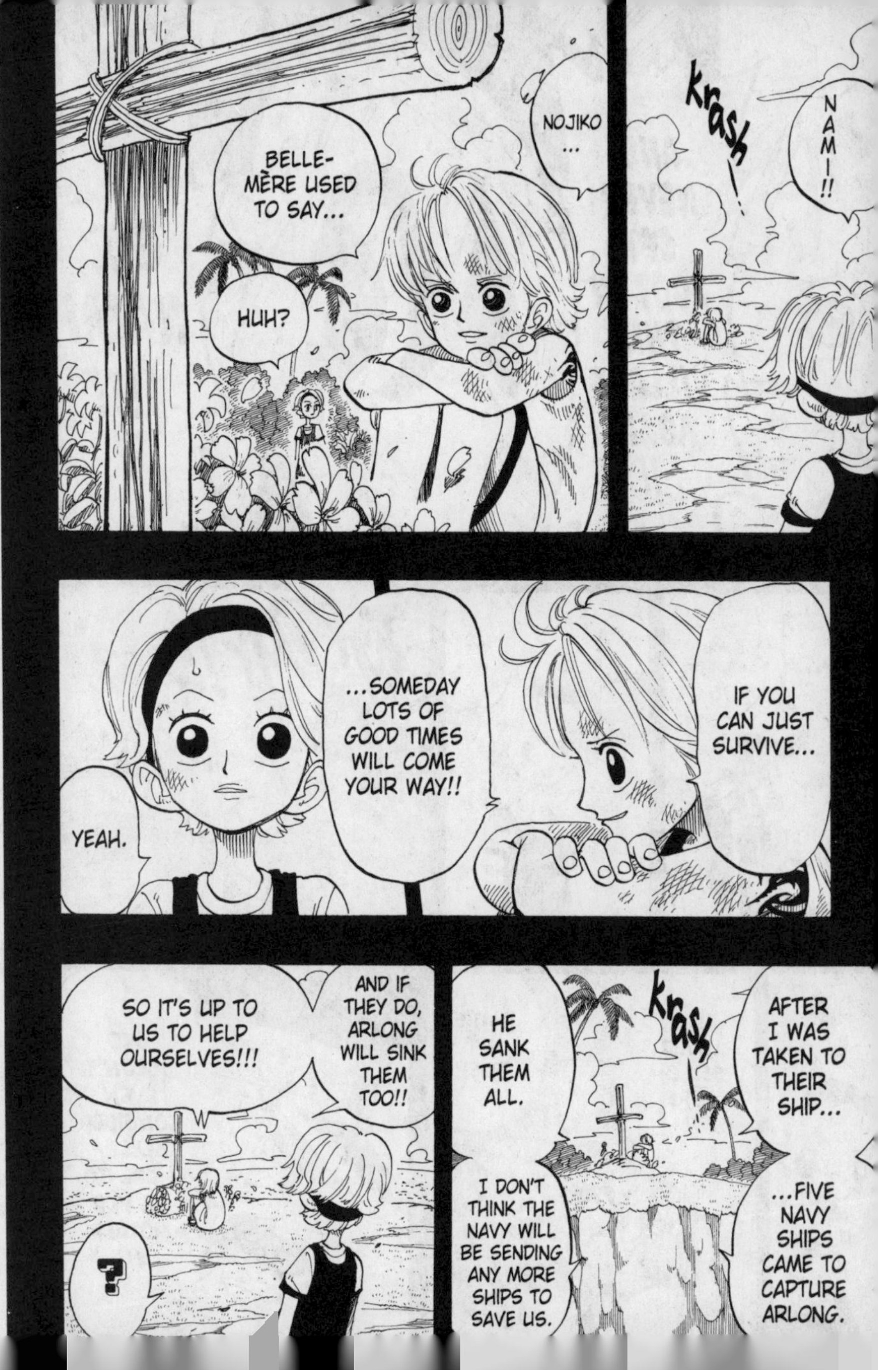
krash
NAMI!!
NOJIKO...
BELLE-MÈRE USED TO SAY...
HUH?
IF YOU CAN JUST SURVIVE...
...SOMEDAY LOTS OF GOOD TIMES WILL COME YOUR WAY!!
YEAH.
AFTER I WAS TAKEN TO THEIR SHIP...
krash
...FIVE NAVY SHIPS CAME TO CAPTURE ARLONG.
HE SANK THEM ALL.
I DON'T THINK THE NAVY WILL BE SENDING ANY MORE SHIPS TO SAVE US.
AND IF THEY DO, ARLONG WILL SINK THEM TOO!!
SO IT'S UP TO US TO HELP OURSELVES!!!
?

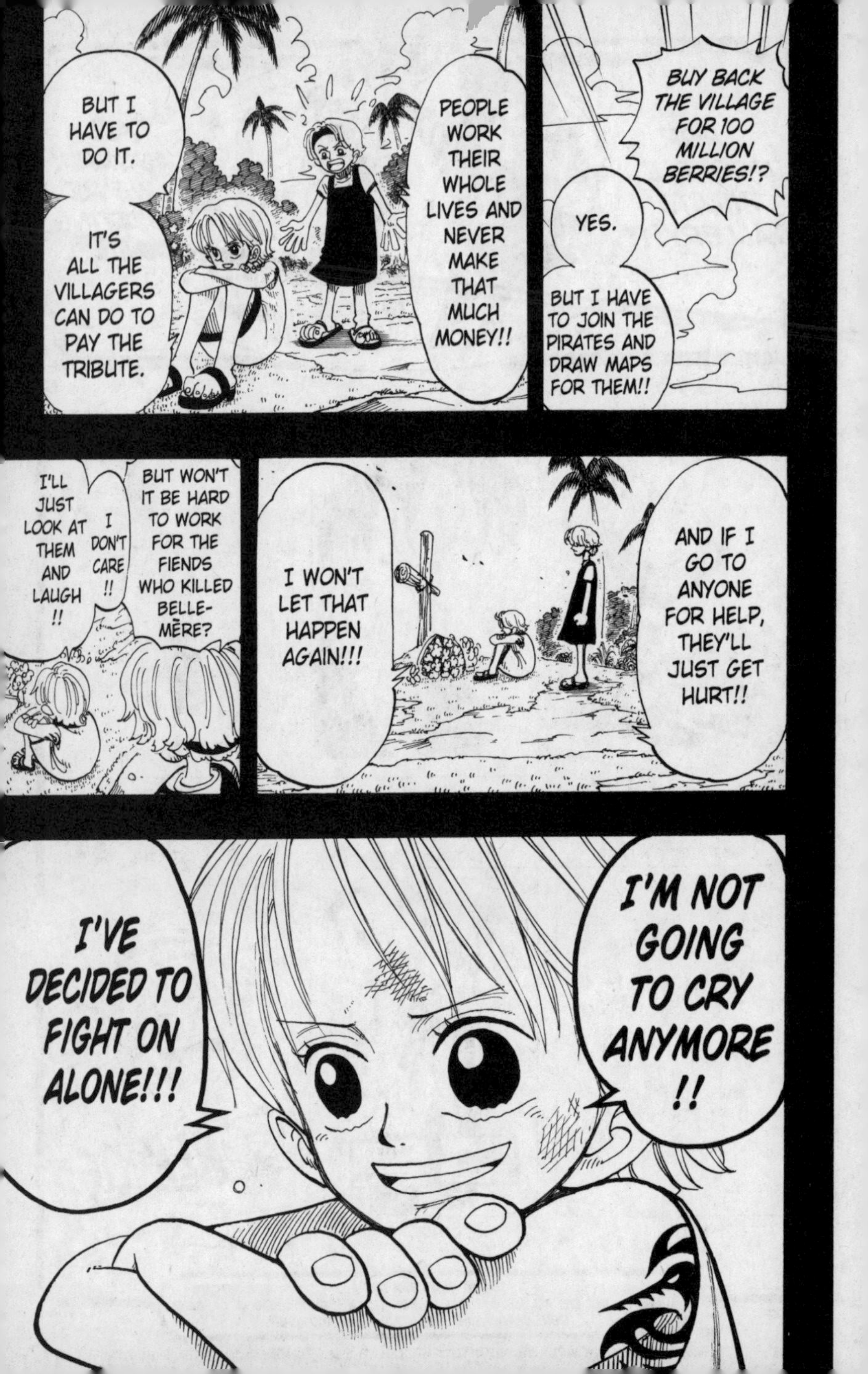
BUY BACK THE VILLAGE FOR 100 MILLION BERRIES!?
YES.
BUT I HAVE TO JOIN THE PIRATES AND DRAW MAPS FOR THEM!!
PEOPLE WORK THEIR WHOLE LIVES AND NEVER MAKE THAT MUCH MONEY!!
BUT I HAVE TO DO IT.
IT'S ALL THE VILLAGERS CAN DO TO PAY THE TRIBUTE.
AND IF I GO TO ANYONE FOR HELP, THEY'LL JUST GET HURT!!
I WON'T LET THAT HAPPEN AGAIN!!!
BUT WON'T IT BE HARD TO WORK FOR THE FIENDS WHO KILLED BELLE-MÈRE?
I DON'T CARE!!
I'LL JUST LOOK AT THEM AND LAUGH!!
I'M NOT GOING TO CRY ANYMORE!!
I'VE DECIDED TO FIGHT ON ALONE!!!

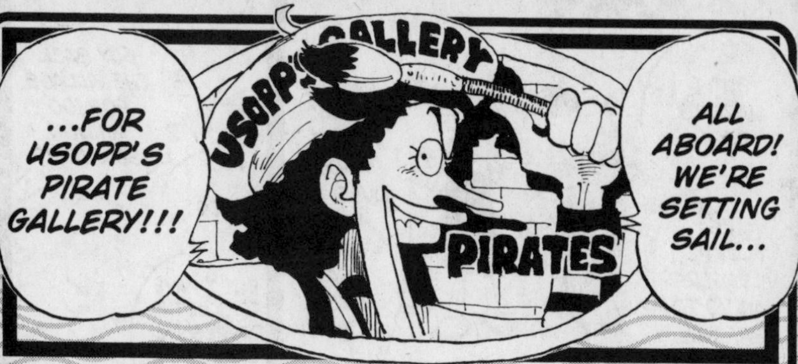
USOPP'S GALLERY
ALL ABOARD! WE'RE SETTING SAIL...
...FOR USOPP'S PIRATE GALLERY!!!
PIRATES

IT'S ALL FUN AND GAMES TO LUFFY!

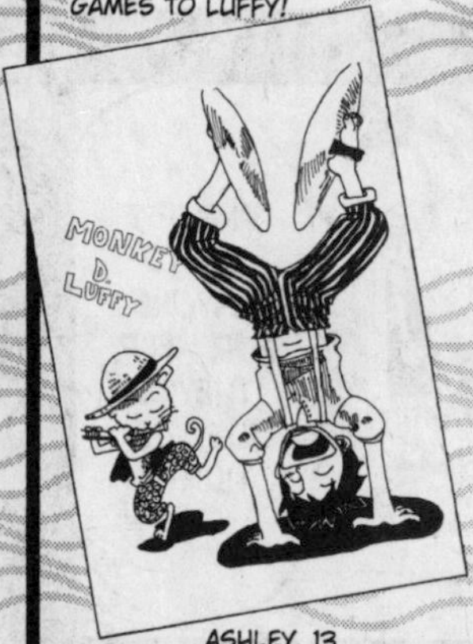
MONKEY D. LUFFY

ASHLEY, 13

OUR HERO LOOKS LOST.

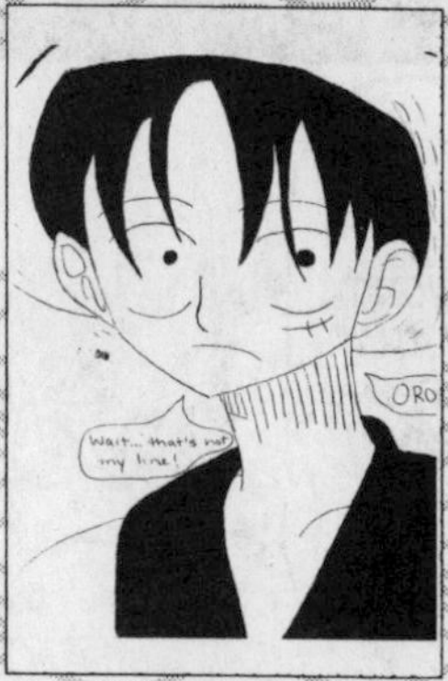
Wait... that's not my line!
ORO

ALLISON, 14

WHAT'S ON YOUR MIND, USOPP?

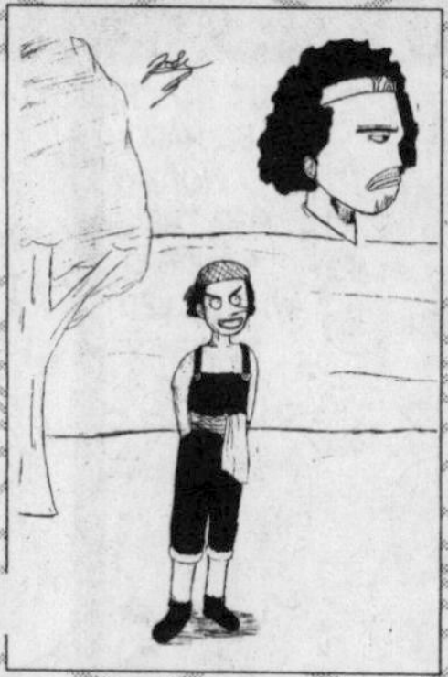

JORDAN, 13

AND THAT'S A FACT.

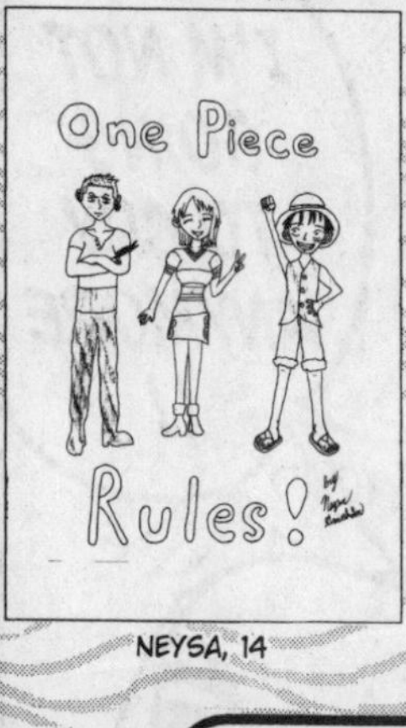
One Piece
Rules!

NEYSA, 14

TWO TOUGH COOKIES.

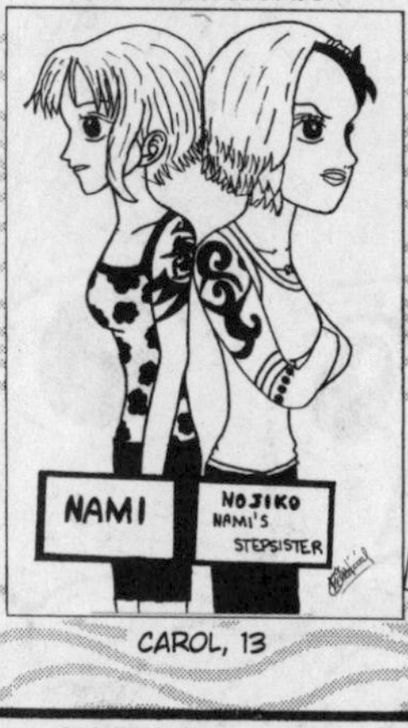
NAMI
NOJIKO
NAMI'S
STEPSISTER

CAROL, 13

THE FUTURE KING OF THE PIRATES.

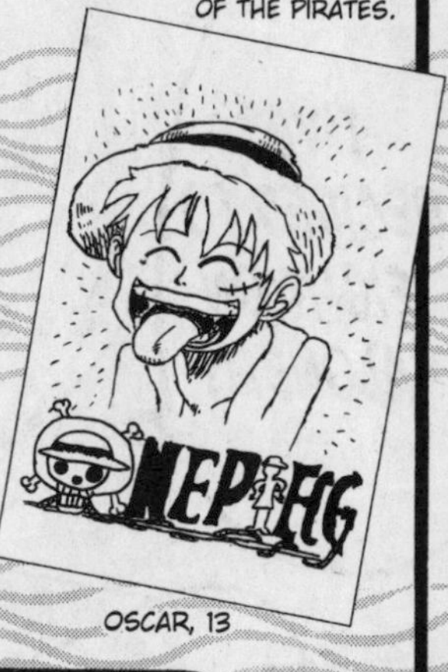

OSCAR, 13

SUBMIT YOUR FAN ART TO:
SHONEN JUMP C/O VIZ MEDIA, LLC P.O. BOX 77010, SAN FRANCISCO, CA, 94107
REMEMBER TO INCLUDE YOUR NAME AND AGE!!

USOPP'S COMMENTS WERE TRANSMITTED THROUGH THE U.S. SHONEN JUMP TEAM—*EDITOR*

# Chapter 80:
# A THIEF IS A THIEF

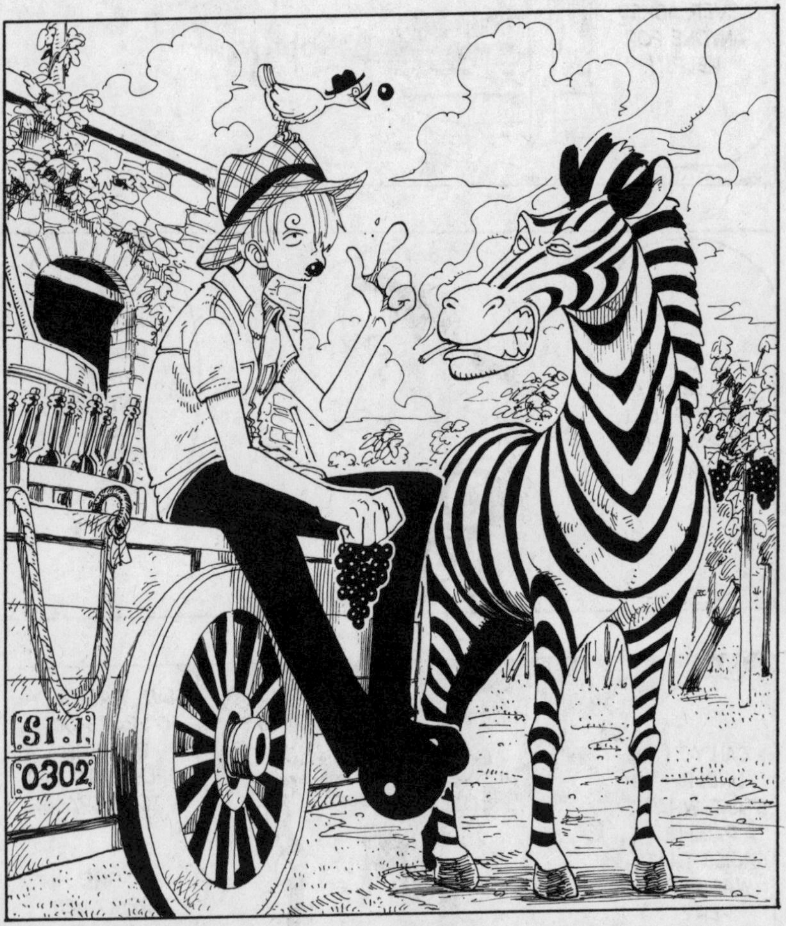
S1.1
0302

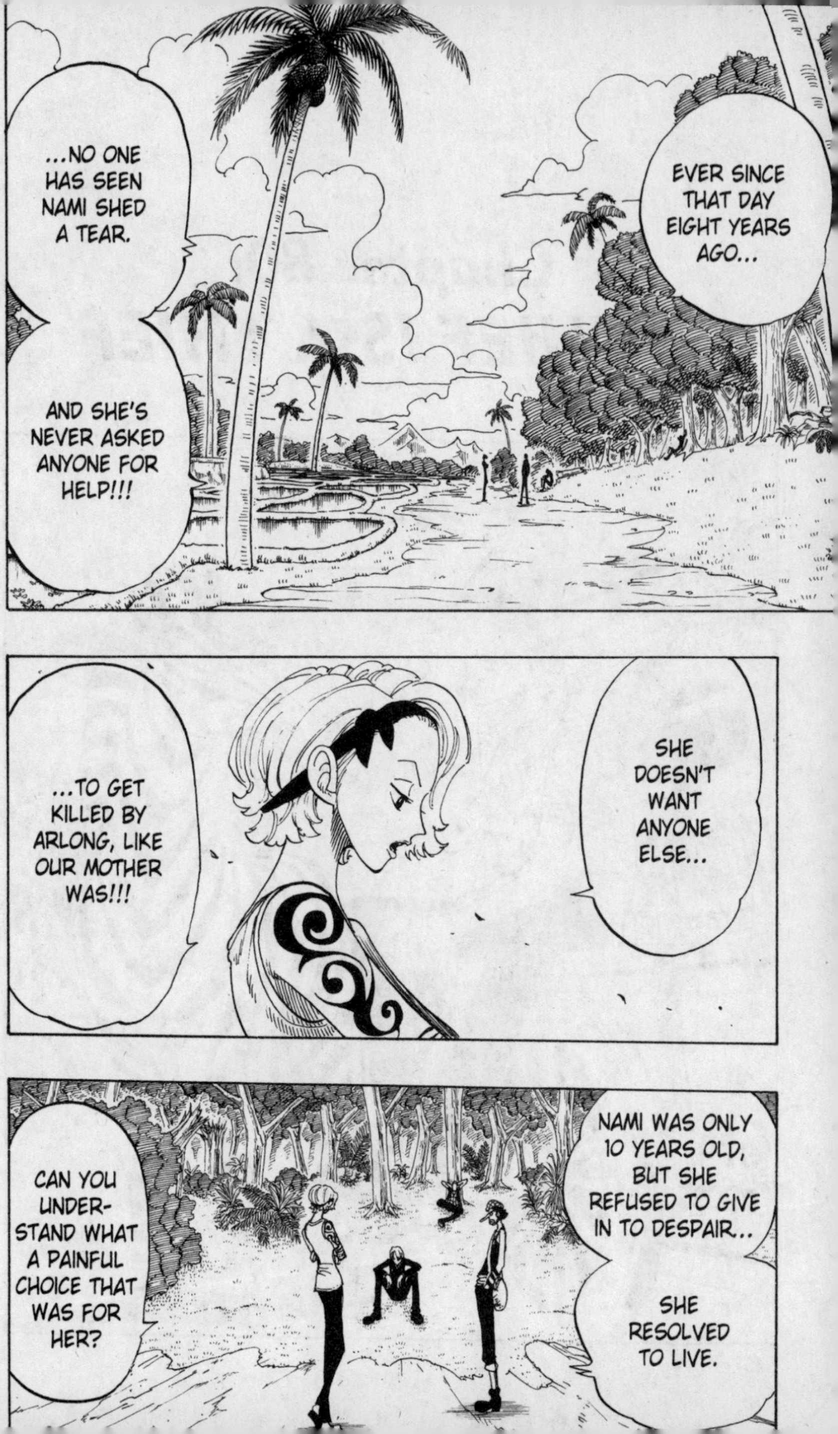
EVER SINCE THAT DAY EIGHT YEARS AGO...
...NO ONE HAS SEEN NAMI SHED A TEAR.
AND SHE'S NEVER ASKED ANYONE FOR HELP!!!
SHE DOESN'T WANT ANYONE ELSE...
...TO GET KILLED BY ARLONG, LIKE OUR MOTHER WAS!!!
NAMI WAS ONLY 10 YEARS OLD, BUT SHE REFUSED TO GIVE IN TO DESPAIR...
SHE RESOLVED TO LIVE.
CAN YOU UNDER-STAND WHAT A PAINFUL CHOICE THAT WAS FOR HER?

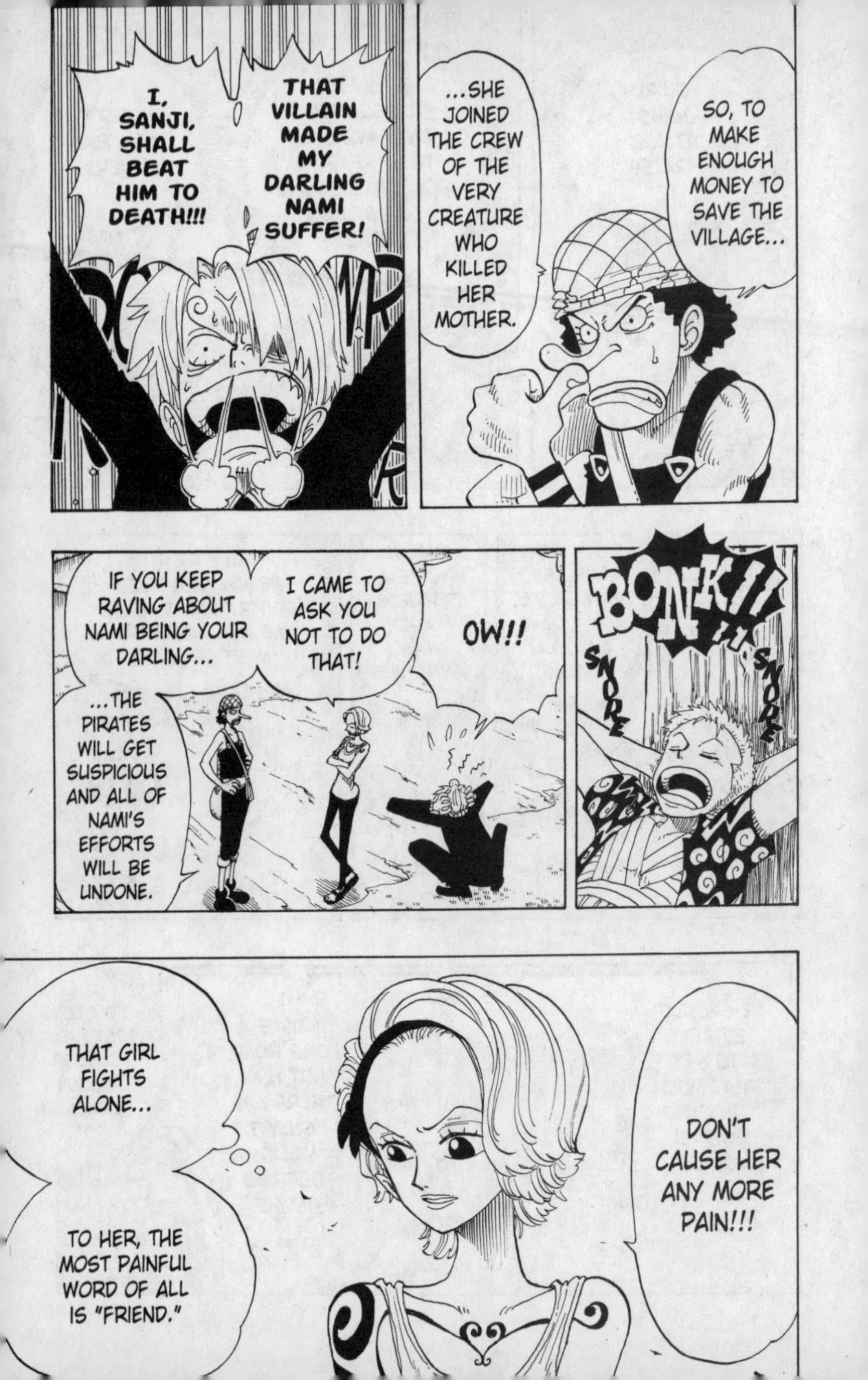
SO, TO MAKE ENOUGH MONEY TO SAVE THE VILLAGE...
...SHE JOINED THE CREW OF THE VERY CREATURE WHO KILLED HER MOTHER.
THAT VILLAIN MADE MY DARLING NAMI SUFFER!
I, SANJI, SHALL BEAT HIM TO DEATH!!!
BONK!!
SNORE
SNORE
OW!!
I CAME TO ASK YOU NOT TO DO THAT!
IF YOU KEEP RAVING ABOUT NAMI BEING YOUR DARLING...
...THE PIRATES WILL GET SUSPICIOUS AND ALL OF NAMI'S EFFORTS WILL BE UNDONE.
DON'T CAUSE HER ANY MORE PAIN!!!
THAT GIRL FIGHTS ALONE...
TO HER, THE MOST PAINFUL WORD OF ALL IS "FRIEND."

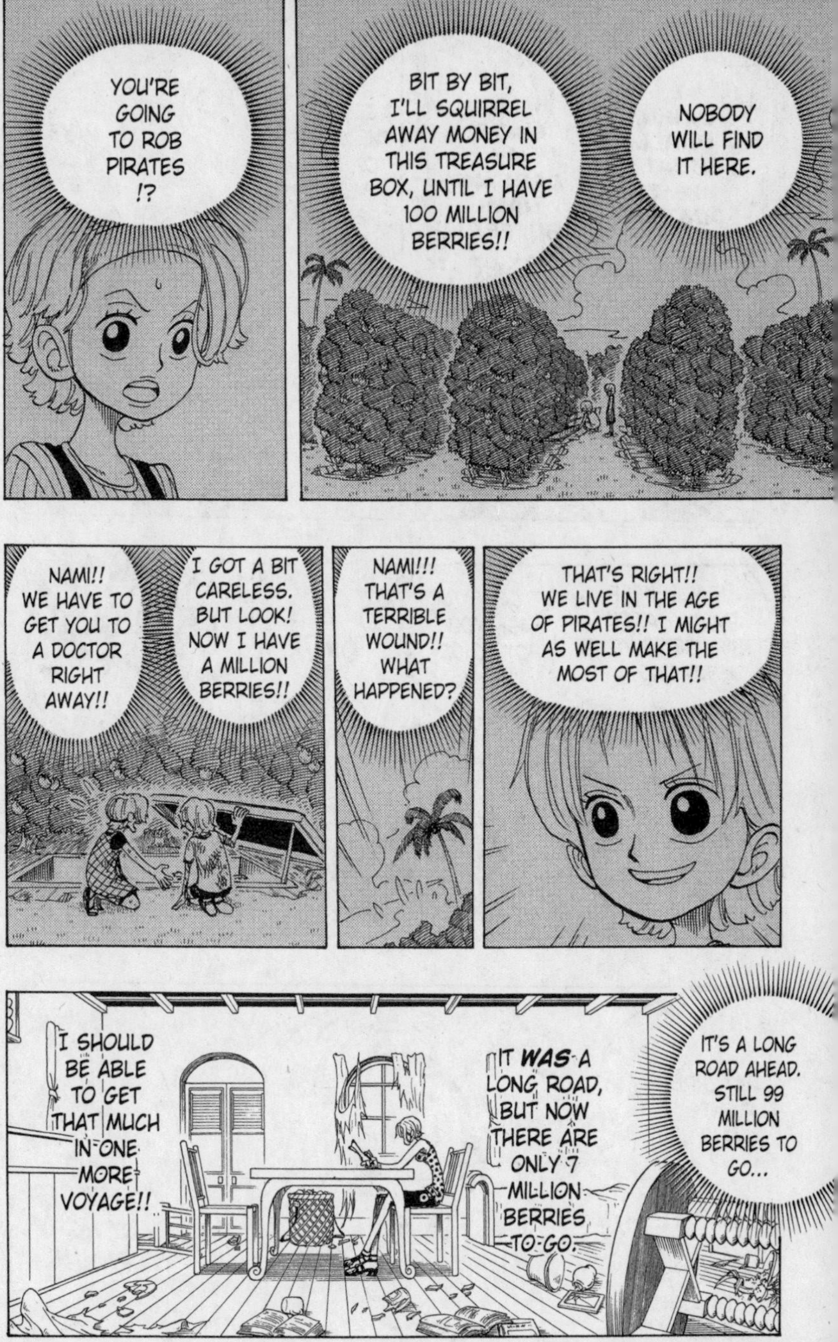

NOBODY WILL FIND IT HERE.
BIT BY BIT, I'LL SQUIRREL AWAY MONEY IN THIS TREASURE BOX, UNTIL I HAVE 100 MILLION BERRIES!!
YOU'RE GOING TO ROB PIRATES !?
THAT'S RIGHT!! WE LIVE IN THE AGE OF PIRATES!! I MIGHT AS WELL MAKE THE MOST OF THAT!!
NAMI!!! THAT'S A TERRIBLE WOUND!! WHAT HAPPENED?
I GOT A BIT CARELESS. BUT LOOK! NOW I HAVE A MILLION BERRIES!!
NAMI!! WE HAVE TO GET YOU TO A DOCTOR RIGHT AWAY!!
IT'S A LONG ROAD AHEAD. STILL 99 MILLION BERRIES TO GO...
IT *WAS* A LONG ROAD, BUT NOW THERE ARE ONLY 7 MILLION BERRIES TO GO.
I SHOULD BE ABLE TO GET THAT MUCH IN ONE MORE VOYAGE!!

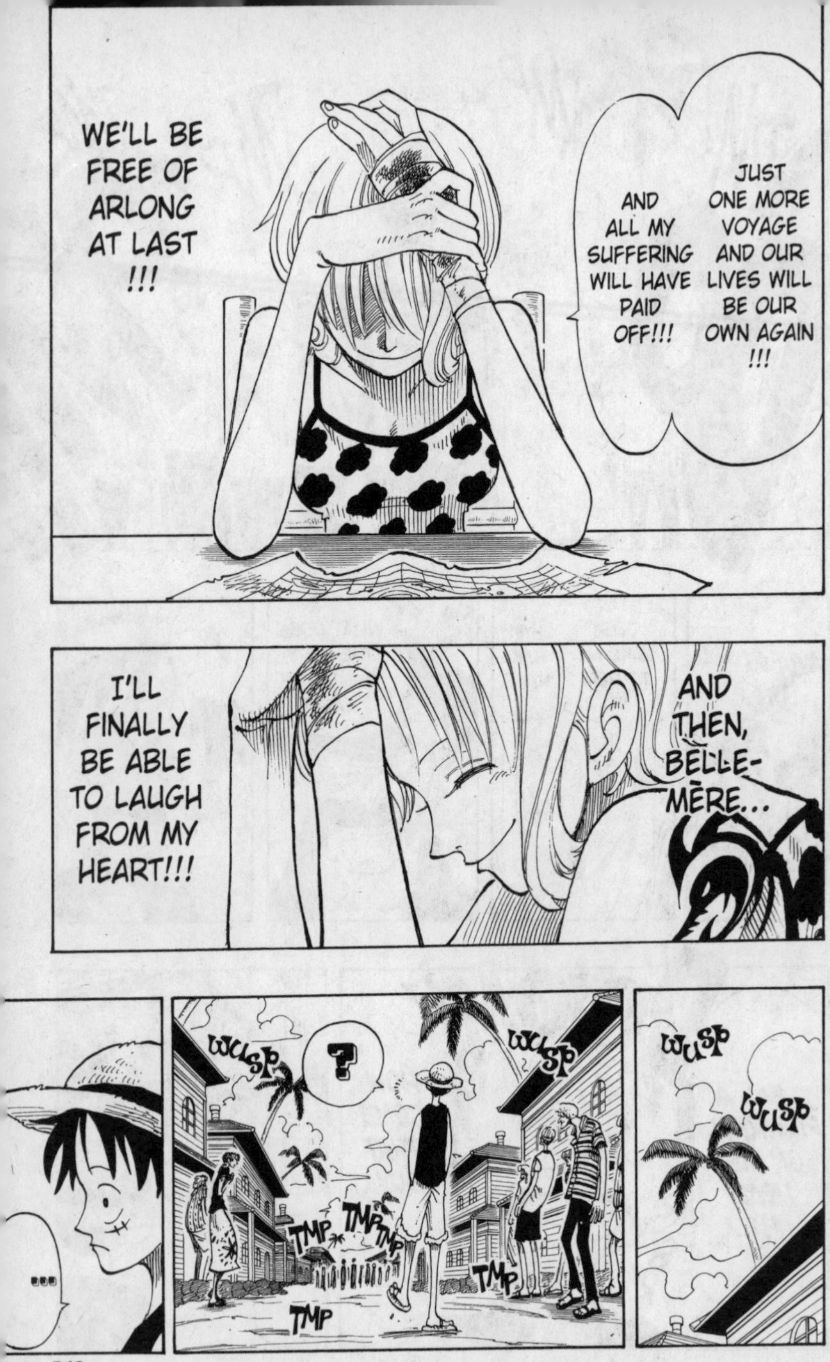
JUST ONE MORE VOYAGE AND OUR LIVES WILL BE OUR OWN AGAIN !!!
AND ALL MY SUFFERING WILL HAVE PAID OFF!!!
WE'LL BE FREE OF ARLONG AT LAST !!!
AND THEN, BELLE-MÈRE...
I'LL FINALLY BE ABLE TO LAUGH FROM MY HEART!!!
WUSP
WUSP
WUSP
?
WUSP
TMP
TMP TMP
TMP
TMP
TMP
...

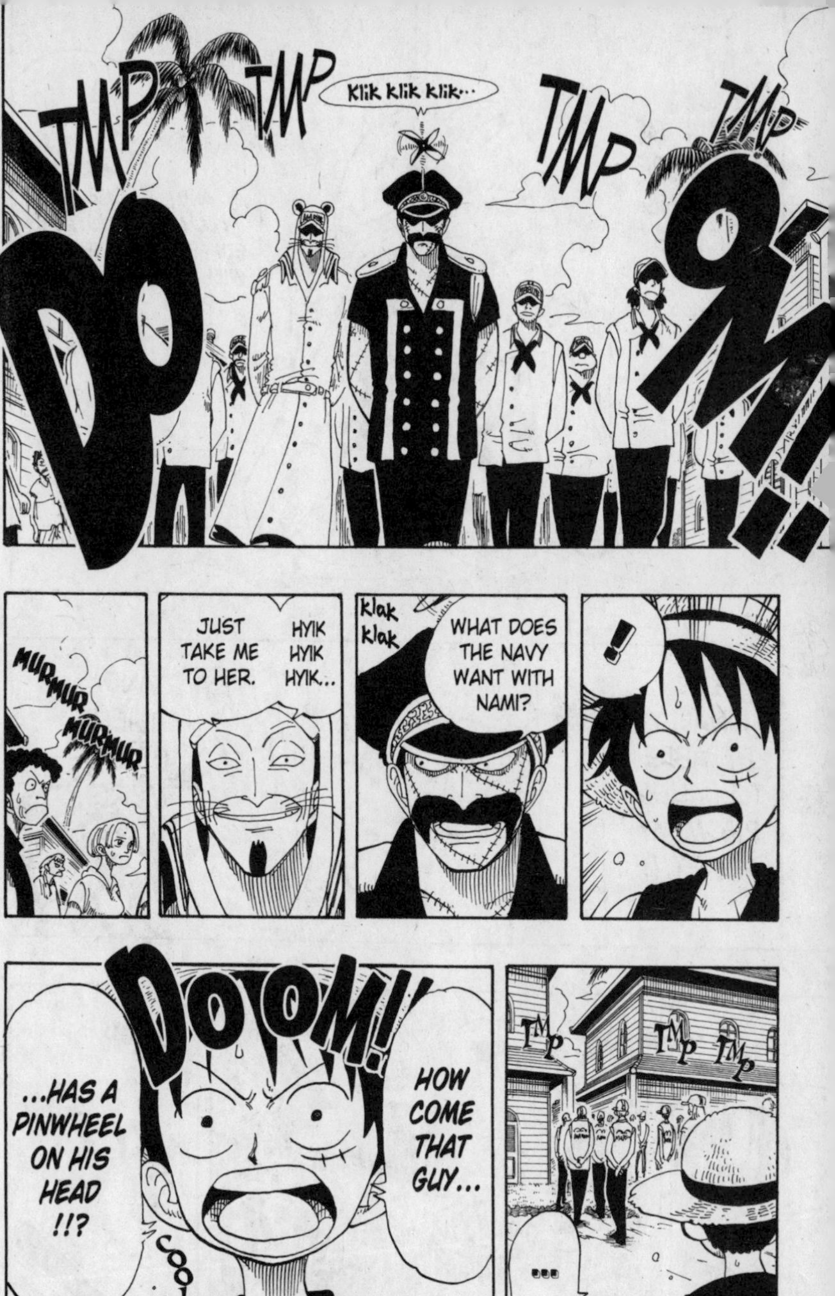
TMP
TMP
Klik klik klik...
TMP
TMP
DOOM!!
!
klak klak
WHAT DOES THE NAVY WANT WITH NAMI?
JUST TAKE ME TO HER.
HYIK HYIK HYIK...
MURMUR
MURMUR
TMP
TMP TMP
...
DOOM!!
HOW COME THAT GUY...
...HAS A PINWHEEL ON HIS HEAD !!?
COOL

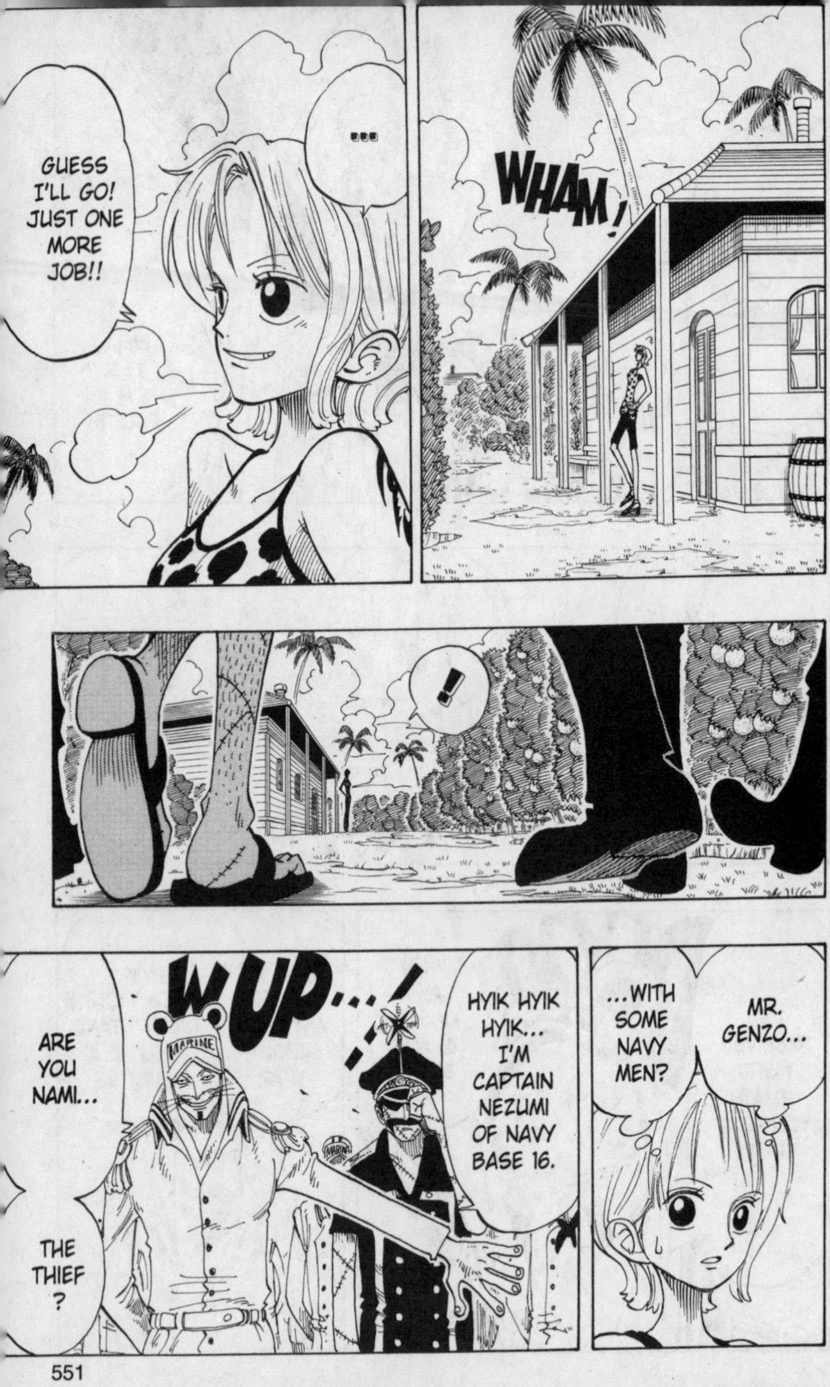
WHAM!
...
GUESS I'LL GO! JUST ONE MORE JOB!!
!
MR. GENZO...
...WITH SOME NAVY MEN?
HYIK HYIK HYIK... I'M CAPTAIN NEZUMI OF NAVY BASE 16.
WUP...!
MARINE
ARE YOU NAMI...
THE THIEF ?

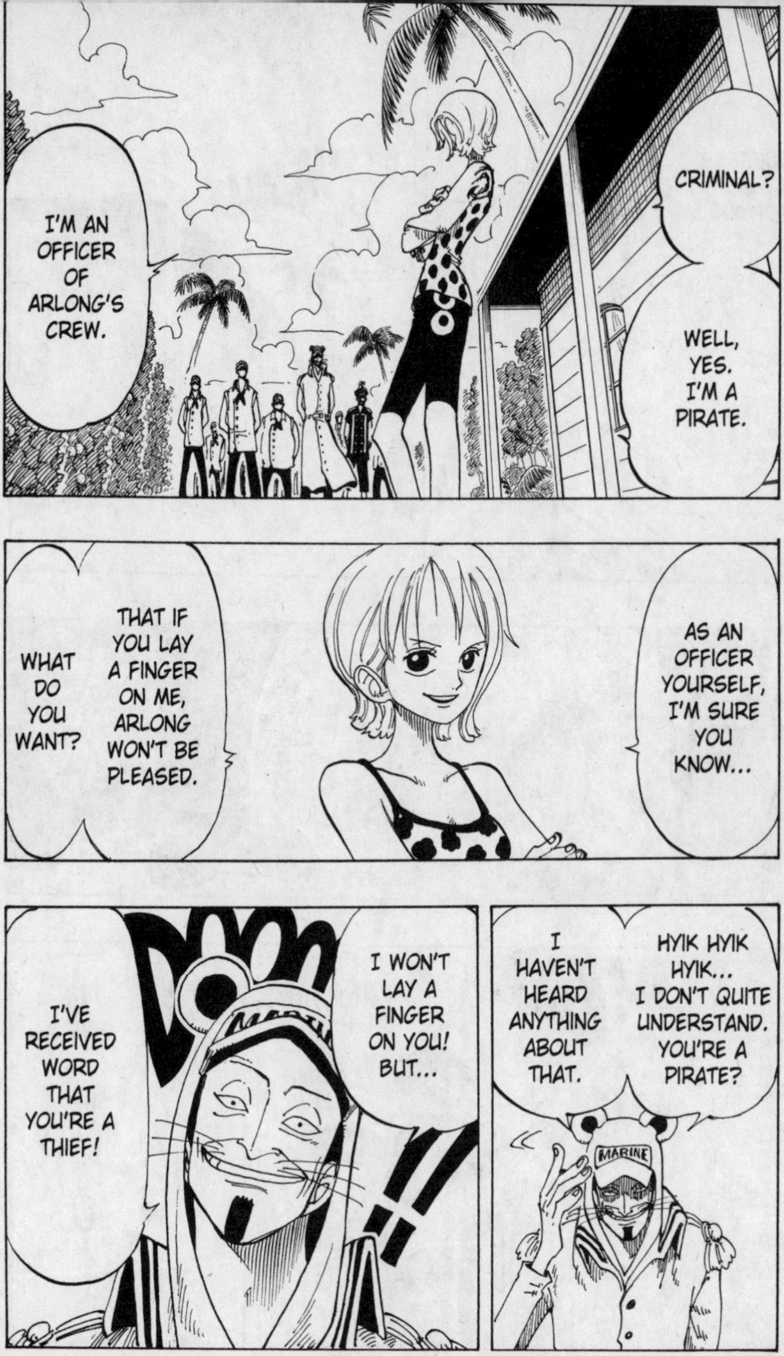
CRIMINAL?
WELL, YES. I'M A PIRATE.
I'M AN OFFICER OF ARLONG'S CREW.
AS AN OFFICER YOURSELF, I'M SURE YOU KNOW...
THAT IF YOU LAY A FINGER ON ME, ARLONG WON'T BE PLEASED.
WHAT DO YOU WANT?
HYIK HYIK HYIK... I DON'T QUITE UNDERSTAND. YOU'RE A PIRATE?
I HAVEN'T HEARD ANYTHING ABOUT THAT.
MARINE
I WON'T LAY A FINGER ON YOU! BUT...
I'VE RECEIVED WORD THAT YOU'RE A THIEF!

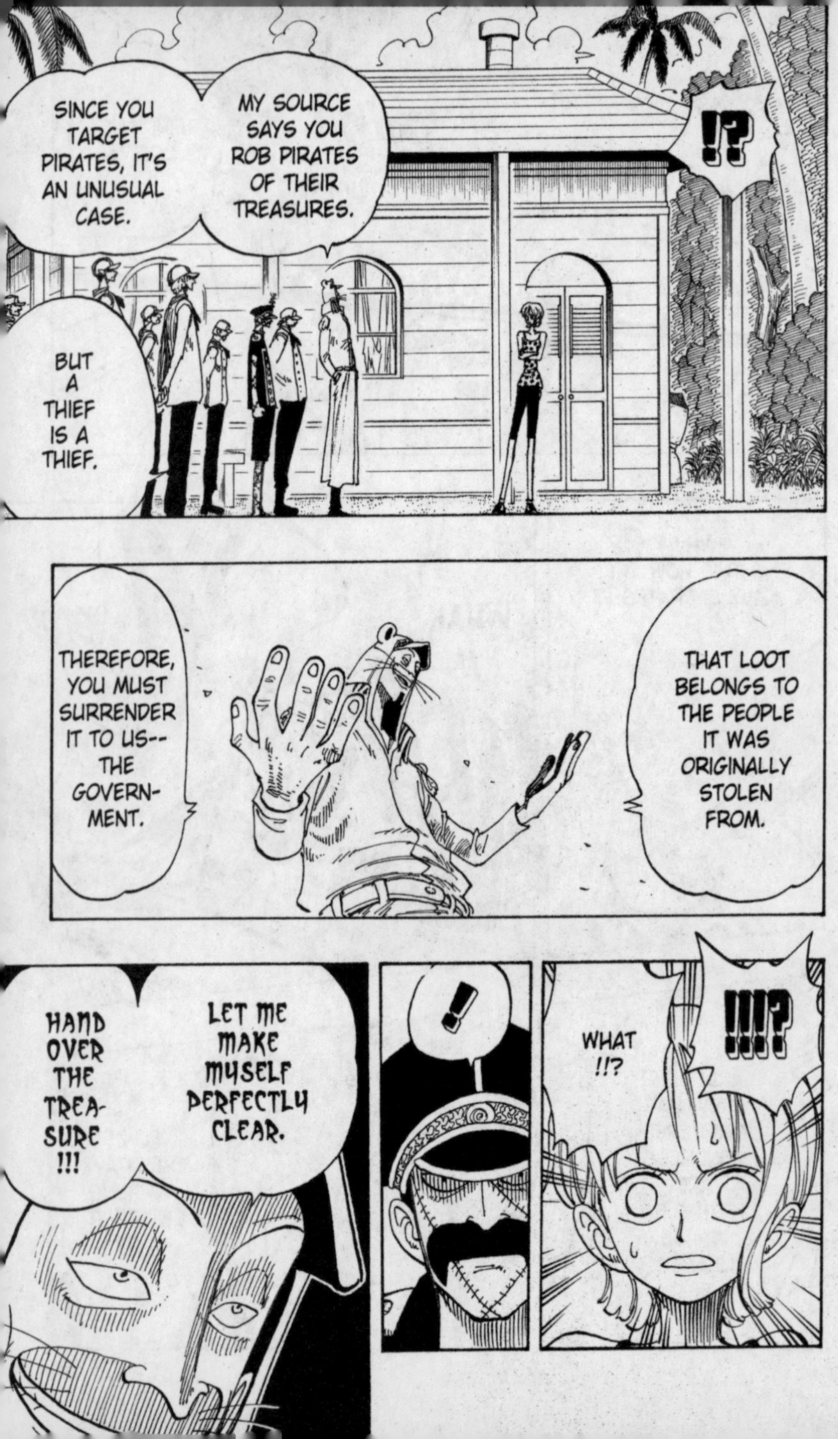
!?
MY SOURCE SAYS YOU ROB PIRATES OF THEIR TREASURES.
SINCE YOU TARGET PIRATES, IT'S AN UNUSUAL CASE.
BUT A THIEF IS A THIEF.
THAT LOOT BELONGS TO THE PEOPLE IT WAS ORIGINALLY STOLEN FROM.
THEREFORE, YOU MUST SURRENDER IT TO US-- THE GOVERNMENT.
!!!?
WHAT !!?
!
LET ME MAKE MYSELF PERFECTLY CLEAR.
HAND OVER THE TREASURE !!!

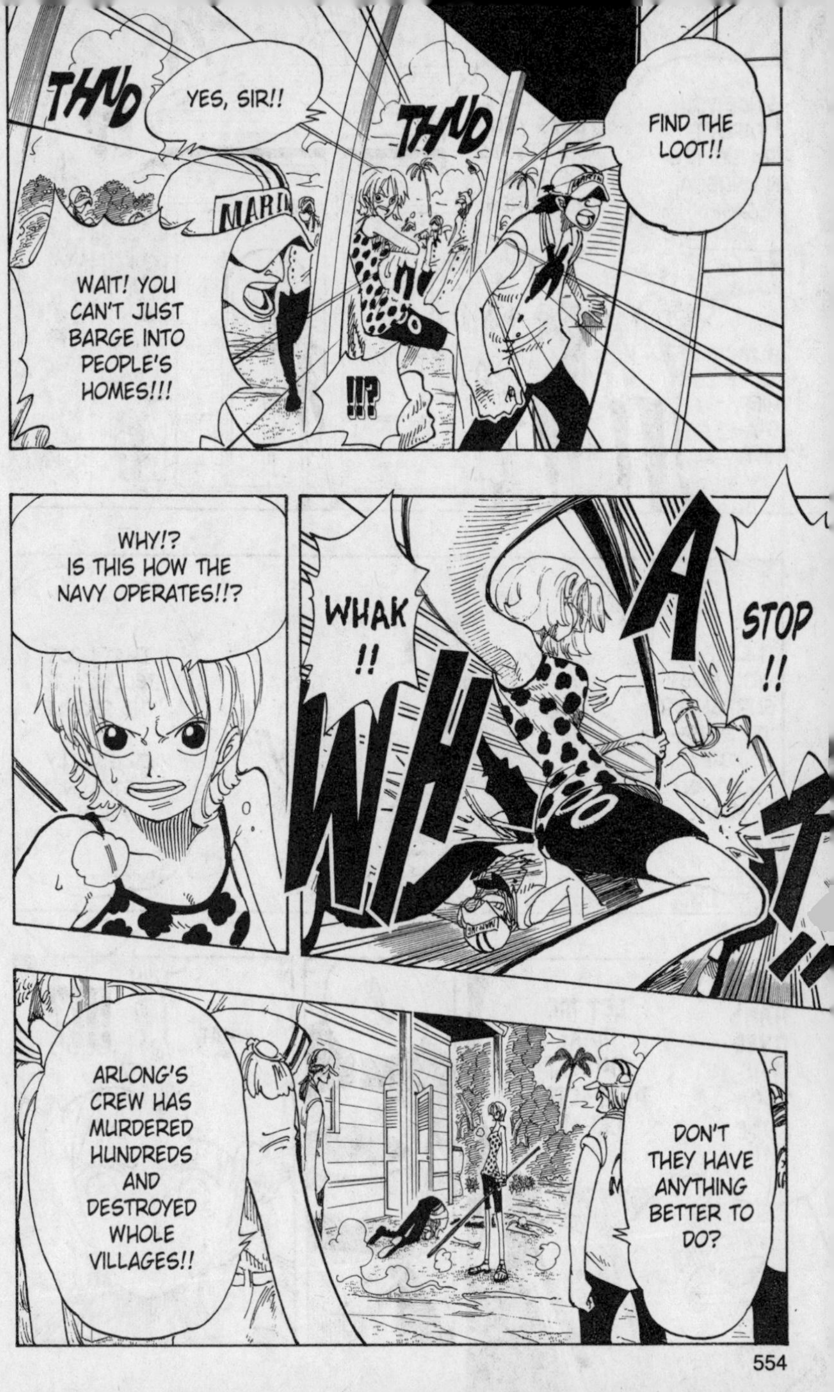
FIND THE LOOT!!
THUD
YES, SIR!!
THUD
WAIT! YOU CAN'T JUST BARGE INTO PEOPLE'S HOMES!!!
!!?
STOP!!
WHAK!!
WHAK!!
WHY!? IS THIS HOW THE NAVY OPERATES!!?
DON'T THEY HAVE ANYTHING BETTER TO DO?
ARLONG'S CREW HAS MURDERED HUNDREDS AND DESTROYED WHOLE VILLAGES!!

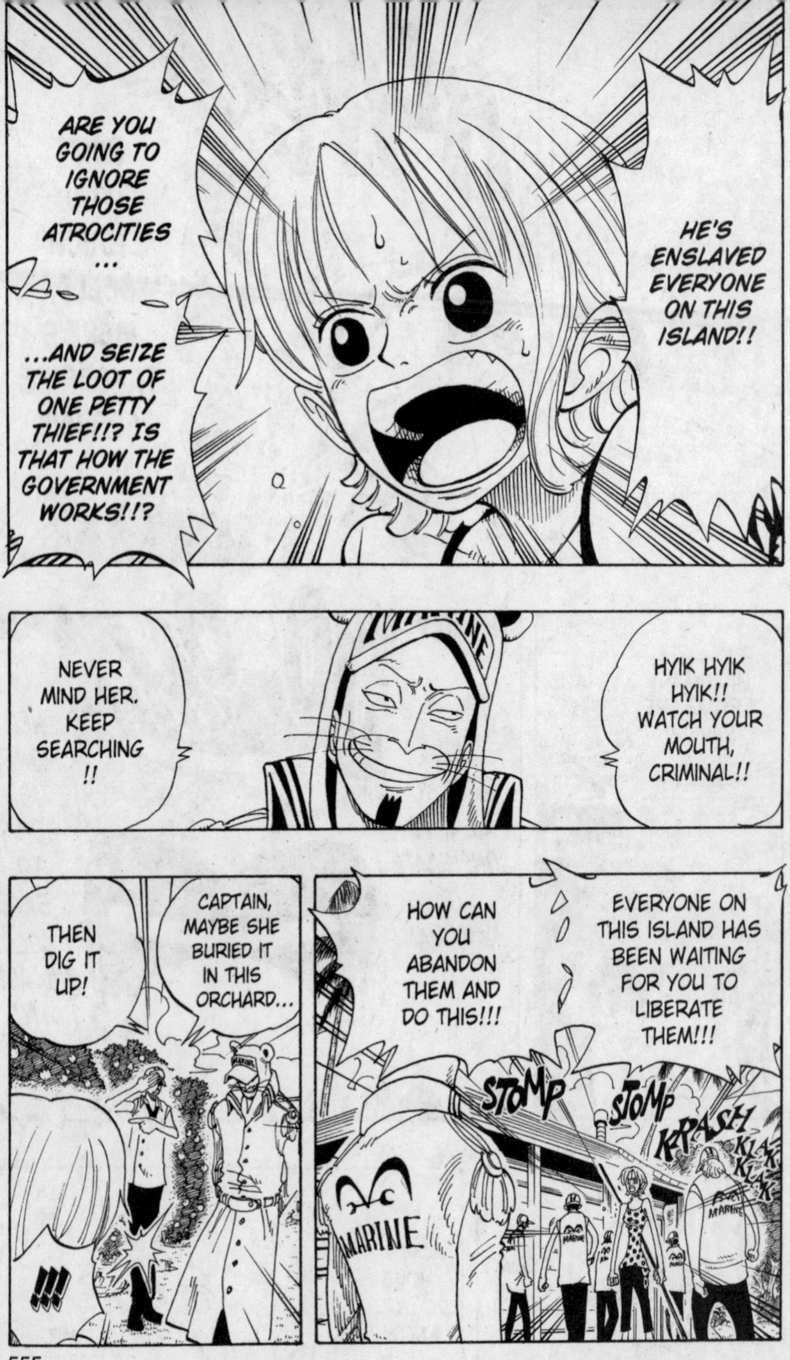
HE'S ENSLAVED EVERYONE ON THIS ISLAND!!
ARE YOU GOING TO IGNORE THOSE ATROCITIES...
...AND SEIZE THE LOOT OF ONE PETTY THIEF!!? IS THAT HOW THE GOVERNMENT WORKS!!?
HYIK HYIK HYIK!! WATCH YOUR MOUTH, CRIMINAL!!
NEVER MIND HER. KEEP SEARCHING!!
MARINE
EVERYONE ON THIS ISLAND HAS BEEN WAITING FOR YOU TO LIBERATE THEM!!!
HOW CAN YOU ABANDON THEM AND DO THIS!!!
STOMP
STOMP
KRASH
KLAK KLAK
MARINE
CAPTAIN, MAYBE SHE BURIED IT IN THIS ORCHARD...
THEN DIG IT UP!
!!!

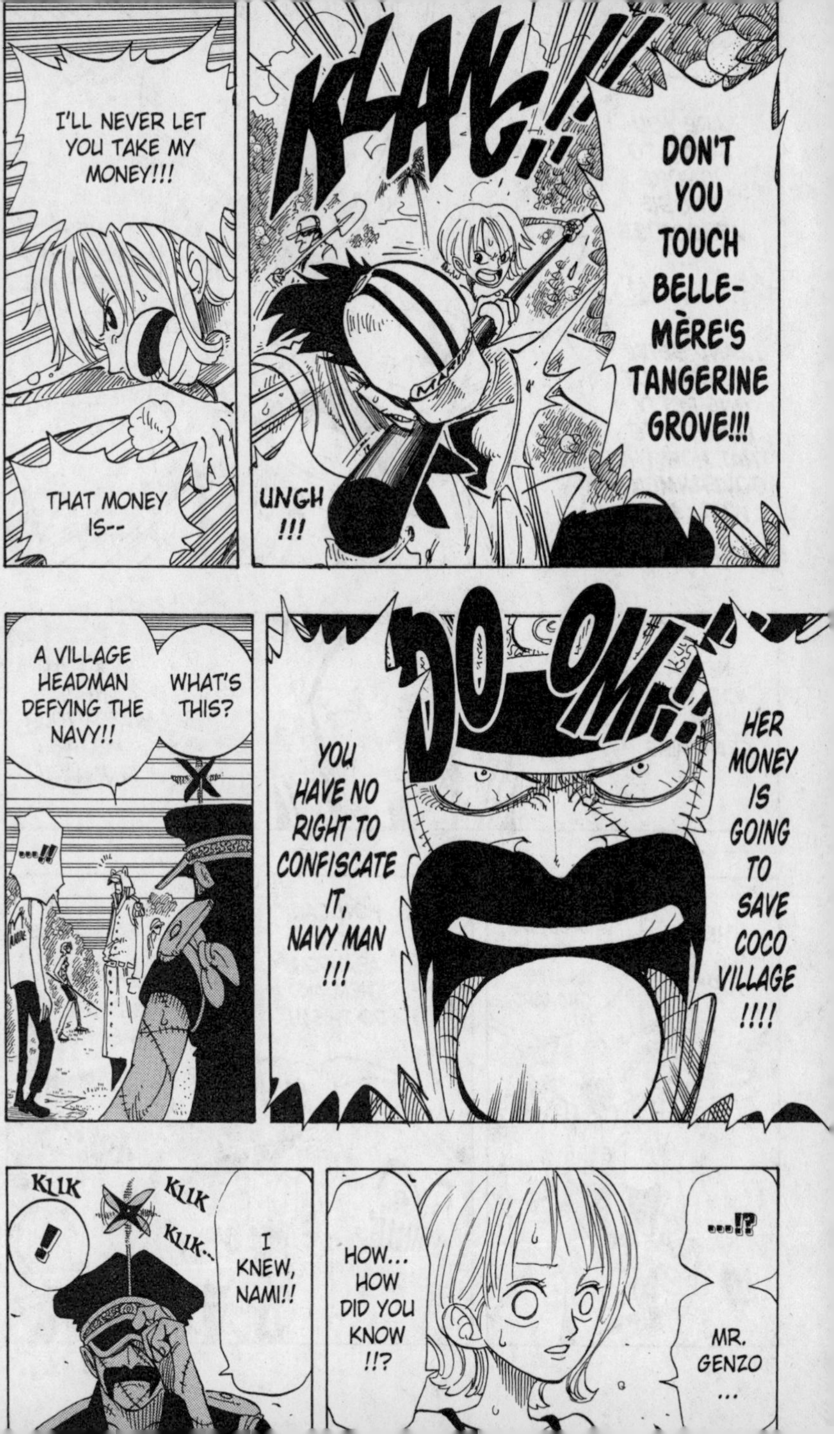
KLANG!!
DON'T YOU TOUCH BELLE-MÈRE'S TANGERINE GROVE!!!
UNGH !!!
I'LL NEVER LET YOU TAKE MY MONEY!!!
THAT MONEY IS--
DO-OM!!
HER MONEY IS GOING TO SAVE COCO VILLAGE !!!!
YOU HAVE NO RIGHT TO CONFISCATE IT, NAVY MAN !!!
WHAT'S THIS?
A VILLAGE HEADMAN DEFYING THE NAVY!!
...!!
...!?
MR. GENZO ...
HOW... HOW DID YOU KNOW !!?
KLIK
KLIK
I KNEW, NAMI!!
KLIK..
KLIK
!

READ THIS WAY

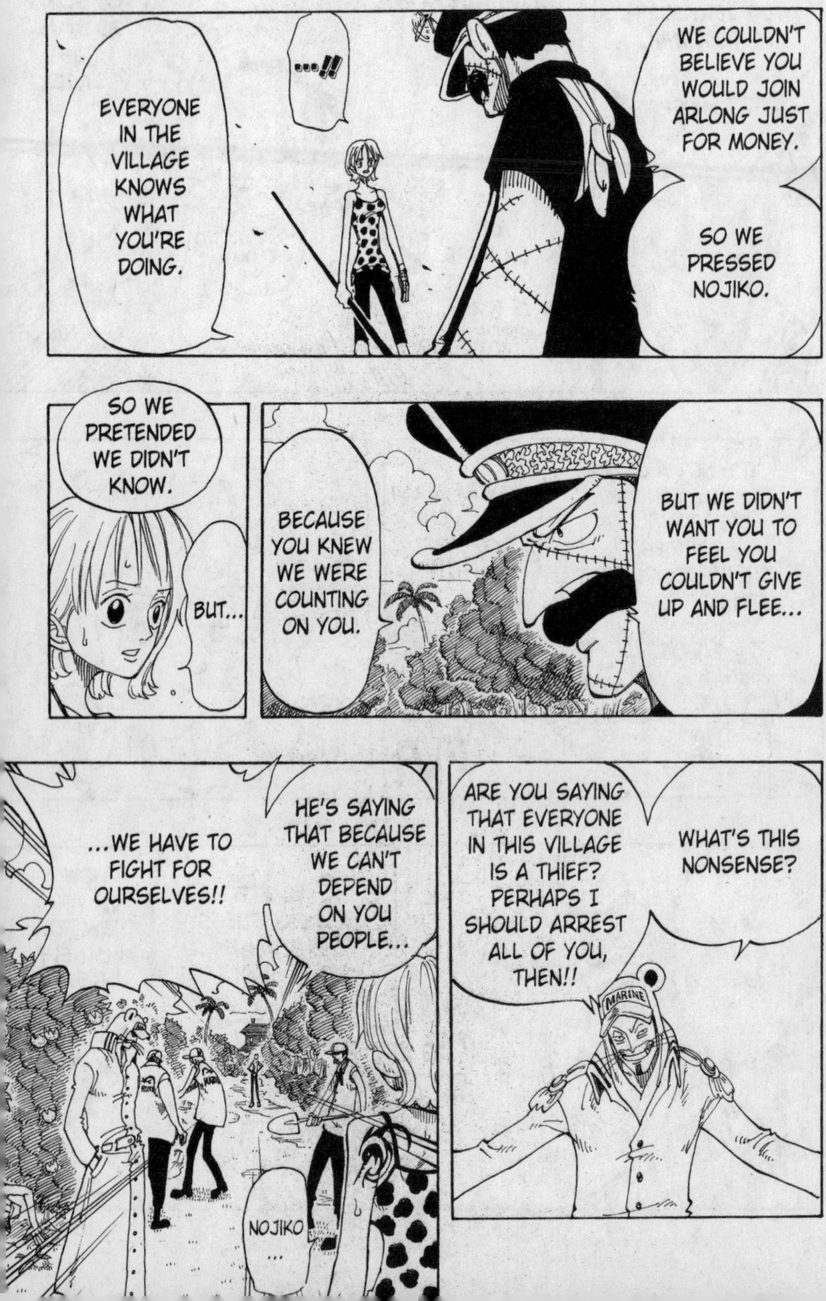
WE COULDN'T BELIEVE YOU WOULD JOIN ARLONG JUST FOR MONEY.
SO WE PRESSED NOJIKO.
...!!
EVERYONE IN THE VILLAGE KNOWS WHAT YOU'RE DOING.
BUT WE DIDN'T WANT YOU TO FEEL YOU COULDN'T GIVE UP AND FLEE...
BECAUSE YOU KNEW WE WERE COUNTING ON YOU.
SO WE PRETENDED WE DIDN'T KNOW.
BUT...
WHAT'S THIS NONSENSE?
ARE YOU SAYING THAT EVERYONE IN THIS VILLAGE IS A THIEF? PERHAPS I SHOULD ARREST ALL OF YOU, THEN!!
MARINE
HE'S SAYING THAT BECAUSE WE CAN'T DEPEND ON YOU PEOPLE...
...WE HAVE TO FIGHT FOR OURSELVES!!
NOJIKO...

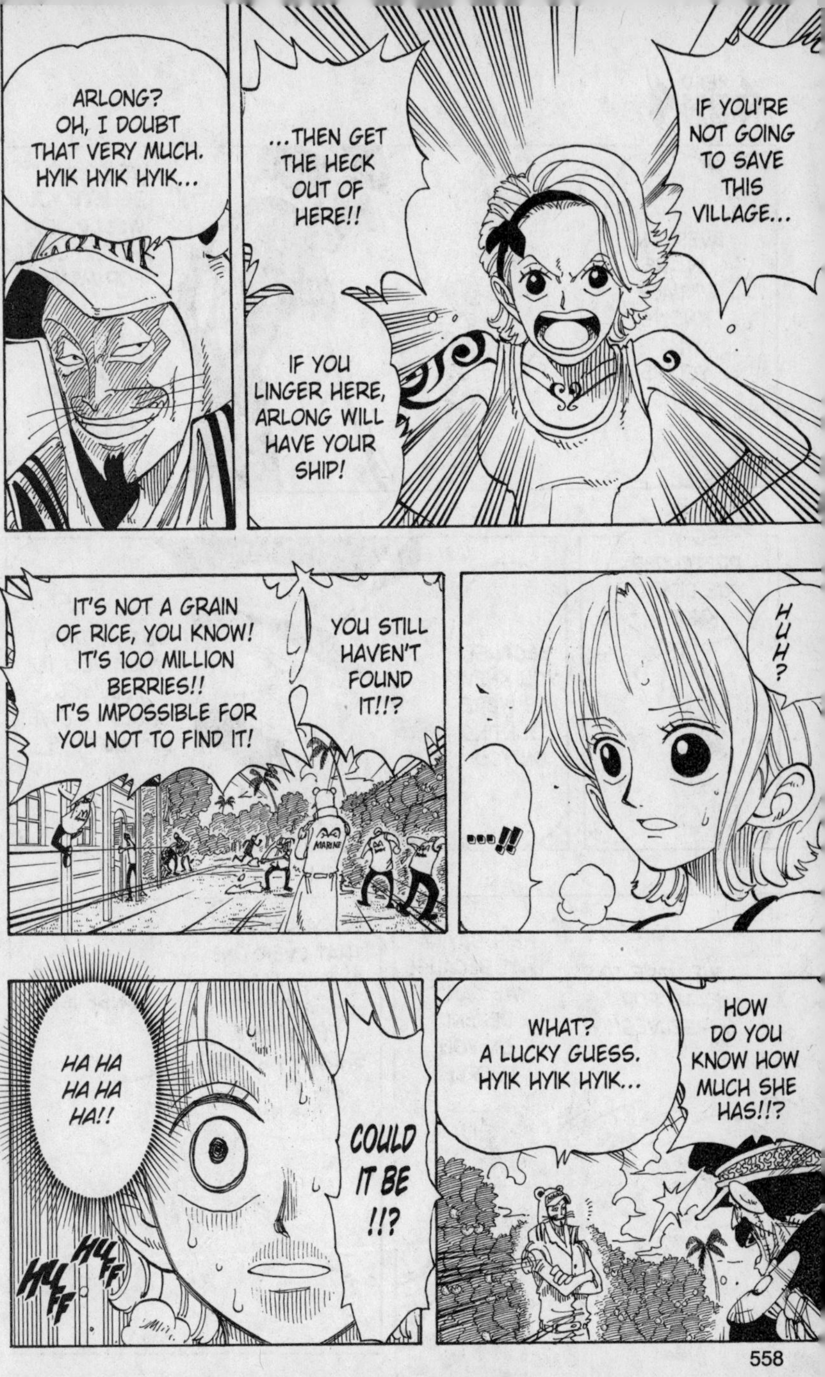
IF YOU'RE NOT GOING TO SAVE THIS VILLAGE...
...THEN GET THE HECK OUT OF HERE!!
IF YOU LINGER HERE, ARLONG WILL HAVE YOUR SHIP!
ARLONG? OH, I DOUBT THAT VERY MUCH. HYIK HYIK HYIK...
HUH?
...!!
YOU STILL HAVEN'T FOUND IT!!?
IT'S NOT A GRAIN OF RICE, YOU KNOW! IT'S 100 MILLION BERRIES!! IT'S IMPOSSIBLE FOR YOU NOT TO FIND IT!
HOW DO YOU KNOW HOW MUCH SHE HAS!!?
WHAT? A LUCKY GUESS. HYIK HYIK HYIK...
COULD IT BE !!?
HA HA HA HA HA!!
HUFF HUFF

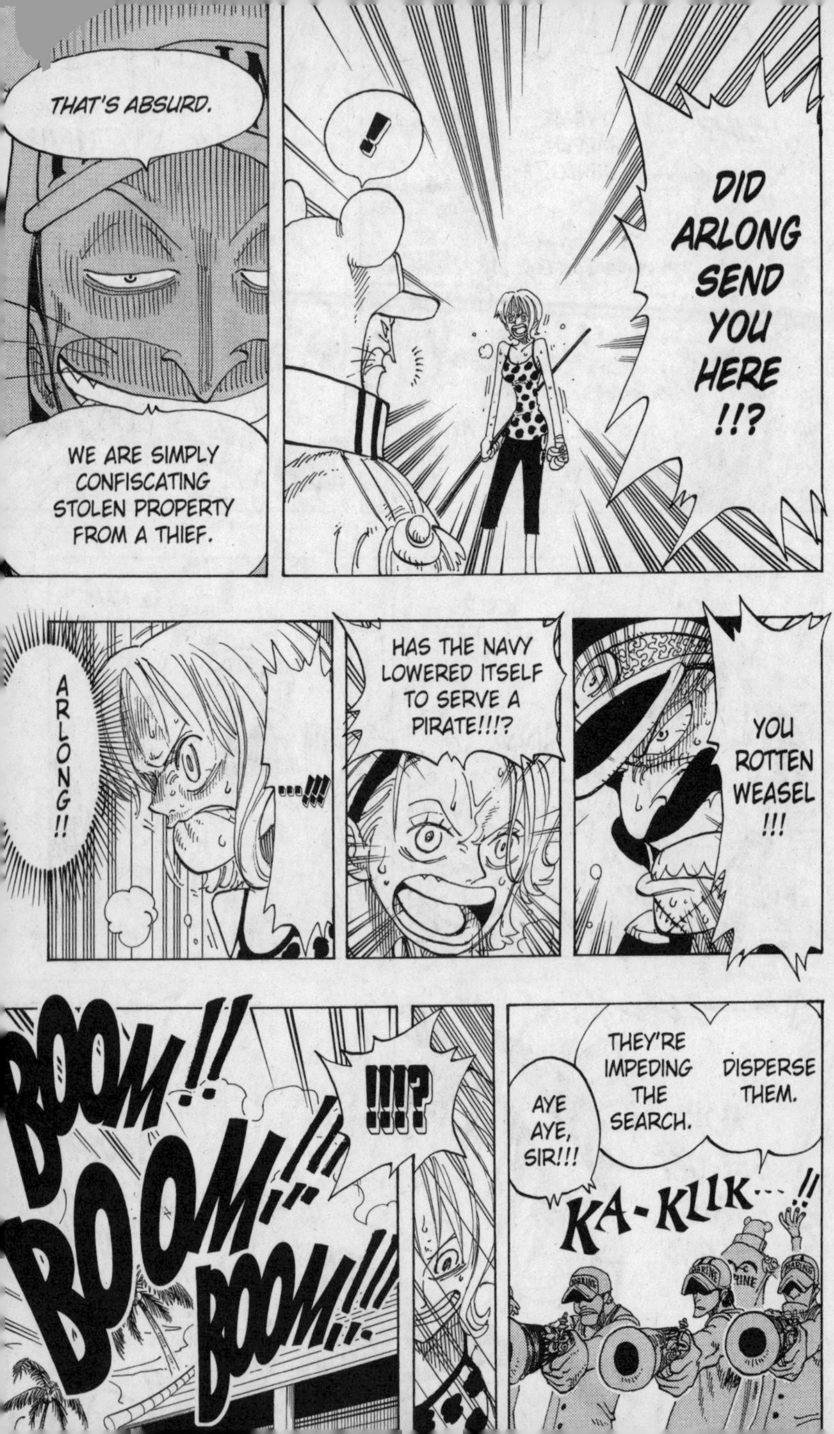
DID ARLONG SEND YOU HERE!!?
!
THAT'S ABSURD.
WE ARE SIMPLY CONFISCATING STOLEN PROPERTY FROM A THIEF.
YOU ROTTEN WEASEL!!!
HAS THE NAVY LOWERED ITSELF TO SERVE A PIRATE!!!?
ARLONG!!
...!!!
DISPERSE THEM.
THEY'RE IMPEDING THE SEARCH.
AYE AYE, SIR!!!
KA-KLIK...!!
!!!?
BOOM!!
BOOM!!
BOOM!!

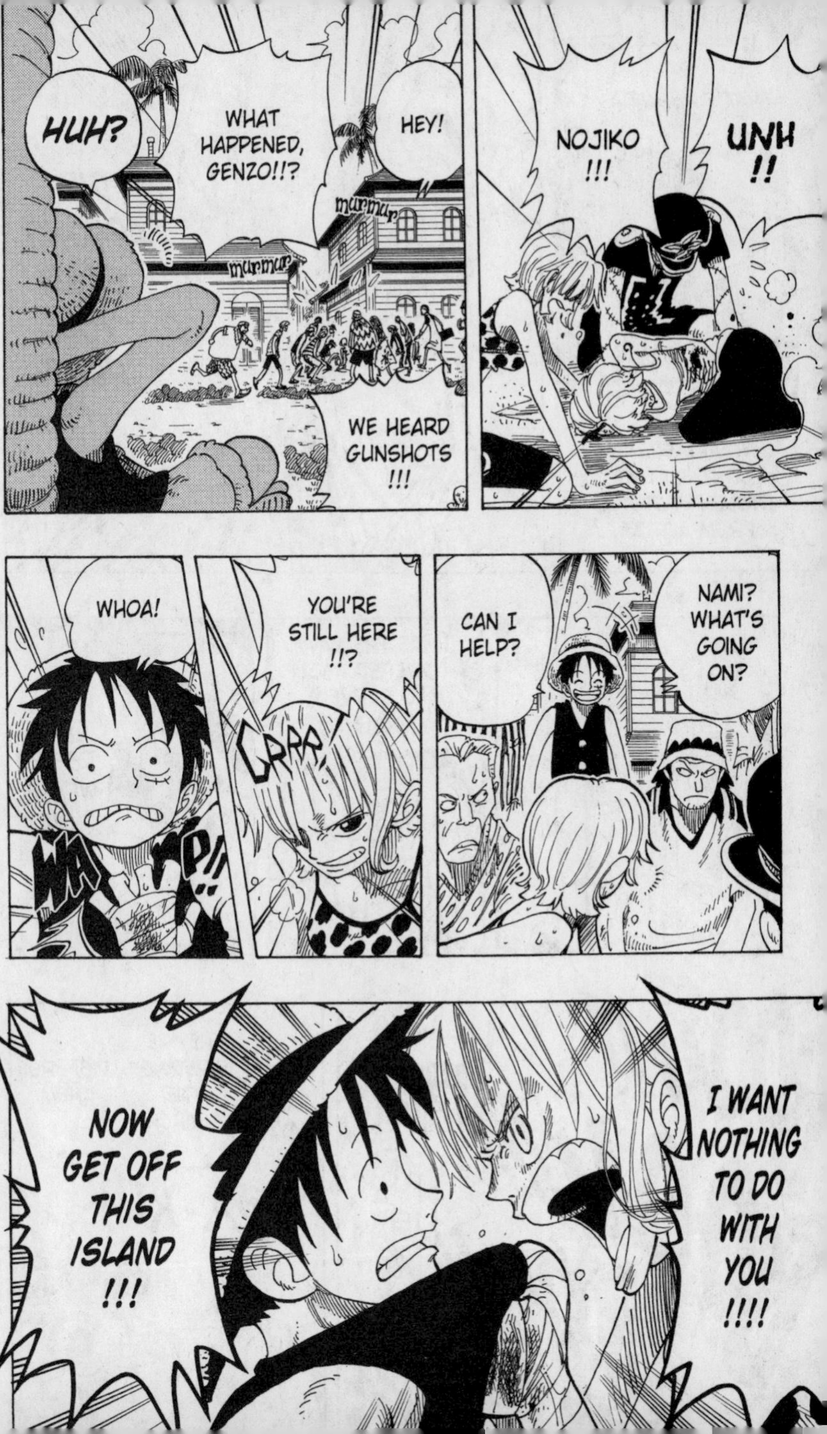
UNH !!
NOJIKO !!!
HEY!
WHAT HAPPENED, GENZO!!?
murmur
murmur
WE HEARD GUNSHOTS !!!
HUH?
NAMI? WHAT'S GOING ON?
CAN I HELP?
YOU'RE STILL HERE !!?
GRRR
WHOA!
I WANT NOTHING TO DO WITH YOU !!!!
NOW GET OFF THIS ISLAND !!!

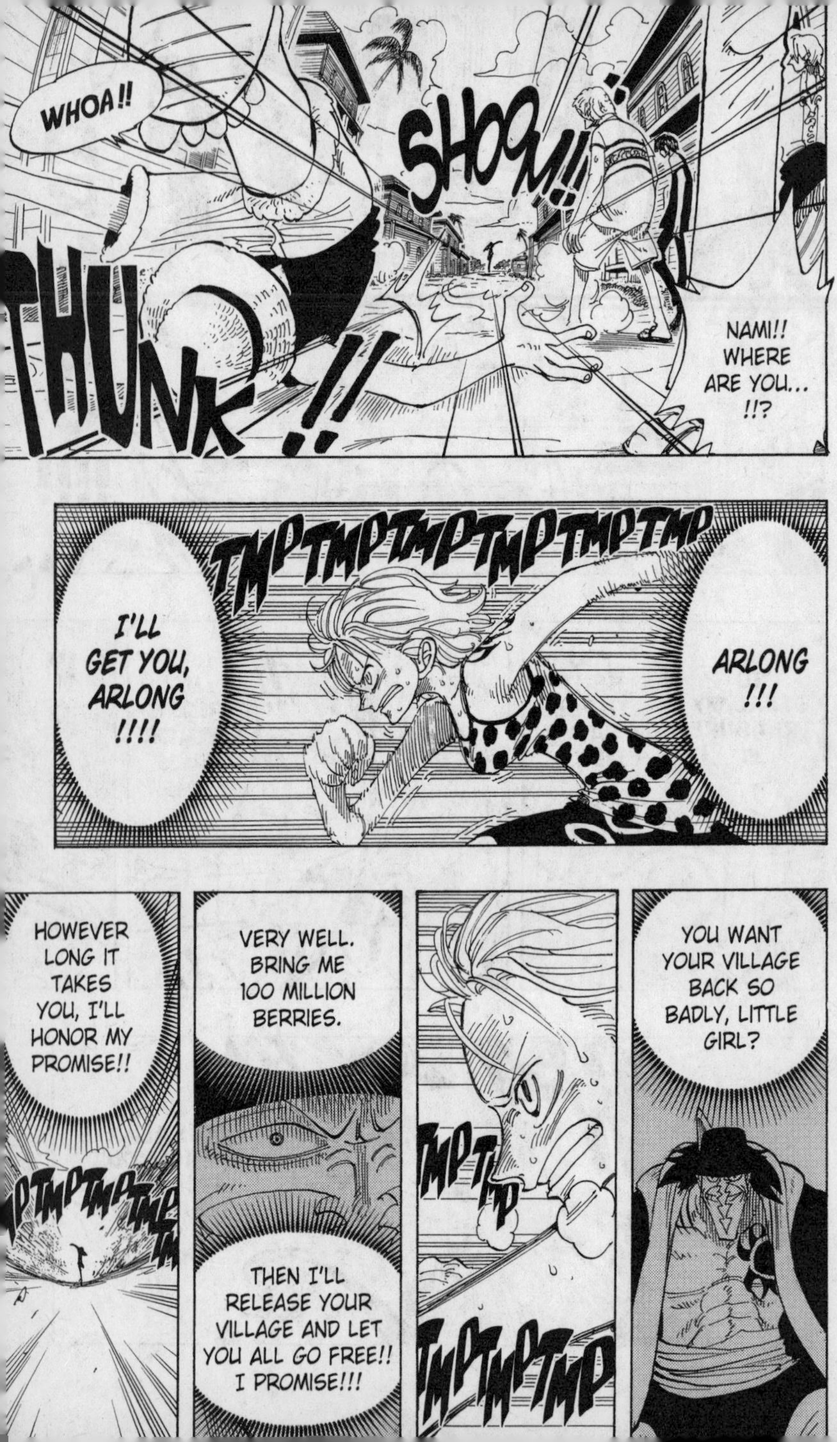
SHOOM!!
NAMI!! WHERE ARE YOU... !!?
WHOA!!
THUNK!!
ARLONG !!!
TMP TMP TMP TMP TMP TMP TMP
I'LL GET YOU, ARLONG !!!!
YOU WANT YOUR VILLAGE BACK SO BADLY, LITTLE GIRL?
TMP TMP
TMP TMP TMP
VERY WELL. BRING ME 100 MILLION BERRIES.
THEN I'LL RELEASE YOUR VILLAGE AND LET YOU ALL GO FREE!! I PROMISE!!!
HOWEVER LONG IT TAKES YOU, I'LL HONOR MY PROMISE!!
TMP TMP TMP TMP

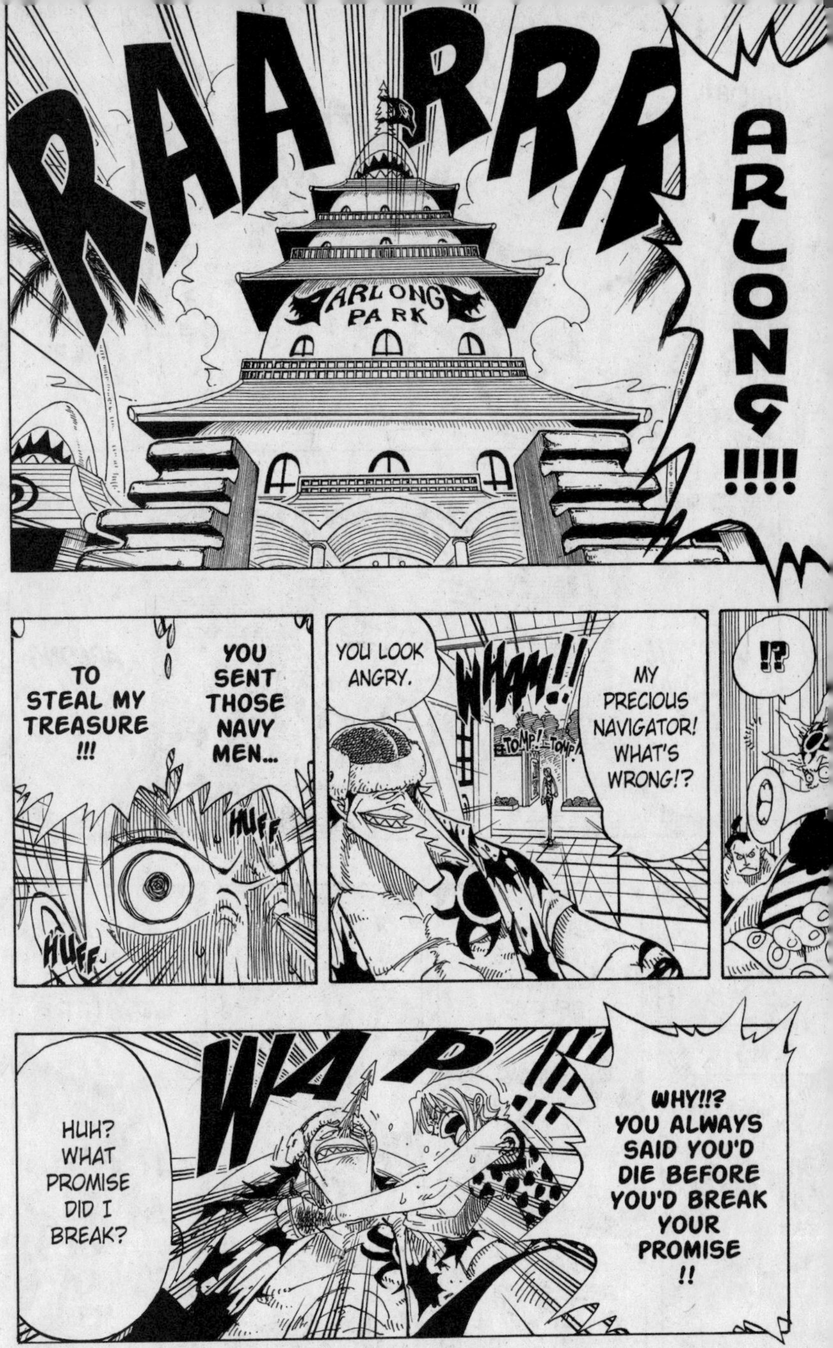
ARLONG!!!!
RAARRR
ARLONG PARK
!?
MY PRECIOUS NAVIGATOR! WHAT'S WRONG!?
WHAM!!
TOMP! TOMP!
YOU LOOK ANGRY.
YOU SENT THOSE NAVY MEN...
TO STEAL MY TREASURE !!!
HUFF
HUFF
WHY!!? YOU ALWAYS SAID YOU'D DIE BEFORE YOU'D BREAK YOUR PROMISE !!
WAP!!!
HUH? WHAT PROMISE DID I BREAK?

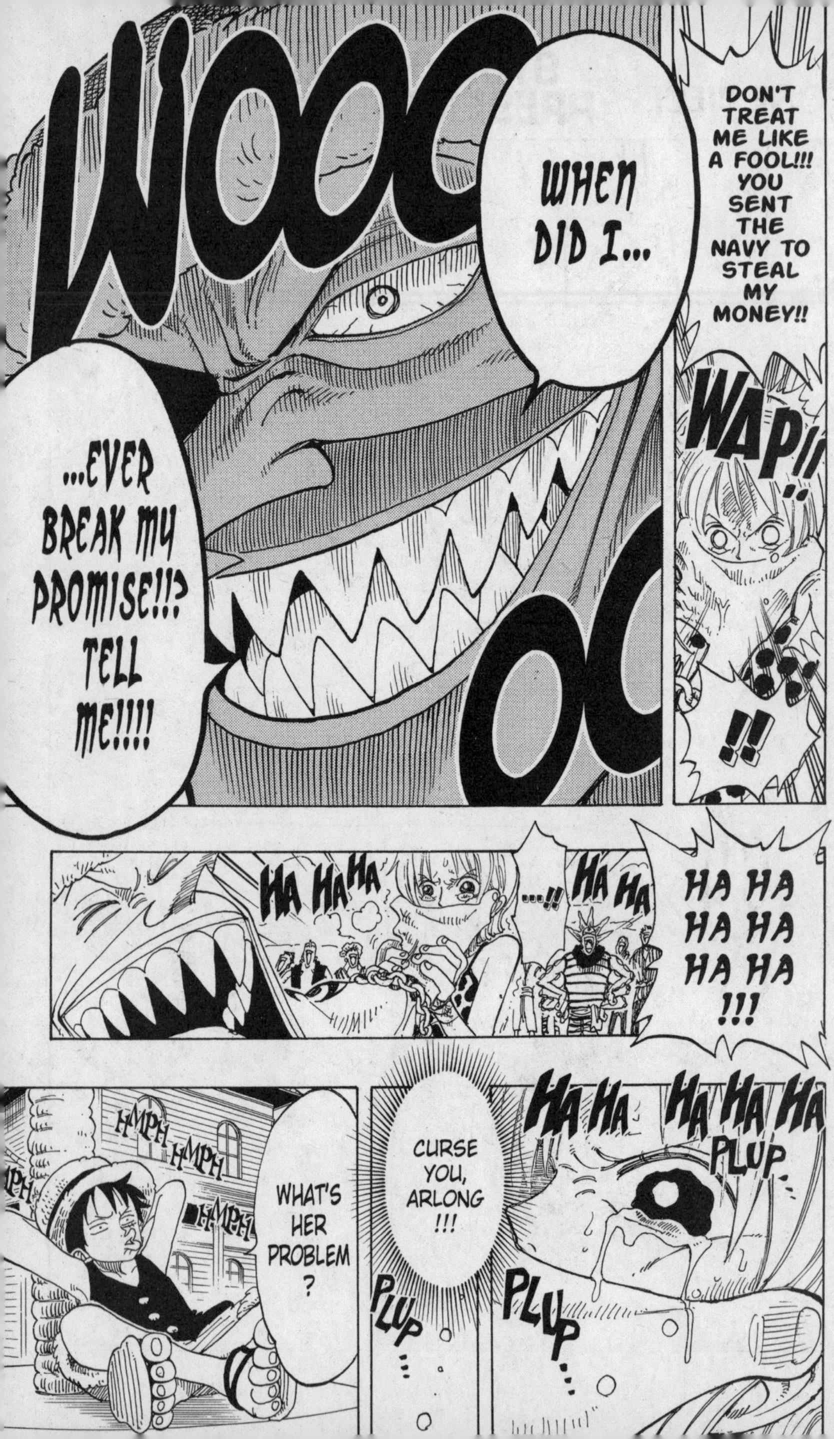
DON'T TREAT ME LIKE A FOOL!!! YOU SENT THE NAVY TO STEAL MY MONEY!!
WAP!!
!!
WOOO
WHEN DID I...
...EVER BREAK MY PROMISE!!? TELL ME!!!!
OO
HA HA HA HA HA HA !!!
HA HA
...!!
HA HA HA
HA HA HA HA HA
PLUP
CURSE YOU, ARLONG!!!
PLUP...
PLUP...
WHAT'S HER PROBLEM?
HMPH HMPH HMPH HMPH

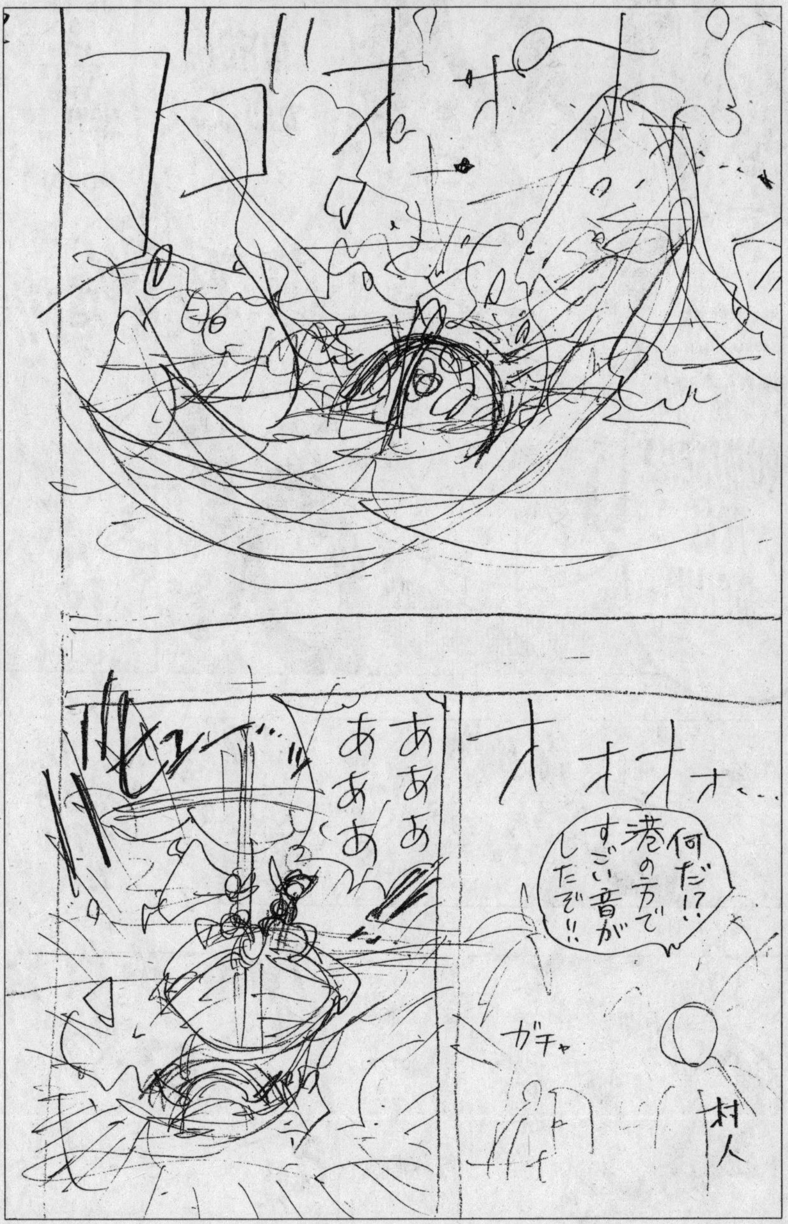
オオオオ…
何だ!? 港の方ですごい音がしたぞ!!
ガチャ
村人
ああああああ

# Chapter 81: TEARS

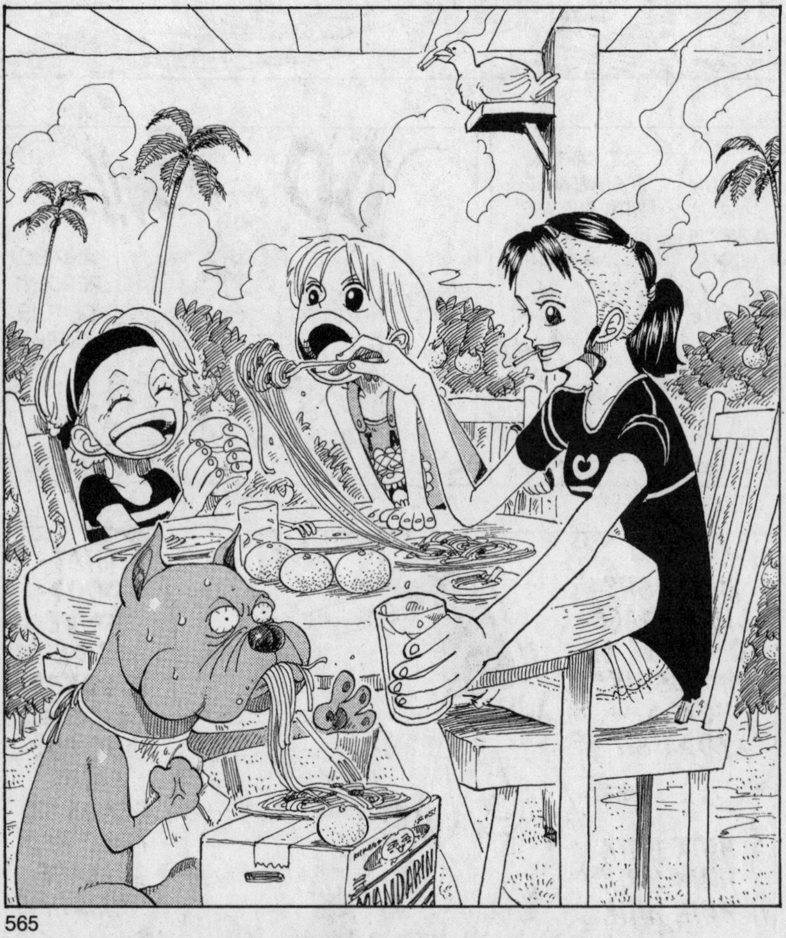
MANDARIN

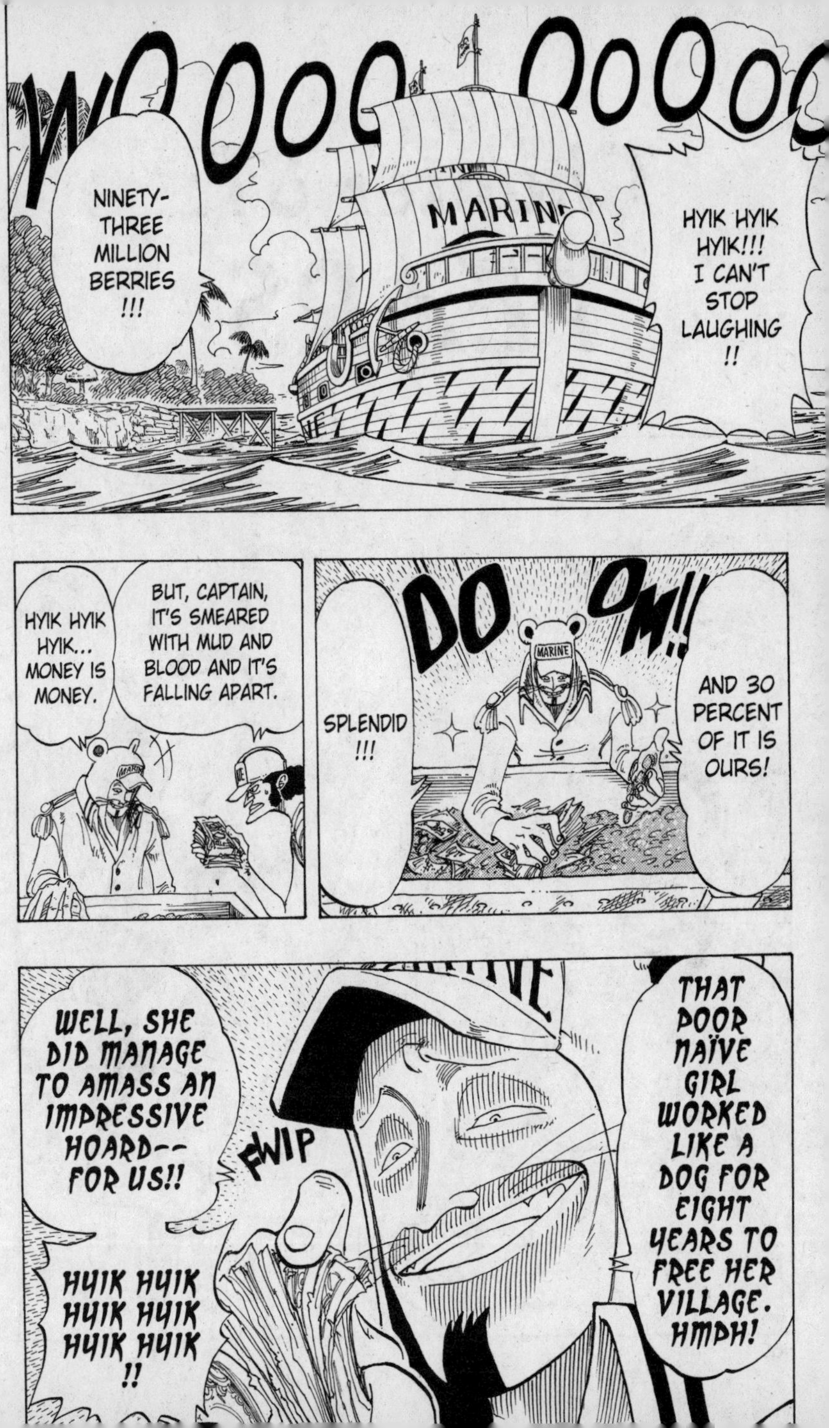
WOOOO OOOOO
HYIK HYIK HYIK!!! I CAN'T STOP LAUGHING!!
NINETY-THREE MILLION BERRIES!!!
MARINE
AND 30 PERCENT OF IT IS OURS!
DOOM!!
MARINE
SPLENDID!!!
BUT, CAPTAIN, IT'S SMEARED WITH MUD AND BLOOD AND IT'S FALLING APART.
HYIK HYIK HYIK... MONEY IS MONEY.
THAT POOR NAÏVE GIRL WORKED LIKE A DOG FOR EIGHT YEARS TO FREE HER VILLAGE. HMPH!
WELL, SHE DID MANAGE TO AMASS AN IMPRESSIVE HOARD--FOR US!!
FWIP
HYIK HYIK HYIK HYIK HYIK HYIK!!

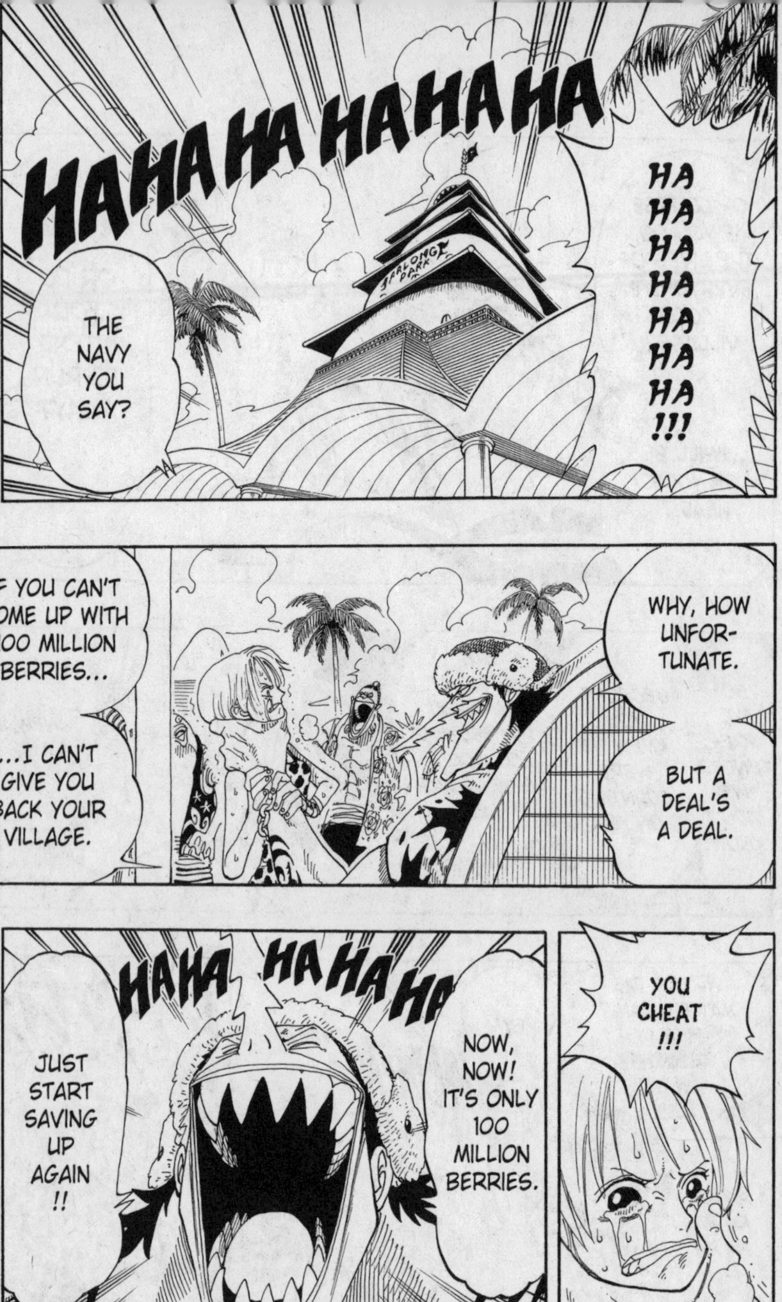
HAHAHAHAHAHAHA
HA HA HA HA HA HA HA!!!
THE NAVY YOU SAY?
WHY, HOW UNFORTUNATE.
BUT A DEAL'S A DEAL.
IF YOU CAN'T COME UP WITH 100 MILLION BERRIES...
...I CAN'T GIVE YOU BACK YOUR VILLAGE.
YOU CHEAT!!!
HAHA HAHAHA
NOW, NOW! IT'S ONLY 100 MILLION BERRIES.
JUST START SAVING UP AGAIN!!

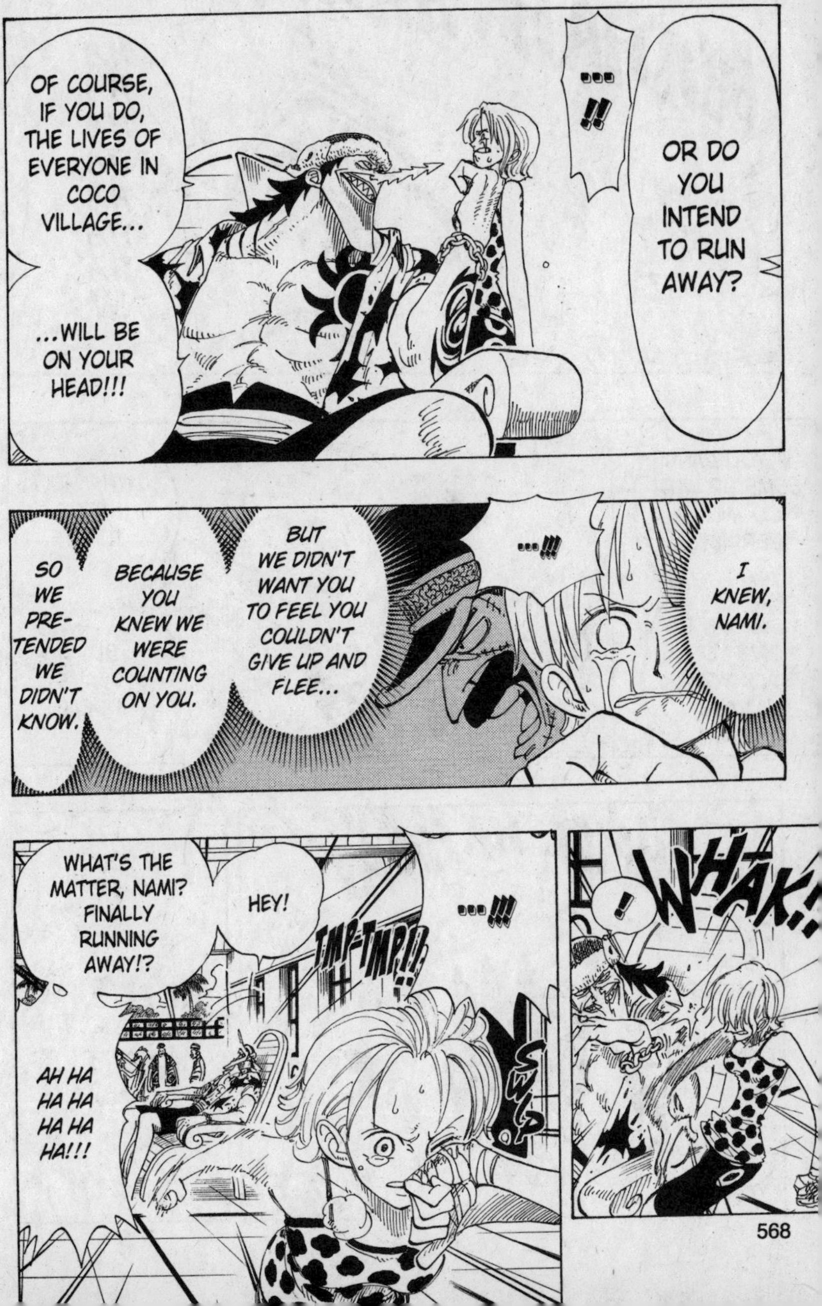
OR DO YOU INTEND TO RUN AWAY?
...!!
OF COURSE, IF YOU DO, THE LIVES OF EVERYONE IN COCO VILLAGE...
...WILL BE ON YOUR HEAD!!!
I KNEW, NAMI.
...!!!
BUT WE DIDN'T WANT YOU TO FEEL YOU COULDN'T GIVE UP AND FLEE...
BECAUSE YOU KNEW WE WERE COUNTING ON YOU.
SO WE PRE-TENDED WE DIDN'T KNOW.
WHAK!!
!
...!!!
TMP-TMP!!
SWIP
HEY!
WHAT'S THE MATTER, NAMI? FINALLY RUNNING AWAY!?
AH HA HA HA HA HA HA!!!

READ THIS WAY

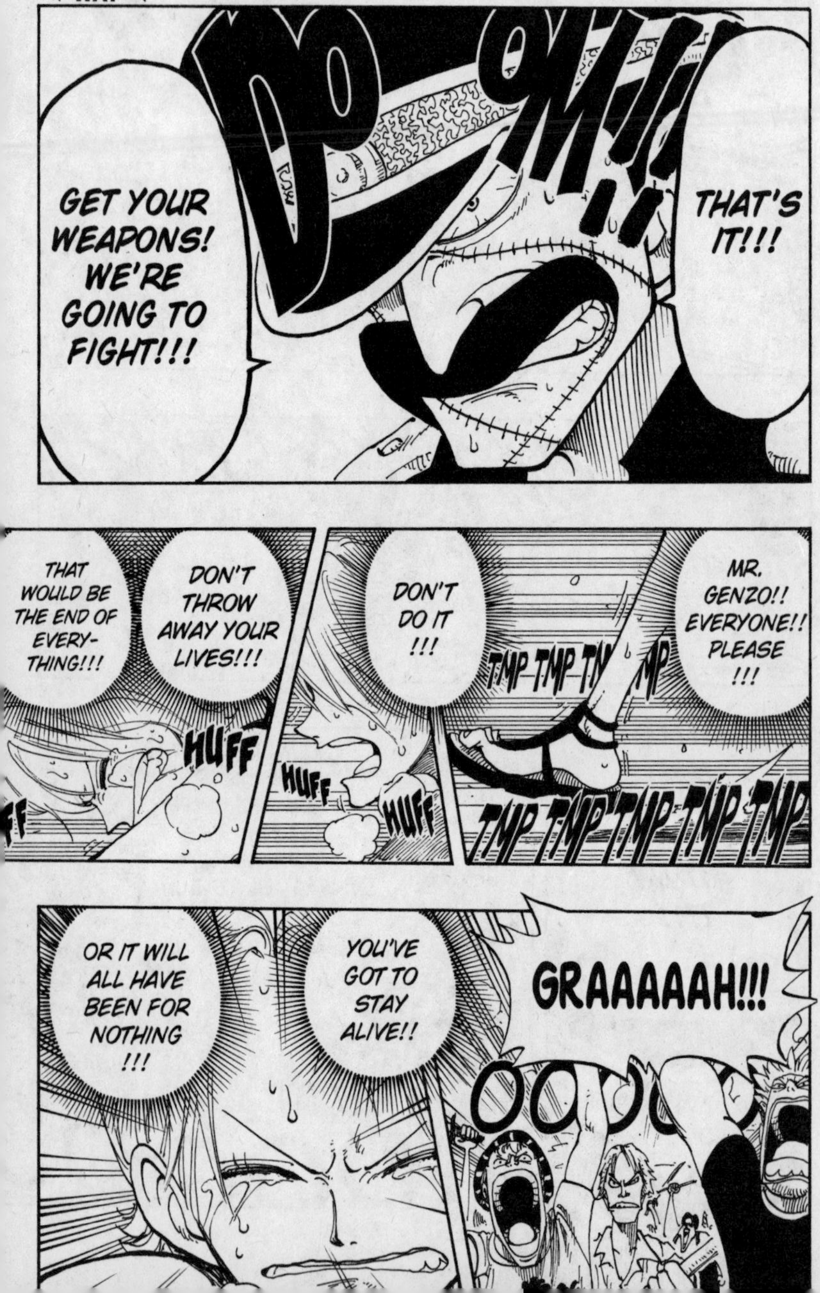
THAT'S IT!!!
DOOM!!
GET YOUR WEAPONS! WE'RE GOING TO FIGHT!!!
MR. GENZO!! EVERYONE!! PLEASE!!!
TMP TMP TMP TMP TMP
DON'T DO IT!!!
HUFF
HUFF
DON'T THROW AWAY YOUR LIVES!!!
THAT WOULD BE THE END OF EVERY-THING!!!
HUFF
GRAAAAAH!!!
YOU'VE GOT TO STAY ALIVE!!
OR IT WILL ALL HAVE BEEN FOR NOTHING!!!

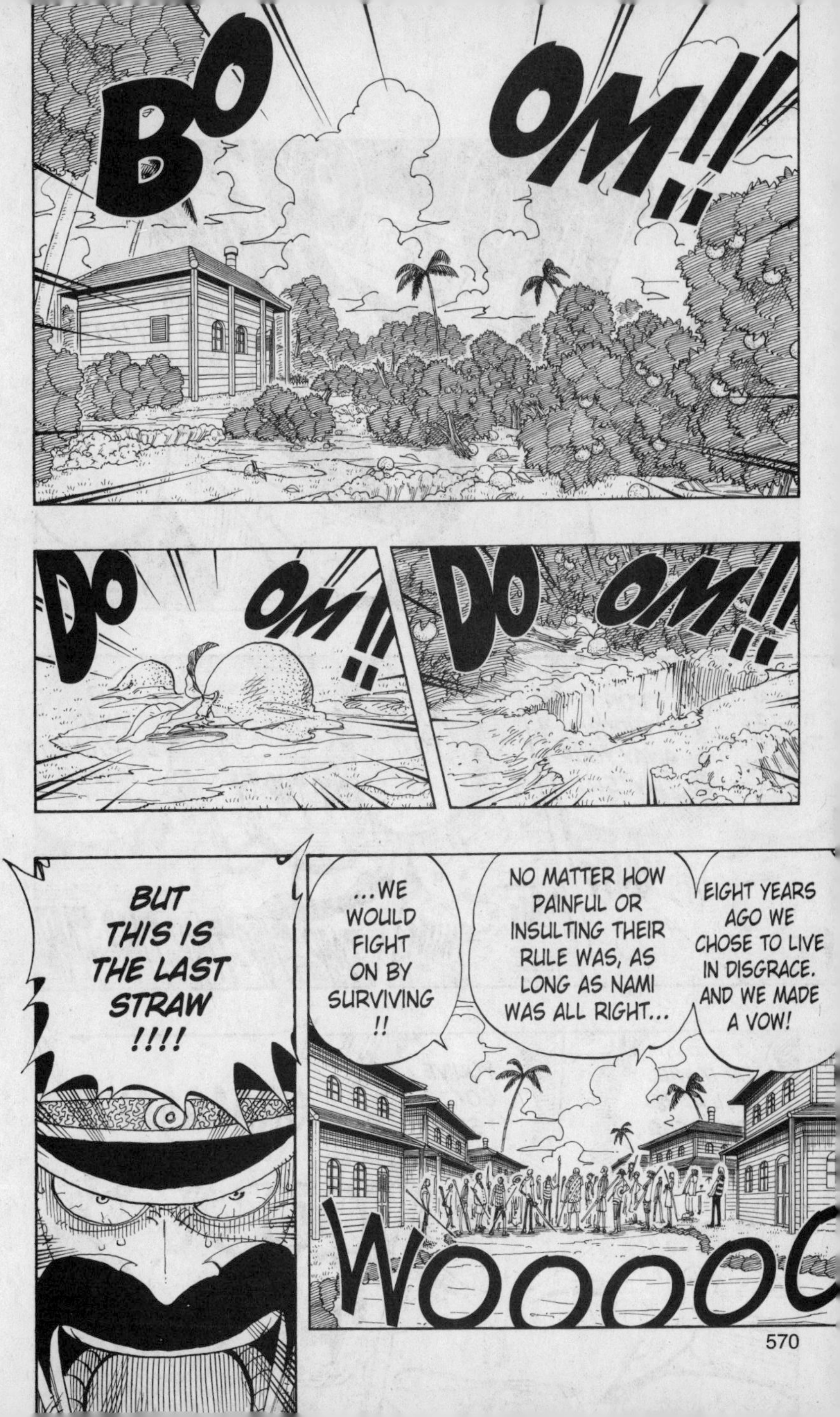
BOOM!!
DOOM!!
DOOM!!
EIGHT YEARS AGO WE CHOSE TO LIVE IN DISGRACE. AND WE MADE A VOW!
NO MATTER HOW PAINFUL OR INSULTING THEIR RULE WAS, AS LONG AS NAMI WAS ALL RIGHT...
...WE WOULD FIGHT ON BY SURVIVING !!
WOOOOO
BUT THIS IS THE LAST STRAW !!!!

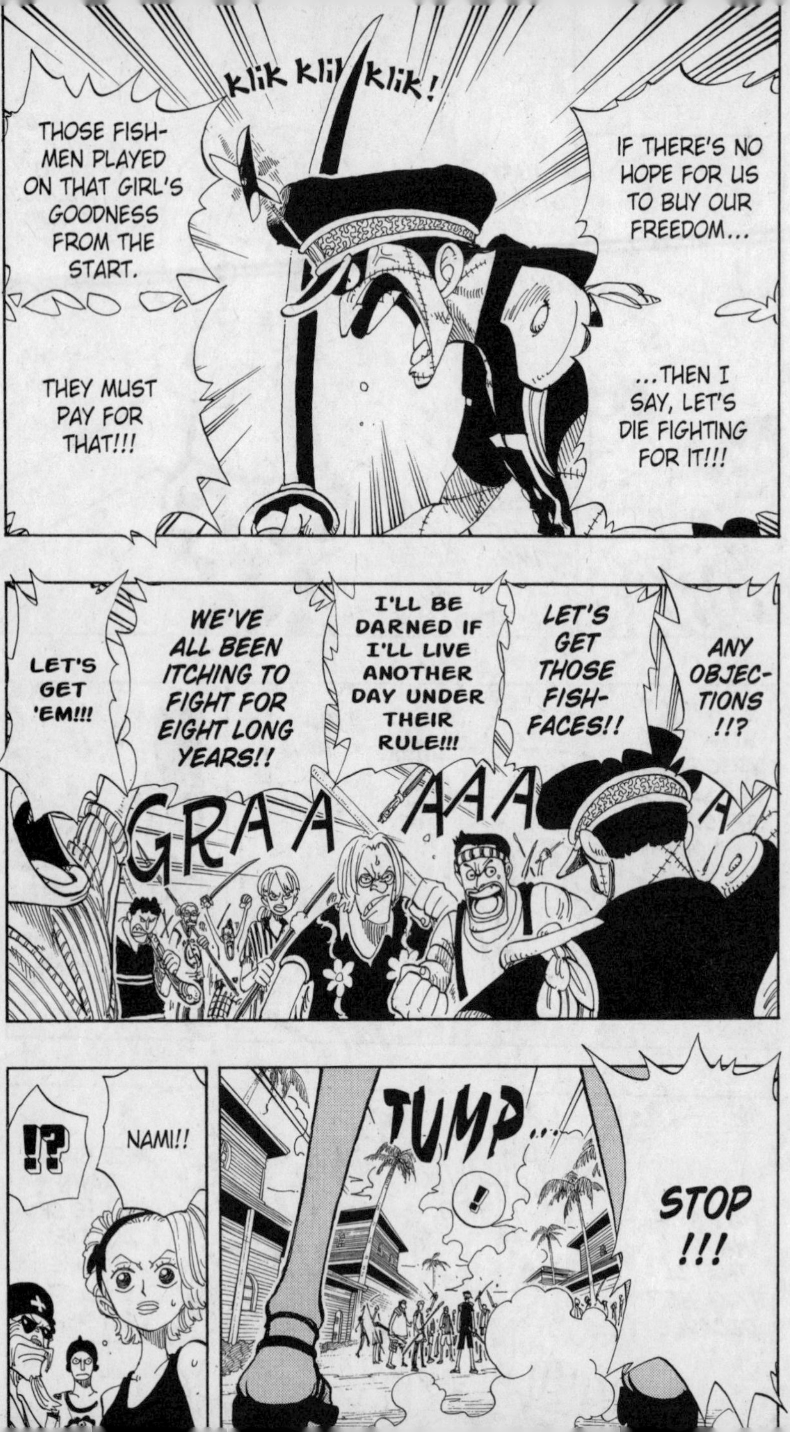
KLIK KLIK KLIK!
IF THERE'S NO HOPE FOR US TO BUY OUR FREEDOM...
...THEN I SAY, LET'S DIE FIGHTING FOR IT!!!
THOSE FISH-MEN PLAYED ON THAT GIRL'S GOODNESS FROM THE START.
THEY MUST PAY FOR THAT!!!
ANY OBJECTIONS!!?
LET'S GET THOSE FISH-FACES!!
I'LL BE DARNED IF I'LL LIVE ANOTHER DAY UNDER THEIR RULE!!!
WE'VE ALL BEEN ITCHING TO FIGHT FOR EIGHT LONG YEARS!!
LET'S GET 'EM!!!
GRAA AAA A
STOP!!!
TUMP...
!
NAMI!!
!?

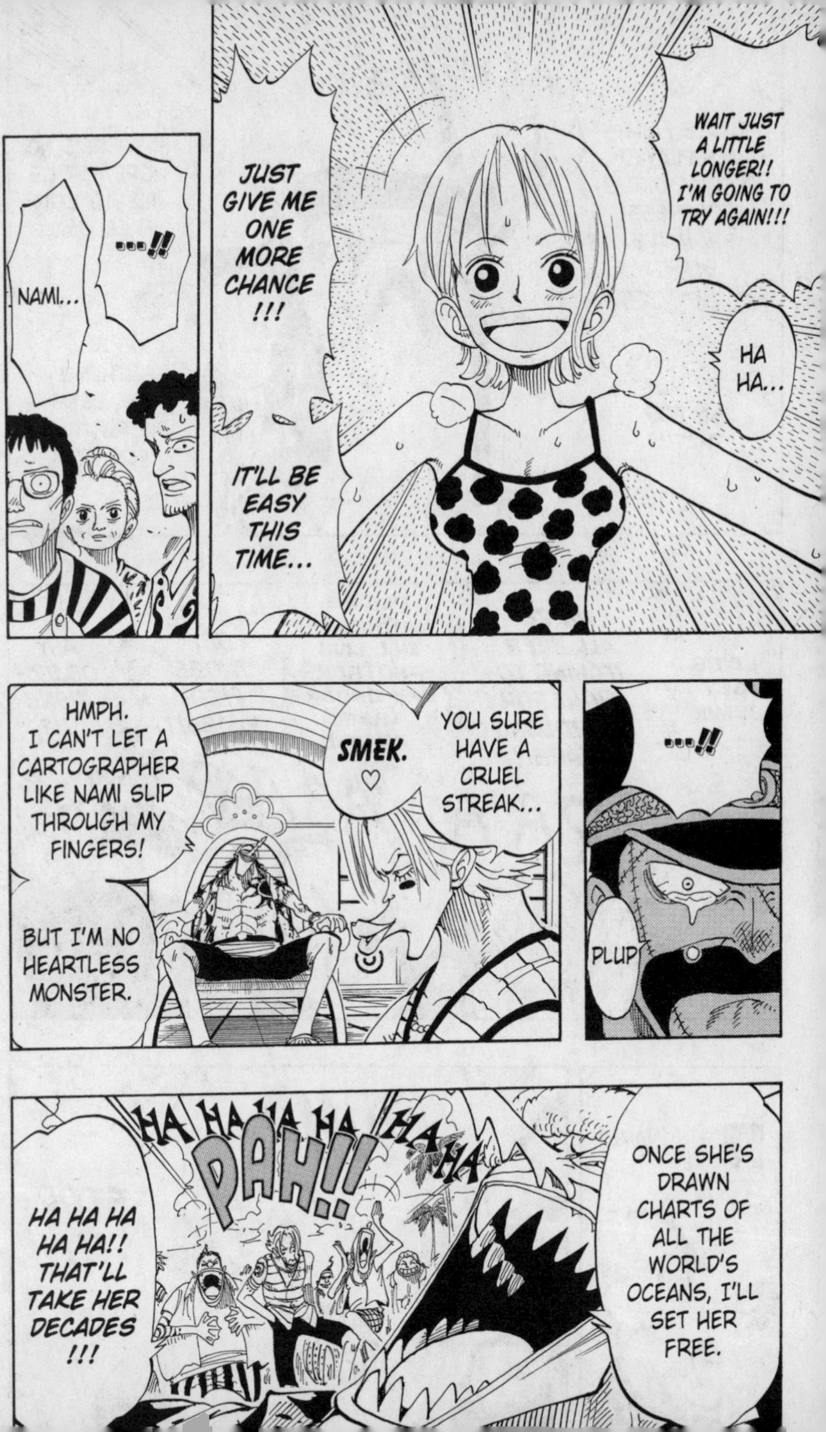
WAIT JUST A LITTLE LONGER!! I'M GOING TO TRY AGAIN!!!
JUST GIVE ME ONE MORE CHANCE !!!
HA HA...
IT'LL BE EASY THIS TIME...
...!!
NAMI...
...!!
PLUP
YOU SURE HAVE A CRUEL STREAK...
SMEK. ♡
HMPH. I CAN'T LET A CARTOGRAPHER LIKE NAMI SLIP THROUGH MY FINGERS!
BUT I'M NO HEARTLESS MONSTER.
ONCE SHE'S DRAWN CHARTS OF ALL THE WORLD'S OCEANS, I'LL SET HER FREE.
HA HA HA HA HA HA
PAH!!
HA HA HA HA!! THAT'LL TAKE HER DECADES !!!

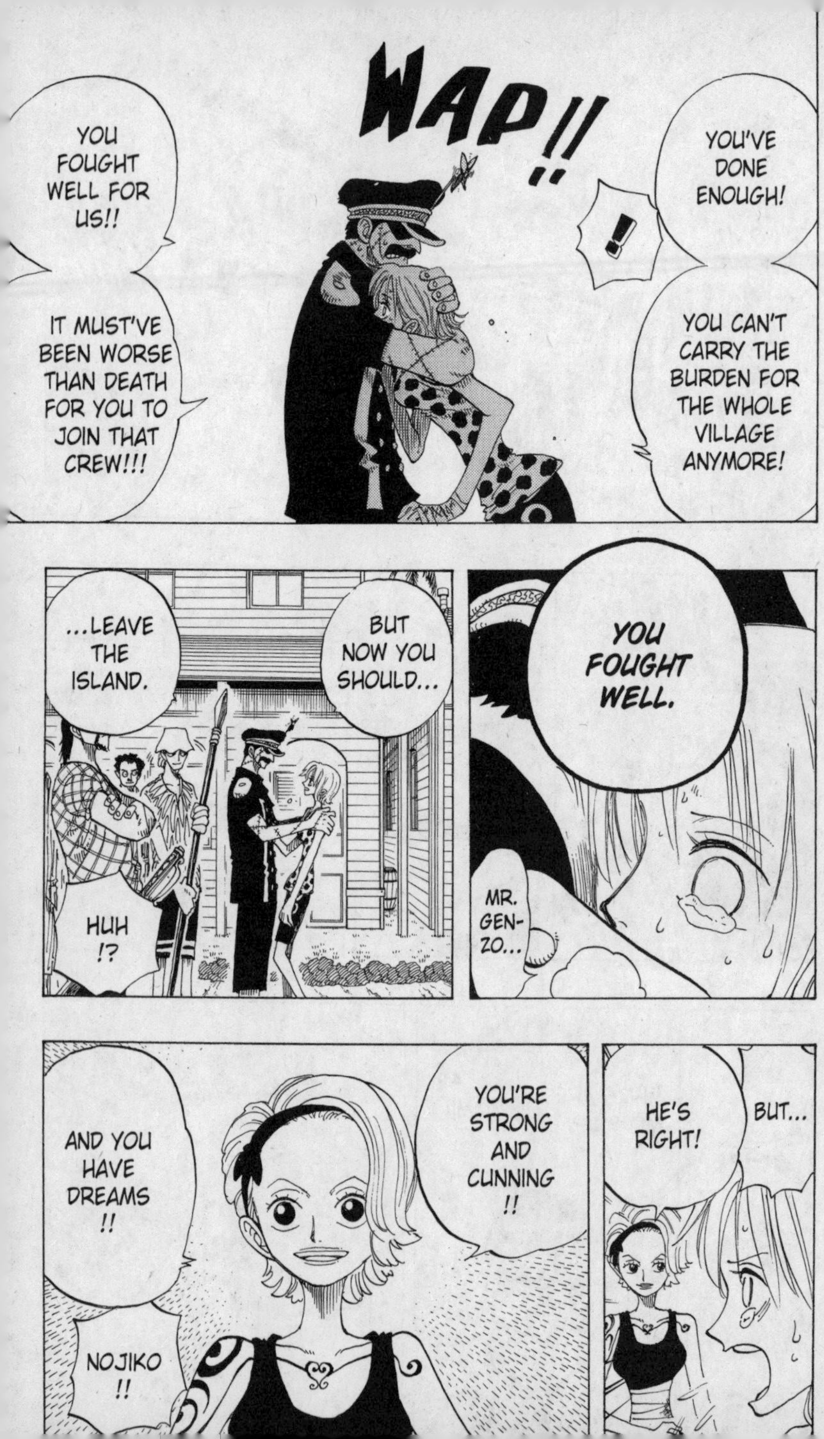
WAP!!
YOU'VE DONE ENOUGH!
YOU CAN'T CARRY THE BURDEN FOR THE WHOLE VILLAGE ANYMORE!
!
YOU FOUGHT WELL FOR US!!
IT MUST'VE BEEN WORSE THAN DEATH FOR YOU TO JOIN THAT CREW!!!
YOU FOUGHT WELL.
MR. GEN-ZO...
BUT NOW YOU SHOULD...
...LEAVE THE ISLAND.
HUH!?
BUT...
HE'S RIGHT!
YOU'RE STRONG AND CUNNING!!
AND YOU HAVE DREAMS!!
NOJIKO!!

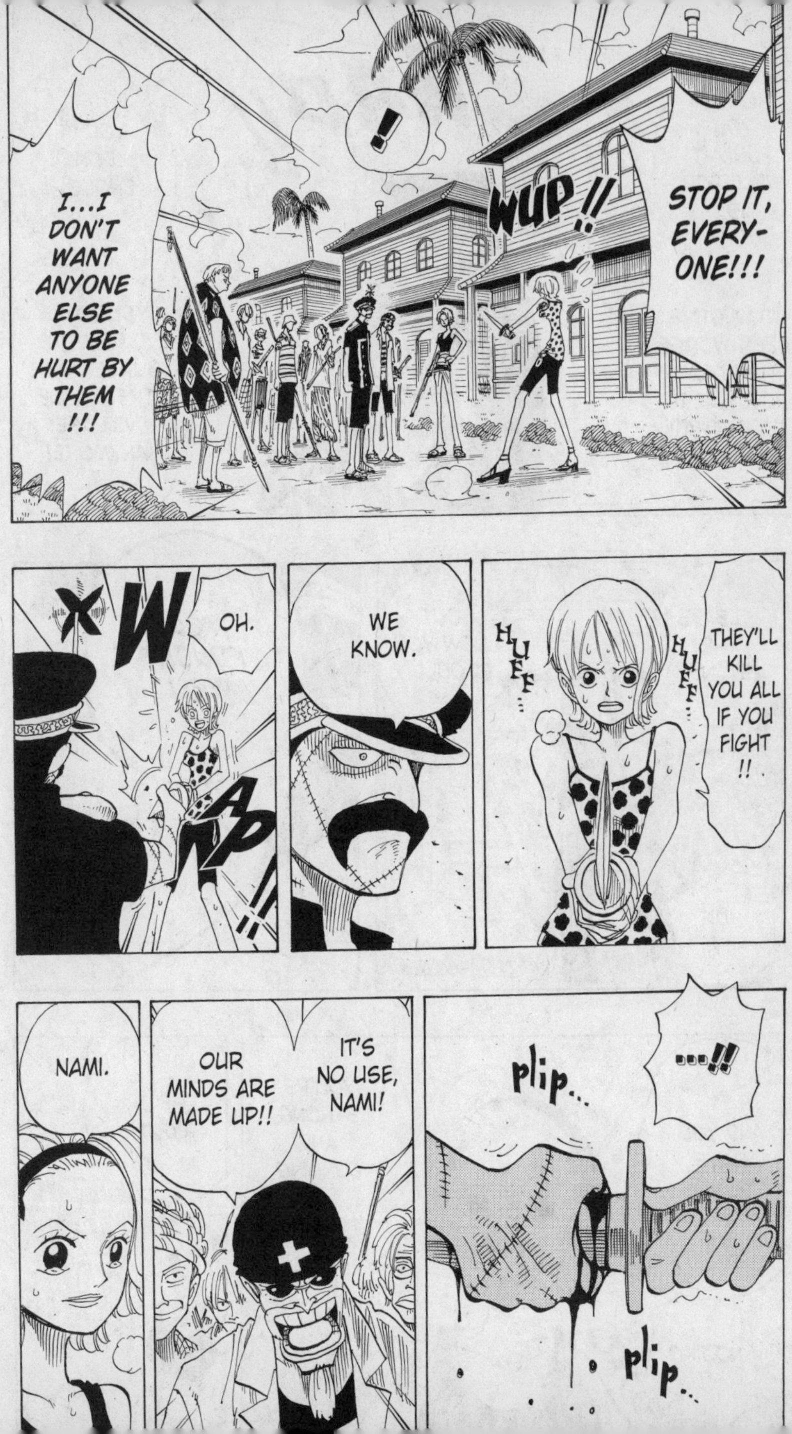
STOP IT, EVERY-ONE!!!
!
WUP!!
I...I DON'T WANT ANYONE ELSE TO BE HURT BY THEM!!!
HUFF... HUFF...
THEY'LL KILL YOU ALL IF YOU FIGHT!!
WE KNOW.
OH.
WAP!!!
...!!
plip...
plip...
IT'S NO USE, NAMI!
OUR MINDS ARE MADE UP!!
NAMI.

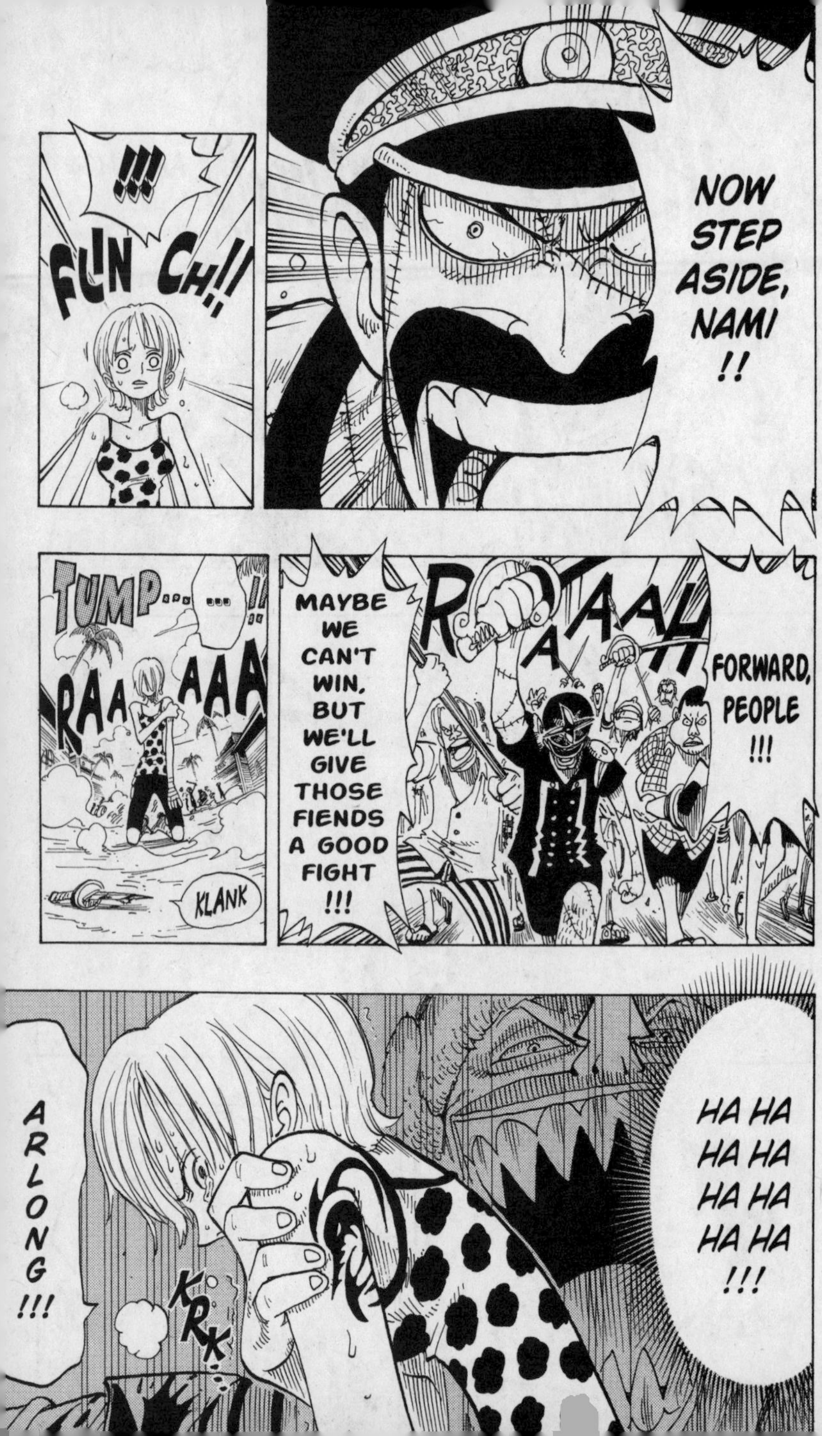
NOW STEP ASIDE, NAMI !!
!!!
FLINCH!!
FORWARD, PEOPLE !!!
RAAAH
MAYBE WE CAN'T WIN, BUT WE'LL GIVE THOSE FIENDS A GOOD FIGHT !!!
TUMP... ...
...!!
RAAAAA
KLANK
HA HA HA HA HA HA HA HA !!!
KRK
ARLONG !!!

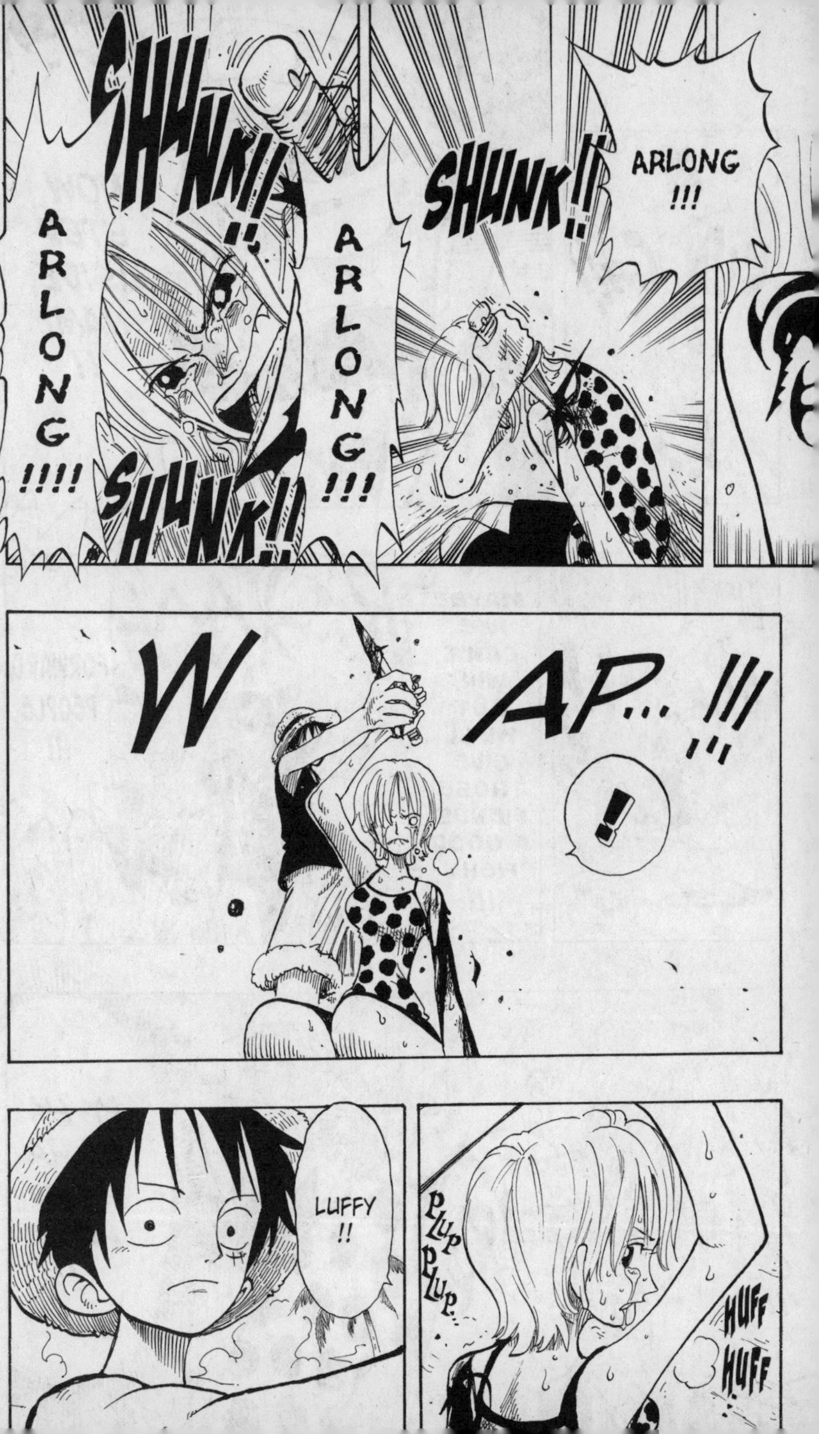
ARLONG !!!
SHUNK!!
ARLONG !!!
SHUNK!!
SHUNK!!
ARLONG !!!!
W AP...!!!
!
HUFF HUFF
PLUP PLUP...
LUFFY !!

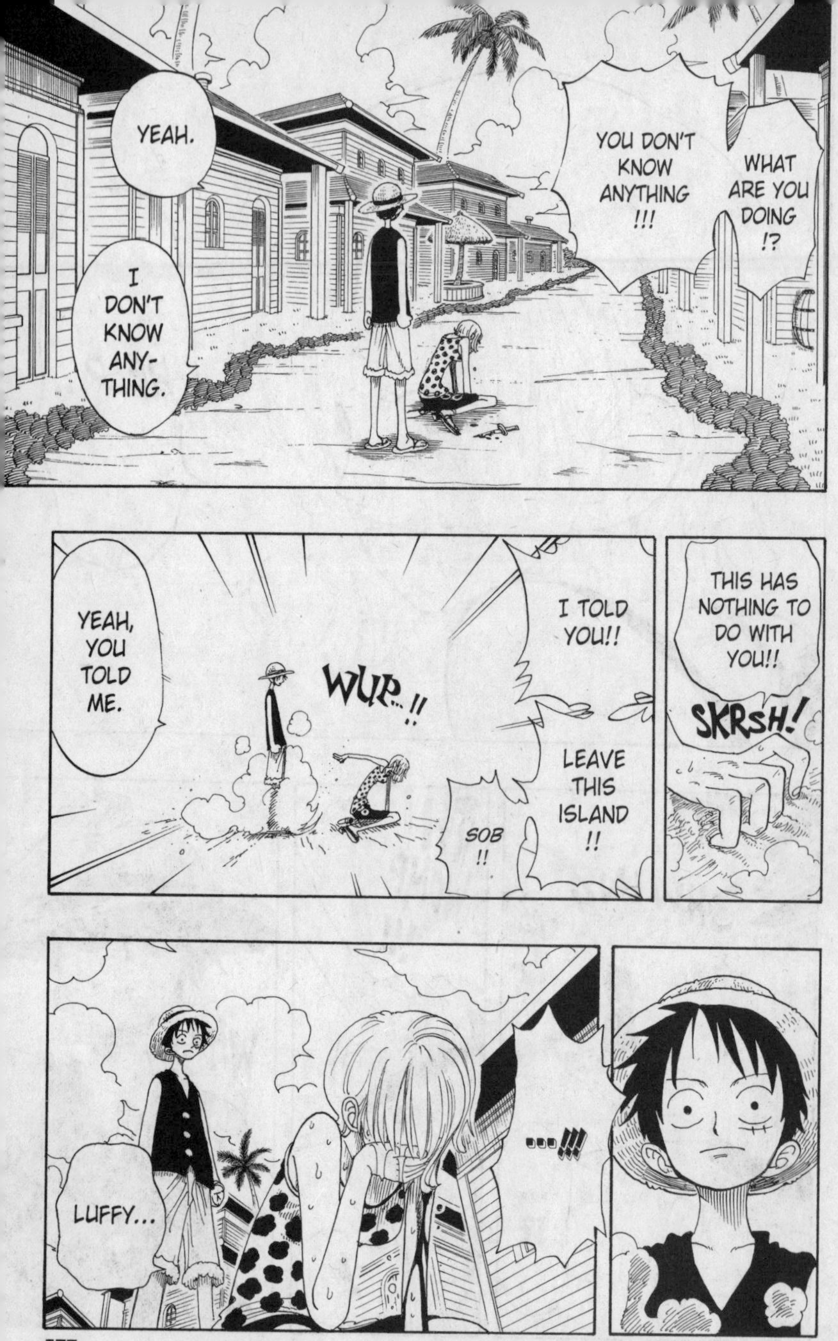
WHAT ARE YOU DOING !?
YOU DON'T KNOW ANYTHING !!!
YEAH.
I DON'T KNOW ANY-THING.
THIS HAS NOTHING TO DO WITH YOU!!
SKRSH!
I TOLD YOU!!
LEAVE THIS ISLAND !!
SOB !!
WUP...!!
YEAH, YOU TOLD ME.
...!!!
LUFFY...

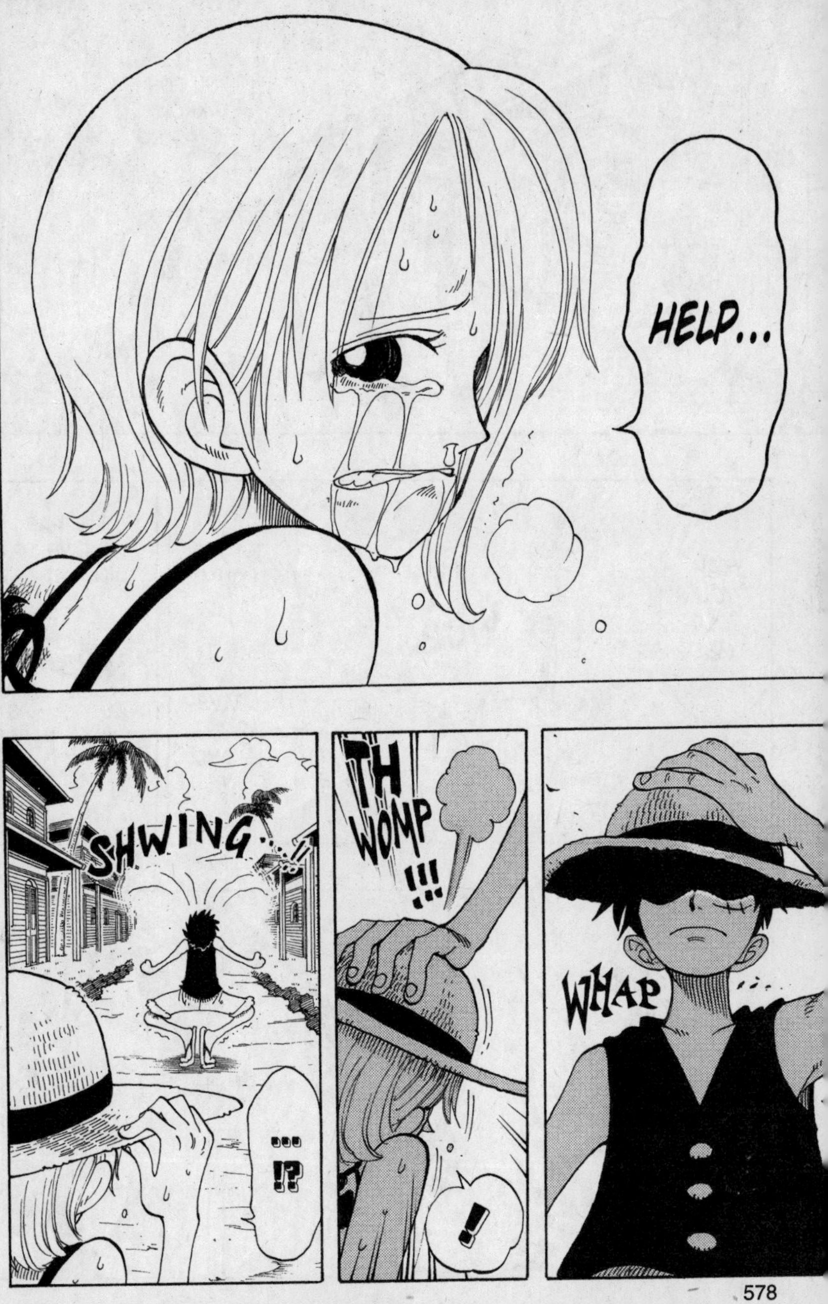
HELP...
WHAP
TH WOMP!!!
!
SHWING...!!
...!?

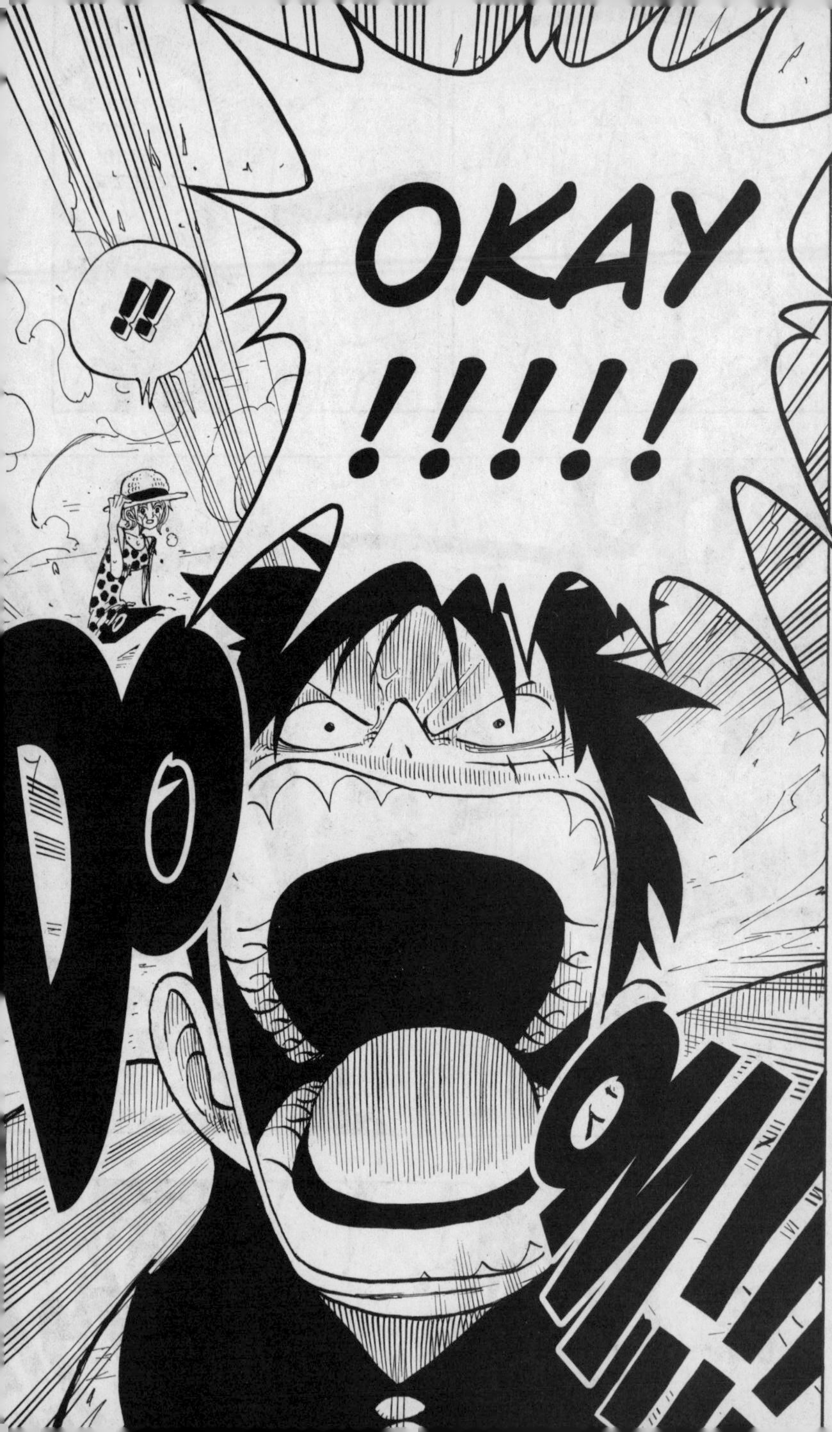
OKAY
!!!!!
!!

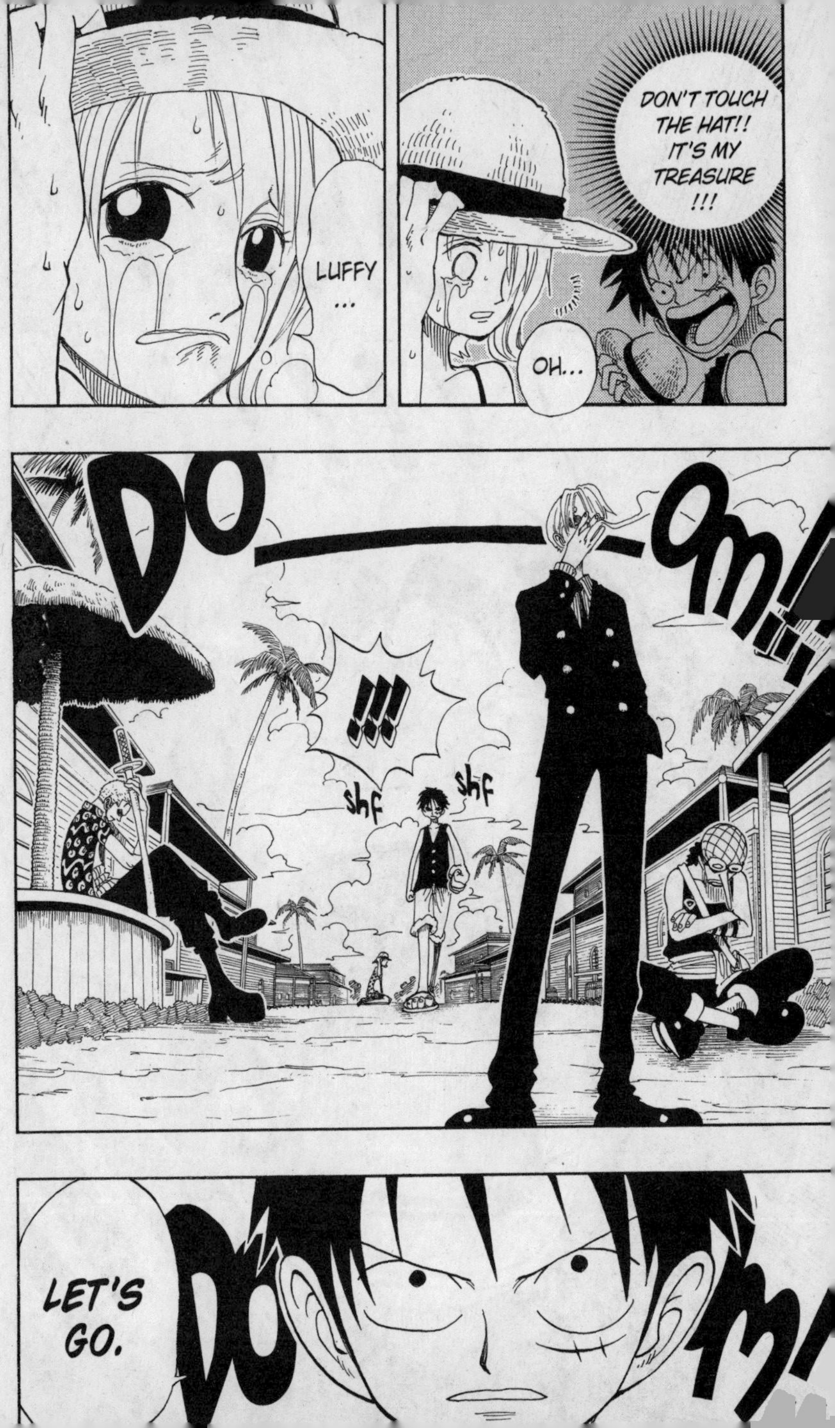

DON'T TOUCH THE HAT!! IT'S MY TREASURE !!!
OH...
LUFFY ...
DO—————OM!!!
!!!
shf
shf
LET'S GO.

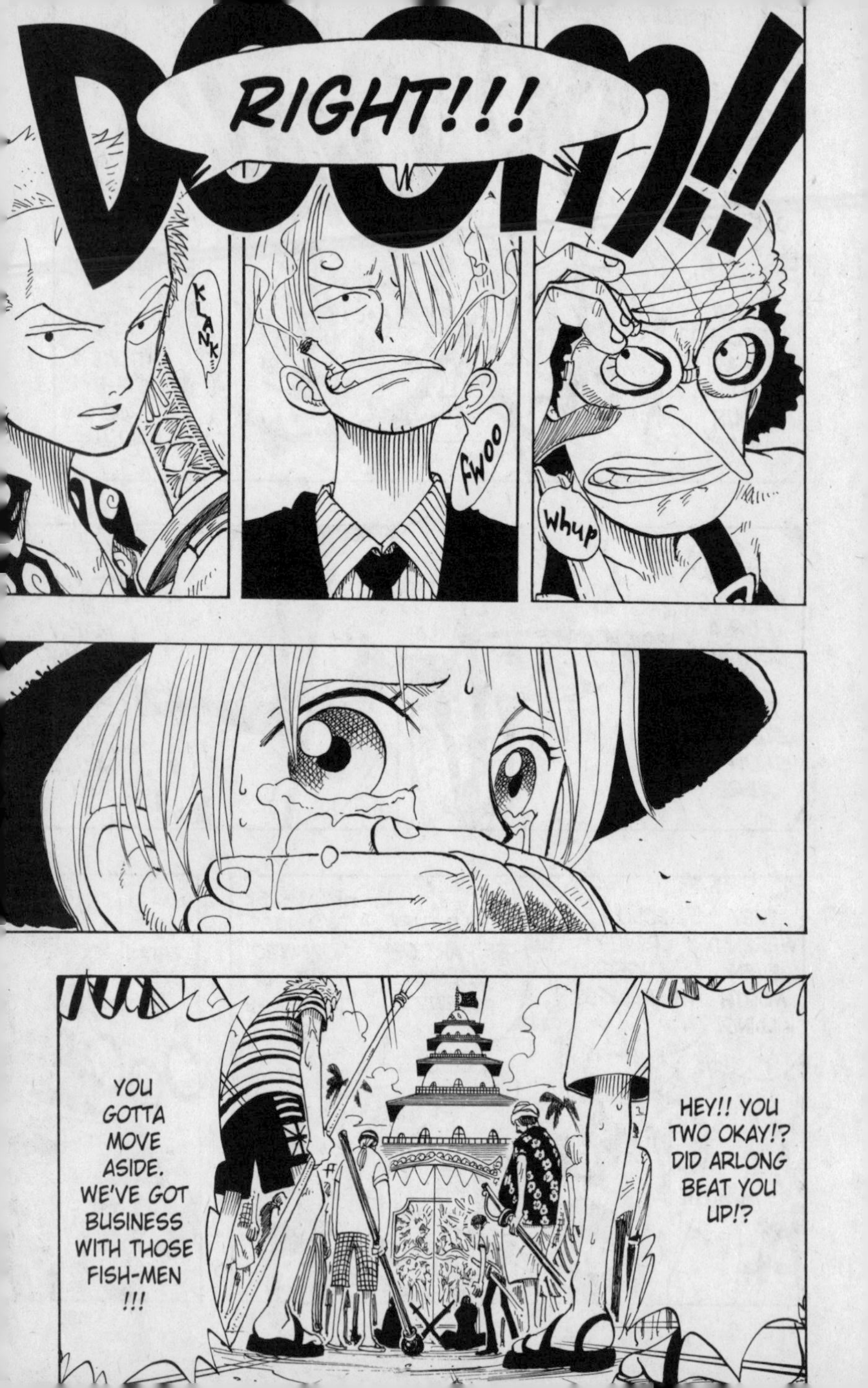
RIGHT!!!
whup
fwoo
KLANK
HEY!! YOU TWO OKAY!? DID ARLONG BEAT YOU UP!?
YOU GOTTA MOVE ASIDE. WE'VE GOT BUSINESS WITH THOSE FISH-MEN !!!

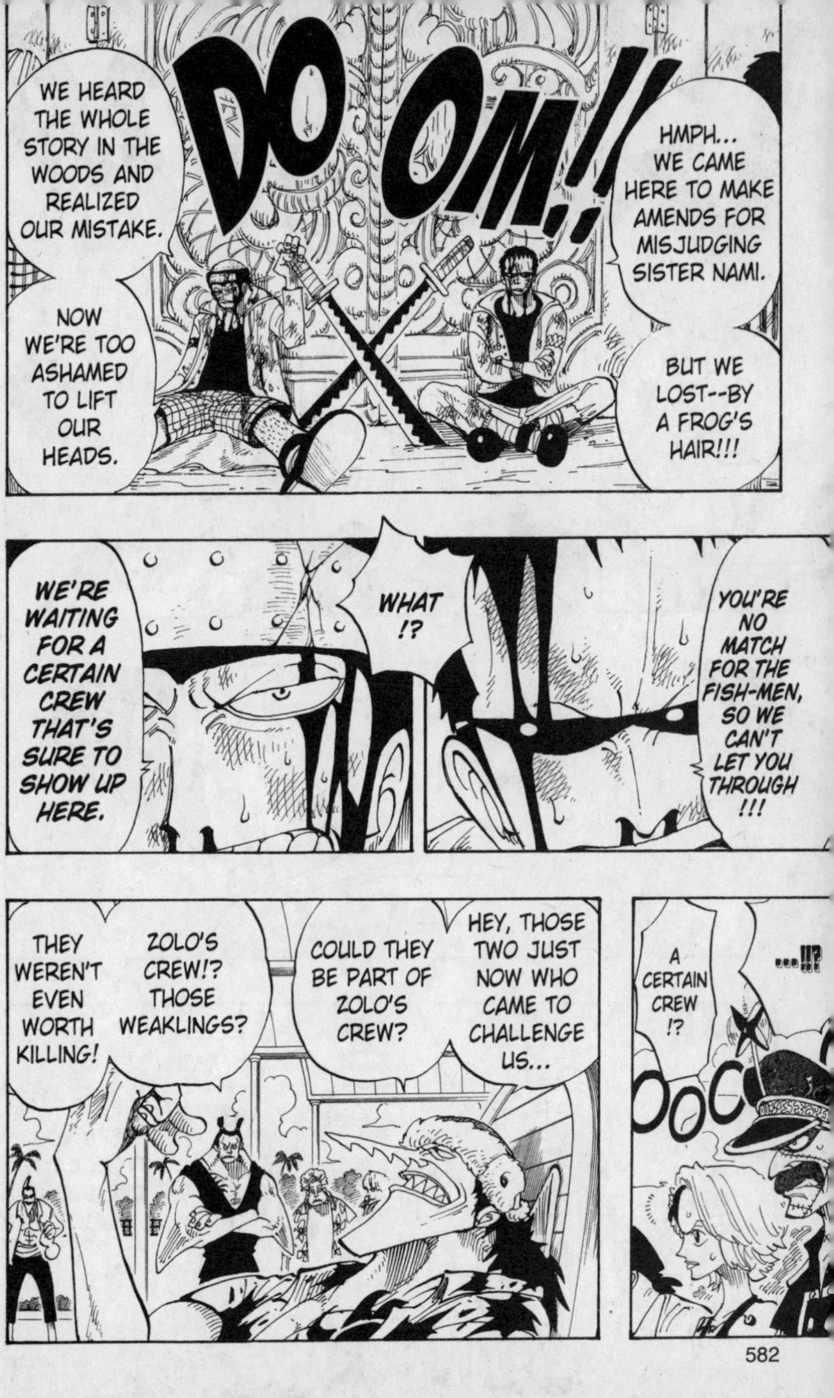
HMPH... WE CAME HERE TO MAKE AMENDS FOR MISJUDGING SISTER NAMI.
DOOM!!
WE HEARD THE WHOLE STORY IN THE WOODS AND REALIZED OUR MISTAKE.
BUT WE LOST--BY A FROG'S HAIR!!!
NOW WE'RE TOO ASHAMED TO LIFT OUR HEADS.
YOU'RE NO MATCH FOR THE FISH-MEN, SO WE CAN'T LET YOU THROUGH !!!
WHAT !?
WE'RE WAITING FOR A CERTAIN CREW THAT'S SURE TO SHOW UP HERE.
...!!?
A CERTAIN CREW !?
HEY, THOSE TWO JUST NOW WHO CAME TO CHALLENGE US...
COULD THEY BE PART OF ZOLO'S CREW?
ZOLO'S CREW!? THOSE WEAKLINGS?
THEY WEREN'T EVEN WORTH KILLING!

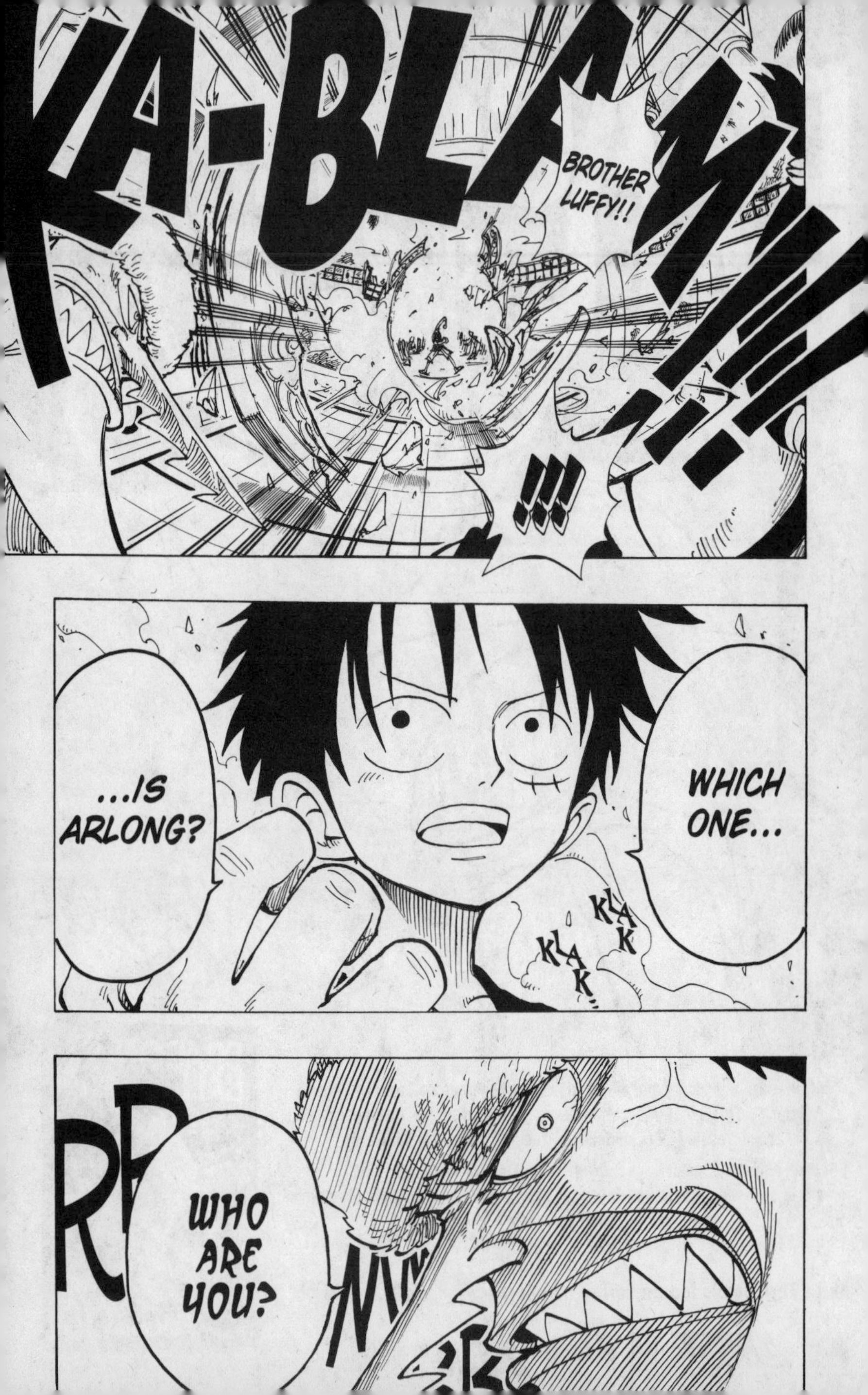
A-BLAM!!!
BROTHER LUFFY!!
!!!
WHICH ONE...
...IS ARLONG?
KLAK
KLAK
WHO ARE YOU?

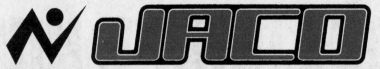
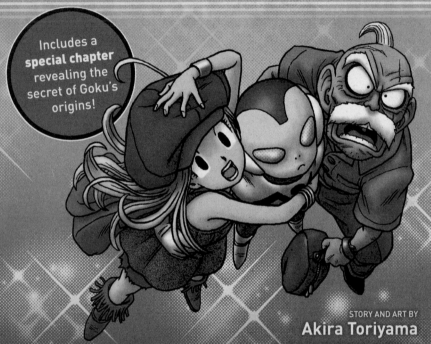
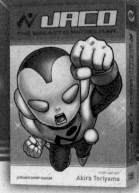

# THE ACTION-PACKED SUPERHERO COMEDY ABOUT ONE MAN'S AMBITION TO BE A HERO FOR FUN!

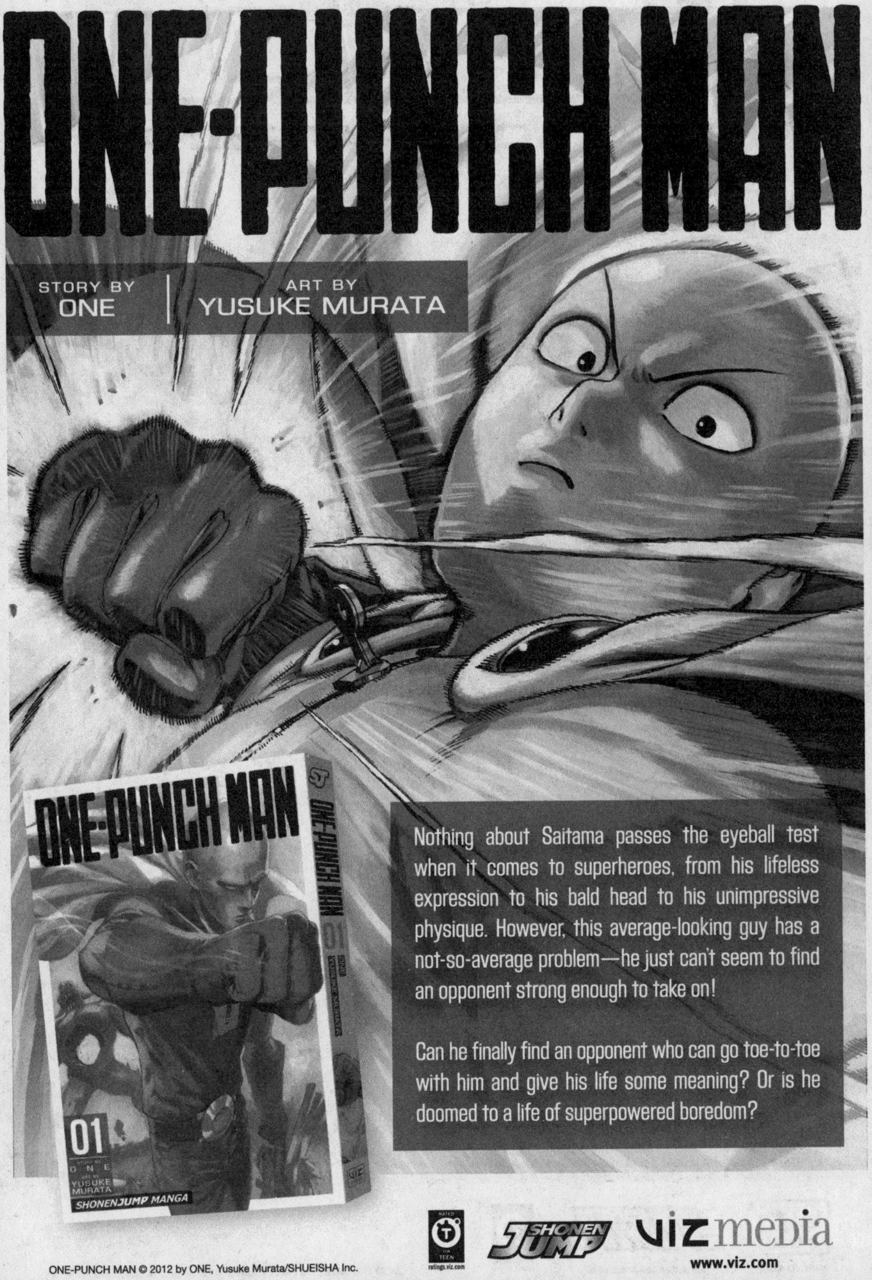

# ONE-PUNCH MAN

**STORY BY**
**ONE**

**ART BY**
**YUSUKE MURATA**

Nothing about Saitama passes the eyeball test when it comes to superheroes, from his lifeless expression to his bald head to his unimpressive physique. However, this average-looking guy has a not-so-average problem—he just can't seem to find an opponent strong enough to take on!

Can he finally find an opponent who can go toe-to-toe with him and give his life some meaning? Or is he doomed to a life of superpowered boredom?

www.viz.com

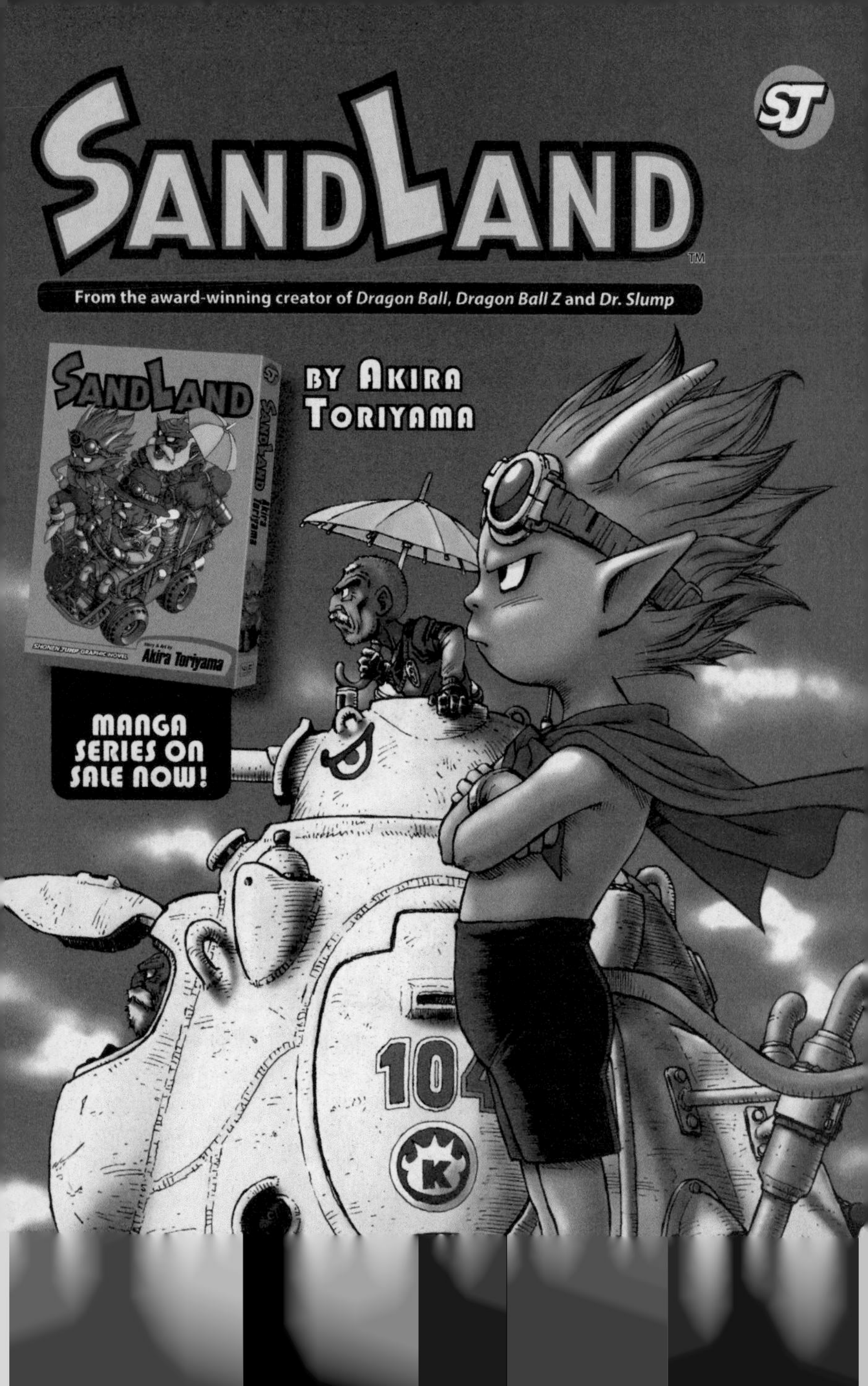
SJ
SANDLAND™
From the award-winning creator of Dragon Ball, Dragon Ball Z and Dr. Slump
BY AKIRA TORIYAMA
SANDLAND
Akira Toriyama
SHONEN JUMP GRAPHIC NOVEL
MANGA SERIES ON SALE NOW!
104
K

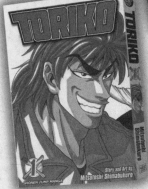

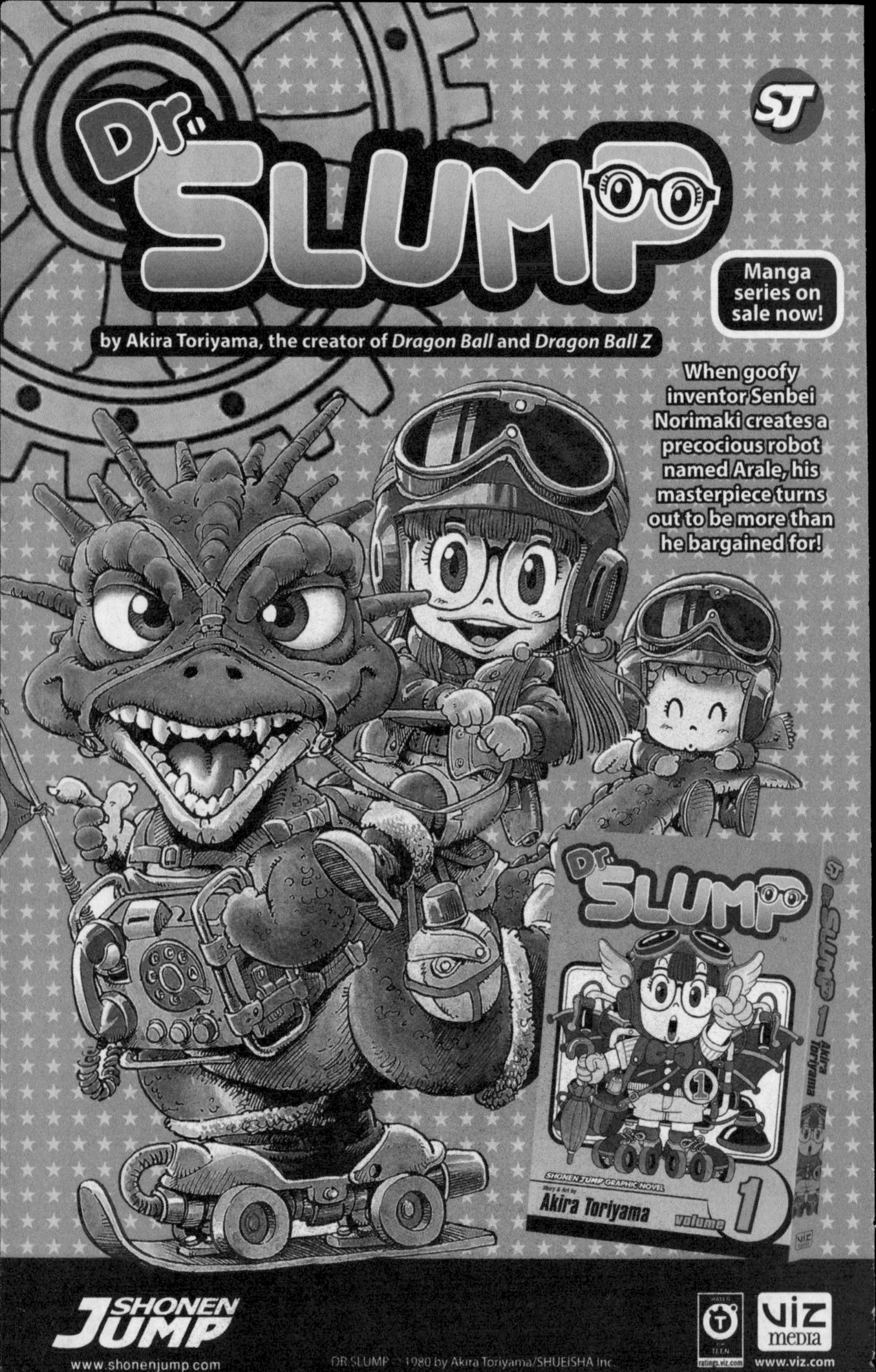

SJ
Dr. SLUMP
Manga series on sale now!
by Akira Toriyama, the creator of *Dragon Ball* and *Dragon Ball Z*
When goofy inventor Senbei Norimaki creates a precocious robot named Arale, his masterpiece turns out to be more than he bargained for!
Dr. SLUMP
SHONEN JUMP GRAPHIC NOVEL
Story & Art by
Akira Toriyama
volume 1
SHONEN JUMP
www.shonenjump.com
DR SLUMP © 1980 by Akira Toriyama/SHUEISHA Inc.
TEEN
ratings.viz.com
VIZ media
www.viz.com

# BAKUMAN。

STORY BY TSUGUMI OHBA
ART BY TAKESHI OBATA

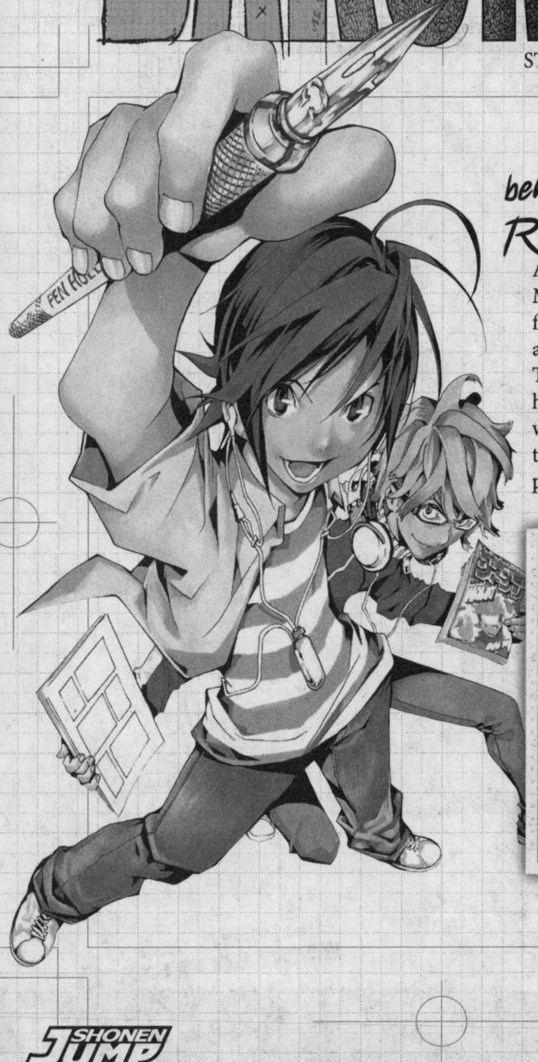
PEN HOL

From the creators of *Death Note*

## The mystery behind manga making REVEALED!

Average student Moritaka Mashiro enjoys drawing for fun. When his classmate and aspiring writer Akito Takagi discovers his talent, he begs to team up. But what exactly does it take to make it in the manga-publishing world?

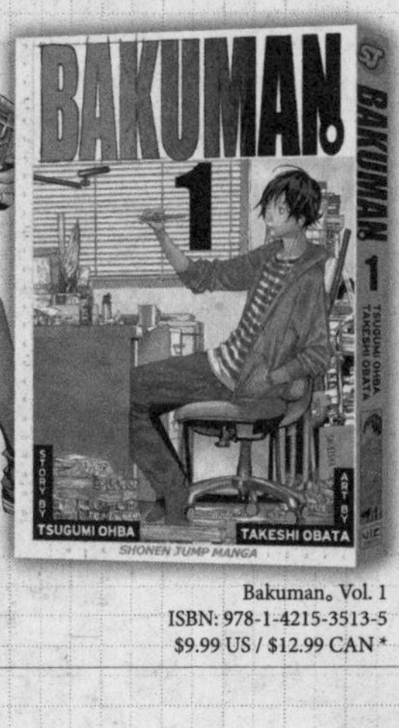
BAKUMAN。
1
STORY BY
TSUGUMI OHBA
ART BY
TAKESHI OBATA
SHONEN JUMP MANGA
BAKUMAN。 1 TSUGUMI OHBA TAKESHI OBATA

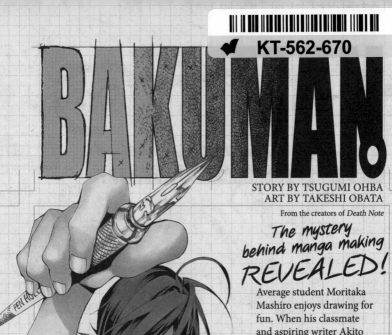

Bakuman。 Vol. 1
ISBN: 978-1-4215-3513-5
$9.99 US / $12.99 CAN *

SHONEN JUMP
www.shonenjump.com


* Prices subject to change

RATED T FOR TEEN
ratings.viz.com

VIZ media
www.viz.com